W0010710

English	Abbr.	Spanish
military		
music		
noun		
nautical		
oneself		
pejorative		
photography		
plural	pl	plural
politics	Pol	política
possessive	poss	posesivo
past participle	pp	participio pasado
preposition	prep	preposición
present participle	pres p	participio de presente
pronoun	pron	pronombre
past tense	pt	tiempo pasado
railroad	Rail	ferrocarril
religion	Relig	religión
school	Schol	enseñanza
singular	sing	singular
someone	s. o.	alguien
something	sth	algo
technical	Tec	técnico
university	Univ	universidad
verb	vb	verbo
intransitive verb	vi	verbo intransitivo
pronominal verb	vpr	verbo pronominal
transitive verb	vt	verbo transitivo
transitive & intransitive verb	vti	verbo transitivo e intransitivo

Oxford Spanish Mini Dictionary
Diccionario Oxford Mini

Spanish–English • English–Spanish
español-inglés • inglés-español

Diccionario Oxford Mini

CUARTA EDICIÓN

español–inglés
inglés–español

OXFORD
UNIVERSITY PRESS

Oxford Spanish Mini Dictionary

FOURTH EDITION

Spanish–English
English–Spanish

OXFORD
UNIVERSITY PRESS

OXFORD
UNIVERSITY PRESS

Great Clarendon Street, Oxford OX2 6DP

Oxford University Press is a department of the University of Oxford.
It furthers the University's objective of excellence in research, scholarship,
and education by publishing worldwide in

Oxford New York

Auckland Cape Town Dar es Salaam Hong Kong Karachi Kuala Lumpur
Madrid Melbourne Mexico City Nairobi New Delhi Shanghai Taipei
Toronto

With offices in
Argentina Austria Brazil Chile Czech Republic France Greece
Guatemala Hungary Italy Japan South Korea Poland Portugal
Singapore Switzerland Thailand Turkey Ukraine Vietnam

Oxford is a registered trade mark of Oxford University Press
in the UK and in certain other countries

Published in the United States
by Oxford University Press Inc., New York

British Library Cataloguing in Publication Data
Data available

Library of Congress Cataloging in Publication Data
Data available

ISBN 978-0-19-953435-7
ISBN 978-0-19-954126-3 (US edition)
ISBN 978-0-19-953490-6 (Spanish cover edition)

10 9 8 7 6 5

Typeset by Interactive Sciences Ltd, Gloucester
Printed and bound in Italy by
L.E.G.O. S.p.A., Lavis (TN)

3833331596283500

Contents/Índice

Contributors/Colaboradores

Fourth Edition/Cuarta edición

Editors/Editores
Joanna Rubery
Nicholas Rollin
Phrasefinder/Frases útiles
Pablo Pérez D'Ors
Carol Styles Carvajal
Oriana Orellana Jordán
Data input/Entrada de datos
Susan Wilkin

Third Edition/Tercera edición

Nicholas Rollin
Carol Styles Carvajal

Second Edition/Segunda edición

Editors/Editores
Carol Styles Carvajal
Michael Britton
Jane Horwood
Phrasefinder/Frases útiles
Idoia Noble
Neil and Roswitha Morris
Data input/Entrada de datos
Susan Wilkin

First Edition/Primera edición

Editor/Editora
Christine Lea

Introduction

This new edition of the *Oxford Spanish Mini Dictionary* is
designed as an effective and practical reference tool for the
student, adult learner, traveller, and business professional.

The wordlist has been revised and updated to reflect recent
additions to both languages. The *Phrasefinder* section has been
expanded. It aims to provide the user with the confidence to
communicate in the most commonly encountered social
situations such as travel, shopping, eating out, and organizing
leisure activities.

Another valuable feature of the dictionary is the special status
given to more complex grammatical words which provide the
basic structure of both languages. Boxed entries in the text for
these *function words* provide extended treatment, including
notes to warn of possible pitfalls.

The dictionary has an easy-to-use, streamlined layout. Bullets
separate each new part of speech within an entry. Nuances
of sense or usage are pinpointed by indicators or by typical
collocates with which the word frequently occurs. Extra help is
given in the form of symbols to mark the register of words and
phrases. An exclamation mark 🔳 indicates colloquial language,
and a cross 🔳 indicates slang.

Each English headword is followed by its phonetic
transcription between slashes. The symbols used are those of
the International Phonetic Alphabet. Pronunciation is also shown
for derivatives and compounds where it is not easily deduced
from that of a headword. The rules for the pronunciation of
Spanish are given on pages xii–xiii.

The swung dash (∼) is used to represent a headword or that part of a headword preceding the vertical bar (|).

In both English and Spanish only irregular plurals are given. Normally Spanish nouns and adjectives ending in an unstressed vowel form the plural by adding s (e.g. *libro, libros*). Nouns and adjectives ending in a stressed vowel or a consonant add es (e.g. *rubí, rubíes, pared, paredes*). An accent on the final syllable is not required when es is added (e.g. *nación, naciones*). Final *z* becomes *ces* (e.g. *vez, veces*).

Spanish nouns and adjectives ending in o form the feminine by changing the final *o* to *a* (e.g. *hermano, hermana*). Most Spanish nouns and adjectives ending in anything other than final *o* do not have a separate feminine form, with the exception of those denoting nationality etc.; these add a to the masculine singular form (e.g. *español, española*). An accent on the penultimate syllable is then not required (e.g. *inglés, inglesa*). Adjectives ending in *án, ón,* or *or* behave like those denoting nationality, with the following exceptions: *inferior, mayor, mejor, menor, peor, superior*, where the feminine has the same form as the masculine. Spanish verb tables will be found at the end of the book.

The Spanish alphabet

In Spanish ñ is considered a separate letter and in the Spanish–English section, therefore, is alphabetized after *ny*.

Introducción

Esta nueva edición del *Diccionario Oxford Mini* ha sido concebida a fin de proporcionar una herramienta de referencia práctica y eficaz al estudiante, joven y adulto, al viajero y a la persona de negocios.

Se ha revisado la lista de palabras con el objeto de incorporar nuevos términos en ambos idiomas. La sección central contiene una lista de *Frases útiles*, que se ha ampliado, destinada a que el usuario adquiera la confianza necesaria para comunicarse en las situaciones más normales de la vida diaria, como las que se encuentran al viajar, hacer compras, comer fuera y organizar actividades recreativas.

Otro valioso aspecto del diccionario es la importancia especial que se da a palabras con una función más compleja dentro de la gramática y que proveen la estructura básica de ambos idiomas. Estos *vocablos clave* están contenidos en recuadros dentro del texto, donde se les da un tratamiento amplio y se incluyen notas para advertir sobre posibles escollos.

El diccionario tiene una presentación clara y es fácil de usar. Símbolos distintivos separan las diferentes categorías gramaticales dentro de cada entrada. Los matices de sentido y de uso se muestran con precisión mediante indicadores o por colocaciones típicas con las que la palabra se usa frecuentemente. Se encuentra ayuda adicional en los signos que indican el registro idiomático de las palabras y frases. Un signo de exclamación 🛈 señala el uso coloquial y una cruz ✖ el uso argot.

....

Cada palabra cabeza de artículo en inglés va seguida de su transcripción fonética entre barras oblicuas. Los símbolos que se usan son los del Alfabeto Fonético Internacional. También aparece la pronunciación de derivados y nombres compuestos cuando no es posible deducirla de la palabra cabeza de artículo. Las reglas sobre pronunciación inglesa se encuentran en la página xiv.

La tilde (∼) se emplea para sustituir la palabra cabeza de artículo o aquella parte de tal palabra que precede a la barra vertical (|).

Tanto en inglés como en español se dan los plurales solamente si son irregulares. Para formar el plural regular en inglés se añade la letra s al sustantivo singular, pero se añade es cuando se trata de una palabra que termina en *ch, sh, s, ss, us, x, o, z* (p.ej. *sash, sashes*). En el caso de una palabra que termine en *y* precedida por una consonante, la *y* se transforma en *ies* (p.ej. *baby, babies*). Para formar el tiempo pasado y el participio pasado se añade *ed* al infinitivo de los verbos regulares ingleses (p.ej. *last, lasted*). En el caso de los verbos ingleses que terminan en e muda se añade sólo la *d* (p.ej. *move, moved*). En el caso de los verbos ingleses que terminan en *y*, se debe cambiar la *y* por *ied* (p.ej. *carry, carried*). Los verbos irregulares se encuentran en el diccionario por orden alfabético remitidos al infinitivo, y también en la lista que aparece en las últimas páginas del diccionario.

Pronunciation of Spanish

Vowels

a   between pronunciation of *a* in English *cat* and *arm*

e   like *e* in English *bed*

i   like *ee* in English *see* but a little shorter

o   like *o* in English *hot* but a little longer

u   like *oo* in English *too*

y   when a vowel is as Spanish **i**

Consonants

b   (1) in initial position or after a nasal consonant is like
        English *b*
        (2) in other positions is between English *b* and English *v*

c   (1) before **e** or **i** is like *th* in English *thin*. In Latin American
        Spanish is like English *s*.
        (2) in other positions is like *c* in English *cat*

ch like *ch* in English *chip*

d   (1) in initial position, after nasal consonants and after **l** is like
        English *d*
        (2) in other positions is like *th* in English *this*

f   like English *f*

g   (1) before **e** or **i** is like *ch* in Scottish *loch*
        (2) in initial position is like *g* in English *get*
        (3) in other positions is like (2) but a little softer

j	like *ch* in Scottish *loch*
k	like English *k*
l	like English *l* but see also **ll**
ll	like *lli* in English *million*
m	like English *m*
n	like English *n*
ñ	like *ni* in English *opinion*
p	like English *p*
q	like English *k*
r	rolled or trilled
s	like *s* in English *sit*
t	like English *t*
v	(1) in initial position or after a nasal consonant is like English *b*
	(2) in other positions is between English *b* and English *v*
w	like Spanish **b** or **v**
x	like English *x*
y	like English *y*
z	like *th* in English *thin*

Pronunciación inglesa

Símbolos fonéticos

Vocales y diptongos

iː	*see*	ɔː	*saw*	eɪ	*page*	ɔɪ	*join*
ɪ	*sit*	ʊ	*put*	əʊ	*home*	ɪə	*near*
e	*ten*	uː	*too*	aɪ	*five*	eə	*hair*
æ	*hat*	ʌ	*cup*	aɪə	*fire*	ʊə	*poor*
ɑː	*arm*	ɜː	*fur*	aʊ	*now*		
ɒ	*got*	ə	*ago*	aʊə	*flour*		

Consonantes

p	*pen*	tʃ	*chin*	s	*so*	n	*no*
b	*bad*	dʒ	*June*	z	*zoo*	ŋ	*sing*
t	*tea*	f	*fall*	ʃ	*she*	l	*leg*
d	*dip*	v	*voice*	ʒ	*measure*	r	*red*
k	*cat*	θ	*thin*	h	*how*	j	*yes*
g	*got*	ð	*then*	m	*man*	w	*wet*

El símbolo ' precede a la sílaba sobre la cual recae el acento tónico.

Aa

a *preposición*

Note that **a** followed by **el** becomes **al**, e.g. *vamos al cine*

····▸ (*dirección*) to. fui a México I went to Mexico. muévete a la derecha move to the right

····▸ (*posición*) se sentaron a la mesa they sat at the table. al lado del banco next to the bank. a orillas del río on the banks of the river

····▸ (*distancia*) queda a 5 km it's 5 km away. a pocos metros de aquí a few meters from here

····▸ (*fecha*) hoy estamos a 5 today is the 5th. ¿a cuánto estamos?, (*LAm*) ¿a cómo estamos? what's the date?

····▸ (*hora, momento*) at. a las 2 at 2 o'clock. a fin de mes at the end of the month. a los 21 años at the age of 21; (*después de*) after 21 years

····▸ (*precio*) ¿a cómo están las peras? how much are the pears? están a 3 euros el kilo they're 3 euros a kilo. salen a 15 euros cada uno they work out at 15 euros each.

····▸ (*medio, modo*) fuimos a pie we went on foot. hecho a mano hand made. pollo al horno (*LAm*) roast chicken

····▸ (*cuando precede al objeto directo de persona*) *no se traduce.* conocí a Juan I met Juan. quieren mucho a sus hijos they love their children very much

····▸ (*con objeto indirecto*) to. se lo di a Juan I gave it to Juan. le vendí el coche a mi amigo I sold my friend the car, I sold the car to my friend. se lo compré a mi madre I bought it from my mother; (*para*) I bought it for my mother

➡ Cuando la preposición **a** se emplea precedida de ciertos verbos como **empezar**, **faltar**, **ir**, **llegar** etc., ver bajo el respectivo verbo

ábaco *m* abacus

abadejo *m* pollack

abadía *f* abbey

abajo *adv* (*down*) below; (*dirección*) down(wards); (*en casa*) downstairs. ● *int* down with. ~ de (*LAm*) under(neath). calle ~ down the street. el ~ firmante the undersigned. escaleras ~ down the stairs. la parte de ~ the bottom (part). más ~ further down

abalanzarse 🔟 *vpr* rush (*hacia* towards)

abanderado *m* standard-bearer; (*Mex, en fútbol*) linesman

abandon|ado *adj* abandoned; (*descuidado*) neglected; (*persona*) untidy. ~ar *vt* leave (*un lugar*); abandon (*persona, cosa*). ● *vi* give

a

up. ~**arse** *vpr* give in; (*descuidarse*) let o.s. go. ~o *m* abandonment; (*estado*) neglect

abani|car 🟥 *vt* fan. ~**co** *m* fan

abaratar *vt* reduce

abarcar 🟥 *vt* put one's arms around, embrace; (*comprender*) embrace

abarrotar *vt* overfill, pack full

abarrotes *mpl* (*LAm*) groceries; (*tienda*) grocer's shop

abast|ecer 🟦 *vt* supply. ~**ecimiento** *m* supply; (*acción*) supplying. ~o *m* supply. no dar ~o be unable to cope (con with)

abati|do *adj* depressed. ~**miento** *m* depression

abdicar 🟥 *vt* give up. ● *vi* abdicate

abdom|en *m* abdomen. ~**inal** *adj* abdominal

abec|é *m* 🔲 alphabet, ABC. ~**edario** *m* alphabet

abedul *m* birch (tree)

abej|a *f* bee. ~**orro** *m* bumblebee

aberración *f* aberration

abertura *f* opening

abeto *m* fir (tree)

abierto *pp* véase **ABRIR**. ● *adj* open

abism|al *adj* abysmal; (*profundo*) deep. ~**al** *vt* throw into an abyss; (*fig, abatir*) humble. ~**arse** *vpr* be absorbed (en in), be lost (en in). ~o *m* abyss. (*fig, diferencia*) world of difference

ablandar *vt* soften. ~**se** *vpr* soften

abnega|ción *f* self-sacrifice. ~**do** *adj* self-sacrificing

abochornar *vt* embarrass. ~**se** *vpr* feel embarrassed

abofetear *vt* slap

aboga|cía *f* law. ~**do** *m* lawyer, solicitor; (*ante tribunal superior*) barrister (*Brit*), attorney (*Amer*).

abolengo *m* ancestry

aboli|ción *f* abolition. ~**cionismo** *m* abolitionism. ~**cionista** *m & f* abolitionist. ~**r** 🟦 *vt* abolish

abolla|dura *f* dent. ~**r** *vt* dent

abolsado *adj* baggy

abomba|do *adj* convex; (*LAm, atontado*) dopey. ~**r** *vt* make convex. ~**rse** *vpr* (*LAm, descomponerse*) go bad

abominable *adj* abominable

abona|ble *adj* payable. ~**do** *adj* paid. ● *m* subscriber. ~**r** *vt* pay; (*en agricultura*) fertilize. ~**rse** *vpr* subscribe.

abono *m* payment; (*estiércol*) fertilizer; (*a un periódico*) subscription

aborda|ble *adj* reasonable; (*persona*) approachable. ~**r** *vt* board (un asunto); ~je approach (una persona); (*Naut*) come alongside; (*Mex, Aviac*) board

aborigen *adj & m* native

aborrec|er 🟦 *vt* loathe. ~**ible** *adj* loathsome. ~**ido** *adj* loathed. ~**imiento** *m* loathing

abort|ar *vi* have a miscarriage. ~**ivo** *adj* abortive. ~o *m* miscarriage; (*voluntario*) abortion. hacerse un ~o have an abortion

abotonar *vt* button (up). ~**se** *vpr* button (up)

abovedado *adj* vaulted

abrasa|dor *adj* burning. ~**r** *vt* burn. ~**rse** *vpr* burn

abraz|ar 🔟 embrace. ~**arse** *vpr* embrace. ~o *m* hug. un ~o con best wishes from

abre|botellas *m invar* bottle-opener. **~cartas** *m invar* paper-knife. **~latas** *m invar* tin opener (Brit), can opener

abrevia|ción *f* abbreviation; (texto abreviado) abridged text. **~do** *adj* brief; (texto) abridged. **~r** *vt* abbreviate; abridge (texto); cut short (viaje etc). ● *vi* be brief. **~tura** *f* abbreviation

abrig|ado *adj* (lugar) sheltered; (persona) well wrapped up. **~ador** *adj* (Mex, ropa) warm. **~ar** [12] *vt* shelter; cherish (esperanza); harbour (duda, sospecha). **~arse** *vpr* (take) shelter; (con ropa) wrap up. **~o** *m* (over)coat; (lugar) shelter

abril *m* April. **~eño** *adj* April

abrillantar *vt* polish

abrir (pp **abierto**) *vt/i* open. **~se** *vpr* open; (extenderse) open out; (el tiempo) clear

abrochar *vt* do up; (con botones) button up

abruma|dor *adj* overwhelming. **~r** *vt* overwhelm

abrupto *adj* steep; (áspero) harsh

abrutado *adj* brutish

absentismo *m* absenteeism

absolu|ción *f* (Relig) absolution; (Jurid) acquittal

absolut|amente *adv* absolutely, completely. **~o** *adj* absolute. en **~o** (not) at all. **~orio** *adj* of acquittal

absolver [2] (pp **absuelto**) *vt* (Relig) absolve; (Jurid) acquit

absor|bente *adj* absorbent; (fig, interesante) absorbing. **~ber** *vt* absorb. **~ción** *f* absorption. **~to** *adj* absorbed

abstemio *adj* teetotal. ● *m* tee-totaller

absten|ción *f* abstention. **~erse** [40] *vpr* abstain, refrain (de from)

abstinencia *f* abstinence

abstra|cción *f* abstraction. **~cto** *adj* abstract. **~er** [41] *vt* abstract. **~erse** *vpr* be lost in thought. **~ído** *adj* absent-minded

absuelto *adj* (Relig) absolved; (Jurid) acquitted

absurdo *adj* absurd. ● *m* absurd thing

abuche|ar *vt* boo. **~o** *m* booing

abuel|a *f* grandmother. **~o** *m* grandfather. **~os** *mpl* grandparents

ab|ulia *f* apathy. **~úlico** *adj* apathetic

abulta|do *adj* bulky. **~r** *vt* (fig, exagerar) exaggerate. ● *vi* be bulky

abunda|ncia *f* abundance. nadar en la **~ncia** be rolling in money. **~nte** *adj* abundant, plentiful. **~r** *vi* be plentiful

aburguesarse *vpr* become middle-class

aburri|do *adj* (con estar) bored; (con ser) boring. **~dor** *adj* (LAm) boring. **~miento** *m* boredom; (cosa pesada) bore. **~r** *vt* bore. **~rse** *vpr* get bored

abus|ar *vi* take advantage. **~ar** de la bebida drink too much. **~ivo** *adj* excessive. **~o** *m* abuse

acá *adv* here. **~ y allá** here and there. de **~ para allá** to and fro. de **~ de ayer** since yesterday. más **~** nearer

acaba|do *adj* finished; (perfecto) perfect. ● *m* finish. **~r** *vt/i* finish. **~rse** *vpr* finish; (agotarse) run out; (morirse) die. **~r con** put an end to. **~r de** (+ infinitivo) have just (+ pp). **~ de llegar** he has just arrived. **~r por** (+ infinitivo) end up (+ gerundio). ¡se **acabó**! that's it!

acabóse *m*. ser el **~** be the end, be the limit

a **acad|emia** f academy. **~émico** adj academic

acallar vt silence

acalora|do adj heated; (persona) hot. **~rse** vpr get hot; (fig, excitarse) get excited

acampar vi camp

acantilado m cliff

acapara|r vt hoard; (monopolizar) monopolize. **~miento** m hoarding; (monopolio) monopolizing

acariciar vt caress; (animal) stroke; (idea) nurture

ácaro m mite

acarre|ar vt transport; (desgracias etc) cause. **~o** m transport

acarton|ado adj (piel) wizened. **~rse** vpr (ponerse rígido) go stiff; (piel) become wizened

acaso adv maybe, perhaps. ● m chance. **~ llueva mañana** perhaps it will rain tomorrow. **por si ~** (just) in case

acata|miento m compliance (de with). **~r** vt comply with

acatarrarse vpr catch a cold, get a cold

acaudalado adj well off

acceder vi agree; (tener acceso) have access

acces|ible adj accessible; (persona) approachable. **~o** m access, entry; (Med, ataque) attack

accesorio adj & m accessory

accident|ado adj (terreno) uneven; (agitado) troubled; (persona) injured. **~al** adj accidental. **~arse** vpr have an accident. **~e** m accident

acci|ón f (incl Jurid) action; (hecho) deed; (Com) share. **~onar** vt work. ● vi gesticulate. **~onista** m & f shareholder

acebo m holly (tree)

acech|ar vt lie in wait for. **~o** m spying. **al ~o** on the look-out

aceit|ar vt oil; (Culin) add oil to. **~e** m oil. **~e de oliva** olive oil. **~e de ricino** castor oil. **~era** f cruet; (para engrasar) oilcan. **~ero** adj oil. **~oso** adj oily

aceitun|a f olive. **~ado** adj olive. **~o** m olive tree

acelera|dor m accelerator. **~r** vt accelerate; (fig) speed up, quicken

acelga f chard

acent|o m accent; (énfasis) stress. **~uación** f accentuation. **~uar** vt stress; (fig) emphasize. **~uarse** vpr become noticeable

acepción f meaning, sense

acepta|ble adj acceptable. **~ción** f acceptance; (éxito) success. **~r** vt accept

acequia f irrigation channel

acera f pavement (Brit), sidewalk (Amer)

acerca de prep about

acerca|miento m approach; (fig) reconciliation. **~r** vt bring near. **~rse** vpr approach

acero m steel. **~ inoxidable** stainless steel

acérrimo adj (fig) staunch

acert|ado adj right, correct; (apropiado) appropriate. **~ar** vt (adivinar) get right, guess. ● vi get right; (en el blanco) hit. **~ar a** happen to. **~ar con** hit on. **~ijo** m riddle

achacar vt attribute

achacoso adj sickly

achaque m ailment

achatar vt flatten

achicar vt make smaller; (fig, fam, empequeñecer) belittle; (Naut) bale out. **~rse** vpr become smaller; (humillarse) be intimidated

achicharra|r vt burn; (fig) pester. **~rse** vpr burn

achichincle m & f (Mex) hanger-on

achicopalado adj (Mex) depressed

achicoria f chicory

achiote m (LAm) annatto

achispa|do adj tipsy. **~rse** vpr get tipsy

achulado adj cocky

acicala|do adj dressed up. **~r** vt dress up. **~rse** vpr get dressed up

acicate m spur

acidez f acidity; (Med) heartburn

ácido adj sour. ● m acid

acierto m success; (idea) good idea; (habilidad) skill

aclama|ción f acclaim; (aplausos) applause. **~r** vt acclaim; (aplaudir) applaud

aclara|ción f explanation. **~r** vt lighten (colores); (explicar) clarify; (enjuagar) rinse. ● vi (el tiempo) brighten up. **~rse** vpr become clear. **~torio** adj explanatory

aclimata|ción f acclimatization, acclimation (Amer). **~r** vt acclimatize, acclimate (Amer). **~rse** vpr become acclimatized, become acclimated (Amer)

acné m acne

acobardar vt intimidate. **~se** vpr lose one's nerve

acocil m (Mex) freshwater shrimp

acog|edor adj welcoming; (ambiente) friendly. **~er** **14** vt welcome; (proteger) shelter; (recibir) receive. **~erse** vpr take refuge. **~ida** f welcome; (refugio) refuge

acolcha|do adj quilted. **~r** vt quilt, pad

acomedido adj (Mex) obliging

acomet|er vt attack; (emprender) undertake. **~ida** f attack

acomod|ado adj well off. **~ador** m usher. **~adora** f usherette. **~ar** vt arrange; (adaptar) adjust. ● vi be suitable. **~arse** vpr settle down; (adaptarse) conform

acompaña|miento m accompaniment. **~nte** m & f companion; (Mus) accompanist. **~r** vt go with; (hacer compañía) keep company; (adjuntar) enclose

acondicionar vt fit out; (preparar) prepare

aconseja|ble adj advisable. **~do** adj advised. **~r** vt advise. **~rse** vpr. **~rse con** consult

acontec|er **11** vi happen. **~imiento** m event

acopla|miento m coupling; (Elec) connection. **~r** vt fit; (Elec) connect; (Rail) couple

acorazado adj armour-plated. ● m battleship

acord|ar **2** vt agree (upon); (decidir) decide; (recordar) remind. **~arse** vpr remember. ● adj in agreement; (Mus) harmonious. ● m chord

acorde|ón m accordion. **~onista** m & f accordionist

acordona|do adj (lugar) cordoned off; (zapatos) lace-up. **~r** vt lace (up); (rodear) cordon off

acorralar vt round up (animales); corner (personas)

acortar vt shorten; cut short (permanencia). **~se** vpr get shorter

acos|ar vt hound; (fig) pester. **~o** m pursuit; (fig) pestering

acostar **2** vt put to bed; (Naut) bring alongside. ● vi (Naut) reach land. ~se vpr go to bed; (echarse) lie down. ~se con (fig) sleep with

acostumbra|do adj (habitual) usual. ~do a used to. ~r vt get used. me ha ~do a levantarme por la noche he's got me used to getting up at night. ● vi. ~r be accustomed to. **acostumbro a** comer a la una I usually have lunch at one o'clock. ~rse vpr become accustomed, get used

acota|ción f (nota) margin note (en el teatro) stage direction; (cota) elevation mark. ~miento m (Mex) hard shoulder

acrecentar 🛽 vt increase. ~se vpr increase

acredita|do adj reputable; (Pol) accredited. ~r vt prove; accredit (diplomático); (garantizar) guarantee; (autorizar) authorize. ~rse vpr make one's name

acreedor adj worthy (de of). ● m creditor

acribillar vt (a balazos) riddle (a with); (a picotazos) cover (a with); (fig, a preguntas etc) bombard (a with)

acr|obacia f acrobatics. ~obacias aéreas aerobatics. ~óbata m & f acrobat. ~obático adj acrobatic

acta f minutes; (certificado) certificate

actitud f posture, position; (fig) attitude, position

activ|ar vt activate; (acelerar) speed up. ~idad f activity. ~o adj active. ● m assets

acto m act; (ceremonia) ceremony. en el ~ immediately

act|or m actor. ~riz f actress

actuación f action; (conducta) behaviour; (Theat) performance

actual adj present; (asunto) top-

ical. ~idad f present; (de asunto) topicality. en la ~idad (en este momento) currently; (hoy en día) nowadays. ~idades fpl current affairs. ~ización f modernization. ~izar 🔟 vt modernize. ~mente adv now, at the present time

actuar 🗷 vi act. ~ de act as

acuarel|a f watercolour. ~ista m & f watercolourist

acuario m aquarium. A~ Aquarius

acuartelar vt quarter, billet; (mantener en cuartel) confine to barracks

acuático adj aquatic

acuchillar vt slash; stab (persona)

acuci|ante adj urgent. ~ar vt urge on; (dar prisa a) hasten. ~oso adj keen

acudir vi. ~ a go to; (asistir) attend; turn up for (a una cita); (en auxilio) go to help

acueducto m aqueduct

acuerdo m agreement. ● vb véase **ACORDAR**. ¡de ~! OK! de ~ con in accordance with. estar de ~ agree. ponerse de ~ agree

acuesto vb véase **ACOSTAR**

acumula|dor m accumulator. ~r vt accumulate. ~rse vpr accumulate

acunar vt rock

acuñar vt mint, coin

acupuntura f acupuncture

acurrucarse 🗷 vpr curl up

acusa|do adj accused; (destacado) marked. ● m accused. ~r vt accuse; (mostrar) show; (denunciar) denounce; acknowledge (recibo)

acuse m. ~ de recibo acknowledgement of receipt

acus|ica m & f 🗊 telltale. ~ón m

acústic|a f acoustics. ∼**o** adj acoustic

adapta|ble adj adaptable. ∼**ción** f adaptation. ∼**dor** m adapter. ∼**r** vt adapt; (ajustar) fit. ∼**rse** vpr adapt o.s.

adecua|do adj suitable. ∼**r** vt adapt, make suitable

adelant|ado adj advanced; (niño) precocious; (reloj) fast. **por** ∼**ado** in advance.. ∼**amiento** m advance(ment); (Auto) overtaking. ∼**ar** vt advance, move forward; (acelerar) speed up; put forward (reloj); (Auto) overtake. ● vi advance, go forward; (reloj) gain, be fast. ∼**arse** vpr advance, move forward; (reloj) gain; (Auto) overtake. ∼**e** adv forward. ● int come in!; (¡siga!) carry on! **más** ∼**e** (lugar) further on; (tiempo) later on. ∼**o** m advance; (progreso) progress

adelgaza|miento m slimming. ∼**r** 🔟 vt make thin; lose (kilos). ● vi lose weight; (adrede) slim. ∼**rse** vpr lose weight; (adrede) slim

ademán m gesture. **en** ∼ **de** as if to. **ademanes** mpl (modales) manners.

además adv besides; (también) also; (lo que es más) what's more. ∼ **de** besides

adentr|arse vpr. ∼**arse en** penetrate into; study thoroughly (tema etc). ∼**o** adv in(side). ∼ **de** (LAm) in(side). **mar** ∼**o** out at sea. **tierra** ∼**o** inland

adepto m supporter

aderez|ar 🔟 vt flavour (bebidas); (condimentar) season; dress (ensalada). ∼**o** m flavouring; (con condimentos) seasoning; (para ensalada) dressing

adeud|ar vt owe. ∼**o** m debit

adhe|rir 4 vt/i stick. ∼**rirse** vpr stick; (fig) follow. ∼**sión** f adhesion; (fig) support. ∼**sivo** adj & m adhesive

adici|ón f addition. ∼**onal** adj additional. ∼**onar** vt add

adicto adj addicted. ● m addict; (seguidor) follower

adiestra|do adj trained. ∼**miento** m training. ∼**r** vt train. ∼**rse** vpr practise

adinerado adj wealthy

adiós int goodbye!; (al cruzarse con alguien) hello!

adit|amento m addition; (accesorio) accessory. ∼**ivo** m additive

adivin|anza f riddle. ∼**ar** vt foretell; (acertar) guess. ∼**o** m fortuneteller

adjetivo adj adjectival. ● m adjective

adjudica|ción f award. ∼**r** 7 vt award. ∼**rse** vpr appropriate. ∼**tario** m winner of an award

adjunt|ar vt enclose. ∼**o** adj enclosed; (auxiliar) assistant. ● m assistant

administra|ción f administration; (gestión) management. ∼**dor** m administrator; (gerente) manager. ∼**dora** f administrator; manageress. ∼**r** vt administer. ∼**tivo** adj administrative

admira|ble adj admirable. ∼**ción** f admiration. ∼**dor** m admirer. ∼**r** vt admire; (sorprender) amaze. ∼**rse** vpr be amazed

admi|sibilidad f admissibility. ∼**sible** adj acceptable. ∼**sión** f admission; (aceptación) acceptance. ∼**tir** vt admit; (aceptar) accept

adobar vt (Culin) pickle; (condimentar) marinade

a

adobe m sun-dried brick

adobo m pickle; (condimento) marinade

adoctrinar vt indoctrinate

adolecer 11 vi. ~ de suffer from

adolescen|cia f adolescence. ~te adj adolescent. • m & f teenager, adolescent

adonde adv where

adónde adv where?

adop|ción f adoption. ~tar vt adopt. ~tivo adj adoptive; (hijo) adopted; (patria) of adoption

adoquín m paving stone; (imbécil) idiot. ~inado m paving. ~inar vt pave

adora|ción f adoration. ~r vt adore

adormec|er 11 vt send to sleep; (fig, calmar) calm, soothe. ~erse vpr fall asleep; (un miembro) go to sleep. ~ido adj sleepy; (un miembro) numb

adormilarse vpr doze

adorn|ar vt adorn (con, de with). ~o m decoration

adosar vt lean (a against); (Mex, adjuntar) to enclose

adqui|rir 4 vt acquire; (comprar) purchase. ~sición f acquisition; (compra) purchase. ~sitivo adj purchasing

adrede adv on purpose

adrenalina f adrenalin

aduan|a f customs. ~ero adj customs. • m customs officer

aducir 47 vt allege

adueñarse vpr take possession

adul|ación f flattery. ~ador adj flattering. • m flatterer. ~ar vt flatter

ad|ulterar vt adulterate. ~ulterio m adultery

adulto adj & m adult, grown-up

advenedizo adj & m upstart

advenimiento m advent, arrival; (subida al trono) accession

adverbio m adverb

advers|ario m adversary. ~idad f adversity. ~o adj adverse, unfavourable

advert|encia f warning. ~ir 4 vt warn; (notar) notice

adviento m Advent

adyacente adj adjacent

aéreo adj air; (foto) aerial; (ferrocarril) overhead

aeróbico adj aerobic

aerodeslizador m hovercraft

aero|ligero m microlight. ~lito m meteorite. ~moza f (LAm) flight attendant. ~puerto m airport. ~sol m aerosol

afab|ilidad f affability. ~le adj affable

afamado adj famous

af|án m hard work; (deseo) desire. ~anador m (Mex) cleaner. ~anar vt ⊠ pinch 🗓. ~anarse vpr strive (en, por to)

afear vt disfigure, make ugly; (censurar) censure

afecta|ción f affectation. ~do adj affected. ~r vt affect

afect|ivo adj sensitive. ~o m (cariño) affection. • a. ~o a attached to. ~uoso adj affectionate. con un ~uoso saludo (en cartas) with kind regards. suyo ~ísimo (en cartas) yours sincerely

afeita|do m shave. ~dora f electric razor. ~r vt shave. ~rse vpr shave, have a shave

afeminado adj effeminate. • m effeminate person

aferrar vt grasp. ~se vpr to

cling (a to)

afianza|miento m (refuerzo) strengthening; (garantía) guarantee. **~rse** 🔟 vpr become established

afiche m (LAm) poster

afición f liking; (conjunto de aficionados) fans. **por ~ón** as a hobby. **~onado** adj keen (a on), fond (a of). ● m fan. **~onar** vt make fond. **~onarse** vpr take a liking to

afila|do adj sharp. **~dor** m knife-grinder. **~r** vt sharpen

afilia|ción f affiliation. **~do** adj affiliated. **~rse** vpr become a member (a of)

afín adj similar; (contiguo) adjacent; (personas) related

afina|ción f (Auto, Mus) tuning. **~do** adj (Mus) in tune. **~dor** m tuner. **~r** vt (afilar) sharpen; (Auto, Mus) tune. **~rse** vpr become thinner

afincarse 🔢 vpr settle

afinidad f affinity; (parentesco) relationship by marriage

afirma|ción f affirmation. **~r** vt make firm; (asentir) affirm. **~rse** vpr steady o.s. **~tivo** adj affirmative

aflicción f affliction

afligi|do adj distressed. **~r** 🔢 vt distress. **~rse** vpr distress o.s.

aflojar vt loosen; (relajar) ease. ● vi let up. **~se** vpr loosen

aflu|encia f flow. **~ente** adj flowing. ● m tributary. **~ir** 🔢 vi flow (a into)

afónico adj hoarse

aforismo m aphorism

aforo m capacity

afortunado adj fortunate, lucky

afrancesado adj Frenchified

afrenta f insult; (vergüenza) disgrace

África f Africa. **~ del Sur** South Africa

africano adj & m African

afrodisíaco adj & m aphrodisiac

afrontar vt bring face to face; (enfrentar) face, confront

afuera adv out(side) **¡~!** out of the way! **~ de** (LAm) outside. **~s** fpl outskirts

agachar vt lower. **~se** vpr bend over

agalla f (de los peces) gill. **~s** fpl (fig) guts

agarradera f (LAm) handle

agarr|ado adj (fig, fam) mean. **~ar** vt grasp; (esp LAm) take; (LAm, pillar) catch. **~arse** vpr hold on; (fam, reñirse) have a fight. **~ón** m tug; (LAm, riña) row

agarrotar vt tie tightly; (el frío) stiffen; garotte (un reo). **~se** vpr go stiff; (Auto) seize up

agasaj|ado m guest of honour. **~ar** vt look after well. **~o** m good treatment

agazaparse vpr crouch

agencia f agency. **~ de viajes** travel agency. **~ inmobiliaria** estate agency (Brit), real estate agency (Amer). **~rse** vpr find (out) for o.s.

agenda f diary (Brit), appointment book (Amer); (programa) agenda

agente m agent; (de policía) policeman. ●**f** agent; (de policía) policewoman. **~ de aduanas** customs officer. **~ de bolsa** stockbroker

ágil adj agile

agili|dad f agility. **~zación** f speeding up. **~zar** vt speed up

agita|ción f waving; (de un líquido) stirring; (*intranquilidad*) agitation. **∼do** *adj* (el mar) rough; (*fig*) agitated. **∼dor** *m* (*Pol*) agitator

agitar *vt* wave; shake (botellas etc); stir (líquidos); (*fig*) stir up. **∼se** *vpr* wave; (el mar) get rough; (*fig*) get excited

aglomera|ción *f* agglomeration; (*de tráfico*) traffic jam. **∼r** *vt* amass. **∼rse** *vpr* form a crowd

agnóstico *adj & m* agnostic

agobi|ante *adj* (trabajo) exhausting; (calor) oppressive. **∼ar** *vt* weigh down; (*fig*, abrumar) overwhelm. **∼o** *m* weight; (cansancio) exhaustion; (opresión) oppression

agolparse *vpr* crowd together

agon|ía *f* death throes; (*fig*) agony. **∼izante** *adj* dying; (luz) failing. **∼izar** 🔟 *vi* be dying

agosto *m* August. hacer su **∼** feather one's nest

agota|do *adj* exhausted; (todo vendido) sold out; (libro) out of print. **∼dor** *adj* exhausting. **∼miento** *m* exhaustion. **∼r** *vt* exhaust. **∼rse** *vpr* be exhausted; (existencias) sell out; (libro) go out of print

agracia|do *adj* attractive; (que tiene suerte) lucky. **∼r** *vt* make attractive

agrada|ble *adj* pleasant, nice. **∼r** *vt/i* please. esto me **∼** I like this

agradec|er 🔟 *vt* thank (persona); be grateful for (cosa). **∼ido** *adj* grateful. ¡muy **∼ido**! thanks a lot! **∼imiento** *m* gratitude

agrado *m* pleasure; (amabilidad) friendliness

agrandar *vt* enlarge; (*fig*) exaggerate. **∼se** *vpr* get bigger

agrario *adj* agrarian, land; (política) agricultural

agrava|nte *adj* aggravating. ● *f* additional problem. **∼r** *vt* aggravate; (aumentar el peso) make heavier. **∼rse** *vpr* get worse

agravi|ar *vt* offend; (perjudicar) wrong. **∼o** *m* offence

agredir 🔢 *vt* attack. **∼ de palabra** insult

agrega|do *m* aggregate; (diplomático) attaché. **∼r** 🔢 *vt* add; appoint (persona). **∼rse** *vpr* to join

agres|ión *f* aggression; (ataque) attack. **∼ividad** *f* aggressiveness. **∼ivo** *adj* aggressive. **∼or** *m* aggressor

agreste *adj* country; (terreno) rough

agriar *regular, o raramente* 🔢 *vt* sour. **∼se** *vpr* turn sour; (*fig*) become embittered

agr|ícola *adj* agricultural. **∼icultor** *m* farmer. **∼icultura** *f* agriculture, farming

agridulce *adj* bitter-sweet; (Culin) sweet-and-sour

agrietar *vt* crack. **∼se** *vpr* crack; (piel) chap

agrio *adj* sour. **∼s** *mpl* citrus fruits

agro|nomía *f* agronomy. **∼pecuario** *adj* farming

agrupa|ción *f* group; (acción) grouping. **∼r** *vt* group. **∼rse** *vpr* form a group

agruras *fpl* (Mex) heartburn

agua *f* water; (lluvia) rain; (marea) tide; (vertiente del tejado) slope. **∼ abajo** downstream. **∼ arriba** upstream. **∼ bendita** holy water. **∼ corriente** running water. **∼ de colonia** eau de cologne. **∼ dulce** fresh water. **∼ mineral con gas** fizzy mineral water. **∼ mineral sin gas** still mineral water. **∼ potable**

drinking water. ~ **salada** salt water. **hacer** ~ (*Naut*) leak. **se me hizo** ~ **la boca** (*LAm*) my mouth watered

aguacate *m* avocado pear; (*árbol*) avocado pear tree

aguacero *m* downpour, heavy shower

aguado *adj* watery; (*Mex, aburrido*) boring

agua|fiestas *m & f invar* spoil-sport, wet blanket. ~**mala** *f* (*Mex*), ~**mar** *m* jellyfish. ~**marina** *f* aquamarine

aguant|ar *vt* put up with, bear; (*sostener*) support. ● *vi* hold out. ~**arse** *vpr* restrain o.s. ~**e** *m* patience; (*resistencia*) endurance

aguar 🔟 *vt* water down

aguardar *vt* wait for. ● *vi* wait

agua|rdiente *m* (cheap) brandy. ~**rrás** *m* turpentine, turps 🔟

agud|eza *f* sharpness; (*fig, perspicacia*) insight; (*fig, ingenio*) wit. ~**izar** 🔟 *vt* sharpen. ~**izarse** *vpr* (*enfermedad*) get worse. ~**o** *adj* sharp; (*ángulo, enfermedad*) acute; (*voz*) high-pitched

agüero *m* omen. **ser de mal** ~ be a bad omen

aguijón *m* sting; (*vara*) goad

águila *f* eagle; (*persona perspicaz*) astute person; (*Mex, de moneda*) heads. **¿~ o sol?** heads or tails?

aguileño *adj* aquiline

aguinaldo *m* Christmas box; (*LAm, paga*) Christmas bonus

aguja *f* needle; (*del reloj*) hand; (*de torre*) steeple. ~**s** *fpl* (*Rail*) points

agujer|ear *vt* make holes in. ~**o** *m* hole

agujetas *fpl* stiffness; (*Mex, de zapatos*) shoe laces. **tener** ~ be stiff

aguzado *adj* sharp

ah *int* ah!, oh!

ahí *adv* there. ~ **nomás** (*LAm*) just there. **de** ~ **que** that is why. **por** ~ that way; (*aproximadamente*) thereabouts

ahija|da *f* god-daughter, godchild. ~**do** *m* godson, godchild. ~**dos** *mpl* godchildren

ahínco *m* enthusiasm; (*empeño*) insistence

ahog|ado *adj* (*en el agua*) drowned; (*asfixiado*) suffocated. ~**ar** 🔟 *vt* (*en el agua*) drown; (*asfixiar*) suffocate; put out (*fuego*). ~**arse** *vpr* (*en el agua*) drown; (*asfixiarse*) suffocate. ~**o** *m* breathlessness; (*fig, angustia*) distress

ahondar *vt* deepen. ● *vi* go deep. ~ **en** (*fig*) examine in depth. ~**se** *vpr* get deeper

ahora *adv* now; (*hace muy poco*) just now; (*dentro de poco*) very soon. ~ **bien** however. ~ **mismo** right now. **de** ~ **en adelante** from now on, in future. **por** ~ for the time being

ahorcar 🔟 *vt* hang. ~**se** *vpr* hang o.s.

ahorita *adv* (*esp LAm fam*) now. ~ **mismo** right now

ahorr|ador *adj* thrifty. ~**ar** *vt* save. ~**arse** *vpr* save o.s. ~**o** *m* saving. ~**os** *mpl* savings

ahuecar 🔟 *vt* hollow; fluff up (*colchón*); deepen (*la voz*)

ahuizote *m* (*Mex*) scourge

ahuma|do *adj* (*Culin*) smoked; (*de colores*) smoky. ~**r** *vt* (*Culin*) smoke; (*llenar de humo*) fill with smoke. ● *vi* smoke. ~**rse** *vpr* become smoky; (*comida*) acquire a smoky taste

ahuyentar *vt* drive away; banish (*pensamientos etc*)

aimará adj & m Aymara. ●m & f Aymara indian

airado adj annoyed

aire m air; (viento) breeze; (corriente) draught; (aspecto) appearance; (Mus) tune, air. ~ acondicionado air-conditioning. al ~ libre outdoors. darse ~s give o.s. airs. ~ar vt air; (ventilar) ventilate; (fig, publicar) make public. ~arse vpr. salir para ~arse go out for some fresh air

airoso adj graceful; (exitoso) successful

aisla|do adj isolated; (Elec) insulated. ~dor adj (Elec) insulating. ~nte adj insulating. ~r 28 vt isolate; (Elec) insulate

ajar vt crumple; (estropear) spoil

ajedre|cista m & f chess-player. ~z m chess

ajeno adj (de otro) someone else's; (de otros) other people's; (extraño) alien

ajetre|ado adj hectic, busy. ~o m bustle

ají m (LAm) chilli; (salsa) chilli sauce

aj|illo m garlic. al ~illo cooked with garlic. ~o m garlic. ~onjolí m sesame

ajuar m furnishings; (de novia) trousseau; (de bebé) layette

ajust|ado adj right; (vestido) tight. ~ar vt fit; (adaptar) adapt; (acordar) agree; settle (una cuenta); (apretar) tighten. ● vi fit. ~arse vpr fit; (adaptarse) adapt o.s.; (acordarse) come to an agreement. ~e m fitting; (adaptación) adjustment; (acuerdo) agreement; (de una cuenta) settlement

al = a + el

ala f wing; (de sombrero) brim. ●m & f (deportes) winger

alaba|nza f praise. ~r vt praise

alacena f cupboard (Brit), closet (Amer)

alacrán m scorpion

alambr|ada f wire fence. ~ado m (LAm) wire fence. ~e m wire. ~e de púas barbed wire

alameda f avenue; (plantío de álamos) poplar grove

álamo m poplar. ~ temblón aspen

alarde m show. hacer ~ de boast of

alarga|do adj long. ~dor m extension. ~r 12 vt lengthen; stretch out (mano etc); (dar) give, pass. ~rse vpr get longer

alarido m shriek

alarm|a f alarm. ~ante adj alarming. ~ar vt alarm, frighten. ~arse vpr be alarmed. ~ista m & f alarmist

alba f dawn

albacea m & f executor

albahaca f basil

albanés adj & m Albanian

Albania f Albania

albañil m builder; (que coloca ladrillos) bricklayer

albarán m delivery note

albaricoque m apricot. ~ro m apricot tree

albedrío m will. libre ~ free will

alberca f tank, reservoir; (Mex, piscina) swimming pool

alberg|ar 12 vt (alojar) put up; (vivienda) house; (dar refugio) shelter. ~arse vpr stay; (refugiarse) shelter. ~ue m accommodation; (refugio) shelter. ~ue de juventud youth hostel

albino adj & m albino

albóndiga f meatball, rissole

albornoz m bathrobe

alborot|ado adj excited; (aturdido) hasty. **~ador** adj rowdy. ● m trouble-maker. **~ar** vt disturb, upset. ● vi make a racket. **~arse** vpr get excited; (el mar) get rough. **~o** m row, uproar

álbum m (pl **~es** o **~s**) album

alcachofa f artichoke

alcald|e m mayor. **~esa** f mayoress. **~ía** f mayoralty; (oficina) mayor's office

alcance m reach; (de arma, telescopio etc) range; (déficit) deficit

alcancía f money-box; (LAm, de niño) piggy bank

alcantarilla f sewer; (boca) drain

alcanzar ⑩ vt (llegar a) catch up; (coger) reach; catch (un autobús); (bala etc) strike, hit. ● vi reach; (ser suficiente) be enough. **~ a** manage

alcaparra f caper

alcázar m fortress

alcoba f bedroom

alcoh|ol m alcohol. **~ol desnaturalizado** methylated spirits, meths. **~ólico** adj & m alcoholic. **~olímetro** m Breathalyser . **~olismo** m alcoholism

alcornoque m cork-oak; (persona torpe) idiot

aldaba f door-knocker

aldea f village. **~no** adj village. ● m villager

alea|ción f alloy. **~r** vt alloy

aleatorio adj uncertain

aleccionar vt instruct

aledaños mpl outskirts

alega|ción f allegation; (LAm, disputa) argument. **~r** ⑫ vt claim; (Jurid) plead. ● vi (LAm) argue. **~ta** f (Mex) argument. **~to** m plea

alegoría f allegory

alegr|ar vt make happy; (avivar) brighten up. **~arse** vpr be happy; (emborracharse) get merry. **~e** adj happy; (achispado) merry, tight. **~ía** f happiness

aleja|do adj distant. **~miento** m removal; (entre personas) estrangement; (distancia) distance. **~r** vt remove; (ahuyentar) get rid of; (fig, apartar) separate. **~rse** vpr move away

alemán adj & m German

Alemania f Germany. **~ Occidental** (historia) West Germany. **~ Oriental** (historia) East Germany

alenta|do adj encouraging. **~r** ❶ vt encourage. ● vi breathe

alerce m larch

al|ergia f allergy. **~érgico** adj allergic

alero m (del tejado) eaves

alerta adj alert. **¡~!** look out! estar **~** be alert; (en guardia) be on the alert. **~r** vt alert

aleta f wing; (de pez) fin

aletarga|do adj lethargic. **~r** ⑫ vt make lethargic. **~rse** vpr become lethargic

alet|azo m (de un ave) flap of the wings; (de un pez) flick of the fin. **~ear** vi flap its wings, flutter

alevosía f treachery

alfab|ético adj alphabetical. **~etizar** ⑩ vt alphabetize; teach to read and write. **~eto** m alphabet. **~eto Morse** Morse code

alfalfa f alfalfa

alfar|ería f pottery. **~ero** m. potter

alféizar m (window)sill

alférez m second lieutenant

alfil m (en ajedrez) bishop

a

alfiler m pin. **~tero** m pincushion; (*estuche*) pin-case

alfombr|a f (*grande*) carpet; (*pequeña*) rug, mat. **~ado** adj (LAm) carpeted. **~ar** vt carpet. **~illa** f rug, mat; (*Med*) type of measles

alforja f saddle-bag

algarabía f hubbub

algas fpl seaweed

álgebra f algebra

álgido adj (*fig*) decisive

algo pron something; (*en frases interrogativas, condicionales*) anything. ● adv rather. ¿~ más? anything else? ¿quieres tomar ~? would you like a drink?; (*de comer*) would you like something to eat?

algod|ón m cotton. **~ón de azúcar** candy floss (Brit), cotton candy (Amer). **~ón hidrófilo** cotton wool. **~onero** adj cotton. ● m cotton plant

alguacil m bailiff

alguien pron someone, somebody; (*en frases interrogativas, condicionales*) anyone, anybody

algún *véase* ALGUNO

alguno adj (*delante de nombres masculinos en singular* algún) some; (*en frases interrogativas, condicionales*) any; (*pospuesto al nombre en frases negativas*) at all. no tiene idea alguna he hasn't any idea at all. alguna que otra vez from time to time. algunas veces, alguna vez sometimes. ● pron one; (*en plural*) some; (*alguien*) someone

alhaja f piece of jewellery; (*fig*) treasure. **~s** fpl jewellery

alharaca f fuss

alhelí m wallflower

alia|do adj allied. ● m ally. **~nza** f alliance; (*anillo*) wedding ring. **~r**

20 vt combine. **~rse** vpr be combined; (*formar una alianza*) form an alliance

alias adv & m alias

alicaído adj (*fig, débil*) weak; (*fig, abatido*) depressed

alicates mpl pliers

aliciente m incentive; (*de un lugar*) attraction

alienado adj mentally ill

aliento m breath; (*ánimo*) courage

aligerar vt make lighter; (*aliviar*) alleviate, ease; (*apresurar*) quicken

alijo m (*de contrabando*) consignment

alimaña f pest. **~s** fpl vermin

aliment|ación f diet; (*acción*) feeding. **~ar** vt feed; (*nutrir*) nourish. ● vi be nourishing. **~arse** vpr feed (con, de on). **~icio** adj nourishing. productos mpl **~icios** foodstuffs. **~o** m food. **~os** mpl (*Jurid*) alimony

alinea|ción f alignment; (*en deportes*) line-up. **~r** vt align, line up

aliñ|ar vt (*Culin*) season; dress (*ensalada*). **~o** m seasoning; (*para ensalada*) dressing

alioli m garlic mayonnaise

alisar vt smooth

alistar vt put on a list; (*Mil*) enlist. **~se** vpr enrol; (*Mil*) enlist; (*LAm, prepararse*) get ready

alivi|ar vt lighten; relieve (*dolor, etc*); (*arg, hurtar*) steal, pinch 🆈. **~arse** vpr (*dolor*) diminish; (*persona*) get better. **~o** m relief

aljibe m tank

allá adv (*over*) there. ¡~ él! that's his business! ~ fuera out there. ~ por 1970 back in 1970. el más ~ the beyond. más ~ further on. más ~ de beyond. por ~ that way

allana|miento m. ~miento (de morada) breaking and entering; (LAm, por la autoridad) raid. ~r vt level; remove (obstáculos); (fig) iron out (dificultades etc); break into (una casa); (LAm, por la autoridad) raid

allega|do adj close. ● m close friend; (pariente) close relative. ~r 🔟 vt collect

allí adv there; (tiempo) then. ~ fuera out there. por ~ that way

alma f soul; (habitante) inhabitant

almac|én m warehouse; (LAm, tienda) grocer's shop; (de un arma) magazine. ~enes mpl department store. ~enaje m storage; (derechos) storage charges. ~enar vt store; stock up with (provisiones)

almanaque m almanac

almeja f clam

almendr|a f almond. ~ado adj almond-shaped. ~o m almond tree

alm|íbar m syrup. ~ibarar vt cover in syrup

almidón m starch. ~onado adj starched; (fig, estirado) starchy

almirante m admiral

almizcle m musk. ~ra f muskrat

almohad|a f pillow. consultar con la ~a sleep on it. ~illa f small cushion. ~ón m large pillow, bolster

almorranas fpl haemorrhoids, piles

alm|orzar 🔢 & 🔟 vt (a mediodía) have for lunch; (desayunar) have for breakfast. ● vi (a mediodía) have lunch; (desayunar) have breakfast. ~uerzo m (a mediodía) lunch; (desayuno) breakfast

alocado adj scatter-brained

aloja|miento m accommoda-

tion. ~r vt put up. ~rse vpr stay

alondra f lark

alpaca f alpaca

alpargata f canvas shoe, espadrille

alpin|ismo m mountaineering, climbing. ~ista m & f mountaineer, climber. ~o adj Alpine

alpiste m birdseed

alquil|ar vt (tomar en alquiler) hire (vehículo), rent (piso, casa); (dar en alquiler) hire (out) (vehículo), rent (out) (piso, casa). se alquila to let (Brit), for rent (Amer.). ~er m (acción — de alquilar un piso etc) renting; (— de alquilar un vehículo) hiring; (precio — por el que se alquila un piso etc) rent; (— por el que se alquila un vehículo) hire charge. de ~er for hire

alquimi|a f alchemy. ~sta m alchemist

alquitrán m tar

alrededor adv around. ~ de around; (con números) about. ~es mpl surroundings; (de una ciudad) outskirts

alta f discharge

altaner|ía f (arrogancia) arrogance. ~o adj arrogant, haughty

altar m altar

altavoz m loudspeaker

altera|ble adj changeable. ~ción f change, alteration. ~r vt change, alter; (perturbar) disturb; (enfadar) anger, irritate. ~rse vpr change, alter; (agitarse) get upset; (enfadarse) get angry; (comida) go off

altercado m argument

altern|ar vt/i alternate. ~arse vpr take turns. ~ativa f alternative. ~ativo adj alternating. ~o adj alternate; (Elec) alternating

Alteza f (título) Highness

a **altibajos** *mpl* (*de terreno*) unevenness; (*fig*) ups and downs

altiplanicie *f,* **altiplano** *m* high
plateau

altisonante *adj* pompous

altitud *f* altitude

altiv|ez *f* arrogance. **~o** *adj* arro-
gant

alto *adj* high; (persona, edificio)
tall; (voz) loud; (*fig, elevado*) lofty;
(*Mus*) (nota) high(-pitched); (*Mus*)
(voz, instrumento) alto; (horas)
early. ● *adv* high; (*de sonidos*)
loud(ly). ● *m* height; (*de un edificio*) top floor; (*viola*) viola; (voz)
alto; (*parada*) stop. ● *int* halt!,
stop! en lo **~** de on the top of.
tiene 3 metros de ~ it is 3
metres high

altoparlante *m* (*esp LAm*) loudspeaker

altruis|mo *m* altruism. **~ta** *adj*
altruistic. ● *m & f* altruist

altura *f* height; (*Aviac, Geog*) altitude; (*de agua*) depth; (*fig, cielo*)
sky. **a estas ~s** at this stage.
tiene 3 metros de ~ it is 3
metres high

alubia *f* (haricot) bean

alucinación *f* hallucination

alud *m* avalanche

aludi|do *adj* in question. **darse
por ~do** take it personally. **no
darse por ~do** turn a deaf ear.
~r *vi* mention

alumbra|do *adj* lit. ● *m* lighting.
~miento *m* lighting; (*parto*) child-
birth. **~r** *vt* light

aluminio *m* aluminium (*Brit*), aluminum (*Amer*)

alumno *m* pupil; (*Univ*) student

aluniza|je *m* landing on the
moon. **~r** ⑩ *vi* land on the moon

alusi|ón *f* allusion. **~vo** *adj*
allusive

alza *f* rise. **~da** *f* (*de caballo*) height; (*Jurid*) appeal. **~do** *adj*
raised; (*Mex, soberbio*) vain; (*pre-
cio*) fixed. **~miento** *m* (*Pol*) uprising. **~r** ⑩ *vt* raise, lift (up); raise
(*precios*). **~rse** *vpr* (*Pol*) rise up

ama *f* lady of the house. **~ de
casa** housewife. **~ de cría** wet-
nurse. **~ de llaves** housekeeper

amab|ilidad *f* kindness. **~le** *adj*
kind; (*simpático*) nice

amaestra|do *adj* trained. **~r** *vt*
train

amag|ar ⑫ *vt* (*mostrar intención
de*) make as if to; (*Mex, amenazar*)
threaten. ● *vi* threaten; (*algo
bueno*) be in the offing. **~o** *m*
threat; (*señal*) sign; (*Med*) symptom

amainar *vi* let up

amalgama *f* amalgam. **~r** *vt*
amalgamate

amamantar *vt/i* breast-feed;
(*animal*) to suckle

amanecer *m* dawn. ● *vi* dawn;
(persona) wake up. **al ~** at dawn,
at daybreak. **~se** *vpr* (*Mex*) stay up
all night

amanera|do *adj* affected. **~rse**
vpr become affected

amansar *vt* tame; break in (un
caballo); soothe (dolor etc). **~se**
vpr calm down

amante *adj* fond. ● *m & f* lover

amapola *f* poppy

amar *vt* love

amara|je *m* landing on water; (*de
astronave*) splash-down. **~r** *vi* land
on water; (astronave) splash down

amarg|ado *adj* embittered. **~ar**
⑫ *vt* make bitter; embitter (persona). **~arse** *vpr* become bitter.
~o *adj* bitter. **~ura** *f* bitterness

amariconado *adj* ① effeminate

amarill|ento adj yellowish; (tez) sallow. **~o** adj & m yellow

amarra|s fpl. soltar las **~s** cast off. **~do** adj (LAm) mean. **~r** vt moor; (esp LAm, atar) tie. **~rse** vpr LAm tie up

amas|ar vt knead; (acumular) to amass. **~ijo** m dough; (acción) kneading; (fig, fam, mezcla) hotch-potch

amate m (Mex) fig tree

amateur adj & m & f amateur

amazona f Amazon; (jinete) horsewoman

ámbar m amber

ambici|ón f ambition. **~onar** vt aspire to. **~onar ser** have an ambition to be. **~oso** adj ambitious. ● m ambitious person

ambidextro adj ambidextrous. ● m ambidextrous person

ambient|ar vt give an atmosphere to. **~arse** vpr adapt o.s. **~e** m atmosphere; (entorno) environment

ambig|üedad f ambiguity. **~uo** adj ambiguous

ámbito m sphere; (alcance) scope

ambos adj & pron both

ambulancia f ambulance

ambulante adj travelling

ambulatorio m out-patients' department

amedrentar vt frighten, scare. **~se** vpr be frightened

amén m amen. ● int amen! **en un decir ~** in an instant

amenaza f threat. **~r** 10 vt threaten

amen|idad f pleasantness. **~izar** 10 vt brighten up. **~o** adj pleasant

América f America. **~ Central**

Central America. **~ del Norte** North America. **~ del Sur** South America. **~ Latina** Latin America

american|a f jacket. **~ismo** m Americanism. **~o** adj American

amerita|do adj (LAm) meritorious. **~r** vt (LAm) deserve

amerizaje m véase AMARAJE

ametralla|dora f machine-gun. **~r** vt machine-gun

amianto m asbestos

amig|a f friend; (novia) girl-friend; (amante) lover. **~able** adj friendly. **~ablemente** adv amicably

am|ígdala f tonsil. **~igdalitis** f tonsillitis

amigo adj friendly. ● m friend; (novio) boyfriend; (amante) lover. **ser ~ de** be fond of. **ser muy ~s** be close friends

amilanar vt daunt. **~se** vpr be daunted

aminorar vt lessen; reduce (velocidad)

amist|ad f friendship. **~ades** fpl friends. **~oso** adj friendly

amn|esia f amnesia. **~ésico** adj amnesiac

amnist|ía f amnesty. **~iar** 20 vt grant an amnesty to

amo m master; (dueño) owner

amodorrarse vpr feel sleepy

amoldar vt mould; (adaptar) adapt; (acomodar) fit. **~se** vpr adapt

amonestar vt rebuke, reprimand; (anunciar la boda) publish the banns

amoniaco, amoníaco m ammonia

amontonar vt pile up; (fig, acumular) accumulate. **~se** vpr pile up; (gente) crowd together

amor *m* love. ~**es** *mpl* (*relaciones amorosas*) love affairs. ~ **propio** pride. **con mil** ~**es**, **de mil** ~**es** with (the greatest of) pleasure. **hacer el** ~ make love. **por (el)** ~ **de Dios** for God's sake

amoratado *adj* purple; (*de frío*) blue

amordazar 10 *vt* gag; (*fig*) silence

amorfo *adj* amorphous, shapeless

amor|ío *m* affair. ~**oso** *adj* loving; (*cartas*) love; (*LAm*), *encantador*) cute

amortajar *vt* shroud

amortigua|dor *adj* deadening. ● *m* (*Auto*) shock absorber. ~**r** 15 *vt* deaden (*ruido*); dim (*luz*); cushion (*golpe*); tone down (*color*)

amortiza|ble *adj* redeemable. ~**ción** *f* (*de una deuda*) repayment; (*de bono etc*) redemption. ~**r** 10 *vt* repay (*una deuda*)

amotinar *vt* incite to riot. ~**se** *vpr* rebel; (*Mil*) mutiny

ampar|ar *vt* help; (*proteger*) protect. ~**arse** *vpr* seek protection; (*de la lluvia*) shelter. ~**o** *m* protection; (*de la lluvia*) shelter. **al** ~**o de** under the protection of

amperio *m* ampere, amp 𝕀

amplia|ción *f* extension; (*photo*) enlargement. ~**r** 20 *vt* enlarge, extend; (*photo*) enlarge

amplifica|ción *f* amplification. ~**dor** *m* amplifier. ~**r** 7 amplify

ampli|o *adj* wide; (*espacioso*) spacious; (*ropa*) loose-fitting. ~**tud** *f* extent; (*espaciosidad*) spaciousness; (*espacio*) space

ampolla *f* (*Med*) blister; (*de medicamento*) ampoule, phial

ampuloso *adj* pompous

amputar *vt* amputate; (*fig*) delete

amueblar *vt* furnish

amuleto *m* charm, amulet

amuralla|do *adj* walled. ~**r** *vt* build a wall around

anacr|ónico *adj* anachronistic. ~**onismo** *m* anachronism

anales *mpl* annals

analfabet|ismo *m* illiteracy. ~**o** *adj & m* illiterate

analgésico *adj* analgesic. ● *m* painkiller

an|álisis *m invar* analysis. ~**álisis de sangre** blood test. ~**alista** *m & f* analyst. ~**alítico** *adj* analytical. ~**alizar** 10 *vt* analyze

an|alogía *f* analogy. ~**álogo** *adj* analogous

anaranjado *adj* orangey

an|arquía *f* anarchy. ~**árquico** *adj* anarchic. ~**arquismo** *m* anarchism. ~**arquista** *adj* anarchistic. ● *m & f* anarchist

anat|omía *f* anatomy. ~**ómico** *adj* anatomical

anca *f* haunch; (*parte superior*) rump; (*fam, nalgas*) bottom. **en** ~**s** (*LAm*) on the crupper

ancestro *m* ancestor

ancho *adj* wide; (*ropa*) loosefitting; (*demasiado grande*) too big; (*ufano*) smug. ● *m* width; (*Rail*) gauge. ~ **de banda** bandwidth. **tiene 3 metros de** ~ it is 3 metres wide

anchoa *f* anchovy

anchura *f* width; (*medida*) measurement

ancian|o *adj* elderly, old. ● *m* elderly man, old man. ~**a** *f* elderly woman, old woman. **los** ~**os** old people

ancla *f* anchor. **echar** ~**s** drop anchor. **levar** ~**s** weigh anchor. ~**r** *vi* anchor

andad|eras *fpl* (Mex) baby-walker. ~**or** *m* baby-walker

Andalucía *f* Andalusia

andaluz *adj & m* Andalusian

andamio *m* platform. ~**s** *mpl* scaffolding

and|anzas *fpl* adventures. ~**ar** 25 *vt* (recorrer) cover, go. ● *vi* walk; (máquina) go, work; (estar) be; (moverse) move. ~**ar a caballo** (LAm) ride a horse. ~**ar en bicicleta** (LAm) ride a bicycle. ¡anda! go on!, come on! ~**ar por** be about. ~**arse** *vpr* (LAm, en imperativo) ¡andate! go away! ● *m* walk. ~**ariego** *adj* fond of walking

andén *m* platform

Andes *mpl.* los ~ the Andes

andin|o *adj* Andean. ~**ismo** *m* (LAm) mountaineering, climbing. ~**ista** *m & f* (LAm) mountaineer, climber

andrajo *m* rag. ~**so** *adj* ragged

anduve *vb* véase **ANDAR**

anécdota *f* anecdote

anecdótico *adj* anecdotal

anegar 12 *vt* flood. ~**se** *vpr* be flooded, flood

anejo *adj* véase **ANEXO**

an|emia *f* anaemia. ~**émico** *adj* anaemic

anest|esia *f* anaesthesia; (droga) anaesthetic. ~**esiar** *vt* anaesthetize. ~**ésico** *adj & m* anaesthetic. ~**esista** *m & f* anaesthetist

anex|ar *vt* annex. ~**o** *adj* attached. ● *m* annexe

anfibio *adj* amphibious. ● *m* amphibian

anfiteatro *m* amphitheatre; (en un teatro) upper circle

anfitri|ón *m* host. ~**ona** *f* hostess

ángel *m* angel; (encanto) charm

angelical *adj*, **angélico** *adj* angelic

angina *f.* ~ **de pecho** angina (pectoris). **tener** ~**s** have tonsillitis

anglicano *adj & m* Anglican

angl|icismo *m* Anglicism. ~**ófilo** *adj & m* Anglophile. ~**ohispánico** *adj* Anglo-Spanish. ~**osajón** *adj & m* Anglo-Saxon

angosto *adj* narrow

angu|ila *f* eel. ~**la** *f* elver, baby eel

ángulo *m* angle; (rincón, esquina) corner; (curva) bend

angusti|a *f* anguish. ~**ar** *vt* distress; (inquietar) worry. ~**arse** *vpr* get distressed; (inquietarse) get worried. ~**oso** *adj* anguished; (que causa angustia) distressing

anhel|ar *vt* (+ nombre) long for; (+ verbo) long to. ~**o** *m* (fig) yearning

anidar *vi* nest

anill|a *f* ring. ~**o** *m* ring. ~**o de boda** wedding ring

ánima *f* soul

anima|ción *f* (de personas) life; (de cosas) liveliness; (bullicio) bustle; (en el cine) animation. ~**do** *adj* lively; (sitio etc) busy. ~**dor** *m* host. ~**dora** *f* hostess; (de un equipo) cheerleader

animadversión *f* ill will

animal *adj* animal; (fig, fam, torpe) stupid. ● *m* animal; (fig, fam, idiota) idiot; (fig, fam, bruto) brute

animar *vt* give life to; (dar ánimo) encourage; (dar vivacidad) liven up. ~**se** *vpr* (decidirse) decide; (ponerse alegre) cheer up. **¿te animas a ir al cine?** do you feel like going to the cinema?

ánimo *m* soul; (mente) mind; (valor) courage; (intención) inten-

a tion. ¡~! come on!, cheer up! dar
~s encourage

animos|idad f animosity. ● **~o** adj
brave; (*resuelto*) determined

aniquilar vt annihilate; (*acabar
con*) ruin

anís m aniseed; (*licor*) anisette

aniversario m anniversary

anoche adv last night, yesterday
evening

anochecer 🔟 vi get dark. ano-
checí en Madrid I was in Madrid
at dusk. ● m nightfall, dusk. al ~
at nightfall

anodino adj bland

an|omalía f anomaly. **~ómalo**
adj anomalous

an|onimato m anonymity.
~ónimo adj anonymous; (*sociedad*) limited. ● m (*carta*) anonymous letter

anormal adj abnormal. ● m & f 🔟
idiot. **~idad** f abnormality

anota|ción f (*nota*) note; (*acción
de poner notas*) annotation. **~r** vt
(*poner nota*) annotate; (*apuntar*)
make a note of; (*LAm*) score (un
gol)

anquilosa|miento m (*fig*) paral-
ysis. **~rse** vpr become paralyzed

ansia f anxiety, worry; (*anhelo*)
yearning. **~r** 🔟 vt long for.
~edad f anxiety. **~oso** adj anx-
ious; (*deseoso*) eager

antagónico adj antagonistic.
~onismo m antagonism. **~onista**
m & f antagonist

antaño adv in days gone by

antártico adj & m Antarctic

ante prep in front of, before;
(*frente a*) in the face of; (*en vista
de*) in view of. ● m elk; (*piel*)
suede. **~anoche** adv the night before last. **~ayer** adv the day before

yesterday. **~brazo** m forearm

ante|cedente adj previous. ● m
antecedent. **~dentes** mpl history,
background. **~dentes penales**
criminal record. **~der** vt precede.
~sor m predecessor; (*antepasado*)
ancestor

antelación f (*advance*) notice.
con ~ in advance

antemano adv. de ~ beforehand

antena f antenna; (*radio, TV*) aerial

anteojeras fpl blinkers. **~o** m
telescope. **~os** mpl binoculars;
(*LAm, gafas*) glasses, spectacles.
~os de sol sunglasses

ante|pasados mpl forebears, an-
cestors. **~poner** 🔢 vt put in front
(a of); (*fig*) put before, prefer.
~proyecto m preliminary sketch;
(*fig*) blueprint

anterior adj previous; (*delantero*)
front. **~idad** f. con ~idad previously. con ~idad a prior to

antes adv before; (*antiguamente*) in
the past; (*mejor*) rather; (*primero*)
first. ~ de before. ~ de que +
subjuntivo before. ~ de que llegue
before he arrives. cuanto ~, lo ~
posible as soon as possible

anti|aéreo adj anti-aircraft.
~biótico adj & m antibiotic. **~ci-
clón** m anticyclone

anticipa|ción f. con ~ación in
advance. con media hora de
~ación half an hour early. **~ado**
adj advance. por ~ado in advance.
~ar vt bring forward; advance (*dinero*). **~arse** vpr be early. **~o** m
(*dinero*) advance; (*fig*) foretaste

anti|conceptivo adj & m contraceptive. ~ **de emergencia** morning-after pill. **~congelante** m antifreeze

anticua|do adj old-fashioned. **~rio** m antique dealer

anticuerpo m antibody

antídoto m antidote

anti|estético adj ugly. **~faz** m mask

antig|ualla f old relic. **~uamente** adv formerly; (*hace mucho tiempo*) long ago. **~üedad** f antiquity; (*objeto*) antique; (*en un empleo*) length of service. **~uo** adj old; (*ruinas*) ancient; (*mueble*) antique

Antillas fpl. las ~ the West Indies

antílope m antelope

antinatural adj unnatural

antipa|tía f dislike; (*cualidad de antipático*) unpleasantness. **~ático** adj unpleasant, unfriendly

anti|semita m & f anti-Semite. **~séptico** adj & m antiseptic. **~social** adj antisocial

antítesis f invar antithesis

antoj|adizo adj capricious. **~arse** vpr fancy. se le ~a un caramelo he fancies a sweet. **~itos** mpl (Mex) snacks bought at street stands. **~o** m whim; (*de embarazada*) craving

antología f anthology

antorcha f torch

ántrax m anthrax

antro m (*fig*) dump, hole. ~ **de perversión** den of iniquity

antrop|ología f anthropology. **~ólogo** m anthropologist

anual adj annual. **~lidad** f annuity. **~lmente** adv yearly. **~rio** m yearbook

anudar vt tie, knot. **~se** vpr tie

anula|ción f annulment, cancellation. **~r** vt annul, cancel. ● adj (*dedo*) ring. ● m ring finger

anunci|ante m & f advertiser. **~ar** vt announce; advertise (*producto comercial*); (*presagiar*) be a sign of. **~o** m announcement; (*para vender algo*) advertisement, advert 🔟; (*cartel*) poster

anzuelo m (fish)hook; (*fig*) bait. tragar el ~ swallow the bait

añadi|dura f addition. por ~dura in addition. **~r** vt add

añejo adj (*vino*) mature

añicos mpl. hacer(se) ~ smash to pieces

año m year. ~ **bisiesto** leap year. ~ **nuevo** new year. al ~ per year, a year. ¿**cuántos** ~s **tiene?** how old is he? **tiene 5** ~s he's 5 (years old). el ~ **pasado** last year. el ~ **que viene** next year. **entrado en** ~s elderly. **los** ~ **60** the sixties

añora|nza f nostalgia. **~r** vt miss

apabulla|nte adj overwhelming. **~r** vt overwhelm

apacible adj gentle; (*clima*) mild

apacigua|r 🔢 vt pacify; (*calmar*) calm; relieve (*dolor* etc). **~rse** vpr calm down

apadrinar vt sponsor; be godfather to (*a un niño*)

apag|ado adj extinguished; (*color*) dull; (*aparato eléctrico, luz*) off; (*persona*) lifeless; (*sonido*) muffled. **~ar** 🔢 vt put out (*fuego, incendio*); turn off, switch off (*aparato eléctrico, luz*); quench (*sed*); muffle (*sonido*). **~arse** vpr (*fuego, luz*) go out; (*sonido*) die away. **~ón** m blackout

apalabrar vt make a verbal agreement; (*contratar*) engage

apalear vt winnow (*grano*); beat

a

apantallar vt (Mex) impress

apañar vt (arreglar) fix; (remendar) mend; (agarrar) grasp, take hold of. **~se** vpr get along, manage

apapachar vt (Mex) cuddle

aparador m sideboard; (Mex, de tienda) shop window

aparato m apparatus; (máquina) machine; (doméstico) appliance; (teléfono) telephone; (radio, TV) set; (ostentación) show, pomp. **~so** adj showy, ostentatious; (caída) spectacular

aparca|miento m car park (Brit), parking lot (Amer). **~r 7** vt/i park

aparear vt mate (animales). **~se** vpr mate

aparecer 11 vi appear. **~se** vpr appear

aparej|ado adj. llevar **~ado**, traer **~ado** mean, entail. **~o** m (avíos) equipment; (de caballo) tack; (de pesca) tackle

aparent|ar vt (afectar) feign; (parecer) look. ● vi show off. **~a 20 años** she looks like she's 20. **~e** adj apparent

apari|ción f appearance; (visión) apparition. **~encia** f appearance; (fig) show. guardar las **~encias** keep up appearances

apartado adj separated; (aislado) isolated. ● m (de un texto) section. **~ (de correos)** post-office box, PO box

apartamento m apartment, flat (Brit)

apart|ar vt separate; (alejar) move away; (quitar) remove; (guardar) set aside. **~arse** vpr leave; (quitarse de en medio) get out of the way; (aislarse) cut o.s. off. **~e** adv apart; (por separado) separately; (además)

besides. ● m aside; (párrafo) new paragraph. **~e de** apart from. **dejar ~e** leave aside. **eso ~e** apart from that

apasiona|do adj passionate; (entusiasta) enthusiastic; (falto de objetividad) biased. ● m. **~do** de lover. **~miento** m passion. **~r** vt excite. **~rse** vpr be mad (por about); (ser parcial) become biased

ap|atía f apathy. **~ático** adj apathetic

apea|dero m (Rail) halt. **~rse** vpr get off

apechugar 12 vi. **1** **~ con** put up with

apedrear vt stone

apeg|ado adj attached (a to). **~o** m **1** attachment. tener **~o** a be fond of

apela|ción f appeal. **~r** vi appeal; (recurrir) resort (a to). ● vt (apodar) call. **~tivo** m (nick)name

apellid|ar vt call. **~arse** vpr be called. ¿cómo te apellidas? what's your surname? **~o** m surname

apelmazarse vpr (lana) get matted

apenar vt sadden; (LAm, avergonzar) embarrass. **~se** vpr be sad; (LAm, avergonzarse) be embarrassed

apenas adv hardly, scarcely; (Mex, sólo) only. ● conj (esp LAm, en cuanto) as soon as. **~ si 1** hardly

ap|éndice m appendix. **~endicitis** f appendicitis

apergaminado adj (piel) wrinkled

aperitivo m (bebida) aperitif; (comida) appetizer

aperos mpl implements; (de labranza) agricultural equipment; (LAm, de un caballo) tack

apertura f opening

apesadumbrar vt upset. **~se** vpr sadden

apestar vt infect. ● vi stink (a of)

apet|ecer 11 vi. ¿te **~ece una copa?** do you fancy a drink? do you feel like a drink? **no me ~ece** I don't feel like it. **~ecible** adj attractive. **~ito** m appetite; (fig) desire. **~itoso** adj appetizing

apiadarse vpr feel sorry (de for)

ápice m (nada, en frases negativas) anything. **no ceder un ~** not give an inch

apilar vt pile up

apiñar vt pack in. **~se** vpr (personas) crowd together; (cosas) be packed tight

apio m celery

aplacar 7 vt placate; soothe (dolor)

aplanar vt level. **~ calles** (LAm fam) loaf around

aplasta|nte adj overwhelming. **~r** vt crush. **~rse** vpr flatten o.s.

aplau|dir vt clap, applaud; (fig) applaud. **~so** m applause; (fig) praise

aplaza|miento m postponement. **~r** 10 vt postpone; defer (pago)

aplica|ble adj applicable. **~ción** f application. **~do** adj (persona) diligent. **~r** 7 vt apply. ● vi (LAm, a un puesto) apply (for). **~rse** vpr apply o.s.

aplom|ado adj composed. **~o** m composure

apocado adj timid

apocar 7 vt belittle (persona). **~se** vpr feel small

apodar vt nickname

apodera|do m representative.

~rse vpr seize

apodo m nickname

apogeo m (fig) height

apolilla|do adj moth-eaten. **~rse** vpr get moth-eaten

apolítico adj non-political

apología f defence

apoltronarse vpr settle o.s. down

apoplejía f stroke

aporrear vt hit, thump; beat up (persona)

aporta|ción f contribution. **~ar** vt contribute. **~e** m (LAm) contribution

aposta adv on purpose

apostar¹ 2 vt/i bet

apostar² vt station. **~se** vpr station o.s.

apóstol m apostle

apóstrofo m apostrophe

apoy|ar vt lean (en against); (descansar) rest; (asentar) base; (reforzar) support. **~arse** vpr lean, rest. **~o** m support

apreci|able adj appreciable; (digno de estima) worthy. **~ación** f appreciation; (valoración) appraisal. **~ar** vt value; (estimar) appreciate. **~o** m appraisal; (fig) esteem

apremi|ante adj urgent, pressing. **~ar** vt urge; (obligar) compel; (dar prisa a) hurry up. ● vi be urgent. **~o** m urgency; (obligación) obligation

aprender vt/i learn. **~se** vpr learn

aprendiz m apprentice. **~aje** m learning; (período) apprenticeship

aprensi|ón f apprehension; (miedo) fear. **~vo** adj apprehensive, fearful

apresar vt seize; (capturar) capture

a **aprestar** vt prepare. ∼**se** vpr prepare

apresura|do adj in a hurry; (hecho con prisa) hurried. ∼**r** vt hurry. ∼**rse** vpr hurry up

apret|ado adj tight; (difícil) difficult; (tacaño) stingy, mean. ∼**ar** **1** vt tighten; press (botón); squeeze (persona); (comprimir) press down. ● vi be too tight. ∼**arse** vpr crowd together. ∼**ón** m squeeze. ∼**ón de manos** handshake

aprieto m difficulty. **verse en un** ∼ be in a tight spot

aprisa adv quickly

aprisionar vt trap

aproba|ción f approval. ∼**r** **2** vt approve (of); pass (examen). ● vi pass

apropia|ción f appropriation. ∼**do** adj appropriate. ∼**rse** vpr. ∼**rse de** appropriate, take

aprovecha|ble adj usable. ∼**do** adj (aplicado) diligent; (ingenioso) resourceful; (oportunista) opportunist. **bien** ∼**do** well spent. ∼**miento** m advantage; (uso) use. ∼**r** vt take advantage of; (utilizar) make use of. ● vi make the most of it. **¡que aproveche!** enjoy your meal! ∼**rse** vpr. ∼**rse de** take advantage of

aprovisionar vt provision (con, de with). ∼**se** vpr stock up

aproxima|ción f approximation; (proximidad) closeness; (en la lotería) consolation prize. ∼**damente** adv roughly, approximately. ∼**do** adj approximate, rough. ∼**r** vt bring near; (fig) bring together (personas). ∼**rse** vpr come closer, approach

apt|itud f suitability; (capacidad) ability. ∼**o** adj (capaz) capable;

(adecuado) suitable

apuesta f bet

apuesto m handsome. ● vb véase **APOSTAR** [1]

apuntalar vt shore up

apunt|ar vt aim (arma); (señalar) point at; (anotar) make a note of, note down; (inscribir) enrol; (en el teatro) prompt. ● vi (con un arma) to aim (a at). ∼**arse** vpr put one's name down; score (triunfo, tanto etc). ∼**e** m note; (bosquejo) sketch. **tomar** ∼**s** take notes

apuñalar vt stab

apur|ado adj difficult; (sin dinero) hard up; (LAm, con prisa) in a hurry. ∼**ar** vt (acabar) finish; drain (vaso etc); (causar vergüenza) embarrass; (LAm, apresurar) hurry. ∼**arse** vpr worry; (LAm, apresurarse) hurry up. ∼**o** m tight spot, difficult situation; (vergüenza) embarrassment; (estrechez) hardship, want; (LAm, prisa) hurry

aquejar vt afflict

aquel adj (f **aquella**, mpl **aquellos**, fpl **aquellas**) that; (en plural) those

aquél pron (f **aquélla**, mpl **aquéllos**, fpl **aquéllas**) that one; (en plural) those

aquello pron that; (asunto) that business

aquí adv here. **de** ∼ from here. **de** ∼ **a 15 días** in a fortnight's time. ∼ **mismo** right here. **de** ∼ **para allá** to and fro. **de** ∼ **que** that is why. **hasta** ∼ until now. **por** ∼ around here

aquietar vt calm (down)

árabe adj & m & f Arab; (lengua) Arabic

Arabia f Arabia. ∼ **Saudita**, ∼ **Saudí** Saudi Arabia

arado m plough. ∼**r** m ploughman

arancel m tariff; (*impuesto*) duty. ~**ario** adj tariff

arándano m blueberry

arandela f washer

araña f spider; (*lámpara*) chandelier. ~**r** vt scratch

arar vt plough

arbitra|je m arbitration; (*en deportes*) refereeing. ~**r** vt/i arbitrate; (*en fútbol etc*) referee; (*en tenis etc*) umpire

arbitr|ariedad f arbitrariness. ~**ario** adj arbitrary. ~**io** m (free) will

árbitro m arbitrator; (*en fútbol etc*) referee; (*en tenis etc*) umpire

árbol m tree; (*eje*) axle; (*palo*) mast. ~ **genealógico** family tree. ~ **de Navidad** Christmas tree

arbol|ado m trees. ~**eda** f wood

arbusto m bush

arca f (*caja*) chest. ~ **de Noé** Noah's ark

arcada f arcade; (*de un puente*) arch; (*náuseas*) retching

arcaico adj archaic

arce m maple (tree)

arcén m (*de autopista*) hard shoulder; (*de carretera*) verge

archipiélago m archipelago

archiv|ador m filing cabinet. ~**ar** vt file (away). ~**o** m file; (*de documentos históricos*) archives. ~**o adjunto** (email) attachment

arcilla f clay

arco m arch; (*Elec, Mat*) arc; (*Mus, arma*) bow; (*LAm, en fútbol*) goal. ~ **iris** rainbow

arder vi burn; (*LAm, escocer*) sting; (*fig, de ira*) seethe. **estar que arde** be very tense

ardid m trick, scheme

ardiente adj burning

ardilla f squirrel

ardor m heat; (*fig*) ardour; (*LAm, escozor*) smarting. ~ **de estómago** heartburn

arduo adj arduous

área f area

arena f sand; (*en deportes*) arena; (*en los toros*) (bull)ring. ~ **movediza** quicksand

arenoso adj sandy

arenque m herring. ~ **ahumado** kipper

arete m (*LAm*) earring

Argel m Algiers. ~**ia** f Algeria

Argentina f Argentina

argentino adj Argentinian, Argentine. ● m Argentinian

argolla f ring. ~ **de matrimonio** (*LAm*) wedding ring

arg|ot m slang. ~**ótico** adj slang

argucia f cunning argument

argüir 🔟 vt (*probar*) prove, show; (*argumentar*) argue. ● vi argue

argument|ación f argument. ~**ar** vt/i argue. ~**o** m argument; (*de libro, película etc*) story, plot

aria f aria

aridez f aridity, dryness

árido adj dry. ~**s** mpl dry goods

Aries m Aries

arisco adj unfriendly

arist|ocracia f aristocracy. ~**ócrata** m & f aristocrat. ~**ocrático** adj aristocratic

aritmética f arithmetic

arma f arm, weapon; (*sección*) section. ~ **de fuego** firearm, ~**s de destrucción masiva** weapons of mass destruction. ~**da** f navy; (*flota*) fleet. ~**do** adj armed (**de** with). ~**dura** f armour; (*de gafas etc*) frame; (*Tec*) framework. ~**mentismo** m build up of arms.

a

~**mento** m arms, armaments; (*acción de armar*) armament. ~**r** vt arm (de with); (*montar*) put together. ~**r un lio** kick up a fuss

armario m cupboard; (*para ropa*) wardrobe (Brit), closet (Amer)

armatoste m huge great thing

armazón m & f frame(work)

armiño m ermine

armisticio m armistice

armonía f harmony

armónica f harmonica, mouth organ

armoni|oso adj harmonious. ~**zar** 🔟 vt harmonize. ● vi harmonize (personas) get on well (con with); (colores) go well (con with)

arn|és m armour. ~**eses** mpl harness

aro m ring, hoop

arom|a m aroma; (*de flores*) scent; (*de vino*) bouquet. ~**ático** adj aromatic

arpa f harp

arpía f harpy; (*fig*) hag

arpillera f sackcloth, sacking

arpón m harpoon

arquear vt arch, bend. ~**se** vpr arch, bend

arque|ología f archaeology. ~**ológico** adj archaeological. ~**ólogo** m archaeologist

arquero m archer; (LAm, en fútbol) goalkeeper

arquitect|o m architect. ~**ónico** adj architectural. ~**ura** f architecture

arrabal m suburb; (*barrio pobre*) poor area. ~**es** mpl outskirts. ~**ero** adj suburban; (*de modales groseros*) common

arraiga|do adj deeply rooted. ~**r**

🔢 vi take root. ~**rse** vpr take root; (*fig*) settle

arran|car 🔢 vt pull up (planta); pull out (diente); (*arrebatar*) snatch; (Auto) start. ● vi start. ~**carse** vpr pull out. ~**que** m sudden start; (Auto) start; (*fig*) outburst

arras fpl security; (*en boda*) coins

arrasar vt level, smooth; raze to the ground (edificio etc); (*llenar*) fill to the brim. ● vi (*en deportes*) sweep to victory; (*en política*) win a landslide victory

arrastr|ar vt pull; (*por el suelo*) drag (along); give rise to (consecuencias). ● vi trail on the ground. ~**arse** vpr crawl; (*humillarse*) grovel. ~**e** m dragging; (*transporte*) haulage. **estar para el ~e** 🔟 be done in

arre int gee up! ~**ar** vt urge on

arrebat|ado adj (*irreflexivo*) impetuous. ~**ar** vt snatch (away); (*fig*) win (over); captivate (corazón etc). ~**o** m (*de cólera etc*) fit; (*éxtasis*) ecstasy

arrech|ar vt (LAm fam, enfurecer) to infuriate. ~**arse** vpr get furious. ~**o** adj furious

arrecife m reef

arregl|ado adj neat; (*bien vestido*) well-dressed; (LAm, amañado) fixed. ~**ar** vt arrange; (*poner en orden*) tidy up; sort out (asunto, problema etc); (*reparar*) mend. ~**arse** vpr (*solucionarse*) get sorted out; (*prepararse*) get ready; (*apañarse*) manage, make do; (*ponerse de acuerdo*) come to an agreement. ~**árselas** manage, get by. ~**o** m (*incl Mus*) arrangement; (*acción de reparar*) repair; (*acuerdo*) agreement; (*solución*) solution. **con**

~o a according to

arrellanarse *vpr* settle o.s. (en into)

arremangar 12 *vt* roll up (mangas); tuck up (falda). **~se** *vpr* roll up one's sleeves

arremeter *vi* charge (contra at); (*atacar*) attack

arremolinarse *vpr* mill about; (*el agua*) to swirl

arrenda|dor *m* landlord. **~dora** *f* landlady. **~miento** *m* renting; (*contrato*) lease; (*precio*) rent. **~r** 1 *vt* (*dar casa en alquiler*) let; (*dar cosa en alquiler*) rent; (*tomar en alquiler*) rent. **~tario** *m* tenant

arreos *mpl* tack

arrepenti|miento *m* repentance, regret. **~rse** 4 *vpr* (*retractarse*) to change one's mind; (*lamentarse*) be sorry. **~rse de** regret; repent of (*pecados*)

arrest|ar *vt* arrest, detain; (*encarcelar*) imprison. **~o** *m* arrest; (*encarcelamiento*) imprisonment

arriar 20 *vt* lower (bandera, vela)

arriba *adv* up; (*dirección*) up(wards); (*en casa*) upstairs. ● *int* up with; (*¡levántate!*) up you get!; (*¡ánimo!*) come on! **¡~ España!** long live Spain! **~ de** (*LAm*) on top of. **~ mencionado** aforementioned. **calle ~** up the street. **de ~** top to bottom. **de ~ abajo** from top to bottom. **de 10 euros para ~** over 10 euros. **escaleras ~** upstairs. **la parte de ~** the top part. **los de ~** those at the top. **más ~** higher up

arrib|ar *vi* (*barco*) reach port; (*esp LAm, llegar*) arrive. **~ista** *m & f* social climber. **~o** *m* (*esp LAm*) arrival

arriero *m* muleteer

arriesga|do *adj* risky; (*person*) daring. **~r** 12 *vt* risk; (*aventurar*)

venture. **~rse** *vpr* take a risk

arrim|ar *vt* bring close(r). **~arse** *vpr* come closer, approach

arrincona|do *adj* forgotten; (*acorralado*) cornered. **~r** *vt* put in a corner; (*perseguir*) corner (*arrumbar*) put aside. **~rse** *vpr* become a recluse

arroba *f* (*Internet*) at (@); measure of weight

arrocero *adj* rice

arrodillarse *vpr* kneel (down)

arrogan|cia *f* arrogance; (*orgullo*) pride. **~te** *adj* arrogant; (*orgulloso*) proud

arroj|ar *vt* throw; (*emitir*) give off, throw out; (*producir*) produce. ● *vi* (*esp LAm, vomitar*) throw up. **~arse** *vpr* throw o.s. **~o** *m* courage

arrollar *vt* roll (up); (*atropellar*) run over; (*vencer*) crush

arropar *vt* wrap up; (*en la cama*) tuck up. **~se** *vpr* wrap (o.s.) up

arroy|o *m* stream; (*de una calle*) gutter. **~uelo** *m* small stream

arroz *m* rice. **~ con leche** rice pudding. **~al** *m* rice field

arruga *f* (*en la piel*) wrinkle, line; (*en tela*) crease. **~r** 12 *vt* wrinkle; crumple (*papel*); crease (*tela*). **~rse** *vpr* (*la piel*) become wrinkled; (*tela*) crease, get creased

arruinar *vt* ruin; (*destruir*) destroy. **~se** *vpr* (*persona*) be ruined

arrullar *vt* lull to sleep. ● *vi* (*palomas*) coo

arrumbar *vt* put aside

arsenal *m* (*astillero*) shipyard; (*de armas*) arsenal; (*fig*) mine

arsénico *m* arsenic

arte *m* (*f en plural*) art; (*habilidad*) skill; (*astucia*) cunning. **bellas ~s** fine arts. **con ~** skilfully. **malas**

~s trickery. **por amor al** ~ for the fun of it

artefacto m device

arteria f artery; (fig, calle) main road

artesan|al adj craft. ~ía f handicrafts. **objeto** m **de** ~ía traditional craft object. ~o m artisan, craftsman

ártico adj Arctic. **Á**~ m. **el Á**~ the Arctic

articula|ción f joint; (pronunciación) articulation. ~**do** adj articulated; (lenguaje) articulate. ~**r** vt articulate

artículo m article. ~s mpl (géneros) goods. ~ **de exportación** export product. ~ **de fondo** editorial, leader

artífice m & f artist; (creador) architect

artifici|al adj artificial. ~o m (habilidad) skill; (dispositivo) device; (engaño) trick

artiller|ía f artillery. ~o m artilleryman, gunner

artilugio m gadget

artimaña f trick

art|ista m & f artist. ~ístico adj artistic

artritis f arthritis

arveja f (LAm) pea

arzobispo m archbishop

as m ace

asa f handle

asado adj roast(ed) ● m roast (meat), joint; (LAm, reunión) barbecue. ~o **a la parrilla** grilled meat; (LAm) barbecued meat

asalariado adj salaried. ● m employee

asalt|ante m attacker; (de un banco) robber. ~**ar** vt storm (forta-

leza); attack (persona); raid (banco etc); (fig) (duda) assail; (fig) (idea etc) cross one's mind. ~o m attack; (robo) robbery; (en boxeo) round

asamblea f assembly; (reunión) meeting

asar vt roast. ~**se** vpr be very hot. ~ **a la parrilla** grill; (LAm) barbecue. ~ **al horno** (sin grasa) bake; (con grasa) roast

asbesto m asbestos

ascend|encia f descent; (LAm, influencia) influence. ~**ente** adj ascending. ~**er** [1] vt promote. ● vi go up, ascend; (cuenta etc) come to, amount to; (ser ascendido) be promoted. ~**iente** m & f ancestor; (influencia) influence

ascens|ión f ascent; (de grado) promotion. **día** m **de la A**~**ión** Ascension Day. ~o m ascent; (de grado) promotion

ascensor m lift (Brit), elevator (Amer). ~**ista** m & f lift attendant (Brit), elevator operator (Amer)

asco m disgust. **dar** ~ **be** disgusting; (fig, causar enfado) be infuriating. **estar hecho un** ~ be disgusting. **me da** ~ it makes me feel sick. **¡qué** ~! how disgusting! **ser un** ~ be disgusting

ascua f ember. **estar en** ~s be on tenterhooks

asea|do adj clean; (arreglado) neat. ~**r** vt (lavar) wash; (limpiar) clean; (arreglar) tidy up

asedi|ar vt besiege; (fig) pester. ~o m siege

asegura|do adj & m insured. ~**dor** m insurer. ~**r** vt secure, make safe; (decir) assure; (concertar un seguro) insure; (preservar) safeguard. ~**rse** vpr make sure

asemejarse *vpr* be alike

asenta|do *adj* situated; (*arraigado*) established. **~r 1** *vt* place; (*asegurar*) settle; (*anotar*) note down; (*Mex, afirmar*) state. **~rse** *vpr* settle; (*estar situado*) be situated; (*esp LAm, sentar cabeza*) settle down

asentir 4 *vi* agree (a to). **~ con la cabeza** nod

aseo *m* cleanliness. **~s** *mpl* toilets

asequible *adj* obtainable; (*precio*) reasonable; (*persona*) approachable

asesin|ar *vt* murder; (*Pol*) assassinate. **~ato** *m* murder; (*Pol*) assassination. **~o** *m* murderer; (*Pol*) assassin

asesor *m* adviser, consultant. **~ar** *vt* advise. **~arse** *vpr.* **~arse con** consult. **~ía** *f* consultancy; (*oficina*) consultant's office

asfalt|ado *adj* asphalt. **~ar** *vt* asphalt. **~o** *m* asphalt

asfixia *f* suffocation. **~nte** *adj* suffocating. **~r** *vt* suffocate. **~rse** *vpr* suffocate

así *adv* (*de esta manera*) like this, like that. ● *adj* such. **~ ~** so-so. **~ como** just as. **~ como ~,** (*LAm*) **~ nomás** just like that. **~ ~ como both ... and. ~ pues** so. **~ que so; (*en cuanto*) as soon as. ~ sea** so be it. **~ y todo** even so. **aun ~** even so. **¿no es ~?** isn't that right? **si es ~** if that is the case. **y ~ (sucesivamente)** and so on

Asia *f* Asia

asiático *adj & m* Asian

asidero *m* handle; (*fig, pretexto*) excuse

asidu|amente *adv* regularly. **~o** *adj & m* regular

asiento *m* seat; (*en contabilidad*) entry. **~ delantero** front seat. **~ trasero** back seat

asignar *vt* assign; allot (*porción, tiempo etc*)

asignatura *f* subject. **~ pendiente** (*en enseñanza*) failed subject; (*fig*) matter still to be resolved

asil|ado *m* inmate; (*Pol*) refugee. **~o** *m* asylum; (*fig*) shelter; (*de ancianos etc*) home. **pedir ~o político** ask for political asylum

asimétrico *adj* asymmetrical

asimila|ción *f* assimilation. **~r** *vt* assimilate

asimismo *adv* also; (*igualmente*) in the same way, likewise

asir 45 *vt* grasp

asist|encia *f* attendance; (*gente*) people (present); (*en un teatro etc*) audience; (*ayuda*) assistance. **~encia médica** medical care. **~enta** *f* (*mujer de la limpieza*) charwoman. **~ente** *m & f* assistant. **~ente social** social worker. **~ido** *adj* assisted. **~ir** *vt* assist, help. ● *vi.* **~ir a** attend, be present at

asma *f* asthma. **~ático** *adj & m* asthmatic

asno *m* donkey; (*fig*) ass

asocia|ción *f* association; (*Com*) partnership. **~do** *adj* associated; (*socio*) associate. ● *m* associate. **~r** *vt* associate; (*Com*) take into partnership. **~rse** *vpr* associate; (*Com*) become a partner

asolar 1 *vt* devastate

asomar *vt* show. ● *vi* appear, show. **~se** *vpr* (*persona*) lean out (a, por of); (*cosa*) appear

asombr|ar *vt* (*pasmar*) amaze; (*sorprender*) surprise. **~arse** *vpr* be amazed; (*sorprenderse*) be surprised. **~o** *m* amazement, surprise.

a

~**oso** adj amazing, astonishing

asomo m sign. **ni por ~** by no means

aspa f cross, X-shape; (de molino) (windmill) sail. **en ~** X-shaped

aspaviento m show, fuss. **~s** mpl gestures. **hacer ~s** make a big fuss

aspecto m look, appearance; (fig) aspect

aspereza f roughness; (de sabor etc) sourness

áspero adj rough; (sabor etc) bitter

aspersión f sprinkling

aspiración f breath; (deseo) ambition

aspirador m, **aspiradora** f vacuum cleaner

aspira|nte m & f candidate. **~r** vt breathe in; (máquina) suck up. ● vi breathe in; (máquina) suck. **~r a** aspire to

aspirina f aspirin

asquear vt sicken. ● vi be sickening. **~se** vpr be disgusted

asqueroso adj disgusting

asta f spear; (de la bandera) flagpole; (cuerno) horn. **a media ~** at half-mast. ●**bandera** f (Mex) flagpole

asterisco m asterisk

astilla f splinter. **~s** fpl firewood

astillero m shipyard

astringente adj & m astringent

astr|o m star. ● vi **~ología** f astrology. **~ólogo** m astrologer. ●**onauta** m & f astronaut. ●**onave** f spaceship. **~onomía** f astronomy. **~ónomo** m astronomer

astu|cia f cleverness; (ardid) cunning trick. **~to** adj astute; (taimado) cunning

asumir vt assume

asunción f assumption. **la A~** the Assumption

asunto m (cuestión) matter; (de una novela) plot; (negocio) business. **~s** mpl exteriores foreign affairs. **el ~ es que** the fact is that

asusta|dizo adj easily frightened. **~r** vt frighten. **~rse** vpr be frightened

ataca|nte m & f attacker. **~r** 7 vt attack

atad|o adj tied. ●m bundle. **~ura** f tie

ataj|ar vi take a short cut; (Mex, en tenis) pick up the balls. ● vt (LAm, agarrar) catch. **~o** m short cut

atañer 22 vt concern

ataque m attack; (Med) fit, attack. **~ al corazón** heart attack. **~ de nervios** fit of hysterics

atar vt tie. **~se** vpr tie up

atarantar vt (LAm) fluster. **~se** vpr (LAm) get flustered

atardecer 11 vi get dark. ● m dusk. **al ~** at dusk

atareado adj busy

atasc|ar 7 vt block; (fig) hinder. **~arse** vpr get stuck; (tubo etc) block. **~o** m blockage; (Auto) traffic jam

ataúd m coffin

atav|iar 20 vt dress up. **~iarse** vpr dress up, get dressed up. **~ío** m dress, attire

atemorizar 10 vt frighten. **~se** vpr be frightened

atención f attention; (cortesía) courtesy, kindness; (interés) interest. **¡~!** look out!. **llamar la ~** attract attention, catch the eye; **prestar ~** pay attention

atender 11 vt attend to; (cuidar) look after. ● vi pay attention

atenerse 40 *vpr* abide (a by)

atentado *m* (*ataque*) attack; (*afrenta*) affront (contra to). ~ contra la vida de uno attempt on s.o.'s life

atentamente *adv* attentively; (*con cortesía*) politely; (*con amabilidad*) kindly. **lo saluda** ~ (*en cartas*) yours faithfully

atentar *vi.* ~ contra threaten. ~ contra la vida de uno make an attempt on s.o.'s life

atento *adj* attentive; (*cortés*) polite; (*amable*) kind

atenua|nte *adj* extenuating. • *f* extenuating circumstance. ~**r** 21 *vt* attenuate; (*hacer menor*) diminish, lessen

ateo *adj* atheistic. • *m* atheist

aterciopelado *adj* velvety

aterra|dor *adj* terrifying. ~**r** *vt* terrify

aterriza|je *m* landing. ~**je** forzoso emergency landing. ~**r** 10 *vt* land

aterrorizar 10 *vt* terrify

atesorar *vt* hoard; amass (fortuna)

atesta|do *adj* packed, full up. • *m* sworn statement. ~**r** *vt* fill up, pack; (*Jurid*) testify

atestiguar 15 *vt* testify to; (*fig*) prove

atiborrar *vt* fill, stuff. ~**se** *vpr* stuff o.s.

ático *m* attic

atina|do *adj* right; (*juicioso*) wise, sensible. ~**r** *vt/i* hit upon; (*acertar*) guess right

atizar 10 *vt* poke; (*fig*) stir up

atlántico *adj* Atlantic. **el** (*océano*) **A**~ the Atlantic (Ocean)

atlas *m* atlas

atl|eta *m & f* athlete. ~**ético** *adj* athletic. ~**etismo** *m* athletics

atmósfera *f* atmosphere

atole *m* (*LAm*) boiled maize drink

atolladero *m* bog; (*fig*) tight corner

atolondra|do *adj* scatterbrained; (*aturdido*) stunned. ~**r** *vt* fluster; (*pasmar*) stun. ~**rse** *vpr* get flustered

at|ómico *adj* atomic. ~**omizador** *m* spray, atomizer

átomo *m* atom

atónito *m* amazed

atonta|do *adj* stunned; (*tonto*) stupid. ~**r** *vt* stun. ~**rse** *vpr* get confused

atorar *vt* (*esp LAm*) to block; (*Mex, sujetar*) secure. ~**se** *vpr* (*esp LAm, atragantarse*) choke; (*atascarse*) get blocked; (*puerta*) get jammed

atormentar *vt* torture. ~**se** *vpr* worry, torment o.s.

atornillar *vt* screw on

atosigar 12 *vt* pester

atraca|dor *m* mugger; (*de banco*) bank robber. ~**r** 7 *vt* dock; (*arrimar*) bring alongside; hold up (banco); mug (persona). • *vi* (barco) dock

atracci|ón *f* attraction. ~**ones** *fpl* entertainment, amusements

atraco *m* hold-up, robbery. ~**ón** *m.* **darse un** ~**ón** stuff o.s. (de with)

atractivo *adj* attractive. • *m* attraction; (*encanto*) charm

atraer 41 *vt* attract

atragantarse *vpr* choke (con on). **la historia se me atraganta** I can't stand history

atrancar 7 *vt* bolt (puerta). ~**se**

a

vpr get stuck
atrapar vt catch; (*encerrar*) trap
atrás adv back; (*tiempo*) previously,
before. años ~ years ago. ~ de
(*LAm*) behind. **dar un paso** ~ step
backwards. **hacia** ~, **para** ~
backwards
atras|ado adj behind; (*reloj*) slow;
(*con deudas*) in arrears; (*país*) backward. **llegar** ~**ado** (*esp LAm*) arrive
late. ~**ar** vt put back (*reloj*); (*demorar*) delay, postpone. ● vi (*reloj*)
be slow. ~**arse** vpr be late; (*reloj*)
be slow; (*quedarse atrás*) fall behind. ~**o** m delay; (*de un reloj*)
slowness; (*de un país*) backwardness. ~**os** mpl (*Com*) arrears
atravesa|do adj lying across. ~**r**
1 vt cross; (*traspasar*) go through
(*poner transversalmente*) lay across.
~**rse** vpr lie across; (*en la garganta*)
get stuck, stick
atrayente adj attractive
atrev|erse vpr dare. ~**erse con**
tackle. ~**ido** adj daring; (*insolente*)
insolent. ~**imiento** m daring; (*descaro*) insolence
atribu|ción f attribution. ~**cio-
nes** fpl authority. ~**uir** **17** vt attribute; confer (*función*). ~**irse** vpr
claim
atribulado adj afflicted
atributo m attribute
atril m lectern; (*Mus*) music stand
atrocidad f atrocity. **¡qué** ~**!**
how awful!
atrofiarse vpr atrophy
atropell|ado adj hasty. ~**ar** vt
knock down; (*por encima*) run
over; (*empujar*) push aside; (*fig*)
outrage, insult. ~**arse** vpr rush.
~**o** m (*Auto*) accident; (*fig*) outrage
atroz adj appalling; (*fig*) atrocious

atuendo m dress, attire
atún m tuna (fish)
aturdi|do adj bewildered; (*por
golpe*) stunned. ~**r** vt bewilder;
(*golpe*) stun; (*ruido*) deafen
auda|cia f boldness, audacity. ~**z**
adj bold
audi|ble adj audible. ~**ción** f
hearing; (*prueba*) audition. ~**encia**
f audience; (*tribunal*) court; (*sesión*)
hearing
auditor m auditor. ~**io** m audience; (*sala*) auditorium
auge m peak; (*Com*) boom
augur|ar vt predict; (*cosas*) augur.
~**io** m prediction. **con nuestros
mejores** ~**ios para** with our best
wishes for. **mal** ~ bad omen
aula f class-room; (*Univ*) lecture
room
aull|ar **23** vi howl. ~**ido** m howl
aument|ar vt increase; magnify
(*imagen*). ● vi increase. ~**o** m increase; (*de sueldo*) rise
aun adv even. ~ **así** even so. ~
cuando although. **más** ~ even
more. **ni** ~ not even
aún adv still, yet. ~ **no ha llegado**
it still hasn't arrived, it hasn't arrived yet
aunar **23** vt join. ~**se** vpr join
together
aunque conj although, (even)
though
aúpa int up! **de** ~ wonderful
aureola f halo
auricular m (*de teléfono*) receiver.
~**es** mpl headphones
aurora f dawn
ausen|cia f absence. **en** ~**cia de**
in the absence of. ~**tarse** vpr
leave. ~**te** adj absent. ● m & f ab-

sentee; (*Jurid*) missing person. ~**tismo** m (*LAm*) absenteeism

auspici|ador m sponsor. ~**ar** vt sponsor. ~**o** m sponsorship; (*signo*) omen. **bajo los** ~**s de** sponsored by

auster|idad f austerity. ~**o** adj austere

austral adj southern

Australia m Australia

australiano adj & m Australian

Austria f Austria

austriaco, **austríaco** adj & m Austrian

aut|enticar 🛂 authenticate. ~**enticidad** f authenticity. ~**éntico** adj authentic

auto m (*Jurid*) decision; (*orden*) order; (*Auto, fam*) car. ~**s** mpl proceedings

auto|abastecimiento m self-sufficiency. ~**biografía** f autobiography

autobús m bus. **en** ~ by bus

autocar m (long-distance) bus, coach (*Brit*)

autocontrol m self-control

autóctono adj indigenous

auto|determinación f self-determination. ~**didacta** adj self-taught. ● m & f self-taught person. ~**escuela** f driving school. ~**financiamiento** m self-financing

autógrafo m autograph

autómata m robot

autom|ático adj automatic. ● m press-stud. ~**atización** f automatization

automotor m diesel train

autom|óvil adj motor. ● m car. ~**ovilismo** m motoring. ~**ovilista** m & f driver, motorist

aut|onomía f autonomy. ~**onómico** adj, ~**ónomo** adj autonomous

autopista f motorway (*Brit*), freeway (*Amer*)

autopsia f autopsy

autor m author. ~**a** f author(ess)

autori|dad f authority. ~**tario** adj authoritarian

autoriza|ción f authorization. ~**do** authorized, official; (*opinión etc*) authoritative. ~**r** 🔟 vt authorize

auto|rretrato m self-portrait. ~**servicio** m self-service restaurant. ~**stop** m hitch-hiking. **hacer** ~**stop** hitch-hike

autosuficiente adj self-sufficient

autovía f dual carriageway

auxili|ar adj auxiliary; (*profesor*) assistant. ● m & f assistant. ● vt help. ~**o** m help. **¡**~**o!** help! **en** ~**o de** in aid of. **pedir** ~**o** shout for help. **primeros** ~**os** first aid

Av. abrev (**Avenida**) Ave

aval m guarantee

avalancha f avalanche

avalar vt guarantee

aval|uar 🔞 vt (*LAm*) value. ~**úo** m valuation

avance m advance; (*en el cine*) trailer. **avances** mpl (*Mex*) trailer

avanzar 🔟 vt move forward. ~ **la pantalla** scroll up. ● vi advance

avar|icia f avarice. ~**icioso** adj, ~**iento** adj greedy; (*tacaño*) miserly. ~**o** adj miserly. ● m miser

avasallar vt dominate

Avda. abrev (**Avenida**) Ave

ave f bird. ~ **de paso** (*incl fig*) bird of passage. ~ **de rapiña** bird of prey

AVE - Alta Velocidad Española *i* A high-speed train service linking Madrid, Seville and Huelva via Cadiz, established in 1992 in time for the international exhibition, Expo 92 in Seville. Lines under construction include: Madrid-Barcelona, with an extension to France, and Barcelona-Valencia. An Ave service linking Madrid and Galicia is planned.

avecinarse *vpr* approach

avejentar *vt* age

avellan|a *f* hazelnut. **~o** *m* hazel (tree)

avemaría *f* Hail Mary

avena *f* oats

avenida *f* (*calle*) avenue

avenir 53 *vt* reconcile. **~se** *vpr* come to an agreement; (*entenderse*) get on well (con with)

aventaja|do *adj* outstanding. **~r** *vt* be ahead of; (*superar*) surpass

avent|ar 1 *vt* fan; winnow (grano etc); (*Mex, lanzar*) throw; (*Mex, empujar*) push. **~arse** *vpr* (*Mex*) throw o.s.; (*atreverse*) dare. **~ón** *m* (*Mex*) ride, lift (*Brit*)

aventur|a *f* adventure. **~a amorosa** love affair. **~ado** *adj* risky. **~ero** *adj* adventurous. ● *m* adventurer

avergonzar 10 & 16 *vt* shame; (*abochornar*) embarrass. **~se** *vpr* be ashamed; (*abochornarse*) be embarrassed

aver|ía *f* (*Auto*) breakdown; (*en máquina*) failure. **~iado** *adj* broken down. **~iarse** 20 *vpr* break down

averigua|ción *f* inquiry; (*Mex, disputa*) argument. **~r** 15 *vt* find out. ● *vi* (*Mex*) argue

aversión *f* aversion (a, hacia,

por to)

avestruz *m* ostrich

avia|ción *f* aviation; (*Mil*) air force. **~dor** *m* (*piloto*) pilot

av|ícola *adj* poultry. **~icultura** *f* poultry farming

avidez *f* eagerness, greed

ávido *adj* eager, greedy

avinagra|do *adj* sour. **~rse** *vpr* go sour; (*fig*) become embittered

avi|ón *m* aeroplane (*Brit*), airplane (*Amer*); (*Mex, juego*) hopscotch. **~onazo** *m* (*Mex*) plane crash

avis|ar *vt* warn; (*informar*) notify, inform; call (médico etc). **~o** *m* warning; (*comunicación*) notice; (*LAm, anuncio, cartel*) advertisement; (*en televisión*) commercial. **estar sobre ~o** be on the alert. **sin previo ~o** without prior warning

avisp|a *f* wasp. **~ado** *adj* sharp. **~ero** *m* wasps' nest; (*fig*) mess. **~ón** *m* hornet

avistar *vt* catch sight of

avivar *vt* stoke up (fuego); brighten up (color); arouse (interés, pasión); intensify (dolor). **~se** *vpr* revive; (*animarse*) cheer up; (*LAm, despabilarse*) wise up

axila *f* armpit, axilla

axioma *m* axiom

ay *int* (*de dolor*) ouch!; (*de susto*) oh!; (*de pena*) oh dear! **¡~ de ti!** poor you!

aya *f* governess, child's nurse

ayer *adv* yesterday. ● *m* past. **antes de ~** the day before yesterday. **~ por la mañana**, (*LAm*) **~ en la mañana** yesterday morning

ayuda *f* help, aid. **~ de cámara** valet. **~nta** *f*, **~nte** *m* assistant; (*Mil*) adjutant. **~r** *vt* help

ayun|ar *vi* fast. **~as** *fpl.* **estar en**

~**as** have had nothing to eat or drink; (*fig, fam*) be in the dark. ~**o** m fasting

ayuntamiento m town council, city council; (*edificio*) town hall

azabache m jet

azad|a f hoe. ~**ón** m (large) hoe

azafata f air hostess

azafate m (LAm) tray

azafrán m saffron

azahar m orange blossom; (*del limonero*) lemon blossom

azar m chance; (*desgracia*) misfortune. **al** ~ at random. **por** ~ by chance. ~**es** mpl ups and downs

azaros|amente adv hazardously. ~**o** adj hazardous, risky; (*vida*) eventful

azorar vt embarrass. ~**rse** vpr be embarrassed

Azores fpl. **las** ~ **the** Azores

azotador m (Mex) caterpillar

azot|ar vt whip, beat; (Mex, *puerta*) slam. ~**e** m whip; (*golpe*) smack; (*fig, calamidad*) calamity

azotea f flat roof

azteca adj & m & f Aztec

Aztecas A Náhuatl-speaking people who in the fourteenth century established a brilliant and tyrannical civilization in central and southern Mexico. Its capital was Tenochtitlán, built on reclaimed marshland, and which became Mexico City. The Aztec empire collapsed in 1521 after defeat by the Spaniards led by Hernán Cortés.

az|úcar m & f sugar. ~**ucarado** adj sweet, sugary. ~**ucarar** vt sweeten. ~**ucarero** m sugar bowl

azucena f (white) lily

azufre m sulphur

azul adj & m blue. ~**ado** adj bluish. ~ **marino** navy blue

azulejo m tile

azuzar [10] vt urge on, incite

Año Nuevo See ▷**Nochevieja**

Bb

bab|a f spittle. ~**ear** vi drool, slobber; (*niño*) dribble. **caérsele la** ~**a a uno** be delighted. ~**eo** m drooling; (*de un niño*) dribbling. ~**ero** m bib

babor m port. **a** ~ to port, on the port side

babosa f slug

babosada f (Mex) drivel

babos|ear vt slobber over; (*niño*) dribble over. ●**vi** (Mex) day dream. ~**o** adj slimy; (LAm, *tonto*) silly

babucha f slipper

baca f luggage rack

bacalao m cod

bache m pothole; (*fig*) bad patch

bachillerato m school-leaving examination

bacteria f bacterium

bagaje m. ~ **cultural** cultural knowledge; (*de un pueblo*) cultural heritage

bahía f bay

bail|able adj dance. ~**aor** m Flamenco dancer. ~**ar** vt/i dance. **ir a** ~**ar** go dancing. ●**arín** m dancer.

~**arina** f dancer; (de ballet) ballerina. ~**e** m dance; (actividad) dancing. ~**e de etiqueta** ball

baja f drop, fall; (Mil) casualty. ~ **por maternidad** maternity leave. **darse de ~** take sick leave. ~**da** f slope; (acto de bajar) descent; (camino) way down. ~**r** vt lower; (llevar abajo) get down; go down (escalera); bow (la cabeza). • vi go down; (temperatura, precio) fall. ~**rse** vpr pull down (pantalones). ~**r(se) de** get out of (coche); get off (autobús, caballo, tren, bicicleta)

bajeza f vile deed

bajío m shallows; (de arena) sandbank; (LAm, terreno bajo) low-lying area

bajo adj low; (de estatura) short, small; (cabeza, ojos) lowered; (humilde) humble, low; (vil) vile, low; (voz) low; (Mus) deep. • m lowland; (Mus) bass. • adv quietly; (volar) low. • prep under. ~ **cero** below zero. **~ la lluvia** in the rain. **los ~s** (LAm) ground floor (Brit); first floor (Amer); **los ~s fondos** the underworld

bajón m sharp drop; (de salud) sudden decline

bala f bullet; (de algodón etc) bale. (LAm, en atletismo) shot. **como una ~** like a shot. **lanzamiento de ~** (LAm) shot put

balada f ballad

balan|ce m balance; (documento) balance sheet; (resultado) outcome. ~**cear** vt balance. ~**cearse** vpr swing. ~**ceo** m swinging. ~**cín** m rocking chair; (de niños) seesaw. ~**za** f scales; (Com) balance

balar vi bleat

balazo m (disparo) shot; (herida) bullet wound

balboa f (unidad monetaria panameña) balboa

balbuc|ear vt/i stammer; (niño) babble. ~**eo** m stammering; (de niño) babbling. ~**ir** 24 vt/i stammer; (niño) babble

balcón m balcony

balda f shelf

balde m bucket. **de ~** free (of charge). **en ~** in vain

baldío adj (terreno) waste

baldosa f (floor) tile; (losa) flagstone

bale|ar adj Balearic. ●**las** (Islas) B~**ares** the Balearics, the Balearic Islands. ● **vt** (LAm) to shoot. ~**o** m (LAm, tiroteo) shooting

balero m (Mex) cup and ball toy; (rodamiento) bearing

balido m bleat; (varios sonidos) bleating

balística f ballistics

baliza f (Naut) buoy; (Aviac) beacon

ballena f whale

ballet /ba'le/ (pl ~s) m ballet

balneario m spa; (con playa) seaside resort

balompié m soccer, football (Brit)

bal|ón m ball. ~**oncesto** m basketball. ~**onmano** m handball. ~**onvolea** m volleyball

balotaje m (LAm) voting

balsa f (de agua) pool; (plataforma flotante) raft

bálsamo m balsam; (fig) balm

---

balseros The name given to illegal immigrants who try to enter a country in small boats or on rafts. It applies particularly to Cubans who try to enter the US by sailing to

Florida and to immigrants attempting to enter Spain by crossing the Straits of Gibraltar.

baluarte m (incl fig) bastion

bambalina f drop curtain. entre ~s behind the scenes

bambole|ar vi sway. ~**arse** vpr sway; (mesa etc) wobble; (barco) rock. ~**o** m swaying; (de mesa etc) wobbling; (de barco) rocking

bambú m (pl ~es) bamboo

banal adj banal. ~**idad** f banality

banan|a f (esp LAm) banana. ~**ero** adj banana. ~**o** m (LAm) banana tree

banc|a f banking; (conjunto de bancos) banks; (en juegos) bank; (LAm, asiento) bench. ~**ario** adj bank, banking. ~**arrota** f bankruptcy. hacer ~**arrota**, ir a la ~**arrota** go bankrupt. ~**o** m (asiento) bench; (Com) bank; (bajío) sandbank; (de peces) shoal

banda f (incl Mus, Radio) band; (Mex, para la raya ancha) stripe; (cinta ancha) sash; (grupo) gang, group. ~ **acha** broadband. ~ **sonora** sound-track. ~**da** f (de pájaros) flock; (de peces) shoal

bandeja f tray

bandejón m (Mex) central reservation (Brit), median strip (Amer)

bander|a f flag. ~**illa** f banderilla. ~**ear** vt stick the banderillas in. ~**ero** m banderillero. ~**ín** m pennant, small flag

bandido m bandit

bando m edict, proclamation; (facción) camp, side. ~**s** mpl banns. pasarse al otro ~ go over to the other side

bandolero m bandit

bandoneón m large accordion

banjo m banjo

banquero m banker

banquete m banquet; (de boda) wedding reception

banquillo m bench; (Jurid) dock; (taburete) footstool

bañ|ador m (de mujer) swimming costume; (de hombre) swimming trunks. ~**ar** vt bath (niño); (Culin, recubrir) coat. ~**arse** vpr go swimming, have a swim; (en casa) have a bath. ~**era** f bath (tub). ~**ista** m & f bather. ~**o** m bath; (en piscina, mar etc) swim; (cuarto) bathroom; (LAm, wáter) toilet; (bañera) bath(tub); (capa) coat(ing)

baqueano (LAm), **baquiano** m guide

bar m bar

baraja f pack of cards. ~**r** vt shuffle; juggle (cifras etc); consider (posibilidades); (Mex, explicar) explain

baranda, **barandilla** f rail; (de escalera) banisters

barat|a f (Mex) sale. ~**ija** f trinket. ~**illo** m junk shop; (géneros) cheap goods. ~**o** adj cheap. ● adv cheap(ly)

barba f chin; (pelo) beard

barbacoa f barbecue; (carne) barbecued meat

barbari|dad f atrocity; (fam, mucho) awful lot 1. ¡qué ~**dad**! how awful! ~**e** f barbarity; (fig) ignorance. ~**smo** m barbarism

bárbaro adj barbaric, cruel; (bruto) uncouth; (fam, estupendo) terrific ~. ● m barbarian. ¡qué ~! how marvellous!

barbear vt (Mex, lisonjear) suck up to

barbecho m. en ~ fallow

barber|ía f barber's (shop). ~**o** m

barber; (*Mex, adulador*) creep

barbilla *f* chin

barbitúrico *m* barbiturate

barbudo *adj* bearded

barca *f* (small) boat. ~ de pasaje ferry. ~za *f* barge

barcelonés *adj* of Barcelona, from Barcelona. ● *m* native of Barcelona

barco *m* boat; (*navío*) ship. ~ cisterna tanker. ~ de vapor steamer. ~ de vela sailing boat. ir en ~ go by boat

barda *f* (*Mex*) wall; (*de madera*) fence

barítono *adj & m* baritone

barman *m* (*pl* ~s) barman

barniz *m* varnish; (*para loza etc*) glaze; (*fig*) veneer. ~ar **10** *vt* varnish; glaze (*loza etc*)

barómetro *m* barometer

bar|ón *m* baron. ~onesa *f* baroness

barquero *m* boatman

barquillo *m* wafer; (*Mex, de helado*) ice-cream cone

barra *f* bar; (*pan*) loaf of French bread; (*palanca*) lever; (*de arena*) sandbank; (*LAm, de hinchas*) supporters. ~ de labios lipstick

barrabasada *f* mischief, prank

barraca *f* hut; (*vivienda pobre*) shack, shanty

barranco *m* ravine, gully; (*despeñadero*) cliff, precipice

barrer *vt* sweep; thrash (*rival*)

barrera *f* barrier. ~ del sonido sound barrier

barriada *f* district; (*LAm, barrio marginal*) slum

barrial *m* (*LAm*) quagmire

barrida *f* sweep; (*LAm, redada*) police raid

barrig|a *f* belly. ~ón *adj*, ~udo *adj* pot-bellied

barril *m* barrel

barrio *m* district, area. ~s bajos poor quarter, poor area. el otro ~ (*fig, fam*) the other world. ~bajero *adj* vulgar, common

barro *m* mud; (*arcilla*) clay; (*arcilla cocida*) earthenware

barroco *adj* Baroque. ● *m* Baroque style

barrote *m* bar

bartola *f*. tirarse a la ~ take it easy

bártulos *mpl* things. liar los ~ pack one's bags

barullo *m* racket; (*confusión*) confusion. a ~ galore

basar *vt* base. ~se *vpr*. ~se en be based on

báscula *f* scales

base *f* base; (*fig*) basis, foundation. a ~ de thanks to; (*mediante*) by means of; (*en una receta*) mainly consisting of. ~ de datos database. partiendo de la ~ de, tomando como ~ on the basis of

básico *adj* basic

basílica *f* basilica

básquetbol, basquetbol *m* (*LAm*) basketball

---

bastante

● *adjetivo/pronombre*

····▸ (*suficiente*) enough. ¿hay ~s sillas? are there enough chairs? ya tengo ~ I have enough already

····▸ (*mucho*) quite a lot. vino ~ gente quite a lot of people came. tiene ~s amigos he has quite a lot of friends ¿te gusta?- sí, ~ do you like it?

— yes, quite a lot
● *adverbio*
····▸ (*suficientemente*) enough. no has estudiado ~ you haven't studied enough. no es lo ~ inteligente he's not clever enough (como para to)
····▸ **bastante** + *adjetivo/adverbio* (*modificando la intensidad*) quite, fairly. parece ~ simpático he looks quite friendly. es ~ fácil de hacer it's quite easy to do. canta ~ bien he sings quite well
····▸ **bastante** *con verbo* (*considerablemente*) quite a lot. el lugar ha cambiado ~ the place has changed quite a lot

bastar *vi* be enough. ¡basta! that's enough! basta con decir que suffice it to say that. basta y sobra that's more than enough

bastardilla *f* italics

bastardo *adj & m* bastard

bastidor *m* frame; (*Auto*) chassis. ~es *mpl* (*en el teatro*) wings. entre ~es behind the scenes

basto *adj* coarse. ~s *mpl* (*naipes*) clubs

bast|ón *m* walking stick; (*de esquí*) ski pole. ~onazo *m* blow with a stick; (*de mando*) staff of office

basur|a *f* rubbish, garbage (*Amer*); (*en la calle*) litter. ~al *m* (*LAm, lugar*) rubbish dump. ~ero *m* dustman (*Brit*), garbage collector (*Amer*); (*sitio*) rubbish dump; (*Mex, recipiente*) dustbin (*Brit*), garbage can (*Amer*)

bata *f* dressing-gown; (*de médico etc*) white coat; (*esp LAm, de baño*) bathrobe

batahola *f* (*LAm*) pandemonium

batall|a *f* battle. ~a campal pitched battle. de ~a everyday. ~ador *adj* fighting. ● *m* fighter. ~ar *vi* battle, fight. ~ón *m* battalion.

batata *f* sweet potato

bate *m* bat. ~ador *m* batter; (*cricket*) batsman. ~ar *vi* bat

batería *f* battery; (*Mus*) drums. ● *m & f* drummer. ~ de cocina kitchen utensils, pots and pans

baterista *m & f* drummer

batido *adj* beaten; (*nata*) whipped. ● *m* batter; (*bebida*) milk shake. ~ra *f* (*food*) mixer

batir *vt* beat; break (*récord*); whip (*nata*). ~ palmas clap. ~se *vpr* fight

batuta *f* baton. llevar la ~ be in command, be the boss

baúl *m* trunk

bauti|smal *adj* baptismal. ~smo *m* baptism, christening. ~zar 10 *vt* baptize, christen. ~zo *m* christening

baya *f* berry

bayeta *f* cloth

bayoneta *f* bayonet

baza *f* (*naipes*) trick; (*fig*) advantage. meter ~ interfere

bazar *m* bazaar

bazofia *f* revolting food; (*fig*) rubbish

beato *adj* blessed; (*piadoso*) devout; (*pey*) overpious

bebé *m* baby

beb|edero *m* drinking trough; (*sitio*) watering place. ~edizo *m* potion; (*veneno*) poison. ~edor *m* heavy drinker. ~er *vt/i* drink. ~ida *f* drink. ~ido *adj* drunk

beca *f* grant, scholarship. ~do *m* (*LAm*) scholarship holder, scholar.

~r **7** vt give a scholarship to.
~rio m scholarship holder, scholar

b **beige** /beis, bes/ adj & m beige

béisbol m, (Mex) **beisbol** m
baseball

belén m crib, nativity scene

belga adj & m & f Belgian

Bélgica f Belgium

bélico adj, **belicoso** adj warlike

bell|eza f beauty. **~o** adj beautiful. **~as artes** fpl fine arts

bellota f acorn

bemol m flat. **tener (muchos)
~es** be difficult

bend|ecir **48** (pero imperativo bendice, futuro, condicional y pp regulares)
vt bless. **~ición** f blessing. **~ito**
adj blessed; (que tiene suerte) lucky;
(feliz) happy

benefactor m benefactor

benefic|encia f charity. **de
~encia** charitable. **~iar** vt benefit.
~iarse vpr benefit. **~iario** m
beneficiary; (de un cheque etc)
payee; (de un beneficio) recipient.
~io m benefit; (ventaja) advantage; (ganancia) profit, gain.
~ioso adj beneficial

benéfico adj beneficial; (de beneficencia) charitable

ben|evolencia f benevolence.
~évolo adj benevolent

bengala f flare. **luz** f **de ~** flare

benigno adj kind; (moderado)
gentle, mild; (tumor) benign

berberecho m cockle

berenjena f aubergine (Brit), eggplant (Amer)

berr|ear vi (animales) bellow;
(niño) bawl. **~ido** m bellow; (de
niño) bawling

berrinche m temper; (de un niño)
tantrum

berro m watercress

besamel(a) f white sauce

bes|ar vt kiss. **~arse** vpr kiss (each
other). **~o** m kiss

bestia f beast; (bruto) brute;
(idiota) idiot. **~ de carga** beast of
burden. **~l** adj bestial, animal; (fig,
fam) terrific. **~lidad** f (acción brutal) horrid thing; (insensatez) stupidity

besugo m red bream

besuquear vt cover with kisses

betabel f (Mex) beetroot

betún m (para el calzado) shoe
polish

biberón m feeding-bottle

Biblia f Bible

bibliografía f bibliography

biblioteca f library; (mueble)
bookcase. **~ de consulta** reference library. **~rio** m librarian

bicarbonato m bicarbonate

bicho m insect, bug; (animal)
small animal, creature. **~ raro** odd
sort

bici f **1** bike. **~cleta** f bicycle. **ir
en ~cleta** cycle. **~moto** (LAm)
moped

bidé, bidet /bi'ðeɪ/ m bidet

bidón m drum, can

bien adv well; (muy) very, quite;
(correctamente) right; (de buena
gana) willingly. ● m good; (efectos)
property. **¡~!** fine!, OK!, good!
¡~... (o) **~** either... or. **¡está ~!**
fine!, alright!; (basta) that is
enough!. **más ~** rather. **¡muy ~!**
good! **no ~** as soon as. **¡qué ~!**
marvellous!, great! **1**. **si ~** although

bienal adj biennial

bien|aventurado adj fortunate.
~estar m well-being. **~hablado**
adj well-spoken. **~hechor** m benefactor. **~intencionado** adj well-

meaning

bienio m two year-period

bienvenid|a f welcome. dar la ~**a** a uno welcome s.o. ~**o** adj welcome. ¡~**o**! welcome!

bifurca|ción f junction. ~**rse** 7 vpr fork; (rail) branch off

b|igamia f bigamy. ~**igamo** adj bigamous. ● m bigamist

bigot|e m moustache. ~**ón** adj (Mex), ~**udo** adj with a big moustache

bikini m bikini

bilingüe adj bilingual

billar m billiards

billete m ticket; (de banco) (bank) note (Brit), bill (Amer). ~ **de ida y vuelta** return ticket (Brit), round-trip ticket (Amer). ~ **sencillo** single ticket (Brit), one-way ticket (Amer). ~**ra** f, ~**ro** m wallet, billfold (Amer)

billón m billion (Brit), trillion (Amer)

bi|mensual adj fortnightly, twice-monthly. ~**mestral** adj two-monthly. ~**mestre** two-month period. ~**motor** adj twin-engined. ● m twin-engined plane

binoculares mpl binoculars

biocarburante m biofuel

bi|ografía f biography. ~**ográfico** adj biographical

bi|ología f biology. ~**ológico** adj biological. ~**ólogo** m biologist

biombo m folding screen

biopsia f biopsy

bioterrorismo m bioterrorism

biplaza m two-seater

biquini m bikini

birlar vt 1 steal, pinch 1

bis m encore. ¡~! encore! vivo en el 3 ~ I live at 3A

bisabuel|a f great-grandmother. ~**o** m great-grandfather. ~**os** mpl great-grandparents

bisagra f hinge

bisiesto adj. año m ~ leap year

bisniet|a f great-granddaughter. ~**o** m great-grandson. ~**os** mpl great-grandchildren

bisonte m bison

bisoño adj inexperienced

bisté, bistec m steak

bisturí m scalpel

bisutería f costume jewellery

bitácora f binnacle

bizco adj cross-eyed

bizcocho m sponge (cake)

bizquear vi squint

blanc|a f white woman; (Mus) minim. ~**o** adj white; (tez) fair. ● m white; (persona) white man; (espacio) blank; (objetivo) target. dar en el ~**o** hit the mark. dejar en ~**o** leave blank. pasar la noche en ~**o** have a sleepless night. ~**ura** f whiteness

blandir 24 vt brandish

bland|o adj soft; (carácter) weak; (cobarde) cowardly; (carne) tender. ~**ura** f softness; (de la carne) tenderness

blanque|ar vt whiten; whitewash (paredes); bleach (tela); launder (dinero). ● vi turn white. ~**o** m whitening; (de dinero) laundering

blasón m coat of arms

bledo m. me importa un ~ I couldn't care less

blinda|je m armour (plating). ~**r** vt armour(-plate)

bloc m (pl ~s) pad

bloque m block; (Pol) bloc. en ~ en bloc. ~**ar** vt block; (Mil) blockade; (Com) freeze. ~**o** m blockade; (Com) freezing

blusa f blouse

bob|ada f silly thing. decir ∼adas talk nonsense. ∼ería f silly thing

bobina f reel; (Elec) coil

bobo adj silly, stupid. ● m idiot, fool

boca f mouth; (fig, entrada) entrance; (de buzón) slot; (de cañón) muzzle. ∼ abajo face down. ∼ arriba face up

bocacalle f junction. la primera ∼ a la derecha the first turning on the right

bocad|illo m (filled) roll; (fam, comida ligera) snack. ∼o m mouthful; (mordisco) bite; (de caballo) bit

boca|jarro. a ∼**jarro** point-blank. ∼**manga** f cuff

bocanada f puff; (de vino etc) mouthful; (ráfaga) gust

bocata f sandwich

bocatería f sandwich bar

bocaza m & f invar big-mouth

boceto m sketch; (de proyecto) outline

bochinche m row; (alboroto) racket. ∼**ro** adj (LAm) rowdy

bochorno m sultry weather; (fig, vergüenza) embarrassment. ¡qué ∼! how embarrassing!. ∼**so** adj oppressive; (fig) embarrassing

bocina f horn; (LAm, auricular) receiver. tocar la ∼ sound one's horn. ∼**zo** m toot

boda f wedding

bodeg|a f cellar; (de vino) wine cellar; (LAm, almacén) warehouse; (de un barco) hold. ∼**ón** m cheap restaurant; (pintura) still life

bodoque m & f (fam, tonto) thick-head; (Mex, niño) kid

bofes mpl lights. echar los ∼ slog away

bofet|ada f slap; (fig) blow. ∼**ón** m punch

boga f (moda) fashion. estar en ∼ be in fashion, be in vogue. ∼**r** 🔢 vt row. ∼**vante** m (crustáceo) lobster

Bogotá f Bogotá

bogotano adj from Bogotá. ● m native of Bogotá

bohemio adj & m Bohemian

bohío m (LAm) hut

boicot m (pl ∼s) boycott. ∼**ear** vt boycott. ∼**eo** m boycott. hacer un ∼ boycott

boina f beret

bola f ball; (canica) marble; (mentira) fib; (Mex, reunión desordenada) rowdy party; (Mex, montón). una ∼ de a bunch of; (Mex, revolución) revolution; (Mex, brillo) shine

boleadoras f fpl bolas

bolear vt (Mex) polish, shine

bolera f bowling alley

bolero m (baile, chaquetilla) bolero; (fig, fam, mentiroso) liar; (Mex, limpiabotos) bootblack

bole|ta f (LAm, de rifa) ticket; (Mex, de notas) (school) report; (Mex, electoral) ballot paper. ∼**taje** m (Mex) tickets. ∼**tería** f (LAm) ticket office; (de teatro, cine) box office. ∼**tero** m (LAm) ticket-seller

boletín m bulletin; (publicación periódica) journal; (de notas) report

boleto m (esp LAm) ticket; (Mex, de avión) (air) ticket. ∼ de ida y vuelta, (Mex) ∼ redondo return ticket (Brit), round-trip ticket (Amer). ∼ sencillo single ticket (Brit), one-way ticket (Amer)

boli m 🔢 Biro (P), ball-point pen

boliche m (juego) bowls; (bolera) bowling alley

bolígrafo m Biro (P), ball-point pen

bolillo m bobbin; (*Mex, pan*) (bread) roll

bolívar m (*unidad monetaria venezolana*) bolívar

Bolivia f Bolivia

boliviano adj Bolivian. ●m Bolivian; (*unidad monetaria de Bolivia*) boliviano

boll|ería f baker's shop. ~o m roll; (*con azúcar*) bun

bolo m skittle; (*Mex, en bautizo*) coins. ~s mpl (*juego*) bowling

bols|a f bag; (*Mex, bolsillo*) pocket; (*Mex, de mujer*) handbag; (*Com*) stock exchange; (*cavidad*) cavity. ~a de agua caliente hot-water bottle. ~illo m pocket. de ~illo pocket. ~o m (*de mujer*) handbag. ~o de mano, ~o de viaje (*overnight*) bag

bomba f bomb; (*máquina*) pump; (*noticia*) bombshell. ~ de aceite (*Auto*) oil pump. ~ de agua (*Auto*) water pump. pasarlo ~ have a marvellous time

bombachos mpl baggy trousers, baggy pants (*Amer*)

bombarde|ar vt bombard; (*desde avión*) bomb. ~o m bombardment; (*desde avión*) bombing. ~ro m (*avión*) bomber

bombazo m explosion

bombear vt pump

bombero m fireman. cuerpo m de ~s fire brigade (*Brit*), fire department (*Amer*)

bombilla f (*light*) bulb; (*LAm, para mate*) pipe for drinking maté

bombín m pump; (*fam, sombrero*) bowler (hat) (*Brit*), derby (*Amer*)

bombo m (*tambor*) bass drum. a ~ y platillos with a lot of fuss

bomb|ón m chocolate; (*Mex, malvavisco*) marshmallow. ~ona f gas cylinder

bonachón adj easygoing; (*bueno*) good-natured

bonaerense adj from Buenos Aires. ● m native of Buenos Aires

bondad f goodness; (*amabilidad*) kindness; (*del clima*) mildness. tenga la ~ de would you be kind enough to. ~oso adj kind

boniato m sweet potato

bonito adj nice; (*mono*) pretty. ¡muy ~!, ¡qué ~! that's nice!, very nice!. ●m bonito

bono m voucher; (*título*) bond. ~ del Tesoro government bond

boñiga f dung

boqueada f gasp. dar la última ~ be dying

boquerón m anchovy

boquete m hole; (*brecha*) breach

boquiabierto adj openmouthed; (*fig*) amazed, dumbfounded. quedarse ~ be amazed

boquilla f mouthpiece; (*para cigarillos*) cigarette-holder; (*filtro de cigarillo*) tip

borbotón m. hablar a borbotones gabble. salir a borbotones gush out

borda|do adj embroidered. ● m embroidery. ~r vt embroider

borde m edge; (*de carretera*) side; (*de plato etc*) rim; (*de un vestido*) hem. al ~e de on the edge of, (*fig*) on the brink of. ●adj (*Esp fam*) stroppy. ~ear vt go round; (*fig*) border on. ~illo m kerb (*Brit*), curb (*esp Amer*)

bordo. a ~ on board

borla f tassel

borrach|era f drunkenness. pegarse una ~era get drunk. ~ín m drunk; (*habitual*) drunkard. ~o adj drunk. ● m drunkard. estar ~o be drunk. **ser ~o** be a drunkard

borrador m rough draft; (de contrato) draft; (para la pizarra) (black)board rubber; (goma) eraser

borrar vt rub out; (tachar) cross out; delete (información)

borrasc|a f depression; (tormenta) storm. **~oso** adj stormy

borrego m year-old lamb; (Mex, noticia falsa) canard

borrico m donkey; (fig, fam) ass

borrón m smudge; (de tinta) inkblot. **~ y cuenta nueva** let's forget about it!

borroso adj blurred; (fig) vague

bos|coso adj wooded. **~que** m wood, forest

bosquej|ar vt sketch; outline (plan). **~o** m sketch; (de plan) outline

bosta f dung

bostez|ar 10 vi yawn. **~o** m yawn

bota f boot; (recipiente) wineskin

botana f (Mex) snack, appetizer

botánic|a f botany. **~o** adj botanical. ● m botanist

botar vt launch; bounce (pelota); (esp LAm, tirar) throw away. ● vi bounce

botarate m irresponsible person; (esp LAm, derrochador) spendthrift

bote m boat; (de una pelota) bounce; (lata) tin, can; (vasija) jar. **~ de la basura** (Mex) rubbish bin (Brit), trash can (Amer). **~ salvavidas** lifeboat. **de ~ en ~** packed

botella f bottle

botica f chemist's (shop) (Brit), drugstore (Amer). **~rio** m chemist (Brit), druggist (Amer)

botijo m earthenware jug

botín m half boot; (de guerra) booty; (de ladrones) haul

botiquín m medicine chest; (de primeros auxilios) first aid kit

bot|ón m button; (yema) bud; (LAm, insignia) badge. **~ones** m invar bellboy (Brit), bellhop (Amer)

bóveda f vault

boxe|ador m boxer. **~ar** vi box. **~o** m boxing

boya f buoy; (corcho) float. **~nte** adj buoyant

bozal m (de perro etc) muzzle; (de caballo) halter

bracear vi wave one's arms; (nadar) swim, crawl

bracero m seasonal farm labourer

braga(s) f(pl) panties, knickers (Brit)

bragueta f flies

bram|ar vi bellow. **~ido** m bellowing

branquia f gill

bras|a f ember. **a la ~a** grilled. **~ero** m brazier

brasier m (Mex) bra

Brasil m. **(el) ~** Brazil

brasile|ño adj & m Brazilian. **~ro** adj & m (LAm) Brazilian

bravío adj wild

brav|o adj fierce; (valeroso) brave; (mar) rough. **¡~!** int well done! **bravo! ~ura** f ferocity; (valor) bravery

braz|a f fathom. **nadar a ~a** swim breast-stroke. **~ada** f (en natación) stroke. **~alete** m bracelet; (brazal) arm-band. **~o** m arm; (de caballo) foreleg; (rama) branch. **~o derecho** right-hand man. **del ~o** arm in arm

brea f tar, pitch

brebaje m potion; (pej) concoction

brecha f opening; (Mil) breach; (Med) gash. ~ generacional generation gap. **estar en la ~** be in the thick of it

brega f struggle. **andar a la ~** work hard

breva f early fig

breve adj short. **en ~** soon, shortly. **en ~s momentos** soon. ~**dad** f shortness

brib|ón m rogue, rascal. ~**onada** f dirty trick

brida f bridle

brigad|a f squad; (Mil) brigade. ~**ier** m brigadier (Brit), brigadier-general (Amer)

brill|ante adj bright; (lustroso) shiny; (persona) brilliant. ● m diamond. ~**ar** vi shine; (centellear) sparkle. ~**o** m shine; (brillantez) brilliance; (centelleo) sparkle. **sacar ~o** polish. ~**oso** adj (LAm) shiny

brinc|ar ⑦ vi jump up and down. ~**o** m jump. **dar un ~o, pegar un ~o** jump

brind|ar vt offer. ● vi. ~**ar por** toast, drink a toast to. ~**is** m toast

br|ío m energy; (decisión) determination. ~**ioso** adj spirited; (garboso) elegant

brisa f breeze

británico adj British. ● m Briton, British person

brocha f paintbrush; (para afeitarse) shaving-brush

broche m clasp, fastener; (joya) brooch; (Mex, para el pelo) hairslide (Brit), barrete (Amer)

brocheta f skewer; (plato) kebab

brócoli m broccoli

brom|a f joke. ~**a pesada** practical joke. **en ~a** in fun. **ni de ~a** no way. ~**ear** vi joke. ~**ista** adj

fond of joking. ● m & f joker

bronca f row; (reprensión) telling-off; (LAm, rabia) foul mood. **dar ~ a uno** bug s.o.

bronce m bronze; (LAm) brass. ~**ado** adj bronze; (por el sol) tanned. ~**ar** vt tan (piel). ~**arse** vpr get a suntan

bronquitis f bronchitis

brot|ar vi (plantas) sprout; (Med) break out; (líquido) gush forth; (lágrimas) well up. ~**e** m shoot; (Med) outbreak

bruces: **de ~** face down(wards). **caer de ~** fall flat on one's face

bruj|a f witch. ~**ería** f witchcraft. ~**o** m wizard, magician. ● adj (Mex) broke

brújula f compass

brum|a f mist; (fig) confusion. ~**oso** adj misty, foggy

brusco adj (repentino) sudden; (de movimiento) brusque

Bruselas f Brussels

brusquedad f roughness; (de movimiento) abruptness

brut|al adj brutal. ~**alidad** f brutality; (estupidez) stupidity. ~**o** adj ignorant; (tosco) rough; (peso, sueldo) gross

bucal adj oral; (lesión) mouth

buce|ar vi dive; (nadar) swim under water. ~**o** m diving; (natación) underwater swimming

bucle m ringlet

budín m pudding

budis|mo m Buddhism. ~**ta** m & f Buddhist

buen véase BUENO

buenaventura f good luck; (adivinación) fortune

bueno adj (delante de nombre mas-

culino en singular **buen**) good; (*agradable*) nice; (*tiempo*) fine. ● *int* well!; (*de acuerdo*) OK!, very well! ¡buena la has hecho! you've gone and done it now! ¡buenas noches! good night! ¡buenas tardes! (*antes del atardecer*) good afternoon!; (*después del atardecer*) good evening! ¡~s días! good morning! estar de buenas be in a good mood. por las buenas willingly. ¡qué bueno! (*LAm*) great!

Buenos Aires *m* Buenos Aires

buey *m* ox

búfalo *m* buffalo

bufanda *f* scarf

bufar *vi* snort

bufete *m* (*mesa*) writing-desk; (*despacho*) lawyer's office

buf|**o** *adj* comic. ● **~ón** *adj* comical. ● *m* buffoon; (*Historia*) jester

buhardilla *f* attic; (*ventana*) dormer window

búho *m* owl

buhonero *m* pedlar

buitre *m* vulture

bujía *f* (*Auto*) spark plug

bulbo *m* bulb

bulevar *m* avenue, boulevard

Bulgaria *f* Bulgaria

búlgaro *adj* & *m* Bulgarian

bull|**a** *f* noise. **~icio** *m* hubbub; (*movimiento*) bustle. **~icioso** *adj* bustling; (*ruidoso*) noisy

bullir 22 *vi* boil; (*burbujear*) bubble; (*fig*) bustle

bulto *m* (*volumen*) bulk; (*forma*) shape; (*paquete*) package; (*maleta etc*) piece of luggage; (*protuberancia*) lump

buñuelo *m* fritter

BUP *abrev* (**Bachillerato Unificado**

Polivalente) secondary school education

buque *m* ship, boat

burbuj|**a** *f* bubble. **~ear** *vi* bubble; (*vino*) sparkle

burdel *m* brothel

burdo *adj* rough, coarse; (*excusa*) clumsy

burgu|**és** *adj* middle-class, bourgeois. ● *m* middle-class person. **~esía** *f* middle class, bourgeoisie

burla *f* taunt; (*broma*) joke; (*engaño*) trick. **~r** *vt* evade. **~rse** *vpr.* **~rse de** mock, make fun of

burlesco *adj* (*en literatura*) burlesque

burlón *adj* mocking

bur|**ocracia** *f* bureaucracy; (*Mex, funcionariado*) civil service. **~ócrata** *m* & *f* bureaucrat; (*Mex, funcionario*) civil servant. **~ocrático** *adj* bureaucratic; (*Mex*) (*empleado*) government

burro *adj* stupid; (*obstinado*) pigheaded. ● *m* donkey; (*fig*) ass

bursátil *adj* stock-exchange

bus *m* bus

busca *f* search. **a la ~ de** in search of. ● *m* beeper

buscador *m* search engine

buscapleitos *m* & *f invar* (*LAm*) trouble-maker

buscar 7 *vt* look for. ● *vi* look. **buscársela** ask for it; **ir a ~ a uno** fetch s.o.

búsqueda *f* search

busto *m* bust

butaca *f* armchair; (*en el teatro etc*) seat

buzo *m* diver

buzón *m* postbox (*Brit*), mailbox (*Amer*)

Cc

C/ abrev (**Calle**) St, Rd

cabal adj exact; (completo) complete. **no estar en sus ~es** not be in one's right mind

cabalga|dura f mount, horse. **~r** [12] vt ride. • vi ride, go riding. **~ta** f ride; (desfile) procession

caballa f mackerel

caballerango m (Mex) groom

caballeresco adj gentlemanly. **literatura** f **caballeresca** books of chivalry

caballer|ía f mount, horse. **~iza** f stable. **~izo** m groom

caballero m gentleman; (de orden de caballería) knight; (tratamiento) sir. **~so** adj gentlemanly

caballete m (del tejado) ridge; (para mesa) trestle; (de pintor) easel

caballito m pony. **~ del diablo** dragonfly. **~ de mar** sea-horse. **~s** mpl (carrusel) merry-go-round

caballo m horse; (del ajedrez) knight; (de la baraja española) queen. **~ de fuerza** horsepower. **a ~** on horseback

cabaña f hut

cabaret /kaba're/ m (pl **~s**) night-club

cabecear vi nod off; (en fútbol) head the ball; (caballo) toss its head

cabecera f (de la cama) headboard; (de la mesa) head; (en un impreso) heading

cabecilla m ringleader

cabello m hair. **~s** mpl hair

caber [28] vi fit (en into). **no cabe duda** there's no doubt

cabestr|illo m sling. **~o** m halter

cabeza f head; (fig, inteligencia) intelligence. **andar de ~** have a lot to do. **~da** f nod. **dar una ~da** nod off. **~zo** m butt; (en fútbol) header

cabida f capacity; (extensión) area; (espacio) room. **dar ~ a** have room for, accommodate

cabina f (de pasajeros) cabin; (de pilotos) cockpit; (electoral) booth; (de camión) cab. **~ telefónica** telephone box (Brit), telephone booth (Amer)

cabizbajo adj crestfallen

cable m cable

cabo m end; (trozo) bit; (Mil) corporal; (mango) handle; (en geografía) cape; (Naut) rope. **al ~ de** after. **de ~ a rabo** from beginning to end. **llevar a ~** carry out

cabr|a f goat. **~iola** f jump, skip. **~itilla** f kid. **~ito** m kid

cábula m (Mex) crook

cacahuate m, (Mex) **cacahuete** m peanut

cacalote m (Mex) crow

cacao m (planta y semillas) cacao; (polvo) cocoa; (fig) confusion

cacarear vt boast about. • vi (gallo) crow; (gallina) cluck

cacería f hunt. **ir de ~** go hunting

cacerola f saucepan, casserole

cacharro m (earthenware) pot; (coche estropeado) wreck; (cosa inútil) piece of junk; (chisme) thing. **~s** mpl pots and pans

cachear vt frisk

cachemir m, **cachemira** f cashmere

cacheo m frisking

cachetada f (LAm) slap

cache|te m slap; (esp LAm, mejilla) cheek. **~tear** vt (LAm) slap. **~tón** adj (LAm) chubby-cheeked

cachimba f pipe

cachiporra f club, truncheon

cachivache m piece of junk. **~s** mpl junk

cacho m bit, piece; (LAm, cuerno) horn

cachondeo m ① joking, joke

cachorro m (perrito) puppy; (de león, tigre) cub

cachucha f (Mex) cup

caciqu|e m cacique, chief; (Pol) local political boss; (hombre poderoso) tyrant. **~il** adj despotic. **~ismo** m despotism

caco m thief

cacofonía f cacophony

cacto m, **cactus** m invar cactus

cada adj invar each, every. **~ uno** each one, everyone. **uno de ~ cinco** one in five. **~ vez más** more and more

cadáver m corpse

cadena f chain; (TV) channel. **~ de fabricación** production line. **~ de montañas** mountain range. **~ perpetua** life imprisonment

cadera f hip

cadete m cadet

caduc|ar ⑦ vi expire. **~idad** f. **fecha** f **de ~idad** sell-by date. **~o** adj outdated

cae|r ㉒ vi fall. **dejar ~r** drop. **este vestido no me ~ bien** this dress doesn't suit me. **hacer ~r** knock over. **Juan me ~ bien** I like Juan. **su cumpleaños cayó en martes** his birthday fell on a Tuesday. **~rse** vpr fall (over). **se le**

cayó he dropped it

café m coffee; (cafetería) café; (Mex, marrón) brown. ●adj. **color ~** coffee-coloured. **~ con leche** white coffee. **~ cortado** coffee with a little milk. **~ negro** (LAm) expresso. **~ solo** black coffee

cafe|ína f caffeine. **~tal** m coffee plantation. **~tera** f coffee-pot. **~tería** f café. **~tero** adj coffee

caíd|a f fall; (disminución) drop; (pendiente) slope. **~o** adj fallen

cafetería In Spain, a place to have a coffee or other drinks, pastries and cakes. *Cafeterías* are frequently combined with *bares* and are very similar. However, *cafeterías* are usually smarter, and serve a wider variety of dishes.

caigo vb véase CAER

caimán m cayman, alligator

caj|a f box; (de botellas) case; (ataúd) coffin; (en tienda) cash desk; (en supermercado) check-out; (en banco) cashier's desk. **~a de ahorros** savings bank. **~a de cambios** gearbox. **~a de caudales**, **~a fuerte** safe. **~a negra** black box. **~a registradora** till. **~ero** m cashier. **~ero automático** cash dispenser. **~etilla** f packet. **~ita** f small box. **~ón** m (de mueble) drawer; (caja grande) crate; (LAm, ataúd) coffin; (Mex, en estacionamiento) parking space. **ser de ~ón** be obvious. **~uela** f (Mex) boot (Brit), trunk (Amer)

cal m lime

cala f cove

calaba|cín m, **~cita** f (Mex) courgette (Brit), zucchini (Amer). **~za** f pumpkin; (fig, fam, idiota) idiot.

dar ~zas a uno give s.o. the brush-off

calabozo m prison; (celda) cell

calado adj soaked. estar ~ hasta los huesos be soaked to the skin. • m (Naut) draught

calamar m squid

calambre m cramp

calami|dad f calamity, disaster. ~toso adj calamitous

calaña f sort

calar vt soak; (penetrar) pierce; (fig, penetrar) see through; rumble (persona); sample (fruta). ~se vpr get soaked; (zapatos) leak; (Auto) stall

calavera f skull; (Mex, Auto) tail light

calcar 7 vt trace; (fig) copy

calcet|a f. hacer ~ knit. ~ín m sock

calcetín m sock

calcinar vt burn

calcio m calcium

calcomanía f transfer

calcula|dor adj calculating. ~dora f calculator. ~r vt calculate; (suponer) reckon, think; (imaginar) imagine

cálculo m calculation; (Med) stone

caldear vt heat, warm. ~se vpr get hot

caldera f boiler

calderilla f small change

caldo m stock; (sopa) clear soup, broth

calefacción f heating. ~ central central heating

caleidoscopio m kaleidoscope

calendario m calendar; (programa) schedule

calent|ador m heater. ~amiento m warming; (en deportes) warm-up. ~ar 1 vt heat; (templar) warm. ~arse vpr get hot; (templarse) warm up; (LAm, enojarse) get mad. ~ura f fever, (high) temperature. ~uriento adj feverish

calibr|ar vt calibrate; (fig) weigh up. ~e m calibre; (diámetro) diameter; (fig) importance

calidad f quality; (condición) capacity. en ~ de as

calidez f (LAm) warmth

cálido adj warm

caliente adj hot; (habitación, ropa) warm; (LAm, enojado) angry

califica|ción f qualification; (evaluación) assessment; (nota) mark. ~do adj (esp LAm) qualified; (mano de obra) skilled. ~r 7 vt qualify; (evaluar) assess; mark (examen etc). ~r de describe as, label

cáliz m chalice; (en botánica) calyx

caliz|a f limestone. ~o adj lime

calla|do adj quiet. ~r vt silence; keep (secreto); hush up (asunto). • vi be quiet, keep quiet, shut up 🔢. ~rse vpr be quiet, keep quiet, shut up 🔢 ¡cállate! be quiet!, shut up! 🔢

calle f street, road; (en deportes, autopista) lane. ~ de dirección única one-way street. ~ mayor high street, main street. de ~ everyday. ~ja f narrow street. ~jear vi hang out on the streets. ~jero adj street. • m street plan. ~jón m alley. ~jón sin salida dead end. ~juela f back street, side street

call|ista m & f chiropodist. ~o m corn, callus. ~os mpl tripe. ~osidad f callus

calm|a f calm. ¡~a! calm down!. en ~a calm. perder la ~a lose one's composure. **~ante** m tranquilizer; (*para el dolor*) painkiller. **~ar** vt calm; (*aliviar*) soothe. ● vi (*viento*) abate. **~arse** vpr calm down; (*viento*) abate. **~o** adj calm. **~oso** adj calm; (*fam, flemático*) slow

calor m heat; (*afecto*) warmth. **hace ~** it's hot. **tener ~** be hot. **~ía** f calorie. **~ífero** adj heat-producing. **~ífico** adj calorific

calumni|a f calumny; (*oral*) slander; (*escrita*) libel. **~ar** vt slander; (*por escrito*) libel. **~oso** adj slanderous; (*cosa escrita*) libellous

caluroso adj warm; (*clima*) hot

calv|a f bald head; (*parte sin pelo*) bald patch. **~icie** f baldness. **~o** adj bald

calza f wedge

calzada f road; (*en autopista*) carriageway

calza|do adj wearing shoes. ● m footwear, shoe. **~dor** m shoehorn. **~r** 🔟 vt put shoes on; (*llevar*) wear. ¿**qué número calza Vd?** what size shoe do you take? ● vi wear shoes. **~rse** vpr put on

calz|ón m shorts. **~ones** mpl shorts; (*LAm, ropa interior*) panties. **~oncillos** mpl underpants

cama f bed. **~ de matrimonio** double bed. **~ individual** single bed. **guardar ~** stay in bed

camada f litter

camafeo m cameo

camaleón m chameleon

cámara f (*aposento*) chamber; (*fotográfica*) camera. **~ fotográfica** camera. **a ~ lenta** in slow motion

camarad|a m & f colleague; (*de colegio*) schoolfriend; (*Pol*) comrade. **~ería** f camaraderie

camarer|a f chambermaid; (*de restaurante etc*) waitress. **~o** m waiter

camarógrafo m cameraman

camarón m shrimp

camarote m cabin

cambi|able adj changeable; (*Com etc*) exchangeable. **~ante** adj variable; (*persona*) moody. **~ar** vt change; (*trocar*) exchange. ● vi change. **~ar de idea** change one's mind. **~arse** vpr change. **~o** m change; (*Com*) exchange rate; (*moneda menuda*) (small) change; (*Auto*) gear. **~o climático** climate change. **en ~o** on the other hand

camello m camel

camellón m (*Mex*) traffic island

camerino m dressing room

camilla f stretcher

camin|ante m traveller. **~ar** vt/i walk. **~ata** f long walk. **~o** m road; (*sendero*) path, track; (*dirección, ruta*) way. **~o de** towards, on the way to. **abrir ~o** make way. **a medio ~o**, **a la mitad del ~o** half-way. **de ~o** on the way

cami|ón m truck, lorry; (*Mex, autobús*) bus. **~onero** m lorry-driver; (*Mex, de autobús*) bus driver. **~oneta** f van; (*LAm, coche familiar*) estate car

Camino de Santiago A pilgrimage route since the Middle Ages across north-western Spain to Santiago de Compostela in Galicia. The city was founded at a place where a shepherd is said to have discovered the tomb of St James the Apostle, and its cathedral reputedly houses the saint's relics.

camis|a f shirt. **~a de fuerza** strait-jacket. **~ería** f shirtmaker's.

~**eta** f T-shirt; (*ropa interior*) vest. ~**ón** m nightdress

camorra f ① row. buscar ~ look for a fight

camote m (*LAm*) sweet potato

campamento m camp. de ~ adj camping

campan|a f bell. ~**ada** f stroke. ~**ario** m bell tower, belfry. ~**illa** f bell

campaña f campaign

campe|ón adj & m champion. ~**onato** m championship

campes|ino adj country. ● m peasant. ~**tre** adj country

camping /'kampɪn/ m (*pl* ~s) camping; (*lugar*) campsite. hacer ~ go camping

camp|iña f countryside. ~**o** m country; (*agricultura, fig*) field; (*de fútbol*) pitch; (*de golf*) course. ~**osanto** m cemetery

camufla|je m camouflage. ~**r** vt camouflage

cana f grey hair, white hair. peinar ~s be getting old

Canadá m. el ~ Canada

canadiense adj & m & f Canadian

canal m (*incl TV*) channel; (*artificial*) canal; (*del tejado*) gutter. ~ de la Mancha English Channel. ~ de Panamá Panama Canal. ~**ón** m (*horizontal*) gutter; (*vertical*) drainpipe

canalla f rabble. ● m (*fig, fam*) swine. ~**da** f dirty trick

canapé m sofa, couch; (*Culin*) canapé

Canarias fpl. las (islas) ~ the Canary Islands, the Canaries

canario adj of the Canary Islands. ● m native of the Canary Islands; (*pájaro*) canary

canast|a f (large) basket. ~**illa** f small basket; (*para un bebé*) layette. ~**illo** m small basket. ~**o** m (large) basket

cancela|ción f cancellation. ~**r** vt cancel; write off (*deuda*)

cáncer m cancer. C~ Cancer

cancha f court; (*LAm, de fútbol, rugby*) pitch, ground

canciller m chancellor; (*LAm, ministro*) Minister of Foreign Affairs

canci|ón f song. ~**ón de cuna** lullaby. ~**onero** m song-book

candado m padlock

candel|a f candle. ~**abro** m candelabra. ~**ero** m candlestick

candente adj (*rojo*) red-hot; (*fig*) burning

candidato m candidate

candid|ez f innocence; (*ingenuidad*) naivety

cándido adj naive

candil m oil lamp. ~**ejas** fpl footlights

candor m innocence; (*ingenuidad*) naivety

canela f cinnamon

cangrejo m crab. ~ de río crayfish

canguro m kangaroo. ●m & f (*persona*) baby-sitter

caníbal adj & m & f cannibal

canica f marble

canijo adj weak; (*Mex, terco*) stubborn; (*Mex, intenso*) incredible

canilla f (*LAm*) shinbone

canino adj canine. ● m canine (tooth)

canje m exchange. ~**ar** vt exchange

cano adj grey. de pelo ~ greyhaired

canoa f canoe

can|ónigo m canon. **~onizar** 10 vt canonize

canoso adj grey-haired

cansa|do adj tired; (que cansa) tiring. **~dor** (LAm) tiring. **~ncio** m tiredness. **~r** vt tire; (aburrir) bore. • vi be tiring; (aburrir) get boring. **~rse** vpr get tired

canta|nte adj singing. • m & f singer. **~or** m Flamenco singer. **~r** vt/i sing. **~rlas claras** speak frankly. • m singing; (poema) poem

cántaro m pitcher. **llover a ~s** pour down

cante m folk song. **~ flamenco, ~ jondo** Flamenco singing

cantera f quarry

cantidad f quantity; (número) number; (de dinero) sum. **una ~ de** lots of

cantimplora f water-bottle

cantina f canteen; (Rail) buffet; (LAm, bar) bar

cant|inela f song. **~o** m singing; (canción) chant; (borde) edge; (de un cuchillo) blunt edge. **~o rodado** boulder; (guijarro) pebble. **de ~o** on edge

canturre|ar vt/i hum. **~o** m humming

canuto m tube

caña f (planta) reed; (del trigo) stalk; (del bambú) cane; (de pescar) rod; (de la bota) leg; (vaso) glass. **~ de azúcar** sugar-cane. **~da** f ravine; (camino) track; (LAm, arroyo) stream

cáñamo m hemp. **~ indio** cannabis

cañ|ería f pipe; (tubería) piping. **~o** m pipe, tube; (de fuente) jet. **~ón** m (de pluma) quill; (de artillería) cannon; (de arma de fuego)

barrel; (desfiladero) canyon. **~onera** f gunboat

caoba f mahogany

ca|os m chaos. **~ótico** adj chaotic

capa f layer; (de pintura) coat; (Culin) coating; (prenda) cloak; (más corta) cape; (en geología) stratum

capaci|dad f capacity; (fig) ability. **~tar** vt qualify, enable; (instruir) train

caparazón m shell

capataz m foreman

capaz adj capable, able

capcioso adj sly, insidious

capellán m chaplain

caperuza f hood; (de bolígrafo) cap

capilla f chapel

capital adj capital, very important. • m (dinero) capital. • f (ciudad) capital. **~ de provincia** county town. **~ino** adj (LAm) of/from the capital. **~ismo** m capitalism. **~ista** adj & m & f capitalist. **~izar** 10 vt capitalize

capit|án m captain; (de pesquero) skipper. **~anear** vt lead, command; (un equipo) skipper; captain

capitel m (de columna) capital

capitulaci|ón f surrender. **~ones** fpl marriage contract

capítulo m chapter; (de serie) episode

capó m bonnet (Brit), hood (Amer)

capón m (pollo) capon

caporal m (Mex) foreman

capot|a f (de mujer) bonnet; (Auto) folding top; (de cochecito) hood. **~e** m cape; (Mex, de coche) bonnet (Brit), hood (Amer)

capricho m whim. **~so** adj capricious, whimsical

Capricornio m Capricorn

cápsula f capsule

captar vt harness (agua); grasp (sentido); capture (atención); win (confianza); (radio) pick up

captura f capture. **~r** vt capture

capucha f hood

capullo m bud; (de insecto) cocoon

caqui m khaki

cara f face; (de una moneda) heads; (de un objeto) side; (aspecto) look, appearance; (descaro) cheek. **~ a** facing. **~ a ~** face to face. **~ dura** véase **CARADURA**. **~ o cruz** heads or tails. **dar la ~ a** face up to. **hacer ~ a** face. **tener mala ~** look ill. **volver la ~** look the other way

carabela f caravel

carabina f carbine; (fig, fam, señora) chaperone

caracol m snail; (de mar) winkle; (LAm, concha) conch; (de pelo) curl. **¡~es!** Good Heavens!. **~a** f conch

carácter m (pl **caracteres**) character; (índole) nature. con **~** a character

característic|a f characteristic. **~o** adj characteristic, typical

caracteriza|do adj characterized; (prestigioso) distinguished. **~r** [10] vt characterize

caradura f cheek, nerve. ● m & f cheeky person

caramba int good heavens!

carámbola f (en billar) cannon; (Mex, choque múltiple) pile-up. **de ~** by pure chance

caramelo m sweet (Brit), candy (Amer); (azúcar fundido) caramel

caraqueño adj from Caracas

carátula f (de disco) sleeve (Brit), jacket (Amer); (de video) case; (de

libro) cover; (Mex, del reloj) face

caravana f caravan; (de vehículos) convoy; (Auto) long line, traffic jam; (remolque) caravan (Brit), trailer (Amer); (Mex, reverencia) bow

caray int [1] good heavens!

carb|ón m coal; (para dibujar) charcoal. **~ de leña** charcoal. **~oncillo** m charcoal. **~onero** adj coal. ● m coal-merchant. **~onizar** [10] vt (fig) burn (to a cinder). **~ono** m carbon

carbura|dor m carburettor. **~nte** m fuel

carcajada f guffaw. **reírse a ~s** roar with laughter. **soltar una ~** burst out laughing

cárcel f prison, jail

carcelero m jailer

carcom|er vt eat away; (fig) undermine. **~erse** vpr be eaten away; (fig) waste away

cardenal m cardinal; (contusión) bruise

cardiaco, cardíaco adj cardiac, heart

cardinal adj cardinal

cardo m thistle

carear vt bring face to face (personas); compare (cosas)

care|cer [11] vi. **~cer de** lack. **~cer de sentido** not to make sense. **~ncia** f lack. **~nte** adj lacking

care|ro adj pricey. **~stía** f (elevado) high cost

careta f mask

carey m tortoiseshell

carga f load; (fig) burden; (acción) loading; (de barco, avión) cargo; (de tren) freight; (de arma) charge; (Elec, ataque) charge; (obligación) obligation. **llevar la ~ de algo** be responsible for sth. **~da** f (Mex,

Pol) supporters. ~**do** *adj* loaded; (*fig*) burdened; (*atmósfera*) heavy; (*café*) strong; (*pila*) charged. ~**mento** *m* load; (*acción*) loading; (*de un barco*) cargo. ~**r** 🔢 *vt* load; (*fig*) burden; (*Elec*, *atacar*) charge; fill (*pluma* etc.). ● *vi* load. ~**r con** carry. ~**rse** *vpr* (*pila*) charge. ~**rse de** to load s.o. down with

cargo *m* (*puesto*) post; (*acusación*) charge. **a ~ de** in the charge of. **hacerse ~ de** take responsibility for. **tener a su ~** be in charge of

carguero *m* (*Naut*) cargo ship

caria|do *adj* decayed. ~**rse** *vpr* decay

caribeño *adj* Caribbean

caricatura *f* caricature

caricia *f* caress; (*a animal*) stroke

caridad *f* charity. **¡por ~!** for goodness sake!

caries *f invar* tooth decay; (*lesión*) cavity

cariño *m* affection; (*caricia*) caress. ~ **mío** my darling. **con mucho ~** (*en carta*) with love from. **tener ~ a** be a fond of. **tomar ~ a** become fond of. ~**so** *adj* affectionate

carisma *m* charisma

caritativo *adj* charitable

cariz *m* look

carmesí *adj & m* crimson

carmín *m* (*de labios*) lipstick; (*color*) red

carnal *adj* carnal. **primo ~** first cousin

carnaval *m* carnival. ~**esco** *adj* carnival

carne *f* meat; (*Anat*, *de frutos*, *pescado*) flesh. ~ **de cerdo** pork. ~ **de cordero** lamb. ~ **de gallina** goose pimples. ~ **molida** (*LAm*), ~ **picada** (*Brit*), ground beef (*Amer*). ~ **de ternera** veal. ~ **de

vaca beef. **me pone la ~ de gallina** it gives me the creeps. **ser de ~ y hueso** be only human

carné, **carnet** *m* card. ~ **de conducir** driving licence (*Brit*), driver's license (*Amer*). ~ **de identidad** identity card. ~ **de manejar** (*LAm*) driving license (*Brit*), driver's license (*Amer*). ~ **de socio** membership card

carnero *m* ram

carnicer|ía *f* butcher's (shop); (*fig*) massacre. ~**o** *adj* carnivorous. ● *m* butcher

carnívoro *adj* carnivorous. ● *m* carnivore

carnoso *adj* fleshy; (*pollo*) meaty

caro *adj* expensive. ● *adv* dear, dearly. **costar ~ a uno** cost s.o. dear.

carpa *f* carp; (*LAm*, *tienda*) tent

carpeta *f* folder, file. ~**zo** *m*. **dar ~zo a** shelve

carpinter|ía *f* carpentry. ~**o** *m* carpenter, joiner

carraspe|ar *vi* clear one's throat. ~**ra** *f*. **tener ~ra** have a frog in one's throat

carrera *f* run; (*prisa*) rush; (*concurso*) race; (*estudios*) degree course; (*profesión*) career; (*de taxi*) journey

carreta *f* cart. ~**da** *f* cartload

carrete *m* reel; (*película*) film

carretear *vi* (*LAm*) taxi

carretera *f* road. ~ **de circunvalación** bypass, ring road. ~ **nacional** A road (*Brit*), highway (*Amer*)

carretilla *f* wheelbarrow

carril *m* lane; (*Rail*) rail

carrito *m* (*en supermercado*, *para equipaje*) trolley (*Brit*), cart (*Amer*)

carro *m* cart; (*LAm*, *coche*) car;

(*Mex*, *vagón*) coach. ~ **de combate** tank. ~**cería** f (*Auto*) bodywork

carroña f carrion

carroza f coach, carriage; (*en desfile de fiesta*) float

carruaje m carriage

carrusel m merry-go-round

cart|a f letter; (*lista de platos*) menu; (*lista de vinos*) list; (*mapa*) map; (*naipe*) card. ~**a blanca** free hand. ~**a de crédito** letter of credit. ~**a verde** green card. ~**earse** vpr correspond

cartel m poster; (*letrero*) sign. ~**era** f hoarding; (*en periódico*) listings; (*LAm en escuela, oficina*) notice board (*Brit*), bulletin board (*Amer*). **de** ~ celebrated

carter|a f wallet; (*de colegial*) satchel; (*para documentos*) briefcase; (*LAm, de mujer*) handbag (*Brit*), purse (*Amer*). ~**ista** m & f pickpocket

cartero m postman, mailman (*Amer*)

cartílago m cartilage

cartilla f first reading book. ~ **de ahorros** savings book. **leerle la** ~ **a uno** tell s.o. off

cartón m cardboard

cartucho m cartridge

cartulina f card

casa f house; (*hogar*) home; (*empresa*) firm. ~ **de huéspedes** boarding-house. ~ **de socorro** first aid post. **ir a** ~ go home. **salir de** ~ go out

casaca f jacket

casado adj married. **los recién** ~**s** the newly-weds

casa|mentero m matchmaker. ~**miento** m marriage; (*ceremonia*) wedding. ~**r** vt marry. ~**rse** vpr get married

cascabel m small bell; (*de serpiente*) rattle

cascada f waterfall

casca|nueces m invar nutcrackers. ~**r** **7** vt crack (nuez, huevo); (*pegar*) beat. ~**rse** vpr crack

cáscara f (*de huevo, nuez*) shell; (*de naranja*) peel; (*de plátano*) skin

cascarrabias adj invar grumpy

casco m helmet; (*de cerámica etc*) piece, fragment; (*cabeza*) scalp; (*de barco*) hull; (*envase*) empty bottle; (*de caballo*) hoof; (*de una ciudad*) part, area

cascote m piece of rubble. ~**s** mpl rubble

caserío m country house; (*poblado*) hamlet

casero adj home-made; (*doméstico*) domestic; (*amante del hogar*) home-loving; (*reunión*) family. ● m owner; (*vigilante*) caretaker

caseta f hut; (*puesto*) stand. ~ **de baño** bathing hut

casete m & f cassette

casi adv almost, nearly; (*en frases negativas*) very nearly. ~ ~ very nearly. ~ **nada** hardly any. **¡~ nada!** is that all? ~ **nunca** hardly ever

casill|a f hut; (*en ajedrez etc*) square; (*en formulario*) box; (*compartimento*) pigeonhole. ~**a electrónica** e-mail address. ~**ero** m pigeonholes; (*compartimento*) pigeonhole

casino m casino; (*club social*) club

caso m case. **el** ~ **es que** the fact is that. **en** ~ **de** in the event of. **en cualquier** ~ in any case, whatever happens. **en ese** ~ in that case. **en todo** ~ in any case. **en último** ~ as a last resort. **hacer** ~ **de** take notice of. **poner por** ~ suppose

caspa f dandruff

casquivana f flirt

cassette m & f cassette

casta f (de animal) breed; (de persona) descent; (grupo social) caste

castaña f chestnut

castañetear vi (dientes) chatter

castaño adj chestnut; (ojos) brown. ● m chestnut (tree)

castañuela f castanet

castellano adj Castilian. ● m (persona) Castilian; (lengua) Castilian, Spanish. ~**parlante** adj Castilian-speaking, Spanish-speaking. ¿habla Vd ~? do you speak Spanish?

---

castellano In Spain the term *castellano*, rather than *español*, refers to the Spanish language as opposed to Catalan, Basque etc. The choice of word has political overtones; *castellano* has separatist connotations and *español* is considered neutral. In Latin America *castellano* is another term for Spanish.

---

castidad f chastity

castig|ar 12 vt punish; (en deportes) penalize. ~**o** m punishment; (en deportes) penalty

castillo m castle

cast|izo adj traditional; (puro) pure. ~**o** adj chaste

castor m beaver

castrar vt castrate

castrense m military

casual adj chance, accidental. ~**idad** f chance, coincidence. dar la ~**idad** happen. de ~**idad** por ~**idad** by chance. ¡qué ~**idad**! what a coincidence!. ~**mente** adv by chance; (precisamente) actually

cataclismo m cataclysm

catador m taster

catalán adj & m Catalan

catalizador m catalyst

cat|alogar 12 vt catalogue; (fig) classify. ~**álogo** m catalogue

Cataluña f Catalonia

catamarán m catamaran

catapulta f catapult

catar vt taste, try

catarata f waterfall, falls; (Med) cataract

catarro m cold

cat|ástrofe m catastrophe. ~**astrófico** adj catastrophic

catecismo m catechism

cátedra f (en universidad) professorship, chair; (en colegio) post of head of department

catedral f cathedral

catedrático m professor; (de colegio) teacher, head of department

categor|ía f category; (clase) class. de ~**oría** important. de primera ~**oría** first-class. ~**órico** adj categorical

cat|olicismo m catholicism. ~**ólico** adj (Roman) Catholic ● m (Roman) Catholic

catorce adj & m fourteen

cauce m river bed; (fig, artificial) channel

caucho m rubber

caudal m (de río) volume of flow; (riqueza) wealth. ~**oso** adj (río) large

caudillo m leader

causa f cause; (motivo) reason; (Jurid) trial. a ~ de, por ~ de because of. ~**r** vt cause

cautel|a f caution. ~**oso** adj cautious, wary

cauterizar 10 vt cauterize

cautiv|ar vt capture; (fig, fascinar) captivate. **~erio** m, **~idad** f captivity. **~o** adj & m captive

cauto adj cautious

cavar vt/i dig

caverna f cave, cavern

caviar m caviare

cavidad f cavity

caza f hunting; (con fusil) shooting; (animales) game. ● m fighter. andar a (la) **~** de be in search of. **~ mayor** game hunting. dar **~** chase, go after. ir de **~** go hunting/shooting. **~dor** m hunter. **~dora** f jacket. **~r** 🔟 vt hunt; (con fusil) shoot; (fig) track down; (obtener) catch, get

caz|o m saucepan; (cucharón) ladle. **~oleta** f (small) saucepan. **~uela** f casserole

cebada f barley

ceb|ar vt fatten (up); bait (anzuelo); prime (arma de fuego). **~o** m bait; (de arma de fuego) charge

ceboll|a f onion. **~eta** f spring onion (Brit), scallion (Amer). **~ino** m chive

cebra f zebra

cece|ar vi lisp. **~o** m lisp

cedazo m sieve

ceder vt give up; (transferir) transfer. ● vi give in; (disminuir) ease off; (romperse) give way, collapse. **ceda el paso** give way (Brit), yield (Amer)

cedro m cedar

cédula f bond. **~ de identidad** identity card

CE(E) abrev (**Comunidad (Económica) Europea**) E(E)C

ceg|ador adj blinding. **~ar** 🔳 & 🔢 vt blind; (tapar) block up. **~arse** vpr be blinded (de by). **~uera** f blindness

ceja f eyebrow

cejar vi give way

celada f ambush; (fig) trap

cela|dor m (de cárcel) prison warder; (de museo etc) security guard. **~r** vt watch

celda f cell

celebra|ción f celebration. **~r** vt celebrate; (alabar) praise. **~rse** vpr take place

célebre adj famous

celebridad f fame; (persona) celebrity

celest|e adj heavenly; (vestido) pale blue. **azul ~e** sky-blue. **~ial** adj heavenly

celibato m celibacy

célibe adj celibate

celo m zeal; (de las hembras) heat; (de los machos) rut; (cinta adhesiva) Sellotape (P) (Brit), Scotch (P) tape (Amer). **~s** mpl jealousy. **dar ~s** make jealous. **tener ~s** be jealous

celofán m cellophane

celoso adj conscientious; (que tiene celos) jealous

celta adj & m (lengua) Celtic. ● m & f Celt

célula f cell

celular adj cellular. ●m (LAm) mobile, cellphone

celulosa f cellulose

cementerio m cemetery

cemento m cement; (hormigón) concrete; (LAm, cola) glue

cena f dinner; (comida ligera) supper

cenag|al m marsh, bog; (fig) tight spot. **~oso** adj boggy

cenar vt have for dinner; (en cena ligera) have for supper. ● vi have dinner; (tomar cena ligera) have supper

cenicero m ashtray

ceniza f ash

censo m census. ~ **electoral** electoral roll

censura f censure; (de prensa etc) censorship. ~**r** vt censure; censor (prensa etc)

centavo adj & m hundredth; (moneda) centavo

centell|a f flash; (chispa) spark. ~**ar**, ~**ear** vi sparkle

centena f hundred. ~**r** m hundred. a ~**res** by the hundred. ~**rio** adj centenarian. ● m centenary; (persona) centenarian

centeno m rye

centésim|a f hundredth. ~**o** adj hundredth

cent|ígrado adj centigrade, Celsius. ● m centigrade. ~**ígramo** m centigram. ~**ilitro** m centilitre. ~**ímetro** m centimetre

céntimo adj hundredth. ● m cent

centinela f sentry

centolla f, **centollo** m spider crab

central adj central. ● f head office. ~ **de correos** general post office. ~ **eléctrica** power station. ~ **nuclear** nuclear power station. ~ **telefónica** telephone exchange. ~**ita** f switchboard

centraliza|ción f centralization. ~**r** 🔟 vt centralize

centrar vt centre

céntrico adj central

centrífugo adj centrifugal

centro m centre. ~ **comercial** shopping centre (Brit), shopping mall (Amer). ~ **de llamadas** call centre

Centroamérica f Central America

centroamericano adj & m Cen-

tral American

ceñi|do adj tight. ~**r** 🄈 & 🟢 vt take (corona); (vestido) cling to. ~**rse** vpr limit o.s. (a to)

ceñ|o m frown. **fruncir el** ~**o** frown. ~**udo** adj frowning

cepill|ar vt brush; (en carpintería) plane. ~**o** m brush; (en carpintería) plane. ~**o de dientes** toothbrush

cera f wax

cerámic|a f ceramics; (materia) pottery; (objeto) piece of pottery. ~**o** adj ceramic

cerca f fence; (de piedra) wall.● adv near, close. ~ **de** prep close to, close up, closely

cercan|ía f nearness, proximity. ~**ías** fpl vicinity. **tren** m **de** ~**ías** local train. ~**o** adj near, close.

cercar 🟢 vt fence in, enclose; (gente) surround; (asediar) besiege

cerciorar vt convince. ~**se** vpr make sure

cerco m (asedio) siege; (círculo) ring; (LAm, valla) fence; (LAm, seto) hedge

cerdo m pig; (carne) pork

cereal m cereal

cerebr|al adj cerebral. ~**o** m brain; (persona) brains

ceremoni|a f ceremony. ~**al** adj ceremonial. ~**oso** adj ceremonious

cerez|a f cherry. ~**o** m cherry tree

cerill|a f match. ~**o** m (Mex) match

cern|er 🔟 vt sieve. ~**erse** vpr hover. ~**idor** m sieve

cero m nought, zero; (fútbol) nil (Brit), zero (Amer); (tenis) love; (persona) nonentity

cerquillo m (LAm, flequillo) fringe (Brit), bangs (Amer)

cerra|do adj shut, closed; (espa-

cio) shut in, enclosed; (*cielo*) overcast; (*curva*) sharp. ~**dura** *f* lock; (*acción de cerrar*) shutting, closing. ~**jero** *m* locksmith. ~**r** 1 *vt* shut, close; (*con llave*) lock; (*cercar*) enclose; turn off (*grifo*); block up (*agujero* etc). ● *vi* shut, close. ~**rse** *vpr* shut, close; (*herida*) heal. ~**r con llave** lock

cerro *m* hill

cerrojo *m* bolt. echar el ~ bolt

certamen *m* competition, contest

certero *adj* accurate

certeza *f*, **certidumbre** *f* certainty

certifica|do *adj* (*carta* etc) registered. ● *m* certificate. ~**r** 7 *vt* certify

certitud *f* certainty

cervatillo *m*, **cervato** *m* fawn

cerve|cería *f* beerhouse, bar; (*fábrica*) brewery. ~**za** *f* beer. ~**za de barril** draught beer. ~**za rubia** lager

cesa|ción *f* cessation, suspension. ~**nte** *adj* redundant. ~**r** *vt* stop. ● *vi* stop, cease; (*dejar un empleo*) resign. sin ~**r** incessantly

cesárea *f* caesarian (section)

cese *m* cessation; (*de un empleo*) dismissal. ~ **del fuego** (*LAm*) ceasefire

césped *m* grass, lawn

cest|a *f* basket. ~**o** *m* basket. ~**o de los papeles** waste-paper basket

chabacano *adj* common; (*chiste* etc) vulgar. ● *m* (*Mex*, *albaricoque*) apricot

chabola *f* shack. ~**s** *fpl* shanty town

cháchara *f* 1 chatter; (*Mex*, *objetos sin valor*) junk

chacharear *vt* (*Mex*) sell. ● *vi* 1 chatter

chacra *f* (*LAm*) farm

chal *m* shawl

chalado *adj* 1 crazy

chalé *m* house (with a garden), villa

chaleco *m* waistcoat, vest (*Amer*). ~ **salvavidas** life-jacket

chalet *m* (*pl* ~s) house (with a garden), villa

chalote *m* shallot

chamac|a *f* (*esp Mex*) girl. ~**o** *m* (*esp Mex*) boy

chamarra *f* sheepskin jacket; (*Mex*, *chaqueta corta*) jacket

chamb|a *f* (*Mex*, *trabajo*) work. **por** ~**a** by fluke. ~**ear** *vi* (*Mex*, *fam*) work

champán *m*, **champaña** *m* & *f* champagne

champiñón *m* mushroom

champú *m* (*pl* ~**es** o ~**s**) shampoo

chamuscar 7 *vt* scorch

chance *m* (*esp LAm*) chance

chancho *m* (*LAm*) pig

chanchullo *m* 1 swindle, fiddle 1

chanclo *m* clog; (*de caucho*) rubber overshoe

chándal *m* (*pl* ~**s**) tracksuit

chantaje *m* blackmail. ~**ar** *vt* blackmail

chanza *f* joke

chapa *f* plate, sheet; (*de madera*) plywood; (*de botella*) metal top; (*carrocería*) bodywork; (*LAm cerradura*) lock. ~**do** *adj* plated. ~**do a la antigua** old-fashioned. ~**do en oro** gold-plated

chaparro *adj* (*LAm*) short, squat

chaparrón *m* downpour

chapopote *m* (*Mex*) tar

chapotear *vi* splash

chapucero adj (persona) slap-dash; (trabajo) shoddy

chapulín m (Mex) locust; (saltamontes) grasshopper

chapurrar, chapurrear vt have a smattering of, speak a little

chapuza f botched job; (trabajo ocasional) odd job

chaquet|a f jacket. **cambiar de ~a** change sides. **~ón** m three-quarter length coat

charc|a f pond, pool. **~o** m puddle, pool

charcutería f delicatessen

charla f chat; (conferencia) talk. **~dor** adj talkative. **~r** vi 🔢 chat. **~tán** adj talkative. ● m chatterbox; (vendedor) cunning hawker; (curandero) charlatan

charol m varnish; (cuero) patent leather. **~a** f (Mex) tray

charr|a f (Mex) horsewoman, cowgirl. **~o** m (Mex) horseman, cowboy

chascar 🔢 vt crack (látigo); click (lengua); snap (dedos). ● vi (madera) creak. **~ con la lengua** click one's tongue

chasco m disappointment

chasis m (Auto) chassis

chasqu|ear vt crack (látigo); click (lengua); snap (dedos). ● vi (madera) creak. **~ con la lengua** click one's tongue. **~ido** m crack; (de la lengua) click; (de los dedos) snap

chatarra f scrap iron; (fig) scrap

chato adj (nariz) snub; (objetos) flat. ● m wine glass

chav|a f (Mex) girl, lass. **~al** m 🔢 boy, lad. **~o** m (Mex) boy, lad.

checa|r 🔢 vt (Mex) check; (Mex, Med) checkup. **~r** 🔢 vt (Mex) check; (vigilar) check up on. **~r tarjeta** clock in

checo adj & m Czech. **~slovaco** adj & m (History) Czechoslovak

chelín m shilling

chelo m cello

cheque m cheque. **~ de viaje** traveller's cheque. **~ar** vt check; (LAm) check in (equipaje). **~o** m check; (Med) checkup. **~ra** f cheque-book

chévere adj (LAm) great

chica f girl; (criada) maid, servant

chicano adj & m Chicano, Mexican-American

> ℹ️
> **Chicano** Chicanos are Mexican Americans, descendants of Mexican immigrants living in US. For long looked down by Americans of European descent, Chicanos have found a new pride in their origins and culture. There are numerous Chicano radio stations and many universities and colleges now offer courses in Chicano studies.

chícharo m (Mex) pea

chicharra f cicada; (timbre) buzzer

chichón m bump

chicle m chewing-gum

chico adj 🔢 small; (esp LAm, de edad) young. ● m boy. **~s** mpl children

chicoria f chicory

chifla|do adj 🔢 crazy, daft. **~r** vt whistle at, boo. ● vi (LAm) whistle; (🔢, gustar mucho) **me chifla el chocolate** I'm mad about chocolate. **~rse** vpr be mad (por about)

chilango adj (Mex) from Mexico City

chile m chilli

Chile *m* Chile
chileno *adj & m* Chilean
chill|ar *vi* scream, shriek; (ratón) squeak; (cerdo) squeal. **~ido** *m* scream, screech. **~ón** *adj* noisy; (colores) loud; (sonido) shrill
chimenea *f* chimney; (*hogar*) fireplace
chimpancé *m* chimpanzee
china *f* Chinese (woman)
China *f* China
chinche *m* drawing-pin (*Brit*), thumbtack (*Amer*); (*insecto*) bedbug; (*fig*) nuisance. **~eta** *f* drawing-pin (*Brit*), thumbtack (*Amer*)
chinela *f* slipper
chino *adj* Chinese; (*Mex rizado*) curly. ● *m* Chinese (man); (*Mex, de pelo rizado*) curly-haired person
chipriota *adj & m & f* Cypriot
chiquero *m* pen; (*LAm, pocilga*) pigsty (*Brit*), pigpen (*Amer*)
chiquillo *adj* childish. ● *m* child, kid [!]
chirimoya *f* custard apple
chiripa *f* fluke
chirri|ar [20] *vi* creak; (frenos) screech; (pájaro) chirp. **~do** *m* creaking; (*de frenos*) screech; (*de pájaros*) chirping
chis *int* sh!, hush!; (*fam, para llamar a uno*) hey!, psst!
chism|e *m* gadget, thingumajig [!]; (*chismorreo*) piece of gossip. **~es** *mpl* things, bits and pieces. **~orreo** *m* gossip. **~oso** *adj* gossipy.● *m* gossip
chisp|a *f* spark; (*pizca*) drop; (*gracia*) wit; (*fig*) sparkle. **estar que echa ~a(s)** be furious. **~eante** *adj* sparkling. **~ear** *vi* spark; (*lloviznar*) drizzle; (*fig*) sparkle. **~orrotear** *vt* throw out sparks; (fuego) crackle; (aceite) spit
chistar *vi*. **ni chistó** he didn't say a word. **sin ~** without saying a word
chiste *m* joke, funny story. **tener ~** be funny
chistera *f* top hat
chistoso *adj* funny
chiva|rse *vpr* tip-off; (niño) tell. **~tazo** *m* tip-off. **~to** *m* informer; (*niño*) telltale
chivo *m* kid; (*LAm, macho cabrío*) billy goat
choca|nte *adj* shocking; (*Mex desagradable*) unpleasant. **~r** [7] *vt* clink (vasos); (*LAm*) crash (vehículo). **¡chócala!** give me five! ● *vi* collide, hit. **~r con, ~r contra** crash into
choch|ear *vi* be gaga. **~o** *adj* gaga; (*fig*) soft
choclo *m* (*LAm*) corn on the cob
chocolate *m* chocolate. **tableta *f* de ~** bar of chocolate
chófer, (*LAm*) **chofer** *m* chauffeur; (*conductor*) driver
cholo *adj & m* (*LAm*) half-breed
chopo *m* poplar
choque *m* collision; (*fig*) clash; (*eléctrico*) shock; (*Auto, Rail etc*) crash, accident; (*sacudida*) jolt
chorizo *m* chorizo
chorro *m* jet, stream; (*caudal pequeño*) trickle; (*fig*) stream. **a ~** (avión) jet. **a ~s** (*fig*) in abundance
chovinista *adj* chauvinistic. ● *m & f* chauvinist
choza *f* hut
chubas|co *m* shower. **~quero** *m* raincoat, anorak
chuchería *f* trinket
chueco *adj* (*LAm*) crooked

chufa f tiger nut

chuleta f chop

chulo adj cocky; (bonito) lovely (Brit), neat (Amer); (Mex, atractivo) cute. ● m tough guy; (proxeneta) pimp

chup|ada f suck; (al helado) lick; (al cigarro) puff. ~**ado** adj skinny; (fam, fácil) very easy. ~**ar** vt suck; puff at (cigarro etc); (absorber) absorb. ~**ete** m dummy (Brit), pacifier (Amer). ~**ón** m sucker; (LAm) dummy (Brit), pacifier (Amer); (Mex, del biberón) teat

churrasco m barbecued steak

churro m fritter; ① mess

chut|ar vi shoot. ~**e** m shot

cianuro m cyanide

cibernética f cibernetics

cicatriz f scar. ~**ar** ⑩ vt/i heal. ~**arse** vpr heal

cíclico adj cyclic(al)

ciclis|mo m cycling. ~**ta** adj cycle. ● m & f cyclist

ciclo m cycle; (de películas, conciertos) season; (de conferencias) series

ciclomotor m moped

ciclón m cyclone

ciego adj blind. ● m blind man, blind person. a ciegas in the dark

cielo m sky; (Relig) heaven; (persona) darling. ¡~**s**! good heavens!, goodness me!

ciempiés m invar centipede

cien adj a hundred. ● **por** ~ one hundred per cent

ciénaga f bog, swamp

ciencia f science; (fig) knowledge. ~**s** fpl (Univ etc) science. ~**s** empresariales business studies. a ~ cierta for certain

cieno m mud

científico adj scientific. ● m

scientist

ciento adj & m a hundred, one hundred. ~**s de** hundreds of. **por** ~ per cent

cierre m fastener; (acción de cerrar) shutting, closing; (LAm, cremallera) zip, zipper (Amer)

cierto adj certain; (verdad) true. **estar en lo** ~ be right. **lo** ~ **es que** the fact is that. **no es** ~ that's not true. ¿**no es** ~? isn't that right? **por** ~ by the way. **si bien es** ~ **que** although

ciervo m deer

cifra f figure, number; (cantidad) sum. **en** ~ coded, in code. ~**do** adj coded. ~**r** vt code; place (esperanzas)

cigala f crayfish

cigarra f cicada

cigarr|illera f cigarette box; (de bolsillo) cigarette case. ~**illo** m cigarette. ~**o** m (cigarrillo) cigarette; (puro) cigar

cigüeña f stork

cilantro m coriander

cil|índrico adj cylindrical. ~**indro** m cylinder

cima f top; (fig) summit

cimbr|ear vt shake. ~**earse** vpr sway. ~**onada** f, ~**onazo** m (LAm) jolt; (de explosión) blast

cimentar ① vt lay the foundations of; (fig, reforzar) strengthen

cimientos mpl foundations

cinc m zinc

cincel m chisel. ~**ar** vt chisel

cinco adj & m five; (en fechas) fifth

cincuent|a adj & m fifty; (quincuagésimo) fiftieth. ~**ón** adj in his fifties

cine m cinema; (local) cinema (Brit), movie theater (Amer). ~**asta** m & f film maker (*Brit*), movie maker (*Amer*). **~matográfico** *adj* film (*Brit*), movie (*Amer*)

cínico *adj* cynical. ● *m* cynic

cinismo *m* cynicism

cinta *f* ribbon; (*película*) film (*Brit*), movie (*Amer*); (*para grabar, en carreras*) tape. **~ aislante** insulating tape. **~ métrica** tape measure. **~ virgen** blank tape

cintur|a *f* waist. **~ón** *m* belt. **~ón de seguridad** safety belt. **~ón salvavidas** lifebelt

ciprés *m* cypress (tree)

circo *m* circus

circuito *m* circuit; (*viaje*) tour. **~ cerrado** closed circuit. **corto ~** short circuit

circula|ción *f* circulation; (*vehículos*) traffic. **~r** *adj* circular. ● *vi* circulate; (*líquidos*) flow; (*conducir*) drive; (*caminar*) walk; (*autobús*) run

círculo *m* circle. **~ vicioso** vicious circle. **en ~** in a circle

circunci|dar *vt* circumcise. **~sión** *f* circumcision

circunferencia *f* circumference

circunflejo *m* circumflex

circunscri|bir (*pp* circunscrito) *vt* confine. **~birse** *vpr* confine o.s. (a to). **~pción** *f* (*distrito*) district. **~pción electoral** constituency

circunspecto *adj* circumspect

circunstancia *f* circumstance

circunv|alar *vt* bypass. **~olar** *vt* 🄶 circle

cirio *m* candle

ciruela *f* plum. **~ pasa** prune

ciru|gía *f* surgery. **~jano** *m* surgeon

cisne *m* swan

cisterna *f* tank, cistern

cita *f* appointment; (*entre chico y chica*) date; (*referencia*) quotation. **~ a ciegas** blind date. **~ flash** speed dating. **~ción** *f* quotation; (*Jurid*) summons. **~do** *adj* aforementioned. **~r** *vt* make an appointment with; (*mencionar*) quote; (*Jurid*) summons. **~rse** *vpr* arrange to meet

cítara *f* zither

ciudad *f* town; (*grande*) city. **~ balneario** (*LAm*) coastal resort. **~ perdida** (*Mex*) shanty town. **~ universitaria** university campus. **~anía** *f* citizenship; (*habitantes*) citizens. **~ano** *adj* civic. ● *m* citizen, inhabitant

cívico *adj* civic

civil *adj* civil. ● *m & f* civil guard; (*persona no militar*) civilian

civiliza|ción *f* civilization. **~r** 🄺 *vt* civilize. **~rse** *vpr* become civilized

civismo *m* community spirit

clam|ar *vi* cry out, clamour. **~or** *m* clamour; (*protesta*) outcry. **~oroso** *adj* noisy; (*éxito*) resounding

clandestino *adj* clandestine, secret; (*referencia*) underground

clara *f* (*de huevo*) egg white

claraboya *f* skylight

clarear *vi* dawn; (*aclarar*) brighten up

clarete *m* rosé

claridad *f* clarity; (*luz*) light

clarifica|ción *f* clarification. **~r** 🄸 *vt* clarify

clar|ín *m* bugle. **~inete** *m* clarinet. **~inetista** *m & f* clarinettist

clarividen|cia *f* clairvoyance; (*fig*) far-sightedness. **~te** *adj* clairvoyant; (*fig*) far-sighted

claro *adj* clear; (*luminoso*) bright;

(colores) light; (líquido) thin. ● m (en bosque) clearing; (espacio) gap. ● adv clearly. ● int of course! ¡~ que sí! yes, of course! ¡~ que no! of course not!

clase f class; (tipo) kind, sort; (aula) classroom. ~ media middle class. ~ obrera working class. ~ social social class. dar ~ teach

clásico adj classical; (típico) classic. ● m classic

clasificación f classification; (deportes) league. ~r **7** vt classify

claustro m cloister; (Univ) staff

claustrofobia f claustrophobia. ~óbico adj claustrophobic

cláusula f clause

clausura f closure

clavado adj fixed; (con clavo) nailed. es ~do a su padre he's the spitting image of his father. ● m (LAm) dive. ~r vt knock in (clavo); stick in (cuchillo); (fijar) fix; (juntar) nail together

clave f key; (Mus) clef; (instrumento) harpsichord. ~cín m harpsichord

clavel m carnation

clavícula f collarbone, clavicle

clavija f peg; (Elec) plug. ~o m nail; (Culin) clove

claxon /'klakson/ m (pl ~s) horn

clemencia f clemency, mercy

clementina f tangerine

cleptómano m kleptomaniac

clerical adj clerical

clérigo m priest

clero m clergy

clic m: hacer ~ en to click on

cliché m cliché; (Foto) negative

cliente m customer; (de médico) patient; (de abogado) client. ~la f

clientele, customers; (de médico) patients

clima m climate; (ambiente) atmosphere. ~ático adj climatic. ~atizado adj air-conditioned

clínica f clinic. ~o adj clinical

cloaca f drain, sewer

clon m clone

cloro m chlorine

club m (pl ~s o ~es) club

coacción f coercion. ~onar vt coerce

coagular vt coagulate; clot (sangre); curdle (leche). ~se vpr coagulate; (sangre) clot; (leche) curdle

coalición f coalition

coartada f alibi. ~r vt hinder; restrict (libertad etc)

cobarde adj cowardly. ● m coward. ~ía f cowardice

cobertizo m shed. ~ura f covering; (en radio, TV) coverage

cobija f (Mex, manta) blanket. ~as fpl (LAm, ropa de cama) bedclothes. ~ar vt shelter. ~arse vpr (take) shelter. ~o m shelter

cobra f cobra

cobrador m collector; (de autobús) conductor. ~r vt collect; (ganar) earn; charge (precio); cash (cheque); (recuperar) recover. ● vi be paid

cobre m copper. ~izo adj coppery

cobro m collection; (de cheque) cashing; (pago) payment. presentar al ~ cash

cocaína f cocaine. ~lero adj (of) coca farming. ● n coca farmer

cocción f cooking; (Tec) firing

cocer **8** & **9** vt/i cook; (hervir) boil; (Tec) fire. ~ido m stew

coche *m* car, automobile (*Amer*); (*de tren*) coach, carriage; (*de bebé*) pram (*Brit*), baby carriage (*Amer*). **~-cama** sleeper. **~ fúnebre** hearse. **~ restaurante** dining-car. **~s de choque** dodgems. **~ra** *f* garage; (*de autobuses*) depot

cochin|ada *f* dirty thing. **~o** *adj* dirty, filthy. ● *m* pig

cociente *m* quotient. **~ intelectual** intelligence quotient, IQ

cocin|a *f* kitchen; (*arte*) cookery, cuisine; (*aparato*) cooker. **~a de gas** gas cooker. **~a eléctrica** electric cooker. **~ar** *vt/i* cook. **~ero** *m* cook

coco *m* coconut; (*árbol*) coconut palm; (*cabeza*) head; (*que mete miedo*) bogeyman. **comerse el ~** think hard

cocoa *f* (*LAm*) cocoa

cocodrilo *m* crocodile

cocotero *m* coconut palm

cóctel *m* (*pl* **~s** o **~es**) cocktail

cod|azo *m* nudge (with one's elbow). **~ear** *vt/i* elbow, nudge. **~earse** *vpr* rub shoulders (con with)

codici|a *f* greed. **~ado** *adj* coveted, sought after. **~ar** *vt* covet. **~oso** *adj* greedy

código *m* code. **~ de la circulación** Highway Code

codo *m* elbow; (*dobladura*) bend. **~ a ~** side by side. **hablar (hasta) por los ~s** talk too much

codorniz *f* quail

coeficiente *m* coefficient. **~ intelectual** intelligence quotient, IQ

coerción *f* constraint

coetáneo *adj & m* contemporary

coexist|encia *f* coexistence. **~ir** *vi* coexist

cofradía *f* brotherhood

cofre *m* chest; (*Mex*, *capó*) bonnet (*Brit*), hood (*Amer*)

coger 14 *vt* (*esp Esp*) take; catch (tren, autobús, pelota, catarro); (*agarrar*) take hold of; (*del suelo*) pick up; pick (frutos etc); (*LAm*, *vulgar*) to screw. **~se** *vpr* trap, catch; (*agarrarse*) hold on

cogollo *m* (*de lechuga etc*) heart; (*brote*) bud

cogote *m* nape; (*LAm*, *cuello*) neck

cohech|ar *vt* bribe. **~o** *m* bribery

cohe|rente *adj* coherent. **~sión** *f* cohesion

cohete *m* rocket

cohibi|do *adj* shy; (*inhibido*) awkward; (*incómodo*) awkward. **~r** *vt* inhibit; (*incomodar*) make s.o. feel embarrassed. **~rse** *vpr* feel inhibited

coima *f* (*LAm*) bribe

coincid|encia *f* coincidence. **dar la ~encia** happen. **~ir** *vt* coincide

coje|ar *vt* limp; (*mueble*) wobble. **~ra** *f* lameness

coj|ín *m* cushion. **~inete** *m* small cushion

cojo *adj* lame; (*mueble*) wobbly. ● *m* lame person

col *f* cabbage. **~es de Bruselas** Brussel sprouts

cola *f* tail; (*fila*) queue; (*para pegar*) glue. **a la ~** at the end. **hacer ~** queue (up) (*Brit*), line up (*Amer*)

colabora|ción *f* collaboration. **~dor** *m* collaborator. **~r** *vi* collaborate

colada *f* washing. **hacer la ~** do the washing

colador *m* strainer

colapso *m* collapse; (*fig*) standstill

colar 🔢 vt strain; pass (moneda falsa etc). ● vi (líquido) seep through; (fig) be believed. ~se vpr slip; (en una cola) jump the queue; (en fiesta) gatecrash

colch|a f bedspread. ~ón m mattress. ~oneta f air bed; (en gimnasio) mat

colear vi wag its tail; (asunto) not be resolved. **vivito y coleando** alive and kicking

colecci|ón f collection. ~onar vt collect. ~onista m & f collector

colecta f collection

colectivo adj collective

colega m & f colleague

colegi|al m schoolboy. ~ala f schoolgirl. ~o m school; (de ciertas profesiones) college. ~o mayor hall of residence

cólera m cholera. ● f anger, fury. **montar en** ~ fly into a rage

colérico adj furious, irate

colesterol m cholesterol

coleta f pigtail

colga|nte adj hanging. ● m pendant. ~r 🔢 & 🔢 vt hang; hang out (ropa lavada); hang up (abrigo etc); put down (teléfono). ● vi hang; (teléfono) hang up. ~rse vpr hang o.s. **dejar a uno** ~**do** let s.o. down

colibrí m hummingbird

cólico m colic

coliflor f cauliflower

colilla f cigarette end

colina f hill

colinda|nte adj adjoining. ~r vt border (con on)

colisión f collision, crash; (fig) clash

collar m necklace; (de perro) collar

colmar vt fill to the brim; try (paciencia); (fig) fulfill. ~ **a uno de atenciones** lavish attention on s.o.

colmena f beehive, hive

colmillo m eye tooth, canine (tooth); (de elefante) tusk; (de carnívoro) fang

colmo m height. **ser el** ~ be the limit, be the last straw

coloca|ción f positioning; (empleo) job, position. ~r 🔢 vt put, place; (buscar empleo) find work for. ~rse vpr find a job

Colombia f Colombia

colombiano adj & m Colombian

colon m colon

colón m (unidad monetaria de Costa Rica y El Salvador) colon

colon|ia f colony; (comunidad) community; (agua de colonia) cologne; (Mex, barrio) residential suburb. ~ia de verano holiday camp. ~iaje m (LAm) colonial period. ~ial adj colonial. ~ialista m & f colonialist. ~ización f colonization. ~izar 🔢 colonize. ~o m colonist, settler; (labrador) tenant farmer

coloqui|al adj colloquial. ~o m conversation; (congreso) conference

color m colour. de ~ colour. en ~(es) (fotos, película) colour. ~ado adj (rojo) red. ~ante m colouring. ~ear vt/i colour. ~ete m blusher. ~ido m colour

colosal adj colossal; (fig, fam, magnífico) terrific

columna f column; (en anatomía) spine. ~ vertebral spinal column; (fig) backbone

columpi|ar vt swing. ~arse vpr swing. ~o m swing

coma f comma; (Mat) point. ● m

(Med) coma

comadre f (madrina) godmother; (amiga) friend. **~ar** vi gossip

comadreja f weasel

comadrona f midwife

comal m (Mex) griddle

command|ancia f command. **~ante** m & f commander. **~o** m command; (Mil, soldado) commando; (de terroristas) cell

comarca f area, region

comba f bend; (juguete) skipping-rope; (de viga) sag. **saltar a la ~** skip. **~rse** vpr bend; (viga) sag

combat|e m combat; (pelea) fight. **~iente** m fighter. **~ir** vt/i fight

combina|ción f combination; (enlace) connection; (prenda) slip. **~r** vt combine; put together (colores)

combustible m fuel

comedia f comedy; (cualquier obra de teatro) play; (LAm, telenovela) soap (opera)

comedi|do adj restrained; (LAm, atento) obliging. **~rse** 5 vpr show restraint

comedor m dining-room; (restaurante) restaurant

comensal m fellow diner

comentar vt comment on; discuss (tema); (mencionar) mention. **~io** m commentary; (observación) comment. **~ios** mpl gossip. **~ista** m & f commentator

comenzar 1 & 10 vt/i begin, start

comer vt eat; (a mediodía) have for lunch; (esp LAm, cenar) have for dinner; (corroer) eat away; (en ajedrez) take. ● vi eat; (a mediodía) have lunch; (esp LAm, cenar) have

dinner. **dar de ~** a feed. **~se** vpr eat (up)

comerci|al adj commercial; (ruta) trade; (nombre, trato) business. ● m (LAm) commercial, ad. **~ante** m trader; (de tienda) shopkeeper. **~ar** vi trade (con with, en in); (con otra persona) do business. **~o** m commerce; (actividad) trade; (tienda) shop; (negocios) business. **~o justo** fair trade

comestible adj edible. **~s** mpl food. **tienda de ~s** grocer's (shop) (Brit), grocery (Amer)

cometa m comet. ● f kite

comet|er vt commit; make (falta). **~ido** m task

comezón m itch

comicios mpl elections

cómico adj comic; (gracioso) funny. ● m comic actor; (humorista) comedian

comida f food; (a mediodía) lunch; (esp LAm, cena) dinner; (acto) meal

comidilla f. **ser la ~ del pueblo** be the talk of the town

comienzo m beginning, start

comillas fpl inverted commas

comil|ón adj greedy. **~ona** f feast

comino m cumin. **(no) me importa un ~** I couldn't care less

comisar|ía f police station. **~io** m commissioner; (deportes) steward

comisión f assignment; (organismo) commission, committee; (Com) commission

comisura f corner. **~ de los labios** corner of the mouth

comité m committee

como prep as; (comparación) like. ● adv about. ● conj as. **~ quieras** as you like. **~ si** as if

cómo *adverbio*

····➤ how. ¿~ se llega? how do you get there? ¿~ es de alto? how tall is it? sé ~ pasó I know how it happened

! Cuando **cómo** va seguido del verbo **llamar** se traduce por *what, p. ej.* ¿~ **te llamas?** what's your name?

····➤ cómo + ser (sugiriendo descripción) ¿~ es su marido? what's her husband like?; (físicamente) what does her husband look like? no sé ~ es la comida I don't know what the food's like

····➤ (por qué) why. ¿~ no actuaron antes? why didn't they act sooner?

····➤ (pidiendo que se repita) sorry?, pardon? ¿~? no te escuché sorry? I didn't hear you

····➤ (en exclamaciones) ¡~ llueve! it's really pouring! ¡~! ¿que no lo sabes? what! you mean you don't know? ¡~ no! of course!

cómoda *f* chest of drawers
comodidad *f* comfort. a su ~ at your convenience
cómodo *adj* comfortable; (*conveniente*) convenient
comoquiera *conj.* ~ que sea however it may be
compacto *adj* compact; (*denso*) dense; (*líneas etc*) close
compadecer **11** *vt* feel sorry for. ~se *vpr.* ~se de feel sorry for
compadre *m* godfather; (*amigo*) friend
compañero *m* companion; (*de trabajo*) colleague; (*de clase*) class-

mate; (*pareja*) partner. ~ía *f* company. en ~ía de with
comparable *adj* comparable. ~ción *f* comparison. ~r *vt* compare. ~tivo *adj & m* comparative
comparecer **11** *vi* appear
comparsa *f* group. ●*m & f* (*en el teatro*) extra
compartim(i)ento *m* compartment
compartir *vt* share
compás *m* (*instrumento*) (pair of) compasses; (*ritmo*) rhythm; (*división*) bar (*Brit*), measure (*Amer*); (*Naut*) compass. a ~ in time
compasión *f* compassion, pity. tener ~ón de feel sorry for. ~vo *adj* compassionate
compatibilidad *f* compatibility. ~le *adj* compatible
compatriota *m & f* compatriot
compendio *m* summary
compensación *f* compensation. ~ción por despido redundancy payment. ~r *vt* compensate
competencia *f* competition; (*capacidad*) competence; (*poder*) authority; (*incumbencia*) jurisdiction. ~te *adj* competent
competición *f* competition. ~dor *m* competitor. ~r **5** *vi* compete
compinche *m* accomplice; (*fam*, *amigo*) friend, mate **!**
complacer **32** *vt* please. ~erse *vpr* be pleased. ~iente *adj* obliging; (*marido*) complaisant
complejidad *f* complexity. ~o *adj & m* complex
complementario *adj* complementary. ~o *m* complement; (*Gram*) object, complement
completar *vt* complete. ~o *adj* complete; (*lleno*) full; (*exhaustivo*)

comprehensive

complexión f build

complica|ción f complication; (esp AmL, implicación) involvement. ~r **7** vt complicate; involve (persona). ~rse vpr become complicated; (implicarse) get involved

cómplice m & f accomplice

complot m (pl ~s) plot

compon|ente adj component. • m component; (miembro) member. ~er **34** vt make up; (Mus, Literatura etc) write, compose; (esp LAm, reparar) mend; (LAm) set (hueso); settle (estómago). ~erse vpr be made up; (arreglarse) get better. ~érselas manage

comporta|miento m behaviour. ~rse vpr behave. ~rse mal misbehave

composi|ción f composition. ~tor m composer

compostura f composure; (LAm, arreglo) repair

compota f stewed fruit

compra f purchase. ~ a plazos hire purchase. hacer la(s) ~(s) do the shopping. ir de ~s go shopping. ~dor m buyer. ~r vt buy. ~venta f buying and selling; (Jurid) sale and purchase contract. negocio m de ~venta second-hand shop

compren|der vt understand; (incluir) include. ~sión f understanding. ~sivo adj understanding

compresa f compress; (de mujer) sanitary towel

compr|esión f compression. ~imido adj compressed. • m pill, tablet. ~imir vt compress

comproba|nte m proof; (recibo) receipt. ~r vt check; (demostrar) prove

comprom|eter vt compromise; (arriesgar) jeopardize. ~eterse vpr compromise o.s.; (obligarse) agree to; (novios) get engaged. ~etido adj (situación) awkward, delicate; (autor) politically committed. ~iso m obligation; (apuro) predicament; (cita) appointment; (acuerdo) agreement. sin ~iso without obligation

compuesto adj compound; (persona) smart. • m compound

computa|ción f (esp LAm) computing. curso m de ~ción computer course. ~dor m, computadora f computer. ~r vt calculate. ~rizar, computerizar **10** vt computerize

cómputo m calculation

comulgar 12 vi take Communion

común adj common; (compartido) joint. en ~ in common. por lo ~ generally. • m el ~ de most

comunal adj communal

comunica|ción f communication. ~do m communiqué. ~do de prensa press release. ~r **7** vt communicate; (informar) inform; (LAm, por teléfono) put through. está ~ndo (teléfono) it's engaged. ~rse vpr communicate; (ponerse en contacto) get in touch. ~tivo adj communicative

comunidad f community. ~ de vecinos residents' association. C~ (Económica) Europea European (Economic) Community. en ~ together

---

Comunidad Autónoma *i*

In 1978 Spain was divided into *comunidades autónomas* or *autonomías*, which have far greater powers than the old

c

regiones. The *comunidades autónomas* are: Andalusia, Aragon, Asturias, Balearic Islands, the Basque Country, Canary Islands, Cantabria, Castilla y León, Castilla-La Mancha, Catalonia, Extremadura, Galicia, Madrid, Murcia, Navarre, La Rioja, Valencia and the North African enclaves of Ceuta and Melilla.

comunión *f* communion; (*Relig*) (Holy) Communion

comunis|mo *m* communism. **~ta** *adj & m & f* communist

con *prep* with; (+ *infinitivo*) by. **~** decir la verdad by telling the truth. **~** que so. **~** tal que as long as

concebir **5** *vt/i* conceive

conceder *vt* concede, grant; award (premio); (*admitir*) admit

concej|al *m* councillor. **~ero** *m* (*LAm*) councillor. **~o** *m* council

concentra|ción *f* concentration; (*Pol*) rally. **~r** *vt* concentrate; assemble (personas). **~rse** *vpr* concentrate

concep|ción *f* conception. **~to** *m* concept; (*opinión*) opinion. bajo ningún **~** in no way

concerniente *adj*. en lo **~** a with regard to

concertar **1** *vt* arrange; agree (upon) (plan)

concesión *f* concession

concha *f* shell; (*carey*) tortoiseshell

conciencia *f* conscience; (*conocimiento*) awareness. **~** limpia clear conscience. **~** sucia guilty conscience. a **~** de que fully aware that. en **~** honestly. tener **~** de be aware of. tomar **~** de become aware of. **~r** *vt* make aware. **~rse**

vpr become aware

concientizar **10** *vt* (*esp LAm*) make aware. **~se** *vpr* become aware

concienzudo *adj* conscientious

concierto *m* concert; (*acuerdo*) agreement; (*Mus*, *composición*) concerto

concilia|ción *f* reconciliation. **~r** *vt* reconcile. **~r** el sueño get to sleep. **~rse** *vpr* gain

concilio *m* council

conciso *m* concise

conclu|ir **17** *vt* finish; (*deducir*) conclude. ● *vi* finish, end. **~sión** *f* conclusion. **~yente** *adj* conclusive

concord|ancia *f* agreement. **~ar** **2** *vt* reconcile. ● *vi* agree. **~e** *adj* in agreement. **~ia** *f* harmony

concret|amente *adv* specifically, to be exact. **~ar** *vt* make specific. **~arse** *vpr* become definite; (*limitarse*) confine o.s. **~o** *adj* concrete; (*determinado*) specific, particular. en **~o** definite; (*concretamente*) to be exact; (*en resumen*) in short. ●*m* (*LAm*, *hormigón*) concrete

concurr|encia *f* concurrence; (*reunión*) audience. **~ido** *adj* crowded, busy. **~ir** *vi* meet; ; (*coincidir*) agree. **~** a (*asistir a*) attend

concurs|ante *m & f* competitor, contestant. **~ar** *vi* compete, take part. **~o** *m* competition; (*ayuda*) help

cond|ado *m* county. **~e** *m* earl, count

condena *f* sentence. **~ción** *f* condemnation. **~do** *m* convicted person. **~r** *vt* condemn; (*Jurid*) convict

condensa|ción *f* condensation.

~r *vt* condense

condesa *f* countess

condescende|ncia *f* condescension; (*tolerancia*) indulgence. ~r **1** *vi* agree; (*dignarse*) condescend

condici|ón *f* condition. a ~ón de (que) on condition that. ~onal *adj* conditional. ~onar *vt* condition

condiment|ar *vt* season. ~o *m* seasoning

condolencia *f* condolence

condominio *m* joint ownership; (*LAm, edificio*) block of flats (*Brit*), condominium (*esp Amer*)

condón *m* condom

condonar *vt* (*perdonar*) reprieve; cancel (deuda)

conducir **47** *vt* drive (vehículo); carry (electricidad, gas, agua). ● *vi* drive; (*fig, llevar*) lead. ¿a qué conduce? what's the point? ~se *vpr* behave

conducta *f* behaviour

conducto *m* pipe, tube; (*en anatomía*) duct. por ~ de through. ~r *m* driver; (*jefe*) leader; (*Elec*) conductor

conduzco *vb véase* **CONDUCIR**

conectar *vt/i* connect

conejo *m* rabbit

conexión *f* connection

confabularse *vpr* plot

confecci|ón *f* (*de trajes*) tailoring; (*de vestidos*) dressmaking. ~ones *fpl* clothing, clothes. de ~ón ready-to-wear. ~onar *vt* make

confederación *f* confederation

conferencia *f* conference; (*al teléfono*) long-distance call; (*Univ*) lecture. ~ en la cima, ~ (en la) cumbre summit conference. ~nte *m & f* lecturer

conferir **4** *vt* confer; award (premio)

confes|ar **1** *vt/i* confess. ~arse *vpr* confess. ~ión *f* confession. ~ionario *m* confessional. ~or *m* confessor

confeti *m* confetti

confia|do *adj* trusting; (*seguro de sí mismo*) confident. ~nza *f* trust; (*en sí mismo*) confidence; (*intimidad*) familiarity. ~r **20** *vt* entrust. ● *vi*. ~r en trust

confiden|cia *f* confidence, secret. ~cial *adj* confidential. ~te *m* confidant. ● *f* confidante

configuraci|ón *f* configuration. ~ar *vt* to configure

conf|ín *m* border. ~ines *mpl* outermost parts. ~inar *vt* confine; (*desterrar*) banish

confirma|ción *f* confirmation. ~r *vt* confirm

confiscar **7** *vt* confiscate

confit|ería *f* sweet-shop (*Brit*), candy store (*Amer*). ~ura *f* jam

conflict|ivo *adj* difficult; (*época*) troubled; (*polémico*) controversial. ~o *m* conflict

confluencia *f* confluence

conform|ación *f* conformation, shape. ~ar *vt* (*acomodar*) adjust. ● *vi* agree. ~arse *vpr* conform. ~e *adj* in agreement; (*contento*) happy, satisfied; (*según*) according (con to). ~e a in accordance with, according to. ● *conj* as. ● *int* OK!. ~idad *f* agreement; (*tolerancia*) resignation. ~ista *m & f* conformist

conforta|ble *adj* comfortable. ~nte *adj* comforting. ~r *vt* comfort

confronta|ción *f* confrontation. ~r *vt* confront

confu|ndir *vt* (*equivocar*) mistake,

confuse; (*mezclar*) mix up, confuse; (*turbar*) embarrass. ~**ndirse** *vpr* become confused; (*equivocarse*) make a mistake. ~**sión** *f* confusion; (*vergüenza*) embarrassment. ~**so** *adj* confused; (*borroso*) blurred

congela|do *adj* frozen. ~**dor** *m* freezer. ~**r** *vt* freeze

congeniar *vi* get on

congestión *f* congestion. ~**onado** *adj* congested. ~**onarse** *vpr* become congested

congoja *f* distress; (*pena*) grief

congraciarse *vpr* ingratiate o.s.

congratular *vt* congratulate

congrega|ción *f* gathering; (*Relig*) congregation. ~**rse** 12 *vpr* gather, assemble

congres|ista *m & f* delegate, member of a congress. ~**o** *m* congress, conference. C~**o** Parliament. C~**o de los Diputados** Chamber of Deputies

cónico *adj* conical

conífer|a *f* conifer. ~**o** *adj* coniferous

conjetura *f* conjecture, guess. ~**r** *vt* conjecture, guess

conjuga|ción *f* conjugation. ~**r** 12 *vt* conjugate

conjunción *f* conjunction

conjunto *adj* joint. ● *m* collection; (*Mus*) band; (*ropa*) suit, outfit. **en** ~ altogether

conjurar *vt* exorcise; avert (*peligro*). ● *vi* plot, conspire

conllevar *vt* to entail

conmemora|ción *f* commemoration. ~**r** *vt* commemorate

conmigo *pron* with me

conmo|ción *f* shock; (*tumulto*) upheaval. ~ **cerebral** concussion. ~**cionar** *vt* shock. ~**ver** 2 *vt*

shake; (*emocionar*) move

conmuta|dor *m* switch; (LAm, de *teléfonos*) switchboard. ~**r** *vt* exchange

connota|ción *f* connotation. ~**do** *adj* (LAm, *destacado*) distinguished. ~**r** *vt* connote

cono *m* cone

conoc|edor *adj & m* expert. ~**er** 11 *vt* know; (*por primera vez*) meet; (*reconocer*) recognize, know. **se conoce que** apparently. **dar a** ~**er** make known. ~**erse** *vpr* know o.s.; (*dos personas*) know each other; (*notarse*) be obvious. ~**ido** *adj* well-known. ● *m* acquaintance. ~**imiento** *m* knowledge; (*sentido*) consciousness. **sin** ~**imiento** unconscious. **tener** ~**imiento de** know about

conozco *vb* véase **CONOCER**

conque *conj* so

conquista *f* conquest. ~**dor** *adj* conquering. ● *m* conqueror; (*de América*) conquistador. ~**r** *vt* conquer, win

consabido *adj* usual, habitual

Conquistadores The collective term for the succession of explorers, soldiers and adventurers who, from the sixteenth century onward led the settlement and exploitation of Spain's Latin American colonies.

consagra|ción *f* consecration. ~**r** *vt* consecrate; (*fig*) devote. ~**rse** *vpr* devote o.s.

consanguíneo *m* blood relation

consciente *adj* conscious

consecuen|cia *f* consequence; (*coherencia*) consistency. **a** ~**cia de** as a result of. ~**te** *adj* consistent

consecutivo *adj* consecutive

conseguir 🔲 & 🔲 *vt* get, obtain; (*lograr*) manage; achieve (*objetivo*)

consej|ero *m* adviser; (*miembro de consejo*) member. **~o** *m* piece of advice; (*Pol*) council. **~o de ministros** cabinet

consenso *m* assent, consent

consenti|do *adj* (*niño*) spoilt. **~miento** *m* consent. **~r** 🔲 *vt* allow; spoil (*niño*). ● *vi* consent

conserje *m* porter, caretaker. **~ría** *f* porter's office

conserva *f* (*mermelada*) preserve; (*en lata*) tinned food. **en ~** tinned (*Brit*), canned. **~ción** *f* conservation; (*de alimentos*) preservation

conservador *adj & m* (*Pol*) conservative

conservar *vt* keep; preserve (*alimentos*). **~se** *vpr* keep; (*costumbre*) survive

conservatorio *m* conservatory

considera|ble *adj* considerable. **~ción** *f* consideration; (*respeto*) respect. **de ~ción** serious. **de mi ~ción** (*LAm, en cartas*) Dear Sir. **~do** *adj* considerate; (*respetado*) respected. **~r** *vt* consider; (*respetar*) respect

consigna *f* order; (*para equipaje*) left luggage office (*Brit*), baggage room (*Amer*); (*eslogan*) slogan

consigo *pron* (*él*) with him; (*ella*) with her; (*Ud, Uds*) with you; (*uno mismo*) with o.s.

consiguiente *adj* consequent. **por ~** consequently

consist|encia *f* consistency. **~ente** *adj* consisting (on of); (*firme*) solid; (*LAm, congruente*) consistent. **~ir** *vi*. **~ en** consist of; (*radicar en*) be due to

consola|ción *f* consolation. **~r**

🔲 *vt* console, comfort. **~rse** *vpr* console o.s.

consolidar *vt* consolidate. **~se** *vpr* consolidate

consomé *m* clear soup, consommé

consonante *adj* consonant. ● *f* consonant

consorcio *m* consortium

conspira|ción *f* conspiracy. **~dor** *m* conspirator. **~r** *vi* conspire

consta|ncia *f* constancy; (*prueba*) proof; (*LAm, documento*) written evidence. **~nte** *adj* constant. **~r** *vi* be clear; (*figurar*) appear, figure; (*componerse*) consist. **hacer ~r** state; (*por escrito*) put on record. **me ~ que** I'm sure that. **que conste que** believe me

constatar *vt* check; (*confirmar*) confirm

constipa|do *m* cold. ● *adj.* **estar ~do** have a cold; (*LAm, estreñido*) be constipated. **~rse** *vpr* catch a cold

constitu|ción *f* constitution; (*establecimiento*) setting up. **~cional** *adj* constitutional. **~ir** 🔲 *vt* constitute; (*formar*) form; (*crear*) set up, establish. **~irse** *vpr* set o.s. up (**en** as). **~tivo** *adj*, **~yente** *adj* constituent

constru|cción *f* construction. **~ctor** *m* builder. **~ir** 🔲 *vt* construct; build (*edificio*)

consuelo *m* consolation

consuetudinario *adj* customary

cónsul *m & f* consul

consulado *m* consulate

consult|a *f* consultation. **horas** *fpl* **de ~a** surgery hours. **obra** *f* **de ~a** reference book. **~ar** *vt* consult. **~orio** *m* surgery

74

consumar vt complete; commit (crimen); carry out (robo); consummate (matrimonio)

consum|ición f consumption; (bebida) drink; (comida) food. ~ición mínima minimum charge. ~ido adj (persona) skinny, wasted. ~idor m consumer. ~ir vt consume. ~irse vpr (persona) waste away; (vela, cigarrillo) burn down; (líquido) dry up. ~ismo m consumerism. ~o m consumption; (LAm, en restaurante etc) (bebida) drink; (comida) food. ~o mínimo minimum charge

contab|ilidad f book-keeping; (profesión) accountancy. ~le m & f accountant

contacto m contact. ponerse en ~ con get in touch with

conta|do adj. al ~ cash. ~s adj pl few. tiene los días ~s his days are numbered. ~dor m meter; (LAm, persona) accountant

contagi|ar vt infect (persona); pass on (enfermedad); (fig) contaminate. ~o m infection; (directo) contagion. ~oso adj infectious; (por contacto directo) contagious

contamina|ción f contamination, pollution. ~r vt contaminate, pollute

contante adj. dinero m ~ cash

contar 2 vt count; tell (relato). se cuenta que it's said that. ● vi count. ~ con rely on, count on. ~se vpr be included (entre among)

contempla|ción f contemplation. sin ~ciones unceremoniously. ~r vt look at; (fig) contemplate

contemporáneo adj & m contemporary

conten|er 40 vt contain; hold (respiración). ~erse vpr contain o.s. ~ido adj contained. ● m contents

content|ar vt please. ~arse vpr. ~arse con be satisfied with, be pleased with. ~o adj (alegre) happy; (satisfecho) pleased

contesta|ción f answer. ~dor m. ~ automático answering machine. ~r vt/i answer; (replicar) answer back

contexto m context

contienda f conflict; (lucha) contest

contigo pron with you

contiguo adj adjacent

continen|tal adj continental. ~te m continent

continu|ación f continuation. a ~ación immediately after. ~ar 21 vt continue, resume. ● vi continue. ~idad f continuity. ~o adj continuous; (frecuente) continual. corriente f ~a direct current

contorno m outline; (de árbol) girth; (de caderas) measurement. ~s mpl surrounding area

contorsión f contortion

contra prep against. en ~ against. ● m cons. ● f snag. llevar la ~ contradict

contraata|car 7 vt/i counterattack. ~que m counter-attack

contrabaj|ista m & f double-bass player. ~o m double-bass; (persona) double-bass player

contraband|ista m & f smuggler. ~o m contraband

contracción f contraction

contrad|ecir 46 vt contradict. ~icción f contradiction. ~ictorio adj contradictory

contraer 41 vt contract. ~ matrimonio marry. **~se** *vpr* contract

contralto *m* counter tenor. ● *f* contralto

contra|mano. a ~ in the wrong direction. **~partida** *f* compensation. **~pelo. a ~** the wrong way

contrapes|ar *vt* counterweight. **~o** *m* counterweight

contraproducente *adj* counterproductive

contraria. llevar la ~a contradict. **~ado** *adj* upset; *(enojado)* annoyed. **~ar** 20 *vt* upset; *(enojar)* annoy. **~edad** *f* setback; *(disgusto)* annoyance. **~o** *adj* contrary (a to); *(dirección)* opposite. **al ~o** on the contrary. **al lo ~o** of contrary to. **de lo ~o** otherwise. **por el ~o** on the contrary. **ser ~o a** be opposed to, be against

contrarrestar *vt* counteract

contrasentido *m* contradiction

contraseña *f* *(palabra)* password; *(en cine)* stub

contrast|ar *vt* check, verify. ● *vi* contrast. **~e** *m* contrast; *(en oro, plata)* hallmark

contratar *vt* contract *(servicio)*; hire, take on *(empleados)*; sign up *(jugador)*

contratiempo *m* setback; *(accidente)* mishap

contrat|ista *m & f* contractor. **~o** *m* contract

contraven|ción *f* contravention. **~ir** 53 *vt* contravene

contraventana *f* shutter

contribu|ción *f* contribution; *(tributo)* tax. **~ir** 17 *vt/i* contribute. **~yente** *m & f* contributor; *(que paga impuestos)* taxpayer

contrincante *m* rival, opponent

control *m* control; *(vigilancia)* check; *(lugar)* checkpoint. **~ar** *vt*

control; *(vigilar)* check. **~arse** *vpr* control s.o.

controversia *f* controversy

contundente *adj* *(arma)* blunt; *(argumento)* convincing

contusión *f* bruise

convalec|encia *f* convalescence. **~er** 11 *vi* convalesce. **~iente** *adj & m & f* convalescent

convalidar *vt* recognize *(título)*

convenc|er 9 *vt* convince. **~imiento** *m* conviction

convención *f* convention. **~onal** *adj* conventional

conveni|encia *f* convenience; *(aptitud)* suitability. **~ente** *adj* suitable; *(aconsejable)* advisable; *(provechoso)* useful. **~o** *m* agreement. **~r** 53 *vt* agree. ● *vi* agree (en on); *(ser conveniente)* be convenient for, suit; *(ser aconsejable)* be advisable

convento *m* *(de monjes)* monastery; *(de monjas)* convent

conversa|ción *f* conversation. **~ciones** *fpl* talks. **~r** *vi* converse, talk

conver|sión *f* conversion. **~so** *adj* converted. **~ir** *vt* convert. **~tible** *adj* convertible. ● *m* *(LAm)* convertible. **~tir** 4 *vt* convert. **~tirse** *vpr*. **~tirse en** turn into; *(Relig)* convert

convic|ción *f* conviction. **~to** *adj* convicted

convida|do *m* guest. **~r** *vt* invite

convincente *adj* convincing

conviv|encia *f* coexistence; *(de parejas)* life together. **~ir** *vi* live together; *(coexistir)* coexist

convocar 7 *vt* call *(huelga, elecciones)*; convene *(reunión)*; summon *(personas)*

convulsión *f* convulsion

conyugal *adj* marital, conjugal; *(vida)* married

cónyuge m spouse. **~s** mpl married couple

coñac m (pl **~s**) brandy

coopera|ción f cooperation. **~r** vi cooperate. **~nte** m & f voluntary aid worker. **~tiva** f cooperative. **~tivo** adj cooperative

coordinar vt coordinate

copa f glass; (deportes, fig) cup; (de árbol) top. **~s** fpl (naipes) hearts. **tomar una ~** have a drink

copia f copy. **~ en limpio** fair copy. **sacar una ~** make a copy. **~r** vt copy

copioso adj copious; (lluvia, nevada etc) heavy

copla f verse; (canción) folksong

copo m flake. **~ de nieve** snowflake. **~s de maíz** cornflakes

coquet|a f flirt; (mueble) dressingtable. **~ear** vi flirt. **~o** adj flirtatious

coraje m courage; (rabia) anger

coral adj choral. ● m coral; (Mus) chorale

coraza f cuirass; (Naut) armourplating; (de tortuga) shell

coraz|ón m heart; (persona) darling. **sin ~ón** heartless. **tener buen ~ón** be good-hearted. **~onada** f hunch; (impulso) impulse

corbata f tie, necktie (esp Amer). **~ de lazo** bow tie

corche|a f quaver. **~te** m fastener, hook and eye; (gancho) hook; (paréntesis) square bracket

corcho m cork. **~lata** f (Mex) (crown) cap

corcova f hump

cordel m cord, string

cordero m lamb

cordial adj cordial, friendly. ● m

tonic. **~idad** f cordiality, warmth

cordillera f mountain range

córdoba m (unidad monetaria de Nicaragua) córdoba

cordón m string; (de zapatos) lace; (cable) cord; (fig) cordon. **~ umbilical** umbilical cord

coreografía f choreography

corista f (bailarina) chorus girl

cornet|a f bugle; (Mex, de coche) horn. **~ín** m cornet

coro m (Mus) choir; (en teatro) chorus

corona f crown; (de flores) wreath, garland. **~ción** f coronation. **~r** vt crown

coronel m colonel

coronilla f crown. **estar hasta la ~** be fed up

corpora|ción f corporation. **~l** adj (castigo) corporal; (trabajo) physical

corpulento adj stout

corral m farmyard. **aves** fpl **de ~** poultry

correa f strap; (de perro) lead; (cinturón) belt

correc|ción f correction; (cortesía) good manners. **~to** adj correct; (cortés) polite

corrector ortográfico m spell checker

corre|dizo adj running. **nudo** m **~dizo** slip knot. **puerta** f **~diza** sliding door. **~dor** m runner; (pasillo) corridor; (agente) agent, broker. **~dor de coches** racing driver

corregir 5 & 14 vt correct

correlación f correlation

correo m post, mail; (persona) courier; (LAm, oficina) post office. **~s** mpl post office. **~ electrónico**

e-mail. echar al ~ post

correr vt run; (mover) move; draw (cortinas). • vi run; (agua, electricidad etc) flow; (tiempo) pass. ~se vpr (apartarse) move along; (colores) run

correspond|encia f correspondence. ~**er** vi correspond; (ser adecuado) be fitting; (contestar) reply; (pertenecer) belong; (incumbir) fall to. ~**erse** vpr (amarse) love one another. ~**iente** adj corresponding

corresponsal m correspondent

corrid|a f run. ~**a de toros** bullfight. de ~**a** from memory. ~**o** adj (continuo) continuous

corriente adj (agua) running; (monedas, publicación, cuenta, año) current; (ordinario) ordinary. • f current; (de aire) draught; (fig) tendency. • m current month. al ~ (al día) up-to-date; (enterado) aware

corr|illo m small group. ~**o** m circle

corroborar vt corroborate

corroer 24 & 37 vt corrode; (en geología) erode; (fig) eat away

corromper vt corrupt, rot (materia). ~**se** vpr become corrupted; (materia) rot; (alimentos) go bad

corrosi|ón f corrosion. ~**vo** adj corrosive

corrupción f corruption; (de materia etc) rot

corsé m corset

corta|do adj cut; (carretera) closed; (leche) curdled; (avergonzado) embarrassed; (confuso) confused. • m coffee with a little milk. ~**dura** f cut. ~**nte** adj sharp; (viento) biting; (frío) bitter. ~**r** vt cut; (recortar) cut out; (aislar, separar, interrumpir) cut off. • vi cut; (novios) break up. ~**rse** vpr cut o.s.; (leche etc) curdle; (fig) be embarrassed. ~**rse el pelo** have one's hair cut. ~**rse las uñas** cut one's nails. ~**uñas** m invar nail-clippers

corte m cut; (de tela) length. ~ **de luz** power cut. ~ **y confección** dressmaking. • f court; (LAm, tribunal) Court of Appeal. **hacer la** ~ court. **la C~s** the Spanish parliament. **la C~ Suprema** the Supreme Court

cortej|ar vt court. ~**o** m (de rey etc) entourage. ~**o fúnebre** cortège, funeral procession

cortés adj polite

cortesía f courtesy

corteza f bark; (de queso) rind; (de pan) crust

cortijo m farm; (casa) farmhouse

cortina f curtain

corto adj short; (apocado) shy. ~ **de short of**. ~ **de alcances** dim, thick. ~ **de vista** short-sighted. a **la corta o a la larga** sooner or later. **quedarse** ~ fall short; (subestimar) underestimate. ~**circuito** m short circuit

Coruña f. **La** ~ Corunna

cosa f thing; (asunto) business; (idea) idea. **como si tal** ~ just like that; (como si no hubiera pasado nada) as if nothing had happened. **decirle a uno cuatro** ~**s** tell s.o. a thing or two

cosecha f harvest; (de vino) vintage. ~**r** vt harvest

coser vt sew; sew on (botón); stitch (herida). • vi sew. ~**se** vpr stick to s.o.

cosmético adj & m cosmetic

cósmico adj cosmic

cosmo|polita adj & m & f cosmopolitan. ~s m cosmos

cosquillas fpl. dar ~ tickle. hacer ~ tickle. tener ~ be ticklish

costa f coast. a ~ de at the expense of. a toda ~ at any cost

costado m side

costal m sack

costar 2 vt cost. ● vi cost; (resultar difícil) to be hard. ~ caro be expensive. cueste lo que cueste at any cost

costarricense adj & m, costarriqueño adj & m Costa Rican

cost|as fpl (Jurid) costs. ~e m cost. ~ear vt pay for; (Naut) sail along the coast

costero adj coastal

costilla f rib; (chuleta) chop

costo m cost. ~so adj expensive

costumbre f custom; (de persona) habit. de ~ usual; (como adv) usually

costur|a f sewing; (línea) seam; (confección) dressmaking. ~era f dressmaker. ~ero m sewing box

cotejar vt compare

cotidiano adj daily

cotill|a f gossip. ~o m gossip

cotiza|ción f quotation, price. ~r 10 vt (en la bolsa) quote. ● vi pay contributions.. ~rse vpr fetch; (en la bolsa) stand at; (fig) be valued

coto m enclosure; (de caza) preserve. ~ de caza game preserve

cotorr|a f parrot; (fig) chatterbox. ~ear vi chatter

coyuntura f joint

coz f kick

cráneo m skull

cráter m crater

crea|ción f creation. ~dor adj

creative. ● m creator. ~r vt create

crec|er 11 vi grow; (aumentar) increase; (río) rise. ~ida f (de río) flood. ~ido adj (persona) grown-up; (número) large, considerable; (plantas) fully-grown. ~iente adj growing; (luna) crescent. ~imiento m growth

credencial f document. ● adj. cartas fpl ~es credentials

credibilidad f credibility

crédito m credit; (préstamo) loan. digno de ~ reliable

credo m creed

crédulo adj credulous

cre|encia f belief. ~er 18 vt/i believe; (pensar) think. ~o que no I don't think so, I think not. ~o que sí I think so. no ~o I don't think so. ¡ya lo ~o! I should think so!. ~erse vpr consider o.s. no me lo ~o I don't believe it. ~ible adj credible

crema f cream; (Culin) custard; (LAm, de la leche) cream. ~ batida (LAm) whipped cream. ~ bronceadora sun-tan cream

cremallera f zip (Brit), zipper (Amer)

crematorio m crematorium

crepitar vi crackle

crepúsculo m twilight

crespo adj frizzy; (LAm, rizado) curly. ● m (LAm) curl

cresta f crest; (de gallo) comb

creyente m believer

cría f breeding; (animal) baby animal. las ~s the young

cria|da f maid, servant. ~dero m (de pollos etc) farm; (de ostras) bed; (de plantas) nursery. ● m servant. ~dor m breeder. ~nza f breeding. ~r 20 vt suckle; grow (plantas); breed (animales); (educar) bring up

(Brit), raise (esp Amer). ~**rse** vpr grow up

criatura f creature; (niño) baby

crim|en m (serious) crime; (asesinato) murder; (fig) crime. ~**inal** adj & m & f criminal

crin f mane

crío m child

criollo adj Creole; (LAm, música, comida) traditional. ●m Creole; (LAm, nativo) Peruvian, Chilean etc

crisantemo m chrysanthemum

crisis f invar crisis

crispar vt twitch; (fam, irritar) annoy. ~**le los nervios a uno** get on s.o.'s nerves

cristal m crystal; (Esp, vidrio) glass; (Esp, de una ventana) pane of glass. **limpiar los** ~**es** (Esp) clean the windows. ~**ino** adj crystalline; (fig) crystal-clear. ~**izar** 10 crystallize. ~**izarse** vpr crystallize

cristian|dad f Christendom. ~**ismo** m Christianity. ~**o** adj Christian. **ser** ~**o** be a Christian. ●m Christian

cristo m crucifix

Cristo m Christ

criterio m criterion; (discernimiento) judgement; (opinión) opinion

cr|ítica f criticism; (reseña) review. ~**iticar** 7 vt criticize. ~**ítico** adj critical. ● m critic

croar vi croak

crom|ado adj chromium-plated. ~**o** m chromium, chrome

crónic|a f chronicle; (de radio, TV) report; (de periódico) feature. ~**a deportiva** sport section. ~**o** adj chronic

cronista m & f reporter

crono|grama m schedule, time-table. ~**logía** f chronology

cron|ometrar vt time. ~**ómetro** m (en deportes) stop-watch

croqueta f croquette

cruce m crossing; (de calles, carreteras) crossroads; (de peatones) (pedestrian) crossing

crucial adj crucial

crucifi|car 7 vt crucify. ~**jo** m crucifix

crucigrama m crossword (puzzle)

crudo adj raw; (fig) harsh. ●m crude (oil)

cruel adj cruel. ~**dad** f cruelty

cruji|do m (de seda, de hojas secas) rustle; (de muebles) creak. ~**r** vi (seda, hojas secas) rustle; (muebles) creak

cruz f cross; (de moneda) tails. ~ **gamada** swastika. **la C~ Roja** the Red Cross

cruza|da f crusade. ~**r** 10 vt cross; exchange (palabras). ~**rse** vpr cross; (pasar en la calle) pass each other. ~**rse con** pass

cuaderno m exercise book; (para apuntes) notebook

cuadra f (caballeriza) stable; (LAm, distancia) block

cuadrado adj & m square

cuadragésimo adj fortieth

cuadr|ar vt square. ● vi suit; (cuentas) tally. ~**arse** vpr (Mil) stand to attention; (fig) dig one's heels in. ~**ilátero** m quadrilateral; (Boxeo) ring

cuadrilla f group; (pandilla) gang

cuadro m square; (pintura) painting; (Teatro) scene; (de números) table; (de mando etc) panel; (conjunto del personal) staff. ~ **de distribución** switchboard. **a** ~**s, de** ~**s** check. **¡qué** ~**!**, **¡vaya un** ~**!**

what a sight!

cuadrúpedo *m* quadruped

cuádruple *adj & m* quadruple

cuajar *vt* congeal (sangre); curdle (leche); (*llenar*) fill up. ● *vi* (nieve) settle; (*fig, fam*) work out. **cuajado** de full of. ~**se** *vpr* coagulate; (sangre) clot; (leche) curdle

cual *pron.* el ~, la ~ etc (*animales y cosas*) that, which; (*personas, sujeto*) who, that; (*personas, objeto*) whom. ● *adj* (*LAm,* qué) what. ~ **si** as if. cada ~ everyone. lo ~ which. por lo ~ because of which. sea ~ sea whatever

cuál *pron* which; (*LAm,* qué) what

cualidad *f* quality

cualquiera *adj* (*delante de nombres* cualquier, *pl* cualesquiera) any. ● *pron* (*pl* cualesquiera) anyone, anybody; (*cosas*) whatever, whichever one. un ~ a nobody. una ~ a slut

cuando *adv* when. ● *conj* when; (*si*) if. ~ más at the most. ~ menos at the least. aun ~ even if. de ~ en ~ from time to time

cuándo *adv & conj* when. ¿de ~ acá?, ¿desde ~? since when? ¡~ no! (*LAm*) as usual!, typical!

cuant|ía *f* quantity; (*extensión*) extent. ~**loso** *adj* abundant. ~**o** *adj* as much ... as, as many ... as. ● *pron* as much as, as many as. ● *adv* as much as. ~**o antes** as soon as possible. ~**o más,** mejor the more the merrier. en ~**o** as soon as. en ~**o a** as far as. por ~**o** since. unos ~**os** a few, some

cuánto *adj* (*interrogativo*) how much?; (*interrogativo en plural*) how many?; (*exclamativo*) what a lot of! ● *pron* how much?; (*en plural*) how many? ● *adv* how much.

¿~ mides? how tall are you? ¿~ tiempo? how long? ¡~ tiempo sin verte! it's been a long time! ¿a ~ estamos? what's the date today? un Sr. no sé ~s Mr So-and-So

cuáquero *m* Quaker

cuarent|a *adj & m* forty; (*cuadragésimo*) fortieth. ~**ena** *f* (*Med*) quarantine. ~**ón** *adj* about forty

cuaresma *f* Lent

cuarta *f* (*palmo*) span

cuartel *m* (*Mil*) barracks. ~ **general** headquarters

cuarteto *m* quartet

cuarto *adj* fourth. ● *m* quarter; (*habitación*) room. ~ **de baño** bathroom. ~ **de estar** living room. ~ **de hora** quarter of an hour. **estar sin un** ~ be broke. **y** ~ (a) quarter past

cuarzo *m* quartz

cuate *m* (*Mex*) twin; (*amigo*) friend; (⬚, *tipo*) guy

cuatro *adj & m* four. ~**cientos** *adj & m* four hundred

Cuba *f* Cuba

cuba|libre *m* rum and Coke (P). ~**no** *adj & m* Cuban

cúbico *adj* cubic

cubículo *m* cubicle

cubiert|a *f* cover; (*neumático*) tyre; (*Naut*) deck. ~**o** *adj* covered; (*cielo*) overcast. ● *m* place setting, piece of cutlery; (*en restaurante*) cover charge. **a** ~**o** under cover

cubilete *m* bowl; (*molde*) mould; (*para los dados*) cup

cubis|mo *m* cubism. ~**ta** *adj & m & f* cubist

cubo *m* bucket; (*Mat*) cube

cubrecama *m* bedspread

cubrir (*pp* cubierto) *vt* cover; fill

(vacante). ~**se** vpr cover o.s.; (ponerse el sombrero) put on one's hat; (el cielo) cloud over, become overcast

cucaracha f cockroach

cuchar|a f spoon. ~**ada** f spoonful. ~**adita** f teaspoonful. ~**illa**, ~**ita** f teaspoon. ~**ón** m ladle

cuchichear vi whisper

cuchill|a f large knife; (de carnicero) cleaver; (hoja de afeitar) razor blade. ~**ada** f stab; (herida) knife wound. ~**o** m knife

cuchitril m (fig) hovel

cuclillas: en ~ adv squatting

cuco adj shrewd; (mono) pretty, nice. ● m cuckoo

cucurucho m cornet

cuello m neck; (de camisa) collar. cortar(le) el ~ a uno cut s.o.'s throat

cuenc|a f (del ojo) (eye) socket; (de río) basin. ~**o** m hollow; (vasija) bowl

cuenta f count; (acción de contar) counting; (cálculo) calculation; (factura) bill; (en banco, relato) account; (de collar) bead. ~ corriente current account, checking account (Amer). dar ~ de give an account of. darse ~ de realize. en resumidas ~s in short. por mi propia ~ on my own account. tener en ~ bear in mind

cuentakilómetros m invar milometer

cuent|ista m & f story-writer; (de mentiras) fibber. ~**o** m story; (mentira) fib, tall story. ~ **de hadas** fairy tale. ● vb véase **CONTAR**

cuerda f rope; (más fina) string; (Mus) string. ~ **floja** tightrope. dar ~ a wind up (un reloj)

cuerdo adj (persona) sane; (acción) sensible

cuerno m horn

cuero m leather; (piel) skin; (del grifo) washer. ~ **cabelludo** scalp. en ~s (vivos) stark naked

cuerpo m body

cuervo m crow

cuesta f slope, hill. ~ abajo downhill. ~ arriba uphill. a ~s on one's back

cuestión f matter; (problema) problem; (cosa) thing

cueva f cave

cuida|do m care; (preocupación) worry. i~**do!** watch out!. tener ~**do** be careful. ~**doso** adj careful. ~**r** vt look after. ~**rse** vpr look after o.s. ~**rse de** be careful to

culata f (de revólver, fusil) butt. ~**zo** m recoil

culebr|a f snake. ~**ón** m soap opera

culinario adj culinary

culminar vi culminate

culo m 🔢 bottom; (LAm vulg) arse (Brit vulg), ass (Amer vulg)

culpa f fault. echar la ~ blame. por ~ de because of. tener la ~ be to blame (de for). ~**bilidad** f guilt. ~**ble** adj guilty. ● m & f culprit. ~**r** vt blame (de for)

cultiv|ar vt farm; grow (plantas); (fig) cultivate. ~**o** m farming; (de plantas) growing

cult|o adj (persona) educated. ● m cult; (homenaje) worship. ~**ura** f culture. ~**ural** adj cultural

culturismo m body-building

cumbre f summit

cumpleaños m invar birthday

cumplido adj perfect; (cortés) polite. ● m compliment. de ~ cour-

cumplimiento | dañar

tesy. **por** ~ out of a sense of duty. **~r** *adj* reliable

cumpli|miento *m* fulfilment; (*de ley*) observance; (*de orden*) carrying out. **~r** *vt* carry out; observe (ley); serve (condena); reach (años); keep (promesa). **hoy cumple 3 años** he's 3 (years old) today. ● *vi* do one's duty. **por** ~ as a mere formality. **~rse** *vpr* expire; (*realizarse*) be fulfilled

cuna *f* cradle; (*fig, nacimiento*) birthplace

cundir *vi* spread; (*rendir*) go a long way

cuneta *f* ditch

cuña *f* wedge

cuñad|a *f* sister-in-law. **~o** *m* brother-in-law

cuño *m* stamp. **de nuevo** ~ new

cuota *f* quota; (*de sociedad etc*) membership, fee; (*LAm, plazo*) instalment; (*Mex, peaje*) toll

cupe *vb* *véase* CABER

cupo *m* cuota; (*LAm, capacidad*) room; (*Mex, plaza*) place

cupón *m* coupon

cúpula *f* dome

cura *f* cure; (*tratamiento*) treatment. ● *m* priest. **~ción** *f* healing. **~ndero** *m* faith-healer. **~r** *vt* (*incl Culin*) cure; dress (herida); (*tratar*) treat; (*fig*) remedy; tan (pieles). **~rse** *vpr* get better

curios|ear *vi* pry; (*mirar*) browse. **~idad** *f* curiosity. **~o** *adj* curious; (*raro*) odd, unusual ● *m* onlooker; (*fisgón*) busybody

curita *f* (*LAm*) (sticking) plaster

curriculum (vitae) *m* curriculum vitae, CV

cursar *vt* issue; (*estudiar*) study

cursi *adj* pretentious, showy

cursillo *m* short course

cursiva *f* italics

curso *m* course; (*Univ etc*) year. **en** ~ under way; (año etc) current

cursor *m* cursor

curtir *vt* tan; (*fig*) harden. **~se** *vpr* become tanned; (*fig*) become hardened

curv|a *f* curve; (*de carretera*) bend. **~ar** *vt* bend; bow (estante). **~arse** *vpr* bend; (estante) bow; (madera) warp. **~ilineo** *adj* curvilinear; (mujer) curvaceous. **~o** *adj* curved

cúspide *f* top; (*fig*) pinnacle

custodi|a *f* safe-keeping; (*Jurid*) custody. **~ar** *vt* guard; (*guardar*) look after. **~o** *m* guardian

cutáneo *adj* skin

cutis *m* skin, complexion

cuyo *pron* (*de persona*) whose, of whom; (*de cosa*) whose, of which. **en** ~ **caso** in which case

Dd

dactilógrafo *m* typist

dado *m* dice. ● *adj* given. ~ **que** since, given that

daltónico *adj* colour-blind

dama *f* lady. ~ **de honor** bridesmaid. **~s** *fpl* draughts (*Brit*), checkers (*Amer*)

damasco *m* damask; (*LAm, fruta*) apricot

danés *adj* Danish. ● *m* Dane; (*idioma*) Danish

danza *f* dance; (*acción*) dancing. **~r** 10 *vt/i* dance

dañar *vt* damage. **~se** *vpr* get

damaged. **～ino** *adj* harmful. **～o** *m* damage; (*a una agencia*) harm. **～os y perjuicios** damages. **hacer ～o** a harm, hurt. **hacerse ～o** hurt o.s.

dar 📘 *vt* give; bear (*frutos*); give out (*calor*); strike (*la hora*). ● *vi* give. **da igual** it doesn't matter. **¡dale!** go on! **da lo mismo** it doesn't matter. **～ a** (*ventana*) look on to; (*edificio*) face. **～ a luz** give birth. **～ con** meet (*persona*); find (*cosa*). **¿qué más da?** it doesn't matter! **～se** *vpr* have (*baño*). **dárselas de** make o.s. out to be. **～se por** consider o.s.

dardo *m* dart

datar *vi*. **～ de** date from

dátil *m* date

dato *m* piece of information. **～s** *mpl* data, information. **～s personales** personal details

---

de *preposición*

> Note that **de** before **el** becomes **del**, e.g. **es del norte**

⋯▸ (*contenido, material*) of. **un vaso de agua** a glass of water. **es de madera** it's made of wood (*pertenencia*) **el coche de Juan** Juan's car. **es de ella** it's hers. **es de María** it's María's. **las llaves del coche** the car keys (*procedencia, origen, época*) from. **soy de Madrid** I'm from Madrid. **una llamada de Lima** a call from Lima. **es del siglo V** it's from the 5th century (*causa, modo*) **se murió de cáncer** he died of cancer. **temblar de miedo** to tremble with fear. **de dos en dos** two by two

⋯▸ (*parte del día, hora*) **de noche** at night. **de madrugada** early in the morning. **las diez de la mañana** ten (o'clock) in the morning. **de 9 a 12** from 9 to 12

⋯▸ (*en oraciones pasivas*) by. **rodeado de agua** surrounded by water. **va seguido de coma** it's followed by a comma. **es de Mozart** it's by Mozart

⋯▸ (*al especificar*) **el cajón de arriba** the top drawer. **la clase de inglés** the English lesson. **la chica de verde** the girl in green. **el de debajo** the one underneath

⋯▸ (*en calidad de*) as. **trabaja de oficinista** he works as a clerk. **vino de chaperón** he came as a chaperon

⋯▸ (*en comparaciones*) than. **pesa más de un kilo** it weighs more than a kilo

⋯▸ (*con superlativo*) **el más alto del mundo** the tallest in the world. **el mejor de todos** the best of all

⋯▸ (*sentido condicional*) if. **de haberlo sabido** if I had known. **de continuar así** if this goes on

> ➡ Cuando la preposición **de** se emplea como parte de expresiones como **de prisa, de acuerdo** etc., y de nombres compuestos como **hombre de negocios, saco de dormir** etc., ver bajo el respectivo nombre

deambular *vi* roam (*por* about)
debajo *adv* underneath. **～ de** under(neath). **el de ～** the one

underneath. por ~ underneath.
por ~ de below

debat|e m debate. **~ir** vt debate

deber vt owe. ● *verbo auxiliar* have to, must; (*en condicional*) should. debo marcharme I must go, I have to go. ● m duty. **~es** mpl homework. **~se** vpr. **~se a** be due to

debido adj due; (*correcto*) proper. **~ a** due to. como es **~** as is proper

débil adj weak; (*sonido*) faint; (*luz*) dim

debili|dad f weakness. **~tar** vt weaken. **~tarse** vpr weaken, get weak

débito m debit. **~ bancario** (*LAm*) direct debit

debut m debut

debutar vi make one's debut

década f decade

deca|dencia f decline. **~dente** adj decadent. **~er** 29 vi decline; (*debilitarse*) weaken. **~ído** adj in low spirits. **~imiento** m decline, weakening

decano m dean; (*miembro más antiguo*) senior member

decapitar vt behead

decena f ten. una **~** de about ten

decencia f decency

decenio m decade

decente adj decent; (*decoroso*) respectable; (*limpio*) clean, tidy

decepci|ón f disappointment. **~onar** vt disappoint

decidi|do adj decided; (*persona*) determined, resolute. **~r** vt decide; settle (*cuestión etc*). ● vi decide. **~rse** vpr make up one's mind

decimal adj & m decimal

décimo adj & m tenth. ● m (*de lotería*) tenth part of a lottery ticket

decir 46 vt say; (*contar*) tell. ● m saying. **~ que no** say no. **~ que sí** say yes. dicho de otro modo in other words. dicho y hecho no sooner said than done. ¿dígame? can I help you? ¡dígame! (*al teléfono*) hello? digamos let's say. es **~** that is to say. mejor dicho rather. ¡no me digas! you don't say!, really! por así **~**, por **~lo así** so to speak, as it were. querer **~** mean. se dice que it is said that, they say that

decisi|ón f decision. **~vo** adj decisive

declara|ción f declaration; (*a autoridad, prensa*) statement. **~ción de renta** income tax return. **~r** vt/i declare. **~rse** vpr declare o.s.; (*epidemia etc*) break out

declinar vt turn down; (*Gram*) decline

declive m slope; (*fig*) decline. en **~** sloping

decola|je m (*LAm*) take-off. **~r** vi (*LAm*) take off

decolorarse vpr become discoloured, fade

decora|ción f decoration. **~do** m (*en el teatro*) set. **~r** vt decorate. **~tivo** adj decorative

decoro m decorum. **~so** adj decent, respectable

decrépito adj decrepit

decret|ar vt decree. **~o** m decree

dedal m thimble

dedica|ción f dedication. **~r** 7 vt dedicate; devote (*tiempo*). **~rse** vpr. **~rse a** devote o.s. to. ¿a qué se dedica? what does he do? **~toria** f dedication

dedo m finger; (*del pie*) toe. **~**

anular ring finger. ～ **corazón** middle finger. ～ **gordo** thumb; (*del pie*) big toe. ～ **índice** index finger. ～ **meñique** little finger. ～ **pulgar** thumb

deduc|ción f deduction. ～**ir** 47 vt deduce; (*descontar*) deduct

defec|to m fault, defect. ～**uoso** adj defective

defen|der 1 vt defend. ～**sa** f defence. ～**derse** vpr defend o.s. ～**sivo** adj defensive. ～**sor** m defender. **abogado** m ～**sor** defence counsel

defeño m (*Mex*) person from the Federal District

deficien|cia f deficiency. ～**cia mental** mental handicap. ～**te** adj poor, deficient. ● m & f ～**te mental** mentally handicapped person

déficit m invar deficit

defini|ción f definition. ～**do** adj defined. ～**r** vt define. ～**tivo** adj definitive. **en** ～**tiva** in all in all

deform|ación f deformation; (*de imagen etc*) distortion. ～**ar** vt deform; distort (*imagen, metal*). ～**arse** vpr go out of shape. ～**e** adj deformed

defraudar vt defraud; (*decepcionar*) disappoint

defunción f death

degenera|ción f degeneration; (*cualidad*) degeneracy. ～**do** adj degenerate. ～**r** vi degenerate

degollar 16 vt cut s.o.'s throat

degradar vt degrade; (*Mil*) demote. ～**se** vpr demean o.s..

degusta|ción f tasting. ～**r** vt taste

dehesa f pasture

deja|dez f slovenliness; (*pereza*) laziness. ～**do** adj slovenly; (*descuidado*) slack, negligent. ～**r** vt leave;

(*abandonar*) abandon; give up (*estudios*); (*prestar*) lend; (*permitir*) let. ～**r a un lado** leave aside. ～**r de stop**

dejo m aftertaste; (*tonillo*) slight accent; (*toque*) touch

del = **de** + **el**

delantal m apron

delante adv in front. ～ **de** in front of. **de** ～ **front**. ～**ra** f front; (*de teatro etc*) front row; (*ventaja*) lead; (*de equipo*) forward line. **llevar la** ～**ra** be in the lead. ～**ro** adj front. ● m forward

delat|ar vt denounce. ～**or** m informer

delega|ción f delegation; (*oficina*) regional office; (*Mex, comisaría*) police station. ～**do** m delegate; (*Com*) agent, representative. ～**r** 12 vt delegate

deleit|ar vt delight. ～**e** m delight

deletrear vt spell (out)

delfín m dolphin

delgad|ez f thinness. ～**o** adj thin; (*esbelto*) slim. ～**ucho** adj skinny

delibera|ción f deliberation. ～**do** adj deliberate. ～**r** vi deliberate (*sobre on*)

delicad|eza f gentleness; (*fragilidad*) frailty; (*tacto*) tact. **falta de** ～**eza** tactlessness. **tener la** ～ **de** have the courtesy to. ～**o** adj delicate; (*refinado*) refined; (*sensible*) sensitive

delici|a f delight. ～**oso** adj delightful; (*sabor etc*) delicious

delimitar vt delimit

delincuen|cia f delinquency. ～**te** m & f criminal, delinquent

delinquir 8 vi commit a criminal offence

delir|ante adj delirious. ～**ar** vi be delirious; (*fig*) talk nonsense. ～**io**

m delirium; (*fig*) frenzy

delito *m* crime, offence

demacrado *adj* haggard

demagogo *m* demagogue

demanda *f* demand; (*Jurid*) lawsuit. **~do** *m* defendant. **~nte** *m* & *f* (*Jurid*) plaintiff. **~r** *vt* (*Jurid*) sue; (*Lam, requerir*) require

demarcación *f* demarcation

demás *adj* rest of the other. ● *pron* rest, others. **lo ~** the rest. **por ~** extremely. **por lo ~** otherwise

demas|ía *f.* **en ~ía** in excess. **~iado** *adj* too much; (*en plural*) too many. ● *adv* too much; (*con adjetivo*) too

demen|cia *f* madness. **~te** *adj* demented, mad

dem|ocracia *f* democracy. **~ócrata** *m* & *f* democrat. **~ocrático** *adj* democratic

demol|er 2 *vt* demolish. **~ición** *f* demolition

demonio *m* devil, demon. ¡**~s**! hell! ¿**cómo ~s**? how the hell? ¡**qué ~s**! what the hell!

demora *f* delay. **~r** *vt* delay. ● *vi* stay on. **~rse** *vpr* be too long; (*Lam, cierto tiempo*) take. **se ~ una hora en llegar** it takes him an hour to get there

demostra|ción *f* demonstration, show. **~r 2** *vt* demonstrate; (*mostrar*) show; (*probar*) prove. **~tivo** *adj* demonstrative

dengue *m* dengue fever

denigrar *vt* denigrate

denominado *adj* named; (*supuesto*) so-called

dens|idad *f* density. **~o** *adj* dense, thick

denta|dura *f* teeth. **~dura postiza** dentures, false teeth. **~l** *adj* dental

dent|era *f.* **darle ~era a uno** set s.o.'s teeth on edge. **~ífrico** *m* toothpaste. **~ista** *m* & *f* dentist

dentro *adv* inside; (*de un edificio*) indoors. **~ de** in. **~ de poco** soon. **por ~** inside

denuncia *f* report; (*acusación*) accusation. **~r** *vt* report; (*periódico etc*) denounce

departamento *m* department; (*Lam, apartamento*) flat (*Brit*), apartment (*Amer*)

depend|encia *f* dependence; (*sección*) section; (*oficina*) office. **~encias** *fpl* buildings. **~er** *vi* depend (**de** on). **~ienta** *f* shop assistant. **~iente** *adj* dependent (*de* on). ● *m* shop assistant

depila|r *vt* depilate. **~torio** *adj* depilatory

deplora|ble *adj* deplorable. **~r** *vt* deplore, regret

deponer 34 *vt* remove from office; depose (*rey*); lay down (*armas*). ● *vi* give evidence

deporta|ción *f* deportation. **~r** *vt* deport

deport|e *m* sport. **hacer ~e** take part in sports. **~ista** *m* sportsman. ● *f* sportswoman. **~ivo** *adj* sports. ● *m* sports car

dep|ositante *m* & *f* depositor. **~ositar** *vt* deposit; (*poner*) put, place. **~ósito** *m* deposit; (*almacén*) warehouse; (*Mil*) depot; (*de líquidos*) tank

depravado *adj* depraved

deprecia|ción *f* depreciation. **~r** *vt* depreciate. **~rse** *vpr* depreciate

depr|esión *f* depression. **~imido** *adj* depressed. **~imir** *vt* depress. **~imirse** *vpr* get depressed

depura|ción f purification. **~do** adj refined. **~r** vt purify; (*Pol*) purge; refine (estilo)

derech|a f (*mano*) right hand; (*lado*) right. **a la ~a** on the right; (*hacia el lado derecho*) to the right. **~ista** adj right-wing. ● m & f right-winger. **~o** adj right; (*vertical*) upright; (*recto*) straight. ● adv straight. **todo ~o** straight on. ● m right; (*Jurid*) law; (*lado*) right side. **~os** mpl dues. **~os de autor** royalties

deriva f drift. **a la ~** drifting, adrift

deriva|do adj derived. ● m derivative, by-product. **~r** vt divert. ● vi. **~r** de derive from, be derived from. **~rse** vpr. **~rse de** be derived from

derram|amiento m spilling. **~amiento de sangre** bloodshed. **~ar** vt spill; shed (lágrimas). **~arse** vpr spill. **~e** m spilling; (*pérdida*) leakage; (*Med*) discharge; (*Med, de sangre*) haemorrhage

derretir 5 vt melt

derribar vt knock down; bring down, overthrow (gobierno etc)

derrocar 7 vt bring down, overthrow (gobierno etc)

derroch|ar vt squander. **~e** m waste

derrot|a f defeat. **~ar** vt defeat. **~ado** adj defeated. **~ero** m course

derrumba|r vt knock down. **~rse** vpr collapse; (*persona*) go to pieces

desabotonar vt unbutton, undo. **~se** vpr come undone; (*persona*) undo

desabrido adj tasteless; (*persona*)

surly; (*LAm*) dull

desabrochar vt undo. **~se** vpr come undone; (*persona*) undo

desacato m defiance; (*Jurid*) contempt of court

desac|ertado adj ill-advised; (*erróneo*) wrong. **~ierto** m mistake

desacreditar vt discredit

desactivar vt defuse

desacuerdo m disagreement

desafiar 20 vt challenge; (*afrontar*) defy

desafina|do adj out of tune. **~r** vi be out of tune. **~rse** vpr go out of tune

desafío m challenge; (*a la muerte*) defiance; (*combate*) duel

desafortunad|amente adv unfortunately. **~o** adj unfortunate

desagrada|ble adj unpleasant. **~r** vt displease. ● vi be unpleasant. **me ~ el sabor** I don't like the taste

desagradecido adj ungrateful

desagrado m displeasure. **con ~** unwillingly

desagüe m drain; (*acción*) drainage. **tubo m de ~** drain-pipe

desahog|ado adj roomy; (*acomodado*) comfortable. **~ar** 12 vt vent. **~arse** vpr let off steam. **~o** m comfort; (*alivio*) relief

desahuci|ar vt declare terminally ill (enfermo); evict (inquilino). **~o** m eviction

desair|ar vt snub. **~e** m snub

desajuste m maladjustment; (*desequilibrio*) imbalance

desala|dora f desalination plant. **~r** vt desalinate

desal|entador adj disheartening. **~entar** 1 vt discourage. **~iento** m discouragement

desaliñado adj slovenly

desalmado adj heartless

desalojar vt (ocupantes) evacuate; (policía) to clear; (LAm) evict (inquilino)

desampar|ado adj helpless; (lugar) unprotected. ~**ar** vt abandon. ~**o** m helplessness; (abandono) lack of protection

desangrar vt bleed. ~**se** vpr bleed

desanima|do adj down-hearted. ~**r** vt discourage. ~**rse** vpr lose heart

desapar|ecer 🔟 vi disappear; (efecto) wear off. ~**ecido** adj missing. ~**o** m missing person. ~**ición** f disappearance

desapego m indifference

desapercibido adj. pasar ~ go unnoticed

desaprobar 🔢 vt disapprove of

desarm|able adj collapsible; (estante) easy to dismantle. ~**ar** vt disarm; (desmontar) dismantle; take apart; (LAm) take down (carpa). ~**e** m disarmament

desarraig|ado adj rootless. ~**ar** 🔢 vt uproot. ~**o** m uprooting

desarregl|ar vt mess up; (alterar) disrupt. ~**o** m disorder

desarroll|ar vt develop. ~**arse** vpr (incl Foto) develop; (suceso) take place. ~**o** m development

desaseado adj dirty; (desordenado) untidy

desasosiego m anxiety; (intranquilidad) restlessness

desastr|ado adj scruffy. ~**e** m disaster. ~**oso** adj disastrous

desatar vt untie; (fig, soltar) unleash. ~**se** vpr come undone; to undo (zapatos)

desatascar 🔢 vt unblock

desaten|der 🔢 vt not pay attention to; neglect (deber etc). ~**to** adj inattentive; (descortés) discourteous

desatin|ado adj silly. ~**o** m silliness; (error) mistake

desatornillar vt unscrew

desautorizar 🔟 vt declare unauthorized; discredit (persona); (desmentir) deny

desavenencia f disagreement

desayun|ar vt have for breakfast.
● vi have breakfast. ~**o** m breakfast

desazón m (fig) unease

desbandarse vpr (Mil) disband; (dispersarse) disperse

desbarajust|ar vt mess up. ~**e** m mess

desbaratar vt spoil; (Mex) mess up (papeles)

desbloquear vt clear; release (mecanismo); unfreeze (cuenta)

desbocado adj (caballo) runaway; (escote) wide

desbordarse vpr overflow; (río) burst its banks

descabellado adj crazy

descafeinado adj decaffeinated.
● m decaffeinated coffee

descalabro m disaster

descalificar 🔢 vt disqualify; (desacreditar) discredit

descalz|ar 🔟 vt take off (zapatos). ~**o** adj barefoot

descampado m open ground. al ~ (LAm) in the open air

descans|ado adj rested; (trabajo) easy. ~**ar** vt/i rest. ~**illo** m landing. ~**o** m rest; (del trabajo) break; (LAm, rellano) landing; (en deportes) half-time; (en el teatro etc) interval

descapotable adj convertible

descarado *adj* cheeky; (*sin vergüenza*) shameless

descarg|a *f* unloading; (*Mil, Elec*) discharge. **~ar** 12 *vt* unload; (*Mil, Elec*) discharge; (*Informática*) download. **~o** *m* (*recibo*) receipt; (*Jurid*) evidence

descaro *m* cheek, nerve

descarriarse 20 *vpr* go the wrong way; (*res*) stray; (*fig*) go astray

descarrila|miento *m* derailment. **~r** *vi* be derailed. **~rse** *vpr* (*LAm*) be derailed

descartar *vt* rule out

descascararse *vpr* (*pintura*) peel; (*taza*) chip

descen|dencia *f* descent; (*personas*) descendants. **~der** 1 *vt* go down (*escalera etc*). ● *vi* (*temperatura*) fall, drop; (*provenir*) be descended (*de* from). **~diente** *m & f* descendent. **~so** *m* descent; (*de temperatura, fiebre etc*) fall, drop

descifrar *vt* decipher; decode (*clave*)

descolgar 2 & 12 *vt* take down; pick up (*el teléfono*). **~se** *vpr* lower o.s.

descolor|ar *vt* discolour, fade. **~ido** *adj* discoloured, faded; (*persona*) pale

descomp|oner 34 *vt* break down; decompose (*materia*); upset (*estómago*); (*esp LAm, estropear*) break; (*esp LAm, desarreglar*) mess up. **~onerse** *vpr* decompose; (*esp LAm, estropearse*) break down; (*persona*) feel sick. **~ostura** *f* (*esp LAm, de máquina*) breakdown; (*esp LAm, náuseas*) sickness; (*esp LAm, diarrea*) diarrhoea; (*LAm, falla*) fault. **~uesto** *adj* decomposed; (*encoleri-*

zado) angry; (*esp LAm, estropeado*) broken. **estar ~uesto** (*del estómago*) have diarrhoea

descomunal *adj* enormous

desconc|ertante *adj* disconcerting. **~ertar** 1 *vt* disconcert; (*dejar perplejo*) puzzle. **~ertarse** *vpr* be put out, be disconcerted

desconectar *vt* disconnect

desconfia|do *adj* distrustful. **~nza** *f* distrust, suspicion. **~r** 20 *vi*. **~r de** mistrust; (*no creer*) doubt

descongelar *vt* defrost; (*Com*) unfreeze

desconoc|er 11 *vt* not know, not recognize. **~ido** *adj* unknown; (*cambiado*) unrecognizable. ● *m* stranger. **~imiento** *m* ignorance

desconsidera|ción *f* lack of consideration. **~do** *adj* inconsiderate

descons|olado *adj* distressed. **~uelo** *m* distress; (*tristeza*) sadness

desconta|do *adj*. **dar por ~do (que)** take for granted (that). **~r** 2 *vt* discount; deduct (*impuestos etc*)

descontento *adj* unhappy (*con* with), dissatisfied (*con* with). ● *m* discontent

descorazonar *vt* discourage. **~se** *vpr* lose heart

descorchar *vt* uncork

descorrer *vt* draw (*cortina*). **~ el cerrojo** unbolt the door

descort|és *adj* rude, discourteous. **~esia** *f* rudeness

descos|er *vt* unpick. **~erse** *vpr* come undone. **~ido** *adj* unstitched

descrédito *m* disrepute. **ir en ~** de damage the reputation of

descremado *adj* skimmed

descri|bir (*pp* descrito) *vt* describe. **~pción** *f* description

descuartizar [10] vt cut up

descubierto adj discovered; (no cubierto) uncovered; (vehículo) open-top; (piscina) open-air; (cielo) clear; (cabeza) bare. ● m overdraft. poner al ~ expose

descubri|miento m discovery. ~r (pp descubierto) vt discover; (destapar) uncover; (revelar) reveal; unveil (estatua). ~rse vpr (quitarse el sombrero) take off one's hat

descuento m discount; (del sueldo) deduction; (en deportes) injury time

descuid|ado adj careless; (aspecto etc) untidy; (desprevenido) unprepared. ~ar vt neglect. ● vi not worry. ¡~a! don't worry!. ~arse vpr be careless ~o m carelessness; (negligencia) negligence

desde prep (lugar etc) from; (tiempo) since, from. ~ ahora from now on. ~ hace un mes a month. ~ luego of course. ~ Madrid hasta Barcelona from Madrid to Barcelona. ~ niño since childhood

desdecirse [45] vpr. ~ de take back (palabras etc); go back on (promesa)

desd|én m scorn. ~eñable adj insignificant. nada ~eñable significant. ~eñar vt scorn

desdicha f misfortune. por ~ unfortunately. ~do adj unfortunate

desdoblar vt (desplegar) unfold

desear vt want; wish (suerte etc). le deseo un buen viaje I hope you have a good journey. ¿qué desea Vd? can I help you?

desech|able adj disposable. ~ar vt throw out; (rechazar) reject. ~o m waste

desembalar vt unpack

desembarcar [7] vt unload. ● vi disembark

desemboca|dura f (de río) mouth; (de calle) opening. ~r vi. ~r en (río) flow into; (calle) lead to

desembolso m payment

desembragar [12] vi declutch

desempaquetar vt unwrap

desempatar vi break a tie. ~e m tie-breaker

desempeñ|ar vt redeem; play (papel); hold (cargo); perform, carry out (deber etc). ~arse vpr (LAm) perform. ~arse bien manage well. ~o m redemption; (de un deber, una función) discharge; (LAm, actuación) performance

desemple|ado adj unemployed. ● m unemployed person. los ~ados the unemployed. ~o m unemployment

desencadenar vt unchain (preso); unleash (perro); (causar) trigger. ~se vpr be triggered off; (guerra etc) break out

desencajar vt dislocate; (desconectar) disconnect. ~se vpr become dislocated

desenchufar vt unplug

desenfad|ado adj uninhibited; (desenvuelto) self-assured. ~o m lack of inhibition; (desenvoltura) self-assurance

desenfocado adj out of focus

desenfren|ado adj unrestrained. ~o m licentiousness

desenganchar vt unhook; uncouple (vagón)

desengañ|ar vt disillusion. ~arse vpr become disillusioned; (darse cuenta) realize. ~o m disillusionment, disappointment

desenlace m outcome

desenmascarar vt unmask

desenredar vt untangle. ~se vpr untangle

desenro|**llar** vt unroll, unwind. ~**scar** 7 vt unscrew

desentend|**erse** 1 vpr want nothing to do with. ~**ido** m. hacerse el ~**ido** (fingir no oír) pretend not to hear; (fingir ignorancia) pretend not to hear

desenterrar 1 vt exhume; (fig) unearth

desentonar vi be out of tune; (colores) clash

desenvoltura f ease; (falta de timidez) confidence

desenvolver 2 (pp desenvuelto) vt unwrap; expound (idea etc). ~se vpr perform; (manejarse) manage

deseo m wish, desire. ~**so** adj eager. estar ~**so** de be eager to

desequilibr|**ado** adj unbalanced. ~**io** m imbalance

des|**ertar** vt desert; (Pol) defect. ~**értico** adj desert-like. ~**ertor** m deserter; (Pol) defector

desespera|**ción** f despair. ~**do** adj desperate. ~**nte** adj infuriating. ~**r** vt drive to despair. ~**rse** vpr despair

desestimar vt (rechazar) reject

desfachat|**ado** adj brazen, shameless. ~**ez** f nerve, cheek

desfallec|**er** 11 vt weaken. ● vi become weak; (desmayarse) faint. ~**imiento** m weakness; (desmayo) faint

desfasado adj out of phase; (idea) outdated; (persona) out of touch

desfavorable adj unfavourable

desfil|**adero** m narrow mountain pass; (cañón) narrow gorge. ~**ar** vi

march (past). ~**e** m procession, parade. ~**e de modelos** fashion show

desgana f, (LAm) **desgano** m (falta de apetito) lack of appetite; (Med) weakness, faintness; (fig) unwillingness

desgarr|**ador** adj heart-rending. ~**ar** vt tear; (fig) break (corazón). ~**o** m tear, rip

desgast|**ar** vt wear away; wear out (ropa). ~**arse** vpr wear away; (ropa) be worn out; (persona) wear o.s. out. ~**e** m wear

desgracia f misfortune; (accidente) accident; **por** ~ unfortunately. **¡qué** ~**!** what a shame!. ~**do** adj unlucky; (pobre) poor. ● m unfortunate person, poor devil 1

desgranar vt shell (habas etc)

desgreñado adj ruffled, dishevelled

deshabitado adj uninhabited; (edificio) unoccupied

deshacer 31 vt undo; strip (cama); unpack (maleta); (desmontar) take to pieces; break (trato); (derretir) melt; (disolver) dissolve. ~**se** vpr come undone; (disolverse) dissolve; (derretirse) melt. ~**se de algo** get rid of sth. ~**se en lágrimas** dissolve into tears. ~**se por hacer algo** go out of one's way to do sth

desheredar vt disinherit

deshidratarse vpr become dehydrated

deshielo m thaw

deshilachado adj frayed

deshincha|**do** adj (neumático) flat. ~**r** vt deflate; (Med) reduce the swelling in. ~**rse** vpr go down

deshollinador m chimney sweep

d

deshon|esto adj dishonest; (obsceno) indecent. **~ra** f disgrace. **~rar** vt dishonour

deshora f. **a ~** out of hours. **comer a ~s** eat between meals

deshuesar vt bone (carne); stone (fruta)

desidia f slackness; (pereza) laziness

desierto adj deserted. • m desert

designar vt designate; (fijar) fix

desigual adj unequal; (terreno) uneven; (distinto) different. **~dad** f inequality

desilusi|ón f disappointment; (pérdida de ilusiones) disillusionment. **~onar** vt disappoint; (quitar las ilusiones) disillusion. **~onarse** vpr be disappointed; (perder las ilusiones) become disillusioned

desinfecta|nte m disinfectant. **~r** vt disinfect

desinflar vt deflate. **~se** vpr go down

desinhibido adj uninhibited

desintegrar vt disintegrate. **~se** vpr disintegrate

desinter|és m lack of interest; (generosidad) unselfishness. **~esado** adj uninterested; (liberal) unselfish

desistir vi. **~ de** give up

desleal adj disloyal. **~tad** f disloyalty

desligar **12** vt untie; (separar) separate; (fig, librar) free. **~se** vpr break away; (de un compromiso) free o.s. (de from)

desliza|dor m (Mex) hang glider. **~r** **10** vt slide, slip. **~se** vpr slide, slip; (patinador) glide; (tiempo) slip by, pass; (fluir) flow

deslucido adj tarnished; (gastado) worn out; (fig) undistinguished

deslumbrar vt dazzle

desmadr|arse vpr get out of control. **~e** m excess

desmán m outrage

desmanchar vt (LAm) remove the stains from

desmantelar vt dismantle; (despojar) strip

desmaquillador m make-up remover

desmay|ado adj unconscious. **~arse** vpr faint. **~o** m faint

desmedido adj excessive

desmemoriado adj forgetful

desmenti|do m denial. **~r** **4** vt deny; (contradecir) contradict

desmenuzar **10** vt crumble; shred (carne etc)

desmerecer **11** vi. **no ~ de** compare favourably with

desmesurado adj excessive; (enorme) enormous

desmonta|ble adj collapsible; (armario) easy to dismantle; (separable) removable. **~r** vt (quitar) remove; (desarmar) dismantle, take apart. • vi dismount

desmoralizar **10** vt demoralize

desmoronarse vpr crumble; (edificio) collapse

desnatado adj skimmed

desnivel m unevenness; (fig) difference, inequality

desnud|ar vt strip; undress, strip (persona). **~arse** vpr undress. **~ez** f nudity. **~o** adj naked; (fig) bare. • m nude

desnutri|ción f malnutrition. **~do** adj undernourished

desobed|ecer **11** vt disobey. **~iencia** f disobedience

desocupa|do adj (asiento etc) vacant, free; (sin trabajo) unemployed; (*ocioso*) idle. **~r** *vt* vacate; (*vaciar*) empty; (*desalojar*) clear

desodorante *m* deodorant

desolado *adj* desolate; (*persona*) sorry, sad

desorbitante *adj* excessive

desorden *m* disorder, untidiness; (*confusión*) confusion. **~ado** *adj* untidy. **~ar** *vt* disarrange, make a mess of

desorganizar 🔟 *vt* disorganize; (*trastornar*) disturb

desorienta|do *adj* confused. **~r** *vt* disorientate. **~rse** *vpr* lose one's bearings

despabila|do *adj* wide awake; (*listo*) quick. **~r** *vt* (*despertar*) wake up; (*avivar*) wise up. **~rse** *vpr* wake up; (*avivarse*) wise up

despach|ar *vt* finish; (*tratar con*) deal with; (*atender*) serve; (*vender*) sell; (*enviar*) send; (*despedir*) fire. **~o** *m* dispatch; (*oficina*) office; (*venta*) sale; (*de localidades*) box office

despacio *adv* slowly

despampanante *adj* stunning

desparpajo *m* confidence; (*descaro*) impudence

desparramar *vt* scatter; spill (*líquidos*)

despavorido *adj* terrified

despecho *m* spite. a **~** de in spite of. por **~** out of spite

despectivo *adj* contemptuous; (*sentido etc*) pejorative

despedazar 🔟 *vt* tear to pieces

despedi|da *f* goodbye, farewell. **~da de soltero** stag-party. **~r** 🗟 *vt* say goodbye to, see off; dismiss (*empleado*); evict (*inquilino*); (*arrojar*) throw; give off (*olor etc*). **~rse** *vpr* say goodbye (**de** to)

despegar 🔃 *vt* unstick. ● *vi* (*avión*) take off. **~ue** *m* take-off

despeinar *vt* ruffle the hair of

despeja|do *adj* clear; (*persona*) wide awake. **~r** *vt* clear; (*aclarar*) clarify. ● *vi* clear. **~rse** *vpr* (*aclararse*) become clear; (*tiempo*) clear up

despellejar *vt* skin

despenalizar *vt* decriminalize

despensa *f* pantry, larder

despeñadero *m* cliff

desperdici|ar *vt* waste. **~o** *m* waste. **~os** *mpl* rubbish

desperta|dor *m* alarm clock. **~r** 🚺 *vt* wake (up); (*fig*) awaken. **~rse** *vpr* wake up

despiadado *adj* merciless

despido *m* dismissal

despierto *adj* awake; (*listo*) bright

despilfarr|ar *vt* waste. **~o** *m* squandering

despintarse *vpr* (*Mex*) run

despista|do *adj* (*con estar*) confused; (*con ser*) absent-minded. **~r** *vt* throw off the scent; (*fig*) mislead. **~rse** *vpr* (*fig*) get confused

despiste *m* mistake; (*confusión*) muddle

desplaza|miento *m* displacement; (*de opinión etc*) swing, shift. **~r** 🔟 *vt* displace. **~rse** *vpr* travel

desplegar 🚹 & 🔢 *vt* open out; spread (*alas*); (*fig*) show

desplomarse *vpr* collapse

despoblado *m* deserted area

despoj|ar *vt* deprive (*persona*); strip (*cosa*). **~os** *mpl* remains; (*de res*) offal; (*de ave*) giblets

despreci|able *adj* despicable; (*cantidad*) negligible. **~ar** *vt* despise; (*rechazar*) scorn. **~o** *m* contempt; (*desaire*) snub

desprender *vt* remove; give off

(olor). **~se** vpr fall off; (fig) part with; (deducirse) follow

despreocupa|do adj unconcerned; (descuidado) careless. **~rse** vpr not worry

desprestigiar vt discredit

desprevenido adj unprepared. pillar a uno **~** catch s.o. unawares

desproporcionado adj disproportionate

desprovisto adj. **~** de lacking in, without

después adv after, afterwards; (más tarde) later; (a continuación) then. **~** de after. **~** de comer after eating. **~** de todo after all. **~** (de) que after. poco **~** soon after

desquit|arse vpr get even (de with). **~e** m revenge

destaca|do adj outstanding. **~r** 🔟 vt emphasize. ● vi stand out. **~rse** vpr stand out. **~rse en** excel at

destajo m. trabajar a **~** do piece-work

destap|ar vt uncover; open (botella). **~arse** vpr reveal one's true self. **~e** m (fig) permissiveness

destartalado adj (coche) clapped-out; (casa) ramshackle

destello m sparkle; (de estrella) twinkle; (fig) glimmer

destemplado adj discordant; (nervios) frayed

desteñir 🔄 & 🔄 vt fade. ● vi fade; (color) run. **~se** vpr fade; (color) run

desterra|do m exile. **~r** 🔟 vt banish

destetar vt wean

destiempo m. a **~** at the wrong moment; (Mus) out of time

destierro m exile

destil|ar vt distil. **~ería** f distillery

destin|ar vt destine; (nombrar) post. **~atario** m addressee. **~o** m (uso) use, function; (lugar) destination; (suerte) destiny. con **~o** a (going) to

destituir 🔟 vt dismiss

destornilla|dor m screwdriver. **~r** vt unscrew

destreza f skill

destroz|ar 🔟 vt destroy; (fig) shatter. **~os** mpl destruction, damage

destru|cción f destruction. **~ir** 🔟 vt destroy

desus|ado adj old-fashioned; (insólito) unusual. **~o** m disuse. caer en **~o** fall into disuse

desvalido adj needy, destitute

desvalijar vt rob; ransack (casa)

desvalorizar 🔟 vt devalue

desván m loft

desvanec|er 🔟 vt make disappear; (borrar) blur; (fig) dispel. **~erse** vpr disappear; (desmayarse) faint. **~imiento** m (Med) faint

desvariar 🔟 vi be delirious; (fig) talk nonsense

desvel|ar vt keep awake. **~arse** vpr stay awake, have a sleepless night. **~o** m sleeplessness

desvencijado adj (mueble) rickety

desventaja f disadvantage

desventura f misfortune. **~do** adj unfortunate

desverg|onzado adj impudent, cheeky. **~üenza** f impudence, cheek

desvestirse 🔄 vt undress

desv|iación f deviation; (Auto) diversion. **~iar** 🔟 vt divert; deflect (pelota). **~iarse** vpr (carretera) branch off; (*del camino*) make a detour; (*del tema*) stray. **~io** *m* diversion

desvivirse *vpr.* **~se por** be completely devoted to; (*esforzarse*) go out of one's way to

detall|ar *vt* relate in detail. **~e** *m* detail; (*fig*) gesture. **al ~e** retail. **entrar en ~es** go into detail. **¡qué ~e!** how thoughtful! **~ista** *m & f* retailer

detect|ar *vt* detect. **~ive** *m* detective

deten|ción *f* stopping; (*Jurid*) arrest; (*en la cárcel*) detention. **~er** 40 *vt* stop; (*Jurid*) arrest; (*encarcelar*) detain; (*retrasar*) delay. **~erse** *vpr* stop; (*entretenerse*) spend a lot of time. **~idamente** *adv* at length. **~ido** *adj* (*Jurid*) under arrest. ● *m* prisoner

detergente *adj & m* detergent

deterior|ar *vt* damage, spoil. **~arse** *vpr* deteriorate. **~o** *m* deterioration

determina|ción *f* determination; (*decisión*) decison. **~nte** *adj* decisive. **~r** *vt* determine; (*decidir*) decide

detestar *vt* detest

detrás *adv* behind; (*en la parte posterior*) on the back. **~ de** behind. **por ~** at the back; (*por la espalda*) from behind

detrimento *m* detriment. **en ~ de** to the detriment of

deud|a *f* debt. **~or** *m* debtor

devalua|ción *f* devaluation. **~r** 21 *vt* devalue. **~se** *vpr* depreciate

devastador *adj* devastating

devoción *f* devotion

devol|ución *f* return; (*Com*) repayment, refund. **~ver** 5 (*pp devuelto*) *vt* return; (*Com*) repay, re-

fund. ● *vi* be sick

devorar *vt* devour

devoto *adj* devout; (*amigo etc*) devoted. ● *m* admirer

di *vb véase* DAR, DECIR

día *m* day. **~ de fiesta** (public) holiday. **~ del santo** saint's day. **~ feriado** (*LAm*), **~ festivo** (public) holiday. **al ~** up to date. **al ~ siguiente** (on) the following day. **¡buenos ~s!** good morning! **de ~** by day. **el ~ de hoy** today. **el ~ de mañana** tomorrow. **un ~ sí y otro no** every other day. **vivir al ~** live from hand to mouth

Día de la raza In Latin America, the anniversary of Columbus's discovery of America, October 12. In Spain it is known as *Día de la Hispanidad*. It is a celebration of the cultural ties shared by Spanish-speaking countries.

diab|etes *f* diabetes. **~ético** *adj* diabetic

diab|lo *m* devil. **~lura** *f* mischief. **~ólico** *adj* diabolical

diadema *f* diadem

diáfano *adj* diaphanous; (*cielo*) clear

diafragma *m* diaphragm

diagn|osis *f* diagnosis. **~osticar** 7 *vt* diagnose. **~óstico** *m* diagnosis

diagonal *adj & f* diagonal

diagrama *m* diagram

dialecto *m* dialect

di|alogar 12 *vi* talk. **~álogo** *m* dialogue; (*Pol*) talks

diamante *m* diamond

diámetro *m* diameter

diana *f* reveille; (*blanco*) bull's-eye

diapositiva f slide, transparency

diario adj daily. ● m newspaper; (libro) diary. a ~o daily. de ~o everyday, ordinary

diarrea f diarrhoea

dibujante m draughtsman. ●f draughtswoman. ~ar vt draw. ~o m drawing. ~os animados cartoons

diccionario m dictionary

dich|a f happiness. por ~a fortunately. ~o adj (tal) such. ● m saying. ~o y hecho no sooner said than done. mejor ~o rather. propiamente ~o strictly speaking. ~oso adj happy; (afortunado) fortunate

diciembre m December

dicta|do m dictation. ~dor m dictator. ~dura f dictatorship. ~men m opinion; (informe) report. ~r vt dictate; pronounce (sentencia etc); (LAm) give (clase)

didáctico adj didactic

dieci|nueve adj & m nineteen. ~ocho adj & m eighteen. ~séis adj & m sixteen. ~siete adj & m seventeen

diente m tooth; (de tenedor) prong; (de ajo) clove. ~ de león dandelion. hablar entre ~s mumble

diestro adj right-handed; (hábil) skillful

dieta f diet

diez adj & m ten

diezmar vt decimate

difamación f (con palabras) slander; (por escrito) libel

diferen|cia f difference; (desacuerdo) disagreement. ~ciar vt differentiate between. ~ciarse vpr differ. ~te adj different; (diversos) various

diferido adj (TV etc) en ~ recorded

difícil adj difficult; (poco probable) unlikely. ~ultad f difficulty. ~ultar vt make difficult

difteria f diphtheria

difundir vt spread; (TV etc) broadcast

difunto adj late, deceased. ● m deceased

difusión f spreading

dige|rir 4 vt digest. ~stión f digestion. ~stivo adj digestive

digital adj digital; (de los dedos) finger

dign|arse vpr deign to. ~atario m dignitary. ~idad f dignity. ~o adj honourable; (decoroso) decent; (merecedor) worthy (de of). ~ de elogio praiseworthy

digo vb véase DECIR

dije vb véase DECIR

dilatar vt expand; (Med) dilate; (prolongar) prolong. ~se vpr expand; (Med) dilate; (extenderse) extend; (Mex, demorarse) be late

dilema m dilemma

diligen|cia f diligence; (gestión) job; (carruaje) stagecoach. ~te adj diligent

dilucidar vt clarify; solve (misterio)

diluir 17 vt dilute

diluvio m flood

dimensión f dimension; (tamaño) size

diminut|ivo adj & m diminutive. ~o adj minute

dimitir vt/i resign

Dinamarca f Denmark

dinamarqués adj Danish. ● m Dane

dinámic|a f dynamics. ~o adj

dynamic

dinamita f dynamite

dínamo m dynamo

dinastía f dynasty

diner|al m fortune. ~o m money. ~o efectivo cash. ~o suelto change

dinosaurio m dinosaur

dios m god. ~a f goddess. ¡D~ mío! good heavens! ¡gracias a D~! thank God!

diploma m diploma. ~acia f diplomacy. ~ado adj qualified. ~arse vpr (LAm) graduate. ~ático adj diplomatic. ● m diplomat

diptongo m diphthong

diputa|ción f delegation. ~ción provincial county council. ~do m deputy; (Pol, en España) member of the Cortes; (Pol, en Inglaterra) Member of Parliament; (Pol, en Estados Unidos) congressman

dique m dike

direc|ción f direction; (señas) address; (los que dirigen) management; (Pol) leadership; (Auto) steering. ~ción prohibida no entry. ~ción única one-way. ~ta f (Auto) top gear. ~tiva f board; (Pol) executive committee. ~tivas fpl guidelines. ~to adj direct; (línea) straight; (tren) through. en ~to (TV etc) live. ~tor m director; (Mus) conductor; (de escuela) headmaster; (de periódico) editor; (gerente) manager. ~tora f (de escuela etc) headmistress. ~torio m board of directors; (LAm, de teléfonos) telephone directory

dirig|ente adj ruling. ● m & f leader; (de empresa) manager. ~ir 14 vt direct; (Mus) conduct; run (empresa etc); address (carta etc). ~irse vpr make one's way; (hablar)

address

disciplina f discipline. ~r vt discipline. ~rio adj disciplinary

discípulo m disciple; (alumno) pupil

disco m disc; (Mus) record; (deportes) discus; (de teléfono) dial; (de tráfico) sign; (Rail) signal. ~ duro hard disk. ~ flexible floppy disk

disconforme adj not in agreement

discord|e adj discordant. ~ia f discord

discoteca f discothèque, disco 🗍; (colección de discos) record collection

discreción f discretion

discrepa|ncia f discrepancy; (desacuerdo) disagreement. ~r vi differ

discreto adj discreet; (moderado) moderate

discrimina|ción f discrimination. ~r vt (distinguir) discriminate between; (tratar injustamente) discriminate against

disculpa f apology; (excusa) excuse. pedir ~s apologize. ~r vt excuse, forgive. ~rse vpr apologize

discurs|ar vi speak (sobre about). ~o m speech

discusión f discussion; (riña) argument

discuti|ble adj debatable. ~r vt discuss; (contradecir) contradict. ● vi argue (por about)

disecar 7 vt stuff; (cortar) dissect

diseminar vt disseminate, spread

disentir 4 vi disagree (de with, en on)

diseña|dor m designer. ~ar vt design. ~o m design; (fig) sketch

disertación f dissertation

disfraz m fancy dress; (*para engañar*) disguise. **~ar** 10 vt dress up; (*para engañar*) disguise. **~arse** vpr. **~arse** de dress up as; (*para engañar*) disguise o.s. as.

disfrutar vt enjoy. ● vi enjoy o.s. **~ de** enjoy

disgust|ar vt displease; (*molestar*) annoy. **~arse** vpr get annoyed, get upset; (*dos personas*) fall out. **~o** m annoyance; (*problema*) trouble; (*riña*) quarrel; (*dolor*) sorrow, grief

disidente adj & m & f dissident

disimular vt conceal. ● vi pretend

disipar vt dissipate; (*derrochar*) squander

dislocarse 7 vpr dislocate

disminu|ción f decrease. **~ir** 17 vi diminish

disolver 2 (*pp disuelto*) vt dissolve. **~se** vpr dissolve

dispar adj different

disparar vt fire; (*Mex, pagar*) buy. ● vi shoot (*contra* at)

disparate m silly thing; (*error*) mistake. **decir ~s** talk nonsense. **¡qué ~!** how ridiculous!

disparidad f disparity

disparo m (*acción*) firing; (*tiro*) shot

dispensar vt give; (*eximir*) exempt. ● vi. **¡Vd dispense!** forgive me

dispers|ar vt scatter, disperse. **~arse** vpr scatter, disperse. **~ión** f dispersion. **~o** adj scattered

dispon|er 34 vt arrange; (*Jurid*) order. ● vi. **~er de** have; (*vender etc*) dispose of. **~erse** vpr prepare (a to). **~ibilidad** f availability. **~ible** adj available

disposición f arrangement; (*aptitud*) talent; (*disponibilidad*) dis-

posal; (*Jurid*) order, decree. **~ de ánimo** frame of mind. **a la ~ de** at the disposal of. **a su ~** at your service

dispositivo m device

dispuesto adj ready; (*persona*) disposed (a to); (*servicial*) helpful

disputa f dispute; (*pelea*) argument

disquete m diskette, floppy disk

dista|ncia f distance. **a ~ncia** from a distance. **guardar las ~ncias** keep one's distance. **~nciar** vt space out; distance (*amigos*). **~nciarse** vpr (*dos personas*) fall out. **~nte** adj distant. **~r** vi be away; (*fig*) be far. **~ 5 kilómetros** it's 5 kilometres away

distin|ción f distinction; (*honor*) award. **~guido** adj distinguished. **~guir** 13 vt/i distinguish. **~guirse** vpr distinguish o.s.; (*diferenciarse*) differ. **~tivo** adj distinctive. ● m badge. **~to** adj different, distinct

distra|cción f amusement; (*descuido*) absent-mindedness, inattention. **~er** 41 vt distract; (*divertir*) amuse. **~erse** vpr amuse o.s.; (*descuidarse*) not pay attention. **~ído** adj (*desatento*) absent-minded

distribu|ción f distribution. **~idor** m distributor. **~ir** 17 vt distribute

distrito m district

disturbio m disturbance

disuadir vt deter, dissuade

diurno adj daytime

divagar 12 vi digress; (*hablar sin sentido*) ramble

diván m settee, sofa

diversi|dad f diversity. **~ficar** 7 vt diversify

diversión f amusement, entertainment; (*pasatiempo*) pastime

diverso *adj* different

diverti|do *adj* amusing; (*que tiene gracia*) funny. **~r** [4] *vt* amuse, entertain. **~rse** *vpr* enjoy o.s.

dividir *vt* divide; (*repartir*) share out

divino *adj* divine

divisa *f* emblem. **~s** *fpl* currency

divisar *vt* make out

división *f* division

divorci|ado *adj* divorced. ● *m* divorcee. **~ar** *vt* divorce. **~arse** *vpr* get divorced. **~o** *m* divorce

divulgar [12] *vt* spread; divulge (*secreto*)

dizque *adv* (*LAm*) apparently; (*supuestamente*) supposedly

do *m* C; (*solfa*) doh

dobl|adillo *m* hem; (*de pantalón*) turn-up (*Brit*), cuff (*Amer*). **~ar** *vt* double; (*plegar*) fold; (*torcer*) bend; turn (*esquina*); dub (*película*). ● *vi* turn; (*campana*) toll. **~arse** *vpr* double; (*curvarse*) bend. **~e** *adj* double. ● *m* double. **el ~e** twice as much (**de, que as**). **~egar** [12] *vt* (*fig*) force to give in. **~egarse** *vpr* give in

doce *adj* & *m* twelve. **~na** *f* dozen

docente *adj* teaching. ● *m* & *f* teacher

dócil *adj* obedient

doctor *m* doctor. **~ado** *m* doctorate

doctrina *f* doctrine

document|ación *f* documentation, papers. **~al** *adj* & *m* documentary. **~o** *m* document. D~o Nacional de Identidad identity

card

dólar *m* dollar

dolarizar *vt* dollarize

dol|er [2] *vi* hurt, ache; (*fig*) grieve. **me duele la cabeza** I have a headache. **le duele el estómago** he has (a) stomach-ache. **~or** *m* pain; (*sordo*) ache; (*fig*) sorrow. **~or de cabeza** headache. **~or de muelas** toothache. **~oroso** *adj* painful

domar *vt* tame; break in (*caballo*)

dom|esticar [7] *vt* domesticate. **~éstico** *adj* domestic

domicili|ar *vt*. **~ar los pagos** pay by direct debit. **~o** *m* address. **~o particular** home address. **reparto a ~** home delivery service

domina|nte *adj* dominant; (*persona*) domineering. **~r** *vt* dominate; (*contener*) control; (*conocer*) have a good command of. ● *vi* dominate. **~rse** *vpr* control o.s.

domingo *m* Sunday

dominio *m* authority; (*territorio*) domain; (*fig*) command

dominó *m* (*pl* **~s**) dominoes; (*ficha*) domino

don *m* talent, gift; (*en un sobre*) Mr. **~** Pedro Pedro

donación *f* donation

donaire *m* grace, charm

dona|nte m & f (de sangre) donor. **~r** vt donate

doncella f maiden; (criada) maid

donde adv where

dónde adv where?; (LAm, cómo) how; ¿hasta ~? how far? ¿por ~? whereabouts?; (por qué camino?) which way? ¿a ~ vas? where are you going? ¿de ~ eres? where are you from?

dondequiera adv. ~ que wherever. por ~ everywhere

doña f (en un sobre) Mrs. ~ María María

dora|do adj golden; (cubierto de oro) gilt. **~r** vt gilt; (Culin) brown

dormi|do adj asleep. quedarse ~do fall asleep; (no despertar) oversleep. **~r 🔲** vt send to sleep. • vi sleep. **~rse** vpr fall asleep. ~ la siesta have an afternoon nap, have a siesta. **~tar** vi doze. **~torio** m bedroom

dors|al adj back. • m (en deportes) number. **~o** m back. nadar de ~ (Mex) do (the) backstroke

dos adj & m two. de ~ en ~ in twos, in pairs. los ~, las ~ both (of them). **~cientos** adj & m two hundred

dosi|ficar 🔲 vt dose; (fig) measure out. **~s** f invar dose

dot|ado adj gifted. **~ar** vt give a dowry; (proveer) provide (de with). **~e** m dowry

doy vb véase DAR

dragar 🔢 vt dredge

drama m drama; (obra de teatro) play. **~turgo** m playwright

drástico adj drastic

droga f drug. **~dicto** m drug addict. **~do** m drug addict. **~r 🔢** vt drug. **~rse** vpr take drugs

droguería f hardware store

ducha f shower. **~rse** vpr have a shower

dud|a f doubt. poner en ~a question. sin ~a (alguna) without a doubt. **~ar** vt/i doubt. **~oso** adj doubtful; (sospechoso) dubious

duelo m duel; (luto) mourning

duende m imp

dueñ|a f owner, proprietress; (de una pensión) landlady. **~o** m owner, proprietor; (de una pensión) landlord

duermo vb véase DORMIR

dul|ce adj sweet; (agua) fresh; (suave) soft, gentle. • m (LAm) sweet. **~zura** f sweetness; (fig) gentleness

duna f dune

dúo m duet, duo

duplica|do adj duplicated. por ~ in duplicate. • m duplicate. **~r 🔢** vt duplicate. **~rse** vpr double

duque m duke. **~sa** f duchess

dura|ción f duration, length. **~dero** adj lasting. **~nte** prep during; (medida de tiempo) for. ~ todo el año all year round. **~r** vi last

durazno m (LAm, fruta) peach

dureza f hardness; (Culin) toughness; (fig) harshness

duro adj hard; (Culin) tough; (fig) harsh. • adv (esp LAm) hard

DVD m (Disco Versátil Digital) DVD. **~teca** f DVD library

Ee

e *conj* and
Ébola *m* ebola
ebrio *adj* drunk
ebullición *f* boiling
eccema *m* eczema
echar *vt* throw; post (carta); give off (olor); pour (líquido); (*expulsar*) expel; (*de recinto*) throw out; fire (empleado); (*poner*) put on; get (gasolina); put out (raíces); show (película). ~ **a** start. ~ **a perder** spoil. ~ **de menos** miss. ~se **atrás** (*fig*) back down. echárselas **de** feign. ~se *vpr* throw o.s.; (*tumbarse*) lie down
eclesiástico *adj* ecclesiastical
eclipse *m* eclipse
eco *m* echo. hacerse ~ de echo
ecología *f* ecology. ~**ista** *m & f* ecologist
economato *m* cooperative store
economía *f* economy; (*ciencia*) economics. ~**ómico** *adj* economic; (*no caro*) inexpensive. ~**omista** *m & f* economist. ~**omizar** [10] *vt/i* economize
ecoturismo *m* ecotourism
ecuación *f* equation
ecuador *m* equator. el E~ the Equator. E~ (*país*) Ecuador
ecuánime *adj* level-headed; (*imparcial*) impartial
ecuatoriano *adj & m* Ecuadorian
ecuestre *adj* equestrian
edad *f* age. ~ avanzada old age. E~ de Piedra Stone Age. E~ Media Middle Ages. ¿qué ~ tiene? how old is he?

edición *f* edition; (*publicación*) publication
edicto *m* edict
edificación *f* building. ~**ante** *adj* edifying. ~**ar** [7] *vt* build; (*fig*) edify. ~**io** *m* building; (*fig*) structure
editar *vt* edit; (*publicar*) publish. ~**or** *adj* publishing. ● *m* editor; (*que publica*) publisher. ~**orial** *adj* editorial. ● *m* leading article. ● *f* publishing house
edredón *m* duvet
educación *f* upbringing; (*modales*) (good) manners; (*enseñanza*) education. falta de ~**ción** rudeness, bad manners. ~**do** *adj* polite. bien ~**do** polite. mal ~**do** rude. ~**r** [7] *vt* bring up; (*enseñar*) educate. ~**tivo** *adj* educational
edulcorante *m* sweetener
EE.UU. *abrev* (**Estados Unidos**) USA
efectivamente *adv* really; (*por supuesto*) indeed. ~**ivo** *adj* effective; (*auténtico*) real. ● *m* cash. ~**o** *m* effect; (*impresión*) impression. en ~**o** really; (*como respuesta*) indeed. ~**os** *mpl* belongings; (*Com*) goods. ~**uar** [21] *vt* carry out; make (viaje, compras etc)
efervescente *adj* effervescent; (*bebidas*) fizzy
eficacia *f* effectiveness; (*de persona*) efficiency. ~**z** *adj* effective; (*persona*) efficient
eficiencia *f* efficiency. ~**te** *adj* efficient
efímero *adj* ephemeral
efusividad *f* effusiveness. ~**vo** *adj* effusive; (*persona*) demonstrative
egipcio *adj & m* Egyptian
Egipto *m* Egypt

ego|ísmo *m* selfishness, egotism. **~ísta** *adj* selfish

egresar *vi* (LAm) graduate; (de colegio) leave school, graduate (Amer)

eje *m* axis; (Tec) axle

ejecu|ción *f* execution; (Mus) performance. **~tar** *vt* carry out; (Mus) perform; (matar) execute. **~tivo** *m* executive

ejempl|ar *adj* exemplary; (ideal) model. ● *m* specimen; (libro) copy; (revista) issue, number. **~ificar 7** *vt* exemplify. **~o** *m* example. **dar (el) ~o** set an example. **por ~o** for example

ejerc|er 9 *vt* exercise; practise (profesión); exert (influencia). ● *vi* practise. **~icio** *m* exercise; (de profesión) practice. **hacer ~icios** take exercise. **~itar** *vt* exercise

ejército *m* army

ejido *m* (Mex) cooperative

ejote *m* (Mex) green bean

---

el *artículo definido masculino* (pl **los**)

The masculine article **el** is also used before feminine nouns which begin with stressed **a** or **ha**, e.g. **el ala derecha, el hada madrina**. Also, **de** followed by **el** becomes **del** and **el** preceded by **a** becomes **al**

....➤ the. **el tren de las seis** the six o'clock train. **el vecino de al lado** the next-door neighbour. **cerca del hospital** near the hospital

....➤ *No se traduce en los siguientes casos:* (con nombre abstracto, genérico) **el tiempo vuela** time flies. **odio el queso** I

hate cheese. **el hilo es muy durable** linen is very durable

....➤ (con colores, días de la semana) **el rojo está de moda** red is in fashion. **el lunes es fiesta** Monday is a holiday

....➤ (con algunas instituciones) **termino el colegio mañana** I finish school tomorrow. **lo ingresaron en el hospital** he was admitted to hospital

....➤ (con nombres propios) **el Sr. Díaz** Mr Díaz. **el doctor Lara** Doctor Lara

....➤ (antes de infinitivo) **es muy cuidadosa en el vestir** she takes great care in the way she dresses. **me di cuenta al verlo** I realized when I saw him

....➤ (con partes del cuerpo, articulos personales) se traduce por un posesivo. **apretó el puño** he clenched his fist. **tienes el zapato desatado** your shoe is undone

....➤ **el + de** **el de Pedro** it's Pedro's. **el del sombrero** the one with the hat

....➤ **el + que** (persona) **el que me atendió** the one who served me. (cosa) **el que se rompió** the one that broke.

....➤ **el + que** + subjuntivo (quienquiera) whoever. **el que gane la lotería** whoever wins the lottery. (cualquiera) whichever. **compra el que sea más barato** buy whichever is cheaper

él *pron* (persona) he; (persona con prep) him; (cosa) it. **es de ~** it's his

elabora|ción *f* elaboration; (fabricación) manufacture. **~r** *vt* elaborate; manufacture (producto);

(*producir*) produce

el|asticidad f elasticity. **~ástico** adj & m elastic

elec|ción f choice; (*de político etc*) election. **~ciones** fpl (*Pol*) election. **~tor** m voter. **~torado** m electorate. **~toral** adj electoral; (*campaña*) election

electrici|dad f electricity. **~sta** m & f electrician

eléctrico adj electric; (*aparato*) electrical

electri|ficar 7 vt electrify. **~zar** 10 vt electrify

electrocutar vt electrocute. **~se** vpr be electrocuted

electrodoméstico adj electrical appliance

electrónic|a f electronics. **~o** adj electronic

elefante m elephant

elegan|cia f elegance. **~te** adj elegant

elegía f elegy

elegi|ble adj eligible. **~do** adj chosen. **~r** 5 & 14 vt choose; (*por votación*) elect

element|al adj elementary; (*esencial*) fundamental. **~o** m element; (*persona*) person, bloke (*Brit, fam*). **~os** mpl (*nociones*) basic principles

elenco m (*en el teatro*) cast

eleva|ción f elevation; (*de precios*) rise, increase; (*acción*) raising. **~dor** m (*Mex*) lift (*Brit*), elevator (*Amer*). **~r** vt raise; (*promover*) promote

elimina|ción f elimination. **~r** vt eliminate; (*Informática*) delete. **~toria** f preliminary heat

élite /e'lit, e'lite/ f elite

ella pron (*persona*) she; (*persona con prep*) her; (*cosa*) it. es de ~s it's theirs. **~s** pron pl they; (*con*

prep) them. es de ~ it's hers

ello pron it

ellos pron pl they; (*con prep*) them. es de ~ it's theirs

elocuen|cia f eloquence. **~te** adj eloquent

elogi|ar vt praise. **~o** m praise

elote m (*Mex*) corncob; (*Culin*) corn on the cob

eludir vt avoid, elude

emanar vi emanate (**de** from); (*originarse*) originate (**de** from, in)

emancipa|ción f emancipation. **~r** vt emancipate. **~rse** vpr become emancipated

embadurnar vt smear

embajad|a f embassy. **~or** m ambassador

embalar vt pack

embaldosar vt tile

embalsamar vt embalm

embalse m reservoir

embaraz|ada adj pregnant. • f pregnant woman. **~ar** 10 vt get pregnant. **~o** m pregnancy; (*apuro*) embarrassment; (*estorbo*) hindrance. **~oso** adj awkward, embarrassing

embar|cación f vessel. **~cadero** m jetty, pier. **~car** 7 vt load (*mercancías etc*). **~carse** vpr board. **~carse en** (*fig*) embark upon

embargo m embargo; (*Jurid*) seizure. **sin ~** however

embarque m loading; (*de pasajeros*) boarding

embaucar 7 vt trick

embelesar vt captivate

embellecer 11 vt make beautiful

embesti|da f charge. **~r** 5 vt/i charge

emblema m emblem

embolsarse vpr pocket

embonar vt (Mex) fit

emborrachar vt get drunk. ~**se** vpr get drunk

emboscada f ambush

embotar vt dull

embotella|miento m (de vehículos) traffic jam. ~**r** vt bottle

embrague m clutch

embriag|arse 12 vpr get drunk. ~**uez** f drunkenness

embrión m embryo

embroll|ar vt mix up; involve (persona). ~**arse** vpr get into a muddle; (en un asunto) get involved. ~**o** m tangle; (fig) muddle

embruj|ado adj bewitched; (casa) haunted. ~**ar** vt bewitch. ~**o** m spell

embrutecer 11 vt brutalize

embudo m funnel

embuste m lie. ~**ro** adj deceitful. • m liar

embuti|do m (Culin) sausage. ~**r** vt stuff

emergencia f emergency

emerger 14 vi appear, emerge

emigra|ción f emigration. ~**nte** adj & m & f emigrant. ~**r** vi emigrate

eminen|cia f eminence. ~**te** adj eminent

emisario m emissary

emi|sión f emission; (de dinero) issue; (TV etc) broadcast. ~**sor** adj issuing; (TV etc) broadcasting. ~**sora** f radio station. ~**tir** vt emit, give out; (TV etc) broadcast; cast (voto); (poner en circulación) issue

emoci|ón f emotion; (excitación) excitement. ¡qué ~**ón**! how exciting!. ~**onado** adj moved.

~**onante** adj exciting; (conmovedor) moving. ~**onar** vt move. ~**onarse** vpr get excited; (conmoverse) be moved

emotivo adj emotional; (conmovedor) moving

empacar 7 vt (LAm) pack

empacho m indigestion

empadronar vt register. ~**se** vpr register

empalagoso adj sickly; (persona) cloying

empalizada f fence

empalm|ar vt connect, join. • vi meet. ~**e** m junction; (de trenes) connection

empan|ada f (savoury) pie; (LAm, individual) pasty. ~**adilla** f pasty

empantanarse vpr become swamped; (coche) get bogged down

empañar vt steam up; (fig) tarnish. ~**se** vpr steam up

empapar vt soak. ~**se** vpr get soaked

empapela|do m wallpaper. ~**r** vt wallpaper

empaquetar vt package

emparedado m sandwich

emparentado adj related

empast|ar vt fill (muela). ~**e** m filling

empat|ar vi draw. ~**e** m draw

empedernido adj confirmed; (bebedor) inveterate

empedrar 1 vt pave

empeine m instep

empeñ|ado adj in debt; (decidido) determined (en to). ~**ar** vt pawn; pledge (palabra). ~**arse** vpr get into debt; (estar decidido a) be determined (en to). ~**o** m pledge; (resolución) determination. **casa** f de ~s pawnshop. ~oso adj (LAm) hardworking

empeorar vt make worse. ● vi get worse. ~se vpr get worse

empequeñecer 🔢 vt become smaller; (fig) belittle

empera|dor m emperor. ~triz f empress

empezar 🔢 & 🔟 vt/i start, begin. para ~ to begin with

empina|do adj (cuesta) steep. ~r vt raise. ~rse vpr (persona) stand on tiptoe

empírico adj empirical

emplasto m plaster

emplaza|miento m (Jurid) summons; (lugar) site. ~r 🔟 vt summon; (situar) site

emple|ada f employee; (doméstica) maid. ~ado m employee. ~ar vt use; employ (persona); spend (tiempo). ~arse vpr get a job. ~o m use; (trabajo) employment; (puesto) job

empobrecer 🔢 vt impoverish. ~se vpr become poor

empoll|ar vt incubate (huevos); (arg, estudiar) cram 🔢. ● vi (ave) sit; (estudiante) ✕ cram. ~ón m ✕ swot (Brit, fam), grind (Amer, fam)

empolvarse vpr powder

empotra|do adj built-in, fitted. ~r vt fit

emprende|dor adj enterprising. ~r vt undertake; set out on (viaje). ~rla con uno pick a fight with s.o.

empresa f undertaking; (Com) company, firm. ~ puntocom dotcom company. ~rio m businessman; (patrón) employer; (de teatro etc) impresario

empuj|ar vt push. ~e m (fig) drive. ~ón m push, shove

empuña|dura f handle

emular vt emulate

en prep in; (sobre) on; (dentro) inside, in; (medio de transporte) by. ~ casa at home. ~ coche by car. ~ 10 días in 10 days. de pueblo ~ pueblo from town to town

enagua f petticoat

enajena|ción f alienation. ~ción mental insanity. ~r vt alienate; (volver loco) derange

enamora|do adj in love. ● m lover. ~r vt win the love of. ~rse vpr fall in love (de with)

enano adj & m dwarf

enardecer 🔢 vt inflame. ~se vpr get excited (por about)

encabeza|do m (Mex) headline. ~miento m heading; (de periódico) headline. ~r 🔟 vt head; lead (revolución etc)

encabritarse vpr rear up

encadenar vt chain; (fig) tie down

encaj|ar vt fit; fit together (varias piezas). ● vi fit; (cuadrar) tally. ~arse vpr put on. ~e m lace; (Com) reserve

encaminar vt direct. ~se vpr make one's way

encandilar vt dazzle; (estimular) stimulate

encant|ado adj enchanted; (persona) delighted. ¡~ado! pleased to meet you! ~ador adj charming. ~amiento m spell. ~ar vt bewitch; (fig) charm, delight. me ~a la leche I love milk. ~o m spell; (fig) delight

encapricharse vpr. ~ con take a fancy to

encarar vt face; (LAm) stand up to (persona). ~se vpr. ~se con stand up to

encarcelar vt imprison

encarecer 11 vt put up the price of. **~se** vpr become more expensive

encarg|ado adj in charge. • m manager, person in charge. **~ar** 12 vt entrust; (pedir) order. **~arse** vpr take charge (de of). **~o** m job; (Com) order; (recado) errand. **hecho de ~o** made to measure

encariñarse vpr. **~ con** take to, become fond of

encarna|ción f incarnation. **~do** adj incarnate; (rojo) red; (uña) ingrowing. • m red

encarnizado adj bitter

encarpetar vt file; (LAm, dar carpetazo) shelve

encarrilar vt put back on the rails; (fig) direct, put on the right track

encasillar vt classify; (fig) pigeonhole

encauzar 10 vt channel

enceguecer vt 11 (LAm) blind

encend|edor m lighter. **~er** 11 vt light; switch on, turn on (aparato eléctrico); start (motor); (fig) arouse. **~erse** vpr light; (aparato eléctrico) come on; (excitarse) get excited; (ruborizarse) blush. **~ido** adj lit; (aparato eléctrico) on; (rojo) bright red. • m (Auto) ignition

encera|do adj waxed. • m (pizarra) blackboard. **~r** vt wax

encerr|ar 1 vt shut in; (con llave) lock up; (fig, contener) contain. **~ona** f trap

enchilar vt (Mex) add chili to

enchinar vt (Mex) perm

enchuf|ado adj switched on. **~ar** vt plug in; fit together (tubos etc). **~e** m socket; (clavija) plug; (de tubos etc) joint; (fam, influen-

cia) contact. **tener ~e** have friends in the right places

encía f gum

enciclopedia f encyclopaedia

encierro m confinement; (cárcel) prison

encim|a adv on top; (arriba) above. **~ de** on, on top of; (sobre) over; (además de) besides, as well as. **por ~** on top; (adj la ligera) superficially. **por ~ de todo** above all. **~ar** vt (Mex) stack up. **~era** f worktop

encina f holm oak

encinta adj pregnant

enclenque adj weak; (enfermizo) sickly

encog|er 14 vt shrink; (contraer) contract. **~se** vpr shrink. **~erse de hombros** shrug one's shoulders

encolar vt glue; (pegar) stick

encolerizar 10 vt make angry. **~se** vpr get furious

encomendar 1 vt entrust

encomi|ar vt praise. **~o** m praise. **~oso** adj (LAm) complimentary

encono m bitterness, ill will

encontra|do adj contrary, conflicting. **~r** 2 vt find; (tropezar con) meet. **~rse** vpr meet; (hallarse) be. **no ~rse** feel uncomfortable

encorvar vt hunch. **~se** vpr stoop

encrespa|do adj (pelo) curly; (mar) rough. **~r** vt curl (pelo); make rough (mar)

encrucijada f crossroads

encuaderna|ción f binding. **~dor** m bookbinder. **~r** vt bind

encub|ierto adj hidden. **~rir** (pp encubierto) vt hide, conceal; cover up (delito); shelter (delincuente)

encuentro m meeting; (en depor-

tes) match; (*Mil*) encounter

encuesta *f* survey; (*investigación*) inquiry

encumbrado *adj* eminent; (*alto*) high

encurtidos *mpl* pickles

endeble *adj* weak

endemoniado *adj* possessed; (*muy malo*) wretched

enderezar 🔟 *vt* straighten out; (*poner vertical*) put upright; (*fig, arreglar*) put right, sort out; (*dirigir*) direct. ~**se** *vpr* straighten out

endeudarse *vpr* get into debt

endiablado *adj* possessed; (*malo*) terrible; (*difícil*) difficult

endosar *vt* endorse (cheque)

endulzar 🔟 *vt* sweeten; (*fig*) soften

endurecer 🔟 *vt* harden. ~**se** *vpr* harden

enemi|go *adj* enemy. ● *m* enemy. ~**stad** *f* enmity. ~**star** *vt* make an enemy of. ~**starse** *vpr* fall out (con with)

en|ergía *f* energy. ~**érgico** *adj* (*persona*) lively; (*decisión*) forceful

energúmeno *m* madman

enero *m* January

enésimo *adj* nth, umpteenth 🔟

enfad|ado *adj* angry; (*molesto*) annoyed. ~**ar** *vt* make cross, anger; (*molestar*) annoy. ~**arse** *vpr* get angry; (*molestarse*) get annoyed. ~**o** *m* anger; (*molestia*) annoyance

énfasis *m invar* emphasis, stress. poner ~ stress, emphasize

enfático *adj* emphatic

enferm|ar *vi* fall ill. ~**arse** *vpr* (*LAm*) fall ill. ~**edad** *f* illness. ~**era** *f* nurse. ~**ería** *f* sick bay; (*carrera*) nursing. ~**ero** *m* (male) nurse

~**izo** *adj* sickly. ~**o** *adj* ill. ● *m* patient

enflaquecer 🔟 *vt* make thin. ● *vi* lose weight

enfo|car 🔟 *vt* shine on; focus (lente); (*fig*) approach. ~**que** *m* focus; (*fig*) approach

enfrentar *vt* face, confront; (*poner frente a frente*) bring face to face. ~**se** *vpr*. ~**se con** confront; (*en deportes*) meet

enfrente *adv* opposite. ~ de opposite. de ~ opposite

enfria|miento *m* cooling; (*catarro*) cold. ~**r** 🔟 *vt* cool (down); (*fig*) cool down. ~**rse** *vpr* go cold; (*fig*) cool off

enfurecer 🔟 *vt* infuriate. ~**se** *vpr* get furious

engalanar *vt* adorn. ~**se** *vpr* dress up

enganchar *vt* hook; hang up (ropa). ~**se** *vpr* get caught; (*Mil*) enlist

engañ|ar *vt* deceive, trick; (*ser infiel*) be unfaithful. ~**arse** *vpr* be wrong, be mistaken; (*no admitir la verdad*) deceive o.s. ~**o** *m* deceit, trickery; (*error*) mistake. ~**oso** *adj* deceptive; (*persona*) deceitful

engarzar 🔟 *vt* string (cuentas); set (joyas)

engatusar 🔟 *vt* coax

engendr|ar *vt* father; (*fig*) breed. ~**o** *m* (*monstruo*) monster; (*fig*) brainchild

englobar *vt* include

engomar *vt* glue

engordar *vt* fatten, gain (kilo). ● *vi* get fatter, put on weight

engorro *m* nuisance

engranaje *m* (*Auto*) gear

engrandecer 🔟 *vt* (*enaltecer*) exalt, raise

engrasar vt grease; (con aceite) oil; (ensuciar) get grease on

engreído adj arrogant

engullir 22 vt gulp down

enhebrar vt thread

enhorabuena f congratulations. dar la ~ congratulate

enigm|a m enigma. ~ático adj enigmatic

enjabonar vt soap. ~se vpr to soap o.s.

enjambre m swarm

enjaular vt put in a cage

enjuag|ar 12 vt rinse. ~ue m rinsing; (para la boca) mouthwash

enjugar 12 vt wipe (away)

enjuiciar vt pass judgement on

enjuto adj (persona) skinny

enlace m connection; (matrimonial) wedding

enlatar vt tin, can

enlazar 10 vt link; tie together (cintas); (Mex, casar) marry

enlodar vt, **enlodazar** 10 vt cover in mud

enloquecer 11 vt drive mad. ● vi go mad. ~se vpr go mad

enlosar vt (con losas) pave; (con baldosas) tile

enmarañar vt tangle (up), entangle; (confundir) confuse. ~se vpr get into a tangle; (confundirse) get confused

enmarcar 7 vt frame

enm|endar vt correct. ~endarse** vpr mend one's way. ~ienda f correction; (de ley etc) amendment

enmohecerse 11 vpr (con óxido) go rusty; (con hongos) go mouldy

enmudecer 11 vi be dumbstruck; (callar) fall silent

ennegrecer 11 vt blacken

ennoblecer 11 vt ennoble; (fig) add style to

enoj|adizo adj irritable. ~ado adj angry; (molesto) annoyed. ~ar vt anger; (molestar) annoy. ~arse vpr get angry; (molestarse) get annoyed. ~o m anger; (molestia) annoyance. ~oso adj annoying

enorgullecerse 11 vpr be proud

enorm|e adj huge, enormous. ~emente adv enormously. ~idad f immensity; (de crimen) enormity

enraizado adj deeply rooted

enrarecido adj rarefied

enred|adera f creeper. ~ar vt tangle (up), entangle; (confundir) confuse; (involucrar) involve. ~arse vpr get tangled; (confundirse) get confused; (persona) get involved (con with). ~o m tangle; (fig) muddle, mess

enrejado m bars

enriquecer 11 vt make rich; (fig) enrich. ~se vpr get rich

enrojecerse 11 vpr (persona) go red, blush

enrolar vt enlist

enrollar vt roll (up), wind (hilo etc)

enroscar 7 vt coil; (atornillar) screw in

ensalad|a f salad. armar una ~a make a mess. ~era f salad bowl. ~illa f Russian salad

ensalzar 10 vt praise; (enaltecer) exalt

ensambla|dura f, **ensamblaje** m (acción) assembling; (efecto) joint. ~r vt join

ensanch|ar vt widen; (agrandar) enlarge. ~arse vpr get wider. ~e m widening

ensangrentar 1 vt stain with blood

ensañarse *vpr.* ~ **con** treat cruelly

ensartar *vt* string (cuentas etc)

ensayar *vt* test; rehearse (obra de teatro etc). ~**o** *m* test, trial; (*composición literaria*) essay

enseguida *adv* at once, immediately

ensenada *f* inlet, cove

enseña|nza *f* education; (*acción de enseñar*) teaching. ~**nza media** secondary education. ~**r** *vt* teach; (*mostrar*) show

enseres *mpl* equipment

ensillar *vt* saddle

ensimismarse *vpr* be lost in thought

ensombrecer 🔟 *vt* darken

ensordecer 🔟 *vt* deafen. ● *vi* go deaf

ensuciar *vt* dirty. ~**se** *vpr* get dirty

ensueño *m* dream

entablar *vt* (*empezar*) start

entablillar *vt* put in a splint

entallar *vt* tailor (un vestido). ● *vi* fit

entarimado *m* parquet; (*plataforma*) platform

ente *m* entity, being; (*fam, persona rara*) weirdo; (*Com*) firm, company

entend|er 🔟 *vt* understand; (*opinar*) believe, think. ● *vi* understand. ~**er de** know about. **a mi** ~**er** in my opinion. **dar a** ~**er** hint. **darse a** ~**er** (*LAm*) make o.s. understood. ~**erse** *vpr* make o.s. understood; (*comprenderse*) be understood. ~**erse con** get on with. ~**ido** *adj* understood; (*enterado*) well-informed. **no darse por** ~**ido** pretend not to understand. ● *interj* agreed!, OK! 🔟. ~**imiento** *m* understanding

entera|do *adj* well-informed; (*que sabe*) aware. **darse por** ~**do** take the hint. ~**r** *vt* inform (**de** of). ~**rse** *vpr.* ~**se de** find out about, hear of. **¡entérate!** listen! **¿te** ~**s?** do you understand?

entereza *f* (*carácter*) strength of character

enternecer 🔟 *vt* (*fig*) move, touch. ~**se** *vpr* be moved, be touched

entero *adj* entire, whole. **por** ~ entirely, completely

enterra|dor *m* gravedigger. ~**r** 🔟 *vt* bury

entibiar *vt* (*enfriar*) cool; (*calentar*) warm (up). ~**se** *vpr* (*enfriarse*) cool down; (*fig*) cool; (*calentarse*) get warm

entidad *f* entity; (*organización*) organization; (*Com*) company; (*importancia*) significance

entierro *m* burial; (*ceremonia*) funeral

entona|ción *f* intonation. ~**r** *vt* intone; sing (nota). ● *vi* (*Mus*) be in tune; (*colores*) match. ~**rse** *vpr* (*emborracharse*) get tipsy

entonces *adv* then. **en aquel** ~ at that time, then

entorn|ado *adj* (*puerta*) ajar; (*ventana*) slightly open. ~**o** *m* environment; (*en literatura*) setting

entorpecer 🔟 *vt* dull; slow down (tráfico); (*dificultar*) hinder

entra|da *f* entrance; (*incorporación*) admission, entry; (*para cine etc*) ticket; (*de datos, Tec*) input; (*de una comida*) starter. **de** ~**da** right away. ~**do** *adj.* ~**do en años** elderly. **ya** ~**da la noche** late at night. ~**nte** *adj* next, coming

entraña *f* (*fig*) heart. ~**s** *fpl* entrails; (*fig*) heart. ~**ble** *adj* (*cariño* deep; (amigo) close. **~r** vt involve

entrar vt (traer) bring in; (llevar) take in. ● vi go in, enter; (venir) come in, enter; (empezar) start, begin; (incorporarse) join. **~ en**, (LAm) **~ a** go into

entre prep (dos personas o cosas) between; (más de dos) among(st)

entre|abierto adj half-open. **~abrir** (pp entreabierto) vt half open. **~acto** m interval. **~cejo** m forehead. fruncir el **~cejo** frown. **~cerrar** **1** vt (LAm) half close. **~cortado** adj (voz) faltering; (respiración) laboured. **~cruzar** **10** vt intertwine

entrega f handing over; (de mercancías etc) delivery; (de novela etc) instalment; (dedicación) commitment. **~r** **12** vt deliver; (dar) give; hand in (deberes); hand over (poder). **~rse** vpr surrender, give o.s. up; (dedicarse) devote o.s. (a to)

entre|lazar **10** vt intertwine. **~més** m hors-d'oeuvre; (en el teatro) short comedy. **~mezclar** vt intermingle

entrena|dor m trainer. **~miento** m training. **~r** vt train. **~rse** vpr train

entre|pierna f crotch; medida inside leg measurement. **~piso** m (LAm) mezzanine. **~sacar** **7** vt pick out; (peluquería) thin out **~suelo** m mezzanine; (de cine) dress circle **~tanto** adv meanwhile, in the meantime **~tejer** vt weave; (entrelazar) interweave

entreten|ción f (LAm) entertainment. **~er** **40** vt entertain, amuse; (detener) delay, keep. **~erse** vpr amuse o.s.; (tardar) delay, linger. **~ido** adj (con ser) entertaining; (con estar) busy. **~imiento** m entertainment

entrever **43** vt make out, glimpse

en:trevista f interview; (reunión) meeting. **~rse** vpr have an interview

entristecer **11** vt sadden, make sad. **~se** vpr grow sad

entromet|erse vpr interfere. **~ido** adj interfering

entumec|erse **11** vpr go numb. **~ido** adj numb

enturbiar vt cloud

entusi|asmar vt fill with enthusiasm; (gustar mucho) delight. **~asmarse** vpr. **~asmarse con** get enthusiastic about. **~asmo** m enthusiasm. **~asta** adj enthusiastic. ● m & f enthusiast

enumerar vt enumerate

envalentonar vt encourage. **~se** vpr become bolder

envas|ado m packaging; (en latas) canning; (en botellas) bottling. **~ar** vt package; (en latas) tin, can; (en botellas) bottle. **~e** m packing; (lata) tin, can; (botella) bottle

envejec|er **11** vt make (look) older. ● vi age, grow old. **~erse** vpr age, grow old

envenenar vt poison

envergadura f importance

envia|do m envoy; (de la prensa) correspondent. **~r** **20** vt send

enviciarse vpr become addicted (con to)

envidi|a f envy; (celos) jealousy. **~ar** vt envy, be envious of. **~oso** adj envious; (celoso) jealous. tener **~a** a envy

envío m sending, dispatch; (de

mercancías) consignment; (*de dinero*) remittance. **~ contra reembolso** cash on delivery. **gastos** *mpl* **de ~** postage and packing (costs)

enviudar *vi* be widowed

env|oltura *f* wrapping. **~olver** 2 (*pp* **envuelto**) *vt* wrap; (*cubrir*) cover; (*rodear*) surround; (*fig, enredar*) involve. **~uelto** *adj* wrapped (up)

enyesar *vt* plaster; (*Med*) put in plaster

épica *f* epic

épico *adj* epic

epid|emia *f* epidemic. **~émico** *adj* epidemic

epil|epsia *f* epilepsy. **~éptico** *adj* epileptic

epílogo *m* epilogue

episodio *m* episode

epístola *f* epistle

epitafio *m* epitaph

época *f* age; (*período*) period. **hacer ~** make history, be epoch-making

equidad *f* equity

equilibr|ado *adj* (well-)balanced. **~ar** *vt* balance. **~io** *m* balance; (*de balanza*) equilibrium. **~ista** *m & f* tightrope walker

equinoccio *m* equinox

equipaje *m* luggage (*esp Brit*), baggage (*esp Amer*)

equipar *vt* equip; (*de ropa*) fit out

equiparar *vt* make equal; (*comparar*) compare

equipo *m* equipment; (*de personas*) team

equitación *f* riding

equivale|nte *adj* equivalent. **~r** 42 *vi* be equivalent; (*significar*) mean

equivoca|ción *f* mistake, error.

~do *adj* wrong. **~rse** *vpr* make a mistake; (*estar en error*) be wrong, be mistaken. **~rse de** be wrong about. **~rse de número** dial the wrong number. **si no me equivoco** if I'm not mistaken

equívoco *adj* equivocal; (*sospechoso*) suspicious ● *m* misunderstanding; (*error*) mistake

era *f* era. ● *vb véase* SER

erario *m* treasury

erección *f* erection

eres *vb véase* SER

erguir 48 *vt* raise. **~se** *vpr* raise

erigir 14 *vt* erect. **~se** *vpr*. **~se en** set o.s. up as; (*llegar a ser*) become

eriza|do *adj* prickly. **~rse** 10 *vpr* stand on end; (*LAm*) (*persona*) get goose pimples

erizo *m* hedgehog; (*de mar*) sea urchin. **~ de mar** sea urchin

ermita *f* hermitage. **~ño** *m* hermit

erosi|ón *f* erosion. **~onar** *vt* erode

er|ótico *adj* erotic. **~otismo** *m* eroticism

err|ar 1 (*la* **i** *inicial pasa a ser* **y**) *vt* miss. ● *vi* wander; (*equivocarse*) make a mistake, be wrong. **~ata** *f* misprint. **~óneo** *adj* erroneous, wrong. **~or** *m* error, mistake. **estar en un ~or** be wrong, be mistaken

eruct|ar *vi* belch. **~o** *m* belch

erudi|ción *f* learning, erudition. **~to** *adj* learned; (*palabra*) erudite

erupción *f* eruption; (*Med*) rash

es *vb véase* SER

esa *adj véase* ESE

ésa *pron véase* ÉSE

esbelto *adj* slender, slim

esboz|ar 10 *vt* sketch, outline. **~o**

m sketch, outline

escabeche *m* brine. **en ~** pickled

escabroso *adj* (terreno) rough; (asunto) difficult; (atrevido) crude

escabullirse 22 *vpr* slip away

escafandra *f* diving-suit

escala *f* scale; (escalera de mano) ladder; (Aviac) stopover. **hacer ~ en** stop at. **vuelo sin ~s** non-stop flight. **~da** *f* climbing; (Pol) escalation. **~r** *vt* climb; break into (una casa). ● *vi* climb, go climbing

escaldar *vt* scald

escalera *f* staircase, stairs; (de mano) ladder. **~ de caracol** spiral staircase. **~ de incendios** fire escape. **~ de tijera** step-ladder. **~ mecánica** escalator

escalfa|do *adj* poached. **~r** *vt* poach

escalinata *f* flight of steps

escalofrío *m* shiver. **tener ~s** be shivering

escalón *m* step, stair; (de escala) rung

escalope *m* escalope

escam|a *f* scale; (de jabón, de la piel) flake. **~oso** *adj* scaly; (piel) flaky

escamotear *vt* make disappear; (robar) steal, pinch

escampar *vi* stop raining

esc|andalizar 10 *vt* scandalize, shock. **~andalizarse** *vpr* be shocked. **~ándalo** *m* scandal; (alboroto) commotion, racket. **armar un ~** make a scene. **~andaloso** *adj* scandalous; (alborotador) noisy

escandinavo *adj* & *m* Scandinavian

escaño *m* bench; (Pol) seat

escapa|da *f* escape; (visita) flying visit. **~r** *vi* escape. **dejar ~r** let

out **~rse** *vpr* escape; (líquido, gas) leak

escaparate *m* (shop) window

escap|atoria *f* (fig) way out. **~e** *m* (de gas, de líquido) leak; (fuga) escape; (Auto) exhaust

escarabajo *m* beetle

escaramuza *f* skirmish

escarbar *vt* scratch; pick (dientes, herida); (fig, escudriñar) pry (en into). **~se** *vpr* pick

escarcha *f* frost. **~do** *adj* (fruta) crystallized

escarlat|a *adj invar* scarlet. **~ina** *f* scarlet fever

escarm|entar 1 *vt* teach a lesson to. ● *vi* learn one's lesson. **~iento** *m* punishment; (lección) lesson

escarola *f* endive

escarpado *adj* steep

escas|ear *vi* be scarce. **~ez** *f* scarcity, shortage; (pobreza) poverty. **~o** *adj* scarce; (poco) little; (muy justo) barely. **~o de** short of

escatimar *vt* be sparing with

escayola *f* plaster

esc|ena *f* scene; (escenario) stage. **~enario** *m* stage; (fig) scene. **~énico** *adj* stage. **~enografía** *f* set design

esc|epticismo *m* scepticism. **~éptico** *adj* sceptical. ● *m* sceptic

esclarecer 11 *vt* (fig) throw light on, clarify

esclav|itud *f* slavery. **~izar** 10 *vt* enslave. **~o** *m* slave

esclusa *f* lock; (de presa) floodgate

escoba *f* broom

escocer 2 & 9 *vi* sting

escocés *adj* Scottish. ● *m* Scot

Escocia *f* Scotland

escog|er 🔢 vt choose. **~ido** adj chosen; (mercancía) choice; (clientela) select

escolar adj school. ● m schoolboy. ● f schoolgirl

escolta f escort

escombros mpl rubble

escond|er vt hide. **~erse** vpr hide. **~idas** fpl (LAm, juego) hide-and-seek. **a ~idas** secretly. **~ite** m hiding place; (juego) hide-and-seek. **~rijo** m hiding place

escopeta f shotgun

escoria f slag; (fig) dregs

escorpión m scorpion

Escorpión m Scorpio

escot|ado adj low-cut. **~e** m low neckline. **pagar a ~e** share the expenses

escozor m stinging

escri|bano m clerk. **~bir** (pp escrito) vt/i write. **~bir a máquina** type. **¿cómo se escribe...?** how do you spell...? **~birse** vpr write to each other. **~to** adj written. **por ~to** in writing. ● m document. **~tor** m writer. **~torio** m desk; (oficina) office; (LAm, en una casa) study. **~tura** f (hand)writing; (Jurid) deed

escrú|pulo m scruple. **~puloso** adj scrupulous

escrut|ar vt scrutinize; count (votos). **~inio** m count

escuadr|a f (instrumento) square; (Mil) squad; (Naut) fleet. **~ón** m squadron

escuálido adj skinny

escuchar vt listen to; (esp LAm, oír) hear. ● vi listen

escudo m shield. **~ de armas** coat of arms

escudriñar vt examine

escuela f school. **~ normal** teachers' training college

escueto adj simple

escuincle m (Mex fam) kid 🔢

escul|pir vt sculpture. **~tor** m sculptor. **~tora** f sculptress. **~tura** f sculpture

escupir vt/i spit

escurr|eplatos m invar plate rack. **~idizo** adj slippery. **~ir** vt drain; wring out (ropa). ● vi drain; (ropa) drip. **~irse** vpr slip

ese pron (f **esa**) that; (mpl **esos**, fpl **esas**) those

ése pron (f **ésa**) that one; (mpl **ésos**, fpl **ésas**) those; (primero de dos) the former

esencia f essence. **~l** adj essential. **lo ~l** the main thing

esf|era f sphere; (de reloj) face. **~érico** adj spherical

esf|orzarse 🔢 & 🔢 vpr make an effort. **~uerzo** m effort

esfumarse vpr fade away; (persona) vanish

esgrim|a f fencing. **~ir** vt brandish; (fig) use

esguince m sprain

eslabón m link

eslavo adj Slavic, Slavonic

eslogan m slogan

esmalt|ar vt enamel. **~e** m enamel. **~e de uñas** nail polish

esmerado adj careful; (persona) painstaking

esmeralda f emerald

esmer|arse vpr take care (en over).

esmero m care

esmoquin (pl **esmóquines**) m dinner jacket, tuxedo (Amer)

esnob adj invar snobbish. ● m & f (pl **~s**) snob. **~ismo** m snobbery

esnórkel m snorkel

eso pron that. ¡~ es! that's it! ~ mismo exactly. a ~ de about. en ~ at that moment. ¿no es ~? isn't that right? por ~ that's why. y ~ que even though

esos adj pl véase **ESE**

ésos pron pl véase **ÉSE**

espabila|do adj bright; (despierto) awake. **~r** vt (avivar) brighten up; (despertar) wake up. **~rse** vpr wake up; (avivarse) wise up; (apresurarse) hurry up

espaci|al adj space. **~ar** vt space out. **~o** m space. **~oso** adj spacious

espada f sword. **~s** fpl (en naipes) spades

espaguetis mpl spaghetti

espald|a f back. a ~s de uno behind s.o.'s back. volver la(s) ~a(s) a uno give s.o. the cold shoulder. ~ mojada wetback. **~illa** f shoulder-blade

espant|ajo m, **~apájaros** m invar scarecrow. **~ar** vt frighten; (ahuyentar) frighten away. **~arse** vpr be frightened; (ahuyentarse) be frightened away. **~o** m terror; (horror) horror. ¡qué ~o! how awful! **~oso** adj horrific; (terrible) terrible

España f Spain

español adj Spanish. ● m (persona) Spaniard; (lengua) Spanish. los ~es the Spanish

esparadrapo m (sticking) plaster

esparcir 9 vt scatter; (difundir) spread. **~rse** vpr be scattered; (difundirse) spread; (divertirse) enjoy o.s.

espárrago m asparagus

espasm|o m spasm. **~ódico** adj spasmodic

espátula f spatula; (en pintura) palette knife

especia f spice

especial adj special. en ~ especially. **~idad** f speciality (Brit), specialty (Amer). **~ista** adj & m & f specialist. **~ización** f specialization. **~izarse** 10 vpr specialize. **~mente** adv especially

especie f kind, sort; (en biología) species. en ~ in kind

especifica|ción f specification. **~r** 7 vt specify

específico adj specific

espect|áculo m sight; (de circo etc) show. **~acular** adj spectacular. **~ador** m & f spectator

espectro m spectre; (en física) spectrum

especula|dor m speculator. **~r** vi speculate

espej|ismo m mirage. **~o** m mirror. **~o retrovisor** (Auto) rear-view mirror

espeluznante adj horrifying

espera f wait. a la ~ waiting (for). **~nza** f hope. **~r** vt hope; (aguardar) wait for; expect (vista, carta, bebé). espero que no I hope not. espero que sí I hope so. ● vi (aguardar) wait. **~rse** vpr hang on; (prever) expect

esperma f sperm

esperpento m fright

espes|ar vt/i thicken. **~arse** vpr thicken. **~o** adj thick. **~or** m thickness

espetón m spit

esp|ía f spy. **~iar** 20 vt spy on. ● vi spy

espiga f (de trigo etc) ear

espina f thorn; (de pez) bone; (en anatomía) spine. ~ dorsal spine

espinaca f spinach

espinazo m spine

espinilla f shin; (Med) blackhead; (LAm, grano) spot

espino m hawthorn. **~so** adj thorny; (fig) difficult

espionaje m espionage

espiral adj & f spiral

esp|iritista m & f spiritualist. **~íritu** m spirit; (mente) mind. **~íritual** adj spiritual

espl|éndido adj splendid; (persona) generous. **~endor** m splendour

espolear vt spur (on)

espolvorear vt sprinkle

esponj|a f sponge. **~oso** adj spongy

espont|aneidad f spontaneity. **~áneo** adj spontaneous

esporádico adj sporadic

espos|a f wife. **~as** fpl handcuffs. **~ar** vt handcuff. **~o** m husband

espuela f spur; (fig) incentive

espum|a f foam; (en bebidas) froth; (de jabón) lather; (de las olas) surf. echar **~a** foam, froth. **~oso** adj (vino) sparkling

esqueleto m skeleton; (estructura) framework

esquema m outline

esqu|í m (pl **~ís**, **~íes**) ski; (deporte) skiing. **~iar** 20 vi ski

esquilar vt shear

esquimal adj & m Eskimo

esquina f corner

esquiv|ar vt avoid; dodge (golpe). **~o** adj elusive

esquizofrénico adj & m schizophrenic

esta adj véase ESTE

ésta pron véase ÉSTE

estab|ilidad f stability. **~le** adj stable

establec|er 11 vt establish. **~erse** vpr settle; (Com) set up. **~imiento** m establishment

establo m cattleshed

estaca f stake

estación f station; (del año) season. **~ de invierno** winter (sports) resort. **~ de servicio** service station

estaciona|miento m parking; (LAm, lugar) car park (Brit), parking lot (Amer). **~r** vt station; (Auto) park. **~rio** adj stationary

estadía f (LAm) stay

estadio m stadium; (fase) stage

estadista m statesman. • f stateswoman

estadístic|a f statistics; (cifra) statistic. **~o** adj statistical

estado m state; (Med) condition. **~ civil** marital status. **~ de ánimo** frame of mind. **~ de cuenta** bank statement. **~ mayor** (Mil) staff. en buen **~** in good condition

Estados Unidos mpl United States

estadounidense adj American, United States. • m & f American

estafa f swindle. **~r** vt swindle

estafeta f (oficina de correos) (sub-)post office

estala|ctita f stalactite. **~gmita** f stalagmite

estall|ar vi explode; (olas) break; (guerra) break out; (fig) burst. **~ar en llanto** burst into tears. **~ar de risa** burst out laughing. **~ido** m explosion; (de guerra etc) outbreak

estamp|a f print; (aspecto) appearance. **~ado** adj printed. • m printing; (motivo) pattern; (tela) cotton print. **~ar** vt stamp;

(imprimir) print

estampido m bang

estampilla f *(LAm, de correos)* (postage) stamp

estanca|do adj stagnant. **~r** [7] vt stem. **~rse** vpr stagnate

estancia f stay; *(cuarto)* large room

estanco adj watertight. ● m tobacconist's (shop)

---

i

estanco In Spain, an establishment selling tobacco, stamps, bus and metro passes and other products whose sale is restricted. Cigarettes etc are sold in bars and cafés but at higher prices. Estancos also sell stationery and sometimes papers.

---

estandarte m standard, banner

estanque m pond; *(depósito de agua)* (water) tank

estanquero m tobacconist

estante m shelf. **~ría** f shelves; *(para libros)* bookcase

estaño m tin

---

estar [27]

● *verbo intransitivo*

· · · ▶ to be ¿cómo estás? how are you?. estoy enfermo I'm ill. está muy cerca it's very near. ¿está Pedro? is Pedro in? ¿cómo está el tiempo? what's the weather like? ya estamos en invierno it's winter already

· · · ▶ *(quedarse)* to stay. sólo ~é una semana I'll only be staying for a week. estoy en un hotel I'm staying in a hotel

· · · ▶ *(con fecha)* ¿a cuánto estamos? what's the date today?

estamos a 8 de mayo it's the 8th of May.

· · · ▶ *(en locuciones)* ¿estamos? all right? ¡ahí está! that's it! ~ por *(apoyar a)* to support; *(LAm, encontrarse a punto de)* to be about to; *(quedar por)* eso está por verse that remains to be seen. son cuentas que están por pagar they're bills still to be paid

● *verbo auxiliar*

· · · ▶ *(con gerundio)* estaba estudiando I was studying

· · · ▶ *(con participio)* está condenado a muerte he's been sentenced to death. está mal traducido it's wrongly translated.

estarse *verbo pronominal* to stay. no se está quieto he won't stay still

---

➡ Cuando el verbo **estar** forma parte de expresiones como **estar de acuerdo, estar a la vista, estar constipado,** etc., ver bajo el respectivo nombre o adjetivo

---

estatal adj state

estático adj static

estatua f statue

estatura f height

estatuto m statute; *(norma)* rule

este adj *(región)* eastern; *(viento, lado)* east. ● m east. ● adj *(f esta)* this; *(mpl estos, fpl estas)* these. ● int *(LAm)* well, er

éste pron *(f ésta)* this one; *(mpl éstos, fpl éstas)* these; *(segundo de dos)* the latter

estela f wake; *(de avión)* trail; *(lápida)* carved stone

estera f mat; *(tejido)* matting

est|éreo *adj* stereo. **~ereofónico** *adj* stereo, stereophonic

estereotipo *m* stereotype

estéril *adj* sterile; (*terreno*) barren

esterilla *f* mat

esterlina *adj.* **libra f ~** pound sterling

estético *adj* aesthetic

estiércol *m* dung; (*abono*) manure

estigma *m* stigma. **~s** *mpl* (*Relig*) stigmata

estil|arse *vpr* be used. **~o** *m* style; (*en natación*) stroke. **~ mariposa** butterfly. **~ pecho** (*LAm*) breaststroke. **por el ~o** of that sort

estilográfica *f* fountain pen

estima *f* esteem. **~do** *adj* (*amigo, colega*) valued. **~do señor** (*en cartas*) Dear Sir. **~r** *vt* esteem; have great respect for (*persona*); (*valorar*) value; (*juzgar*) consider

est|imulante *adj* stimulating. ● *m* stimulant. **~imular** *vt* stimulate; (*incitar*) incite. **~imulo** *m* stimulus

estir|ado *adj* stretched; (*persona*) haughty. **~ar** *vt* stretch; (*fig*) stretch out. **~ón** *m* pull, tug; (*crecimiento*) sudden growth

estirpe *m* stock

esto *pron neutro* this; (*este asunto*) this business. **en ~** at this point. **en ~ de** in this business of. **por ~** therefore

estofa|do *adj* stewed. ● *m* stew. **~r** *vt* stew

estómago *m* stomach. **dolor** *m* **de ~** stomach ache

estorb|ar *vt* obstruct; (*molestar*) bother. ● *vi* be in the way. **~o** *m* hindrance; (*molestia*) nuisance

estornud|ar *vi* sneeze. **~o** *m* sneeze

estos *adj mpl véase* **ESTE**

éstos *pron mpl véase* **ÉSTE**

estoy *vb véase* **ESTAR**

estrabismo *m* squint

estrado *m* stage; (*Mus*) bandstand

estrafalario *adj* eccentric; (*ropa*) outlandish

estrago *m* devastation. **hacer ~os** devastate

estragón *m* tarragon

estrambótico *adj* eccentric; (*ropa*) outlandish

estrangula|dor *m* strangler; (*Auto*) choke. **~r** *vt* strangle

estratagema *f* stratagem

estrat|ega *m & f* strategist. **~egia** *f* strategy. **~égico** *adj* strategic

estrato *m* stratum

estrech|ar *vt* make narrower; take in (*vestido*); embrace (*persona*). **~ar la mano a uno** shake hands with s.o. **~arse** *vpr* become narrower; (*abrazarse*) embrace. **~ez** *f* narrowness; **~eces** *fpl* financial difficulties. **~o** *adj* narrow; (*vestido etc*) tight; (*fig, íntimo*) close. **~o de miras** narrow-minded. ● *m* strait(s)

estrella *f* star. **~ de mar** starfish. **~ado** *adj* starry

estrellar *vt* smash; crash (*coche*). **~se** *vpr* crash (*contra* into)

estremec|er 🔢 *vt* shake. **~erse** *vpr* shake; (*de emoción etc*) tremble (*de* with). **~imiento** *m* shaking

estren|ar *vt* wear for the first time (*vestido etc*); show for the first time (*película*). **~arse** *vpr* make one's début. **~o** *m* (*de película*) première; (*de obra de teatro*) first night; (*de persona*) debut

estreñi|do *adj* constipated. **~miento** *m* constipation

estrés m stress
estría f groove; (de la piel) stretch mark
estribillo m (incl Mus) refrain
estribo m stirrup; (de coche) step. **perder los ~s** lose one's temper
estribor m starboard
estricto adj strict
estridente adj strident, raucous
estrofa f stanza, verse
estropajo m scourer
estropear vt damage; (plan) spoil; ruin (ropa). **~se** vpr be damaged; (averiarse) break down; (ropa) get ruined; (fruta etc) go bad; (fracasar) fail
estructura f structure. **~l** adj structural
estruendo m roar; (de mucha gente) uproar
estrujar vt squeeze; wring (out) (ropa); (fig) drain
estuario m estuary
estuche m case
estudi|ante m & f student. **~antil** adj student. **~ar** vt study. **~o** m study; (de artista) studio. **~oso** adj studious
estufa f heater; (Mex, cocina) cooker
estupefac|iente m narcotic. **~to** adj astonished
estupendo adj marvellous; (persona) fantastic; **¡~!** that's great!
est|upidez f stupidity; (acto) stupid thing. **~úpido** adj stupid
estupor m amazement
estuve vb véase ESTAR
etapa f stage. **por ~s** in stages
etéreo adj ethereal
etern|idad f eternity. **~o** adj eternal
étic|a f ethics. **~o** adj ethical

etimología f etymology
etiqueta f ticket, tag; (ceremonial) etiquette. **de ~** formal
étnico adj ethnic
eucalipto m eucalyptus
eufemismo m euphemism
euforia f euphoria
euro m euro. **~escéptico** adj & m Eurosceptic
Europa f Europe
euro|peo adj & m European. **~zona** f eurozone
eutanasia f euthanasia
evacua|ción f evacuation. **~r** 21 vt evacuate
evadir vt avoid; evade (impuestos). **~se** vpr escape
evalua|ción f evaluation. **~r** 21 vt assess; evaluate (datos)
evangeli|o m gospel. **~sta** m & f evangelist; (Mex, escribiente) scribe
evapora|ción f evaporation. **~rse** vpr evaporate; (fig) disappear
evasi|ón f evasion; (fuga) escape. **~vo** adj evasive
evento m event; (caso) case
eventual adj possible. **~idad** f eventuality
eviden|cia f evidence. **poner en ~cia a uno** show s.o. up. **~ciar** vt show. **~ciarse** vpr be obvious. **~te** adj obvious. **~temente** adv obviously
evitar vt avoid; (ahorrar) spare; (prevenir) prevent
evocar 7 vt evoke
evoluci|ón f evolution. **~onar** vi evolve; (Mil) manoeuvre
ex prefijo ex-, former
exacerbar vt exacerbate
exact|amente adv exactly. **~itud** f exactness. **~o** adj exact; (preciso) accurate; (puntual) punc-

tual. ¡~! exactly!

exagera|ción f exaggeration. **~do** adj exaggerated. **~r** vt/i exaggerate

exalta|do adj exalted; (excitado) (over)excited; (fanático) hotheaded. **~r** vt exalt. **~rse** vpr get excited

exam|en m exam, examination. **~inar** vt examine. **~inarse** vpr take an exam

exasperar vt exasperate. **~se** vpr get exasperated

excarcela|ción f release (from prison). **~r** vt release

excava|ción f excavation. **~dora** f digger. **~r** vt excavate

excede|ncia f leave of absence. **~nte** adj & m surplus. **~r** vi exceed. **~rse** vpr go too far

excelen|cia f excellence; (tratamiento) Excellency. **~te** adj excellent

exc|entricidad f eccentricity. **~éntrico** adj & m eccentric

excepci|ón f exception. **~onal** adj exceptional. a **~ón de, con ~ón de** except (for)

except|o prep except (for). **~uar** 21 vt except

exces|ivo adj excessive. **~o** m excess. **~o de equipaje** excess luggage (esp Brit), excess baggage (esp Amer)

excita|ción f excitement. **~r** vt excite; (incitar) incite. **~rse** vpr get excited

exclama|ción f exclamation. **~r** vi exclaim

exclu|ir 17 vt exclude. **~sión** f exclusion. **~siva** f sole right; (reportaje) exclusive (story). **~sivo** adj exclusive

excomu|lgar 12 vt excommunicate. **~nión** f excommunication

excremento m excrement

excursi|ón f excursion, outing. **~onista** m & f day-tripper

excusa f excuse; (disculpa) apology. presentar sus **~s** apologize. **~r** vt excuse

exento adj exempt; (libre) free

exhalar vt exhale, breath out; give off (olor etc)

exhaust|ivo adj exhaustive. **~o** adj exhausted

exhibi|ción f exhibition; (demostración) display. **~cionista** m & f exhibitionist. **~r** vt exhibit **~rse** vpr show o.s.; (hacerse notar) draw attention to o.s.

exhumar vt exhume; (fig) dig up

exig|encia f demand. **~ente** adj demanding. **~ir** 14 vt demand

exiguo adj meagre

exil|(i)ado adj exiled. ● m exile. **~(i)arse** vpr go into exile. **~io** m exile

exim|ente m reason for exemption; (Jurid) grounds for acquittal. **~ir** vt exempt

existencia f existence. **~s** fpl stock. **~lismo** m existentialism

exist|ente adj existing. **~ir** vi exist

éxito m success. no tener **~** fail. tener **~** be successful

exitoso adj successful

éxodo m exodus

exonerar vt exonerate

exorbitante adj exorbitant

exorci|smo m exorcism. **~zar** 10 vt exorcise

exótico adj exotic

expan|dir vt expand; (fig) spread. **~dirse** vpr expand. **~sión** f expansion. ~**sivo** adj expansive

expatria|**do** adj & m expatriate.
~**rse** vpr emigrate; (exiliarse) go
into exile

expectativa f prospect; (esperanza) expectation. estar a la ~
be waiting

expedi|**ción** f expedition; (de documento) issue; (de mercancías) dispatch. ~**ente** m record, file; (Jurid) proceedings. ~**r** 5 vt issue; (enviar) dispatch, send. ~**to** adj clear; (LAm, fácil) easy

expeler vt expel

expend|**edor** m dealer. ~**edor automático** vending machine. ~**io** m (LAm) shop; (venta) sale

expensas fpl (Jurid) costs. a ~ de at the expense of. a mis ~ at my expense

experiencia f experience

experiment|**al** adj experimental.
~**ar** vt test, experiment with; (sentir) experience. ~**o** m experiment

experto adj & m expert

expiar 20 vt atone for

expirar vi expire

explanada f levelled area;
(paseo) esplanade

explayarse vpr speak at length;
(desahogarse) unburden o.s. (con to)

explica|**ción** f explanation. ~**r** 7 vt explain. ~**rse** vpr understand; (hacerse comprender) explain o.s. no me lo explico I can't understand it

explícito adj explicit

explora|**ción** f exploration.
~**dor** m explorer; (muchacho) boy scout. ~**r** vt explore

explosi|**ón** f explosion; (fig) outburst. ~**onar** vt blow up. ~**vo**

adj & m explosive

explota|**ción** f working; (abuso) exploitation. ~**r** vt work (mina); farm (tierra); (abusar) exploit. • vi explode

expone|**nte** m exponent. ~**r** 34 vt expose; display (mercancías); present (tema); set out (hechos); exhibit (cuadros etc); (arriesgar) risk. • vi exhibit. ~**rse** vpr. ~**se a** que run the risk of

exporta|**ción** f export. ~**dor** m exporter. ~**r** vt export

exposición f exposure; (de cuadros etc) exhibition; (de hechos) exposition

expres|**ar** vt express. ~**arse** vpr express o.s. ~**ión** f expression.
~**ivo** adj expressive; (cariñoso) affectionate

expreso adj express. • m express; (café) expresso

exprimi|**dor** m squeezer. ~**r** vt squeeze

expropiar vt expropriate

expuesto adj on display; (lugar etc) exposed; (peligroso) dangerous. estar ~ a be exposed to

expuls|**ar** vt expel; throw out (persona); send off (jugador).
~**ión** f expulsion

exquisito adj exquisite; (de sabor) delicious

éxtasis m invar ecstasy

extend|**er** 1 vt spread (out); (ampliar) extend; issue (documento). ~**erse** vpr spread; (paisaje etc) extend, stretch. ~**ido** adj spread out; (generalizado) widespread; (brazos) outstretched

extens|**amente** adv widely; (detalladamente) in full. ~**ión** f extension; (área) expanse; (largo) length.

~o adj extensive

extenuar 21 vt exhaust

exterior adj external, exterior; (del extranjero) foreign; (aspecto etc) outward. ● m outside, exterior; (países extranjeros) abroad

extermin|ación f extermination. ~ar vt exterminate. ~io m extermination

externo adj external; (signo etc) outward. ● m day pupil

extin|ción f extinction. ~guidor m (LAm) fire extinguisher. ~guir 13 vt extinguish. ~guirse vpr die out; (fuego) go out. ~to adj (raza etc) extinct. ~tor m fire extinguisher

extirpar vt eradicate; remove (tumor)

extorsión f extortion

extra adj invar extra; (de buena calidad) good-quality; (huevos) large. paga f ~ bonus

extracto m extract

extradición f extradition

extraer 41 vt extract

extranjer|ía f (Esp) la ley de ~ immigration law. ~o adj foreign. ● m foreigner; (países) foreign countries. del ~ from abroad. en el ~, por el ~ abroad

extrañ|ar vt surprise; (encontrar extraño) find strange; (LAm, echar de menos) miss. ~arse vpr be surprised (de at). ~eza f strangeness; (asombro) surprise. ~o adj strange. ● m stranger

extraoficial adj unofficial

extraordinario adj extraordinary

extrarradio m outlying districts

extraterrestre adj extraterrestrial. ● m alien

extravagan|cia f oddness, ec-centricity. ~te adj odd, eccentric

extrav|iado adj lost. ~iar 20 vt lose. ~iarse vpr get lost; (objetos) go missing. ~ío m loss

extremar vt take extra (precauciones); tighten up (vigilancia). ~se vpr make every effort

extremeño adj from Extremadura

extrem|idad f end. ~idades fpl extremities. ~ista adj & m & f extremist. ~o adj extreme. ● m end; (colmo) extreme. en ~o extremely. en último ~o as a last resort

extrovertido adj & m extrovert

exuberan|cia f exuberance. ~te adj exuberant

eyacular vt/i ejaculate

Ff

fa m F; (solfa) fah

fabada f bean and pork stew

fábrica f factory. marca f de ~ trade mark

fabrica|ción f manufacture. ~ción en serie mass production. ~nte m & f manufacturer. ~r 7 vt manufacture

fábula f fable; (mentira) fabrication

fabuloso adj fabulous

facci|ón f faction. ~ones fpl (de la cara) features

faceta f facet

facha f (fam, aspecto) look. ~da f façade

fácil adj easy; (probable) likely

facili|dad f ease; (*disposición*) aptitude. **~dades** fpl facilities. **~tar** vt facilitate; (*proporcionar*) provide

factible adj feasible

factor m factor

factura f bill, invoice. **~r** vt (*hacer la factura*) invoice; (*al embarcar*) check in

faculta|d f faculty; (*capacidad*) ability; (*poder*) power. **~tivo** adj optional

faena f job. **~s domésticas** housework

faisán m pheasant

faja f (*de tierra*) strip; (*corsé*) corset; (*Mil etc*) sash

fajo m bundle; (*de billetes*) wad

falda f skirt; (*de montaña*) side

falla f fault; (*defecto*) flaw. **~ humana** (*LAm*) human error. **~r** vi fail. **me falló** he let me down. **sin ~r** without fail. ● vt (*errar*) miss

fallec|er 11 vi die. **~ido** m deceased

fallido adj vain; (*fracasado*) unsuccessful

fallo m (*defecto*) fault; (*error*) mistake. **~ humano** human error; (*en certamen*) decision; (*Jurid*) ruling

falluca f (*Mex*) smuggled goods

fals|ear vt falsify, distort. **~ificación** f forgery. **~ificador** m forger. **~ificar** 7 vt forge. **~o** adj false; (*falsificado*) forged; (*joya*) fake

falt|a f lack; (*ausencia*) absence; (*escasez*) shortage; (*defecto*) fault, defect; (*culpa*) fault; (*error*) mistake; (*en fútbol etc*) foul; (*en tenis*) fault. **a ~a de** for lack of. **echar en ~a** miss. **hacer ~a** be necessary. **me hace ~a** I need. **sacar ~as** find fault. **~o** adj lacking (de in)

faltar *verbo intransitivo*

❗ cuando el verbo **faltar** va precedido del complemento indirecto **le** (o **les, nos** etc) el sujeto en español pasa a ser el objeto en inglés p.ej: **les falta experiencia** they lack experience

····➤ (*no estar*) to be missing **¿quién falta?** who's missing? **falta una de las chicas** one of the girls is missing. **al abrigo le faltan 3 botones** the coat has three buttons missing. **~ a algo** (*no asistir*) to be absent from sth; (*no acudir*) to miss sth

····➤ (*no haber suficiente*) **va a ~ leche** there won't be enough milk. **nos faltó tiempo** we didn't have enough time

····➤ (*no tener*) **le falta cariño** he lacks affection

····➤ (*hacer falta*) **le falta sal** it needs more salt. **¡es lo que nos faltaba!** that's all we needed!

····➤ (*quedar*) **¿te falta mucho?** are you going to be much longer? **falta poco para Navidad** it's not long until Christmas. **aún falta mucho** (*distancia*) there's a long way to go yet **¡no faltaba más!** of course!

fama f fame; (*reputación*) reputation

famélico adj starving

familia f family; (*hijos*) children. **~ numerosa** large family. **~r** adj familiar; (*de la familia*) family; (*sin ceremonia*) informal; (*lenguaje*) colloquial. ● m & f relative. **~ridad** f familiarity. **~rizarse** 10 vpr become familiar (**con** with)

famoso *adj* famous

fanático *adj* fanatical. • *m* fanatic

fanfarr|ón *adj* boastful. • *m* braggart. ~**onear** *vi* show off

fango *m* mud. ~**so** *adj* muddy

fantasía *f* fantasy. de ~ fancy; (*joya*) imitation

fantasma *m* ghost

fantástico *adj* fantastic

fardo *m* bundle

faringe *f* pharynx

farmac|éutico *m* chemist (*Brit*), pharmacist, druggist (*Amer*). ~**ia** *f* (*ciencia*) pharmacy; (*tienda*) chemist's (shop) (*Brit*), pharmacy

faro *m* lighthouse; (*Aviac*) beacon; (*Auto*) headlight

farol *m* lantern; (*de la calle*) street lamp. ~**a** *f* street lamp

farr|a *f* partying. ~**ear** *vi* (*LAm*) go out partying

farsa *f* farce. ~**nte** *m & f* fraud

fascículo *m* instalment

fascinar *vt* fascinate

fascis|mo *m* fascism

fase *f* phase

fastidi|ar *vt* annoy; (*estropear*) spoil. ~**arse** *vpr* (*máquina*) break down; hurt (*pierna*); (*LAm, molestarse*) get annoyed. **¡para que te** ~**es!** so there!. ~**o** *m* nuisance; (*aburrimiento*) boredom. ~**oso** *adj* annoying

fatal *adj* fateful; (*mortal*) fatal; (*fam, pésimo*) terrible. ~**idad** *f* fate; (*desgracia*) misfortune

fatig|a *f* fatigue. ~**ar** [12] *vt* tire. ~**arse** *vpr* get tired. ~**oso** *adj* tiring

fauna *f* fauna

favor *m* favour. **a** ~ **de, en** ~ **de** in favour of. **haga el** ~ **de** would

you be so kind as to, please. **por** ~ please

favorec|er [11] *vt* favour; (*vestido, peinado etc*) suit. ~**ido** *adj* favoured

favorito *adj & m* favourite

fax *m* fax

faxear *vt* fax

faz *f* face

fe *f* faith. **dar** ~ **de** certify. **de buena** ~ in good faith

febrero *m* February

febril *adj* feverish

fecha *f* date. **a estas** ~**s** now; (*todavía*) still. **hasta la** ~ so far. **poner la** ~ date. ~**r** *vt* date

fecund|ación *f* fertilization. ~**ación artificial** artificial insemination. ~**ar** *vt* fertilize. ~**o** *adj* fertile; (*fig*) prolific

federa|ción *f* federation. ~**l** *adj* federal

felici|dad *f* happiness. ~**dades** *fpl* best wishes; (*congratulaciones*) congratulations. ~**tación** *f* letter of congratulation. **¡**~**taciones!** (*LAm*) congratulations! ~**tar** *vt* congratulate

feligrés *m* parishioner

feliz *adj* happy; (*afortunado*) lucky. **¡Felices Pascuas!** Happy Christmas! **¡F**~ **Año Nuevo!** Happy New Year!

felpudo *m* doormat

fem|enil *adj* (*Mex*) women's. ~**enino** *adj* feminine; (*equipo*) women's; (*en biología*) female. • *adj* feminine. ~**inista** *adj & m & f* feminist.

fen|omenal *adj* phenomenal. ~**ómeno** *m* phenomenon; (*monstruo*) freak

feo *adj* ugly; (*desagradable*) nasty. • *adv* (*LAm*) (*mal*) bad

feria f fair; (verbena) carnival; (Mex, cambio) small change. ~**do** m (LAm) public holiday

ferment|ar vt/i ferment. ~**o** m ferment

fero|cidad f ferocity. ~**z** adj fierce

férreo adj iron; (disciplina) strict

ferreter|ía f hardware store, ironmonger's (Brit). ~**o** m hardware dealer, ironmonger (Brit)

ferro|carril m railway (Brit), railroad (Amer). ~**viario** adj rail. ● m railwayman (Brit), railroader (Amer)

fértil adj fertile

fertili|dad f fertility. ~**zante** m fertilizer. ~**zar** [10] vt fertilize

ferv|iente adj fervent. ~**or** m fervour

festej|ar vt celebrate; entertain (persona). ~**o** m celebration

festiv|al m festival. ~**idad** f festivity. ~**o** adj festive. ● m public holiday

fétido adj stinking

feto m foetus

fiable adj reliable

fiado m. al ~ on credit. ~**r** m (Jurid) guarantor

fiambre m cold meat. ~**ría** f (LAm) delicatessen

fianza f (dinero) deposit; (objeto) surety. bajo ~ on bail

fiar [20] vt (vender) sell on credit; (confiar) confide. ● vi give credit. ~**se** vpr. ~**se de** trust

fibra f fibre. ~ de vidrio fibreglass

ficción f fiction

fich|a f token; (tarjeta) index card; (en juegos) counter. ~**ar** vt open a file on. estar ~**ado** have a (police) record. ~**ero** m card index; (en informática) file

fidedigno adj reliable

fidelidad f faithfulness

fideos mpl noodles

fiebre f fever. ~ aftosa foot-and-mouth disease. ~ del heno hay fever. ~ porcina swine fever. tener ~ have a temperature

fiel adj faithful; (memoria, relato etc) reliable. ● m believer

fieltro m felt

fier|a f wild animal. ~**o** adj fierce

fierro m (LAm) metal bar; (hierro) iron

fiesta f party; (día festivo) holiday. ~**s** fpl celebrations

fiestas A fiesta in Spain can be a day of local celebrations, a larger event for a town or city, or a national holiday to commemorate a saint's day or a historical event. Famous Spanish fiestas include The Fallas in Valencia, the Sanfermines in Pamplona, and the Feria de Sevilla. In Latin America fiestas patrias are a period of one or more days when each country celebrates its independence. There are usually military parades, firework displays, and cultural events typical of the country.

figura f figure; (forma) shape. ~**r** vi appear; (destacar) show off. ~**rse** vpr imagine. ¡figúrate! just imagine!

fij|ación f fixing; (obsesión) fixation. ~**ar** vt fix; establish (residencia). ~**arse** vpr (poner atención) pay attention; (percatarse) notice. ¡fíjate! just imagine! ~**o** adj fixed; (firme) stable; (permanente) permanent. ● adv. mirar ~**o** stare

fila f line; (de soldados etc) file; (en el teatro, cine etc) row; (cola)

queue. **ponerse en ~** line up
filántropo m philanthropist
filat|elia f stamp collecting, philately. **~élico** adj philatelic. ● m stamp collector, philatelist
filete m fillet
filial adj filial. ● f subsidiary
Filipinas fpl. **las (islas) ~** the Philippines
filipino adj Philippine, Filipino
filmar vt film; shoot (película)
filo m edge; (de hoja) cutting edge. **al ~ de las doce** at exactly twelve o'clock. **sacar ~ a** sharpen
filología f philology
filón m vein; (fig) gold-mine
fil|osofía f philosophy. **~ósofo** m philosopher
filtr|ar vt filter. **~arse** vpr filter; (dinero) disappear; (noticia) leak. **~o** m filter; (bebida) philtre. **~ solar** sunscreen
fin m end; (objetivo) aim. **~ de semana** weekend. **a ~ de** in order to. **a ~ de cuentas** at the end of the day. **a ~ de que** in order that. **a ~es de** at the end of. **al ~ y al cabo** after all. **dar ~ a** end. **en ~** in short. **por ~** finally. **sin ~** endless
final adj final. ● m end. ● f final. **~idad** f aim. **~ista** m & f finalist. **~izar** 10 vt finish. ● vi end
financi|ación f financing; (fondos) funds; (facilidades) credit facilities. **~ar** vt finance. **~ero** adj financial. ● m financier
finca f property; (tierras) estate; (rural) farm; (de recreo) country house
fingir 14 vt feign; (simular) simulate. ● vi pretend. **~se** vpr pretend to be
finlandés adj Finnish. ● m (per-

sona) Finn; (lengua) Finnish
Finlandia f Finland
fino adj fine; (delgado) thin; (oído) acute; (de modales) refined; (sutil) subtle
firma f signature; (acto) signing; (empresa) firm
firmar vt/i sign
firme adj firm; (estable) stable, steady; (color) fast. ● m (pavimento) (road) surface. ● adv hard. **~za** f firmness
fisc|al adj fiscal, tax. ● m & f public prosecutor. **~o** m treasury
fisg|ar 12 vi snoop (around). **~ón** adj nosy. ● m snooper
físic|a f physics. **~o** adj physical. ● m physique; (persona) physicist
fisonomista m & f. **ser buen ~** be good at remembering faces
fistol m (Mex) tiepin
flaco adj thin, skinny; (débil) weak
flagelo m scourge
flagrante adj flagrant. **en ~** red-handed
flama f (Mex) flame
flamante adj splendid; (nuevo) brand-new
flamear vi flame; (bandera etc) flap
flamenco adj flamenco; (de Flandes) Flemish. ● m (ave) flamingo; (música etc) flamenco; (idioma) Flemish

---

i **flamenco** Flamenco is performed in three forms: guitar, singing and dancing. Originally a gypsy art form, it also has Arabic and North African influences. Modern flamenco blends traditional forms with rock, jazz and salsa. In its pure form the music and lyrics are improvised, but tourists are more likely to see rehearsed performances.

flan m crème caramel

flaqueza f thinness; (*debilidad*) weakness

flauta f flute

flecha f arrow. ~**zo** m love at first sight

fleco m fringe; (*Mex, en el pelo*) fringe (*Brit*), bangs (*Amer*)

flem|a f phlegm. ~**ático** adj phlegmatic

flequillo m fringe (*Brit*), bangs (*Amer*)

fletar vt charter; (*LAm, transportar*) transport

flexible adj flexible

flirte|ar vi flirt. ~**o** m flirting

floj|ear vi flag; (*holgazanear*) laze around. ~**o** adj loose; (*poco fuerte*) weak; (*perezoso*) lazy

flor f flower. la ~ **y nata** the cream. ~**a** f flora. ~**ecer** 11 vi flower, bloom; (*fig*) flourish. ~**eciente** adj (*fig*) flourishing. ~**ero** m flower vase. ~**ista** m & f florist

flot|a f fleet. ~**ador** m float; (*de niño*) rubber band. ~**ar** vi float. ~**e. a** ~**e** afloat

fluctua|ción f fluctuation. ~**r** 21 vi fluctuate

flu|idez f fluidity; (*fig*) fluency. ~**ido** adj fluid; (*fig*) fluent. ● m fluid. ~**ir** 17 vi flow

fluoruro m fluoride

fluvial adj river

fobia f phobia

foca f seal

foco m focus; (*lámpara*) floodlight;

(*LAm, de coche*) (head)light; (*Mex, bombilla*) light bulb

fogón m cooker; (*LAm, fogata*) bonfire

folio m sheet

folklórico adj folk

follaje m foliage

follet|ín m newspaper serial. ~**o** m pamphlet

follón m 1 mess; (*alboroto*) row; (*problema*) trouble

fomentar vt promote; boost (*ahorro*); stir up (*odio*)

fonda f (*pensión*) boarding-house; (*LAm, restaurant*) cheap restaurant

fondo m bottom; (*de calle, pasillo*) end; (*de sala etc*) back; (*de escenario, pintura etc*) background. ~ **de reptiles** slush fund. ~**s** mpl funds, money. **a** ~ thoroughly

fonétic|a f phonetics. ~**o** adj phonetic

fontanero m plumber

footing /'futin/ m jogging

forastero m stranger

forcejear vi struggle

forense adj forensic. ● m & f forensic scientist

forjar vt forge. ~**se** vpr forge; build up (*ilusiones*)

forma f form; (*contorno*) shape; (*modo*) way; (*Mex, formulario*) form. ~**s** fpl conventions. **de todas** ~**s** anyway. **estar en** ~ be in good form. ~**ción** f formation; (*educación*) training. ~**l** adj formal; (*de fiar*) reliable; (*serio*) serious. ~**lidad** f formality; (*fiabilidad*) reliability; (*seriedad*) seriousness. ~**r** vt form; (*componer*) make up; (*enseñar*) train. ~**rse** vpr form; (*desarrollarse*) develop; (*educarse*) to be educated. ~**to** m format

formidable adj formidable; (*muy*

grande) enormous

fórmula *f* formula. **~ de cortesía** polite expression

formular *vt* formulate; make (queja etc). **~io** *m* form

fornido *adj* well-built

forr|ar *vt* (en el interior) line; (en el exterior) cover. **~o** *m* lining; (cubierta) cover

fortale|cer ⑪ *vt* strengthen. **~za** *f* strength; (Mil) fortress; (fuerza moral) fortitude

fortuito *adj* fortuitous; (encuentro) chance

fortuna *f* fortune; (suerte) luck

forz|ar ② & ⑩ *vt* force; strain (vista). **~osamente** *adv* necessarily. **~oso** *adj* necessary

fosa *f* ditch; (tumba) grave. **~s fpl nasales** nostrils

fósforo *m* phosphorus; (cerilla) match

fósil *adj & m* fossil

foso *m* ditch; (en castillo) moat; (de teatro) pit

foto *f* photo. **sacar ~s** take photos

fotocopia *f* photocopy. **~dora** *f* photocopier. **~r** *vt* photocopy

fotogénico *adj* photogenic

fot|ografía *f* photography; (Foto) photograph. **~ografiar** ⑳ *vt* photograph. **~ógrafo** *m* photographer

foul /faʊl/ *m* (pl ~s) (LAm) foul

frac *m* (pl ~s o fraques) tails

fracas|ar *vi* fail. **~o** *m* failure

fracción *f* fraction; (Pol) faction

fractura *f* fracture. **~r** *vt* fracture. **~rse** *vpr* fracture

fragan|cia *f* fragrance. **~te** *adj* fragrant

frágil *adj* fragile

fragmento *m* fragment; (de canción etc) extract

fragua *f* forge. **~r** ⑮ *vt* forge; (fig) concoct. ● *vi* set

fraile *m* friar; (monje) monk

frambuesa *f* raspberry

franc|és *adj* French. ● *m* (persona) Frenchman; (lengua) French. **~esa** *f* Frenchwoman

Francia *f* France

franco *adj* frank; (evidente) marked; (Com) free. ● *m* (moneda) franc

francotirador *m* sniper

franela *f* flannel

franja *f* border; (banda) stripe; (de terreno) strip

franque|ar *vt* clear; (atravesar) cross; pay the postage on (carta). **~o** *m* postage

franqueza *f* frankness

frasco *m* bottle; (de mermelada etc) jar

frase *f* phrase; (oración) sentence. **~ hecha** set phrase

fratern|al *adj* fraternal. **~idad** *f* fraternity

fraud|e *m* fraud. **~ulento** *adj* fraudulent

fray *m* brother, friar

frecuen|cia *f* frequency. **con ~cia** frequently. **~tar** *vt* frequent. **~te** *adj* frequent

frega|dero *m* sink. **~r** ① & ⑫ *vt* scrub; wash (los platos); mop (el suelo); (LAm, fam, molestar) annoy

freír ⑤① (pp **frito**) *vt* fry. **~se** *vpr* fry; (persona) roast

frenar *vt* brake; (fig) check

frenético *adj* frenzied; (furioso) furious

freno *m* (de caballería) bit; (Auto)

brake; (*fig*) check

frente *m* front. ~ a opposite. ~ a
~ face to face. al ~ at the head;
(*hacia delante*) forward. chocar de
~ crash head on. de ~ a (*LAm*) facing. hacer ~ a face (*cosa*); stand
up to (*persona*). ●*f* forehead. arrugar la ~ frown

fresa *f* strawberry

fresc|o *adj* (*frío*) cool; (*reciente*)
fresh; (*descarado*) cheeky. ●*m* fresh
air; (*frescor*) coolness; (*mural*)
fresco; (*persona*) impudent person.
al ~o in the open air. hacer ~o
be cool. tomar el ~o get some
fresh air. ~or *m* coolness. ~ura *f*
freshness; (*frío*) coolness; (*descaro*)
cheek

frialdad *f* coldness; (*fig*) indifference

fricci|ón *f* rubbing; (*fig, Tec*) fric-
tion; (*masaje*) massage. ~onar *vt*
rub

frigidez *f* frigidity

frígido *adj* frigid

frigorífico *m* fridge, refrigerator

frijol *m* (*LAm*) bean. ~es refritos
(*Mex*) fried purée of beans

frío *adj & m* cold. tomar ~ catch
cold. hacer ~ be cold. tener ~
be cold

frito *adj* fried; (fam, *harto*) fed up.
me tiene ~ I'm sick of him

fr|ivolidad *f* frivolity. ~ívolo *adj*
frivolous

fronter|a *f* border, frontier. ~izo
adj border; (*país*) bordering

frontón *m* pelota court; (*pared*)
fronton

frotar *vt* rub; strike (cerilla)

fructífero *adj* fruitful

fruncir 9 *vt* gather (tela). ~ el
ceño frown

frustra|ción *f* frustration. ~r *vt*
frustrate. ~rse *vpr* (*fracasar*) fail.
quedar ~do be disappointed

frut|a *f* fruit. ~al *adj* fruit. ~ería *f*
fruit shop. ~ero *m* fruit seller; (*recipiente*) fruit bowl. ~icultura *f*
fruit-growing. ~o *m* fruit

fucsia *f* fuchsia. ●*m* fuchsia

fuego *m* fire. ~s artificiales fireworks. a ~ lento on a low heat.
tener ~ have a light

fuente *f* fountain; (*manantial*)
spring; (*plato*) serving dish; (*fig*)
source

fuera *adv* out; (*al exterior*) outside;
(*en otra parte*) away; (*en el extranjero*) abroad. ~ de outside; (*excepto*) except for, besides. por ~
on the outside. ●*vb véase* IR Y SER

fuerte *adj* strong; (*color*) bright;
(*sonido*) loud; (*dolor*) severe;
(*duro*) hard; (*grande*) large; (*lluvia,
nevada*) heavy. ●*m* fort; (*fig*)
strong point. ●*adv* hard; (*con hablar etc*) loudly; (*llover*) heavily;
(*mucho*) a lot

fuerza *f* strength; (*poder*) power;
(*en física*) force; (*Mil*) forces. ~ de
voluntad will-power. a ~ de by
(dint of). a la ~ by necessity. por
~ by force; (*por necesidad*) by necessity. tener ~s para have the
strength to

fuese *vb véase* IR Y SER

fug|a *f* flight, escape; (*de gas etc*)
leak; (*Mus*) fugue. ~arse 12 *vpr*
flee, escape. ~az *adj* fleeting.
~itivo *adj & m* fugitive

fui *vb véase* IR, SER

fulano *m* so-and-so. ~, mengano
y zutano every Tom, Dick and
Harry

fulminar *vt* (*fig, con mirada*) look
daggers at

fuma|dor *adj* smoking. • *m* smoker. ~**r** *vt/i* smoke. ~**r en pipa** smoke a pipe. ~**rse** *vpr* smoke. ~**rada** *f* puff of smoke

func|ión *f* function; (*de un cargo etc*) duty; (*de teatro*) show, performance. ~**onal** *adj* functional. ~**onar** *vi* work, function. no ~**ona** out of order. ~**onario** *m* civil servant

funda *f* cover. ~ **de almohada** pillowcase

funda|ción *f* foundation. ~**mental** *adj* fundamental. ~**mentar** *vt* base (en on). ~**mento** *m* foundation. ~**r** *vt* found; (*fig*) base. ~**rse** *vpr* be based

fundi|ción *f* melting; (*de metales*) smelting; (*taller*) foundry. ~**r** *vt* melt; smelt (metales); cast (objeto); blend (colores); (*fusionar*) merge; (*Elec*) blow; (*LAm*) seize up (motor). ~**rse** *vpr* melt; (*unirse*) merge

fúnebre *adj* funeral; (*sombrío*) gloomy

funeral *adj* funeral. • *m* funeral. ~**es** *mpl* funeral

funicular *adj* & *m* funicular

furg|ón *m* van. ~**oneta** *f* van

fur|ia *f* fury; (*violencia*) violence. ~**ibundo** *adj* furious. ~**ioso** *adj* furious. ~**or** *m* fury

furtivo *adj* furtive. cazador ~ poacher

furúnculo *m* boil

fusible *m* fuse

fusil *m* rifle. ~**ar** *vt* shoot

fusión *f* melting; (*unión*) fusion; (*Com*) merger

fútbol *m*, (*Mex*) **futbol** *m* football

futbolista *m* & *f* footballer

futur|ista *adj* futuristic. • *m* & *f* futurist. ~**o** *adj* & *m* future

Gg

gabardina *f* raincoat

gabinete *m* (*Pol*) cabinet; (*en museo etc*) room; (*de dentista, médico etc*) consulting room

gaceta *f* gazette

gafa *f* hook. ~**s** *fpl* glasses, spectacles. ~**s de sol** sunglasses

gaf|ar *vt* ⚠ bring bad luck to. ~**e** *m* jinx

gaita *f* bagpipes

gajo *m* segment

gala *f* gala. ~**s** *fpl* finery, best clothes. estar de ~ be dressed up. hacer ~ de show off

galán *m* (*en el teatro*) (romantic) hero; (*enamorado*) lover

galante *adj* gallant. ~**ar** *vt* court. ~**ría** *f* gallantry

galápago *m* turtle

galardón *m* award

galaxia *f* galaxy

galera *f* galley

galer|ía *f* gallery. ~**ía comercial** (shopping) arcade. ~**ón** *m* (*Mex*) hall

Gales *m* Wales. país de ~ Wales

gal|és *adj* Welsh. • *m* Welshman; (*lengua*) Welsh. ~**esa** *f* Welshwoman

galgo *m* greyhound

Galicia *f* Galicia

galimatías *m invar* gibberish

gallard|ía *f* elegance. ~**o** *adj* elegant

gallego adj & m Galician

galleta f biscuit (Brit), cookie (Amer)

gall|ina f hen, chicken; (fig, fam) coward. ~o m cock

galón m gallon; (cinta) braid; (Mil) stripe

galop|ar vi gallop. ~e m gallop

gama f scale; (fig) range

gamba f prawn (Brit), shrimp (Amer)

gamberro m hooligan

gamuza f (piel) chamois leather; (de otro animal) suede

gana f wish, desire; (apetito) appetite. de buena ~ willingly. de mala ~ reluctantly. no me da la ~ I don't feel like it. tener ~s de (+ infinitivo) feel like (+ gerundio)

ganad|ería f cattle raising; (ganado) livestock. ~o m livestock. ~o lanar sheep. ~o porcino pigs. ~o vacuno cattle

gana|dor adj winning. • m winner. ~ncia f gain; (Com) profit. ~r vt earn; (en concurso, juego etc) win; (alcanzar) reach. • vi (vencer) win; (mejorar) improve. ~rle a uno beat s.o. ~rse la vida earn a living. salir ~ndo come out better off

ganch|illo m crochet. hacer ~illo crochet. ~o m hook; (LAm, colgador) hanger. tener ~o be very attractive

ganga f bargain

ganso m goose

garabat|ear vt/i scribble. ~o m scribble

garaje m garage

garant|e m & f guarantor. ~ía f guarantee. ~izar [10] vt guarantee

garapiña f (Mex) pineapple squash. ~do adj. almendras fpl ~das sugared almonds

garbanzo m chick-pea

garbo m poise; (de escrito) style. ~so adj elegant

garganta f throat; (valle) gorge

gárgaras fpl. hacer ~ gargle

garita f hut; (de centinela) sentry box

garra f (de animal) claw; (de ave) talon

garrafa f carafe

garrafal adj huge

garrapata f tick

garrapat|ear vi scribble. ~o m scribble

garrote m club, cudgel; (tormento) garrotte

gar|úa f (LAm) drizzle. ~uar vi [21] (LAm) drizzle

garza f heron

gas m gas. con ~ fizzy. sin ~ still

gasa f gauze

gaseosa f fizzy drink

gas|óleo m diesel. ~olina f petrol (Brit), gasoline (Amer), gas (Amer). ~olinera f petrol station (Brit), gas station (Amer)

gast|ado adj spent; (vestido etc) worn out. ~ador m spendthrift. ~ar vt spend; (consumir) use; (malgastar) waste; (desgastar) wear out; wear (vestido etc); crack (broma). ~arse vpr wear out. ~o m expense; (acción de gastar) spending

gastronomía f gastronomy

gat|a f cat. a ~as on all fours. ~ear vi crawl

gatillo m trigger

gat|ito m kitten. ~o m cat. dar ~o por liebre take s.o. in

gaucho m Gaucho

gaucho A peasant of the pampas of Argentina, Uruguay and Brazil. Modern gauchos work as foremen on farms and ranches and take part in rodeos. Traditionally, a gaucho's outfit was characterized by its baggy trousers, leather chaps, and *chiripá*, a waist-high garment. They also used *boleadoras* for catching cattle.

gaveta *f* drawer

gaviota *f* seagull

gazpacho *m* gazpacho

gelatina *f* gelatine; (*jalea*) jelly

gema *f* gem

gemelo *m* twin. ~**s** *mpl* (*anteojos*) binoculars; (*de camisa*) cuff-links

gemido *m* groan

Géminis *m* Gemini

gemir 5 *vi* moan; (*animal*) whine, howl

gen *m*, **gene** *m* gene

geneal|ogía *f* genealogy. ~**ógico** *adj* genealogical. árbol *m* ~**ógico** family tree

generaci|ón *f* generation. ~**onal** *adj* generational

general *adj* general. en ~ in general. por lo ~ generally. ●*m* general. ~**izar** 10 *vt/i* generalize. ~**mente** *adv* generally

generar *vt* generate

género *m* type, sort; (*en biología*) genus; (*Gram*) gender; (*en literatura etc*) genre; (*producto*) product; (*tela*) material. ~**s** de punto knitwear. ~ **humano** mankind

generos|idad *f* generosity. ~**o** *adj* generous

genétic|a *f* genetics. ~**o** *adj* genetic

geni|al *adj* brilliant; (*divertido*) funny. ~**o** *m* temper; (*carácter*) nature; (*talento, persona*) genius

genital *adj* genital. ~**es** *mpl* genitals

genoma *m* genome

gente *f* people; (*nación*) nation; (*fam, familia*) family, folks; (*Mex, persona*) person. ●*adj* (*LAm*) respectable; (*amable*) kind

gentil *adj* charming. ~**eza** *f* kindness. tener la ~**eza** de be kind enough to

gentío *m* crowd

genuflexión *f* genuflection

genuino *adj* genuine

ge|ografía *f* geography. ~**ográfico** *adj* geographical.

ge|ología *f* geology. ~**ólogo** *m* geologist

geom|etría *f* geometry. ~**étrico** *adj* geometrical

geranio *m* geranium

geren|cia *f* management. ~**ciar** *vt* (*LAm*) manage. ~**te** *m & f* manager

germen *m* germ

germinar *vi* germinate

gestación *f* gestation

gesticula|ción *f* gesticulation. ~**r** *vi* gesticulate

gesti|ón *f* step; (*administración*) management. ~**onar** *vt* take steps to arrange; (*dirigir*) manage

gesto *m* expression; (*ademán*) gesture; (*mueca*) grimace

gibraltareño *adj* & *m* Gibraltarian

gigante *adj* gigantic. ● *m* giant. ~**sco** *adj* gigantic

gimn|asia *f* gymnastics. ~**asio** *m* gymnasium, gym 1. ~**asta** *m & f* gymnast. ~**ástico** *adj* gymnastic

gimotear *vi* whine

ginebra f gin

ginec|ólogo m gynaecologist

gira f tour. ~r vt spin; draw (cheque); transfer (dinero). • vi rotate, go round; (en camino) turn

girasol m sunflower

gir|atorio adj revolving. ~o m turn; (Com) draft; (locución) expression. ~o postal money order

gitano adj & m gypsy

glacia|l adj icy. ~r m glacier

glándula f gland

glasear vt glaze; (Culin) ice

glob|al adj global; (fig) overall. ~alización f globalization. ~o m globe; (juguete) balloon

glóbulo m globule

gloria f glory; (placer) delight. ~rse vpr boast (de about)

glorieta f square; (Auto) roundabout (Brit), (traffic) circle (Amer)

glorificar 7 vt glorify

glorioso adj glorious

glotón adj gluttonous. • m glutton

gnomo /'nomo/ m gnome

gob|ernación f government. Ministerio m de la G~ernación Home Office (Brit), Department of the Interior (Amer). ~ernador adj governing. • m governor. ~ernante adj governing. • m & f leader. ~ernar 1 vt govern. ~ierno m government

goce m enjoyment

gol m goal

golf m golf

golfo m gulf; (niño) urchin; (holgazán) layabout

golondrina f swallow

golos|ina f titbit; (dulce) sweet. ~o adj fond of sweets

golpe m blow; (puñetazo) punch;

(choque) bump; (de emoción) shock; (arg, atraco) job 1; (en golf, en tenis, de remo) stroke. ~ de estado coup d'etat. ~ de fortuna stroke of luck. ~ de vista glance. ~ militar military coup. de ~ suddenly. de un ~ in one go. ~ar vt hit; (dar varios golpes) beat; (con mucho ruido) bang; (con el puño) punch. • vi knock

goma f rubber; (para pegar) glue; (banda) rubber band; (de borrar) eraser. ~ de mascar chewing gum. ~ espuma foam rubber

googlear ® vt/i 1 to google

gord|a f (Mex) small thick tortilla. ~o adj (persona) (con ser) fat; (con estar) have put on weight; (carne) fatty; (grueso) thick; (grande) large, big. • m first prize. ~ura f fatness; (grasa) fat

gorila f gorilla

gorje|ar vi chirp. ~o m chirping

gorra f cap. ~ de baño (LAm) bathing cap

gorrión m sparrow

gorro m cap; (de niño) bonnet. ~ de baño bathing cap

got|a f drop; (Med) gout. ni ~a nothing. ~ear vi drip. ~era f leak

gozar 10 vt enjoy. • vi. ~ de enjoy

gozne m hinge

gozo m pleasure; (alegría) joy. ~so adj delighted

graba|ción f recording. ~do m engraving, print; (en libro) illustration. ~dora f tape-recorder. ~r vt engrave; record (discos etc)

graci|a f grace; (favor) favour; (humor) wit. ~as fpl thanks. ¡~as! thank you!, thanks! dar las ~as thank. hacer ~a amuse; (gustar) please. ¡muchas ~as! thank you

very much! **tener** ~a be funny.
~**oso** adj funny. ● m fool, comic
character

grada f step. ~**as** fpl stand(s).
~**ación** f gradation. ~**o** m degree;
(en enseñanza) year (Brit), grade
(Amer). **de buen** ~**o** willingly

gradua|ción f graduation; (de al-
cohol) proof. ~**do** m graduate. ~**l**
adj gradual. ~**r** 🔢 vt graduate; (regular) adjust. ~**rse** vpr graduate

gráfic|a f graph. ~**o** adj graphic.
● m graph

gram|ática f grammar. ~**atical**
adj grammatical

gramo m gram, gramme (Brit)

gran adj véase GRANDE

grana f (color) deep red

granada f pomegranate; (Mil)
grenade

granate m (color) maroon

Gran Bretaña f Great Britain

grande adj (delante de nombre en singular **gran**) big, large; (alto) tall;
(fig) great; (LAm, de edad) grown
up. ~**za** f greatness

grandioso adj magnificent

granel m. a ~ in bulk; (suelto)
loose; (fig) in abundance

granero m barn

granito m granite; (grano) small
grain

graniz|ado m iced drink. ~**ar** 🔟
vi hail. ~**o** m hail

granj|a f farm. ~**ero** m farmer

grano m grain; (semilla) seed; (de
café) bean; (Med) spot. ~**s** mpl cer-
eals

granuja m & f rogue

grapa f staple. ~**r** vt staple

gras|a f grease; (Culin) fat. ~**iento**
adj greasy

gratifica|ción f (de sueldo)

bonus (recompensa) reward. ~**r** 🔟
vt reward

grat|is adv free. ~**itud** f gratitude.
~**o** adj pleasant ~**uito** adj free;
(fig) uncalled for

grava|men m tax; (carga) bur-
den; (sobre inmueble) encum-
brance. ~**r** vt tax; (cargar) burden

grave adj serious; (voz) deep; (sonido) low; (acento) grave. ~**dad** f
gravity

gravilla f gravel

gravitar vi gravitate; (apoyarse)
rest (sobre on); (peligro) hang
(sobre over)

gravoso adj costly

graznar vi (cuervo) caw; (pato)
quack; honk (ganso)

Grecia f Greece

gremio m union

greña f mop of hair

gresca f rumpus; (riña) quarrel

griego adj & m Greek

grieta f crack

grifo m tap, faucet (Amer)

grilletes mpl shackles

grillo m cricket. ~**s** mpl shackles

gringo m (LAm) foreigner; (norteamericano) Yankee 🔟

gripe f flu

gris adj grey. ● m grey; (fam, policía) policeman

grit|ar vi shout. ~**ería** f, ~**erío** m
uproar. ~**o** m shout; (de dolor, sorpresa) cry; (chillido) scream. **dar**
~**s** shout

grosella f redcurrant. ~ **negra**
blackcurrant

groser|ía f rudeness; (ordinariez)
coarseness; (comentario etc) coarse
remark; (palabra) swearword. ~**o**
adj coarse; (descortés) rude

grosor m thickness

g

grotesco *adj* grotesque

grúa *f* crane

grueso *adj* thick; (*persona*) fat, stout. • *m* thickness; (*fig*) main body

grumo *m* lump

gruñi|do *m* grunt; (*de perro*) growl. ~**r** 🔢 *vi* grunt; (*perro*) growl

grupa *f* hindquarters

grupo *m* group

gruta *f* grotto

guacamole *m* guacamole

guadaña *f* scythe

guaje *m* (*Mex*) gourd

guajolote *m* (*Mex*) turkey

guante *m* glove

guapo *adj* good-looking; (*chica*) pretty; (*elegante*) smart

guarda *m & f* guard; (*de parque etc*) keeper. ~**barros** *m invar* mudguard. ~**bosque** *m* gamekeeper. ~**costas** *m invar* coastguard vessel. ~**espaldas** *m invar* bodyguard. ~**meta** *m* goalkeeper. ~**r** *vt* keep; (*proteger*) protect; (*en un lugar*) put away; (*reservar*) save, keep. ~**rse** *vpr*. ~**rse de** (+ *infinitivo*) avoid (+ *gerundio*). ~**rropa** *m* wardrobe; (*en local público*) cloakroom. ~**vallas** *m invar* (*LAm*) goalkeeper

guardería *f* nursery

guardia *f* guard; (*policía*) policewoman; (*de médico*) shift. G~ Civil Civil Guard. ~ **municipal** police. **estar de** ~ be on duty. **estar en** ~ be on one's guard. **montar la** ~ mount guard. • *m* policeman. ~ **jurado** *m & f* security guard. ~ **de tráfico** *m* traffic policeman. • *f* traffic policewoman

guardián *m* guardian; (*de parque etc*) keeper; (*de edificio*) security guard

guar|ecer 🔟 *vt* (*albergar*) give shelter to. ~**ecerse** *vpr* take shelter. ~**ida** *f* den, lair; (*de personas*) hideout

guarn|ecer 🔟 *vt* (*adornar*) adorn; (*Culin*) garnish. ~**ición** *f* adornment; (*de caballo*) harness; (*Culin*) garnish; (*Mil*) garrison; (*de piedra preciosa*) setting

guas|a *f* joke. ~**ón** *adj* humorous. • *m* joker

Guatemala *f* Guatemala

guatemalteco *adj & m* Guatemalan

guateque *m* party, bash

guayab|a *f* guava; (*dulce*) guava jelly. ~**era** *f* lightweight jacket

gubernatura *f* (*Mex*) government

güero *adj* (*Mex*) fair

guerr|a *f* war; (*método*) warfare. **dar** ~**a** annoy. ~**ero** *adj* warlike; (*belicoso*) fighting. • *m* warrior. ~**illa** *f* band of guerrillas. ~**illero** *m* guerrilla

guía *m & f* guide. • *f* guidebook; (*de teléfonos*) directory

guiar 🔟 *vt* guide; (*llevar*) lead; (*Auto*) drive. ~**se** *vpr* be guided (*por by*)

guijarro *m* pebble

guillotina *f* guillotine

guind|a *f* morello cherry. ~**illa** *f* chilli

guiñapo *m* rag; (*fig, persona*) wreck

guiñ|ar *vt/i* wink. ~**o** *m* wink. **hacer** ~**os** wink

guión *m* hyphen, dash; (*de película etc*) script. ~**onista** *m & f* scriptwriter

guirnalda *f* garland

guisado *m* stew

135

guisante *m* pea. ~ de olor
sweet pea

guis|ar *vt/i* cook. **~o** *m* stew

guitarr|a *f* guitar. **~ista** *m & f*
guitarist

gula *f* gluttony

gusano *m* worm; (*larva de mosca*)
maggot

---

gustar

● *verbo intransitivo*

! Cuando el verbo **gustar** va
precedido del complemento
indirecto **le** (o **les, nos** etc), el
sujeto en español pasa a ser el
objeto en inglés. **me gusta
mucho la música** I like music
very much. **le gustan los hela-
dos** he likes ice cream. **a Juan
no le gusta** Juan doesn't like it
(or her etc)

····▸ **gustar** + *infinitivo*. les gusta
ver televisión they like watch-
ing television

····▸ **gustar que** + *subjuntivo*. me
~ía que vinieras I'd like you
to come. no le gusta que lo
corrijan he doesn't like being
corrected. ¿te ~ía que te lo
comprara? would you like me
to buy it for you?

····▸ **gustar de algo** to like sth.
gustan de las fiestas they like
parties

····▸ (*tener acogida*) to go down
well. ese tipo de cosas que
siempre gusta those sort of
things always go down well. el
libro no gustó the book
didn't go down well

····▸ (*en frases de cortesía*) to
wish. como guste as you

wish. **cuando gustes** whenever you wish

● *verbo transitivo*

····▸ (*LAm, querer*) ¿gusta un
café? would you like a coffee?
¿gustan pasar? would you like
to come in? ● **gustarse** *verbo pronominal* to like each other

gusto *m* taste; (*placer*) pleasure. a
~ comfortable. a mí ~ to my lik-
ing. buen ~ good taste. con
mucho ~ with pleasure. dar ~
please. mucho ~ pleased to meet
you. ~so *adj* tasty; (*de buen grado*)
willingly

gutural *adj* guttural

g
h

Hh

ha *vb* véase **HABER**

haba *f* broad bean

Habana *f* La ~ Havana

habano *m* (*puro*) Havana

haber *verbo auxiliar* **30** have. ● *v* impersonal (*presente* & *pl* **hay**, *imperfecto*
s & *pl* **había**, *pretérito* *s* & *pl* **hubo**).
hay una carta para ti there's a let-
ter for you. hay 5 bancos en la
plaza there are 5 banks in the
square. hay que hacerlo it must
be done, you have to do it. he
aquí here is, here are. no hay de
qué don't mention it, not at all.
¿qué hay? (¿qué pasa?) what's the
matter?; (¿qué tal?) how are you?

habichuela *f* bean

hábil *adj* skilful; (*listo*) clever; (*día*)
working; (*Jurid*) competent

habili|dad *f* skill; (*astucia*) clever-

ness; (Jurid) competence. **~tar** vt
qualify

habita|ción f room; (dormitorio)
bedroom; (en biología) habitat.
**~ción de matrimonio, ~ción
doble** double room. **~ción individual, ~ción sencilla** single room.
~do adj inhabited. **~nte** m inhabitant. **~r** vt live in. ● vi live

hábito m habit

habitual|l adj usual, habitual;
(cliente) regular. **~r** 21 vt accustom. **~rse** vpr. **~rse a** get used to

habla f speech; (idioma) language;
(dialecto) dialect. **al ~** (al teléfono)
speaking. **ponerse al ~ con** get in
touch with. **~dor** adj talkative. ● m
chatterbox. **~duría** f rumour.
~durías fpl gossip. **~nte** adj
speaking. ● m & f speaker. **~r** vt
speak. ● vi speak, talk (con to);
(Mex, por teléfono) call. **¡ni ~r!** out
of the question! **se ~ español**
Spanish spoken

hacend|ado m landowner; (LAm)
farmer. **~oso** adj hard-working

hacer 31

● verbo transitivo

····▸ to do. **¿qué haces?** what are
you doing? **~ los deberes** to
do one's homework. **no sé qué
~** I don't know what to do.
hazme un favor can you do
me a favour?

····▸ (fabricar, preparar, producir)
to make. **me hizo un vestido**
she made me a dress. **~ un
café** to make a (cup of) coffee.
no hagas tanto ruido don't
make so much noise

····▸ (construir) to build (casa,
puente)

····▸ **hacer que uno haga algo** to

make s.o. do sth. **haz que se
vaya** make him leave. **hizo
que se equivocara** he made
her go wrong

····▸ **hacer hacer algo** to have
sth done. **hizo arreglar el
techo** he had the roof repaired

➡️ Cuando el verbo **hacer**
se emplea en expresiones
como **hacer una pregunta,
hacer trampa** etc., ver bajo el
respectivo nombre

● verbo intransitivo

····▸ (actuar, obrar) to do. **hiciste bien en llamar** you did
the right thing to call **¿cómo
haces para parecer tan
joven?** what do you do to
look so young?

····▸ (fingir, simular) **hacer
como que** to pretend. **hizo
como que no me conocía** he
pretended not to know me.
haz como que estás dormido
pretend you're asleep

····▸ **hacer de** (en teatro) to play
the part of; (ejercer la función
de) to act as

····▸ (LAm, sentar) **tanta sal
hace mal** so much salt is not
good for you. **dormir le hizo
bien** the sleep did him good.
el pepino me hace mal cucumber doesn't agree with me

verbo impersonal

····▸ (hablando del tiempo atmosférico) to be. **hace sol** it's
sunny. **hace 3 grados** it's 3
degrees

····▸ (con expresiones temporales)
hace una hora que espero
I've been waiting for an hour.

llegó hace 3 días he arrived 3 days ago. **hace mucho tiempo** a long time ago. **hasta hace poco** until recently

● **hacerse** *verbo pronominal*

····▸ (*para sí*) to make o.s. (falda, café)

····▸ (*hacer que otro haga*) **se hizo la permanente** she had her hair permed. **me hice una piscina** I had a pool built

····▸ (*convertirse en*) to become. **se hicieron amigos** they became friends

····▸ (*acostumbrarse*) ∼**se a algo** to get used to sth

····▸ (*fingirse*) to pretend. ∼**se el enfermo** to pretend to be ill

····▸ (*moverse*) to move. **hazte para atrás** move back

····▸ **hacerse de** (*LAm*) to make (amigo, dinero)

hacha *f* axe; (*antorcha*) torch
hacia *prep* towards; (*cerca de*) near; (*con tiempo*) at about. ∼ **abajo** downwards. ∼ **arriba** upwards. ∼ **atrás** backwards. ∼ **las dos** (at) about two o'clock
hacienda *f* country estate; (*en LAm*) ranch; **la ∼ pública** the Treasury. **Ministerio m de H∼** Ministry of Finance; (*en Gran Bretaña*) Exchequer; (*en Estados Unidos*) Treasury
hada *f* fairy. **el ∼ madrina** the fairy godmother
hago *vb véase* **HACER**
Haití *m* Haiti
halag|ar 12 *vt* flatter. ∼**üeño** *adj* flattering; (*esperanzador*) promising
halcón *m* falcon
halla|r *vt* find; (*descubrir*) discover.

∼**rse** *vpr* be. ∼**zgo** *m* discovery
hamaca *f* hammock; (*asiento*) deck-chair
hambr|e *f* hunger; (*de muchos*) famine. **tener** ∼**e** be hungry. ∼**iento** *adj* starving
hamburguesa *f* hamburger
harag|án *adj* lazy, idle. ● *m* layabout. ∼**anear** *vi* laze around
harap|iento *adj* in rags. ∼**o** *m* rag
harina *f* flour
hart|ar *vt* (*fastidiar*) annoy. **me estás** ∼**ando** you're annoying me. ∼**arse** *vpr* (*llenarse*) gorge o.s. (*de* on); (*cansarse*) get fed up (*de* with). ∼**o** *adj* (*cansado*) tired; (*fastidiado*) fed up (*de* with). ● *adv* (*LAm*) (*muy*) very; (*mucho*) a lot
hasta *prep* as far as; (*en el tiempo*) until, till; (*Mex*) not until. ● *adv* even. **¡∼ la vista!** goodbye!, see you! 1 **¡∼ luego!** see you later! **¡∼ mañana!** see you tomorrow! **¡∼ pronto!** see you soon!
hast|iar 20 *vt* (*cansar*) weary, tire; (*aburrir*) bore. ∼**iarse** *vpr* get fed up (*de* with). ∼**io** *m* weariness; (*aburrimiento*) boredom
haya *f* beech (tree). ● *vb véase* **HABER**
hazaña *f* exploit
hazmerreír *m* laughing stock
he *vb véase* **HABER**
hebilla *f* buckle
hebra *f* thread; (*fibra*) fibre
hebreo *adj & m* Hebrew
hechi|cera *f* witch. ∼**cería** *f* witchcraft. ∼**cero** *m* wizard. ∼**zar** 10 *vt* cast a spell on; (*fig*) captivate. ∼**zo** *m* spell; (*fig*) charm
hech|o *pp de* hacer. ● *adj* (*manufacturado*) made; (*terminado*) done; (*vestidos etc*) ready-made; (*Culin*)

done. ● m fact; (acto) deed; (cuestión) matter; (suceso) event. de ~o in fact. ~ura f making; (forma) form; (del cuerpo) build; (calidad de fabricación) workmanship

hed|er 🔟 vi stink. ~iondez f stench. ~iondo adj stinking, smelly. ~or m stench

hela|da f frost. ~dera f (LAm) fridge, refrigerator. ~dería f ice-cream shop. ~do adj freezing; (congelado) frozen; (LAm, bebida) chilled. ● m ice-cream. ~r 🔟 vt/i freeze. anoche heló there was a frost last night. ~rse vpr freeze

helecho m fern

hélice f propeller

helicóptero m helicopter

hembra f female; (mujer) woman

hemorr|agia f haemorrhage. ~oides fpl haemorrhoids

hendidura f crack, split; (en geología) fissure

heno m hay

heráldica f heraldry

hered|ar vt/i inherit. ~era f heiress. ~ero m heir. ~itario adj hereditary

herej|e m heretic. ~ía f heresy

herencia f inheritance; (fig) heritage

heri|da f injury; (con arma) wound. ~do adj injured; (con arma) wounded; (fig) hurt. ● m injured person. ~r 🔟 vt injure; (con arma) wound; (fig) hurt. ~rse vpr hurt o.s.

herman|a f sister. ~a política sister-in-law. ~astra f stepsister. ~astro m stepbrother. ~o m brother. ~o político brother-in-law. ~os mpl brothers; (chicos y chicas) brothers and sisters. ~os gemelos twins

hermético adj hermetic; (fig) watertight

hermos|o adj beautiful; (espléndido) splendid. ~ura f beauty

héroe m hero

hero|ico adj heroic. ~ína f heroine; (droga) heroin. ~ísmo m heroism

herr|adura f horseshoe. ~amienta f tool. ~ero m blacksmith

herv|idero m (fig) hotbed; (multitud) throng. ~ir 🔟 vt/i boil. ~or m (fig) ardour. romper el ~ come to the boil

hiberna|ción f hibernation. ~r vi hibernate

híbrido adj & m hybrid

hice vb véase HACER

hidalgo m nobleman

hidrata|nte adj moisturizing. ~r vt hydrate; (crema etc) moisturize

hidráulico adj hydraulic

hidr|oavión m seaplane. ~oeléctrico adj hydroelectric. ~ofobia f rabies. ~ófobo adj rabid. ~ógeno m hydrogen

hiedra f ivy

hielo m ice

hiena f hyena

hierba f grass; (Culin, Med) herb. mala ~ weed. ~buena f mint.

hierro m iron

hígado m liver

higi|ene f hygiene. ~énico adj hygienic

hig|o m fig. ~uera f fig tree

hij|a f daughter. ~astra f stepdaughter. ~astro m stepson. ~o m son. ~os mpl sons; (chicos y chicas) children

hilar vt spin. ~ delgado split hairs

hilera f row; (Mil) file

hilo *m* thread; (*Elec*) wire; (*de líquido*) trickle; (*lino*) linen

hilv|án *m* tacking. **∼anar** *vt* tack; (*fig*) put together

himno *m* hymn. **∼ nacional** anthem

hincapié *m*. hacer **∼ en** stress, insist on

hincar **7** *vt* drive (estaca) (en into). **∼se** *vpr*. **∼se de rodillas** kneel down

hincha *f* **1** grudge. ● *m & f* (*fam, aficionado*) fan

hincha|do *adj* inflated; (*Med*) swollen. **∼r** *vt* inflate, blow up. **∼rse** *vpr* swell up; (*fig, fam, comer mucho*) gorge o.s. **∼zón** *f* swelling

hinojo *m* fennel

hiper|mercado *m* hypermarket. **∼sensible** *adj* hypersensitive. **∼tensión** *f* high blood pressure

hípic|a *f* horse racing. **∼o** *adj* horse

hipn|osis *f* hypnosis. **∼otismo** *m* hypnotism. **∼otizar** **10** *vt* hypnotize

hipo *m* hiccup. tener **∼** have hiccups

hipo|alérgeno *adj* hypoallergenic. **∼condríaco** *adj & m* hypochondriac

hip|ocresía *f* hypocrisy. **∼ócrita** *adj* hypocritical. ● *m & f* hypocrite

hipódromo *m* racecourse

hipopótamo *m* hippopotamus

hipoteca *f* mortgage. **∼r** **7** *vt* mortgage

hip|ótesis *f invar* hypothesis. **∼otético** *adj* hypothetical

hiriente *adj* offensive, wounding

hirsuto *adj* (*barba*) bristly; (*pelo*) wiry

hispánico *adj* Hispanic

Hispanidad - Día de la
See ▷**DÍA DE LA RAZA**

Hispanoamérica *f* Spanish America

hispano|americano *adj* Spanish American. **∼hablante** *adj* Spanish-speaking

hist|eria *f* hysteria. **∼érico** *adj* hysterical

hist|oria *f* history; (*relato*) story; (*excusa*) tale, excuse. pasar a la **∼oria** go down in history. **∼oriador** *m* historian. **∼órico** *adj* historical. **∼orieta** *f* tale; (*con dibujos*) strip cartoon

hito *m* milestone

hizo *vb véase* HACER

hocico *m* snout

hockey /'(x)oki/ *m* hockey. **∼ sobre hielo** ice hockey

hogar *m* home; (*chimenea*) hearth. **∼eño** *adj* domestic; (*persona*) home-loving

hoguera *f* bonfire

hoja *f* leaf; (*de papel, metal etc*) sheet; (*de cuchillo, espada etc*) blade. **∼ de afeitar** razor blade. **∼lata** *f* tin

hojaldre *m* puff pastry

hojear *vt* leaf through

hola *int* hello!

Holanda *f* Holland

holand|és *adj* Dutch. ● *m* Dutchman; (*lengua*) Dutch. **∼esa** *f* Dutchwoman. los **∼eses** the Dutch

holg|ado *adj* loose; (*fig*) comfortable. **∼ar** **2** & **12** *vi*. huelga decir que needless to say. **∼azán** *adj* lazy. ● *m* idler. **∼ura** *f* looseness; (*fig*) comfort

hollín *m* soot

hombre m man; (*especie humana*) man(kind). ● *int* Good Heavens!; (*de duda*) well. ~ **de negocios** businessman. ~ **rana** frogman

hombr|era f shoulder pad. ~**o** m shoulder

homenaje m homage, tribute. **rendir** ~ **a** pay tribute to

home|ópata m homoeopath. ~**opatía** f homoeopathy. ~**opático** adj homoeopathic

homicid|a adj murderous. ● m & f murderer. ~**io** m murder

homosexual adj & m & f homosexual. ~**idad** f homosexuality

hond|o adj deep. ~**onada** f hollow

Honduras f Honduras

hondureño adj & m Honduran

honest|idad f honesty. ~**o** adj honest

hongo m fungus; (*LAm, Culin*) mushroom; (*venenoso*) toadstool

hon|or m honour. ~**orable** adj honourable. ~**orario** adj honorary. ~**orarios** mpl fees. ~**ra** f honour; (*buena fama*) good name. ~**radez** f honesty. ~**rado** adj honest. ~**rar** vt honour

hora f hour; (*momento puntual*) time; (*cita*) appointment. ~ **pico**, ~ **punta** rush hour. ~**s** fpl **de trabajo** working hours. ~**s** fpl **extraordinarias** overtime. ~**s libres** free time. **a estas** ~**s** now. **¿a qué** ~**?** (at) what time? **a última** ~ at the last moment. **de última** ~ last-minute. **en buena** ~ at the right time. **media** ~ half an hour. **pedir** ~ to make an appointment. **¿qué** ~ **es?** what time is it?

horario adj hourly. ● m timetable. ~ **de trabajo** working hours

horca f gallows

horcajadas fpl. **a** ~ astride

horchata f tiger-nut milk

horizont|al adj & f horizontal. ~**e** m horizon

horma f mould; (*para fabricar calzado*) last; (*para conservar su forma*) shoe-tree. **de** ~ **ancha** broad-fitting

hormiga f ant

hormigón m concrete

hormigue|ar vi tingle; (*bullir*) swarm. **me** ~**a la mano** I've got pins and needles in my hand. ~**o** m tingling; (*fig*) anxiety

hormiguero m anthill; (*de gente*) swarm

hormona f hormone

horn|ada f batch. ~**illa** f (*LAm*) burner. ~**illo** m burner; (*cocina portátil*) portable electric cooker. ~**o** m oven; (*para cerámica etc*) kiln; (*Tec*) furnace

horóscopo m horoscope

horquilla f pitchfork; (*para el pelo*) hairpin

horr|endo adj awful. ~**ible** adj horrible. ~**ipilante** adj terrifying. ~**or** m horror; (*atrocidad*) atrocity. **¡qué** ~**or!** how awful!. ~**orizar** 🔟 vt horrify. ~**orizarse** vpr be horrified. ~**oroso** adj horrifying

hort|aliza f vegetable. ~**elano** m market gardener

hosco adj surly

hospeda|je m accommodation. ~**r** vt put up. ~**rse** vpr stay

hospital m hospital. ~**ario** adj hospitable. ~**idad** f hospitality

hostal m boarding-house

hostería f inn

hostia f (*Relig*) host

hostigar 🔢 vt whip; (*fig, molestar*) pester

hostil adj hostile. ~**idad** f hostility

hotel m hotel. ~**ero** adj hotel. ● m hotelier

hoy adv today. ~ (en) día nowadays. ~ **por** ~ at the present time. **de** ~ **en adelante** from now on

hoy|**o** m hole. ~**uelo** m dimple

hoz f sickle

hube vb véase HABER

hucha f money box

hueco adj hollow; (palabras) empty; (voz) resonant; (persona) superficial. ● m hollow; (espacio) space; (vacío) gap

huelg|**a** f strike. ~**a de brazos caídos** sit-down strike. ~**a de hambre** hunger strike. **declararse en** ~**a** come out on strike. ~**uista** m & f striker

huella f footprint; (de animal etc) track. ~ **de carbono** carbon footprint. ~ **digital** fingerprint

huelo vb véase OLER

huérfano adj orphaned. ● m orphan. ~ **de** without

huert|**a** f market garden (Brit), truck farm (Amer); (terreno de regadío) irrigated plain. ~**o** m vegetable garden; (de árboles frutales) orchard

hueso m bone; (de fruta) stone

huésped m guest; (que paga) lodger

huesudo adj bony

huev|**a** f roe. ~**o** m egg. ~**o duro** hard-boiled egg. ~**o escalfado** poached egg. ~**o estrellado**, ~**o frito** fried egg. ~**o pasado por agua** boiled egg. ~**os revueltos** scrambled eggs. ~**o tibio** (Mex) boiled egg

hui|**da** f flight, escape. ~**dizo** adj (tímido) shy; (esquivo) elusive

huipil m (Mex) traditional embroidered smock

huir vi 🔟 flee, run away; (evitar). ~ **de** avoid. **me huye** he avoids me

huitlacoche m (Mex) edible black fungus

hule m oilcloth; (Mex, goma) rubber

human|**idad** f mankind; (fig) humanity. ~**itario** adj humanitarian. ~**o** adj human; (benévolo) humane

humareda f cloud of smoke

humed|**ad** f dampness; (en meteorología) humidity; (gotitas de agua) moisture. ~**ecer** 🔟 vt moisten. ~**ecerse** vpr become moist

húmedo adj damp; (clima) humid; (labios) moist; (mojado) wet

humi|**ldad** f humility. ~**lde** adj humble. ~**llación** f humiliation. ~**llar** vt humiliate. ~**llarse** vpr lower o.s.

humo m smoke; (vapor) steam; (gas nocivo) fumes. ~**s** mpl airs

humor m mood, temper; (gracia) humour. **estar de mal** ~ be in a bad mood. ~**ista** m & f humorist. ~**ístico** adj humorous

hundi|**miento** m sinking. ~**r** vt sink; destroy (persona). ~**rse** vpr sink; (edificio) collapse

húngaro adj & m Hungarian

Hungría f Hungary

huracán m hurricane

huraño adj unsociable

hurgar 12 vi rummage (en through). ~se vpr. ~se la nariz pick one's nose

hurra int hurray!

hurtadillas fpl. a ~ stealthily

hurt|ar vt steal. ~o m theft; (cosa robada) stolen object

husmear vt sniff out; (fig) pry into

huyo vb véase **HUIR**

Ii

iba véase **IR**

ibérico adj Iberian

iberoamericano adj & m Latin American

iceberg /iθ'ber/ m (pl ~s) iceberg

ictericia f jaundice

ida f outward journey; (partida) departure. de ~ y vuelta (billete) return (Brit), round-trip (Amer); (viaje) round

idea f idea; (opinión) opinion. cambiar de ~ change one's mind. no tener la más remota ~, no tener la menor ~ not have the slightest idea, not have a clue 1

ideal adj & m ideal. ~ista m & f idealist. ~izar 10 vt idealize

idear vt think up, conceive; (inventar) invent

ídem pron & adv the same

idéntico adj identical

identi|dad f identity. ~ficación f identification. ~ficar 7 vt identify. ~ficarse vpr identify o.s. ~ficarse con identify with

ideolo|gía f ideology. ~ógico adj ideological

idílico adj idyllic

idilio m idyll

idiom|a m language. ~ático adj idiomatic

idiosincrasia f idiosyncrasy

idiot|a adj idiotic. ● m & f idiot. ~ez f stupidity

idolatrar vt worship; (fig) idolize

ídolo m idol

idóneo adj suitable (para for)

iglesia f church

iglú m igloo

ignora|ncia f ignorance. ~nte adj ignorant. ● m ignoramus. ~r vt not know, be unaware of; (no hacer caso de) ignore

igual adj equal; (mismo) the same; (similar) like; (llano) even; (liso) smooth. ● adv the same. ● m equal. ~ que (the same) as. al ~ que the same as. da ~, es ~ it doesn't matter. sin ~ unequalled

igual|ar vt make equal; equal (éxito, récord); (allanar) level. ~arse vpr be equal. ~dad f equality. ~mente adv equally; (también) also, likewise; (respuesta de cortesía) the same to you

ilegal adj illegal

ilegible adj illegible

ilegítimo adj illegitimate

ileso adj unhurt

ilícito adj illicit

ilimitado adj unlimited

ilógico adj illogical

ilumina|ción f illumination; (alumbrado) lighting. ~r vt light (up). ~rse vpr light up

ilusi|ón f illusion; (sueño) dream; (alegría) joy. hacerse ~ones build up one's hopes. me hace ~ón I'm thrilled; I'm looking forward to (algo en el futuro). **~onado** adj excited. **~onar** vt give false hope. **~onarse** vpr have false hopes

ilusionis|mo m conjuring. **~ta** m & f conjurer

iluso adj naive. ● m dreamer. **~rio** adj illusory

ilustra|ción f learning; (dibujo) illustration. **~do** adj learned; (con dibujos) illustrated. **~r** vt explain; (instruir) instruct; (añadir dibujos etc) illustrate. **~rse** vpr acquire knowledge. **~tivo** adj illustrative

ilustre adj illustrious

imagen f image; (TV etc) picture

imagina|ble adj imaginable. **~ción** f imagination. **~r** vt imagine. **~rse** vpr imagine. **~rio** m imaginary. **~tivo** adj imaginative

imán m magnet

imbécil adj stupid. ● m & f idiot

imborrable adj indelible; (recuerdo etc) unforgettable

imita|ción f imitation. **~r** vt imitate

impacien|cia f impatience. **~tarse** vpr lose one's patience. **~te** adj impatient

impacto m impact; (huella) mark. **~ de bala** bullet hole

impar adj odd

imparcial adj impartial. **~idad** f impartiality

impartir vt impart, give

impasible adj impassive

impávido adj fearless; (impasible) impassive

impecable adj impeccable

impedi|do adj disabled. **~mento** m impediment. **~r** **5** vt prevent; (obstruir) hinder

impenetrable adj impenetrable

impensa|ble adj unthinkable. **~do** adj unexpected

impera|r vi prevail. **~tivo** adj imperative; (necesidad) urgent

imperceptible adj imperceptible

imperdible m safety pin

imperdonable adj unforgivable

imperfec|ción f imperfection. **~to** adj imperfect

imperi|al adj imperial. **~alismo** m imperialism. **~o** m empire; (poder) rule. **~oso** adj imperious

impermeable adj waterproof. ● m raincoat

impersonal adj impersonal

impertinen|cia f impertinence. **~te** adj impertinent

imperturbable adj imperturbable

ímpetu m impetus; (impulso) impulse; (violencia) force

impetuos|idad f impetuosity. **~o** adj impetuous

implacable adj implacable

implantar vt introduce

implementación f implementation

implica|ción f implication. **~r** **7** vt implicate; (significar) imply

implícito adj implicit

implorar vt implore

impon|ente adj imposing; **1** terrific. **~er** **34** vt impose; (requerir) demand; deposit (dinero). **~erse** vpr (hacerse obedecer) assert o.s.; (hacerse respetar) command respect; (prevalecer) prevail. **~ible** adj taxable

importa|ción f importation; (artículo) import. **~ciones** fpl imports. **~dor** adj importing. ● m importer

importa|ncia f importance.

~nte adj important; (en cantidad) considerable; **~r** vt import; (ascender a) amount to. ● vi be important, matter. **¿le ~ría...?** would you mind...? **no ~** it doesn't matter

importe m price; (total) amount
importun|ar vt bother. **~o** adj troublesome; (inoportuno) inopportune

imposib|ilidad f impossibility. **~le** adj impossible. **hacer lo ~le para** do all one can to
imposición f imposition; (impuesto) tax
impostor m impostor
impoten|cia f impotence. **~te** adj impotent
impracticable adj impracticable; (intransitable) unpassable
imprecis|ión f vagueness; (error) inaccuracy. **~o** adj imprecise
impregnar vt impregnate; (empapar) soak
imprenta f printing; (taller) printing house, printer's
imprescindible adj indispensable, essential
impresi|ón f impression; (acción de imprimir) printing; (tirada) edition; (huella) imprint. **~onable** adj impressionable. **~onante** adj impressive; (espantoso) frightening. **~onar** vt impress; (negativamente) shock; (conmover) move; (Foto) expose. **~onarse** vpr be impressed; (negativamente) be shocked; (conmover) be moved
impresionis|mo m impressionism. **~ta** adj & m & f impressionist
impreso adj printed. ● m form. **~s** mpl printed matter. **~ra** f printer
imprevis|ible adj unforeseeable.

~to adj unforeseen
imprimir (pp **impreso**) vt print (libro etc)
improbab|ilidad f improbability. **~le** adj unlikely, improbable
improcedente adj inadmissible; (conducta) improper; (despido) unfair
improductivo adj unproductive
improperio m insult. **~s** mpl abuse
impropio adj improper
improvis|ación f improvisation. **~ado** adj improvised. **~ar** vt improvise. **~o** adj. **de ~o** unexpectedly
impruden|cia f imprudence. **~te** adj imprudent
impúdica f indecency; (desvergüenza) shamelessness. **~údico** adj indecent; (desvergonzado) shameless. **~udor** m indecency; (desvergüenza) shamelessness
impuesto adj imposed. ● m tax. **~ a la renta** income tax. **~ sobre el valor agregado** (LAm), **~ sobre el valor añadido** VAT, value added tax
impuls|ar vt propel; drive (persona); boost (producción etc). **~ividad** f impulsiveness. **~ivo** adj impulsive. **~o** m impulse
impun|e adj unpunished. **~idad** f impunity
impur|eza f impurity. **~o** adj impure
imputa|ción f charge. **~r** vt attribute; (acusar) charge
inaccesible adj inaccessible
inaceptable adj unacceptable
inactiv|idad f inactivity. **~o** adj inactive
inadaptado adj maladjusted

inadecuado adj inadequate; (inapropiado) unsuitable

inadmisible adj inadmissible; (inaceptable) unacceptable

inadvertido adj distracted. pasar ~ go unnoticed

inagotable adj inexhaustible

inaguantable adj unbearable

inaltera|ble adj impassive; (color) fast; (convicción) unalterable. ~do adj unchanged

inapreciable adj invaluable; (imperceptible) imperceptible

inapropiado adj inappropriate

inasequible adj out of reach

inaudito adj unprecedented

inaugura|ción f inauguration. ~l adj inaugural. ~r vt inaugurate

inca adj & m & f Inca. ~ico adj Inca

Incas Founded in the twelfth century, the Andean empire of the Quechua-speaking Incas grew and extended from southern Colombia to Argentina and central Chile. Its capital was Cuzco. The Incas built an extensive road network and impressive buildings, including Machu Picchu. The empire collapsed in 1533 after defeat by the Spaniards led by Francisco Pizarro.

incalculable adj incalculable

incandescente adj incandescent

incansable adj tireless

incapa|cidad f incapacity; (física) disability. ~citado adj disabled. ~citar vt incapacitate. ~z adj incapable

incauto adj unwary; (fácil de engañar) gullible

incendi|ar vt set fire to. ~arse

vpr catch fire. ~ario adj incendiary. ● m arsonist. ~o m fire

incentivo m incentive

incertidumbre f uncertainty

incesante adj incessant

incest|o m incest. ~uoso adj incestuous

inciden|cia f incidence; (efecto) impact; (incidente) incident. ~tal adj incidental. ~te m incident

incidir vi fall (en into); (influir) influence

incienso m incense

incierto adj uncertain

incinera|dor m incinerator. ~r vt incinerate; cremate (cadáver)

incipiente adj incipient

incisi|ón f incision. ~vo adj incisive. ● m incisor

incitar vt incite

inclemen|cia f harshness. ~te adj harsh

inclina|ción f slope; (de la cabeza) nod; (fig) inclination. ~r vt tilt; (inducir) incline. ~rse vpr lean; (en saludo) bow; (tender) be inclined (a to)

inclu|ido adj included; (precio) inclusive. ~ir 17 vt include; (en cartas) enclose. ~sión f inclusion. ~sive adv inclusive. hasta el lunes ~sive up to and including Monday. ~so adv even

incógnito adj unknown. de ~ incognito

incoheren|cia f incoherence. ~te adj incoherent

incoloro adj colourless

incomestible adj, **incomible** adj uneatable, inedible

incomodar vt inconvenience; (causar vergüenza) make feel uncomfortable. ~se vpr feel uncomfortable; (*enojarse*) get angry

incómodo *adj* uncomfortable; (*inconveniente*) inconvenient

incomparable *adj* incomparable

incompatib|ilidad *f* incompatibility. **~le** *adj* incompatible

incompeten|cia *f* incompetence. **~te** *adj & m & f* incompetent

incompleto *adj* incomplete

incompren|dido *adj* misunderstood. **~sible** *adj* incomprehensible. **~sión** *f* incomprehension

incomunicado *adj* cut off; (*preso*) in solitary confinement

inconcebible *adj* inconceivable

inconcluso *adj* unfinished

incondicional *adj* unconditional

inconfundible *adj* unmistakable

incongruente *adj* incoherent; (*contradictorio*) inconsistent

inconmensurable *adj* immeasurable

inconscien|cia *f* unconsciousness; (*irreflexión*) recklessness. **~te** *adj* unconscious; (*irreflexivo*) reckless

inconsecuente *adj* inconsistent

inconsistente *adj* flimsy

inconsolable *adj* inconsolable

inconstan|cia *f* lack of perseverance. **~te** *adj* changeable; (*persona*) lacking in perseverance; (*voluble*) fickle

incontable *adj* countless

incontenible *adj* irrepressible

incontinen|cia *f* incontinence. **~te** *adj* incontinent

inconvenien|cia *f* inconvenience. **~te** *adj* inconvenient; (*inapropiado*) inappropriate; (*incorrecto*) improper. ● *m* problem; (*desventaja*) drawback

incorpora|ción *f* incorporation.

~r *vt* incorporate; (*Culin*) add. **~rse** *vpr* sit up; join (*sociedad, regimiento etc*)

incorrecto *adj* incorrect; (*descortés*) discourteous

incorregible *adj* incorrigible

incorruptible *adj* incorruptible

incrédulo *adj* sceptical; (*mirada, gesto*) incredulous

increíble *adj* incredible

increment|ar *vt* increase. **~o** *m* increase

incriminar *vt* incriminate

incrustar *vt* encrust

incuba|ción *f* incubation. **~dora** *f* incubator. **~r** *vt* incubate; (*fig*) hatch

incuestionable *adj* unquestionable

inculcar 🔢 *vt* inculcate

inculpar *vt* accuse

inculto *adj* uneducated

incumplimiento *m* non-fulfilment; (*de un contrato*) breach

incurable *adj* incurable

incurrir *vi* ~ en incur (*gasto*); fall into (*error*); commit (*crimen*)

incursión *f* raid

indagar 🔢 *vt* investigate

indebido *adj* unjust; (*uso*) improper

indecen|cia *f* indecency. **~te** *adj* indecent

indecible *adj* indescribable

indecis|ión *f* indecision. **~o** *adj* (*con ser*) indecisive; (*con estar*) undecided

indefenso *adj* defenceless

indefini|ble *adj* indefinable. **~do** *adj* indefinite; (*impreciso*) undefined

indemnizar 🔢 *vt* compensate

independ|encia *f* independence. **~iente** *adj* independent. **~izarse** [10] *vpr* become independent

indes|cifrable *adj* indecipherable. **~criptible** *adj* indescribable

indeseable *adj* undesirable

indestructible *adj* indestructible

indetermina|ble *adj* indeterminable. **~do** *adj* indeterminate; (*tiempo*) indefinite

India *f.* la ~ India

indica|ción *f* indication; (*señal*) signal. **~ciones** *fpl* directions. **~dor** *m* indicator; (*Tec*) gauge. **~r** [7] *vt* show, indicate; (*apuntar*) point at; (*hacer saber*) point out; (*aconsejar*) advise. **~tivo** *adj* indicative. ● *m* indicative; (*al teléfono*) dialling code

índice *m* index; (*dedo*) index finger; (*catálogo*) catalogue; (*indicación*) indication; (*aguja*) pointer

indicio *m* indication, sign; (*vestigio*) trace

indiferen|cia *f* indifference. **~te** *adj* indifferent. me es **~te** it's all the same to me

indígena *adj* indigenous. ● *m & f* native

indigen|cia *f* poverty. **~te** *adj* needy

indigest|ión *f* indigestion. **~o** *adj* indigestible

indign|ación *f* indignation. **~ado** *adj* indignant. **~ar** *vt* make indignant. **~arse** *vpr* become indignant. **~o** *adj* unworthy; (*despreciable*) contemptible

indio *adj & m* Indian

indirect|a *f* hint. **~o** *adj* indirect

indisciplinado *adj* undisciplined

indiscre|ción *f* indiscretion. **~to** *adj* indiscreet

indiscutible *adj* unquestionable

indisoluble *adj* indissoluble

indispensable *adj* indispensable

indisp|oner [34] *vt* (*enemistar*) set against. **~onerse** *vpr* fall out; (*ponerse enfermo*) fall ill. **~osición** *f* indisposition. **~uesto** *adj* indisposed

individu|al *adj* individual; (*cama*) single. ● *m* (*en tenis etc*) singles. **~alidad** *f* individuality. **~alista** *m & f* individualist. **~alizar** [10] *vt* individualize. **~o** *m* individual

indocumentado *m* person without identity papers; (*inmigrante*) illegal immigrant

índole *f* nature; (*clase*) type

indolen|cia *f* indolence. **~te** *adj* indolent

indoloro *adj* painless

indomable *adj* untameable

inducir [47] *vt* induce. ~ a error be misleading

indudable *adj* undoubted

indulgen|cia *f* indulgence. **~te** *adj* indulgent

indult|ar *vt* pardon. **~o** *m* pardon

industria *f* industry. **~l** *adj* industrial. ● *m & f* industrialist. **~lización** *f* industrialization. **~lizar** [10] *vt* industrialize

inédito *adj* unpublished; (*fig*) unknown

inefable *adj* indescribable

ineficaz *adj* ineffective; (*sistema etc*) inefficient

ineficiente *adj* inefficient

ineludible *adj* inescapable, unavoidable

inept|itud *f* ineptitude. **~o** *adj* inept

inequívoco *adj* unequivocal

inercia *f* inertia

inerte *adj* inert; (*sin vida*) lifeless

inesperado adj unexpected

inestable adj unstable

inestimable adj inestimable

inevitable adj inevitable

inexistente adj non-existent

inexorable adj inexorable

inexper|iencia f inexperience. ~to adj inexperienced

inexplicable adj inexplicable

infalible adj infallible

infam|ar vt defame. ~atorio adj defamatory. ~e adj infamous; (fig, fam, muy malo) awful. ~ia f infamy

infancia f infancy

infant|a f infanta, princess. ~e m infante, prince. ~ería f infantry. ~il adj children's; (población) child; (actitud etc) childish, infantile

infarto m heart attack

infec|ción f infection. ~cioso adj infectious. ~tar vt infect. ~tarse vpr become infected. ~to adj infected; ⊺ disgusting

infeli|cidad f unhappiness. ~z adj unhappy

inferior adj inferior. ● m & f inferior. ~idad f inferiority

infernal adj infernal, hellish

infestar vt infest; (fig) inundate

infi|delidad f unfaithfulness. ~el adj unfaithful

infierno m hell

infiltra|ción f infiltration. ~rse vpr infiltrate

ínfimo adj lowest; (calidad) very poor

infini|dad f infinity. ~tivo m infinitive. ~to adj infinite. ● m. el ~to the infinite; (en matemáticas) infinity. ~dad de countless

inflación f inflation

inflama|ble adj (in)flammable.

~ción f inflammation. ~r vt set on fire; (fig, Med) inflame. ~rse vpr catch fire; (Med) become inflamed

inflar vt inflate; blow up (globo); (fig, exagerar) exaggerate

inflexi|ble adj inflexible. ~ón f inflexion

influ|encia f influence (en on). ~ir 17 vt influence. ● vi. ~ en influence. ~jo m influence. ~yente adj influential

informa|ción f information; (noticias) news; (en aeropuerto etc) information desk; (de teléfonos) directory enquiries. ~dor m informant

informal adj informal; (persona) unreliable

inform|ante m & f informant. ~ar vt/i inform. ~arse vpr find out. ~ática f information technology, computing. ~ativo adj informative; (programa) news. ~atizar 10 vt computerize

informe adj shapeless. ● m report. ~s fpl references, information

infracción f infringement. ~ de tráfico traffic offence

infraestructura f infrastructure

infranqueable adj impassable; (fig) insuperable

infrarrojo adj infrared

infringir 14 vt infringe

infructuoso adj fruitless

ínfulas fpl. darse ~ give o.s. airs. tener ~ de fancy o.s. as

infundado adj unfounded

infu|ndir vt instil. ~sión f infusion

ingeni|ar vt invent. ~árselas para find a way to

ingenier|ía f engineering. ~o m engineer

ingenio m ingenuity; (*agudeza*) wit; (LAm, de azúcar) refinery. **~so** adj ingenious

ingenu|idad f naivety. **~o** adj naïve

Inglaterra f England

ingl|és adj English. ● m Englishman; (*lengua*) English. **~esa** f Englishwoman. **los ~eses** the English

ingrat|itud f ingratitude. **~o** adj ungrateful; (*desagradable*) thankless

ingrediente m ingredient

ingres|ar vt deposit. ● vi. **~ar en** come in, enter; join (sociedad). **~o** m entrance; (de dinero) deposit; (en sociedad, hospital) admission. **~os** mpl income

inh|ábil adj unskilful; (no apto) unfit. **~abilidad** f unskilfulness; (para cargo) ineligibility

inhabitable adj uninhabitable

inhala|dor m inhaler. **~r** vt inhale

inherente adj inherent

inhibi|ción f inhibition. **~r** vt inhibit

inhóspito adj inhospitable

inhumano adj inhuman

inici|ación f beginning. **~al** adj & f initial. **~ar** vt initiate; (comenzar) begin, start. **~ativa** f initiative. **~o** m beginning

inigualado adj unequalled

ininterrumpido adj uninterrupted

injert|ar vt graft. **~to** m graft

injuri|a f insult. **~ar** vt insult. **~oso** adj insulting

injust|icia f injustice. **~o** adj unjust, unfair

inmaculado adj immaculate

inmaduro adj unripe; (persona) immature

inmediaciones fpl. **las ~** the vicinity, the surrounding area

inmediat|amente adv immediately. **~o** adj immediate; (contiguo) next. **de ~o** immediately

inmejorable adj excellent

inmemorable adj immemorial

inmens|idad f immensity. **~o** adj immense

inmersión f immersion

inmigra|ción f immigration. **~nte** adj & m & f immigrant. **~r** vt immigrate

inminen|cia f imminence. **~te** adj imminent

inmiscuirse 17 vpr interfere

inmobiliario adj property

inmolar vt sacrifice

inmoral adj immoral. **~idad** f immorality

inmortal adj immortal. **~izar** 10 vt immortalize

inmóvil adj immobile

inmovilizador m immobilizer

inmueble adj. **bienes ~s** property

inmund|icia f filth. **~o** adj filthy

inmun|e adj immune. **~idad** f immunity. **~ización** f immunization. **~izar** 10 vt immunize

inmuta|ble adj unchangeable. **~rse** vpr be perturbed. **sin ~rse** unperturbed

innato adj innate

innecesario adj unnecessary

innegable adj undeniable

innova|ción f innovation. **~r** vi innovate. ● vt make innovations in

innumerable adj innumerable

inocen|cia f innocence. **~tada** f practical joke. **~te** adj innocent. **~tón** adj naïve

inocuo adj innocuous

inodoro adj odourless. • m toilet

inofensivo adj inoffensive

inolvidable adj unforgettable

inoperable adj inoperable

inoportuno adj untimely; (comentario) ill-timed

inoxidable adj stainless

inquiet|ar vt worry. **~arse** vpr get worried. **~o** adj worried; (agitado) restless. **~ud** f anxiety

inquilino m tenant

inquirir [4] vt enquire into, investigate

insaciable adj insatiable

insalubre adj unhealthy

insatisfecho adj unsatisfied; (descontento) dissatisfied

inscri|bir (pp inscrito) vt (en registro) register; (en curso) enrol; (grabar) inscribe. **~birse** vpr register. **~pción** f inscription; (registro) registration

insect|icida m insecticide. **~o** m insect

insegur|idad f insecurity. **~o** adj insecure; (ciudad) unsafe, dangerous

insemina|ción f insemination. **~r** vt inseminate

insensato adj foolish

insensible adj insensitive

inseparable adj inseparable

insertar vt insert

insidi|a f malice. **~oso** adj insidious

insigne adj famous

insignia f badge; (bandera) flag

insignificante adj insignificant

insinua|ción f insinuation. **~ante** adj insinuating. **~r** [21] vt imply; insinuate (algo ofensivo). **~rse** vpr. **~rsele a** make a pass at

insípido adj insipid

insist|encia f insistence. **~ente** adj insistent. **~ir** vi insist; (hacer hincapié) stress

insolación f sunstroke

insolen|cia f rudeness, insolence. **~te** adj rude, insolent

insólito adj unusual

insolven|cia f insolvency. **~te** adj a & f insolvent

insomn|e adj sleepless. • m & f insomniac. **~io** m insomnia

insondable adj unfathomable

insoportable adj unbearable

insospechado adj unexpected

insostenible adj untenable

inspec|ción f inspection. **~cionar** vt inspect. **~tor** m inspector

inspira|ción f inspiration. **~r** vt inspire. **~rse** vpr be inspired

instala|ción f installation. **~r** vt install. **~rse** vpr settle

instancia f request. en última **~** as a last resort

instant|ánea f snapshot. **~áneo** adj instantaneous; (café etc) instant. **~e** m instant. a cada **~e** constantly. al **~e** immediately

instaura|ción f establishment. **~r** vt establish

instiga|ción f instigation. **~dor** m instigator. **~r** [12] vt instigate; (incitar) incite

instint|ivo adj instinctive. **~o** m instinct

institu|ción f institution. **~cional** adj institutional. **~ir** [17] vt establish. **~to** m institute; (en enseñanza) (secondary) school. **~triz** f governess

instru|cción f education; (Mil) training. **~cciones** fpl instruction. **~ctivo** adj instructive; (película etc) educational. **~ctor** m instructor. **~ir** ⓱ vt instruct, teach; (Mil) train

instrument|ación f instrumentation. **~al** adj instrumental. **~o** m instrument; (herramienta) tool

insubordina|ción f insubordination. **~r** vt stir up. **~rse** vpr rebel

insuficien|cia f insufficiency; (inadecuación) inadequacy. **~te** adj insufficient

insufrible adj insufferable

insular adj insular

insulina f insulin

insulso adj tasteless; (fig) insipid

insult|ar vt insult. **~o** m insult

insuperable adj insuperable; (inmejorable) unbeatable

insurgente adj insurgent

insurrec|ción f insurrection. **~to** adj insurgent

intachable adj irreproachable

intacto adj intact

intangible adj intangible

integra|ción f integration. **~l** adj integral; (completo) complete; (incorporado) built-in; (pan) wholemeal (Brit), wholewheat (Amer). **~r** vt make up

integridad f integrity; (entereza) wholeness

íntegro adj complete; (fig) upright

intelect|o m intellect. **~ual** adj & m & f intellectual

inteligen|cia f intelligence. **~te** adj intelligent

inteligible adj intelligible

intemperie f. a la **~** in the open

intempestivo adj untimely

intenci|ón f intention. con doble **~ón** implying sth else. **~onado** adj deliberate. bien **~onado** well-meaning. mal **~onado** malicious.

~onal adj intentional

intens|idad f intensity. **~ificar** ⑦ vt intensify. **~ivo** adj intensive. **~o** adj intense

intent|ar vt try. **~o** m attempt; (Mex, propósito) intention

inter|calar vt insert. **~cambio** m exchange. **~ceder** vt intercede

interceptar vt intercept

interdicto m ban

inter|és m interest; (egoísmo) self-interest. **~esado** adj interested; (parcial) biassed; (egoísta) selfish. **~esante** adj interesting. **~esar** vt interest; (afectar) concern. **~esarse** vpr take an interest (por in)

interfaz m & f interface

interfer|encia f interference. **~ir** ④ vi interfere

interfono m intercom

interino adj temporary; (persona) acting. ● m stand-in

interior adj interior; (comercio etc) domestic. ● m inside. Ministerio del I **~** Interior Ministry

interjección f interjection

inter|locutor m speaker. **~mediario** adj & m intermediary. **~medio** adj intermediate. ● m interval

interminable adj interminable

intermitente adj intermittent. ● m indicator

internacional adj international

intern|ado m (Escol) boarding-school. **~ar** vt (en manicomio) commit; (en hospital) admit. **~arse** vpr penetrate

internauta m & f netsurfer

Internet m Internet

interno adj internal; (en enseñanza) boarding. ● m boarder

interponer 34 *vt* interpose. ~se *vpr* intervene

int|erpretación *f* interpretation. ~erpretar *vt* interpret; (*Mús etc*) play. ~érprete *m* interpreter; (*Mus*) performer

interroga|ción *f* interrogation; (*signo*) question mark. ~r 12 *vt* question. ~tivo *adj* interrogative

interru|mpir *vt* interrupt; cut off (*suministro*); cut short (*viaje etc*); block (*tráfico*). ~pción *f* interruption. ~ptor *m* switch

inter|sección *f* intersection. ~urbano *adj* inter-city; (*llamada*) long-distance

intervalo *m* interval; (*espacio*) space. a ~s at intervals

interven|ir 53 *vt* control; (*Med*) operate on. ● *vi* intervene; (*participar*) take part. ~tor *m* inspector; (*Com*) auditor

intestino *m* intestine

intim|ar *vi* become friendly. ~idad *f* intimacy

intimidar *vt* intimidate

íntimo *adj* intimate; (*amigo*) close. ● *m* close friend

intolera|ble *adj* intolerable. ~nte *adj* intolerant

intoxicar 7 *vt* poison

intranquilo *adj* worried

intransigente *adj* intransigent

intransitable *adj* impassable

intransitivo *adj* intransitive

intratable *adj* impossible

intrépido *adj* intrepid

intriga *f* intrigue. ~nte *adj* intriguing. ~r 12 *vt* intrigue

intrincado *adj* intricate

intrínseco *adj* intrinsic

introduc|ción *f* introduction. ~r 47 *vt* introduce; (*meter*) insert.

~irse *vpr* get into

intromisión *f* interference

introvertido *adj* introverted. ● *m* introvert

intruso *m* intruder

intui|ción *f* intuition. ~r 17 *vt* sense. ~tivo *adj* intuitive

inunda|ción *f* flooding. ~r 1 *vt* flood

inusitado *adj* unusual

in|útil *adj* useless; (*vano*) futile. ~utilidad *f* uselessness

invadir *vt* invade

inv|alidez *f* invalidity; (*Med*) disability. ~álido *adj* & *m* invalid

invariable *adj* invariable

invas|ión *f* invasion. ~or *adj* invading. ● *m* invader

invencible *adj* invincible

inven|ción *f* invention. ~tar *vt* invent

inventario *m* inventory

invent|iva *f* inventiveness. ~ivo *adj* inventive. ~or *m* inventor

invernadero *m* greenhouse

invernal *adj* winter

inverosímil *adj* implausible

inver|sión *f* inversion; (*Com*) investment. ~sionista *m* & *f* investor

inverso *adj* inverse; (*contrario*) opposite. a la inversa the other way round. a la inversa de contrary to

inversor *m* investor

invertir 4 *vt* reverse; (*Com*) invest; put in (*tiempo*)

investidura *f* investiture

investiga|ción *f* investigation; (*Univ*) research. ~dor *m* investigator; (*Univ*) researcher. ~r 12 *vt* investigate; (*Univ*) research

investir 5 *vt* invest

invicto *adj* unbeaten

invierno *m* winter

inviolable *adj* inviolate

invisible *adj* invisible

invita|ción *f* invitation. **~do** *m* guest. **~r** *vt* invite. **te invito a una copa** I'll buy you a drink

invocar **7** *vt* invoke

involuntario *adj* involuntary

invulnerable *adj* invulnerable

inyec|ción *f* injection. **~tar** *vt* inject

---

ir **49**

● *verbo intransitivo*

····▷ to go. **fui a verla** I went to see her. **ir a pie** to go on foot. **ir en coche** to go by car. **vamos a casa** let's go home. **fue (a) por el pan** he went to get some bread

! Cuando la acción del verbo **ir** significa trasladarse hacia o con el interlocutor la traducción es *to come*, p.ej: **¡ya voy!** *I'm coming!* **yo voy contigo** *I'll come with you*

····▷ *(estar)* to be. **iba con su novio** she was with her boyfriend. **¿cómo te va?** how are you?

····▷ *(sentar)* to suit. **ese color no le va** that colour doesn't suit her. **no me va ni me viene** I don't mind at all

····▷ *(Méx, apoyar)* **irle a** to support. **le va al equipo local** he supports the local team

····▷ *(en exclamaciones)* **¡vamos!** come on! **¡vaya!** what a surprise!; *(contrariedad)* oh, dear! **¡vaya noche!** what a night!

¡qué va! nonsense!

➡ Cuando el verbo intransitivo se emplea con expresiones como **ir de paseo, ir de compras, ir tirando** etc., ver bajo el respectivo nombre, verbo etc.

● *verbo auxiliar*

····▷ **ir a** + *infinitivo* (*para expresar futuro, propósito*) to be going to + *infinitive*; *(al prevenir)* **no te vayas a caer** be careful you don't fall. **no vaya a ser que llueva** in case it rains; *(en sugerencias)* **vamos a dormir** let's go to sleep. **vamos a ver** let's see

····▷ **ir** + *gerundio*. **ve arreglándote** start getting ready. **el tiempo va mejorando** the weather is gradually getting better.

● *irse verbo pronominal*

····▷ to go. **se ha ido a casa** he's gone home

····▷ *(marcharse)* to leave. **se fue sin despedirse** he left without saying goodbye. **se fue de casa** she left home

---

ira *f* anger. **~cundo** *adj* irascible

Irak *m* Iraq

Irán *m* Iran

iraní *adj & m & f* Iranian

iraquí *adj & m & f* Iraqi

iris *m (del ojo)* iris

Irlanda *f* Ireland

irland|és *adj* Irish. ● *m* Irishman; *(lengua)* Irish. **~esa** *f* Irishwoman. **los ~eses** the Irish

ir|onía *f* irony. **~ónico** *adj* ironic

irracional *adj* irrational

irradiar vt radiate

irreal adj unreal. ~**idad** f unreality

irrealizable adj unattainable

irreconciliable adj irreconcilable

irreconocible adj unrecogniz-able

irrecuperable adj irretrievable

irreflexión f impetuosity

irregular adj irregular. ~**idad** f ir-regularity

irreparable adj irreparable

irreprimible adj irrepressible

irreprochable adj irreproachable

irresistible adj irresistible

irrespetuoso adj disrespectful

irresponsable adj irresponsible

irriga|ción f irrigation. ~**r** 🔟 vt irrigate

irrisorio adj derisory

irrita|ble adj irritable. ~**ción** f ir-ritation. ~**r** vt irritate. ~**rse** vpr get annoyed

irrumpir vi burst (en in)

isla f island. las I~s Británicas the British Isles

islámico adj Islamic

islandés adj Icelandic. • m Ice-lander; (lengua) Icelandic

Islandia f Iceland

isleño adj island. • m islander

Israel m Israel

israelí adj & m Israeli

Italia f Italy

italiano adj & m Italian

itinerario adj itinerary

IVA abrev (impuesto sobre el valor agregado (LAm), impuesto sobre el valor añadido) VAT

izar 🔟 vt hoist

izquierd|a f. la ~**a** the left hand; (Pol) left. a la ~**a** on the left; (con movimiento) to the left. de ~**a**

left-wing. ~**ista** m & f leftist. ~**o** adj left

Jj

ja int ha!

jabalí m (pl ~es) wild boar

jabalina f javelin

jab|ón m soap. ~**onar** vt soap. ~**onoso** adj soapy

jaca f pony

jacinto m hyacinth

jactarse vpr boast

jadea|nte adj panting. ~**r** vi pant

jaguar m jaguar

jaiba f (LAm) crab

jalar vt (LAm) pull

jalea f jelly

jaleo m row, uproar. armar un ~ kick up a fuss

jalón m (LAm, tirón) pull; (Mex fam trago) drink; (Mex, tramo) stretch

jamás adv never. nunca ~ never ever

jamelgo m nag

jamón m ham. ~ de York boiled ham. ~ serrano cured ham

Japón m. el ~ Japan

japonés adj & m Japanese

jaque m check. ~ mate check-mate

jaqueca f migraine

jarabe m syrup

jardín m garden. ~ de la infan-cia, (Mex) ~ de niños kindergar-ten, nursery school

jardiner|ía f gardening. ~**o** m gardener

jarr|a f jug. en ~as with hands on hips. ~o m jug. caer como un ~o de agua fría come as a shock. ~ón m vase

jaula f cage

jauría f pack of hounds

jazmín m jasmine

jef|a f boss. ~atura f leadership; (sede) headquarters. ~e m boss; (Pol etc) leader. ~e de camareros head waiter. ~e de estación station-master. ~e de ventas sales manager

jengibre m ginger

jer|arquía f hierarchy. ~árquico adj hierarchical

jerez m sherry. al ~ with sherry

jerez Sherry is produced in an area around Jerez de la Frontera near Cádiz. Sherries are drunk worldwide as an aperitif, and in Spain as an accompaniment to tapas. The main types are: the pale *fino* and *manzanilla* and the darker *oloroso* and *amontillado*. It is from *Jerez* that sherry takes its English name.

jerga f coarse cloth; (argot) jargon

jerigonza f jargon; (galimatías) gibberish

jeringa f syringe; (LAm fam, molestia) nuisance. ~r 12 vt (fig, fam, molestar) annoy

jeroglífico m hieroglyph(ic)

jersey m (pl ~s) jersey

Jesucristo m Jesus Christ. antes de ~ BC, before Christ

jesuita adj & m Jesuit

Jesús m Jesus. • int good heavens!; (al estornudar) bless you!

jícara f (Mex) gourd

jilguero m goldfinch

jinete m & f rider

jipijapa m panama hat

jirafa f giraffe

jirón m shred, tatter

jitomate m (Mex) tomato

jorna|da f working day; (viaje) journey; (etapa) stage. ~l m day's wage. ~lero m day labourer

joroba f hump. ~do adj hunchbacked. • m hunchback. ~r vt 🗓 annoy

jota f letter J; (danza) jota, popular dance. ni ~ nothing

joven (pl jóvenes) adj young. • m young man. • f young woman

jovial adj jovial

joy|a f jewel. ~as fpl jewellery. ~ería f jeweller's (shop). ~ero m jeweller; (estuche) jewellery box

juanete m bunion

jubil|ación f retirement. ~ado adj retired. ~ar vt pension off. ~arse vpr retire. ~eo m jubilee

júbilo m joy

judaísmo m Judaism

judía f Jewish woman; (alubia) bean. ~ blanca haricot bean. ~ escarlata runner bean. ~ verde French bean

judicial adj judicial

judío adj Jewish. • m Jewish man

judo m judo

juego m play; (de mesa, niños) game; (de azar) gambling; (conjunto) set. estar en ~ be at stake. estar fuera de ~ be offside. hacer ~ match. ~s mpl malabares juggling. J~s mpl Olímpicos Olympic Games. • vb véase JUGAR

juerga f spree

jueves m invar Thursday

juez m judge. ~ de instrucción examining magistrate. ~ de línea linesman

juga|dor m player; (habitual, por dinero) gambler. **~r** 3 vt play. ●vi play; (apostar fuerte) gamble. **~rse** vpr risk. **~r al fútbol**, (LAm) **~r fútbol** play football

juglar m minstrel

jugo m juice; (de carne) gravy; (fig) substance. **~so** adj juicy; (fig) substantial

juguet|e m toy. **~ear** vi play. **~ón** adj playful

juicio m judgement; (opinión) opinion; (razón) reason. **a mi ~** in my opinion. **~so** adj wise

juliana f vegetable soup

julio m July

junco m rush, reed

jungla f jungle

junio m June

junt|a f meeting; (consejo) board, committee; (Pol) junta; (Tec) joint. **~ar** vt join; (reunir) collect. **~arse** vpr join; (gente) meet. **~o** adj joined; (en plural) together. **~o a** next to. **~ura** f joint

jura|do adj sworn. ● m jury; (miembro de jurado) juror. **~mento** m oath. **prestar ~mento** take an oath. **~r** vt/i swear. **~r en falso** commit perjury. **jurárselas a uno** have it in for s.o.

jurel m (type of) mackerel

jurídico adj legal

juris|dicción f jurisdiction. **~prudencia** f jurisprudence

justamente adj exactly; (con justicia) fairly

justicia f justice

justifica|ción f justification. **~r** 7 vt justify

justo adj fair, just; (exacto) exact;

(ropa) tight. ● adv just. **~ a tiempo** just in time

juven|il adj youthful. **~tud** f youth; (gente joven) young people

juzga|do m (tribunal) court. **~r** 12 vt judge. **a ~r por** judging by

Kk

kilo m, **kilogramo** m kilo, kilogram

kil|ometraje m distance in kilometres, mileage. **~ométrico** adj 1 endless. **~ómetro** m kilometre. **~ómetro cuadrado** square kilometre

kilovatio m kilowatt

kiosco m kiosk

Ll

la artículo definido femenino (pl **las**)

····▶ the. **la flor azul** the blue flower. **la casa de al lado** the house next door. **cerca de la iglesia** near the church No se traduce en los siguientes casos:

····▶ (con nombre abstracto, genérico) **la paciencia es una virtud** patience is a virtue. **odio la leche** I hate milk. **la madera es muy versátil** wood is very versatile

····▶ (con algunas instituciones)

termino la universidad mañana I finish university tomorrow. no va nunca a la iglesia he never goes to church. está en la cárcel he's in jail

····▸ (con nombres propios) la Sra. Díaz Mrs Díaz. la doctora Lara doctor Lara

····▸ (con partes del cuerpo, artículos personales) se traduce por un posesivo. apretó la mano le clenched his fist. tienes la camisa desabrochada your shirt is undone

····▸ la + de. es la de Ana it's Ana's. la del sombrero the one with the hat

····▸ la + que (persona) la que me atendió the one who served me. (cosa) la que se rompió the one that broke

····▸ la + que + subjuntivo (quienquiera) whoever. la que gane pasará a la final whoever wins will go to the final. (cualquiera) whichever. compra la que sea más barata buy whichever is cheaper

laberinto m labyrinth, maze
labia f gift of the gab
labio m lip
labor f work. ~es de aguja needlework. ~es de ganchillo crochet. ~es de punto knitting. ~es domésticas housework. ~able adj working. ~ar vi work
laboratorio m laboratory
laborioso adj laborious
laborista adj Labour. ● m & f member of the Labour Party
labra|do adj worked; (madera) carved; (metal) wrought; (tierra)

ploughed. ~**dor** m farmer; (obrero) farm labourer. ~**nza** f farming. ~**r** vt work; carve (madera); cut (piedra); till (la tierra). ~**rse** vpr. ~**rse** un porvenir carve out a future for o.s.
labriego m peasant
laca f lacquer
lacayo m lackey
lacio adj straight; (flojo) limp
lacón m shoulder of pork
lacónico adj laconic
lacr|ar vt seal. ~**e** m sealing wax
lactante adj (niño) still on milk
lácteo adj milky. **productos** mpl ~**s** dairy products
ladear vt tilt. ~**se** vpr lean
ladera f slope
ladino adj astute
lado m side. **al** ~ near. **al** ~ **de** next to, beside. **de** ~ sideways. **en todos** ~**s** everywhere. **los de** ~ the next door neighbours. **por otro** ~ on the other hand. **por todos** ~**s** everywhere. **por un** ~ on the one hand
ladr|ar vi bark. ~**ido** m bark
ladrillo m brick
ladrón m thief, robber; (de casas) burglar
lagart|ija f (small) lizard. ~**o** m lizard
lago m lake
lágrima f tear
lagrimoso adj tearful
laguna f small lake; (fig, omisión) gap
laico adj lay
lament|able adj deplorable; (que da pena) pitiful; (pérdida) sad. ~**ar** vt be sorry about. ~**arse** vpr lament; (quejarse) complain. ~**o** m moan

lamer vt lick

lámina f sheet; (ilustración) plate; (estampa) picture card

lamina|do adj laminated. ~r vt laminate

lámpara f lamp. ~ de pie standard lamp

lamparón m stain

lampiño adj beardless; (cuerpo) hairless

lana f wool. de ~ wool(len)

lanceta f lancet

lancha f boat. ~ motora motor boat. ~ salvavidas lifeboat

langost|a f (de mar) lobster; (insecto) locust. ~ino m king prawn

languide|cer 11 vi languish. ~z f languor

lánguido adj languid; (decaído) listless

lanilla f nap; (tela fina) flannel

lanudo adj woolly; (perro) shaggy

lanza f lance, spear

lanza|llamas m invar flamethrower. ~miento m throw; (acción de lanzar) throwing; (de proyectil, de producto) launch. ~miento de peso, (LAm) ~miento de bala shot put. ~r 1 vt throw; (de un avión) drop; launch (proyectil, producto). ~rse vpr throw o.s.

lapicero m (propelling) pencil

lápida f tombstone; (placa conmemorativa) memorial tablet

lapidar vt stone

lápiz m pencil. ~ de labios lipstick. a ~ in pencil

lapso m lapse

laptop m laptop

larg|a f. a la ~a in the long run. dar ~as put off. ~ar 12 vt (Naut) let out; (fam, dar) give; 1 deal

(bofetada etc). ~arse vpr 1 beat it 1. ~o adj long. ● m length. ¡~o! go away! a lo ~o lengthwise. a lo ~o de along. tener 100 metros de ~o be 100 metres long

laring|e f larynx. ~itis f laryngitis

larva f larva

las artículo definido fpl the. véase tb **LA**. ● pron them. ~ de those, the ones. ~ de Vd your ones, yours. ~ que whoever, the ones

láser m laser

lástima f pity; (queja) complaint. da ~ verlo así it's sad to see him like that. ella me da ~ I feel sorry for her. ¡qué ~! what a pity!

lastim|ado adj hurt. ~ar vt hurt. ~arse vpr hurt o.s. ~ero adj doleful. ~oso adj pitiful

lastre m ballast; (fig) burden

lata f tinplate; (envase) tin (esp Brit), can; (fam, molestia) nuisance. dar la ~ be a nuisance. ¡qué ~! what a nuisance!

latente adj latent

lateral adj side, lateral

latido m beating; (cada golpe) beat

latifundio m large estate

latigazo m (golpe) lash; (chasquido) crack

látigo m whip

latín m Latin. saber ~ 1 know what's what 1

latino adj Latin. L~américa f Latin America. ~americano adj & m Latin American

latir vi beat; (herida) throb

latitud f latitude

latón m brass

latoso adj annoying; (pesado) boring

laúd m lute

laureado adj honoured; (premiado) prize-winning

laurel m laurel; (Culin) bay

lava f lava

lava|ble adj washable. ∼**bo** m wash-basin; (retrete) toilet. ∼**dero** m sink. ∼**do** m washing. ∼**do de cerebro** brainwashing. ∼**do en seco** dry-cleaning. ●m (Mex, fregadero) sink. ∼**dora** f washing machine. ∼**ndería** f laundry. ∼**ndería automática** launderette, laundromat (esp Amer). ∼**platos** m & f invar dishwasher. ∼**r** vt wash. ∼**r en seco** dry-clean. ∼**rse** vpr have a wash. ∼**rse las manos** (incl fig) wash one's hands. ∼**tiva** f enema. ∼**vajillas** m invar dishwasher; (detergente) washing-up liquid (Brit), dishwashing liquid (Amer)

laxante adj & m laxative

lazada f bow

lazarillo m guide for a blind person

lazo m knot; (lazada) bow; (fig, vínculo) tie; (con nudo corredizo) lasso; (Mex, cuerda) rope

le pron (acusativo, él) him; (acusativo, Vd) you; (dativo, él) (to) him; (dativo, ella) (to) her; (dativo, cosa) (to) it; (dativo, Vd) (to) you

leal adj loyal; (fiel) faithful. ∼**tad** f loyalty; (fidelidad) faithfulness

lección f lesson

leche f milk; (golpe) bash. ∼ **condensada** condensed milk. ∼ **desnatada** skimmed milk. ∼ **en polvo** powdered milk. ∼ **sin desnatar** whole milk. **tener mala** ∼ be spiteful. ∼**ra** f (vasija) milk jug. ∼**ría** f dairy. ∼**ro** adj milk; dairy. ●m milkman

lecho m (en literatura) bed. ∼ **de**

río river bed

lechoso adj milky

lechuga f lettuce

lechuza f owl

lect|or m reader; (Univ) language assistant. ∼**ura** f reading

leer 18 vt/i read

legación f legation

legado m legacy; (enviado) legate

legajo m bundle, file

legal adj legal. ∼**idad** f legality. ∼**izar** 10 vt legalize; (certificar) authenticate. ∼**mente** adv legally

legar 12 vt bequeath

legible adj legible

legi|ón f legion. ∼**onario** m legionary. ∼**onella** f legionnaire's disease

legisla|ción f legislation. ∼**dor** m legislator. ∼**r** vi legislate. ∼**tura** f term (of office); (año parlamentario) session; (LAm, cuerpo) legislature

leg|itimidad f legitimacy. ∼**ítimo** adj legitimate; (verdadero) real

lego adj lay; (ignorante) ignorant. ●m layman

legua f league

legumbre f vegetable

lejan|ía f distance. ∼**o** adj distant

lejía f bleach

lejos adv far. ∼ **de** far from. **a lo** ∼ in the distance. **desde** ∼ from a distance, from afar

lema m motto

lencería f linen; (de mujer) lingerie

lengua f tongue; (idioma) language. **irse de la** ∼ talk too much. **morderse la** ∼ hold one's tongue

lenguado *m* sole
lenguaje *m* language
lengüeta *f* (*de zapato*) tongue.
~**da** *f*, ~**zo** *m* lick
lente *f* lens. ~**s** *mpl* glasses. ~**s de
contacto** contact lenses
lentej|a *f* lentil. ~**uela** *f* sequin
lentilla *f* contact lens
lent|itud *f* slowness. ~**o** *adj* slow
leña *f* firewood. ~**ador** *m* wood-
cutter. ~**o** *m* log
Leo *m* Leo
le|ón *m* lion. ~**ona** *f* lioness
leopardo *m* leopard
leotardo *m* thick tights
lepr|a *f* leprosy. ~**oso** *m* leper
lerdo *adj* dim; (*torpe*) clumsy
les *pron* (*acusativo*) them; (*acusativo,
Vds*) you; (*dativo*) (to) them; (*dativo, Vds*) (to) you
lesbiana *f* lesbian
lesi|ón *f* wound. ~**onado** *adj* in-
jured. ~**onar** *vt* injure; (*dañar*)
damage
letal *adj* lethal
let|árgico *adj* lethargic. ~**argo** *m*
lethargy
letr|a *f* letter; (*escritura*) handwrit-
ing; (*de una canción*) words, lyrics.
~**a de cambio** bill of exchange.
~**a de imprenta** print. ~**ado** *adj*

learned. ~**ero** *m* notice; (*cartel*)
poster
letrina *f* latrine
leucemia *f* leukaemia
levadura *f* yeast. ~ **en polvo**
baking powder
levanta|miento *m* lifting; (*su-
blevación*) uprising. ~**r** *vt* raise, lift;
(*construir*) build; (*recoger*) pick up.
~**rse** *vpr* get up; (*ponerse de pie*)
stand up; (*erguirse, sublevarse*)
rise up
levante *m* east; (*viento*) east wind
levar *vt*. ~ **anclas** weigh anchor
leve *adj* light; (*sospecha etc*) slight;
(*enfermedad*) mild; (*de poca importancia*) trivial. ~**dad** *f* lightness;
(*fig*) slightness
léxico *m* vocabulary
lexicografía *f* lexicography
ley *f* law; (*parlamentaria*) act
leyenda *f* legend
liar 20 *vt* tie; (*envolver*) wrap up;
roll (*cigarrillo*); (*fig, confundir*) confuse; (*fig, enredar*) involve. ~**se** *vpr*
get involved
libanés *adj & m* Lebanese
libelo *m* (*escrito*) libellous article;
(*Jurid*) petition
libélula *f* dragonfly
libera|ción *f* liberation. ~**dor** *adj*
liberating. ● *m* liberator
liberal *adj & m & f* liberal. ~**idad** *f*
liberality
liber|ar *vt* free. ~**tad** *f* freedom.
~**tad de cultos** freedom of worship. ~**tad de imprenta** freedom
of the press. ~**tad provisional**
bail. ~**tad** free. ~**tador** *m* liberator. ~**tar** *vt* free
libertino *m* libertine
libido *f* libido
libio *adj & m* Libyan

libra f pound. ~ **esterlina** pound sterling

Libra m Libra

libra|dor m (Com) drawer. ~**r** vt free; (de un peligro) save. ~**rse** vpr free o.s. ~**rse de** get rid of

libre adj free. **estilo** ~ (en natación) freestyle. ~ **de impuestos** tax-free

librea f livery

libr|ería f bookshop (Brit), bookstore (Amer); (mueble) bookcase. ~**ero** m bookseller; (Mex, mueble) bookcase. ~**eta** f notebook. ~**o** m book. ~**o de bolsillo** paperback. ~**o de ejercicios** exercise book. ~**o de reclamaciones** complaints book

licencia f permission; (documento) licence. ~**do** m graduate; (Mex, abogado) lawyer. ~ **para manejar** (Mex) driving licence. ~**r** vt (Mil) discharge; (echar) dismiss. ~**tura** f degree

licencioso adj licentious

licitar vt bid for

lícito adj legal; (permisible) permissible

licor m liquor; (dulce) liqueur

licua|dora f blender. ~**r** 21 liquefy; (Culin) blend

lid f fight. **en buena** ~ by fair means. ~**es** fpl matters

líder m leader

liderato m, **liderazgo** f leadership

lidia f bullfighting; (lucha) fight. ~**r** vt/i fight

liebre f hare

lienzo m linen; (del pintor) canvas; (muro, pared) wall

liga f garter; (alianza) league; (LAm, gomita) rubber band. ~**dura** f bond; (Mus) slur; (Med) ligature.

~**mento** m ligament. ~**r** 12 vt bind; (atar) tie; (Mus) slur. ● vi mix. ~**r con** (fig) pick up. ~**rse** vpr (fig) commit o.s.

liger|eza f lightness; (agilidad) agility; (rapidez) swiftness; (de carácter) fickleness. ~**o** adj light; (rápido) quick; (ágil) agile; (superficial) superficial; (de poca importancia) slight. ● adv quickly. **a la** ~**a** lightly, superficially

liguero m suspender belt

lija f dogfish; (papel de lija) sandpaper. ~**r** vt sand

lila f lilac. ● m (color) lilac

lima f file; (fruta) lime. ~**duras** fpl filings. ~**r** vt file (down)

limita|ción f limitation. ~**do** adj limited. ~**r** vt limit. ~**r con** border on. ~**tivo** adj limiting

límite m limit. ~ **de velocidad** speed limit

limítrofe adj bordering

lim|ón m lemon; (Mex) lime. ~**onada** f lemonade

limosn|a f alms. **pedir** ~**a** beg. ~**ear** vi beg

limpia|botas m invar bootblack. ~**parabrisas** m invar windscreen wiper (Brit), windshield wiper (Amer). ~**pipas** m invar pipe-cleaner. ~**r** vt clean; (enjugar) wipe. ~**vidrios** m invar (LAm) window cleaner

limpi|eza f cleanliness; (acción de limpiar) cleaning. ~**eza en seco** dry-cleaning. ~**o** adj clean; (cielo) clear; (fig, honrado) honest; (neto) net. **pasar a** ~**o**, (LAm) **pasar en** ~**o** make a fair copy. ● adv fairly. **jugar** ~**o** play fair

linaje m lineage; (fig, clase) kind

lince m lynx

linchar vt lynch

lind|ar vi border (con on). ~**e** f

boundary. **~ero** m border
lindo adj pretty, lovely. **de lo ~** 🔢 a lot
línea f line. **en ~** online. **en ~s generales** broadly speaking. **guardar la ~** watch one's figure
lingote m ingot
lingü|ista m & f linguist. **~ística** f linguistics. **~ístico** adj linguistic
lino m flax; (*tela*) linen
linterna f lantern; (*de bolsillo*) torch, flashlight (*Amer*)
lío m bundle; (*jaleo*) fuss; (*embrollo*) muddle; (*amorío*) affair
liquida|ción f liquidation; (*venta especial*) sale. **~r** vt liquify; (*Com*) liquidate; settle (*cuenta*)
líquido adj liquid; (*Com*) net. ● m liquid; (*Com*) cash
lira f lyre; (*moneda italiana*) lira
líric|a f lyric poetry. **~o** adj lyric(al)
lirio m iris
lirón m dormouse; (*fig*) sleepyhead. **dormir como un ~** sleep like a log
lisiado adj crippled
liso adj smooth; (*pelo*) straight; (*tierra*) flat; (*sencillo*) plain
lisonj|a f flattery. **~eador** adj flattering. ● m flatterer. **~ear** vt flatter. **~ero** adj flattering
lista f stripe; (*enumeración*) list. **~ de correos** poste restante. **a ~s** striped. **pasar ~** take the register. **~do** adj striped
listo adj clever; (*preparado*) ready
listón m strip; (*en saltos*) bar; (*Mex, cinta*) ribbon
litera f (*en barco, tren*) berth; (*en habitación*) bunk bed
literal adj literal
litera|rio adj literary. **~tura** f literature

litig|ar 🔢 vi dispute; (*Jurid*) litigate. **~io** m dispute; (*Jurid*) litigation
litografía f (*arte*) lithography; (*cuadro*) lithograph
litoral adj coastal. ● m coast
litro m litre
lituano adj & m Lithuanian
liturgia f liturgy
liviano adj fickle; (*LAm, de poco peso*) light
lívido adj livid
llaga f wound; (*úlcera*) ulcer
llama f flame; (*animal*) llama
llamada f call
llama|do adj called. ●m (*LAm*) call. **~miento** m call. **~r** vt call; (*por teléfono*) phone. ● vi call; (*golpear en la puerta*) knock; (*tocar el timbre*) ring. **~r por teléfono** phone, telephone. **~rse** vpr be called. **¿cómo te ~s?** what's your name?
llamarada f sudden blaze; (*fig, de pasión etc*) outburst
llamativo adj flashy; (*color*) loud; (*persona*) striking
llamear vi blaze
llano adj flat, level; (*persona*) natural; (*sencillo*) plain. ● m plain
llanta f (*Auto*) (wheel) rim; (*LAm, neumático*) tyre
llanto m crying
llanura f plain
llave f key; (*para tuercas*) spanner; (*LAm, del baño etc*) tap (*Amer*), faucet (*Amer*); (*Elec*) switch. **~ inglesa** monkey wrench. **cerrar con ~** lock. **echar la ~** lock up. **~ro** m key-ring
llega|da f arrival. **~r** 🔢 vi arrive, come; (*alcanzar*) reach; (*bastar*) be enough. **~r a** (*conseguir*) manage

to. ~r a saber find out. ~r a ser become. ~r hasta go as far as

llen|ar *vt* fill (up); (*rellenar*) fill in; (*cubrir*) cover (*de* with). ~o *adj* full. ● *m* (*en el teatro etc*) full house. de ~ entirely

lleva|dero *adj* tolerable. ~r *vt* carry; (*inducir, conducir*) lead; (*acompañar*) take; wear (*ropa*). ¿cuánto tiempo ~s aquí? how long have you been here? llevo 3 años estudiando inglés I've been studying English for 3 years. ~rse *vpr* take away; win (*premio etc*); (*comprar*) take. ~rse bien get on well together

llor|ar *vi* cry; (*ojos*) water. ~iquear *vi* whine. ~iqueo *m* whining. ~o *m* crying. ~ón *adj* whining. ● *m* cry-baby. ~oso *adj* tearful

llov|er 2 *vi* rain. ~izna *f* drizzle. ~iznar *vi* drizzle

llueve *vb véase* **LLOVER**

lluvi|a *f* rain; (*fig*) shower. ~oso *adj* rainy; (*clima*) wet

lo *articulo definido neutro.* ~ importante what is important, the important thing. ● *pron* (*él*) him; (*cosa*) it. ~ que what, that which

loa *f* praise. ~ble *adj* praiseworthy. ~r *vt* praise

lobo *m* wolf

lóbrego *adj* gloomy

lóbulo *m* lobe

local *adj* local. ● *m* premises. ~idad *f* locality; (*de un espectáculo*) seat; (*entrada*) ticket. ~izador *m* pager; (*de reserva*) booking reference. ~izar 10 *vt* find, locate

loción *f* lotion

loco *adj* mad, crazy. ● *m* lunatic. ~ de alegría mad with joy. estar ~ por be crazy about. volverse ~

go mad

locomo|ción *f* locomotion. ~tora *f* locomotive

locuaz *adj* talkative

locución *f* expression

locura *f* madness; (*acto*) crazy thing. con ~ madly

locutor *m* broadcaster

lod|azal *m* quagmire. ~o *m* mud

lógic|a *f* logic. ~o *adj* logical

logr|ar *vt* get; win (*premio*). ~ hacer manage to do. ~o *m* achievement; (*de premio*) winning; (*éxito*) success

loma *f* small hill

lombriz *f* worm

lomo *m* back; (*de libro*) spine. ~ de cerdo loin of pork

lona *f* canvas

loncha *f* slice; (*de tocino*) rasher

londinense *adj* from London. ● *m* Londoner

Londres *m* London

loneta *f* thin canvas

longaniza *f* sausage

longev|idad *f* longevity. ~o *adj* long-lived

longitud *f* length; (*en geografía*) longitude

lonja *f* slice; (*de tocino*) rasher; (*Com*) market

loro *m* parrot

los *articulo definido mpl* the. *véase tb* **EL**. ● *pron* them. ~ de Antonio Antonio's. ~ que whoever, the ones

losa *f* (*baldosa*) flagstone. ~ sepulcral tombstone

lote *m* share; (*de productos*) batch; (*terreno*) plot (*Brit*), lot (*Amer*)

lotería *f* lottery

loto *m* lotus

loza f crockery; (*fina*) china

lozano adj fresh; (vegetación) lush; (persona) healthy-looking

lubina f sea bass

lubrica|nte adj lubricating. ● m lubricant. **∼r 7** vt lubricate

lucero m bright star. **∼ del alba** morning star

lucha f fight; (*fig*) struggle. **∼dor** m fighter. **∼r** vi fight; (*fig*) struggle

lucid|ez f lucidity. **∼o** adj splendid

lúcido adj lucid

luciérnaga f glow-worm

lucimiento m brilliance

lucio m pike

lucir 11 vt (*fig*) show off. ● vi shine; (joya) sparkle; (*LAm, mostrarse*) look. **∼se** vpr (*fig*) shine, excel; (*presumir*) show off

lucr|ativo adj lucrative. **∼o** m gain

luego adv then; (*más tarde*) later (on); (*Mex, pronto*) soon. ● conj therefore. **∼ que** as soon as. **desde ∼** of course

lugar m place; (*espacio libre*) room. **∼ común** cliché. **dar ∼ a** give rise to. **en ∼ de** instead of. **en primer ∼** first. **hacer ∼** make room. **tener ∼** take place. **∼eño** adj local, village

lugarteniente m deputy

lúgubre adj gloomy

lujo m luxury. **∼so** adj luxurious. **de ∼** luxury

lumbago m lumbago

lumbre f fire; (*luz*) light

luminoso adj luminous; (*fig*) bright; (letrero) illuminated

luna f moon; (*espejo*) mirror. **∼ de miel** honeymoon. **claro de ∼** moonlight. **estar en la ∼** be miles away. **∼r** adj lunar. ●m mole;

(*en tela*) spot

lunes m invar Monday

lupa f magnifying glass

lustr|abotas m invar (*LAm*) bootblack. **∼ar** vt shine, polish. **∼e** m shine; (*fig, esplendor*) splendour. **dar ∼e a**, **sacar ∼e a** polish. **∼oso** adj shining

luto m mourning. **estar de ∼** be in mourning

luz f light; (*electricidad*) electricity. **luces altas** (*LAm*) headlights on full beam. **luces bajas** (*LAm*), **luces cortas** dipped headlights. **luces antiniebla** fog light. **luces largas** headlights on full beam. **a la ∼ de** in the light of. **a todas luces** obviously. **dar a ∼** give birth. **hacer a ∼** shed light on. **sacar a la ∼** bring to light

Mm

macabro adj macabre

macaco m macaque (monkey)

macanudo adj 1 great 1

macarrones mpl macaroni

macerar vt macerate (fruta); marinade (carne etc)

maceta f mallet; (*tiesto*) flowerpot

machacar 7 vt crush. ● vi go on (sobre about)

machamartillo. **a ∼** adj ardent; (*como adv*) firmly

machet|azo m blow with a machete; (*herida*) wound from a machete. **∼e** m machete

mach|ista m male chauvinist. **∼o** adj male; (*varonil*) macho

machu|car **7** *vt* bruise; (*aplastar*) crush. ~**cón** *m* (*LAm*) bruise

macizo *adj* solid. • *m* mass; (*de plantas*) bed

madeja *f* skein

madera *m* (*vino*) Madeira. • *f* wood; (*naturaleza*) nature. ~**ble** *adj* yielding timber. ~**men** *m* woodwork

madero *m* log; (*de construcción*) timber

madona *f* Madonna

madr|astra *f* stepmother. ~**e** *f* mother. ~**eperla** *f* mother-of-pearl. ~**eselva** *f* honeysuckle

madrigal *m* madrigal

madriguera *f* den; (*de conejo*) burrow

madrileño *adj* of Madrid. • *m* person from Madrid

madrina *f* godmother; (*en una boda*) matron of honour

madrug|ada *f* dawn. de ~**ada** at dawn. ~**ador** *adj* who gets up early. • *m* early riser. ~**ar** **12** *vi* get up early

madur|ación *f* maturing; (*de fruta*) ripening. ~**ar** *vt/i* mature; (*fruta*) ripen. ~**ez** *f* maturity; (*de fruta*) ripeness. ~**o** *adj* mature; (*fruta*) ripe

maestr|ía *f* skill; (*Univ*) master's degree. ~**o** *m* master; (*de escuela*) schoolteacher

mafia *f* mafia

magdalena *f* fairy cake (*Brit*), cup cake (*Amer*)

magia *f* magic

mágico *adj* magic; (*maravilloso*) magical

magist|erio *m* teaching (profession); (*conjunto de maestros*) teachers. ~**rado** *m* magistrate; (*juez*) judge. ~**ral** *adj* teaching; (*bien* hecho) masterly. ~**ratura** *f* magistracy

magn|animidad *f* magnanimity. ~**ánimo** *adj* magnanimous. ~**ate** *m* magnate, tycoon

magnavoz *m* (*Mex*) megaphone

magnético *adj* magnetic

magneti|smo *m* magnetism. ~**zar** **10** *vt* magnetize

magn|ificar *vt* extol; (*LAm*) magnify (*objeto*). ~**ificencia** *f* magnificence. ~**ífico** *adj* magnificent. ~**itud** *f* magnitude

magnolia *f* magnolia

mago *m* magician; (*en cuentos*) wizard

magro *adj* lean; (*tierra*) poor

magulla|dura *f* bruise. ~**r** *vt* bruise. ~**rse** *vpr* bruise

mahometano *adj* Islamic

maíz *m* maize, corn (*Amer*)

majada *f* sheepfold; (*estiércol*) manure; (*LAm*) flock of sheep

majader|ía *f* silly thing. ~**o** *m* idiot. • *adj* stupid

majest|ad *f* majesty. ~**uoso** *adj* majestic

majo *adj* nice

mal *adv* badly; (*poco*) poorly; (*difícilmente*) hardly; (*equivocadamente*) wrongly; (*desagradablemente*) bad. • *adj*. estar ~ be ill; (*anímicamente*) be in a bad way; (*incorrecto*) be wrong. estar ~ de (*escaso de*) be short of. *véase tb* **MALO**. • *m* evil; (*daño*) harm; (*enfermedad*) illness. ~ que bien somehow (or other). de ~ en peor from bad to worse. hacer ~ en be wrong to. ¡menos ~! thank goodness!

malabaris|mo *m* juggling. ~**ta** *m* & *f* juggler

mala|consejado *adj* ill-advised.

~**costumbrado** adj spoilt.
~**crianza** (LAm) rudeness. ~**gra-
decido** adj ungrateful

malagueño adj of Málaga. • m
person from Málaga

malaria f malaria

Malasia f Malaysia

malavenido adj incompatible

malaventura adj unfortunate

malayo adj Malay(an)

malbaratar vt sell off cheap;
(malgastar) squander

malcarado adj nasty looking

malcriado adj (niño) spoilt

maldad f evil; (acción) wicked
thing

maldecir 🔢 (pero imperativo mal-
dice, futuro y condicional regulares, pp
maldecido o **maldito**) vt curse. •
vi curse; speak ill (de of)

maldi|ciente adj backbiting; (que
blasfema) foul-mouthed. ~**ción** f
curse. ~**to** adj damned. ¡~**to** sea!
damn (it)!

maleab|ilidad f malleability.
~**le** adj malleable

malea|nte m criminal. ~**r** vt
damage; (pervertir) corrupt. ~**rse**
vpr be spoilt; (pervertirse) be corrupted

malecón m breakwater; (embarca-
dero) jetty; (Rail) embankment;
(LAm, paseo marítimo) seafront

maledicencia f slander

mal|eficio m curse. ~**éfico** adj
evil

malestar m discomfort; (fig) uneasiness

maleta f (suit)case. hacer la ~**a**
pack (one's case). ~**ero** m porter;
(Auto) boot, trunk (Amer). ~**ín** m
small case; (para documentos)
briefcase

mal|evolencia f malevolence.
~**évolo** adj malevolent

maleza f weeds; (matorral) under-
growth

mal|gastar vt waste. ~**hablado**
adj foul-mouthed. ~**hechor** m
criminal. ~**humorado** adj bad-
tempered

malici|a f malice; (picardía) mis-
chief. ~**arse** vpr suspect. ~**oso** adj
malicious; (pícaro) mischievous

maligno adj malignant; (persona)
evil

malla f mesh; (de armadura) mail;
(de gimnasia) leotard

Mallorca f Majorca

mallorquín adj & m Majorcan

malmirado adj (con estar)
frowned upon

malo adj (delante de nombre masculino
en singular **mal**) bad; (enfermo) ill. ~
de difficult to. estar de ~**as** (LAm,
malhumorado) be in a bad mood;
(LAm, con mala suerte) be out of
luck. lo ~ es que the trouble is
that. por las malas by force

malogr|ar vt waste; (estropear)
spoil. ~**arse** vpr fall through

maloliente adj smelly

malpensado adj nasty, malicious

malsano adj unhealthy

malsonante adj ill-sounding;
(grosero) offensive

malt|a f malt. ~**eada** f (LAm) milk
shake. ~**ear** vt malt

maltr|atar vt ill-treat; (pegar)
batter; mistreat (juguete etc).
~**echo** adj battered

malucho adj 🔢 under the weather

malva f mallow. (color de) ~ adj
invar mauve

malvado *adj* wicked

malvavisco *m* marshmallow

malversa|ción *f* embezzlement. **~dor** *adj* embezzling. ● *m* embezzler. **~r** *vt* embezzle

Malvinas *fpl*. las (islas) ~ the Falklands, the Falkland Islands

mama *f* mammary gland; (*de mujer*) breast

mamá *f* mum; (*usado por niños*) mummy

mama|da *f* sucking. **~r** *vt* suck; (*fig*) grow up with. ● *vi* (*bebé*) feed; (*animal*) suckle. dar de ~ breastfeed

mamario *adj* mammary

mamarracho *m* clown; (*cosa ridícula*) (ridiculous) sight; (*cosa mal hecha*) botch; (*cosa fea*) mess. ir hecho un ~ look a sight

mameluco *m* (*LAm*) overalls; (*de niño*) rompers

mamífero *adj* mammalian. ● *m* mammal

mamila *f* (*Mex*) feeding bottle

mamotreto *m* (*libro*) hefty volume; (*armatoste*) huge thing

mampara *f* screen

mampostería *f* masonry

mamut *m* mammoth

manada *f* herd; (*de lobos*) pack; (*de leones*) pride. en ~ in crowds

mana|ntial *m* spring; (*fig*) source. **~r** *vi* flow; (*fig*) abound. ● *vt* drip with

manaza *f* big hand

mancha *f* stain; (*en la piel*) blotch. **~do** *adj* stained; (*sucio*) dirty; (*animal*) spotted. **~r** *vt* stain; (*ensuciar*) dirty. **~rse** *vpr* get stained; (*ensuciarse*) get dirty

manchego *adj* de la Mancha. ● *m* person from la Mancha

manchón *m* large stain

mancilla *f* blemish. **~r** *vt* stain

manco *adj* (*de una mano*) one-handed; (*de las dos manos*) handless; (*de un brazo*) one-armed; (*de los dos brazos*) armless

mancomun|adamente *adv* jointly. **~ar** *vt* unite; (*Jurid*) make jointly liable. **~arse** *vpr* unite. **~idad** *f* union

manda *f* (*Mex*) religious offering

manda|dero *m* messenger. **~do** *m* (*LAm*) shopping; (*diligencia*) errand. hacer los **~dos** (*LAm*) do the shopping. **~miento** *m* order; (*Relig*) commandment. **~r** *vt* order; (*enviar*) send; (*gobernar*) rule. ● *vi* be in command. ¿mande? (*Mex*) pardon?

mandarin|a *f* (*naranja*) mandarin (orange). **~o** *m* mandarin tree

mandat|ario *m* attorney; (*Pol*) head of state. **~o** *m* mandate; (*Pol*) term of office

mandíbula *f* jaw

mando *m* command. ~ a distancia remote control. al ~ de in charge of. altos ~s *mpl* high-ranking officers

mandolina *f* mandolin

mandón *adj* bossy

manducar **7** *vt* **1** stuff oneself with

manecilla *f* hand

manej|able *adj* manageable. **~ar** *vt* use; handle (asunto etc); (*fig*) manage; (*LAm*, *conducir*) drive. **~arse** *vpr* get by. **~o** *m* handling. **~os** *mpl* scheming

manera *f* way. **~s** *fpl* manners. de alguna ~ somehow. de ~ que so (that). de ninguna ~ by no means. de otra ~ otherwise. de todas **~s** anyway

m

manga f sleeve; (tubo de goma) hose; (red) net; (para colar) filter; (LAm, de langostas) swarm

mango m handle; (fruta) mango. **~near** vt boss about. ● vi (entrometerse) interfere

manguera f hose(pipe)

manguito m muff

maní m (pl ~es) (LAm) peanut

manía f mania; (antipatía) dislike. **tener la ~ de** have an obsession with

maniaco adj, **maníaco** adj maniac(al). ● m maniac

maniatar vt tie the s.o.'s hands

maniático adj maniac(al); (obsesivo) obsessive; (loco) crazy; (delicado) finicky

manicomio m lunatic asylum

manicura f manicure; (mujer) manicurist

manido adj stale

manifesta|ción f manifestation, sign; (Pol) demonstration. **~nte** m demonstrator. **~r 1** vt show; (Pol) state. **~rse** vpr show; (Pol) demonstrate

manifiesto adj clear; (error) obvious; (verdad) manifest. ● m manifesto

manilargo adj light-fingered

manilla f (de cajón etc) handle; (de reloj) hand. **~r** m handlebar(s)

maniobra f manoeuvre. **~r** vt operate; (Rail) shunt. ● vt/i manoeuvre. **~s** fpl (Mil) manoeuvres

manipula|ción f manipulation. **~r** vt manipulate

maniquí m dummy. ● m & f model

mani|rroto adj & m spendthrift. **~ta** f, (LAm) **~to** m little hand

manivela f crank

manjar m delicacy

mano f hand; (de animales) front foot; (de perros, gatos) front paw. **~ de obra** work force. **¡~s arriba!** hands up! **a ~** by hand; (próximo) handy. **a ~ derecha** on the right. **de segunda ~** second hand. **echar una ~** lend a hand. **tener buena ~ para** be good at. ● m (LAm, fam) mate (Brit), buddy (Amer)

manojo m bunch

manose|ar vt handle. **~o** m handling

manotada f, **manotazo** m slap

manote|ar vi gesticulate. **~o** m gesticulation

mansalva: **a ~** adv without risk

mansarda f attic

mansión f mansion. **~ señorial** stately home

manso adj gentle; (animal) tame

manta f blanket

manteca f fat. **~oso** adj greasy

mantel m tablecloth; (del altar) altar cloth. **~ería** f table linen

manten|er 40 vt support; (conservar) keep; (sostener) maintain. **~erse** vpr support o.s.; (permanecer) remain. **~se de/con** live off. **~imiento** m maintenance

mantequ|era f butter churn. **~illa** f butter

mant|illa f mantilla. **~o** m cloak. **~ón** m shawl

manual adj & m manual

manubrio m crank; (LAm, de bicicleta) handlebars

manufactura f manufacture. **~r** vt manufacture, make

manuscrito adj handwritten. ● m manuscript

manutención f maintenance

manzana f apple; (de edificios)

block. ~**r** m (apple) orchard. ~ **de Adán** (LAm) Adam's apple

manzan|illa f camomile tea. ●m manzanilla, pale dry sherry. ~**o** m apple tree

maña f skill. ~**s** fpl cunning

mañan|a f morning. ~**a por la** ~**a** tomorrow morning. **pasado** ~**a** the day after tomorrow. **en la** ~**a** (LAm), **por la** ~**a** in the morning. ● m future. ● adv tomorrow. ~**ero** adj who gets up early. ● m early riser

mañoso adj clever; (astuto) crafty; (LAm, caprichoso) difficult

mapa m map

mapache m racoon

maqueta f scale model

maquiladora f (Mex) cross-border assembly plant

maquilla|je m make-up. ~**r** vt make up. ~**rse** vpr make up

máquina f machine; (Rail) engine. ~ **de afeitar** shaver. ~ **de escribir** typewriter. ~ **fotográfica** camera

maquin|ación f machination. ~**al** adj mechanical. ~**aria** f machinery. ~**ista** m & f operator; (Rail) engine driver

mar m & f sea. **alta** ~ high seas. **a** ~ **de** 🔢 lots of

maraña f thicket; (enredo) tangle; (embrollo) muddle

maratón m & f marathon

maravill|a f wonder. **a las mil** ~**as, de** ~**as** marvellously. **contar/decir** ~**as** speak wonderfully of. **hacer** ~**as** work wonders. ~**ar** vt astonish. ~**arse** vpr be astonished (de at). ~**oso** adj marvellous, wonderful

marca f mark; (de coches etc) make; (de alimentos, cosméticos)

brand; (Deportes) record. ~ **de fábrica** trade mark. **de** ~ brand name; (fig) excellent. **de** ~ **mayor** 🔢 absolute. ~**do** adj marked. ~**dor** m marker; (Deportes) scoreboard. ~**r** 🔢 vt mark; (señalar) show; score (un gol); dial (número de teléfono). ● vi score

marcha f (incl Mus) march; (Auto) gear; (desarrollo) course; (partida) departure. **a toda** ~ at full speed. **dar/hacer** ~ **atrás** put into reverse. **poner en** ~ start; (fig) set in motion

marchante m (f **marchanta**) art dealer; (Mex, en mercado) stall holder

marchar vi go; (funcionar) work, go; (Mil) march. ~**se** vpr leave

marchit|ar vt wither. ~**arse** vpr wither. ~**o** adj withered

marcial adj martial

marciano adj & m Martian

marco m frame; (moneda alemana) mark; (deportes) goal-posts

marea f tide. ~**do** adj sick; (en el mar) seasick; (aturdido) dizzy; (borracho) drunk. ~**r** vt make feel sick; (aturdir) make feel dizzy; (confundir) confuse. ~**rse** vpr feel sick; (en un barco) get seasick; (estar aturdido) feel dizzy; (irse la cabeza) feel faint; (emborracharse) get slightly drunk; (confundirse) get confused

marejada f swell; (fig) wave

mareo m sickness; (en el mar) seasickness; (aturdimiento) dizziness; (confusión) muddle

marfil m ivory

margarina f margarine

margarita f daisy; (cóctel) margarita

marg|en m margin; (de un ca-

mino) side. ●*f* (*de un río*) bank.
~**inado** *adj* excluded. ●*m* outcast.
al ~**en** (*fig*) outside. ~**inal** *adj*
marginal. ~**inar** *vt* (*excluir*) exclude; (*fijar márgenes*) set margins

mariachi *m* (*Mex*) (*música popular
de Jalisco*) Mariachi music; (*conjunto*) Mariachi band; (*músico*)
Mariachi musician

> **mariachi** The word can
> mean the traditional Mex-
> ican musical ensemble, the musi-
> cians and the lively mestizo music
> they play. *Mariachis* wearing cos-
> tumes based on those worn by
> *charros* can be seen in the Plaza
> Garibaldi, in Mexico City, where
> they are hired for parties, or to
> sing *mañanitas* or serenades.

maric|a *m* 🔲 sissy 🔲. ~**ón** *m* 🔲
homosexual, queer 🔲; (*LAm, cobarde*) wimp
marido *m* husband
mariguana *f*, **marihuana** *f* marijuana
marimacho *m* mannish woman
marimba *f* (*type of*) drum (*LAm,
especie de xilófon*) marimba
marin|a *f* navy; (*barcos*) fleet;
(*cuadro*) seascape. ~**a de guerra**
navy. ~**a mercante** merchant
navy. ~**ería** *f* seamanship; (*marine-
ros*) sailors. ~**ero** *adj* marine;
(*barco*) seaworthy. ● *m* sailor. a la
~**era** in tomato and garlic sauce.
~**o** *adj* marine
marioneta *f* puppet. ~**s** *fpl* puppet show
maripos|a *f* butterfly. ~**a noc-
turna** moth. ~**ear** *vi* be fickle;
(*galantear*) flirt. ~**ón** *m* flirt
mariquita *f* ladybird (*Brit*), lady-
bug (*Amer*). ●*m* 🔲 sissy 🔲

mariscador *m* shell-fisher
mariscal *m* marshal
maris|car *vt* fish for shellfish.
~**co** *m* seafood, shellfish. ~**quero**
m (*pescador de mariscos*) seafood
fisherman; (*vendedor de mariscos*)
seafood seller
marital *adj* marital; (*vida*) married
marítimo *adj* maritime; (*ciudad
etc*) coastal, seaside
marmita *f* cooking pot
mármol *m* marble
marmota *f* marmot
maroma *f* rope; (*Mex, voltereta*)
somersault
marqu|és *m* marquess. ~**esa** *f*
marchioness. ~**esina** *f* glass canopy; (*en estadio*) roof
marran|a *f* sow. ~**ada** *f* filthy
thing; (*cochinada*) dirty trick. ~**o**
adj filthy. ● *m* hog
marrón *adj & m* brown
marroqu|í *adj & m & f* Moroccan.
● *m* (*leather*) morocco. ~**inería** *f*
leather goods
Marruecos *m* Morocco
marsopa *f* porpoise
marsupial *adj & m* marsupial
marta *f* marten
martajar *vt* (*Mex*) crush (*maíz*)
Marte *m* Mars
martes *m invar* Tuesday. ~ **de carnaval** Shrove Tuesday
martill|ar *vt* hammer. ~**azo** *m*
blow with a hammer. ~**ear** *vt*
hammer. ~**eo** *m* hammering. ~**o**
m hammer
martín *m* **pescador** kingfisher
martinete *m* (*del piano*) hammer;
(*ave*) heron
martingala *f* (*ardid*) trick
mártir *m & f* martyr
martir|io *m* martyrdom; (*fig*) tor-

ment. **~izar** 🔟 vt martyr; (*fig*) torment, torture

marxis|mo m Marxism. **~ta** adj & m & f Marxist

marzo m March

más adv & adj (*comparativo*) more; (*superlativo*) most. **~** caro dearer. **~** doloroso more painful. el **~** caro the dearest. el **~** (*de dos*) the dearer. el **~** curioso the most curious; (*de dos*) the more curious. • prep plus. • m (*sign*). **~** bien rather. **~** de (*cantidad indeterminada*) more than. **~** o menos more or less. **~** que more than. **~** y **~** more and more. a lo (*a* (the) most. dos **~** dos two plus two. de **~** too many. es **~** moreover. nadie **~** nobody else. no **~** no more

masa f mass; (*Culin*) dough. en **~** en masse

masacre f massacre

masaj|e m massage. **~ear** vt massage. **~ista** m masseur. • f masseuse

mascada f (*Mex*) scarf

mascar 🔽 vt chew

máscara f mask

mascar|ada f masquerade. **~illa** f mask. **~ón** m (*Naut*) figurehead

mascota f mascot

masculin|idad f masculinity. **~o** adj masculine; (*sexo*) male. • m masculine

mascullar 🔢 vt mumble

masilla f putty

masivo adj massive, large-scale

mas|ón m Freemason. **~onería** f Freemasonry. **~ónico** adj Masonic

masoqui|smo m masochism. **~ta** adj masochistic. • m & f masochist

mastica|ción f chewing. **~r** 🔽

vt chew

mástil m (*Naut*) mast; (*de bandera*) flagpole; (*de guitarra, violín*) neck

mastín m mastiff

mastodonte m mastodon; (*fig*) giant

masturba|ción f masturbation. **~rse** vpr masturbate

mata f (*arbusto*) bush; (*LAm, planta*) plant

matad|ero m slaughterhouse. **~or** adj killing. • m (*torero*) matador

matamoscas m invar fly swatter

mata|nza f killing. **~r** vt kill (*personas*); slaughter (*reses*). **~rife** m butcher. **~rse** vpr kill o.s.; (*en un accidente*) be killed; (*Mex, para un examen*) cram. **~rse trabajando** work like mad

mata|polillas m invar moth killer. **~rratas** m invar rat poison

matasanos m invar quack

matasellos m invar postmark

mate adj matt. • m (*ajedrez*) (check)mate (*LAm, bebida*) maté

matemáti|cas f pl mathematics, maths (*Brit*), math (*Amer*). **~o** adj mathematical. • m mathematician

materia f matter; (*material*) material; (*LAm, asignatura*) subject. **~** prima raw material. en **~** de on the question of

material adj & m material. **~idad** f material nature. **~ismo** m materialism. **~ista** adj materialistic. • m & f materialist; (*Mex, constructor*) building contractor. **~izar** 🔟 vt materialize. **~izarse** vpr materialize. **~mente** adv materially; (*absolutamente*) absolutely

matern|al adj maternal; (*amor*) motherly. **~idad** f motherhood; (*hospital*) maternity hospital; (*sala*)

maternity ward. ~**o** adj motherly; (lengua) mother

matin|al adj morning. ~**ée** m matinée

matiz m shade; (fig) nuance. ~**ación** f combination of colours. ~**ar** 10 vt blend (colores); (introducir variedad) vary; (teñir) tinge (de with)

mat|ón m bully; (de barrio) thug. ~**onismo** m bullying; (de barrio) thuggery

matorral m scrub; (conjunto de matas) thicket

matraca f rattle. **dar** ~ pester

matraz m flask

matriarca f matriarch. ~**do** m matriarchy. ~**l** adj matriarchal

matr|ícula f (lista) register, list; (inscripción) registration; (Auto) registration number; (placa) licence plate. ~**icular** vt register. ~**icularse** vpr enrol, register

matrimoni|al adj matrimonial. ~**o** m marriage; (pareja) married couple

matriz f matrix; (molde) mould; (útero) womb, uterus

matrona f matron; (partera) midwife

matutino adj morning

maull|ar vi miaow. ~**ido** m miaow

mausoleo m mausoleum

maxilar adj maxillary. ● m jaw(bone)

máxim|a f maxim. ~**e** adv especially. ~**o** adj maximum; (punto) highest. ● m maximum

maya f daisy. ●adj Mayan. ●m & f (persona) Maya

mayo m May

mayonesa f mayonnaise

mayor adj (más grande, comparativo) bigger; (más grande, superlativo) biggest; (de edad, comparativo) older; (de edad, superlativo) oldest; (adulto) grown-up; (principal) main, major; (Mus) major. ● m & f (adulto) adult. **al por** ~ wholesale. ~**al** m foreman. ~**azgo** m entailed estate

mayordomo m butler

mayor|ía f majority. ~**ista** m & f wholesaler. ~**itario** adj majority; (socio) principal. ~**mente** adv especially

mayúscul|a f capital (letter). ~**o** adj capital; (fig, grande) big

mazacote m hard mass

mazapán m marzipan

mazmorra f dungeon

mazo m mallet; (manojo) bunch; (LAm, de naipes) pack (Brit), deck (Amer)

mazorca f cob. ~ **de maíz** corncob

me pron (acusativo) me; (dativo) (to) me; (reflexivo) (to) myself

mecánic|a f mechanics. ~**o** adj mechanical. ● m mechanic

mecani|smo m mechanism. ~**zación** f mechanization. ~**zar** 10 vt mechanize

mecanograf|ía f typing. ~**iado** adj typed, typewritten. ~**iar** 20 vt type

mecanógrafo m typist

mecate m (Mex) string; (más grueso) rope

mecedora f rocking chair

mecenas m & f invar patron

mecer 9 vt rock; swing (columpio). ~**se** vpr rock; (en un columpio) swing

mecha f (de vela) wick; (de explosivo) fuse. ~**s** fpl highlights

mechar vt stuff, lard

mechero m (cigarette) lighter

mechón m (de pelo) lock

medall|a f medal. **~ón** m medallion; (relicario) locket

media f stocking; (promedio) average. **a ~s** half each

mediación f mediation

mediado adj half full; (a mitad de) halfway through. **~s** mpl. **a ~s de marzo** in mid-March

mediador m mediator

medialuna f (pl mediaslunas) croissant

median|amente adv fairly. **~a** f (Auto) central reservation (Brit), median strip (Amer). **~era** f party wall. **~ero** adj (muro) party. **~o** adj medium; (mediocre) average, mediocre

medianoche f (pl medianoches) midnight; (Culin) type of roll

mediante prep through, by means of

mediar vi mediate; (llegar a la mitad) be halfway through; (interceder) intercede (por for)

medic|ación f medication. **~amento** m medicine. **~ina** f medicine. **~inal** adj medicinal

medición f measurement

médico adj medical. • m doctor. **~ de cabecera** GP, general practitioner

medid|a f measurement; (unidad) measure; (disposición) measure, step; (prudencia) moderation. **a la ~a** made to measure. **a ~a que** as. **en cierta ~a** to a certain extent. **~or** m (LAm) meter

medieval adj medieval. **~ista** m & f medievalist

medio adj half (a); (mediano) average. **dos horas y media** two and a half hours. **~ litro** half a litre. **las dos y media** half past two. • m middle; (Math) (manera) means; (en deportes) half(-back). **en ~** in the middle (de of). **por ~ de** through. **~ ambiente** m environonment

medioambiental adj environmental

mediocr|e adj mediocre. **~idad** f mediocrity

mediodía m midday, noon; (sur) south

medioevo m Middle Ages

Medio Oriente m Middle East

medir 5 vt measure; weigh up (palabras etc). • vi measure, be. **¿cuánto mide de alto?** how tall is it? **~se** vpr (moderarse) measure o.s.; (Mex, probarse) try on

medita|bundo adj thoughtful. **~ción** f meditation. **~r** vt think about. • vi meditate

mediterráneo adj Mediterranean

Mediterráneo m Mediterranean

médium m & f medium

médula f marrow

medusa f jellyfish

megáfono m megaphone

megalómano m megalomaniac

mejicano adj & m Mexican

Méjico m Mexico

mejilla f cheek

mejillón m mussel

mejor adj & adv (comparativo) better; (superlativo) best. **~ dicho** rather. **a lo ~** perhaps. **tanto ~** so much the better. **~a** f improvement. **~able** adj improvable. **~amiento** m improvement

mejorana f marjoram

mejorar vt improve, better. • vi

get better. ~**se** *vpr* get better

mejunje *m* mixture

melancolía *f* melancholy.
~**ólico** *adj* melancholic

melaza *f* molasses

melen|a *f* long hair; (*de león*)
mane. ~**udo** *adj* long-haired

melindr|es *mpl* affectation. hacer
~**es** con la comida be picky
about food. ~**oso** *adj* affected

mellizo *adj* & *m* twin

melocot|ón *m* peach. ~**onero** *m*
peach tree

mel|odía *f* melody. ~**ódico** *adj*
melodic. ~**odioso** *adj* melodious

melodram|a *m* melodrama.
~**ático** *adj* melodramatic

melómano *m* music lover

melón *m* melon

meloso *adj* sickly-sweet; (*canción*)
slushy

membran|a *f* membrane. ~**oso**
adj membranous

membrete *m* letterhead

membrill|ero *m* quince tree.
~**o** *m* quince

memo *adj* stupid. ● *m* idiot

memorable *adj* memorable

memorando *m*, **memorándum**
m notebook; (*nota*) memorandum,
memo

memori|a *f* memory; (*informe*)
report; (*tesis*) thesis. ~**as** *fpl* (*autobiografía*) memoirs. de ~**a** by
heart; (*citar*) from memory. ~**al** *m*
memorial. ~**ón** *m* good memory.
~**zación** *f* memorizing. ~**zar** 🔟 *vt*
memorize

menaje *m* household goods. ~
de cocina kitchenware

menci|ón *f* mention. ~**onado** *adj*
aforementioned. ~**onar** *vt* mention

mendi|cidad *f* begging. ~**gar**
🔢 *vt* beg for. ● *vi* beg. ~**go** *m*
beggar

mendrugo *m* piece of stale
bread

mene|ar *vt* wag (*rabo*); shake (*ca-
beza*); wiggle (*caderas*). ~**arse** *vpr*
move; (*con inquietud*) fidget; (*balancearse*) swing. ~**o** *m* movement;
(*sacudida*) shake

menester *m* occupation. ser ~
be necessary. ~**oso** *adj* needy

menestra *f* vegetable stew

mengano *m* so-and-so

mengua *f* decrease; (*falta*) lack.
~**do** *adj* diminished. ~**nte** *adj*
(*luna*) waning; (*marea*) ebb. ~**r** 🔢
vt/i decrease, diminish

meningitis *f* meningitis

menjurje *m* mixture

menopausia *f* menopause

menor *adj* (*más pequeño, comparativo*) smaller; (*más pequeño, superlativo*) smallest; (*más joven, comparativo*) younger; (*más joven,
superlativo*) youngest; (*Mus*) minor.
● *m* & *f* (*menor de edad*) minor. al ~
por ~ retail

menos *adj* (*comparativo*) less;
(*comparativo, con plural*) fewer;
(*superlativo*) least; (*superlativo, con
plural*) fewest. ● *adv* (*comparativo*)
less; (*superlativo*) least. ● *prep* except. al ~ at least. a ~ que unless. las dos ~ diez ten to two. ni
mucho ~ far from it. por lo ~ at
least. ~**cabar** *vt* lessen; (*fig, estropear*) damage. ~**cabo** *m* lessening.
~**preciable** *adj* contemptible.
~**preciar** *vt* despise. ~**precio** *m*
contempt

mensaje *m* message. ~**ro** *m*
messenger

menso *adj* (*LAm, fam*) stupid

menstru|ación f menstruation. **~al** adj menstrual. **~ar** 21 vi menstruate

mensual adj monthly. **~idad** f monthly pay; (*cuota*) monthly payment

mensurable adj measurable

menta f mint

mental adj mental. **~idad** f mentality. **~mente** adv mentally

mentar 1 vt mention, name

mente f mind

mentecato adj stupid. ● m idiot

mentir 4 vi lie. **~a** f lie. **~ijillas** fpl. de **~ijillas** for a joke. **~oso** adj lying. ● m liar

mentís m invar denial

mentor m mentor

menú m menu

menud|ear vi happen frequently; (*Mex, Com*) sell retail. **~encia** f trifle. **~encias** fpl (*LAm*) giblets. **~eo** m (*Mex*) retail trade. **~illos** mpl giblets. **~o** adj small; (*lluvia*) fine. a **~o** often. **~os** mpl giblets

meñique adj (*dedo*) little. ● m little finger

meollo m (*médula*) marrow; (*de tema etc*) heart

merca|chifle m hawker; (*fig*) profiteer. **~der** m merchant. **~dería** f (*LAm*) merchandise. **~do** m market. M**~do Común** Common Market. **~do negro** black market

mercan|cía(s) f(,pl) goods, merchandise. **~te** adj merchant. ● m merchant ship. **~til** adj mercantile, commercial. **~tilismo** m mercantilism

merced f favour. su/vuestra **~** your honour

mercenario adj & m mercenary

mercer|ía f haberdashery (*Brit*), notions (*Amer*).

mercurial adj mercurial

mercurio m mercury

merec|edor adj worthy (de of). **~er** 11 vt deserve. **~erse** vpr deserve. **~idamente** adv deservedly. **~ido** adj well deserved. **~imiento** m (*mérito*) merit

merend|ar 1 vt have as an afternoon snack. ● vi have an afternoon snack. **~ero** m snack bar; (*lugar*) picnic area

merengue m meringue

meridi|ano m midday; (*fig*) dazzling. ● m meridian. **~onal** adj southern. ● m southerner

merienda f afternoon snack

merino adj merino

mérito m merit; (*valor*) worth

meritorio adj praiseworthy. ● m unpaid trainee

merluza f hake

merma f decrease. **~r** vt/i decrease, reduce

mermelada f jam

mero adj mere; (*Mex, verdadero*) real. ● adv (*Mex, precisamente*) exactly; (*Mex, casi*) nearly. ● m grouper

merode|ador m prowler. **~ar** vi prowl

mes m month

mesa f table; (*para escribir o estudiar*) desk. poner la **~** lay the table

mesarse vpr tear at one's hair

meser|a f (*LAm*) waitress. **~o** m (*LAm*) waiter

meseta f plateau; (*descansillo*) landing

Mesías m Messiah

mesilla f, **mesita** f small table. **~**

m

de noche bedside table

mesón m inn

mesoner|a f landlady. **~o** m landlord

mestiz|aje m crossbreeding. **~o** adj (persona) half-caste; (animal) cross-bred. ● m (persona) half-caste; (animal) cross-breed

mesura f moderation. **~do** adj moderate

meta f goal; (de una carrera) finish

metabolismo m metabolism

metafisic|a f metaphysics. **~o** adj metaphysical

met|áfora f metaphor. **~afórico** adj metaphorical

met|al m metal; (de la voz) timbre. **~ales** mpl (instrumentos de latón) brass. **~álico** adj (objeto) metal; (sonido) metallic

metal|urgia f metallurgy. **~úrgico** adj metallurgical

metamorfosis f invar metamorphosis

metedura de pata f blunder

mete|órico adj meteoric. **~orito** m meteorite. **~oro** m meteor. **~orología** f meteorology. **~orológico** adj meteorological. **~orólogo** m meteorologist

meter vt put; score (un gol); (en redar) involve; (causar) make. **~se** vpr get involved (en in); (entrometerse) meddle. **~se con uno** pick a quarrel with s.o.

meticulos|idad f meticulousness. **~o** adj meticulous

metida de pata f (LAm) blunder

metido m reprimand. ● adj. **~** en años getting on. estar **~** en algo be involved in sth. estar muy **~** con uno be well in with s.o.

metódico adj methodical

metodis|mo m Methodism. **~ta** adj & m & f Methodist

método m method

metodología f methodology

metraje m length. de largo **~** (película) feature

metrall|a f shrapnel. **~eta** f submachine gun

métric|a f metrics. **~o** adj metric; (verso) metrical

metro m metre; (tren) underground (Brit), subway (Amer). **~** cuadrado square metre

metrónomo m metronome

metr|ópoli f metropolis. **~opolitano** adj metropolitan. ● m metropolitan; (tren) underground (Brit), subway (Amer)

mexicano adj & m Mexican

México m Mexico. **~** D. F. Mexico City

mezcal m (Mex) mescal

mezc|la f (acción) mixing; (substancia) mixture; (argamasa) mortar. **~lador** m mixer. **~lar** vt mix; shuffle (los naipes). **~larse** vpr mix; (intervenir) interfere. **~olanza** f mixture

mezquin|dad f meanness. **~o** adj mean; (escaso) meagre. ● m mean person

mezquita f mosque

mi adj my. ● m (Mus) E; (solfa) mi

mí pron me

miau m miaow

mica f (silicato) mica

mico m (long-tailed) monkey

micro|bio m microbe. **~biología** f microbiology. **~cosmos** m invar microcosm. **~film(e)** m microfilm

micrófono m microphone

microonda f microwave. **~s** m invar microwave oven

microordenador *m* microcomputer

micros|cópico *adj* microscopic. **~copio** *m* microscope. **~urco** *m* long-playing record

miedo *m* fear (a for). **dar ~** frighten. **morirse de ~** be scared to death. **tener ~** be frightened. **~so** *adj* fearful

miel *f* honey

miembro *m* limb; (*persona*) member

mientras *conj* while. ● *adv* meanwhile. **~ que** whereas. **~ tanto** in the meantime

miércoles *m invar* Wednesday. **~ de ceniza** Ash Wednesday

mierda *f* (🆘) shit

mies *f* ripe, grain

miga *f* crumb; (*fig, meollo*) essence. **~jas** *fpl* crumbs; (*sobras*) scraps. **~r** 🔢 *vt* crumble

migra|ción *f* migration. **~torio** *adj* migratory

mijo *m* millet

mil *adj & m* a/one thousand. **~es de thousands of.** **~ novecientos noventa y nueve** nineteen ninety-nine. **~ euros** a thousand euros

milagro *m* miracle. **~so** *adj* miraculous

milen|ario *adj* millenial. **~io** *m* millennium

milésimo *adj & m* thousandth

mili *f* 🆒 military service. **~cia** *f* soldiering; (*gente armada*) militia

mili|gramo *m* milligram. **~litro** *m* millilitre

milímetro *m* millimetre

militante *adj & m & f* activist

militar *adj* military. ● *m* soldier. **~ismo** *m* militarism. **~ista** *adj* militaristic. ● *m & f* militarist.

~izar 🔟 *vt* militarize

milla *f* mile

millar *m* thousand. **a ~es** by the thousand

mill|ón *m* million. **un ~ón de libros** a million books. **~onada** *f* fortune. **~onario** *m* millionaire. **~onésimo** *adj & m* millionth

milonga *f* popular dance and music from the River Plate region

milpa *f* (Mex) maize field, cornfield (Amer)

milpies *m invar* woodlouse

mimar *vt* spoil

mimbre *m & f* wicker. **~arse** *vpr* sway. **~ra** *f* osier. **~ral** *m* osierbed

mimetismo *m* mimicry

mímic|a *f* mime. **~o** *adj* mimic

mimo *m* mime; (adj *un niño*) spoiling; (*caricia*) cuddle

mimosa *f* mimosa

mina *f* mine. **~r** *vt* mine; (*fig*) undermine

minarete *m* minaret

mineral *m* mineral; (*mena*) ore. **~ogía** *f* mineralogy. **~ogista** *m & f* mineralogist

miner|ía *f* mining. **~o** *adj* mining. ● *m* miner

miniatura *f* miniature

minifundio *m* smallholding

minimizar 🔟 *vt* minimize

mínim|o *adj & m* minimum. **como ~ at least.** **~um** *m* minimum

minino *m* 🆒 cat, puss 🆒

minist|erial *adj* ministerial; (reunión) cabinet. **~erio** *m* ministry. **~ro** *m* minister

minor|ía *f* minority. **~idad** *f* minority. **~ista** *m & f* retailer

minuci|a *f* trifle. **~osidad** *f* thoroughness. **~oso** *adj* thorough; (de-

*tallado) detailed

minúscul|a f lower case letter.
~o adj tiny

minuta f draft copy; (*de abogado*)
bill

minut|ero m minute hand. **~o** m
minute

mío adj & pron mine. **un amigo ~** a
friend of mine

miop|e adj short-sighted. ● m & f
short-sighted person. **~ía** f short-
sightedness

mira f sight; (*fig, intención*) aim. **a
la ~** on the lookout. **con ~s a**
with a view to. **~da** f look. **echar
una ~da** a glance at. **~do** adj
careful with money; (*comedido*)
considerate. **bien ~do** highly re-
garded. **no estar bien ~do** be
frowned upon. **~dor** m viewpoint.
~miento m consideration. **~r** vt
look at; (*observar*) watch; (*considerar*) consider. **~r fijamente** a stare
at. ●**vi** look (edificio etc). **~ hacia**
face. **~rse** vpr (*personas*) look at
each other

mirilla f peephole

miriñaque m crinoline

mirlo m blackbird

mirón adj nosey. ●m nosey-parker;
(*espectador*) onlooker

mirto m myrtle

misa f mass. **~l** m missal

misántropo m misanthropist

miscelánea f miscellany; (*Mex,
tienda*) corner shop (*Brit*), small general store (*Amer*)

miser|able adj very poor; (*lasti-
moso*) miserable; (*tacaño*) mean.
~ía f extreme poverty; (*suciedad*)
squalor

misericordi|a f pity; (*piedad*)
mercy. **~oso** adj merciful

mísero adj miserable; (*tacaño*)

mean; (*malvado*) wicked

misil m missile

misi|ón f mission. **~onero** m mis-
sionary

misiva f missive

mism|ísimo adj very same. **~o**
adj same; (*después de pronombre
personal*) myself, yourself, himself,
herself, itself, ourselves, yourselves,
themselves; (*enfático*) very. ● adv.
ahora ~ right now. **aquí ~** right
here. **lo ~** the same

misterio m mystery. **~so** adj
mysterious

mística f mysticism. **~o** adj mystical. ●m mystic

mistifica|ción f mystification.
~r 7 vt mystify

mitad f half; (*centro*) middle. cortar algo por la **~** cut sth in half

mitigar 12 vt mitigate; quench
(sed); relieve (dolor etc)

mitin m, **mitín** m meeting

mito m myth. **~logía** f myth-
ology. **~lógico** adj mythological

mitón m mitten

mitote m (*Mex*) Aztec dance

mixt|o adj mixed. **educación
mixta** coeducation

mobbing m harassment

mobiliario m furniture

moce|dad f youth. **~río** m young
people. **~tón** m strapping lad.
~tona f strapping girl

mochales adj invar. **estar ~** be
round the bend

mochila f rucksack

mocho adj blunt. ● m butt end

mochuelo m little owl

moción f motion

moco m mucus. **limpiarse los ~s**
blow one's nose

moda f fashion. **estar de ~** be in

fashion. ~l adj modal. ~les mpl
manners. ~lidad f kind

model|ado m modelling. ~ador
m modeller. ~ar vt model; (fig,
configurar) form. ~o m & f model

módem m modem

modera|ción f moderation.
~do adj moderate. ~r vt moderate; reduce (velocidad). ~rse vpr
control oneself

modern|idad f modernity.
~ismo m modernism. ~ista m & f
modernist. ~izar 10 vt modernize.
~o adj modern; (a la moda) fash-
ionable

modest|ia f modesty. ~o adj
modest

módico adj moderate

modifica|ción f modification.
~r 7 vt modify

modismo m idiom

modist|a f dressmaker. ~o m de-
signer

modo m manner, way; (Gram)
mood; (Mus) mode. ~ de ser character. de ~ que so that. de ningún ~ certainly not. de todos ~s
anyhow. ni ~ (LAm) no way

modorra f drowsiness

modula|ción f modulation.
~dor m modulator. ~r vt modu-
late

módulo m module

mofa f mockery. ~rse vpr. ~rse
de make fun of

mofeta f skunk

moflet|e m chubby cheek. ~udo
adj with chubby cheeks

mohín m grimace. hacer un ~
pull a face

moho m mould; (óxido) rust. ~so
adj mouldy; (metales) rusty

moisés m Moses basket

mojado adj wet

mojar vt wet; (empapar) soak; (humedecer) moisten, dampen

mojigat|ería f prudishness. ~o
m prude. ● adj prudish

mojón m boundary post; (señal)
signpost

molar m molar

mold|e m mould; (aguja) knitting
needle. ~ear vt mould, shape; (fig)
form. ~ura f moulding

mole f mass, bulk. ● m (Mex, salsa)
chili sauce with chocolate and ses-
ame

mol|écula f molecule. ~ecular
adj molecular

mole|dor adj grinding. ● m
grinder. ~r 2 grind

molest|ar vt annoy; (incomodar)
bother. ¿le ~a que fume? do you
mind if I smoke? ● vi be a nuisance. no ~ar do not disturb.
~arse vpr bother; (ofenderse) take
offence. ~ia f bother, nuisance;
(inconveniente) inconvenience; (incomodidad) discomfort. ~o adj annoying; (inconveniente) inconvenient; (ofendido) offended

molicie f softness; (excesiva comodidad) easy life

molido adj ground; (fig, muy cansado) worn out

molienda f grinding

molin|ero m miller. ~ete m toy
windmill. ~illo m mill; (juguete)
toy windmill. ~ m de
agua watermill. ~o m. ~ de viento
windmill

molleja f gizzard

mollera f (de la cabeza) crown;
(fig, sesera) brains

molusco m mollusc

moment|áneamente adv momen-
tarily. ~áneo adj (breve) mo-

mentary; (*pasajero*) temporary. **~o**
m moment; (*ocasión*) time. **al ~o**
at once. **de ~o** for the moment
momi|a *f* mummy. **~ficar 7** *vt*
mummify. **~ficarse** *vpr* become
mummified
monacal *adj* monastic
monada *f* beautiful thing; (*niño
bonito*) cute kid; (*acción tonta*) silli-
ness
monaguillo *m* altar boy
mon|arca *m & f* monarch. **~ar-
quía** *f* monarchy. **~árquico** *adj*
monarchical
monasterio *m* monastery
mond|a *f* peeling; (*piel*) peel.
~adientes *m invar* toothpick.
~adura *f* peeling; (*piel*) peel. **~ar**
vt peel (*fruta etc*). **~o** *adj* (*sin pelo*)
bald
mondongo *m* innards
moned|a *f* coin; (*de un país*) cur-
rency. **~ero** *m* purse (*Brit*), change
purse (*Amer*)
monetario *adj* monetary
mongolismo *m* Down's syndrome
monigote *m* weak character;
(*muñeco*) rag doll; (*dibujo*) doodle
monitor *m* monitor
monj|a *f* nun. **~e** *m* monk. **~il**
adj nun's; (*como de monja*) like a
nun
mono *m* monkey; (*sobretodo*)
overalls. ● *adj* pretty
monocromo *adj & m* mono-
chrome
monóculo *m* monocle
mon|ogamia *f* monogamy.
~ógamo *adj* monogamous
monogra|fía *f* monograph.
~ma *m* monogram
mon|ologar 12 *vi* soliloquize.
~ólogo *m* monologue

monoplano *m* monoplane
monopoli|o *m* monopoly. **~zar**
10 *vt* monopolize
monos|ilábico *adj* monosyllabic.
~ílabo *m* monosyllable
monoteís|mo *m* monotheism.
~ta *adj* monotheistic. ● *m & f*
monotheist
mon|otonía *f* monotony.
~ótono *adj* monotonous
monseñor *m* monsignor
monstruo *m* monster. **~sidad** *f*
monstrosity; (*atrocidad*) atrocity.
~so *adj* monstrous
monta *f* mounting; (*valor*) total
value
montacargas *m invar* service lift
(*Brit*), service elevator (*Amer*)
monta|dor *m* fitter. **~je** *m*
assembly; (*Cine*) montage; (*teatro*)
staging, production
montañ|a *f* mountain. **~a rusa**
roller coaster. **~ero** *adj* mountain-
eer. **~és** *adj* mountain. ● *m* high-
lander. **~ismo** *m* mountaineering.
~oso *adj* mountainous
montaplatos *m invar* dumb
waiter
montar *vt* ride; (*subirse a*) get on;
(*ensamblar*) assemble; cock (*arma*);
set up (*una casa, un negocio*). ● *vi*
ride; (*subirse*) mount. **~ a caballo**
ride a horse
monte *m* (*montaña*) mountain;
(*terreno inculto*) scrub; (*bosque*)
woodland. **~ de piedad** pawnshop
montepío *m* charitable fund for
dependents
montés *adj* wild
montevideano *adj & m*
Montevidean
montículo *m* hillock
montón *m* heap, pile. **a montones** in abundance. **un ~ de**

loads of

montura f mount; (silla) saddle

monument|al adj monumental; (fig, muy grande) enormous. **~o** m monument

monzón m & f monsoon

moño a f ribbon. **~o** m bun; (LAm, lazo) bow

moque|o m runny nose. **~ro** 🔟 handkerchief

moqueta f fitted carpet

moquillo m distemper

mora f mulberry; (de zarzamora) blackberry; (Jurid) default

morada f dwelling

morado adj purple

morador m inhabitant

moral m mulberry tree. ●f morals. ●adj moral. **~eja** f moral. **~idad** f morality. **~ista** m & f moralist. **~izador** adj moralizing. **~izar** 🔟 vt moralize

morar vi live

moratoria f moratorium

mórbido adj soft; (malsano) morbid

morbo m illness. **~sidad** f morbidity. **~so** adj unhealthy

morcilla f black pudding

morda|cidad f sharpness. **~z** adj scathing

mordaza f gag

morde|dura f 🔟 bite. **~r** 🔟 vt bite; (Mex, exigir soborno a) extract a bribe from. ●vi bite. **~rse** vpr bite o.s. **~rse las uñas** bite one's nails

mordi|da f (Mex) bribe. **~sco** m bite. **~squear** vt nibble (at)

moreno adj (con ser) dark; (de pelo obscuro) dark-haired; (de raza negra) dark-skinned; (con estar) brown, tanned

morera f white mulberry tree

moretón m bruise

morfema m morpheme

morfin|a f morphine. **~ómano** m morphine addict

morfolo|gía f morphology. **~ógico** adj morphological

moribundo adj dying

morir 🟥 (pp muerto) vi die; (fig, extinguirse) die away; (fig, terminar) end. **~ ahogado** drown. **~se** vpr die. **~se de hambre** starve to death; (fig) be starving. **se muere por una flauta** she's dying to have a flute

morisco adj Moorish. ● m Moor

morm|ón m Mormon. **~ónico** adj Mormon. **~onismo** m Mormonism

moro adj Moorish. ● m Moor

morral m (mochila) rucksack; (de cazador) gamebag; (para caballos) nosebag

morrillo m nape of the neck

morriña f homesickness

morro m snout

morrocotudo adj (🔟, tremendo) terrible; (estupendo) terrific 🔟

morsa f walrus

mortaja f shroud

mortal adj & m & f mortal. **~idad** f mortality. **~mente** adv mortally

mortandad f loss of life; (Mil) carnage

mortecino adj failing; (color) pale

mortero m mortar

mortífero adj deadly

mortifica|ción f mortification. **~r** 🗷 vt (atormentar) torment. **~rse** vpr distress o.s.

mortuorio adj death

mosaico m mosaic; (Mex, baldosa) floor tile

mosca f fly. **~rda** f blowfly. **~rdón** m botfly; (de cuerpo azul)

bluebottle
moscatel *adj* muscatel
moscón *m* botfly; (*mosca de cuerpo azul*) bluebottle
moscovita *adj* & *m* & *f* Muscovite
mosque|arse *vpr* get cross. ~**o** *m* resentment
mosquete *m* musket. ~**ro** *m* musketeer
mosquit|ero *m* mosquito net. ~**o** *m* mosquito
mostacho *m* moustache
mostaza *f* mustard
mosto *m* must, grape juice
mostrador *m* counter
mostrar 2 *vt* show. ~**se** *vpr* (show oneself to) be. se mostró muy amable he was very kind
mota *f* spot, speck
mote *m* nickname
motea|do *adj* speckled. ~**r** *vt* speckle
motejar *vt* call
motel *m* motel
motete *m* motet
motín *m* riot; (*de tropas, tripulación*) mutiny
motiv|ación *f* motivation. ~**ar** *vt* motivate. ~**o** *m* reason. con ~ de because of
motocicl|eta *f* motor cycle, motor bike ⓘ. ~**ista** *m* & *f* motorcyclist
motoneta *f* (*LAm*) (motor) scooter
motor *adj* motor. ● *m* motor, engine. ~ de arranque starter motor. ~**a** *f* motor boat. ~**ismo** *m* motorcycling. ~**ista** *m* & *f* motorist; (*de una moto*) motorcyclist. ~**izar** 10 *vt* motorize
motriz *adj* motor
move|dizo *adj* movable; (*poco*

firme) unstable; (*persona*) fickle. ~**r** 2 *vt* move; shake (la cabeza); (*provocar*) cause. ~**se** *vpr* move; (*darse prisa*) hurry up
movi|ble *adj* movable. ~**do** *adj* moved; (*Foto*) blurred
móvil *adj* mobile; (*Esp, teléfono*) mobile phone, cellphone. ● *m* motive
movili|dad *f* mobility. ~**zación** *f* mobilization. ~**zar** 10 *vt* mobilize
movimiento *m* movement, motion; (*agitación*) bustle
moza *f* young girl. ~**lbete** *m* lad
mozárabe *adj* Mozarabic. ● *m* & *f* Mozarab
moz|o *m* young boy. ~**uela** *f* young girl. ~**uelo** *m* young boy/lad
mucam|a *f* (*LAm*) servant. ~**o** *m* (*LAm*) servant
muchach|a *f* girl; (*sirvienta*) servant, maid. ~**o** *m* boy, lad
muchedumbre *f* crowd
mucho *adj* a lot of; (*en negativas, preguntas*) much, a lot of. ~**s** a lot of; (*en negativas, preguntas*) many, a lot of. ● *pron* a lot; (*personas*) many (people). como ~ at the most. ni ~ menos by no means. por ~ que however much. ● *adv* a lot, very much; (*tiempo*) long, a long time
mucos|idad *f* mucus. ~**o** *adj* mucous
muda *f* change of clothing; (*de animales*) shedding. ~**ble** *adj* changeable; (*personas*) fickle. ~**nza** *f* change, removal (*Brit*). ~**r** *vt* change; shed (piel). ~**rse** *vpr* (*de ropa*) change one's clothes; (*de casa*) move (house)
mudéjar *adj* & *m* & *f* Mudejar
mud|ez *f* dumbness. ~**o** *adj*

dumb; (*callado*) silent
mueble *adj* movable. • *m* piece of furniture. **~s** *mpl* furniture
mueca *f* grimace, face. hacer una ~ pull a face
muela *f* back tooth, molar; (*piedra de afilar*) grindstone; (*piedra de molino*) millstone. ~ del juicio wisdom tooth
muelle *adj* soft. • *m* spring; (*Naut*) wharf; (*malecón*) jetty
muérdago *m* mistletoe
muero *vb véase* **MORIR**
muert|e *f* death; (*homicidio*) murder. **~o** *adj* dead. • *m* dead person
muesca *f* nick; (*ranura*) slot
muestra *f* sample; (*prueba*) proof; (*modelo*) model; (*señal*) sign. **~rio** *m* collection of samples
muestro *vb véase* **MOSTRAR**
muevo *vb véase* **MOVER**
mugi|do *m* moo. **~r** 🔟 *vi* moo
mugr|e *m* dirt. **~iento** *adj* dirty, filthy
mugrón *m* sucker
mujer *f* woman; (*esposa*) wife. • *int* my dear! **~iego** *adj* fond of the women. • *m* womanizer. **~zuela** *f* prostitute
mula *f* mule. **~da** *f* drove of mules
mulato *adj* of mixed race (*black and white*). • *m* person of mixed race
mulero *m* muleteer
muleta *f* crutch; (*toreo*) stick with a red flag
mulli|do *adj* soft. **~r** 🔢 *vt* soften
mulo *m* mule
multa *f* fine. **~r** *vt* fine
multi|color *adj* multicoloured. **~copista** *m* duplicator. **~cultural** *adj* multicultural. **~forme** *adj*

multiform. **~lateral** *adj* multilateral. **~lingüe** *adj* multilingual. **~millonario** *m* multimillionaire
múltiple *adj* multiple
multiplic|ación *f* multiplication. **~ar** 🔟 *vt* multiply. **~arse** *vpr* multiply. **~idad** *f* multiplicity
múltiplo *m* multiple
multitud *f* multitude, crowd. **~inario** *adj* mass; (*concierto*) with mass audience
mund|ano *adj* wordly; (*de la sociedad elegante*) society. **~ial** *adj* world-wide. la segunda guerra **~ial** the Second World War. **~illo** *m* world, circles. **~o** *m* world. todo el **~o** everybody
munición *f* ammunition; (*provisiones*) supplies
municip|al *adj* municipal. **~alidad** *f* municipality. **~io** *m* municipality; (*ayuntamiento*) town council
muñe|ca *f* (*en anatomía*) wrist; (*juguete*) doll; (*maniquí*) dummy. **~co** *m* doll. **~quera** *f* wristband
muñón *m* stump
mural *adj* mural, wall. • *m* mural. **~lla** *f* (*city*) wall. **~r** *vt* wall
murciélago *m* bat
murga *f* street band
murmullo *m* (*incl fig*) murmur
murmura|ción *f* gossip. **~dor** *adj* gossiping. • *m* gossip. **~r** *vi* murmur; (*criticar*) gossip
muro *m* wall
murria *f* depression
mus *m* card game
musa *f* muse
musaraña *f* shrew
muscula|r *adj* muscular. **~tura** *f* muscles
músculo *m* muscle
musculoso *adj* muscular

m

muselina f muslin

museo m museum. ~ de arte art gallery

musgo m moss. ~so adj mossy

música f music

musical adj & m musical

músico adj musical. ● m musician

music|ología f musicology. ~ólogo m musicologist

muslo m thigh

mustio adj (plantas) withered; (cosas) faded; (personas) gloomy; (Mex, hipócrita) two-faced

musulmán adj & m Muslim

muta|bilidad f mutability. ~ción f mutation

mutila|ción f mutilation. ~do adj crippled. ● m cripple. ~r vt mutilate; maim (persona)

mutis m (en el teatro) exit. ~mo m silence

mutu|alidad f mutuality; (asociación) friendly society. ~amente adv mutually. ~o adj mutual

muy adv very; (demasiado) too

Nn

nabo m turnip

nácar m mother-of-pearl

nac|er 11 vi be born; (pollito) hatch out; (planta) sprout. ~ido adj born. recien ~ido newborn. ~iente adj (sol) rising. ~imiento m birth; (de río) source; (belén) crib. lugar m de ~imiento place of birth

naci|ón f nation. ~onal adj national. ~onalidad f nationality.

~onalismo m nationalism. ~onalista m & f nationalist. ~onalizar 10 vt nationalize. ~onalizarse vpr become naturalized

nada pron nothing, not anything. ● adv not at all. ¡~ de eso! nothing of the sort! antes que ~ first of all. ¡de ~! (después de 'gracias') don't mention it! para ~ (not) at all. por ~ del mundo not for anything in the world

nada|dor m swimmer. ~r vi swim. ~r de espalda(s) do (the) backstroke

nadería f trifle

nadie pron no one, nobody

nado m (Mex) swimming. ● adv a ~ swimming

naipe m (playing) card. juegos mpl de ~s card games

nalga f buttock. ~s fpl bottom. ~da f (Mex) smack on the bottom

nana f lullaby

naranj|a f orange. ~ada f orangeade. ~al m orange grove. ~ero m orange tree

narcótico adj & m narcotic

nariz f nose. ¡narices! rubbish!

narra|ción f narration. ~dor m narrator. ~r vt tell. ~tivo adj narrative

nasal adj nasal

nata f cream

natación f swimming

natal adj native; (pueblo etc) home. ~idad f birth rate

natillas fpl custard

nativo adj & m native

nato adj born

natural adj natural. ● m native. ~eza f nature. ~eza muerta still life. ~idad f naturalness. ~ista m & f naturalist. ~izar 10 vt naturalize. ~**izarse** *vpr* become naturalized. ~**mente** *adv* naturally. ● *int* of course!

naufrag|ar 12 *vi* (barco) sink; (persona) be shipwrecked; (*fig*) fail. ~**io** *m* shipwreck

náufrago *adj* shipwrecked. ● *m* shipwrecked person

náuseas *fpl* nausea. dar ~s a uno make s.o. feel sick. **sentir** ~s feel sick

náutico *adj* nautical

navaja *f* penknife; (*de afeitar*) razor. ~**zo** *m* slash

naval *adj* naval

nave *f* ship; (*de iglesia*) nave. ~ **espacial** spaceship. **quemar las** ~s burn one's boats

navega|ble *adj* navigable; (barco) seaworthy. ~**ción** *f* navigation; (*tráfico*) shipping. ~**dor** *m* (*Informática*) browser. ~**nte** *m & f* navigator. ~**r** 12 *vi* sail; (*Informática*) browse

Navidad *f* Christmas. ~**eño** *adj* Christmas. **en** ~**ades** at Christmas. **¡feliz** ~**ad!** Happy Christmas! **por** ~**ad** at Christmas

nazi *adj & m & f* Nazi. ~**smo** *m* Nazism

neblina *f* mist

nebuloso *adj* misty; (*fig*) vague

necedad *f* foolishness. **decir** ~**es** talk nonsense. **hacer una** ~ do sth stupid

necesari|amente *adv* necessarily. ~**o** *adj* necessary

necesi|dad *f* need; (*cosa esencial*) necessity; (*pobreza*) poverty. ~**dades** *fpl* hardships. **no hay** ~**dad** there's no need. **por** ~**dad** (out) of necessity. ~**tado** *adj* in need (de of). ~**tar** *vt* need. ● *vi*. ~**tar de** need

necio *adj* silly. ● *m* idiot

néctar *m* nectar

nectarina *f* nectarine

nefasto *adj* unfortunate; (*consecuencia*) disastrous; (*influencia*) harmful

nega|ción *f* denial; (*Gram*) negative. ~**do** *adj* useless. ~**r** 1 & 12 *vt* deny; (*rehusar*) refuse. ~**rse** *vpr* refuse (a to). ~**tiva** *f* (*acción*) denial; (*acción de rehusar*) refusal. ~**tivo** *adj & m* negative

negligen|cia *f* negligence. ~**te** *adj* negligent

negoci|able *adj* negotiable. ~**ación** *f* negotiation. ~**ante** *m & f* dealer. ~**ar** *vt/i* negotiate. ~**ar en** trade in. ~**o** *m* business; (*Com, trato*) deal. ~**os** *mpl* business. **hombre** *m* **de** ~**os** businessman

negr|a *f* black woman; (*Mus*) crotchet. ~**o** *adj* black; (*ojos*) dark. ● *m* (*color*) black; (*persona*) black man. ~**ura** *f* blackness. ~**uzco** *adj* blackish

nen|a *f* little girl. ~**o** *m* little boy

nenúfar *m* water lily

neocelandés *adj* from New Zealand. ● *m* New Zealander

neón *m* neon

nepotismo *m* nepotism

nervio *m* nerve; (*tendón*) sinew; (*en botánica*) vein. ~**sidad** *f*, ~**sismo** *m* nervousness; (*impaciencia*) impatience. ~**so** *adj* nervous; (*de temperamento*) highly-strung. **ponerse** ~**so** get nervous

neto *adj* clear; (*verdad*) simple; (*Com*) net

neumático *adj* pneumatic. ● *m* tyre

neumonía *f* pneumonia

neur|algia *f* neuralgia. ~**ología** *f* neurology. ~**ólogo** *m* neurologist. ~**osis** *f* neurosis. ~**ótico** *adj*

n

neurotic

neutr|al adj neutral. **~alidad** f neutrality. **~alizar 10** vt neutralize. **~o** adj neutral; (Gram) neuter

neva|da f snowfall. **~r 1** vi snow. **~sca** f blizzard

nevera f refrigerator, fridge (Brit)

nevisca f light snowfall

nexo m link

ni conj. **~...** ~ neither... nor. ~ aunque not even if. ~ siquiera not even. **sin...~** ... without ... or...

Nicaragua f Nicaragua

nicaragüense adj & m & f Nicaraguan

nicho m niche

nicotina f nicotine

nido m nest; (de ladrones) den

niebla f fog. **hay ~** it's foggy. **un día de ~** a foggy day

niet|a f granddaughter. **~o** m grandson. **~os** mpl grandchildren

nieve f snow; (Mex, helado) sorbet

niki m polo shirt

nimi|edad f triviality. **~o** adj insignificant

ninfa f nymph

ningún véase **NINGUNO**

ninguno adj (delante de nombre masculino en singular ningún) no; (con otro negativo) any. **de ninguna manera, de ningún modo** by no means. **en ninguna parte** nowhere. **sin ningún amigo** without any friends. ●pron (de dos) neither; (de más de dos) none; (nadie) no-one, nobody

niñ|a f (little) girl. **~era** f nanny. **~ería** f childish thing. **~ez** f childhood. **~o** adj childish. ● m (little) boy **de ~o** as a child. **desde ~o** from childhood

níquel m nickel

níspero m medlar

nitidez f clarity; (de foto, imagen) sharpness

nítido adj clear; (foto, imagen) sharp

nitrógeno m nitrogen

nivel m level; (fig) standard. ~ **de vida** standard of living. **~ar** vt level. **~arse** vpr become level

no adv not; (como respuesta) no. **¿~?** isn't it? **¡a que ~!** I bet you don't! **¡cómo ~!** of course! **Felipe ~ tiene hijos** Felipe has no children. **¡que ~!** certainly not!

noble adj & m & f noble. **~mente** adv nobly. **~za** f nobility

noche f night. ~ **vieja** New Year's Eve. **de ~** at night. **hacerse de ~** get dark. **hacer ~** spend the night. **media ~** midnight. **en la ~** (LAm), **por la ~** at night

> **Nochevieja** In Spain and other Spanish-speaking countries, where it is known as Año Nuevo, it is customary to see the New Year in by eating twelve grapes for good luck, one at each chime of the clock at midnight.

Nochebuena f Christmas Eve

noción f notion. **nociones** fpl rudiments

nocivo adj harmful

nocturno adj nocturnal; (clase) evening; (tren etc) night. ● m nocturne

nodriza f wet nurse

nogal m walnut tree; (madera) walnut

nómada adj nomadic. ● m & f nomad

nombr|ado adj famous; (susodicho) aforementioned. **~amiento** m appointment. **~ar** vt appoint; (citar) mention. **~e** m name; (Gram) noun; (fama) renown. **~e de pila** Christian name. **en ~e de** in the name of. **no tener ~e** be unspeakable. **poner de ~e** call

nomeolvides m invar forget-me-not

nómina f payroll

nomina|l adj nominal. **~tivo** adj & m nominative. **~tivo a** (cheque etc) made out to

non adj odd. ● m odd number. **pares y ~es** odds and evens

nono adj ninth

nordeste adj (región) north-eastern; (viento) north-easterly. ● m northeast

nórdico adj Nordic. ● m Northern European

noria f water-wheel; (en una feria) big wheel (Brit), Ferris wheel (Amer)

norma f rule

normal adj normal. ● f teachers' training college. **~idad** f normality (Brit), normalcy (Amer). **~izar** 10 vt normalize. **~mente** adv normally, usually

noroeste adj (región) north-western; (viento) north-westerly. ● m northwest

norte adj (región) northern; (viento, lado) north. ● m north; (fig, meta) aim

Norteamérica f (North) America

norteamericano adj & m (North) American

norteño adj northern. ● m northerner

Noruega f Norway

noruego adj & m Norwegian

nos pron (acusativo) us; (dativo) (to) us; (reflexivo) (to) ourselves; (recíproco) (to) each other

nosotros pron we; (con prep) us

nost|algia f nostalgia; (de casa, de patria) homesickness. **~álgico** adj nostalgic

nota f note; (de examen etc) mark. **de ~** famous. **de mala ~** notorious. **digno de ~** notable. **~ble** adj notable. **~ción** f notation. **~r** vt notice. **es de ~r** it should be noted. **hacerse ~r** stand out

notario m notary

notici|a f (piece of) news. **~as** fpl news. **atrasado de ~as** behind with the news. **tener ~as de** hear from. **~ario**, (LAm) **~ero** m news

notifica|ción f notification. **~r** 7 vt notify

notori|edad f notoriety. **~o** adj well-known; (evidente) obvious; (notable) marked

novato adj inexperienced. ● m novice

novecientos adj & m nine hundred

noved|ad f newness; (cosa nueva) innovation; (cambio) change; (moda) latest fashion. **llegar sin ~ad** arrive safely. **~oso** adj novel

novel|a f novel. **~ista** m & f novelist

noveno adj ninth

noventa adj & m ninety; (nonagésimo) ninetieth

novia f girlfriend; (prometida) fiancée; (en boda) bride. **~r** vi (LAm) go out together. **~zgo** m engagement

novicio m novice

noviembre m November

novill|a f heifer. **~o** m bullock. **hacer ~os** play truant

novio m boyfriend; (*prometido*) fiancé; (*en boda*) bridegroom. **los** ~**s** the bride and groom

nub|arrón m large dark cloud. ~**e** f cloud; (*de insectos etc*) swarm. ~**lado** adj cloudy, overcast. ● m cloud. ~**lar** vt cloud. ~**larse** vpr become cloudy; (*vista*) cloud over. ~**oso** adj cloudy

nuca f back of the neck

nuclear adj nuclear

núcleo m nucleus

nudillo m knuckle

nudis|mo m nudism. ~**ta** m & f nudist

nudo m knot; (*de asunto etc*) crux. **tener un** ~ **en la garganta** have a lump in one's throat. ~**so** adj knotty

nuera f daughter-in-law

nuestro adj our. ● pron ours. ~ **amigo** our friend. **un coche** ~ a car of ours

nueva f (piece of) news. ~**s** fpl news. ~**mente** adv again

Nueva Zelanda f, (LAm) **Nueva Zelandia** f New Zealand

nueve adj & m nine

nuevo adj new. **de** ~ again. **estar** ~ be as good as new

nuez f walnut. ~ **de Adán** Adam's apple. ~ **moscada** nutmeg

nul|idad f nullity; (*fam, persona*) dead loss ⊞. ~**o** adj useless; (*Jurid*) null and void

num|eración f numbering. ~**eral** adj & m numeral. ~**erar** vt number. ~**érico** adj numerical

número m number; (*arábigo, romano*) numeral; (*de zapatos etc*) size; (*billete de lotería*) lottery ticket; (*de publicación*) issue. **sin** ~ countless

numeroso adj numerous

nunca adv never. ~ (**ja**)**más** never again. **casi** ~ hardly ever. **como** ~ like never before. **más que** ~ more than ever

nupcial adj nuptial. **banquete** ~ wedding breakfast

nutria f otter

nutri|ción f nutrition. ~**do** adj nourished, fed; (*fig*) large; (*aplausos*) loud; (*fuego*) heavy. ~**r** vt nourish, feed; (*fig*) feed. ~**tivo** adj nutritious. **valor** m ~**tivo** nutritional value

nylon m nylon

Ññ

ñapa f (LAm) extra goods given free

ñato adj (LAm) snub-nosed

ñoñ|ería f, ~**ez** f insipidity. ~**o** adj insipid; (*tímido*) bashful; (*quisquilloso*) prudish

Oo

o conj or. ~ **bien** rather. ~... ~ either ... or

oasis m invar oasis

obed|ecer ⊞ vt/i obey. ~**iencia** f obedience. ~**iente** adj obedient

obes|idad f obesity. ~**o** adj obese

obispo m bishop

obje|ción f objection. **~tar** vt/i object

objetivo adj objective. ● m objective; (foto etc) lens

objeto m object. **~r** m objector. **~ de conciencia** conscientious objector

oblicuo adj oblique

obliga|ción f obligation; (Com) bond. **~do** adj obliged; (forzoso) obligatory; **~r 12** vt force, oblige. **~rse** vpr. **~rse a** undertake to. **~torio** adj obligatory

oboe m oboe. ● m & f (músico) oboist

obra f work; (acción) deed; (de teatro) play; (construcción) building work. **~ maestra** masterpiece. **en ~s** under construction. **por ~ de** thanks to. **~r** vt do

obrero adj labour; (clase) working. ● m workman; (de fábrica, construcción) worker

obscen|idad f obscenity. **~o** adj obscene

obscu... véase **oscu...**

obsequi|ar vt lavish attention on. **~ar con** give, present with. **~o** m gift, present; (agasajo) attention. **~oso** adj obliging

observa|ción f observation. **hacer una ~ción** make a remark. **~dor** m observer. **~ncia** f observance. **~r** vt observe; (notar) notice. **~torio** m observatory

obses|ión f obsession. **~ionar** vt obsess. **~ivo** adj obsessive. **~o** adj obsessed

obst|aculizar 10 vt hinder; hold up (tráfico). **~áculo** m obstacle

obstante: no **~** adv however, nevertheless; (como prep) in spite of

obstar vi. eso no obsta para que vaya that should not prevent him

from going

obstina|do adj obstinate. **~rse** vpr. **~rse en** (+ infinitivo) insist on (+ gerundio)

obstru|cción f obstruction. **~ir 17** vt obstruct

obtener 40 vt get, obtain

obtura|dor m (Foto) shutter. **~r** vt plug; fill (muela etc)

obvio adj obvious

oca f goose

ocasi|ón f occasion; (oportunidad) opportunity. **aprovechar la ~ón** take the opportunity. **con ~ón de** on the occasion of. **de ~ón** bargain; (usado) second-hand. **en ~ones** sometimes. **perder una ~ón** miss a chance. **~onal** adj chance. **~onar** vt cause

ocaso m sunset; (fig) decline

occident|al adj western. ● m & f westerner. **~e** m west

océano m ocean

ochenta adj & m eighty

ocho adj & m eight. **~cientos** adj & m eight hundred

ocio m idleness; (tiempo libre) leisure time. **~sidad** f idleness. **~so** adj idle; (inútil) pointless

oct|agonal adj octagonal. **~ágono** m octagon

octano m octane

octav|a f octave. **~o** adj & m eighth

octogenario adj & m octogenarian

octubre m October

ocular adj eye

oculista m & f ophthalmologist, ophthalmic optician

ocult|ar vt hide. **~arse** vpr hide. **~o** adj hidden; (secreto) secret

ocupa|ción f occupation. **~do**

adj occupied; (persona) busy. **estar ~do** (asiento) be taken; (línea telefónica) be engaged (Brit) be busy (Amer). **~nte** m & f occupant. **~r** vt occupy, take up (espacio). **~rse** vpr look after

ocurr|encia f occurrence, event; (idea) idea; (que tiene gracia) witty remark. **~ir** vi happen. ¿qué ~e? what's the matter? **~irse** vpr occur. **se me ~e que** it occurs to me that

oda f ode

odi|ar vt hate. **~o** m hatred. **~oso** adj hateful; (persona) horrible

oeste adj (región) western; (viento, lado) west. ● m west

ofen|der vt offend; (insultar) insult. **~derse** vpr take offence. **~sa** f offence. **~siva** f offensive. **~sivo** adj offensive

oferta f offer; (en subasta) bid. **~s de empleo** situations vacant. **en ~** on (special) offer

oficial adj official. ● m skilled worker; (Mil) officer

oficin|a f office. **~a de colocación** employment office. **~a de turismo** tourist office. **horas fpl de ~a** business hours. **~ista** m & f office worker

oficio m trade. **~so** adj (no oficial) unofficial

ofrec|er 11 vt offer; give (fiesta, banquete etc); (prometer) promise. **~erse** vpr volunteer. **~imiento** m offer

ofrenda f offering. **~r** vt offer

ofuscar 7 vt blind; (confundir) confuse. **~se** vpr get worked up

oí|ble adj audible. **~do** m ear; (sentido) hearing. **al ~do** in one's ear. **de ~das** by hearsay. **conocer**

de ~das have heard of. **de ~do** by ear. **duro de ~do** hard of hearing

oigo vb véase **OIR**

oír 50 vt hear. **¡oiga!** listen!; (al teléfono) hello!

ojal m buttonhole

ojalá int I hope so! ● conj if only

ojea|da f glance. **dar una ~da a, echar una ~da a** have a quick glance at. **~r** vt have a look at

ojeras fpl rings under one's eyes

ojeriza f ill will. **tener ~ a** have a grudge against

ojo m eye; (de cerradura) keyhole; (de un puente) span. **¡~!** careful!

ola f wave

olé int bravo!

olea|da f wave. **~je** m swell

óleo m oil; (cuadro) oil painting

oleoducto m oil pipeline

oler 2 (las formas que empiecen por ue se escriben hue) vt smell. ● vi smell (a of). **me huele mal** (fig) it sounds fishy to me

olfat|ear vt sniff; scent (rastro). **~o** m (sense of) smell; (fig) intuition

olimpiada f, **olimpíada** f Olympic games, Olympics

olímpico adj Olympic; (fig, fam) total

oliva f olive. **~ar** m olive grove. **~o** m olive tree

olla f pot, casserole. **~ a/de presión, ~ exprés** pressure cooker

olmo m elm (tree)

olor m smell. **~oso** adj sweet-smelling

olvid|adizo adj forgetful. **~ar** vt forget. **~arse** vpr forget. **~arse de** forget. **se me ~ó** I forgot. **~o** m oblivion; (acto) omission

ombligo *m* navel

omi|sión *f* omission. ~**tir** *vt* omit

ómnibus *adj* omnibus

omnipotente *adj* omnipotent

omóplato *m* shoulder blade

once *adj & m* eleven

ond|a *f* wave. ~**a corta** short wave. ~**a larga** long wave. **longitud** *f* **de** ~**a** wavelength. ~**ear** *vi* wave; (agua) ripple. ~**ulación** *f* undulation; (del pelo) wave. ~**ular** *vi* wave

onomásti|co *adj* (índice) of names. ● *m* (LAm) saint's day

onomástica See ▷SANTO

ONU *abrev* (**Organización de las Naciones Unidas**) UN

OPA *f* take-over bid

opac|ar **7** (LAm) make opaque; (deslucir) mar; (anular) overshadow. ~**o** *adj* opaque; (fig) dull

opci|ón *f* option. ~**onal** *adj* optional

open-jaw *m* open jaws ticket

ópera *f* opera

opera|ción *f* operation; (Com) transaction; ~ **retorno** (Esp) return to work (after the holidays). ~**dor** *m* operator; (TV) cameraman, (Mex, obrero) machinist. ~**r** *vt* operate on; work (milagro etc); (Mex) operate (máquina). ● *vi* operate; (Com) deal. ~**rse** *vpr* take place; (Med) have an operation. ~**torio** *adj* operative

opereta *f* operetta

opin|ar *vi* express one's opinion. ● *vt* think. ~ **que** think that. ¿**qué opinas?** what do you think? ~**ión** *f* opinion. **la** ~**ión pública** public opinion

opio *m* opium

opone|nte *adj* opposing. ● *m & f* opponent. ~**r** *vt* oppose; offer (resistencia); raise (objeción). ~**rse** *vpr* be opposed; (dos personas) oppose each other

oporto *m* port (wine)

oportun|idad *f* opportunity; (cualidad de oportuno) timeliness; (LAm, ocasión) occasion. ~**ista** *m & f* opportunist. ~**o** *adj* opportune; (apropiado) suitable

oposi|ción *f* opposition. ~**ciones** *fpl* public examination. ~**tor** *m* candidate; (Pol) opponent

opres|ión *f* oppression; (ahogo) difficulty in breathing. ~**ivo** *adj* oppressive. ~**or** *m* oppressor

oprimir *vt* squeeze; press (botón etc); (ropa) be too tight for; (fig) oppress

optar *vi* choose. ~ **por** opt for

óptic|a *f* optics; (tienda) optician's (shop). ~**o** *adj* optic(al). ● *m* optician

optimis|mo *m* optimism. ~**ta** *adj* optimistic. ● *m & f* optimist

óptimo *adj* ideal; (condiciones) perfect

opuesto *adj* opposite; (opiniones) conflicting

opulen|cia *f* opulence. ~**to** *adj* opulent

oración *f* prayer; (Gram) sentence

ora|dor *m* speaker. ~**l** *adj* oral

órale *int* (Mex) come on!; (de acuerdo) OK!

orar *vi* pray (por for)

órbita *f* orbit

orden *f* order. ~ **del día** agenda. **órdenes** *fpl* **sagradas** Holy Orders. **a sus órdenes** (esp Mex) can I help you? ~ **de arresto** arrest warrant. **en** ~ in order. **por** ~ in turn.

o

~**ado** adj tidy

ordenador m computer

ordena|nza f ordinance. ● m (Mil) orderly. ~**r** vt put in order; (mandar) order; (Relig) ordain; (LAm, en restaurante) order

ordeñar vt milk

ordinario adj ordinary; (grosero) common; (de mala calidad) poor-quality

orear vt air

orégano m oregano

oreja f ear

orfanato m orphanage

orfebre m goldsmith, silversmith

orfeón m choral society

orgánico adj organic

organillo m barrel-organ

organismo m organism

organista m & f organist

organiza|ción f organization. ~**dor** m organizer. ~**r** 10 vt organize. ~**rse** vpr get organized

órgano m organ

orgasmo m orgasm

orgía f orgy

orgullo m pride. ~**so** adj proud

orientación f orientation; (guía) guidance; (Archit) aspect

oriental adj & m & f oriental

orientar vt position; advise (persona). ~**se** vpr point; (persona) find one's bearings

oriente m east

orificio m hole

orig|en m origin. dar ~**en** a give rise to. ~**inal** adj original; (excéntrico) odd. ~**inalidad** f originality. ~**inar** vt give rise to. ~**inario** adj original; (nativo) native. ser ~**inario de** come from. ~**inarse** vpr originate; (incendio) start

orilla f (del mar) shore; (de río) bank; (borde) edge. **a** ~**s del mar** by the sea

orina f urine. ~**l** m chamber-pot. ~**r** vi urinate

oriundo adj native. **ser** ~ **de** (persona) come from; (especie etc) native to

ornamental adj ornamental

ornitología f ornithology

oro m gold. ~**s** mpl Spanish card suit. ~ **de ley** 9 carat gold. **hacerse de** ~ make a fortune. **prometer el** ~ **y el moro** promise the moon

orquesta f orchestra. ~**l** adj orchestral. ~**r** vt orchestrate

orquídea f orchid

ortiga f nettle

ortodoxo adj orthodox

ortografía f spelling

ortopédico adj orthopaedic

oruga f caterpillar

orzuelo m sty

os pron (acusativo) you; (dativo) (to) you; (reflexivo) (to) yourselves; (recíproco) (to) each other

osad|ía f boldness. ~**o** adj bold

oscila|ción f swinging; (de precios) fluctuation; (Tec) oscillation. ~**r** vi swing; (precio) fluctuate; (Tec) oscillate

oscur|ecer 11 vi get dark. ● vt darken; (fig) obscure. ~**ecerse** vpr grow dark; (nublarse) cloud over. ~**idad** f darkness; (fig) obscurity. ~**o** adj dark; (fig) obscure. **a** ~**as** in the dark

óseo adj bone

oso m bear. ~ **de felpa**, ~ **de peluche** teddy bear

ostensible adj obvious

ostent|ación f ostentation. ~**ar**

vt show off; (*mostrar*) show. **~oso** *adj* ostentatious

osteópata *m & f* osteopath

ostión *m* (*esp Mex*) oyster

ostra *f* oyster

ostracismo *m* ostracism

Otan *abrev* (**Organización del Tratado del Atlántico Norte**) NATO, North Atlantic Treaty Organization

otitis *f* inflammation of the ear

otoño *m* autumn (*Brit*), fall (*Amer*)

otorga|miento *m* granting. **~r** [12] *vt* give; grant (*préstamo*); (*Jurid*) draw up (*testamento*)

otorrinolaringólogo *m* ear, nose and throat specialist

otro, otra

● *adjetivo*

····➤ another; (*con artículo, posesivo*) other. **come ~ pedazo** have another piece. **el ~ día** the other day. **mi ~ coche** my other car. **otra cosa** something else. **otra persona** somebody else. **otra vez** again

····➤ (*en plural*) other; (*con numeral*) another. **en otras ocasiones** on other occasions. **~s 3 vasos** another 3 glasses

····➤ (*siguiente*) next. **al ~ día** the next day. **me bajo en la otra estación** I get off at the next station

● *pronombre*

····➤ (*cosa*) another one. **lo cambié por ~** I changed it for another one

····➤ (*persona*) someone else. **invitó a ~** she invited someone else

····➤ (*en plural*) (some) others. **tengo ~s en casa** I have

(some) others at home. **~s piensan lo contrario** others think the opposite

····➤ (*con artículo*) **el ~** the other one. **los ~s** the others. **uno detrás del ~** one after the other. **los ~s no vinieron** the others didn't come. **esta semana no, la otra** not this week, next week. **de un día para el ~** from one day to the next

 Para usos complementarios ver **uno, tanto**

ovación *f* ovation

oval *adj*, **ovalado** *adj* oval

óvalo *m* oval

ovario *m* ovary

oveja *f* sheep; (*hembra*) ewe

overol *m* (*LAm*) overalls

ovillo *m* ball. **hacerse un ~** curl up

OVNI *abrev* (**objeto volante no identificado**) UFO

ovulación *f* ovulation

oxida|ción *f* rusting. **~r** *vi* rust. **~rse** *vpr* go rusty

óxido *m* rust; (*en química*) oxide

oxígeno *m* oxygen

oye *vb véase* **oír**

oyente *adj* listening. ● *m & f* listener; (*Univ*) occasional student

ozono *m* ozone

Pp

pabellón m pavilion; (en jardín) summerhouse; (en hospital) block; (de instrumento) bell; (bandera) flag

pacer 11 vi graze

pachucho adj (fruta) overripe; (persona) poorly

pacien|cia f patience. perder la ~cia lose patience. ~te adj & m & f patient

pacificar 7 vt pacify. ~se vpr calm down

pacífico adj peaceful. el (Océano) P~ the Pacific (Ocean)

pacifis|mo m pacifism. ~ta adj & m & f pacifist

pact|ar vi agree, make a pact. ~o m pact, agreement

padec|er 11 vt/i suffer (de from); (soportar) bear. ~er del corazón have heart trouble. ~imiento m suffering

padrastro m stepfather

padre adj 1 terrible; (Mex, estupendo) great. ● m father. ~s mpl parents

padrino m godfather; (en boda) man who gives away the bride

padrón m register. ~ electoral (LAm) electoral roll

paella f paella

paga f payment; (sueldo) pay. ~dero adj payable

pagano adj & m pagan

pagar 12 vt pay; pay for (compras). ● vi pay. ~é m IOU

página f page

pago m payment

país m country; (ciudadanos) na-

tion. ~ natal native land. el P~ Vasco the Basque Country. los P~es Bajos the Low Countries

paisaje m landscape, scenery

paisano m compatriot

paja f straw; (en texto) padding

pájaro m bird. ~ carpintero woodpecker

paje m page

pala f shovel; (para cavar) spade; (para basura) dustpan; (de pimpón) bat

palabr|a f word; (habla) speech. pedir la ~a ask to speak. tomar la ~a take the floor. ~ota f swear-word. decir ~otas swear

palacio m palace

paladar m palate

palanca f lever; (fig) influence. ~ de cambio (de velocidades) gear lever (Brit), gear shift (Amer)

palangana f washbasin (Brit), washbowl (Amer)

palco m (en el teatro) box

palestino adj & m Palestinian

paleta f (de pintor) palette; (de albañil) trowel

paleto m yokel

paliativo adj & m palliative

palide|cer 11 vi turn pale. ~z f paleness

pálido adj pale. ponerse ~ turn pale

palillo m (de dientes) toothpick; (para comer) chopstick

paliza f beating

palma f (de la mano) palm; (árbol) palm (tree); (de dátiles) date palm. dar ~s clap. ~da f pat; (LAm) slap. ~das fpl applause

palmera f palm tree

palmo m span; (fig) few inches. ~ a ~ inch by inch

palmote|ar vi clap. ~**o** m clapping, applause

palo m stick; (de valla) post; (de golf) club; (golpe) blow; (de naipes) suit; (mástil) mast

paloma f pigeon; (blanca, símbolo) dove

palomitas fpl popcorn

palpar vt feel

palpita|ción f palpitation. ~**nte** adj throbbing. ~**r** vi beat; (latir con fuerza) pound; (vena, sien) throb

palta f (LAm) avocado (pear)

paludismo m malaria

pamela f (woman's) broad-brimmed dress hat

pamp|a f pampas. ~**ero** adj of the pampas

pan m bread; (barra) loaf. ~ **integral** wholewheat bread, wholemeal bread (Brit). ~ **tostado** toast. ~ **rallado** breadcrumbs. **ganarse el** ~ earn one's living

pana f corduroy

panader|ía f bakery; (tienda) baker's (shop). ~**o** m baker

panal m honeycomb

panameño adj & m Panamanian

pancarta f banner, placard

panda m panda

pander|eta f (small) tambourine. ~**o** m tambourine

pandilla f gang

panecillo m (bread) roll

panel m panel

panfleto m pamphlet

pánico m panic. **tener** ~ be terrified (a of)

panor|ama m panorama. ~**ámico** adj panoramic

panque m (Mex) sponge cake

pantaletas fpl (Mex) panties, knickers (Brit)

pantalla f screen; (de lámpara) (lamp)shade

pantalón m, **pantalones** mpl trousers. ~ **a la cadera** bumsters

pantano m marsh; (embalse) reservoir. ~**so** adj marshy

pantera f panther

panti m (Mex), **pantimedias** fpl tights (Brit), pantyhose (Amer)

pantomima f pantomime

pantorrilla f calf

pantufla f slipper

panz|a f belly. ~**udo** adj potbellied

pañal m nappy (Brit), diaper (Amer)

paño m material; (de lana) woollen cloth; (trapo) cloth. ~ **de cocina** dishcloth; (para secar) tea towel. ~ **higiénico** sanitary towel. **en** ~**s menores** in one's underclothes

pañuelo m handkerchief; (de cabeza) scarf

papa m pope. ●f (LAm) potato. ~**s fritas** (LAm) chips (Brit), French fries (Amer); (de paquete) crisps (Brit), chips (Amer)

papá m dad(dy). ~**s** mpl parents. **P~ Noel** Father Christmas

papada f (de persona) double chin

papagayo m parrot

papalote m (Mex) kite

papanatas m invar simpleton

paparrucha f (tontería) silly thing

papaya f papaya, pawpaw

papel m paper; (en el teatro etc) role. ~ **carbón** carbon paper. ~ **de calcar** tracing paper. ~ **de envolver** wrapping paper. ~ **de plata** silver paper. ~ **higiénico** toilet paper. **~ pintado** wallpaper. **~ secante** blotting paper. **~eo** m paperwork. **~era** f waste-paper basket. **~ería** f stationer's (shop). **~eta** f (para votar) (ballot) paper

paperas fpl mumps

paquete m packet; (bulto) parcel; (LAm, de papas fritas) bag; (Mex, problema) headache. **~ postal** parcel

Paquistán m Pakistan

paquistaní adj & m Pakistani

par adj (número) even. ● m couple; (dos cosas iguales) pair. a **~es** two by two. de **~ en ~** wide open. **~es y nones** odds and evens. sin **~** without equal. ● f par. a la **~** (Com) at par. a la **~ que** at the same time

---

para preposición

····▸ for. es **~** ti it's for you. **~** siempre for ever. ¿**~** qué? what for? **~** mi cumpleaños for my birthday

····▸ (con infinitivo) to. es muy tarde **~** llamar it's too late to call. salió **~** divertirse he went out to have fun. lo hago **~** ahorrar I do it (in order) to save money

····▸ (dirección) iba **~** la oficina he was going to the office. empújalo **~** atrás push it back. ¿vas **~** casa? are you going home?

····▸ (tiempo) by. debe estar listo **~** el 5 it must be ready by the 5th. **~** entonces by then

····▸ (LAm, hora) to. son 5 **~** la una it's 5 to one

····▸ **~** que so (that). grité **~** que me oyera I shouted so

(that) he could hear me.

Note that **para que** is always followed by a verb in the subjunctive

parabienes mpl congratulations

parábola f (narración) parable

parabólica f satellite dish

para|brisas m invar windscreen (Brit), windshield (Amer). **~caídas** m invar parachute. **~caidista** m & f parachutist; (Mil) paratrooper. **~choques** m invar bumper (Brit), fender (Amer) (Rail) buffer

parad|a f (acción) stop; (lugar) bus stop; (de taxis) rank; (Mil) parade. **~ero** m whereabouts; (LAm, lugar) bus stop. **~o** adj stationary; (desempleado) unemployed. estar **~** (LAm, de pie) be standing

paradoja f paradox

parador m state-owned hotel

---

parador (nacional de turismo) A national chain of hotels in Spain. They are often converted castles, palaces and monasteries. They provide a high standard of accommodation but are relatively inexpensive and often act as showcases for local craftsmanship and cooking.

---

parafina f paraffin

paraguas m invar umbrella

Paraguay m Paraguay

paraguayo adj & m Paraguayan

paraíso m paradise; (en el teatro) gallery

paralel|a f parallel (line). **~as** fpl parallel bars. **~o** adj & m parallel

par|álisis f invar paralysis. **~alítico** adj paralytic. **~alizar** 🔟 vt paralyse

parámetro m parameter

paramilitar adj paramilitary

páramo m bleak upland

parangón m comparison

paraninfo m main hall

paranoi|a f paranoia. **~co** adj paranoiac

parar vt/i stop. **sin ~** continuously. **~se** vpr stop; (LAm, ponerse de pie) stand

pararrayos m invar lightning conductor

parásito adj parasitic. • m parasite

parcela f plot. **~r** vt divide into plots

parche m patch

parcial adj partial. **a tiempo ~** part-time. **~idad** f prejudice

parco adj laconic; (sobrio) frugal

parear vt put into pairs

parec|er m opinion. al **~er** apparently. a mi **~er** in my opinion. • vi 🔢 seem; (asemejarse) look like; (tener aspecto de) look. me **~e** I think. **~e fácil** it looks easy. ¿qué te **~e?** what do you think? según **~e** apparently. **~erse** vpr look alike. **~ido** adj similar. **bien ~ido** good-looking. • m similarity

pared f wall. **~ por medio** next door. **~ón** m (de fusilamiento) wall. **llevar al ~ón** shoot

parej|a f pair; (hombre y mujer) couple; (compañero) partner. **~a de hecho** legalised partnership of unmarried couple. **~o** adj the same; (LAm, sin desniveles) even; (LAm, liso) smooth; (Mex, equitativo) equal. • adv (LAm) evenly

parente|la f relations. **~sco** m relationship

paréntesis m invar parenthesis, bracket (Brit); (intervalo) break. **entre ~** in brackets (Brit), in parenthesis: (fig) by the way

paria m & f outcast

paridad f equality; (Com) parity

pariente m & f relation, relative

parir vt give birth to. • vi give birth

parisiense adj & m & f, **parisino** adj & m Parisian

parking /'parkin/ m car park (Brit), parking lot (Amer)

parlament|ar vi talk. **~ario** adj parliamentary. • m member of parliament (Brit), congressman (Amer). **~o** m parliament

parlanchín adj talkative. • m chatterbox

parlante m (LAm) loudspeaker

paro m stoppage; (desempleo) unemployment; (subsidio) unemployment benefit; (LAm, huelga) strike. **~ cardíaco** cardiac arrest

parodia f parody

parpadear vi blink; (luz) flicker

párpado m eyelid

parque m park. **~ de atracciones** funfair. **~ eólico** wind farm. **~ infantil** playground. **~ zoológico** zoo, zoological gardens

parquímetro m parking meter

parra f grapevine

párrafo m paragraph

parrilla f grill; (LAm, Auto) luggage rack. **a la ~** grilled. **~da** f grill

párroco m parish priest

parroqui|a f parish; (iglesia) parish church. **~no** m parishioner

parte m (informe) report. **dar ~** report. **de mi ~** for me •f part; (porción) share; (Jurid) party; (Mex,

P

repuesto) spare (part). **de ~** de from. **¿de ~ de quién?** (al teléfono) who's speaking? **en cualquier ~** anywhere. **en gran ~** largely. **en ~** partly. **en todas ~s** everywhere. **la mayor ~** the majority. **la ~ superior** the top. **ninguna ~** nowhere. **por otra ~** on the other hand. **por todas ~s** everywhere

partera f midwife

partición f division; (Pol) partition

participa|ción f participation; (noticia) announcement; (de lotería) share. **~nte** adj participating. ● m & f participant. **~r** vt announce. ● vi take part

participio m participle

particular adj particular; (clase) private, nada de ~ nothing special. ● m private individual.

partida f departure; (en registro) entry; (documento) certificate; (de mercancías) consignment; (juego) game; (de gente) group

partidario adj & m partisan. **~ de** in favour of

parti|do m (Pol) party; (encuentro) match, game; (LAm, de ajedrez) game. **~r** vt cut; (romper) break; crack (nueces). ● vi leave. **a ~r de** from. **~ de** the start from. **~rse** vpr (romperse) break; (dividirse) split

partitura f (Mus) score

parto m labour. **estar de ~** be in labour

parvulario m kindergarten, nursery school (Brit)

pasa f raisin. **~ de Corinto** currant

pasa|da f passing; (de puntos) row. **de ~da** in passing. **~dero** adj passable. **~dizo** m passage.

~do adj past; (día, mes etc) last; (anticuado) old-fashioned; (comida) bad, off. **~do mañana** the day after tomorrow. **~dos tres días** after three days. **~dor** m bolt; (de pelo) hair-slide

pasaje m passage; (pasajeros) passengers; (LAm, de avión etc) ticket. **~ro** adj passing. ● m passenger

pasamano(s) m handrail; (barandilla de escalera) banister(s)

pasamontañas m invar balaclava

pasaporte m passport

pasar vt pass; (atravesar) go through; (filtrar) strain; spend (tiempo); show (película); (tolerar) tolerate; give (mensaje, enfermedad). ● vi pass; (suceder) happen; (ir) go; (venir) come; (tiempo) go by. **~ de** have no interest in. **~lo bien** have a good time. **~ frío** be cold. **~ la aspiradora** vacuum. **~ por alto** leave out. **lo que pasa es que** the fact is that. **pase lo que pase** whatever happens. **¡pase Vd!** come in!, go in! **¡que lo pases bien!** have a good time! **¿qué pasa?** what's the matter?, what's happening? **~se** vpr pass; (dolor) go away; (flores) wither; (comida) go bad; spend (tiempo); (excederse) go too far

pasarela f footbridge; (Naut) gangway

pasatiempo m hobby, pastime

Pascua f (fiesta de los hebreos) Passover; (de Resurrección) Easter; (Navidad) Christmas. **~s** fpl Christmas

pase m pass

pase|ante m & f passer-by. **~ar** vt walk (perro); (exhibir) show off. ● vi walk. **ir a ~ar, salir a ~ar** walk. **~arse** vpr walk. **~o** m walk; (en coche etc) ride; (calle) avenue. **~o**

marítimo promenade. **dar un ～o,
ir de ～** go for a walk. **¡vete a ～o!**
⚠ get lost! ⚠

pasillo m corridor; (de cine, avión)
aisle

pasión f passion

pasivo adj passive

pasm|ar vt astonish. **～arse** vpr be
astonished

paso m step; (acción de pasar)
passing; (camino) way; (entre montañas) pass; (estrecho) strait(s). **～
a nivel** level crossing (Brit), grade
crossing (Amer). **～ de cebra** zebra
crossing. **～ de peatones** pedestrian crossing. **～ elevado** flyover
(Brit), overpass (Amer). **a cada ～** at
every turn. **a dos ～s** very near. **de
～** in passing. **de ～** por just passing
through. **oír ～s** hear footsteps. **prohibido el ～** no entry

pasota m & f drop-out

pasta f paste; (masa) dough; (sl,
dinero) dough ⚠. **～s** fpl pasta;
(pasteles) pastries. **～ de dientes**,
～ dentífrica toothpaste

pastel m cake; (empanada) pie;
(lápiz) pastel. **～ería** f cake shop

pasteurizado adj pasteurized

pastilla f pastille; (de jabón) bar;
(de chocolate) piece

pasto m pasture; (hierba) grass;
(LAm, césped) lawn. **～r** m shepherd; (Relig) minister. **～ra** f shepherdess

pata f leg; (pie de perro, gato)
paw; (de ave) foot. **～ arriba** upside down. **a cuatro ～s** on all
fours. **meter la ～** put one's foot
in it. **tener mala ～** have bad luck.
～da f kick. **～lear** vi stamp one's
feet; (niño) kick

patata f potato. **～s fritas** chips
(Brit), French fries (Amer); (de bolsa)

(potato) crisps (Brit), (potato) chips
(Amer)

patente adj obvious. ● f licence

patern|al adj paternal; (cariño
etc) fatherly. **～idad** f paternity.
～o adj paternal; (cariño etc)
fatherly

patético adj moving

patillas fpl sideburns

patín m skate; (con ruedas) roller
skate. **patines en línea** Rollerblades (P)

patina|dor m skater. **～je** m skating. **～r** vi skate; (resbalar) slide;
(coche) skid

patio m patio. **～ de butacas** stalls
(Brit), orchestra (Amer)

pato m duck

patológico adj pathological

patoso adj clumsy

patraña f hoax

patria f homeland

patriarca m patriarch

patrimonio m patrimony; (fig)
heritage

patri|ota adj patriotic. ● m & f
patriot. **～otismo** m patriotism

patrocin|ar vt sponsor. **～io** m
sponsorship

patrón m (jefe) boss; (de pensión
etc) landlord; (en costura) pattern

patrulla f patrol; (fig, cuadrilla)
group. **～r** vt/i patrol

pausa f pause. **～do** adj slow

pauta f guideline

paviment|ar vt pave. **～o** m
pavement

pavo m turkey. **～ real** peacock

pavor m terror

payas|ada f buffoonery. **～o** m
clown

paz f peace

P

peaje m toll

peatón m pedestrian

peca f freckle

peca|do m sin; (defecto) fault. ~**dor** m sinner. ~**minoso** adj sinful. ~**r 7** vi sin

pech|o m chest; (de mujer) breast; (fig, corazón) heart. **dar el** ~**o a un niño** breast-feed a child. **tomar a** ~**o** take to heart. ~**uga** f breast

pecoso adj freckled

peculiar adj peculiar, particular. ~**idad** f peculiarity

pedal m pedal. ~**ear** vi pedal

pedante adj pedantic

pedazo m piece, bit. **a** ~**s** in pieces. **hacer(se)** ~**s** smash

pediatra m & f paediatrician

pedicuro m chiropodist

pedi|do m order; (LAm, solicitud) request. ~**r 5** vt ask for; (Com, en restaurante) order. ● vi ask. ~**r prestado** borrow

pega|dizo adj catchy. ~**joso** adj sticky

pega|mento m glue. ~**r 12** vt stick (on); (coser) sew on; give (enfermedad etc); (juntar) join; (golpear) hit; (dar) give. ~**r fuego a** set fire to ● vi stick. ~**rse** vpr stick; (pelearse) hit each other. ~**tina** f sticker

pein|ado m hairstyle. ~**ar** vt comb. ~**arse** vpr comb one's hair. ~**e** m comb. ~**eta** f ornamental comb

p.ej. abrev (por ejemplo) e.g.

pelado adj (fruta) peeled; (cabeza) bald; (terreno) bare

pela|je m (de animal) fur; (fig, aspecto) appearance. ~**mbre** m (de animal) fur; (de persona) thick hair

pelar vt peel; shell (habas); skin (tomates); pluck (ave)

peldaño m step; (de escalera de mano) rung

pelea f fight; (discusión) quarrel. ~**r** vi fight; (discutir) quarrel. ~**rse** vpr fight; (discutir) quarrel

peletería f fur shop

peliagudo adj difficult, tricky

pelícano m pelican

película f film (esp Brit), movie (esp Amer). ~ **de dibujos animados** cartoon (film)

peligro m danger; (riesgo) hazard, risk. **poner en** ~ endanger. ~**so** adj dangerous

pelirrojo adj red-haired

pellejo m skin

pellizc|ar 7 vt pinch. ~**o** m pinch

pelma m & f, **pelmazo** m bore, nuisance

pelo m hair. **no tener** ~**s en la lengua** be outspoken. **tomar el** ~ **a uno** pull s.o.'s leg

pelota f ball. ~ **vasca** pelota. **hacer la** ~ **a uno** suck up to s.o.

pelotera f squabble

peluca f wig

peludo adj hairy

peluquer|ía f hairdresser's. ~**o** m hairdresser

pelusa f down

pena f sadness; (lástima) pity; (LAm, vergüenza) embarrassment; (Jurid) sentence. ~ **de muerte** death penalty. **a duras** ~**s** with difficulty. **da** ~ **que** it's a pity that. **me da** ~ it makes me sad. **merecer la** ~ **be** worthwhile. **pasar** ~**s** suffer hardship. **¡qué** ~! what a pity! **valer la** ~ be worthwhile

penal adj penal; (derecho) criminal. ● m prison; (LAm, penalty)

penalty. **~idad** f suffering; (*Jurid*)
penalty. **~ty** m penalty

pendiente adj hanging; (*cuenta*)
outstanding; (*asunto etc*) pending.
● m earring. ● f slope

péndulo m pendulum

pene m penis

penetra|nte adj penetrating; (*so-
nido*) piercing; (*viento*) bitter. **~r**
vt penetrate; (*fig*) pierce. ● vi. **~r**
en penetrate; (*entrar*) go into

penicilina f penicillin

pen|ínsula f peninsula. **~insular**
adj peninsular

penique m penny

penitencia f penitence; (*castigo*)
penance

penoso adj painful; (*difícil*) difficult; (*LAm*, *tímido*) shy; (*LAm*, *embarazoso*) embarrassing

pensa|do adj. **bien ~do** all
things considered. **menos ~do**
least expected. **~dor** m thinker.
~miento m thought. **~r 1** vt
think; (*considerar*) consider.
cuando menos se piensa when
least expected. **¡ni ~rlo!** no way!
pienso que sí I think so. ● vi
think. **~r en** think about. **~tivo**
adj thoughtful

pensi|ón f pension; (*casa de hués-
pedes*) guest-house. **~ón completa** full board. **~onista** m & f
pensioner; (*huésped*) lodger

penúltimo adj & m penultimate,
last but one

penumbra f half-light

penuria f shortage. **pasar ~s** suffer hardship

peñ|a f rock; (*de amigos*) group;
(*LAm*, *club*) folk club. **~ón** m rock.
el P~ón de Gibraltar The Rock
(of Gibraltar)

peón m labourer; (*en ajedrez*)

pawn; (*en damas*) piece

peonza f (spinning) top

peor adj (*comparativo*) worse; (*superlativo*) worst. ●adv worse. **de
mal en ~** from bad to worse. **lo
~** the worst thing. **tanto ~** so
much the worse

pepin|illo m gherkin. **~o** m cu-
cumber. **(no) me importa un ~o**
I couldn't care less

pepita f pip; (*de oro*) nugget

pequeñ|ez f smallness; (*minucia*)
trifle. **~o** adj small, little; (*de edad*)
young; (*menor*) younger. ●m little
one. **es el ~o** he's the youngest

pera f (*fruta*) pear. **~l** m pear
(tree)

percance m mishap

percatarse vpr. **~ de** notice

perc|epción f perception. **~ibir**
vt perceive; earn (*dinero*)

percha f hanger; (*de aves*) ● perch

percusión f percussion

perde|dor adj losing. ● m loser.
~r 1 vt lose; (*malgastar*) waste;
miss (*tren etc*). ● vi lose. **~rse** vpr
get lost; (*desaparecer*) disappear;
(*desperdiciarse*) be wasted; (*estropearse*) be spoilt. **echar(se) a ~r**
spoil

pérdida f loss; (*de líquido*) leak;
(*de tiempo*) waste

perdido adj lost

perdiz f partridge

perd|ón m pardon, forgiveness.
pedir ~ón apologize. ●int sorry!
~onar vt excuse, forgive; (*Jurid*)
pardon. **¡~one (Vd)!** sorry!

perdura|ble adj lasting. **~r** vi
last

perece|dero adj perishable. **~r
11** vi perish

peregrin|ación f pilgrimage.

~o adj strange. ● m pilgrim

perejil m parsley

perengano m so-and-so

perenne adj everlasting; (planta) perennial

perez|a f laziness. ~**oso** adj lazy

perfec|ción f perfection. a la ~**ción** perfectly, to perfection. ~**cionar** vt perfect; (mejorar) improve. ~**cionista** m & f perfectionist. ~**to** adj perfect; (completo) complete

perfil m profile; (contorno) outline. ~**ado** adj well-shaped

perfora|ción f perforation. ~**dora** f punch. ~**r** vt pierce, perforate; punch (papel, tarjeta etc)

perfum|ar vt perfume. ~**arse** vpr put perfume on. ~**e** m perfume, scent. ~**ería** f perfumery

pericia f skill

perif|eria f (de ciudad) outskirts. ~**érico** adj (barrio) outlying. ● m (Mex, carretera) ring road

perilla f (barba) goatee

perímetro m perimeter

periódic|o adj periodic(al). ● m newspaper

periodis|mo m journalism. ~**ta** m & f journalist

período m, **periodo** m period

periquito m budgerigar

periscopio m periscope

perito adj & m expert

perju|dicar ⁊ vt damage; (desfavorecer) not suit. ~**dicial** adj damaging. ~**icio** m damage. en ~**icio** de to the detriment of

perla f pearl. de ~s adv very well

permane|cer ⑪ vi remain. ~**ncia** f permanence; (estancia) stay. ~**nte** adj permanent. ● f perm. ● m (Mex) perm

permi|sivo adj permissive. ~**so** m permission; (documento) licence; (Mil etc) leave. ~**so de conducir** driving licence (Brit), driver's license (Amer). con ~**so** excuse me. ~**tir** vt allow, permit. ¿me ~**te**? may I? ~**tirse** vpr allow s.o.

pernicioso adj pernicious; (persona) wicked

perno m bolt

pero conj but. ● m fault; (objeción) objection

perogrullada f platitude

perpendicular adj & f perpendicular

perpetrar vt perpetrate

perpetu|ar ㉑ vt perpetuate. ~**o** adj perpetual

perplejo adj perplexed

perr|a f (animal) bitch; (moneda) coin, penny (Brit), cent (Amer); (rabieta) tantrum. estar sin una ~**a** be broke. ~**era** f dog pound; (vehículo) dog catcher's van. ~**o** adj awful. ● m dog. ~**o galgo** greyhound. de ~**os** awful

persa adj & m & f Persian

perse|cución f pursuit; (política etc) persecution. ~**guir** ⑤ & ⑬ vt pursue; (por ideología etc) persecute

persevera|nte adj persevering. ~**r** vi persevere

persiana f blind; (LAm, contraventana) shutter

persignarse vpr cross o.s.

persist|ente adj persistent. ~**ir** vi persist

person|a f person. ~**as** fpl people. ~**aje** m (persona importante) important figure; (de obra literaria) character. ~**al** adj personal. ● m staff. ~**alidad** f personality. ~**arse** vpr appear in person. ~**ifi-**

car **7** vt personify

perspectiva f perspective

perspica|cia f shrewdness; (de vista) keen eyesight. ~z adj shrewd; (vista) keen

persua|dir vt persuade. ~sión f persuasion. ~sivo adj persuasive

pertenecer **11** vi belong

pértiga f pole. salto m con ~ pole vault

pertinente adj relevant

perturba|ción f disturbance. ~ción del orden público breach of the peace. ~r vt disturb; disrupt (orden)

Perú m. el ~ Peru

peruano adj & m Peruvian

perver|so adj evil. ● m evil person. ~tir **4** vt pervert

pesa f weight. ●~dez f weight; (de cabeza etc) heaviness; (lentitud) sluggishness; (cualidad de fastidioso) tediousness; (cosa fastidiosa) bore, nuisance

pesadilla f nightmare

pesado adj heavy; (sueño) deep; (viaje) tiring; (duro) hard; (aburrido) boring, tedious

pésame m sympathy, condolences

pesar vt weigh. ●vi be heavy. ● m sorrow; (remordimiento) regret. a ~ de (que) in spite of. pese a (que) in spite of

pesca f fishing; (peces) fish; (pescado) catch. ir de ~ go fishing. ~da f hake. ~dería f fish shop. ~dilla f whiting. ~do m fish. ~dor adj fishing. ● m fisherman. ~r **7** vt catch. ● vi fish

pescuezo m neck

pesebre m manger

pesero m (Mex) minibus

peseta f peseta

pesimista adj pessimistic. ● m & f pessimist

pésimo adj very bad, awful

peso m weight; (moneda) peso. ~ bruto gross weight. ~ neto net weight. al ~ by weight. de ~ influential

pesquero adj fishing

pestañ|a f eyelash. ~ear vi blink

peste f plague; (hedor) stench. ~icida m pesticide

pestillo m bolt; (de cerradura) latch

petaca f cigarette case; (Mex, maleta) suitcase

pétalo m petal

petardo m firecracker

petición f request; (escrito) petition

petirrojo m robin

petrificar **7** vt petrify

petr|óleo m oil. ~olero adj oil. ● m oil tanker

petulante adj smug

peyorativo adj pejorative

pez f fish; (substancia negruzca) pitch. ~ espada swordfish

pezón m nipple

pezuña f hoof

piadoso adj compassionate; (devoto) devout

pian|ista m & f pianist. ~o m piano. ~o de cola grand piano

piar **20** vi chirp

picad|a f. caer en ~a (LAm) nosedive. ~o adj perforated; (carne) minced (Brit), ground (Amer); (ofendido) offended; (mar) choppy; (diente) bad. ●m. caer en ~o nosedive. ~ura f bite, sting; (de polilla) moth hole

picaflor m (LAm) hummingbird

picante adj hot; (chiste etc) risqué

picaporte m door-handle; (aldaba) knocker

picar ⊘ vt (ave) peck; (insecto, pez) bite; (abeja, avispa) sting; (comer poco) pick at; mince (Brit), grind (Amer) (carne); chop (up) (cebolla etc); (Mex, pinchar) prick. ● vi itch; (ave) peck; (insecto, pez) bite; (sol) scorch; (comida) be hot

picardía f craftiness; (travesura) naughty thing

pícaro adj crafty; (niño) mischievous. ● m rogue

picazón f itch

pichón m pigeon; (Mex, novato) beginner

pico m beak; (punta) corner; (herramienta) pickaxe; (cima) peak. **y ~** (con tiempo) a little after; (con cantidad) a little more than. **~tear** vt peck; (fam, comer) pick at

picudo adj pointed

pido vb véase PEDIR

pie m foot; (Bot, de vaso) stem. **~ cuadrado** square foot. **a cuatro ~s** on all fours. **al ~ de la letra** literally. **a ~** on foot. **a ~(s) juntillas** (fig) firmly. **buscarle tres ~s al gato** split hairs. **de ~** standing (up). **de ~s a cabeza** from head to toe. **en ~** standing (up). **ponerse de ~** stand up

piedad f pity; (Relig) piety

piedra f stone; (de mechero) flint

piel f skin; (cuero) leather

pienso vb véase PENSAR

pierdo vb véase PERDER

pierna f leg

pieza f piece; (parte) part; (obra teatral) play; (moneda) coin; (habitación) room. **~ de recambio** spare part

pijama m pyjamas

pila f (montón) pile; (recipiente) basin; (eléctrica) battery. **~ bautismal** font. **~r** m pillar

píldora f pill

pillaje m pillage. **~r** vt catch

pillo adj wicked. ● m rogue

pilotar vt pilot. **~o** m pilot

pimentero m (vasija) pepperpot. **~entón** m paprika; (LAm, fruto) pepper. **~ienta** f pepper. **grano m de ~ienta** peppercorn. **~iento** m pepper

pináculo m pinnacle

pinar m pine forest

pincel m paintbrush. **~ada** f brush-stroke. **la última ~ada** (fig) the finishing touch

pinchar vt pierce, prick; puncture (neumático); (fig, incitar) push; (Med, fam) give an injection to. **~azo** m prick; (en neumático) puncture. **~itos** mpl kebab(s); (tapas) savoury snacks. **~o** m point

ping-pong m table tennis, ping-pong

pingüino m penguin

pino m pine (tree)

pinta f spot; (fig, aspecto) appearance. **tener ~a de** look like. **~ada** f graffiti. **~ar** vt paint. **no ~a nada** (fig) it doesn't count. **~arse** vpr put on make-up. **~or** m painter. **~oresco** adj picturesque. **~ura** f painting; (material) paint

pinza f (clothes-)peg (Brit), clothespin (Amer); (de cangrejo etc) claw. **~s** fpl tweezers

piña f pine cone; (fruta) pineapple. **~ón** m (semilla) pine nut

pío adj pious. ● m chirp. **no decir ni ~** not say a word

piojo m louse

pionero m pioneer

pipa f pipe; (semilla) seed; (de girasol) sunflower seed

pique m resentment; (rivalidad) rivalry. **irse a ~** sink

piquete m picket; (Mex, herida) prick; (Mex, de insecto) sting

piragua f canoe

pirámide f pyramid

pirata adj invar pirate. ● m & f pirate

Pirineos mpl. los **~the** Pyrenees

piropo m flattering comment

pirueta f pirouette

piruli m lollipop

pisa|da f footstep; (huella) footprint. **~papeles** m invar paperweight. **~r** vt tread on. ● vi tread

piscina f swimming pool

Piscis m Pisces

piso m floor; (vivienda) flat (Brit), apartment (Amer); (de autobús) deck

pisotear vt trample (on)

pista f track; (fig, indicio) clue. **~ de aterrizaje** runway. **~ de baile** dance floor. **~ de carreras** racing track. **~ de hielo** ice-rink. **~ de tenis** tennis court

pistol|a f pistol. **~era** f holster. **~ero** m gunman

pistón m piston

pit|ar, (LAm) **~ear** vt whistle at; (conductor) hoot at; award (falta). ● vi blow a whistle; (Auto) sound one's horn. **~ido** m whistle

pitill|era f cigarette case. **~o** m cigarette

pito m whistle; (Auto) horn

pitón m python

pitorre|arse vpr. **~arse de** make fun of. **~o** m teasing

pitorro m spout

piyama m (LAm) pyjamas

pizarr|a f slate; (en aula) blackboard. **~ón** m (LAm) blackboard

pizca f ① tiny piece; (de sal) pinch. **ni ~** not at all

placa f plate; (con inscripción) plaque; (distintivo) badge. **~ de matrícula** number plate

place|ntero adj pleasant. **~r** 32 vi. haz lo que te plazca do as you please. **me ~** hacerlo I'm pleased to do it. ● m pleasure

plácido adj placid

plaga f (also fig) plague. **~do** adj. **~do de** filled with

plagio m plagiarism

plan m plan. **en ~ de** as a

plana f page. **en primera ~** on the front page

plancha f iron; (lámina) sheet. **a la ~** grilled. **tirarse una ~** put one's foot in it. **~do** m ironing. **~r** vt iron. ● vi do the ironing

planeador m glider

planear vt plan. ● vi glide

planeta m planet

planicie f plain

planifica|ción f planning. **~r** 7 vt plan

planilla f (LAm) payroll; (personal) staff

plano adj flat. ● m plane; (de edificio) plan; (de ciudad) street plan. **primer ~** foreground; (Foto) close-up

planta f (del pie) sole; (en botánica, fábrica) plant; (plano) ground plan; (piso) floor. **~ baja** ground floor (Brit), first floor (Amer)

planta|ción f plantation. **~r** vt plant; deal (golpe). **~r en la calle** throw out. **~rse** vpr stand; (fig) stand firm

plantear vt (exponer) expound; (causar) create; raise (cuestión)

plantilla f (insole); (nómina) payroll; (personal) personnel

plaqué m plating. **de ~** plated

plástico adj & m plastic

plata f silver; (fig, fam, dinero) money. **~ de ley** hallmarked silver

plataforma f platform

plátano m plane (tree); (fruta) banana. **platanero** m banana tree

platea f stalls (Brit), orchestra (Amer)

plateado adj silver-plated; (color de plata) silver

plá|tica f talk. **~aticar 7** vi (Mex) talk. ● vt (Mex) tell

platija f plaice

platillo m saucer; (Mus) cymbal. **~ volador** (LAm), **~ volante** flying saucer

platino m platinum. **~s** mpl (Auto) points

plato m plate; (comida) dish; (parte de una comida) course

platónico adj platonic

playa f beach; (fig) seaside

plaza f square; (mercado) market (place); (sitio) place; (empleo) job. **~ de toros** bullring

plazco vb véase **PLACER**

plazo m period; (pago) instalment; (fecha) date. **comprar a ~s** buy on hire purchase (Brit), buy on the installment plan (Amer)

plazuela f little square

pleamar f high tide

pleb|e f common people. **~eyo** adj & m plebeian. **~iscito** m plebiscite

plega|ble adj pliable; (silla) folding. **~r 1 & 12** vt fold. **~rse** vpr

bend; (fig) yield

pleito m (court) case; (fig) dispute

plenilunio m full moon

plen|itud f fullness; (fig) height. **~o** adj full. **en ~o día** in broad daylight. **en ~o verano** at the height of the summer

plieg|o m sheet. **~ue** m fold; (en ropa) pleat

plisar vt pleat

plom|ero m (LAm) plumber. **~o** m lead; (Elec) fuse. **con ~o** leaded. **sin ~o** unleaded

pluma f feather; (para escribir) pen. **~ atómica** (Mex) ballpoint pen. **~ estilográfica** fountain pen. **~je** m plumage

plum|ero m feather duster; (para plumas, lápices etc) pencil-case. **~ón** m down; (edredón) down-filled quilt

plural adj & m plural. **en ~** in the plural

pluri|empleo m having more than one job. **~partidismo** m multi-party system. **~étnico** adj multiethnic

plus m bonus

pluscuamperfecto m pluperfect

plusvalía f capital gain

pluvial adj rain

pobla|ción f population; (ciudad) city, town; (pueblo) village. **~do** adj populated. ● m village. **~r 2** vt populate; (habitar) inhabit. **~rse** vpr get crowded

pobre adj poor. ● m & f poor person; (fig) poor thing. **¡~cito!** poor (little) thing! **¡~ de mí!** poor (old) me! **~za** f poverty

pocilga f pigsty

poción f potion

poco

● *adjetivo/pronombre*

····▸ poco, poca little, not much. tiene poca paciencia he has little patience. ¿cuánta leche queda? - poca how much milk is there left? - not much

····▸ pocos, pocas few. muy ~s días very few days. unos ~s dólares a few dollars. compré unos ~s I bought a few. aceptaron a muy ~s very few (people) were accepted

····▸ a ~ de llegar soon after he arrived. ¡a ~ ! (*Mex*) really? dentro de ~ soon. a ~ ~, (*LAm*) gradually, little by little. hace ~ recently, not long ago. por ~ nearly. un ~ (*cantidad*) a little; (*tiempo*) a while. un ~ de a (little) bit of, a little, some

● *adverbio*

····▸ (*con verbo*) not much. lee muy ~ he doesn't read very much

····▸ (*con adjetivo*) un lugar ~ conocido a little known place. es ~ inteligente he's not very intelligent

! Cuando **poco** modifica a un adjetivo, muchas veces el inglés prefiere el uso del prefijo *un-*, p. ej. **poco amistoso** *unfriendly*. **poco agradecido** *ungrateful*

podar *vt* prune

poder 33 *verbo auxiliar* be able to. no voy a ~ terminar I won't be able to finish. no pudo venir he couldn't come. ¿puedo hacer algo? can I do anything? ¿puedo pasar? may I come in? no ~ con not be able to cope with; (*no aguantar*) not be able to stand. no ~ más be exhausted; (*estar harto de algo*) not be able to manage any more. no ~ menos que have no alternative but. puede que it is possible that. puede ser it is possible. ¿se puede ...? may I...? ● *m* power. en el ~ in power. ~es públicos authorities. ~oso *adj* powerful

podrido *adj* rotten

po|ema *m* poem. ~esía *f* poetry; (*poema*) poem. ~eta *m & f* poet. ~ético *adj* poetic

polaco *adj* Polish. ● *m* Pole; (*lengua*) Polish

polar *adj* polar. estrella ~ polestar

polea *f* pulley

pol|émica *f* controversy. ~emizar 10 *vi* argue

polen *m* pollen

policía *f* police (*force*); (*persona*) policewoman. ● *m* policeman. ~co *adj* police; (*novela etc*) detective

policromo *adj*, **policromo** *adj* polychrome

polideportivo *m* sports centre

polietileno *m* polythene

poligamia *f* polygamy

polígono *m* polygon

polilla *f* moth

polio(mielitis) *f* polio(myelitis)

polític|a *f* politics; (*postura*) policy; (*mujer*) politician. ~ interior domestic policy. ~o *adj* political, familia ~a in-laws. ● *m* politician

póliza *f* (*de seguros*) policy

poll|o *m* chicken; (*gallo joven*) chick. ~uelo *m* chick

polo *m* pole; (*helado*) ice lolly (*Brit*),

Popsicle (P) *(Amer)*; *(juego)* polo.
P~ norte North Pole

Polonia f Poland

poltrona f armchair

polución f pollution

polv|areda f dust cloud; *(fig, escándalo)* uproar. ~era f compact. ~o m powder; *(suciedad)* dust. ~os mpl powder. en ~o powdered. estar hecho ~o be exhausted. quitar el ~o dust

pólvora f gunpowder; *(fuegos artificiales)* fireworks

polvoriento adj dusty

pomada f ointment

pomelo m grapefruit

pómez adj. piedra f ~ pumice stone

pomp|a f bubble; *(esplendor)* pomp. ~as fúnebres funeral. ~oso adj pompous; *(espléndido)* splendid

pómulo m cheekbone

ponchar vt *(Mex)* puncture

ponche m punch

poncho m poncho

ponderar vt *(alabar)* speak highly of

poner 34 vt put; put on *(ropa, obra de teatro, TV etc)*; lay *(la mesa, un huevo)*; set *(examen, deberes)*; *(contribuir)* contribute; give *(nombre)*; make *(nervioso)*; pay *(atención)*; show *(película, interés)*; open *(una tienda)*; equip *(una casa)*. ~ con *(al teléfono)* put through to. ~ por escrito put in writing. ~ una multa fine. pongamos let's suppose. ● vi lay. ~se vpr *(volverse)* get; put on *(ropa)*; *(sol)* set. ~se a start to. ~se a mal con uno fall out with s.o.

pongo vb véase **PONER**

poniente m west; *(viento)* west wind

pont|ificar 7 vi pontificate. ~ífice m pontiff

popa f stern

popote m *(Mex)* (drinking) straw

popul|acho m masses. ~ar adj popular; *(costumbre)* traditional; *(lenguaje)* colloquial. ~aridad f popularity. ~arizar 10 vt popularize.

póquer m poker

poquito m. un ~ a little bit. ● adv a little

---

por preposición

····> for. es ~ tu bien it's for your own good. lo compró por 5 dólares he bought it for 5 dollars. si no fuera por ti if it weren't for you. vino por una semana he came for a week

➤ Para expresiones como **por la mañana, por la noche** etc., ver bajo el respectivo nombre

····> *(causa)* because of. se retrasó ~ la lluvia he was late because of the rain. no hay trenes ~ la huelga there aren't any trains because of the strike

····> *(medio, agente)* by. lo envié ~ correo I sent it by post. fue destruida ~ las bombas it was destroyed by the bombs

····> *(a través de)* through. entró ~ la ventana he got in through the window. me enteré ~ un amigo I found out through a friend. ~ todo el país throughout the country

····▶ (a lo largo de) along. caminar ~ la playa to walk along the beach. cortar ~ la línea de puntos cut along the dotted line

····▶ (proporción) per. cobra 30 dólares ~ hora he charges 30 dollars per hour. uno ~ persona one per person. 10 ~ ciento 10 per cent

····▶ (Mat) times. dos ~ dos (son) cuatro two times two is four

····▶ (modo) in. ~ escrito in writing. pagar ~ adelantado to pay in advance

➡️ Para expresiones como **por dentro, por fuera** etc., ver bajo el respectivo adverbio

····▶ (en locuciones) ~ más que no matter how much. ¿~ qué? why? ~ si in case. ~ supuesto of course

porcelana f china
porcentaje m percentage
porcino adj pig
porción f portion; (de chocolate) piece
pordiosero m beggar
porfia|do adj stubborn. ~r 20 vi insist
pormenor m detail
pornogr|afía f pornography. ~áfico adj pornographic
poro m pore; (Mex, puerro) leek. ~so adj porous
porque conj because; (para que) so that
porqué m reason

porquería f filth; (basura) rubbish; (grosería) dirty trick
porra f club
porrón m wine jug (with a long spout)
portaaviones m invar aircraft carrier
portada f (de libro) title page; (de revista) cover
portadocumentos m invar (LAm) briefcase
portador m bearer
portaequipaje(s) m invar boot (Brit), trunk (Amer); (encima del coche) roof-rack
portal m hall; (puerta principal) main entrance. ~es mpl arcade
porta|ligas m invar suspender belt. ~monedas m invar purse
portarse vpr behave
portátil adj portable. ●m portable computer, laptop
portavoz m spokesman. ●f spokeswoman
portazo m bang. dar un ~ slam the door
porte m transport; (precio) carriage; (LAm, tamaño) size. ~ador m carrier
portento m marvel
porteño adj from Buenos Aires
porter|ía f porter's lodge; (en deportes) goal. ~o m caretaker, porter; (en deportes) goalkeeper. ~o automático entryphone
pórtico m portico
portorriqueño adj & m Puerto Rican
Portugal m Portugal
portugués adj & m Portuguese
porvenir m future
posada f inn. dar ~ give shelter
posar vt put. ● vi pose. ~se vpr

P

(pájaro) perch; (avión) land

posdata f postscript

pose|edor m owner; (de récord, billete, etc) holder. **~er** [18] vt own; hold (récord); have (conocimientos). **~sión** f possession. **~sionarse** vpr. **~sionarse de** take possession of. **~sivo** adj possessive

posgraduado adj & m postgraduate

posguerra f post-war years

posib|ilidad f possibility. **~le** adj possible. **de ser ~le** if possible. **en lo ~le** as far as possible. **si es ~le** if possible

posición f position; (en sociedad) social standing

positivo adj positive

poso m sediment

posponer [34] vt put after; (diferir) postpone

posta f. **a ~** on purpose

postal adj postal. • f postcard

poste m pole; (de valla) post

póster m (pl ~s) poster

postergar [12] vt pass over; (diferir) postpone

posteri|dad f posterity. **~or** adj back; (años) later; (capítulos) subsequent. **~ormente** adv later

postigo m door; (contraventana) shutter

postizo adj false, artificial. • m hairpiece

postrarse vpr prostrate o.s.

postre m dessert, pudding (Brit)

postular vt postulate; (LAm) nominate (candidato)

póstumo adj posthumous

postura f position, stance

potable adj drinkable; (agua) drinking

potaje m vegetable stew

potasio m potassium

pote m pot

poten|cia f power. **~cial** adj & m potential. **~te** adj powerful

potro m colt; (en gimnasia) horse

pozo m well; (hoyo seco) pit; (de mina) shaft; (fondo común) pool

práctica f practice. **en la ~** in practice

practica|nte m & f nurse. **~r** [7] vt practise; play (deportes); (ejecutar) carry out

práctico adj practical; (conveniente, útil) handy. • m practitioner

prad|era f meadow; (terreno grande) prairie. **~o** m meadow

pragmático adj pragmatic

preámbulo m preamble

precario adj precarious; (medios) scarce

precaución f precaution; (cautela) caution. **con ~** cautiously

precaverse vpr take precautions

precede|ncia f precedence; (prioridad) priority. **~nte** adj preceding. • m precedent. **~r** vt/i precede

precepto m precept. **~r** m tutor

precia|do adj valued; (don) valuable. **~rse** vpr. **~rse de** pride o.s. on

precio m price. **~ de venta al público** retail price. **al ~ de** at the cost of. **no tener ~** be priceless. **¿qué ~ tiene?** how much is it?

precios|idad f (cosa preciosa) beautiful thing. **¡es una ~idad!** it's beautiful! **~o** adj precious; (bonito) beautiful

precipicio m precipice

precipita|ción f precipitation; (prisa) rush. **~damente** adv hastily. **~do** adj hasty. **~r** vt (apre-

surar) hasten; (*arrojar*) hurl. ~rse
vpr throw o.s.; (*correr*) rush; (*actuar
sin reflexionar*) act rashly

precis|amente adj exactly. ~ar
vt require; (*determinar*) determine.
~ión f precision. ~o adj precise;
(*necesario*) necessary. si es ~o if
necessary

preconcebido adj preconceived

precoz adj early; (niño) precocious

precursor m forerunner

predecesor m predecessor

predecir 46, (*pero imperativo* pre-
dice, *futuro y condicional regulares*) vt
foretell

predestinado adj predestined

prédica f sermon

predicar 7 vt/i preach

predicción f prediction; (*del
tiempo*) forecast

predilec|ción f predilection.
~to adj favourite

predisponer 34 vt predispose

predomin|ante adj predomin-
ant. ~ar vi predominate. ~io m
predominance

preeminente adj pre-eminent

prefabricado adj prefabricated

prefacio m preface

prefer|encia f preference; (*Auto*)
right of way. de ~encia prefer-
ably. ~ente adj preferential. ~ible
adj preferable. ~ido adj favourite.
~ir 4 vt prefer

prefijo m prefix; (*telefónico*) dialling code

pregonar vt announce

pregunta f question. hacer una
~ ask a question. ~r vt/i ask (*por
about*). ~rse vpr wonder

prehistórico adj prehistoric

preju|icio m prejudice. ~zgar 12
vt prejudge

preliminar adj & m preliminary

preludio m prelude

premarital adj, **prematrimonial**
adj premarital

prematuro adj premature

premedita|ción f premedita-
tion. ~r vt premeditate

premi|ar vt give a prize to; (*re-
compensar*) reward. ~o m prize;
(*recompensa*) reward. ~o gordo
jackpot

premonición f premonition

prenatal adj antenatal

prenda f garment; (*garantía*)
surety; (*en juegos*) forfeit. en ~ de
as a token of. ~r vt captivate.
~rse vpr fall in love (de with)

prende|dor m brooch. ~r vt
capture; (*sujetar*) fasten; light (cigarrillo); (*LAm*) turn on (gas, radio,
etc). ● vi catch; (*arraigar*) take
root. ~rse vpr (*encenderse*) catch
fire

prensa f press. ~r vt press

preñado adj pregnant; (*fig*) full

preocupa|ción f worry. ~do adj
worried. ~r vt worry. ~rse vpr
worry. ~rse de look after

prepara|ción f preparation.
~do adj prepared. ● m prepar-
ation. ~r vt prepare. ~rse vpr get
ready. ~tivos mpl preparations.
~torio adj preparatory

preposición f preposition

prepotente adj arrogant; (*actitud*) high-handed

prerrogativa f prerogative

presa f (*cosa*) prey; (*embalse*) dam

presagi|ar vt presage. ~o m
omen

presbiteriano adj & m Presbyterian. ~ítero m priest

prescindir vi. ~ de do without;

(*deshacerse de*) dispense with

prescri|bir (*pp* prescrito) *vt* describe. **~pción** *f* prescription

presencia *f* presence; (*aspecto*) appearance. **en ~** de in the presence of. **~r** *vt* be present at; (*ver*) witness

presenta|ble *adj* presentable. **~ción** *f* presentation; (*de una persona a otra*) introduction. **~dor** *m* presenter. **~r** *vt* present; (*ofrecer*) offer; (*entregar*) hand in; (*hacer conocer*) introduce; show (película). **~rse** *vpr* present o.s.; (*hacerse conocer*) introduce o.s.; (*aparecer*) turn up

presente *adj* present; (*actual*) this. ● *m* present. **los ~s** those present. **tener ~** remember

presenti|miento *m* premonition. **~r** 4 *vt* have a feeling (que that)

preservar *vt* preserve. **~tivo** *m* condom

presiden|cia *f* presidency; (*de asamblea*) chairmanship. **~cial** *adj* presidential. **~ta** *f* (woman) president. **~te** *m* president; (*de asamblea*) chairman. **~te del gobierno** prime minister

presidi|ario *m* convict. **~o** *m* prison

presidir *vt* be president of; preside over (tribunal); chair (reunión, comité)

presi|ón *f* pressure. **a ~ón** under pressure. **hacer ~ón** press. **~onar** *vt* press; (*fig*) put pressure on

preso *adj*. **estar ~** be in prison. **llevarse a uno ~** take s.o. away under arrest. ● *m* prisoner

presta|do *adj* (*de uno*) lent; (*a uno*) borrowed. **pedir ~do** bor-

row. **~mista** *m & f* moneylender

préstamo *m* loan; (*acción de pedir prestado*) borrowing; (*acción de prestar*) lending

prestar *vt* lend; give (ayuda etc); pay (atención). **~se** *vpr*. **~se a** be open to; (*ser apto*) be suitable (para for)

prestidigita|ción *f* conjuring. **~dor** *m* conjurer

prestigio *m* prestige. **~so** *adj* prestigious

presu|mido *adj* conceited. **~mir** *vi* show off; boast (de about). **~nción** *f* conceit; (*suposición*) presumption. **~nto** *adj* alleged. **~ntuoso** *adj* conceited

presup|oner 34 *vt* presuppose. **~uesto** *m* budget; (*precio estimado*) estimate

preten|cioso *adj* pretentious. **~der** *vt* try to; (*afirmar*) claim; (*solicitar*) apply for; (*cortejar*) court. **~diente** *m* pretender; (*a una mujer*) suitor. **~sión** *f* pretension; (*aspiración*) aspiration

pretérito *m* preterite, past

pretexto *m* pretext. **con el ~ de** on the pretext of

prevalecer 11 *vi* prevail (sobre over)

preven|ción *f* prevention; (*prejuicio*) prejudice. **~ido** *adj* ready; (*precavido*) cautious. **~ir** 53 *vt* prevent; (*advertir*) warn. **~tiva** *f* (Mex) amber light. **~tivo** *adj* preventive

prever 43 *vt* foresee; (*planear*) plan

previo *adj* previous

previs|ible *adj* predictable. **~ión** *f* forecast; (*prudencia*) precaution

prima *f* (*pariente*) cousin; (*cantidad*) bonus

primario *adj* primary

primavera f spring. **~l** adj spring

primer adj véase PRIMERO. **~a** f (Auto) first (gear); (en tren etc) first class. **~o** adj (delante de nombre masculino en singular **primer**) first; (mejor) best; (principal) leading. **la ~a fila** the front row. **lo ~o es** the most important thing is. **~a enseñanza** primary education. **a ~os de** at the beginning of. **de ~a** first-class. ● n (the) first. ● adv first

primitivo adj primitive

primo m cousin; ① fool. **hacer el ~** be taken for a ride

primogénito adj & m first-born, eldest

primor m delicacy; (cosa) beautiful thing

primordial adj fundamental; (interés) paramount

princesa f princess

principal adj main. **lo ~ es** que the main thing is

príncipe m prince

principi|ante m & f beginner. **~o** m beginning; (moral, idea) principle; (origen) origin. **al ~o** at first. **a ~o(s) de** at the beginning of. **desde el ~o** from the start. **en ~o** in principle. **~os** mpl (nociones) rudiments

prión m prion

prioridad f priority

prisa f hurry, haste. **darse ~** hurry (up). **de ~** quickly. **tener ~** be in a hurry

prisi|ón f prison; (encarcelamiento) imprisonment. **~onero** m prisoner

prismáticos mpl binoculars

priva|ción f deprivation. **~da** f (Mex) private road. **~do** adj (particular) private. **~r** vt deprive (de of). **~tivo** adj exclusive (de to)

privilegi|ado adj privileged; (muy bueno) exceptional. **~o** m privilege

pro prep. **en ~ de** for, in favour of. ● m advantage. **los ~s y los contras** the pros and cons

proa f bow

probab|ilidad f probability. **~le** adj probable, likely. **~lemente** adv probably

proba|dor m fitting-room. **~r** ② vt try; try on (ropa); (demostrar) prove. ● vi try. **~rse** vpr try on

probeta f test-tube

problema m problem. **hacerse ~as** (LAm) worry

procaz adj indecent

proced|encia f origin. **~ente** adj (razonable) reasonable. **~ente de** (coming) from. **~er** m conduct. ● vi proceed. **~er contra** start legal proceedings against. **~er de** come from. **~imiento** m procedure; (sistema) process; (Jurid) proceedings

proces|ador m. **~ de textos** word processor. **~al** adj procedural. **costas ~ales** legal costs. **~amiento** m processing; (Jurid) prosecution. **~amiento de textos** word-processing.. **~ar** vt process; (Jurid) prosecute

procesión f procession

proceso m process; (Jurid) trial; (transcurso) course

proclamar vt proclaim

procrea|ción f procreation. **~r** vt procreate

procura|dor m attorney, solicitor; (asistente) clerk (Brit), paralegal (Amer). **~r** vt try; (obtener) obtain

prodigar ⑫ vt lavish

prodigio m prodigy; (maravilla) wonder; (milagro) miracle. **~so** adj prodigious

pródigo *adj* prodigal

produc|ción *f* production. **~ir** [47] *vt* produce; (*causar*) cause. **~irse** *vpr* (*suceder*) happen. **~tivo** *adj* productive. **~to** *m* product. **~tos agrícolas** farm produce. **~tos alimenticios** foodstuffs. **~tos de belleza** cosmetics. **~tos de consumo** consumer goods. **~tor** *m* producer.

proeza *f* exploit

profan|ación *f* desecration. **~ar** *vt* desecrate. **~o** *adj* profane

profecía *f* prophecy

proferir [4] *vt* utter; hurl (*insultos* etc)

profes|ión *f* profession. **~ional** *adj* professional. **~or** *m* teacher; (*en universidad*) lecturer. **~orado** *m* teaching profession; (*conjunto de profesores*) staff

prof|eta *m* prophet. **~etizar** [10] *vt/i* prophesize

prófugo *adj & m* fugitive

profund|idad *f* depth. **~o** *adj* deep; (*fig*) profound. **poco ~o** shallow

progenitor *m* ancestor

programa *m* programme; (*de estudios*) syllabus. **~ concurso** quiz show. **~ de entrevistas** chat show. **~ción** *f* programming; (*TV* etc) programmes; (*en periódico*) TV guide. **~r** *vt* programme. **~dor** *m* computer programmer

progres|ar *vi* (make) progress. **~ión** *f* progression. **~ista** *adj* progressive. **~ivo** *adj* progressive. **~o** *m* progress. **hacer ~os** make progress

prohibi|ción *f* prohibition. **~do** *adj* forbidden. **prohibido fumar** no smoking. **~r** *vt* forbid. **~tivo** *adj* prohibitive

prójimo *m* fellow man

prole *f* offspring

proletari|ado *m* proletariat. **~o** *adj & m* proletarian

prol|iferación *f* proliferation. **~iferar** *vi* proliferate. **~ífico** *adj* prolific

prolijo *adj* long-winded

prólogo *m* prologue

prolongar [12] *vt* prolong; (*alargar*) lengthen. **~se** *vpr* go on

promedio *m* average. **como ~** on average

prome|sa *f* promise. **~ter** *vt* promise. ● *vi* show promise. **~terse** *vpr* (*novios*) get engaged. **~tida** *f* fiancée. **~tido** *adj* promised; (*novios*) engaged. ● *m* fiancé

prominente *f* prominence

promiscu|idad *f* promiscuity. **~o** *adj* promiscuous

promo|ción *f* promotion. **~tor** *m* promoter. **~ver** [2] *vt* promote; (*causar*) cause

promulgar [12] *vt* promulgate

pronombre *m* pronoun

pron|osticar [7] *vt* predict; forecast (*tiempo*). **~óstico** *m* prediction; (*del tiempo*) forecast; (*Med*) prognosis

pront|itud *f* promptness. **~o** *adj* quick. ● *adv* quickly; (*dentro de poco*) soon; (*temprano*) early. **de ~o** suddenly. **por lo ~o** for the time being. **tan ~ como** as soon as

pronuncia|ción *f* pronunciation. **~miento** *m* revolt. **~r** *vt* pronounce; deliver (*discurso*). **~rse** *vpr* (*declararse*) declare o.s.; (*sublevarse*) rise up

propagación *f* propagation

propaganda *f* propaganda;

(anuncios) advertising

propagar 12 *vt/i* propagate. ~**se** *vpr* spread

propasarse *vpr* go too far

propens|ión *f* inclination. ~**o** *adj* inclined

propici|ar *vt* favour; *(provocar)* bring about. ~**o** *adj* favourable

propie|dad *f* property. ~**tario** *m* owner

propina *f* tip

propio *adj* own; *(característico)* typical; *(natural)* natural; *(apropiado)* proper. el ~ médico the doctor himself

proponer 34 *vt* propose; put forward (persona). ~**se** *vpr*. ~**se** hacer intend to do

proporci|ón *f* proportion. ~**onado** *adj* proportioned. ~**onal** *adj* proportional. ~**onar** *vt* provide

proposición *f* proposition

propósito *m* intention. a ~ *(adrede)* on purpose; *(de paso)* by the way. a ~ de with regard to

propuesta *f* proposal

propuls|ar *vt* propel; *(fig)* promote. ~**ión** *f* propulsion. ~**ión a chorro** jet propulsion

prórroga *f* extension

prorrogar 12 *vt* extend

prosa *f* prose. ~**ico** *adj* prosaic

proscri|bir *(pp* proscrito) *vt* exile; *(prohibir)* ban. ~**to** *adj* banned. ● *m* exile; *(bandido)* outlaw

proseguir 5 & 13 *vt/i* continue

prospecto *m* prospectus; *(de fármaco)* directions for use

prosper|ar *vi* prosper; *(persona)* do well. ~**idad** *f* prosperity

próspero *adj* prosperous. ¡P~

Año Nuevo! Happy New Year!

prostit|ución *f* prostitution. ~**uta** *f* prostitute

protagonista *m & f* protagonist

prote|cción *f* protection. ~**ctor** *adj* protective. ● *m* protector; *(benefactor)* patron. ~**ger** 14 *vt* protect. ~**gida** *f* protégée. ~**gido** *adj* protected. ● *m* protégé

proteína *f* protein

protesta *f* protest; *(manifestación)* demonstration; *(Mex, promesa)* promise; *(Mex, juramento)* oath

protestante *adj & m & f* Protestant

protestar *vt/i* protest

protocolo *m* protocol

provecho *m* benefit. ¡buen ~! enjoy your meal! de ~ useful. en ~ de to the benefit of. sacar ~ de benefit from

proveer 18 *(pp* proveído y provisto) *vt* supply, provide

provenir 53 *vi* come (de from)

proverbi|al *adj* proverbial. ~**o** *m* proverb

provinci|a *f* province. ~**l** *adj*, ~**no** *adj* provincial

provisional *adj* provisional

provisto *adj* provided (de with)

provoca|ción *f* provocation. ~**r** 7 *vt* provoke; *(causar)* cause. ~**tivo** *adj* provocative

proximidad *f* proximity

próximo *adj* next; *(cerca)* near

proyec|ción *f* projection. ~**tar** *vt* hurl; cast (luz); show (película). ~**til** *m* missile. ~**to** *m* plan. ~**to de ley** bill. en ~**to** planned. ~**tor** *m* projector

pruden|cia *f* prudence; *(cuidado)* caution. ~**te** *adj* prudent, sensible

p

prueba f proof; (examen) test; (de ropa) fitting. a ~ on trial. a ~ de proof against. a ~ de agua waterproof. poner a ~ test

pruebo vb véase PROBAR

psicoan|álisis f psychoanalysis. ~**alista** m & f psychoanalyst. ~**alizar** ⑩ vt psychoanalyse

psic|ología f psychology. ~**ológico** adj psychological. ~**ólogo** m psychologist. ~**ópata** m & f psychopath. ~**osis** f invar psychosis

psiqu|e f psyche. ~**iatra** m & f psychiatrist. ~**iátrico** adj psychiatric

psíquico adj psychic

ptas, pts abrev (**pesetas**) pesetas

púa f sharp point; (espina) thorn; (de erizo) quill; (de peine) tooth; (Mus) plectrum

pubertad f puberty

publica|ción f publication. ~**r** ⑦ vt publish

publici|dad f publicity; (Com) advertising. ~**tario** adj advertising

público adj public. ● m public; (de espectáculo etc) audience

puchero m cooking pot; (guisado) stew. hacer ~s (fig, fam) pout

pude vb véase PODER

pudor m modesty. ~**oso** adj modest

pudrir (pp podrido) vt rot; (fig, molestar) annoy. ~**se** vpr rot

puebl|ecito m small village. ~**erino** m country bumpkin. ~**o** m town; (aldea) village; (nación) nation, people

puedo vb véase PODER

puente m bridge; (fig, fam) long weekend. ~ **colgante** suspension bridge. ~ **levadizo** drawbridge. hacer ~ ⑫ have a long weekend

puente Puentes are very important in Spain and Latin America. Hacer Puente means that when a working day falls between two public holidays, it too is taken as a holiday.

puerco adj filthy; (grosero) coarse. ● m pig. ~ **espín** porcupine

puerro m leek

puerta f door; (en deportes) goal; (de ciudad, en jardín) gate. ~ **principal** main entrance. a ~ **cerrada** behind closed doors

puerto m port; (fig, refugio) refuge; (entre montañas) pass. ~ **franco** free port

puertorriqueño adj & m Puerto Rican

pues adv (entonces) then; (bueno) well. ● conj since

puest|a f setting; (en juegos) bet. ~**a de sol** sunset. ~**a en escena** staging. ~**a en marcha** starting. ~**o** adj put; (vestido) dressed. ● m place; (empleo) position, job; (en mercado etc) stall. ● conj. ~**o que** since

pugn|a f struggle. ~**r** vi. ~**r por** strive to

puja f struggle (por to); (en subasta) bid. ~**r** vt struggle; (en subasta) bid

pulcro adj neat

pulga f flea. tener malas ~**s** be bad-tempered

pulga|da f inch. ~**r** m thumb; (del pie) big toe

puli|do adj polished; (modales) refined. ~**r** vt polish; (suavizar) smooth

pulla f gibe

pulm|ón m lung. ~**onar** adj pulmonary. ~**onía** f pneumonia

pulpa f pulp

pulpería f (LAm) grocer's shop (Brit), grocery store (Amer)

púlpito m pulpit

pulpo m octopus

pulque m (Mex) pulque, alcoholic Mexican drink. **~ría** f bar

pulsa|ción f pulsation. **~dor** m button. **~r** vt press; (Mus) pluck

pulsera f bracelet

pulso m pulse; (firmeza) steady hand. echar un ~ arm wrestle. tomar el ~ a uno take s.o.'s pulse

pulular vi teem with

puma m puma

puna f puna, high plateau

punitivo adj punitive

punta f point; (extremo) tip. estar de ~ be in a bad mood. ponerse de ~ con uno fall out with s.o. sacar ~ a sharpen

puntada f stitch

puntaje m (LAm) score

puntal m prop, support

puntapié m kick

puntear vt mark; (Mus) pluck (LAm, en deportes) lead

puntería f aim; (destreza) markmanship

puntiagudo adj pointed; (afilado) sharp

puntilla f (encaje) lace. en ~s (LAm), de ~s on tiptoe

punto m point; (señal, trazo) dot; (de examen) mark; (lugar) spot, place; (de taxis) stand; (momento) moment; (punto final) full stop (Brit), period (Amer); (puntada) stitch. ~ de vista point of view. ~ com dot-com. ~ final full stop (Brit), period (Amer). ~ muerto (Auto) neutral (gear). ~ y aparte full stop, new paragraph (Brit),

period, new paragraph (Amer). ~ y coma semicolon. a ~ on time; (listo) ready. a ~ de on the point of. de ~ knitted. dos ~s colon. en ~ exactly. hacer ~ knit. hasta cierto ~ to a certain extent

puntuación f punctuation; (en deportes, acción) scoring; (en deportes, número de puntos) score

puntual adj punctual; (exacto) accurate. **~idad** f punctuality; (exactitud) accuracy

puntuar 21 vt punctuate; mark (Brit), grade (Amer) (examen). ● vi score (points)

punza|da f sharp pain; (fig) pang. **~nte** adj sharp. **~r** 10 vt prick

puñado m handful. a ~s by the handful

puñal m dagger. **~ada** f stab

puñ|etazo m punch. **~o** m fist; (de ropa) cuff; (mango) handle. de su ~o (y letra) in his own handwriting

pupa f (fam, en los labios) cold sore

pupila f pupil

pupitre m desk

puré m purée; (sopa) thick soup. ~ de papas (LAm), ~ de patatas mashed potatoes

pureza f purity

purga f purge. **~torio** m purgatory

puri|ficación f purification. **~ificar** 7 vt purify. **~sta** m & f purist. **~tano** adj puritanical. ● m puritan

puro adj pure; (cielo) clear. de pura casualidad by sheer chance. de ~ tonto out of sheer stupidity. ● m cigar

púrpura f purple

pus m pus

puse vb véase **PONER**

pusilánime adj fainthearted
puta f (vulg) whore

Qq

que pron rel (personas, sujeto) who; (personas, complemento) whom; (cosas) which, that. ● conj that. ¡∼ tengan Vds buen viaje! have a good journey! ¡∼ venga! let him come! ∼ venga o no venga whether he comes or not. creo ∼ tiene razón I think (that) he is right. más ∼ more than. lo ∼ what. ∼ tú if I were you

qué adj (con sustantivo) what; (con a o adv) how. ● pron what. ¡∼ bonito! how nice!. ¿en ∼ piensas? what are you thinking about?

quebra|da f gorge; (paso) pass. ∼dizo adj fragile. ∼do adj broken; (Com) bankrupt. ● m (Math) fraction. ∼ntar vt break; disturb (paz). ∼nto m (pérdida) loss; (daño) damage. ∼r **1** vt break. ● vi break; (Com) go bankrupt. ∼rse vpr break

quechua adj Quechua. ● m & f Quechuan. ● m (lengua) Quechua.

quedar vi stay, remain; (estar) be; (haber todavía) be left. ∼ bien come off well. ∼se vpr stay. ∼ con arrange to meet. ∼ en agree to. ∼ en nada come to nothing. ∼ por (+ infinitivo) remain to be (+ pp)

quehacer m work. ∼es domésticos household chores

queja f complaint; (de dolor) moan. ∼rse vpr complain (de

about); (gemir) moan. ∼ido m moan

quema|do adj burnt; (LAm, bronceado) tanned; (fig) annoyed. ∼dor m burner. ∼dura f burn. ∼r vt/i burn. ∼rse vpr burn o.s.; (consumirse) burn up; (con el sol) get sunburnt. ∼rropa adv. a ∼rropa point-blank

quena f Indian flute

quepo vb véase CABER

querella f (riña) quarrel, dispute; (Jurid) criminal action

quer|er **33** vt want; (amar) love; (necesitar) need. ∼er decir mean. ● m love; (amante) lover. como quiera however. cuando quiera que whenever. donde quiera wherever. ¿quieres darme ese libro? would you pass me that book? ¿quieres un helado? would you like an ice-cream? quisiera ir a la playa I'd like to go to the beach. sin ∼er without meaning to. ∼ido adj dear; (amado) loved

querosén m, **queroseno** m kerosene

querubín m cherub

ques|adilla f (Mex) tortilla filled with cheese. ∼o m cheese

quetzal m (unidad monetaria ecuatoriana) quetzal

quicio m frame. sacar de ∼ a uno infuriate s.o.

quiebra f (Com) bankruptcy

quien pron rel (sujeto) who; (complemento) whom

quién pron interrogativo (sujeto) who; (tras preposición) ¿con ∼? who with?, to whom? ¿de ∼ son estos libros? whose are these books?

quienquiera pron whoever

quiero vb véase QUERER

quiet|o adj still; (inmóvil) motionless; (carácter etc) calm. **~ud** f stillness

quijada f jaw

quilate m carat

quilla f keel

quimera f (fig) illusion

químic|a f chemistry. **~o** adj chemical. ● m chemist

quince adj & m fifteen. **~ días** a fortnight. **~na** f fortnight. **~nal** adj fortnightly

quincuagésimo adj fiftieth

quiniela f pools coupon. **~s** fpl (football) pools

quinientos adj & m five hundred

quinquenio m (period of) five years

quinta f (casa) villa

quintal m a hundred kilograms

quinteto m quintet

quinto adj & m fifth

quiosco m kiosk; (en jardín) summerhouse; (en parque etc) bandstand

quirúrgico adj surgical

quise vb véase QUERER

quisquill|a f trifle; (camarón) shrimp. **~oso** adj irritable; (exigente) fussy

quita|esmalte m nail polish remover. **~manchas** m invar stain remover. **~nieves** m invar snow plough. **~r** vt remove, take away; take off (ropa); (robar) steal. **~ndo** (fam, a excepción de) apart from. **~rse** vpr get rid of (dolor); take off (ropa). **~rse de** (no hacerlo más) stop. **~rse de en medio** get out of the way. **~sol** m sunshade

quizá(s) adv perhaps

quórum m quorum

Rr

rábano m radish. **~ picante** horseradish. **me importa un ~** I couldn't care less

rabi|a f rabies; (fig) rage. **~ar** vi (de dolor) be in great pain; (estar enfadado) be furious. **dar ~a** infuriate. **~eta** f tantrum

rabino m rabbi

rabioso adj rabid; (furioso) furious

rabo m tail

racha f gust of wind; (fig) spate. **pasar por una mala ~** go through a bad patch

racial adj racial

racimo m bunch

ración f share, ration; (de comida) portion

raciona|l adj rational. **~lizar** 🔟 vt rationalize. **~r** vt (limitar) ration; (repartir) ration out

racis|mo m racism. **~ta** adj racist

radar m radar

radiación f radiation

radiactiv|idad f radioactivity. **~o** adj radioactive

radiador m radiator

radiante adj radiant; (brillante) brilliant

radical adj & m & f radical

radicar 🔟 vi lie (en in). **~se** vpr settle

radio m radius; (de rueda) spoke; (LAm) radio. ● f radio. **~actividad** f radioactivity. **~activo** adj radioactive. **~difusión** f broadcasting. **~emisora** f radio station. **~escucha** m & f listener. **~grafía** f radiography

radi|ólogo m radiologist. **~ote-rapia** f radiotherapy

radioyente m & f listener

raer 38 vt scrape; (*quitar*) scrape off

ráfaga f (*de viento*) gust; (*de ametralladora*) burst

rafia f raffia

raído adj threadbare

raíz f root. **a ~ de** as a result of. **echar raíces** (*fig*) settle

raja f split; (*Culin*) slice. **~r** vt split. **~rse** vpr split; (*fig*) back out

rajatabla. a ~ rigorously

ralea f sort

ralla|dor m grater. **~r** vt grate

ralo adj (*pelo*) thin

rama f branch. **~je** m branches. **~l** m branch

rambla f watercourse; (*avenida*) avenue

ramera f prostitute

ramifica|ción f ramification. **~rse** 7 vpr branch out

ram|illete m bunch. **~o** m branch; (*de flores*) bunch, bouquet

rampa f ramp, slope

rana f frog

ranch|era f (*Mex*) folk song. **~ero** m cook; (*Mex, hacendado*) rancher. **~o** m (*LAm, choza*) hut; (*LAm, casucha*) shanty; (*Mex, hacienda*) ranch

rancio adj rancid; (*vino*) old; (*fig*) ancient

rango m rank

ranúnculo m buttercup

ranura f groove; (*para moneda*) slot

rapar vt shave; crop (*pelo*)

rapaz adj rapacious; (*ave*) of prey

rape m monkfish

rapidez f speed

rápido adj fast, quick. ● adv quickly. ● m (*tren*) express. **~s** mpl rapids

rapiña f robbery. **ave** f **de ~** bird of prey

rapsodia f rhapsody

rapt|ar vt kidnap. **~o** m kidnapping; (*de ira etc*) fit

raqueta f racquet

rar|eza f rarity; (*cosa rara*) oddity. **~o** adj rare; (*extraño*) odd. **es ~o que** it is strange that. **¡qué ~o!** how strange!

ras. a ~ de level with

rasca|cielos m invar skyscraper. **~r** 7 vt scratch; (*raspar*) scrape

rasgar 12 vt tear

rasgo m characteristic; (*gesto*) gesture; (*de pincel*) stroke. **~s** mpl (*facciones*) features

rasguear vt strum

rasguñ|ar vt scratch. **~o** m scratch

raso adj (*cucharada etc*) level; (*vuelo etc*) low. **al ~** in the open air. ● m satin

raspa|dura f scratch; (*acción*) scratching. **~r** vt scratch; (*rozar*) scrape

rastr|a. a ~as dragging. **~ear** vt track. **~ero** adj creeping. **~illar** vt rake. **~illo** m rake. **~o** m track; (*señal*) sign. **ni ~o** not a trace

rata f rat

ratero m petty thief

ratifica|ción f ratification. **~r** 7 vt ratify

rato m moment, short time. **~s libres** spare time. **a ~s** at times. **a cada ~** (*LAm*) always. **hace un ~** a moment ago. **pasar un mal ~** have a rough time

rat|ón m mouse. **~onera** f

mousetrap; (madriguera) mouse hole

raudal m torrent. a ~les in abundance

raya f line; (lista) stripe; (de pelo) parting. a ~s striped. **pasarse de la** ~ go too far. ~r vt scratch. ~r **en** border on

rayo m ray; (descarga eléctrica) lightning. ~ **de luna** moonbeam. ~ **láser** laser beam. ~s X X-rays

raza f race; (de animal) breed. **de** ~ (caballo) thoroughbred; (perro) pedigree

razón f reason. a ~**ón de** at the rate of. **tener** ~**ón** be right. ~**onable** adj reasonable. ~**onar** vt reason out. ● vi reason

RDSI abrev (Red Digital de Servicios Integrados) ISDN

re m D; (solfa) re

reac|ción f reaction; (LAm, Pol) right wing. ~**ción en cadena** chain reaction. ~**cionario** adj & m reactionary. ~**tor** m reactor; (avión) jet

real adj real; (de rey etc) royal; (hecho) true. ● m real, old Spanish coin

realidad f reality; (verdad) truth. **en** ~ in fact. **hacerse** ~ come true

realis|mo m realism. ~**ta** adj realistic. ● m & f realist

realiza|ción f fulfilment. ~**r** 🔟 vt carry out; make (viaje); fulfil (ilusión); (vender) sell. ~**rse** vpr (sueño, predicción etc) come true; (persona) fulfil o.s.

realzar 🔟 vt (fig) enhance

reanimar vt revive. ~**se** vpr revive

reanudar vt resume; renew (amistad)

reavivar vt revive

rebaja f reduction. **en** ~s in the sale. ~**do** adj (precio) reduced. ~**r** vt lower; lose (peso)

rebanada f slice

rebaño m herd; (de ovejas) flock

rebasar vt exceed; (dejar atrás) leave behind; (Mex, Auto) overtake

rebatir vt refute

rebel|arse vpr rebel. ~**de** adj rebellious; (grupo) rebel. ● m rebel. ~**día** f rebelliousness. ~**ión** f rebellion

rebosa|nte adj brimming (de with). ~**r** vi overflow; (abundar) abound

rebot|ar vi bounce; (rechazar) repel. ● vi bounce; (bala) ricochet. ~**e** m bounce, rebound. **de** ~**e** on the rebound

reboz|ar 🔟 vt wrap up; (Culin) coat in batter. ~**o** m (LAm) shawl

rebusca|do adj affected; (complicado) over-elaborate. ~**r** 🔽 vt search through

rebuznar vi bray

recado m errand; (mensaje) message

reca|er 🟚 vi fall back; (Med) relapse; (fig) fall. ~**ída** f relapse

recalcar 🔽 vt stress

recalcitrante adj recalcitrant

recalentar 🔟 vt reheat; (demasiado) overheat

recámara f small room; (de arma de fuego) chamber; (Mex, dormitorio) bedroom

recambio m (Mec) spare (part); (de pluma etc) refill. **de** ~ spare

recapitular vt sum up

recarg|ar 🔢 vt overload; (aumentar) increase; recharge (batería); top up (móvil). ~**o** m increase

recat|ado adj modest. **~o** m prudence; (*modestia*) modesty. **sin ~o** openly

recauda|ción f (*cantidad*) takings. **~dor** m tax collector. **~r** vt collect

recel|ar vt suspect. ● vi be suspicious (de of). **~o** m distrust; (*temor*) fear. **~oso** adj suspicious

recepci|ón f reception. **~onista** m & f receptionist

receptáculo m receptacle

receptor m receiver

recesión f recession

receta f recipe; (*Med*) prescription

rechaz|ar 🔟 vt reject; defeat (*moción*); repel (*ataque*); (*no aceptar*) turn down. **~o** m rejection

rechifla f booing

rechinar vi squeak. **le rechinan los dientes** he grinds his teeth

rechoncho adj stout

recib|imiento m (*acogida*) welcome. **~ir** vt receive; (*acoger*) welcome. ● vi entertain. **~irse** vpr graduate. **~o** m receipt. **acusar ~o** acknowledge receipt

reci|én adv recently; (*LAm, hace poco*) just. **~ casado** newly married. **~ nacido** newborn. **~ente** adj recent; (*Culin*) fresh

recinto m enclosure; (*local*) premises

recio adj strong; (*voz*) loud. ● adv hard; (*en voz alta*) loudly

recipiente m receptacle. ● m & f recipient

recíproco adj reciprocal; (*sentimiento*) mutual

recita|l m recital; (*de poesías*) reading. **~r** vt recite

reclama|ción f claim; (*queja*) complaint. **~r** vt claim. ● vi appeal

réclame m (*LAm*) advertisement

reclamo m (*LAm*) complaint

reclinar vi lean. **~se** vpr lean

reclus|ión f imprisonment. **~o** m prisoner

recluta m & f recruit. **~miento** m recruitment. **~r** vt recruit

recobrar vt recover. **~se** vpr recover

recodo m bend

recog|er 🔢 vt collect; pick up (*cosa caída*); (*cosechar*) harvest. **~erse** vpr withdraw; (*ir a casa*) go home; (*acostarse*) go to bed. **~ida** f collection; (*cosecha*) harvest

recomenda|ción f recommendation. **~r** 🔟 vt recommend; (*encomendar*) entrust

recomenzar 🔟 & 🔟 vt/i start again

recompensa f reward. **~r** vt reward

reconcilia|ción f reconciliation. **~r** vt reconcile. **~rse** vpr be reconciled

reconoc|er 🔢 vt recognize; (*admitir*) acknowledge; (*examinar*) examine. **~imiento** m recognition; (*admisión*) acknowledgement; (*agradecimiento*) gratitude; (*examen*) examination

reconozco vb véase RECONOCER

reconquista f reconquest. **~r** vt reconquer; (*fig*) win back

---

Reconquista The period
in Spain's history during
which the Christian kingdoms
slowly recovered the territories
occupied by the Moslem Moors
of North Africa. The Moorish invasion began in 711 AD and was
halted in 718. The expulsion of

the last Moorish ruler of Granada in 1492 completed the *Reconquista*.

reconsiderar *vt* reconsider

reconstruir **17** *vt* reconstruct

récord /'rekor/ *m* (*pl* ~s) record

recordar **2** *vt* remember; (*hacer acordar*) remind. ● *vi* remember. **que yo recuerde** as far as I remember. **si mal no recuerdo** if I remember rightly

recorr|er *vt* tour (país); go round (zona, museo); cover (distancia). ~ **mundo** travel all around the world. ~**ido** *m* journey; (*trayecto*) route

recort|ar *vt* cut (out). ~**e** *m* cutting (out); (*de periódico etc*) cutting

recostar **2** *vt* lean. ~**se** *vpr* lie down

recoveco *m* bend; (*rincón*) nook

recre|ación *f* recreation. ~**ar** *vt* recreate; (*divertir*) entertain. ~**arse** *vpr* amuse o.s. ~**ativo** *adj* recreational. ~**o** *m* recreation; (*en escuela*) break

recrudecer **11** *vi* intensify

recta *f* straight line. ~ **final** home stretch

rect|angular *adj* rectangular. ~**ángulo** *adj* rectangular; (*triángulo*) right-angled. ● *m* rectangle

rectifica|ción *f* rectification. ~**r** **7** *vt* rectify

rect|itud *f* straightness; (*fig*) honesty. ~**o** *adj* straight; (*fig, justo*) fair; (*fig, honrado*) honest. **todo** ~**o** straight on. ● *m* rectum

rector *adj* governing. ● *m* rector

recubrir (*pp* recubierto) *vt* cover (con, de with)

recuerdo *m* memory; (*regalo*) souvenir. ~**s** *mpl* (*saludos*) regards. ● *vb véase* RECORDAR

recupera|ción *f* recovery. ~**r** *vt* recover. ~**r el tiempo perdido** make up for lost time. ~**rse** *vpr* recover

recur|rir *vi*. ~**rir a** resort to (cosa); turn to (persona). ~**so** *m* resort; (*medio*) resource; (*Jurid*) appeal. ~**sos** *mpl* resources

red *f* (*malla*) net; (*para equipaje*) luggage rack; (*Com*) chain; (*Elec, gas*) mains. **la R**~ the Net

redac|ción *f* writing; (*lenguaje*) wording; (*conjunto de redactores*) editorial staff; (*oficina*) editorial office; (*Escol, Univ*) essay. ~**tar** *vt* write. ~**tor** *m* writer; (*de periódico*) editor

redada *f* catch; (*de policía*) raid

redecilla *f* small net; (*para el pelo*) hairnet

redentor *adj* redeeming

redimir *vt* redeem

redoblar *vt* redouble; step up (vigilancia)

redomado *adj* utter

redond|a *f* (*de imprenta*) roman (type); (*Mus*) semibreve (Brit), whole note (Amer). **a la** ~**a** around. ~**ear** *vt* round off. ~**el** *m* circle; (*de plaza de toros*) arena. ~**o** *adj* round; (*completo*) complete; (*Mex, boleto*) return, round-trip (Amer). **en** ~**o** round; (*categóricamente*) flatly

reduc|ción *f* reduction. ~**ido** *adj* reduced; (*limitado*) limited; (*pequeño*) small; (*precio*) low. ~**ir** **47** *vt* reduce. ~**irse** *vpr* be reduced; (*fig*) amount

reduje *vb véase* REDUCIR

redundan|cia *f* redundancy. ~**te** *adj* redundant

reduzco *vb véase* REDUCIR

reembols|ar vt reimburse. **~o** m repayment. **contra ~o** cash on delivery

reemplaz|ar 10 vt replace. **~o** m replacement

refacci|ón f (LAm) refurbishment; (Mex, Mec) spare part. **~onar** vt (LAm) refurbish. **~onaria** f (Mex) repair shop

referencia f reference; (información) report. **con ~ a** with reference to. **hacer ~ a** refer to

referéndum m (pl **~s**) referendum

referir 4 vt tell; (remitir) refer. **~se** vpr refer. **por lo que se refiere a** as regards

refiero vb véase REFERIR

refilón. de ~ obliquely

refin|amiento m refinement. **~ar** vt refine. **~ería** f refinery

reflector m reflector; (proyector) searchlight

reflej|ar vt reflect. **~o** adj reflex. **•** m reflection; (Med) reflex; (en el pelo) highlights

reflexi|ón f reflection. **sin ~ón** without thinking. **~onar** vi reflect. **~vo** adj (persona) thoughtful; (Gram) reflexive

reforma f reform. **~s** fpl (reparaciones) repairs. **~r** vt reform. **~rse** vpr reform

reforzar 2 & 10 vt reinforce

refrac|ción f refraction. **~tario** adj heat-resistant

refrán m saying

refregar 1 & 12 vt scrub

refresc|ar 7 vt refresh; (enfriar) cool. **•** vi get cooler. **~arse** vpr refresh o.s. **~o** m cold drink. **~os** mpl refreshments

refrigera|ción f refrigeration; (aire acondicionado) air-

conditioning; (de motor) cooling. **~r** vt refrigerate; air-condition (lugar); cool (motor). **~dor** m refrigerator

refuerzo m reinforcement

refugi|ado m refugee. **~arse** vpr take refuge. **~o** m refuge, shelter

refunfuñar vi grumble

refutar vt refute

regadera f watering-can; (Mex, ducha) shower

regala|do adj as a present, free; (cómodo) comfortable. **~r** vt give

regalo m present, gift

regañ|adientes. a ~adientes reluctantly. **~ar** vt scold. **•** vi moan; (dos personas) quarrel. **~o** m (reprensión) scolding

regar 1 & 12 vt water

regata f boat race; (serie) regatta

regate|ar vt haggle over; (economizar) economize on. **•** vi haggle; (en deportes) dribble. **~o** m haggling; (en deportes) dribbling

regazo m lap

regenerar vt regenerate

régimen m (pl **regímenes**) regime; (Med) diet; (de lluvias) pattern

regimiento m regiment

regi|ón f region. **~onal** adj regional

regir 5 & 14 vt govern. **•** vi apply, be in force

registr|ado adj registered. **~ar** vt register; (Mex) check in (equipaje); (grabar) record; (examinar) search. **~arse** vpr register; (darse) be reported. **~o** m (acción de registrar) registration; (libro) register; (cosa anotada) entry; (inspección) search. **~o civil** (oficina) registry office

regla f ruler; (norma) rule; (mens-

truación) period. **en** ～ in order.
por ～ general as a rule. ～**mentación** f regulation. ～**mentar** vt
regulate. ～**mentario** adj regulation; (horario) set. ～**mento** m regulations

regocij|arse vpr be delighted.
～**o** m delight

regode|arse vpr (+ gerundio) delight in (+ gerund). ～**o** m delight

regordete adj chubby

regres|ar vi return; (LAm) send
back (persona). ～**arse** vpr (LAm)
return. ～**ivo** adj backward. ～**o** m
return

regula|ble adj adjustable. ～**dor**
m control. ～**r** adj regular; (mediano) average; (no bueno) so-so.
● vt regulate; adjust (volumen
etc). ～**ridad** f regularity. **con**
～**ridad** regularly

rehabilita|ción f rehabilitation;
(en empleo etc) reinstatement. ～**r**
vt rehabilitate; (en cargo) reinstate

rehacer 🟦 vt redo; (repetir) repeat; rebuild (vida). ～**se** vpr recover

rehén m hostage

rehogar 🟦 vt sauté

rehuir 🟦 vt avoid

rehusar vt/i refuse

reimpr|esión f reprinting.
～**imir** (pp reimpreso) vt reprint

reina f queen. ～**do** m reign.
～**nte** adj ruling; (fig) prevailing.
～**r** vi reign; (fig) prevail

reincidir vi (Jurid) reoffend

reino m kingdom. **R～ Unido**
United Kingdom

reintegr|ar vt reinstate (persona); refund (cantidad). ～**arse** vpr
return. ～**o** m refund

reír 🟦 vi laugh. ～**se** vpr laugh.
～**se de** laugh at. **echarse a** ～

burst out laughing

reivindica|ción f claim. ～**r** 🟦
vt claim; (rehabilitar) restore

rej|a f grille; (verja) railing. **entre**
～**as** behind bars. ～**illa** f grille,
grating; (red) luggage rack

rejuvenecer 🟦 vt/i rejuvenate.
～**se** vpr be rejuvenated

relaci|ón f connection; (trato) relation(ship); (relato) account; (lista)
list. **con** ～**ón a, en** ～**ón a** in relation to. ～**onado** adj related. **bien**
～**onado** well-connected. ～**onar** vt
relate (con to). ～**onarse** vpr be
connected; (tratar) mix (con with)

relaja|ción f relaxation; (aflojamiento) slackening. ～**do** adj relaxed. ～**r** vt relax; (aflojar) slacken.
～**rse** vpr relax

relamerse vpr lick one's lips

relámpago m (flash of) lightning

relatar vt tell, relate

relativ|idad f relativity. ～**o** adj
relative

relato m tale; (relación) account

relegar 🟦 vt relegate. ～ **al olvido** consign to oblivion

relev|ante adj outstanding. ～**ar**
vt relieve; (substituir) replace. ～**o** m
relief. **carrera** f **de** ～**os** relay race

relieve m relief; (fig) importance.
de ～ important. **poner de** ～ emphasize

religi|ón f religion. ～**osa** f nun.
～**oso** adj religious. ● m monk

relinch|ar vi neigh. ～**o** m neigh

reliquia f relic

rellano m landing

rellen|ar vt refill; (Culin) stuff; fill
in (formulario). ～**o** adj full up;
(Culin) stuffed. ● m filling; (Culin)
stuffing

reloj m clock; (de bolsillo o pulsera)

watch. ~ **de caja** grandfather clock. ~ **de pulsera** wrist-watch. ~ **de sol** sundial. ~ **despertador** alarm clock. ~**ería** f watchmaker's (shop). ~**ero** m watchmaker

reluci|ente adj shining. ~**r** 11 vi shine; (destellar) sparkle

relumbrar vi shine

remach|ar vt rivet. ~**e** m rivet

remangar 12 vt roll up

remar vi row

remat|ado adj (total) complete. ~**ar** vt finish off; (agotar) use up; (Com) sell off cheap; (LAm, subasta) auction; (en tenis) smash. ~**e** m end; (fig) finishing touch; (LAm, subastar) auction; (en tenis) smash. **de** ~**e** completely

remedar vt imitate

remedi|ar vt remedy; repair (daño); (fig, resolver) solve. **no lo pude** ~**ar** I couldn't help it. ~**o** m remedy; (fig) solution; (LAm, medicamento) medicine. **como último** ~**o** as a last resort. **no hay más** ~**o** there's no other way. **no tener más** ~**o** have no choice

remedo m poor imitation

rem|endar 11 vt repair. ~**iendo** m patch

remilg|ado adj fussy; (afectado) affected. ~**o** m fussiness; (afectación) affectation. ~**oso** adj (Mex) fussy

reminiscencia f reminiscence

remisión f remission; (envío) sending; (referencia) reference

remit|e m sender's name and address. ~**ente** m sender. ~**ir** vt send; (referir) refer ● vi diminish

remo m oar

remojar vt soak; (fig, fam) celebrate. ~**o** m soaking. **poner a** ~**o** soak

remolacha f beetroot. ~ **azucarera** sugar beet

remolcar 7 vt tow

remolino m swirl; (de aire etc) whirl

remolque m towing; (cabo) towrope; (vehículo) trailer. **a** ~ on tow. **dar** ~ a a tow

remontar vt overcome. ~ **el vuelo** soar up; (avión) gain height. ~**se** vpr soar up; (en el tiempo) go back to

remord|er 2 vi. **eso le remuerde** he feels guilty for it. **me remuerde la conciencia** I have a guilty conscience. ~**imiento** m remorse. **tener** ~**imientos** feel remorse

remoto adj remote; (época) distant

remover 2 vt stir (líquido); turn over (tierra); (quitar) remove; (fig, activar) revive

remunera|ción f remuneration. ~**r** vt remunerate

renac|er 11 vi be reborn; (fig) revive. ~**imiento** m rebirth. **R**~**imiento** Renaissance

renacuajo m tadpole; (fig) tiddler

rencilla f quarrel

rencor m bitterness. **guardar** ~ a have a grudge against. ~**oso** adj resentful

rendi|ción f surrender. ~**do** adj submissive; (agotado) exhausted

rendija f crack

rendi|miento m performance; (Com) yield. ~**r** 5 vt yield; (agotar) exhaust; (pagar) (homenaje); present (informe). ● vi pay; (producir) produce. ~**rse** vpr surrender

renegar 1 & 12 vt deny. ● vi grumble. ~ **de** renounce (fe etc); disown (personas)

renglón *m* line; (*Com*) item. a ∼ seguido straight away

reno *m* reindeer

renombr|ado *adj* renowned. ∼e *m* renown

renova|ción *f* renewal; (*de edificio*) renovation; (*de mobiliario*) complete change. ∼r *vt* renew; renovate (edificio); change (mobiliario)

rent|a *f* income; (*Mex, alquiler*) rent. ∼a vitalicia (life) annuity. ∼able *adj* profitable. ∼ar *vt* yield; (*Mex, alquilar*) rent, hire. ∼ista *m & f* person of independent means

renuncia *f* renunciation; (*dimisión*) resignation. ∼r *vi.* ∼r a renounce, give up; (*dimitir*) resign

reñi|do *adj* hard-fought. estar ∼do con be incompatible with (cosa); be on bad terms with (persona). ∼r **5** & **22** *vt* scold. ● *vi* quarrel

reo *m & f* (*Jurid*) accused; (*condenado*) convicted offender; (*pez*) sea trout

reojo *m* mirar de ∼ look out of the corner of one's eye at

reorganizar **10** *vt* reorganize

repar|ación *f* repair; (*acción*) repairing (*fig, compensación*) reparation. ∼ar *vt* repair; (*fig*) make amends for; (*notar*) notice. ● *vi.* ∼ar en notice; (*hacer caso de*) pay attention to. ∼o *m* fault; (*objeción*) objection. poner ∼os raise objections

repart|ición *f* distribution. ∼idor *m* delivery man. ∼imiento *m* distribution. ∼ir *vt* distribute, share out; deliver (cartas, leche etc); hand out (folleto, premio). ∼o *m* distribution; (*de cartas, leche etc*) delivery; (*actores*) cast

repas|ar *vt* go over; check (cuenta); revise (texto); (*leer a la ligera*) glance through; (*coser*) mend. ● *vi* revise. ∼o *m* revision; (*de ropa*) mending. dar un ∼o look through

repatria|ción *f* repatriation. ∼r *vt* repatriate

repele|nte *adj* repulsive. ● *m* insect repellent. ∼r *vt* repel

repent|e. de ∼ suddenly. ∼ino *adj* sudden

repercu|sión *f* repercussion. ∼tir *vi* reverberate; (*fig*) have repercussions (en on)

repertorio *m* repertoire

repetil|ción *f* repetition; (*de programa*) repeat. ∼damente *adv* repeatedly. ∼r **5** *vt* repeat; have a second helping of (plato); (*imitar*) copy. ∼r have a second helping of

repi|car **7** *vt* ring (campanas). ∼que *m* peal

repisa *f* shelf. ∼ de chimenea mantlepiece

repito *vb véase* **REPETIR**

replegarse **1** & **12** *vpr* withdraw

repleto *adj* full up. ∼ de gente packed with people

réplica *adj* reply; (*copia*) replica

replicar **7** *vi* reply

repollo *m* cabbage

reponer **34** *vt* replace; revive (obra de teatro); (*contestar*) reply. ∼se *vpr* recover

report|aje *m* report; (*LAm, entrevista*) interview. ∼ar *vt* yield; (*LAm, denunciar*) report. ∼e *m* (*Mex, informe*) report; (*Mex, queja*) complaint. ∼ero *m* reporter

repos|ado *adj* quiet; (*sin prisa*) unhurried. ∼ar *vi* rest; (*líquido*) settle. ∼o *m* rest

repostar *vt* replenish. ● *vi* (avión)

r

refuel; (Auto) fill up. **~ería** f pastrymaking

reprender vt reprimand

represalia f reprisal. tomar **~s** retaliate

representa|ción f representation; (en el teatro) performance. en **~ción de** representing. **~nte** m representative. **~r** vt represent; perform (obra de teatro); play (papel); (aparentar) look. **~rse** vpr imagine. **~tivo** adj representative

represi|ón f repression. **~vo** adj repressive

reprimenda f reprimand

reprimir vt supress. **~se** vpr control o.s.

reprobar 2 vt condemn; (LAm, Univ, etc) fail

reproch|ar vt reproach. **~e** m reproach

reproduc|ción f reproduction. **~ir** 47 vt reproduce. **~tor** adj reproductive; (animal) breeding

reptil m reptile

rep|ública f republic. **~ublicano** adj & m republican

repudiar vt condemn; (Jurid) repudiate

repuesto m (Mec) spare (part). de **~** spare

repugna|ncia f disgust. **~nte** adj repugnant; (olor) disgusting. **~r** vt disgust

repuls|a f rebuff. **~ión** f repulsion. **~ivo** adj repulsive

reputa|ción f reputation. **~do** adj reputable. **~r** vt consider

requeri|miento m request; (necesidad) requirement. **~r** 4 vt require; summons (persona)

requesón m curd cheese

requete... prefijo (fam) extremely

requis|a f requisition; (confiscación) seizure; (inspección) inspection; (Mil) requisition. **~ar** vt requisition; (confiscar) seize; (inspeccionar) inspect. **~ito** m requirement

res f animal. **~ lanar** sheep. **~ vacuna** (vaca) cow; (toro) bull; (buey) ox. carne de **~** (Mex) beef

resabido adj well-known; (persona) pedantic

resaca f undercurrent; (después de beber) hangover

resaltar vi stand out. hacer **~** emphasize

resarcir 9 vt repay; (compensar) compensate. **~se** vpr make up for

resbal|adilla f (Mex) slide. **~adizo** adj slippery. **~ar** vi slip; (Auto) skid; (líquido) trickle. **~arse** vpr slip; (Auto) skid; (líquido) trickle. **~ón** m slip; (de vehículo) skid. **~oso** adj (LAm) slippery

rescat|ar vt rescue; (fig) recover. **~e** m ransom; (recuperación) recovery; (salvamento) rescue

rescoldo m embers

resecar 7 vt dry up. **~se** vpr dry up

resenti|do adj resentful. **~miento** m resentment. **~rse** vpr feel the effects; (debilitarse) be weakened; (ofenderse) take offence (de at)

reseña f summary; (de persona) description; (en periódico) report, review. **~r** vt describe; (en periódico) report on, review

reserva f reservation; (provisión) reserve(s). de **~** in reserve. **~ción** f (LAm) reservation. **~do** adj reserved. **~r** vt reserve; (guardar) keep, save. **~rse** vpr save o.s.

resfria|do m cold. **~rse** vpr catch

a cold

resguard|ar vt protect. **~arse** vpr protect o.s.; (fig) take care. **~o** m protection; (garantía) guarantee; (recibo) receipt

resid|encia f residence; (Univ) hall of residence (Brit), dormitory (Amer); (de ancianos etc) home. **~encial** adj residential. **~ente** adj & m & f resident. **~ir** vi reside; (fig) lie (en in)

residu|al adj residual. **~o** m residue. **~os** mpl waste

resigna|ción f resignation. **~rse** vpr resign o.s. (a to)

resist|encia f resistence. **~ente** adj resistent. **~ir** vt resist; (soportar) bear. ● vi resist. ya no resisto más I can't take it any more

resol|ución f resolution; (solución) solution; (decisión) decision. **~ver** ② (pp resuelto) resolve; solve (problema etc). **~verse** vpr resolve itself; (resultar bien) work out; (decidir) decide

resona|ncia f resonance. tener **~ncia** cause a stir. **~nte** adj resonant; (fig) resounding. **~r** ② vi resound

resorte m spring; (Mex, elástico) elastic. tocar (todos los) **~s** (fig) pull strings

respald|ar vt back; (escribir) endorse. **~arse** vpr lean back. **~o** m backing; (de asiento) back

respect|ar vi. en lo que **~a** a with regard to. en lo que a mí **~a** as far as I'm concerned. **~ivo** adj respective. **~o** m respect. al **~o** on this matter. (con) **~o a** with regard to

respet|able adj respectable. ● m audience. **~ar** vt respect. **~o** m respect. faltar al **~o** a be disres-

pectful to. **~uoso** adj respectful

respir|ación f breathing; (ventilación) ventilation. **~ar** vi breathe; (fig) breathe a sigh of relief. **~o** m breathing; (fig) rest

respland|ecer ⑪ vi shine. **~eciente** adj shining. **~or** m brilliance; (de llamas) glow

responder vi answer; (replicar) answer back; (reaccionar) respond. **~ de** be responsible for. **~ por** uno vouch for s.o.

responsab|ilidad f responsibility. **~le** adj responsible

respuesta f reply, answer

resquebrajar vt crack. **~se** vpr crack

resquemor m (fig) uneasiness

resquicio m crack; (fig) possibility

resta f subtraction

restablecer ⑪ vt restore. **~se** vpr recover

rest|ante adj remaining. lo **~nte** the rest. **~ar** vt take away; (substraer) subtract. ● vi be left

restaura|ción f restoration. **~nte** m restaurant. **~r** vt restore

restitu|ción f restitution. **~ir** ⑰ vt return; (restaurar) restore

resto m rest, remainder; (en matemática) remainder. **~s** mpl remains; (de comida) leftovers

restorán m restaurant

restregar ⑧ & ⑫ vt rub

restri|cción f restriction. **~ngir** ⑭ vt restrict, limit

resucitar vt resuscitate; (fig) revive. ● vi return to life

resuello m breath; (respiración) heavy breathing

resuelto adj resolute

resulta|do m result (en in). **~r** vi result; (salir) turn out; (dar resul-

tado) work; (*ser*) be; (*costar*)
come to

resum|en *m* summary. **en ∼en**
in short. **∼ir** *vt* summarize; (*recapitular*) sum up

resur|gir ⁵ *vi* reemerge; (*fig*) revive. **∼gimiento** *m* resurgence.
∼rección *f* resurrection

retaguardia *f* (*Mil*) rearguard

retahíla *f* string

retar *vt* challenge

retardar *vt* slow down; (*demorar*)
delay

retazo *m* remnant; (*fig*) piece, bit

reten|ción *f* retention. **∼er** ⁴⁰ *vt*
keep; (*en la memoria*) retain; (*no dar*) withhold

reticencia *f* insinuation; (*reserva*)
reluctance

retina *f* retina

retir|ada *f* withdrawal. **∼ado** *adj*
remote; (*vida*) secluded; (*jubilado*)
retired. **∼ar** *vt* move away; (*quitar*)
remove; withdraw (dinero); (*jubilar*) pension off. **∼arse** *vpr* draw
back; (*Mil*) withdraw; (*jubilarse*) retire; (*acostarse*) go to bed. **∼o** *m*
retirement; (*pensión*) pension;
(*lugar apartado*) retreat; (*LAm, de apoyo, fondos*) withdrawal

reto *m* challenge

retocar ⁷ *vt* retouch

retoño *m* shoot; (*fig*) kid

retoque *m* (*acción*) retouching;
(*efecto*) finishing touch

retorc|er ² & ⁹ *vt* twist; wring
(ropa). **∼erse** *vpr* get twisted up;
(*de dolor*) writhe. **∼ijón** *m* (*LAm*)
stomach cramp

retóric|a *f* rhetoric; (*grandilocuencia*) grandiloquence. **∼o** *m* rhetorical

retorn|ar *vt/i* return. **∼o** *m* return

retortijón *m* twist; (*de tripas*)
stomach cramp

retractarse *vpr* retract. **∼ de lo
dicho** withdraw what one said

retransmitir *vt* repeat (radio,
TV), broadcast. **∼ en directo**
broadcast live

retras|ado *adj* (*con ser*) mentally
handicapped; (*con estar*) behind;
(*reloj*) slow; (*poco desarrollado*)
backward; (*anticuado*) old-
fashioned. **∼ar** *vt* delay; put back
(reloj); (*retardar*) slow down; (*posponer*) postpone. ● *vi* (*reloj*) be
slow. **∼arse** *vpr* be late; (*reloj*) be
slow. **∼o** *m* delay; (*poco desarrollo*)
backwardness; (*de reloj*) slowness.
traer ∼o be late. **∼os** *mpl* arrears

retrato *m* portrait; (*fig, descripción*) description. **ser el vivo ∼ de**
be the living image of

retrete *m* toilet

retribu|ción *f* payment; (*recompensa*) reward. **∼ir** ¹⁷ *vt* pay; (*recompensar*) reward; (*LAm*) return
(favor)

retroce|der *vi* move back; (*fig*)
back down. **∼so** *m* backward
movement; (*de arma de fuego*) recoil; (*Med*) relapse

retrógrado *adj* & *m* (*Pol*) reactionary

retrospectivo *adj* retrospective

retrovisor *m* rear-view mirror

retumbar *vt* echo; (*trueno etc*)
boom

reum|a *m*, **reúma** *m* rheumatism.
∼ático *adj* rheumatic. **∼atismo** *m*
rheumatism

reun|ión *f* meeting; (*entre amigos*) reunion. **∼ir** ²³ *vt* join
together; (*recoger*) gather
(together); raise (fondos). **∼rse** *vpr*
meet; (amigos etc) get together

revalidar vt confirm; (Mex, estudios) validate

revalorizar 🔟 vt, (LAm) **revaluar** 🟤 vt revalue; increase (pensiones). **~se** vpr appreciate

revancha f revenge; (en deportes) return match. tomar la ~ get one's own back

revela|ción f revelation. **~do** m developing. **~dor** adj revealing. **~r** vt reveal; (Foto) develop

revent|ar 🔟 vi burst; (tener ganas) be dying to. **~arse** vpr burst. **~ón** m burst; (Auto) blow out; (Mex, fiesta) party

reveren|cia f reverence; (de hombre, niño) bow; (de mujer) curtsy. **~ciar** vt revere. **~do** adj (Relig) reverend. **~te** adj reverent

revers|ible adj reversible. **~o** m reverse; (de papel) back

revertir 🟤 vi revert (a to)

revés m wrong side; (de prenda) inside; (contratiempo) setback; (en deportes) backhand. al ~ the other way round; (con lo de arriba abajo) upside down; (con lo de dentro fuera) inside out

revesti|miento m coating. **~r** 🟤 vt cover

revis|ar vt check; overhaul (mecanismo); service (coche etc); (LAm, equipaje) search. **~ión** f check(ing); (Med) checkup; (de coche etc) service; (LAm, de equipaje) inspection. **~or** m inspector

revista f magazine; (inspección) inspection; (artículo) review; (espectáculo) revue. pasar ~ a inspect

revivir vi revive

revolcar 🟤 & 🟥 vt knock over. **~se** vpr roll around

revolotear vi flutter

revoltijo m, **revoltillo** m mess

revoltoso adj rebellious; (niño) naughty

revoluci|ón f revolution. **~onar** vt revolutionize. **~onario** adj & m revolutionary

revolver 🟤 (pp revuelto) vt mix; stir (líquido); (desordenar) mess up

revólver m revolver

revuelo m fluttering; (fig) stir

revuelt|a f revolt; (conmoción) disturbance. **~o** adj mixed up; (líquido) cloudy; (mar) rough; (tiempo) unsettled; (huevos) scrambled

rey m king. los ~es the king and queen. los R~es Magos the Three Wise Men

reyerta f brawl

rezagarse 🟥 vpr fall behind

rez|ar 🔟 vt say. ● vi pray; (decir) say. **~o** m praying; (oración) prayer

rezongar 🟥 vi grumble

ría f estuary

riachuelo m stream

riada f flood

ribera f bank

ribete m border; (fig) embellishment

rico adj rich; (Culin, fam) good, nice. ● m rich person

rid|ículo adj ridiculous. **~iculizar** 🔟 vt ridicule

riego m watering; (irrigación) irrigation

riel m rail

rienda f rein

riesgo m risk. correr (el) ~ de run the risk of

rifa f raffle. **~r** vt raffle

rifle m rifle

rigidez f rigidity; (fig) inflexibility

rígido adj rigid; (fig) inflexible

rig|or m strictness; (*exactitud*) exactness; (*de clima*) severity. de ~or compulsory. en ~or strictly speaking. ~**uroso** adj rigorous

rima f rhyme. ~r vt/i rhyme

rimbombante adj resounding; (*lenguaje*) pompous; (*fig, ostentoso*) showy

rímel m mascara

rin m (Mex) rim

rincón m corner

rinoceronte m rhinoceros

riña f quarrel; (*pelea*) fight

riñón m kidney

río m river; (*fig*) stream. ~ abajo downstream. ~ arriba upstream.
● v *véase* REÍR

riqueza f wealth; (*fig*) richness. ~**s** fpl riches

ris|a f laugh. desternillarse de ~a split one's sides laughing. la ~a laughter. ~**otada** f guffaw. ~**ueño** adj smiling; (*fig*) cheerful

rítmico adj rhythmic(al)

ritmo m rhythm; (*fig*) rate

rit|o m rite; (*fig*) ritual. ~**ual** adj & m ritual

rival adj & m & f rival. ~**idad** f rivalry. ~**izar** 10 vi rival

riz|ado adj curly. ~**ar** 10 vt curl; ripple (agua). ~**o** m curl; (*en agua*) ripple

róbalo m bass

robar vt steal (cosa); rob (banco); (*raptar*) kidnap

roble m oak (tree)

robo m theft; (*de banco, museo*) robbery; (*en vivienda*) burglary

robusto adj robust

roca f rock

roce m rubbing; (*señal*) mark; (*fig, entre personas*) regular contact; (*Pol*) friction. tener un ~ con uno have a brush with s.o.

rociar 20 vt spray

rocín m nag

rocío m dew

rodaballo m turbot

rodaja f slice. en ~**s** sliced

roda|je m (*de película*) shooting; (*de coche*) running in. ~r 2 vt shoot (película); run in (coche). ● vi roll; (*coche*) run; (*hacer una película*) shoot

rode|ar vt surround; (*LAm*) round up (ganado). ~**arse** vpr surround o.s. (de with). ~**o** m detour; (*de ganado*) round-up. andar con ~**os** beat about the bush. sin ~**os** plainly

rodill|a f knee. ponerse de ~**as** kneel down. ~**era** f knee-pad

rodillo m roller; (*Culin*) rolling-pin

roe|dor m rodent. ~r 37 vt gnaw

rogar 2 & 12 vt/i beg; (*Relig*) pray; se ruega a los Sres. pasajeros... passengers are requested.... se ruega no fumar please do not smoke

roj|izo adj reddish. ~**o** adj & m red. ponerse ~**o** blush

roll|izo adj plump; (*bebé*) chubby. ~**o** m roll; (*de cuerda*) coil; (*Culin, rodillo*) rolling-pin; (*fig, fam, pesadez*) bore

romance adj Romance. ● m (*idilio*) romance; (*poema*) ballad

roman|o adj & m Roman. a la ~**a** (*Culin*) (deep-)fried in batter

rom|anticismo m romanticism. ~**ántico** adj romantic

romería f pilgrimage; (*LAm, multitud*) mass

romero m rosemary

romo adj blunt; (*nariz*) snub

rompe|cabezas m invar puzzle;

(de piezas) jigsaw (puzzle). ~**olas** m invar breakwater

romp|er *(pp* **roto)** *vt* break; tear (hoja, camisa etc); break off (relaciones etc). ● *vi* break; (novios) break up. ~**er** a burst out. ~**erse** *vpr* break

ron m rum

ronc|ar 7 *vi* snore. ~**o** *adj* hoarse

roncha f lump; *(por alergia)* rash

ronda f round; *(patrulla)* patrol; *(serenata)* serenade. ● *vt* patrol. ● *vi* be on patrol; *(merodear)* hang around

ronqu|era f hoarseness. ~**ido** m snore

ronronear *vi* purr

roña f *(suciedad)* grime. ~**oso** *adj* dirty; *(oxidado)* rusty; *(tacaño)* mean

rop|a f clothes, clothing. ~**a blanca** linen, underwear. ~**a de cama** bedclothes. ~**a interior** underwear. ~**aje** m robes; *(excesivo)* heavy clothing. ~**ero** m wardrobe

ros|a *adj invar* pink. ● f rose. ● m pink. ~**áceo** *adj* pinkish. ~**ado** *adj* pink; *(mejillas)* rosy. ● m *(vino)* rosé. ~**al** m rose-bush

rosario m rosary; *(fig)* series

ros|ca f *(de tornillo)* thread; *(de pan)* roll; *(bollo)* type of doughnut. ~**co** m roll. ~**quilla** f type of doughnut

rostro m face

rota|ción f rotation. ~**r** *vt/i* rotate. ~**rse** *vpr* take turns. ~**tivo** *adj* rotary

roto *adj* broken

rótula f kneecap

rotulador m felt-tip pen

rótulo m sign; *(etiqueta)* label; *(logotipo)* logo

rotundo *adj* categorical

rotura f tear; *(grieta)* crack

rozadura f scratch

rozagante *adj* *(LAm)* healthy

rozar 10 *vt* rub against; *(ligeramente)* brush against; *(raspar)* graze. ~**se** *vpr* rub; *(con otras personas)* mix

Rte. *abrev* **(Remite(nte))** sender

rubéola f German measles

rubí m ruby

rubicundo *adj* ruddy

rubio *adj* *(pelo)* fair; *(persona)* fair-haired; *(tabaco)* Virginia

rubor m blush; *(Mex, cosmético)* blusher. ~**izarse 10** *vpr* blush

rúbrica f *(de firma)* flourish; *(firma)* signature; *(título)* heading

rudeza f roughness

rudiment|ario *adj* rudimentary. ~**os** *mpl* rudiments

rueca f distaff

rueda f wheel; *(de mueble)* castor; *(de personas)* ring; *(Culin)* slice. ~**de prensa** press conference

ruedo m edge; *(redondel)* bullring

ruego m request; *(súplica)* entreaty. ● *vb véase* **ROGAR**

rufián m pimp; *(granuja)* rogue

rugby m rugby

rugi|do m roar. ~**r 14** *vi* roar

ruibarbo m rhubarb

ruido m noise. ~**so** *adj* noisy; *(fig)* sensational

ruin *adj* despicable; *(tacaño)* mean

ruin|a f ruin; *(colapso)* collapse. ~**oso** *adj* ruinous

ruiseñor m nightingale

ruleta f roulette

rulo m curler

rumano *adj & m* Romanian

rumbo m direction; *(fig)* course;

(*fig, esplendidez*) lavishness. con ~ a in the direction of. ~**so** *adj* lavish

rumia|nte *adj & m* ruminant. ~**r** *vt* chew; (*fig*) brood over. • *vi* ruminate

rumor *m* rumour; (*ruido*) murmur. ~**earse** *vpr* se ~**ea** que rumour has it that. ~**oso** *adj* murmuring

runrún *m* (*de voces*) murmur; (*de motor*) whirr

ruptura *f* breakup; (*de relaciones etc*) breaking off; (*de contrato*) breach

rural *adj* rural

ruso *adj & m* Russian

rústico *adj* rural; (*de carácter*) coarse. en rústica paperback

ruta *f* route; (*fig*) course

rutina *f* routine. ~**rio** *adj* routine; (*trabajo*) monotonous

Ss

....

S.A. *abrev* (**Sociedad Anónima**) Ltd, plc, Inc (*Amer*)

sábado *m* Saturday

sábana *f* sheet

sabañón *m* chilblain

sabático *adj* sabbatical

sab|elotodo *m & f invar* know-all [1]. ~**er** 38 *vt* know; (*ser capaz de*) be able to, know how to; (*enterarse de*) find out. • *vi* know. ~**er** a taste of. hacer ~**er** let know. ¡qué sé yo! how should I know? que yo sepa as far as I know. ¿~**es** nadar? can you swim? un no sé qué a certain sth. ¡yo qué sé! how should I know? ¡vete a ~**er**! who

knows? ~**er** *m* knowledge. ~**ido** *adj* well-known. ~**iduría** *f* wisdom; (*conocimientos*) knowledge

sabi|endas. a ~ knowingly; (*a propósito*) on purpose. ~**hondo** *m* know-all. ~**o** *adj* learned; (*prudente*) wise

sabor *m* taste, flavour; (*fig*) flavour. ~**ear** *vt* taste; (*fig*) savour

sabot|aje *m* sabotage. ~**eador** *m* saboteur. ~**ear** *vt* sabotage

sabroso *adj* tasty; (*chisme*) juicy; (*LAm, agradable*) pleasant

sabueso *m* (*perro*) bloodhound; (*fig, detective*) detective

saca|corchos *m invar* corkscrew. ~**puntas** *m invar* pencil-sharpener

sacar 7 *vt* take out; put out (*parte del cuerpo*); (*quitar*) remove; take (*foto*); win (*premio*); get (billete, entrada); withdraw (*dinero*); reach (*solución*); draw (conclusión); make (*copia*). ~ **adelante** bring up (*niño*); carry on (*negocio*)

sacarina *f* saccharin

sacerdo|cio *m* priesthood. ~**te** *m* priest

saciar *vt* satisfy; quench (*sed*)

saco *m* sack; (*LAm, chaqueta*) jacket. ~ **de dormir** sleeping-bag

sacramento *m* sacrament

sacrific|ar 7 *vt* sacrifice; slaughter (*res*); put to sleep (*perro, gato*). ~**arse** *vpr* sacrifice o.s. ~**io** *m* sacrifice; (*de res*) slaughter

sacr|ilegio *m* sacrilege. ~**ilego** *adj* sacrilegious

sacudi|da *f* shake; (*movimiento brusco*) jolt, jerk; (*fig*) shock. ~**da eléctrica** electric shock. ~**r** *vt* shake; (*golpear*) beat. ~**rse** *vpr* shake off; (*fig*) get rid of

sádico *adj* sadistic. • *m* sadist

sadismo | salvo

sadismo m sadism

safari m safari

sagaz adj shrewd

Sagitario m Sagittarius

sagrado adj (lugar) holy, sacred; (altar, escrituras) holy; (fig) sacred

sal f salt. • vb véase **SALIR**

sala f room; (en casa) living room; (en hospital) ward; (para reuniones etc) hall; (en teatro) house; (Jurid) courtroom. ~ de embarque departure lounge. ~ de espera waiting room. ~ de estar living room. ~ de fiestas nightclub

salado adj salty; (agua del mar) salt; (no dulce) savoury; (fig) witty

salario m wage

salchich|a f (pork) sausage. ~ón m salami

sald|ar vt settle (cuenta); (vender) sell off. ~o m balance. ~os mpl sales. venta de ~os clearance sale

salero m salt-cellar

salgo vb véase **SALIR**

sali|da f departure; (puerta) exit, way out; (de gas, de líquido) leak; (de astro) rising; (Com, venta) sale; (chiste) witty remark; (fig) way out; ~da de emergencia emergency exit. ~ente adj (Archit) projecting; (pómulo etc) prominent. ~r 52 vi leave; (ir afuera) go out; (Informática) exit; (revista etc) be published; (resultar) turn out; (astro) rise; (aparecer) appear. ~r adelante get by. ~rse vpr leave; (recipiente, líquido etc) leak. ~rse con la suya get one's own way

saliva f saliva

salmo m psalm

salm|ón m salmon. ~onete m red mullet

salón m living-room, lounge. ~ de

actos assembly hall. ~ de clases classroom. ~ de fiestas dancehall

salpica|dera f (Mex) mudguard. ~dero m (Auto) dashboard. ~dura f splash; (acción) splashing. ~r 7 vt splash; (fig) sprinkle

sals|a f sauce; (para carne asada) gravy; (Mus) salsa. ~ verde parsley sauce. ~era f sauce-boat

salt|amontes m invar grasshopper. ~ar vt jump (over); (fig) miss out. • vi jump; (romperse) break; (líquido) spurt out; (desprenderse) come off; (pelota) bounce; (estallar) explode. ~eador m highwayman. ~ear vt (Culin) sauté

salt|o m jump; (al agua) dive. ~o de agua waterfall. ~o mortal somersault. de un ~o with one jump. ~ón adj (ojos) bulging

salud f health. • int cheers!; (LAm, al estornudar) bless you! ~able adj healthy

salud|ar vt greet, say hello to; (Mil) salute. lo ~a atentamente (en cartas) yours faithfully. ~ con la mano wave. ~o m greeting; (Mil) salute. ~os mpl best wishes

salva f salvo. una ~ de aplausos a burst of applause

salvación f salvation

salvado m bran

salvaguardia f safeguard

salvaje adj (planta, animal) wild; (primitivo) savage. • m & f savage

salva|mento m rescue. ~r vt save, rescue; (atravesar) cross (recorrer); travel (fig) overcome. ~rse vpr save o.s. ~vidas m & f invar lifeguard. • m lifebelt. chaleco m ~vidas life-jacket

salvo adj safe. • adv & prep except (for). a ~ out of danger. poner a ~ put in a safe place. ~ que unless. ~**conducto** m safe-conduct.

San adj Saint, St. ~ **Miguel** St Michael

sana|r vt cure. • vi recover; heal (herida). ~**torio** m sanatorium

sanci|ón f sanction. ~**onar** vt sanction

sandalia f sandal

sandía f watermelon

sándwich /'saŋgwitʃ/ m (pl ~s, ~es) sandwich

sangr|ante adj bleeding; (fig) flagrant. ~**ar** vt/i bleed. ~**e** f blood. a ~ **e fría** in cold blood

sangría f (bebida) sangria

sangriento adj bloody

sangu|ijuela f leech. ~**íneo** adj blood

san|idad f health. ~**itario** adj sanitary. •m (Mex) toilet. ~**o** adj healthy; (mente) sound. ~**o y salvo** safe and sound. **cortar por lo** ~**o** settle things once and for all

santiamén m. **en un** ~ in an instant

sant|idad f sanctity. ~**ificar** **7** vt sanctify. ~**iguarse** **15** vpr cross o.s. ~**o** adj holy; (delante de nombre) Saint, St. • m saint; (día) saint's day, name day. ~**uario** m sanctuary. ~**urrón** adj sanctimonious

> **santo** Most first names in Spanish-speaking countries are those of saints. A person's *santo* (also known as *onomástico* in Latin America and *onomástica* in Spain) is the saint's day of the saint they are named after. As well as celebrating their calendar birthday many people also celebrate their *santo*.

saña f viciousness. **con** ~ viciously

sapo m toad

saque m (en tenis) service; (inicial en fútbol) kick-off. ~ **de banda** throw-in; (en rugby) line-out. ~ **de esquina** corner (kick)

saque|ar vt loot. ~**o** m looting

sarampión m measles

sarape m (Mex) colourful blanket

sarc|asmo m sarcasm. ~**ástico** adj sarcastic

sardina f sardine

sargento m sergeant

sarpullido m rash

sartén f or m frying-pan (Brit), fry-pan (Amer)

sastre m tailor. ~**ría** f tailoring; (tienda) tailor's (shop)

Sat|anás m Satan. ~**ánico** adj satanic

satélite m satellite

satinado adj shiny

sátira f satire

satírico adj satirical. • m satirist

satisf|acción f satisfaction. ~**acer** **31** vt satisfy; (pagar) pay; (gustar) please; meet (gastos, requisitos). ~**acerse** vpr satisfy o.s.; (vengarse) take revenge. ~**actorio** adj satisfactory. ~**echo** adj satisfied. ~**echo de sí mismo** smug

satura|ción f saturation. ~**r** vt saturate

Saturno m Saturn

sauce m willow. ~ **llorón** weeping willow

sauna f, (LAm) **sauna** m sauna

saxofón m, **saxófono** m saxophone

sazona|do adj ripe; (Culin) seasoned. ~**r** vt ripen; (Culin) season

se *pronombre*

● (*en lugar de le, les*) **se lo di** (*a él*) I gave it to him; (*a ella*) I gave it to her; (*a usted, ustedes*) I gave it to you; (*a ellos, ellas*) I gave it to them. **se lo compré** I bought it for him (*or her etc*). **se lo quité** I took it away from him (*or her etc*). **se lo dije** I told him (*or her etc*)

····▸ (*reflexivo*) **se secó** (*él*) he dried himself; (*ella*) she dried herself; (*usted*) you dried yourself. (*sujeto no humano*) it dried itself. **se secaron** (*ellos, ellas*) they dried themselves. (*ustedes*) you dried yourselves. (*con partes del cuerpo*) **se lavó la cara** (*él*) he washed his face; (*con efectos personales*) **se limpian los zapatos** they clean their shoes

····▸ (*recíproco*) each other, one another. **se ayudan mucho** they help each other a lot. **no se hablan** they don't speak to each other

····▸ (*cuando otro hace la acción*) **va a operarse** she's going to have an operation. **se cortó el pelo** he had his hair cut

····▸ (*enfático*) **se bebió el café** he drank his coffee. **se subió al tren** he got on the train

➡ **se** also forms part of certain pronominal verbs such as **equivocarse, arrepentirse, caerse** etc., which are treated under the respective entries

····▸ (*voz pasiva*) **se construyeron muchas casas** many houses were built. **se vendió**

rápidamente it was sold very quickly

····▸ (*impersonal*) **antes se escuchaba más radio** people used to listen to the radio more in the past. **no se puede entrar** you can't get in. **se está bien aquí** it's very nice here

····▸ (*en instrucciones*) **sírvase frío** serve cold

sé *vb véase* SABER *y* SER

sea *vb véase* SER

seca|dor *m* drier; (*de pelo*) hairdrier. ~**nte** *adj* drying. ● *m* blotting-paper. ~**r** **7** *vt* dry. ~**rse** *vpr* dry; (*río etc*) dry up; (*persona*) dry o.s.

sección *f* section

seco *adj* dry; (*frutos, flores*) dried; (*flaco*) thin; (*respuesta*) curt. **a secas** just. **en** ~ (*bruscamente*) suddenly. **lavar en** ~ dry-clean

secretar|ía *f* secretariat; (*Mex, ministerio*) ministry. ~**io** *m* secretary; (*Mex, Pol*) minister

secreto *adj & m* secret

secta *f* sect. ~**rio** *adj* sectarian

sector *m* sector

secuela *f* consequence

secuencia *f* sequence

secuestr|ar *vt* confiscate; kidnap (*persona*); hijack (*avión*). ~**o** *m* seizure; (*de persona*) kidnapping; (*de avión*) hijack(ing)

secundar *vt* second, help. ~**io** *adj* secondary

sed *f* thirst. ● *vb véase* SER. **tener** ~ be thirsty. **tener** ~ **de** (*fig*) be hungry for

seda *f* silk. ~ **dental** dental floss

sedante *adj & m* sedative

sede *f* seat; (*Relig*) see; (*de organismo*) headquarters; (*de congreso,*

juegos etc) venue
sedentario *adj* sedentary
sedici|ón *f* sedition. **~oso** *adj* seditious
sediento *adj* thirsty
seduc|ción *f* seduction. **~ir** 🔲 *vt* seduce; (*atraer*) attract. **~tor** *adj* seductive. ● *m* seducer
seglar *adj* secular. ● *m* layman
segrega|ción *f* segregation. **~r** 🔲 *vt* segregate
segui|da *f*, en **~da** immediately. **~do** *adj* continuous; (*en plural*) consecutive. **~** de followed by. ● *adv* straight; (*LAm, a menudo*) often. todo **~do** straight ahead. **~dor** *m* follower; (*en deportes*) supporter. **~r** 🔲 & 🔲 *vt* follow. ● *vi* (*continuar*) continue; (*por un camino*) go on. **~r adelante** carry on
según *prep* according to. ● *adv* it depends; (*a medida que*) as
segund|a *f* (*Auto*) second gear; (*en tren, avión etc*) second class. **~o** *adj* & *m* second
segur|amente *adv* certainly; (*muy probablemente*) surely. **~idad** *f* security; (*ausencia de peligro*) safety; (*certeza*) certainty; (*aplomo*) confidence. **~idad en sí mismo** self-confidence. **~idad social** social security. **~o** *adj* safe; (*cierto*) certain, sure; (*estable*) secure; (*de fiar*) reliable. ● *adv* for certain. ● *m* insurance; (*dispositivo de seguridad*) safety device. **~o de sí mismo** self-confident. **~o contra terceros** third-party insurance
seis *adj* & *m* six. **~cientos** *adj* & *m* six hundred
seísmo *m* earthquake
selec|ción *f* selection. **~cionar** *vt* select, choose. **~tivo** *adj* selective.

~to *adj* selected; (*fig*) choice
sell|ar *vt* stamp; (*cerrar*) seal. **~o** *m* stamp; (*precinto*) seal; (*fig, distintivo*) hallmark; (*LAm, en moneda*) reverse
selva *f* forest; (*jungla*) jungle
semáforo *m* (*Auto*) traffic lights; (*Rail*) signal; (*Naut*) semaphore
semana *f* week. **S~** Santa Holy Week. **~l** *adj* weekly. **~rio** *adj* & *m* weekly

Semana Santa The most famous Holy Week celebrations in the Spanish-speaking world are held in Sevilla between Palm Sunday and Easter Sunday. Lay brotherhoods, *cofradías*, process through the city in huge parades. During the processions they sing *saetas*, flamenco verses mourning Christ's passion.

semántic|a *f* semantics. **~o** *adj* semantic
semblante *m* face; (*fig*) look
sembrar 🔲 *vt* sow; (*fig*) scatter
semeja|nte *adj* similar; (*tal*) such. ● *m* fellow man. **~nza** *f* similarity. a **~nza de** like. **~r** *vi*. **~r a** resemble
semen *m* semen. **~tal** *adj* stud. ● *m* stud animal
semestr|al *adj* half-yearly. **~e** *m* six months
semi|circular *adj* semicircular. **~círculo** *m* semicircle. **~final** *f* semifinal
semill|a *f* seed. **~ero** *m* seedbed; (*fig*) hotbed
seminario *m* (*Univ*) seminar; (*Relig*) seminary
sémola *f* semolina
senado *m* senate. **~r** *m* senator

sencill|ez f simplicity. **~o** adj simple; (para viajar) single ticket; (disco) single; (LAm, dinero suelto) change

senda f, **sendero** m path

sendos adj pl each

seno m bosom. **~ materno** womb

sensaci|ón f sensation; (percepción, impresión) feeling. **~onal** adj sensational

sensat|ez f good sense. **~o** adj sensible

sensi|bilidad f sensibility. **~ble** adj sensitive; (notable) notable; (lamentable) lamentable. **~tivo** adj (órgano) sense

sensual adj sensual. **~idad** f sensuality

senta|do adj sitting (down); **dar algo por ~do** take something for granted. **~dor** adj (LAm) flattering. **~r 1** vt sit; (establecer) establish. ● vi suit; (de medidas) fit; (comida) agree with. **~rse** vpr sit (down)

sentencia f (Jurid) sentence. **~r** vt sentence (a to)

sentido adj heartfelt; (sensible) sensitive. ● m sense; (dirección) direction; (conocimiento) consciousness. **~ común** common sense. **~ del humor** sense of humour. **~ único** one-way. **doble ~** double meaning. **no tener ~** not make sense. **perder el ~** faint. **sin ~** senseless

sentim|ental adj sentimental. **~iento** m feeling; (sentido) sense; (pesar) regret

sentir 4 vt feel; (oír) hear; (lamentar) be sorry for. **lo siento mucho** I'm really sorry. ● m (opinión) opinion. **~se** vpr feel; (Mex, ofenderse) be offended

seña f sign. **~s** fpl (dirección) address; (descripción) description. **dar ~s de** show signs of

señal f signal; (letrero, aviso) sign; (telefónica) tone; (Com) deposit. **dar ~es de** show signs of. **en ~ de** as a token of. **~ado** adj (hora, día) appointed. **~ar** vt signal; (poner señales en) mark; (apuntar) point out; (manecilla, aguja) point to; (determinar) fix. **~arse** vpr stand out

señor m man, gentleman; (delante de nombre propio) Mr; (tratamiento directo) sir. **~a** f lady, woman; (delante de nombre propio) Mrs; (esposa) wife; (tratamiento directo) madam. **el ~** Mr. **muy ~ mío** Dear Sir. **¡no ~!** certainly not!. **~ial** adj (casa) stately. **~ita** f young lady; (delante de nombre propio) Miss; (tratamiento directo) miss. **~ito** m young gentleman

señuelo m lure

sepa vb véase **SABER**

separa|ción f separation. **~do** adj separate. **por ~do** separately. **~r** vt separate; (de empleo) dismiss. **~rse** vpr separate; (amigos) part. **~tista** adj & m & f separatist

septentrional adj north(ern)

septiembre m September

séptimo adj seventh

sepulcro m sepulchre

sepult|ar vt bury. **~ura** f burial; (tumba) grave. **~urero** m gravedigger

sequ|edad f dryness. **~ía** f drought

séquito m entourage; (fig) train

---

ser **39**

● verbo intransitivo

····▸ to be. **es bajo** he's short. **es abogado** he's a lawyer.

ábreme, soy yo open up, it's me. ¿cómo es? (como persona) what's he like?; (físicamente) what does he look like? era invierno it was winter

····▸ ser de (indicando composición) to be made of. es de hierro it's made of iron. (provenir de) to be from. es de México he's from Mexico. (pertenecer a) to belong to. el coche es de Juan the car belongs to Juan, it's Juan's car

····▸ (sumar) ¿cuánto es todo? how much is that altogether? son 40 dólares that's 40 dollars. somos 10 there are 10 of us

····▸ (con la hora) son las 3 it's 3 o'clock. ~ía la una it must have been one o'clock

····▸ (tener lugar) to be held. ~á en la iglesia it will be held in the church

····▸ (ocurrir) to happen ¿dónde fue el accidente? where did the accident happen? me contó cómo fue he told me how it happened

····▸ (en locuciones) a no ~ que unless. como sea no matter what. cuando sea whenever. donde sea wherever. ¡eso es! that's it! es que the thing is. lo que sea anything. no sea que, no vaya a ~ que in case. o sea in other words. sea ... sea ... either ... or ... sea como sea at all costs

● nombre masculino being; (persona) person. el ~ humano the human being. un ~ amargado a bitter person. los ~es queridos the loved ones

seren|ar vt calm down. ~**arse** vpr calm down. ~**ata** f serenade. ~**idad** f serenity. ~**o** adj serene; (cielo) clear; (mar) calm

seri|al m serial. ~**e** f series. fuera de ~**e** (fig) out of this world. producción f en ~**e** mass production

seri|edad f seriousness. ~**o** adj serious; (confiable) reliable; en ~**o** seriously. poco ~**o** frivolous

sermón m sermon; (fig) lecture

serp|enteante adj winding. ~**entear** vi wind. ~**iente** f snake. ~**iente de cascabel** rattlesnake

serr|ar 1 vt saw. ~**in** m sawdust. ~**uchar** vt (LAm) saw. ~**ucho** m (hand)saw

servi|cial adj helpful. ~**cio** m service; (conjunto) toilet; (aseo) toilet; ~**cio a domicilio** delivery service. ~**dor** m servant. su (seguro) ~**dor** (en cartas) yours faithfully. ~**dumbre** f servitude; (criados) servants, staff. ~**l** adj servile

servidor m server; (criado) servant

servilleta f napkin, serviette

servir 5 vt serve; (en restaurante) wait on. ● vi serve; (ser útil) be of use. ~**se** vpr help o.s. ~**se de** use. no ~ de nada be useless. para ~**le** at your service. sírvase sentarse please sit down

sesent|a adj & m sixty. ~**ón** adj & m sixty-year-old

seseo m pronunciation of the Spanish c as an s

sesión f session; (en el cine, teatro) performance

seso m brain

seta f mushroom

sete|cientos adj & m seven hundred. **~nta** adj & m seventy. **~ntón** adj & m seventy-year-old

setiembre m September

seto m fence; (de plantas) hedge. **~ vivo** hedge

seudónimo m pseudonym

sever|idad f severity; (de profesor etc) strictness. **~o** adj severe; (profesor etc) strict

sevillan|as fpl popular dance from Seville. **~o** m person from Seville

sexo m sex

sext|eto m sextet. **~o** adj sixth

sexual adj sexual. **~idad** f sexuality

si m (Mus) B; (solfa) te. ● conj if; (dubitativo) whether; **~ no** otherwise. **por ~** (acaso) in case

sí¹ pron reflexivo (él) himself; (ella) herself; (de cosa) itself; (uno) oneself; (Vd) yourself; (ellos, ellas) themselves; (Vds) yourselves; (recíproco) each other

sí² adv yes. ● m consent

sida m Aids

sidra f cider

siembra f sowing; (época) sowing time

siempre adv always; (LAm, todavía) still; (Mex, por fin) after all. **~ que** if; (cada vez) whenever. **como ~** as usual. **de ~** the usual thing. **para ~** for ever

sien f temple

siento vb véase SENTAR y SENTIR

sierra f saw; (cordillera) mountain range

siesta f nap, siesta

siete adj & m seven

sífilis f syphilis

sifón m U-bend; (de soda) syphon

sigilo m stealth; (fig) secrecy

sigla f abbreviation

siglo m century; (época) age. hace **~s que no escribe** he hasn't written for ages

significa|ción f significance. **~do** adj (conocido) well-known. ● m meaning; (importancia) significance. **~r 7** vt mean; (expresar) express. **~tivo** adj meaningful; (importante) significant

signo m sign. **~ de admiración** exclamation mark. **~ de interrogación** question mark

sigo vb véase SEGUIR

siguiente adj following, next. **lo ~** the following

sílaba f syllable

silb|ar vt/i whistle. **~ato** m, **~ido** m whistle

silenci|ador m silencer. **~ar** vt hush up. **~o** m silence. **~oso** adj silent

sill|a f chair; (de montar) saddle (Relig) see **~a de ruedas** wheelchair. **~ín** m saddle. **~ón** m armchair

silueta f silhouette; (dibujo) outline

silvestre adj wild

simb|ólico adj symbolic(al). **~olismo** m symbolism. **~olizar 10** vt symbolize

símbolo m symbol

sim|etría f symmetry. **~étrico** adj symmetric(al)

similar adj similar (a to)

simp|atía f friendliness; (cariño) affection. **~ático** adj nice, likeable; (ambiente) pleasant. **~atizante** m & f sympathizer. **~atizar 10** vi get on (well together)

simpl|e adj simple; (*mero*) mere. ~**eza** f simplicity; (*tontería*) stupid thing; (*insignificancia*) trifle. ~**icidad** f simplicity. ~**ificar** 7 vt simplify. ~**ista** adj simplistic. ~**ón** m simpleton

simula|ción f simulation. ~**r** vt simulate; (*fingir*) feign

simultáneo adj simultaneous

sin prep without. ~ **saber** without knowing. ~ **querer** accidentally

sinagoga f synagogue

sincer|idad f sincerity. ~**o** adj sincere

sincronizar 10 vt synchronize

sindica|l adj (trade-)union. ~**lista** m & f trade-unionist. ~**to** m trade union

síndrome m syndrome

sinfín m endless number (de of)

sinfonía f symphony

singular adj singular; (*excepcional*) exceptional. ~**izarse** vpr stand out

siniestro adj sinister. ● m disaster; (*accidente*) accident

sinnúmero m endless number (de of)

sino m fate. ● conj but

sinónimo adj synonymous. ● m synonym (de for)

sintaxis f syntax

síntesis f invar synthesis; (*resumen*) summary

sint|ético adj synthetic. ~**etizar** 10 vt synthesize; (*resumir*) summarize

síntoma f symptom

sintomático adj symptomatic

sinton|ía f tuning; (*Mus*) signature tune. ~**izar** 10 vt (*con la radio*) tune (in) to

sinvergüenza m & f crook

siquiera conj even if. ● adv at least. **ni** ~ not even

sirena f siren; (*en cuentos*) mermaid

sirio adj & m Syrian

sirvient|a f maid. ~**e** m servant

sirvo vb véase **SERVIR**

sísmico adj seismic

sismo m earthquake

sistem|a m system. **por** ~**a** as a rule. ~**ático** adj systematic

sitiar vt besiege; (*fig*) surround

sitio m place; (*espacio*) space; (*Mil*) siege; (*Mex, parada de taxi*) taxi rank. **en cualquier** ~ anywhere. ~ **web** website

situa|ción f situation; (*estado, condición*) position. ~**r** 21 vt place, put; locate (*edificio*). ~**rse** vpr be successful, establish o.s.

slip /es'lip/ m (pl ~s) underpants, briefs

smoking /es'mokin/ m (pl ~s) dinner jacket (*Brit*), tuxedo (*Amer*)

sobaco m armpit

sobar vt handle; knead (*masa*)

soberan|ía f sovereignty. ~**o** adj sovereign; (*fig*) supreme. ● m sovereign

soberbi|a f pride; (*altanería*) arrogance. ~**o** adj proud; (*altivo*) arrogant

soborn|ar vt bribe. ~**o** m bribe

sobra f surplus. **de** ~ more than enough. ~**s** fpl leftovers. **de** ~**do** more than enough. ~**nte** adj surplus. ~**r** vi be left over; (*estorbar*) be in the way

sobre prep on; (*encima de*) on top of; (*más o menos*) about; (*por encima de*) above; (*sin tocar*) over. ~ **todo** above all, especially. ● m envelope. ~**cargar** 12 vt overload. ~**coger** 14 vt startle; (*conmover*)

move. ~**cubierta** f dustcover.
~**dosis** f invar overdose. ~**entender 1** vt understand, infer. ~**girar** vt (LAm) overdraw. ~**giro** m (LAm) overdraft. ~**humano** adj superhuman. ~**llevar** vt bear. ~**mesa** f de ~mesa after-dinner. ~**natural** adj supernatural. ~**nombre** m nickname. ~**pasar** vt exceed. ~**peso** m (LAm) excess baggage. ~**poner 34** vt superimpose. ~**ponerse** vpr overcome. ~**saliente** adj (fig) outstanding. ● m excellent mark. ~**salir 52** vi stick out; (fig) stand out. ~**saltar** vt startle. ~**salto** m fright. ~**sueldo** m bonus. ~**todo** m overcoat. ~**venir 53** vi happen. ~**viviente** adj surviving. ● m & f survivor. ~**vivir** vi survive. ~**volar** vt fly over

sobriedad f moderation; (de estilo) simplicity

sobrin|a f niece. ~**o** m nephew. ~**os** (varones) nephews; (varones y mujeres) nieces and nephews

sobrio adj moderate, sober

socavar vt undermine

soci|able adj sociable. ~**al** adj social. ~**aldemócrata** m & f social democrat. ~**alismo** m socialism. ~**alista** adj & m & f socialist. ~**edad** f society; (Com) company. ~**edad anónima** limited company. ~**o** m member; (Com) partner. ~**ología** f sociology. ~**ólogo** m sociologist

socorr|er vt help. ~**o** m help

soda f (bebida) soda (water)

sodio m sodium

sofá m sofa, settee

sofistica|ción f sophistication. ~**do** adj sophisticated

sofo|cante adj suffocating; (fig) stifling. ~**car 7** vt smother

(fuego); (fig) stifle. ~**carse** vpr get upset

soga f rope

soja f soya (bean)

sojuzgar 12 vt subdue

sol m sun; (luz) sunlight; (Mus) G; (solfa) soh. al ~ in the sun. día m de ~ sunny day. hace ~, hay ~ it is sunny. tomar el ~ sunbathe

solamente adv only

solapa f lapel; (de bolsillo etc) flap. ~**do** adj sly

solar adj solar. ● m plot

solariego adj (casa) ancestral

soldado m soldier. ~ **raso** private

solda|dor m welder; (utensilio) soldering iron. ~**r 2** vt weld, solder

soleado adj sunny

soledad f solitude; (aislamiento) loneliness

solemn|e adj solemn. ~**idad** f solemnity

soler 2 vi be in the habit of. suele despertarse a las 6 he usually wakes up at 6 o'clock

sol|icitante m applicant. ~ de asilo asylum seeker. ~**icitar** vt request, ask for; apply for (empleo). ~**ícito** adj solicitous. ~**icitud** f request; (para un puesto) application; (formulario) application form; (preocupación) concern

solidaridad f solidarity

solid|ez f solidity; (de argumento etc) soundness. ~**ificarse 7** vpr solidify

sólido adj solid; (argumento etc) sound. ● m solid

soliloquio m soliloquy

solista m & f soloist

solitario adj solitary; (aislado) lonely. ● m loner; (juego, diamante) solitaire

s

solloz|ar 10 vi sob. **~o** m sob

solo adj (sin compañía) alone; (aislado) lonely; (sin ayuda) by oneself; (único) only; (Mus) solo; (café) black. ● m solo; (juego) solitaire. **a solas** alone

sólo adv only. **~ que** except that. **no ~... sino también** not only... but also.... **tan ~** only

solomillo m sirloin

soltar 2 vt let go of; (dejar ir) release; (dejar caer) drop; (dejar salir, decir) let out; give (golpe etc). **~se** vpr come undone; (librarse) break loose

solter|a f single woman. **~o** adj single. ● m bachelor

soltura f looseness; (fig) ease, fluency

solu|ble adj soluble. **~ción** f solution. **~cionar** vt solve; settle (huelga, asunto)

solvente adj & m solvent

sombr|a f shadow; (lugar sin sol) shade. **a la ~a** in the shade. **~eado** adj shady

sombrero m hat. **~ hongo** bowler hat

sombrío adj sombre

somero adj superficial

someter vt subdue; subject (persona); (presentar) submit. **~se** vpr give in

somn|oliento adj sleepy. **~ífero** m sleeping-pill

somos vb véase SER

son m sound. ● vb véase SER

sonámbulo m sleepwalker. **ser ~** walk in one's sleep

sonar 2 vt blow; ring (timbre). ●vi sound; (timbre, teléfono etc) ring; (despertador) go off; (Mus) play; (fig, ser conocido) be familiar. **~ a** sound like. **~se** vpr blow one's nose

sonde|ar vt sound out; explore (espacio); (Naut) sound. **~o** m poll; (Naut) sounding

soneto m sonnet

sonido m sound

sonoro adj sonorous; (ruidoso) loud

sonr|eír 51 vi smile. **~eírse** vpr smile. **~isa** f smile

sonroj|arse vpr blush. **~o** m blush

sonrosado adj rosy, pink

sonsacar 7 vt wheedle out

soñ|ado adj dream. **~ador** m dreamer. **~ar** 2 vi dream (con of). **¡ni ~arlo!** not likely!

sopa f soup

sopesar vt (fig) weigh up

sopl|ar vt blow; blow out (vela); blow off (polvo); (inflar) blow up. ● vi blow. **~ete** m blowlamp. **~o** m puff

soport|al m porch. **~ales** mpl arcade. **~ar** vt support; (fig) bear, put up with. **~e** m support

soprano f soprano

sor f sister

sorb|er vt sip; (con ruido) slurp; (absorber) absorb. **~ por la nariz** sniff. **~ete** m sorbet, water-ice. **~o** m (pequeña cantidad) sip; (trago grande) gulp

sordera f deafness

sórdido adj squalid; (asunto) sordid

sordo adj deaf; (ruido etc) dull. ● m deaf person. **hacerse el ~** turn a deaf ear. **~mudo** adj deaf and dumb

soroche m (LAm) mountain sickness

sorpre|ndente adj surprising.

~nder *vt* surprise. ~nderse *vpr* be surprised. ~sa *f* surprise

sorte|ar *vt* draw lots for; (*fig*) avoid. ~o *m* draw. por ~o by drawing lots

sortija *f* ring; (*de pelo*) ringlet

sortilegio *m* sorcery; (*embrujo*) spell

sos|egar **11** & **12** *vt* calm. ~iego *m* calmness

soslayo, de ~ sideways

soso *adj* tasteless; (*fig*) dull

sospech|a *f* suspicion. ~ar *vt* suspect. ● *vi*. ~ de suspect. ~oso *adj* suspicious. ● *m* suspect

sost|én *m* support; (*prenda femenina*) bra **11**, brassière. ~ener **40** *vt* support; bear (*peso*); (*sujetar*) hold; (*sustentar*) maintain; (*alimentar*) sustain. ~enerse *vpr* support o.s.; (*continuar*) remain. ~enido *adj* sustained; (*Mus*) sharp. ● *m* (*Mus*) sharp

sota *f* (*de naipes*) jack

sótano *m* basement

soviético *adj* (*Historia*) Soviet

soy *vb véase* SER

Sr. *abrev* (Señor) Mr. ~a. *abrev* (Señora) Mrs. ~ta. *abrev* (Señorita) Miss

su *adj* (*de él*) his; (*de ella*) her; (*de animal, objeto*) its; (*de uno*) one's; (*de Vd*) your; (*de ellos, de ellas*) their; (*de Vds*) your

suav|e *adj* smooth; (*fig*) gentle; (color, sonido) soft; (tabaco, sedante) mild. ~idad *f* smoothness, softness. ~izante *m* conditioner; (*para ropa*) softener. ~izar **10** *vt* smooth, soften

subalimentado *adj* underfed

subarrendar **11** *vt* sublet

subasta *f* auction. ~r *vt* auction

sub|campeón *m* runner-up. ~consciencia *f* subconscious. ~consciente *adj* & *m* subconscious. ~continente *m* subcontinent. ~desarrollado *adj* underdeveloped. ~director *m* assistant manager

súbdito *m* subject

sub|dividir *vt* subdivide. ~estimar *vt* underestimate

subi|da *f* rise; (*a montaña*) ascent; (*pendiente*) slope. ~do *adj* (color) intense. ~r *vt* go up; climb (montaña); (*llevar*) take up; (*aumentar*) raise; turn up (radio, calefacción). ● *vi* go up. ~r a get into (coche); get on (autobús, avión, barco, tren); (*aumentar*) rise. ~ a pie walk up. ~rse *vpr* climb up. ~rse a get on (tren etc)

súbito *adj* sudden. de ~ suddenly

subjetivo *adj* subjective

subjuntivo *adj* & *m* subjunctive

subleva|ción *f* uprising. ~rse *vpr* rebel

sublim|ar *vt* sublimate. ~e *adj* sublime

submarino *adj* underwater. ● *m* submarine

subordinado *adj* & *m* subordinate

subrayar *vt* underline

subsanar *vt* rectify; overcome (dificultad); make up for (carencia)

subscri|bir *vt* (*pp* subscrito) sign. ~birse *vpr* subscribe (a to). ~pción *f* subscription

subsidi|ario *adj* subsidiary. ~o *m* subsidy. ~o de desempleo, ~ de paro unemployment benefit

subsiguiente *adj* subsequent

subsist|encia *f* subsistence. ~ir *vi* subsist; (*perdurar*) survive

substraer **41** *vt* take away

s

subterráneo adj underground

subtítulo m subtitle

suburb|ano adj suburban. ~**io** m suburb; (barrio pobre) depressed area

subvenci|ón f subsidy. ~**onar** vt subsidize

subver|sión f subversion. ~**sivo** adj subversive. ~**tir** 4 vt subvert

succi|ón f suction. ~**onar** vt suck

suce|der vi happen; (seguir) ~ a follow. • vt (substituir) succeed. lo que ~**de** es que the trouble is that. ¿qué ~**de**? what's the matter? ~**sión** f succession. ~**sivo** adj successive; (consecutivo) consecutive. en lo ~**sivo** in future. ~**so** m event; (incidente) incident. ~**sor** m successor

suciedad f dirt; (estado) dirtiness

sucinto adj concise; (prenda) scanty

sucio adj dirty; (conciencia) guilty. en ~ in rough

sucre m (unidad monetaria del Ecuador) sucre

suculento adj succulent

sucumbir vi succumb (a to)

sucursal f branch (office)

Sudáfrica f South Africa

sudafricano adj & m South African

Sudamérica f South America

sudamericano adj & m South American

sudar vi sweat

sud|este m south-east. ~**oeste** m south-west

sudor m sweat

Suecia f Sweden

sueco adj Swedish. • m (persona) Swede; (lengua) Swedish. hacerse el ~ pretend not to hear

suegr|a f mother-in-law. ~**o** m father-in-law. mis ~**os** my in-laws

suela f sole

sueldo m salary

suelo m ground; (dentro de edificio) floor; (territorio) soil; (en la calle etc) road surface. • vb véase **SOLER**

suelto adj loose; (cordones) undone; (sin pareja) odd; (lenguaje) fluent. con el pelo ~ with one's hair down. • m change

sueño m sleep; (lo soñado, ilusión) dream. tener ~ be sleepy

suerte f luck; (destino) fate; (azar) chance. de otra ~ otherwise. de ~ que so. echar ~**s** draw lots. por ~ fortunately. tener ~ be lucky

suéter m sweater, jersey

suficien|cia f (aptitud) aptitude; (presunción) smugness. ~**te** adj enough, sufficient; (presumido) smug. ~**temente** adv sufficiently

sufijo m suffix

sufragio m (voto) vote

sufri|miento m suffering. ~**r** vt suffer; undergo (cambio); have (accident). • vi suffer

suge|rencia f suggestion. ~**rir** 4 vt suggest. ~**stión** f (en psicología) suggestion. es pura ~**stión** it's all in one's mind. ~**stionable** adj impressionable. ~**stionar** vt influence. ~**stivo** adj (estimulante) stimulating; (atractivo) sexy

suicid|a adj suicidal. • m & f suicide victim; (fig) maniac. ~**arse** vpr commit suicide. ~**io** m suicide

Suiza f Switzerland

suizo adj & m Swiss

suje|ción f subjection. con ~ a in accordance with. ~**tador** m bra 🇬🇧, brassière. ~**tapapeles** m invar paper-clip. ~**tar** vt fasten; (agarrar) hold. **~tarse** *vpr.* **~se** a hold on to; (*someterse*) abide by. **~to** *adj* fastened; (*susceptible*) subject (a to). ● *m* individual; (*Gram*) subject.

suma *f* sum; (*Math*) addition; (*combinación*) combination. **en ~** in short. **~mente** *adv* extremely. **~r** *vt* add (up); (*totalizar*) add up to. ● *vi* add up. **~rse** *vpr.* **~rse a** join in

sumario *adj* brief; (*Jurid*) summary. ●*m* table of contents; (*Jurid*) pre-trial proceedings

sumergi|ble *adj* submersible. **~r** 🔟 *vt* submerge

suministr|ar *vt* supply. **~o** *m* supply; (*acción*) supplying

sumir *vt* sink; (*fig*) plunge

sumis|ión *f* submission. **~o** *adj* submissive

sumo *adj* great; (*supremo*) supreme. **a lo ~** at the most

suntuoso *adj* sumptuous

supe *vb véase* SABER

superar *vt* surpass; (*vencer*) overcome; beat (marca); (*dejar atrás*) get over. **~se** *vpr* better o.s.

superchería *f* swindle

superfici|al *adj* superficial. **~e** *f* surface; (*extensión*) area. **de ~e** surface

superfluo *adj* superfluous

superior *adj* superior; (*más alto*) higher; (*mejor*) better; (*piso*) upper. ● *m* superior. **~idad** *f* superiority

superlativo *adj & m* superlative

supermercado *m* supermarket

superstici|ón *f* superstition. **~oso** *adj* superstitious

supervis|ar *vt* supervise. **~ión** *f* supervision. **~or** *m* supervisor

superviv|encia *f* survival. **~iente** *adj* surviving. ● *m & f* survivor

suplantar *vt* supplant

suplement|ario *adj* supplementary. **~o** *m* supplement

suplente *adj & m & f* substitute

súplica *f* entreaty; (*Jurid*) request

suplicar 🔟 *vt* beg

suplicio *m* torture

suplir *vt* make up for; (*reemplazar*) replace

supo|ner 🔢 *vt* suppose; (*significar*) mean; involve (gasto, trabajo). **~sición** *f* supposition

suprem|acía *f* supremacy. **~o** *adj* supreme

supr|esión *f* suppression; (*de impuesto*) abolition; (*de restricción*) lifting. **~imir** *vt* suppress; abolish (impuesto); lift (restricción); delete (párrafo)

supuesto *adj* supposed; (*falso*) false; (*denominado*) so-called. ●*m* assumption. **¡por ~!** of course!

sur *m* south; (*viento*) south wind

surc|ar 🔟 *vt* plough; cut through (agua). **~o** *m* furrow; (*de rueda*) rut

surfear *vi* (*Informática*) surf

surgir 🔟 *vi* spring up; (*elevarse*) loom up; (*aparecer*) appear; (*dificultad, oportunidad*) arise

surrealis|mo *m* surrealism. **~ta** *adj & m & f* surrealist

surti|do *adj* well-stocked; (*variado*) assorted. ●*m* assortment, selection. **~dor** *m* (*de gasolina*) petrol pump (*Brit*), gas pump (*Amer*). **~r** *vt* supply; have (efecto). **~rse** *vpr* provide o.s. (de with)

susceptib|ilidad *f* sensitivity. **~le** *adj* susceptible; (*sensible*) sensitive

suscitar *vt* provoke; arouse

s

(curiosidad, interés)

suscr... *véase* SUBSCR...

susodicho *adj* aforementioned

suspen|der *vt* suspend; stop (tratamiento); call off (viaje); (*en examen*) fail; (*colgar*) hang (de from). ∼**se** *m* suspense. novela de ∼**se** thriller. ∼**sión** *f* suspension. ∼**so** *m* fail; (*LAm, en libro, película*) suspense. en ∼**so** suspended

suspir|ar *vi* sigh. ∼**o** *m* sigh

sust... *véase* SUBST...

sustanci|a *f* substance. ∼**al** *adj* substantial. ∼**oso** *adj* substantial

sustantivo *m* noun

sustent|ación *f* support. ∼**ar** *vt* support; (*alimentar*) sustain; (*mantener*) maintain. ∼**o** *m* support; (*alimento*) sustenance

substitu|ción *f* substitution; (*permanente*) replacement. ∼**ir** 🆄 *vt* substitute, replace. ∼**to** *m* substitute; (*permanente*) replacement

susto *m* fright

susurr|ar *vi* (*persona*) whisper; (*agua*) murmur; (*hojas*) rustle

sutil *adj* fine; (*fig*) subtle. ∼**eza** *f* subtlety

suyo *adj & pron* (*de él*) his; (*de ella*) hers; (*de animal*) its; (*de Vd*) yours; (*de ellos, de ellas*) theirs; (*de Vds*) yours. un amigo ∼ a friend of his, a friend of theirs, etc

Tt

tabac|alera *f* (state) tobacco monopoly. ∼**o** *m* tobacco; (*cigarrillos*) cigarettes

tabern|a *f* bar. ∼**ero** *m* barman; (*dueño*) landlord

tabique *m* partition wall; (*Mex, ladrillo*) brick

tabl|a *f* plank; (*del suelo*) floorboard; (*de vestido*) pleat; (*índice*) index; (*gráfico, en matemática etc*) table. hacer ∼**as** (*en ajedrez*) draw. ∼**a** de surf surfboard. ∼**ado** *m* platform; (*en el teatro*) stage. ∼**ao** *m* place where flamenco shows are held. ∼**ero** *m* board. ∼**ero** de mandos dashboard

tableta *f* tablet; (*de chocolate*) bar

tabl|illa *f* splint; (*Mex, de chocolate*) bar. ∼**ón** *m* plank. ∼**ón** de anuncios notice board (*esp Brit*), bulletin board (*Amer*)

tabú *m* (*pl* ∼**es**, ∼**s**) taboo

tabular *vt* tabulate

taburete *m* stool

tacaño *adj* mean

tacha *f* stain, blemish. sin ∼ unblemished; (*conducta*) irreproachable. ∼**r** *vt* (*con raya*) cross out; (*Jurid*) impeach. ∼ de accuse of

tácito *adj* tacit

taciturno *adj* taciturn; (*triste*) glum

taco *m* plug; (*LAm, tacón*) heel; (*de billar*) cue; (*de billetes*) book; (*fig, fam, lío*) mess; (*palabrota*) swearword; (*Mex, Culin*) taco, filled tortilla

tacón *m* heel

táctic|a *f* tactics. ∼**o** *adj* tactical

táctil *adj* tactile

tacto *m* touch; (*fig*) tact

tahúr *m* card-sharp

tailandés *adj & m* Thai

Tailandia *f* Thailand

taimado *adj* sly

taj|ada *f* slice. sacar ~ada profit. ~ante *adj* categorical; (*tono*) sharp. ~ear *vt* (*LAm*) slash. ~o *m* cut; (*en mina*) face

tal *adj* such. de ~ manera in such a way. un ~ someone called. ● *pron*. como ~ as such. y ~ and things like that. ● *adv*. con ~ de que as long as. ~ como the way. ~ para cual **1** two of a kind. ~ vez maybe. ¿qué ~? how are you? ¿qué ~ es ella? what's she like?

taladr|ar *vt* drill. ~o *m* drill

talante *m* mood. de buen ~ (estar) in a good mood; (*ayudar*) willingly

talar *vt* fell

talco *m* talcum powder

talega *f*, **talego** *m* sack

talento *m* talent; (*fig*) talented person

talismán *m* talisman

talla *f* carving; (*de diamante etc*) cutting; (*estatura*) height; (*tamaño*) size. ~do *m* carving; (*de diamante etc*) cutting. ~dor *m* carver; (*cortador*) cutter; (*LAm, de naipes*) dealer. ~r *vt* carve; sculpt (*escultura*); cut (*diamante*); (*Mex, restregar*) scrub. ~rse *vpr* (*Mex*) rub o.s.

tallarín *m* noodle

talle *m* waist; (*figura*) figure

taller *m* workshop; (*de pintor etc*) studio; (*Auto*) garage

tallo *m* stem, stalk

tal|ón *m* heel; (*recibo*) counterfoil;

(*cheque*) cheque. ~onario *m* receipt book; (*de cheques*) cheque book

tamal *m* (*LAm*) tamale

tamaño *adj* such a. ● *m* size. de ~ natural life-size

tambalearse *vpr* (*persona*) stagger; (*cosa*) wobble

también *adv* also, too

tambor *m* drum. ~ del freno brake drum. ~ilear *vi* drum

tamiz *m* sieve. ~ar **10** *vt* sieve

tampoco *adv* neither, nor, not either. yo ~ fui I didn't go either

tampón *m* tampon; (*para entintar*) ink-pad

tan *adv* so. ~... como as... as. ¿qué ~...? (*LAm*) how...?

tanda *f* group; (*de obreros*) shift

tang|ente *adj & f* tangent. ~ible *adj* tangible

tango *m* tango

tanque *m* tank

tante|ar *vt* estimate; sound up (*persona*); (*ensayar*) test; (*fig*) weigh up; (*LAm, palpar*) feel. ● *vi* (*LAm*) feel one's way. ~o *m* estimate; (*prueba*) test; (*en deportes*) score

tanto *adj* (*en singular*) so much; (*en plural*) so many; (*comparación en singular*) as much; (*comparación en plural*) as many. ● *pron* so much; (*en plural*) so many. ● *adv* so; (*con verbo*) so much. hace ~ tiempo it's been so long. ~... como both ...and. ¿qué ~...? (*LAm*) how much...? ~ como as well as; (*cantidad*) as much as. ~ más... cuanto que all the more ... because. ~ si... como si whether ... or. a ~s de sometime in. en ~, entre ~ meanwhile. en ~ que while. entre ~ meanwhile. hasta

~ que until. no es para ~ it's not as bad as all that. otro ~ the same; (el doble) as much again. por (lo) ~ therefore. ●m certain amount; (punto) point; (gol) goal. estar al ~ de be up to date with

tañer 22 vi peal

tapa f lid; (de botella) top; (de libro) cover. ~s fpl savoury snacks. ~**dera** f cover, lid; (fig) cover. ~r vt cover; (abrigar) wrap up; (obturar) plug. ~**rrabo(s)** m invar loincloth

---

i

tapas In Spain these are small portions of food served in bars and cafés with a drink. There is a wide variety, including Spanish omelette, seafood, different kinds of cooked potatoes, cheese, ham, chorizo etc. The practice of going out for a drink and tapas is known as tapeo.

---

tapete m (de mesa) table cover; (Mex, alfombra) rug

tapia f wall. ~r vt enclose

tapi|cería f tapestry; (de muebles) upholstery. ~z m tapestry. ~zar 10 vt upholster (muebles)

tapón m stopper; (Tec) plug

taqu|igrafía f shorthand

taquill|a f ticket office; (fig, dinero) takings. ~ero adj box-office

tara f (peso) tare; (defecto) defect

tarántula f tarantula

tararear vt/i hum

tarda|nza f delay. ~r vt take. ●vi (retrasarse) be late; (emplear mucho tiempo) take a long time. a más ~r at the latest. sin ~r without delay

tard|e adv late. ● f (antes del atardecer) afternoon; (después del atardecer) evening. en la ~e (LAm), por la ~e in the afternoon. ~ío adj late

tarea f task, job

tarifa f rate; (en transporte) fare; (lista de precios) tariff

tarima f dais

tarjeta f card. ~ de crédito credit card. ~ de fidelidad loyalty card. ~ postal postcard. T~ Sanitaria Europea European Health Insurance Card. t~ SIM SIM card. ~ telefónica telephone card

tarro m jar; (Mex, taza) mug

tarta f cake; (con base de masa) tart. ~ helada ice-cream gateau

tartamud|ear vi stammer. ~o adj. es ~o he stammers

tasa f valuation; (impuesto) tax; (índice) rate. ~r vt value; (limitar) ration

tasca f bar

tataarabuel|a f great-great-grandmother. ~o m great-great-grandfather. ~os mpl great-great-grandparents

tatua|je m (acción) tattooing; (dibujo) tattoo. ~r 21 vt tattoo

taurino adj bullfighting

Tauro m Taurus

tauromaquia f bullfighting

taxi m taxi. ~ista m & f taxi-driver

taz|a f cup. ~ón m bowl

te pron (acusativo) you; (dativo) (to) you; (reflexivo) (to) yourself

té m tea; (LAm, reunión) tea party

teatr|al adj theatre; (exagerado) theatrical. ~o m theatre; (literatura) drama

tebeo m comic

tech|ado m roof. ~ar vt roof. ~o m (interior) ceiling; (LAm, tejado) roof. ~umbre f roof

tecl|a f key. **~ado** m keyboard.
~ear vt key in

técnica f technique

tecnicismo m technical nature;
(palabra) technical term

técnico adj technical. ● m techni-
cian; (en deportes) trainer

tecnolog|ía f technology.
~ógico adj technological

tecolote m (Mex) owl

teja f tile. **~s de pizarra** slates.
~do m roof. **a toca ~** cash

teje|dor m weaver. **~r** vt weave;
(hacer punto) knit

tejemaneje m 🔟 intrigue. **~s**
mpl scheming

tejido m material; (Anat, fig) tissue. **~s** mpl textiles

tejón m badger

tela f material, fabric; (de araña)
web; (en líquido) skin

telar m loom. **~es** mpl textile mill

telaraña f spider's web, cobweb

tele f 🔟 TV, telly

tele|banca f telephone banking.
~comunicación f telecommunica-
tion. **~diario** m television news.
~dirigido adj remote-controlled;
(misil) guided. **~férico** m cable-car

tel|efonear vt/i telephone. **~efó-
nico** adj telephone. **~efonista** m &
f telephonist

teléfono m telephone. **~ celular**
(LAm) mobile phone, cellular
phone. **~ móvil** (Esp) mobile
phone, cellular phone. **~ satélite**
satphone

tel|egrafía f telegraphy.
~égrafo m telegraph. **~egrama**
m telegram

telenovela f television soap
opera

teleobjetivo m telephoto lens

telep|atía f telepathy. **~ático** adj
telepathic

telesc|ópico adj telescopic.
~opio m telescope

telesilla m & f chair-lift

telespectador m viewer

telesquí m ski-lift

televi|dente m & f viewer. **~sar**
vt televise. **~sión** f television.
~sor m television (set)

télex m invar telex

telón m curtain

tema m subject; (Mus) theme

tembl|ar 🔝 vi shake; (de miedo)
tremble; (de frío) shiver. **~or** m
shaking; (de miedo) trembling; (de
frío) shivering; **~or de tierra** earth
tremor. **~oroso** adj trembling

tem|er vt be afraid (of). ● vi be
afraid. **~erse** vpr be afraid. **~era-
rio** adj reckless. **~eroso** adj frightened. **~ible** adj fearsome. **~or** m
fear

témpano m floe

temperamento m tempera-
ment

temperatura f temperature

tempest|ad f storm. **~uoso** adj
stormy

templ|ado adj (tibio) warm;
(clima, tiempo) mild; (valiente) courageous. **~anza** f mildness. **~ar** vt
temper; (calentar) warm up. **~e** m
tempering; (coraje) courage;
(humor) mood

templo m temple

tempora|da f season. **~l** adj
temporary. ● m storm

tempran|ero adj (frutos) early.
ser ~ero be an early riser. **~o** adj
& adv early

tenacidad f tenacity

tenacillas fpl tongs

tenaz adj tenacious

tenaza f, **tenazas** fpl pliers; (de chimenea, Culin) tongs; (de cangrejo) pincer

tende|ncia f tendency. ~**nte** adj. ~**nte a** aimed at. ~**r 1** vt spread (out); hang out (ropa a secar); (colocar) lay. ● vi tend (a to). ~**rse** vpr lie down

tender|ete m stall. ~**o** m shopkeeper

tendido adj spread out; (ropa) hung out; (persona) lying down. ● m (en plaza de toros) front rows

tendón m tendon

tenebroso adj gloomy; (asunto) sinister

tenedor m fork; (poseedor) holder

---

tener 40

● verbo transitivo

! El presente del verbo **tener** admite dos traducciones: to have y to have got, este último de uso más extendido en el inglés británico

⋯▸ to have. ¿tienen hijos? do you have any children?, have you got any children? no tenemos coche we don't have a car, we haven't got a car. tiene gripe he has (the) flu, he's got (the) flu

⋯▸ to be. (dimensiones, edad) tiene 1 metro de largo it's 1 meter long. tengo 20 años I'm 20 (years old)

⋯▸ (sentir) tener + nombre to be + adjective. ~ **celos** to be jealous. ~ **frío** to be cold

⋯▸ (sujetar, sostener) to hold. tenme la escalera hold the ladder for me

⋯▸ (indicando estado) tiene las manos sucias his hands are dirty. me tiene preocupada I'm worried about him. me tuvo esperando he kept me waiting

⋯▸ (llevar puesto) to be wearing, to have on. ¡qué zapatos más elegantes tienes! those are very smart shoes you're wearing! tienes el suéter al revés you have your sweater on inside out

⋯▸ (considerar) ~ a uno por algo to think s.o. is sth. lo tenía por tímido I thought he was shy

● verbo auxiliar

⋯▸ ~ **que** hacer algo to have to do sth. tengo que irme I have to go

⋯▸ tener + participio pasado. tengo pensado comprarlo I'm thinking of buying it. tenía entendido otra cosa I understood something else

⋯▸ (LAm, con expresiones temporales) tienen 2 años de estar aquí they've been here for 2 months. tiene mucho tiempo sin verlo she hasn't seen him for a long time

⋯▸ (en locuciones) aquí tiene here you are. ¿qué tienes? what's the matter with you? ¿y eso qué tiene? (LAm) and what's wrong with that?

● **tenerse** verbo pronominal

⋯▸ (sostenerse) no podía ~**se** en pie (de cansancio) he was dead on his feet; (de borracho) he could hardly stand

····▶ (considerarse) to consider o.s. **se tiene por afortunado** he considers himself lucky

tengo vb véase TENER

teniente m lieutenant

tenis m tennis. ~ **de mesa** table tennis. ~**ta** m & f tennis player

tenor m sense; (Mus) tenor. **a** ~ **de** according to

tens|ión f tension; (arterial) blood pressure; (Elec) voltage; (estrés) strain. ~**o** adj tense

tentación f temptation

tentáculo m tentacle

tenta|dor adj tempting. ~**r** 🖬 vt tempt; (palpar) feel

tentativa f attempt

tenue adj thin; (luz, voz) faint; (color) subdued

teñi|r 🖬 & 🟪 vt dye; (fig) tinge (de with). ~**rse** vpr dye one's hair

teología f theology

te|oría f theory. ~**órico** adj theoretical

tequila f tequila

terap|euta m & f therapist. ~**éutico** adj therapeutic. ~**ia** f therapy

terc|er adj véase TERCERO. ~**era** f (Auto) third (gear). ~**ero** adj (delante de nombre masculino en singular **tercer**) third. ● m third party. ~**io** m third

terciopelo m velvet

terco adj obstinate

tergiversar vt distort

termal adj thermal

térmico adj thermal

termina|ción f ending; (conclusión) conclusion. ~**l** adj & m terminal. ~**nte** adj categorical. ~**r** vt finish, end. ~ **por end up.** ~**rse** vpr come to an end

término m end; (palabra) term;

(plazo) period. ~ **medio** average. **dar** ~ **a** finish off. **en primer** ~ first of all. **en último** ~ as a last resort. **estar en buenos** ~**s con** be on good terms with. **llevar a** ~ carry out

terminología f terminology

termita f termite

termo m Thermos (P) flask, flask

termómetro m thermometer

termo|nuclear adj thermonuclear. ~**stato** m thermostat

terner|a f (carne) veal. ~**o** m calf

ternura f tenderness

terquedad f stubbornness

terrado m flat roof

terraplén m embankment

terrateniente m & f landowner

terraza f terrace; (balcón) balcony; (terrado) flat roof

terremoto m earthquake

terre|no adj earthly. ● m land; (solar) plot (fig) field. ~**stre** adj land; (Mil) ground

terrible adj terrible. ~**mente** adv awfully

territori|al adj territorial. ~**o** m territory

terrón m (de tierra) clod; (Culin) lump

terror m terror. ~**ífico** adj terrifying. ~**ismo** m terrorism. ~**ista** m & f terrorist

terso adj smooth

tertulia f gathering

tesina f dissertation

tesón m tenacity

tesor|ería f treasury. ~**ero** m treasurer. ~**o** m treasure; (tesorería) treasury; (libro) thesaurus

testaferro m figurehead

testa|mento m will. T~**mento** (Relig) Testament. ~**r** vi make a will

t

testarudo adj stubborn

testículo m testicle

testi|ficar ⑦ vt/i testify. ~**go** m witness. ~**go ocular**, ~**go presencial** eyewitness. **ser** ~**go de** witness. ~**monio** m testimony

teta f tit (fam o vulg); (de biberón) teat

tétanos m tetanus

tetera f (para el té) teapot

tetilla f nipple; (de biberón) teat

tétrico adj gloomy

textil adj & m textile

text|o m text. ~**ual** adj textual; (traducción) literal; (palabras) exact

textura f texture

tez f complexion

ti pron you

tía f aunt; Ⓣ woman

tiara f tiara

tibio adj lukewarm

tiburón m shark

tiempo m time; (atmosférico) weather; (Mus) tempo; (Gram) tense; (en partido) half. **a su** ~ in due course. **a** ~ in time. **¿cuánto** ~? how long? **hace buen** ~ the weather is fine. **hace** ~ some time ago. **mucho** ~ a long time. **perder el** ~ waste time

tienda f shop (esp Brit), store (esp Amer); (de campaña) tent. ~ **de comestibles**, ~ **de ultramarinos** grocer's (shop) (Brit), grocery store (Amer)

tiene vb véase TENER

tienta. **andar a** ~s feel one's way

tierno adj tender; (joven) young

tierra f land; (planeta, Elec) earth; (suelo) ground; (en geología) soil, earth; (LAm, polvo) dust. **por** ~ overland, by land

tieso adj stiff; (engreído) conceited

tiesto m flowerpot

tifón m typhoon

tifus m typhus; (fiebre tifoidea) typhoid (fever)

tigre m tiger. ~**sa** f tigress

tijera f, **tijeras** fpl scissors; (de jardín) shears

tijeretear vt snip

tila f (infusión) lime tea

tild|ar vt. ~**ar de** (fig) brand as. ~**e** f tilde

tilo m lime(-tree)

timar vt swindle

timbal m kettledrum; (Culin) timbale, meat pie. ~**es** mpl (Mus) timpani

timbr|ar vt stamp. ~**e** m (sello) fiscal stamp; (Mex) postage stamp; (Elec) bell; (sonido) timbre

timidez f shyness

tímido adj shy

timo m swindle

timón m rudder; (rueda) wheel; (fig) helm

tímpano m eardrum

tina f tub. ~**co** m (Mex) water tank. ~**ja** f large earthenware jar

tinglado m mess; (asunto) racket

tinieblas fpl darkness; (fig) confusion

tino f good sense; (tacto) tact

tint|a f ink. **de buena** ~ on good authority. ~**e** m dyeing; (color) dye; (fig) tinge. ~**ero** m ink-well

tintinear vi tinkle; (vasos) chink, clink

tinto adj (vino) red

tintorería f dry cleaner's

tintura f dyeing; (color) dye

tío m uncle; Ⓣ man. ~**s** mpl uncle and aunt

tiovivo m merry-go-round

típico adj typical

tipo m type; (fam, persona) person; (figura de mujer) figure; (figura de hombre) build; (Com) rate

tip|ografía f typography. **∼ográfico** adj typographic(al)

tira f strip. la ∼ de lots of

tirabuzón m corkscrew; (de pelo) ringlet

tirad|a f distance; (serie) series; (de periódico etc) print-run. de una ∼a in one go. ∼o adj (barato) very cheap; (fam, fácil) very easy. ∼or m (asa) handle

tiran|ía f tyranny. **∼izar** 10 vt tyrannize. **∼o** adj tyrannical. ● m tyrant

tirante adj tight; (fig) tense; (relaciones) strained. ● m strap. ∼s mpl braces (esp Brit), suspenders (Amer)

tirar vt throw; (desechar) throw away; (derribar) knock over; drop (bomba); fire (cohete); (imprimir) print. ● vi (disparar) shoot. ∼ a tend to (be); (parecerse a) resemble. ∼ abajo knock down. ∼ de pull. a todo ∼ at the most. ir tirando get by. ∼se vpr throw o.s.; (tumbarse) lie down

tirita f (sticking) plaster

tiritar vi shiver (de with)

tiro m throw; (disparo) shot. ∼ libre free kick. a ∼ within range. errar el ∼ miss. pegarse un ∼ shoot o.s.

tiroides m thyroid (gland)

tirón m tug. de un ∼ in one go

tirote|ar vt shoot at. **∼o** m shooting

tisana f herb tea

tisú m (pl ∼s, ∼es) tissue

títere m puppet. ∼s mpl puppet show

titilar vi (estrella) twinkle

titiritero m puppeteer; (acróbata) acrobat

titube|ante adj faltering; (fig) hesitant. **∼ar** vi falter. **∼o** m hesitation

titula|do adj (libro) entitled; (persona) qualified. **∼r** m headline; (persona) holder. ● vt call. **∼rse** vpr be called; (persona) graduate

título m title; (académico) qualification; (Univ) degree. a ∼ de as, by way of

tiza f chalk

tiz|nar vt dirty. **∼ne** m soot

toall|a f towel. **∼ero** m towel-rail

tobillo m ankle

tobogán m slide; (para la nieve) toboggan

tocadiscos m invar record-player

toca|do adj touched 1. ● m headdress. **∼dor** m dressing-table. **∼nte** adj. en lo ∼nte a with regard to. **∼r** 7 vt touch; (palpar) feel; (Mus) play; ring (timbre); (mencionar) touch on; (barco) stop at. ● vi ring; (corresponder a uno). te ∼ a ti it's your turn. en lo que ∼ a as for. **∼rse** vpr touch; (personas); touch each other

tocayo m namesake

tocino m bacon

tocólogo m obstetrician

todavía adv still; (con negativos) yet. ∼ no not yet

---

todo , **toda**

● adjetivo

····▸ (la totalidad) all. ∼ el vino all the wine. ∼s los edificios all the buildings. ∼ ese dinero all that money. ∼ el mundo

t

everyone. (*como adv*) está toda sucia it's all dirty

····▸ (*entero*) whole. ~ **el día** the whole day, all day. ~ **toda su familia** his whole family. ~ **el tiempo** the whole time, all the time

····▸ (*cada, cualquiera*) every. ~ **tipo de coche** every type of car. ~**s los días** every day

····▸ (*enfático*) a toda velocidad at top speed. es ~ **un caballero** he's a real gentleman

····▸ (*en locuciones*) ante ~ above all. a ~ esto meanwhile. con ~ even so. del ~ totally. ~ lo contrario quite the opposite

➡ Para expresiones como **todo recto, todo seguido** etc., ver bajo el respectivo adjetivo

● *pronombre*

····▸ all; (*todas las cosas*) everything. eso es ~ that's all. lo perdieron ~ they lost everything. quiere comprar ~ he wants to buy everything

····▸ **todos, todas** all; (*todo el mundo*) everyone. los compró ~s he bought them all, he bought all of them. ~s queríamos ir we all wanted to go. vinieron ~s everyone came

● *nombre masculino* **el/un** ~ the/a whole

toldo *m* awning

tolera|ncia *f* tolerance. ~**nte** *adj* tolerant. ~**r** *vt* tolerate

toma *f* taking; (*de universidad etc*) occupation; (*de agua*) dose; (*de agua*) intake; (*Elec*) socket; (*LAm, acequia*) irrigation channel. ● *int* well!, fancy

that! ~ **de corriente** power point. ~**dura** *f*. ~**dura de pelo** hoax. ~**r** *vt* take; catch (autobús, tren); occupy (universidad etc); (*beber*) drink, have; (*comer*) eat, have. ● *vi* take; (*esp LAm, beber*) drink; (*LAm, dirigirse*) go. ~**r a bien** take well. ~**r a mal** take badly. ~**r en serio** take seriously. ~**rla con uno** pick on s.o. ~**r por** take for. ~ **y daca** give and take. ¿qué va a ~**r**? what would you like? ~**rse** *vpr* take; (*beber*) drink, have; (*comer*) eat, have

tomate *m* tomato

tomillo *m* thyme

tomo *m* volume

ton: **sin** ~ **ni son** without rhyme or reason

tonad|a *f* tune; (*canción*) popular song; (*LAm, acento*) accent. ~**illa** *f* tune

tonel *m* barrel. ~**ada** *f* ton. ~**aje** *m* tonnage

tónic|a *f* trend; (*bebida*) tonic water. ~**o** *adj* tonic; (*sílaba*) stressed. ● *m* tonic

tonificar **7** *vt* invigorate

tono *m* tone; (*Mus, modo*) key; (*color*) shade

tont|ería *f* silliness; (*cosa*) silly thing; (*dicho*) silly remark. **dejarse de** ~**erías** stop fooling around. ~**o** *adj* silly. ● *m* fool, idiot; (*payaso*) clown. **hacer el** ~**o** act the fool. **hacerse el** ~**o** act dumb

topacio *m* topaz

topar *vi*. ~ **con** run into

tope *m* maximum. ● *m* end; (*de tren*) buffer; (*Mex, Auto*) speed bump. **hasta los** ~**s** crammed full. **ir a** ~ go flat out

tópico *adj* trite. **de uso** ~ (*Med*) for external use only. ● *m* cliché

topo m mole

topogr|afía f topography. **~áfico** adj topographical

toque m touch; (sonido) sound; (de campana) peal; (de reloj) stroke. **~ de queda** curfew. dar los últimos **~s** put the finishing touches. **~tear** vt fiddle with

toquilla f shawl

tórax m invar thorax

torcer ② & ⑨ vt twist; (doblar) bend; wring out (ropa). ● vi turn. **~se** vpr twist

tordo adj dapple grey. ● m thrush

tore|ar vt fight; (evitar) dodge. ● vi fight (bulls). **~o** m bullfighting. **~ro** m bullfighter

torment|a f storm. **~o** m torture. **~oso** adj stormy

tornado m tornado

tornasolado adj irridescent

torneo m tournament

tornillo m screw

torniquete m (Med) tourniquet; (entrada) turnstile

torno m lathe; (de alfarero) wheel. **en ~ a** around

toro m bull. **~s** mpl bullfighting. **ir a los ~s** go to a bullfight

---

(la fiesta de) los toros
Bullfighting is popular in Spain and some Latin American countries. The season runs from March to October in Spain, from November to March in Latin America. The bullfighters who take part in a **corrida** gather in **cuadrillas**. The principal bullfighter or **matador** is assisted by **peones**.

---

toronja f (LAm) grapefruit

torpe adj clumsy; (estúpido) stupid

torpedo m torpedo

torpeza f clumsiness; (de inteligencia) slowness. **una ~** a blunder

torre f tower; (en ajedrez) castle, rook; (Elec) pylon; (edificio) tower block (Brit), apartment block (Amer)

torren|cial adj torrential. **~te** m torrent; (circulatorio) bloodstream; (fig) flood

tórrido adj torrid

torsión f twisting

torso m torso

torta f tart; (LAm, de verduras) pie; (golpe) slap, punch; (Mex, bocadillo) filled roll. **no entender ni ~** not understand a thing. **pegarse un ~zo** have a bad accident

tortícolis f stiff neck

tortilla f omelette; (Mex, de maíz) tortilla. **~ española** potato omelette. **~ francesa** plain omelette

tórtola f turtle-dove

tortuoso adj winding; (fig) devious

tortura f torture. **~r** vt torture

tos f cough. **~ ferina** whooping cough

tosco adj crude; (persona) coarse

toser vi cough

tost|ada f piece of toast. **~adas** fpl toast; (Mex, de tortilla) fried tortillas. **~ado** adj (pan) toasted; (café) roasted; (persona, color) tanned. **~ar** vt toast (pan); roast (café); tan (piel)

total adj total. ● adv after all. **~ que** so, to cut a long story short. ● m total; (totalidad) whole. **~idad** f whole. **~itario** adj totalitarian. **~izar** ⑩ vt total

tóxico adj toxic

toxi|cómano m drug addict. **~na** f toxin

t

tozudo adj stubborn

traba f catch; (fig, obstáculo) obstacle. poner ~s a hinder

trabaj|ador adj hard-working. ● m worker. ~ar vt work; knead (masa). ● vi work (de as); (actor) act. ¿en qué ~as? what do you do? ~o m work. costar ~o be difficult. ~oso adj hard

trabalenguas m invar tongue-twister

traba|r vt (sujetar) fasten; (unir) join; (entablar) strike up. ~rse vpr get stuck. trabársele la lengua get tongue-tied

trácala m (Mex) cheat. ●f (Mex) trick

tracción f traction

tractor m tractor

tradici|ón f tradition. ~onal adj traditional

traduc|ción f translation. ~ir 🔟 vt translate (a into). ~tor m translator

traer 🔟 vt bring; (llevar) carry; (causar) cause. traérselas be difficult

trafica|nte m & f dealer. ~r 🔟 vi deal

tráfico m traffic; (Com) trade

traga|luz m skylight. ~perras f invar slot-machine. ~r 🔟 vt swallow; (comer mucho) devour; (soportar) put up with. no lo trago I can't stand him. ~rse vpr swallow; (fig) swallow up

tragedia f tragedy

trágico adj tragic. ● m tragedian

trag|o m swallow, gulp; (pequeña porción) sip; (fig, disgusto) blow; (LAm, bebida alcohólica) drink. echar(se) un ~ have a drink. ~ón adj greedy. ●m glutton.

trai|ción f treachery; (Pol) trea-

son. ~cionar vt betray. ~cionero adj treacherous. ~dor adj treacherous. ● m traitor

traigo vb véase **TRAER**

traje m dress; (de hombre) suit. ~ de baño swimming-costume. ~ de etiqueta, ~ de noche evening dress. ●vb véase **TRAER**

traj|ín m coming and going; (ajetreo) hustle and bustle. ~inar vi bustle about

trama f weft; (fig, argumento) plot. ~r vt weave; (fig) plot

tramitar vt negotiate

trámite m step. ~s mpl procedure

tramo m (parte) section; (de escalera) flight

tramp|a f trap; (fig) trick. hacer ~a cheat. ~illa f trapdoor

trampolín m trampoline; (de piscina) springboard; (rígido) diving board

tramposo adj cheating. ● m cheat

tranca f bar. ~r vt bar

trance m moment; (hipnótico etc) trance

tranco m stride

tranquil|idad f peace; (de espíritu) peace of mind. con ~ calmly. ~izar 🔟 vt calm down; (reconfortar) reassure. ~o adj calm; (lugar) quiet; (conciencia) clear. estáte ~o don't worry

transa|cción f transaction; (acuerdo) settlement. ~r vi (LAm) compromise

transatlántico adj transatlantic. ● m (ocean) liner

transbord|ador m ferry. ~ar vt transfer. ~o m transfer. hacer ~o change (en at)

transcri|bir (pp transcrito) vt transcribe. ~pción f transcription

transcur|rir vi pass. ~**so** m course

transeúnte m & f passer-by

transfer|encia f transfer. ~**ir** [4] vt transfer

transforma|ción f transformation. ~**dor** m transformer. ~**r** vt transform

transfusión f transfusion

transgre|dir vt transgress. ~**sión** f transgression

transición f transition

transigir [14] vi give in, compromise

transistor m transistor

transita|ble adj passable. ~**r** vi go

transitivo adj transitive

tránsito m transit; (tráfico) traffic

transitorio adj transitory

transmi|sión f transmission; (radio, TV) broadcast ~**sor** m transmitter. ~**sora** f broadcasting station. ~**tir** vt transmit; (radio, TV) broadcast; (fig) pass on

transparen|cia f transparency. ~**tar** vt show. ~**te** adj transparent

transpira|ción f perspiration. ~**r** vi transpire; (sudar) sweat

transport|ar vt transport. ~**e** m transport. empresa f de ~**es** removals company

transversal adj transverse. una calle ~ a la Gran Vía a street which crosses the Gran Vía

tranvía m tram

trapear vt (LAm) mop

trapecio m trapeze; (Math) trapezium

trapo m cloth. ~**s** mpl rags; (fam, ropa) clothes a todo ~ out of control

tráquea f windpipe, trachea

traquete|ar vt bang, rattle; (persona) rush around. ~**o** m banging, rattle

tras prep after; (detrás) behind

trascende|ncia f significance; (alcance) implication. ~**ntal** adj transcendental; (importante) important. ~**r** [1] vi (saberse) become known; (extenderse) spread

trasero adj back, rear. • m (de persona) bottom

trasfondo m background

traslad|ar vt move; transfer (empleado etc); (aplazar) postpone. ~**o** m transfer; (copia) copy. (mudanza) removal. dar ~**o** notify

trasl|úcido adj translucent. ~**ucirse** [11] vpr be translucent; (dejarse ver) show through; (fig, revelarse) be revealed. ~**uz** m. al ~**uz** against the light

trasmano. a ~ out of the way

trasnochar vt (acostarse tarde) go to bed late; (no acostarse) stay up all night; (no dormir) be unable to sleep

traspas|ar vt go through; (transferir) transfer; go beyond (límite). se ~**a** for sale. ~**o** m transfer

traspié m trip; (fig) slip. dar un ~ stumble; (fig) slip up

trasplant|ar vt transplant. ~**e** m transplant

trasto m piece of junk. • ~**s** mpl junk

trastorn|ado adj mad. ~**ar** vt upset; (volver loco) drive mad; (fig, fam, gustar mucho) delight. ~**arse**

vpr get upset; (*volverse loco*) go mad. **~o** *m* (*incl Med*) upset; (*Pol*) disturbance; (*fig*) confusion

trat|able *adj* friendly; (*Med*) treatable. **~ado** *m* treatise; (*acuerdo*) treaty. **~amiento** *m* treatment; (*título*) title. **~ante** *m & f* dealer. **~ar** *vt* (*incl Med*) treat; deal with (*asunto etc*); (*manejar*) handle; (*de tú, de Vd*) address (de as). ● *vi* deal (with). **~ar con** have to do with; (*Com*) deal in. **~ar de** be about; (*intentar*) try. ¿de qué se **~a?** what's it about? **~o** *m* treatment; (*acuerdo*) agreement; (*título*) title; (*relación*) relationship. ¡**~o** hecho! agreed! **~os** *mpl* dealings

traum|a *m* trauma. **~ático** *adj* traumatic

través: a **~** de through; (*lado a lado*) crossways

travesaño *m* crossbeam; (*de portería*) crossbar

travesía *f* crossing; (*calle*) side-street

trav|esura *f* prank. **~ieso** *adj* (*niño*) mischievous, naughty

trayecto *m* (*tramo*) stretch; (*ruta*) route; (*viaje*) journey. **~ria** *f* trajectory; (*fig*) course

traz|a *f* (*aspecto*) appearance. **~as** *fpl* signs. **~ado** *m* plan. **~ar** 🔟 *vt* draw; (*bosquejar*) sketch. **~o** *m* stroke; (*línea*) line

trébol *m* clover. **~es** *mpl* (*en naipes*) clubs

trece *adj & m* thirteen

trecho *m* stretch; (*distancia*) distance; (*tiempo*) while. a **~s** here and there. de **~** en **~** at intervals

tregua *f* truce; (*fig*) respite

treinta *adj & m* thirty

tremendo *adj* terrible; (*extraordinario*) terrific

tren *m* train. **~ de aterrizaje** landing gear. **~ de vida** lifestyle

tren|cilla *f* braid. **~za** *f* braid; (*de pelo*) plait. **~zar** 🔟 *vt* plait

trepa|dor *adj* climbing. **~dora** *f* climber. **~r** *vt/i* climb. **~rse** *vpr.* **~rse a** climb (*árbol*); climb onto (*silla etc*)

tres *adj & m* three. **~cientos** *adj & m* three hundred. **~illo** *m* three-piece suite; (*Mus*) triplet

treta *f* trick

tri|angular *adj* triangular. **~ángulo** *m* triangle

trib|al *adj* tribal. **~u** *f* tribe

tribuna *f* platform; (*de espectadores*) stand. **~l** *m* court; (*de examen etc*) board; (*fig*) tribunal

tribut|ar *vt* pay. **~o** *m* tribute; (*impuesto*) tax

triciclo *m* tricycle

tricolor *adj* three-coloured

tricotar *vt/i* knit

tridimensional *adj* three-dimensional

trig|al *m* wheat field. **~o** *m* wheat

trigésimo *adj* thirtieth

trigueño *adj* olive-skinned; (*pelo*) dark blonde

trilla|do *adj* (*fig, manoseado*) trite; (*fig, conocido*) well-known. **~r** *vt* thresh

trilogía *f* trilogy

trimestr|al *adj* quarterly. **~e** *m* quarter; (*en enseñanza*) term

trin|ar *vi* warble. estar que trina be furious

trinchar *vt* carve

trinchera *f* ditch; (*Mil*) trench; (*abrigo*) trench coat

trineo *m* sledge

trinidad *f* trinity

trino *m* warble

trío m trio

tripa f intestine; (fig, vientre) tummy, belly. ~s fpl (de máquina etc) parts, workings. **revolver las** ~s turn one's stomach

triple adj triple. ● m. el ~e (de) three times as much (as). ~icado adj. por ~icado in triplicate. ~icar 7 vt treble

tripula|ción f crew. ~nte m & f member of the crew. ~r vt man

tris m. estar en un ~ be on the point of

triste adj sad; (paisaje, tiempo etc) gloomy; (fig, insignificante) miserable. ~za f sadness

triturar vt crush

triunf|al adj triumphal. ~ante adj triumphant. ~ar vi triumph (de, sobre over). ~o m triumph

trivial adj trivial. ~idad f triviality

trizas, hacer algo ~ smash sth to pieces. hacerse ~ smash

trocear vt cut up, chop

trocha f narrow path; (LAm, rail) gauge

trofeo m trophy

tromba f whirlwind; (marina) waterspout. ~ de agua heavy downpour

trombón m trombone

trombosis f invar thrombosis

trompa f horn; (de orquesta) French horn; (de elefante) trunk; (hocico) snout; (en anatomía) tube. coger una ~ 🔢 get drunk. ~zo m bump

trompet|a f trumpet; (músico) trumpet player; (Mil) trumpeter. ~illa f ear-trumpet

trompo m (juguete) (spinning) top

tronar vt (Mex) shoot. ● vi thunder

tronchar vt bring down; (fig) cut short. ~se de risa laugh a lot

tronco m trunk. dormir como un ~ sleep like a log

trono m throne

trop|a f troops. ~el m mob

tropez|ar 1 & 10 vi trip; (fig) slip up. ~ar con run into. ~ón m stumble; (fig) slip

tropical adj tropical

trópico adj tropical. ● m tropic

tropiezo m slip; (desgracia) hitch

trot|ar vi trot. ~e m trot; (fig) toing and froing. al ~e at a trot; (de prisa) in a rush. de mucho ~e hard-wearing

trozo m piece, bit. a ~s in bits

trucha f trout

truco m trick. coger el ~ get the knack

trueno m thunder; (estampido) bang

trueque m exchange; (Com) barter

trufa f truffle

truhán m rogue

truncar 7 vt truncate; (fig) cut short

tu adj your

tú pron you

tuba f tuba

tubérculo m tuber

tuberculosis f tuberculosis

tub|ería f pipes; (oleoducto etc) pipeline. ~o m tube. ~o de ensayo test tube. ~o de escape (Auto) exhaust (pipe). ~ular adj tubular

tuerca f nut

tuerto adj one-eyed, blind in one eye. ● m one-eyed person

tuétano m marrow; (fig) heart. hasta los ~s completely

tufo m stench

tugurio m hovel

tul m tulle

tulipán m tulip

tulli|do adj paralysed. **~r** 🔲 vt cripple

tumba f grave, tomb

tumb|ar vt knock over, knock down (estructura); (fig, fam, en examen) fail. **~arse** vpr lie down. **~o** m jolt. dar un **~o** tumble. **~ona** f sun lounger

tumor m tumour

tumulto m turmoil; (Pol) riot

tuna f prickly pear; (de estudiantes) student band

tunante m & f rogue

túnel m tunnel

túnica f tunic

tupé m toupee; (fig) nerve

tupido adj thick

turba f peat; (muchedumbre) mob

turbado adj upset

turbante m turban

turbar vt upset; (molestar) disturb. **~se** vpr be upset

turbina f turbine

turbi|o adj cloudy; (vista) blurred; (asunto etc) shady. **~ón** m squall

turbulen|cia f turbulence; (disturbio) disturbance. **~te** adj turbulent

turco adj Turkish. ● m Turk; (lengua) Turkish

tur|ismo m tourism; (coche) car. hacer **~** travel around. **~ cultural** cultural heritage tourism. **~ patrimonial** (LAm) heritage tourism. **~ista** m & f tourist. **~ístico** adj tourist

turn|arse vpr take turns (para to). **~o** m turn; (de trabajo) shift. de **~** on duty

turquesa f turquoise

Turquía f Turkey

turrón m nougat

tutear vt address as tú. **~se** vpr be on familiar terms

tutela f (Jurid) guardianship; (fig) protection

tutor m guardian; (en enseñanza) form master

tuve vb véase TENER

tuyo adj & pron yours. un amigo **~** a friend of yours

Uu

u conj or

ubic|ar vt (LAm) place; (localizar) find. **~arse** vpr (LAm) be situated; (orientarse) find one's way around

ubre f udder

Ud. abrev (Usted) you

UE abrev (Unión Europea) EU

uf int phew!; (de repugnancia) ugh!

ufan|arse vpr be proud (con, de of); (jactarse) boast (con, de about). **~o** adj proud

úlcera f ulcer

últimamente adv (recientemente) recently; (finalmente) finally

ultim|ar vt complete; (LAm, matar) kill. **~átum** m ultimatum

último adj last; (más reciente) latest; (más lejano) furthest; (más alto) top; (más bajo) bottom; (definitivo) final. ● m last one. estar en las últimas be on one's last legs; (sin dinero) be down to one's last penny. por **~** finally. vestido a la última dressed in the latest fashion

ultra *adj* ultra, extreme

ultraj|ante *adj* offensive. ~**e** *m* insult, outrage

ultramar *m*. de ~ overseas; (productos) foreign. ~**inos** *mpl* groceries. tienda de ~s grocer's (shop) (*Brit*), grocery store (*Amer*)

ultranza. a ~ (*con decisión*) decisively; (*extremo*) out-and-out

ultravioleta *adj invar* ultraviolet

umbilical *adj* umbilical

umbral *m* threshold

---

un , **una** *artículo indefinido*

! The masculine article **un** is also used before feminine nouns which begin with stressed **a** or **ha**, e.g. **un alma piadosa**, **un hada madrina**

····▸ (*en sing*) a; (*antes de sonido vocálico*) an. **un perro** a dog. **una hora** an hour

····▸ **unos**, **unas** (*cantidad incierta*) some. compré ~os libros I bought some books. (*cantidad cierta*) these ~os ojos preciosos she has beautiful eyes. tiene ~os hijos muy buenos her children are very good. (*en aproximaciones*) about. en ~as 3 horas in about 3 hours

➡ For further information see **uno**

---

un|ánime *adj* unanimous. ~**animidad** *f* unanimity

undécimo *adj* eleventh

ungüento *m* ointment

únic|amente *adv* only. ~**o** *adj* only; (*fig, incomparable*) unique

unicornio *m* unicorn

unid|ad *f* unit; (*cualidad*) unity. ~**ad de disco** disk drive. ~**o** *adj* united

unifica|ción *f* unification. ~**r** 🔢 *vt* unite, unify

uniform|ar *vt* standardize. ~**e** *adj* & *m* uniform. ~**idad** *f* uniformity

unilateral *adj* unilateral

uni|ón *f* union; (*cualidad*) unity; (*Tec*) joint. ~**r** *vt* join; (*líquidos*) join together; (*caminos*) converge; (*compañías*) merge

unísono *m* unison. al ~ in unison

univers|al *adj* universal. ~**idad** *f* university. ~**itario** *adj* university. ~**o** *m* universe

---

uno , **una**
● *adjetivo*

Note that **uno** becomes **un** before masculine nouns

one. **una peseta** one peseta. **un dólar** one dollar. **ni una persona** not one person, not a single person. **treinta y un años** thirty one years

● *pronombre*

····▸ one. **es mío** one (of them) is mine. **es la una** it's one o'clock. **se ayudan el ~ al otro** they help one another, they help each other. **lo que sienten el ~ por el otro** what they feel for each other

····▸ (*fam, alguien*) someone. **le pregunté a ~** I asked someone

····▸ **unos**, **unas** some. **no tenía vasos así es que le presté ~s** she didn't have any glasses so I lent her some. **a ~s les** gusta, a otros no some like it, others don't. los ~s a los otros one another, each other ····➤ (*impersonal*) you. ~ no sabe qué decir you don't know what to say

untar *vt* grease; (*cubrir*) spread; (*fig, fam, sobornar*) bribe

uña *f* nail; (*de animal*) claw; (*casco*) hoof

uranio *m* uranium

Urano *m* Uranus

urban|idad *f* politeness. ~**ismo** *m* town planning. ~**ización** *f* development. ~**izar** 10 *vt* develop. ~**o** *adj* urban

urbe *f* big city

urdir *vt* (*fig*) plot

urg|encia *f* urgency; (*emergencia*) emergency. ~**encias** A & E, (*Amer*) emergency room. ~**ente** *adj* urgent; (*carta*) express. ~**ir** 14 *vi* be urgent.

urinario *m* urinal

urna *f* urn; (*Pol*) ballot box

urraca *f* magpie

URSS *abrev* (*Historia*) USSR

Uruguay *m*. el ~ Uruguay

uruguayo *adj* & *m* Uruguayan

us|ado *adj* (*con estar*) used; (*ropa etc*) worn; (*con ser*) secondhand. ~**ar** *vt* use; (*llevar*) wear. ~**arse** *vpr* (*LAm*) be in fashion. ~**o** *m* use; (*costumbre*) custom. al ~**o** de in the style of

usted *pron* you. ~**es** you

usual *adj* usual

usuario *adj* user

usur|a *f* usury. ~**ero** *m* usurer

usurpar *vt* usurp

utensilio *m* utensil; (*herramienta*) tool

útero *m* womb, uterus

útil *adj* useful. ~**es** *mpl* implements; (*equipo*) equipment

utili|dad *f* usefulness. ~**dades** *fpl* (*LAm*) profits. ~**zación** *f* use, utilization. ~**zar** 10 *vt* use, utilize

utopía *f* Utopia

uva *f* grape. ~ **pasa** raisin. mala ~ bad mood

Vv

vaca *f* cow. carne de ~ beef

vacaciones *fpl* holiday(s), vacation(s) (*Amer*). de ~ on holiday, on vacation (*Amer*)

vacante *adj* vacant. • *f* vacancy

vaciar 20 *vt* empty; (*ahuecar*) hollow out; (*en molde*) cast

vacila|ción *f* hesitation. ~**nte** *adj* unsteady; (*fig*) hesitant. ~**r** *vi* hesitate (11, *bromear*) tease; (*LAm, divertirse*) have fun

vacío *adj* empty; (*frívolo*) frivolous. • *m* empty space; (*estado*) emptiness; (*en física*) vacuum; (*fig*) void

vacuna *f* vaccine. ~**ción** *f* vaccination. ~**r** *vt* vaccinate

vacuno *adj* bovine

vad|ear *vt* ford. ~**o** *m* ford

vaga|bundear *vi* wander. ~**bundo** *adj* vagrant; (*perro*) stray. niño ~ street urchin. • *m* tramp, vagrant. ~**ncia** *f* vagrancy; (*fig*) laziness. ~**r** 12 *vi* wander (about)

vagina *f* vagina

vago *adj* vague; (*holgazán*) lazy. • *m* layabout

vag|ón *m* coach, carriage; (*de mer-*

cancias) wagon. **~ón restaurante** dining-car. **~oneta** f small freight wagon; (*Mex, para pasajeros*) van

vaho m breath; (*vapor*) steam. **~s** mpl inhalation

vain|a f sheath; (*de semillas*) pod. **~illa** f vanilla

vaiv|én m swinging; (*de tren etc*) rocking. **~enes** mpl (*fig, de suerte*) swings

vajilla f dishes, crockery

vale m voucher; (*pagaré*) IOU. **~dero** adj valid

valenciano adj from Valencia

valentía f bravery, courage

valer 42 vt be worth; (*costar*) cost; (*fig, significar*) mean. ● vi be worth; (*costar*) cost; (*servir*) be of use; (*ser valedero*) be valid; (*estar permitido*) be allowed. **~ la pena** be worthwhile, be worth it. **¿cuánto vale?** how much is it? no **~ para nada** be useless. **eso no me vale** (*Mex, fam*) I don't give a damn about that. **¡vale!** all right!, OK! 1

valeroso adj courageous

valgo vb véase **VALER**

valía f worth

validez f validity. **dar ~ a** validate

válido adj valid

valiente adj brave; (*en sentido irónico*) fine. ● m brave person

valija f suitcase. **~ diplomática** diplomatic bag

valioso adj valuable

valla f fence; (*en atletismo*) hurdle

valle m valley

val|or m value, worth; (*coraje*) courage. **objetos** mpl **de ~or** valuables. **sin ~or** worthless. **~ores** mpl securities. **~oración** f valu-

ation. **~orar** vt value

vals m invar waltz

válvula f valve

vampiro m vampire

vanagloriarse vpr boast

vandalismo m vandalism

vándalo m & f vandal

vanguardi|a f vanguard. **de ~** (*en arte, música etc*) avant-garde

van|idad f vanity. **~idoso** adj vain. **~o** adj vain; (*inútil*) futile; (*palabras*) empty. **en ~** in vain

vapor m steam, vapour; (*Naut*) steamer. **al ~** (*Culin*) steamed. **~izador** m vaporizer. **~izar** 10 vaporize

vaquer|o m cowherd, cowboy. **~os** mpl jeans

vara f stick; (*de autoridad*) staff; (*medida*) yard

varar vi run aground

varia|ble adj & f variable. **~ción** f variation. **~do** adj varied. **~nte** f variant; (*Auto*) by-pass. **~ntes** fpl hors d'oeuvres. **~r** 20 vt change; (*dar variedad a*) vary. ● vi vary; (*cambiar*) change

varicela f chickenpox

variedad f variety

varilla f stick; (*de metal*) rod

varios adj several

varita f wand

variz f (*pl* varices, (*LAm*) **várices**) varicose vein

var|ón adj male. ● m man; (*niño*) boy. **~onil** adj manly

vasco adj & m Basque

vaselina f Vaseline (P), petroleum jelly

vasija f vessel, pot

vaso m glass; (*en anatomía*) vessel

vástago m shoot; (*descendiente*) descendant

vasto adj vast

vaticin|ar vt forecast. **~io** m prediction, forecast

vatio m watt

vaya vb véase **IR**

Vd. abrev (**Usted**) you

vecin|al adj local. **~dad** f neighbourhood; (vecinos) residents; (Mex, edificio) tenement house. **~dario** m neighbourhood; (vecinos) residents. **~o** adj neighbouring. ● m neighbour; (de barrio, edificio) resident

ve|da f close season. **~do** m reserve. **~do de caza** game reserve. **~r** vt prohibit

vega f fertile plain

vegeta|ción f vegetation. **~l** adj & m plant, vegetable. **~r** vi grow; (persona) vegetate. **~riano** adj & m vegetarian

vehemente adj vehement

vehículo m vehicle

veinte adj & m twenty

veinti|cinco adj & m twenty-five. **~cuatro** adj & m twenty-four. **~dós** adj & m twenty-two. **~nueve** adj & m twenty-nine; **~ocho** adj & m twenty-eight. **~séis** adj & m twenty-six. **~siete** adj & m twenty-seven. **~trés** adj & m twenty-three. **~uno** adj & m (delante de nombre masculino **veintiún**) twenty-one

vejación f humiliation

vejar vt ill-treat

veje|storio m old crock; (LAm, cosa) old relic. **~z** f old age

vejiga f bladder

vela f (Naut) sail; (de cera) candle; (vigilia) vigil. **pasar la noche en ~** have a sleepless night

velada f evening

vela|do adj veiled; (Foto) exposed.

~r vt watch over; hold a wake over (difunto); (encubrir) veil; (Foto) expose. ● vi stay awake. **~r por** look after. **~rse** vpr (Foto) get exposed

velero m sailing-ship

veleta f weather vane

vell|o m hair; (pelusa) down. **~ón** m fleece

velo m veil

veloc|idad f speed; (Auto, Mec) gear. **a toda ~idad** at full speed. **~ímetro** m speedometer. **~ista** m & f sprinter

velódromo m cycle-track

veloz adj fast, quick

vena f vein; (en madera) grain. **estar de/en ~** be in the mood

venado m deer; (Culin) venison

vencedor adj winning. ● m winner

venc|er 🖲 vt defeat; (superar) overcome. ● vi win; (pasaporte) expire. **~erse** vpr collapse; (LAm, pasaporte) expire. **~ido** adj beaten; (pasaporte) expired; (Com, atrasado) in arrears. **darse por ~ido** give up. **~imiento** m due date; (de pasaporte) expiry date

venda f bandage. **~je** m dressing. **~r** vt bandage

vendaval m gale

vende|dor adj selling. ● m seller; (en tienda) salesperson. **~dor ambulante** pedlar. **~r** vt sell. **se ~** for sale. **~rse** vpr (persona) sell out

vendimia f grape harvest

veneciano adj Venetian

veneno m poison; (malevolencia) venom. **~so** adj poisonous

venera|ble adj venerable. **~ción** f reverence. **~r** vt revere

venéreo adj venereal

venezolano adj & m Venezuelan

Venezuela f Venezuela

venga|nza f revenge. **~r** 12 vt avenge. **~rse** vpr take revenge (de, por for) (en on). **~tivo** adj vindictive

vengo vb véase **VENIR**

venia f (permiso) permission. **~l** adj venial

veni|da f arrival; (vuelta) return. **~dero** adj coming. **~r** 53 vi come. **~r bien** suit. **la semana que viene** next week. **¡venga!** come on!

venta f sale; (posada) inn. **en ~** for sale

ventaj|a f advantage. **~oso** adj advantageous

ventan|a f (inc informática) window; (de la nariz) nostril. **~illa** f window

ventarrón m 🛈 strong wind

ventila|ción f ventilation. **~dor** m fan. **~r** vt air

vent|isca f blizzard. **~olera** f gust of wind. **~osa** f sucker. **~osidad** f wind, flatulence. **~oso** adj windy

ventrílocuo m ventriloquist

ventur|a f happiness; (suerte) luck. **a la ~a** with no fixed plan. **echar la buena ~a** a uno tell s.o.'s fortune. **por ~a** fortunately; (acaso) perhaps. **~oso** adj happy, lucky

Venus m Venus

ver 43 vt see; watch (televisión). ● vi see. **a mi modo de ~** in my view. **a ~** let's see. **dejarse ~** show. **no lo puedo ~** I can't stand him. **no tener nada que ~ con** have nothing to do with. **vamos a ~** let's see. **ya lo veo** that's obvious. **ya ~emos** we'll see. **~se** vpr

see o.s.; (encontrarse) find o.s.; (dos personas) meet; (LAm, parecer) look

veran|eante m & f holidaymaker, vacationer (Amer). **~ear** vi spend one's summer holiday. **~eo** m. **ir de ~eo** spend one's summer holiday. **lugar m de ~eo** summer resort. **~iego** adj summer. **~o** m summer

vera|s. **de ~** really; (verdadero) real. **~z** adj truthful

verbal adj verbal

verbena f (fiesta) fair; (baile) dance

verbo m verb. **~so** adj verbose

verdad f truth. **¿~?** isn't it?, aren't they?, won't it? etc. **a decir ~** to tell the truth. **de ~** really. **~eramente** adv really. **~ero** adj true; (fig) real

verd|e adj green; (fruta) unripe; (chiste) dirty. ● m green; (hierba) grass. **~or** m greenness

verdugo m executioner; (fig) tyrant

verdu|lería f greengrocer's (shop). **~lero** m greengrocer

vereda f path; (LAm, acera) pavement (Brit), sidewalk (Amer)

veredicto m verdict

verg|onzoso adj shameful; (tímido) shy. **~üenza** f shame; (bochorno) embarrassment. **¡es una ~üenza!** it's a disgrace! **me da ~üenza** I'm ashamed. **tener/embarrassed**. **tener ~üenza** be ashamed/embarrassed

verídico adj true

verifica|ción f verification. **~r** 7 vt check. **~rse** vpr take place; (resultar verdad) come true

verja f (cerca) railings; (puerta) iron gate

vermú m, **vermut** m vermouth

verosímil adj likely; (relato) credible

verruga f wart

versa|do adj versed. ~r vi. ~ **sobre** deal with

versátil adj versatile; (fig) fickle

versión f version; (traducción) translation

verso m verse; (poema) poem

vértebra f vertebra

verte|dero m dump; (desagüe) drain. ~r **1** vt pour; (derramar) spill ● vi flow

vertical adj & f vertical

vértice f vertex

vertiente f slope

vertiginoso adj dizzy

vértigo m (Med) vertigo. **dar** ~ make dizzy

vesícula f vesicle. ~ **biliar** gall bladder

vespertino adj evening

vestíbulo m hall; (de hotel, teatro) foyer

vestido m dress

vestigio m trace. ~s mpl remains

vest|imenta f clothes. ~ir **5** vt (llevar) wear; dress (niño etc). ● vi dress. ~ir de wear. ~irse vpr get dressed. ~irse de wear; (disfrazarse) dress up as. ~uario m wardrobe; (en gimnasio etc) changing room (Brit), locker room (Amer)

vetar vt veto

veterano adj veteran

veterinari|a f veterinary science. ~o adj veterinary. ● m vet **1**, veterinary surgeon (Brit), veterinarian (Amer)

veto m veto

vez f time; (turno) turn. **a la** ~ at the same time. **alguna** ~ some-

times; (en preguntas) ever. **algunas veces** sometimes. **a su** ~ in turn. **a veces** sometimes. **cada** ~ each time. **cada** ~ **más** more and more. **de una** ~ in one go. **de una** ~ **para siempre** once and for all. **de** ~ **en cuando** from time to time. **dos veces** twice. **en** ~ **de** instead of. **érase una** ~, **había una** ~ once upon a time there was. **otra** ~ again. **pocas veces**, **rara** ~ seldom. **una** ~ (que) once

vía f road; (Rail) line; (en anatomía) tract; (fig) way. ~ **férrea** railway (Brit), railroad (Amer). ~ **rápida** fast lane. **estar en** ~s de be in the process of. ● prep vía. ~ **aérea** by air. ~ **de comunicación** means of communication.

viab|ilidad f viability. ~le adj viable

viaducto m viaduct

viaj|ante m & f commercial traveller. ~ar vi travel. ~e m journey; (corto) trip. ~e de novios honeymoon. ¡buen ~e! have a good journey!. **estar de** ~ be away. **salir de** ~ go on a trip. ~ero m traveller; (pasajero) passenger

víbora f viper

vibra|ción f vibration. ~nte adj vibrant. ~r vt/i vibrate

vicario m vicar

viceversa adv vice versa

vici|ado adj (texto) corrupt; (aire) stale. ~ar vt corrupt; (estropear) spoil. ~o m vice; (mala costumbre) bad habit. ~oso adj dissolute; (círculo) vicious

víctima f victim; (de un accidente) casualty

victori|a f victory. ~oso adj victorious

vid f vine

vida f life; (*duración*) lifetime. ¡∼ mía! my darling! de por ∼ for life. en mi ∼ never (in my life). estar con ∼ be still alive

vídeo m, (*LAm*) **video** m video; (*cinta*) videotape; (*aparato*) video recorder

videojuego m video game

vidri|era f stained glass window; (*puerta*) glass door; (*LAm, escaparate*) shop window. ∼ería f glass works. ∼ero m glazier. ∼o m glass; (*LAm, en ventana*) window pane. limpiar los ∼os clean the windows. ∼oso adj glassy

vieira f scallop

viejo adj old. ● m old person

viene vb véase VENIR

viento m wind. hacer ∼ be windy

vientre m stomach; (*cavidad*) abdomen; (*matriz*) womb; (*intestino*) bowels; (*de vasija etc*) belly

viernes m invar Friday. V∼ Santo Good Friday

viga f beam; (*de metal*) girder

vigen|cia f validity. ∼te adj valid; (*ley*) in force. entrar en ∼cia come into force

vigésimo adj twentieth

vigía f watch-tower. ● m & f (*persona*) lookout

vigil|ancia f vigilance. ∼ante adj vigilant. ● m & f security guard; (*nocturno*) watchman. ∼ar vt keep an eye on. ● vi be vigilant; (*vigía*) keep watch. ∼ia f vigil; (*Relig*) fasting

vigor m vigour; (*vigencia*) force. entrar en ∼ come into force. ∼oso adj vigorous

vil adj vile. ∼eza f vileness; (*acción*) vile deed

villa f (*casa*) villa; (*Historia*) town. la V∼ Madrid

villancico m (Christmas) carol

villano adj villanous; (*Historia*) peasant

vilo, en ∼ in the air

vinagre m vinegar. ∼ra f vinegar bottle. ∼ras fpl cruet. ∼ta f vinaigrette

vincular vt bind

vínculo m tie, bond

vindicar ⑦ vt (*rehabilitar*) vindicate

vine vb véase VENIR

vinicult|or m wine-grower. ∼ura f wine growing

vino m wine. ∼ de la casa house wine. ∼ de mesa table wine. ∼ tinto red wine

viñ|a f vineyard. ∼atero m (*LAm*) wine-grower. ∼edo m vineyard

viola f viola

viola|ción f violation; (*de una mujer*) rape. ∼r vt violate; break (*ley*); rape (*mujer*)

violen|cia f violence; (*fuerza*) force. ∼tarse vpr get embarrassed. ∼to adj violent; (*fig*) awkward

violeta adj invar & f violet

violín m violin. ● m & f (*músico*) violinist. ∼ista m & f violinist. ∼ón m double bass. ∼onc(h)elista m & f cellist. ∼onc(h)elo m cello

viraje m turn. ∼r vt turn. ● vi turn; (*fig*) change direction. ∼r bruscamente swerve

virg|en adj. ser ∼en be a virgin. ● f virgin. ∼inal adj virginal. ∼inidad f virginity

Virgo m Virgo

viril adj virile. ∼idad f virility

virtu|al adj virtual. ∼d f virtue; (*capacidad*) power. en ∼ de by virtue of. ∼oso adj virtuous. ● m

virtuoso
viruela f smallpox
virulento adj virulent
virus m invar virus
visa f (LAm) visa. ~**ado** m visa. ~**r** vt endorse
vísceras fpl entrails
viscoso adj viscous
visera f visor; (de gorra) peak
visib|ilidad f visibility. ~**le** adj visible
visillo m (cortina) net curtain
visi|ón f vision; (vista) sight. ~**onario** adj & m visionary
visita f visit; (visitante) visitor; (invitado) guest; (Internet) hit. ~**nte** m & f visitor. ~**r** vt visit
vislumbrar vt glimpse
viso m sheen; (aspecto) appearance
visón m mink
visor m viewfinder
víspera f day before, eve
vista f sight, vision; (aspecto, mirada) look; (panorama) view. apartar la ~ look away. a primera ~, a simple ~ at first sight. con ~s a with a view to. en ~ de in view of. estar a la ~ be obvious. hacer la ~ gorda turn a blind eye. perder la ~ lose one's sight. tener a la ~ have in front of one. volver la ~ atrás look back. ~**zo** m glance. dar/echar un ~**zo** a glance at
visto adj seen; (poco original) common (considerado) considered. ~ que since. bien ~ acceptable. está ~ que it's obvious that. mal ~ unacceptable. por lo ~ apparently. • vb véase **VESTIR**. ~ **bueno** m approval. ~**so** adj colourful, bright
visual adj visual. campo ~ field of

vision
vital adj vital. ~**icio** adj life; (cargo) held for life. ~**idad** f vitality
vitamina f vitamin
viticult|or m wine-grower. ~**ura** f wine growing
vitorear vt cheer
vítreo adj vitreous
vitrina f showcase; (en casa) glass cabinet; (LAm, escaparate) shop window
viud|a f widow. ~**ez** f widowhood. ~**o** adj widowed. • m widower
viva m cheer. ~**cidad** f liveliness. ~**mente** adv vividly. ~**z** adj lively
víveres mpl supplies
vivero m nursery; (de peces) hatchery; (de moluscos) bed
viveza f vividness; (de inteligencia) sharpness; (de carácter) liveliness
vívido adj vivid
vividor m pleasure seeker
vivienda f housing; (casa) house; (piso) flat (Brit), apartment (esp Amer). sin ~ homeless
viviente adj living
vivificar 🔽 vt (animar) enliven
vivir vt live through. • vi live; (estar vivo) be alive. ¡viva! hurray! ¡viva el rey! long live the king! • m life. ~ de live on. de mal ~ dissolute
vivisección f vivisection
vivo adj alive; (viviente) living; (color) bright; (listo) clever; (fig) lively. • m sharp operator
vocab|lo m word. ~**ulario** m vocabulary
vocación f vocation
vocal adj vocal. • f vowel. • m & f member. ~**ista** m & f vocalist
voce|ar vt call (mercancías); (fig)

proclaim; (*Mex*) page (persona). ●
vi shout. ~**río** *m* shouting. ~**ro**
(*LAm*) spokeperson

vociferar *vi* shout

vola|dor *adj* flying. ● *m* rocket.
~**ndas.** en ~**ndas** in the air.
~**nte** *adj* flying. ● *m* (*Auto*)
steering-wheel; (*nota*) note; (*rehi-
lete*) shuttlecock. ~**r 2** *vt* blow up.
● *vi* fly; (*fam, desaparecer*) disappear

volátil *adj* volatile

volcán *m* volcano. ~**ico** *adj* vol-
canic

volcar 2 & 7 *vt* knock over; (*vaciar*) empty out; turn over (*molde*).
● *vi* overturn. ~**se** *vpr* fall over; (*vehículo*) overturn; (*fig*) do one's utmost. ~**se** en throw o.s. into

vóleibol *m*, (*Mex*) **volibol** *m* vol-
leyball

voltaje *m* voltage

volte|ar *vt* turn over; (*en el aire*)
toss; ring (*campanas*); (*LAm*) turn
over (*colchón* etc). ~**arse** *vpr* (*LAm*)
turn around; (*carro*) overturn.
~**reta** *f* somersault

voltio *m* volt

voluble *adj* (*fig*) fickle

volum|en *m* volume. ~**inoso** *adj*
voluminous

voluntad *f* will; (*fuerza de voluntad*) willpower; (*deseo*) wish; (*intención*) intention. **buena** ~ goodwill.
mala ~ ill will

voluntario *adj* voluntary. ● *m*
volunteer

voluptuoso *adj* voluptuous

volver 2 (*pp* **vuelto**) *vt* turn; (*de
arriba a abajo*) turn over; (*devolver*)
restore. ● *vi* return; (*fig*) revert. ~ **a
hacer algo** do sth again. ~ **en
sí** come round. ~**se** *vpr* turn

round; (*hacerse*) become

vomit|ar *vt* bring up. ● *vi* be sick,
vomit. ~**ivo** *adj* disgusting

vómito *m* vomit; (*acción*) vomit-
ing

voraz *adj* voracious

vos *pron* (*LAm*) you. ~**otros** *pron*
you; (*reflexivo*) yourselves

vot|ación *f* voting; (*voto*) vote.
~**ante** *m & f* voter. ~**ar** *vt* vote for.
● *vi* vote (**por** for). ~**o** *m* vote;
(*Relig*) vow

voy *vb véase* **IR**

voz *f* voice; (*rumor*) rumour; (*palabra*) word. ~ **pública** public opinion. **a media** ~ softly. **a una** ~
unanimously. **dar voces** shout. **en**
~ **alta** loudly

vuelco *m* upset. **el corazón me
dio un** ~ my heart missed a beat

vuelo *m* flight; (*acción*) flying; (*de
ropa*) flare. **al** ~ in flight; (*fig*) in
passing

vuelta *f* turn; (*curva*) bend;
(*paseo*) walk; (*revolución*) revolution; (*regreso*) return; (*dinero*)
change. **a la** ~ on one's return. **a
la** ~ **de la esquina** round the corner. **dar la** ~ **al mundo** go round
the world. **dar una** ~ go for a
walk. **estar de** ~ be back

vuelvo *vb véase* **VOLVER**

vuestro *adj* your. ● *pron* yours. **un
amigo** ~ a friend of yours

vulg|ar *adj* vulgar; (*persona*) com-
mon. ~**aridad** *f* vulgarity. ~**ari-
zar 10** *vt* popularize. ~**o** *m* common people

vulnerable *adj* vulnerable

Ww

wáter /'(g)water/ m toilet
Web m /'(g)web/. **el ~** the Web
whisky /'(g)wiski/ m whisky

Xx

xenofobia f xenophobia
xilófono m xylophone

Yy

y conj and
ya adv already; (ahora) now; (con negativos) any more; (para afirmar) yes, sure; (en seguida) immediately; (pronto) soon. ● **~ mismo** (LAm) right away. ● int of course! **~ no** no longer. **~ que** since. **¡~!, ~!** oh sure!
yacaré m (LAm) alligator
yac|er 44 vi lie. **~imiento** m deposit; (de petróleo) oilfield
yanqui m & f American, Yank(ee)
yate m yacht
yegua f mare
yelmo m helmet
yema f (en botánica) bud; (de huevo) yolk; (golosina) sweet. **~ del dedo** fingertip

yerba f (LAm) grass; (Med) herb
yergo vb véase **ERGUIR**
yermo adj uninhabited; (no cultivable) barren. ● m wasteland
yerno m son-in-law
yerro m mistake. ● vb véase **ERRAR**
yeso m plaster; (mineral) gypsum
yo pron I. **~ mismo** myself. **¿quién, ~?** who, me? **soy ~** it's me
yodo m iodine
yoga m yoga
yogur m yog(h)urt
yuca f yucca
yugo m yoke
Yugoslavia f Yugoslavia
yugoslavo adj & m Yugoslav
yunque m anvil
yunta f yoke

Zz

zafarrancho m (confusión) mess; (riña) quarrel
zafarse vpr escape; get out of (obligación etc); (Mex, dislocarse) dislocate
zafiro m sapphire
zaga f rear; (en deportes) defence. **a la ~** behind
zaguán m hall
zaherir 4 vt hurt
zahorí m dowser
zaino adj (caballo) chestnut; (vaca) black
zalamer|ía f flattery. **~o** adj flattering. ● m flatterer
zamarra f (piel) sheepskin; (prenda) sheepskin jacket

zamarrear vt shake

zamba f South American dance

zambulli|da f dive; (baño) dip. ~**rse** vpr dive

zamparse vpr gobble up

zanahoria f carrot

zancad|a f stride. ~**illa** f trip. hacer una ~**illa** a uno trip s.o. up

zanc|o m stilt. ~**udo** adj long-legged; (ave) wading. ● m (LAm) mosquito

zanganear vi idle

zángano m drone. ●m & f (persona) idler

zangolotear vt shake. ● vi rattle; (persona) fidget

zanja f ditch; (para tuberías etc) trench. ~**r** vt (fig) settle

zapat|a f tap with one's feet. ~**ería** f shoe shop; (arte) shoe-making. ~**ero** m shoemaker; (el que remienda zapatos) cobbler. ~**illa** f slipper; (de deportes) trainer. ~**illa de ballet** ballet shoe. ~**o** m shoe

zarand|a f sieve. ~**ear** vt (sacudir) shake

zarcillo m earring

zarpa f paw

zarpar vi set sail, weigh anchor

zarza f bramble. ~**mora** f blackberry

zarzuela f Spanish operetta

zarzuela A musical drama consisting of alternating passages of dialogue, songs, choruses, and dancing that originated in Spain in the seventeenth century. Also popular in Latin America, its name derives from the Palacio de la Zarzuela, the Madrid palace where the Royal family now lives.

zigzag m zigzag. ~**uear** vi zigzag

zinc m zinc

zócalo m skirting-board; (pedestal) plinth; (Mex, plaza) main square

zodiaco m, **zodíaco** m zodiac

zona f zone; (área) area

zoo m zoo. ~**logía** f zoology. ~**lógico** adj zoological

zoólogo m zoologist

zopenco adj stupid. ● m idiot

zoquete m blockhead

zorr|a f vixen. ~**illo** m (LAm) skunk.. ~**o** m fox

zorzal m thrush

zozobra f (fig) anxiety. ~**r** vi founder

zueco m clog

zumb|ar m 🗓 give (golpe etc). ● vi buzz. ~**ido** m buzzing

zumo m juice

zurci|do m darning. ~**r** 🗓 vt darn

zurdo adj left-handed; (mano) left

zurrar vt (fig, fam, dar golpes) beat (up)

zutano m so-and-so

Phrasefinder/Frases útiles

Useful phrases — Expresiones útiles

yes, please/no, thank you	sí, por favor/no, gracias
sorry	perdone
excuse me	disculpe
I'm sorry, I don't understand	perdone, pero no le entiendo
you're welcome!	¡de nada!, ¡no hay de qué!

Meeting people — Saludos

hello/goodbye	hola/adiós
how are you?	¿cómo está usted?
nice to meet you	mucho gusto

Asking questions	**Preguntas**
do you speak English/Spanish?	¿habla usted inglés/español?
what's your name?	¿cómo se llama?
where are you from?	¿de dónde es?
how much is it?	¿cuánto es?
where is...?	¿dónde está...?
can I have...?	¿me da...?
would you like...?	¿quiere usted...?

About you	**Información personal**
my name is...	me llamo...
I'm American/I'm Mexican	soy americano/-a/mexicano/-a
I don't speak Spanish/English	no hablo español/inglés
I live near Seville/Chester	vivo cerca de Sevilla/Chester
I'm a student	soy estudiante
I work in an office	trabajo en una oficina

Emergencies	**Emergencias**
can you help me, please?	¿me ayuda, por favor?
I'm lost	me he perdido
I'm ill	no me encuentro bien
call an ambulance	llamen a una ambulancia

Reading signs	**Carteles y señales**
no entry	prohibido el paso
no smoking	prohibido fumar
fire exit	salida de emergencia
for sale	en venta
push	empujar
pull	tirar, (*LAm*) jalar
press	apretar, pulsar

2

Going Places/Viajes

By rail and underground / En tren y en metro

where can I buy a ticket?	¿dónde se sacan los billetes, (*LAm*) boletos?
what time is the next train to Barcelona/New York?	¿a qué hora sale el próximo tren para Barcelona/Nueva York?
do I have to change?	¿tengo que hacer algún transbordo?
can I take my bike on the train?	¿puedo llevar la bicicleta en el tren?
which platform for the train to San Sebastian/Bath?	¿de qué andén sale el tren para San Sebastián/Bath?
a single/return, (*Amer*) round trip to Baltimore/Valencia, please	un billete, (*LAm*) boleto de ida/ida y vuelta para Baltimore/Valencia, por favor
I'd like an all-day ticket	quiero un billete, (*LAm*) boleto que valga para todo el día
I'd like to reserve a seat	quisiera reservar una plaza
is there a student/senior citizen discount?	¿hacen descuentos para estudiantes/jubilados?
is this the train for Seville/Manchester?	¿éste es el tren para Sevilla/Manchester?
what time does the train arrive in Madrid/Washington?	¿a qué hora llega el tren a Madrid/Washington?
have I missed the train?	¿he perdido el tren?
which line do I need to take for the Prado/London Eye?	¿qué línea se coge, (*LAm*) toma para ir al Prado/London Eye?

YOU WILL HEAR:	OIRÁS:
el tren va a llegar al andén número 2	the train is arriving at platform 2
hay un tren que sale para Madrid a las 10	there's a train to Madrid at 10 o'clock
el tren llegará con retraso/puntual	the train is delayed/on time
la próxima parada es..., (LAm) el próximo paradero es...	the next stop is...
su billete, (LAm) boleto no es válido	your ticket isn't valid

MORE USEFUL WORDS:	MÁS PALABRAS ÚTILES:
underground station, (Amer) subway station	estación de metro
timetable	horario
connection	transbordo
seat reservation	reserva de plaza/asiento
express train	tren expreso
local train	tren de cercanías
high-speed train	tren de alta velocidad

DID YOU KNOW...?	¿SABÍAS QUE...?
In some of the larger Spanish train stations, you will need to take a ticket and wait for your number to be called before you can speak to a clerk.	En Inglaterra se puede ir del aeropuerto de Heathrow al centro de Londres en menos de veinte minutos gracias a un tren que se llama Heathrow Express.

At the airport	En el aeropuerto
when's the next flight to Paris/Rome?	¿cuándo sale el próximo vuelo para París/Roma?
what time do I have to check in?	¿a qué hora tengo que facturar, (*LAm*) chequear, (*Mex*) registrar el equipaje?
where do I check in?	¿dónde puedo facturar, (*LAm*) chequear, (*Mex*) registrar el equipaje?
I'd like to confirm my flight	quisiera confirmar mi vuelo
I'd like a window seat/an aisle seat	quisiera un asiento de ventanilla/pasillo
I want to change/cancel my reservation	quiero cambiar/cancelar mi reserva
can I carry this in my hand, (*Amer*) carry-on luggage?	¿puedo llevar ésto como equipaje de mano?
my luggage hasn't arrived	mi equipaje no ha llegado

YOU WILL HEAR:	OIRÁS:
el vuelo BA7057 saldrá con retraso/ha sido cancelado	flight BA7057 is delayed/cancelled
vaya a la puerta (de embarque), (*Mex*) sala de abordar 29	please go to gate 29
su tarjeta de embarque, (*Mex*) pase de abordar, por favor	your boarding card, please

MORE USEFUL WORDS:	MÁS PALABRAS ÚTILES:
arrivals	llegadas
departures	salidas
baggage claim	recogida de equipajes

Asking how to get there · Cómo llegar a los sitios

how do I get to the airport?	¿cómo se llega al aeropuerto?
how long will it take to get there?	¿cuánto tiempo se tarda en llegar?
how far is it from here?	¿a qué distancia está?
which bus do I take for the cathedral?	¿qué autobús debo coger, (*LAm*) tomar, para ir a la catedral?
where does this bus go?	¿a dónde va este autobús?
does this bus/train go to...?	¿éste autobús/tren va a ...?
where should I get off?	¿dónde me tengo que bajar?
how much is it to the town centre?	¿cuánto cuesta ir al centro de la ciudad?
what time is the last bus?	¿a qué hora sale el último autobús?
where's the nearest underground station, (*Amer*) subway station?	¿dónde está la estación de metro más cercana?
is this the turning for...?	¿es ésta la calle para...?
can you call me a taxi?	¿me puede pedir un taxi?

YOU WILL HEAR:	OIRÁS:
tome la primera (calle) a la derecha	take the first turning, (*Amer*) turn on the right
al llegar al semáforo/después de pasar la iglesia, gire a la izquierda	turn left at the traffic lights/ just past the church

Disabled travellers · Viajeros discapacitados

I'm disabled	soy minusválido
is there wheelchair access?	¿hay un acceso para sillas de ruedas?
are guide dogs permitted?	¿se permite la entrada de perros lazarillo?

On the road | Por carretera

where's the nearest petrol station, (Amer) gas station?	¿dónde está la gasolinera más cercana?
what's the best way to get there?	¿cuál es la mejor forma de llegar?
I've got a puncture, (Amer) flat tire	he tenido un pinchazo, (Mex) se nos ponchó una llanta
I'd like to hire, (Amer) rent a bike/car	quisiera alquilar, (Mex) rentar una bicicleta/un coche
where can I park around here?	¿dónde puedo aparcar por aquí?
there's been an accident	ha habido un accidente
my car's broken down	se me ha estropeado el coche, (LAm) se me descompuso el carro
the car won't start	el coche, (LAm) carro no arranca
where's the nearest garage?	¿dónde está el taller más cercano?
pump number six, please	surtidor, (Andes, Ven) bomba número seis, por favor
fill it up, please	llénelo, por favor
can I wash my car here?	¿tienen túnel de lavado?
can I park here?	¿aquí se puede aparcar, (LAm) estacionar, (Col) parquear?
there's a problem with the brakes/lights	les pasa algo a los frenos/los faros
the clutch/gearstick isn't working	no funciona el embrague/cambio de marchas, (LAm) la palanca de cambios, (Mex) de velocidades
take the third exit off the roundabout, (Amer) traffic circle	en la rotonda, vaya por la tercera salida
turn right at the next junction	gire a la derecha en el próximo cruce
slow down	vaya más despacio
I can't drink – I'm driving	tengo que conducir, (LAm) manejar así que no puedo beber, (LAm) tomar
can I buy a road map here?	¿venden mapas de carreteras?

YOU WILL HEAR: OIRÁS:

enséñeme su carnet de conducir, (LAm) licencia, (Col) pase, (Chi) carné, (Ur) libreta de manejar, (Per) su brevete, (Arg) registro	can I see your driving licence?
tiene que rellenar un parte de accidente	you need to fill out an accident report
esta carretera es de un solo sentido	this road is one-way
está prohibido aparcar, (LAm) estacionar aquí	you can't park here

MORE USEFUL WORDS: MÁS PALABRAS ÚTILES:

diesel	diésel
unleaded	sin plomo
motorway, (Amer) expressway	autopista
toll	peaje, (Mex) cuota
satnav, (Amer) GPS	navegación vía satélite
speed camera	radar de tráfico, (Chi) fotorradar
roundabout	rotonda, glorieta
crossroads	cruce
dual carriageway, (Amer) divided highway	vía de doble sentido
exit	salida
traffic lights	semáforo
driver	conductor, -ora, chofer (or esp Spain) chófer

DID YOU KNOW...?   ¿SABÍAS QUE...?

The speed limits on Spanish roads are as follows: motorway 120 km/h (74 mph), open roads 90-100 km/h (56-62 mph) , towns and villages 50 km/h (31 mph).	Para entrar en coche hasta el centro de Londres hay que pagar una tasa de circulación especial; hay un sistema electrónico para detectar a los infractores.

COMMON SPANISH ROAD SIGNS

Aparcamiento, (*LAm*) estacionamiento, (*Col*) parqueadero	Parking
Atención: Paso a nivel de tren	Beware: level crossing
Autopista	Motorway, (*Amer*) Expressway
Autovía	Dual carriageway, (*Amer*) Divided highway
Cambio de sentido, (*Mex*) retorno	Change of direction
Casco urbano	Urban area
Ceda el Paso	Give Way, (*Amer*) Yield
(*LAm*) Cuidado: Cruce de ferrocarril/vía férrea	Beware: level crossing
Desvío	Detour
Dirección Única, (*LAm*) calle de sentido único	One-way street
Obras	Roadworks, (*Amer*) Men working
Peligro	Danger
Vado permanente	No parking (at any time)
Zona de residentes	Parking only for people with resident cards
Zona peatonal	Pedestrian area

SEÑALES DE TRÁFICO CORRIENTES EN PAÍSES DE HABLA INGLESA

Cattle	Ganado
Contraflow	Carril en sentido contrario
Ford	Vado, (*LAm*) Acceso
Get in lane	Incorpórese al carril
Give way	Ceda el Paso
Keep clear	No estacionar
No overtaking, (*Amer*) Do not pass	Prohibido adelantar, (*Mex*) rebasar
Pedestrians crossing	Peatones cruzando
Red route – no stopping	Prohibido parar
Reduce speed now	Reduzca su velocidad
Stop	Stop, (*LAm*) pare

Keeping in touch/Comunicación

On the phone Por teléfono

where can I buy a phone card?	¿dónde puedo comprar una tarjeta telefónica?
may I use your phone?	¿podría usar su teléfono?
do you have a mobile, (*Amer*) cell phone?	¿tiene usted un móvil, (*LAm*) un celular?
what is your phone number?	¿cuál es su número (de teléfono)?
what is the area code for Santiago/Cardiff?	¿cuál es el prefijo, (*LAm*) código de Santiago/Cardiff?
I want to make a phone call	quiero hacer una llamada
I'd like to reverse the charges, (*Amer*) call collect	quisiera hacer una llamada a cobro revertido, (*LAm*) una llamada por cobrar
the line's engaged/busy	está comunicando, (*LAm*) está ocupado
there's no answer	no contestan
hello, this is Natalia	hola, soy, (*esp LAm*) habla Natalia
is Juan there, please?	¿está Juan, por favor?
who's calling?	¿de parte de quién?
sorry, wrong number	perdone, se ha confundido
just a moment, please	un momentito, por favor
would you like to hold?	¿le importa esperar?
it's a business/personal call	es una llamada personal/de negocios
I'll put you through to him/her	le pongo (*or* le paso, comunico) con él/ella
s/he cannot come to the phone at the moment	en este momento está ocupado/-a
please tell him/her I called	dígale que he llamado, (*LAm*) que llamé, por favor
I'd like to leave a message for him/her	quisiera dejarle un mensaje

I'll try again later	volveré a llamar más tarde
please tell him/her that María called	dígale que ha llamado, (*LAm*) que llamó María, por favor
can he/she call me back?	¿le puede decir que me llame?
my home number is...	mi número de casa es...
my business number is...	mi número del trabajo es...
my fax number is...	mi número de fax es...
we were cut off	se ha cortado, (*LAm*) se cortó
I'll call you later	te llamaré más tarde
I need to top up my phone	tengo que recargar el saldo
the battery's run out	me he quedado sin batería
I'm running low on credit	se me está gastando el saldo
send me a text	mándame un mensaje
there's no signal here	aquí no hay cobertura
you're breaking up	te oigo fatal, (*LAm*) te escucho muy mal
could you speak a little louder?	¿podría hablar un poco más alto?

YOU WILL HEAR:	OIRÁS:
sí, diga, dígame, (*LAm*) aló, (*Mex*) bueno	hello
llámame al móvil, (*LAm*) al celular	call me on my mobile, (*Amer*) cell phone
¿quiere dejar un mensaje/recado?	would you like to leave a message?

MORE USEFUL WORDS:	MÁS PALABRAS ÚTILES:
text message	mensaje (de texto)/SMS
top-up card	tarjeta de saldo, (*LAm*) de prepago
phone box, (*Amer*) phone booth	cabina de teléfono
dial	marcar, (*LAm*) discar
directory enquiries	información de direcciones/guía

Writing Por carta

what's your address?	¿cuál es su dirección?
where is the nearest post office?	¿dónde está la oficina de correos más cercana?, (LAm) ¿dónde está el correo más cercano?
could I have a stamp for Argentina/Italy, please?	¿me da un sello, (LAm) una estampilla, (Mex) un timbre para Argentina/Italia, por favor?
I'd like to send a parcel	quisiera mandar un paquete
where is the nearest postbox, (Amer) mailbox?	¿dónde está el buzón más cercano?
dear Isabel/Fred	querida/querido Isabel/Fred
dear Sir or Madam	muy señor mío
yours sincerely	atentamente
yours faithfully	le envía un cordial saludo
best wishes	un abrazo

YOU WILL HEAR:	OIRÁS:
¿Quiere mandarlo por envío urgente?	Would you like to send it first class?
¿Contiene objetos de valor?	Is it valuable?

MORE USEFUL WORDS:	MÁS PALABRAS ÚTILES:
letter	carta
postcode, (Amer) ZIP code	código postal
airmail	correo aéreo
postcard	postal
fragile	frágil
urgent	urgente
registered post, (Amer) mail	correo certificado

On line   En línea

are you on the Internet?	¿está conectado/-a a Internet?
what's your e-mail address?	¿cuál es su dirección de correo electrónico?
I'll e-mail it to you on Tuesday	se lo mandaré por correo electrónico el martes
I looked it up on the Internet	lo he buscado, (*LAm*) lo busqué en Internet
the information is on their website	la información está en su sitio web
my e-mail address is jane dot smith at new99 dot com	mi correo electrónico es jane punto smith arroba new99 punto com
can I check my e-mail here?	¿puedo mirar el correo (electrónico)?
I have broadband/dial-up	tengo banda ancha/ conexión por módem
do you have wireless internet access?	¿tienen wi-fi?
I'll send you the file as an attachment	le mandaré el archivo como (archivo) adjunto, (*LAm also*) anexo

YOU WILL SEE:	VERÁS:
buscar	search
hacer doble clic en el icono	double-click on the icon
abrir la aplicación	open (up) the application
descargar archivo	download file

MORE USEFUL WORDS:	MÁS PALABRAS ÚTILES:
subject (of an email)	asunto (de un email)
password	contraseña
social networking site	red de contacto en línea
search engine	buscador
mouse	ratón, (*LAm also*) mouse
keyboard	teclado

13

Meeting up   Citas, encuentros

what shall we do this evening?	¿qué hacemos esta tarde?
do you want to go out tonight?	¿quieres que salgamos esta noche?
where shall we meet?	¿dónde quedamos, (*LAm*) nos encontramos?
I'll see you outside the café at 6 o'clock	nos vemos a las 6 a la puerta de la cafetería
see you later	hasta luego
I can't today, I'm busy	hoy no puedo, estoy ocupado/-a
I'm sorry, I've got something planned	lo siento, tengo otros planes
let's meet for a coffee in town	¿nos tomamos un café por ahí?
would you like to see a show/film (*Amer*) movie?	¿quieres que vayamos al teatro/cine?
what about next week instead?	¿qué tal si lo dejamos para la semana que viene?
shall we go for something to eat?	¿vamos a tomar, (*LAm*) comer algo?

YOU WILL HEAR:	OIRÁS:
encantado/-a	nice to meet you
¿te invito a una copa?	can I buy you a drink?

MORE USEFUL WORDS:	MÁS PALABRAS ÚTILES:
bar	bar
bar (*serving counter in a bar/pub*)	barra
meal	comida
snack	algo para picar
date	cita
cigarette	pitillo

Food and Drink/Comer y beber

Booking a restaurant	Reservar mesa en un restaurante
can you recommend a good restaurant?	¿me puede recomendar un buen restaurante?
I'd like to reserve a table for four	quisiera reservar una mesa para cuatro
a reservation for tomorrow evening at eight o'clock	una reserva para mañana a las ocho de la tarde

Ordering	Pedir la comida
could we see the menu/wine list, please?	¿nos enseña el menú/la carta de vinos, por favor?
do you have a vegetarian/children's menu?	¿tienen un menú especial para vegetarianos/niños?
as a starter... and to follow...	de primero.. y de segundo...
could we have some more bread?	¿nos puede traer más pan?
what would you recommend?	¿qué recomienda?
I'd like a white coffee	quisiera un café con leche
...black coffee	...café solo, (LAm) café negro
...a decaffeinated coffee	...un café descafeinado
could I have the bill, (Amer) check?	¿me trae la cuenta, por favor?

YOU WILL HEAR	OIRÁS
¿Ya han decidido lo que van a pedir?	Are you ready to order?
¿Quieren entrada/un aperitivo?	Would you like a starter/aperitif?
¿Qué van a pedir de segundo plato?	What will you have as main course?
¿Quieren postre/café?	Would you like a dessert/coffee?
¿Algo más?	Anything else?
¡Buen provecho!	Enjoy your meal!
El servicio (no) está incluido.	Service is (not) included.

15

The menu La carta/El menú

starters	de primero	de primero	starters
hors d'oeuvres	entremeses, (Mex) botanas	entremeses, botanas (Mex)	hors d'oeuvres
omelette	omelette, tortilla	omelette, tortilla	omelette
soup	sopa	sopa	soup

fish	pescado	pescado	fish
bass	lubina	anguila	eel
cod	bacalao	arenque	herring
eel	anguila	atún	tuna
hake	merluza	bacalao	cod
herring	arenque	calamares	squid
monkfish	rape	camarones (LAm)	prawns, shrimps
mullet	mújol, (LAm) lisa	gambas	prawns, shrimps
mussels	mejillones	lenguado	sole
oyster	ostra, (Mex) ostión	lisa (LAm)	mullet
		lubina	bass
prawns	gambas	mejillones	mussels
salmon	salmón	merluza	hake
sardines	sardinas	mújol	mullet
shrimps	gambas	ostra, (Mex) ostión	oyster
sole	lenguado		
squid	calamares	rape	monkfish
trout	trucha	róbalo	bass
tuna	atún	rodaballo	turbot
turbot	rodaballo	trucha	trout

meat	carne	carne	meat
beef	carne de vaca	bistec, filete	steak
chicken	pollo	carne de vaca, de res (Mex)	beef
duck	pato		

16

goose	ganso		cerdo	pork
hare	liebre		codorniz	quail
ham	jamón		conejo	rabbit
kidneys	riñones		cordero	lamb
lamb	cordero		ganso	goose
liver	hígado		hígado	liver
pork	cerdo		jamón	ham
quail	codorniz		liebre	hare
rabbit	conejo		pato	duck
steak	bistec, filete		pollo	chicken
tenderloin	lomo		puerco (*Mex*)	pork
turkey	pavo		riñones	kidneys
veal	ternera		solomillo (*Esp*)	sirloin steak
venison	venado		ternera	veal
white meat	carne blanca		venado	venison

vegetables	**verduras**		**verduras**	**vegetables**
artichoke	alcachofa		alcachofa	artichoke
asparagus	ésparragos		arvejas (*LAm*)	peas
aubergine	berenjena		apio	celery
beans	frijoles		batata	sweet potato
carrots	zanahorias		berenjena	aubergine
cabbage	col, repollo		camote (*LAm*)	sweet potato
celery	apio		cebollas	onions
endive	endivia		champiñones	mushrooms
lettuce	lechuga		chícharos (*Mex*)	peas
mushrooms	champiñones		col, repollo	cabbage
peas	guisantes, (*LAm*) arvejas		coliflor	cauliflower
			ésparragos	asparagus
pepper	pimiento		frijoles	beans
potatoes	patatas, (*LAm*) papas		guisantes	peas
runner bean	habichuela		haba	broad bean

17

tomato	tomate, (Mex) jitomate	jitomate (Mex)	tomato
		papas	potatoes
sweet potato	batata, camote (LAm)	patatas	potatoes
		pimiento	pepper
zucchini	calabacines	zanahorias	carrots

the way it's cooked	cómo se prepara	cómo se prepara	the way it's cooked
boiled	cocido -da	a la parilla	grilled
roast	asado -da	a la plancha	griddled
fried	frito -ta	asado -da	roast
pureed	puré de	bien cocido	well done
grilled	a la parilla	bien hecho	well done
griddled	a la plancha	cocido -da	boiled
stewed	estofado -da, guisado -da	estofado -da	stewed
		guisado -da	stewed
rare	poco hecho	frito -ta	fried
well done	bien hecho	poco hecho	rare

deserts	postres	postres	deserts
ice cream	helados	fruta	fruit
fruits	fruta	helados	ice cream
pie	tarta, (LAm) pay	pastel, (LAm) pay	pie
tart	tarta	tarta	tart

other		otros	
bread	pan	aceite de oliva	olive oil
butter	mantequilla	ajo	garlic
cheese	queso	arroz	rice
cheeseboard	tabla de quesos	condimento	seasoning
garlic	ajo	mantequilla	butter
mayonnaise	mayonesa	mayonesa	mayonnaise
mustard	mostaza	mostaza	mustard
olive oil	aceite de oliva	pan	bread

18

pepper	pimienta	pimienta	pepper
rice	arroz	queso	cheese
salt	sal	sal	salt
sauce	salsa	salsa	sauce
seasoning	condimento	tabla de quesos	cheeseboard
vinegar	vinagre	vinagre	vinegar

drinks	bebidas	bebidas	drinks
beer	cerveza	agua mineral	mineral water
bottle	botella	bebida no alcohólica	soft drink
carbonated	con gas		
half-bottle	media botella	botella	botella
liqueur	licor	cerveza	beer
mineral water	agua mineral	con gas	carbonated
red wine	vino tinto	licor	liqueur
rosé	vino rosado	media botella	half-bottle
soft drink	bebida no alcohólica	sin gas	still
		vino	wine
still	sin gas	vino blanco	white wine
house wine	vino de la casa	vino de la casa	house wine
table wine	vino de mesa	vino de mesa	table wine
white wine	vino blanco	vino rosado	rosé
wine	vino	vino tinto	red wine

19

Places to stay/Alojamiento

Camping | Campings

can we pitch our tent here?	¿podemos montar la tienda (de campaña) aquí?
can we park our caravan here?	¿podemos aparcar la caravana aquí?, (LAm) ¿podemos estacionar el tráiler aquí?
what are the facilities like?	¿cómo son las instalaciones?
how much is it per night?	¿cuánto cobran por (pasar la) noche?
where do we park the car?	¿dónde podemos aparcar, (esp LAm) estacionar?
we're looking for a campsite	estamos buscando un camping

At the hotel | Hoteles ★★★

I'd like a double/ single room with bath	quisiera una habitación individual/ doble con baño
we have a reservation in the name of Morris	tenemos una reserva a nombre de Morris
we'll be staying three nights, from Friday to Sunday	nos quedaremos tres noches, de viernes a domingo
how much does the room cost?	¿cuánto cuesta la habitación?
I'd like to see the room	quisiera ver la habitación
what time is breakfast?	¿a qué hora se sirve el desayuno?
can I leave this in your safe?	¿puedo dejar esto en la caja fuerte?
bed and breakfast	(lugar donde dan) alojamiento y desayuno
we'd like to stay another night	nos gustaría quedarnos una noche más
please call me at 7:30	¿me podría despertar a las 7:30, por favor?
are there any messages for me?	¿hay algún mensaje para mí?

Hostels Albergues

could you tell me where the youth hostel is?	¿me podría indicar dónde está el albergue?
what time does the hostel close?	¿a qué hora cierra el albergue?
I'll be staying in a hostel	me alojaré en un albergue
the hostel we're staying in is great value	el albergue donde nos alojamos ofrece una buena relación calidad-precio
I know a really good hostel in Dublin	conozco un albergue estupendo en Dublín
I'd like to go backpacking in Australia	me gustaría irme a Australia con la mochila al hombro

Rooms to rent Alquiler de habitaciones

I'm looking for a room with a reasonable rent	quiero alquilar, (Mex) rentar una habitación que tenga un precio razonable
I'd like to rent an apartment for a few weeks	me gustaría alquilar, (Mex) rentar un apartamento para unas cuantas semanas
where do I find out about rooms to rent?	¿dónde me puedo informar sobre alquileres, (Mex) rentas de habitaciones?
what's the weekly rent?	¿cuánto cuesta el alquiler, (Mex) la renta semanal?
I'm staying with friends at the moment	en este momento estoy alojado en casa de unos amigos
I rent an apartment on the outskirts of town	vivo en un apartamento alquilado, (Mex) rentado en las afueras
the room's fine — I'll take it	la habitación está muy bien, me la quedo
the deposit is one month's rent in advance	como depósito, se paga un mes de alquiler, (Mex) renta por adelantado

Shopping/Las compras

At the bank   En el banco

I'd like to change some money	quisiera cambiar dinero
I want to change some dollars into euros	quisiera cambiar dólares a euros
do you take Eurocheques?	¿aceptan Eurocheques?
what's the exchange rate today?	¿a cuánto está hoy el cambio?
I prefer traveller's cheques, (Amer) traveler's checks to cash	prefiero cheques de viaje que dinero en metálico, (esp LAm) en efectivo
I'd like to transfer some money from my account	quisiera hacer una transferencia desde mi cuenta corriente
I'll get some money from the cash machine	sacaré dinero del cajero (automático)
I'm with another bank	no soy cliente/-a de este banco

Finding the right shop   Dar con la tienda adecuada

where's the main shopping district?	¿dónde está la zona de tiendas?
where can I buy batteries/postcards?	¿dónde puedo comprar unas pilas/postales?
where's the nearest pharmacy/bookshop?	¿dónde está la farmacia/librería más cercana?
is there a good food shop around here?	¿hay una buena tienda de comestibles por aquí?
what time do the shops open/close?	¿a qué hora abren/cierran las tiendas?
where did you get those?	¿dónde los/las ha comprado?
I'm looking for presents for my family	estoy buscando regalos para mi familia
we'll do our shopping on Saturday	(nosotros) haremos las compras el sábado
I love shopping	me encanta ir de compras

Are you being served? ¿Lo/La atienden?

how much does that cost?	¿cuánto cuesta?
can I try it on?	¿me lo puedo probar?
could you wrap it for me, please?	¿me lo envuelve, por favor?
can I pay by credit card/cheque, (Amer) check?	¿puedo pagar con tarjeta/cheque?
do you have this in another colour, (Amer) color?	¿tiene éste/-a en otro color?
could I have a bag, please?	¿me da una bolsa, por favor?
I'm just looking	sólo estoy mirando
I'll think about it	me lo voy a pensar
I'd like a receipt, please	¿me da el recibo, por favor?
I need a bigger/smaller size	necesito una talla más grande/más pequeña
I take a size 10/a medium	uso la talla 38/mediana
it doesn't suit me	no me queda bien
I'm sorry, I don't have any change/anything smaller	perdone, pero no tengo cambio/billetes más pequeños
that's all, thank you	nada más, gracias

Changing things Devoluciones

can I have a refund?	¿me podría devolver el dinero?
can you mend it for me?	¿me lo/la podrían arreglar?
can I speak to the manager?	quisiera hablar con el encargado/la encargada
it doesn't work	no funciona
I'd like to change it, please	quisiera cambiarlo/-a, por favor
I bought this here yesterday	compré esto ayer

23

Currency Convertor		Convertidor de divisas	
€/$	£/$	£/$	€/$
0.25		0.25	
0.5		0.5	
0.75		0.75	
1		1	
1.5		1.5	
2		2	
3		3	
5		5	
10		10	
20		20	
30		30	
40		40	
50		50	
100		100	
200		200	
1000		1000	

Sports and leisure/Deportes y ocio

Keeping fit — Mantenerse en forma

where can we play tennis/squash?	¿dónde se puede jugar al tenis/squash, (*LAm*) jugar tenis/squash?
where is the local sports centre, (*Amer*) center?	¿hay por aquí cerca un polideportivo?
what's the charge per day?	¿cuánto cobran (al día)?
is there a reduction for children/a student discount?	¿hacen descuentos a niños/estudiantes?
I'm looking for a swimming pool/tennis court	estoy buscando una piscina, (*Mex*) alberca/un club de tenis
are there any yoga/pilates classes here?	¿hay clases de yoga/pilates?
I want to do aerobics	quiero hacer aerobic
is there a hotel gym?	¿hay gimnasio en este hotel?
you have to be a member	(para entrar) hace falta ser socio
I would like to go fishing/riding	me gustaría ir a pescar/montar a caballo
I love swimming	me encanta nadar

Watching sport — Ver espectáculos deportivos

is there a match, (*Amer*) game on Saturday?	¿hay un partido el sábado?
which teams are playing?	¿quién está jugando?
where can I get tickets?	¿dónde se compran las entradas?
I'd like to see a match	me gustaría ver un partido
my favourite, (*Amer*) favorite team is...	mi equipo favorito es el...
let's watch the match, (*Amer*) game on TV	veamos el partido por la tele
who's winning?	¿quién gana?
the reds are winning 3-1	los rojos van ganando 3 a 1

SPORTS AND PASTIMES

American football/football	fútbol americano
badminton	bádminton
basketball	baloncesto, (*LAm*) básquetbol
cycling	ciclismo
football/soccer	fútbol
golf	golf
hiking	montañismo
horse-riding	equitación
paddle tennis	pádel, (*LAm*) paddle
pelota	pelota
roller-blading	patinaje
running	correr
sailing	vela
surfing	surf
swimming	natación

DEPORTES Y PASATIEMPOS

bádminton	badminton
baloncesto, (*LAm*) básquetbol	basketball
ciclismo	cycling
correr	running
equitación	horse-riding
fútbol americano	American football/football
fútbol	football/soccer
golf	golf
montañismo	hiking
natación	swimming
pádel, (*LAm*) paddle	paddle tennis
patinaje	roller-blading
pelota	pelota
surf	surfing
vela	sailing

································

Movies/theatres/clubs — Cine/Teatro/Discotecas

what's on?	¿qué ponen, (*esp LAm*) dan (en el cine/teatro)?
when does the box office open/close?	¿a qué hora abren/cierran la taquilla, (*LAm*) boletería?
what time does the concert/performance start?	¿a qué hora empieza el concierto/la representación?
when does it finish?	¿a qué hora termina?
are there any seats left for tonight?	¿quedan entradas para esta noche?
how much are the tickets?	¿cuánto cuestan las entradas?
where can I get a programme, (*Amer*) program?	¿dónde puedo conseguir un programa?
I want to book tickets for tonight's performance	quiero reservar entradas para esta noche
I'll book seats in the circle	reservaré entradas de platea
I'd rather have seats in the stalls, (*Amer*) orchestra	prefiero el patio de butacas
somewhere in the middle, but not too far back	que sean centrales, pero no demasiado atrás
four, please	cuatro, por favor
for Saturday	para el sábado
we'd like to go to a club	nos gustaría ir a una discoteca

Hobbies — Aficiones y hobbies

what do you do at, (*Amer*) on weekends?	¿qué hace los fines de semana?
I like reading/listening to music/going out	me gusta leer/escuchar música/salir
do you like watching TV/shopping/travelling?	¿te gusta ver la tele/ir de compras/viajar?
I read a lot	leo mucho
I collect musical instruments	colecciono instrumentos musicales

27

Good timing/A tiempo

Telling the time   La hora

what time is it?	¿qué hora es?
it's 2 o'clock	son las 2
at about 8 o'clock	hacia las 8
from 10 o'clock onwards	a partir de las 10
at 5 o'clock in the morning/afternoon	a las cinco de la mañana/tarde
it's five past/quarter past/half past one	es la una y cinco/y cuarto/y media
it's twenty-five to/quarter to one	es la una menos veinticinco/menos cuarto/(LAm) son veinticinco/un cuarto para la una
a quarter/three quarters of an hour	un cuarto/tres cuartos de hora

Days and dates   Días y fechas

Sunday, Monday, Tuesday, Wednesday, Thursday, Friday, Saturday
domingo, lunes, martes, miércoles, jueves, viernes, sábado

January, February, March, April, May, June, July, August, September, October, November, December
enero, febrero, marzo, abril, mayo, junio, julio, agosto, septiembre, octubre, noviembre, diciembre

what's the date?	¿qué fecha es hoy?
it's the second of June	(es el) dos de junio
we meet up every Monday	nos vemos todos los lunes
we're going away in August	nos vamos fuera en agosto
on November 8th	el 8 de noviembre

Public holidays and special days	Fiestas y celebraciones especiales
Bank holiday	día festivo en el Reino Unido
Bank holiday Monday	lunes de puente
New Year's Day (Jan 1)	Año Nuevo (1 de enero)
Epiphany (Jan 6)	Reyes (6 de enero)
St Valentine's Day (Feb 14)	San Valentín (14 de febrero)
Shrove Tuesday/Pancake Day	Martes de Carnaval
Ash Wednesday	Miércoles de Ceniza
Holy Week	Semana Santa
Good Friday	Viernes Santo
Easter	Pascua (de Resurrección)
Easter Monday	lunes de Pascua
May Day (May 1)	1 de mayo, día del trabajador
Independence Day	4 de julio, fiesta de la independencia de los EEUU
Thanksgiving	día de Acción de Gracias, fiesta típica de EEUU y Canadá
Halloween (Oct 31)	Halloween (fiesta de fantasmas y brujas que se celebra la víspera de Todos los Santos)
All Saints' Day	Todos los Santos
Guy Fawkes Day/ Bonfire Night (Nov 5)	fiesta de Guy Fawkes (5 de noviembre: se celebra que el católico Guy Fawkes fracasó en su intento de incendiar el parlamento)
Remembrance Sunday	fiesta en recuerdo a los caídos en las dos guerras mundiales
St Nicholas' Day (Dec 6)	San Nicolás (6 de diciembre)
Christmas Eve (Dec 24)	Nochebuena (24 de diciembre)
Christmas Day (Dec 25)	Navidad (25 de diciembre)
Boxing Day (Dec 26)	día de fiesta que sigue al día de Navidad
New Year's Eve (Dec 31)	Nochevieja (31 de diciembre)

29

Health and Beauty/Salud y belleza

At the doctor's	En el médico
can I see a doctor?	¿podría verme un médico?
I don't feel well	no me encuentro, (LAm) no me siento bien
it hurts here	me duele aquí
I have a migraine/stomach ache	tengo migrañas/dolor de tripa, (LAm) de estómago
are there any side effects?	¿tiene efectos secundarios?
I have a sore ankle/wrist/knee	me he hecho daño, (LAm) me hice daño en el tobillo/la muñeca/la rodilla

YOU WILL HEAR:	OIRÁS:
necesita pedir cita (or pedir hora)	you need to make an appointment
siéntese, por favor	please take a seat
¿tiene una Tarjeta Sanitaria Europea (TSE)?	do you have a European Health Insurance Card (EHIC)?
¿tiene seguro médico?	do you have Health Insurance?
tengo que tomarle la tensión, (LAm) presión	I need to take your blood pressure

MORE USEFUL WORDS:	MÁS PALABRAS ÚTILES:
nurse	enfermera/-o
antibiotics	antibióticos
medicine	medicina
infection	infección
treatment	tratamiento
rest	reposo

At the pharmacy — En la farmacia

can I have some painkillers?	¿me puede dar un analgésico?
I have asthma/hay fever/eczema	tengo asma/alergia al polen/eccema
I've been stung by a wasp/bee	me ha picado una avispa/abeja
I've got a cold/cough/the flu	tengo catarro/tos/gripe
I need something for diarrhoea/ stomachache	necesito algo para la diarrea/ el dolor de estómago
I'm pregnant	estoy embarazada

YOU WILL HEAR: — OIRÁS:

¿lo ha tomado alguna vez?/ ¿ha tomado alguna vez este medicamento?	have you taken this/these before?/ have you taken this medicine before?
su receta estará lista en diez minutos	your prescription will be ready in ten minutes
tómese con las comidas/ tres veces al día	take at mealtimes/ three times a day
¿tiene alguna alergia?	are you allergic to anything?
¿está tomando otros medicamentos?	are you taking any other medication?

MORE USEFUL WORDS: — MÁS PALABRAS ÚTILES:

plasters, (*Amer*) Band-Aid™	tiritas, (*LAm*) curitas
insect repellent	repelente contra insectos
contraception	anticonceptivos
sun cream	crema de sol
aftersun	loción aftersun, (*LAm*) para después de asolearse
dosage	dosis

31

At the hairdresser's/salon   En la peluquería

I'd like a cut and blow dry	¿me puede cortar y secar?
just a trim please	corte nada más que las puntas, por favor
a grade 3 back and sides	lo quiero al 3 por detrás y por los lados
I'd like my hair washed first please	lavar y cortar, por favor
can I have a manicure/pedicure/facial?	¿hacen la manicura/la pedicura/tratamiento facial?
how much is a head/back massage?	¿cuánto cuesta el masaje de cabeza/espalda?
can I see a price list?	¿puedo ver la lista de precios?
do you offer reflexology/aromatherapy treatments?	¿hacen reflexología/aromaterapia?

YOU WILL HEAR: OIRÁS:

¿quiere que le seque el pelo?	would you like your hair blow-dried?
¿dónde quiere la raya, (*Col, Ven*) la carrera, (*Chi*) la partidura?	where is your parting, (*Amer*) part?
¿quiere que le corte a (*LAm*) en capas?	would you like your hair layered?

MORE USEFUL WORDS: MÁS PALABRAS ÚTILES:

dry/greasy/fine/flyaway/frizzy	seco/graso/fino/lacio/crespo
highlights	mechas, (*Mex*) luces, (*Chi, Mex*) rayitos, (*Col*) mechones, (*RPl*) claritos
extensions	extensiones
sunbed	solarium, (*LAm also*) cama solar
leg/arm/bikini wax	depilación a la cera en las piernas/los brazos/las ingles

32

At the dentist's   En el dentista

I have toothache	me duele un diente
I'd like an emergency appointment	necesito una cita de urgencia
I have cracked a tooth	se me ha roto, (*LAm*) se me rompió un diente
my gums are bleeding	me sangran las encías

YOU WILL HEAR: OIRÁS:

abra la boca	open your mouth
necesita un empaste, (*Chi, Mex*) una tapadura, (*RPI*) una emplomadura, (*Col*) una calza	you need a filling
tenemos que hacer una radiografía	we need to take an X-ray
enjuáguese, por favor	please rinse

MORE USEFUL WORDS: MÁS PALABRAS ÚTILES:

anaesthetic	anestesia
root canal treatment	endodoncia
injection	inyección
floss	hilo dental

DID YOU KNOW...?   ¿SABÍAS QUE...?

Spanish hairdressers will normally wash your hair before your haircut. If you don't want them to do so, you should tell them beforehand.	Antiguamente, las peluquerías se anunciaban con un poste pintado con bandas rojas y blancas en espiral.

33

Weights & measures/Pesos y medidas

Length/Longitud

inches/pulgadas	0.39	3.9	7.8	11.7	15.6	19.7	39
cm/centímetros	1	10	20	30	40	50	100

Distance/Distancia

miles/millas	0.62	6.2	12.4	18.6	24.9	31	62
km/km	1	10	20	30	40	50	100

Weight/Peso

pounds/libras	2.2	22	44	66	88	110	220
kg/kilos	1	10	20	30	40	50	100

Capacity/Capacidad

gallons/galones	0.22	2.2	4.4	6.6	8.8	11	22
litres/litros	1	10	20	30	40	50	100

Temperature/Temperatura

°C	0	5	10	15	20	25	30	37	38	40
°F	32	41	50	59	68	77	86	98.4	100	104

Clothing and shoe sizes/Tallas de ropa y calzado

Women's clothing sizes/Ropa de señora

UK	8	10	12	14	16	18
US	6	8	10	12	14	16
Continent	36	38	40	42	44	46

Men's clothing sizes/Ropa de caballero

UK/US	36	38	40	42	44	46
Continent	46	48	50	52	54	56

Men's and women's shoes/Calzado de señora y caballero

UK women	4	5	6	7	7.5	8			
UK men			6	7	8	9	10	11	
US	6.5	7.5	8.5	9.5	10.5	11.5	12.5	13.5	14.5
Continent	37	38	39	40	41	42	43	44	45

Aa

a /ə/, stressed form /eɪ/

before vowel sound or silent 'h' **an**

indefinite article

⋯▸ un (*m*), una (*f*). **a problem** un problema. **an apple** una manzana. **have you got a pencil?** ¿tienes un lápiz?

! Feminine singular nouns beginning with stressed or accented *a* or *ha* take the article *un* instead of *una*, e.g. *un águila, un hada*

⋯▸ (*when talking about prices and quantities*) por. **30 miles an hour** 30 millas por hora. **twice a week** dos veces por semana, dos veces a la semana

! There are many cases in which **a** is not translated, such as when talking about people's professions, in exclamations, etc: **she's a lawyer** *es abogada.* **what a beautiful day!** *¡qué día más precioso!* **have you got a car?** ¿tienes coche? **half a cup** media taza

A & E /eɪ·ænd'iː/ *n* urgencias *fpl*

aback /ə'bæk/ *adv.* **be taken ~** quedar desconcertado

abandon /ə'bændən/ *vt* abandonar. ● *n* abandono *m*, desenfado *m*. **~ed** *a* abandonado

abashed /ə'bæʃt/ *adj* confuso

abate /ə'beɪt/ *vi* disminuir; (*storm etc*) calmarse

abattoir /'æbətwɑː(r)/ *n* matadero *m*

abbess /'æbɪs/ *n* abadesa *f*

abbey /'æbɪ/ *n* abadía *f*

abbot /'æbət/ *n* abad *m*

abbreviat|e /ə'briːvɪeɪt/ *vt* abreviar. **~ion** /-'eɪʃn/ *n* abreviatura *f*; (*act*) abreviación *f*

abdicat|e /'æbdɪkeɪt/ *vt/i* abdicar. **~ion** /-'eɪʃn/ *n* abdicación *f*

abdom|en /'æbdəmən/ *n* abdomen *m*. **~inal** /-'dɒmnl/ *adj* abdominal

abduct /æb'dʌkt/ *vt* secuestrar. **~ion** /-ʃn/ *n* secuestro *m*

abhor /əb'hɔː(r)/ *vt* (*pt* abhorred) aborrecer. **~rence** /-'hɒrəns/ *n* aborrecimiento *m*. **~rent** /-'hɒrənt/ *adj* aborrecible

abide /ə'baɪd/ *vt* (*pt* abided) soportar. ● *vi* (*old use, pt* abode) morar. □ **~ by** *vt* atenerse a; cumplir (*promise*)

ability /ə'bɪlətɪ/ *n* capacidad *f*; (*cleverness*) habilidad *f*

abject /'æbdʒekt/ *adj* (*wretched*) miserable

ablaze /ə'bleɪz/ *adj* en llamas

able /'eɪbl/ *adj* (*-er, -est*) capaz. **be ~** poder; (*know how to*) saber. **~-bodied** /-'bɒdɪd/ *adj* sano, no discapacitado

ably /'eɪblɪ/ *adv* hábilmente

abnormal /æb'nɔːml/ *adj* anormal. **~ity** /-'mælətɪ/ *n* anormalidad f

aboard /əˈbɔːd/ adv a bordo. ● prep a bordo de

abode /əˈbəud/ see ABIDE. ● n (old use) domicilio m

aboli|sh /əˈbɒlɪʃ/ vt abolir. ~tion /æbəˈlɪʃn/ n abolición f

abominable /əˈbɒmɪnəbl/ adj abominable

aborigin|al /æbəˈrɪdʒənl/ adj & n aborigen (m & f), indígena (m & f). ~es /-iːz/ npl aborígenes mpl

abort /əˈbɔːt/ vt hacer abortar. ~ion /-ʃn/ n aborto m provocado; (fig) aborto m. have an ~ion hacerse un aborto. ~ive adj fracasado

abound /əˈbaund/ vi abundar (in en)

about /əˈbaut/ adv (approximately) alrededor de; (here and there) por todas partes; (in existence) por aquí. ~ here por aquí. be ~ to estar a punto de. ● prep sobre; (around) alrededor de; (somewhere in) en. talk ~ hablar de. ~-face, ~-turn n (fig) cambio m rotundo

above /əˈbʌv/ adv arriba. ● prep encima de; (more than) más de. ~ all sobre todo. ~ board adj legítimo. ~ mentioned adj susodicho

abrasi|on /əˈbreɪʒn/ n abrasión f. ~ve /-sɪv/ adj abrasivo

abreast /əˈbrest/ adv. march four ~ marchar en columna de cuatro en fondo. keep ~ of mantenerse al corriente de

abroad /əˈbrɔːd/ adv (be) en el extranjero; (go) al extranjero; (far and wide) por todas partes

abrupt /əˈbrʌpt/ adj brusco. ~ly adv (suddenly) repentinamente; (curtly) bruscamente

abscess /ˈæbsɪs/ n absceso m

abscond /əbˈskɒnd/ vi fugarse

absen|ce /ˈæbsəns/ n ausencia f; (lack) falta f. ~t /ˈæbsənt/ adj ausente. ~t-minded /-ˈmaɪndɪd/ adj distraído. ~t-mindedness n distracción f, despiste m. ~tee /-ˈtiː/ n ausente m & f. ~teeism n absentismo m, ausentismo m (LAm)

absolute /ˈæbsəluːt/ adj absoluto. ~ly adv absolutamente

absolve /əbˈzɒlv/ vt (from sin) absolver; (from obligation) liberar

absor|b /əbˈzɔːb/ vt absorber. ~bent /-bent/ adj absorbente. ~bent cotton n (Amer) algodón m hidrófilo. ~ption /əbˈzɔːpʃən/ n absorción f

abstain /əbˈsteɪn/ vi abstenerse (from de)

abstemious /əbˈstiːmɪəs/ adj abstemio

abstention /əbˈstenʃn/ n abstención f

abstract /ˈæbstrækt/ adj abstracto. ● n (summary) resumen m; (painting) cuadro m abstracto. ● /əbˈstrækt/ vt extraer; (summarize) resumir. ~ion /-ʃn/ n abstracción f

absurd /əbˈsɜːd/ adj absurdo. ~ity n absurdo m, disparate m

abundan|ce /əˈbʌndəns/ n abundancia f. ~t adj abundante

abus|e /əˈbjuːz/ vt (misuse) abusar de; (ill-treat) maltratar; (insult) insultar. ● /əˈbjuːs/ n abuso m; (insults) insultos mpl. ~ive /əˈbjuːsɪv/ adj injurioso

abysmal /əˈbɪzməl/ adj 🔢 pésimo

abyss /əˈbɪs/ n abismo m

academic /ækəˈdemɪk/ adj académico; (pej) teórico. ● n universitario *m*, catedrático *m*

academy /əˈkædəmɪ/ *n* academia *f*.

accelerat|e /əkˈseləreɪt/ *vt* acelerar. • *vi* acelerar; (*Auto*) apretar el acelerador. **~ion** /-ˈreɪʃn/ *n* aceleración *f*. **~or** *n* acelerador *m*

accent /ˈæksənt/ *n* acento *m*

accept /əkˈsept/ *vt* aceptar. **~able** *adj* aceptable. **~ance** *n* aceptación *f*; (*approval*) aprobación *f*

access /ˈækses/ *n* acceso *m*. **~ible** /əkˈsesəbl/ *adj* accesible; (*person*) tratable

accession /ækˈseʃn/ *n* (*to power, throne etc*) ascenso *m*; (*thing added*) adquisición *f*

accessory /əkˈsesərɪ/ *adj* accesorio. • *n* accesorio *m*, complemento *m*; (*Jurid*) cómplice *m & f*

accident /ˈæksɪdənt/ *n* accidente *m*; (*chance*) casualidad *f*. by ~ sin querer; (*by chance*) por casualidad. **~al** /-ˈdentl/ *adj* accidental, fortuito. **~ally** /-ˈdentəlɪ/ *adv* sin querer; (*by chance*) por casualidad. **~-prone** *adj* propenso a los accidentes

acclaim /əˈkleɪm/ *vt* aclamar. • *n* aclamación *f*

accolade /ˈækəleɪd/ *n* (*praise*) encomio *m*

accommodat|e /əˈkɒmədeɪt/ *vt* (*give hospitality to*) alojar; (*adapt*) acomodar; (*oblige*) complacer. **~ing** *adj* complaciente. **~ion** /-ˈdeɪʃn/ *n*, **~ions** *npl* (*Amer*) alojamiento *m*

accompan|iment /əˈkʌmpənɪmənt/ *n* acompañamiento *m*. **~ist** *n* acompañante *m & f*. **~y** /əˈkʌmpənɪ/ *vt* acompañar

accomplice /əˈkʌmplɪs/ *n* cómplice *m & f*

accomplish /əˈkʌmplɪʃ/ *vt* (*complete*) acabar; (*achieve*) realizar; (*carry out*) llevar a cabo. **~ed** *adj* consumado. **~ment** *n* realización *f*; (*ability*) talento *m*; (*thing achieved*) triunfo *m*, logro *m*

accord /əˈkɔːd/ *vi* concordar. • *vt* conceder. • *n* acuerdo *m*; (*harmony*) armonía *f*. of one's own ~ espontáneamente. **~ance** *n*. in ~ance with de acuerdo con. **~ing** *adv*. **~ing** to según. **~ingly** *adv* en conformidad; (*therefore*) por consiguiente

accordion /əˈkɔːdɪən/ *n* acordeón *m*

accost /əˈkɒst/ *vt* abordar

account /əˈkaʊnt/ *n* cuenta *f*; (*description*) relato *m*. **~s** *npl* (*in business*) contabilidad *f*. on ~ of a causa de. on no ~ de ninguna manera. on this ~ por eso. take into ~ tener en cuenta. • *vt* considerar. □ ~ **for** *vt* dar cuenta de, explicar

accountan|cy /əˈkaʊntənsɪ/ *n* contabilidad *f*. **~t** *n* contable *m & f*, contador *m* (*LAm*)

accumulat|e /əˈkjuːmjʊleɪt/ *vt* acumular. • *vi* acumularse. **~ion** /-ˈleɪʃn/ *n* acumulación *f*

accura|cy /ˈækjərəsɪ/ *n* exactitud *f*, precisión *f*. **~te** /-ət/ *adj* exacto, preciso

accus|ation /ækjuːˈzeɪʃn/ *n* acusación *f*. **~e** /əˈkjuːz/ *vt* acusar

accustom /əˈkʌstəm/ *vt* acostumbrar. **~ed** *adj*. be ~ed (to) estar acostumbrado (a). get ~ed (to) acostumbrarse (a)

ace /eɪs/ *n* as *m*

ache /eɪk/ *n* dolor *m*. • *vi* doler. my leg ~s me duele la pierna

achieve /əˈtʃiːv/ *vt* realizar; lograr

a (success). **~ment** n realización f; (feat) proeza f; (thing achieved) logro m

acid /'æsɪd/ adj & n ácido (m). **~ic** adj /ə'sɪdɪk/ adj ácido. **~ rain** n lluvia f ácida

acknowledge /ək'nɒlɪdʒ/ vt reconocer. **~ receipt of** acusar recibo de. **~ment** n reconocimiento m; (Com) acuse m de recibo

acne /'æknɪ/ n acné m

acorn /'eɪkɔːn/ n bellota f

acoustic /ə'kuːstɪk/ adj acústico. **~s** npl acústica f

acquaint /ə'kweɪnt/ vt. **~ s.o. with** poner a uno al corriente de. **be ~ed with** conocer (person); saber (fact). **~ance** n conocimiento m; (person) conocido m

acquiesce /ækwɪ'es/ vi consentir (in en). **~nce** n aquiescencia f, consentimiento m

acqui|re /ə'kwaɪə(r)/ vt adquirir; aprender (language). **~re a taste for** tomar gusto a. **~sition** /ækwɪ'zɪʃn/ n adquisición f. **~sitive** /-'kwɪzətɪv/ adj codicioso

acquit /ə'kwɪt/ vt (pt acquitted) absolver. **~tal** n absolución f

acre /'eɪkə(r)/ n acre m

acrid /'ækrɪd/ adj acre

acrimonious /ækrɪ'məʊnɪəs/ adj cáustico, mordaz

acrobat /'ækrəbæt/ n acróbata m & f. **~ic** /-'bætɪk/ adj acrobático. **~ics** npl acrobacia f

acronym /'ækrənɪm/ n acrónimo m, siglas fpl

across /ə'krɒs/ adv & prep (side to side) de un lado a otro; (on other side) al otro lado de; (crosswise) a través. **it is 20 metres ~** tiene 20 metros de ancho. **go or walk ~** atravesar, cruzar

act /ækt/ n acto m; (action) acción f; (in variety show) número m; (decree) decreto m. ● vt hacer (part, role). ● vi actuar; (pretend) fingir. **~ as** actuar de; (object) servir de. **~ for** representar. **~ing** adj interino. ● n (of play) representación f; (by actor) interpretación f; (profession) profesión f de actor

action /'ækʃn/ n acción f; (Jurid) demanda f; (plot) argumento m. **out of ~** (on sign) no funciona. **put out of ~** inutilizar. **take ~** tomar medidas **~ replay** n repetición f de la jugada

activate /'æktɪveɪt/ vt activar

activ|e /'æktɪv/ adj activo; (energetic) lleno de energía; (volcano) en actividad. **~ist** n activista m & f. **~ity** /-'tɪvətɪ/ n actividad f

act|or /'æktə(r)/ n actor m. **~ress** /-trɪs/ n actriz f

actual /'æktʃʊəl/ adj verdadero. **~ly** adv en realidad, efectivamente; (even) incluso

acute /ə'kjuːt/ adj agudo. **~ly** adv agudamente

ad /æd/ n ① anuncio m, aviso m (LAm)

AD /eɪ'diː/ abbr (= Anno Domini) d. de J.C.

Adam's apple /ædəmz'æpl/ n nuez f (de Adán)

adapt /ə'dæpt/ vt adaptar. ● vi adaptarse. **~ability** /ə'bɪlətɪ/ n adaptabilidad f. **~able** /-əbl/ adj adaptable. **~ation** /ædæp'teɪʃn/ n adaptación f; (of book etc) versión f. **~or** /ə'dæptə(r)/ n (Elec, with several sockets) enchufe m múltiple; (Elec, for different sockets) adaptador m

add /æd/ vt añadir. ● vi sumar. □ **~ up** vt sumar; (fig) tener sentido.

up to equivaler a

adder /'ædə(r)/ n víbora f

addict /'ædɪkt/ n adicto m; (fig) entusiasta m & f. **~ed** /ə'dɪktɪd/ adj **~ed to** adicto a; (fig) fanático de. **~ion** /ə'dɪkʃn/ n (Med) dependencia f; (fig) afición f. **~ive** /ə'dɪktɪv/ adj que crea adicción; (fig) que crea hábito

addition /ə'dɪʃn/ n suma f. **in ~** además. **~al** adj suplementario

address /ə'dres/ n dirección f; (on form) domicilio m; (speech) discurso m. ● vt poner la dirección en; (speak to) dirigirse a. **~ book** n libreta f de direcciones. **~ee** /ædre'siː/ n destinatario m

adept /'ædept/ adj & n experto (m)

adequa|cy /'ædɪkwəsɪ/ n suficiencia f. **~te** /-ət/ adj suficiente, adecuado. **~tely** adv suficientemente, adecuadamente

adhere /əd'hɪə(r)/ vi adherirse (to a); observar (rule). **~nce** /-rəns/ n adhesión f; (to rules) observancia f

adhesi|on /əd'hiːʒn/ n adherencia f. **~ve** /-sɪv/ adj & n adhesivo (m)

adjacent /ə'dʒeɪsnt/ adj contiguo

adjective /'ædʒɪktɪv/ n adjetivo m

adjourn /ə'dʒɜːn/ vt aplazar; suspender (meeting etc). ● vi suspenderse

adjust /ə'dʒʌst/ vt ajustar (machine); (arrange) arreglar. ● vi. **~ (to)** adaptarse (a). **~able** adj ajustable. **~ment** n adaptación f; (Tec) ajuste m

administer /əd'mɪnɪstə(r)/ vt administrar

administrat|ion /ədmɪnɪ'streɪʃn/ n administración f. **~ive** /əd'mɪnɪstrətɪv/ adj administrativo. **~or** /əd'mɪnɪstreɪtə(r)/ n administrador m

admirable /'ædmərəbl/ adj admirable

admiral /'ædmərəl/ n almirante m

admir|ation /ædmə'reɪʃn/ n admiración f. **~e** /əd'maɪə(r)/ vt admirar. **~er** /əd'maɪərə(r)/ n admirador m

admission /əd'mɪʃn/ n admisión f; (entry) entrada f

admit /əd'mɪt/ vt (pt admitted) dejar entrar; (acknowledge) admitir, reconocer. **~ to** confesar. **be ~ted (to hospital etc)** ingresar. **~tance** n entrada f. **~tedly** adv es verdad que

admonish /əd'mɒnɪʃ/ vt reprender; (advise) aconsejar

ado /ə'duː/ n alboroto m; (trouble) dificultad f. **without more or further ~** en seguida, sin más

adolescen|ce /ædə'lesns/ n adolescencia f. **~t** adj & n adolescente (m & f)

adopt /ə'dɒpt/ vt adoptar. **~ed** adj (child) adoptivo. **~ion** /-ʃn/ n adopción f

ador|able /ə'dɔːrəbl/ adj adorable. **~ation** /ædə'reɪʃn/ n adoración f. **~e** /ə'dɔː(r)/ vt adorar

adorn /ə'dɔːn/ vt adornar. **~ment** n adorno m

adrift /ə'drɪft/ adj & adv a la deriva

adult /'ædʌlt/ adj & n adulto (m)

adulter|er /ə'dʌltərə(r)/ n adúltero m. **~ess** /-ɪs/ n adúltera f. **~y** n adulterio m

advance /əd'vɑːns/ vt adelantar. ● vi adelantarse. ● n adelanto m. **in ~** con anticipación, por adelantado. **~d** adj avanzado; (studies) superior

advantage /əd'vɑːntɪdʒ/ n ventaja f. **take ~ of** aprovecharse de; abusar de (person). **~ous** /ædvən**

'teɪdʒəs/ adj ventajoso

advent /'ædvənt/ n venida f. A~ n adviento m

adventur|e /əd'ventʃə(r)/ n aventura f. ~er n aventurero m. ~ous adj (person) aventurero; (thing) arriesgado m. (fig, bold) audaz

adverb /'ædvɜːb/ n adverbio m

adversary /'ædvəsərɪ/ n adversario m

advers|e /'ædvɜːs/ adj adverso, contrario, desfavorable. ~ity /əd'vɜːsətɪ/ n infortunio m

advert /'ædvɜːt/ n ① anuncio m, aviso m (LAm). ~ise /'ædvətaɪz/ vt anunciar. ● vi hacer publicidad; (seek, sell) poner un anuncio. ~isement /əd'vɜːtɪsmənt/ n anuncio m, aviso m (LAm). ~iser /'ædvətaɪzə(r)/ n anunciante m & f

advice /əd'vaɪs/ n consejo m; (report) informe m

advis|able /əd'vaɪzəbl/ adj aconsejable. ~e /əd'vaɪz/ vt aconsejar; (inform) avisar. ~e against aconsejar en contra de. ~er n consejero m; (consultant) asesor m. ~ory adj consultivo

advocate /'ædvəkət/ n defensor m; (Jurid) abogado m. ● /'ædvəkeɪt/ vt recomendar

aerial /'eərɪəl/ adj aéreo. ● n antena f

aerobics /eə'rəʊbɪks/ npl aeróbica f

aerodrome /'eərədrəʊm/ n aeródromo m

aerodynamic /eərəʊdaɪ'næmɪk/ adj aerodinámico

aeroplane /'eərəpleɪn/ n avión m

aerosol /'eərəsɒl/ n aerosol m

aesthetic /iːs'θetɪk/ adj estético

afar /ə'fɑː(r)/ adv lejos

affable /'æfəbl/ adj afable

affair /ə'feə(r)/ n asunto m. (love) ~ aventura f, amorío m. ~s npl (business) negocios mpl

affect /ə'fekt/ vt afectar; (pretend) fingir. ~ation /æfek'teɪʃn/ n afectación f. ~ed adj afectado, amanerado

affection /ə'fekʃn/ n cariño m. ~ate /-ət/ adj cariñoso

affiliate /ə'fɪlɪeɪt/ vt afiliar

affirm /ə'fɜːm/ vt afirmar. ~ative /-ətɪv/ adj afirmativo. ● n respuesta f afirmativa

afflict /ə'flɪkt/ vt afligir. ~ion /-ʃn/ n aflicción f, pena f

affluen|ce /'æfluəns/ n riqueza f. ~t adj rico

afford /ə'fɔːd/ vt permitirse; (provide) dar. he can't ~ a car no le alcanza el dinero para comprar un coche

affront /ə'frʌnt/ n afrenta f, ofensa f. ● vt afrentar, ofender

afield /ə'fiːld/ adv. far ~ muy lejos

afloat /ə'fləʊt/ adv a flote

afraid /ə'freɪd/ adj. be ~ tener miedo (of a); (be sorry) sentir, lamentar

afresh /ə'freʃ/ adv de nuevo

Africa /'æfrɪkə/ n África f. ~n adj & n africano (m). ~n-American adj & n norteamericano (m) de origen africano

after /'ɑːftə(r)/ adv después; (behind) detrás. ● prep después de; (behind) detrás de. it's twenty ~ four (Amer) son las cuatro y veinte. be ~ (seek) andar en busca de. ● conj después de que. ● adj posterior. ~-effect n consecuencia f, efecto m secundario. ~math /'ɑːftəmæθ/ n secuelas fpl. ~noon /-'nuːn/ n tarde f. ~shave n loción

f para después de afeitarse.
~thought *n* ocurrencia *f* tardía.
~wards /-wədz/ *adv* después

again /ə'gen/ *adv* otra vez; (*besides*) además. **do ~** volver a hacer, hacer otra vez. **~ and ~** una y otra vez

against /ə'genst/ *prep* contra; (*in opposition to*) en contra de, contra

age /eɪdʒ/ *n* edad *f*. **at four years of ~** a los cuatro años. **under ~** menor de edad. **~s** *npl* 🔟 siglos *mpl*. ● *vt/i* (*pres p* **ageing**) envejecer. **~d** /eɪdʒd/ *adj* de ... años. **~d 10** de 10 años. **~d** /'eɪdʒɪd/ *adj* viejo, anciano

agency /'eɪdʒənsɪ/ *n* agencia *f*; (*department*) organismo *m*

agenda /ə'dʒendə/ *n* orden *m* del día

agent /'eɪdʒənt/ *n* agente *m* & *f*; (*representative*) representante *m* & *f*

aggravat|e /'ægrəveɪt/ *vt* agravar; (*fam, irritate*) irritar. **~ion** /-'veɪʃn/ *n* agravación *f*; (*fam, irritation*) irritación *f*

aggress|ion /ə'greʃn/ *n* agresión *f*. **~ive** *adj* agresivo. **~iveness** *n* agresividad *f*. **~or** *n* agresor *m*

aggrieved /ə'griːvd/ *adj* apenado, ofendido

aghast /ə'gɑːst/ *adj* horrorizado

agile /'ædʒaɪl/ *adj* ágil. **~ity** /ə'dʒɪlətɪ/ *n* agilidad *f*

aging /'eɪdʒɪŋ/ *adj* envejecido. ● *n* envejecimiento *m*

agitat|e /'ædʒɪteɪt/ *vt* agitar. **~ed** *adj* nervioso. **~ion** /-'teɪʃn/ *n* agitación *f*, excitación *f*. **~or** *n* agitador *m*

ago /ə'gəʊ/ *adv*. **a long time ~** hace mucho tiempo. **3 days ~** hace 3 días

agon|ize /'ægənaɪz/ *vi* atormen-

tarse. **~izing** *adj* (*pain*) atroz; (*experience*) angustioso. **~y** *n* dolor *m* (*agudo*); (*mental*) angustia *f*

agree /ə'griː/ *vt* acordar. ● *vi* estar de acuerdo; (*of figures*) concordar; (*get on*) entenderse. □ **~ on** *vt* acordar (date, details). □ **~ with** *vt* (*of food etc*) sentarle bien a. **~able** /ə'grɪəbl/ *adj* agradable. **be ~able** (*willing*) estar de acuerdo. **~d** *adj* (time, place) convenido. **~ment** /-mənt/ *n* acuerdo *m*. **in ~ment** de acuerdo

agricultur|al /ægrɪ'kʌltʃərəl/ *adj* agrícola. **~e** /'ægrɪkʌltʃə(r)/ *n* agricultura *f*

aground /ə'graʊnd/ *adv*. **run ~** (*of ship*) varar, encallar

ahead /ə'hed/ *adv* delante; (*in time*) antes de. **be ~** ir delante

aid /eɪd/ *vt* ayudar. ● *n* ayuda *f*. **in ~ of** a beneficio de

AIDS /eɪdz/ *n* sida *m*

ailment /'eɪlmənt/ *n* enfermedad *f*

aim /eɪm/ *vt* apuntar; (*fig*) dirigir. ● *vi* apuntar; (*fig*) pretender. ● *n* puntería *f*; (*fig*) objetivo *m*. **~less** *adj*, **~lessly** *adv* sin objeto, sin rumbo

air /eə(r)/ *n* aire *m*. **be on the ~** (*Radio, TV*) estar en el aire. **put on ~s** darse aires. ● *vt* airear. **~ bag** *n* (*Auto*) bolsa *f* de aire. **~ base** *n* base *f* aérea. **~borne** *adj* en el aire; (*Mil*) aerotransportado. **~-conditioned** *adj* climatizado, con aire acondicionado. **~ conditioning** *n* aire *m* acondicionado. **~craft** *n* (*pl invar*) avión *m*. **~craft carrier** *n* portaaviones *m*. **~field** *n* aeródromo *m*. **A~ Force** *n* fuerzas *fpl* aéreas. **~ freshener** *n* ambientador *m*. **~gun** *n* escopeta *f* de aire comprimido. **~ hostess** *n* azafata f, aeromoza f (LAm). ~**line** n línea f aérea. ~**mail** n correo m aéreo. ~**plane** n (Amer) avión m. ~**port** n aeropuerto m. ~**sick** adj mareado (en un avión). ~**tight** adj hermético. ~ **traffic controller** n controlador m aéreo. ~**y** adj (-ier, -iest) aireado; (manner) desenfadado

aisle /ail/ n nave f lateral; (gangway) pasillo m

ajar /əˈdʒɑː(r)/ adj entreabierto

alarm /əˈlɑːm/ n alarma f. ●vt asustar. ~**clock** n despertador m. ~**ist** n alarmista m & f

Albania /ælˈbeɪnɪə/ n Albania f. ~**n** adj & n albanés (m)

albatross /ˈælbətrɒs/ n albatros m

album /ˈælbəm/ n álbum m

alcohol /ˈælkəhɒl/ n alcohol m. ~**ic** /-ˈhɒlɪk/ adj & n alcohólico (m)

alcove /ˈælkəʊv/ n nicho m

ale /eɪl/ n cerveza f

alert /əˈlɜːt/ adj vivo; (watchful) vigilante. ●n alerta f. on the ~ alerta. ●vt avisar

algebra /ˈældʒɪbrə/ n álgebra f

Algeria /ælˈdʒɪərɪə/ n Argelia f. ~**n** adj & n argelino (m)

alias /ˈeɪlɪəs/ n (pl -ases) alias m. ●adv alias

alibi /ˈælɪbaɪ/ n (pl -is) coartada f

alien /ˈeɪlɪən/ n extranjero m. ●adj ajeno, ~**ate** /-eɪt/ vt enajenar. ~**ation** /-ˈneɪʃn/ n enajenación f

alienat|e /ˈeɪlɪəneɪt/ vt enajenar. ~**ion** /-ˈneɪʃn/ n enajenación f

alight /əˈlaɪt/ adj ardiendo; (light) encendido

align /əˈlaɪn/ vt alinear. ~**ment** n alineación f

alike /əˈlaɪk/ adj parecido, seme-

jante. **look** or **be** ~ parecerse. ●adv de la misma manera

alive /əˈlaɪv/ adj vivo. ~ **with** lleno de

alkali /ˈælkəlaɪ/ n (pl -is) álcali m. ~**ne** adj alcalino

---

all /ɔːl/

● adjective todo, -da; (pl) todos, -das. ~ **day** todo el día. ~ **the windows** todas las ventanas. ~ **four of us went** fuimos los cuatro

● pronoun

····▸ (everything) todo. that's ~ eso es todo. I did ~ I could to persuade her hice todo lo que pude para convencerla

····▸ (after pronoun) todo, -da; (pl) todos, -das. he helped us ~ nos ayudó a todos

····▸ all of todo, -da, (pl) todos, -das. ~ **of the paintings** todos los cuadros. ~ **of the milk** toda la leche

····▸ (in phrases) all in all en general. not at all (in no way) de ninguna manera; (after thanks) de nada, no hay de qué. it's not at ~ bad no está nada mal. I don't like it at ~ no me gusta nada

● adverb

····▸ (completely) completamente. she was ~ alone estaba completamente sola. I got ~ dirty me ensucié todo/toda. I don't know him ~ that well no lo conozco tan bien

····▸ (in scores) the score was one ~ iban empatados uno a uno

····▸ (in phrases) to be all for sth

estar completamente a favor de algo. **to be all in** 🖭 estar rendido

all-around /ɔ:ləˈraʊnd/ adj (Amer) completo

allay /əˈleɪ/ vt aliviar (pain); aquietar (fears etc)

all-clear /ɔ:lˈklɪə(r)/ n fin m de (la) alarma; (permission) visto m bueno

allegation /ælɪˈgeɪʃn/ n alegato m. **~e** /əˈledʒ/ vt alegar. **~ed** adj presunto. **~edly** /-ɪdlɪ/ adv según se dice, supuestamente

allegiance /əˈliːdʒəns/ n lealtad f

allegory /ˈælɪgərɪ/ n alegoría f

allergic /əˈlɜːdʒɪk/ adj alérgico (to a). **~y** /ˈælədʒɪ/ n alergia f

alleviate /əˈliːvɪeɪt/ vt aliviar

alley /ˈælɪ/ (pl -eys) n callejuela f

alliance /əˈlaɪəns/ n alianza f

alligator /ˈælɪgeɪtə(r)/ n caimán m

allocate /ˈæləkeɪt/ vt asignar; (share out) repartir. **~ion** /-ˈkeɪʃn/ n asignación f; (distribution) reparto m

allot /əˈlɒt/ vt (pt allotted) asignar. **~ment** n asignación f; (land) parcela f

allow /əˈlaʊ/ vt permitir; (grant) conceder; (reckon on) prever; (agree) admitir. ◻ **~ for** vt tener en cuenta. **~ance** /əˈlaʊəns/ n concesión f; (pension) pensión f; (Com) rebaja f. **make ~ances for** ser indulgente con (person); (take into account) tener en cuenta

alloy /ˈælɔɪ/ n aleación f

all: **~ right** adj & adv bien. ● int ¡vale!, ¡okey! (esp LAm), ¡órale! (Mex). **~round** adj completo

allusion /əˈluːʒn/ n alusión f

ally /ˈælaɪ/ n aliado m. ● /əˈlaɪ/ vt. **~ o.s.** aliarse (with con)

almighty /ɔːlˈmaɪtɪ/ adj todopoderoso

almond /ˈɑːmənd/ n almendra f

almost /ˈɔːlməʊst/ adv casi

alone /əˈləʊn/ adj solo. ● adv sólo, solamente

along /əˈlɒŋ/ prep por, a lo largo de. ● adv. **~ with** junto con. **all ~** todo el tiempo. **come ~** venga. **~side** /-ˈsaɪd/ adv (Naut) al costado. ● prep al lado de

aloof /əˈluːf/ adv apartado. ● adj reservado

aloud /əˈlaʊd/ adv en voz alta

alphabet /ˈælfəbet/ n alfabeto m. **~ical** /-ˈbetɪkl/ adj alfabético

Alps /ælps/ npl. **the ~** los Alpes

already /ɔːlˈredɪ/ adv ya

Alsatian /ælˈseɪʃn/ n pastor m alemán

also /ˈɔːlsəʊ/ adv también; (moreover) además

altar /ˈɔːltə(r)/ n altar m

alter /ˈɔːltə(r)/ vt cambiar. ● vi cambiarse. **~ation** /-ˈreɪʃn/ n modificación f; (to garment) arreglo m

alternate /ɔːlˈtɜːnət/ adj alterno; (Amer) see **ALTERNATIVE**. ● /ˈɔːltəneɪt/ vt/i alternar. **~ly** /ɔːlˈtɜːnətlɪ/ adv alternativamente

alternative /ɔːlˈtɜːnətɪv/ adj alternativo. n alternativa f. **~ly** adv en cambio, por otra parte

although /ɔːlˈðəʊ/ conj aunque

altitude /ˈæltɪtjuːd/ n altitud f

altogether /ɔːltəˈɡeðə(r)/ adv completamente; (on the whole) en total

aluminium /æljʊˈmɪnɪəm/, **aluminum** /əˈluːmɪnəm/ (Amer) n aluminio m a **always** /'ɔ:lweɪz/ adv siempre

am /æm/ see BE

a.m. abbr (= ante meridiem) de la mañana

amalgamate /ə'mælgəmeɪt/ vt amalgamar. • vi amalgamarse

amass /ə'mæs/ vt acumular

amateur /'æmətə(r)/ adj & n amateur (m & f). **~ish** adj (pej) torpe, chapucero

amaze /ə'meɪz/ vt asombrar. **~ed** adj asombrado, estupefacto. be **~ed at** quedarse asombrado de, asombrarse de. **~ement** n asombro m. **~ing** adj increíble

ambassador /æm'bæsədə(r)/ n embajador m

ambigu|ity /æmbɪ'gju:əti/ n ambigüedad f. **~ous** /æm'bɪgjuəs/ adj ambiguo

ambiti|on /æm'bɪʃn/ n ambición f. **~ous** /-ʃəs/ adj ambicioso

ambivalent /æm'bɪvələnt/ adj ambivalente

amble /'æmbl/ vi andar despacio, andar sin prisa

ambulance /'æmbjʊləns/ n ambulancia f

ambush /'æmbʊʃ/ n emboscada f. • vt tender una emboscada a

amen /ɑː'men/ int amén

amend /ə'mend/ vt enmendar. **~ment** n enmienda f. **~s** npl. make **~s** reparar

amenities /ə'mi:nətiz/ npl servicios mpl; (of hotel, club) instalaciones fpl

America /ə'merɪkə/ n (continent) América; (North America) Estados mpl Unidos, Norteamérica f. **~n** adj & n americano (m); (North American) estadounidense (m & f), norteamericano (m). **~nism** n americanismo m

American dream El *i* sueño americano se basa en la idea de que cualquier persona en los Estados Unidos puede prosperar mediante el trabajo duro. Para los inmigrantes y las minorías, el concepto abarca la libertad y la igualdad de derechos.

amiable /'eɪmɪəbl/ adj simpático

amicable /'æmɪkəbl/ adj amistoso

amid(st) /ə'mɪd(st)/ prep entre, en medio de

ammonia /ə'məʊnɪə/ n amoníaco m, amoniaco m

ammunition /æmjʊ'nɪʃn/ n municiones fpl

amnesty /'æmnəsti/ n amnistía f

amok /ə'mɒk/ adv. run **~** volverse loco

among(st) /ə'mʌŋ(st)/ prep entre

amount /ə'maʊnt/ n cantidad f; (total) total m, suma f. □ **~ to** vt sumar; (fig) equivaler a, significar

amp(ere) /'æmp(eə(r))/ n amperio m

amphibi|an /æm'fɪbɪən/ n anfibio m. **~ous** /-əs/ adj anfibio

amphitheatre /'æmfɪθɪətə(r)/ n anfiteatro m

ampl|e /'æmpl/ adj (-er, -est) amplio; (enough) suficiente; (plentiful) abundante. **~y** adv ampliamente, bastante

amplif|ier /'æmplɪfaɪə(r)/ n amplificador m. **~y** /'æmplɪfaɪ/ vt amplificar

amputat|e /'æmpjʊteɪt/ vt amputar. **~ion** /-'teɪʃn/ n amputación f

amus|e /ə'mju:z/ vt divertir. **~ed** adj (expression) divertido. keep s.o. **~ed** entretener a uno. **~ement** n diversión f. **~ing** adj divertido

an /ən, æn/ *see* A

anaemi|a /ə'ni:mɪə/ n anemia f. **~c** *adj* anémico

anaesthe|tic /ænɪs'θetɪk/ n anestésico m. **~tist** /ə'ni:sθitɪst/ n anestesista m & f

anagram /'ænəgræm/ n anagrama m

analogy /ə'nælədʒɪ/ n analogía f

analy|se /'ænəlaɪz/ vt analizar. **~sis** /ə'næləsɪs/ n (pl -ses /-siːz/) análisis m. **~st** /'ænəlɪst/ n analista m & f. **~tic(al)** /ænə'lɪtɪk(əl)/ adj analítico

anarch|ist /'ænəkɪst/ n anarquista m & f. **~y** n anarquía f

anatom|ical /ænə'tɒmɪkl/ adj anatómico. **~y** /ə'nætəmɪ/ n anatomía f

ancest|or /'ænsestə(r)/ n antepasado m. **~ral** /-'sestrəl/ adj ancestral. **~ry** /'ænsestrɪ/ n ascendencia f

anchor /'æŋkə(r)/ n ancla f. ● vt anclar; (fig) sujetar. ● vi anclar. **~man** n (on TV) presentador m. **~woman** n (on TV) presentadora f

ancient /'eɪnʃənt/ adj antiguo, viejo

ancillary /æn'sɪlərɪ/ adj auxiliar

and /ənd, ænd/ conj y; (before i- and hi-) e. bread **~** butter pan m con mantequilla. go **~** see him vete a verlo. more **~** more cada vez más. try **~** come trata de venir

anecdot|al /ænɪk'dəʊtl/ adj anecdótico. **~e** /'ænɪkdəʊt/ n anécdota f

anew /ə'njuː/ adv de nuevo

angel /'eɪndʒl/ n ángel m. **~ic** /æn'dʒelɪk/ adj angélico

anger /'æŋgə(r)/ n ira f. ● vt enfa-

dar, (esp LAm) enojar

angle /'æŋgl/ n ángulo m; (fig) punto m de vista. **~r** /'æŋglə(r)/ n pescador m

Anglican /'æŋglɪkən/ adj & n anglicano (m)

angr|ily /'æŋgrɪlɪ/ adv con enfado, (esp LAm) con enojo. **~y** /'æŋgrɪ/ adj (-ier, -iest) enfadado, (esp LAm) enojado. get **~y** enfadarse, enojarse (esp LAm)

anguish /'æŋgwɪʃ/ n angustia f

animal /'ænɪməl/ adj & n animal (m)

animat|e /'ænɪmeɪt/ vt animar. **~ion** /-'meɪʃn/ n animación f

animosity /ænɪ'mɒsətɪ/ n animosidad f

ankle /'æŋkl/ n tobillo m. **~ boot** botín m. **~ sock** calcetín m corto

annexe /'æneks/ n anexo m

annihilat|e /ə'naɪəleɪt/ vt aniquilar. **~ion** /-'leɪʃn/ n aniquilación f

anniversary /ænɪ'vɜːsərɪ/ n aniversario m

announce /ə'naʊns/ vt anunciar, comunicar. **~ment** n anuncio m; (official) comunicado m. **~r** n (Radio, TV) locutor m

annoy /ə'nɔɪ/ vt molestar. **~ance** n molestia m. **~ed** adj enfadado, enojado (LAm). **~ing** adj molesto

annual /'ænjʊəl/ adj anual. n anuario m. **~ly** adv cada año

annul /ə'nʌl/ vt (pt annulled) anular. **~ment** n anulación f

anonymous /ə'nɒnɪməs/ adj anónimo

anorak /'ænəræk/ n anorac m

another /ə'nʌðə(r)/ adj & pron otro. **~** 10 minutes 10 minutos más. in **~** way de otra manera. one **~** el uno al otro; (pl) unos a otros

answer /'ɑːnsə(r)/ n respuesta f; (solution) solución f. • vt contestar; escuchar, oír (prayer). ~ **the door** abrir la puerta. • vi contestar. □ ~ **back** vi contestar. □ ~ **for** vt ser responsable de. ~**able** adj responsable. ~**ing machine** n contestador m automático

ant /ænt/ n hormiga f

antagoni|sm /æn'tægənɪzəm/ n antagonismo m. ~**stic** /-'nɪstɪk/ adj antagónico, opuesto. ~**ze** /æn'tægənaɪz/ vt provocar la enemistad de

Antarctic /æn'tɑːktɪk/ adj antártico. • n the ~ la región antártica

antelope /'æntɪləʊp/ n antílope m

antenatal /'æntɪneɪtl/ adj prenatal

antenna /æn'tenə/ n (pl -nae /-niː/) (of insect etc) n antena f; (pl -nas) (of radio, TV) antena f

anthem /'ænθəm/ n himno m

anthology /æn'θɒlədʒɪ/ n antología f

anthrax /'ænθræks/ n ántrax m

anthropolog|ist /ænθrə'pɒlədʒɪst/ n antropólogo m. ~**y** n antropología f

anti-... /ænti/ pref anti... ~**aircraft** /-'eəkrɑːft/ adj antiaéreo

antibiotic /ˌæntɪbaɪ'ɒtɪk/ adj & n antibiótico (m)

anticipat|e /æn'tɪsɪpeɪt/ vt anticiparse a; (foresee) prever; (forestall) prevenir. ~**ion** /-'peɪʃn/ n (foresight) previsión f; (expectation) expectativa f

anti: ~**climax** /-'klaɪmæks/ n decepción f. ~**clockwise** /-'klɒkwaɪz/ adv & adj en sentido contrario al de las agujas del reloj

antidote /'æntɪdəʊt/ n antídoto m

antifreeze /'æntɪfriːz/ n anticongelante m

antiperspirant /ænti'pɜːspɪrənt/ n antitranspirante m

antiquated /'æntɪkweɪtɪd/ adj anticuado

antique /æn'tiːk/ adj antiguo. • n antigüedad f. ~ **dealer** anticuario m. ~ **shop** tienda f de antigüedades

antiquity /æn'tɪkwətɪ/ n antigüedad f

anti: ~**septic** /-'septɪk/ adj & n antiséptico (m). ~**social** /-'səʊʃl/ adj antisocial

antlers /'æntləz/ npl cornamenta f

anus /'eɪnəs/ n ano m

anvil /'ænvɪl/ n yunque m

anxi|ety /æŋ'zaɪətɪ/ n ansiedad f; (worry) inquietud f; (eagerness) anhelo m. ~**ous** /'æŋkʃəs/ adj inquieto; (eager) deseoso. ~**ously** adv con inquietud; (eagerly) con impaciencia

any /'enɪ/ adj algún; (negative) ningún m; (whatever) cualquier; (every) todo. **at** ~ **moment** en cualquier momento. **have you** ~ **wine?** ¿tienes vino? • pron alguno; (negative) ninguno. **have we** ~? ¿tenemos algunos? **not** ~ ninguno. • adv (a little) un poco, algo. **is it** ~ **better?** ¿está algo mejor?

anybody /'enɪbɒdɪ/ pron alguien; (after negative) nadie. ~ **can do it** cualquiera puede hacerlo

anyhow /'enɪhaʊ/ adv de todas formas; (in spite of all) a pesar de todo; (badly) de cualquier manera

anyone /'enɪwʌn/ pron see **ANYBODY**

anything /'enɪθɪŋ/ pron algo; (whatever) cualquier cosa; (after negative) nada. ~ **but** todo menos

anyway /'enɪweɪ/ adv de todas formas

anywhere /'enɪweə(r)/ adv en cualquier parte; (after negative) en ningún sitio. ~ **else** en cualquier otro lugar. ~ **you go** dondequiera que vayas

apart /ə'pɑːt/ adv aparte; (separated) separado. ~ **from** aparte de. come ~ romperse. take ~ desmontar

apartheid /ə'pɑːtheɪt/ n apartheid m

apartment /ə'pɑːtmənt/ n (Amer) apartamento m, piso m. ~ **building** n (Amer) edificio m de apartamentos, casa f de pisos

apath|etic /æpə'θetɪk/ adj apático. ~**y** /'æpəθɪ/ n apatía f

ape /eɪp/ n mono m. • vt imitar

aperitif /ə'peratɪf/ n aperitivo m

aperture /'æpətʃʊə(r)/ n abertura f

apex /'eɪpeks/ n ápice m

aphrodisiac /æfrə'dɪzɪæk/ adj & n afrodisíaco (m), afrodisíaco (m)

apologetic /əpɒlə'dʒetɪk/ adj lleno de disculpas. be ~**etic** disculparse. ~**ize** /ə'pɒlədʒaɪz/ vi disculparse (for de). ~**y** /ə'pɒlədʒɪ/ n disculpa f

apostle /ə'pɒsl/ n apóstol m

apostrophe /ə'pɒstrəfɪ/ n apóstrofo m

appal /ə'pɔːl/ vt (pt appalled) horrorizar. ~**ling** adj espantoso

apparatus /æpə'reɪtəs/ n aparato m

apparel /ə'pærəl/ n (Amer) ropa f

apparent /ə'pærənt/ adj aparente; (clear) evidente. ~**ly** adv por lo visto

apparition /æpə'rɪʃn/ n aparición f

appeal /ə'piːl/ vi apelar; (attract) atraer. • n llamamiento m; (attraction) atractivo m; (Jurid) apelación f. ~**ing** adj atrayente

appear /ə'pɪə(r)/ vi aparecer; (seem) parecer; (in court) comparecer. ~**ance** n aparición f; (aspect) aspecto m; (in court) comparecencia f

appease /ə'piːz/ vt aplacar; (pacify) apaciguar

append /ə'pend/ vt adjuntar

appendicitis /əpendɪ'saɪtɪs/ n apendicitis f

appendix /ə'pendɪks/ n (pl -ices -ɪsiːz/) (of book) apéndice m. (pl -ixes) (organ) apéndice m

appetite /'æpɪtaɪt/ n apetito m

applau|d /ə'plɔːd/ vt/i aplaudir. ~**se** /ə'plɔːz/ n aplausos mpl. round of ~**se** aplauso m

apple /'æpl/ n manzana f. ~ **tree** n manzano m

appliance /ə'plaɪəns/ n aparato m. electrical ~ electrodoméstico m

applic|able /'æplɪkəbl/ adj aplicable; (relevant) pertinente. ~**ant** /'æplɪkənt/ n candidato m, solicitante m & f. ~**ation** /æplɪ'keɪʃn/ n aplicación f; (request) solicitud f. ~**ation form** formulario m (de solicitud)

appl|ied /ə'plaɪd/ adj aplicado. ~**y** /ə'plaɪ/ vt aplicar; vi aplicarse; (ask) presentar una solicitud. ~**y for** solicitar (job etc)

appoint /ə'pɔɪnt/ vt nombrar; (fix) señalar. ~**ment** n cita f

apprais|al /ə'preɪzl/ n evaluación f. ~**e** /ə'preɪz/ vt evaluar

appreciable /ə'priːʃəbl/ adj (considerable) considerable

appreciat|e /ə'priːʃɪeɪt/ vt (value)

apreciar; (*understand*) comprender; (*be grateful for*) agradecer. ~ion /-'eɪʃn/ n aprecio m; (*gratitude*) agradecimiento m. ~ive /ə'priːʃɪətɪv/ adj agradecido

apprehen|sion /æprɪ'henʃn/ n (*fear*) recelo f. ~sive adj aprensivo

apprentice /ə'prentɪs/ n aprendiz m. ● vt. be ~d to s.o. estar de aprendiz con uno. ~ship n aprendizaje m

approach /ə'prəʊtʃ/ vt acercarse a. ● vi acercarse. ● n acercamiento m; (*to problem*) enfoque m; (*access*) acceso m

appropriate /ə'prəʊprɪət/ adj apropiado. ● /ə'prəʊprɪeɪt/ vt apropiarse de. ~ly /-ətlɪ/ adv apropiadamente

approv|al /ə'pruːvl/ n aprobación f. on ~al a prueba. ~e /ə'pruːv/ vt/i aprobar. ~ingly adv con aprobación

approximat|e /ə'prɒksɪmət/ adj aproximado. ● /ə'prɒksɪmeɪt/ vt aproximarse a. ~ely /-ətlɪ/ adv aproximadamente. ~ion /-'meɪʃn/ n aproximación f

apricot /'eɪprɪkɒt/ n albaricoque m, chabacano m (Mex)

April /'eɪprəl/ n abril m. ~ fool! ¡incentón!

apron /'eɪprən/ n delantal m

apt /æpt/ adj apropiado. be ~ to tener tendencia a. ~itude /'æptɪtjuːd/ n aptitud f. ~ly adv acertadamente

aquarium /ə'kweərɪəm/ n (pl -ums) acuario m

Aquarius /ə'kweərɪəs/ n Acuario m

aquatic /ə'kwætɪk/ adj acuático

aqueduct /'ækwɪdʌkt/ n acueducto m

Arab /'ærəb/ adj & n árabe (m & f). ~ian /ə'reɪbɪən/ adj árabe. ~ic /'ærəbɪk/ adj & n árabe (m). ~ic numerals npl números mpl arábigos

arable /'ærəbl/ adj cultivable

arbitrary /'ɑːbɪtrərɪ/ adj arbitrario

arbitrat|e /'ɑːbɪtreɪt/ vi arbitrar. ~ion /-'treɪʃn/ n arbitraje m. ~or n árbitro m

arc /ɑːk/ n arco m

arcade /ɑː'keɪd/ n arcada f; (*around square*) soportales mpl; (*shops*) galería f

arch /ɑːtʃ/ n arco m. ● vt arquear. ● vi arquearse

archaeolog|ical /ɑːkɪə'lɒdʒɪkl/ adj arqueológico. ~ist /ɑːkɪ'ɒlədʒɪst/ n arqueólogo m. ~y /ɑːkɪ'ɒlədʒɪ/ n arqueología f

archaic /ɑː'keɪɪk/ adj arcaico

archbishop /ɑːtʃ'bɪʃəp/ n arzobispo m

archer /'ɑːtʃə(r)/ n arquero m. ~y n tiro m con arco

architect /'ɑːkɪtekt/ n arquitecto m. ~ure /-tʃə(r)/ n arquitectura f. ~ural /-'tektʃərəl/ adj arquitectónico

archives /'ɑːkaɪvz/ npl archivo m

archway /'ɑːtʃweɪ/ n arco m

Arctic /'ɑːktɪk/ adj ártico. ● n. the ~ el Ártico

ard|ent /'ɑːdənt/ adj fervoroso; (*supporter, lover*) apasionado. ~our /-ədə(r)/ n fervor m; (*love*) pasión f

arduous /'ɑːdjʊəs/ adj arduo

are /ɑː(r)/ see BE

area /'eərɪə/ n (Math) superficie f; (*of country*) zona f; (*of city*) barrio m

arena /ə'riːnə/ n arena f; (*scene of activity*) ruedo m

aren't /ɑːnt/ = are not

Argentin|a /ɑ:dʒən'ti:nə/ n Argentina f. **~ian** /-'tɪnɪən/ adj & n argentino (m)

argu|able /'ɑ:gjʊəbl/ adj discutible. **~e** /'ɑ:gju:/ vi discutir; (reason) razonar. **~ment** /'ɑ:gjʊmənt/ n disputa f; (reasoning) argumento m. **~mentative** /ɑ:gjʊ'mentətɪv/ adj discutidor

arid /'ærɪd/ adj árido

Aries /'eəri:z/ n Aries m

arise /ə'raɪz/ vi (pt arose, pp arisen) surgir (from de)

aristocra|cy /ærɪ'stɒkrəsɪ/ n aristocracia f. **~t** /'ærɪstəkræt/ n aristócrata m & f. **~tic** /-'krætɪk/ adj aristocrático

arithmetic /ə'rɪθmətɪk/ n aritmética f

ark /ɑ:k/ n (Relig) arca f

arm /ɑ:m/ n brazo m; (of garment) manga f. **~s** npl armas fpl. ● vt armar

armament /'ɑ:məmənt/ n armamento m

arm: **~band** n brazalete m. **~chair** n sillón m

armed /ɑ:md/ adj armado. **~ robbery** n robo m a mano armada

armful /'ɑ:mfʊl/ n brazada f

armour /'ɑ:mə(r)/ n armadura f. **~ed** /'ɑ:məd/ adj blindado. **~y** /'ɑ:mərɪ/ n arsenal m

armpit /'ɑ:mpɪt/ n sobaco m, axila f

army /'ɑ:mɪ/ n ejército m

aroma /ə'rəʊmə/ n aroma m

arose /ə'rəʊz/ see ARISE

around /ə'raʊnd/ adv alrededor. (near) cerca. all **~** por todas partes. ● prep alrededor de; (with time) a eso de

arouse /ə'raʊz/ vt despertar

arrange /ə'reɪndʒ/ vt arreglar;

(fix) fijar. **~ment** n arreglo m; (agreement) acuerdo m. **~ments** npl (plans) preparativos mpl

arrears /ə'rɪəz/ npl atrasos mpl. in **~** atrasado en el pago (with de)

arrest /ə'rest/ vt detener. ● n detención f. under **~** detenido

arriv|al /ə'raɪvl/ n llegada f. new **~al** recién llegado m. **~e** /ə'raɪv/ vi llegar

arrogan|ce /'ærəgəns/ n arrogancia f. **~t** adj arrogante. **~tly** adv con arrogancia

arrow /'ærəʊ/ n flecha f

arse /ɑ:s/ n (vulgar) culo m

arsenal /'ɑ:sənl/ n arsenal m

arsenic /'ɑ:snɪk/ n arsénico m

arson /'ɑ:sn/ n incendio m provocado. **~ist** n incendiario m

art¹ /ɑ:t/ n arte m. A**~s** npl (Univ) Filosofía y Letras fpl. fine **~s** bellas artes fpl

art² /ɑ:t/ (old use, with thou) see ARE

artery /'ɑ:tərɪ/ n arteria f

art gallery n museo m de arte, pinacoteca f; (commercial) galería f de arte

arthritis /ɑ:'θraɪtɪs/ n artritis f

article /'ɑ:tɪkl/ n artículo m. **~ of clothing** prenda f de vestir

articulat|e /ɑ:'tɪkjʊlət/ adj (utterance) articulado; (person) que sabe expresarse. ● /ɑ:'tɪkjʊleɪt/ vt/i articular. **~ed lorry** n camión m articulado. **~ion** /-'leɪʃn/ n articulación f

artificial /ɑ:tɪ'fɪʃl/ adj artificial. **~ respiration** respiración f artificial

artillery /ɑ:'tɪlərɪ/ n artillería f

artist /'ɑ:tɪst/ n artista m & f. **~tic** /ɑ:'tɪstɪk/ adj artístico. **~ry** /'ɑ:tɪstrɪ/ n arte m, habilidad f

as /æz, əz/ adv & conj como; (since) ya que; (while) mientras. **~ big**

tan grande como. ~ **far** ~ (*distance*) hasta; (*qualitative*) en cuanto a. ~ **far** ~ **I** (*know* que yo sepa. ~ **if** como si. ~ **long** ~ mientras. ~ **much** ~ tanto como. ~ **soon** ~ tan pronto como. ~ **well** también

asbestos /æz'bestos/ n amianto m, asbesto m

ascen|d /ə'send/ vt/i subir. **A~sion** /ə'senʃn/ n. the **A~sion** la Ascensión. ~**t** /ə'sent/ n subida f

ascertain /æsə'teɪn/ vt averiguar

ash /æʃ/ n ceniza f. ● n. ~ (*tree*) fresno m

ashamed /ə'ʃeɪmd/ adj avergonzado (of de). be ~ of s.o. avergonzarse de uno

ashore /ə'ʃɔː(r)/ adv a tierra. go ~ desembarcar

ash: ~**tray** n cenicero m. **A~ Wednesday** n Miércoles m de Ceniza

Asia /'eɪʃə/ n Asia f. ~**n** adj & n asiático (m). ~**tic** /-ɪ'ætɪk/ adj asiático

aside /ə'saɪd/ adv a un lado. ● n (*in theatre*) aparte m

ask /ɑːsk/ vt pedir; hacer (*question*); (*invite*) invitar. ~ **about** enterarse de. ~ **s.o. to do something** pedirle a uno que haga algo. □ ~ **after** vt preguntar por. □ ~ **for** vt. ~ **for help** pedir ayuda. ~ **for trouble** buscarse problemas. □ ~ **in** vt. ~ **s.o. in** invitar a uno a pasar

askew /ə'skjuː/ adv & adj torcido

asleep /ə'sliːp/ adv & adj dormido. **fall** ~ dormirse

asparagus /ə'spærəgəs/ n espárrago m

aspect /'æspekt/ n aspecto m

asphalt /'æsfælt/ n asfalto m. ● vt

asfaltar

aspir|ation /æspə'reɪʃn/ n aspiración f. ~**e** /əs'paɪə(r)/ vi aspirar

aspirin /'æsprɪn/ n aspirina f

ass /æs/ n asno m; (*fig, fam*) imbécil m; (*Amer vulgar*) culo m

assassin /ə'sæsɪn/ n asesino m. ~**ate** /-eɪt/ vt asesinar. ~**ation** /-'eɪʃn/ n asesinato m

assault /ə'sɔːlt/ n (*Mil*) ataque m; (*Jurid*) atentado m. ● vt asaltar

assemble /ə'sembl/ vt reunir; (*Mec*) montar. ● vi reunirse. ~**y** n reunión f; (*Pol etc*) asamblea f. ~**y line** n línea f de montaje

assent /ə'sent/ n asentimiento m. ● vi asentir

assert /ə'sɜːt/ vt afirmar; hacer valer (*one's rights*). ~**ion** /-ʃn/ n afirmación f. ~**ive** adj positivo, firme

assess /ə'ses/ vt evaluar; (*determine*) determinar; fijar (*tax etc*). ~**ment** n evaluación f

asset /'æset/ n (*advantage*) ventaja f. ~**s** npl (*Com*) bienes mpl

assign /ə'saɪn/ vt asignar; (*appoint*) nombrar. ~**ment** n asignación f; (*mission*) misión f; (*task*) función f; (*for school*) trabajo m

assimilate /ə'sɪmɪleɪt/ vt asimilar. ● vi asimilarse

assist /ə'sɪst/ vt/i ayudar. ~**ance** n ayuda f. ~**ant** n ayudante m & f; (*shop*) dependienta f, dependiente m. ● adj auxiliar, adjunto

associat|e /ə'səʊʃɪeɪt/ vt asociar. ● vi asociarse. ● /ə'səʊʃɪət/ adj asociado. ● n colega m & f; (*Com*) socio m. ~**ion** /-'eɪʃn/ n asociación f.

assort|ed /ə'sɔːtɪd/ adj surtido. ~**ment** n surtido m

assum|e /ə'sjuːm/ vt suponer; tomar (*power, attitude*); asumir (role, burden). **~ption** /əˈsʌmpʃn/ n suposición f

assur|ance /əˈʃʊərəns/ n seguridad f; (insurance) seguro m. **~e** /əˈʃʊə(r)/ vt asegurar. **~ed** adj seguro

asterisk /ˈæstərɪsk/ n asterisco m

asthma /ˈæsmə/ n asma f. **~tic** /-ˈmætɪk/ adj & n asmático (m)

astonish /əˈstɒnɪʃ/ vt asombrar. **~ed** adj asombrado. **~ing** adj asombroso. **~ment** n asombro m

astound /əˈstaʊnd/ vt asombrar. **~ed** adj atónito. **~ing** adj increíble

astray /əˈstreɪ/ adv. go **~** extraviarse. lead **~** llevar por mal camino

astrology /əˈstrɒlədʒɪ/ n astrología f

astronaut /ˈæstrənɔːt/ n astronauta m & f

astronom|er /əˈstrɒnəmə(r)/ n astrónomo m. **~ical** /æstrəˈnɒmɪkl/ adj astronómico. **~y** /əˈstrɒnəmɪ/ n astronomía f

astute /əˈstjuːt/ adj astuto

asylum /əˈsaɪləm/ n asilo m. lunatic **~** manicomio m. **~ seeker** n solicitante m & f de asilo

at /æt/ preposition

••••▸ (location) en. she's at the office está en la oficina. at home en casa. call me at the office llámame a la oficina

For translations of phrases such as **at the top, at the front of, at the back of** see entries **top, front** etc

••••▸ (at the house of) en casa

de. I'll be at Rachel's estaré en casa de Rachel

••••▸ (Comput: @) arroba f

••••▸ (talking about time) at 7 o'clock a las siete. **at night** por la noche, de noche, en la noche (LAm). **at Christmas** en Navidad

••••▸ (talking about age) a. **at six (years of age)** a los seis años

••••▸ (with measurements, numbers etc) a. **at 60 miles an hour** a 60 millas por hora. **at a depth of** a una profundidad de. **three at a time** de tres en tres

For translations of phrasal verbs with **at**, such as **look at**, see entries for those verbs

ate /et/ see EAT

atheis|m /ˈeɪθɪɪzəm/ n ateísmo m. **~t** n ateo m

athlet|e /ˈæθliːt/ n atleta m & f. **~ic** /-ˈletɪk/ adj atlético. **~ics** npl atletismo m; (Amer, Sport) deportes mpl

Atlantic /ætˈlæntɪk/ adj atlántico. **●n. the ~ (Ocean)** el (Océano) Atlántico

atlas /ˈætləs/ n atlas m

ATM abbr (= automated teller machine) cajero m automático

atmospher|e /ˈætməsfɪə(r)/ n atmósfera f; (fig) ambiente m. **~ic** /-ˈferɪk/ adj atmosférico

atom /ˈætəm/ n átomo m. **~ic** /əˈtɒmɪk/ adj atómico

atroci|ous /əˈtrəʊʃəs/ adj atroz. **~ty** /əˈtrɒsɪtɪ/ n atrocidad f

attach /əˈtætʃ/ vt sujetar; adjuntar (document etc). **be ~ed to** (be fond of) tener cariño a. **~ment** n (affection) cariño m; (tool)

accesorio m; (to email) archivo m
adjunto

attack /əˈtæk/ n ataque m. ● vt/i
atacar. ∼er n agresor m

attain /əˈteɪn/ vt conseguir. ∼able
adj alcanzable

attempt /əˈtempt/ vt intentar. ● n
tentativa f; (attack) atentado m

attend /əˈtend/ vt asistir a; (escort)
acompañar. ● vi prestar atención.
□ ∼ **to** vt (look after) ocuparse de.
∼ance n asistencia f; (people present) concurrencia f.

atten|tion /əˈtenʃn/ n atención f.
∼tion! (Mil) ¡firmes! pay ∼tion
prestar atención. ∼tive adj atento

attic /ˈætɪk/ n desván m

attire /əˈtaɪə(r)/ n atavío m

attitude /ˈætɪtjuːd/ n postura f

attorney /əˈtɜːnɪ/ n (pl -eys)
(Amer) abogado m

attract /əˈtrækt/ vt atraer. ∼ion
/-ʃn/ n atracción f; (charm) atractivo m. ∼ive adj atractivo; (interesting) atrayente

attribute /əˈtrɪbjuːt/ vt atribuir.
● /ˈætrɪbjuːt/ n atributo m

aubergine /ˈəʊbəʒiːn/ n berenjena f

auction /ˈɔːkʃn/ n subasta f. ● vt
subastar. ∼eer /-əˈnɪə(r)/ n subas-
tador m

audaci|ous /ɔːˈdeɪʃəs/ adj audaz.
∼ty /ɔːˈdæsətɪ/ n audacia f

audible /ˈɔːdəbl/ adj audible

audience /ˈɔːdɪəns/ n (at play,
film) público m; (TV) audiencia f;
(interview) audiencia f

audiovisual /ɔːdɪəʊˈvɪʒuəl/ adj
audiovisual

audit /ˈɔːdɪt/ n revisión f de cuentas. ● vt revisar

audition /ɔːˈdɪʃn/ n audición f.

● vt hacerle una audición a. ● vi dar
una audición (for para)

auditor /ˈɔːdɪtə(r)/ n interventor
m de cuentas

auditorium /ɔːdɪˈtɔːrɪəm/ (pl
-riums or -ria /-rɪə/) n sala f, audi-
torio m

augment /ɔːɡˈment/ vt aumentar

augur /ˈɔːɡə(r)/ vt augurar. it ∼s
well es de buen agüero

August /ˈɔːɡəst/ n agosto m

aunt /ɑːnt/ n tía f

au pair /əʊˈpeə(r)/ n chica f au
pair

aura /ˈɔːrə/ n aura f, halo m

auster|e /ɔːˈstɪə(r)/ adj austero.
∼ity /ɔːˈsterətɪ/ n austeridad f

Australia /ɒˈstreɪlɪə/ n Australia f.
∼n adj & n australiano (m)

Austria /ˈɒstrɪə/ n Austria f. ∼n
adj & n austríaco (m)

authentic /ɔːˈθentɪk/ adj auténtico. ∼ate /-keɪt/ vt autenticar.
∼ity /-ənˈtɪsətɪ/ n autenticidad f

author /ˈɔːθə(r)/ n autor m. ∼ess
/-ɪs/ n autora f

authoritative /ɔːˈθɒrɪtətɪv/ adj
autorizado; (manner) autoritario

authority /ɔːˈθɒrətɪ/ n autoridad
f; (permission) autorización f

authoriz|ation /ɔːθəraɪˈzeɪʃn/ n
autorización f. ∼e /ˈɔːθəraɪz/ vt autorizar

autobiography /ɔːtəʊbaɪˈɒɡrəfɪ/ n autobiografía f

autograph /ˈɔːtəɡrɑːf/ n autógrafo m. ● vt firmar, autografiar

automat|e /ˈɔːtəmeɪt/ vt automa-
tizar. ∼ic /-ˈmætɪk/ adj automático.
∼ion /-ˈmeɪʃn/ n automatización f.
∼on /ɔːˈtɒmətən/ n (pl -tons or -ta
/-tə/) autómata m

automobile /ˈɔːtəməbiːl/ n

(*Amer*) coche *m*, carro *m* (*LAm*), automóvil *m*

autonom|ous /ɔːˈtɒnəməs/ *adj* autónomo. **~y** *n* autonomía *f*

autopsy /ˈɔːtɒpsɪ/ *n* autopsia *f*

autumn /ˈɔːtəm/ *n* otoño *m*. **~al** /ɔːˈtʌmnəl/ *adj* otoñal

auxiliary /ɔːɡˈzɪlɪərɪ/ *adj* & *n* auxiliar (*m* & *f*)

avail /əˈveɪl/ *n*. **to no** ~ inútil

availab|ility /əveɪləˈbɪlətɪ/ *n* disponibilidad *f*. **~le** /əˈveɪləbl/ *adj* disponible

avalanche /ˈævəlɑːnʃ/ *n* avalancha *f*

avaric|e /ˈævərɪs/ *n* avaricia *f*. **~ious** /-ˈrɪʃəs/ *adj* avaro

avenue /ˈævənjuː/ *n* avenida *f*; (*fig*) vía *f*

average /ˈævərɪdʒ/ *n* promedio *m*. **on** ~ por término medio. ● *adj* medio

avers|e /əˈvɜːs/ *adj*. **be** ~**e to** ser reacio a. **~ion** /-ʃn/ *n* repugnancia *f*

avert /əˈvɜːt/ *vt* (*turn away*) apartar; (*ward off*) desviar

aviation /eɪvɪˈeɪʃn/ *n* aviación *f*

avid /ˈævɪd/ *adj* ávido

avocado /ævəˈkɑːdəʊ/ *n* (*pl* -*os*) aguacate *m*

avoid /əˈvɔɪd/ *vt* evitar. **~able** *adj* evitable. **~ance** *n* el evitar

await /əˈweɪt/ *vt* esperar

awake /əˈweɪk/ *vt/i* (*pt* awoke, *pp* awoken) despertar. ● *adj* despierto. **wide** ~ completamente despierto; (*fig*) despabilado. **~n** /əˈweɪkən/ *vt/i* despertar. **~ning** *n* el despertar

award /əˈwɔːd/ *vt* otorgar; (*Jurid*) adjudicar. ● *n* premio *m*; (*Jurid*) adjudicación *f*; (*scholarship*) beca *f*

aware /əˈweə(r)/ *adj*. **be** ~ **of** sth ser consciente de algo, darse cuenta de algo. **~ness** *n* conciencia *f*

awash /əˈwɒʃ/ *adj* inundado

away /əˈweɪ/ *adv* (*absent*) fuera. **far** ~ muy lejos. ● *adj* ~ **match** partido *m* fuera de casa

awe /ɔː/ *n* temor *m*. **~-inspiring** *adj* impresionante. **~some** /-səm/ *adj* imponente

awful /ˈɔːfʊl/ *adj* terrible, malísimo. **feel** ~ sentirse muy mal

awkward /ˈɔːkwəd/ *adj* difícil; (*inconvenient*) inoportuno; (*clumsy*) desmañado; (*embarrassed*) incómodo. **~ness** *n* dificultad *f*; (*discomfort*) molestia *f*; (*clumsiness*) torpeza *f*

awning /ˈɔːnɪŋ/ *n* toldo *m*

awoke /əˈwəʊk/, **awoken** /əˈwəʊkən/ *see* AWAKE

axe /æks/ *n* hacha *f*. ● *vt* (*pres p* axing) cortar con hacha; (*fig*) recortar

axis /ˈæksɪs/ *n* (*pl* axes /-iːz/) eje *m*

axle /ˈæksl/ *n* eje *m*

Bb

BA /biːˈeɪ/ *abbr see* BACHELOR

babble /ˈbæbl/ *vi* balbucir; (*chatter*) parlotear; (*stream*) murmurar.

baboon /bəˈbuːn/ *n* mandril *m*

baby /ˈbeɪbɪ/ *n* niño *m*, bebé *m*. ● **buggy**, **~ carriage** (*Amer*) cochecito *m*. **~ish** /ˈbeɪbɪɪʃ/ *adj* infantil. **~-sit** *vi* cuidar a los niños, hacer de canguro. **~-sitter** *n* baby sitter *m* & *f*, canguro *m* & *f*

bachelor /'bætʃələ(r)/ *n* soltero *m*. B~ **of Arts (BA)** licenciado *m* en filosofía y letras. B~ **of Science (BSc)** licenciado *m* en ciencias

back /bæk/ *n* espalda *f*; (of car) parte *f* trasera; (of chair) respaldo *m*; (of cloth) revés *m*; (of house) parte *f* de atrás; (of animal, book) lomo *m*; (of hand, document) dorso *m*; (football) defensa *m* & *f*. in the ~ **of beyond** en el quinto infierno. ● *adj* trasero. the ~ **door** la puerta trasera. ● *adv* atrás; (returned) de vuelta. ● *vt* apoyar; (betting) apostar a; (car) dar marcha atrás a (car). ● *vi* retroceder; (car) dar marcha atrás. □ ~ **down** *vi* volverse atrás. □ ~ **out** *vi* retirarse. □ ~ **up** *vt* apoyar; (Comp) hacer una copia de seguridad de. ~**ache** *n* dolor *m* de espalda. ~**bone** *n* columna *f* vertebral; (fig) pilar *m*. ~**date** /-'deɪt/ *vt* antedatar. ~**er** *n* partidario *m*; (Com) financiador *m*. ~**fire** /-'faɪə(r)/ *vi* petardear; (fig) fallar. his **plan** ~**fired on him** le salió el tiro por la culata. ~**ground** *n* fondo *m*; (environment) antecedentes *mpl*. ~**hand** *n* (Sport) revés *m*. ~**ing** *n* apoyo *m*. ~**lash** *n* reacción *f*; (fig) reacción *f* adversa *mpl*. ~**log** *n* atrasos *mpl*. ~**side** /-'saɪd/ *n* 🄸 trasero *m*. ~**stage** /-'steɪdʒ/ *adj* de bastidores. ● *adv* entre bastidores. ~**stroke** *n* (tennis etc) revés *m*; (swimming) estilo *m* espalda, estilo *m* dorso (Mex). ~**up** *n* apoyo *m*; (Comp) copia *f* de seguridad. ~**ward** /-wəd/ *adj* (step etc) hacia atrás; (retarded) retrasado; (undeveloped) atrasado. ● *adv* (Amer) see **BACKWARDS**. ~**wards** *adv* hacia atrás; (fall) de espaldas; (back to front) al revés. go ~**wards and forwards** ir de acá para allá. ~**water** *n* agua *f* estan-

cada; (fig) lugar *m* apartado

bacon /'beɪkən/ *n* tocino *m*

bacteria /bæk'tɪərɪə/ *npl* bacterias *fpl*

bad /bæd/ *adj* (**worse, worst**) malo, (before masculine singular noun) mal; (serious) grave; (harmful) nocivo; (language) indecente. **feel** ~ sentirse mal

bade /beɪd/ see **BID**

badge /bædʒ/ *n* distintivo *m*, chapa *f*

badger /'bædʒə(r)/ *n* tejón *m*. ● *vt* acosar

bad: ~**ly** *adv* mal; **want** ~**ly** desear muchísimo. ~**ly injured** gravemente herido. ~**ly off** mal de dinero. ~**mannered** /-'mænəd/ *adj* mal educado

badminton /'bædmɪntən/ *n* bádminton *m*

bad-tempered /bæd'tempəd/ *adj* (always) de mal carácter; (temporarily) de mal humor

baffle /'bæfl/ *vt* desconcertar. ~**d** *adj* perplejo

bag /bæg/ *n* bolsa *f*; (handbag) bolso *m*. ● *vt* (*pt* **bagged**) ensacar; (take) coger (esp Spain), agarrar (LAm). ~**s** *npl* (luggage) equipaje *m*

baggage /'bægɪdʒ/ *n* equipaje *m*. ~ **room** *n* (Amer) consigna *f*

baggy /'bægɪ/ *adj* (clothes) holgado

bagpipes /'bægpaɪps/ *npl* gaita *f*

baguette /bæ'get/ *n* baguette *f*

bail[1] /beɪl/ *n* fianza *f*. ● *vt* poner en libertad bajo fianza. ~ **s.o. out** pagar la fianza a uno

bail[2] *vt*. ~ **out** (Naut) achicar

bait /beɪt/ *n* cebo *m*

bak|e /beɪk/ *vt* cocer al horno. ● *vi* cocerse. ~**er** *n* panadero *m*. ~**ery**

n panadería *f*

balance /'bæləns/ *n* equilibrio *m*; (Com) balance *m*; (sum) saldo *m*; (scales) balanza *f*; (remainder) resto *m*. ●*vt* equilibrar (load); mantener en equilibrio (object); nivelar (budget). ●*vi* equilibrarse; (Com) cuadrar. ~d *adj* equilibrado

balcony /'bælkənɪ/ *n* balcón *m*

bald /bɔːld/ *adj* (-er, -est) calvo, pelón (Mex)

bale /beɪl/ *n* bala *f*, fardo *m*. ●*vi.* ~ out lanzarse en paracaídas

Balearic /bælɪ'ærɪk/ *adj.* the ~ Islands las Islas *fpl* Baleares

ball /bɔːl/ *n* bola *f*; (tennis etc) pelota *f*; (football etc) balón *m*, pelota *f* (esp LAm); (of yarn) ovillo *m*; (dance) baile *m*

ballad /'bæləd/ *n* balada *f*

ballast /'bæləst/ *n* lastre *m*

ball bearing *n* cojinete *m* de bolas

ballerina /bælə'riːnə/ *f* bailarina *f*

ballet /'bæleɪ/ *n* ballet *m*. ~ dancer *n* bailarín *m* de ballet, bailarina *f* de ballet

balloon /bə'luːn/ *n* globo *m*

ballot /'bælət/ *n* votación *f*. ~ box *n* urna *f*. ~ paper *n* papeleta *f*.

ball: ~point. ~point (pen) bolígrafo *m*, pluma *f* atómica (Mex). ~room *n* salón *m* de baile

bamboo /bæm'buː/ *n* bambú *m*

ban /bæn/ *vt* (*pt* banned) prohibir. ~ s.o. from sth prohibir algo a uno. ●*n* prohibición *f*

banal /bə'nɑːl/ *adj* banal. ~ity /-'nælətɪ/ *n* banalidad *f*

banana /bə'nɑːnə/ *n* plátano *m*

band /bænd/ *n* (strip) banda *f*. ●*n* (Mus) orquesta *f*; (military, brass)

banda *f*. □ ~ together *vi* juntarse

bandage /'bændɪdʒ/ *n* venda *f*. ●*vt* vendar

Band-Aid /'bændeɪd/ *n* (Amer, ®) tirita *f*, curita *f* (LAm)

B & B /'biːənbiː/ *abbr* (= bed and breakfast) cama *f* y desayuno; (place) pensión *f*

bandit /'bændɪt/ *n* bandido *m*

band: ~stand *n* quiosco *m* de música. ~wagon *n*. jump on the ~wagon (fig) subirse al carro

bandy /'bændɪ/ *adj* (-ier, -iest) patizambo

bang /bæŋ/ *n* (noise) ruido *m*; (blow) golpe *m*; (of gun) estampido *m*; (of door) golpe *m*. ●*vt* (strike) golpear. ~ the door dar un portazo. ●*adv* exactamente. ●*int* ¡pum! ~s *npl* (Amer) flequillo *m*, cerquillo *m* (LAm), fleco *m* (Mex)

banger /'bæŋə(r)/ *n* petardo *m*; (Ⓔ, Culin) salchicha *f*

bangle /'bæŋgl/ *n* brazalete *m*

banish /'bænɪʃ/ *vt* desterrar

banisters /'bænɪstəz/ *npl* pasamanos *m*

banjo /'bændʒəʊ/ *n* (*pl* -os) banjo *m*

bank /bæŋk/ *n* (Com) banco *m*; (of river) orilla *f*. ●*vt* depositar. ●*vi* (in flying) ladearse. □ ~ on *vt* contar con. □ ~ with *vi* tener una cuenta con. ~ card *n* tarjeta *f* bancaria; (Amer) tarjeta *f* de crédito (expedida por un banco). ~er *n* banquero *m*. ~ holiday *n* día *m* festivo, día *m* feriado (LAm). ~ing *n* (Com) banca *f*. ~note *n* billete *m* de banco

bankrupt /'bæŋkrʌpt/ *adj & n* quebrado (*m*). go ~ quebrar. ●*vt* hacer quebrar. ~cy /-rʌpsɪ/ *n* bancarrota *f*, quiebra *f*

bank statement *n* estado *m*

de cuenta

banner /'bænə(r)/ n bandera f; (in demonstration) pancarta f

banquet /'bæŋkwɪt/ n banquete m

banter /'bæntə(r)/ n chanza f

bap /bæp/ n panecillo m blando

baptism /'bæptɪzəm/ n bautismo m; (act) bautizo m

Baptist /'bæptɪst/ n bautista m & f

baptize /bæp'taɪz/ vt bautizar

bar /baː(r)/ n barra f; (on window) reja f; (of chocolate) tableta f; (of soap) pastilla f; (pub) bar m; (Mus) compás m; (Jurid) abogacía f; (fig) obstáculo m. ● vt (pt barred) atrancar (door); (exclude) excluir; (prohibit) prohibir. ● prep excepto

barbar|ian /baː'beərɪən/ adj & n bárbaro (m). ~ic /baː'bærɪk/ adj bárbaro

barbecue /'baːbɪkjuː/ n barbacoa f. ● vt asar a la parrilla

barbed wire /baːbd 'waɪə(r)/ n alambre m de púas

barber /'baːbə(r)/ n peluquero m, barbero m

barbwire /baːb'waɪə(r)/ n (Amer) see BARBED WIRE

bare /beə(r)/ adj (-er, -est) desnudo; (room) con pocos muebles; (mere) simple; (empty) vacío. ● vt desnudar; (uncover) descubrir. ~ one's teeth mostrar los dientes. ~back adv a pelo. ~faced adj descarado. ~foot adj descalzo. ~headed /-'hedɪd/ adj descubierto. ~ly adv apenas

bargain /'baːgɪn/ n (agreement) pacto m; (good buy) ganga f. ● vi negociar; (haggle) regatear. □ ~ for vt esperar, contar con

barge /baːdʒ/ n barcaza f. ● vi. ~ in irrumpir

baritone /'bærɪtəʊn/ n barítono m

bark /baːk/ n (of dog) ladrido m; (of tree) corteza f. ● vi ladrar

barley /'baːlɪ/ n cebada f

bar: ~maid n camarera f. ~man /-mən/ n camarero m, barman m

barmy /'baːmɪ/ adj 🔲 chiflado

barn /baːn/ n granero m

barometer /bə'rɒmɪtə(r)/ n barómetro m

baron /'bærən/ n barón m. ~ess /-ɪs/ n baronesa f

barracks /'bærəks/ npl cuartel m

barrage /'bæraːʒ/ n (Mil) barrera f; (dam) presa f. a ~ of questions un aluvión de preguntas

barrel /'bærəl/ n barril m; (of gun) cañón m

barren /'bærən/ adj estéril

barrette /bə'ret/ n (Amer) pasador m

barricade /bærɪ'keɪd/ n barricada f. ● vt cerrar con barricadas

barrier /'bærɪə(r)/ n barrera f

barrister /'bærɪstə(r)/ n abogado m

bartender /'baːtendə(r)/ n (Amer) (male) camarero m, barman m; (female) camarera f

barter /'baːtə(r)/ n trueque m. ● vt trocar

base /beɪs/ n base f. ● vt basar. ~ball n béisbol m, beisbol m (Mex)

basement /'beɪsmənt/ n sótano m

bash /bæʃ/ vt golpear. ● n golpe m. have a ~ 🔲 probar

bashful /'bæʃfl/ adj tímido

basic /'beɪsɪk/ adj básico, fundamental. ~ally adv fundamentalmente

basin /ˈbeɪsn/ n (for washing) palangana f; (for food) cuenco m; (of river) cuenca f

basis /ˈbeɪsɪs/ n (pl bases/-siːz/) base f

bask /bɑːsk/ vi asolearse; (fig) gozar (in de)

basket /ˈbɑːskɪt/ n cesta f; (big) cesto m. ~**ball** n baloncesto m, básquetbol m (LAm)

bass[1] /beɪs/ adj bajo. ●n (Mus) bajo m

bass[2] /bæs/ n (fish) lubina f

bassoon /bəˈsuːn/ n fagot m

bastard /ˈbɑːstəd/ n bastardo m. you ~! (vulgar) ¡cabrón! (vulgar)

bat /bæt/ n (for baseball, cricket) bate m; (for table tennis) raqueta f; (mammal) murciélago m. off one's own ~ por sí solo. ●vt (pt batted) golpear. without ~ting an eyelid sin pestañear. ●vi batear

batch /bætʃ/ n (of people) grupo m; (of papers) pila f; (of goods) remesa f; (of bread) hornada f; (Comp) lote m

bated /ˈbeɪtɪd/ adj. with ~ breath con aliento entrecortado

bath /bɑːθ/ n (pl -s /bɑːðz/) baño m; (tub) bañera f, tina f (LAm). ~s npl (swimming pool) piscina f, alberca f (Mex). have a ~, take a ~ (Amer) bañarse. ●vt bañar. ●vi bañarse

bathe /beɪð/ vt bañar. ●vi bañarse. ●n baño m. ~**r** n bañista m & f

bathing /ˈbeɪðɪŋ/ n baños mpl. ~ **costume**, ~ **suit** n traje m de baño

bathroom /ˈbɑːθrʊm/ n cuarto m de baño; (Amer, toilet) servicio m, baño m (LAm)

batsman /ˈbætsmən/ n (pl -men) bateador m

battalion /bəˈtæliən/ n batallón m

batter /ˈbætə(r)/ vt (beat) apalear; (cover with batter) rebozar. ●n batido m para rebozar; (Amer, for cake) masa f. ~**ed** /ˈbætəd/ adj (car etc) estropeado; (wife etc) maltratado

battery /ˈbætərɪ/ n (Mil, Auto) batería f; (of torch, radio) pila f

battle /ˈbætl/ n batalla f; (fig) lucha f. ●vi luchar. ~**field** n campo m de batalla. ~**ship** n acorazado m

bawl /bɔːl/ vt/i gritar

bay /beɪ/ n (on coast) bahía f. keep at ~ mantener a raya

bayonet /ˈbeɪənet/ n bayoneta f

bay window /beɪ ˈwɪndəʊ/ n ventana f salediza

bazaar /bəˈzɑː(r)/ n bazar m

BC abbr (= **before Christ**) a. de C., antes de Cristo

---

be /biː/

present **am, are, is**; past **was, were**; past participle **been**

● intransitive verb

! Spanish has two verbs meaning be, ser and estar. See those entries for further information about the differences between them.

····▸ (position, changed condition or state) estar. where is the library? ¿dónde está la biblioteca? she's tired está cansada. how are you? ¿cómo estás?

····▸ (identity, nature or permanent characteristics) ser. she.she's tall es alta. he's Scottish es escocés. I'm a journalist soy periodista. he's very kind es muy bondadoso

····▸ (*feel*) to be + *adjective* tener + *sustantivo*. to be cold/hot tener frío/calor. he's hungry/thirsty tiene hambre/sed

····▸ (*age*) he's thirty tiene treinta años

····▸ (*weather*) it's cold/hot hace frío/calor. it was 40 degrees hacía 40 grados

● *auxiliary verb*

····▸ (*in tenses*) estar. I'm working trabajando. they were singing estaban cantando, cantaban

····▸ (*in tag questions*) it's a beautiful house, isn't it? es una casa preciosa, ¿verdad? or ¿no? or ¿no es cierto?

····▸ (*in short answers*) are you disappointed? - yes, I am ¿estás desilusionado? - sí (,lo estoy). I'm surprised, aren't you? estoy sorprendido, ¿tú no?

····▸ (*in passive sentences*) it was built in 1834 fue construido en 1834, se construyó en 1834. she was told that ... le dijeron que..., se le dijo que ...

! Note that passive sentences in English are often translated using the pronoun se or using the third person plural.

beach /biːtʃ/ *n* playa *f*
beacon /ˈbiːkən/ *n* faro *m*
bead /biːd/ *n* cuenta *f*; (*of glass*) abalorio *m*
beak /biːk/ *n* pico *m*
beaker /ˈbiːkə(r)/ *n* taza *f* (*alta y*

sin asa)

beam /biːm/ *n* (*of wood*) viga *f*; (*of light*) rayo *m*; (*Naut*) bao *m*. ● *vt* emitir. ● *vi* irradiar; (*smile*) sonreír

bean /biːn/ *n* alubia *f*, frijol *m* (*LAm*); (*broad bean*) haba *f*; (*of coffee*) grano *m*

bear /beə(r)/ *vt* (*pt* bore, *pp* borne) llevar; parir (niño); (*endure*) soportar. ~ **right** torcer a la derecha. ~ **in mind** tener en cuenta. □ ~ **with** *vt* tener paciencia con. ● *n* oso *m*. ~**able** *adj* soportable

beard /biəd/ *n* barba *f*. ~**ed** *adj* barbudo

bearer /ˈbeərə(r)/ *n* portador *m*; (*of passport*) titular *m & f*

bearing /ˈbeərɪŋ/ *n* comportamiento *m*; (*relevance*) relación *f*; (*Mec*) cojinete *m*. **get one's ~s** orientarse. **lose one's ~s** desorientarse

beast /biːst/ *n* bestia *f*; (*person*) bruto *m*. ~**ly** *adj* (**-ier**, **-iest**) bestial; T horrible

beat /biːt/ *vt* (*pt* beat, *pp* beaten) (*hit*) pegar; (*defeat*) derrotar; (*better*) sobrepasar; batir (record); (*baffle*) dejar perplejo. ~ **it** X largarse. ● *vi* (*heart*) latir. ● *n* latido *m*; (*Mus*) ritmo *m*; (*of policeman*) ronda *f*. □ ~ **up** *vt* darle una paliza a; (*Culin*) batir. ~ **up on** (*Amer, fam*) darle una paliza a. ~**er** *n* batidor *m*. ~**ing** *n* paliza *f*

beautician /bjuːˈtɪʃn/ *n* esteticista *m & f*

beautiful /ˈbjuːtɪfl/ *adj* hermoso. ~**ly** *adv* maravillosamente

beauty /ˈbjuːtɪ/ *n* belleza *f*. ~ **salon**, ~ **shop** (*Amer*) salón *m* de belleza. ~ **spot** *n* (*on face*) lunar *m*; (*site*) lugar *m* pintoresco

beaver /ˈbiːvə(r)/ *n* castor *m*

became | being

became /bɪˈkeɪm/ *see* BECOME

because /bɪˈkɒz/ *conj* porque.
● *adv.* ~ **of** por, a causa de

beckon /ˈbekən/ *vt/i.* ~ **(to)** hacer señas (a)

become /bɪˈkʌm/ *vi* (*pt* became, *pp* become) hacerse, llegar a ser, volverse, convertirse en. **what has** ~ **of her?** ¿qué es de ella?

bed /bed/ *n* cama *f*; (*layer*) estrato *m*; (*of sea, river*) fondo *m*; (*of flowers*) macizo *m*. **go to** ~ acostarse. ● *vi* (*pt* bedded). ~ **and breakfast (B & B)** cama y desayuno; (*place*) pensión *f*. ~**bug** *n* chinche *f*. ~**clothes** *npl*, ~**ding** *n* ropa *f* de cama, cobijas *fpl* (LAm)

> **Bed and breakfast** Los
> bed & breakfast o B&B
> son casas privadas o pequeños hoteles que ofrecen alojamiento y desayuno a precios generalmente módicos.

bed: ~**room** *n* dormitorio *m*, cuarto *m*, habitación *f*, recámara *f* (Mex). ~**-sitter** /-ˈsɪtə(r)/ *n* habitación *f* con cama y uso de cocina y baño compartidos, estudio *m*. ~**spread** *n* colcha *f*. ~**time** *n* hora *f* de acostarse

bee /biː/ *n* abeja *f*; (Amer, social gathering) círculo *m*

beech /biːtʃ/ *n* haya *f*

beef /biːf/ *n* carne *f* de vaca, carne *f* de res (Mex). ● *vi* 🅧 quejarse. ~**burger** *n* hamburguesa *f*. ~**y** *adj* (-ier, -iest) musculoso

bee: ~**hive** *n* colmena *f*. ~**line** *n*. **make a** ~**line for** ir en línea recta hacia

been /biːn/ *see* BE

beer /bɪə(r)/ *n* cerveza *f*

beet /biːt/ *n* (Amer) remolacha *f*,

betabel *f* (Mex)

beetle /ˈbiːtl/ *n* escarabajo *m*

beetroot /ˈbiːtruːt/ *n invar* remolacha *f*, betabel *f* (Mex)

befall /bɪˈfɔːl/ *vt* (*pt* befell, *pp* befallen) ocurrirle a. ● *vi* ocurrir

before /bɪˈfɔː(r)/ *prep* (*time*) antes de; (*place*) delante de. ~ **leaving** antes de marcharse. ● *adv* (*place*) delante; (*time*) antes. **a week** ~ una semana antes. **the week** ~ la semana anterior. ● *conj* (*time*) antes de que. ● **he leaves** antes de que se vaya. ~**hand** *adv* de antemano

befriend /bɪˈfrend/ *vt* hacerse amigo de

beg /beg/ *vt/i* (*pt* begged) mendigar; (*entreat*) suplicar; (*ask*) pedir. ● **s.o.'s pardon** pedir perdón a uno. **I** ~ **your pardon!** ¡perdone Vd! **I** ~ **your pardon?** ¿cómo?

began /bɪˈɡæn/ *see* BEGIN

beggar /ˈbeɡə(r)/ *n* mendigo *m*

begin /bɪˈɡɪn/ *vt/i* (*pt* began, *pp* begun, *pres p* beginning) comenzar, empezar. ~**ner** *n* principiante *m & f*. ~**ning** *n* principio *m*

begrudge /bɪˈɡrʌdʒ/ *vt* envidiar; (*give*) dar de mala gana

begun /bɪˈɡʌn/ *see* BEGIN

behalf /bɪˈhɑːf/ *n*. **on** ~ **of, in** ~ **of** (Amer) de parte de, en nombre de

behave /bɪˈheɪv/ *vi* comportarse, portarse. ~ **(o.s.)** portarse bien. ~**iour** /bɪˈheɪvjə(r)/ *n* comportamiento *m*

behead /bɪˈhed/ *vt* decapitar

behind /bɪˈhaɪnd/ *prep* detrás de, atrás de (LAm). ● *adv* detrás; (*late*) atrasado. ● *n* 🅘 trasero *m*.

beige /beɪʒ/ *adj & n* beige (*m*)

being /ˈbiːɪŋ/ *n* ser *m*. **come into** ~ nacer

belated /bɪˈleɪtɪd/ adj tardío

belch /beltʃ/ vi eructar. □ ~ **out** vt arrojar (smoke)

belfry /ˈbelfrɪ/ n campanario m

Belgi|an /ˈbeldʒən/ adj & n belga (m & f). **~um** /ˈbeldʒəm/ n Bélgica f

belie|f /bɪˈliːf/ n (trust) fe f; (opinion) creencia f. **~ve** /bɪˈliːv/ vt/i creer. **~ve in** creer en. **make ~ve** fingir

belittle /bɪˈlɪtl/ vt menospreciar (achievements); denigrar (person)

bell /bel/ n campana f; (on door, bicycle) timbre m

belligerent /bɪˈlɪdʒərənt/ adj beligerante

bellow /ˈbeləʊ/ vt gritar. ● vi bramar. **~s** npl fuelle m

bell pepper n (Amer) pimiento m

belly /ˈbelɪ/ n barriga f

belong /bɪˈlɒŋ/ vi pertenecer (to a); (club) ser socio (to de); (have as usual place) ir. **~ings** /bɪˈlɒŋɪŋz/ npl pertenencias fpl. **personal ~ings** efectos mpl personales

beloved /bɪˈlʌvɪd/ adj querido

below /bɪˈləʊ/ prep debajo de, abajo de (LAm); (fig) inferior a. ● adv abajo

belt /belt/ n cinturón m; (area) zona f. ● vt (fig) rodear; ⊠ darle una paliza a. □ ~**way** n (Amer) carretera f de circunvalación

bench /bentʃ/ n banco m

bend /bend/ n curva f. ● vt (pt & pp bent) doblar; torcer (arm, leg). ● vi doblarse; (road) torcerse. □ ~ **down** vi inclinarse □ ~ **over** vi agacharse

beneath /bɪˈniːθ/ prep debajo de; (fig) inferior a. ● adv abajo

beneficial /benɪˈfɪʃl/ adj provechoso

beneficiary /benɪˈfɪʃərɪ/ n beneficiario m

benefit /ˈbenɪfɪt/ n provecho m, ventaja f; (allowance) subsidio m; (for unemployed) subsidio m; (perk) beneficio m. ● vt (pt benefited, pres p benefiting) beneficiar. ● vi beneficiarse

benevolent /bəˈnevələnt/ adj benévolo

benign /bɪˈnaɪn/ adj benigno

bent /bent/ see **BEND**. ● n inclinación f. ● adj torcido; (⊠, corrupt) corrompido

bereave|d /bɪˈriːvd/ n. **the ~d** la familia del difunto. **~ment** n pérdida f; (mourning) luto m

beret /ˈbereɪ/ n boina f

berry /ˈberɪ/ n baya f

berserk /bəˈsɜːk/ adj. **go ~** volverse loco

berth /bɜːθ/ n litera f; (anchorage) amarradero m. **give a wide ~ to** evitar. ● vt/i atracar

beside /bɪˈsaɪd/ prep al lado de. **be ~ o.s.** estar fuera de sí

besides /bɪˈsaɪdz/ prep además de; (except) excepto. ● adv además

besiege /bɪˈsiːdʒ/ vt sitiar, asediar; (fig) acosar

best /best/ adj (el) mejor. **the ~ thing is to...** lo mejor es... ● adv mejor. **like ~** preferir. ● n lo mejor. **at ~** a lo más. **do one's ~** hacer todo lo posible. **make the ~ of** contentarse con. **~ man** n padrino m (de boda)

bestow /bɪˈstəʊ/ vt conceder

bestseller /bestˈselə(r)/ n éxito m de librería, bestseller m

bet /bet/ n apuesta f. ● vt/i (pt bet or betted) apostar

betray /bɪˈtreɪ/ vt traicionar. **~al** n traición f

better /'betə(r)/ adj & adv mejor. ~ off en mejores condiciones; (richer) más rico. get ~ mejorar. all the ~ tanto mejor. I'd ~ be off me tengo que ir. the ~ part de la mayor parte de. • vt mejorar; (beat) sobrepasar. ~ o.s. superarse. • n superior m. get the ~ of vencer a. my ~s mis superiores mpl

between /bɪ'twiːn/ prep entre. • adv en medio

beverage /'bevərɪdʒ/ n bebida f

beware /bɪ'weə(r)/ vi tener cuidado. • int ¡cuidado!

bewilder /bɪ'wɪldə(r)/ vt desconcertar. ~ment n aturdimiento m

bewitch /bɪ'wɪtʃ/ vt hechizar; (delight) cautivar

beyond /bɪ'jɒnd/ prep más allá de; (fig) fuera de. ~ doubt sin lugar a duda. • adv más allá

bias /'baɪəs/ n tendencia f; (prejudice) prejuicio m. • vt (pt biased) influir en. ~ed adj parcial

bib /bɪb/ n babero m

Bible /'baɪbl/ n Biblia f

biblical /'bɪblɪkl/ adj bíblico

bibliography /bɪblɪ'ɒɡrəfɪ/ n bibliografía f

biceps /'baɪseps/ n invar bíceps m

bicker /'bɪkə(r)/ vi altercar

bicycle /'baɪsɪkl/ n bicicleta f

bid /bɪd/ n (offer) oferta f; (attempt) tentativa f. • vi hacer una oferta. • vt (pt & pp bid, pres p bidding) ofrecer; (pt bid, pp bidden, pres p bidding) mandar; dar (welcome, good day etc). ~der n postor m. ~ding n (at auction) ofertas fpl; (order) mandato m

bide /baɪd/ vt. ~ one's time esperar el momento oportuno

bifocals /baɪ'fəʊklz/ npl gafas fpl

bifocales, anteojos mpl bifocales (LAm)

big /bɪɡ/ adj (bigger, biggest) grande, (before singular noun) gran. • adv. talk ~ fanfarronear

bigam|ist /'bɪɡəmɪst/ n bígamo m. ~ous /'bɪɡəməs/ adj bígamo. ~y n bigamia f

big-headed /-'hedɪd/ adj engreído

bigot /'bɪɡət/ n fanático m. ~ed adj fanático

bike /baɪk/ n 🔲 bici f 🔲

bikini /bɪ'kiːnɪ/ n (pl -is) bikini m

bile /baɪl/ n bilis f

bilingual /baɪ'lɪŋɡwəl/ adj bilingüe

bill /bɪl/ n cuenta f; (invoice) factura f; (notice) cartel m; (Amer, banknote) billete m; (Pol) proyecto m de ley; (of bird) pico m

billet /'bɪlɪt/ n (Mil) alojamiento m. • vt alojar

billfold /'bɪlfəʊld/ n (Amer) cartera f, billetera f

billiards /'bɪlɪədz/ n billar m

billion /'bɪlɪən/ n billón m; (Amer) mil millones mpl

bin /bɪn/ n recipiente m; (for rubbish) cubo m de basura, bote m de basura (Mex); (for waste paper) papelera f

bind /baɪnd/ vt (pt bound) atar; encuadernar (book); (Jurid) obligar. • n 🔲 lata f. ~ing n (of books) encuadernación f; (braid) ribete m

binge /bɪndʒ/ n 🔲, (of food) comilona f; (of drink) borrachera f. go on a ~ ir de juerga

bingo /'bɪŋɡəʊ/ n bingo m

binoculars /bɪ'nɒkjʊləz/ npl gemelos mpl

biofuel /'baɪəʊfjuːəl/ n biocarburante m

biograph|er /baɪ'ɒɡrəfə(r)/ n

biógrafo m. **~y** n biografía f

biolog|ical /baɪəˈlɒdʒɪkl/ adj biológico. **~ist** /baɪˈɒlədʒɪst/ n biólogo m. **~y** /baɪˈɒlədʒɪ/ n biología f

bioterrorism /baɪəʊˈterərɪzm/ n bioterrorismo m

birch /bɜːtʃ/ n (tree) abedul m

bird /bɜːd/ n ave f; (small) pájaro m; (sl, girl) chica f

Biro /ˈbaɪərəʊ/ n (pl -os) (®) bolígrafo m

birth /bɜːθ/ n nacimiento m. **give ~** dar a luz. **~ certificate** n partida f de nacimiento. **~ control** n control m de la natalidad. **~day** n cumpleaños m. **~mark** n marca f de nacimiento. **~place** n lugar m de nacimiento. **~ rate** n natalidad f

biscuit /ˈbɪskɪt/ n galleta f

bisect /baɪˈsekt/ vt bisecar

bishop /ˈbɪʃəp/ n obispo m; (Chess) alfil m

bit /bɪt/ see **BITE**. ● n trozo m; (quantity) poco m; (of horse) bocado m; (Mec) broca f; (Comp) bit m

bitch /bɪtʃ/ n perra f; (fam, woman) bruja f [1]

bit|e /baɪt/ vt/i (pt bit, pp bitten) morder; (insect) picar. **~ one's nails** morderse las uñas. ● n mordisco m; (mouthful) bocado m; (of insect etc) picadura f. **~ing** /ˈbaɪtɪŋ/ adj mordaz

bitter /ˈbɪtə(r)/ adj amargo; (of weather) glacial. ● n cerveza f amarga. **~ly** adv amargamente. **it's ~ly cold** hace un frío glacial. **~ness** n amargor m; (resentment) amargura f

bizarre /bɪˈzɑː(r)/ adj extraño

black /blæk/ adj (-er, -est) negro. **~ and blue** amoratado. ● n negro m; (coffee) solo, negro m (LAm). ● vt

ennegrecer; limpiar (shoes). **~ out** vi desmayarse. **~ and white** n blanco y negro m. **~-and-white** adj en blanco y negro f. **~berry** /-bərɪ/ n zarzamora f. **~bird** n mirlo m. **~board** n pizarra f. **~currant** /-ˈkʌrənt/ n grosella f negra. **~en** vt ennegrecer. **~ eye** n ojo m morado. **~list** vt poner en la lista negra. **~mail** n chantaje m. ● vt chantajear. **~mailer** n chantajista m & f. **~out** n apagón m; (Med) desmayo m; (of news) censura f. **~smith** n herrero m

bladder /ˈblædə(r)/ n vejiga f

blade /bleɪd/ n (of knife, sword) hoja f. **~ of grass** brizna f de hierba

blame /bleɪm/ vt echar la culpa a. **be to ~** tener la culpa. ● n culpa f. **~less** adj inocente

bland /blænd/ adj (-er, -est) suave

blank /blæŋk/ adj (page, space) en blanco; (cassette) virgen; (cartridge) sin bala; (fig) vacío. ● n blanco m

blanket /ˈblæŋkɪt/ n manta f, cobija f (LAm), frazada f (LAm); (fig) capa f. ● vt (pt blanketed) (fig) cubrir (in, with de)

blare /bleə(r)/ vi sonar muy fuerte. ● n estrépito m

blasphem|e /blæsˈfiːm/ vt/i blasfemar. **~ous** /ˈblæsfəməs/ adj blasfemo. **~y** /ˈblæsfəmɪ/ n blasfemia f

blast /blɑːst/ n explosión f; (gust) ráfaga f; (sound) toque m. ● vt volar. **~ed** adj maldito. **~-off** n (of missile) despegue m

blatant /ˈbleɪtnt/ adj patente; (shameless) descarado

blaze /bleɪz/ n llamarada f; (of light) resplandor m; (fig) arranque m. ● vi arder en llamas; (fig) brillar

blazer /'bleɪzə(r)/ n chaqueta f

bleach /bliːtʃ/ n lejía f, cloro m (LAm), blanqueador m (LAm). ●vt blanquear; decolorar (hair).

bleak /bliːk/ adj (-er, -est) desolado; (fig) sombrío

bleat /bliːt/ n balido m. ●vi balar

bleed /bliːd/ vt/i (pt bled /bled/) sangrar

bleep /bliːp/ n pitido m

blemish /'blemɪʃ/ n mancha f

blend /blend/ n mezcla f. ●vt mezclar. ●vi combinarse. ~er n licuadora f

bless /bles/ vt bendecir. ~ you! (on sneezing) ¡Jesús!, ¡salud! (Mex). ~ed /'blesɪd/ adj bendito. ~ing n bendición f; (advantage) ventaja f

blew /bluː/ see BLOW

blight /blaɪt/ n añublo m, tizón m, (fig) plaga f. ●vt añublar, atizonar; (fig) destrozar

blind /blaɪnd/ adj ciego. ~ alley callejón m sin salida. ●n persiana f; (fig) pretexto m. ●vt dejar ciego; (dazzle) deslumbrar. ~fold adj & adv con los ojos vendados. ●n venda f. ●vt vendar los ojos a. ~ly adv a ciegas. ~ness n ceguera f

blink /blɪŋk/ vi parpadear; (light) centellear. ~ers npl (on horse) anteojeras fpl

bliss /blɪs/ n felicidad f. ~ful adj feliz

blister /'blɪstə(r)/ n ampolla f

blizzard /'blɪzəd/ n ventisca f

bloated /'bləʊtɪd/ adj hinchado (with de)

blob /blɒb/ n (drip) gota f; (stain) mancha f

bloc /blɒk/ n (Pol) bloque m

block /blɒk/ n bloque m; (of wood) zoquete m; (of buildings) manzana f, cuadra f (LAm). in ~ letters en letra de imprenta. ~ of flats edificio m de apartamentos, casa f de pisos. ●vt bloquear. ~ade /blɒ'keɪd/ n bloqueo m. ●vt bloquear. ~age /-ɪdʒ/ n obstrucción f. ~head n Ⅱ zopenco m

bloke /bləʊk/ n Ⅱ tipo m, tío m Ⅱ

blond /blɒnd/ adj & n rubio (m), güero m (Mex fam). ~e adj & n rubia (f), güera (f) (Mex fam)

blood /blʌd/ n sangre f. ~bath n masacre m. ~-curdling /-kɜːdlɪŋ/adj horripilante. ~hound n sabueso m. ~ pressure n tensión f arterial. high ~ pressure hipertensión f. ~shed n derramamiento m de sangre. ~shot adj sanguinolento; (eye) inyectado de sangre. ~stream n torrente m sanguíneo. ~thirsty adj sanguinario. ~y adj (-ier, -iest) sangriento; (stained) ensangrentado; Ⅹ maldito

bloom /bluːm/ n flor f. ●vi florecer

blossom /'blɒsəm/ n flor f. ●vi florecer. ~ (out) into (fig) llegar a ser

blot /blɒt/ n borrón m. ●vt (pt blotted) manchar; (dry) secar. □ ~ out vt oscurecer

blotch /blɒtʃ/ n mancha f. ~y adj lleno de manchas

blotting-paper /'blɒtɪŋ/ n papel m secante

blouse /blaʊz/ n blusa f

blow /bləʊ/ vt (pt blew, pp blown) soplar; fundir (fuse); tocar (trumpet). ●vi soplar; (fuse) fundirse; (sound) sonar. ●n golpe m. □ ~ down vt derribar. □ ~ out vt apagar (candle). □ ~ over vi pasar. □ ~ up vt inflar; (explode) volar;

(Photo) ampliar. vi (explode) estallar; (burst) reventar. ~-dry vt secar con secador. ~lamp n soplete m. ~out n (of tyre) reventón m. ~torch n soplete m

blue /bluː/ adj (-er, -est) azul; (joke) verde. ● n azul m. out of the ~ totalmente inesperado. ~s npl. have the ~s tener tristeza. ~bell n campanilla f. ~berry n arándano m. ~bottle n moscarda f. ~print n plano m; (fig, plan) programa m

bluff /blʌf/ n (poker) farol m, bluff m (LAm), blof m (Mex). ● vt engañar. ● vi tirarse un farol, hacer un blof (LAm), blofear (Mex)

blunder /ˈblʌndə(r)/ vi cometer un error. ● n metedura f de pata

blunt /blʌnt/ adj desafilado; (person) directo, abrupto. ● vt desafilar. ~ly adv francamente

blur /blɜː(r)/ n impresión f indistinta. ● vt (pt blurred) hacer borroso

blurb /blɜːb/ n resumen m publicitario

blurt /blɜːt/ vt. ~ out dejar escapar

blush /blʌʃ/ vi ruborizarse. ● n rubor m

boar /bɔː(r)/ n verraco m. wild ~ jabalí m

board /bɔːd/ n tabla f, tablero m; (for notices) tablón m de anuncios, tablero m de anuncios (LAm); (blackboard) pizarra f; (food) pensión f; (of company) junta f. ~ and lodging casa y comida. full ~ pensión f completa. go by the ~ ser abandonado. ● vt alojar; ~ a ship embarcarse. ● vi alojarse (with en casa de); (at school) ser interno. ~er n huésped m & f; (school) interno m. ~ing card n tarjeta f de embarque. ~ing

house n casa f de huéspedes, pensión f. ~ing pass n see ~ING CARD. ~ing school n internado m

boast /bəʊst/ vt enorgullecerse de. ● vi jactarse. ● n jactancia f. ~ful adj jactancioso

boat /bəʊt/ n barco m; (small) bote m, barca f

bob /bɒb/ vi (pt bobbed) menearse, subir y bajar. □ ~ up vi presentarse súbitamente

bobbin /ˈbɒbɪn/ n carrete m; (in sewing machine) canilla f, bobina f

bobby pin /ˈbɒbɪ/ n (Amer) horquilla f, pasador m (Mex). ~ sox /sɒks/ npl (Amer) calcetines mpl cortos

bobsleigh /ˈbɒbsleɪ/ n bob (sleigh) m

bode /bəʊd/ vi. ~ well/ill ser de buen/mal agüero

bodice /ˈbɒdɪs/ n corpiño m

bodily /ˈbɒdɪlɪ/ adj físico, corporal. ● adv físicamente

body /ˈbɒdɪ/ n cuerpo m; (dead) cadáver m. ~guard n guardaespaldas m. ~ part n pedazo m de cuerpo. ~work n carrocería f

bog /bɒg/ n ciénaga f. □ ~ down vt (pt bogged). get ~ged down empantanarse

boggle /ˈbɒgl/ vi sobresaltarse. the mind ~s uno se queda atónito

bogus /ˈbəʊgəs/ adj falso

boil /bɔɪl/ vt/i hervir. be ~ing hot estar ardiendo; (weather) hacer mucho calor. ● n furúnculo m. □ ~ away vi evaporarse. □ ~ down to vt reducirse a. □ ~ over vi rebosar. ~ed adj hervido; (egg) pasado por agua. ~er n caldera f. ~er suit n mono m, overol m (LAm)

boisterous /ˈbɔɪstərəs/ adj ruidoso, bullicioso

bold /bəʊld/ adj (-er, -est) audaz.
~**ly** adv con audacia, audazmente

Bolivia /bə'lɪvɪə/ n Bolivia f. ~**n**
adj & n boliviano (m)

bolster /'bəʊlstə(r)/ □ ~ **up** vt
sostener

bolt /bəʊlt/ n (on door) cerrojo m;
(for nut) perno m; (lightning) rayo
m; (leap) fuga f. ● vt echar el cerrojo
a (a door); engullir (food). ● vi fugarse. ● adv. ~ **upright** rígido

bomb /bɒm/ n bomba f. ● vt bombardear. ~**ard** /bɒm'bɑːd/ vt bombardear ~**er** /'bɒmə(r)/ n (plane)
bombardero m; (terrorist) terrorista
m & f. ~**ing** /bɒmɪŋ/ n bombardeo
m. ~**shell** n bomba f

bond /bɒnd/ n (agreement) obligación f; (link) lazo m; (Com) bono m.
● vi (stick) adherirse. ~**age** /-ɪdʒ/ n
esclavitud f

bone /bəʊn/ n hueso m; (of fish)
espina f. ● vt deshuesar; quitar las
espinas a (fish). ~**-dry** adj completamente seco. ~ **idle** adj holgazán

bonfire /'bɒnfaɪə(r)/ n hoguera f,
fogata f

bonnet /'bɒnɪt/ n gorra f; (Auto)
capó m, capote m (Mex)

bonus /'bəʊnəs/ n (payment) boni-
ficación f; (fig) ventaja f

bony /'bəʊnɪ/ adj (-ier, -iest) huesudo; (fish) lleno de espinas

boo /buː/ int ¡bu! ● vt/i abuchear

boob /buːb/ n (fam, mistake) metedura f de pata. ● vi 🔢 meter la
pata

book /bʊk/ n libro m; (of cheques
etc) talonario m, chequera f; (notebook) libreta f; (exercise book) cuaderno m, libreta f, (pl) (Com) cuentas
fpl. ● vt (enter) registrar; (reserve)
reservar. ● vi reservar. ~**case** n bi-

blioteca f, librería f, librero m (Mex).
~**ing** n reserva f, reservación f
(LAm). ~**ing office** n (in theatre)
taquilla f, boletería f (LAm). ~**keep-
ing** n contabilidad f. ~**let** /'bʊklɪt/
n folleto m. ~**maker** n corredor m
de apuestas. ~**mark** n señal f.
~**seller** n librero m. ~**shop**, (Amer)
~**store** n librería f. ~**worm** n (fig)
ratón m de biblioteca

boom /buːm/ vi retumbar; (fig)
prosperar. ● n estampido m, (Com)
boom m

boost /buːst/ vt estimular; reforzar
(morale). ● n empuje m. ~**er** n
(Med) revacunación f. ~**er cable** n
(Amer) cable m de arranque

boot /buːt/ n bota f; (Auto) maletero m, cajuela f (Mex). □ ~ **up** vt
(Comp) cargar

booth /buːð/ n cabina f; (at fair)
puesto m

booze /buːz/ vi 🔢 beber mucho.
● n 🔢 alcohol m

border /'bɔːdə(r)/ n borde m;
(frontier) frontera f; (in garden)
arriate m. □ ~ **on** vt lindar con.
~**line** n línea f divisoria. ~**line
case** n caso m dudoso

bor|e /bɔː(r)/ see **BEAR**. ● vt
(annoy) aburrir; (Tec) taladrar. ● vi
taladrar. ● n (person) pelmazo m;
(thing) lata f. ~**ed** adj aburrido. be
~**ed** estar aburrido. **get** ~**ed** abu-
rrirse. ~**edom** /'bɔːdəm/ n aburri-
miento m. ~**ing** adj aburrido, pesado

born /bɔːn/ adj nato. **be** ~ nacer

borne /bɔːn/ see **BEAR**

borough /'bʌrə/ n municipio m

borrow /'bɒrəʊ/ vt pedir prestado

boss /bɒs/ n 🔢 jefe m. ● vt. ~
(about) 🔢 dar órdenes a. ~**y** adj
mandón

botan|ical /bə'tænɪkl/ adj botánico. **~ist** /'bɒtənɪst/ n botánico m. **~y** /'bɒtənɪ/ n botánica f

both /bəʊθ/ adj & pron ambos (mpl), los dos (mpl). ● adv al mismo tiempo, a la vez. ~ Ann and Brian came tanto Ann como Bob vinieron.

bother /'bɒðə(r)/ vt (inconvenience) molestar; (worry) preocupar. ~ it! ¡caramba! ● vi molestarse. ~ about preocuparse de. ~ doing tomarse la molestia de hacer. ● n molestia f

bottle /'bɒtl/ n botella, mamila f (Mex); (for baby) biberón m. ● vt embotellar. □ ~ **up** vt (fig) reprimir. **~neck** n (traffic jam) embotellamiento m. ~ **opener** n abrebotellas m, destapador m (LAm)

bottom /'bɒtəm/ n fondo m; (of hill) pie m; (buttocks) trasero m. ● adj de más abajo; (price) más bajo; (lip, edge) inferior. **~less** adj sin fondo

bough /baʊ/ n rama f

bought /bɔːt/ see BUY

boulder /'bəʊldə(r)/ n canto m

bounce /baʊns/ vt hacer rebotar. ● vi rebotar; (person) saltar; Ⓣ (cheque) ser rechazado. ● n rebote m

bound /baʊnd/ see BIND. ● vi saltar. ● n (jump) salto m. ~s npl (limits) límites mpl. out of ~s zona f prohibida. ● adj. be ~ for dirigirse a. ~ to obligado a; (certain) seguro de

boundary /'baʊndərɪ/ n límite m

bouquet /bʊ'keɪ/ n ramo m; (of wine) buqué m, aroma m

bout /baʊt/ n período m; (Med) ataque m; (Sport) encuentro m

bow¹ /bəʊ/ n (weapon, Mus) arco

m; (knot) lazo m, moño m (LAm)

bow² /baʊ/ n reverencia f; (Naut) proa f. ● vi inclinarse. ● vt inclinar

bowels /'baʊəlz/ npl intestinos mpt, (fig) entrañas fpl

bowl /bəʊl/ n (container) cuenco m; (for washing) palangana f; (ball) bola f. ● vt (cricket) arrojar. ● vi (cricket) arrojar la pelota. □ ~ **over** vt derribar

bowl: **~er** n (cricket) lanzador m. **~er** (hat) sombrero m de hongo, bombín m, bolos mpl. **~ing** n bolos mpl. **~ing alley** n bolera f

bow tie /bəʊ 'taɪ/ n corbata f de lazo, pajarita f

box /bɒks/ n caja f; (for jewels etc) estuche m; (in theatre) palco m. ● vt boxear contra. ~ **s.o.'s ears** dar una manotada a uno. ● vi boxear. **~er** n boxeador m. **~ing** n boxeo m. **B~ing Day** n el 26 de diciembre. ~ **office** n taquilla f, boletería f (LAm). ~ **room** n trastero m

boy /bɔɪ/ n chico m, muchacho m; (young) niño m

boy: ~ **band** n grupo m pop de chicos. **~friend** n novio m. **~hood** n niñez f. **~ish** adj de muchacho; (childish) infantil

boycott /'bɔɪkɒt/ vt boicotear. ● n boicoteo m

bra /brɑː/ n sostén m, sujetador m, brasier m (Mex)

brace /breɪs/ n abrazadera f. ● vt asegurar. ~ **o.s.** prepararse. **~s** npl tirantes mpl; (Amer, dental) aparato(s) m(pl)

bracelet /'breɪslɪt/ n pulsera f

bracken /'brækən/ n helecho m

bracket /'brækɪt/ n soporte m; (group) categoría f; (parenthesis) paréntesis m. **square ~s** corchetes mpl. ● vt poner entre paréntesis;

(*join together*) agrupar

brag /bræg/ vi (pt **bragged**) jactarse (*about de*)

braid /breɪd/ n galón m; (*Amer, in hair*) trenza f

brain /breɪn/ n cerebro m. ● vt romper la cabeza a. ∼**child** n invento m. ∼**drain** n 🔄 fuga f de cerebros. ∼**storm** n ataque m de locura; (*Amer, brainwave*) idea f genial. ∼**wash** vt lavar el cerebro. ∼**wave** n idea f genial. ∼**y** adj (**-ier, -iest**) inteligente

brake /breɪk/ n freno m. ● vt/i frenar. ∼ **fluid** n líquido m de freno. ∼ **lights** npl luces fpl de freno

bramble /'bræmbl/ n zarza f

bran /bræn/ n salvado m

branch /brɑːntʃ/ n rama f; (*of road*) bifurcación f; (*Com*) sucursal m; (*fig*) ramo m. □ ∼ **off** vi bifurcarse. □ ∼ **out** vi ramificarse

brand /brænd/ n marca f. ● vt marcar; (*label*) tildar de

brandish /'brændɪʃ/ vt blandir

brand: ∼ name: n marca f. ∼**-new** /-'njuː/ adj flamante

brandy /'brændɪ/ n coñac m

brash /bræʃ/ adj descarado

brass /brɑːs/ n latón m. get down to ∼ **tacks** (*fig*) al grano. ∼ **band** n banda f de música

brassière /'bræsjeə(r)/ n see **BRA**

brat /bræt/ n (*pej*) mocoso m

bravado /brə'vɑːdəʊ/ n bravata f

brave /breɪv/ adj (**-er, -est**) valiente. ● n (*North American Indian*) guerrero m indio. the ∼ npl los valientes. ● vt afrontar. ∼**ry** /-ərɪ/ n valentía f, valor m

brawl /brɔːl/ n alboroto m. ● vi pelearse

brazen /'breɪzn/ adj descarado

Brazil /brə'zɪl/ n Brasil m. ∼**ian** /-jən/ adj & n brasileño (m)

breach /briːtʃ/ n infracción f, violación f; (*of contract*) incumplimiento m; (*gap*) brecha f. ∼ **of the peace** alteración f del orden público. ● vt abrir una brecha en

bread /bred/ n pan m. a loaf of ∼ un pan. ∼**crumbs** npl migajas fpl; (*Culin*) pan m rallado, pan m molido (*Mex*)

breadth /bredθ/ n anchura f

breadwinner /'bredwɪnə(r)/ n sostén m de la familia

break /breɪk/ vt (pt **broke**, pp **broken**) romper; infringir, violar (*law*); batir (*record*); comunicar (*news*); interrumpir (*journey*). ● vi romperse; (*news*) divulgarse. ● n ruptura f; (*interval*) intervalo m; (*fam, chance*) oportunidad f; (*in weather*) cambio m. □ ∼ **away** vi escapar. □ ∼ **down** vt derribar; analizar (*figures*). vi estropearse, descomponerse (*LAm*); (*Auto*) averiarse; (*cry*) deshacerse en lágrimas. □ ∼ **in** vi (*intruder*) entrar (*para robar*). □ ∼ **into** vt entrar (*para robar*) (house etc); (*start doing*) ponerse a. □ ∼ **off** vi interrumpirse. □ ∼ **out** vi (war, disease) estallar; (*run away*) escaparse. □ ∼ **up** vi romperse; (band, lovers) separarse; (schools) terminar. ∼**able** adj frágil. ∼**age** /-ɪdʒ/ n rotura f. ∼**down** n (*Tec*) falla f; (*Med*) colapso m, crisis f nerviosa; (*of figures*) análisis f. ∼**er** n (*wave*) ola f grande

breakfast /'brekfəst/ n desayuno m. **have** ∼ desayunar

break: ∼through n adelanto m. ∼**water** n rompeolas m

breast /brest/ n pecho m. (*of chicken etc*) pechuga f. (*estilo m*)

~stroke n braza f, (estilo m) pecho m (LAm)

breath /breθ/ n aliento m, respiración f. be out of ~ estar sin aliento. hold one's ~ aguantar la respiración. under one's ~ a media voz

breath|e /briːð/ vt/i respirar. ~er n descanso m, pausa f. ~ing n respiración f

breathtaking /ˈbreθteɪkɪŋ/ adj impresionante

bred /bred/ see BREED

breed /briːd/ vt (pt bred) criar; (fig) engendrar. ● vi reproducirse. ● n raza f

breez|e /briːz/ n brisa f. ~y adj de mucho viento

brew /bruː/ vt hacer (beer); preparar (tea). ● vi hacer cerveza; (tea) reposar; (fig) prepararse. ● n infusión f. ~er n cervecero m. ~ery n cervecería f, fábrica f de cerveza

bribe /braɪb/ n soborno m. ● vt sobornar. ~ry /braɪbərɪ/ n soborno m

brick /brɪk/ n ladrillo m. ~layer n albañil m

bridal /ˈbraɪdl/ adj nupcial

bride /braɪd/ n novia f. ~groom n novio m. ~smaid /ˈbraɪdzmeɪd/ n dama f de honor

bridge /brɪdʒ/ n puente m; (of nose) caballete m; (Cards) bridge m. ● vt tender un puente sobre. ~ a gap llenar un vacío

bridle /ˈbraɪdl/ n brida f. ~ path n camino m de herradura

brief /briːf/ adj (-er, -est) breve. ● n (Jurid) escrito m. ● vt dar instrucciones a. ~case n maletín m, portafolio(s) m (LAm). ~ly adv brevemente. ~s npl (man's) calzoncillos mpl; (woman's) bragas fpl, calzo-

nes mpl (LAm), pantaletas fpl (Mex)

brigade /brɪˈgeɪd/ n brigada f

bright /braɪt/ adj (-er, -est) brillante, claro; (clever) listo; (cheerful) alegre. ~en vt aclarar; hacer más alegre (house etc). ● vi (weather) aclararse; (face) illuminarse

brillian|ce /ˈbrɪljəns/ n brillantez f, brillo m. ~t adj brillante

brim /brɪm/ n borde m; (of hat) ala f. □ ~ over vi (pt brimmed) desbordarse

brine /braɪn/ n salmuera f

bring /brɪŋ/ vt (pt brought) traer; (lead) llevar. □ ~ about vt causar. □ ~ back vt devolver. □ ~ down vt derribar. □ ~ off vt lograr. □ ~ on vt causar. □ ~ out vt sacar; lanzar (product); publicar (book). □ ~ round/to vt hacer volver en sí. □ ~ up vt (Med) vomitar; educar (children); plantear (question)

brink /brɪŋk/ n borde m

brisk /brɪsk/ adj (-er, -est) enérgico, vivo

bristle /ˈbrɪsl/ n cerda f. ● vi erizarse

Brit|ain /ˈbrɪtən/ n Gran Bretaña f. ~ish /ˈbrɪtɪʃ/ adj británico. ● npl the ~ish los británicos. ~on /ˈbrɪtən/ n británico m

Brittany /ˈbrɪtənɪ/ n Bretaña f

brittle /ˈbrɪtl/ adj quebradizo

broach /brəʊtʃ/ vt abordar

broad /brɔːd/ adj (-er, -est) ancho. in ~ daylight a plena luz del día. ~band n banda f ancha. ~ bean n haba f. ~cast n emisión f. ● vt (pt broadcast) emitir. ● vi hablar por la radio. ~caster n locutor m. ~casting n radio-difusión f. ~en vt ensanchar. ● vi ensancharse. ~ly adv en general. ~-minded /-ˈmaɪndɪd/ adj de miras amplias, tolerante

broccoli /ˈbrɒkəlɪ/ n invar brécol m

brochure /ˈbrəʊʃə(r)/ n folleto m

broil /brɔɪl/ vt (Amer) asar a la parrilla. ~er n (Amer) parrilla f

broke /brəʊk/ see BREAK. ● adj 🏮 sin blanca, en la ruina

broken /ˈbrəʊkən/ see BREAK. ● adj roto

broker /ˈbrəʊkə(r)/ n corredor m

brolly /ˈbrɒlɪ/ n 🏮 paraguas m

bronchitis /brɒŋˈkaɪtɪs/ n bronquitis f

bronze /brɒnz/ n bronce m. ● adj de bronce

brooch /brəʊtʃ/ n broche m

brood /bruːd/ n cría f; (humorous) prole m. ● vi empollar; (fig) meditar

brook /brʊk/ n arroyo m. ● vt soportar

broom /bruːm/ n escoba f. ~stick n palo m de escoba

broth /brɒθ/ n caldo m

brothel /ˈbrɒθl/ n burdel m

brother /ˈbrʌðə(r)/ n hermano m. ~hood n fraternidad f. ~-in-law (pl ~s-in-law) n cuñado m. ~ly adj fraternal

brought /brɔːt/ see BRING

brow /braʊ/ n frente f; (of hill) cima f. ~beat vt (pt -beaten, pp -beat) intimidar

brown /braʊn/ adj (-er, -est) marrón, café (Mex); (hair) castaño; (skin) bronceado. ● n marrón m, café m (Mex). ● vt poner moreno; (Culin) dorar. ~bread n pan m integral. ~ sugar /braʊn ˈʃʊgə(r)/ n azúcar m moreno, azúcar f prieta

browse /braʊz/ vi (in a shop) curiosear; (animal) pacer; (Comp) navegar. ~r (Comp) browser m,

navegador m

bruise /bruːz/ n magulladura f. ● vt magullar; machucar (fruit)

brunch /brʌntʃ/ n 🏮 desayuno m tardío

brunette /bruːˈnet/ n morena f

brunt /brʌnt/ n. bear o take the ~ of sth sufrir algo

brush /brʌʃ/ n cepillo m; (large) escoba; (for decorating) brocha f; (artist's) pincel; (skirmish) escaramuza f. ● vt cepillar. □ ~ against vt rozar. □ ~ aside vt rechazar. □ ~ off (rebuff) vt desairar. □ ~ up (on) vt refrescar

brusque /bruːsk/ adj brusco. ~ly adv bruscamente

Brussels /ˈbrʌslz/ n Bruselas f. ~ sprout n col f de Bruselas

brutal /ˈbruːtl/ adj brutal. ~ity /-ˈtælətɪ/ n brutalidad f. ~ly adv brutalmente

brute /bruːt/ n bestia f. ~ force fuerza f bruta

BSc abbr see BACHELOR

BSE abbr (bovine spongiform encephalopathy) EBE f

bubbl|e /ˈbʌbl/ n burbuja f. ● vi burbujear. □ ~ over vi desbordarse. ~ly adj burbujeante

buck /bʌk/ adj macho. ● n (deer) ciervo m; (Amer fam) dólar m. pass the ~ pasar la pelota

bucket /ˈbʌkɪt/ n balde m, cubo m, cubeta f (Mex)

buckle /ˈbʌkl/ n hebilla f. ● vt abrochar. ● vi torcerse

bud /bʌd/ n brote m. ● vi (pt budded) brotar.

Buddhis|m /ˈbʊdɪzəm/ n budismo m. ~t adj & n budista (m & f)

budding /ˈbʌdɪŋ/ adj (fig) en ciernes

buddy /ˈbʌdɪ/ n 🗉 amigo m, cuate m (Mex)

budge /bʌdʒ/ vt mover. ● vi moverse

budgerigar /ˈbʌdʒərɪgɑː(r)/ n periquito m

budget /ˈbʌdʒɪt/ n presupuesto m

buffalo /ˈbʌfələʊ/ n (pl -oes or -o) búfalo m

buffer /ˈbʌfə(r)/ n parachoques m

buffet¹ /ˈbʌfeɪ/ n (meal) buffet m; (in train) bar m

buffet² /ˈbʌfɪt/ n golpe m

bug /bʌg/ n bicho m; 🗈 (germ) microbio m; (fam, device) micrófono m oculto. ● vt (pt bugged) 🗈 ocultar un micrófono en; (bother) molestar

buggy /ˈbʌgɪ/ n. baby ~ sillita f de paseo (plegable); (Amer) cochecito m

bugle /ˈbjuːgl/ n corneta f

build /bɪld/ vt/i (pt built) construir. ● n (of person) figura f, tipo m. □ ~ up vt/i fortalecer; (increase) aumentar. ~er n (contractor) contratista m & f; (labourer) albañil m. ~ing n edificio m; (construction) construcción f. ~up n aumento m; (of gas etc) acumulación f

built /bɪlt/ see **BUILD.** ~-in adj empotrado. ~-up area n zona f urbanizada

bulb /bʌlb/ n bulbo m; (Elec) bombilla f, foco m (Mex)

Bulgaria /bʌlˈgeərɪə/ n Bulgaria f. ~n adj & n búlgaro (m)

bulge /bʌldʒ/ n protuberancia f. ● vi pandearse. ~ing adj abultado; (eyes) saltón

bulk /bʌlk/ n bulto m, volumen m. in ~ a granel; (loose) suelto. the ~ of la mayor parte de. ~y adj voluminoso

bull /bʊl/ n toro m. ~dog n bulldog m. ~dozer /-dəʊzə(r)/ n bulldozer m

bullet /ˈbʊlɪt/ n bala f

bulletin /ˈbʊlətɪn/ n anuncio m; (journal) boletín m. ~ board n (Amer) tablón m de anuncios, tablero m de anuncios (LAm)

bulletproof /ˈbʊlɪtpruːf/ adj a prueba de balas

bullfight /ˈbʊlfaɪt/ n corrida f (de toros). ~er n torero m. ~ing n (deporte m de) los toros

bull: ~ring n plaza f de toros. ~'s-eye n diana f. ~shit n (vulgar) sandeces fpl 🗈, gilipolleces fpl ✕

bully /ˈbʊlɪ/ n matón m. ● vt intimidar. ~ing n intimidación f

bum /bʌm/ n (fam, backside) trasero m; (Amer fam, tramp) holgazán m

bumblebee /ˈbʌmblbiː/ n abejorro m

bump /bʌmp/ vt chocar contra. ● vi dar sacudidas. ● n (blow) golpe m; (jolt) sacudida f. □ ~ into vt chocar contra; (meet) encontrar.

bumper /ˈbʌmpə(r)/ n parachoques m. ● adj récord. ~ edition n edición f especial

bun /bʌn/ n bollo m; (bread roll) panecillo m, bolillo m (Mex); (hair) moño m, chongo m (Mex)

bunch /bʌntʃ/ n (of people) grupo m; (of bananas, grapes) racimo m; (of flowers) ramo m

bundle /ˈbʌndl/ n bulto m; (of papers) legajo m. □ ~ up vt atar

bungalow /ˈbʌŋgələʊ/ n casa f de un solo piso

bungle /ˈbʌŋgl/ vt echar a perder

bunk /bʌŋk/ n litera f

bunker /ˈbʌŋkə(r)/ n carbonera f;

(Golf, Mil) búnker m

bunny /'bʌnɪ/ n conejito m

buoy /'bɔɪ/ n boya f. □~ **up** vt hacer flotar; (fig) animar

buoyant /'bɔɪənt/ adj flotante; (fig) optimista

burden /'bɜːdn/ n carga f. ●vt cargar (with de)

bureau /'bjʊərəʊ/ n (pl -eaux /-əʊz/) agencia f; (desk) escritorio m; (Amer, chest of drawers) cómoda f

bureaucra|cy /bjʊə'rɒkrəsɪ/ n burocracia f. ~**t** /'bjʊərəkræt/ n burócrata m & f. ~**tic** /-'krætɪk/ adj burocrático

burger /'bɜːgə(r)/ n 🔲 hamburguesa f

burgl|ar /'bɜːglə(r)/ n ladrón m. ~**ar alarm** n alarma f antirrobo. ~**ary** n robo m (en casa o edificio). ~**e** /'bɜːgl/ vt entrar a robar en. **we were** ~**ed** nos entraron a robar

burial /'berɪəl/ n entierro m

burly /'bɜːlɪ/ adj (-ier, -iest) corpulento

burn /bɜːn/ vt (pt burned or burnt) quemar. ●vi quemarse. ●n quemadura f. ~**er** n quemador m. □~ **down** vt incendiar. vi incendiarse

burnt /bɜːnt/ see BURN

burp /bɜːp/ n 🔲 eructo m. ●vi 🔲 eructar

burrow /'bʌrəʊ/ n madriguera f. ●vt excavar

burst /bɜːst/ vt (pt burst) reventar. ●vi reventarse. ~ **into tears** echarse a llorar. ~ **out laughing** echarse a reír. ●n (Mil) ráfaga f; (of activity) arrebato; (of applause) salva f

bury /'berɪ/ vt enterrar; (hide) ocultar

bus /bʌs/ n (pl buses) autobús m, camión m (Mex)

bush /bʊʃ/ n arbusto m; (land) monte m. ~**y** adj espeso

business /'bɪznɪs/ n negocio m; (Com) negocios mpl; (profession) ocupación f; (fig) asunto m. **mind one's own** ~ ocuparse de sus propios asuntos. ~**like** adj práctico, serio. ~**man** /-mən/ n hombre m de negocios. ~**woman** n mujer f de negocios

busker /'bʌskə(r)/ n músico m ambulante

bus stop n parada f de autobús, paradero m de autobús (LAm)

bust /bʌst/ n busto m; (chest) pecho m. ●vt (pt busted or bust) 🔲 romper. ●vi romperse. ●adj roto. **go** ~ 🔲 quebrar

bust-up /'bʌstʌp/ n 🔲 riña f

busy /'bɪzɪ/ adj (-ier, -iest) ocupado; (street) concurrido. **be** ~ (Amer) (phone) estar comunicando, estar ocupado (LAm). ●vt. ~ **o.s. with** ocuparse de. ~**body** n entrometido m

but /bʌt/ conj pero; (after negative) sino. ●prep menos. ~ **for** si no fuera por. **last** ~ **one** penúltimo

butcher /'bʊtʃə(r)/ n carnicero m. ●vt matar; (fig) hacer una carnicería con

butler /'bʌtlə(r)/ n mayordomo m

butt /bʌt/ n (of gun) culata f; (of cigarette) colilla f; (target) blanco m; (Amer fam, backside) trasero m. ●vi topar. □~ **in** vi interrumpir

butter /'bʌtə(r)/ n mantequilla f. ●vt untar con mantequilla. ~**cup** n ranúnculo m. ~**fingers** n manazas m, torpe m. ~**fly** n mariposa f; (swimming) estilo m mariposa

buttock /'bʌtək/ n nalga f

button /'bʌtn/ n botón m. ● vt abotonar. ● vi abotonarse. ~hole n ojal m. ● vt (fig) detener

buy /baɪ/ vt/i (pt bought) comprar. ● n compra f. ~er n comprador m

buzz /bʌz/ n zumbido m. ● vi zumbar. □ ~ **off** vi ⊠ largarse. ~er n timbre m

by /baɪ/ prep por; (near) cerca de; (before) antes de; (according to) según. ~ and large en conjunto, en general. ~ car en coche. ~ oneself por sí solo

bye /baɪ/, **bye-bye** /ˈbaɪbaɪ/ int 🗓 ¡adiós!

by: ~-**election** n elección f parcial. ~**law** n reglamento m (local). ~**pass** n carretera f de circunvalación. ● vt eludir; (road) circunvalar. ~**product** n subproducto m ~**stander** /-stændə(r)/ n espectador m

byte /baɪt/ n (Comp) byte m, octeto m

Cc

cab /kæb/ n taxi m; (of lorry, train) cabina f

cabaret /ˈkæbəreɪ/ n cabaret m

cabbage /ˈkæbɪdʒ/ n col f, repollo m

cabin /ˈkæbɪn/ n (house) cabaña f; (in ship) camarote m; (in plane) cabina f

cabinet /ˈkæbɪnɪt/ n (cupboard) armario m; (for display) vitrina f. C~ (Pol) gabinete m

cable /ˈkeɪbl/ n cable m. ~ car n teleférico m. ~ TV n televisión f

por cable, cablevisión f (LAm)

cackle /ˈkækl/ n (of hen) cacareo m; (laugh) risotada f. ● vi cacarear; (laugh) reírse a carcajadas

cactus /ˈkæktəs/ n (pl -ti /-taɪ/ or -tuses) cacto m

caddie, caddy /ˈkædɪ/ n (golf) portador m de palos

cadet /kəˈdet/ n cadete m

cadge /kædʒ/ vt/i gorronear

café /ˈkæfeɪ/ n cafetería f

cafeteria /kæfɪˈtɪərɪə/ n restaurante m autoservicio

caffeine /ˈkæfiːn/ n cafeína f

cage /keɪdʒ/ n jaula f. ● vt enjaular

cake /keɪk/ n pastel m, tarta f; (sponge) bizcocho m. ~ of soap pastilla f de jabón

calamity /kəˈlæmɪtɪ/ n calamidad f

calcium /ˈkælsɪəm/ n calcio m

calculat|e /ˈkælkjʊleɪt/ vt/i calcular. ~**ion** /-ˈleɪʃn/ n cálculo m. ~**or** n calculadora f

calculus /ˈkælkjʊləs/ n (Math) cálculo m

calendar /ˈkælɪndə(r)/ n calendario m

calf /kɑːf/ n (pl calves) (animal) ternero m; (of leg) pantorilla f

calibre /ˈkælɪbə(r)/ n calibre m

call /kɔːl/ vt/i llamar. ● n llamada f; (shout) grito m; (visit) visita f. be on ~ estar de guardia. long-distance ~ llamada f de larga distancia, conferencia f. □ ~ **back** vt hacer volver; (on phone) volver a llamar. vi volver; (on phone) volver a llamar. □ ~ **for** vt pedir; (fetch) ir a buscar. □ ~ **off** vt suspender. □ ~ **on** vt pasar a visitar. □ ~ **out** vi dar voces. □ ~ **together** vt convocar. □ ~ **up** vt (Mil) llamar al servicio militar; (phone) llamar. ~

box *n* cabina *f* telefónica. ~ **centre** *n* centro *m* de llamadas. ~**er** *n* visita *f*; (*phone*) persona que llama *m.* ~**ing** *n* vocación *f*

callous /ˈkæləs/ *adj* insensible, cruel

calm /kɑːm/ *adj* (-er, -est) tranquilo; (*sea*) en calma. ● *n* tranquilidad *f*, calma *f*. ● *vt* calmar. ● *vi* calmarse. ~ **down** *vi* tranquilizarse. *vt* calmar. ~**ly** *adv* con calma

calorie /ˈkælərɪ/ *n* caloría *f*

calves /kɑːvz/ *npl see* CALF

camcorder /ˈkæmkɔːdə(r)/ *n* videocámara *f*, camcórder *m*

came /keɪm/ *see* COME

camel /ˈkæml/ *n* camello *m*

camera /ˈkæmərə/ *n* cámara *f*, máquina *f* fotográfica ~**man** /-mæn/ *n* camarógrafo *m*, cámara *m*

camouflage /ˈkæməflɑːʒ/ *n* camuflaje *m*. ● *vt* camuflar

camp /kæmp/ *n* campamento *m*. ● *vi* acampar. go ~**ing** hacer camping

campaign /kæmˈpeɪn/ *n* campaña *f*. ● *vi* hacer campaña

camp: ~**bed** *n* catre *m* de tijera. ~**er** *n* campista *m & f*; (*vehicle*) cámper *m*. ~**ground** *n* (*Amer*) *see* ~**SITE**. ~**ing** *n* camping *m*. ~**site** *n* camping *m*

campus /ˈkæmpəs/ *n* (*pl* -puses) campus *m*, ciudad *f* universitaria

can¹ /kæn/ /kən/

negative **can't, cannot** (formal); past **could**

auxiliary verb

····▸ (*be able to*) poder. I ~'t lift it no lo puedo levantar. she

says she ~ come dice que puede venir

····▸ (*be allowed to*) poder. ~ I smoke? ¿puedo fumar?

····▸ (*know verbs of*) saber. ~ you swim? ¿sabes nadar?

····▸ (*with verbs of perception*) *not translated.* I ~'t see you no te veo. I ~ hear you better now ahora te oigo mejor

····▸ (*in requests*) ~ I have a glass of water, please? ¿me trae un vaso de agua, por favor?. ~ I have a kilo of cheese, please? ¿me da un kilo de queso, por favor?

····▸ (*in offers*) ~ I help you? ¿te ayudo?; (*in shop*) ¿lo/la atienden?

can² /kæn/ *n* lata *f*, bote *m*. ● *vt* (*pt* canned) enlatar. ~**ned music** música *f* grabada

Canad|a /ˈkænədə/ *n* (el) Canadá *m*. ~**ian** /kəˈneɪdɪən/ *adj & n* canadiense (*m & f*)

canal /kəˈnæl/ *n* canal *m*

Canaries /kəˈneərɪz/ *npl* = CANARY ISLANDS

canary /kəˈneərɪ/ *n* canario *m*. C~ **Islands** *npl* the C~ Islands las Islas Canarias

cancel /ˈkænsl/ *vt* (*pt* cancelled) cancelar; anular (*command, cheque*); (*delete*) tachar. ~**lation** /-ˈleɪʃn/ *n* cancelación *f*

cancer /ˈkænsə(r)/ *n* cáncer *m*. C~ *n* (*in astrology*) Cáncer *m*. ~**ous** *adj* canceroso

candid /ˈkændɪd/ *adj* franco

candidate /ˈkændɪdeɪt/ *n* candidato *m*

candle /ˈkændl/ *n* vela *f*. ~**stick** *n* candelero *m*

candour /'kændə(r)/ n franqueza f

candy /'kændɪ/ n (Amer) caramelo m, dulce f (LAm). **~floss** /-flɒs/ n algodón m de azúcar

cane /keɪn/ n caña f; (for baskets) mimbre m; (stick) bastón m; (for punishment) palmeta f. ● vt castigar con palmeta

canister /'kænɪstə(r)/ n bote m

cannabis /'kænəbɪs/ n cáñamo m índico, hachís m, cannabis m

cannibal /'kænɪbl/ n caníbal m. **~ism** n canibalismo m

cannon /'kænən/ n invar cañón m. **~ ball** n bala f de cañón

cannot /'kænət/ see CAN¹

canoe /kə'nu:/ n canoa f, piragua f. ● vi ir en canoa

canon /'kænən/ n canon m; (person) canónigo m. **~ize** vt canonizar

can opener n abrelatas m

canopy /'kænəpɪ/ n dosel m

can't /kɑ:nt/ see CAN¹

cantankerous /kæn'tæŋkərəs/ adj mal humorado

canteen /kæn'ti:n/ n cantina f; (of cutlery) juego m de cubiertos

canter /'kæntə(r)/ n medio galope m. ● vi ir a medio galope

canvas /'kænvəs/ n lona f; (artist's) lienzo m

canvass /'kænvəs/ vi hacer campaña, solicitar votos. **~ing** n solicitación f (de votos)

canyon /'kænjən/ n cañón m

cap /kæp/ n gorra f; (lid) tapa f; (of cartridge) cápsula f; (of pen) capuchón m. ● vt (pt capped) tapar, poner cápsula a; (outdo) superar

capab|ility /keɪpə'bɪlətɪ/ n capacidad f. **~le** /'keɪpəbl/ adj capaz

capacity /kə'pæsətɪ/ n capacidad f; (function) calidad f

cape /keɪp/ n (cloak) capa f; (headland) cabo m

capital /'kæpɪtl/ adj capital. **~ letter** mayúscula f. ● n (money) capital f; (town) capital m. **~ism** n capitalismo m. **~ist** adj & n capitalista (m & f.) **~ize** vt capitalizar; escribir con mayúsculas (word). ● vi. **~ize on** aprovechar

capitulat|e /kə'pɪtʃuleɪt/ vi capitular. **~ion** n -'leɪʃn/ n capitulación f

> **Capitol** El Capitolio o sede del Congreso (Congress) de EE.UU., en Washington DC. Situado en *Capitol Hill*, a menudo la prensa emplea este nombre para hacer referencia al Congreso de EE.UU.

Capricorn /'kæprɪkɔ:n/ n Capricornio m

capsize /kæp'saɪz/ vt hacer volcar. ● vi volcarse

capsule /'kæpsju:l/ n cápsula f

captain /'kæptɪn/ n capitán m; (of plane) comandante m & f. ● vt capitanear

caption /'kæpʃn/ n (heading) título m; (of cartoon etc) leyenda f

captivate /'kæptɪveɪt/ vt encantar

captiv|e /'kæptɪv/ adj & n cautivo (m). **~ity** /-'tɪvətɪ/ n cautiverio m, cautividad f

capture /'kæptʃə(r)/ vt capturar; atraer (attention); (Mil) tomar. ● n apresamiento m; (Mil) toma f

car /kɑ:(r)/ n coche m, carro m (LAm); (Amer, of train) vagón m

caramel /'kærəmel/ n azúcar m quemado; (sweet) caramelo m, dulce m (LAm)

caravan /ˈkærəvæn/ n caravana f

carbohydrate /kɑːbəʊˈhaɪdreɪt/ n hidrato m de carbono

carbon /ˈkɑːbən/ n carbono m; (paper) carbón m. ~ **copy** n copia f al carbón. ~ **dioxide** /daɪˈɒksaɪd/ n anhídrido m carbónico. ~ **foot print** n huella f de carbono. ~ **monoxide** /məˈnɒksaɪd/ n monóxido de carbono

carburettor /kɑːbjʊˈretə(r)/ n carburador m

carcass /ˈkɑːkəs/ n cuerpo m de animal muerto; (for meat) res f muerta

card /kɑːd/ n tarjeta f; (for games) carta f; (membership) carnet m; (records) ficha f. ~**board** n cartón m

cardigan /ˈkɑːdɪgən/ n chaqueta f de punto, rebeca f

cardinal /ˈkɑːdɪnəl/ adj cardinal. ● n cardenal m

care /keə(r)/ n cuidado m; (worry) preocupación f; (protection) cargo m. ~ **of** a cuidado de, en casa de. **take** ~ tener cuidado. **take** ~ **of** cuidar de (person); ocuparse de (matter). ● vi interesarse. □ ~ **about** vt preocuparse por. □ ~ **for** vt cuidar de; (like) querer

career /kəˈrɪə(r)/ n carrera f. ● vi correr a toda velocidad

care:: ~**free** adj despreocupado. ~**ful** adj cuidadoso; (cautious) prudente. **be** ~**ful** tener cuidado. ~**fully** adv con cuidado. ~**less** adj negligente; (not worried) indiferente. ~**lessly** adv descuidadamente. ~**lessness** n descuido m. ~**r** n persona que cuida de un discapacitado

caress /kəˈres/ n caricia f. ● vt aca-

riciar

caretaker /ˈkeəteɪkə(r)/ n vigilante m; (of flats etc) portero m

car ferry n transbordador m de coches

cargo /ˈkɑːgəʊ/ n (pl -oes) carga f

Caribbean /kærɪˈbiːən/ adj caribeño. **the** ~ **(Sea)** n el mar Caribe

caricature /ˈkærɪkətʃʊə(r)/ n caricatura f. ● vt caricaturizar

carnage /ˈkɑːnɪdʒ/ n carnicería f, matanza f

carnation /kɑːˈneɪʃn/ n clavel m

carnival /ˈkɑːnɪvl/ n carnaval m

carol /ˈkærəl/ n villancico m

carousel /kærəˈsel/ n tiovivo m, carrusel m (LAm); (for baggage) cinta f transportadora

carp /kɑːp/ n invar carpa f. □ ~ **at** vi quejarse de

car park n aparcamiento m, estacionamiento m

carpent|er /ˈkɑːpɪntə(r)/ n carpintero m. ~**ry** /-trɪ/ n carpintería f

carpet /ˈkɑːpɪt/ n alfombra f. ~ **sweeper** n cepillo m mecánico

carriage /ˈkærɪdʒ/ n coche m; (Mec) carro m; (transport) transporte m; (cost, bearing) porte m; (of train) vagón m. ~**way** n calzada f

carrier /ˈkærɪə(r)/ n transportista m & f; (company) empresa f de transportes; (Med) portador m. ~ **bag** n bolsa f

carrot /ˈkærət/ n zanahoria f

carry /ˈkærɪ/ vt llevar; transportar (goods); (involve) llevar consigo, implicar. ● vi (sounds) llegar, oírse. □ ~ **off** vt llevarse. □ ~ **on** vi seguir, continuar. □ ~ **out** vt realizar; cumplir (promise, threat). ~ **cot** n cuna f portátil

carsick /ˈkɑːsɪk/ adj mareado (por viajar en coche)

cart /kɑːt/ n carro m; (Amer, supermarket, airport) carrito m. ● vt acarrear; (fam, carry) llevar

carton /ˈkɑːtən/ n caja f de cartón

cartoon /kɑːˈtuːn/ n caricatura f, chiste m; (strip) historieta f; (film) dibujos mpl animados

cartridge /ˈkɑːtrɪdʒ/ n cartucho m

carve /kɑːv/ vt tallar; trinchar (meat)

cascade /kæsˈkeɪd/ n cascada f. ● vi caer en cascadas

case /keɪs/ n caso m; (Jurid) proceso m; (crate) cajón m; (box) caja f; (suitcase) maleta f, petaca f (Mex). in any ∼ en todo caso. in ∼ he comes por si viene. in ∼ of en caso de

cash /kæʃ/ n dinero m efectivo. pay (in) ∼ pagar al contado. ● vt cobrar. ∼ in (on) aprovecharse de. ∼ desk n caja f. ∼ dispenser n cajero m automático

cashier /kæˈʃɪə(r)/ n cajero m

cashpoint /ˈkæʃpɔɪnt/ n cajero m automático

casino /kəˈsiːnəʊ/ n (pl -os) casino m

cask /kɑːsk/ n barril m

casket /ˈkɑːskɪt/ n cajita f; (Amer) ataúd m, cajón m (LAm)

casserole /ˈkæsərəʊl/ n cacerola f; (stew) guiso m, guisado m (Mex)

cassette /kəˈset/ n cassette m & f

cast /kɑːst/ vt (pt cast) arrojar; fundir (metal); emitir (vote). ● n lanzamiento m; (in play) reparto m; (mould) molde m

castanets /kæstəˈnets/ npl castañuelas fpl

castaway /ˈkɑːstəweɪ/ n náufrago m

caster /ˈkɑːstə(r)/ n ruedecita f. ∼ sugar n azúcar m extrafino

Castile /kæˈstiːl/ n Castilla f. ∼ian /kæˈstɪliən/ adj & n castellano (m)

cast: ∼ iron n hierro m fundido. ∼-iron adj (fig) sólido

castle /ˈkɑːsl/ n castillo m; (Chess) torre f

cast-offs /ˈkɑːstɒfs/ npl desechos mpl

castrate /kæˈstreɪt/ vt castrar. ∼ion /-ʃn/ n castración f

casual /ˈkæʒʊəl/ adj casual; (meeting) fortuito; (work) ocasional; (attitude) despreocupado; (clothes) informal, de sport. ∼ly adv de paso

casualty /ˈkæʒʊəltɪ/ n (injured) herido m; (dead) víctima f; (in hospital) urgencias fpl. ∼ies npl (Mil) bajas fpl

cat /kæt/ n gato m

Catalan /ˈkætələn/ adj & n catalán (m)

catalogue /ˈkætəlɒg/ n catálogo m. ● vt catalogar

Catalonia /kætəˈləʊnɪə/ n Cataluña f

catalyst /ˈkætəlɪst/ n catalizador m

catamaran /kætəməˈræn/ n catamarán m

catapult /ˈkætəpʌlt/ n catapulta f; (child's) tirachinas f, resortera f (Mex)

catarrh /kəˈtɑː(r)/ n catarro m

catastrophe /kəˈtæstrəfɪ/ n catástrofe m. ∼ic /kætəˈstrɒfɪk/ adj catastrófico

catch /kætʃ/ vt (pt caught) coger (esp Spain), agarrar, tomar (train, bus); (unawares) sorprender, pillar; (understand) entender; contagiarse de (disease). ∼ a cold resfriarse.

~ **sight of** avistar. • vi (*get stuck*)
engancharse; (*fire*) prenderse. • n
(*by goalkeeper*) parada f; (*of fish*)
pesca f; (*on door*) pestillo m; (*on
window*) cerradura f. ◻ ~ **on** vi ①
hacerse popular. ◻ ~ **up** vi poner
al día. ◻ ~ **up with** alcanzar; ponerse al corriente de (*news* etc).
~**ing** adj contagioso. ~**phrase** |
eslogan m. ~**y** adj pegadizo

categor|ical /ˌkætɪˈɡɒrɪkl/ adj ca-
tegórico. ~**y** /ˈkætɪɡərɪ/ n categoría f

cater /ˈkeɪtə(r)/ vi encargarse del
servicio de comida. ~ **for** proveer
a (*needs*). ~**er** n proveedor m

caterpillar /ˈkætəpɪlə(r)/ n oruga
f, azotador m (*Mex*)

cathedral /kəˈθiːdrəl/ n catedral f

catholic /ˈkæθəlɪk/ adj universal.
C~ adj & n católico (m). **C~ism** /kə
ˈθɒlɪsɪzəm/ n catolicismo m

cat: ~**nap** n sueñecito m.
C~seyes npl (®) catafaros mpl

cattle /ˈkætl/ npl ganado m

catwalk /ˈkætwɔːk/ n pasarela f

Caucasian /kɔːˈkeɪʒən/. n, a male
~ (*Amer*) un hombre de raza
blanca

caught /kɔːt/ see CATCH

cauliflower /ˈkɒlɪflaʊə(r)/ n coliflor f

cause /kɔːz/ n causa f, motivo m.
• vt causar

caution /ˈkɔːʃn/ n cautela f;
(*warning*) advertencia f. • vt advertir; (*Jurid*) amonestar. ~**us** /-ʃəs/
adj cauteloso, prudente

cavalry /ˈkævlrɪ/ n caballería f

cave /keɪv/ n cueva f. ◻ ~ **in** vi
hundirse. ~**man** n troglodita m

cavern /ˈkævən/ n caverna f

caviare /ˈkævɪɑː(r)/ n caviar m

cavity /ˈkævɪtɪ/ n cavidad f; (*in*

tooth*) caries f

CCTV abbr (closed circuit television) CCTV m

CD abbr (= **compact disc**) CD m. ~
player (reproductor m de)
compact-disc m. ~**-ROM** n
CD-ROM m

cease /siːs/ vt/i cesar. ~**fire** n alto
m el fuego

cedar /ˈsiːdə(r)/ n cedro m

ceiling /ˈsiːlɪŋ/ n techo m

celebrat|e /ˈselɪbreɪt/ vt celebrar.
• vi divertirse. ~**ed** adj célebre.
~**ion** /-ˈbreɪʃn/ n celebración f;
(*party*) fiesta f

celebrity /sɪˈlebrətɪ/ n celebridad f

celery /ˈselərɪ/ n apio m

cell /sel/ n celda f; (*in plants, electricity*) célula f

cellar /ˈselə(r)/ n sótano m; (*for
wine*) bodega f

cello /ˈtʃelaʊ/ n (pl -os) violon-
c(h)elo m, chelo m

Cellophane /ˈseləfeɪn/ n (®) celofán m (®)

cellphone /ˈselfəʊn/ n celular m
(*LAm*), móvil m (*Esp*)

cellul|ar /ˈseljʊlə(r)/ adj celular. ~
phone n teléfono celular m (*LAm*),
teléfono móvil m (*Esp*). ~**oid** n ce-
luloide m

Celsius /ˈselsɪəs/ adj. 20 degrees
~ 20 grados centígrados or Cel-
sio(s)

cement /sɪˈment/ n cemento m.
• vt cementar

cemetery /ˈsemətrɪ/ n cementerio m

cens|or /ˈsensə(r)/ n censor m. • vt
censurar. ~**ship** n censura f. ~**ure**
/ˈsenʃə(r)/ vt censurar

census /ˈsensəs/ n censo m

cent /sent/ n (S) centavo m; (€) céntimo m

centenary /sen'ti:nərɪ/ n centenario m

centi|grade /'sentɪɡreɪd/ adj centígrado. **~litre** n centilitro m. **~metre** n centímetro m. **~pede** /-pi:d/ n ciempiés m

central /'sentrəl/ adj central; (of town) céntrico. **~ heating** n calefacción f central. **~ize** vt centralizar

centre /'sentə(r)/ n centro m. ● vt (pt centred) centrar. ● vi centrarse (on en)

century /'sentʃərɪ/ n siglo m

cereal /'sɪərɪəl/ n cereal m

ceremon|ial /serɪ'məʊnɪəl/ adj & n ceremonial m. **~y** /'serɪmənɪ/ n ceremonia f

certain /'sɜːtn/ adj cierto. for **~** seguro. make **~** of asegurarse de. **~ly** adv desde luego

certificate /sə'tɪfɪkət/ n certificado m; (of birth, death etc) partida f

certify /'sɜːtɪfaɪ/ vt certificar

chafe /tʃeɪf/ vt rozar. ● vi rozarse

chaffinch /'tʃæfɪntʃ/ n pinzón m

chagrin /'ʃæɡrɪn/ n disgusto m

chain /tʃeɪn/ n cadena f. ● vt encadenar. **~ reaction** n reacción f en cadena. **~-smoker** n fumador m que siempre tiene un cigarrillo encendido. **~ store** n tienda f de una cadena

chair /tʃeə(r)/ n silla f; (Univ) cátedra f. ● vt presidir. **~-lift** n telesquí m, telesilla m (LAm). **~man** /-mən/ n presidente m

chalet /'ʃæleɪ/ n chalé m

chalk /tʃɔ:k/ n (in geology) creta f; (stick) tiza f, gis m (Mex)

challeng|e /'tʃælɪndʒ/ n desafío

m; (fig) reto m. ● vt desafiar; (question) poner en duda. **~ing** adj estimulante

chamber /'tʃeɪmbə(r)/ n (old use) cámara f. **~maid** n camarera f. **~pot** n orinal m

champagne /ʃæm'peɪn/ n champaña m, champán m

champion /'tʃæmpɪən/ n campeón m. ● vt defender. **~ship** n campeonato m

chance /tʃɑ:ns/ n casualidad f; (likelihood) posibilidad f; (opportunity) oportunidad f; (risk) riesgo m. by **~** por casualidad. ● adj fortuito

chancellor /'tʃɑ:nsələ(r)/ n canciller m; (Univ) rector m. **C~** of the Exchequer Ministro m de Hacienda

chandelier /ʃændə'lɪə(r)/ n araña f (de luces)

chang|e /tʃeɪndʒ/ vt cambiar; (substitute) reemplazar. **~ one's mind** cambiar de idea. ● vi cambiarse. ● n cambio m; (coins) cambio m, sencillo m (LAm), feria f (Mex); (money returned) cambio m, vuelta f, vuelto m (LAm). **~eable** adj cambiable; (weather) variable. **~ing room** n (Sport) vestuario m, vestidor m (Mex); (in shop) probador m

channel /'tʃænl/ n canal m; (TV) medio m. ● vt (pt channelled) acanalar; (fig) encauzar. **the (English) C~** el Canal de la Mancha. **C~ Islands** npl. **the C~ Islands** las islas Anglonormandas. **C~ Tunnel** n. **the C~ Tunnel** el Eurotúnel

chant /tʃɑ:nt/ n canto m. ● vt/i cantar

chaos /'keɪɒs/ n caos m. **~tic** /-'ɒtɪk/ adj caótico

chap /tʃæp/ n 1 tipo m, tío m 1. ● vt (pt chapped) agrietar. ● vi agrietarse

chapel /'tʃæpl/ n capilla f

chaperon /'ʃæpərəʊn/ n acompañante f

chapter /'tʃæptə(r)/ n capítulo m

char /tʃɑː(r)/ vt (pt charred) carbonizar

character /'kærəktə(r)/ n carácter m; (in book, play) personaje m. **in ~** característico. **~istic** /-'rɪstɪk/ adj típico. **~ize** vt caracterizar

charade /ʃə'rɑːd/ n farsa f. **~s** npl (game) charada f

charcoal /'tʃɑːkəʊl/ n carbón m vegetal; (for drawing) carboncillo m

charge /tʃɑːdʒ/ n precio m; (Elec, Mil) carga f; (Jurid) acusación f; (task, custody) encargo m; (responsibility) responsabilidad f. **in ~ of** responsable de, encargado de. **the person in ~** la persona responsable. **take ~ of** encargarse de. ● vt pedir; (Elec, Mil) cargar; (Jurid) acusar. ● vi cargar; (animal) embestir (at contra)

charit|able /'tʃærɪtəbl/ adj caritativo. **~y** /'tʃærɪtɪ/ n caridad f; (society) institución f benéfica

charm /tʃɑːm/ n encanto m; (spell) hechizo m; (on bracelet) dije m, amuleto m. ● vt encantar. **~ing** adj encantador

chart /tʃɑːt/ n (for navigation) carta f de navegación; (table) tabla f

charter /'tʃɑːtə(r)/ n carta f. ● vt alquilar (bus, train); fletar (plane, ship). **~ flight** n vuelo m chárter

chase /tʃeɪs/ vt perseguir. ● vi correr (after tras). ● n persecución f. □ **~ away**, □ **~ off** vt ahuyentar

chassis /'ʃæsɪ/ n chasis m

chastise /tʃæs'taɪz/ vt castigar

chastity /'tʃæstətɪ/ n castidad f

chat /tʃæt/ n charla f, conversación f (LAm), plática f (Mex). ● vi (pt chatted) charlar, conversar (LAm), platicar (Mex)

chatter /'tʃætə(r)/ n charla f. ● vi charlar. **his teeth are ~ing** le castañetean los dientes. **~box** n parlanchín m

chauffeur /'ʃəʊfə(r)/ n chófer m

chauvinis|m /'ʃəʊvɪnɪzəm/ n patriotería f; (male) machismo m. **~t** n patriotero m; (male) machista m

cheap /tʃiːp/ adj (-er, -est) barato; (poor quality) de baja calidad; (rate) económico. **~(ly)** adv barato, a bajo precio

cheat /tʃiːt/ vt defraudar; (deceive) engañar. ● vi (at cards) hacer trampas. ● n trampa f; (person) tramposo m

check /tʃek/ vt comprobar; (examine) inspeccionar; (curb) frenar. ● vi comprobar. ● n comprobación f; (of tickets) control m; (curb) freno m; (Chess) jaque m; (pattern) cuadro m; (Amer, bill) cuenta f; (Amer, cheque) cheque m. □ **~ in** vi registrarse; (at airport) facturar el equipaje, chequear el equipaje (LAm), registrar el equipaje (Mex). □ **~ out** vi pagar la cuenta y marcharse. □ **~ up** vi confirmar. □ **~ up on** vi investigar. **~book** n (Amer) see CHEQUEBOOK. **~ered** /'tʃekəd/ adj (Amer) see CHEQUERED

checkers /'tʃekəz/ n (Amer) damas fpl

check: **~mate** n jaque m mate. ● vt dar mate a. **~out** n caja f. **~point** n control m. **~up** n chequeo m, revisión f

cheek /tʃiːk/ n mejilla f; (fig) descaro m. **~bone** n pómulo m. **~y** adj descarado

cheep /tʃiːp/ vi piar

cheer /tʃɪə(r)/ n alegría f; (applause) viva m. ~s! ¡salud! • vt alegrar; (applaud) aplaudir. • vi alegrarse; (applaud) aplaudir. ~ up! ¡anímate! ~ful adj alegre

cheerio /tʃɪərɪˈəʊ/ int 🔟 ¡adiós!, ¡hasta luego!

cheerless /ˈtʃɪəlɪs/ adj triste

cheese /tʃiːz/ n queso m

cheetah /ˈtʃiːtə/ n guepardo m

chef /ʃef/ n jefe m de cocina

chemical /ˈkemɪkl/ adj químico. • n producto m químico

chemist /ˈkemɪst/ n farmacéutico m; (scientist) químico m. ~'s (shop) n química f. ~'s (shop) farmacia f

cheque /tʃek/ n cheque m, talón m. ~book n chequera f, talonario m

cherish /ˈtʃerɪʃ/ vt cuidar; (love) querer; abrigar (hope)

cherry /ˈtʃerɪ/ n cereza f. ~ tree n cerezo m

chess /tʃes/ n ajedrez m. ~board n tablero m de ajedrez

chest /tʃest/ n pecho m; (box) cofre m, cajón m

chestnut /ˈtʃesnʌt/ n castaña f. • adj castaño. ~ tree n castaño m

chest of drawers n cómoda f

chew /tʃuː/ vt masticar. ~ing gum n chicle m

chic /ʃiːk/ adj elegante

chick /tʃɪk/ n polluelo m. ~en /ˈtʃɪkɪn/ n pollo m. • adj 🔟 cobarde. □ ~en out vi 🔟 acobardarse. ~enpox /ˈtʃɪkɪnpɒks/ n varicela f. ~pea n garbanzo m

chicory /ˈtʃɪkərɪ/ n (in coffee) achicoria f; (in salad) escarola f

chief /tʃiːf/ n jefe m. • adj principal. ~ly adv principalmente

chilblain /ˈtʃɪlbleɪn/ n sabañón m

child /tʃaɪld/ n (pl **children** /ˈtʃɪldrən/) niño m; (offspring) hijo m. ~birth n parto m. ~hood n niñez f. ~ish adj infantil. ~less adj sin hijos. ~like adj ingenuo, de niño

Chile /ˈtʃɪlɪ/ n Chile m. ~an adj & n chileno (m)

chill /tʃɪl/ n frío m; (illness) resfriado m. • adj frío. • vt enfriar; refrigerar (food)

chilli /ˈtʃɪlɪ/ n (pl -ies) chile m

chilly /ˈtʃɪlɪ/ adj frío

chime /tʃaɪm/ n carillón m. • vt tocar (bells); dar (hours). • vi repicar

chimney /ˈtʃɪmnɪ/ n (pl -eys) chimenea f. ~ sweep n deshollinador m

chimpanzee /tʃɪmpænˈziː/ n chimpancé m

chin /tʃɪn/ n barbilla f

china /ˈtʃaɪnə/ n porcelana f

China /ˈtʃaɪnə/ n China f. ~ese /-ˈniːz/ adj & n chino (m)

chink /tʃɪŋk/ n (crack) grieta f; (sound) tintín m. • vi tintinear

chip /tʃɪp/ n pedacito m; (splinter) astilla f; (Culin) patata f frita, papa f frita (LAm); (in gambling) ficha f; (Comp) chip m. have a ~ on one's shoulder guardar rencor. • vt (pt chipped) desportillar. □ ~ in vi 🔟 interrumpir; (with money) contribuir

chiropodist /kɪˈrɒpədɪst/ n callista m & f, pedicuro m

chirp /tʃɜːp/ n pío m. • vi piar. ~y adj alegre

chisel /ˈtʃɪzl/ n formón m. • vt (pt chiselled) cincelar

chivalr|ous /ˈʃɪvəlrəs/ adj caballeroso. ~y /-rɪ/ n caballerosidad f

chlorine /ˈklɔːriːn/ n cloro m

chock /tʃɒk/ n cuña f. **~-a-block** adj. **~-full** adj atestado

chocolate /'tʃɒklət/ n chocolate m; (individual sweet) bombón m, chocolate m (LAm)

choice /tʃɔɪs/ n elección f; (preference) preferencia f. ● adj escogido

choir /'kwaɪə(r)/ n coro m

choke /tʃəʊk/ vt sofocar. ● vi sofocarse. ● n (Auto) choke m, estárter m, ahogador m (Mex)

cholera /'kɒlərə/ n cólera m

cholesterol /kə'lestərɒl/ n colesterol m

choose /tʃuːz/ vt/i (pt chose, pp chosen) elegir, escoger. **~y** adj 🔲 exigente

chop /tʃɒp/ vt (pt chopped) cortar. ● n (Culin) chuleta f. □ **~ down** vt talar. □ **~ off** vt cortar. **~per** n hacha f; (butcher's) cuchilla f. **~py** adj picado

chord /kɔːd/ n (Mus) acorde f.

chore /tʃɔː(r)/ n tarea f, faena f. **household ~s** npl quehaceres mpl domésticos

chorus /'kɔːrəs/ n coro m; (of song) estribillo m

chose /tʃəʊz/, **chosen** /'tʃəʊzn/ see CHOOSE

Christ /kraɪst/ n Cristo m

christen /'krɪsn/ vt bautizar. **~ing** n bautizo m

Christian /'krɪstʃən/ adj & n cristiano (m). **~ity** /krɪstɪ'ænətɪ/ n cristianismo m. **~ name** n nombre m de pila

Christmas /'krɪsməs/ n Navidad f. Merry **~!** ¡Feliz Navidad!, ¡Felices Pascuas! Father **~** Papá m Noel. ● adj de navidad, navideño. **~ card** n tarjeta f de Navidad f. **~ day** n día m de Navidad. **~ Eve** n Nochebuena f. **~ tree** n árbol m de Navidad

chrom|e /krəʊm/ n cromo m. **~ium** /'krəʊmɪəm/ n cromo m

chromosome /'krəʊməsəʊm/ n cromosoma m

chronic /'krɒnɪk/ adj crónico; (fam, bad) terrible

chronicle /'krɒnɪkl/ n crónica f. ● vt historiar

chronological /krɒnə'lɒdʒɪkl/ adj cronológico

chubby /'tʃʌbɪ/ adj (-ier, -iest) regordete; (person) gordinflón 🔲

chuck /tʃʌk/ 🔲 tirar. □ **~ out** vt tirar

chuckle /'tʃʌkl/ n risa f ahogada. ● vi reírse entre dientes

chug /tʃʌg/ vi (pt chugged) (of motor) traquetear

chum /tʃʌm/ n amigo m, compinche m, cuate m (Mex)

chunk /tʃʌŋk/ n trozo m grueso. **~y** adj macizo

church /tʃɜːtʃ/ n iglesia f. **~yard** n cementerio m

churn /tʃɜːn/ n (for milk) lechera f, cántara f; (for making butter) mantequera f. ● vt agitar. □ **~ out** vt producir en profusión

chute /ʃuːt/ n tobogán m

cider /'saɪdə(r)/ n sidra f

cigar /sɪ'gɑː(r)/ n puro m

cigarette /sɪgə'ret/ n cigarrillo m. **~ end** n colilla f. **~ holder** n boquilla f. **~ lighter** n mechero m, encendedor f

cinecamera /'sɪnɪkæmərə/ n tomavistas m, filmadora f (LAm)

cinema /'sɪnəmə/ n cine m

cipher /'saɪfə(r)/ n (Math, fig) cero m; (code) clave f

circle /'sɜːkl/ n círculo m; (in theatre) anfiteatro m. ● vt girar alrededor de. • vi dar vueltas

circuit /ˈsɜːkɪt/ n circuito m

circular /ˈsɜːkjʊlə(r)/ adj & n circular (f)

circulat|e /ˈsɜːkjʊleɪt/ vt hacer circular. • vi circular. ~ion /-ˈleɪʃn/ n circulación f; (number of copies) tirada f

circumcise /ˈsɜːkəmsaɪz/ vt circuncidar

circumference /səˈkʌmfərəns/ n circunferencia f

circumstance /ˈsɜːkəmstəns/ n circunstancia f. ~s (means) npl situación f económica

circus /ˈsɜːkəs/ n circo m

cistern /ˈsɪstən/ n cisterna f

cite /saɪt/ vt citar

citizen /ˈsɪtɪzn/ n ciudadano m; (inhabitant) habitante m & f

citrus /ˈsɪtrəs/ n. ~ fruits cítricos mpl

city /ˈsɪtɪ/ n ciudad f; the C~ el centro m financiero de Londres

> **City** - the Área ubicada dentro de los límites de la antigua ciudad de Londres. Actualmente es el centro financiero de la capital donde tienen sus sedes centrales muchas instituciones financieras. A menudo, cuando se habla de The City, se está refiriendo a ésas y no a la zona propiamente dicha.

civic /ˈsɪvɪk/ adj cívico

civil /ˈsɪvl/ adj civil; (polite) cortés

civilian /sɪˈvɪlɪən/ adj & n civil (m & f)

civiliz|ation /sɪvɪlaɪˈzeɪʃn/ n civilización f. ~ed /ˈsɪvɪlaɪzd/ adj civilizado.

civil: ~ **partnership** n matrimonio m de homosexuales. ~

servant n funcionario m (del Estado), burócrata m & f (Mex.)

service n administración f pública. ~ **war** n guerra f civil

clad /klæd/ see CLOTHE

claim /kleɪm/ vt reclamar; (assert) pretender. • n reclamación f; (right) derecho m; (Jurid) demanda f

clairvoyant /kleəˈvɔɪənt/ n clarividente m & f

clam /klæm/ n almeja f. • vi (pt clammed). ~ **up** 🔲 ponerse muy poco comunicativo

clamber /ˈklæmbə(r)/ vi trepar a gatas

clammy /ˈklæmɪ/ adj (-ier, -iest) húmedo

clamour /ˈklæmə(r)/ n clamor m. • vi. ~ **for** pedir a gritos

clamp /klæmp/ n abrazadera f; (Auto) cepo m. • vt sujetar con abrazadera; poner cepo a (car). ~ **down on** vt reprimir

clan /klæn/ n clan m

clang /klæŋ/ n sonido m metálico

clap /klæp/ vt (pt clapped) aplaudir; batir (hands). • vi aplaudir. • n palmada f; (of thunder) trueno m

clarif|ication /klærɪfɪˈkeɪʃn/ n aclaración f. ~y /ˈklærɪfaɪ/ vt aclarar. • vi aclararse

clarinet /klærɪˈnet/ n clarinete m

clarity /ˈklærətɪ/ n claridad f

clash /klæʃ/ n choque m; (noise) estruendo m; (contrast) contraste m; (fig) conflicto m. • vt golpear. • vi encontrarse; (colours) desentonar

clasp /klɑːsp/ n cierre m. • vt agarrar; apretar (hand)

class /klɑːs/ n clase f. **evening** ~ n clase nocturna. • vt clasificar

classic /ˈklæsɪk/ adj & n clásico (m). ~**al** adj clásico. ~**s** npl estudios mpl clásicos

classif|ication /klæsɪfɪˈkeɪʃn/ n clasificación f. **~y** /ˈklæsɪfaɪ/ vt clasificar

class: ~room n aula f, clase f. **~y** adj 🅓 elegante

clatter /ˈklætə(r)/ n ruido m; (of train) traqueteo m. ● vi hacer ruido

clause /klɔːz/ n cláusula f; (Gram) oración f

claustrophobia /ˌklɔːstrəˈfəʊbɪə/ n claustrofobia f

claw /klɔː/ n garra f; (of cat) uña f; (of crab) pinza f. ● vt arañar

clay /kleɪ/ n arcilla f

clean /kliːn/ adj (-er, -est) limpio; (stroke) bien definido. ● adv completamente. ● vt limpiar. ○ **~ up** vt hacer la limpieza. **~er** n persona f que hace la limpieza. **~liness** /ˈklenlɪnɪs/ n limpieza f

cleans|e /klenz/ vt limpiar. **~er** n producto m de limpieza; (for skin) crema f de limpieza. **~ing cream** n crema f de limpieza

clear /klɪə(r)/ adj (-er, -est) claro; (transparent) transparente; (without obstacles) libre; (profit) neto; (sky) despejado. **keep ~ of** evitar. ● adv claramente. ● vt despejar; liquidar (goods); (Jurid) absolver; (jump over) saltar por encima de; quitar, levantar (LAm) (table). ○ **~ off** vi 🅧, **~ out** vi (🅧, go away) largarse. ○ **~ up** vt (tidy) ordenar; aclarar (mystery). ● vi (weather) despejarse. **~ance** n (removal of obstructions) despeje m; (authorization) permiso m; (by security) acreditación f. **~ing** n claro m. **~ly** adv evidentemente. **~way** n carretera f en la que no se permite parar

cleavage /ˈkliːvɪdʒ/ n escote m

clef /klef/ n (Mus) clave f

clench /klentʃ/ vt apretar

clergy /ˈklɜːdʒɪ/ n clero m. **~man** /-mən/ n clérigo m

cleric /ˈklerɪk/ n clérigo m. **~al** adj clerical; (of clerks) de oficina

clerk /klɑːk/ n empleado m; (Amer, salesclerk) vendedor m

clever /ˈklevə(r)/ adj (-er, -est) inteligente; (skilful) hábil. **~ly** adv inteligentemente; (with skill) hábilmente. **~ness** n inteligencia f

cliché /ˈkliːʃeɪ/ n lugar m común m, cliché m

click /klɪk/ n golpecito m. ● vi chascar; 🅓 llevarse bien. **~ on sth** hacer clic en algo. ● vt chasquear

client /ˈklaɪənt/ n cliente m

cliff /klɪf/ n acantilado m

climat|e /ˈklaɪmət/ n clima m. **~e change** n cambio m climático. **~ic** /-ˈmætɪk/ adj climático

climax /ˈklaɪmæks/ n clímax m; (orgasm) orgasmo m

climb /klaɪm/ vt subir (stairs); trepar (tree); escalar (mountain). ● vi subir. ○ **~ down** vi bajar; (fig) ceder. **~er** n (Sport) alpinista m & f, andinista m & f (LAm); (plant) trepadora f

clinch /klɪntʃ/ vt cerrar (deal)

cling /klɪŋ/ vi (pt clung) agarrarse; (stick) pegarse

clinic /ˈklɪnɪk/ n centro m médico; (private hospital) clínica f. **~al** adj clínico

clink /klɪŋk/ n tintineo m. ● vt hacer tintinear. ● vi tintinear

clip /klɪp/ n (fastener) clip m; (for paper) sujetapapeles m; (for hair) horquilla f. ● vt (pt clipped) (cut) cortar; (join) sujetar. **~pers** /ˈklɪpəz/ npl (for hair) maquinilla f para cortar el pelo; (for nails) cortauñas m. **~ping** n recorte m

cloak /kləʊk/ n capa f. **~room** n guardarropa m; (toilet) lavabo m, baño m (LAm)

clock /klɒk/ n reloj m. **~wise** a/adv en el sentido de las agujas del reloj. **~work** n mecanismo m de relojería. like **~work** con precisión

clog /klɒg/ n zueco m. ● vt (pt clogged) atascar

cloister /ˈklɔɪstə(r)/ n claustro m

clone /kləʊn/ n clon m

close¹ /kləʊs/ adj (-er, -est) cercano; (together) apretado; (friend) íntimo; (weather) bochornoso; (link etc) estrecho; (game, battle) reñido. have a **~** shave (fig) escaparse de milagro. ● adv cerca

close² /kləʊz/ vt cerrar. ● vi cerrarse; (end) terminar. **~ down** vt/i cerrar. ● n fin m. **~d** adj cerrado

closely /ˈkləʊslɪ/ adv estrechamente; (at a short distance) de cerca; (with attention) detenidamente; (precisely) rigurosamente

closet /ˈklɒzɪt/ n (Amer) armario m; (for clothes) armario m, closet m (LAm)

close-up /ˈkləʊsʌp/ n (Cinema etc) primer plano m

closure /ˈkləʊʒə(r)/ n cierre m

clot /klɒt/ n (Med) coágulo m; 𝔼 tonto m. ● vi (pt clotted) cuajarse; (blood) coagularse

cloth /klɒθ/ n tela f; (duster) trapo m; (tablecloth) mantel m

clothe /kləʊð/ vt (pt clothed or clad) vestir. **~es** /kləʊðz/ npl ropa. **~espin**, **~espeg** (Amer) n pinza f (para tender la ropa). **~ing** n ropa f

cloud /klaʊd/ n nube f. ● **~ over** vi nublarse. **~y** adj (-ier, -iest) nu-

blado; (liquid) turbio

clout /klaʊt/ n bofetada f. ● vt abofetear

clove /kləʊv/ n clavo m. **~ of garlic** n diente m de ajo

clover /ˈkləʊvə(r)/ n trébol m

clown /klaʊn/ n payaso m. ● vi hacer el payaso

club /klʌb/ n club m; (weapon) porra f; (golf club) palo m de golf; (at cards) trébol m. ● vt (pt clubbed) aporrear. □ **~ together** vi contribuir con dinero (to para)

cluck /klʌk/ vi cloquear

clue /kluː/ n pista f; (in crosswords) indicación f. not to have a **~** no tener la menor idea

clump /klʌmp/ n grupo m. ● vt agrupar

clums|iness /ˈklʌmzɪnɪs/ n torpeza f. **~y** /ˈklʌmzɪ/ adj (-ier, -iest) torpe

clung /klʌŋ/ see CLING

cluster /ˈklʌstə(r)/ n grupo m. ● vi agruparse

clutch /klʌtʃ/ vt agarrar. ● n (Auto) embrague m

clutter /ˈklʌtə(r)/ n desorden m. ● vt. **~ (up)** abarrotar. **~ed** /ˈklʌtəd/ adj abarratado de cosas

coach /kəʊtʃ/ n autocar m, autobús m; (of train) vagón m; (horse-drawn) coche m; (Sport) entrenador m. ● vt (Sport) entrenar

coal /kəʊl/ n carbón m

coalition /kəʊəˈlɪʃn/ n coalición f

coarse /kɔːs/ adj (-er, -est) grueso; (material) basto; (person, language) ordinario

coast /kəʊst/ n costa f. ● vi (with cycle) deslizarse sin pedalear; (with car) n en punto muerto. **~al** adj costero. **~guard** n guardacostas m. **~line** n litoral m

coat /kəʊt/ n abrigo m; (*jacket*) chaqueta f; (*of animal*) pelo m; (*of paint*) mano f. ● vt cubrir, revestir. **~hanger** n percha f, gancho m (LAm). **~ing** n capa f. **~ of arms** n escudo m de armas

coax /kəʊks/ vt engatusar

cobbler /'kɒblə(r)/ n zapatero m (remendón)

cobblestone /'kɒbəlstəʊn/ n adoquín m

cobweb /'kɒbweb/ n telaraña f

cocaine /kə'keɪn/ n cocaína f

cock /kɒk/ n (*cockerel*) gallo m; (*male bird*) macho m. ● vt amartillar (*gun*); aguzar (*ears*). **~erel** /'kɒkərəl/ n gallo m. **~-eyed** /-aɪd/ adj 🔢 torcido

cockney /'kɒknɪ/ adj & n (pl **-eys**) londinense (m & f) (del este de Londres)

cockpit /'kɒkpɪt/ n (*in aircraft*) cabina f del piloto

cockroach /'kɒkrəʊtʃ/ n cucaracha f

cocktail /'kɒkteɪl/ n cóctel m

cock-up /'kɒkʌp/ n 🔢 lío m

cocky /'kɒkɪ/ adj (**-ier**, **-iest**) engreído

cocoa /'kəʊkəʊ/ n cacao m; (*drink*) chocolate m, cocoa f (LAm)

coconut /'kəʊkənʌt/ n coco m

cocoon /kə'ku:n/ n capullo m

cod /kɒd/ n invar bacalao m

code /kəʊd/ n código m; (*secret*) clave f; **in ~** en clave

coeducational /kəʊedʒʊ 'keɪʃənl/ adj mixto

coerc|e /kəʊ'ɜ:s/ vt coaccionar. **~ion** /-ʃn/ n coacción f

coffee /'kɒfɪ/ n café m. **~ bean** n grano m de café. **~ maker** n cafetera f. **~pot** n cafetera f

coffin /'kɒfɪn/ n ataúd m, cajón m (LAm)

cog /kɒg/ n diente m; (*fig*) pieza f

coherent /kəʊ'hɪərənt/ adj coherente

coil /kɔɪl/ vt enrollar. ● n rollo m; (*one ring*) vuelta f

coin /kɔɪn/ n moneda f. ● vt acuñar

coincide /kəʊɪn'saɪd/ vi coincidir. **~nce** /kəʊ'ɪnsɪdəns/ n casualidad f. **~ntal** /kəʊɪnsɪ'dentl/ adj casual

coke /kəʊk/ n (*coal*) coque m. **C~** ⑧ Coca-Cola f ⑧

colander /'kʌləndə(r)/ n colador m

cold /kəʊld/ adj (**-er**, **-est**) frío. **be ~** (*person*) tener frío. **it is ~** (*weather*) hace frío. ● n frío m; (*Med*) resfriado m. **have a ~** estar resfriado. **~-blooded** /-'blʌdɪd/ adj (*animal*) de sangre fría; (*murder*) a sangre fría. **~-shoulder** /-'ʃəʊldə(r)/ vt tratar con frialdad. **~ sore** n herpes m labial. **~ storage** n conservación f en frigorífico

coleslaw /'kəʊlslɔ:/ n ensalada f de col

collaborat|e /kə'læbəreɪt/ vi colaborar. **~ion** /-'reɪʃn/ n colaboración f. **~or** n colaborador m

collaps|e /kə'læps/ vi derrumbarse; (*Med*) sufrir un colapso. ● n derrumbamiento m; (*Med*) colapso m. **~ible** /-əbl/ adj plegable

collar /'kɒlə(r)/ n cuello m; (*for animals*) collar m. ● vt 🔢 hurtar. **~bone** n clavícula f

colleague /'kɒli:g/ n colega m & f

collect /kə'lekt/ vt reunir; (*hobby*) coleccionar, juntar (LAm); (*pick up*) recoger; cobrar (rent). ● vi (*people*) reunirse; (*things*) acumularse. **~ion** /-ʃn/ n colección f; (*in church*) colecta f; (*of post*) recogida *f.* ~**or** *n* coleccionista *m*

college /'kɒlɪdʒ/ *n* colegio *m*; *(of art, music etc)* escuela *f*; *(Amer)* universidad *f*

colli|de /kə'laɪd/ *vi* chocar. ~**sion** /-'lɪʒn/ *n* choque *m*

colloquial /kə'ləʊkwɪəl/ *adj* coloquial

Colombia /kə'lʌmbɪə/ *n* Colombia *f*. ~**n** *adj* & *n* colombiano *(m)*

colon /'kəʊlən/ *n* (Gram) dos puntos *mpl*; *(Med)* colon *m*

colonel /'kɜːnl/ *n* coronel *m*

colon|ial /kə'ləʊnɪəl/ *adj* colonial. ~**ize** /'kɒlənaɪz/ *vt* colonizar. ~**y** /'kɒlənɪ/ *n* colonia *f*

colossal /kə'lɒsl/ *adj* colosal

colour /'kʌlə(r)/ *n* color *m*. off ~ *(fig)* indispuesto. ● *adj* de color(es), en color(es) ● *vt* colorear; *(dye)* teñir. ~**blind** *adj* daltónico. ~**ed** /'kʌləd/ *adj* de color. ~**ful** *adj* lleno de color; *(fig)* pintoresco. ~**ing** *n* color; *(food colouring)* colorante *m*. ~**less** *adj* incoloro

column /'kɒləm/ *n* columna *f*. ~**ist** *n* columnista *m* & *f*

coma /'kəʊmə/ *n* coma *m*

comb /kəʊm/ *n* peine *m*. ● *vt* *(search)* registrar. ~ one's hair peinarse

combat /'kɒmbæt/ *n* combate *m*. ● *vt* (*pt* combated) combatir

combination /kɒmbɪ'neɪʃn/ *n* combinación *f*

combine /kəm'baɪn/ *vt* combinar. ● *vi* combinarse. ● /'kɒmbaɪn/ *n* asociación *f*. ~ **harvester** *n* cosechadora *f*

combustion /kəm'bʌstʃən/ *n* combustión *f*

come /kʌm/ *vi* (*pt* came, *pp* come) venir; *(occur)* pasar. □ ~ **across** *vt* encontrarse con (person); encon-

trar (object). □ ~ **apart** *vi* deshacerse. □ ~ **away** *vi* (leave) salir; *(become detached)* salirse. □ ~ **back** *vi* volver. □ ~ **by** *vt* obtener. □ ~ **down** *vi* bajar. □ ~ **in** *vi* entrar; *(arrive)* llegar. □ ~ **into** *vt* entrar en; heredar (money). □ ~ **off** *vi* desprenderse; *(succeed)* tener éxito. *vt.* ~ **off it!** [] ¡no me vengas con eso! □ ~ **on** *vi* *(start to work)* encenderse. ~ **on, hurry up!** ¡vamos, date prisa! □ ~ **out** *vi* salir. □ ~ **round** *vi* *(after fainting)* volver en sí; *(be converted)* cambiar de idea; *(visit)* venir. □ ~ **to** *vt* llegar a (decision etc). □ ~ **up** *vi* subir; *(fig)* surgir. □ ~ **up with** *vt* proponer (idea). ~**back** *n* retorno *m*; *(retort)* réplica *f*

comedian /kə'miːdɪən/ *n* cómico *m*

comedy /'kɒmədɪ/ *n* comedia *f*

comet /'kɒmɪt/ *n* cometa *m*

comfort /'kʌmfət/ *n* comodidad *f*; *(consolation)* consuelo *m*. ● *vt* consolar. ~**able** *adj* cómodo. ~**er** *n* *(for baby)* chupete *m*, chupón *m* *(LAm)*; *(Amer, for bed)* edredón *m*

comic /'kɒmɪk/ *adj* cómico. ● *n* cómico *m*; *(periodical)* revista *f* de historietas, tebeo *m*. ~**al** *adj* cómico. ~ **strip** *n* tira *f* cómica

coming /'kʌmɪŋ/ *n* llegada *f*. ~**s and goings** idas *fpl* y venidas. ● *adj* próximo; *(week, month etc)* que viene

comma /'kɒmə/ *n* coma *f*

command /kə'mɑːnd/ *n* orden *f*; *(mastery)* dominio *m*. ● *vt* ordenar; imponer (respect)

commandeer /kɒmən'dɪə(r)/ *vt* requisar

command: ~**er** *n* comandante *m*. ~**ing** *adj* imponente. ~**ment** *n* mandamiento *m*

commando /kə'mɑːndəʊ/ n (pl -os) comando m

commemorat|e /kə'meməreɪt/ vt conmemorar. **~ion** /-'reɪʃn/ n conmemoración f. **~ive** /-ɪv/ adj conmemorativo

commence /kə'mens/ vt dar comienzo a. ● vi iniciarse

commend /kə'mend/ vt alabar. **~able** adj loable. **~ation** /kɒmen'deɪʃn/ n elogio m

comment /'kɒment/ n observación f. ● vi hacer observaciones (on sobre)

commentary /'kɒməntrɪ/ n comentario m; (Radio, TV) reportaje m

commentat|e /'kɒmənteɪt/ vi narrar. **~or** n (Radio, TV) locutor m

commerc|e /'kɒmɜːs/ n comercio m. **~ial** /kə'mɜːʃl/ adj comercial. ● n anuncio m; aviso m (LAm). **~ialize** vt comercializar

commiserat|e /kə'mɪzəreɪt/ vi compadecerse (with de). **~ion** /-'reɪʃn/ n conmiseración f

commission /kə'mɪʃn/ n comisión f. out of **~** fuera de servicio. ● vt encargar; (Mil) nombrar oficial

commissionaire /kəmɪʃə'neə(r)/ n portero m

commit /kə'mɪt/ vt (pt committed) cometer; (entrust) confiar. **~ o.s.** comprometerse. **~ment** n compromiso m

committee /kə'mɪtɪ/ n comité m

commodity /kə'mɒdətɪ/ n producto m, artículo m

common /'kɒmən/ adj (-er, -est) común; (usual) corriente; (vulgar) ordinario. ● n. in **~** en común. **~er** n plebeyo m. **~ law** n derecho m consuetudinario. **~ly** adv comúnmente. **C~ Market** n Mercado m Común. **~place** adj banal.

● n banalidad f. **~ room** n sala f común, salón m común. **C~s** n. the (House of) **C~s** la Cámara de los Comunes. **~ sense** n sentido m común. **C~wealth** n. the **C~wealth** la Mancomunidad f Británica

commotion /kə'məʊʃn/ n confusión f

commune /'kɒmjuːn/ n comuna f

communicat|e /kə'mjuːnɪkeɪt/ vt comunicar. ● vi comunicarse. **~ion** /-'keɪʃn/ n comunicación f. **~ive** /-ətɪv/ adj comunicativo

communion /kə'mjuːnɪən/ n comunión f

communis|m /'kɒmjʊnɪzəm/ n comunismo m. **~t** n comunista m & f

community /kə'mjuːnətɪ/ n comunidad f. **~ centre** n centro m social

commute /kə'mjuːt/ vi viajar diariamente (entre el lugar de residencia y el trabajo). ● vt (Jurid) conmutar. **~r** n viajero m diario

compact /kəm'pækt/ adj compacto. ● /'kɒmpækt/ n (for powder) polvera f. **~ disc**, **~ disk** /'kɒmpækt/ n disco m compacto,

compact-disc m. • **disc player** n
(reproductor m de) compact-disc

companion /kəmˈpænɪən/ n
compañero m. **~ship** n compañía f

company /ˈkʌmpənɪ/ n compañía
f; (guests) visita f; (Com) sociedad f

compar|able /ˈkɒmpərəbl/ adj
comparable. **~ative** /kəm
ˈpærətɪv/ adj comparativo; (fig) re-
lativo. • n (Gram) comparativo m.
~e /kəmˈpeə(r)/ vt comparar.
~ison /kəmˈpærɪsn/ n comparación f

compartment /kəmˈpɑːtmənt/
n compartim(i)ento m

compass /ˈkʌmpəs/ n brújula f.
~es npl compás m

compassion /kəmˈpæʃn/ n compasión f. **~ate** /-ət/ adj compasivo

compatible /kəmˈpætəbl/ adj
compatible

compel /kəmˈpel/ vt (pt com-
pelled) obligar. **~ling** adj irresistible

compensat|e /ˈkɒmpənseɪt/ vt
compensar; (for loss) indemnizar.
• vi. **~e for sth** compensar algo.
~ion /-ˈseɪʃn/ n compensación f;
(financial) indemnización f

compère /ˈkɒmpeə(r)/ n presentador m. • vt presentar

compete /kəmˈpiːt/ vi competir

competen|ce /ˈkɒmpətəns/ n
competencia f. **~t** adj competente

competit|ion /kɒmpəˈtɪʃn/ n
(contest) concurso m; (Sport) competición f, competencia f (LAm);
(Com) competencia f. **~ive** /kəm
ˈpetətɪv/ adj competidor; (price)
competitivo. **~or** /kəmˈpetɪtə(r)/ n
competidor m; (in contest) concursante m & f

compile /kəmˈpaɪl/ vt compilar

complacen|cy /kəmˈpleɪsənsɪ/ n

autosuficiencia f. **~t** adj satisfecho
de sí mismo

complain /kəmˈpleɪn/ vi. **~**
(about) quejarse (de). • vt. **~ that**
quejarse de que. **~t** n queja f;
(Med) enfermedad f

complement /ˈkɒmplɪmənt/ n
complemento m. • vt complementar. **~ary** /-ˈmentrɪ/ adj complementario

complet|e /kəmˈpliːt/ adj com-
pleto; (finished) acabado; (down-
right) total. • vt acabar; llenar (a
form). **~ely** adv completamente.
~ion /-ʃn/ n finalización f

complex /ˈkɒmpleks/ adj complejo. • n complejo m

complexion /kəmˈplekʃn/ n tez
f; (fig) aspecto m

complexity /kəmˈpleksətɪ/ n
complejidad f

complicat|e /ˈkɒmplɪkeɪt/ vt
complicar. **~ed** adj complicado.
~ion /-ˈkeɪʃn/ n complicación f

compliment /ˈkɒmplɪmənt/ n
cumplido m; (amorous) piropo m.
• vt felicitar. **~ary** /-ˈmentrɪ/ adj
halagador; (given free) de regalo.
~s npl saludos mpl

comply /kəmˈplaɪ/ vi. **~ with**
conformarse con

component /kəmˈpəʊnənt/ adj &
n componente (m)

compos|e /kəmˈpəʊz/ vt compo-
ner. be **~ed of** estar compuesto
de. **~er** n compositor m. **~ition**
/kɒmpəˈzɪʃn/ n composición f

compost /ˈkɒmpɒst/ n abono m

composure /kəmˈpəʊʒə(r)/ n serenidad f

compound /ˈkɒmpaʊnd/ n compuesto m; (enclosure) recinto m.
• adj compuesto; (fracture)

complicado

comprehen|d /kɒmprɪˈhend/ vt comprender. **~sion** /kɒmprɪˈhenʃn/ n comprensión f. **~sive** /kɒmprɪˈhensɪv/ adj extenso; (insurance) contra todo riesgo. **~sive (school)** n instituto m de enseñanza secundaria

compress /ˈkɒmpres/ n (Med) compresa f. ● /kəmˈpres/ vt comprimir. **~ion** /-ˈpreʃn/ n compresión f

comprise /kəmˈpraɪz/ vt comprender

compromis|e /ˈkɒmprəmaɪz/ n acuerdo m, compromiso m, arreglo m. ● vt comprometer. ● vi llegar a un acuerdo. **~ing** adj (situation) comprometido

compuls|ion /kəmˈpʌlʃn/ n (force) coacción f; (obsession) compulsión f. **~ive** /kəmˈpʌlsɪv/ adj compulsivo. **~ory** /kəmˈpʌlsərɪ/ adj obligatorio

comput|e /kəmˈpjuːt/ vb calcular. **comput|er** n ordenador m, computadora f (LAm). **~erize** vt computarizar, computerizar. **~er studies** n, **~ing** n informática f, computación f

comrade /ˈkɒmreɪd/ n camarada m & f

con /kɒn/ vt (pt conned) 🅴 estafar. ● n (fraud) estafa f; (objection) see PRO

concave /ˈkɒnkeɪv/ adj cóncavo

conceal /kənˈsiːl/ vt ocultar

concede /kənˈsiːd/ vt conceder

conceit /kənˈsiːt/ n vanidad f. **~ed** adj engreído

conceiv|able /kənˈsiːvəbl/ adj concebible. **~e** /kənˈsiːv/ vt/i concebir

concentrat|e /ˈkɒnsəntreɪt/ vt

concentrar. ● vi concentrarse (on en). **~ion** /-ˈtreɪʃn/ n concentración f

concept /ˈkɒnsept/ n concepto m

conception /kənˈsepʃn/ n concepción f

concern /kənˈsɜːn/ n asunto m; (worry) preocupación f; (Com) empresa f. ● vt tener que ver con; (deal with) tratar de. as far as I'm **~ed** en cuanto a mí. be **~ed** about preocuparse por. **~ing** prep acerca de

concert /ˈkɒnsət/ n concierto m. **~ed** /kənˈsɜːtɪd/ adj concertado

concertina /kɒnsəˈtiːnə/ n concertina f

concerto /kənˈtʃɜːtəʊ/ n (pl -os or -ti /-tɪ/) concierto m

concession /kənˈseʃn/ n concesión f

concise /kənˈsaɪs/ adj conciso

conclu|de /kənˈkluːd/ vt/i concluir. **~ding** adj final. **~sion** /-ʃn/ n conclusión f. **~sive** /-sɪv/ adj decisivo. **~sively** adv concluyentemente

concoct /kənˈkɒkt/ vt confeccionar; (fig) inventar. **~ion** /-ʃn/ n mezcla f; (drink) brebaje m

concrete /ˈkɒnkriːt/ n hormigón m, concreto m (LAm). ● adj concreto

concussion /kənˈkʌʃn/ n conmoción f cerebral

condemn /kənˈdem/ vt condenar. **~ation** /kɒndemˈneɪʃn/ n condena f

condens|ation /kɒndenˈseɪʃn/ n condensación f. **~e** /kənˈdens/ vt condensar. ● vi condensarse

condescend /kɒndɪˈsend/ vi dignarse (to a). **~ing** adj superior

condition /kənˈdɪʃn/ n condición

f. on ~ that a condición de que. ● *vt* condicionar. ~al *adj* condicional. ~er *n* (*for hair*) suavizante *m*, enjuague *m* (*LAm*)

condo /'kɒndəʊ/ *n* (*pl* -os) (*Amer fam*) see **CONDOMINIUM**

condolences /kən'dəʊlənsɪz/ *npl* pésame *m*

condom /'kɒndɒm/ *n* condón *m*

condominium /kɒndə'mɪnɪəm/ *n* (*Amer*) apartamento *m*, piso *m* (en régimen de propiedad horizontal)

condone /kən'dəʊn/ *vt* condonar

conduct /kən'dʌkt/ *vt* llevar a cabo (*business, experiment*); conducir (*electricity*); dirigir (*orchestra*). ● /'kɒndʌkt/ *n* conducta *f*. ~or /kən'dʌktə(r)/ *n* director *m*; (*of bus*) cobrador *m*. ~ress /kən'dʌktrɪs/ *n* cobradora *f*

cone /kəʊn/ *n* cono *m*; (*for ice cream*) cucurucho *m*, barquillo *m* (*Mex*)

confectionery /kən'fekʃənrɪ/ *n* productos *mpl* de confitería

confederation /kənfedə'reɪʃn/ *n* confederación *f*

conference /'kɒnfərəns/ *n* congreso *m*; an international ~ on ... un congreso internacional sobre ...

confess /kən'fes/ *vt* confesar. ● *vi* confesarse. ~ion /-ʃn/ *n* confesión *f*

confetti /kən'fetɪ/ *n* confeti *m*

confide /kən'faɪd/ *vt/i* confiar

confiden|ce /'kɒnfɪdəns/ *n* confianza *f*; (*self-confidence*) confianza en sí mismo; (*secret*) confidencia *f*. ~ce trick *n* estafa *f*, timo *m*. ~t /'kɒnfɪdənt/ *adj* seguro de sí mismo. be ~t of confiar en

confidential /kɒnfɪ'denʃl/ *adj* confidencial. ~ity /-denʃɪ'ælətɪ/ *n*

confidencialidad *f*

configur|ation /kənfɪgə'reɪʃn/ *n* configuración *f*. ~e /kən'fɪgə(r)/ *vt* configurar

confine /kən'faɪn/ *vt* confinar; (*limit*) limitar. ~ment *n* (*imprisonment*) prisión *f*

confirm /kən'fɜːm/ *vt* confirmar. ~ation /kɒnfə'meɪʃn/ *n* confirmación *f*. ~ed *adj* inveterado

confiscat|e /'kɒnfɪskeɪt/ *vt* confiscar. ~ion /-'keɪʃn/ *n* confiscación *f*

conflict /'kɒnflɪkt/ *n* conflicto *m*. ● /kən'flɪkt/ *vi* chocar. ~ing /kən'flɪktɪŋ/ *adj* contradictorio

conform /kən'fɔːm/ *vi* conformarse. ~ist *n* conformista *m & f*

confound /kən'faʊnd/ *vt* confundir. ~ed *adj* Ⓣ maldito

confront /kən'frʌnt/ *vt* hacer frente a; (*face*) enfrentarse con. ~ation /kɒnfrʌn'teɪʃn/ *n* confrontación *f*

confus|e /kən'fjuːz/ *vt* confundir. ~ed *adj* confundido. get ~ed confundirse. ~ing *adj* confuso. ~ion /-ʒn/ *n* confusión *f*

congeal /kən'dʒiːl/ *vi* coagularse

congest|ed /kən'dʒestɪd/ *adj* congestionado. ~ion /-tʃən/ *n* congestión *f*

congratulat|e /kən'grætjʊleɪt/ *vt* felicitar. ~ions /-'leɪʃnz/ *npl* enhorabuena *f*, felicitaciones *fpl* (*LAm*)

congregat|e /'kɒŋgrɪgeɪt/ *vi* congregarse. ~ion /-'geɪʃn/ *n* asamblea *f*; (*Relig*) fieles *mpl*, feligreses *mpl*

congress /'kɒŋgres/ *n* congreso *m*. C~ (*Amer*) el Congreso. ~man /-mən/ *n* (*Amer*) miembro *m* del Congreso. ~woman *n* (*Amer*) miembro *f* del Congreso.

Congress El Congreso es el organismo legislativo de EE.UU. Se reúne en el Capitolio (*Capitol*) y está compuesto por dos cámaras: El Senado y la Cámara de Representantes. Se renueva cada dos años y su función es elaborar leyes que deben ser aprobadas, primero, por las dos cámaras y posteriormente por el Presidente.   *i*

conifer /ˈkɒnɪfə(r)/ *n* conífera *f*

conjugat|e /ˈkɒndʒʊɡeɪt/ *vt* conjugar. ∼**ion** /-ˈɡeɪʃn/ *n* conjugación *f*

conjunction /kənˈdʒʌŋkʃn/ *n* conjunción *f*

conjur|e /ˈkʌndʒə(r)/ *vi* hacer juegos de manos. ● *vt*. □ ∼ **e up** *vt* evocar. ∼**er**, ∼**or** *n* prestidigitador *m*

conk /kɒŋk/ *vi*. ∼ **out** 🄴 fallar; (person) desmayarse

conker /ˈkɒŋkə(r)/ *n* 🄴 castaña *f* de Indias

conman /ˈkɒnmæn/ *n* (*pl* -men) 🄴 estafador *m*, timador *m*

connect /kəˈnekt/ *vt* conectar; (*associate*) relacionar. ● *vi* (*be fitted*) estar conectado (to a). □ ∼ **with** *vt* (train) enlazar con. ∼**ed** *adj* unido; (*related*) relacionado. be ∼**ed with** tener que ver con, estar emparentado con. ∼**ion** /-ʃn/ *n* conexión *f*; (Rail) enlace *m*; (*fig*) relación *f*. in ∼**ion** with a propósito de, con respecto a

connive /kəˈnaɪv/ *vi*. ∼ **at** ser cómplice en

connoisseur /kɒnəˈsɜː(r)/ *n* experto *m*

connotation /kɒnəˈteɪʃn/ *n* connotación *f*

conquer /ˈkɒŋkə(r)/ *vt* conquistar; (*fig*) vencer. ∼**or** *n* conquistador *m*

conquest /ˈkɒŋkwest/ *n* conquista *f*

conscience /ˈkɒnʃəns/ *n* conciencia *f*

conscientious /kɒnʃɪˈenʃəs/ *adj* concienzudo

conscious /ˈkɒnʃəs/ *adj* consciente; (*deliberate*) intencional. ∼**ly** *adv* a sabiendas. ∼**ness** *n* consciencia *f*; (Med) conocimiento *m*

conscript /ˈkɒnskrɪpt/ *n* recluta *m & f*, conscripto *m* (LAm). ● /kənˈskrɪpt/ *vt* reclutar. ∼**ion** /kənˈskrɪpʃn/ *n* reclutamiento *m*, conscripción *f* (LAm)

consecrate /ˈkɒnsɪkreɪt/ *vt* consagrar

consecutive /kənˈsekjʊtɪv/ *adj* sucesivo

consensus /kənˈsensəs/ *n* consenso *m*

consent /kənˈsent/ *vi* consentir. ● *n* consentimiento *m*

consequen|ce /ˈkɒnsɪkwəns/ *n* consecuencia *f*. ∼**t** *adj* consiguiente. ∼**tly** *adv* por consiguiente

conservation /kɒnsəˈveɪʃn/ *n* conservación *f*, preservación *f*. ∼**ist** *n* conservacionista *m*

conservative /kənˈsɜːvətɪv/ *adj* conservador; (*modest*) prudente, moderado. **C**∼ *adj & n* conservador (*m*)

conservatory /kənˈsɜːvətrɪ/ *n* invernadero *m*

conserve /kənˈsɜːv/ *vt* conservar

consider /kənˈsɪdə(r)/ *vt* considerar; (*take into account*) tomar en cuenta. ∼**able** *adj* considerable. ∼**ably** *adv* considerablemente

considerat|e /kənˈsɪdərət/ *adj*

considerado. **~ion** /-'reɪʃn/ n consideración f. **take sth into ~ion** tomar algo en cuenta

considering /kənˈsɪdərɪŋ/ prep teniendo en cuenta. ● *conj.* ~ **(that)** teniendo en cuenta que

consign /kənˈsaɪn/ vt consignar; (send) enviar. **~ment** n envío m

consist /kənˈsɪst/ vi. ~ **of** consistir en. **~ency** n consistencia f; (fig) coherencia f. **~ent** adj coherente; (unchanging) constante. **~ent with** compatible con. **~ently** adv constantemente

consolation /kɒnsəˈleɪʃn/ n consuelo m

console /kənˈsəʊl/ vt consolar. ● /ˈkɒnsəʊl/ n consola f

consolidate /kənˈsɒlɪdeɪt/ vt consolidar

consonant /ˈkɒnsənənt/ n consonante f

conspicuous /kənˈspɪkjʊəs/ adj (easily seen) visible; (showy) llamativo; (noteworthy) notable

conspir|acy /kənˈspɪrəsɪ/ n conspiración f. **~ator** /kənˈspɪrətə(r)/ n conspirador m. **~e** /kənˈspaɪə(r)/ vi conspirar

constable /ˈkʌnstəbl/ n agente m & f de policía

constant /ˈkɒnstənt/ adj constante. **~ly** adv constantemente

constellation /kɒnstəˈleɪʃn/ n constelación f

consternation /kɒnstəˈneɪʃn/ n consternación f

constipat|ed /ˈkɒnstɪpeɪtɪd/ adj estreñido. **~ion** /-ˈpeɪʃn/ n estreñimiento m

constituen|cy /kənˈstɪtjʊənsɪ/ n distrito m electoral. **~t** n (Pol) elector m. ● adj constituyente, constitutivo

constitut|e /ˈkɒnstɪtjuːt/ vt constituir. **~ion** f. **~ional** /-ˈtjuːʃənl/ adj constitucional. ● n paseo m

constrict /kənˈstrɪkt/ vt apretar. **~ion** /-ʃn/ n constricción f

construct /kənˈstrʌkt/ vt construir. **~ion** /-ʃn/ n construcción f. **~ive** adj constructivo

consul /ˈkɒnsl/ n cónsul m & f. **~ate** /ˈkɒnsjʊlət/ n consulado m

consult /kənˈsʌlt/ vt/i consultar. **~ancy** n asesoría. **~ant** n asesor m; (Med) especialista m & f; (Tec) consejero m técnico. **~ation** /kɒnslˈteɪʃn/ n consulta f

consume /kənˈsjuːm/ vt consumir. **~r** n consumidor m. ● adj de consumo

consummate /ˈkɒnsəmət/ adj consumado. ● /ˈkɒnsəmeɪt/ vt consumar

consumption /kənˈsʌmpʃn/ n consumo m

contact /ˈkɒntækt/ n contacto m. ● vt ponerse en contacto con. ~ **lens** n lentilla f, lente f de contacto (LAm)

contagious /kənˈteɪdʒəs/ adj. contagioso

contain /kənˈteɪn/ vt contener. ~ **o.s.** contenerse. **~er** n recipiente m; (Com) contenedor m

contaminat|e /kənˈtæmɪneɪt/ vt contaminar. **~ion** /-ˈneɪʃn/ n contaminación f

contemplate /ˈkɒntəmpleɪt/ vt contemplar; (consider) considerar

contemporary /kənˈtempərərɪ/ adj & n contemporáneo (m)

contempt /kənˈtempt/ n desprecio m. **~ible** adj despreciable. **~uous** /-tjʊəs/ adj desdeñoso

contend /kənˈtend/ vt competir.

~er n aspirante m & f (for a)
content /kən'tent/ adj satisfecho.
● /'kɒntent/ n contenido m. ● /kən'tent/ vt contentar. **~ed** /kən'tentɪd/ adj satisfecho. **~ment** /kən'tentmənt/ n satisfacción f. **~s** /'kɒntents/ n contenido m; (of book) índice m de materias

contest /'kɒntest/ n (competition) concurso m; (Sport) competición f, competencia f (LAm). ● /kən'test/ vt disputar. **~ant** /kən'testənt/ n concursante m & f

context /'kɒntekst/ n contexto m

continent /'kɒntɪnənt/ n continente m. the C**~** Europa f. **~al** /-'nentl/ adj continental. **~al quilt** n edredón m

contingen|cy /kən'tɪndʒənsɪ/ n contingencia f. **~t** adj & n contingente (m)

continu|al /kən'tɪnjʊəl/ adj continuo. **~ally** adv continuamente. **~ation** /-'eɪʃn/ n continuación f. **~e** /kən'tɪnjuː/ vt/i continuar, seguir. **~ed** adj continuo. **~ity** /kɒntɪ'njuːətɪ/ n continuidad f. **~ous** /kən'tɪnjʊəs/ adj continuo. **~ously** adv continuamente

contort /kən'tɔːt/ vt retorcer. **~ion** /-ʃn/ n contorsión f. **~ionist** /-ʃənɪst/ n contorsionista m & f

contour /'kɒntʊə(r)/ n contorno m

contraband /'kɒntrəbænd/ n contrabando m

contracepti|on /kɒntrə'sepʃn/ n anticoncepción f. **~ve** /-tɪv/ adj & n anticonceptivo (m)

contract /'kɒntrækt/ n contrato m. ● /kən'trækt/ vt contraer. ● vi contraerse. **~ion** /kən'trækʃn/ n contracción f. **~or** /kən'træktə(r)/ n contratista m & f

contradict /kɒntrə'dɪkt/ vt contradecir. **~ion** /-ʃn/ n contradicción f. **~ory** adj contradictorio

contraption /kən'træpʃn/ n 🄒 artilugio m

contrary /'kɒntrərɪ/ adj contrario. the **~** lo contrario. on the **~** al contrario. ● adv. **~** to contrariamente a. ● /kən'treərɪ/ adj (obstinate) terco

contrast /'kɒntrɑːst/ n contraste m. ● /kən'trɑːst/ vt/i contrastar. **~ing** adj contrastante

contravene /kɒntrə'viːn/ vt contravenir

contribut|e /kən'trɪbjuːt/ vt contribuir con. ● vi contribuir. **~e to** escribir para (newspaper). **~ion** /kɒntrɪ'bjuːʃn/ n contribución f. **~or** /kən'trɪbjuːtə(r)/ n contribuyente m & f; (to newspaper) colaborador m

contrite /'kɒntraɪt/ adj arrepentido, pesaroso

contriv|e /kən'traɪv/ vt idear. **~e to** conseguir. **~ed** adj artificioso

control /kən'trəʊl/ vt (pt controlled) controlar. ● n control m. **~ler** n director m. **~s** npl (Mec) mandos mpl

controvers|ial /kɒntrə'vɜːʃl/ adj controvertido. **~y** /'kɒntrəvɜːsɪ/ n controversia f

conundrum /kə'nʌndrəm/ n adivinanza f

convalesce /kɒnvə'les/ vi convalecer. **~nce** n convalecencia f

convector /kən'vektə(r)/ n estufa f de convección

convene /kən'viːn/ vt convocar. ● vi reunirse

convenien|ce /kən'viːnɪəns/ n conveniencia f, comodidad f. all modern **~ces** todas las comodidades. at your **~ce** según le convenga. ~ces npl servicios mpl, baños mpl (LAm). ~t adj conveniente; (place) bien situado; (time) oportuno. be ~t convenir. ~tly adv convenientemente

convent /'kɒnvənt/ n convento m

convention /kən'venʃn/ n convención f. ~al adj convencional

converge /kən'vɜːdʒ/ vi converger

conversation /kɒnvə'seɪʃn/ n conversación f. ~al adj familiar, coloquial.

converse /kən'vɜːs/ vi conversar. ● /'kɒnvɜːs/ adj inverso. ● n lo contrario. ~ly adv a la inversa

conver|sion /kən'vɜːʃn/ n conversión f. ~t /kən'vɜːt/ vt convertir. ● /'kɒnvɜːt/ n converso m. ~tible /kən'vɜːtɪbl/ adj convertible. ● n (Auto) descapotable m, convertible m (LAm)

convex /'kɒnveks/ adj convexo

convey /kən'veɪ/ vt transportar (goods, people); comunicar (idea, feeling). ~or belt n cinta f transportadora, banda f transportadora (LAm)

convict /kən'vɪkt/ vt condenar. ● /'kɒnvɪkt/ n presidiario m. ~ion /kən'vɪkʃn/ n condena f; (belief) creencia f

convinc|e /kən'vɪns/ vt convencer. ~ing adj convincente

convoluted /'kɒnvəluːtɪd/ adj (argument) intrincado

convoy /'kɒnvɔɪ/ n convoy m

convuls|e /kən'vʌls/ vt convulsionar. be ~ed with laughter desternillarse de risa. ~ion /-ʃn/ n convulsión f

coo /kuː/ vi arrullar

cook /kʊk/ vt hacer, preparar. ● vi cocinar; (food) hacerse. ● n coci-

nero m. ◻ ~ **up** vt 🛈 inventar. ~**book** n libro m de cocina. ~**er** n cocina f, estufa f (Mex). ~**ery** n cocina f

cookie /'kʊkɪ/ n (Amer) galleta f

cool /kuːl/ adj (-er, -est) fresco; (calm) tranquilo; (unfriendly) frío. ● n fresco m; 🅇 calma f. ● vt enfriar. ● vi enfriarse. ◻ ~ **down** vi (person) calmarse. ~**ly** adv tranquilamente

coop /kuːp/ n gallinero m. ◻ ~ **up** vt encerrar

co-op /'kəʊɒp/ n cooperativa f

cooperat|e /kəʊ'ɒpəreɪt/ vi cooperar. ~**ion** /-'reɪʃn/ n cooperación f. ~**ive** /kəʊ'ɒpərətɪv/ adj cooperativo. ● n cooperativa f

co-opt /kəʊ'ɒpt/ vt cooptar

co-ordinat|e /kəʊ'ɔːdɪneɪt/ vt coordinar. ● /kəʊ'ɔːdɪnət/ n (Math) coordenada f. ~**es** npl prendas fpl para combinar. ~**ion** /kəʊɔːdɪ'neɪʃn/ n coordinación f

cop /kɒp/ n 🛈 poli m & f 🛈, tira m & f (Mex, fam)

cope /kəʊp/ vi arreglárselas. ~ **with** hacer frente a

copious /'kəʊpɪəs/ adj abundante

copper /'kɒpə(r)/ n cobre m; (coin) perra f; 🛈 poli m & f 🛈, tira m & f (Mex, fam). ● adj de cobre

copy /'kɒpɪ/ n copia f; (of book, newspaper) ejemplar m. ● vt copiar. ~**right** n derechos mpl de reproducción

coral /'kɒrəl/ n coral m

cord /kɔːd/ n cuerda f; (fabric) pana f; (Amer, Elec) cordón m, cable m

cordial /'kɔːdɪəl/ adj cordial. ● n refresco m (concentrado)

cordon /'kɔːdn/ n cordón m. ◻ ~ **off** vt acordonar

core /kɔː(r)/ n (of apple) corazón m; (of Earth) centro m; (of problem) meollo m

cork /kɔːk/ n corcho m. ~**screw** n sacacorchos m

corn /kɔːn/ n (wheat) trigo m; (Amer) maíz m; (hard skin) callo m

corned beef /kɔːnd 'biːf/ n carne f de vaca en lata

corner /'kɔːnə(r)/ n ángulo m; (inside) rincón m; (outside) esquina f; (football) córner m. • vt arrinconar; (Com) acaparar

cornet /'kɔːnɪt/ n (Mus) corneta f; (for ice cream) cucurucho m, barquillo m (Mex)

corn: ~**flakes** npl copos mpl de maíz. ~**flour** n maizena f (®)

Cornish /'kɔːnɪʃ/ adj de Cornualles

cornstarch /'kɔːnstɑːtʃ/ n (Amer) maizena f (®)

corny /'kɔːnɪ/ adj (fam, trite) gastado

coronation /kɒrə'neɪʃn/ n coronación f

coroner /'kɒrənə(r)/ n juez m de primera instancia

corporal /'kɔːpərəl/ n cabo m. • adj corporal

corporate /'kɔːpərət/ adj corporativo

corporation /kɔːpə'reɪʃn/ n corporación f; (Amer) sociedad f anónima

corps /kɔː(r)/ n (pl corps /kɔːz/) cuerpo m

corpse /kɔːps/ n cadáver m

corpulent /'kɔːpjʊlənt/ adj corpulento

corral /kə'rɑːl/ n corral m

correct /kə'rekt/ adj correcto; (time) exacto. • vt corregir. ~**ion** /-ʃn/ n corrección f

correspond /kɒrɪ'spɒnd/ vi corresponder; (write) escribirse. ~**ence** n correspondencia f. ~**ent** n corresponsal m & f

corridor /'kɒrɪdɔː(r)/ n pasillo m

corro|de /kə'rəʊd/ vt corroer. • vi corroerse. ~**sion** /-ʒn/ n corrosión f. ~**sive** /-sɪv/ adj corrosivo

corrugated /'kɒrəgeɪtɪd/ adj ondulado. ~ **iron** n chapa f de zinc

corrupt /kə'rʌpt/ adj corrompido. • vt corromper. ~**ion** /-ʃn/ n corrupción f

corset /'kɔːsɪt/ n corsé m

cosmetic /kɒz'metɪk/ adj & n cosmético (m)

cosmic /'kɒzmɪk/ adj cósmico

cosmopolitan /kɒzmə'pɒlɪtən/ adj & n cosmopolita (m & f)

cosmos /'kɒzmɒs/ n cosmos m

cosset /'kɒsɪt/ vt (pt cosseted) mimar

cost /kɒst/ vt (pt cost) costar; (pt costed) calcular el costo de (LAm), calcular el coste de (LAm). • n coste m, costo m (LAm). to one's ~ a sus expensas. ~**s** npl (Jurid) costas fpl

Costa Rica /kɒstə'riːkə/ n Costa Rica. ~**n** adj & n costarricense (m & f), costarriqueño (m & f)

cost: ~-**effective** adj rentable. ~**ly** adj (-ier, -iest) costoso

costume /'kɒstjuːm/ n traje m; (for party, disguise) disfraz m

cosy /'kəʊzɪ/ adj (-ier, -iest) acogedor. • n cubreteras m

cot /kɒt/ n cuna f

cottage /'kɒtɪdʒ/ n casita f. ~ **cheese** n requesón m. ~ **pie** n pastel m de carne cubierta con puré

cotton /'kɒtn/ n algodón m; (thread) hilo m; (Amer) see ~

WOOL □ ~ **on** vi 🔊 comprender. ~ **bud** n bastoncillo m, cotonete m (Mex). ~ **candy** n (Amer) algodón m de azúcar. ~ **swab** n (Amer) hisopo m. ~ **wool** n algodón m hidrófilo

couch /kaʊtʃ/ n sofá m

cough /kɒf/ vi toser. ●n tos f. ~ **up** vt 🔊 pagar. ~ **mixture** n jarabe m para la tos

could /kʊd/ pt of **CAN¹**

couldn't /ˈkʊdnt/ = **could not**

council /ˈkaʊnsl/ n consejo m; (of town) ayuntamiento m. ~ **house** n vivienda f subvencionada. ~**lor** n concejal m

counsel /ˈkaʊnsl/ n consejo m; (pl invar) (Jurid) abogado m. ●vt (pt counselled) aconsejar. ~**ling** n terapia f de apoyo. ~**lor** n consejero m

count /kaʊnt/ n recuento m; (nobleman) conde m. ●vt/i contar. □ ~ **on** vt contar. ~**down** n cuenta f atrás

counter /ˈkaʊntə(r)/ n (in shop) mostrador m; (in bank, post office) ventanilla f; (token) ficha f. ●adv. ~ **to** en contra de. ●adj opuesto. ●vt oponerse a; parar (blow)

counter... /ˈkaʊntə(r)/ pref contra.... ~**act** /-ˈækt/ vt contrarrestar. ~**attack** n contraataque m. ●vt/i contraatacar. ~**balance** n contrapeso m. ●vt/i contrapesar. ~**clockwise** /-ˈklɒkwaɪz/ a/adv (Amer) en sentido contrario al de las agujas del reloj

counterfeit /ˈkaʊntəfɪt/ adj falsificado. ●n falsificación f. ●vt falsificar

counterfoil /ˈkaʊntəfɔɪl/ n matriz f, talón m (LAm)

counter-productive /ˌkaʊntəprəˈdʌktɪv/ adj contraproducente

countess /ˈkaʊntɪs/ n condesa f

countless /ˈkaʊntlɪs/ adj innumerable

country /ˈkʌntri/ n (native land) país m; (countryside) campo m; (Mus) (música f) country m. ~**-and-western** /-enˈwestən/ (música f) country m. ~**man** /-mən/ n (of one's own country) compatriota m. ~**side** n campo m; (landscape) paisaje m

county /ˈkaʊnti/ n condado m

coup /kuː/ n golpe m

couple /ˈkʌpl/ n (of things) par m; (of people) pareja f; (married) matrimonio m. a ~ of un par de

coupon /ˈkuːpɒn/ n cupón m

courage /ˈkʌrɪdʒ/ n valor m. ~**ous** /kəˈreɪdʒəs/ adj valiente

courgette /kʊəˈʒet/ n calabacín m

courier /ˈkʊriə(r)/ n mensajero m; (for tourists) guía m & f

course /kɔːs/ n curso m; (behaviour) conducta f; (in navigation) rumbo m; (Culin) plato m; (for golf) campo m. in due ~ a su debido tiempo. in the ~ of en el transcurso de, durante. of ~ claro, por supuesto. of ~ not claro que no, por supuesto que no

court /kɔːt/ n corte f; (tennis) pista f; cancha f (LAm); (Jurid) tribunal m. ●vt cortejar; buscar (danger)

courteous /ˈkɜːtɪəs/ adj cortés

courtesy /ˈkɜːtəsɪ/ n cortesía f

courtier /ˈkɔːtɪə(r)/ n (old use) cortesano m

court:: ~ **martial** n (pl ~s martial) consejo m de guerra. -**martial** vt (pt ~martialled) juzgar en consejo de guerra. ~**ship** n cortejo m. ~**yard** n patio *m*

cousin /'kʌzn/ *n* primo *m*. **first** ~ primo carnal. **second** ~ primo segundo

cove /kəʊv/ *n* ensenada *f*, cala *f*

Coventry /'kɒvntrɪ/ *n*. **send s.o. to** ~ hacer el vacío a uno

cover /'kʌvə(r)/ *vt* cubrir. ● *n* cubierta *f*; (*shelter*) abrigo *m*; (*lid*) tapa *f*; (*for furniture*) funda *f*; (*pretext*) pretexto *m*; (*of magazine*) portada *f*. ~ **up** *vt* cubrir; (*fig*) ocultar. ~**age** *n* cobertura *f*. ~ **charge** *n* precio del cubierto. ~**ing** *n* cubierta *f*. ~**ing letter** *n* carta *f* adjunta

covet /'kʌvɪt/ *vt* codiciar

cow /kaʊ/ *n* vaca *f*

coward /'kaʊəd/ *n* cobarde *m*. ~**ice** /'kaʊədɪs/ *n* cobardía *f*. ~**ly** *adj* cobarde

cowboy /'kaʊbɔɪ/ *n* vaquero *m*

cower /'kaʊə(r)/ *vi* encogerse, acobardarse

coxswain /'kɒksn/ *n* timonel *m*

coy /kɔɪ/ *adj* (**-er**, **-est**) (*shy*) tímido; (*evasive*) evasivo

crab /kræb/ *n* cangrejo *m*, jaiba *f* (*LAm*)

crack /kræk/ *n* grieta *f*; (*noise*) crujido *m*; (*of whip*) chasquido *m*; (*drug*) crack *m*. ● *adj* de primera. ● *vt* agrietar; chasquear (*whip*, *fingers*); cascar (*nut*); gastar (*joke*); resolver (*problem*). ● *vi* agrietarse. **get** ~**ing** 🆒 darse prisa. ~ **down on** *vt* 🆒 tomar medidas enérgicas contra

cracker /'krækə(r)/ *n* (*Culin*) cracker *f*, galleta *f* (*salada*); (*Christmas cracker*) sorpresa *f* (que estalla al abrirla)

crackle /'krækl/ *vi* crepitar. ● *n* crepitación *f*, crujido *m*

crackpot /'krækpɒt/ *n* 🆒 chiflado *m*

cradle /'kreɪdl/ *n* cuna *f*. ● *vt* acunar

craft /krɑːft/ *n* destreza *f*; (*technique*) arte *f*; (*cunning*) astucia *f*. ● *n invar* (*boat*) barco *m*

craftsman /'krɑːftsmən/ *n* (*pl* -men) artesano *m*. ~**ship** *n* artesanía *f*

crafty /'krɑːftɪ/ *adj* (**-ier**, **-iest**) astuto

cram /kræm/ *vt* (*pt* crammed) rellenar. ~ **with** llenar de. ● *vi* (*for exams*) memorizar, empollar 🅧, zambutir (*Mex*)

cramp /kræmp/ *n* calambre *m*

cramped /kræmpt/ *adj* apretado

crane /kreɪn/ *n* grúa *f*. ● *vt* estirar (*neck*)

crank /kræŋk/ *n* manivela *f*; (*person*) excéntrico *m*. ~**y** *adj* excéntrico

cranny /'krænɪ/ *n* grieta *f*

crash /kræʃ/ *n* accidente *m*; (*noise*) estruendo *m*; (*collision*) choque *m*; (*Com*) quiebra *f*. ● *vt* estrellar. ● *vi* quebrar con estrépito; (*have accident*) tener un accidente; (*two cars etc*) estrellarse, chocar; (*fail*) fracasar. ~ **course** *n* curso *m* intensivo. ~ **helmet** *n* casco *m* protector. ~**-land** *vi* hacer un aterrizaje forzoso

crass /kræs/ *adj* craso, burdo

crate /kreɪt/ *n* cajón *m*. ● *vt* embalar

crater /'kreɪtə(r)/ *n* cráter *m*

crav|e /kreɪv/ *vt* ansiar. ~**ing** *n* ansia *f*

crawl /krɔːl/ *vi* (*baby*) gatear; (*move slowly*) avanzar lentamente; (*drag o.s.*) arrastrarse. ~ **to** humillarse ante. ~ **with** hervir de. ● *n* *(swimming)* crol *m*. at a ~ a paso lento

crayon /'kreɪən/ *n* lápiz *m* de color; *(made of wax)* lápiz *m* de cera, crayola *f* (®), crayón *m* (Mex)

craze /kreɪz/ *n* manía *f*. ~y /'kreɪzɪ/ *adj* (-ier, -iest) loco. be ~y about estar loco por

creak /kriːk/ *n* crujido *m*; *(of hinge)* chirrido *m*. ● *vi* crujir; *(hinge)* chirriar

cream /kriːm/ *n* crema *f*; *(fresh)* nata *f*, crema *f* (LAm). ● *adj (colour)* color crema. ● *vt (beat)* batir. ~ **cheese** *n* queso *m* para untar, queso *m* crema (LAm). ~y *adj* cremoso

crease /kriːs/ *n* raya *f*, pliegue *m* (Mex); *(crumple)* arruga *f*. ● *vt* plegar; *(wrinkle)* arrugar. ● *vi* arrugarse

creat|e /kriː'eɪt/ *vt* crear. ~ion /-ʃn/ *n* creación *f*. ~ive *adj* creativo. ~or *n* creador *m*

creature /'kriːtʃə(r)/ *n* criatura *f*

crèche /kreʃ/ *n* guardería *f* (infantil)

credib|ility /kredə'bɪlətɪ/ *n* credibilidad *f*. ~le /'kredəbl/ *adj* creíble

credit /'kredɪt/ *n* crédito *m*; *(honour)* mérito *m*. take the ~ for atribuirse el mérito de. ● *vt (pt credited)* acreditar; *(believe)* creer. ~ s.o. with atribuir a uno. ~ **card** *n* tarjeta *f* de crédito. ~or *n* acreedor *m*

creed /kriːd/ *n* credo *m*

creek /kriːk/ *n* ensenada *f*. up the ~ 🅇 en apuros

creep /kriːp/ *vi (pt crept)* arrastrarse; *(plant)* trepar. ● *n* 🅣 adulador. ~s *n* /kriːps/ *npl*. give s.o. the ~s poner los pelos de punta a uno. ~er *n* enredadera *f*

cremat|e /krɪ'meɪt/ *vt* incinerar. ~ion /-ʃn/ *n* cremación *f*. ~orium /kremə'tɔːrɪəm/ *n (pl -ia /-ɪə/)* crematorio *m*

crept /krept/ see **CREEP**

crescendo /krɪ'ʃendəʊ/ *n (pl -os)* crescendo *m*

crescent /'kresnt/ *n* media luna *f*; *(street)* calle *f* en forma de media luna

crest /krest/ *n* cresta *f*; *(on coat of arms)* emblema *m*

crevice /'krevɪs/ *n* grieta *f*

crew /kruː/ *n* tripulación *f*; *(gang)* pandilla *f*. ~ **cut** *n* corte *m* al rape

crib /krɪb/ *n (Amer)* cuna *f*; *(Relig)* belén *m*. ● *vt/i (pt cribbed)* copiar

crick /krɪk/ *n* calambre *m*; *(in neck)* tortícolis *f*

cricket /'krɪkɪt/ *n (Sport)* críquet *m*; *(insect)* grillo *m*

crim|e /kraɪm/ *n* delito *m*; *(murder)* crimen *m*; *(acts)* delincuencia *f*. ~inal /'krɪmɪnl/ *adj & n* criminal (*m & f*)

crimson /'krɪmzn/ *adj & n* carmesí (*m*)

cringe /krɪndʒ/ *vi* encogerse; *(fig)* humillarse

crinkle /'krɪŋkl/ *vt* arrugar. ● *vi* arrugarse. ● *n* arruga *f*

cripple /'krɪpl/ *n* lisiado *m*. ● *vt* lisiar; *(fig)* paralizar

crisis /'kraɪsɪs/ *n (pl crises /-siːz/)* crisis *f*

crisp /krɪsp/ *adj* (-er, -est) *(Culin)* crujiente; *(air)* vigorizador. ~s *npl* patatas *fpl* fritas, papas *fpl* fritas (LAm) (de bolsa)

crisscross /'krɪskrɒs/ *adj* entrecruzado. ● *vt* entrecruzar. ● *vi* entrecruzarse

criterion /kraɪ'tɪərɪən/ *n (pl -ia /-ɪə/)* criterio *m*

critic /ˈkrɪtɪk/ n crítico m. **∼al** adj crítico. **∼ally** adv críticamente; (ill) gravemente

critici|sm /ˈkrɪtɪsɪzəm/ n crítica f. **∼ze** /ˈkrɪtɪsaɪz/ vt/i criticar

croak /krəʊk/ n (of person) gruñido m; (of frog) canto m. ● vi gruñir; (frog) croar

Croat /ˈkrəʊæt/ n croata m & f. **∼ia** /krəʊˈeɪʃə/ n Croacia f. **∼ian** adj croata

crochet /ˈkrəʊʃeɪ/ n crochet m, ganchillo m. ● vt tejer a crochet or a ganchillo

crockery /ˈkrɒkərɪ/ n loza f

crocodile /ˈkrɒkədaɪl/ n cocodrilo m. **∼ tears** npl lágrimas fpl de cocodrilo

crocus /ˈkrəʊkəs/ n (pl **-es**) azafrán m de primavera

crook /krʊk/ n 🄸 sinvergüenza m & f. **∼ed** /ˈkrʊkɪd/ adj torcido, chueco (LAm); (winding) tortuoso; (dishonest) deshonesto

crop /krɒp/ n cosecha f; (haircut) corte m de pelo muy corto. ● vt (pt cropped) cortar. □ **∼ up** vi surgir

croquet /ˈkrəʊkeɪ/ n croquet m

cross /krɒs/ n cruz f; (of animals) cruce m. ● vt cruzar; (oppose) contrariar. **∼ s.o.'s mind** ocurrírsele a uno. **∼ o.s.** santiguarse. ● adj enfadado, enojado (esp LAm). □ **∼ out** vt tachar. **∼bar** n travesaño m. **∼-examine** /-ɪɡˈzæmɪn/ vt interrogar. **∼-eyed** adj bizco. **∼fire** n fuego m cruzado. **∼ing** n (by boat) travesía f; (on road) cruce m peatonal. **∼ly** adv con enfado, con enojo (esp LAm). **∼-purposes** /-ˈpɜːpəsɪz/ npl. **talk at ∼-purposes** hablar sin entenderse. **∼-reference** /-ˈrefrəns/ n remisión f. **∼roads** n invar cruce m.

∼-section /-ˈsekʃn/ n sección f transversal; (fig) muestra f representativa. **∼walk** n (Amer) paso de peatones. **∼word** n **∼word** (puzzle) crucigrama m

crotch /krɒtʃ/ n entrepiernas fpl

crouch /kraʊtʃ/ vi agacharse

crow /krəʊ/ n cuervo m. **as the ∼ flies** en línea recta. ● vi cacarear. **∼bar** n palanca f

crowd /kraʊd/ n muchedumbre f. ● vt amontonar; (fill) llenar. ● vi amontonarse; (gather) reunirse. **∼ed** adj atestado

crown /kraʊn/ n corona f; (of hill) cumbre f; (of head) coronilla f. ● vt coronar

crucial /ˈkruːʃl/ adj crucial

crucifix /ˈkruːsɪfɪks/ n crucifijo m. **∼ion** /-ˈfɪkʃn/ n crucifixión f

crucify /ˈkruːsɪfaɪ/ vt crucificar

crude /kruːd/ adj (-er, -est) (raw) crudo; (rough) tosco; (vulgar) ordinario

cruel /ˈkruːəl/ adj (crueller, cruellest) cruel. **∼ty** n crueldad f

cruet /ˈkruːɪt/ n vinagrera f

cruise /kruːz/ n crucero m. ● vi hacer un crucero; (of car) circular lentamente. **∼r** n crucero m

crumb /krʌm/ n miga f

crumble /ˈkrʌmbl/ vt desmenuzar. ● vi desmenuzarse; (collapse) derrumbarse

crummy /ˈkrʌmɪ/ adj (-ier, -iest) 🄳 miserable

crumpet /ˈkrʌmpɪt/ n bollo m blando

crumple /ˈkrʌmpl/ vt arrugar. ● vi arrugarse

crunch /krʌntʃ/ vt hacer crujir; (bite) masticar. **∼y** adj crujiente

crusade /kruːˈseɪd/ n cruzada f.

~r n cruzado m

crush /krʌʃ/ vt aplastar; arrugar (clothes). ● n (crowd) aglomeración f. **have a ~ on** ⬜ estar chiflado por

crust /krʌst/ n corteza f. ~**y** adj (bread) de corteza dura

crutch /krʌtʃ/ n muleta f; (between legs) entrepiernas fpl

crux /krʌks/ n (pl cruxes). **the ~** (of the matter) el quid (de la cuestión)

cry /kraɪ/ n grito m. **be a far ~ from** (fig) distar mucho de. ● vi llorar; (call out) gritar. □ ~ **off** vi echarse atrás, rajarse. ~**baby** n llorón m

crypt /krɪpt/ n cripta f

cryptic /krɪptɪk/ adj enigmático

crystal /krɪstl/ n cristal m. ~**lize** vi cristalizarse

cub /kʌb/ n cachorro m. C~ (Scout) n lobato m

Cuba /kjuːbə/ n Cuba f. ~**n** adj & n cubano (m)

cubbyhole /kʌbɪhəʊl/ n cuchitril m

cub|e /kjuːb/ n cubo m. ~**ic** adj cúbico

cubicle /kjuːbɪkl/ n cubículo m; (changing room) probador m

cuckoo /kʊkuː/ n cuco m, cuclillo m

cucumber /kjuːkʌmbə(r)/ n pepino m

cuddl|e /kʌdl/ vt abrazar. ● vi abrazarse. ● n abrazo m. ~**y** adj adorable

cue /kjuː/ n (Mus) entrada f; (in theatre) pie m; (in snooker) taco m

cuff /kʌf/ n puño m; (Amer, of trousers) vuelta f, dobladillo m; (blow) bofetada f. **speak off the ~** hablar de improviso. ● vt abofetear. ~**link**

n gemelo m, mancuerna f (Mex)

cul-de-sac /kʌldəsæk/ n callejón m sin salida

culinary /kʌlɪnərɪ/ adj culinario

cull /kʌl/ vt sacrificar en forma selectiva (animals)

culminat|e /kʌlmɪneɪt/ vi culminar. ~**ion** /-ˈneɪʃn/ n culminación f

culprit /kʌlprɪt/ n culpable m & f

cult /kʌlt/ n culto m

cultivat|e /kʌltɪveɪt/ vt cultivar. ~**ion** /-ˈveɪʃn/ n cultivo m

cultur|al /kʌltʃərəl/ adj cultural. ~**e** /kʌltʃə(r)/ n cultura f; (Bot etc) cultivo m. ~**ed** adj cultivado; (person) culto

cumbersome /kʌmbəsəm/ adj incómodo; (heavy) pesado

cunning /kʌnɪŋ/ adj astuto. ● n astucia f

cup /kʌp/ n taza f; (trophy) copa f

cupboard /kʌbəd/ n armario m

curator /kjʊəˈreɪtə(r)/ n (of museum) conservador m

curb /kɜːb/ n freno m; (Amer) bordillo m (de la acera), borde m de la banqueta (Mex). ● vt refrenar

curdle /kɜːdl/ vt cuajar. ● vi cuajarse; (go bad) cortarse

cure /kjʊə(r)/ vt curar. ● n cura f

curfew /kɜːfjuː/ n toque m de queda

curio|sity /kjʊərɪˈɒsətɪ/ n curiosidad f. ~**us** /kjʊərɪəs/ adj curioso

curl /kɜːl/ vt rizar, enchinar (Mex). ~ **o.s. up** acurrucarse. ● vi (hair) rizarse, enchinarse (Mex); (paper) ondularse. ● n rizo m, chino m (Mex). ~**er** n rulo m, chino m (Mex). ~**y** adj (-ier, -iest) rizado, chino (Mex)

currant /kʌrənt/ n pasa f de Corinto

currency /'kʌrənsɪ/ n moneda f

current /'kʌrənt/ n corriente (f); (existing) actual. ~ **affairs** npl sucesos de actualidad. ~**ly** adv actualmente

curriculum /kə'rɪkjʊləm/ n (pl -la) programa m de estudios. ~ **vitae** n currículum m vitae

curry /'kʌrɪ/ n curry m. ● vt preparar al curry

curse /kɜːs/ n maldición f; (oath) palabrota f. ● vt maldecir. ● vi decir palabrotas

cursory /'kɜːsərɪ/ adj superficial

curt /kɜːt/ adj brusco

curtain /'kɜːtn/ n cortina f; (in theatre) telón m

curtsey, curtsy /'kɜːtsɪ/ n reverencia f. ● vi hacer una reverencia

curve /kɜːv/ n curva f. ● vi estar curvado. (road) torcerse

cushion /'kʊʃn/ n cojín m, almohadón m

cushy /'kʊʃɪ/ adj (-ier, -iest) 🔲 fácil

custard /'kʌstəd/ n natillas fpl

custody /'kʌstədɪ/ n custodia f; **be in** ~ Jurid estar detenido

custom /'kʌstəm/ n costumbre f; (Com) clientela f. ~**ary** /-ərɪ/ adj acostumbrado. ~**er** n cliente m. ~**s** npl aduana f. ~**s officer** n aduanero m

cut /kʌt/ vt/i (pt cut, pres p cutting) cortar; reducir (prices). ● n corte m; (reduction) reducción f. □ ~ **across** vt cortar camino por. □ ~ **back, ~ down** vt reducir. □ ~ **in** vi interrumpir. □ ~ **off** vt cortar; (phone) desconectar; (fig) aislar. □ ~ **out** vt recortar; (omit) suprimir. □ ~ **through** vt cortar camino por. □ ~ **up** vt cortar en pedazos

cute /kjuːt/ adj (-er, -est) 🔲

mono, amoroso (LAm); (Amer, attractive) guapo, buen mozo (LAm)

cutlery /'kʌtlərɪ/ n cubiertos mpl

cutlet /'kʌtlɪt/ n chuleta f

cut: ~**-price,** (Amer) ~**-rate** a precio reducido. ~**-throat** adj despiadado. ~**ting** adj cortante; (remark) mordaz. ● n (from newspaper) recorte m; (of plant) esqueje m

CV n (= curriculum vitae) currículum m (vitae)

cyberspace /'saɪbəspeɪs/ ciberespacio m

cycl|e /'saɪkl/ n ciclo m; (bicycle) bicicleta f. ● vi ir en bicicleta. ~**ing** n ciclismo m. ~**ist** n ciclista m & f

cylind|er /'sɪlɪndə(r)/ n cilindro m. ~**er head** (Auto) culata f. ~**rical** /-'lɪndrɪkl/ adj cilíndrico

cymbal /'sɪmbl/ n címbalo m

cynic /'sɪnɪk/ n cínico m. ~**al** adj cínico. ~**ism** /-sɪzəm/ n cinismo m

Czech /tʃek/ adj & n checo (m). ~**oslovakia** /-ə'vækɪə/ n (History) Checoslovaquia f. ~ **Republic** n. the ~ **Republic** n la República Checa

Dd

dab /dæb/ vt (pt dabbed) tocar ligeramente. ● n toque m suave. **a** ~ **of** un poquito de

dad /dæd/ n 🔲 papá m. ~**dy** n papi m. ~**dy-long-legs** n invar (cranefly) típula f; (Amer, harvestman) segador m, falangio m

daffodil /'dæfədɪl/ n narciso m

daft /dɑːft/ *adj* (**-er, -est**) 🔁 tonto

dagger /'dægə(r)/ *n* daga *f*, puñal *m*

daily /'deɪli/ *adj* diario. ● *adv* diariamente, cada día

Dáil Éireann Es el nombre de la cámara baja del Parlamento de la República de Irlanda. Se pronuncia /dɔɪl/ y consta de 166 representantes o diputados, comúnmente llamados TDs, que representan 41 circunscripciones. Se eligen por medio del sistema de representación proporcional. Según la Constitución debe haber un diputado por cada 20.000 a 30.000 personas.

---

dainty /'deɪnti/ *adj* (**-ier, -iest**) delicado

dairy /'deəri/ *n* vaquería *f*; (*shop*) lechería *f*

daisy /'deɪzi/ *n* margarita *f*

dam /dæm/ *n* presa *f*, represa *f* (*LAm*)

damage /'dæmɪdʒ/ *n* daño *m*; **~s** (*npl, Jurid*) daños *mpl* y perjuicios *mpl*. ● *vt* (*fig*) dañar, estropear. **~ing** *adj* perjudicial

dame /deɪm/ *n* (*old use*) dama *f*; (*Amer, sl*) chica *f*

damn /dæm/ *vt* condenar; (*curse*) maldecir. ● *int* 🔁 ¡caray! 🔁. ● *adj* maldito. ● *n* **I don't give a ~** (*no*) me importa un comino

damp /dæmp/ *n* humedad *f*. ● *adj* (**-er, -est**) húmedo. ● *vt* mojar. **~ness** *n* humedad *f*

dance /dɑːns/ *vt/i* bailar. ● *n* baile *m*. **~e hall** *n* salón *m* de baile. **~er** *n* bailador *m*; (*professional*) bailarín *m*. **~ing** *n* baile *m*

dandelion /'dændɪlaɪən/ *n* diente *m* de león

dandruff /'dændrʌf/ *n* caspa *f*

dandy /'dændi/ *n* petimetre *m*

Dane /deɪn/ *n* danés *m*

danger /'deɪndʒə(r)/ *n* peligro *m*; (*risk*) riesgo *m*. **~ous** *adj* peligroso

dangle /'dæŋgl/ *vt* balancear. ● *vi* suspender, colgar

Danish /'deɪnɪʃ/ *adj* danés. ● *m* (*language*) danés *m*

dar|e /deə(r)/ *vt* desafiar. ● *vi* atreverse a. **I ~ say** probablemente. ● *n* desafío *m*. **~edevil** *n* atrevido *m*. **~ing** *adj* atrevido

dark /dɑːk/ *adj* (**-er, -est**) oscuro; (*skin, hair*) moreno. ● *n* oscuridad *f*; (*nightfall*) atardecer. **in the ~** a oscuras. **~en** *vt* oscurecer. ● *vi* oscurecerse. **~ness** *n* oscuridad *f*. **~room** *n* cámara *f* oscura

darling /'dɑːlɪŋ/ *adj* querido. ● *n* cariño *m*

darn /dɑːn/ *vt* zurcir

dart /dɑːt/ *n* dardo *m*. ● *vi* lanzarse; (*run*) precipitarse. **~board** *n* diana *f*. **~s** *npl* los dardos *mpl*

dash /dæʃ/ *vi* precipitarse. ● *vt* tirar; (*break*) romper; defraudar (*hopes*). ● *n* (*small amount*) poquito *m*; (*punctuation mark*) guión *m*. □ **~ off** *vi* marcharse apresuradamente. **~ out** *vi* salir corriendo. **~board** *n* tablero *m* de mandos

data /'deɪtə/ *npl* datos *mpl*. **~base** *n* base *f* de datos. **~ processing** *n* proceso *m* de datos

date /deɪt/ *n* fecha *f*; (*appointment*) cita *f*; (*fruit*) dátil *m*. **to ~** hasta la fecha. ● *vt* fechar; *vi* datar; datar (*remains*); (*be old-fashioned*) quedar anticuado. **~d** *adj* pasado de moda

daub /dɔːb/ *vt* embadurnar

daughter | decimal

daughter /'dɔːtə(r)/ n hija f. **~-in-law** n nuera f

dawdle /'dɔːdl/ vi andar despacio; (waste time) perder el tiempo

dawn /dɔːn/ n amanecer m. ● vi amanecer; (fig) nacer. it ~ed on me that caí en la cuenta de que

day /deɪ/ n día m; (whole day) jornada f; (period) época f. **~break** n amanecer m. **~ care center** n (Amer) guardería f infantil. **~dream** n ensueño m. ● vi soñar despierto. **~light** n luz f del día. **~time** n día m

daze /deɪz/ vt aturdir. ● n aturdimiento m. in a ~ aturdido. **~d** adj aturdido

dazzle /'dæzl/ vt deslumbrar

dead /ded/ adj muerto; (numb) dormido. ● adv justo; ([]], completely) completamente. **~ beat** adj rendido. **~ slow** muy lento. **stop ~** parar en seco. **~en** vt amortiguar (sound, blow); calmar (pain). **~ end** n callejón m sin salida. **~line** n fecha f tope, plazo m de entrega. **~lock** n punto m muerto. **~ly** adj (-ier, -iest) mortal

deaf /def/ adj (-er, -est) sordo. **~en** vt ensordecer. **~ness** n sordera f

deal /diːl/ n (agreement) acuerdo m; (treatment) trato m. a good ~ bastante. a great ~ (of) muchísimo. ● vt (pt dealt) dar (a blow, cards). ● vi (cards) dar, repartir. □ ~ in vt comerciar en. □ ~ out vt repartir, distribuir. □ ~ with vt tratar con (person); tratar de (subject); ocuparse de (problem). **~er** n comerciante m. **drug ~er** traficante m & f de drogas

dean /diːn/ n deán m; (Univ) decano m

dear /dɪə(r)/ adj (-er, -est) querido; (expensive) caro. ● n querido m. ● adv caro. ● int. oh **~**! ¡ay por Dios! **~ me!** ¡Dios mío! **~ly** adv (pay) caro; (very much) muchísimo

death /deθ/ n muerte f. **~ sentence** n pena f de muerte. **~ trap** n lugar m peligroso

debat|able /dɪ'beɪtəbl/ adj discutible. **~e** /dɪ'beɪt/ n debate m. ● vt debatir, discutir

debauchery /dɪ'bɔːtʃərɪ/ vt libertinaje m

debit /'debɪt/ n débito m. ● vt debitar, cargar. **~ card** tarjeta f de cobro automático

debris /'debriː/ n escombros mpl

debt /det/ n deuda f. be in ~ tener deudas. **~or** n deudor m

debut /'debjuː/ n debut m

decade /dekeɪd/ n década f

decaden|ce /'dekədəns/ n decadencia f. **~t** adj decadente

decay /dɪ'keɪ/ vi descomponerse; (tooth) cariarse. ● n decomposición f; (of tooth) caries f

deceased /dɪ'siːst/ adj difunto

deceit /dɪ'siːt/ n engaño m. **~ful** adj falso. **~fully** adv falsamente

deceive /dɪ'siːv/ vt engañar

December /dɪ'sembə(r)/ n diciembre m

decen|cy /'diːsənsɪ/ n decencia f. **~t** adj decente; (fam, good) bueno; (fam, kind) amable. **~tly** adv decentemente

deception /dɪ'sepʃn/ n engaño m. **~ve** /-tɪv/ adj engañoso

decibel /'desɪbel/ n decibel(io) m

decide /dɪ'saɪd/ vt/i decidir. **~d** adj resuelto; (unquestionable) indudable

decimal /'desɪml/ adj & n decimal (m). **~ point** n coma f (decimal), punto *m* decimal

decipher /dɪˈsaɪfə(r)/ *vt* descifrar

decis|ion /dɪˈsɪʒn/ *n* decisión *f*. **~ive** /dɪˈsaɪsɪv/ *adj* decisivo; (*manner*) decidido

deck /dek/ *n* (*Naut*) cubierta *f*; (*Amer, of cards*) baraja *f*; (*of bus*) piso *m*. ● *vt* adornar. **~chair** *n* tumbona *f*, silla *f* de playa

declar|ation /deklǝˈreɪʃn/ *n* declaración *f*. **~e** /dɪˈkleǝ(r)/ *vt* declarar

decline /dɪˈklaɪn/ *vt* rehusar; (*Gram*) declinar. ● *vi* disminuir; (*deteriorate*) deteriorarse. ● *n* decadencia *f*; (*decrease*) disminución *f*

decode /diːˈkǝʊd/ *vt* descifrar

decompose /diːkǝmˈpǝʊz/ *vi* descomponerse

décor /ˈdeɪkɔː(r)/ *n* decoración *f*

decorat|e /ˈdekǝreɪt/ *vt* adornar, decorar (*LAm*); empapelar y pintar (*room*). **~ion** /-ˈreɪʃn/ *n* (*act*) decoración *f*; (*ornament*) adorno *m*. **~ive** /-ǝtɪv/ *adj* decorativo. **~or** *n* pintor *m* decorador

decoy /ˈdiːkɔɪ/ *n* señuelo *m*. ● /dɪˈkɔɪ/ *vt* atraer con señuelo

decrease /dɪˈkriːs/ *vt/i* disminuir. ● /ˈdiːkriːs/ *n* disminución *f*

decree /dɪˈkriː/ *n* decreto *m*. ● *vt* decretar

decrepit /dɪˈkrepɪt/ *adj* decrépito

decriminalize /diːˈkrɪmɪnǝlaɪz/ *vt* despenalizar

dedicat|e /ˈdedɪkeɪt/ *vt* dedicar. **~ion** /-ˈkeɪʃn/ *n* dedicación *f*

deduce /dɪˈdjuːs/ *vt* deducir

deduct /dɪˈdʌkt/ *vt* deducir. **~ion** /-ʃn/ *n* deducción *f*

deed /diːd/ *n* hecho *m*; (*Jurid*) escritura *f*

deem /diːm/ *vt* juzgar, considerar

deep /diːp/ *adj* (-er, -est) *adv* profundo. ● *adv* profundamente. be **~** in thought estar absorto en sus pensamientos. **~en** *vt* hacer más profundo. ● *vi* hacerse más profundo. **~freeze** *n* congelador *m*, freezer *m* (*LAm*). **~ly** *adv* profundamente

deer /dɪǝ(r)/ *n invar* ciervo *m*

deface /dɪˈfeɪs/ *vt* desfigurar

default /dɪˈfɔːlt/ *vi* faltar. ● *n* opción por defecto. by **~** in rebeldía

defeat /dɪˈfiːt/ *vt* vencer; (*frustrate*) frustrar. ● *n* derrota *f*. **~ism** *n* derrotismo *m*. **~ist** *n* derrotista *n & (m & f)*

defect /ˈdiːfekt/ *n* defecto *m*. ● /dɪˈfekt/ *vi* desertar. **~** to pasar a. **~ion** /dɪˈfekʃn/ *n* (*Pol*) deserción *f*. **~ive** /dɪˈfektɪv/ *adj* defectuoso

defence /dɪˈfens/ *n* defensa *f*. **~less** *adj* indefenso

defen|d /dɪˈfend/ *vt* defender. **~dant** *n* (*Jurid*) acusado *m*. **~sive** /-sɪv/ *adj* defensivo. ● *n* defensiva *f*

defer /dɪˈfɜː(r)/ *vt* (*pt* deferred) aplazar. **~ence** /ˈdefǝrǝns/ *n* deferencia *f*. **~ential** /defǝˈrenʃl/ *adj* deferente

defian|ce /dɪˈfaɪǝns/ *n* desafío *m*. in **~ce** of a despecho de. **~t** *adj* desafiante. **~tly** *adv* con actitud desafiante

deficien|cy /dɪˈfɪʃǝnsɪ/ *n* falta *f*. **~t** *adj* deficiente. be **~t** in carecer de

deficit /ˈdefɪsɪt/ *n* déficit *m*

define /dɪˈfaɪn/ *vt* definir

definite /ˈdefɪnɪt/ *adj* (*final*) definitivo; (*certain*) seguro; (*clear*) claro; (*firm*) firme. **~ly** *adv* seguramente; (*definitively*) definitivamente

definition /defɪˈnɪʃn/ *n* definición *f*

definitive /dɪˈfɪnətɪv/ adj definitivo

deflate /dɪˈfleɪt/ vt desinflar. ● vi desinflarse

deflect /dɪˈflekt/ vt desviar

deform /dɪˈfɔːm/ vt deformar. ~ed adj deforme. ~ity n deformidad f

defrost /diːˈfrɒst/ vt descongelar. ● vi descongelarse

deft /deft/ adj (-er, -est) hábil. ~ly adv hábilmente f

defuse /diːˈfjuːz/ vt desactivar (bomb); (fig) calmar

defy /dɪˈfaɪ/ vt desafiar

degenerate /dɪˈdʒenəreɪt/ vi degenerar. ● /dɪˈdʒenərət/ adj & n degenerado (m)

degrad|ation /degrəˈdeɪʃn/ n degradación f. ~e /dɪˈɡreɪd/ vt degradar

degree /dɪˈgriː/ n grado m; (Univ) licenciatura f; (rank) rango m. to a certain ~ hasta cierto punto

deign /deɪn/ vi. ~ to dignarse

deity /ˈdiːɪti/ n deidad f

deject|ed /dɪˈdʒektɪd/ adj desanimado. ~ion /-ʃn/ n abatimiento m

delay /dɪˈleɪ/ vt retrasar, demorar (LAm). ● vi tardar, demorar (LAm). ● n retraso m, demora f (LAm)

delegat|e /ˈdelɪgeɪt/ vt/i delegar. ● /ˈdelɪgət/ n delegado m. ~ion /-ˈgeɪʃn/ n delegación f

delet|e /dɪˈliːt/ vt tachar. ~ion /-ʃn/ n supresión f

deliberat|e /dɪˈlɪbəreɪt/ vt/i deliberar. ● /dɪˈlɪbərət/ adj intencionado; (steps etc) pausado. ~ely adv a propósito. ~ion /-ˈreɪʃn/ n deliberación f

delica|cy /ˈdelɪkəsi/ n delicadeza f; (food) manjar m. ~te /ˈdelɪkət/ adj delicado

delicatessen /delɪkəˈtesn/ n charcutería f, salchichonería f (Mex)

delicious /dɪˈlɪʃəs/ adj delicioso

delight /dɪˈlaɪt/ n placer m. ● vt encantar. ● vi deleitarse. ~ed adj encantado. ~ful adj delicioso

deliri|ous /dɪˈlɪrɪəs/ adj delirante. ~um /-əm/ n delirio m

deliver /dɪˈlɪvə(r)/ vt entregar; (distribute) repartir; (aim) lanzar; (Med) he ~ed the baby la asistió en el parto. ~ance n liberación f. ~y n entrega f; (of post) reparto m; (Med) parto m

delta /ˈdeltə/ n (of river) delta m

delude /dɪˈluːd/ vt engañar. ~ o.s. engañarse

deluge /ˈdeljuːdʒ/ n diluvio m

delusion /dɪˈluːʒn/ n ilusión f

deluxe /dɪˈlʌks/ adj de lujo

delve /delv/ vi hurgar. ~ into (investigate) ahondar en

demand /dɪˈmɑːnd/ vt exigir. ● n petición f, pedido m (LAm); (claim) exigencia f; (Com) demanda f. in ~ muy popular, muy solicitado. on ~ a solicitud. ~ing adj exigente. ~s npl exigencias fpl

demented /dɪˈmentɪd/ adj demente

demo /ˈdeməʊ/ n (pl -os) 🅸 manifestación f

democra|cy /dɪˈmɒkrəsi/ n democracia f. ~t /ˈdeməkræt/ n demócrata m & f. D~t a & n (in US) demócrata (m & f). ~tic /deməˈkrætɪk/ adj democrático

demoli|sh /dɪˈmɒlɪʃ/ vt derribar. ~tion /deməˈlɪʃn/ n demolición f

demon /ˈdiːmən/ n demonio m

demonstrat|e /ˈdemənstreɪt/ vt demostrar. ● vi manifestarse, hacer una manifestación. ~ion /-ˈstreɪʃn/ n demostración f; (Pol)

manifestación f. **~or**
/'demənstreɪtə(r)/n (Pol) manifestante m & f; (marketing) demostrador m

demoralize /dɪˈmɒrəlaɪz/ vt desmoralizar

demote /dɪˈməʊt/ vt bajar de categoría

demure /dɪˈmjʊə(r)/ adj recatado

den /den/ n (of animal) guarida f, madriguera f

denial /dɪˈnaɪəl/ n denegación f; (statement) desmentimiento m

denim /ˈdenɪm/ n tela f vaquera or de jeans, mezclilla (Mex) f. **~s** npl vaqueros mpl, jeans mpl, tejanos mpl, pantalones mpl de mezclilla (Mex)

Denmark /ˈdenmɑːk/ n Dinamarca f

denote /dɪˈnəʊt/ vt denotar

denounce /dɪˈnaʊns/ vt denunciar

dens|e /dens/ adj (-er, -est) espeso; (person) torpe. **~ely** adv densamente. **~ity** n densidad f

dent /dent/ n abolladura f. **●vt** abollar

dental /ˈdentl/ adj dental. **~ floss** /flɒs/ n hilo m or seda f dental. **~ surgeon** n dentista m & f

dentist /ˈdentɪst/ n dentista m & f. **~ry** n odontología f

dentures /ˈdentʃəz/ npl dentadura f postiza

deny /dɪˈnaɪ/ vt negar; desmentir (rumour); denegar (request)

deodorant /diːˈəʊdərənt/ adj & n desodorante (m)

depart /dɪˈpɑːt/ vi partir, salir. **~ from** (deviate from) apartarse de

department /dɪˈpɑːtmənt/ n departamento m; (Pol) ministerio m, secretaría f (Mex). **~ store** n grandes almacenes mpl, tienda f de departamentos (Mex)

departure /dɪˈpɑːtʃə(r)/ n partida f; (of train etc) salida f

depend /dɪˈpend/ vi depender. **~ on** depender de. **~able** adj digno de confianza. **~ant** /dɪˈpendənt/ n familiar m & f dependiente. **~ence** n dependencia f. **~ent** adj dependiente. be **~ent** on depender de

depict /dɪˈpɪkt/ vt representar; (in words) describir

deplete /dɪˈpliːt/ vt agotar

deplor|able /dɪˈplɔːrəbl/ adj deplorable. **~e** /dɪˈplɔː(r)/ vt deplorar

deploy /dɪˈplɔɪ/ vt desplegar

deport /dɪˈpɔːt/ vt deportar. **~ation** /-ˈteɪʃn/ n deportación f

depose /dɪˈpəʊz/ vt deponer

deposit /dɪˈpɒzɪt/ vt (pt deposited) depositar. **●n** depósito m

depot /ˈdepəʊ/ n depósito m; (Amer) estación f de autobuses

deprav|ed /dɪˈpreɪvd/ adj depravado. **~ity** /dɪˈprævətɪ/ n depravación f

depress /dɪˈpres/ vt deprimir; (press down) apretar. **~ed** adj deprimido. **~ing** adj deprimente. **~ion** /-ʃn/ n depresión f

depriv|ation /deprɪˈveɪʃn/ n privación f. **~e** /dɪˈpraɪv/ vt. **~e of** privar de. **~d** adj carenciado

depth /depθ/ n profundidad f. be out of one's **~** perder pie; (fig) meterse en honduras. **in ~** a fondo

deput|ize /ˈdepjʊtaɪz/ vi. **~ize for** sustituir a. **~y** /ˈdepjʊtɪ/ n sustituto m. **~y chairman** n vicepresidente m

derail /dɪˈreɪl/ vt hacer descarrilar. **~ment** n descarrilamiento m

derelict /ˈderəlɪkt/ adj abandonado y en ruinas

deri|de /dɪˈraɪd/ vt mofarse de.

~sion /dɪˈrɪʒn/ n mofa f. ~sive /dɪˈraɪsɪv/ adj burlón. ~sory /-ˈraɪsərɪ/ adj (offer etc) irrisorio

deriv|ation /derɪˈveɪʃn/ n derivación f. ~ative /-ˈrɪvətɪv/ n derivado m. ~e /dɪˈraɪv/ vt/i derivar

derogatory /dɪˈrɒɡətrɪ/ adj despectivo

descen|d /dɪˈsend/ vt/i descender, bajar. ~dant n descendiente m & f. ~t n descenso m, bajada f; (lineage) ascendencia f

descri|be /dɪsˈkraɪb/ vt describir. ~ption /-ˈkrɪpʃn/ n descripción f. ~ptive /-ˈkrɪptɪv/ adj descriptivo

desecrate /ˈdesɪkreɪt/ vt profanar

desert¹ /dɪˈzɜːt/ vt abandonar. ● vi (Mil) desertar. ~er /dɪˈzɜːtə(r)/ n desertor m

desert² /ˈdezət/ adj & n desierto (m)

deserts /dɪˈzɜːts/ npl lo merecido. get one's just ~ llevarse su merecido

deserv|e /dɪˈzɜːv/ vt merecer. ~ing adj (cause) meritorio

design /dɪˈzaɪn/ n diseño m; (plan) plan m. ~s (intentions) propósitos mpl. ● vt diseñar; (plan) planear

designate /ˈdezɪɡneɪt/ vt designar

designer /dɪˈzaɪnə(r)/ n diseñador m; (fashion ~) diseñador m de modas. ● adj (clothes) de diseño exclusivo

desirable /dɪˈzaɪərəbl/ adj deseable

desire /dɪˈzaɪə(r)/ n deseo m. ● vt desear

desk /desk/ n escritorio m; (at school) pupitre m; (in hotel) recepción f; (Com) caja f. ~top publishing n autoedición f, edición f electrónica

desolat|e /ˈdesələt/ adj desolado; (uninhabited) deshabitado. ~ion /-ˈleɪʃn/ n desolación f

despair /dɪˈspeə(r)/ n desesperación f. be in ~ estar desesperado. ● vi. ~ of desesperarse de

despatch /dɪˈspætʃ/ vt, n see DISPATCH

desperat|e /ˈdespərət/ adj desesperado. ~ely adv desesperadamente. ~ion /-ˈreɪʃn/ n desesperación f

despicable /dɪˈspɪkəbl/ adj despreciable

despise /dɪˈspaɪz/ vt despreciar

despite /dɪˈspaɪt/ prep a pesar de

despondent /dɪˈspɒndənt/ adj abatido

despot /ˈdespɒt/ n déspota m

dessert /dɪˈzɜːt/ n postre m. ~spoon n cuchara f de postre

destination /destɪˈneɪʃn/ n destino m

destiny /ˈdestɪnɪ/ n destino m

destitute /ˈdestɪtjuːt/ adj indigente

destroy /dɪˈstrɔɪ/ vt destruir. ~er n destructor m

destruct|ion /dɪˈstrʌkʃn/ n destrucción f. ~ve /-ɪv/ adj destructivo

desultory /ˈdesəltrɪ/ adj desganado

detach /dɪˈtætʃ/ vt separar. ~able adj separable. ~ed adj (aloof) distante; (house) no adosado. ~ment n desprendimiento m; (Mil) destacamento m; (aloofness) indiferencia f

detail /ˈdiːteɪl/ n detalle m. explain sth in ~ explicar algo detalladamente. ● vt detallar; (Mil) destacar. ~ed adj detallado

detain /dɪˈteɪn/ vt detener; (delay) retener. ~ee /diːteɪˈniː/ n detenido m

detect /dɪ'tekt/ vt percibir; (*discover*) descubrir. ~ive n (*private*) detective m; (*in police*) agente m & f. ~or n detector m

detention /dɪ'tenʃn/ n detención f

deter /dɪ'tɜː(r)/ vt (*pt* deterred) disuadir; (*prevent*) impedir

detergent /dɪ'tɜːdʒənt/ adj & n detergente (m)

deteriorat|e /dɪ'tɪərɪəreɪt/ vi deteriorarse. ~ion /-'reɪʃn/ n deterioro m

determin|ation /dɪtɜːmɪ'neɪʃn/ n determinación f. ~e /dɪ'tɜːmɪn/ vt determinar; (*decide*) decidir. ~ed adj determinado; (*resolute*) decidido

deterrent /dɪ'terənt/ n elemento m de disuasión

detest /dɪ'test/ vt aborrecer. ~able adj odioso

detonat|e /'detəneɪt/ vt hacer detonar. • vi detonar. ~ion /-'neɪʃn/ n detonación f. ~or n detonador m

detour /'diːtʊə(r)/ n rodeo m; (*Amer, of transport*) desvío m, desviación f. • vt (*Amer*) desviar

detract /dɪ'trækt/ vi. ~ from disminuir

detriment /'detrɪmənt/ n. to the ~ of en perjuicio de. ~al /-'mentl/ adj perjudicial

devalue /diː'væljuː/ vt desvalorizar

devastat|e /'devəsteɪt/ vt devastar. ~ing adj devastador; (*fig*) arrollador. ~ion /-'steɪʃn/ n devastación f

develop /dɪ'veləp/ vt desarrollar; contraer (illness); urbanizar (land). • vi desarrollarse; (*appear*) aparecer. ~ing adj (*country*) en vías de desarrollo. ~ment n desarrollo m. (new) ~ment novedad f

deviant /'diːvɪənt/ adj desviado

deviat|e /'diːvɪeɪt/ vi desviarse. ~ion /-'eɪʃn/ n desviación f

device /dɪ'vaɪs/ n dispositivo m; (*scheme*) estratagema f

devil /'devl/ n diablo m

devious /'diːvɪəs/ adj taimado

devise /dɪ'vaɪz/ vt idear

devoid /dɪ'vɔɪd/ adj. be ~ of carecer de

devolution /diːvə'luːʃn/ n descentralización f; (*of power*) delegación f

devot|e /dɪ'vəʊt/ vt dedicar. ~ed adj (*couple*) unido; (*service*) leal. ~ee /devə'tiː/ n partidario m. ~ion /-ʃn/ n devoción f

devour /dɪ'vaʊə(r)/ vt devorar

devout /dɪ'vaʊt/ adj devoto

dew /djuː/ n rocío m

dexterity /dek'sterətɪ/ n destreza f

diabet|es /daɪə'biːtiːz/ n diabetes f. ~ic /-'betɪk/ adj & n diabético (m)

diabolical /daɪə'bɒlɪkl/ adj diabólico

diagnos|e /'daɪəgnəʊz/ vt diagnosticar. ~is /-'nəʊsɪs/ n (*pl* -oses/-siːz/) diagnóstico m

diagonal /daɪ'ægənl/ adj & n diagonal (f)

diagram /'daɪəgræm/ n diagrama m

dial /'daɪəl/ n cuadrante m; (*on clock, watch*) esfera f; (*on phone*) disco m. • vt (*pt* dialled) marcar, discar (LAm)

dialect /'daɪəlekt/ n dialecto m

dialling: ~ code n prefijo m, código m de la zona (LAm). ~ tone n tono m de marcar, tono n de discado (LAm)

dialogue /'daɪəlɒg/ n diálogo m

dial tone n (*Amer*) *see* **DIALLING TONE**

diameter /daɪˈæmɪtə(r)/ n diámetro m

diamond /ˈdaɪəmənd/ n diamante m; (*shape*) rombo m. **~s** npl (*Cards*) diamantes mpl

diaper /ˈdaɪəpə(r)/ n (*Amer*) pañal m

diaphragm /ˈdaɪəfræm/ n diafragma m

diarrhoea /daɪəˈrɪə/ n diarrea f

diary /ˈdaɪərɪ/ n diario m; (*book*) agenda f

dice /daɪs/ n invar dado m. ● vt (*Culin*) cortar en cubitos

dictate /dɪkˈteɪt/ vt/i dictar. **~ion** /dɪkˈteɪʃn/ n dictado m. **~or** n dictador m. **~orship** n dictadura f

dictionary /ˈdɪkʃənərɪ/ n diccionario m

did /dɪd/ *see* **DO**

didn't /ˈdɪdnt/ = **did not**

die /daɪ/ vi (*pres p* dying) morir. be dying to morirse por. □ **~ down** vi irse apagando. □ **~ out** vi extinguirse

diesel /ˈdiːzl/ n (*fuel*) gasóleo m. **~ engine** n motor m diesel

diet /ˈdaɪət/ n alimentación f; (*restricted*) régimen m. be on a **~** estar a régimen. ● vi estar a régimen

differ /ˈdɪfə(r)/ vi ser distinto; (*disagree*) no estar de acuerdo. **~ence** /ˈdɪfrəns/ n diferencia f; (*disagreement*) desacuerdo m. **~ent** /ˈdɪfrənt/ adj distinto, diferente. **~ently** adv de otra manera

difficult /ˈdɪfɪkəlt/ adj difícil. **~y** n dificultad f

diffuse /dɪˈfjuːs/ adj difuso. ● /dɪˈfjuːz/ vt difundir. ● vi difundirse. **~ion** /-ʒn/ n difusión f

dig /dɪg/ n (*poke*) empujón m; (*poke with elbow*) codazo m; (*remark*) indirecta f. **~s** npl ⓵ alojamiento m ● vt (*pt* dug, *pres p* digging) cavar; (*thrust*) empujar. ● vi cavar. □ **~ out** vt extraer. □ **~ up** vt desenterrar

digest /ˈdaɪdʒest/ n resumen m. ● /daɪˈdʒest/ vt digerir. **~ion** /-ˈdʒestʃn/ n digestión f. **~ive** /-ˈdʒestɪv/ adj digestivo

digger /ˈdɪgə(r)/ n (*Mec*) excavadora f

digit /ˈdɪdʒɪt/ n dígito m; (*finger*) dedo m. **~al** /ˈdɪdʒɪtl/ adj digital

dignified /ˈdɪgnɪfaɪd/ adj solemne

dignitary /ˈdɪgnɪtərɪ/ n dignatario m

dignity /ˈdɪgnətɪ/ n dignidad f

digress /daɪˈgres/ vi divagar. **~ from** apartarse de. **~ion** /-ʃn/ n digresión f

dike /daɪk/ n dique m

dilapidated /dɪˈlæpɪdeɪtɪd/ adj ruinoso

dilate /daɪˈleɪt/ vt dilatar. ● vi dilatarse

dilemma /daɪˈlemə/ n dilema m

diligent /ˈdɪlɪdʒənt/ adj diligente

dilute /daɪˈljuːt/ vt diluir

dim /dɪm/ adj (dimmer, dimmest) (light) débil; (room) oscuro; (fam, stupid) torpe. ● vt (*pt* dimmed) atenuar. **~ one's headlights** (*Amer*) poner las (luces) cortas or de cruce, poner las (luces) bajas (*LAm*). ● vi (light) irse atenuando

dime /daɪm/ n (*Amer*) moneda de diez centavos

dimension /daɪˈmenʃn/ n dimensión f

diminish /dɪˈmɪnɪʃ/ vt/i disminuir

dimple /ˈdɪmpl/ n hoyuelo m

din /dɪn/ n jaleo m

dine /daɪn/ vi cenar. **~r** n comensal m & f; (Amer, restaurant) cafetería f

dinghy /'dɪŋgɪ/ n bote m; (inflatable) bote m neumático

dingy /'dɪndʒɪ/ adj (-ier, -iest) miserable, sucio

dinner /'dɪnə(r)/ n cena f, comida f (LAm). **have** ~ cenar, comer (LAm). ~ **party** n cena f, comida f (LAm)

dinosaur /'daɪnəsɔ:(r)/ n dinosaurio m

dint /dɪnt/ n. **by** ~ **of** a fuerza de

dip /dɪp/ vt (pt dipped) meter; (in liquid) mojar. ~ **one's headlights** poner las (luces) cortas or cruce, poner las (luces) bajas (LAm). ● vi bajar. ● n (slope) inclinación f; (in sea) baño m. □ ~ **into** vt hojear (book)

diphthong /'dɪfθɒŋ/ n diptongo m

diploma /dɪ'pləʊmə/ n diploma m

diploma|cy /dɪ'pləʊməsɪ/ n diplomacia f. **~t** /'dɪpləmæt/ n diplomático m. **~tic** /-'mætɪk/ adj diplomático

dipstick /'dɪpstɪk/ n (Auto) varilla f del nivel de aceite

dire /daɪə(r)/ adj (-er, -est) terrible; (need, poverty) extremo

direct /dɪ'rekt/ adj directo. ● adv directamente. ● vt dirigir; (show the way) indicar. ~**ion** /-ʃn/ n dirección f. ~**ions** npl instrucciones fpl. ~**ly** adv directamente; (at once) en seguida. ● conj 🄴 en cuanto. ~**or** n director m; (of company) directivo m

directory /dɪ'rektərɪ/ n guía f; (Comp) directorio m

dirt /dɜ:t/ n suciedad f. ~**y** adj

(-ier, -iest) sucio. ● vt ensuciar

disab|ility /dɪsə'bɪlətɪ/ n invalidez f. ~**le** /dɪs'eɪbl/ vt incapacitar. ~**led** adj minusválido

disadvantage /dɪsəd'vɑ:ntɪdʒ/ n desventaja f. ~**d** adj desfavorecido

disagree /dɪsə'gri:/ vi no estar de acuerdo (with con). ~ **with** (food, climate) sentarle mal a. ~**able** adj desagradable. ~**ment** n desacuerdo m; (quarrel) riña f

disappear /dɪsə'pɪə(r)/ vi desaparecer. ~**ance** n desaparición f

disappoint /dɪsə'pɔɪnt/ vt decepcionar. ~**ing** adj decepcionante. ~**ment** n decepción f

disapprov|al /dɪsə'pru:vl/ n desaprobación f. ~**e** /dɪsə'pru:v/ vi. ~**e of** desaprobar. ~**ing** adj de reproche

disarm /dɪs'ɑ:m/ vt desarmar. ● vi desarmarse. ~**ament** n desarme m

disarray /dɪsə'reɪ/ n desorden m

disast|er /dɪ'zɑ:stə(r)/ n desastre m. ~**rous** /-strəs/ adj catastrófico

disband /dɪs'bænd/ vt disolver. ● vi disolverse

disbelief /dɪsbɪ'li:f/ n incredulidad f

disc /dɪsk/ n disco m

discard /dɪs'kɑ:d/ vt descartar; abandonar (beliefs etc)

discern /dɪ'sɜ:n/ vt percibir. ~**ing** adj exigente; (ear, eye) educado

discharge /dɪs'tʃɑ:dʒ/ vt descargar; cumplir (duty); (Mil) licenciar. ● /'dɪstʃɑ:dʒ/ n descarga f; (Med) secreción f; (Mil) licenciamiento m

disciple /dɪ'saɪpl/ n discípulo m

disciplin|ary /dɪsə'plɪnərɪ/ adj disciplinario. ~**e** /'dɪsɪplɪn/ n disciplina f. ● vt disciplinar; (punish) sancionar

disc jockey /'dɪskdʒɒkɪ/ n pinchadiscos *m* & *f*

disclaim /dɪs'kleɪm/ *vt* desconocer. **~er** *n* (*Jurid*) descargo *m* de responsabilidad

disclos|e /dɪs'kləʊz/ *vt* revelar. **~ure** /-ʒə(r)/ *n* revelación *f*

disco /'dɪskəʊ/ *n* (*pl* -os) 🄳 discoteca *f*

discolour /dɪs'kʌlə(r)/ *vt* decolorar. ● *vi* decolorarse

discomfort /dɪs'kʌmfət/ *n* malestar *m*; (*lack of comfort*) incomodidad *f*

disconcert /dɪskən'sɜːt/ *vt* desconcertar

disconnect /dɪskə'nekt/ *vt* separar; (*Elec*) desconectar

disconsolate /dɪs'kɒnsələt/ *adj* desconsolado

discontent /dɪskən'tent/ *n* descontento *m*. **~ed** *adj* descontento

discontinue /dɪskən'tɪnjuː/ *vt* interrumpir

discord /'dɪskɔːd/ *n* discordia *f*; (*Mus*) disonancia *f*. **~ant** /-'skɔːdənt/ *adj* discorde; (*Mus*) disonante

discotheque /'dɪskətek/ *n* discoteca *f*

discount /'dɪskaʊnt/ *n* descuento *m*. ● /dɪs'kaʊnt/ *vt* hacer caso omiso de; (*Com*) descontar

discourag|e /dɪs'kʌrɪdʒ/ *vt* desanimar; (*dissuade*) disuadir. **~ing** *adj* desalentador

discourteous /dɪs'kɜːtɪəs/ *adj* descortés

discover /dɪs'kʌvə(r)/ *vt* descubrir. **~y** *n* descubrimiento *m*

discredit /dɪs'kredɪt/ *vt* (*pt* discredited) desacreditar. ● *n* descrédito *m*

discreet /dɪs'kriːt/ *adj* discreto. **~ly** *adv* discretamente

discrepancy /dɪs'krepənsɪ/ *n* discrepancia *f*

discretion /dɪs'kreʃn/ *n* discreción *f*

discriminat|e /dɪs'krɪmɪneɪt/ *vt* discriminar. **~e between** distinguir entre. **~ing** *adj* perspicaz. **~ion** /-'neɪʃn/ *n* discernimiento *m*; (*bias*) discriminación *f*

discus /'dɪskəs/ *n* disco *m*

discuss /dɪ'skʌs/ *vt* discutir. **~ion** /-ʃn/ *n* discusión *f*

disdain /dɪs'deɪn/ *n* desdén *m*. **~ful** *adj* desdeñoso

disease /dɪ'ziːz/ *n* enfermedad *f*

disembark /dɪsɪm'bɑːk/ *vi* desembarcar

disenchant|ed /dɪsɪn'tʃɑːntɪd/ *adj* desilusionado. **~ment** *n* desencanto *m*

disentangle /dɪsɪn'tæŋgl/ *vt* desenredar

disfigure /dɪs'fɪgə(r)/ *vt* desfigurar

disgrace /dɪs'greɪs/ *n* vergüenza *f*. ● *vt* deshonrar. **~ful** *adj* vergonzoso

disgruntled /dɪs'grʌntld/ *adj* descontento

disguise /dɪs'gaɪz/ *vt* disfrazar. ● *n* disfraz *m*. **in ~** disfrazado

disgust /dɪs'gʌst/ *n* repugnancia *f*, asco *m*. ● *vt* dar asco a. **~ed** *adj* indignado; (*stronger*) asqueado. **~ing** *adj* repugnante, asqueroso

dish /dɪʃ/ *n* plato *m*. **wash** o **do the ~es** fregar los platos, lavar los trastes (*Mex*). □ **~ up** *vt/i* servir. **~cloth** *n* bayeta *f*

disheartening /dɪs'hɑːtnɪŋ/ *adj* desalentador

dishonest /dɪs'ɒnɪst/ *adj* deshonesto. **~y** *n* falta *f* de honradez

dishonour /dɪs'ɒnə(r)/ *n* deshonra *f*

d

dish: ~ **soap** n (Amer) lavavajillas m. ~ **towel** n paño m de cocina. ~**washer** n lavaplatos m, lavavajillas m. ~**washing liquid** n (Amer) see ~ **SOAP**

disillusion /dɪsɪ'luːʒn/ vt desilusionar. ~**ment** n desilusión f

disinfect /dɪsɪn'fekt/ vt desinfectar. ~**ant** n desinfectante m

disintegrate /dɪs'ɪntɪɡreɪt/ vt desintegrar. ● vi desintegrarse

disinterested /dɪs'ɪntrəstɪd/ adj desinteresado

disjointed /dɪs'dʒɔɪntɪd/ adj inconexo

disk /dɪsk/ n disco m. ~ **drive** (Comp) unidad f de discos. ~**ette** /dɪs'ket/ n disquete m

dislike /dɪs'laɪk/ n aversión f. I ~ dogs no me gustan los perros

dislocate /'dɪsləkeɪt/ vt dislocar(se) (limb)

dislodge /dɪs'lɒdʒ/ vt sacar

disloyal /dɪs'lɔɪəl/ adj desleal. ~**ty** n deslealtad f

dismal /'dɪzməl/ adj triste; (bad) fatal

dismantle /dɪs'mæntl/ vt desmontar

dismay /dɪs'meɪ/ n consternación f. ● vt consternar

dismiss /dɪs'mɪs/ vt despedir; (reject) rechazar. ~**al** n despido m; (of idea) rechazo m

dismount /dɪs'maʊnt/ vi desmontar

disobe|dience /dɪsə'biːdɪəns/ n desobediencia f. ~**dient** adj desobediente. ~**y** /dɪsə'beɪ/ vt/i desobedecer

disorder /dɪs'ɔːdə(r)/ n desorden m; (ailment) afección f. ~**ly** adj desordenado

disorganized /dɪs'ɔːɡənaɪzd/ adj desorganizado

disorientate /dɪs'ɔːrɪənteɪt/ vt desorientar

disown /dɪs'əʊn/ vt repudiar

disparaging /dɪs'pærɪdʒɪŋ/ adj despreciativo

dispatch /dɪs'pætʃ/ vt despachar. ● n despacho m. ~ **rider** n mensajero m

dispel /dɪs'pel/ vt (pt dispelled) disipar

dispens|able /dɪs'pensəbl/ adj prescindible. ~**e** vt distribuir; (Med) preparar. □ ~ **with** vt prescindir de

dispers|al /dɪs'pɜːsl/ n dispersión f. ~**e** /dɪs'pɜːs/ vt dispersar. ● vi dispersarse

dispirited /dɪs'pɪrɪtɪd/ adj desanimado

display /dɪs'pleɪ/ vt exponer (goods); demostrar (feelings). ● n exposición f; (of feelings) demostración f

displeas|e /dɪs'pliːz/ vt desagradar. be ~**ed with** estar disgustado con. ~**ure** /-'pleʒə(r)/ n desagrado m

dispos|able /dɪs'pəʊzəbl/ adj desechable. ~**al** /dɪs'pəʊzl/ n (of waste) eliminación f. at s.o.'s ~**al** a la disposición de uno. ~**e of** /dɪs'pəʊz/ vt deshacerse de

disproportionate /dɪsprə'pɔːʃənət/ adj desproporcionado

disprove /dɪs'pruːv/ vt desmentir (claim); refutar (theory)

dispute /dɪs'pjuːt/ vt discutir. ● n disputa f. in ~ en disputado

disqualif|ication /dɪskwɒlɪfɪ'keɪʃn/ n descalificación f. ~**y** /dɪs'kwɒlɪfaɪ/ vt incapacitar; (Sport) descalificar

disregard /dɪsrɪ'ɡɑːd/ vt no hacer caso de. ● n indiferencia f (for a)

disreputable /dɪsˈrepjʊtəbl/ adj de mala fama

disrespect /dɪsrɪˈspekt/ n falta f de respeto

disrupt /dɪsˈrʌpt/ vt interrumpir; trastornar (plans). **~ion** /-ʃn/ n trastorno m. **~ive** adj (influence) perjudicial, negativo

dissatis|faction /dɪsætɪsˈfækʃn/ n descontento m. **~fied** /dɪˈsætɪsfaɪd/ adj descontento

dissect /dɪˈsekt/ vt disecar

dissent /dɪˈsent/ vi disentir. ● n disentimiento m

dissertation /dɪsəˈteɪʃn/ n (Univ) tesis f

dissident /ˈdɪsɪdənt/ adj & n disidente (m & f)

dissimilar /dɪˈsɪmɪlə(r)/ adj distinto

dissolute /ˈdɪsəluːt/ adj disoluto

dissolve /dɪˈzɒlv/ vt disolver. ● vi disolverse

dissuade /dɪˈsweɪd/ vt disuadir

distan|ce /ˈdɪstəns/ n distancia f. from a **~ce** desde lejos. in the **~ce** a lo lejos. **~t** adj distante, lejano; (aloof) distante

distaste /dɪsˈteɪst/ n desagrado m. **~ful** adj desagradable

distil /dɪsˈtɪl/ vt (pt distilled) destilar. **~lery** /dɪsˈtɪləri/ n destilería f

distinct /dɪsˈtɪŋkt/ adj distinto; (clear) claro; (marked) marcado. **~ion** /-ʃn/ n distinción f; (in exam) sobresaliente m. **~ive** adj distintivo

distinguish /dɪsˈtɪŋgwɪʃ/ vt/i distinguir. **~ed** adj distinguido

distort /dɪsˈtɔːt/ vt torcer. **~ion** /-ʃn/ n deformación f

distract /dɪsˈtrækt/ vt distraer. **~ed** adj distraído. **~ion** /-ʃn/ n distracción f; (confusion) aturdimiento m

distraught /dɪsˈtrɔːt/ adj consternado, angustiado

distress /dɪsˈtres/ n angustia f. ● vt afligir. **~ed** adj afligido. **~ing** adj penoso

distribut|e /dɪˈstrɪbjuːt/ vt repartir, distribuir. **~ion** /-ˈbjuːʃn/ n distribución f. **~or** n distribuidor m; (Auto) distribuidor m (del encendido)

district /ˈdɪstrɪkt/ n zona f, región f; (of town) barrio m

distrust /dɪsˈtrʌst/ n desconfianza f. ● vt desconfiar de

disturb /dɪsˈtɜːb/ vt molestar; (perturb) inquietar; (move) desordenar; (interrupt) interrumpir. **~ance** n disturbio m; (tumult) alboroto m. **~ed** adj trastornado. **~ing** adj inquietante

disused /dɪsˈjuːzd/ adj fuera de uso

ditch /dɪtʃ/ n zanja f; (for irrigation) acequia f. ● vt 🄴 abandonar

dither /ˈdɪðə(r)/ vi vacilar

ditto /ˈdɪtəʊ/ adv ídem

divan /dɪˈvæn/ n diván m

dive /daɪv/ vi tirarse (al agua), zambullirse; (rush) meterse (precipitadamente). ● n (into water) zambullida f; (Sport) salto m (de trampolín); (of plane) descenso m en picado, descenso m en picada (LAm); (🄳, place) antro m. **~r** n saltador m; (underwater) buzo m

diverge /daɪˈvɜːdʒ/ vi divergir. **~nt** adj divergente

divers|e /daɪˈvɜːs/ adj diverso. **~ify** vt diversificar. **~ity** n diversidad f

diver|sion /daɪˈvɜːʃn/ n desvío m; desviación f; (distraction) diversión f. **~t** /daɪˈvɜːt/ vt desviar; (entertain) divertir

divide /dɪˈvaɪd/ vt dividir. ● vi dividirse. ∼**d highway** n (Amer) autovía f, carretera f de doble pista

dividend /ˈdɪvɪdend/ n dividendo m

divine /dɪˈvaɪn/ adj divino

division /dɪˈvɪʒn/ n división f

divorce /dɪˈvɔːs/ n divorcio m. ● vt divorciarse de. get ∼d divorciarse. ● vi divorciarse. ∼e /dɪvɔːˈsiː/ n divorciado m

divulge /daɪˈvʌldʒ/ vt divulgar

DIY abbr see **DO-IT-YOURSELF**

dizz|iness /ˈdɪzɪnɪs/ n vértigo m. ∼**y** adj (-ier, -iest) mareado. be or feel ∼**y** marearse

DJ abbr see **DISC JOCKEY**

do /duː//dʊ, də/

3rd person singular present **does**; past **did**; past participle **done**

● transitive verb

····▸ hacer. he does what he wants hace lo que quiere. to do one's homework hacer los deberes. to do the cooking preparar la comida, cocinar. well done! ¡muy bien!

····▸ (clean) lavar (dishes). limpiar (windows)

····▸ (as job) what does he do? ¿en qué trabaja?

····▸ (swindle) estafar. I've been done! ¡me han estafado!

····▸ (achieve) she's done it! ¡lo ha logrado!

● intransitive verb

····▸ hacer. do as you're told! ¡haz lo que se te dice!

····▸ (fare) how are you doing?

(with a task) ¿qué tal te va? how do you do?, (as greeting) mucho gusto, encantado

····▸ (perform) she did well/badly le fue bien/mal

····▸ (be suitable) will this do? ¿esto sirve?

····▸ (be enough) ser suficiente, bastar. one box will do con una caja basta, con una caja es suficiente

● auxiliary verb

····▸ (to form interrogative and negative) do you speak Spanish? ¿hablas español?. I don't want to no quiero. don't shut the door no cierres la puerta

····▸ (in tag questions) you eat meat, don't you? ¿comes carne, ¿verdad? or ¿no? he lives in London, doesn't he? vive en Londres, ¿no? or ¿verdad? or ¿no es cierto?

····▸ (in short answers) do you like it? - yes, I do ¿te gusta? - sí. who wrote it? - I did ¿quién lo escribió? - yo

····▸ (emphasizing) do come in! ¡pase Ud!. don't you exaggerate! ¡cómo exageras! □ **do away with** vt abolir. □ **do in** vt (sl, kill) eliminar. □ **do up** vt abrochar (coat etc); arreglar (house). □ **do with** vt (need) (with can, could) necesitar; (expressing connection) it has nothing to do with that no tiene nada que ver con eso. □ **do without** vt prescindir de

docile /ˈdəʊsaɪl/ adj dócil

dock /dɒk/ n (Naut) dársena f; (wharf, quay) muelle m; (Jurid) banquillo m de los acusados. ∼**s** npl (port) puerto m. ● vt cortar (tail);

atracar (ship). ● vi (ship) atracar.
~er n estibador m. **~yard** n astillero m

doctor /'dɒktə(r)/ n médico m,
doctor m

doctrine /'dɒktrɪn/ n doctrina f

document /'dɒkjʊmənt/ n documento m. **~ary** /-'mentri/ adj & n
documental m

dodge /dɒdʒ/ vt esquivar. ● vi esquivarse. ● n treta f. **~ems**
/'dɒdʒəmz/ npl autos mpl de choque. **~y** adj (**-ier, -iest**) (awkward)
difícil

doe /dəʊ/ n (rabbit) coneja f; (hare)
liebre f hembra; (deer) cierva f

does /dʌz/ see **DO**

doesn't /'dʌznt/ = **does not**

dog /dɒg/ n perro m. ● vt (pt dogged) perseguir

dogged /'dɒgɪd/ adj obstinado

doghouse /'dɒghaʊs/ n (Amer)
casa f del perro. **in the ~** ⬛ en
desgracia

dogma /'dɒgmə/ n dogma m.
~tic /-'mætɪk/ adj dogmático

do|ings npl actividades fpl. **~-it-
yourself** /du:ɪtjə'self/ n bricolaje m

dole /dəʊl/ n ⬛ subsidio m de
paro, subsidio m de desempleo. **on
the ~** ⬛ parado, desempleado.
□ **~ out** vt distribuir

doleful /'dəʊlfl/ adj triste

doll /dɒl/ n muñeca f

dollar /'dɒlə(r)/ n dólar m

dollarization /dɒlərar'zeɪʃn/ n
dolarización f

dollop /'dɒləp/ n ⬛ porción f

dolphin /'dɒlfɪn/ n delfín m

domain /dəʊ'meɪn/ n dominio m

dome /dəʊm/ n cúpula f

domestic /də'mestɪk/ adj doméstico; (trade, flights, etc) nacional.

~ated /də'mestɪkeɪtɪd/ adj (animal) domesticado. **~ science** n
economía f doméstica

domin|ance /'dɒmɪnəns/ n dominio m. **~ant** adj dominante.
~ate /-eɪt/ vt/i dominar. **~ation**
/-'neɪʃn/ n dominación f. **~eering**
adj dominante

Dominican Republic /də
'mɪnɪkən/ n República f Dominicana

dominion /də'mɪnjən/ n dominio m

domino /'dɒmɪnəʊ/ n (pl **-oes**)
ficha f de dominó. **~es** npl (game)
dominó m

donat|e /dəʊ'neɪt/ vt donar. **~ion**
/-ʃn/ n donativo m, donación f

done /dʌn/ see **DO**

donkey /'dɒŋkɪ/ n burro m, asno
m. **~'s years** ⬛ siglos mpl

donor /'dəʊnə(r)/ n donante m & f

don't /dəʊnt/ = **do not**

doodle /'du:dl/ vi/t garrapatear

doom /du:m/ n destino m; (death)
muerte f. ● vt. **be ~ed** to estar
condenado a

door /dɔ:(r)/ n puerta f. **~bell** n
timbre m. **~ knob** n pomo m (de
la puerta). **~mat** n felpudo m.
~step n peldaño m. **~way** n (en
trada f

dope /dəʊp/ n ⬛ droga f; (sl, idiot)
imbécil m. ● vt ⬛ drogar

dormant /'dɔ:mənt/ adj aletargado, (volcano) inactivo

dormice /'dɔ:maɪs/ see **DOR-
MOUSE**

dormitory /'dɔ:mɪtrɪ/ n dormitorio m

dormouse /'dɔ:maʊs/ n (pl
-mice) lirón m

DOS /dɒs/ abbr (= **disc-operating
system**) DOS m

dosage | drain

dos|age /ˈdəʊsɪdʒ/ n dosis f. **~e**
/dəʊs/ n dosis f

dot /dɒt/ n punto m. **on the ~** en
punto. **~·com** n punto m com.
~-com company empresa f punt
tocom

dote /dəʊt/ vi. **~ on** adorar

dotty /ˈdɒtɪ/ adj (-ier, -iest) 🔢 chiflado

double /ˈdʌbl/ adj doble. ● adv al
doble. ● n doble m; (person) doble
m & f. **at the ~** corriendo. ● vt doblar; redoblar (efforts etc.) ● vi doblarse. **~ bass** /beɪs/ n contrabajo
m. **~ bed** n cama f de matrimonio,
cama f de doa plazas (LAm). **~
chin** n papada f. **~ click** vt hacer
doble clic en. **~-cross** /-ˈkrɒs/ vt
traicionar. **~-decker** /-ˈdekə(r)/ n
autobús m de dos pisos. **~ Dutch**
n 🔢 chino m. **~ glazing** /ˈɡleɪzɪŋ/
n doble ventana f. **~s** npl (tennis)
dobles mpl

doubly /ˈdʌblɪ/ adv doblemente

doubt /daʊt/ n duda f. ● vt dudar;
(distrust) dudar de. **~ful** adj dudoso. **~less** adv sin duda

dough /dəʊ/ n masa f; (sl, money)
pasta f 🔢, lana f (LAm fam). **~nut**
n donut m, dona f (Mex)

dove /dʌv/ n paloma f

down /daʊn/ adv abajo. **~ with**
abajo, muera. ● vt bajar. **go ~** bajar;
(sun) ponerse. ● prep abajo. ● adj 🔢
deprimido. ● vt derribar; (fam,
drink) beber. ● n (feathers) plumón
m. **~ and out** adj en la miseria.
~cast adj abatido. **~fall** n perdi-
ción f; (of king, dictator) caída f.
~-hearted /-ˈhɑːtɪd/ adj abatido.
~hill /-ˈhɪl/ adv cuesta abajo.
~load /-ˈləʊd/ vt (Comp) bajar.
~market /-ˈmɑːkɪt/ adj (newspaper) popular; (store) barato. **~
payment** n depósito m. **~pour** n

aguacero m. **~right** adj completo.
● adv completamente. ● adj colli-
nas fpl. **~stairs** /-ˈsteəz/ adv abajo.
● /-ˈsteəz/ adj de abajo. **~stream**
adv río abajo. **~-to-earth** /-tʊˈɜːθ/
adj práctico. **~town** /-ˈtaʊn/ n centro m (de la ciudad). ● adv. **go
~town** ir al centro. **~ under** adv
en las antípodas; (in Australia) en
Australia. **~ward** /-wəd/ adj & adv.
~wards adv hacia abajo

dowry /ˈdaʊərɪ/ n dote f

doze /dəʊz/ vi dormitar

dozen /ˈdʌzn/ n docena f. a **~
eggs** una docena de huevos. **~s
of** 🔢 miles de, muchos

Dr /ˈdɒktə(r)/ abbr (Doctor)

drab /dræb/ adj monótono

draft /drɑːft/ n borrador m; (Com)
letra f de cambio; (Amer, Mil) reclutamiento m; (Amer, of air) corriente
f de aire. ● vt redactar el borrador
de; (Amer, conscript) reclutar

drag /dræg/ vt (pt dragged) arrastrar. ● n 🔢 lata f

dragon /ˈdræɡən/ n dragón m.
~fly n libélula f

drain /dreɪn/ vt vaciar (tank,
glass); drenar (land); (fig) agotar.
● vi escurrirse. ● n (pipe) sumidero
m, resumidero m (LAm); (plughole)
desagüe m. **~board** (Amer), **~ing**

board n escurridero m

drama /ˈdrɑːmə/ n drama m; (art) arte m teatral. **~tic** /drəˈmætɪk/ adj dramático. **~tist** /ˈdræmətɪst/ n dramaturgo m. **~tize** /ˈdræmətaɪz/ vt adaptar al teatro; (fig) dramatizar

drank /dræŋk/ see DRINK

drape /dreɪp/ vt cubrir; (hang) colgar. **~s** npl (Amer) cortinas fpl

drastic /ˈdræstɪk/ adj drástico

draught /drɑːft/ n corriente f de aire. **~ beer** n cerveza f de barril. **~s** npl (game) juego m de damas fpl. **~y** adj lleno de corrientes de aire

draw /drɔː/ vt (pt drew, pp drawn) tirar; (attract) atraer; dibujar (picture); trazar (line). **~ the line** trazar el límite. ● vi (Art) dibujar; (Sport) empatar. **~ near** acercarse. ● n (Sport) empate m; (in lottery) sorteo m. □ **~ in** vi (days) acortarse. □ **~ out** vt sacar (money). □ **~ up** vi pararse. vt redactar (document); acercar (chair). **~back** n desventaja f. **~bridge** n puente m levadizo

drawer /drɔː(r)/ n cajón m; gaveta f (Mex). **~s** npl calzones mpl

drawing /ˈdrɔːɪŋ/ n dibujo m. **~pin** n tachuela f, chincheta f, chinche f. **~ room** n salón m

drawl /drɔːl/ n habla f lenta

drawn /drɔːn/ see DRAW

dread /dred/ n terror m. ● vt temer. **~ful** adj terrible. **~fully** adv terriblemente

dream /driːm/ n sueño m. ● vt/i (pt dreamed or dreamt /dremt/) soñar. □ **~ up** vt idear. adj ideal. **~er** n soñador m

dreary /ˈdrɪərɪ/ adj (-ier, -iest) triste; (boring) monótono

dredge /dredʒ/ n draga f. ● vt dra-

gar. **~r** n draga f

dregs /dregz/ npl posos mpl, heces fpl; (fig) hez f

drench /drentʃ/ vt empapar

dress /dres/ n vestido m; (clothing) ropa f. ● vt vestir; (decorate) adornar; (Med) vendar. ● vi vestirse. □ **~ up** vi ponerse elegante. **~ as** disfrazarse de. **~ circle** n primer palco m

dressing /ˈdresɪŋ/ n (sauce) aliño m; (bandage) vendaje m. **~-down** /ˈdaun/ n rapapolvo m, reprensión f. **~ gown** n bata f. **~ room** n vestidor m; (in theatre) camarín m. **~ table** n tocador m

dress: ~maker n modista m & f. **~making** n costura f. **~ rehearsal** n ensayo m general

drew /druː/ see DRAW

dribble /ˈdrɪbl/ vi (baby) babear; (in football) driblar, driblear

drie|d /draɪd/ adj (food) seco; (milk) en polvo. **~r** /ˈdraɪə(r)/ n secador m

drift /drɪft/ vi ir a la deriva; (snow) amontonarse. ● n (movement) dirección f; (of snow) montón m

drill /drɪl/ n (tool) taladro m; (of dentist) torno m; (training) ejercicio m. ● vt taladrar, perforar; (train) entrenar. ● vi entrenarse

drink /drɪŋk/ vt/i (pt drank, pp drunk) beber, tomar (LAm). ● n bebida f. **~able** adj bebible; (water) potable. **~er** n bebedor m. **~ing water** n agua f potable

drip /drɪp/ vi (pt dripped) gotear. ● n gota f; (Med) goteo m intravenoso; (fam, person) soso m. **~-dry** /-ˈdraɪ/ adj de lava y pon. **~ping** adj. be **~ping** wet estar chorreando

drive /draɪv/ vt (pt drove, pp

driven) conducir, manejar (*LAm*) (car etc). ~ **s.o. mad** volver loco a uno. ~ **s.o. to do sth** llevar a uno a hacer algo. ● *vi* conducir, manejar (*LAm*). □ ~ **at** querer decir. ~ **in** (in *car*) entrar en coche. ● *n* paseo *m*; (*road*) calle *f*; (*private road*) camino *m* de entrada; (*fig*) empuje *m*. ~**r** *n* conductor *m*, chofer *m* (*LAm*). ~**r's license** *n* (*Amer*) see **DRIVING LICENSE**

drivel /ˈdrɪvl/ *n* tonterías *fpl*

driving /ˈdraɪvɪŋ/ *n* conducción *f*. ~ **licence** *n* permiso *m* de conducir, licencia *f* de conducción (*LAm*), licencia *f* (de manejar) (*Mex*). ~ **test** *n* examen *m* de conducir, examen *m* de manejar (*LAm*)

drizzle /ˈdrɪzl/ *n* llovizna *f*. ● *vi* lloviznar

drone /drəʊn/ *n* zumbido *m*. ● *vi* zumbar

drool /druːl/ *vi* babear

droop /druːp/ *vi* inclinarse; (flowers) marchitarse

drop /drɒp/ *n* gota *f*; (*fall*) caída *f*; (*decrease*) descenso *m*. ● *vt* (*pt* dropped) dejar caer; (lower) bajar. ● *vi* caer. □ ~ **in on** pasar por casa de. □ ~ **off** *vi* (*sleep*) dormirse. □ ~ **out** *vi* retirarse; (student) abandonar los estudios. ~**out** *n* marginado *m*

drought /draʊt/ *n* sequía *f*

drove /drəʊv/ see **DRIVE**. ● *n* manada *f*

drown /draʊn/ *vt* ahogar. ● *vi* ahogarse

drowsy /ˈdraʊzɪ/ *adj* soñoliento

drudgery /ˈdrʌdʒərɪ/ *n* trabajo *m* pesado

drug /drʌg/ *n* droga *f*; (*Med*) medicamento *m*. ● *vt* (*pt* drugged) drogar. ~ **addict** *n* drogadicto *m*.

~**gist** *n* (*Amer*) farmacéutico *m*. ~**store** *n* (*Amer*) farmacia *f* (que vende otros artículos también)

drum /drʌm/ *n* tambor *m*; (*for oil*) bidón *m*. ● *vi* (*pt* drummed) tocar el tambor. ● *vt*. ~ **sth into s.o.** hacerle aprender algo a uno a fuerza de repetírselo. ~**mer** *n* tambor *m*; (in group) batería *f*. ~**s** *npl* batería *f*. ~**stick** *n* baqueta *f*; (*Culin*) muslo *m*

drunk /drʌŋk/ see **DRINK**. ● *adj* borracho. **get** ~ emborracharse. ● *n* borracho *m*. ~**ard** /-əd/ *n* borracho *m*. ~**en** *adj* borracho

dry /draɪ/ *adj* (drier, driest) seco. ● *vt* secar. ● *vi* secarse. □ ~ **up** *vi* (stream) secarse; (funds) agotarse. ~**-clean** *vt* limpiar en seco. ~**-cleaner's** tintorería *f*. ~**er** *n* see **DRIER**

DTD *abbrev* **Document Type Definition** DTD *m*

dual /ˈdjuːəl/ *adj* doble. ~ **carriageway** *n* autovía *f*, carretera *f* de doble pista

dub /dʌb/ *vt* (*pt* dubbed) doblar (film)

dubious /ˈdjuːbɪəs/ *adj* dudoso; (person) sospechoso

duchess /ˈdʌtʃɪs/ *n* duquesa *f*

duck /dʌk/ *n* pato *m*. ● *vt* sumergir; bajar (head). ● *vi* agacharse. ~**ling** /ˈdʌklɪŋ/ *n* patito *m*

duct /dʌkt/ *n* conducto *m*

dud /dʌd/ *adj* inútil; (cheque) sin fondos

due /djuː/ *adj* debido; (expected) esperado. ~ **to** debido a. ● *adv*. ~ **north** derecho hacia el norte. ~**s** *npl* derechos *mpl*

duel /ˈdjuːəl/ *n* duelo *m*

duet /djuːˈet/ *n* dúo *m*

duffel, duffle /ˈdʌfl/: ~ **bag** *n* bolsa *f* de lona. ~ **coat** *n* trenca *f*

dug | dynasty

dug /dʌg/ *see* DIG

duke /djuːk/ *n* duque *m*

dull /dʌl/ *adj* (**-er**, **-est**) (weather) gris; (colour) apagado; (person, play, etc) pesado; (sound) sordo

dumb /dʌm/ *adj* (**-er**, **-est**) mudo; 🗩 estúpido. □ ~ **down** *vt* reducir el valor intelectual de. ~**found** /dʌm'faʊnd/ *vt* pasmar

dummy /'dʌmɪ/ *n* muñeco *m*; (of tailor) maniquí *m*; (for baby) chupete *m*. ● *adj* falso. ~ **run** prueba *f*

dump /dʌmp/ *vt* tirar, botar (LAm). ● *n* vertedero *m*; (Mil) depósito *m*; 🗩 lugar *m* desagradable. **be down in the** ~**s** estar deprimido

dumpling /'dʌmplɪŋ/ *n* bola *f* de masa hervida

Dumpster /'dʌmpstə(r)/ *n* (Amer, ®) contenedor *m* (para escombros)

dumpy /'dʌmpɪ/ *adj* (**-ier**, **-iest**) regordete

dunce /dʌns/ *n* burro *m*

dung /dʌŋ/ *n* (manure) estiércol *m*

dungarees /dʌŋgə'riːz/ *npl* mono *m*, peto *m*

dungeon /'dʌndʒən/ *n* calabozo *m*

dunk /dʌŋk/ *vt* remojar

dupe /djuːp/ *vt* engañar. ● *n* inocentón *m*

duplicat|e /'djuːplɪkət/ *adj & n* duplicado (*m*). ● /'djuːplɪkeɪt/ *vt* duplicar; (on machine) reproducir. ~**ing machine**, ~**or** *n* multicopista *f*

durable /'djʊərəbl/ *adj* durable

duration /djʊ'reɪʃn/ *n* duración *f*

duress /djʊ'res/ *n*. **under** ~ bajo coacción

during /'djʊərɪŋ/ *prep* durante

dusk /dʌsk/ *n* anochecer *m*

dust /dʌst/ *n* polvo *m*. ● *vt* quitar el polvo a; (sprinkle) espolvorear

(with con). ~**bin** *n* cubo *m* de la basura, bote *m* de la basura (Mex). ~ **cloth** (Amer), ~**er** *n* trapo *m*. ~**jacket** *n* sobrecubierta *f*. ~**man** /-mən/ *n* basurero *m*. ~**pan** *n* recogedor *m*. ~**y** *adj* (**-ier**, **-iest**) polvoriento

Dutch /dʌtʃ/ *adj* holandés. ● *n* (language) holandés *m*. **the** ~ (people) los holandeses. ~**man** /-mən/ *n* holandés *m*. ~**woman** *n* holandesa *f*

duty /'djuːtɪ/ *n* deber *m*; (tax) derechos *mpl* de aduana. **on** ~ de servicio. ~**-free** /-'friː/ *adj* libre de impuestos

duvet /'djuːveɪ/ *n* edredón *m*

DVD *abbr* (= **digital video disc**) DVD *m*

dwarf /dwɔːf/ *n* (*pl* **-s** or **dwarves**) enano *m*

dwell /dwel/ *vi* (*pt* **dwelt** or **dwelled**) morar. □ ~ **on** *vt* detenerse en. ~**ing** *n* morada *f*

dwindle /'dwɪndl/ *vi* disminuir

dye /daɪ/ *vt* (*pres p* **dyeing**) teñir. ● *n* tinte *m*

dying /'daɪɪŋ/ *see* DIE

dynamic /daɪ'næmɪk/ *adj* dinámico. ~**s** *npl* dinámica *f*

dynamite /'daɪnəmaɪt/ *n* dinamita *f*. ● *vt* dinamitar

dynamo /'daɪnəməʊ/ *n* (*pl* **-os**) dínamo *f*, dínamo *f*, dinamo *m* (LAm), dínamo *m* (LAm)

dynasty /'dɪnəstɪ/ *n* dinastía *f*

d

Ee

E *abbr* (= **East**) E

each /iːtʃ/ *adj* cada. ● *pron* cada uno. ~ **one** cada uno. ~ **other** uno a otro, el uno al otro. **they love** ~ **other** se aman

eager /'iːgə(r)/ *adj* impaciente; (*enthusiastic*) ávido. ~**ness** *n* impaciencia *f*; (*enthusiasm*) entusiasmo *m*

eagle /'iːgl/ *n* águila *f*

ear /ɪə(r)/ *n* oído *m*; (*outer*) oreja *f*; (*of corn*) espiga *f*. ~**ache** *n* dolor *m* de oído. ~**drum** *n* tímpano *m*

earl /ɜːl/ *n* conde *m*

early /'ɜːlɪ/ *adj* (-ier, -iest) temprano; (*before expected time*) prematuro. ● *adv* temprano; (*ahead of time*) con anticipación

earn /ɜːn/ *vt* ganar; (*deserve*) merecer

earnest /'ɜːnɪst/ *adj* serio. **in** ~ en serio

earnings /'ɜːnɪŋz/ *npl* ingresos *mpl*; (*Com*) ganancias *fpl*

ear: ~**phone** *n* audífono *m*. ~**ring** *n* pendiente *m*, arete *m* (*LAm*). ~**shot** *n*. **within** ~**shot** al alcance del oído

earth /ɜːθ/ *n* tierra *f*. **the E**~ (*planet*) la Tierra. ● *vt* (*Elec*) conectar a tierra. ~**quake** *n* terremoto *m*

earwig /'ɪəwɪg/ *n* tijereta *f*

ease /iːz/ *n* facilidad *f*; (*comfort*) tranquilidad *f*. **at** ~ a gusto; (*Mil*) en posición de descanso. **ill at** ~ molesto. **with** ~ fácilmente. ● *vt* calmar; aliviar (pain). ● *vi* calmarse;

(*lessen*) disminuir

easel /'iːzl/ *n* caballete *m*

easily /'iːzɪlɪ/ *adv* fácilmente

east /iːst/ *n* este *m*. ● *adj* este, oriental; (*wind*) del este. ● *adv* hacia el este.

Easter /'iːstə(r)/ *n* Semana *f* Santa; (*Relig*) Pascua *f* de Resurrección. ~ **egg** *n* huevo *m* de Pascua

east: ~**erly** /-əlɪ/ *adj* (wind) del este. ~**ern** /-ən/ *adj* oriental, oriental. ~**ward** /-wəd/, ~**wards** *adv* hacia el este

easy /'iːzɪ/ *adj* (-ier, -iest) fácil. ● *adv.* **go** ~ **on sth** 🄴 no pasarse con algo. **take it** ~ tomarse las cosas con calma. ● *int* ¡despacio! ~**chair** *n* sillón *m*. ~**going** /-'gəʊɪŋ/ *adj* acomodadizo

eat /iːt/ *vt/i* (*pt* ate, *pp* eaten) comer. □ ~ **into** *vt* corroer. ~**er** *n* comedor *m*

eaves /iːvz/ *npl* alero *m*. ~**drop** *vi* (*pt* -dropped). ~**drop (on)** escuchar a escondidas

ebb /eb/ *n* reflujo *m*. ● *vi* bajar; (*fig*) decaer

ebola /i:'bəʊlə/ *n* Ébola *m*

ebony /'ebənɪ/ *n* ébano *m*

EC /i:'si:/ *abbr* (= European Community) CE *f* (Comunidad *f* Europea)

eccentric /ɪk'sentrɪk/ *adj* & *n* excéntrico (*m*). ~**ity** /eksən'trɪsətɪ/ *n* excentricidad *f*

echo /'ekəʊ/ *n* (*pl* -oes) eco *m*. ● *vi* hacer eco

eclipse /ɪ'klɪps/ *n* eclipse *m*. ● *vt* eclipsar

ecolog|ical /i:kə'lɒdʒɪkl/ *adj* ecológico. ~**y** *n* ecología *f*

e-commerce /i:'kɒmɜːs/ *n* comercio *m* electrónico

econom|ic /i:kə'nɒmɪk/ *adj* eco-

nómico; ~ **refugee** refugiado *m*
económico. ~**ical** *adj* económico.
~**ics** *n* economía *f.* ~**ist** /ɪ
'kɒnəmɪst/ *n* economista *m & f.*
~**ize** /ɪ'kɒnəmaɪz/ *vi* economizar.
~**ize on sth** economizar algo. ~**y**
/ɪ'kɒnəmɪ/ *n* economía *f*

ecsta|sy /'ekstəsɪ/ *n* éxtasis *f.*
~**tic** /ɪk'stætɪk/ *adj* extático

Ecuador /'ekwədɔː(r)/ *n* Ecuador
m. ~**ean** /ekwə'dɔːrɪən/ *adj & n*
ecuatoriano (*m*)

edg|e /edʒ/ *n* borde *m; (of knife)*
filo *m; (of town)* afueras *fpl.* **have
the** ~**e on** /llevar la ventaja. **be
on** ~**e** nervioso □. ● *vt* ribetear. ●
vi avanzar cautelosamente. ~**eways**
adv de lado. ~**y** *adj* nervioso

edible /'edɪbl/ *adj* comestible

edit /'edɪt/ *vt* dirigir (newspaper);
preparar una edición de (text); editar (film). ~**ion** /ɪ'dɪʃn/ *n* edición *f.*
~**or** /ˈ (of newspaper)* director *m;
(of text)* redactor *m.* ~**orial**
/ˈtɔːrɪəl/ *adj* editorial. ● *n* artículo *m*
de fondo

educat|e /'edʒʊkeɪt/ *vt* educar.
~**ed** *adj* culto. ~**ion** /ˈ'keɪʃn/ *n*
educación *f. (knowledge, culture)*
cultura *f.* ~**ional** /ˈ'keɪʃənl/ *adj* instructivo

EC /iːˈsiː/ *abbr* (= European Com-

mission) CE *f* (Comisión *f* Europea)

eel /iːl/ *n* anguila *f*

eerie /'ɪərɪ/ *adj* (-**ier**, -**iest**) misterioso

effect /ɪ'fekt/ *n* efecto *m.* **in** ~
efectivamente. **take** ~ entrar en
vigor. ~**ive** *adj* eficaz; (striking) impresionante; (real) efectivo.
~**ively** *adv* eficazmente. ~**iveness**
n eficacia *f*

effeminate /ɪ'femɪnət/ *adj* afeminado

efficien|cy /ɪ'fɪʃənsɪ/ *n* eficiencia
f; (Mec) rendimiento *m.* ~**t** *adj* eficiente. ~**tly** *adv* eficientemente

effort /'efət/ *n* esfuerzo *m.* ~**less**
adj fácil

e.g. /iːˈdʒiː/ *abbr* (= exempli gratia) p.ej., por ejemplo

egg /eg/ *n* huevo *m.* □ ~ **on** *vt* □
incitar. ~**cup** *n* huevera *f.* ~**plant**
n (Amer) berenjena *f.* ~**shell** *n* cáscara *f* de huevo

ego /'iːgəʊ/ *n* (pl -**os**) yo *m.* ~**ism**
n egoísmo *m.* ~**ist** *n* egoísta *m & f.*
~**centric** /iːgəʊ'sentrɪk/ *adj* egocéntrico. ~**tism** *n* egotismo *m.*
~**tist** *n* egotista *m & f*

eh /eɪ/ *int* □ ¡eh!

eiderdown /'aɪdədaʊn/ *n* edredón *m*

eight /eɪt/ *adj & n* ocho (*m*). ~**een**
/er'tiːn/ *adj & n* dieciocho (*m*).
~**eenth** *adj* decimoctavo. ● *n* dieciochavo *m.* ~**h** /eɪtθ/ *adj & n* octavo (*m*). ~**ieth** /'eɪtɪəθ/ *adj* octogésimo. ● *n* ochentavo *m.* ~**y** /'eɪtɪ/
adj & n ochenta (*m*)

either /'aɪðə(r)/ *adj* cualquiera de
los dos; (negative) ninguno de los
dos; (each) cada. ● *pron* uno u otro;
(with negative) ni uno ni otro. ● *adv*
(negative) tampoco. ● *conj* o. ~

e

Tuesday or Wednesday o el martes o el miércoles; (with negative) ni el martes ni el miércoles

eject /ɪˈdʒekt/ vt expulsar

eke /iːk/ vt. ~ **out** hacer alcanzar (resources). ~ **out a living** ganarse la vida a duras penas

elaborate /ɪˈlæbərət/ adj complicado. ●/ɪˈlæbəreɪt/ vt elaborar. ●/ɪˈlæbəreɪt/ vi explicarse

elapse /ɪˈlæps/ vi transcurrir

elastic /ɪˈlæstɪk/ adj & n elástico (m). ~ **band** n goma f (elástica), liga f (Mex)

elated /ɪˈleɪtɪd/ adj regocijado. ~**ion** /-ʃn/ n regocijo m

elbow /ˈelbəʊ/ n codo m. ●vt dar un codazo a

elder /ˈeldə(r)/ adj mayor. ●n mayor m & f; (tree) saúco m. ~**ly** /ˈeldəlɪ/ adj mayor, anciano

eldest /ˈeldɪst/ adj & n mayor (m & f)

elect /ɪˈlekt/ vt elegir. ~ **to do** decidir hacer. ●adj electo. ~**ion** /-ʃn/ n elección f. ~**or** n elector m. ~**oral** adj electoral. ~**orate** /-ət/ n electorado m

electric /ɪˈlektrɪk/ adj eléctrico. ~**al** adj eléctrico. ~ **blanket** n manta f eléctrica. ~**ian** /ɪlekˈtrɪʃn/ n electricista m & f. ~**ity** /ɪlek-ˈtrɪsəti/ n electricidad f

electrify /ɪˈlektrɪfaɪ/ vt electrificar; (fig) electrizar

electrocute /ɪˈlektrəkjuːt/ vt electrocutar

electrode /ɪˈlektrəʊd/ n electrodo m

electron /ɪˈlektrɒn/ n electrón m

electronic /ɪlekˈtrɒnɪk/ adj electrónico. ~ **mail** n correo m electrónico. ~**s** n electrónica f

elegan|ce /ˈelɪgəns/ n elegancia f.

~**t** adj elegante. ~**tly** adv elegantemente

element /ˈelɪmənt/ n elemento m. ~**ary** /-ˈmentrɪ/ adj elemental. ~**ary school** n (Amer) escuela f primaria

elephant /ˈelɪfənt/ n elefante m

elevat|e /ˈelɪveɪt/ vt elevar. ~**ion** /-ˈveɪʃn/ n elevación f. ~**or** n (Amer) ascensor m

eleven /ɪˈlevn/ adj & n once (m). ~**th** adj undécimo. ●n onceavo m

elf /elf/ n (pl **elves**) duende m

eligible /ˈelɪdʒəbl/ adj elegible. **be** ~ **for** tener derecho a

eliminat|e /ɪˈlɪmɪneɪt/ vt eliminar. ~**ion** /-ˈneɪʃn/ n eliminación f

élite /erˈliːt/ n elite f, élite f

ellip|se /ɪˈlɪps/ n elipse f. ~**tical** adj elíptico

elm /elm/ n olmo m

elope /ɪˈləʊp/ vi fugarse con el amante

eloquen|ce /ˈeləkwəns/ n elocuencia f. ~**t** adj elocuente

El Salvador /el ˈsælvədɔː(r)/ n El Salvador

else /els/ adv. **somebody** ~ otra persona. **everybody** ~ todos los demás. **nobody** ~ ningún otro, nadie más. **nothing** ~ nada más. **or** ~ o bien. **somewhere** ~ en otra parte. ~**where** adv en otra parte

elu|de /ɪˈluːd/ vt eludir. ~**sive** /-sɪv/ adj esquivo

elves /elvz/ see ELF

emaciated /ɪˈmeɪʃɪeɪtɪd/ adj consumido

email, e-mail /ˈiːmeɪl/ n correo m electrónico, correo-e m. ●vt mandar por correo electrónico, emailear. ~ **address** n casilla f electrónica, dirección f de correo electrónico

emancipat|e /ɪ'mænsɪpeɪt/ vt emancipar. **~ion** /-'peɪʃn/ n emancipación f

embankment /ɪm'bæŋkmənt/ n terraplén m; (of river) dique m

embargo /ɪm'bɑːgəʊ/ n (pl -oes) embargo m

embark /ɪm'bɑːk/ vi embarcarse. **~ on** (fig) emprender. **~ation** /embɑː'keɪʃn/ n embarque m

embarrass /ɪm'bærəs/ vt avergonzar. **~ed** adj avergonzado. **~ing** adj embarazoso. **~ment** n vergüenza f

embassy /'embəsi/ n embajada f

embellish /ɪm'belɪʃ/ vt adornar. **~ment** n adorno m

embers /'embəz/ npl ascuas fpl

embezzle /ɪm'bezl/ vt desfalcar. **~ment** n desfalco m

emblem /'embləm/ n emblema m

embrace /ɪm'breɪs/ vt abrazar; (fig) abarcar. ● vi abrazarse. ● n abrazo m

embroider /ɪm'brɔɪdə(r)/ vt bordar. **~y** n bordado m

embroil /ɪm'brɔɪl/ vt enredar

embryo /'embrɪəʊ/ n (pl -os) embrión m. **~nic** /-'ɒnɪk/ adj embrionario

emend /ɪ'mend/ vt enmendar

emerald /'emərəld/ n esmeralda f

emerge /ɪ'mɜːdʒ/ vi salir. **~nce** /-əns/ n aparición f

emergency /ɪ'mɜːdʒənsɪ/ n emergencia f; (Med) urgencia f. **in an ~** en caso de emergencia. **~ exit** n salida f de emergencia. **~ room** n urgencias fpl

emigra|nt /'emɪgrənt/ n emigrante m & f. **~te** /'emɪgreɪt/ vi emigrar. **~tion** /-'greɪʃn/ n

emigración f

eminen|ce /'emɪnəns/ n eminencia f. **~t** adj eminente.

emi|ssion /ɪ'mɪʃn/ n emisión f. **~t** vt (pt emitted) emitir

emoti|on /ɪ'məʊʃn/ n emoción f. **~onal** adj emocional; (person) emotivo; (moving) conmovedor. **~ve** /ɪ'məʊtɪv/ adj emotivo

empathy /'empəθɪ/ n empatía f

emperor /'empərə(r)/ n emperador m

empha|sis /'emfəsɪs/ n (pl ~ses /-siːz/) énfasis m. **~size** /'emfəsaɪz/ vt enfatizar. **~tic** /ɪm'fætɪk/ adj (gesture) enfático; (assertion) categórico

empire /'empaɪə(r)/ n imperio m

empirical /ɪm'pɪrɪkl/ adj empírico

employ /ɪm'plɔɪ/ vt emplear. **~ee** /emplɔɪ'iː/ n empleado m. **~er** n patrón m. **~ment** n empleo m. **~ment agency** n agencia f de trabajo

empower /ɪm'paʊə(r)/ vt autorizar (to a hacer)

empress /'emprɪs/ n emperatriz f

empty /'emptɪ/ adj vacío; (promise) vano. **on an ~y stomach** con el estómago vacío. ● n [T] envase m (vacío). ● vt vaciar. ● vi vaciarse

emulate /'emjʊleɪt/ vt emular

emulsion /ɪ'mʌlʃn/ n emulsión f

enable /ɪ'neɪbl/ vt. **~ s.o. to do sth** permitir a uno hacer algo

enact /ɪ'nækt/ vt (Jurid) decretar; (in theatre) representar

enamel /ɪ'næml/ n esmalte m. ● vt (pt enamelled) esmaltar

enchant /ɪn'tʃɑːnt/ vt encantar. **~ing** adj encantador. **~ment** n encanto m

encircle /ɪn'sɜːkl/ vt rodear

enclave /ˈenkleɪv/ n enclave m

enclose /ɪnˈkləʊz/ vt cercar (land); (Com) adjuntar. ∼ed adj (space) cerrado; (Com) adjunto. ∼ure /ɪnˈkləʊʒə(r)/ n cercamiento m

encode /ɪnˈkəʊd/ vt codificar, cifrar

encore /ˈɒŋkɔː(r)/ int ¡otra! ● n bis m, repetición f

encounter /ɪnˈkaʊntə(r)/ vt encontrar. ● n encuentro m

encourage /ɪnˈkʌrɪdʒ/ vt animar; (stimulate) fomentar. ∼ment n ánimo m. ∼ing adj alentador

encroach /ɪnˈkrəʊtʃ/ vi. ∼ on invadir (land); quitar (time)

encyclopaedia /ɪnsaɪkləˈpiːdɪə/ n enciclopedia f. ∼c adj enciclopédico

end /end/ n fin m; (furthest point) extremo m. in the ∼ por fin. make ∼s meet poder llegar a fin de mes. put an ∼ to poner fin a. no ∼ of muchísimos. on ∼ de pie; (consecutive) seguido. ● vt/i terminar, acabar

endanger /ɪnˈdeɪndʒə(r)/ vt poner en peligro. ∼ed adj (species) en peligro

endearing /ɪnˈdɪərɪŋ/ adj simpático

endeavour /ɪnˈdevə(r)/ n esfuerzo m, intento m. ● vi. ∼ to esforzarse por

ending /ˈendɪŋ/ n fin m

endless /ˈendlɪs/ adj interminable

endorse /ɪnˈdɔːs/ vt endosar; (fig) aprobar. ∼ment n endoso m; (fig) aprobación f; (Auto) nota f de inhabilitación

endur|ance /ɪnˈdjʊərəns/ n resistencia f. ∼e /ɪnˈdjʊə(r)/ vt aguantar. ∼ing adj perdurable

enemy /ˈenəmɪ/ n & a enemigo (m)

energ|etic /enəˈdʒetɪk/ adj enérgico. ∼y /ˈenədʒɪ/ n energía f. ∼y-efficient adj energéticamente eficiente

enforce /ɪnˈfɔːs/ vt hacer cumplir (law); hacer valer (claim). ∼d adj forzado

engage /ɪnˈgeɪdʒ/ vt emplear (staff); captar (attention); (Mec) hacer engranar. ● vi (Mec) engranar. ∼e in dedicarse a. ∼ed adj prometido, comprometido (LAm); (busy) ocupado. be ∼ed (of phone) estar comunicando, estar ocupado (LAm). get ∼ed prometerse, comprometerse (LAm). ∼ement n compromiso m

engine /ˈendʒɪn/ n motor m; (of train) locomotora f. ∼ driver n maquinista m

engineer /endʒɪˈnɪə(r)/ n ingeniero m; (mechanic) mecánico m; (Amer, Rail) maquinista m. ● vt (contrive) fraguar. ∼ing n ingeniería f

England /ˈɪŋglənd/ n Inglaterra f

English /ˈɪŋglɪʃ/ adj inglés. ● n (language) inglés m. ● npl. the ∼ los ingleses. ∼man /-mən/ n inglés m. ∼woman n inglesa f

engrav|e /ɪnˈgreɪv/ vt grabar. ∼ing n grabado m

engrossed /ɪnˈgrəʊst/ adj absorto

engulf /ɪnˈgʌlf/ vt envolver

enhance /ɪnˈhɑːns/ vt realzar; aumentar (value)

enigma /ɪˈnɪgmə/ n enigma m. ∼tic /enɪgˈmætɪk/ adj enigmático

enjoy /ɪnˈdʒɔɪ/ vt. I ∼ reading me gusta la lectura. ∼ o.s. divertirse. ∼able adj agradable. ∼ment n placer m

enlarge /ɪnˈlɑːdʒ/ vt agrandar;

(*Photo*) ampliar. ● vi agrandarse. ∼ upon extenderse sobre. ∼ment n. (*Photo*) ampliación f

enlighten /ɪnˈlaɪtn/ vt ilustrar. ∼ment n. the E∼ment el siglo de la luces

enlist /ɪnˈlɪst/ vt alistar; conseguir (support). ● vi alistarse

enliven /ɪnˈlaɪvn/ vt animar

enorm|ity /ɪˈnɔːmətɪ/ n enormidad f. ∼ous /ɪˈnɔːməs/ adj enorme. ∼ously adv enormemente

enough /ɪˈnʌf/ adj & adv bastante. ● n bastante m, suficiente m. ● int ¡basta!

enquir|e /ɪnˈkwaɪə(r)/ vt/i preguntar. ∼e about informarse de. ∼y n pregunta f; (*investigation*) investigación f

enrage /ɪnˈreɪdʒ/ vt enfurecer

enrol /ɪnˈrəʊl/ vt (*pt* enrolled) inscribir, matricular (student). ● vi inscribirse, matricularse

ensue /ɪnˈsjuː/ vi seguir

ensure /ɪnˈʃʊə(r)/ vt asegurar

entail /ɪnˈteɪl/ vt suponer; acarrear (expense)

entangle /ɪnˈtæŋgl/ vt enredar. ∼ment n enredo m

enter /ˈentə(r)/ vt entrar en, entrar a (*esp LAm*); presentarse a (competition); inscribirse en (race); (*write*) escribir. ● vi entrar

enterpris|e /ˈentəpraɪz/ n empresa f; (*fig*) iniciativa f. ∼ing adj emprendedor

entertain /entəˈteɪn/ vt entretener; recibir (guests); abrigar (ideas, hopes); (*consider*) considerar. ∼ing adj entretenido. ∼ment n entretenimiento m; (*show*) espectáculo m

enthral /ɪnˈθrɔːl/ vt (*pt* enthralled) cautivar

enthuse /ɪnˈθjuːz/ vi. ∼ over en-

tusiasmarse por

enthusias|m /ɪnˈθjuːzɪæzəm/ n entusiasmo m. ∼t n entusiasta m & f. ∼tic /-ˈæstɪk/ adj entusiasta. ∼tically adv con entusiasmo

entice /ɪnˈtaɪs/ vt atraer

entire /ɪnˈtaɪə(r)/ adj entero. ∼ly adv completamente. ∼ty /ɪnˈtaɪərətɪ/ n. in its ∼ty en su totalidad

entitle /ɪnˈtaɪtl/ vt titular; (*give a right*) dar derecho a. be ∼d to tener derecho a. ∼ment n derecho m

entity /ˈentətɪ/ n entidad f

entrails /ˈentreɪlz/ npl entrañas fpl

entrance /ˈentrəns/ n entrada f. ● /ɪnˈtrɑːns/ vt encantar

entrant /ˈentrənt/ n participante m & f; (*in exam*) candidato m

entreat /ɪnˈtriːt/ vt suplicar. ∼y n súplica f

entrenched /ɪnˈtrentʃt/ adj (position) afianzado

entrust /ɪnˈtrʌst/ vt confiar

entry /ˈentrɪ/ n entrada f

entwine /ɪnˈtwaɪn/ vt entrelazar

enumerate /ɪˈnjuːməreɪt/ vt enumerar

envelop /ɪnˈveləp/ vt envolver

envelope /ˈenvələʊp/ n sobre m

enviable /ˈenvɪəbl/ adj envidiable

envious /ˈenvɪəs/ adj envidioso

environment /ɪnˈvaɪərənmənt/ n medio m ambiente. ∼al /-ˈmentl/ adj ambiental

envisage /ɪnˈvɪzɪdʒ/ vt prever; (*imagine*) imaginar

envision /ɪnˈvɪʒn/ vt (*Amer*) prever

envoy /ˈenvɔɪ/ n enviado m

envy /ˈenvɪ/ n envidia f. ● vt envidiar

enzyme /ˈenzaɪm/ n enzima f

ephemeral /ɪˈfemərəl/ adj

efímero

epic /'epɪk/ n épica f. ● adj épico

epidemic /epɪ'demɪk/ n epidemia f. ● adj epidémico

epilep|sy /'epɪlepsɪ/ n epilepsia f. ~**tic** /-'leptɪk/ adj & n epiléptico (m)

epilogue /'epɪlɒg/ n epílogo m

episode /'epɪsəʊd/ n episodio m

epitaph /'epɪtɑːf/ n epitafio m

epitom|e /ɪ'pɪtəmɪ/ n personificación f, epítome m. ~**ize** vt ser la personificación de

epoch /'iːpɒk/ n época f

equal /'iːkwəl/ adj & n igual (m & f). ~ **to** (a task) a la altura de. ● (pt **equalled**) ser igual a; (Math) ser. ~**ity** /ɪ'kwɒlətɪ/ n igualdad f. ~**ize** vt igualar. ● vi (Sport) empatar. ~**izer** n (Sport) gol m del empate. ~**ly** adv igualmente; (share) por igual

equation /ɪ'kweɪʒn/ n ecuación f

equator /ɪ'kweɪtə(r)/ n ecuador m. ~**ial** /ekwə'tɔːrɪəl/ adj ecuatorial

equilibrium /iːkwɪ'lɪbrɪəm/ n equilibrio m

equinox /'iːkwɪnɒks/ n equinoccio m

equip /ɪ'kwɪp/ vt (pt **equipped**) equipar. ~ **sth** with proveer algo de. ~**ment** n equipo m

equivalen|ce /ɪ'kwɪvələns/ n equivalencia f. ~**t** adj & n equivalente (m). be ~**t** to equivaler a

equivocal /ɪ'kwɪvəkl/ adj equívoco

era /'ɪərə/ n era f

eradicate /ɪ'rædɪkeɪt/ vt erradicar, extirpar

erase /ɪ'reɪz/ vt borrar. ~**r** n goma f (de borrar)

erect /ɪ'rekt/ adj erguido. ● vt levantar. ~**ion** /-ʃn/ n construcción

f; (physiology) erección f

ero|de /ɪ'rəʊd/ vt erosionar. ~**sion** /-ʒn/ n erosión f

erotic /ɪ'rɒtɪk/ adj erótico

err /ɜː(r)/ vi errar; (sin) pecar

errand /'erənd/ n recado m, mandado m (LAm)

erratic /ɪ'rætɪk/ adj desigual; (person) voluble

erroneous /ɪ'rəʊnɪəs/ adj erróneo

error /'erə(r)/ n error m

erudit|e /'eruːdaɪt/ adj erudito. ~**ion** /-'dɪʃn/ n erudición f

erupt /ɪ'rʌpt/ vi entrar en erupción; (fig) estallar. ~**ion** /-ʃn/ n erupción f

escalat|e /'eskəleɪt/ vt intensificar. ● vi intensificarse. ~**ion** /-'leɪʃn/ n intensificación f. ~**or** n escalera f mecánica

escapade /eska'peɪd/ n aventura f

escape /ɪ'skeɪp/ vi escaparse. ● vt evitar. ● n fuga f; (of gas, water) escape m. have a narrow ~ escapar por un pelo. ~**ism** /-ɪzəm/ n escapismo m

escort /'eskɔːt/ n acompañante m; (Mil) escolta f ● /ɪ'skɔːt/ vt acompañar; (Mil) escoltar

Eskimo /'eskɪməʊ/ n (pl -os or invar) esquimal m & f

especial /ɪ'speʃl/ adj especial. ~**ly** adv especialmente

espionage /'espɪənɑːʒ/ n espionaje m

Esq. /ɪ'skwaɪə(r)/ abbr (= Esquire) (in address) E. Ashton, ~ Sr. Don E. Ashton

essay /'eseɪ/ n ensayo m; (at school) composición f

essence /'esns/ n esencia f. in ~ esencialmente

essential /ɪˈsenʃl/ adj esencial. • n elemento m esencial. **~ly** adv esencialmente

establish /ɪˈstæblɪʃ/ vt establecer. **~ment** n establecimiento m. the E**~ment** los que mandan

estate /ɪˈsteɪt/ n finca f; (housing estate) complejo m habitacional, urbanización f, fraccionamiento m (Mex); (possessions) bienes mpl. **~ agent** n agente m inmobiliario. **~ car** n ranchera f, (coche m) familiar m, camioneta f (LAm)

esteem /ɪˈstiːm/ n estima f

estimat|e /ˈestɪmət/ n cálculo m; (Com) presupuesto m. • /ˈestɪmeɪt/ vt calcular. **~ion** /-ˈmeɪʃn/ n estimación f; (opinion) opinión f

estranged /ɪsˈtreɪndʒd/ adj alejado

estuary /ˈestʃʊəri/ n estuario m

etc /et'setrə/ abbr (= et cetera) etc.

etching /ˈetʃɪŋ/ n aguafuerte m

etern|al /ɪˈtɜːnl/ adj eterno. **~ity** /-əti/ n eternidad f

ether /ˈiːθə(r)/ n éter m

ethic /ˈeθɪk/ n ética f. **~al** adj ético. **~s** npl ética f

ethnic /ˈeθnɪk/ adj étnico

etiquette /ˈetɪket/ n etiqueta f

etymology /etɪˈmɒlədʒi/ n etimología f

EU /iːˈjuː/ abbr (European Union) UE (Unión Europea)

euphemism /ˈjuːfəmɪzəm/ n eufemismo m

euphoria /juːˈfɔːrɪə/ n euforia f

euro /ˈjʊərəʊ/ n euro m

Europe /ˈjʊərəp/ n Europa f. **~an** /-ˈpɪən/ adj & n europeo m. **~an Health Insurance Card** n Tarjeta f Sanitaria Europea. **~an Union** n Unión f Europea

euthanasia /juːθəˈneɪzɪə/ n eutanasia f

evacuat|e /ɪˈvækjʊeɪt/ vt evacuar; desocupar (building). **~ion** /-ˈeɪʃn/ n evacuación f

evade /ɪˈveɪd/ vt evadir

evaluat|e /ɪˈvæljʊeɪt/ vt evaluar. **~tion** /-ˈeɪʃn/ vt evaluación f

evangelical /iːvænˈdʒelɪkl/ adj evangélico

evaporat|e /ɪˈvæpəreɪt/ vi evaporarse. **~ion** /-ˈreɪʃn/ n evaporación f

evasi|on /ɪˈveɪʒn/ n evasión f. **~ve** /ɪˈveɪsɪv/ adj evasivo

eve /iːv/ n víspera f

even /ˈiːvn/ adj (flat, smooth) plano; (colour) uniforme; (distribution) equitativo; (number) par. get **~** with desquitarse con. • vt nivelar. □ **~ up** vt equilibrar. • adv aun, hasta, incluso. **~ if** aunque. **~ so** aun así. not **~** ni siquiera

evening /ˈiːvnɪŋ/ n tarde f; (after dark) noche f. **~ class** n clase f nocturna

event /ɪˈvent/ n acontecimiento m; (Sport) prueba f. in the **~ of** en caso de. **~ful** adj lleno de acontecimientos

eventual /ɪˈventʃʊəl/ adj final, definitivo. **~ity** /-ˈælətɪ/ n eventualidad f. **~ly** adv finalmente

ever /ˈevə(r)/ adv (negative) nunca, jamás; (at all times) siempre. have you **~** been to Greece? ¿has estado (alguna vez) en Grecia?, **~** after desde entonces. **~** since desde entonces. **~** so 🆃 muy. for **~** para siempre. hardly **~** casi nunca. **~green** adj de hoja perenne. • n árbol m de hoja perenne. **~lasting** adj eterno.

every /ˈevri/ adj cada, todo. **~**

e (margin tab)

child todos los niños. ~ one cada uno. ~ other day un día sí y otro no. ~body pron todos, todo el mundo. ~day adj de todos los días. ~one pron todos, todo el mundo. ~thing pron todo. ~where adv (be) en todas partes, (go) a todos lados

evict /ɪ'vɪkt/ vt desahuciar. ~ion /-ʃn/ n desahucio m

eviden|ce /'evɪdəns/ n evidencia f; (proof) pruebas fpl; (Jurid) testimonio m; give ~ce prestar declaración. ~ce of señales de. in ~ce visible. ~t adj evidente. ~tly adv evidentemente

evil /'iːvl/ adj malvado. ● n mal m

evo|cative /ɪ'vɒkətɪv/ adj evocador. ~ke /ɪ'vəʊk/ vt evocar

evolution /iːvə'luːʃn/ n evolución f

evolve /ɪ'vɒlv/ vt desarrollar. ● vi evolucionar

ewe /juː/ n oveja f

exact /ɪg'zækt/ adj exacto. ● vt exigir (from a). ~ing adj exigente. ~ly adv exactamente

exaggerat|e /ɪg'zædʒəreɪt/ vt exagerar. ~ion /-'reɪʃn/ n exageración f

exam /ɪg'zæm/ n examen m. ~ination /ɪgzæmɪ'neɪʃn/ n examen m. ~ine /ɪg'zæmɪn/ vt examinar; interrogar (witness). ~iner n examinador m

example /ɪg'zɑːmpl/ n ejemplo m. for ~ por ejemplo. make an ~ of s.o. darle un castigo ejemplar a uno

exasperat|e /ɪg'zæspəreɪt/ vt exasperar. ~ing adj exasperante. ~ion /-'reɪʃn/ n exasperación f

excavat|e /'ekskəveɪt/ vt excavar. ~ion /-'veɪʃn/ n excavación f

exceed /ɪk'siːd/ vt exceder. ~ingly adv sumamente

excel /ɪk'sel/ vi (pt excelled) sobresalir. ● vt. ~ o.s. lucirse. ~lence /'eksələns/ n excelencia f. ~lent adj excelente

except /ɪk'sept/ prep menos, excepto. ~ for si no fuera por. ● vt exceptuar. ~ing prep con excepción de

exception /ɪk'sepʃn/ n excepción f. take ~ to ofenderse por. ~al adj excepcional. ~ally adv excepcionalmente

excerpt /'eksɜːpt/ n extracto m

excess /ɪk'ses/ n exceso m. ● /'ekses/ adj excedente. ~ fare suplemento m. ~ luggage exceso m de equipaje. ~ive adj excesivo

exchange /ɪk'stʃeɪndʒ/ vt cambiar. ● n intercambio m; (of money) cambio m. (telephone) ~ central f telefónica

excise /'eksaɪz/ n impuestos mpl interos. ● /ek'saɪz/ vt quitar

excit|able /ɪk'saɪtəbl/ adj excitable. ~e /ɪk'saɪt/ vt emocionar; (stimulate) excitar. ~ed adj entusiasmado. get ~ed entusiasmarse. ~ement n emoción f; (enthusiasm) entusiasmo m. ~ing adj emocionante

exclaim /ɪk'skleɪm/ vi/t exclamar. ~mation /eksklə'meɪʃn/ n exclamación f. ~mation mark n signo m de admiración f

exclu|de /ɪk'skluːd/ vt excluir. ~sion /-ʒən/ n exclusión f. ~sive /ɪk'skluːsɪv/ adj exclusivo; (club) selecto. ~sive of excluyendo. ~sively adv exclusivamente

excruciating /ɪk'skruːʃɪeɪtɪŋ/ adj atroz, insoportable

excursion /ɪk'skɜːʃn/ n excursión f

excus|able /ɪkˈskjuːzəbl/ adj perdonable. **∼e** /ɪkˈskjuːz/ vt perdonar. **∼e from** dispensar de. **∼e me!** ¡perdón! ● /ɪkˈskjuːs/ n excusa f

ex-directory /eksdɪˈrektərɪ/ adj que no figura en la guía telefónica, privado (Mex)

execute /ˈeksɪkjuːt/ vt ejecutar. **∼ion** /eksɪˈkjuːʃn/ n ejecución f. **∼ioner** n verdugo m

executive /ɪgˈzekjʊtɪv/ adj & n ejecutivo (m)

exempt /ɪgˈzempt/ adj exento (from de). ● vt dispensar. **∼ion** /-ʃn/ n exención f

exercise /ˈeksəsaɪz/ n ejercicio m. ● vt ejercer. ● vi hacer ejercicio. **∼ book** n cuaderno m

exert /ɪgˈzɜːt/ vt ejercer. **∼ o.s.** hacer un gran esfuerzo. **∼ion** /-ʃn/ n esfuerzo m

exhale /eksˈheɪl/ vt/i exhalar

exhaust /ɪgˈzɔːst/ vt agotar. ● n (Auto) tubo m de escape. **∼ed** adj agotado. **∼ion** /-stʃən/ n agotamiento m. **∼ive** adj exhaustivo

exhibit /ɪgˈzɪbɪt/ vt mostrar; (fig) mostrar. ● n objeto m expuesto; (Jurid) documento m. **∼ion** /eksɪˈbɪʃn/ n exposición f. **∼ionist** n exhibicionista m & f. **∼or** /ɪgˈzɪbɪtə(r)/ n expositor m

exhilarat|ing /ɪgˈzɪləreɪtɪŋ/ adj excitante. **∼ion** /-ˈreɪʃn/ n regocijo m

exhort /ɪgˈzɔːt/ vt exhortar

exile /ˈeksaɪl/ n exilio m; (person) exiliado m. ● vt desterrar

exist /ɪgˈzɪst/ vi existir. **∼ence** n existencia f. **in ∼ence** existente

exit /ˈeksɪt/ n salida f

exorbitant /ɪgˈzɔːbɪtənt/ adj

exorbitante

exorcis|e /ˈeksɔːsaɪz/ vt exorcizar. **∼m** /-sɪzəm/ n exorcismo m. **∼t** n exorcista m & f

exotic /ɪgˈzɒtɪk/ adj exótico

expand /ɪkˈspænd/ vt expandir; (develop) desarrollar. ● vi expandirse

expanse /ɪkˈspæns/ n extensión f

expansion /ɪkˈspænʃn/ n expansión f

expatriate /eksˈpætrɪət/ adj & n expatriado m

expect /ɪkˈspekt/ vt esperar; (suppose) suponer; (demand) contar con. **I ∼ so** supongo que sí. **∼ancy** n esperanza f **life ∼ancy** esperanza f de vida. **∼ant** adj expectante. **∼ant mother** n futura madre f

expectation /ekspek'teɪʃn/ n expectativa f

expedient /ɪkˈspiːdɪənt/ adj conveniente. ● n expediente m

expedition /ekspɪˈdɪʃn/ n expedición f

expel /ɪkˈspel/ vt (pt expelled) expulsar

expend /ɪkˈspend/ vt gastar. **∼able** adj prescindible. **∼iture** /-ɪtʃə(r)/ n gastos mpl

expens|e /ɪkˈspens/ n gasto m. **at s.o.'s ∼e** a costa de uno. **∼es** mpl. (Com) gastos mpl. **∼ive** adj caro

experience /ɪkˈspɪərɪəns/ n experiencia f. ● vt experimentar. **∼d** adj con experiencia; (driver) experimentado

experiment /ɪkˈsperɪmənt/ n experimento m. ● vi experimentar. **∼al** /-ˈmentl/ adj experimental

expert /ˈekspɜːt/ adj & n experto (m). **∼ise** /ekspɜːˈtiːz/ n pericia f. **∼ly** adv hábilmente

expir|e /ik'spaɪə(r)/ vi (passport, ticket) caducar; (contract) vencer. **∼y** n vencimiento m, caducidad f

expla|in /ik'spleɪn/ vt explicar. **∼nation** /eksplə'neɪʃn/ n explicación f **∼natory** /iks'plænətərɪ/ adj explicativo

explicit /ik'splɪsɪt/ adj explícito

explode /ik'spləʊd/ vt hacer explotar. ● vi estallar

exploit /'eksplɔɪt/ n hazaña f. /ik'splɔɪt/ vt explotar. **∼ation** /eksplɔɪ'teɪʃn/ n explotación f

explor|ation /eksplə'reɪʃn/ n exploración f **∼atory** /iks'splɒrətrɪ/ adj exploratorio. **∼e** /ik'splɔː(r)/ vt explorar. **∼er** n explorador m

explosi|on /ik'spləʊʒn/ n explosión f. **∼ve** /-sɪv/ adj & n explosivo (m)

export /ik'spɔːt/ vt exportar. ● /'ekspɔːt/ n exportación f; (item) artículo m de exportación. **∼er** /iks'pɔːtə(r)/ exportador m

expos|e /ik'spəʊz/ vt exponer; (reveal) descubrir. **∼ure** /-ʒə(r)/ n exposición f **die of ∼ure** morir de frío

express /ik'spres/ vt expresar. ● adj expreso; (letter) urgente. ● adv (by express post) por correo urgente. ● n (train) rápido m, expreso m. **∼ion** n expresión f. **∼ive** adj expresivo. **∼ly** adv expresadamente. **∼way** n (Amer) autopista f

expulsion /ik'spʌlʃn/ n expulsión f

exquisite /'ekskwɪzɪt/ adj exquisito

exten|d /ik'stend/ vt extender; (prolong) prolongar; ampliar (house). ● vi extenderse. **∼sion** /-ʃn/ n extensión f; (of road, time) prolongación f; (building) anejo m.

∼sive /-sɪv/ adj extenso. **∼sively** adv extensamente. **∼t** n extensión f; (fig) alcance f. **to a certain ∼t** hasta cierto punto

exterior /ik'stɪərɪə(r)/ adj & n exterior (m)

exterminat|e /ik'stɜːmɪneɪt/ vt exterminar. **∼ion** /-'neɪʃn/ n exterminio m

external /ik'stɜːnl/ adj externo

extinct /ik'stɪŋkt/ adj extinto. **∼ion** /-ʃn/ n extinción f

extinguish /ik'stɪŋgwɪʃ/ vt extinguir. **∼er** n extintor m, extinguidor m (LAm)

extol /ik'stəʊl/ vt (pt extolled) alabar

extort /ik'stɔːt/ vt sacar por la fuerza. **∼ion** /-ʃn/ n exacción f. **∼ionate** /-ənət/ adj exorbitante

extra /'ekstrə/ adj de más. ● adv extraordinariamente. ● n suplemento m; (Cinema) extra m & f

extract /'ekstrækt/ n extracto m. ● /ik'strækt/ vt extraer. **∼ion** /ik'strækʃn/ n extracción f

extradit|e /'ekstrədaɪt/ vt extraditar. **∼ion** /-'dɪʃn/ n extradición f

extra∼ordinary /ik'strɔːdnrɪ/ adj extraordinario. **∼sensory** /ekstrə'sensərɪ/ adj extrasensorial

extravagan|ce /ik'strævəgəns/ n prodigalidad f; (of gestures, dress) extravagancia f. **∼t** adj pródigo; (behaviour) extravagante. **∼za** n gran espectáculo m

extrem|e /ik'striːm/ adj & n extremo (m). **∼ely** adv extremadamente. **∼ist** n extremista m & f

extricate /'ekstrɪkeɪt/ vt desenredar, librar

extrovert /'ekstrəvɜːt/ n extrovertido m

exuberan|ce /ig'zjuːbərəns/ n

exuberancia f. **~t** adj exuberante

exude /ɪgˈzjuːd/ vt rezumar

exult /ɪgˈzʌlt/ vi exultar. **~ation** /egzʌlˈteɪʃn/ n exultación f

eye /aɪ/ n ojo m. **keep an ~ on** no perder de vista. **see ~ to ~ with** s.o. estar de acuerdo con uno. ● vt (pt **eyed**, pres p **eyeing**) mirar. **~ball** n globo m ocular. **~brow** n ceja f. **~drops** npl colirio m. **~lash** n pestaña f. **~lid** n párpado m. **~-opener** n 🛈 revelación f. **~-shadow** n sombra f de ojos. **~sight** n vista f. **~sore** n (fig, fam) monstruosidad f, adefesio m. **~witness** n testigo m ocular

Ff

fable /ˈfeɪbl/ n fábula f

fabric /ˈfæbrɪk/ n tejido m, tela f

fabricate /ˈfæbrɪkeɪt/ vt inventar. **~ation** /-ˈkeɪʃn/ n invención f

fabulous /ˈfæbjʊləs/ adj fabuloso

facade /fəˈsɑːd/ n fachada f

face /feɪs/ n cara f, rostro m; (of watch) esfera f, carátula f (Mex); (aspect) aspecto m. **~ down(wards)** boca abajo. **~ up(wards)** boca arriba. **in the ~ of** frente a. **lose ~** quedar mal. **pull ~s** hacer muecas. ● vt mirar hacia; (house) dar a; (confront) enfrentarse con. ● vi volverse. □ **~ up to** vt enfrentarse con. **~ flannel** n paño m (para lavarse la cara). **~less** adj anónimo. **~ lift** n cirugía f estética en la cara

facetious /fəˈsiːʃəs/ adj burlón

facial /ˈfeɪʃl/ adj facial

facile /ˈfæsaɪl/ adj superficial, simplista

facilitate /fəˈsɪlɪteɪt/ vt facilitar

facility /fəˈsɪlɪtɪ/ n facilidad f

fact /fækt/ n hecho m. **as a matter of ~, in ~** en realidad, de hecho

faction /ˈfækʃn/ n facción f

factor /ˈfæktə(r)/ n factor m

factory /ˈfæktərɪ/ n fábrica f

factual /ˈfæktʃʊəl/ adj basado en hechos, factual

faculty /ˈfækəltɪ/ n facultad f

fad /fæd/ n manía f, capricho m

fade /feɪd/ vi (colour) desteñirse; (flowers) marchitarse; (light) apagarse; (memory, sound) desvanecerse

fag /fæg/ n (fam, chore) faena f; (sl, cigarette) cigarrillo m, pitillo m

Fahrenheit /ˈfærənhaɪt/ adj Fahrenheit

fail /feɪl/ vi fracasar; (brakes) fallar; (in an exam) suspender, ser reprobado (LAm). **he ~ed to arrive** no llegó. ● vt suspender, ser reprobado en (LAm) (exam); suspender, reprobar (LAm) (candidate). ● n. **without ~** sin falta. **~ing** n defecto m. ● prep. **~ing that, ...** si eso no resulta.... **~ure** /ˈfeɪljə(r)/ n fracaso m

faint /feɪnt/ adj (-er, -est) (weak) débil; (indistinct) indistinto. **feel ~** estar mareado. **the ~est idea** la más remota idea. ● vi desmayarse. ● n desmayo m. **~-hearted** /-ˈhɑːtɪd/ adj pusilánime, cobarde. **~ly** adv (weakly) débilmente; (indistinctly) indistintamente; (slightly) ligeramente

fair /feə(r)/ adj (-er, -est) (just) justo; (weather) bueno; (amount) razonable; (hair) rubio, güero (Mex fam); (skin) blanco. ● adv limpio. ● n feria f. **~-haired** /·'heəd/ adj rubio, güero (Mex fam). **~ly** adv (justly) justamente; (rather) bastante. **~ness** n justicia f. in all **~ness** sinceramente. **~ play** n juego m limpio. **~ trade** n comercio m justo

fairy /'feərɪ/ n hada f. **~ story**, **~ tale** n cuento m de hadas

faith /feɪθ/ n (trust) confianza f; (Relig) fe f. **~ful** adj fiel. **~fully** adv fielmente. yours **~fully** (in letters) (le saluda) atentamente

fake /feɪk/ n falsificación f; (person) farsante m. ● adj falso. ● vt falsificar

falcon /'fɔːlkən/ n halcón m

Falkland Islands /'fɔːlklənd/ npl. the Falkland Islands, the Falklands las (Islas) Malvinas

fall /fɔːl/ vi (pt fell, pp fallen) caer; (decrease) bajar. ● n caída f; (Amer, autumn) otoño m; (in price) bajada f. □ **~ apart** vi deshacerse. □ **~ back on** vt recurrir a. □ **~ down** vi (fall) caerse. □ **~ for** vt 🄸 enamorarse de (person); dejarse engañar por (trick). □ **~ in** vi (Mil) formar filas. □ **~ off** vi caerse; (diminish) disminuir. □ **~ out** vi (quarrel) reñir (with con); (drop out) caerse; (Mil) romper filas. □ **~ over** vi caerse. □ **~ through** vi no salir adelante

fallacy /'fæləsɪ/ n falacia f

fallible /'fælɪbl/ adj falible

fallout /'fɔːlaʊt/ n lluvia f radiactiva. **~ shelter** n refugio m antinuclear

fallow /'fæləʊ/ adj en barbecho

false /fɔːls/ adj. **~ alarm** n falsa alarma. **~hood** n mentira f. **~ly** adv falsamente. **~ teeth** npl dentadura f postiza

falsify /'fɔːlsɪfaɪ/ vt falsificar

falter /'fɔːltə(r)/ vi vacilar

fame /feɪm/ n fama f. **~d** adj famoso

familiar /fə'mɪlɪə(r)/ adj familiar. the name sounds **~** el nombre me suena. be **~ with** conocer. **~ity** /·'ærətɪ/ n familiaridad f. **~ize** vt familiarizar

family /'fæmlɪ/ n familia f. ● adj de (la) familia, familiar. **~ tree** n árbol m genealógico

famine /'fæmɪn/ n hambre f, hambruna f

famished /'fæmɪʃt/ adj hambriento

famous /'feɪməs/ adj famoso

fan /fæn/ n abanico m; (Mec) ventilador m; (enthusiast) aficionado m; (of group, actor) fan m & f; (of sport, team) hincha m & f. ● vt (pt fanned) abanicar; avivar (interest). □ **~ out** vi desparramarse en forma de abanico

fanatic /fə'nætɪk/ n fanático m. **~al** adj fanático. **~ism** /-sɪzəm/ n fanatismo m

fan belt n correa f de ventilador, banda f del ventilador (Mex)

fanciful /'fænsɪfl/ adj (imaginative) imaginativo; (impractical) extravagante

fancy /'fænsɪ/ n imaginación f; (liking) gusto m. take a **~** to tomar cariño a (person); aficionarse a (thing). ● adj de lujo. ● vt (imagine) imaginar; (believe) creer; (fam, want) apetecer a. **~ dress** n disfraz m

fanfare /'fænfeə(r)/ n fanfarria f

fang /fæŋ/ n (of animal) colmillo m; (of snake) diente m

fantasize /'fæntəsaɪz/ vi fantasear

fantastic /fæn'tæstɪk/ adj fantástico

fantasy /'fæntəsi/ n fantasía f

far /fɑː(r)/ adv lejos; (much) mucho. as ~ as hasta. as ~ as I know que yo sepa. by ~ con mucho. ● adj (further, furthest or farther, farthest) lejano. ~ away lejano

farc|e /fɑːs/ n farsa f. ~ical adj ridículo

fare /feə(r)/ n (on bus) precio m del billete, precio m del boleto (LAm); (on train, plane) precio m del billete, precio m del pasaje (LAm); (food) comida f

Far East /fɑːˈriːst/ n Extremo or Lejano Oriente m

farewell /feəˈwel/ int & n adiós (m)

far-fetched /fɑːˈfetʃt/ adj improbable

farm /fɑːm/ n granja f. ● vt cultivar. □ ~ out vt encargar (a terceros). ● vi ser agricultor. ~er n agricultor m, granjero m. ~house n granja f. ~ing n agricultura f. ~yard n corral m

far: ~-off adj lejano. ~-reaching /fɑːˈriːtʃɪŋ/ adj trascendental. ~-sighted /fɑːˈsaɪtɪd/ adj con visión del futuro; (Med, Amer) hipermétrope

farther, farthest /ˈfɑːðə(r), ˈfɑːðəst/ see **FAR**

fascinat|e /ˈfæsɪneɪt/ vt fascinar. ~ed adj fascinado. ~ing adj fascinante. ~ion /-ˈneɪʃn/ n fascinación f

fasc|ism /ˈfæʃɪzəm/ n fascismo m. ~t adj & n fascista (m & f)

fashion /ˈfæʃn/ n (manner) manera f; (vogue) moda f. be in/out of ~ estar de moda/estar pasado de moda. ~able adj de moda

fast /fɑːst/ adj (-er, -est) rápido; (clock) adelantado; (secure) fijo; (colours) sólido. ● adv rápidamente;

(securely) firmemente. ~ asleep profundamente dormido. ● vi ayunar. ● n ayuno m

fasten /ˈfɑːsn/ vt sujetar; cerrar (case); abrochar (belt etc). ● vi (case) cerrarse; (belt etc) cerrarse. ~er, ~ing n (on box, window) cierre m; (on door) cerrojo m

fat /fæt/ n grasa f. ● adj (fatter, fattest) gordo; (meat) que tiene mucha grasa; (thick) grueso. get ~ engordar

fatal /ˈfeɪtl/ adj mortal; (fateful) fatídico. ~ity /fəˈtælətɪ/ n muerto m. ~ly adv mortalmente

fate /feɪt/ n destino m; (one's lot) suerte f. ~d adj predestinado. ~ful adj fatídico

father /ˈfɑːðə(r)/ n padre m. ~hood n paternidad f. ~-in-law m (pl ~s-in-law) suegro m. ~ly adj paternal

fathom /ˈfæðəm/ n braza f. ● vt. ~ (out) comprender

fatigue /fəˈtiːg/ n fatiga f. ● vt fatigar

fat|ten vt. ~ten (up) cebar (animal). ~tening adj que engorda. ~ty adj graso, grasoso (LAm). ● n ⊞ gordinflón m

fatuous /ˈfætjʊəs/ adj fatuo

faucet /ˈfɔːsɪt/ n (Amer) grifo m, llave f (LAm)

fault /fɔːlt/ n defecto m; (blame) culpa f; (tennis) falta f; (in geology) falla f. at ~ culpable. ● vt encontrarle defectos a. ~less adj impecable. ~y adj defectuoso

favour /ˈfeɪvə(r)/ n favor m. ● vt favorecer; (support) estar a favor de; (prefer) preferir. ~able adj favorable. ~ably adv favorablemente. ~ite adj & n preferido (m). ~itism n favoritismo m

fawn /fɔːn/ n cervato m. ● adj beige, beis. ● vi. ~ **on** adular

fax /fæks/ n fax m. ● vt faxear

fear /fɪə(r)/ n miedo m. ● vt temer. ~**ful** adj (frightening) espantoso; (frightened) temeroso. ~**less** adj intrépido. ~**some** /-səm/ adj espantoso

feasib|ility /fiːzə'bɪlətɪ/ n viabilidad f. ~**le** /'fiːzəbl/ adj factible; (likely) posible

feast /fiːst/ n (Relig) fiesta f; (meal) banquete m

feat /fiːt/ n hazaña f

feather /'feðə(r)/ n pluma f. ~**weight** n peso m pluma

feature /'fiːtʃə(r)/ n (on face) rasgo m; (characteristic) característica f; (in newspaper) artículo m; ~ (film) película f principal, largometraje m. ● vt presentar; (give prominence to) destacar

February /'febrʊərɪ/ n febrero m

fed /fed/ see **FEED**

feder|al /'fedərəl/ adj federal. ~**ation** /fedə'reɪʃn/ n federación f

fed up adj 🗉 harto (with de)

fee /fiː/ n (professional) honorarios mpl; (enrolment) derechos mpl; (club) cuota f

feeble /'fiːbl/ adj (-er, -est) débil

feed /fiːd/ vt (pt fed) dar de comer a; (supply) alimentar. ● vi comer. ● n (for animals) pienso m; (for babies) comida f. ~**back** n reacción f

feel /fiːl/ vt (pt felt) sentir; (touch) tocar; (think) considerar. do you ~ it's a good idea? ¿te parece buena idea? ~ **as if** tener la impresión de que. ~ **hot/hungry** tener calor/ hambre. ~ **like** (fam, want) tener ganas de. ● n sensación f. **get the ~ of sth** acostumbrarse a algo. ~**er** n (of insect) antena f. ~**ing** n

sentimiento m; (physical) sensación f

feet /fiːt/ see **FOOT**

feign /feɪn/ vt fingir

feint /feɪnt/ n finta f

fell /fel/ see **FALL**. ● vt derribar; talar (tree)

fellow /'feləʊ/ n 🗉 tipo m; (comrade) compañero m; (of society) socio m. ~ **countryman** n compatriota m. ~ **passenger/traveller** n compañero m de viaje

felony /'felən/ n delito m grave

felt /felt/ see **FEEL**. ● n fieltro m

female /'fiːmeɪl/ adj hembra; (voice, sex etc) femenino. ● n mujer f; (animal) hembra f

femini|ne /'femənɪn/ adj & n femenino (m). ~**nity** /-'nɪnətɪ/ n feminidad f. ~**st** adj & n feminista m & f

fenc|e /fens/ n cerca f, cerco m (LAm). ● vt. ~**e (in)** encerrar, cercar. ● vi (Sport) practicar la esgrima. ~**er** n esgrimidor m. ~**ing** n (Sport) esgrima f

fend /fend/ vi. ~ **for o.s.** valerse por sí mismo. □ ~ **off** vt defenderse de

fender /'fendə(r)/ n rejilla f; (Amer, Auto) guardabarros m, salpicadera f (Mex)

ferment /fə'ment/ vt/i fermentar. ~**ation** /-'teɪʃn/ n fermentación f

fern /fɜːn/ n helecho m

feroci|ous /fə'rəʊʃəs/ adj feroz. ~**ty** /fə'rɒsətɪ/ n ferocidad f

ferret /'ferɪt/ n hurón m. ● vi (pt ferreted) ~ **about** husmear. ● vt. ~ **out** descubrir

ferry /'ferɪ/ n ferry m. ● vt transportar

fertil|e /'fɜːtaɪl/ adj fértil. ~**ity** /-'tɪlətɪ/ n fertilidad f. ~**ize**

/ˈfɜːtəlaɪz/ vt fecundar, abonar (soil). ∼izer n fertilizante m

ferv|ent /ˈfɜːvənt/ adj ferviente. ∼our /-və(r)/ n fervor m

fester /ˈfestə(r)/ vi enconarse

festival /ˈfestəvl/ n fiesta f; (of arts) festival m

festiv|e /ˈfestɪv/ adj festivo. the ∼e season n las Navidades. ∼ity /feˈstɪvətɪ/ n festividad f

fetch /fetʃ/ vt (go for) ir a buscar; (bring) traer; (be sold for) venderse en. ∼ing adj atractivo

fête /feɪt/ n fiesta f. ● vt festejar

fetish /ˈfetɪʃ/ n fetiche m

fetter /ˈfetə(r)/ vt encadenar

feud /fjuːd/ n contienda f

feudal /ˈfjuːdl/ adj feudal. ∼ism n feudalismo m

fever /ˈfiːvə(r)/ n fiebre f. ∼ish adj febril

few /fjuː/ adj pocos. a ∼ houses algunas casas. ● n pocos mpl. a ∼ unos (pocos). a good ∼, quite a ∼ 🔲 muchos. ● adj & n menos. ∼est adj el menor número de

fiancé /fɪˈɒnseɪ/ n novio m. ∼e /fɪˈɒnseɪ/ n novia f

fiasco /fɪˈæskəʊ/ n (pl -os) fiasco m

fib /fɪb/ n 🔲 mentirita f. ● vi 🔲 mentir, decir mentirillas

fibre /ˈfaɪbə(r)/ n fibra f. ∼glass n fibra f de vidrio

fickle /ˈfɪkl/ adj inconstante

ficti|on /ˈfɪkʃn/ n ficción f. (works of) ∼ novelas fpl. ∼onal adj novelesco. ∼tious /fɪkˈtɪʃəs/ adj ficticio

fiddle /ˈfɪdl/ n 🔲 violín m; (fam, swindle) trampa f. ● vt 🔲 falsificar. ∼ with juguetear con

fidget /ˈfɪdʒɪt/ vi (pt fidgeted) moverse, ponerse nervioso. ∼ with

juguetear con. ● n persona f inquieta. ∼y adj inquieto

field /fiːld/ n campo m. ∼ day n. have a ∼ day hacer su agosto. ∼ glasses npl gemelos mpl. F∼ Marshal n mariscal m de campo. ∼ trip n viaje m de estudio. ∼work n investigaciones fpl en el terreno

fiend /fiːnd/ n demonio m. ∼ish adj diabólico

fierce /fɪəs/ adj (-er, -est) feroz; (attack) violento. ∼ly adv (growl) con ferocidad; (fight) con fiereza

fiery /ˈfaɪərɪ/ adj (-ier, -iest) ardiente; (temper) exaltado

fifteen /fɪfˈtiːn/ adj & n quince (m). ∼th adj decimoquinto. ● n quinceavo m

fifth /fɪfθ/ adj & n quinto (m)

fif|tieth /ˈfɪftɪəθ/ adj quincuagésimo. ● n cincuentavo m. ∼y adj & n cincuenta (m). ∼y-∼y adv mitad y mitad, a medias. ● adj. a ∼y-∼y chance una posibilidad de cada dos

fig /fɪg/ n higo m

fight /faɪt/ vi (pt fought) luchar; (quarrel) disputar. ● vt luchar contra. ● n pelea f; (struggle) lucha f; (quarrel) disputa f; (Mil) combate m. □ ∼ back vi defenderse. □ ∼ off vt rechazar (attack); luchar contra (illness). ∼er n luchador m; (airplane) avión m de caza. ∼ing n luchas fpl

figment /ˈfɪgmənt/ n. ∼ of the imagination producto m de la imaginación

figurative /ˈfɪgjʊrətɪv/ adj figurado

figure /ˈfɪgə(r)/ n (number) cifra f; (person) figura f; (shape) forma f; (of woman) tipo m. ● vt imaginar;

(*Amer fam*, reckon) calcular. ● *vi* figurar. that ~s (*fam*) es lógico. □ ~ **out** *vt* entender. ~**head** *n* testaferro *m*, mascarón *m* de proa. ~ **of speech** *n* figura *f* retórica

filch /filtʃ/ *vt* 🄔 hurtar

file /faɪl/ *n* (*tool, for nails*) lima *f*; (*folder*) carpeta *f*; (*set of papers*) expediente *m*; (*Comp*) archivo *m*; (*row*) fila *f*. **in single** ~ en fila india. ● *vt* archivar (papers); limar (metal, nails). ● ~ **in** *vi* entrar en fila. ~ **past** *vt* desfilar ante

filing cabinet /'faɪlɪŋ/ *n* archivador *m*

fill /fil/ *vt* llenar. ● *vi* llenarse. ● *n*. **eat one's** ~ hartarse de comer. **have had one's** ~ **of** estar harto de □ ~ **in** *vt* rellenar (form, hole). □ ~ **out** *vt* rellenar (form). *vi* (*get fatter*) engordar. □ ~ **up** *vt* llenar. *vi* llenarse

fillet /'filit/ *n* filete *m*. ● *vt* (*pt* **filleted**) cortar en filetes (meat); quitar la espina a (fish)

filling /'filiŋ/ *n* (*in tooth*) empaste *m*, tapadura *f* (Mex). ~ **station** *n* gasolinera *f*

film /film/ *n* película *f*. ● *vt* filmar. ~ **star** *n* estrella *f* de cine

filter /'filtə(r)/ *n* filtro *m*. ● *vt* filtrar. ● *vi* filtrarse. ~-**tipped** *adj* con filtro

filth /filθ/ *n* mugre *f*. ~**y** *adj* mugriento

fin /fin/ *n* aleta *f*

final /'faɪnl/ *adj* último; (*conclusive*) decisivo. ● *n* (Sport) final *f*. ~**s** *npl* (Schol) exámenes *mpl* de fin de curso

finale /fɪ'nɑːlɪ/ *n* final *m*

final|ist *n* finalista *m & f*. ~**ize** *vt* ultimar. ~**ly** *adv* (*lastly*) finalmente, por fin

financ|e /'faɪnæns/ *n* finanzas *fpl*. ● *vt* financiar. ~**ial** /far'nænʃl/ *adj* financiero; (*difficulties*) económico

find /faɪnd/ *vt* (*pt* **found**) encontrar. □ ~ **out** *vt* descubrir. ● *vi* (*learn*) enterarse. ~**ings** *npl* conclusiones *fpl*

fine /faɪn/ *adj* (-er, -est) (*delicate*) fino; (*excellent*) excelente. ● *adv* muy bien. ● *n* multa *f*. ● *vt* multar. ~ **arts** *npl* bellas artes *fpl*. ~**ly** *adv* (*cut*) en trozos pequeños; (*adjust*) con precisión

finger /'fiŋgə(r)/ *n* dedo *m*. ● *vt* tocar. ~**nail** *n* uña *f*. ~**print** *n* huella *f* digital. ~**tip** *n* punta *f* del dedo

finish /'finiʃ/ *vt/i* terminar, acabar. ~ **doing** terminar de hacer. ● *n* fin *m*; (*of race*) llegada *f*

finite /'faɪnaɪt/ *adj* finito

Fin|land /'finlənd/ *n* Finlandia *f*. ~**n** *n* finlandés *m*. ~**nish** *adj* & *n* finlandés (*m*)

fiord /fjɔːd/ *n* fiordo *m*

fir /fɜː(r)/ *n* abeto *m*

fire /faɪə(r)/ *n* fuego *m*; (*conflagration*) incendio *m*. ● *vt* disparar (gun); (*dismiss*) despedir; avivar (imagination). ● *vi* disparar. ~ **alarm** *n* alarma *f* contra incendios. ~**arm** *n* arma *f* de fuego. ~ **brigade**, ~ **department** (Amer) *n* cuerpo *m* de bomberos. ~ **engine** *n* coche *m* de bomberos, carro *m* de bomberos (Mex). ~**escape** *n* escalera *f* de incendios. ~ **extinguisher** *n* extintor *m*, extinguidor *m* (LAm). ~**fighter** *n* bombero *m*. ~**man** /-mən/ *n* bombero *m*. ~**place** *n* chimenea *f*. ~**side** *n* hogar *m*. ~ **truck** *n* (Amer) see ~ **ENGINE**. ~**wood** *n* leña *f*. ~**work** *n* fuego *m* artificial

firm /fɜːm/ *n* empresa *f*. ● *adj* (-er,

-est) firme. ~**ly** adv firmemente

first /fɜːst/ adj primero, (before masculine singular noun) primer. ●n primero m. ●adv primero; (first time) por primera vez. ~ **of all** primero. ~ **aid** n primeros auxilios mpl. ~ **aid kit** n botiquín m. ~ **class** /-ˈklɑːs/ adv (travel) en primera clase. ~**-class** adj de primera clase. ~ **floor** n primer piso m; (Amer) planta f baja. F~ **Lady** n (Amer) Primera Dama f. ~**ly** adv en primer lugar. ~ **name** n nombre m de pila. ~**-rate** /-ˈreɪt/ adj excelente

fish /fɪʃ/ n (pl invar or -es) pez m; (as food) pescado m. ●vi pescar. **go** ~**ing** ir de pesca. □ ~ **out** vt sacar. ~**erman** n pescador m. ~**ing** n pesca f. ~**ing pole** (Amer), ~**ing rod** n caña f de pesca. ~**monger** n pescadero m. ~ **shop** n pescadería f. ~**y** adj (smell) a pescado; (fam, questionable) sospechoso

fission /ˈfɪʃn/ n fisión f

fist /fɪst/ n puño m

fit /fɪt/ adj (fitter, fittest) (healthy) en forma; (good enough) adecuado; (able) capaz. ●n (attack) ataque m; (of clothes) corte m. ●vt (pt fitted) (adapt) adaptar; (be the right size for) quedarle bien a; (install) colocar. ●vi encajar; (in certain space) caber; (clothes) quedarle bien a uno. □ ~ **in** vi caber. ~**ful** adj irregular. ~**ness** n salud f; (Sport) (buena) forma f física. ~**ting** adj apropiado. ●n (of clothes) prueba f. ~**ting room** n probador m

five /faɪv/ adj & n cinco (m).

fix /fɪks/ vt fijar; (mend, deal with) arreglar. ●n. **in a** ~ en un aprieto. ~**ed** adj fijo. ~**ture** /ˈfɪkstʃə(r)/ n

(Sport) partido m

fizz /fɪz/ vi burbujear. ●n efervescencia f. ~**le** /fɪzl/ vi. **le out** fracasar. ~**y** adj efervescente; (water) con gas

fjord /fjɔːd/ n fiordo m

flabbergasted /ˈflæbəɡɑːstɪd/ adj estupefacto

flabby /ˈflæbɪ/ adj flojo

flag /flæɡ/ n bandera f. ●vi (pt flagged) (weaken) flaquear; (conversation) languidecer

flagon /ˈflæɡən/ n botella f grande, jarro m

flagpole /ˈflæɡpəʊl/ n asta f de bandera

flagrant /ˈfleɪɡrənt/ adj flagrante

flair /fleə(r)/ n don m (for de)

flak|e /fleɪk/ n copo m; (of paint, metal) escama f. ●vi descharse. ~**y** adj escamoso

flamboyant /flæmˈbɔɪənt/ adj (clothes) vistoso; (manner) extravagante

flame /fleɪm/ n llama f. **go up in** ~**s** incendiarse

flamingo /fləˈmɪŋɡəʊ/ n (pl -o(e)s) flamenco m

flammable /ˈflæməbl/ adj inflamable

flan /flæn/ n tartaleta f

flank /flæŋk/ n (of animal) ijada f; (of person) costado m; (Mil, Sport) flanco m

flannel /ˈflænl/ n franela f; (for face) paño m (para lavarse la cara).

flap /flæp/ vi (pt flapped) ondear; (wings) aletear; ●vt batir (wings); agitar (arms). ●n (cover) tapa f; (of pocket) cartera f; (of table) ala f. **get into a** ~ 🄵 ponerse nervioso

flare /fleə(r)/ ●n llamarada f; (Mil)

flash | float

bengala *f*; (*in skirt*) vuelo *m*. □ ~ **up** *vi* llamear; (*fighting*) estallar; (*person*) encolerizarse

flash /flæʃ/ ● *vi* destellar. ● *vt* (*aim torch*) dirigir; (*flaunt*) hacer ostentación de. ~ **past** pasar como un rayo. ● *n* destello *m*; (*Photo*) flash *m*. ~**back** *n* escena *f* retrospectiva. ~**light** *n* (*Amer, torch*) linterna *f*. ~**y** *adj* ostentoso

flask /flɑːsk/ *n* frasco *m*; (*vacuum flask*) termo *m*

flat /flæt/ *adj* (**flatter, flattest**) plano; (*tyre*) desinflado; (*refusal*) categórico; (*fare, rate*) fijo; (*Mus*) bemol. ● *adv* (*Mus*) demasiado bajo. ~ **out** (*at top speed*) a toda velocidad. ● *n* (*rooms*) apartamento *m*, piso *m*; 🔲 pinchazo *m*; (*Mus*) (*Auto, esp Amer*) bemol *m*. ~**ly** *adv* categóricamente. ~**ten** *vt* allanar, aplanar

flatter /flætə(r)/ *vt* adular. ~**ing** *adj* (*person*) lisonjero; (*clothes*) favorecedor. ~**y** *n* adulación *f*

flaunt /flɔːnt/ *vt* hacer ostentación de

flavour /ˈfleivə(r)/ *n* sabor *m*. ● *vt* sazonar. ~**ing** *n* condimento *m*

flaw /flɔː/ *n* defecto *m*. ~**less** *adj* perfecto

flea /fliː/ *n* pulga *f*

fleck /flek/ *n* mancha *f*, pinta *f*

fled /fled/ *see* FLEE

flee /fliː/ *vi* (*pt* **fled**) huir. ● *vt* huir de

fleece /fliːs/ *n* vellón *m*. ● *vt* 🔲 desplumar

fleet /fliːt/ *n* flota *f*; (*of cars*) parque *m* móvil

fleeting /ˈfliːtɪŋ/ *adj* fugaz

Flemish /ˈflemɪʃ/ *adj* & *n* flamenco (*m*)

flesh /fleʃ/ *n* carne *f*. **in the** ~ en

persona

flew /fluː/ *see* FLY

flex /fleks/ *vt* doblar; flexionar (*muscle*). ● *n* (*Elec*) cable *m*

flexib|ility /fleksəˈbilətɪ/ *n* flexibilidad *f*. ~**le** /ˈfleksəbl/ *adj* flexible

flexitime /ˈfleksɪtaɪm/, (*Amer*) **flextime** /ˈflekstaɪm/ *n* horario *m* flexible

flick /flik/ *n* golpecito *m*. ● *vt* dar un golpecito a. □ ~ **through** *vt* hojear

flicker /ˈflikə(r)/ *vi* parpadear. ● *n* parpadeo *m*; (*of hope*) resquicio *m*

flies /flaiz/ *npl* (*on trousers*) bragueta *f*

flight /flait/ *n* vuelo *m*; (*fleeing*) huida *f*, fuga *f*. ~ **of stairs** tramo *m* de escalera *f*. **take** (**to**) ~ darse a la fuga. ~ **attendant** *n* (*male*) sobrecargo *m*, aeromozo *m* (*LAm*); (*female*) azafata *f*, aeromoza *f* (*LAm*). ~**-deck** *n* cubierta *f* de vuelo

flimsy /ˈflimzi/ *adj* (**-ier, -iest**) flojo, débil, poco sólido

flinch /flintʃ/ *vi* retroceder (*from ante*)

fling /fliŋ/ *vt* (*pt* **flung**) arrojar. ● *n* (*love affair*) aventura *f*; (*wild time*) juerga *f*

flint /flint/ *n* pedernal *m*; (*for lighter*) piedra *f*

flip /flip/ *vt* (*pt* **flipped**) dar un golpecito a. ● *n* golpecito *m*. □ ~ **through** *vt* hojear

flippant /ˈflipənt/ *adj* poco serio

flipper /ˈflipə(r)/ *n* aleta *f*

flirt /flɜːt/ *vi* coquetear. ● *n* (*woman*) coqueta *f*; (*man*) coqueto *m*

flit /flit/ *vi* (*pt* **flitted**) revolotear

float /fləʊt/ *vi* flotar. ● *vt* hacer flotar; introducir en Bolsa (*company*).

● n flotador m; (cash) caja f chica

flock /flɒk/ n (of birds) bandada f; (of sheep) rebaño m. ● vi congregarse

flog /flɒg/ vt (pt **flogged**) (beat) azotar; (fam, sell) vender

flood /flʌd/ n inundación f; (fig) avalancha f. ● vt inundar. ● vi (building etc) inundarse; (river) desbordar. **~light** n foco m. ● vt (pt ~**lit**) iluminar (con focos)

floor /flɔː(r)/ n suelo m; (storey) piso m; (for dancing) pista f. ● vt derribar; (baffle) confundir

flop /flɒp/ vi (pt **flopped**) dejarse caer pesadamente; (fam, fail) fracasar. ● n 🄵 fracaso m. **~py** adj flojo. ● n see **~PY DISK**. **~py disk** n disquete m, floppy (disk) m

floral /ˈflɔːrəl/ adj floral

florid /ˈflɒrɪd/ adj florido

florist /ˈflɒrɪst/ n florista m & f

flounder /ˈflaʊndə(r)/ vi (in water) luchar para mantenerse a flote; (speaker) quedar sin saber qué decir

flour /flaʊə(r)/ n harina f

flourish /ˈflʌrɪʃ/ vi florecer; (business) prosperar. ● vt blandir. ● n ademán m elegante; (in handwriting) rasgo m. **~ing** adj próspero

flout /flaʊt/ vt burlarse de

flow /fləʊ/ vi fluir; (blood) correr; (hang loosely) caer. ● n flujo m; (stream) corriente f; (of traffic, information) circulación f. **~ chart** n organigrama m

flower /flaʊə(r)/ n flor f. ● vi florecer, florear (Mex). **~ bed** n macizo m de flores. **~y** adj florido

flown /fləʊn/ see **FLY**

flu /fluː/ n gripe f

fluctuat|e /ˈflʌktjʊeɪt/ vi fluctuar. **~ion** /-ˈeɪʃn/ n fluctuación f

flue /fluː/ n tiro m

fluen|cy /ˈfluːənsɪ/ n fluidez f. **~t** adj (style) fluido; (speaker) elocuente. **be ~t in a language** hablar un idioma con fluidez. **~tly** adv con fluidez

fluff /flʌf/ n pelusa f. **~y** adj (-ier, -iest) velloso

fluid /ˈfluːɪd/ adj & n fluido (m)

flung /flʌŋ/ see **FLING**

fluorescent /flʊəˈresnt/ adj fluorescente

flush /flʌʃ/ vi ruborizarse. ● vt. **~ the toilet** tirar de la cadena, jalarle a la cadena (LAm). ● n (blush) rubor m

fluster /ˈflʌstə(r)/ vt poner nervioso

flute /fluːt/ n flauta f

flutter /ˈflʌtə(r)/ vi ondear; (bird) revolotear. ● n (of wings) revoloteo m; (fig) agitación f

flux /flʌks/ n flujo m. **be in a state of ~** estar siempre cambiando

fly /flaɪ/ vi (pt **flew**, pp **flown**) volar; (passenger) ir en avión; (flag) flotar; (rush) correr. ● vt pilotar, pilotear (LAm) (aircraft); transportar en avión (passengers, goods); izar (flag). ● n mosca f; (of trousers) see **FLIES**. **~ing** adj volante. ● n **flying visit** visita f relámpago. ● n (activity) aviación f. **~leaf** n guarda f. **~over** n paso m elevado

foal /fəʊl/ n potro m

foam /fəʊm/ n espuma f. ● vi espumar. **~ rubber** n goma f espuma, hule m espuma (Mex)

fob /fɒb/ vt (pt **fobbed**). **~ sth off onto s.o.** (palm off) encajarle algo a uno

focal /ˈfəʊkl/ adj focal

focus /ˈfəʊkəs/ n (pl -**cuses** or -**ci** /-saɪ/) foco m; (fig) centro m. **in ~**

f

enfocado. out of ~ desenfocado. ● *vt* (*be focused*) enfocar (*fig*) concentrar. ● *vi* enfocar; (*fig*) concentrarse (on en)

fodder /'fɒdə(r)/ *n* forraje *m*

foe /fəʊ/ *n* enemigo *m*

foetus /'fi:təs/ *n* (*pl* -tuses) feto *m*

fog /fɒg/ *n* niebla *f*

fog|gy *adj* (-ier, -iest) nebuloso. it is ~gy hay niebla. ~horn *n* sirena *f* de niebla

foible /'fɔɪbl/ *n* punto *m* débil

foil /fɔɪl/ *vt* (*thwart*) frustrar. ● *n* papel *m* de plata

foist /fɔɪst/ *vt* encajar (on a)

fold /fəʊld/ *vt* doblar; cruzar (arms). ● *vi* doblarse; (*fail*) fracasar. ● *n* pliegue *m*. (*for sheep*) redil *m*. ~er *n* carpeta *f*. ~ing *adj* plegable

foliage /'fəʊlɪɪdʒ/ *n* follaje *m*

folk /fəʊk/ *n* gente *f*. ● *adj* popular. ~lore /-lɔ:(r)/ *n* folklore *m*. ~ music *n* música *f* folklórica; (*modern*) música *f* folk. ~s *npl* (*one's relatives*) familia *f*

follow /'fɒləʊ/ *vt/i* seguir. □ ~ up *vt* seguir. ~er *n* seguidor *m*. ~ing *n* partidarios *mpl*. ● *adj* siguiente. ● *prep* después de

folly /'fɒlɪ/ *n* locura *f*

fond /fɒnd/ *adj* (-er, -est) (*loving*) cariñoso; (*hope*) vivo. be ~ of s.o. tener(le) cariño a uno. be ~ of sth estar aficionado a algo

fondle /'fɒndl/ *vt* acariciar

fondness /'fɒndnɪs/ *n* cariño *m*; (*for things*) afición *f*

font /fɒnt/ *n* pila *f* bautismal

food /fu:d/ *n* comida *f*. ~ processor *n* robot *m* de cocina

fool /fu:l/ *n* idiota *m* & *f*. ● *vt* engañar. □ ~ about *vi* hacer payasadas.

~hardy *adj* temerario. ~ish *adj* tonto. ~ishly *adv* tontamente. ~ishness *n* tontería *f*. ~proof *adj* infalible

foot /fʊt/ *n* (*pl* feet) pie *m*; (*measure*) pie *m* (= 30,48cm); (*of animal, furniture*) pata *f*. get under s.o.'s feet estorbar a uno. on ~ a pie. on/to one's feet de pie. put one's ~ in it meter la pata. ● *vt* pagar (bill). ~age /-ɪdʒ/ *n* (*of film*) secuencia *f*. ~-and-mouth disease *n* fiebre *f* aftosa. ~ball *n* (*ball*) balón *m*; (*game*) fútbol *m*; (*American ~ball*) fútbol *m* americano. ~baller *n* futbolista *m* & *f*. ~bridge *n* puente *m* para peatones. ~hills *npl* estribaciones *fpl*. ~hold *n* punto *m* de apoyo. ~ing *n* pie *m*. on an equal ~ing en igualdad de condiciones. ~lights *npl* candilejas *fpl*. ~man /-mən/ *n* lacayo *m*. ~note *n* nota *f* (al pie de la página). ~path *n* (*in country*) senda *f*; (*in town*) acera *f*, banqueta *f* (Mex). ~print *n* huella *f*. ~step *n* paso *m*. ~wear *n* calzado *m*

for /fɔː(r)/ /fə(r)/

● *preposition*

····▸ (*intended for*) para. it's ~ my mother es para mi madre. she works ~ a multinational trabaja para una multinacional

····▸ (*on behalf of*) por. I did it ~ you lo hice por ti

➡ See entries **para** and **por** for further information

····▸ (*expressing purpose*) para. I use it ~ washing the car lo uso para limpiar el coche. what ~? ¿para qué?. to go out ~ a meal salir a comer fuera

····▸ (*in favour of*) a favor de. are you ~ or against the idea? ¿estás a favor o en contra de la idea?

····▸ (*indicating cost, in exchange for*) por. I bought it ~ 30 pounds lo compré por 30 libras. she left him ~ another man lo dejó por otro. thanks ~ everything gracias por todo. what's the Spanish ~ toad? ¿cómo se dice toad' en español?

····▸ (*expressing duration*) he read ~ two hours leyó durante dos horas. how long are you going ~? ¿por cuánto tiempo vas? I've been waiting ~ three hours hace tres horas que estoy esperando, llevo tres horas esperando

····▸ (*in the direction of*) para. the train ~ Santiago el tren para Santiago

● *conjunction* (*because*) porque, pues (*literary usage*). she left at once, ~ it was getting late se fue en seguida, porque o pues se hacía tarde

forage /'fɒrɪdʒ/ *vi* forrajear. ● *n* forraje *m*

forbade /fə'bæd/ see **FORBID**

forbearance /fɔː'beərəns/ *n* paciencia *f*

forbid /fə'bɪd/ *vt* (*pt* forbade, *pp* forbidden) prohibir (s.o. to do a uno hacer). ~ s.o. sth prohibir algo a uno. ~**ding** *adj* imponente

force /fɔːs/ *n* fuerza *f*. by ~ a la fuerza. come into ~ entrar en vigor. the ~s las fuerzas *fpl* armadas. ● *vt* forzar; (*compel*) obligar (s.o. to do sth a uno a hacer

algo). ~ on imponer a. ~ open forzar. ~**d** *adj* forzado. ~**-feed** *vt* alimentar a la fuerza. ~**ful** *adj* enérgico

forceps /'fɔːseps/ *n* fórceps *m*

forcibl|e /'fɔːsəbl/ *adj* a la fuerza. ~**y** *adv* a la fuerza

ford /fɔːd/ *n* vado *m* ● *vt* vadear

fore /fɔː(r)/ *adj* anterior. ● *n*. come to the ~ hacerse evidente

forearm /'fɔːrɑːm/ *n* antebrazo *m*

foreboding /fɔː'bəʊdɪŋ/ *n* presentimiento *m*

forecast /'fɔːkɑːst/ *vt* (*pt* forecast) pronosticar (weather); prever (result). ● *n* pronóstico *m*. weather ~ pronóstico *m* del tiempo

forecourt /'fɔːkɔːt/ *n* patio *m* delantero

forefinger /'fɔːfɪŋɡə(r)/ *n* (dedo *m*) índice *m*

forefront /'fɔːfrʌnt/ *n* vanguardia *f*. in the ~ a la vanguardia

forego /fɔː'ɡəʊ/ *vt* (*pt* forewent, *pp* foregone) see **FORGO**

foregone /'fɔːɡɒn/ *adj*. ~ conclusion resultado *m* previsto

foreground /'fɔːɡraʊnd/ *n*. in the ~ en primer plano

forehead /'fɒrɪd/ *n* frente *f*

foreign /'fɒrən/ *adj* extranjero; (trade) exterior; (travel) al extranjero, en el extranjero. ~**er** *n* extranjero *m*

foreman /'fɔːmən/ *n* (*pl* -men /-mən/) *n* capataz *m*

foremost /'fɔːməʊst/ *adj* primero. ● *adv*. first and ~ ante todo

forerunner /'fɔːrʌnə(r)/ *n* precursor *m*

foresee /fɔː'siː/ *vt* (*pt* -saw, *pp* -seen) prever. ~**able** *adj* previsible

foresight /'fɔːsaɪt/ *n* previsión *f*

f

forest /'forist/ n bosque m

forestall /fɔː'stɔːl/ vt (prevent) prevenir; (preempt) anticiparse a

forestry /'foristri/ n silvicultura f

foretaste /'fɔːteist/ n anticipo m

foretell /fɔː'tel/ vt (pt foretold) predecir

forever /fə'revə(r)/ adv para siempre; (always) siempre

forewarn /fɔː'wɔːn/ vt advertir

forewent /fɔː'went/ see FOREGO

foreword /'fɔːwɜːd/ n prefacio m

forfeit /'fɔːfit/ n (penalty) pena f; (in game) prenda f. ● vt perder; perder el derecho a (property)

forgave /fə'geiv/ see FORGIVE

forge /fɔːdʒ/ n fragua f. ● vt fraguar; (copy) falsificar. □ ~ ahead vi adelantarse rápidamente. ~r n falsificador m. ~ry n falsificación f

forget /fə'get/ vt (pt forgot, pp forgotten) olvidar, olvidarse de. ● vi olvidarse (about de). I forgot se me olvidó. ~ful adj olvidadizo

forgive /fə'giv/ vt (pt forgave, pp forgiven) perdonar. ~ s.o. for sth perdonar algo a uno. ~ness n perdón m

forgo /fɔː'gəʊ/ vt (pt forwent, pp forgone) renunciar a

fork /fɔːk/ n tenedor m; (for digging) horca f; (in road) bifurcación f. ● vi (road) bifurcarse. □ ~ out vt 🅘 desembolsar, aflojar 🅘. ~-lift truck n carretilla f elevadora

forlorn /fə'lɔːn/ adj (hope, attempt) desesperado; (smile) triste

form /fɔːm/ n forma f; (document) formulario m; (Schol) clase f. ● vt formar. ● vi formarse

formal /'fɔːml/ adj formal; (person) formalista; (dress) de etiqueta. ~ity /-'mælətɪ/ n formalidad f. ~ly adv oficialmente

format /'fɔːmæt/ n formato m. ● vt (pt formatted) (Comp) formatear

formation /fɔː'meiʃn/ n formación f

former /'fɔːmə(r)/ adj anterior; (first of two) primero. ● n. the ~ el primero m, la primera f, los primeros mpl, las primeras fpl. ~ly adv antes

formidable /'fɔːmidəbl/ adj formidable

formula /'fɔːmjʊlə/ n (pl -ae /-iː/ or -as) fórmula f. ~te /-leit/ vt formular

forsake /fə'seik/ vt (pt forsook, pp forsaken) abandonar

fort /fɔːt/ n fuerte m

forth /fɔːθ/ adv. and so ~ y así sucesivamente. ~coming /-'kʌmiŋ/ adj próximo, venidero; (sociable) comunicativo. ~right adj directo. ~with /-'wiθ/ adv inmediatamente

fortieth /'fɔːtiiθ/ adj cuadragésimo. ● n cuadragésima parte f

fortnight /'fɔːtnait/ n quince días mpl, quincena f. ~ly adj bimensual. ● adv cada quince días

fortress /'fɔːtris/ n fortaleza f

fortunate /'fɔːtʃənət/ adj afortunado. be ~ tener suerte. ~ly adv afortunadamente

fortune /'fɔːtʃuːn/ n fortuna f. ~-teller n adivino m

forty /'fɔːtɪ/ adj & n cuarenta (m). ~ winks un sueñecito

forum /'fɔːrəm/ n foro m

forward /'fɔːwəd/ adj (movement) hacia adelante; (advanced) precoz; (pert) impertinente. ● n (Sport) delantero m. ● adv adelante. go ~ avanzar. ● vt hacer seguir (letter); enviar (goods). ~s adv adelante

forwent /fɔː'went/ see FORGO

fossil /'fɒsl/ adj & n fósil (m)

foster /'fɒstə(r)/ vt (*promote*) fomentar; criar (child). ~ **child** n hijo m adoptivo

fought /fɔːt/ see FIGHT

foul /faʊl/ adj (-er, -est) (smell) nauseabundo; (weather) pésimo; (person) asqueroso; (dirty) sucio; (language) obsceno; n (Sport) falta f. ●vt contaminar; (entangle) enredar. ~ **play** n (Sport) jugada f sucia; (crime) delito m

found /faʊnd/ see FIND. ●vt fundar.

foundation /faʊn'deɪʃn/ n fundación f; (basis) fundamento m. (cosmetic) base f (de maquillaje). ●~s npl (of building) cimientos mpl

founder /'faʊndə(r)/ n fundador m. ●vi (ship) hundirse

fountain /'faʊntɪn/ n fuente f. ~ **pen** n pluma f (estilográfica) f, estilográfica f

four /fɔː(r)/ adj & n cuatro (m). ~**fold** adj cuádruple. ●adv cuatro veces. ~**some** /-səm/ n grupo m de cuatro personas ~**teen** /'fɔːtiːn/ adj & n catorce (m). ~**teenth** adj & n decimocuarto (m). ~**th** /fɔːθ/ adj & n cuarto (m). ~**-wheel drive** n tracción f integral

fowl /faʊl/ n ave f

fox /fɒks/ n zorro m, zorra f. ●vt [T] confundir

foyer /'fɔɪeɪ/ n (of theatre) foyer m; (of hotel) vestíbulo m

fraction /'frækʃn/ n fracción f

fracture /'fræktʃə(r)/ n fractura f. ●vt fracturar. ~ **fracturarse**

fragile /'frædʒaɪl/ adj frágil

fragment /'frægmənt/ n fragmento m. ~**ary** /-ərɪ/ adj fragmentario

fragran|ce /'freɪɡrəns/ n fragan-

cia f. ~**t** adj fragante

frail /freɪl/ adj (-er, -est) frágil

frame /freɪm/ n (of picture, door, window) marco m; (of spectacles) montura f; (fig, structure) estructura f. ●vt enmarcar (picture); formular (plan, question); (fam, incriminate unjustly) incriminar falsamente. ~**work** n estructura f; (context) marco m

France /frɑːns/ n Francia f

frank /fræŋk/ adj franco. ●vt franquear. ~**ly** adv francamente

frantic /'fræntɪk/ adj frenético. ~ **with** loco de

fratern|al /frə'tɜːnl/ adj fraternal. ~**ity** /frə'tɜːnɪtɪ/ n fraternidad f; (club) asociación f. ~**ize** /'frætənaɪz/ vi fraternizar

fraud /frɔːd/ n fraude m; (person) impostor m. ~**ulent** /-jʊlənt/ adj fraudulento

fraught /frɔːt/ adj (tense) tenso. ~ **with** cargado de

fray /freɪ/ n riña f

freak /friːk/ n fenómeno m; (monster) monstruo m. ●adj anormal. ~**ish** adj anormal

freckle /'frekl/ n peca f. ~**d** adj pecoso

free /friː/ adj (freer /'friːə(r)/, freest /'friːɪst/) libre; (gratis) gratuito. ~ **of charge** gratis. ●vt (pt freed) (set at liberty) poner en libertad; (relieve from) liberar (from/ of de); (untangle) desenredar. ~**dom** n libertad f. ~**hold** n propiedad f absoluta. ~ **kick** n tiro m libre. ~**lance** adj & adv por cuenta propia. ~**ly** adv libremente. ~**mason** n masón m. ~**-range** adj (eggs) de granja. ~**speech** n libertad f de expresión. ~**style** n estilo m libre. ~**way** n (Amer) autopista f

freez|e /friːz/ vt (pt froze, pp frozen) helar; congelar (food, wages). • vi helarse; (become motionless) quedarse inmóvil. • n (on wages, prices) congelación f. **~er** n congelador m. **~ing** adj glacial. **~ing (point)** punto m de congelación f. below **~ing** bajo cero

freight /freɪt/ n (goods) mercancías fpl. **~er** n buque m de carga

French /frentʃ/ adj francés. • n (language) francés m. • npl. the **~** (people) los franceses. **~ fries** npl patatas fpl fritas, papas fpl fritas (LAm). **~man** /-mən/ n francés m. **~ window** n puerta f ventana. **~woman** francesa f

frenz|ied /frenzɪd/ adj frenético. **~y** n frenesí m

frequency /friːkwənsɪ/ n frecuencia f

frequent /frɪˈkwent/ vt frecuentar. • /friːkwənt/ adj frecuente. **~ly** adv frecuentemente

fresh /freʃ/ adj (-er, -est) fresco; (different, additional) nuevo; (water) dulce. **~en** vi refrescar. □ **~en up** vi (person) refrescarse. **~er** n 🄸 see **~MAN**. **~ly** adv recientemente. **~man** /-mən/ n estudiante m de primer año. **~ness** n frescura f

fret /fret/ vi (pt fretted) preocuparse. **~ful** adj (discontented) quejoso; (irritable) irritable

friction /frɪkʃn/ n fricción f

Friday /fraɪdeɪ/ n viernes m

fridge /frɪdʒ/ n 🄸 frigorífico m, nevera f, refrigerador m (LAm)

fried /fraɪd/ see **FRY**. • adj frito

friend /frend/ n amigo m. **~liness** n simpatía f. **~ly** adj (-ier, -iest) simpático. **~ship** n amistad f

fries /fraɪz/ npl see **FRENCH FRIES**

frieze /friːz/ n friso m

frigate /frɪgat/ n fragata f

fright /fraɪt/ n miedo m; (shock) susto m. **~en** vt asustar. □ **~ off** vt ahuyentar. **~ened** adj asustado. be **~ened** tener miedo (of de.) **~ful** adj espantoso, horrible. **~fully** adv terriblemente

frigid /frɪdʒɪd/ adj frígido

frill /frɪl/ n volante m, olán m (Mex). **~s** npl (fig) adornos mpl. with no **~s** sencillo

fringe /frɪndʒ/ n (sewing) fleco m; (ornamental border) franja f; (of hair) flequillo m, cerquillo m (LAm), fleco m (Mex); (of area) periferia f; (of society) margen m

fritter /frɪtə(r)/ vt. □ **~ away** vt desperdiciar (time); malgastar (money)

frivol|ity /frɪˈvɒlɪtɪ/ n frivolidad f. **~ous** /frɪvələs/ adj frívolo

fro /frəʊ/ see **TO AND FRO**

frock /frɒk/ n vestido m

frog /frɒg/ n rana f. have a **~ in** one's throat tener carraspera. **~man** /-mən/ n hombre m rana. **~spawn** n huevos mpl de rana

frolic /frɒlɪk/ vi (pt frolicked) retozar

from /frɒm//frəm/ prep de; (indicating starting point) desde; (habit, conviction) por; **~** then on a partir de ahí

front /frʌnt/ n parte f delantera; (of building) fachada f; (of clothes) delantera f; (Mil, Pol) frente f; (of book) principio m; (fig, appearance) apariencia f; (seafront) paseo m marítimo, malecón m (LAm). in **~** of delante de. • adj delantero; (first) primero. **~al** adj frontal; (attack) de frente. **~ door** n puerta f principal

frontier /frʌntɪə(r)/ n frontera f

front page n (of newspaper) primera plana f

frost /frɒst/ n (freezing) helada f; (frozen dew) escarcha f. ~**bite** n congelación f. ~**bitten** adj congelado. ~**ed** adj (glass) esmerilado. ~**ing** n (Amer) glaseado m. ~**y** adj (weather) helado; (night) de helada; (fig) glacial

froth /frɒθ/ n espuma f. ● vi espumar. ~**y** adj espumoso

frown /fraʊn/ vi fruncir el entrecejo ● n ceño m. □ ~ **on** vt desaprobar.

froze /frəʊz/ see FREEZE. ~**n** /'frəʊzn/ see FREEZE. ● adj congelado; (region) helado

frugal /'fruːɡl/ adj frugal

fruit /fruːt/ n (in botany) fruto m; (as food) fruta f. ~**ful** /'fruːtfl/ adj fértil; (fig) fructífero. ~**ion** /fruː'ɪʃn/ n. come to ~**ion** realizarse. ~**less** adj infructuoso. ~ **salad** n macedonia f de frutas. ~**y** adj que sabe a fruta

frustrat|e /frʌ'streɪt/ vt frustrar. ~**ion** /-ʃn/ n frustración f. ~**ed** adj frustrado. ~**ing** adj frustrante

fry /fraɪ/ vt (pt fried) freír. ● vi freírse. ~**ing pan** n sárten f, sartén m (LAm)

fudge /fʌdʒ/ n dulce m de azúcar

fuel /'fjuːəl/ n combustible m

fugitive /'fjuːdʒɪtɪv/ adj & n fugitivo (m)

fulfil /fʊl'fɪl/ vt (pt fulfilled) cumplir (con) (promise, obligation); satisfacer (condition); hacer realidad (ambition). ~**ment** n (of promise, obligation) cumplimiento m; (of conditions) satisfacción f; (of hopes, plans) realización f

full /fʊl/ adj (-er, -est) lleno; (bus, hotel) completo; (account) deta-

llado. at ~ speed a máxima velocidad. be ~ (up) (with food) no poder más. ● n. in ~ sin quitar nada. to the ~ completamente. write in ~ escribir con todas las letras. ~**back** n (Sport) defensa m & f. ~**blown** /fʊl'bləʊn/ adj verdadero. ~**fledged** /-'fledʒd/ adj (Amer) see FULLY-FLEDGED. ~ **moon** n luna f llena. ~**scale** /-'skeɪl/ adj (drawing) de tamaño natural; (fig) amplio. ~ **stop** n punto m. ~**-time** adj (employment) de jornada completa. ● /-'taɪm/ adv a tiempo completo. ~**y** adv completamente. ~**-fledged** /-'fledʒd/ adj (chick) capaz de volar; (lawyer, nurse) hecho y derecho

fulsome /'fʊlsəm/ adj excesivo

fumble /'fʌmbl/ vi buscar (a tientas)

fume /fjuːm/ vi despedir gases; (fig, be furious) estar furioso. ~**s** npl gases mpl

fumigate /'fjuːmɪɡeɪt/ vt fumigar

fun /fʌn/ n (amusement) diversión f; (merriment) alegría f. for ~ en broma. have ~ divertirse. make ~ of burlarse de

function /'fʌŋkʃn/ n (purpose, duty) función f; (reception) recepción f. ● vi funcionar. ~**al** adj funcional

fund /fʌnd/ n fondo m. ● vt financiar

fundamental /fʌndə'mentl/ adj fundamental. ~**ist** adj & n fundamentalista (m & f)

funeral /'fjuːnərəl/ n entierro m, funerales mpl. ~ **director** n director m de pompas fúnebres

funfair /'fʌnfeə(r)/ n feria f; (permanent) parque m de atracciones, parque m de diversiones (LAm)

fungus /ˈfʌŋɡəs/ n (pl -gi /-ɡaɪ/) hongo m

funnel /ˈfʌnl/ n (for pouring) embudo m; (of ship) chimenea f

funn|ily /ˈfʌnɪlɪ/ adv (oddly) curiosamente. ~y adj (-ier, -iest) divertido, gracioso; (odd) curioso, raro

fur /fɜː(r)/ n pelo m; (pelt) piel f

furious /ˈfjʊərɪəs/ adj furioso. ~ly adv furiosamente

furlough /ˈfɜːləʊ/ n (Amer) permiso m. **on** ~ de permiso

furnace /ˈfɜːnɪs/ n horno m

furnish /ˈfɜːnɪʃ/ vt amueblar, amoblar (LAm); (supply) proveer. ~ings npl muebles mpl, mobiliario m

furniture /ˈfɜːnɪtʃə(r)/ n muebles mpl, mobiliario m. **a piece of** ~ un mueble

furrow /ˈfʌrəʊ/ n surco m

furry /ˈfɜːrɪ/ adj peludo

furthe|r /ˈfɜːðə(r)/ adj más lejano; (additional) nuevo. ● adv más lejos; (more) además. ● vt fomentar. ~rmore adv además. ~st adj más lejano. ● adv más lejos

furtive /ˈfɜːtɪv/ adj furtivo

fury /ˈfjʊərɪ/ n furia f

fuse /fjuːz/ vt (melt) fundir; (fig, unite) fusionar. ● **the lights** fundir los plomos. ● vi fundirse; (fig) fusionarse. ● n fusible m, plomo m; (of bomb) mecha f. ~**box** n caja f de fusibles

fuselage /ˈfjuːzəlɑːʒ/ n fuselaje m

fusion /ˈfjuːʒn/ n fusión f

fuss /fʌs/ n (commotion) jaleo m. **kick up a** ~ armar un lío, armar una bronca. **make a** ~ **of** tratar con mucha atención. ● vi preocuparse. ~y adj (-ier, -iest) (finicky) remilgado; (demanding) exigente

futil|e /ˈfjuːtaɪl/ adj inútil, vano. ~**ity** /fjuːˈtɪlətɪ/ n inutilidad f

futur|e /ˈfjuːtʃə(r)/ adj futuro. ● n futuro m. **in** ~ de ahora en adelante. ~**istic** /fjuːtʃəˈrɪstɪk/ adj futurista

fuzz /fʌz/ n pelusa f. ~y adj (hair) crespo; (photograph) borroso

Gg

gab /ɡæb/ n. **have the gift of the** ~ tener un pico de oro

gabardine /ɡæbəˈdiːn/ n gabardina f

gabble /ˈɡæbl/ vi hablar atropelladamente

gable /ˈɡeɪbl/ n aguilón m

gad /ɡæd/ vi (pt gadded). ~ **about** callejear

gadget /ˈɡædʒɪt/ n chisme m

Gaelic /ˈɡeɪlɪk/ adj & n gaélico (m)

gaffe /ɡæf/ n plancha f, metedura f de pata, metida f de pata (LAm)

gag /ɡæɡ/ n mordaza f; (joke) chiste m. ● vt (pt gagged) amordazar. ● vi hacer arcadas

gaiety /ˈɡeɪətɪ/ n alegría f

gaily /ˈɡeɪlɪ/ adv alegremente

gain /ɡeɪn/ vt ganar; (acquire) adquirir; (obtain) conseguir. ● vi (clock) adelantar. ● n ganancia f; (increase) aumento m

gait /ɡeɪt/ n modo m de andar

gala /ˈɡɑːlə/ n fiesta f. ~ **performance** (función f de) gala f

galaxy /ˈɡæləksɪ/ n galaxia f

gale /ɡeɪl/ n vendaval m

gall /ɡɔːl/ n bilis f; (fig) hiel f; (impudence) descaro m

gallant /ˈɡælənt/ adj (brave) valiente; (*chivalrous*) galante. **~ry** *n* valor *m*

gall bladder /'gɔːlblædə(r)/ *n* vesícula *f* biliar

gallery /'gælərɪ/ *n* galería *f*

galley /'gælɪ/ *n* (*ship*) galera *f*; (*ship's kitchen*) cocina *f* **~ (proof)** *n* galerada *f*

gallivant /'gælɪvænt/ *vi* 🔲 callejear

gallon /'gælən/ *n* galón *m* (*imperial = 4,546l; Amer = 3,785l*)

gallop /'gæləp/ *n* galope *m*. ● *vi* (*pt* **galloped**) galopar

gallows /'gæləʊz/ *n* horca *f*

galore /gə'lɔː(r)/ *adj* en abundancia

galvanize /'gælvənaɪz/ *vt* galvanizar

gambl|e /'gæmbl/ *vi* jugar. **~e on** contar con. ● *vt* jugarse. ● *n* (*venture*) empresa *f* arriesgada; (*bet*) apuesta *f*; (*risk*) riesgo *m*. **~er** *n* jugador *m*. **~ing** *n* juego *m*

game /geɪm/ *n* juego *m*; (*match*) partido *m*; (*animals, birds*) caza *f*. ● *adj* valiente. **~ for** listo para. **~keeper** *n* guardabosque *m*. **~s** *n* (*in school*) deportes *mpl*

gammon /'gæmən/ *n* jamón *m* fresco

gamut /'gæmət/ *n* gama *f*

gander /'gændə(r)/ *n* ganso *m*

gang /gæŋ/ *n* pandilla *f*; (*of workmen*) equipo *m*. **~master** *n* contratista de mano de obra indocumentada. □ **~ up** *vi* unirse (**on** contra)

gangling /'gæŋglɪŋ/ *adj* larguirucho

gangrene /'gæŋgriːn/ *n* gangrena *f*

gangster /'gæŋstə(r)/ *n* bandido *m*, gángster *m & f*

gangway /'gæŋweɪ/ *n* pasillo *m*; (*of ship*) pasarela *f*

gaol /dʒeɪl/ *n* cárcel *f*. **~er** *n* carcelero *m*

gap /gæp/ *n* espacio *m*; (*in fence, hedge*) hueco *m*; (*in time*) intervalo *m*; (*in knowledge*) laguna *f*; (*difference*) diferencia *f*

---

gap year En Gran Bretaña, es el periodo, entre el final de los estudios secundarios y el ingreso a la universidad, que muchos estudiantes destinan a obtener experiencia laboral relacionada con sus futuras carreras. Otros emprenden actividades no relacionadas con los estudios y para algunos es la oportunidad para ahorrar dinero o viajar.

i

g

---

gap|e /geɪp/ *vi* quedarse boquiabierto; (*be wide open*) estar muy abierto. **~ing** *adj* abierto; (*person*) boquiabierto

garage /'gærɑːʒ/ *n* garaje *m*, garage *m* (*LAm*), cochera *f* (*Mex*); (*petrol station*) gasolinera *f*; (*for repairs, sales*) taller *m*, garage *m* (*LAm*)

garbage /'gɑːbɪdʒ/ *n* basura *f*. **~ can** *n* (*Amer*) cubo *m* de la basura, bote *m* de la basura (*Mex*). **~ collector, ~ man** *n* (*Amer*) basurero *m*

garble /'gɑːbl/ *vt* tergiversar, embrollar

garden /'gɑːdn/ *n* (*of flowers*) jardín *m*; (*of vegetables/fruit*) huerto *m*. ● *vi* trabajar en el jardín. **~er** /'gɑːdnə(r)/ *n* jardinero *m*. **~ing** *n* jardinería *f*; (*vegetable growing*) horticultura *f*

gargle /'gɑːgl/ *vi* hacer gárgaras

gargoyle /'gɑːgɔɪl/ *n* gárgola *f*

garish /'geərɪʃ/ *adj* chillón

garland /'ɡɑːlənd/ n guirnalda f

garlic /'ɡɑːlɪk/ n ajo m

garment /'ɡɑːmənt/ n prenda f (de vestir)

garnish /'ɡɑːnɪʃ/ vt adornar, decorar. ● n adorno m

garret /'ɡærət/ n buhardilla f

garrison /'ɡærɪsn/ n guarnición f

garrulous /'ɡærələs/ adj hablador

garter /'ɡɑːtə(r)/ n liga f

gas /ɡæs/ n (pl gases) gas m; (anaesthetic) anestésico m; (Amer, petrol) gasolina f ● vt (pt gassed) asfixiar con gas

gash /ɡæʃ/ n tajo m. ● vt hacer un tajo de

gasket /'ɡæskɪt/ n junta f

gas: ∼ mask n careta f antigás. **∼ meter** n contador m de gas

gasoline /'ɡæsəliːn/ n (Amer) gasolina f

gasp /ɡɑːsp/ vi jadear; (with surprise) dar un grito ahogado. ● n exclamación f, grito m

gas: ∼ ring n hornillo m de gas. **∼ station** n (Amer) gasolinera f

gastric /'ɡæstrɪk/ adj gástrico

gate /ɡeɪt/ n puerta f; (of metal) verja f; (barrier) barrera f

gate: ∼crash vt colarse en. **∼crasher** n intruso m (que ha entrado sin ser invitado). **∼way** n puerta f

gather /'ɡæðə(r)/ vt reunir (people, things); (accumulate) acumular; (pick up) recoger, recoger (flowers); (fig, infer) deducir; (sewing) fruncir. ∼ speed acelerar. ● vi (people) reunirse; (things) acumularse. ∼ing n reunión f

gaudy /'ɡɔːdɪ/ adj (-ier, -iest) chillón

gauge /ɡeɪdʒ/ n (measurement) medida f; (Rail) entrevía f; (instrument) indicador m. ● vt medir; (fig) estimar

gaunt /ɡɔːnt/ adj descarnado; (from illness) demacrado

gauntlet /'ɡɔːntlɪt/ n. **run the ∼** of aguantar el acoso de

gauze /ɡɔːz/ n gasa f

gave /ɡeɪv/ see GIVE

gawky /'ɡɔːkɪ/ adj (-ier, -iest) torpe

gawp /ɡɔːp/ vi. **∼ at** mirar como un tonto

gay /ɡeɪ/ adj (-er, -est) (fam, homosexual) homosexual, gay ⊤; (dated, joyful) alegre

gaze /ɡeɪz/ vi. **∼ (at)** mirar (fijamente). ● n mirada f (fija)

gazelle /ɡə'zel/ n (pl invar or -s) gacela f

GB abbr see **GREAT BRITAIN**

gear /ɡɪə(r)/ n equipo m; (Tec) engranaje m; (Auto) marcha f, cambio m. **in ∼** engranado. **out of ∼** desengranado. **change ∼, shift ∼** (Amer) cambiar de marcha. ● vt adaptar. **∼box** n (Auto) caja f de cambios

geese /ɡiːs/ see GOOSE

gel /dʒel/ n gel m

gelatine /'dʒelətiːn/ n gelatina f

gelignite /'dʒelɪɡnaɪt/ n gelignita f

gem /dʒem/ n piedra f preciosa

Gemini /'dʒemɪnaɪ/ n Géminis mpl

gender /'dʒendə(r)/ n género m

gene /dʒiːn/ n gen m, gene m

genealogy /dʒiːnɪ'ælədʒɪ/ n genealogía f

general /'dʒenərəl/ adj general. ● n general m. **in ∼** en general. **∼ election** n elecciones fpl generales. **∼ization** /-'zeɪʃn/ n generalización f

f. ~**ize** vt/i generalizar. ~ **know-ledge** n cultura f general. ~**ly** adv generalmente. ~ **practitioner** n médico m de cabecera

generat|e /'dʒenəreɪt/ vt generar. ~**ion** /-'reɪʃn/ n generación f. ~**ion gap** n brecha f generacional. ~**or** n generador m

genero|sity /dʒenə'rɒsəti/ n generosidad f. ~**us** /'dʒenərəs/ adj generoso; (plentiful) abundante

genetic /dʒɪ'netɪk/ adj genético. ~**s** n genética f.

Geneva /dʒɪ'niːvə/ n Ginebra f

genial /'dʒiːnɪəl/ adj simpático, afable

genital /'dʒenɪtl/ adj genital. ~**s** npl genitales mpl

genitive /'dʒenɪtɪv/ adj & n genitivo (m)

genius /'dʒiːnɪəs/ n (pl -uses) genio m

genocide /'dʒenəsaɪd/ n genocidio m

genome /'dʒiːnəʊm/ n genoma m

genre /ʒɑːnʳ/ n género m

gent /dʒent/ n 🔲 señor m. ~**s** n aseo m de caballeros

genteel /dʒen'tiːl/ adj distinguido

gentl|e /'dʒentl/ adj (-er, -est) (person) dulce; (murmur, breeze) suave; (hint) discreto. ~**eman** n señor m; (well-bred) caballero m. ~**eness** n amabilidad f

genuine /'dʒenjʊɪn/ adj verdadero; (person) sincero

geograph|er /dʒɪ'ɒɡrəfə(r)/ n geógrafo m. ~**ical** /dʒɪə'ɡræfɪkl/ adj geográfico. ~**y** /dʒɪ'ɒɡrəfɪ/ n geografía f

geolog|ical /dʒɪə'lɒdʒɪkl/ adj geológico. ~**ist** /dʒɪ'ɒlədʒɪst/ n geólogo m. ~**y** /dʒɪ'ɒlədʒɪ/ n geología f

geometr|ic(al) /dʒɪə'metrɪk(l)/ adj geométrico. ~**y** /dʒɪ'ɒmətrɪ/ n geometría f

geranium /dʒə'reɪnɪəm/ n geranio m

geriatric /dʒerɪ'ætrɪk/ adj (patient) anciano; (ward) de geriatría. ~**s** n geriatría f

germ /dʒɜːm/ n microbio m, germen m

German /'dʒɜːmən/ adj & n alemán (m). ~**ic** /dʒɜː'mænɪk/ adj germánico. ~ **measles** n rubéola f. ~**y** n Alemania f

germinate /'dʒɜːmɪneɪt/ vi germinar

gesticulate /dʒe'stɪkjʊleɪt/ vi hacer ademanes, gesticular

gesture /'dʒestʃə(r)/ n gesto m, ademán m; (fig) gesto m. ● vi hacer gestos

---

get /ɡet/

past **got**; past participle **got, gotten** (Amer); present participle **getting**

● transitive verb

····▶ (obtain) conseguir, obtener. did you get the job? ¿conseguiste el trabajo?

····▶ (buy) comprar. I got it in the sales lo compré en las rebajas

····▶ (achieve, win) sacar. she got very good marks sacó muy buenas notas

····▶ (receive) recibir. I got a letter from Alex recibí una carta de Alex

····▶ (fetch) ir a buscar. ~ your coat vete a buscar tu abrigo

····▸ (*experience*) llevarse. **I got a terrible shock** me llevé un shock espantoso

····▸ (*fam, understand*) entender. **I don't ~ what you mean** no entiendo lo que quieres decir

····▸ (*ask or persuade*) **to ~ s.o. to do sth** hacer que uno haga algo

> Note that *hacer que* is followed by the subjunctive form of the verb

····▸ (*cause to be done or happen*) **I must ~ this watch fixed** tengo que llevar a arreglar este reloj. **they got the roof mended** hicieron arreglar el techo

● *intransitive verb*

····▸ (*arrive, reach*) llegar. **I got there late** llegué tarde. **how do you ~ to Paddington?** ¿cómo se llega a Paddington?

····▸ (*become*) **to ~ tired** cansarse. **she got very angry** se puso furiosa. **it's ~ting late** se está haciendo tarde

➡ For translations of expressions such as **get better**, **get old** see **better**, **old** etc. See also **got**

····▸ **to get to do sth** (*manage to*) llegar a. **did you ~ to see him?** ¿llegaste a verlo? □ **get along** *vi* (*manage*) arreglárselas; (*progress*) hacer progresos. □ **get along with** *vt* llevarse bien con. □ **get at** *vt* (*reach*) llegar a; (*imply*) querer decir. □ **get away** *vi* salir; (*escape*) escaparse. □ **get back** *vi*

volver. *vt* (*recover*) recobrar. □ **get by** *vi* (*manage*) arreglárselas; (*pass*) pasar. □ **get down** *vi* bajar. *vt* (*make depressed*) deprimir. □ **get in** *vi* entrar. □ **get into** *vt* entrar en; subir a (car). □ **get off** *vt* bajar(se) de (train etc). *vi* (*from train etc*) bajarse; (*Jurid*) salir absuelto. □ **get on** *vi* (*progress*) hacer progresos; (*succeed*) tener éxito. *vt* subirse a (train etc). □ **get on with** *vt* (*be on good terms with*) llevarse bien con; (*continue*) seguir con. □ **get out** *vi* salir. *vt* (*take out*) sacar. □ **get out of** *vt* (*fig*) librarse de. □ **get over** *vt* reponerse de (illness). □ **get round** *vt* soslayar (difficulty etc); engatusar (person). □ **get through** *vi* pasar; (*on phone*) comunicarse (to con). □ **get together** *vi* (*meet up*) reunirse. *vt* (*assemble*) reunir. □ **get up** *vi* levantarse; (*climb*) subir

geyser /ˈgiːzə(r)/ *n* géiser *m*

ghastly /ˈgɑːstlɪ/ *adj* (**-ier, -iest**) horrible

gherkin /ˈgɜːkɪn/ *n* pepinillo *m*

ghetto /ˈgetəʊ/ *n* (*pl* **-os**) gueto *m*

ghost /ɡəʊst/ *n* fantasma *m*. **~ly** *adj* espectral

giant /ˈdʒaɪənt/ *n* gigante *m*. ● *adj* gigantesco

gibberish /ˈdʒɪbərɪʃ/ *n* jerigonza *f*

gibe /dʒaɪb/ *n* pulla *f*

giblets /ˈdʒɪblɪts/ *npl* menudillos *mpl*

giddiness /ˈgɪdɪnɪs/ *n* vértigo *m*. **~y** *adj* (**-ier, -iest**) mareado. **be/feel ~y** estar/sentirse mareado

gift /gɪft/ *n* regalo *m*; (*ability*) don

m. ~**ed** *adj* dotado de talento.
~-**wrap** *vt* envolver para regalo

gigantic /dʒaɪˈɡæntɪk/ *adj* gigantesco.

giggle /ˈɡɪɡl/ *vi* reírse tontamente.
●*n* risita *f*

gild /ɡɪld/ *vt* dorar

gills /ɡɪlz/ *npl* agallas *fpl*

gilt /ɡɪlt/ *n* dorado *m.* ●*adj* dorado

gimmick /ˈɡɪmɪk/ *n* truco *m*

gin /dʒɪn/ *n* ginebra *f*

ginger /ˈdʒɪndʒə(r)/ *n* jengibre *m.*
●*adj* rojizo. **he has** ~ **hair** es pelirrojo. ~**bread** *n* pan *m* de jengibre

gipsy /ˈdʒɪpsɪ/ *n* gitano *m*

giraffe /dʒɪˈrɑːf/ *n* jirafa *f*

girder /ˈɡɜːdə(r)/ *n* viga *f*

girdle /ˈɡɜːdl/ *n* (belt) cinturón *m*;
(corset) corsé *m*

girl /ɡɜːl/ *n* chica *f*, muchacha *f*;
(child) niña *f.* ~ **band** *n* grupo *m*
pop de chicas. ~**friend** *n* amiga *f*;
(of boy) novia *f.* ~**ish** *adj* de niña;
(boy) afeminado. ~ **scout** *n* (Amer)
exploradora *f*, guía *f*

giro /ˈdʒaɪrəʊ/ *n* (pl -os) giro *m*
(bancario)

girth /ɡɜːθ/ *n* circunferencia *f*

gist /dʒɪst/ *n* lo esencial

give /ɡɪv/ *vt* (pt gave, pp given)
dar; (deliver) entregar; regalar
(present); prestar (aid, attention).
~ **o.s. to** darse a. ●*vi* dar; (yield)
ceder; (stretch) dar de sí. ●*n* elasticidad *f.* □ ~ **away** *vt* regalar; revelar (secret). □ ~ **back** *vt* devolver.
□ ~ **in** *vi* ceder. □ ~ **off** *vt* emitir.
□ ~ **out** *vt* distribuir. (become used
up) agotarse. □ ~ **up** *vt* renunciar
a; (yield) ceder. ~ **up doing sth**
dejar de hacer algo. ~ **o.s. up** entregarse (**to** a). *vi* rendirse. ~**n**
/ˈɡɪvn/ see **GIVE.** ●*adj* dado. ~**n**
name *n* nombre *m* de pila

glacier /ˈɡlæsɪə(r)/ *n* glaciar *m*

glad /ɡlæd/ *adj* contento. **be** ~
alegrarse (**about** de). ~**den** *vt* alegrar

gladly /ˈɡlædlɪ/ *adv* alegremente;
(willingly) con mucho gusto

glamo|rous /ˈɡlæmərəs/ *adj* glamoroso. ~**ur** /ˈɡlæmə(r)/ *n* glamour *m*

glance /ɡlɑːns/ *n* ojeada *f.* ●*vi.* ~
at dar un vistazo a

gland /ɡlænd/ *n* glándula *f*

glar|e /ɡleə(r)/ *vi* (light) deslumbrar; (stare angrily) mirar airadamente. ●*n* resplandor *m*; (stare)
mirada *f* airada. ~**ing** *adj* deslumbrante; (obvious) manifiesto

glass /ɡlɑːs/ *n* (material) cristal *m*,
vidrio *m*; (without stem or for wine)
vaso *m*; (with stem) copa *f*; (for
beer) caña *f*; (mirror) espejo *m.*
~**es** *npl* (spectacles) gafas *fpl*, lentes
fpl (LAm), anteojos *mpl* (LAm). ~**y** *adj*
vítreo

glaze /ɡleɪz/ *vt* poner cristal(es) or
vidrio(s) a (windows, doors); vidriar
(pottery). ●*vi.* ~ (**over**) (eyes) vidriarse. ●*n* barniz *m*; (for pottery)
esmalte *m*

gleam /ɡliːm/ *n* destello *m.* ●*vi*
destellar

glean /ɡliːn/ *vt* espigar; recoger
(information)

glee /ɡliː/ *n* regocijo *m*

glib /ɡlɪb/ *adj* de mucha labia;
(reply) fácil

glide /ɡlaɪd/ *vi* deslizarse; (plane)
planear. ~**er** *n* planeador *m.* ~**ing**
n planeo *m*

glimmer /ˈɡlɪmə(r)/ *n* destello *m.*
●*vi* destellar

glimpse /ɡlɪmps/ *n.* **catch a** ~ **of**
vislumbrar, ver brevemente. ●*vt*
vislumbrar

g

glint /glɪnt/ n destello m. ● vi destellar

glisten /ˈglɪsn/ vi brillar

glitter /ˈglɪtə(r)/ vi brillar. ● n brillo m

gloat /gləʊt/ vi. ~ on/over regodearse sobre

glob|al /ˈgləʊbl/ adj (worldwide) mundial; (all-embracing) global. ~alization n globalización f. ~al warming n calentamiento m global. ~e /gləʊb/ n globo m

gloom /gluːm/ n oscuridad f; (sadness, fig) tristeza f. ~y adj (-ier, -iest) triste; (pessimistic) pesimista

glor|ify /ˈglɔːrɪfaɪ/ vt glorificar. ~ious /ˈglɔːrɪəs/ adj espléndido; (deed, hero etc) glorioso. ~y /ˈglɔːrɪ/ n gloria f

gloss /glɒs/ n lustre m. ~ (paint) (pintura f al or de) esmalte m. ◻ ~ over vt (make light of) minimizar; (cover up) encubrir

glossary /ˈglɒsərɪ/ n glosario m

glossy /ˈglɒsɪ/ adj brillante

glove /glʌv/ n guante m. ~ compartment n (Auto) guantera f

glow /gləʊ/ vi brillar. ● n brillo m. ~ing /ˈgləʊɪŋ/ adj incandescente; (account) entusiasta; (complexion) rojo

glucose /ˈgluːkəʊs/ n glucosa f

glue /gluː/ n cola f, goma f de pegar. ● vt (pres p gluing) pegar

glum /glʌm/ adj (glummer, glummest) triste

glutton /ˈglʌtn/ n glotón m

gnarled /nɑːld/ adj nudoso

gnash /næʃ/ vt. ~ one's teeth rechinar los dientes

gnat /næt/ n jején m, mosquito m

gnaw /nɔː/ vt roer. ● vi. ~ at roer

gnome /nəʊm/ n gnomo m

---

go /gəʊ/

3rd pers sing present **goes**; past **went**; past participle **gone**

● intransitive verb

····▸ ir. I'm going to France voy a Francia. to go shopping ir de compras. to go swimming ir a nadar

····▸ (leave) irse. we're going on Friday nos vamos el viernes

····▸ (work, function) (engine, clock) funcionar

····▸ (become) irse. to go deaf quedarse sordo. to go mad volverse loco. his face went red se puso colorado

····▸ (stop) (headache, pain) irse (+ me/te/le). the pain's gone se me ha ido el dolor

····▸ (turn out, progress) ir. everything's going very well todo va muy bien. how did the exam go? ¿qué tal te fue en el examen?

····▸ (match, suit) combinar. the jacket and the trousers go well together la chaqueta y los pantalones combinan bien.

····▸ (cease to function) (bulb, fuse) fundirse. the brakes have gone los frenos no funcionan

● auxiliary verb to be going to + infinitive ir a + infinitivo. it's going to rain va a llover. she's going to win! ¡va a ganar!

● noun (pl goes)

····▸ (turn) turno m. you have three goes tienes tres turnos. it's your go te toca a ti

····▸ (attempt) to have a go at

doing sth intentar hacer algo. have another go inténtalo de nuevo

····▸ (*energy, drive*) empuje *m*. she has a lot of go tiene mucho empuje

····▸ (*in phrases*) I've been on the go all day no he parado en todo el día. to make a go of sth sacar algo adelante *etc.* □ **go across** *vt/vi* cruzar. □ **go after** *vi* perseguir. □ **go away** *vi* irse. □ **go back** *vi* volver. □ **go back on** *vt* faltar a (a promise etc). □ **go by** *vi* pasar. □ **go down** *vi* bajar; (*sun*) ponerse. □ **go for** *vt* (*fam, attack*) atacar. □ **go in** *vi* entrar. □ **go in for** *vt* presentarse para (exam); participar en (competition). □ **go off** *vi* (*leave*) irse; (*go bad*) pasarse; (*explode*) estallar; (*lights*) apagarse. □ **go on** *vi* seguir; (*happen*) pasar; (*be switched on*) encenderse, prenderse (*LAm*). □ **go out** *vi* salir; (*fire, light*) apagarse. □ **go over** *vt* (*check*) revisar; (*revise*) repasar. □ **go through** *vt* pasar por; (*search*) registrar; (*check*) examinar. □ **go up** *vt/vi* subir. □ **go without** *vt* pasar sin

goad /ɡəʊd/ *vt* aguijonear

go-ahead /ˈɡəʊəhed/ *n* luz *f* verde. ●*adj* dinámico

goal /ɡəʊl/ *n* (*Sport*) gol *m*; (*objective*) meta *f*. ~**ie** /ˈɡəʊlɪ/ *n* 🔲, ~**keeper** *n* portero *m*, arquero *m* (*LAm*). ~**post** *n* poste *m* de la portería, poste *m* del arco (*LAm*)

goat /ɡəʊt/ *n* cabra *f*

gobble /ˈɡɒbl/ *vt* engullir

goblin /ˈɡɒblɪn/ *n* duende *m*

god /ɡɒd/ *n* dios *m*. **G~** *n* Dios *m*. ~**child** *n* ahijado *m*. ~**-daughter** *n* ahijada *f*. ~**dess** /ˈɡɒdes/ *n* diosa *f*. ~**father** *n* padrino *m*. ~**forsaken** *adj* olvidado de Dios. ~**mother** *n* madrina *f*. ~**send** *n* beneficio *m* inesperado. ~**son** *n* ahijado *m*

going /ˈɡəʊɪŋ/ *n* camino *m*; (*racing*) (estado *m* del) terreno *m*. it is slow/hard ~ es lento/difícil. ●*adj* (price) actual; (concern) en funcionamiento

gold /ɡəʊld/ *n* oro *m*. ●*adj* de oro. ~**en** *adj* de oro; (*in colour*) dorado; (opportunity) único. ~**en wedding** *n* bodas *fpl* de oro. ~**fish** *n invar* pez *m* de colores. ~**mine** *n* mina *f* de oro; (*fig*) fuente *f* de gran riqueza. ~**-plated** /-ˈpleɪtɪd/ *adj* chapado en oro. ~**smith** *n* orfebre *m*

golf /ɡɒlf/ *n* golf *m*. ~ **ball** *n* pelota *f* de golf. ~ **club** *n* palo *m* de golf; (*place*) club *m* de golf. ~**course** *n* campo *m* de golf. ~**er** *n* jugador *m* de golf

gondola /ˈɡɒndələ/ *n* góndola *f*

gone /ɡɒn/ *see* **GO**. ●*adj* pasado. ~ six o'clock después de las seis

gong /ɡɒŋ/ *n* gong(o) *m*

good /ɡʊd/ *adj* (**better**, **best**) bueno, (*before masculine singular noun*) buen. ~ **afternoon** *n* buenas tardes. ~ **evening** (*before dark*) buenas tardes; (*after dark*) buenas noches. ~ **morning** buenos días. ~ **night** buenas noches. as ~ as (*almost*) casi. have a ~ time divertirse. have a ~ time divertirse. a ~ bien *m*. for ~ para siempre. it is no ~ shouting es inútil gritar etc. ~**bye** /-ˈbaɪ/ *int* ¡adiós! ●*n* adiós *m*. say ~bye to despedirse de. ~**-for-nothing** /-fənʌθɪŋ/ *adj* & *n* inútil (*m*). **G~ Friday** *n* Viernes *m* Santo. ~**-looking**

/·'lʊkɪŋ/ adj guapo, buen mozo m (LAm), buena moza f (LAm). **~ness** n bondad f. **~ness!**, **~ness** gracious!, **~ness me!**, my **~ness!** ¡Dios mío! **~s** npl mercancías fpl. **~will** /-'wɪl/ n buena voluntad f. **~y** n (Culin, fam) golosina f; (in film) bueno m

gooey /'guːɪ/ adj (**gooier, gooiest**) ▣ pegajoso; (fig) sentimental

goofy /'guːfɪ/ adj (Amer) necio

google (®) /'guːgl/ vt, vi ▣ googlear ▣

goose /guːs/ n (pl **geese**) oca f, ganso m. **~berry** /'gʊzbərɪ/ n uva f espina, grosella f espinosa. **~flesh** n, **~pimples** npl carne f de gallina

gore /gɔː(r)/ n sangre f. ● vt cornear

gorge /gɔːdʒ/ n (of river) garganta f. ● vt. ~ o.s. hartarse (on de)

gorgeous /'gɔːdʒəs/ adj precioso; (splendid) magnífico

gorilla /gə'rɪlə/ n gorila m

gorse /gɔːs/ n aulaga f

gory /'gɔːrɪ/ adj (**-ier, -iest**) ▣ sangriento

gosh /gɒʃ/ int ¡caramba!

go-slow /gəʊ'sləʊ/ n huelga f de celo, huelga f pasiva

gospel /'gɒspl/ n evangelio m

gossip /'gɒsɪp/ n (chatter) chismorreo m; (person) chismoso m. ● vi (pt **gossiped**) (chatter) chismorrear; (repeat scandal) contar chismes

got /gɒt/ see **GET**. have ~ tener. I've ~ to do it tengo que hacerlo.

gotten /'gɒtn/ see **GET**

gouge /gaʊdʒ/ vt abrir (hole). □ ~ out vt sacar

gourmet /'gʊəmeɪ/ n gastrónomo m

govern /'gʌvən/ vt/i gobernar.

~ess n institutriz f. **~ment** n gobierno m. **~or** n gobernador m

gown /gaʊn/ n vestido m; (of judge, teacher) toga f

GP abbr see **GENERAL PRACTITIONER**

GPS abbrev **Global Positioning System** GPS m

grab /græb/ vt (pt **grabbed**) agarrar

grace /greɪs/ n gracia f. **~ful** adj elegante

gracious /'greɪʃəs/ adj (kind) amable; (elegant) elegante

grade /greɪd/ n clase f, categoría f; (of goods) clase f, calidad f; (on scale) grado m; (school mark) nota f; (Amer, class) curso m, año m

gradient /'greɪdɪənt/ n pendiente f, gradiente f (LAm)

gradual /'grædʒʊəl/ adj gradual. **~ly** adv gradualmente, poco a poco

graduat|e /'grædjʊət/ n (Univ) licenciado. ● /'grædjʊeɪt/ vi licenciarse. **~ion** /-'eɪʃn/ n graduación f

graffiti /grə'fiːtɪ/ npl graffiti mpl, pintadas fpl

graft /grɑːft/ n (Med, Bot) injerto m; (Amer fam, bribery) chanchullos mpl. ● vt injertar

grain /greɪn/ n grano m

gram /græm/ n gramo m

gramma|r /'græmə(r)/ n gramática f. **~tical** /grə'mætɪkl/ adj gramatical

gramme /græm/ n gramo m

grand /grænd/ adj (**-er, -est**) magnífico; (fam, excellent) estupendo. **~child** /n nieto m. **~daughter** /n nieta f. **~eur** /'grændʒə(r)/ n grandiosidad f. **~father** n abuelo m. **~father clock** n reloj m de caja. **~iose** /'grændɪəʊs/ adj grandioso;

~**mother** n abuela f. ~**parents** npl abuelos mpl. ~ **piano** n piano m de cola. ~**son** n nieto m. ~**stand** /'grænstænd/ n tribuna f

granite /'grænɪt/ n granito m

granny /'grænɪ/ n ⊞ abuela f

grant /grɑːnt/ vt conceder; (give) donar; (admit) admitir (that que). **take for** ~**ed** dar por sentado. ● n concesión f; (Univ) beca f

granule /'grænuːl/ n gránulo m

grape /greɪp/ n uva f. ~**fruit** n invar pomelo m, toronja f (LAm)

graph /grɑːf/ n gráfica f

graphic /'græfɪk/ adj gráfico. ~**s** npl diseño m gráfico; (Comp) gráficos mpl

grapple /'græpl/ vi. ~ **with** forcejear con; (mentally) lidiar con

grasp /grɑːsp/ vt agarrar. ● n (hold) agarro m; (fig) comprensión f. ~**ing** adj avaro

grass /grɑːs/ n hierba f. ~**hopper** n saltamontes m. ~ **roots** npl base f popular. ● adj de las bases. ~**y** adj cubierto de hierba

grate /greɪt/ n rejilla f; (fireplace) chimenea f. ● vt rallar. ● vi rechinar; (be irritating) ser crispante

grateful /'greɪtfl/ adj agradecido. ~**ly** adv con gratitud

grater /'greɪtə(r)/ n rallador m

grati|fied /'grætɪfaɪd/ adj contento. ~**y** /'grætɪfaɪ/ vt satisfacer; (please) agradar a. ~**ying** adj agradable

grating /'greɪtɪŋ/ n reja f

gratitude /'grætɪtjuːd/ n gratitud f

gratuitous /grə'tjuːɪtəs/ adj gratuito

gratuity /grə'tjuːətɪ/ n (tip) propina f

grave /greɪv/ n sepultura f. ● adj (-er, -est) (serious) grave

gravel /'grævl/ n grava f

gravely /'greɪvlɪ/ adv (seriously) seriamente; (solemnly) con gravedad

grave: ~**stone** n lápida f. ~**yard** n cementerio m

gravitate /'grævɪteɪt/ vi gravitar

gravity /'grævətɪ/ n gravedad f

gravy /'greɪvɪ/ n salsa f

gray /greɪ/ adj & n (Amer) see GREY

graze /greɪz/ vi (eat) pacer. ● vt (touch) rozar; (scrape) raspar. ● n rasguño m

greas|e /griːs/ n grasa f. ● vt engrasar. ~**eproof paper** n papel m encerado or de cera. ~**y** adj (hands) grasiento; (food) graso; (hair, skin) graso, grasoso (LAm)

great /greɪt/ adj (-er, -est) grande, (before singular noun) gran; (fam, very good) estupendo. G~ **Britain** n Gran Bretaña f. ~**grandfather** /-'grænfɑːðə(r)/ n bisabuelo m. ~**grandmother** /-'grænmʌðə(r)/ n bisabuela f. ~**ly** adv (very) muy; (much) mucho

Greece /griːs/ n Grecia f

greed /griːd/ n avaricia f; (for food) glotonería f. ~**y** adj avaro; (for food) glotón

Greek /griːk/ adj & n griego (m)

green /griːn/ adj (-er, -est) verde. ● n verde m; (grass) césped m. ~ **belt** n zona f verde. ~ **card** n (Amer) permiso m de residencia y trabajo. ~**ery** n verdor m. ~**gage** /-geɪdʒ/ n claudia f. ~**grocer** n verdulero m. ~**house** n invernadero m. **the** ~**house effect** el efecto invernadero. ~ **light** n luz f verde. ~**s** npl verduras fpl

g

Green Card En EE.UU., documento oficial que toda persona que no sea ciudadana norteamericana debe obtener para residir y trabajar en este país. En el Reino Unido, es el documento que se debe obtener de la compañía de seguros, cuando se lleva un automóvil al extranjero, a fin de que siga vigente la cobertura de la póliza. *i*

greet /griːt/ vt saludar; (receive) recibir. ~**ing** n saludo m

gregarious /grɪˈɡeərɪəs/ adj gregario; (person) sociable

grenade /grɪˈneɪd/ n granada f

grew /gruː/ see **GROW**

grey /greɪ/ adj (-er, -est) gris. have ~ **hair** ser canoso. ●n gris m. ~**hound** n galgo m

grid /grɪd/ n reja f; (Elec, network) red f; (on map) cuadriculado m

grief /griːf/ n dolor m. **come to** ~ (person) acabar mal; (fail) fracasar

grievance /ˈgriːvns/ n queja f formal

grieve /griːv/ vt apenar. ●vi afligirse. ~ **for** llorar

grievous /ˈgriːvəs/ adj doloroso; (serious) grave. ~ **bodily harm** (Jurid) lesiones fpl (corporales) graves

grill /grɪl/ n parrilla f. ●vt asar a la parrilla; (Ⅱ, interrogate) interrogar

grille /grɪl/ n rejilla f

grim /grɪm/ adj (grimmer, grimmest) severo

grimace /ˈgrɪməs/ n mueca f. ●vi hacer muecas

grim|e /graɪm/ n mugre f. ~**y** adj mugriento

grin /grɪn/ vt (pt grinned) sonreír. ●n sonrisa f (abierta)

grind /graɪnd/ vt (pt ground) moler (coffee, corn etc); (pulverize) pulverizar; (sharpen) afilar; (Amer) picar, moler (meat)

grip /grɪp/ vt (pt gripped) agarrar; (interest) captar. ●n agarro m; (hold) apretón m; (strength of hand) apretón m; (hairgrip) horquilla f, pasador m (Mex). **come to** ~**s with** entender (subject)

grisly /ˈgrɪzlɪ/ adj (-ier, -iest) horrible

gristle /ˈgrɪsl/ n cartílago m

grit /grɪt/ n arenilla f; (fig) agallas fpl. ●vt (pt gritted) echar arena en (road). ~ **one's teeth** (fig) acorazarse

groan /grəʊn/ vi gemir. ●n gemido m

grocer /ˈgrəʊsə(r)/ n tendero m, abarrotero m (Mex). ~**ies** npl comestibles mpl. ~**y** n tienda f de comestibles, tienda f de abarrotes (Mex)

groggy /ˈgrɒgɪ/ adj (weak) débil; (unsteady) inseguro; (ill) malucho

groin /grɔɪn/ n ingle f

groom /gruːm/ n mozo m de caballos; (bridegroom) novio m. ●vt almohazar (horses); (fig) preparar

groove /gruːv/ n ranura f; (in record) surco m

grope /grəʊp/ vi (find one's way) moverse a tientas. ~ **for** buscar a tientas

gross /grəʊs/ adj (-er, -est) (coarse) grosero; (Com) bruto; (fat) grueso; (flagrant) flagrante. ●n invar gruesa f. ~**ly** adv (very) enormemente

grotesque /grəʊˈtesk/ adj grotesco

ground /graʊnd/ see **GRIND**. ●n suelo m; (area) terreno m; (reason) razón f; (Amer, Elec) toma f de tierra. ● vt fundar (theory); retirar de servicio (aircraft). **~s** npl jardines mpl; (sediment) poso m. **~ beef** n (Amer) carne f picada, carne f molida. **~ cloth** n (Amer) see **~SHEET. ~ floor** n planta f baja. **~ing** n base f, conocimientos mpl (in de). **~less** adj infundado. **~sheet** n suelo m impermeable (de una tienda de campaña). **~work** n trabajo m preparatorio

group /gruːp/ n grupo m. ● vt agrupar. ● vi agruparse

grouse /graʊs/ n invar (bird) urogallo m. ● vi 🔟 rezongar

grovel /ˈgrɒvl/ vi (pt grovelled) postrarse; (fig) arrastrarse

grow /grəʊ/ vi (pt grew, pp grown) crecer; (become) volverse, ponerse. ● vt cultivar. **~ a beard** dejarse (crecer) la barba. □ **~ up** vi hacerse mayor. **~ing** adj (quantity) cada vez mayor; (influence) creciente

growl /graʊl/ vi gruñir. ● n gruñido m

grown /grəʊn/ see GROW. ● adj adulto. **~-up** adj & n adulto (m)

growth /grəʊθ/ n crecimiento m; (increase) aumento m; (development) desarrollo m; (Med) bulto m, tumor m

grub /grʌb/ n (larva) larva f; (fam, food) comida f

grubby /ˈgrʌbɪ/ adj (-ier, -iest) mugriento

grudge /grʌdʒ/ vt see BEGRUDGE. ● n rencilla f. **bear/have a ~ against s.o.** guardarle rencor a uno. **~ingly** adv de mala gana

gruelling /ˈgruːəlɪŋ/ adj agotador

gruesome /ˈgruːsəm/ adj horrible

gruff /grʌf/ adj (-er, -est) (manners) brusco; (voice) ronco

grumble /ˈgrʌmbl/ vi rezongar

grumpy /ˈgrʌmpɪ/ adj (-ier, -iest) malhumorado

grunt /grʌnt/ vi gruñir. ● n gruñido m

guarant|ee /ˌgærənˈtiː/ n garantía f. ● vt garantizar. **~or** n garante m & f

guard /gɑːd/ vt proteger; (watch) vigilar. ● n (vigilance, Mil group) guardia f; (person) guardia m; (on train) jefe m de tren. □ **~ against** vt evitar; protegerse contra (risk). **~ed** adj cauteloso. **~ian** /-ɪən/ n guardián m; (of orphan) tutor m

Guatemala /gwɑːtəˈmɑːlə/ n Guatemala f. **~n** adj & n guatemalteco (m)

guer(r)illa /gəˈrɪlə/ n guerrillero m. **~ warfare** n guerrilla f

guess /ges/ vt/i adivinar; (suppose) suponer. ● n conjetura f. **~work** n conjeturas fpl

guest /gest/ n invitado m; (in hotel) huésped m. **~house** n casa f de huéspedes

guffaw /gʌˈfɔː/ n carcajada f. ● vi reírse a carcajadas

guidance /ˈgaɪdəns/ n (advice) consejos mpl; (information) información f

guide /gaɪd/ n (person) guía m & f; (book) guía f. **Girl G~** exploradora f, guía f. ● vt guiar. **~book** n guía f. **~ dog** n perro m guía, perro m lazarillo. **~d missile** n proyectil m teledirigido. **~lines** npl pauta f

guild /gɪld/ n gremio m

guile /gaɪl/ n astucia f

guillotine /ˈgɪlətiːn/ n guillotina f

guilt /gɪlt/ n culpa f; (Jurid) culpabilidad f. **~y** adj culpable

guinea pig /ˈgɪnɪ/ n conejillo m

g

de Indias, cobaya f

guitar /gɪˈtɑː(r)/ n guitarra f. **~ist** n guitarrista m & f

gulf /ɡʌlf/ n (part of sea) golfo m; (gap) abismo m

gull /ɡʌl/ n gaviota f

gullet /ˈɡʌlɪt/ n garganta f, gaznate m 🔲

gullible /ˈɡʌləbl/ adj crédulo

gully /ˈɡʌlɪ/ n (ravine) barranco m

gulp /ɡʌlp/ vt. ▢ **~ (down)** tragarse de prisa. ● vi tragar saliva. ● n trago m

gum /ɡʌm/ n (in mouth) encía f; (glue) goma f de pegar; (for chewing) chicle m. ● vt (pt gummed) engomar

gun /ɡʌn/ n (pistol) pistola f; (rifle) fusil m, escopeta f; (artillery piece) cañón m. ● vt (pt gunned) ▢ **~ down** vt abatir a tiros. **~fire** n tiros mpl

gun: ~man /-mən/ n pistolero m, gatillero m (Mex). **~powder** n pólvora f. **~shot** n disparo m

gurgle /ˈɡɜːɡl/ vi (liquid) gorgotear; (baby) gorjear

gush /ɡʌʃ/ vi. **~ (out)** salir a borbotones. ● n (of liquid) chorro m; (fig) torrente m

gusset /ˈɡʌsɪt/ n entretela f

gust /ɡʌst/ n ráfaga f

gusto /ˈɡʌstəʊ/ n entusiasmo m

gusty /ˈɡʌstɪ/ adj borrascoso

gut /ɡʌt/ n intestino m. ● vt (pt gutted) destripar; (fire) destruir. **~s** npl tripas fpl; (fam, courage) agallas fpl

gutter /ˈɡʌtə(r)/ n (on roof) canalón m, canaleta f; (in street) cuneta f; (fig, slum) arroyo m

guttural /ˈɡʌtərəl/ adj gutural

guy /ɡaɪ/ n (fam, man) tipo m 🔲

tío m 🔲

guzzle /ˈɡʌzl/ vt (drink) chupar 🔲; (eat) tragarse

gym /dʒɪm/ n 🔲 (gymnasium) gimnasio m; (gymnastics) gimnasia f

gymnasium /dʒɪmˈneɪzɪəm/ n gimnasio m

gymnast /ˈdʒɪmnæst/ n gimnasta m & f. **~ics** /dʒɪmˈnæstɪks/ npl gimnasia f

gymslip /ˈdʒɪmslɪp/ n túnica f (de gimnasia)

gynaecolog|ist /ˌɡaɪnɪˈkɒlədʒɪst/ n ginecólogo m. **~y** n ginecología f

gypsy /ˈdʒɪpsɪ/ n gitano m

gyrate /dʒaɪəˈreɪt/ vi girar

Hh

haberdashery /ˈhæbədæʃərɪ/ n mercería f; (Amer, clothes) ropa f y accesorios mpl para caballeros

habit /ˈhæbɪt/ n costumbre f; (Relig, costume) hábito m. **be in the ~ of** (+ gerund) tener la costumbre de (+ infinitivo), soler (+ infinitivo). **get into the ~ of** (+ gerund) acostumbrarse a (+ infinitivo)

habitable /ˈhæbɪtəbl/ adj habitable

habitat /ˈhæbɪtæt/ n hábitat m

habitation /ˌhæbɪˈteɪʃn/ n habitación f

habitual /həˈbɪtjʊəl/ adj habitual; (liar) inveterado. **~ly** adv de costumbre

hack /hæk/ n (old horse) jamelgo

m; (writer) escritorzuelo *m*. ● *vt* cortar. ~**er** *n* (Comp) pirata *m* informático

hackneyed /'hæknɪd/ adj manido

had /hæd/ see HAVE

haddock /'hædək/ *n* invar eglefino *m*

haemorrhage /'hemərɪdʒ/ *n* hemorragia *f*

haemorrhoids /'hemərɔɪdz/ *npl* hemorroides *fpl*

hag /hæg/ *n* bruja *f*

haggard /'hægəd/ adj demacrado

hail /heɪl/ *n* granizo *m*. ● *vi* granizar. ● *vt* (greet) saludar; llamar (taxi). □ ~ **from** *vt* venir de. ~**stone** *n* grano *m* de granizo

hair /heə(r)/ *n* pelo *m*. ~**band** *n* cinta *f*, banda *f* (Mex). ~**brush** *n* cepillo *m* (para el pelo). ~**cut** *n* corte *m* de pelo. **have a** ~**cut** cortarse el pelo. ~**do** *n* 🔟 peinado *m*. ~**dresser** *n* peluquero *m*. ~**dresser's (shop)** *n* peluquería *f*. ~**dryer** *n* secador *m*, secadora *f* (Mex). ~**grip** *n* horquilla *f*, pasador *m* (Mex). ~**pin** *n* horquilla *f*. ~**pin bend** *n* curva *f* cerrada. ~**raising** adj espeluznante. ~**spray** *n* laca *f*, fijador *m* (para el pelo). ~**style** *n* peinado *m*. ~**y** adj (-ier, -iest) peludo

half /hɑːf/ *n* (pl halves) mitad *f*. ● adj medio. ~ **a dozen** media docena *f*. ~ **an hour** media hora *f*. ● adv medio, a medias. ~**hearted** /-'hɑːtɪd/ adj poco entusiasta. ~**-mast** /-'mɑːst/ *n*. **at** ~**-mast** a media asta. ~ **term** *n* vacaciones *fpl* de medio trimestre. ~**-time** *n* (Sport) descanso *m*, medio tiempo *m* (LAm). ~**way** adj medio. ● adv a medio camino

hall /hɔːl/ *n* (entrance) vestíbulo *m*;

(for public events) sala *f*, salón *m*. ~ **of residence** residencia *f* universitaria, colegio *m* mayor. ~**mark** /-mɑːk/ *n* (on gold, silver) contraste *m*; (fig) sello *m* (distintivo)

hallo /hə'ləʊ/ int see HELLO

Hallowe'en /hæləʊ'iːn/ *n* víspera *f* de Todos los Santos

hallucination /həluːsɪ'neɪʃn/ *n* alucinación *f*

halo /'heɪləʊ/ *n* (pl -oes) aureola *f*

halt /hɔːlt/ *n*. **come to a** ~ pararse. ● *vt* parar. ● *vi* pararse

halve /hɑːv/ *vt* reducir a la mitad; (divide into halves) partir por la mitad

halves /hɑːvz/ see HALF

ham /hæm/ *n* jamón *m*

hamburger /'hæmbɜːgə(r)/ *n* hamburguesa *f*

hammer /'hæmə(r)/ *n* martillo *m*. ● *vt* martill(e)ar

hammock /'hæmək/ *n* hamaca *f*

hamper /'hæmpə(r)/ *n* cesta *f*. ● *vt* estorbar

hamster /'hæmstə(r)/ *n* hámster *m*

hand /hænd/ *n* mano *f*; (of clock, watch) manecilla *f*; (worker) obrero *m*. **by** ~ a mano. **lend a** ~ echar una mano. **on** ~ a mano. **on the one** ~... **on the other** ~ por un lado... por otro. **out of** ~ fuera de control. **to** ~ a mano. ● *vt* pasar. □ ~ **down** *vt* pasar. □ ~ **in** *vt* entregar. □ ~ **over** *vt* entregar. □ ~ **out** *vt* distribuir. ~**bag** *n* bolso *m*, cartera *f* (LAm), bolsa *f* (Mex). ~**brake** *n* (in car) freno *m* de mano. ~**cuffs** *npl* esposas *fpl*. ~**ful** *n* puñado *m*; (fam, person) persona *f* difícil

handicap /'hændɪkæp/ *n* desventaja *f*; (Sport) hándicap *m*. ~**ped** adj minusválido

handicraft /'hændɪkrɑːft/ n artesanía f

handkerchief /'hæŋkətʃɪf/ n (pl -fs or -chieves /-'tʃiːvz/) pañuelo m

handle /'hændl/ n (of door) picaporte m; (of drawer) tirador m; (of implement) mango m; (of cup, bag, jug) asa f. • vt manejar; (touch) tocar. **~bars** npl manillar m, manubrio m (LAm).

h- **handsome** /'hænsəm/ adj (good-looking) guapo, buen mozo, buena moza (LAm); (generous) generoso

handwriting /'hændraɪtɪŋ/ n letra f

handy /'hændɪ/ adj (-ier, -iest) (useful) práctico; (person) diestro; (near) a mano. come in ~ venir muy bien. **~man** n hombre m habilidoso

hang /hæŋ/ vt (pt hung) colgar; (pt hanged) (capital punishment) ahorcar. • vi colgar; (clothing) caer. • n. get the ~ of sth coger el truco de algo. □ **~ about**. □ **~ around** vi holgazanear. □ **~ on** vi (wait) esperar. □ **~ out** vt tender (washing). □ **~ up** vi (also telephone) colgar

hangar /'hæŋə(r)/ n hangar m

hang: **~er** n (for clothes) percha f. **~glider** n tabla f delta, deslizador m (Mex). **~over** (after drinking) resaca f. **~up** n 🆃 complejo m

hankie, hanky /'hæŋkɪ/ n 🆃 pañuelo m

haphazard /hæp'hæzəd/ adj fortuito. **~ly** adv al azar

happen /'hæpən/ vi pasar, suce-

der, ocurrir. if he ~s to come si acaso viene. **~ing** n acontecimiento m

happ|ily /'hæpɪlɪ/ adv alegremente; (fortunately) afortunadamente. **~iness** n felicidad f. **~y** adj (-ier, -iest) feliz; (satisfied) contento

harass /'hærəs/ vt acosar. **~ment** n acoso m

harbour /'hɑːbə(r)/ n puerto m

hard /hɑːd/ adj (-er, -est) duro; (difficult) difícil. • adv (work) mucho; (pull) con fuerza. ~ done by tratado injustamente. **~boiled egg** /-'bɔɪld/ n huevo m duro. **~disk** n disco m duro. **~en** vt endurecer. • vi endurecerse. **~headed** /-'hedɪd/ adj realista

hardly /'hɑːdlɪ/ adv apenas. ~ ever casi nunca

hard: **~ness** n dureza f. **~ship** n apuro m. **~ shoulder** n arcén m, acotamiento m (Mex). **~ware** n /-weə(r)/ ferretería f; (Comp) hardware m. **~ware store** n (Amer) ferretería f. **~working** /-'wɜːkɪŋ/ adj trabajador

hardy /'hɑːdɪ/ adj (-ier, -iest) fuerte; (plants) resistente

hare /heə(r)/ n liebre f

hark /hɑːk/ vi escuchar. □ **~ back to** vt volver a

harm /hɑːm/ n daño m. there is no ~ in asking con preguntar no se pierde nada. • vt hacer daño a (person); dañar (thing); perjudicar (interests). **~ful** adj perjudicial. **~less** adj inofensivo

harmonica /hɑː'mɒnɪkə/ n armónica f

harmon|ious /hɑː'məʊnɪəs/ adj armonioso. **~y** /'hɑːmənɪ/ n armonía f

harness /'hɑːnɪs/ n arnés m. ●vt poner el arnés a (horse); (fig) aprovechar

harp /hɑːp/ n arpa f. ●vi. ~ on (about) machacar (con)

harpoon /hɑː'puːn/ n arpón m

harpsichord /'hɑːpsɪkɔːd/ n clavicémbalo m, clave m

harrowing /'hærəʊɪŋ/ adj desgarrador

harsh /hɑːʃ/ adj (-er, -est) duro, severo; (light) fuerte; (climate) riguroso. ~ly adv severamente. ~ness n severidad f

harvest /'hɑːvɪst/ n cosecha f. ●vt cosechar

has /hæz/ see HAVE

hassle /'hæsl/ n 🄲 lío m 🄲, rollo m 🄲. ●vt (harass) fastidiar

hast|e /heɪst/ n prisa f, apuro m (LAm). make ~e darse prisa. ~ily /'heɪstɪlɪ/ adv de prisa. ~y /'heɪstɪ/ adj (-ier, -iest) rápido; (rash) precipitado

hat /hæt/ n sombrero m

hatch /hætʃ/ n (for food) ventanilla f; (Naut) escotilla f. ●vt empollar (eggs); tramar (plot). ●vi salir del cascarón. ~back n coche m con tres/cinco puertas; (door) puerta f trasera

hatchet /'hætʃɪt/ n hacha f

hat|e /heɪt/ n odio m. ●vt odiar. ~eful adj odioso. ~red /'heɪtrɪd/ n odio m

haughty /'hɔːtɪ/ adj (-ier, -iest) altivo

haul /hɔːl/ vt arrastrar; transportar (goods). ●n (catch) redada f; (stolen goods) botín m; (journey) recorrido m. ~age /-ɪdʒ/ n transporte m. ~er n (Amer), ~ier n transportista m & f

haunt /hɔːnt/ vt frecuentar; (ghost) rondar. ●n sitio m preferido. ~ed adj (house) embrujado; (look) angustiado

---

have /hæv/həv, əv/

3rd person singular present **has,** past **had**

● *transitive verb*

····▸ tener. I ~ three sisters tengo tres hermanas. do you ~ a credit card? ¿tiene una tarjeta de crédito?

····▸ (in requests) can I ~ a kilo of apples, please? ¿me da un kilo de manzanas, por favor?

····▸ (eat) comer. I had a pizza comí una pizza

····▸ (drink) tomar. come and ~ a drink ven a tomar una copa

····▸ (smoke) fumar (cigarette)

····▸ (hold, organize) hacer (party, meeting)

····▸ (get, receive) I had a letter from Tony yesterday recibí una carta de Tony ayer. we've had no news of her no hemos tenido noticias suyas

····▸ (illness) tener (flu, headache). to ~ a cold estar resfriado, tener catarro

····▸ to have sth done: we had it painted hicimos pintar. I had my hair cut me corté el pelo

····▸ to have it in for s.o. tenerle manía a uno

● *auxiliary verb*

····▸ haber. I've seen her already ya la he visto, ya la vi (LAm)

····▸ to have just done sth acabar de hacer algo. I've just

seen her acabo de verla

····> **to have to do sth** tener que hacer algo. **I ~ to** or **I've got to go to the bank** tengo que ir al banco

····> (in tag questions) **you've met her, ~n't you?** ya la conoces, ¿no? or ¿verdad? or ¿no es cierto?

····> (in short answers) **you've forgotten something - have I?** has olvidado algo - ¿sí?

haven /'heɪvn/ n puerto m; (refuge) refugio m

haversack /'hævəsæk/ n mochila f

havoc /'hævək/ n estragos mpl

hawk /hɔːk/ n halcón m

hawthorn /'hɔːθɔːn/ n espino m

hay /heɪ/ n heno m. **~ fever** n fiebre f del heno. **~stack** n almiar m. **~wire** adj. **go ~wire** (plans) desorganizarse; (machine) estropearse

hazard /'hæzəd/ n riesgo m. **~ous** adj arriesgado

haze /heɪz/ n neblina f

hazel /'heɪzl/ n avellano m. **~nut** n avellana f

hazy /'heɪzɪ/ adj (-ier, -iest) nebuloso

he /hiː/ pron él

head /hed/ n cabeza f; (of family, government) jefe m; (of organization) director m; (of beer) espuma f. **~s or tails** cara o cruz. ● adj principal. ● vt encabezar, cabecear (ball). □ **~ for** vt dirigirse a. **~ache** n dolor m de cabeza. **~er** n (football) cabezazo m. **~first** /-'fɜːst/ adv de cabeza. **~ing** n título m, encabezamiento m. **~lamp** n faro m, foco m (LAm). **~land** /-lənd/ n promontorio m. **~line** n

titular m. **the news ~lines** el resumen informativo. **~long** adv de cabeza; (precipitately) precipitadamente. **~master** n director m. **~mistress** /-'vn/ adj & adv de frente. **~phones** npl auriculares mpl, cascos mpl. **~quarters** /-'kwɔːtəz/ n (of business) oficina f central; (Mil) cuartel m general. **~strong** adj testarudo. **~teacher** /-'tiːtʃə(r)/ n director m. **~y** adj (-ier, -iest) (scent) embriagador

heal /hiːl/ vt curar. ● vi cicatrizarse

health /helθ/ n salud f. **~y** adj sano

heap /hiːp/ n montón m. ● vt amontonar.

hear /hɪə(r)/ vt/i (pt heard /hɜːd/) oír. **~, ~!** ¡bravo! **~ about** oír hablar de. **~ from** recibir noticias de. **~ing** n oído m; (Jurid) vista f. **~ing-aid** n audífono m. **~say** n rumores mpl

hearse /hɜːs/ n coche m fúnebre

heart /hɑːt/ n corazón m. **at ~** en el fondo. **by ~** de memoria. **lose ~** descorazonarse. **~ache** n congoja f. **~ attack** n ataque m al corazón, infarto m. **~break** n congoja f. **~breaking** adj desgarrador. **~burn** n ardor m de estómago. **~felt** adj sincero

hearth /hɑːθ/ n hogar m

heart: ~ily adv de buena gana. **~less** adj cruel. **~y** adj (welcome) caluroso; (meal) abundante

heat /hiːt/ n calor m; (contest) (prueba f) eliminatoria f. ● vt calentar. ● vi calentarse. **~ed** adj (fig) acalorado. **~er** n calentador m

heath /hiːθ/ n brezal m, monte m

heathen /'hiːðn/ n & a pagano m.

heather /'heðə(r)/ n brezo m

heat: ∼ing n calefacción f. ∼stroke n insolación f. ∼wave n ola f de calor

heave /hi:v/ vt (lift) levantar; exhalar (sigh); (fam, throw) tirar. ● vi (pull) tirar, jalar (LAm); (🔲, retch) dar arcadas

heaven /'hevn/ n cielo m. ∼ly adj celestial; (astronomy) celeste; (fam, excellent) divino

heav|ily /'hevɪlɪ/ adv pesadamente; (smoke, drink) mucho. ∼y adj (-ier, -iest) pesado; (rain) fuerte; (traffic) denso. ∼yweight n peso m pesado

heckle /'hekl/ vt interrumpir

hectic /'hektɪk/ adj febril

he'd /hi:d/ = he had, he would

hedge /hedʒ/ n seto m (vivo). ● vi escaparse por la tangente. ∼hog n erizo m

heed /hi:d/ vt hacer caso de. ● n. take ∼ tener cuidado

heel /hi:l/ n talón m.; (of shoe) tacón m

hefty /'heftɪ/ adj (-ier, -iest) (sturdy) fuerte; (heavy) pesado

heifer /'hefə(r)/ n novilla f

height /haɪt/ n altura f.; (of person) estatura f.; (of fame, glory) cumbre f. ∼en vt elevar; (fig) aumentar

heir /eə(r)/ n heredero m. ∼ess n heredera f. ∼loom n reliquia f heredada

held /held/ see HOLD

helicopter /'helɪkɒptə(r)/ n helicóptero m

hell /hel/ n infierno m

he'll /hi:l/ = he will

hello /hə'ləʊ/ int ¡hola!; (Telephone, caller) ¡oiga!, ¡bueno! (Mex); (Telephone, person answering) ¡dígal, ¡bueno! (Mex). say ∼ to saludar

helm /helm/ n (Naut) timón m

helmet /'helmɪt/ n casco m

help /help/ vt/i ayudar. he cannot ∼ laughing no puede menos de reír. ∼ o.s. to servirse. it cannot be ∼ed no hay más remedio. ● n ayuda f. ● int ¡socorro! ∼er n ayudante m. ∼ful adj útil; (person) amable. ∼ing n porción f. ∼less adj (unable to manage) incapaz; (defenceless) indefenso

hem /hem/ n dobladillo m

hemisphere /'hemɪsfɪə(r)/ n hemisferio m

hen /hen/ n (chicken) gallina f.; (female bird) hembra f

hence /hens/ adv de aquí. ∼forth adv de ahora en adelante

henpecked /'henpekt/ adj dominado por su mujer

her /hɜː(r)/ pron (direct object) la; (indirect object) le; (after prep) ella. I know ∼ la conozco. ● adj su, sus pl

herb /hɜːb/ n hierba f. ∼al adj de hierbas

herd /hɜːd/ n (of cattle, pigs) manada f; (of goats) rebaño m. ● vt arrear. ∼ together reunir

here /hɪə(r)/ adv aquí, acá (esp LAm). ∼! (take this) ¡tenga! ∼abouts /-ə'baʊts/ adv por aquí. ∼after /-'ɑːftə(r)/ adv en el futuro. ∼by /-'baɪ/ adv por este medio

hereditary /hɪ'redɪtərɪ/ adj hereditario

here|sy /'herəsɪ/ n herejía f. ∼tic n hereje m & f

herewith /hɪə'wɪθ/ adv adjunto

heritage /'herɪtɪdʒ/ n herencia f.; (fig) patrimonio m. ∼ tourism n turismo m cultural, turismo m patrimonial (LAm)

hermetically /hɜː'metɪklɪ/ adv. ∼ sealed herméticamente cerrado

hermit /'hɜːmɪt/ n ermitaño m, eremita m

hernia /'hɜːnɪə/ n hernia f

hero /'hɪərəʊ/ n (pl -oes) héroe m. **~ic** /hɪ'rəʊɪk/ adj heroico

heroin /'herəʊɪn/ n heroína f

hero|**ine** /'herəʊɪn/ n heroína f. **~ism** /'herəʊɪzm/ n heroísmo m

heron /'herən/ n garza f (real)

herring /'herɪŋ/ n arenque m

hers /hɜːz/ poss pron (el) suyo m, (la) suya f, (los) suyos mpl, (las) suyas fpl

herself /hɜː'self/ pron ella misma; (reflexive) se; (after prep) sí misma

he's /hiːz/ = **he is**, **he has**

hesit|**ant** /'hezɪtənt/ adj vacilante. **~ate** /-teɪt/ vi vacilar. **~ation** /-'teɪʃn/ n vacilación f

heterosexual /hetərəʊ'seksjuəl/ adj & n heterosexual (m & f)

het up /het'ʌp/ adj 🛇 nervioso

hew /hjuː/ vt (pp hewed or hewn) cortar; (cut into shape) tallar

hexagon /'heksəgən/ n hexágono m. **~al** /-'ægənl/ adj hexagonal

hey /heɪ/ int ¡eh!; (expressing dismay, protest) ¡oye!

heyday /'heɪdeɪ/ n apogeo m

hi /haɪ/ int ¡hola!

hibernat|**e** /'haɪbəneɪt/ vi hibernar. **~ion** /-'neɪʃn/ n hibernación f

hiccough, hiccup /'hɪkʌp/ n hipo m. **have (the) ~s** tener hipo. • vi hipar

hide /haɪd/ vt (pt hid, pp hidden) esconder. • vi esconderse. • n piel f; (tanned) cuero m. **~-and-seek** /'haɪdnsiːk/ n. **play ~-and-seek** jugar al escondite, jugar a las escondidas (LAm)

hideous /'hɪdɪəs/ adj (dreadful) horrible; (ugly) feo

hideout /'haɪdaʊt/ n escondrijo m

hiding /'haɪdɪŋ/ n (🛇, thrashing) paliza f. **go into ~** esconderse. **~ place** n escondite m, escondrijo m

hierarchy /'haɪərɑːkɪ/ n jerarquía f

hieroglyphics /haɪərə'glɪfɪks/ n jeroglíficos mpl

hi-fi /'haɪfaɪ/ adj de alta fidelidad. • n equipo m de alta fidelidad, hi-fi m

high /haɪ/ adj (-er, -est) alto; (ideals) elevado; (wind) fuerte; (fam, drugged) drogado, colocado 🛇; (voice) agudo; (meat) pasado. • n alto nivel m. **a (new) ~** un récord. • adv alto. **~er education** n enseñanza f superior. **~-handed** /-'hændɪd/ adj prepotente. **~ heels** npl zapatos mpl de tacón alto. **~lands** /-ləndz/ npl tierras fpl altas. **~-level** adj de alto nivel. **~light** n punto m culminante. • vt destacar; (Art) realzar. **~ly** adv muy; (paid) muy bien. **~ly strung** adj nervioso. **H~ness** n (title) alteza f. **~-rise** adj (building) alto. **~ school** n (Amer) instituto m, colegio m secundario. **~ street** n calle f principal. **~-strung** adj (Amer) nervioso. **~way** n carretera f

---

High School En EE.UU., el último ciclo del colegio secundario, generalmente para alumnos de edades comprendidas entre los 14 y los 18 años. En Gran Bretaña, algunos colegios secundarios también reciben el nombre de high schools. ⓘ

---

hijack /'haɪdʒæk/ vt secuestrar. • n secuestro m. **~er** n secuestrador

hike /haɪk/ n caminata f. • vi ir de

caminata. ~r n excursionista m & f

hilarious /hɪˈleərɪəs/ adj muy divertido

hill /hɪl/ n colina f; (slope) cuesta f. ~side n ladera f. ~y adj accidentado

hilt /hɪlt/ n (of sword) puño m. to the ~ (fig) totalmente

him /hɪm/ pron (direct object) lo, le (only Spain) (indirect object) le; (after prep) él. I know ~ lo/le conozco. ~self pron él mismo; (reflexive) se; (after prep) sí mismo

hind|er /ˈhɪndə(r)/ vt estorbar. ~rance /ˈhɪndrəns/ n obstáculo m

hindsight /ˈhaɪnsaɪt/ n. with ~ retrospectivamente

Hindu /ˈhɪnduː/ n & a hindú (m & f). ~ism n hinduismo m

hinge /hɪndʒ/ n bisagra f

hint /hɪnt/ n indirecta f; (advice) consejo m. • vi soltar una indirecta. ~ at dar a entender

hip /hɪp/ n cadera f

hippie /ˈhɪpɪ/ n hippy m & f

hippopotamus /hɪpəˈpɒtəməs/ n (pl -muses or -mi /-maɪ/) hipopótamo m

hire /ˈhaɪə(r)/ vt alquilar (thing); contratar (person). • n alquiler m. ~ car n alquiler m de coches. ~ purchase n compra f a plazos

his /hɪz/ adj su, sus. • poss pron (el) suyo m, (la) suya f, (los) suyos mpl, (las) suyas fpl

Hispan|ic /hɪˈspænɪk/ adj hispánico. • n (Amer) hispano m. ~ist /ˈhɪspənɪst/ n hispanista m & f

hiss /hɪs/ n silbido. • vt/i silbar

histor|ian /hɪˈstɔːrɪən/ n historiador m. ~ic(al) /hɪˈstɒrɪk(l)/ adj histórico. ~y /ˈhɪstərɪ/ n historia f

hit /hɪt/ vt (pt hit, pres p hitting) golpear (object); pegarle a (per-

son); (collide with) chocar con; (affect) afectar. ~ it off with hacer buenas migas con. ▫ ~ on vt dar con. • n (blow) golpe m; (success) éxito m. (Internet) visita f

hitch /hɪtʃ/ vt (fasten) enganchar. • n (snag) problema m. ~ a lift, ~ a ride (Amer) see ~HIKE. ~hike vi hacer autostop, hacer dedo, ir de aventón (Mex). ~hiker n autoestopista m & f

hither /ˈhɪðə(r)/ adv aquí, acá. ~ and thither acá y allá. ~to adv hasta ahora

hit-or-miss /hɪtɔːˈmɪs/ adj (approach) poco científico

hive /haɪv/ n colmena f

hoard /hɔːd/ vt acumular. • n provisión f; (of money) tesoro m

hoarding /ˈhɔːdɪŋ/ n valla f publicitaria

hoarse /hɔːs/ adj (-er, -est) ronco. ~ly adv con voz ronca

hoax /həʊks/ n engaño m. • vt engañar

hob /hɒb/ n (of cooker) hornillos mpl, hornillas fpl (LAm)

hobble /ˈhɒbl/ vi cojear, renguear (LAm)

hobby /ˈhɒbɪ/ n pasatiempo m. ~horse n (toy) caballito m (de niño); (fixation) caballo m de batalla

hockey /ˈhɒkɪ/ n hockey m; (Amer) hockey m sobre hielo

hoe /həʊ/ n azada f. • vt (pres p hoeing) azadonar

hog /hɒg/ n (Amer) cerdo m. • vt (pt hogged) 🔲 acaparar

hoist /hɔɪst/ vt levantar; izar (flag). • n montacargas m

hold /həʊld/ vt (pt held) tener; (grasp) coger (esp Spain), agarrar; (contain) contener; mantener (interest); (believe) creer. ● vi mantenerse. ● n (influence) influencia f; (Naut, Aviat) bodega f. □ ~ **back** vt (contain) contener. □ ~ on vi (stand firm) resistir; (wait) esperar. □ ~ **on to** vt (keep) guardar; (cling to) agarrarse a. □ ~ **out** vt (offer) ofrecer. vi (resist) resistir. □ ~ **up** vt (raise) levantar; (support) sostener; (delay) retrasar; (rob) atracar. ~**all** n bolsa f (de viaje). ~**er** n tenedor m; (of post) titular m; (wallet) funda f. ~**up** atraco m

hole /həʊl/ n agujero m; (in ground) hoyo m; (in road) bache m. ● vt agujerear

holiday /'hɒlɪdeɪ/ n vacaciones fpl; (public) fiesta f. **go on** ~ ir de vacaciones. ~**maker** n veraneante m & f

holiness /'həʊlɪnɪs/ n santidad f

Holland /'hɒlənd/ n Holanda f

hollow /'hɒləʊ/ adj & n hueco (m)

holly /'hɒlɪ/ n acebo m

holocaust /'hɒləkɔːst/ n holocausto m

holster /'həʊlstə(r)/ n pistolera f

holy /'həʊlɪ/ adj (-ier, -iest) santo, sagrado. **H~ Ghost** n, **H~ Spirit** n Espíritu m Santo. ~ **water** n agua f bendita

homage /'hɒmɪdʒ/ n homenaje m. **pay** ~ **to** rendir homenaje a

home /həʊm/ n casa f; (for old people) residencia f de ancianos; (native land) patria f. ● adj (cooking) casero; (address) particular; (background) familiar; (Pol) interior; (match) de casa. ● adv. (at) ~ en casa. ~**land** n patria f. ~**land security** seguridad f nacional. ~**less** adj sin hogar. ~**ly** adj (-ier, -iest) casero; (Amer, ugly) feo. ~**-made**

adj hecho en casa. ~ **page** n (Comp) página f frontal. ~**sick** adj. **be** ~**sick** echar de menos a su familia/su país, extrañar a su familia/su país (LAm). ~ **town** n ciudad f natal. ~**work** n deberes mpl

homicide /'hɒmɪsaɪd/ n homicidio m

homoeopathic /həʊmɪəʊ'pæθɪk/ adj homeopático

homogeneous /hɒməʊ'dʒiːnɪəs/ adj homogéneo

homosexual /həʊməʊ'seksjʊəl/ adj & n homosexual (m)

honest /'ɒnɪst/ adj honrado; (frank) sincero. ~**ly** adv honradamente. ~**y** n honradez f

honey /'hʌnɪ/ n miel f. ~**comb** n panal m. ~**moon** n luna f de miel. ~**suckle** n madreselva f

honorary /'ɒnərərɪ/ adj honorario

honour /'ɒnə(r)/ n honor m. ● vt honrar; cumplir (con) (promise). ~**able** adj honorable

hood /hʊd/ n capucha f; (car roof) capota f; (Amer, car bonnet) capó m, capote m (Mex)

hoodwink /'hʊdwɪŋk/ vt engañar

hoof /huːf/ n (pl hoofs or hooves) (of horse) casco m, pezuña f (Mex); (of cow) pezuña f

hook /hʊk/ n gancho m; (on garment) corchete m; (for fishing) anzuelo m. **let s.o. off the** ~ dejar salir a uno del atolladero. **off the** ~ (telephone) descolgado. ● vt. ~**ed on** 🅳 adicto a. □ ~**up** vt enganchar. ~**ed** adj (tool) en forma de gancho; (nose) aguileño

hookey /'hʊkɪ/ n. **play** ~ (Amer fam) faltar a clase, hacer novillos

hooligan /'huːlɪɡən/ n vándalo m, gamberro m

hoop /hu:p/ n aro m

hooray /hʊˈreɪ/ int & n ¡viva! (m)

hoot /hu:t/ n (of horn) bocinazo m; (of owl) ululato m. ● vi tocar la bocina; (owl) ulular

Hoover /ˈhu:və(r)/ n (®) aspiradora f. ● vt pasar la aspiradora por, aspirar (LAm)

hooves /hu:vz/ see HOOF

hop /hɒp/ vi (pt hopped) saltar a la pata coja; (frog, rabbit) brincar, saltar; (bird) dar saltitos. ● n salto m; (flight) etapa f. ~(s) (plant) lúpulo m

hope /həʊp/ n esperanza f. ● vt/i esperar. ~ for esperar. ~ful adj (optimistic) esperanzado; (promising) esperanzador. ~fully adv con optimismo; (it is hoped) se espera. ~less adj desesperado

horde /hɔ:d/ n horda f

horizon /həˈraɪzn/ n horizonte m

horizontal /hɒrɪˈzɒntl/ adj horizontal. ~ly adv horizontalmente

hormone /ˈhɔ:məʊn/ n hormona f

horn /hɔ:n/ n cuerno m, asta f, cacho m (LAm); (of car) bocina f; (Mus) trompa f. ~ed adj con cuernos

hornet /ˈhɔ:nɪt/ n avispón m

horoscope /ˈhɒrəskəʊp/ n horóscopo m

horrible /ˈhɒrəbl/ adj horrible

horrid /ˈhɒrɪd/ adj horrible

horrific /həˈrɪfɪk/ adj horroroso

horrify /ˈhɒrɪfaɪ/ vt horrorizar

horror /ˈhɒrə(r)/ n horror m

hors-d'oeuvre /ɔ:ˈdɜ:vr/ n (pl -s /-ˈdɜ:vr/) entremés m, botana f (Mex)

horse /hɔ:s/ n caballo m. ~back n. on ~back a caballo. ~power n (unit) caballo m (de fuerza). ~ra-

cing n carreras fpl de caballos. ~shoe n herradura f

horticultural /ˌhɔ:tɪˈkʌltʃərəl/ adj hortícola. ~e /ˈhɔ:tɪkʌltʃə(r)/ n horticultura f

hose /həʊz/ n manguera f, manga f. ● vt. ~ down lavar (con manguera). ~pipe n manga f

hosiery /ˈhəʊziəri/ n calcetería f

hospice /ˈhɒspɪs/ n residencia f para enfermos desahuciados

hospitable /hɒˈspɪtəbl/ adj hospitalario

hospital /ˈhɒspɪtl/ n hospital m

hospitality /hɒspɪˈtæləti/ n hospitalidad f

host /həʊst/ n (master of house) anfitrión m; (Radio, TV) presentador m; (multitude) gran cantidad f; (Relig) hostia f

hostage /ˈhɒstɪdʒ/ n rehén m

hostel /ˈhɒstl/ n (for students) residencia f; (for homeless people) hogar m

hostess /ˈhəʊstɪs/ n anfitriona f

hostile /ˈhɒstaɪl/ adj hostil. ~ity /-ˈtɪləti/ n hostilidad f

hot /hɒt/ adj (hotter, hottest) caliente; (weather, day) caluroso; (climate) cálido; (Culin) picante; (news) de última hora. be/feel ~ tener calor. get ~ calentarse. it is ~ hace calor. ~bed n (fig) semillero m

hotchpotch /ˈhɒtʃpɒtʃ/ n mezcolanza f

hot dog n perrito m caliente

hotel /həʊˈtel/ n hotel m. ~ier /-ɪeɪ/ n hotelero m

hot: ~house n invernadero m. ~plate n placa f, hornilla f (LAm). ~-water bottle /-ˈwɔ:tə(r)/ n bolsa f de agua caliente

hound /haʊnd/ n perro m de caza.

• vt perseguir

hour /aʊə(r)/ n hora f. ~**ly** adj
(rate) por hora. • adv (every hour)
cada hora; (by the hour) por hora

house /haʊs/ n (pl -s /ˈhaʊzɪz/)
casa f; (Pol) cámara f. • /haʊz/ vt
alojar; (keep) guardar. ~**hold** n
casa f. ~**holder** n dueño m de una
casa. ~**keeper** n ama f de llaves.
~**maid** n criada f, mucama f (LAm).
~-**proud** adj meticuloso. ~**warm-
ing** (party) n fiesta de
inauguración de una casa. ~**wife**
n ama f de casa. ~**work** n tareas
fpl domésticas

housing /ˈhaʊzɪŋ/ n alojamiento
m. ~ **development** (Amer), ~ **estate** n complejo m habitacional, urbanización f

hovel /ˈhɒvl/ n casucha f

hover /ˈhɒvə(r)/ vi (bird, threat
etc) cernerse; (loiter) rondar.
~**craft** n (pl invar or -crafts) aerodeslizador m

how /haʊ/ adv cómo. ~ about a
walk? ¿qué te parece si damos un
paseo? ~ are you? ¿cómo está
Vd? ~ do you do? (in introduc-
tion) mucho gusto. ~ long? (in
time) ¿cuánto tiempo? ~ long is
the room? ¿cuánto mide de largo
el cuarto? ~ often? ¿cuántas
veces?

however /haʊˈevə(r)/ adv (nevertheless) no obstante, sin embargo;
(with verb) de cualquier manera
que (+ subjunctive); (with adjective or
adverb) por... que (+ subjunctive). ~
much it rains por mucho que
llueva

howl /haʊl/ n aullido. • vi aullar

hp abbr see HORSEPOWER

HP abbr see HIRE-PURCHASE

hub /hʌb/ n (of wheel) cubo m;

(fig) centro m

hubcap /ˈhʌbkæp/ n tapacubos m

huddle /ˈhʌdl/ vi apiñarse

hue /hju:/ n (colour) color m

huff /hʌf/ n. be in a ~ estar enfu-
rruñado

hug /hʌg/ vt (pt hugged) abrazar.
• n abrazo m

huge /hju:dʒ/ adj enorme. ~**ly** adv
enormemente

hulk /hʌlk/ n (of ship) barco m
viejo

hull /hʌl/ n (of ship) casco m

hullo /həˈləʊ/ int see HELLO

hum /hʌm/ vt/i (pt hummed) (person) canturrear; (insect, engine)
zumbar. • n zumbido m

human /ˈhju:mən/ adj & n humano
(m). ~ **being** n ser m humano. ~**e**
/hju:ˈmeɪn/ adj humano. ~**itarian**
/hju:mænɪˈteərɪən/ adj humanita-
rio. ~**ity** /hju:ˈmænətɪ/ n humanidad f

humbl|e /ˈhʌmbl/ adj (-er, -est)
humilde. • vt humillar. ~**y** adv hu-
mildemente

humdrum /ˈhʌmdrʌm/ adj monótono

humid /ˈhju:mɪd/ adj húmedo.
~**ity** /hju:ˈmɪdətɪ/ n humedad f

humiliat|e /hju:ˈmɪlɪeɪt/ vt humi-
llar. ~**ion** /-ˈeɪʃn/ n humillación f

humility /hju:ˈmɪlətɪ/ n humil-
dad f

humongous /hju:ˈmʌŋgəs/ adj
🅶 de primera

humo|rist /ˈhju:mərɪst/ n humo-
rista m & f. ~**rous** /-rəs/ adj humo-
rístico. ~**rously** adv con gracia.
~**ur** /ˈhju:mə(r)/ n humor m.
sense of ~ **ur** sentido m del humor

hump /hʌmp/ n (of person, camel)
joroba f; (in ground) montículo m

hunch /hʌntʃ/ vt encorvar. ● n presentimiento m; (lump) joroba f. ~**back** n jorobado m

hundred /'hʌndrəd/ adj ciento, (before noun) cien. one ~ **and** ninety-eight ciento noventa y ocho. two ~ doscientos. three ~ pages trescientas páginas. four ~ cuatrocientos. five ~ quinientos. ● n ciento m. ~**s of** centenares de. ~**th** adj & n centésimo (m). ~**weight** n 50,8kg; (Amer) 45,36kg

hung /hʌŋ/ see HANG

Hungar|ian /hʌŋ'geərɪən/ adj & n húngaro (m). ~**y** /'hʌŋgərɪ/ n Hungría f

hung|er /'hʌŋgə(r)/ n hambre f. ● vi. ~**er for** tener hambre de. ~**rily** /'hʌŋgrəlɪ/ adv ávidamente. ~**ry** adj (-ier, -iest) hambriento. be ~**ry** tener hambre

hunk /hʌŋk/ n (buen) pedazo m

hunt /hʌnt/ vt cazar. ● vi cazar. ~ **for** buscar. ● n caza f. ~**er** n cazador m. ~**ing** n caza f. go ~**ing** ir de caza

hurl /hɜːl/ vt lanzar

hurrah /hʊ'rɑː/, **hurray** /hʊ'reɪ/ int & n ¡viva! (m)

hurricane /'hʌrɪkən/ n huracán m

hurr|ied /'hʌrɪd/ adj apresurado. ~**iedly** adv apresuradamente. ~**y** vi darse prisa, apurarse (LAm). ● vt meter prisa a, apurar (LAm). ● n prisa f. be in a ~**y** tener prisa, estar apurado (LAm)

hurt /hɜːt/ vt (pt hurt) hacer daño a, lastimar (LAm). ~ **s.o.'s** feelings ofender a uno. ● vi doler. my head ~**s** me duele la cabeza. ~**ful** adj hiriente

hurtle /'hɜːtl/ vt ir volando. ● vi. ~ **along** mover rápidamente

husband /'hʌzbənd/ n marido m, esposo m

hush /hʌʃ/ vt acallar. ● n silencio m. □ ~ **up** vt acallar (affair). ~-**hush** adj 🄸 super secreto

husk /hʌsk/ n cáscara f

husky /'hʌskɪ/ adj (-ier, -iest) (hoarse) ronco

hustle /'hʌsl/ vt (jostle) empujar. ● vi (hurry) darse prisa, apurarse (LAm). ● n empuje m

hut /hʌt/ n cabaña f

hutch /hʌtʃ/ n conejera f

hybrid /'haɪbrɪd/ adj & n híbrido (m)

hydrangea /haɪ'dreɪndʒə/ n hortensia f

hydrant /'haɪdrənt/ n. (fire) ~ n boca f de riego, boca f de incendios (LAm)

hydraulic /haɪ'drɔːlɪk/ adj hidráulico

hydroelectric /haɪdrəʊɪ'lektrɪk/ adj hidroeléctrico

hydrofoil /'haɪdrəfɔɪl/ n hidrodeslizador m

hydrogen /'haɪdrədʒən/ n hidrógeno m

hyena /haɪ'iːnə/ n hiena f

hygien|e /'haɪdʒiːn/ n higiene f. ~**ic** /haɪ'dʒiːnɪk/ adj higiénico

hymn /hɪm/ n himno m

hyper... /'haɪpə(r)/ pref hiper...

hyphen /'haɪfn/ n guión m. ~**ate** /-eɪt/ vt escribir con guión

hypno|sis /hɪp'nəʊsɪs/ n hipnosis f. ~**tic** /-'nɒtɪk/ adj hipnótico. ~**tism** /'hɪpnətɪzəm/ n hipnotismo m. ~**tist** /'hɪpnətɪst/ n hipnotista m & f. ~**tize** /'hɪpnətaɪz/ vt hipnotizar

hypochondriac /haɪpə'kɒndrɪæk/ n hipocondríaco m

hypocri|sy /hɪ'pɒkrəsɪ/ n hipo-

h

cresía f. ~te /'hɪpəkrɪt/ n hipócrita m & f. ~tical /hɪpə'krɪtɪkl/ adj hipócrita

hypodermic /haɪpə'dɜːmɪk/ adj hipodérmico. ● n hipodérmica f

hypothe|sis /haɪ'pɒθəsɪs/ n (pl -theses/-siːz/) hipótesis f. ~tical /-ə'θetɪkl/ adj hipotético

hysteri|a /hɪ'stɪərɪə/ n histerismo m. ~cal /-'terɪkl/ adj histérico. ~cs /hɪ'sterɪks/ npl histerismo m. have ~cs ponerse histérico; (laugh) morir de risa

Ii

I /aɪ/ pron yo

ice /aɪs/ n hielo m. ● vt helar; glasear (cake). ● vi. ~ (up) helarse, congelarse. ~berg /-bɜːg/ n iceberg m. ~ box n (compartment) congelador; (Amer fam, refrigerator) frigorífico m, refrigerador m (LAm). ~cream n helado m. ~ cube n cubito m de hielo

Iceland /'aɪslənd/ n Islandia f

ice: ~ lolly polo m, paleta f helada (LAm). ~ rink n pista f de hielo. ~ skating n patinaje n sobre hielo

icicle /'aɪsɪkl/ n carámbano m

icing /'aɪsɪŋ/ n glaseado m

icon /'aɪkɒn/ n icono m

icy /'aɪsɪ/ adj (-ier, -iest) helado; (fig) glacial

I'd /aɪd/ = I had. I would

idea /aɪ'dɪə/ n idea f

ideal /aɪ'dɪəl/ adj & n ideal (m). ~ism n idealismo m. ~ist n idea-

lista m & f. ~istic /-'lɪstɪk/ adj idealista. ~ize vt idealizar. ~ly adv idealmente

identical /aɪ'dentɪkl/ adj idéntico. ~ twins npl gemelos mpl idénticos, gemelos mpl (LAm)

identif|ication /aɪdentɪfɪ'keɪʃn/ n identificación f. ~y /aɪ'dentɪfaɪ/ vt identificar. ● vi. ~y with identificarse con

identity /aɪ'dentɪtɪ/ n identidad f. ~ card n carné m de identidad. ~ theft n robo m de identidad

ideolog|ical /aɪdɪə'lɒdʒɪkl/ adj ideológico. ~y /aɪdɪ'ɒlədʒɪ/ n ideología f

idiocy /'ɪdɪəsɪ/ n idiotez f

idiom /'ɪdɪəm/ n locución f. ~atic /-'mætɪk/ adj idiomático

idiot /'ɪdɪət/ n idiota m & f. ~ic /-'ɒtɪk/ adj idiota

idle /'aɪdl/ adj (-er, -est) ocioso; (lazy) holgazán; (out of work) desocupado; (machine) parado. ● vi (engine) andar al ralentí. ~ness n ociosidad f; (laziness) holgazanería f

idol /'aɪdl/ n ídolo m. ~ize vt idolatrar

idyllic /ɪ'dɪlɪk/ adj idílico

i.e. abbr (= id est) es decir

if /ɪf/ conj si

igloo /'ɪgluː/ n iglú m

ignit|e /ɪg'naɪt/ vt encender. ● vi encenderse. ~ion /-'nɪʃn/ n ignición f; (Auto) encendido m. ~ion key n llave f de contacto

ignoramus /ɪgnə'reɪməs/ n (pl -muses) ignorante

ignoran|ce /'ɪgnərəns/ n ignorancia f. ~t adj ignorante

ignore /ɪg'nɔː(r)/ vt no hacer caso de; hacer caso omiso de (warning)

ill /ɪl/ adj enfermo. ● adv mal. ● n mal m

I'll /aɪl/ = **I will**

ill: **~-advised** /-əd'vaɪzd/ adj imprudente. **~ at ease** /-ət'i:z/ adj incómodo. **~-bred** /-'bred/ adj mal educado

illegal /ɪ'li:gl/ adj ilegal

illegible /ɪ'ledʒəbl/ adj ilegible

illegitima|cy /ɪlɪ'dʒɪtɪməsɪ/ n ilegitimidad f. **~te** /-ət/ adj ilegítimo

illitera|cy /ɪ'lɪtərəsɪ/ n analfabetismo m. **~te** /-ət/ adj analfabeto

illness /'ɪlnɪs/ n enfermedad f

illogical /ɪ'lɒdʒɪkl/ adj ilógico

illuminat|e /ɪ'lu:mɪneɪt/ vt iluminar. **~ion** /-'neɪʃn/ n iluminación f

illusion /ɪ'lu:ʒn/ n ilusión f. **~sory** /-sərɪ/ adj ilusorio

illustrat|e /'ɪləstreɪt/ vt ilustrar. **~ion** /-'streɪʃn/ n ilustración f; (example) ejemplo m

illustrious /ɪ'lʌstrɪəs/ adj ilustre

ill will /ɪl'wɪl/ n mala voluntad f

I'm /aɪm/ = **I am**

image /'ɪmɪdʒ/ n imagen f. **~ry** n imágenes fpl

imagin|able /ɪ'mædʒɪnəbl/ adj imaginable. **~ary** adj imaginario. **~ation** /-'neɪʃn/ n imaginación f. **~ative** adj imaginativo. **~e** /ɪ'mædʒɪn/ vt imaginar(se)

imbalance /ɪm'bæləns/ n desequilibrio m

imbecile /'ɪmbəsi:l/ n imbécil m & f

imitat|e /'ɪmɪteɪt/ vt imitar. **~ion** /-'teɪʃn/ n imitación f. ● adj de imitación. **~or** n imitador m

immaculate /ɪ'mækjʊlət/ adj inmaculado

immatur|e /ɪmə'tjʊə(r)/ adj inmaduro. **~ity** n inmadurez f

immediate /ɪ'mi:dɪət/ adj inmediato. **~ly** adv inmediatamente.

● conj en cuanto (+ subjunctive)

immens|e /ɪ'mens/ adj inmenso. **~ely** adv inmensamente; (fam, very much) muchísimo

immers|e /ɪ'mɜ:s/ vt sumergir. **~ion** /-ʃn/ n inmersión f. **~ion heater** n calentador m de inmersión

immigra|nt /'ɪmɪgrənt/ adj & n inmigrante (m & f). **~tion** /-'greɪʃn/ n inmigración f

imminent /'ɪmɪnənt/ adj inminente

immobil|e /ɪ'məʊbaɪl/ adj inmóvil. **~ize** /-bɪlaɪz/ vt inmovilizar. **~izer** /-bɪlaɪzə(r)/ n inmovilizador m

immoderate /ɪ'mɒdərət/ adj inmoderado

immodest /ɪ'mɒdɪst/ adj inmodesto

immoral /ɪ'mɒrəl/ adj inmoral. **~ity** /ɪmə'rælətɪ/ n inmoralidad f

immortal /ɪ'mɔ:tl/ adj inmortal. **~ity** /-'tælətɪ/ n inmortalidad f. **~ize** vt inmortalizar

immun|e /ɪ'mju:n/ adj inmune (to a). **~ity** n inmunidad f. **~ization** /ɪmjʊnaɪ'zeɪʃn/ n inmunización f. **~ize** /'ɪmjʊnaɪz/ vt inmunizar

imp /ɪmp/ n diablillo m

impact /'ɪmpækt/ n impacto m

impair /ɪm'peə(r)/ vt perjudicar

impale /ɪm'peɪl/ vt atravesar (on con)

impart /ɪm'pɑ:t/ vt comunicar (news); impartir (knowledge)

impartial /ɪm'pɑ:ʃl/ adj imparcial. **~ity** /-ɪ'ælətɪ/ n imparcialidad f

impassable /ɪm'pɑ:səbl/ adj (road) intransitable

impassive /ɪm'pæsɪv/ adj impasible

impatien|ce /ɪm'peɪʃəns/ n impaciencia f. ~t adj impaciente. get ~t impacientarse. ~tly adv con impaciencia

impeccable /ɪm'pekəbl/ adj impecable

impede /ɪm'piːd/ vt estorbar

impediment /ɪm'pedɪmənt/ obstáculo m. (speech) ~ n defecto m del habla

impending /ɪm'pendɪŋ/ adj inminente

impenetrable /ɪm'penɪtrəbl/ adj impenetrable

imperative /ɪm'perətɪv/ adj imprescindible. ● n (Gram) imperativo m

imperceptible /ɪmpə'septəbl/ adj imperceptible

imperfect /ɪm'pɜːfɪkt/ adj imperfecto. ~ion /ɪmpə'fekʃn/ n imperfección f

imperial /ɪm'pɪərɪəl/ adj imperial. ~ism n imperialismo m

impersonal /ɪm'pɜːsənl/ adj impersonal

impersonat|e /ɪm'pɜːsəneɪt/ vt hacerse pasar por; (mimic) imitar. ~ion /-'neɪʃn/ n imitación f. ~or n imitador m

impertinen|ce /ɪm'pɜːtɪnəns/ n impertinencia f. ~t adj impertinente

impervious /ɪm'pɜːvɪəs/ adj. ~ to impermeable a

impetuous /ɪm'petjʊəs/ adj impetuoso

impetus /'ɪmpɪtəs/ n ímpetu m

implacable /ɪm'plækəbl/ adj implacable

implant /ɪm'plɑːnt/ vt implantar

implement /'ɪmplɪmənt/ n instrumento m, implemento m (LAm). ● /'ɪmplɪment/ vt implementar

implementation /ɪmplɪmen'teɪʃn/ n implementación f

implicat|e /'ɪmplɪkeɪt/ vt implicar. ~ion /-'keɪʃn/ n implicación f

implicit /ɪm'plɪsɪt/ adj (implied) implícito; (unquestioning) absoluto

implore /ɪm'plɔː(r)/ vt implorar

imply /ɪm'plaɪ/ vt (involve) implicar; (insinuate) dar a entender, insinuar

impolite /ɪmpə'laɪt/ adj mal educado

import /ɪm'pɔːt/ vt importar.
● /'ɪmpɔːt/ n importación f; (item) artículo m de importación; (meaning) significación f

importan|ce /ɪm'pɔːtəns/ n importancia f. ~t adj importante

importer /ɪm'pɔːtə(r)/ n importador m

impos|e /ɪm'pəʊz/ vt imponer.
● vi. ~e on abusar de la amabilidad de. ~ing adj imponente. ~ition /ɪmpə'zɪʃn/ n imposición f; (fig) abuso m

impossib|ility /ɪmpɒsə'bɪlətɪ/ n imposibilidad f. ~le /ɪm'pɒsəbl/ adj imposible

impostor /ɪm'pɒstə(r)/ n impostor m

impoten|ce /'ɪmpətəns/ n impotencia f. ~t adj impotente

impound /ɪm'paʊnd/ vt confiscar

impoverished /ɪm'pɒvərɪʃt/ adj empobrecido

impractical /ɪm'præktɪkl/ adj poco práctico

impregnable /ɪm'pregnəbl/ adj inexpugnable

impregnate /'ɪmpregneɪt/ vt impregnar (with con, de)

impress /ɪm'pres/ vt impresionar; (make good impression) causar una buena impresión a. ● vi impresionar

impression /ɪmˈpreʃn/ n impresión f. **~able** adj impresionable. **~ism** n impresionismo m

impressive /ɪmˈpresɪv/ adj impresionante

imprint /ˈɪmprɪnt/ n impresión f. • /ɪmˈprɪnt/ vt imprimir

imprison /ɪmˈprɪzn/ vt encarcelar. **~ment** n encarcelamiento m

improbab|ility /ɪmprɒbəˈbɪlətɪ/ n improbabilidad f. **~le** /ɪmˈprɒbəbl/ adj improbable

impromptu /ɪmˈprɒmptju:/ adj improvisado. • adv de improviso

improper /ɪmˈprɒpə(r)/ adj impropio; (incorrect) incorrecto

improve /ɪmˈpru:v/ vt mejorar. • vi mejorar. **~ment** n mejora f

improvis|ation /ɪmprəvaɪˈzeɪʃn/ n improvisación f. **~e** /ˈɪmprəvaɪz/ vt/i improvisar

impuden|ce /ˈɪmpjʊdəns/ n insolencia f. **~t** adj insolente

impuls|e /ˈɪmpʌls/ n impulso m. on **~e** sin reflexionar. **~ive** adj irreflexivo

impur|e /ɪmˈpjʊə(r)/ adj impuro. **~ity** n impureza f

in /ɪn/ prep en; (within) dentro de. **~ a firm manner** de una manera terminante. **~ an hour's** (time) dentro de una hora. **~ doing** al hacer. **~ so far as** en la medida en que. **~ the evening** por la tarde. **~ the rain** bajo la lluvia. **~ the sun** al sol. one **~ ten** uno de cada diez. the best **~ the world** el mejor del mundo. **~** adv (inside) dentro; (at home) en casa. come **~** entrar. the **~s and outs of** los detalles de

inability /ɪnəˈbɪlətɪ/ n incapacidad f

inaccessible /ɪnækˈsesəbl/ adj inaccesible

inaccura|cy /ɪnˈækjʊrəsɪ/ n inexactitud f. **~te** /-ət/ adj inexacto

inactiv|e /ɪnˈæktɪv/ adj inactivo. **~ity** /-ˈtɪvətɪ/ n inactividad f

inadequa|cy /ɪnˈædɪkwəsɪ/ n insuficiencia f. **~te** /-ət/ adj insuficiente

inadvertently /ɪnədˈvɜ:təntlɪ/ adv sin querer

inadvisable /ɪnədˈvaɪzəbl/ adj desaconsejable

inane /ɪˈneɪm/ adj estúpido

inanimate /ɪnˈænɪmət/ adj inanimado

inappropriate /ɪnəˈprəʊprɪət/ adj inoportuno

inarticulate /ɪnɑ:ˈtɪkjʊlət/ adj incapaz de expresarse claramente

inattentive /ɪnəˈtentɪv/ adj desatento

inaudible /ɪnˈɔ:dəbl/ adj inaudible

inaugurate /ɪnˈɔ:gjʊreɪt/ vt inaugurar

inborn /ˈɪnbɔ:n/ adj innato

inbred /ɪnˈbred/ adj (inbred) innato; (social group) endogámico

Inc /ɪŋk/ abbr (Amer) (= **Incorporated**) S.A., Sociedad Anónima

incalculable /ɪnˈkælkjʊləbl/ adj incalculable

incapable /ɪnˈkeɪpəbl/ adj incapaz

incapacit|ate /ɪnkəˈpæsɪteɪt/ vt incapacitar. **~y** n incapacidad f

incarcerate /ɪnˈkɑ:səreɪt/ vt encarcelar

incarnat|e /ɪnˈkɑ:nət/ adj encarnado. **~ion** /-ˈneɪʃn/ n encarnación f

incendiary /ɪnˈsendɪərɪ/ adj incendiario. **~ bomb** bomba f incendiaria

incense /ˈɪnsens/ n incienso m.
● /ɪnˈsens/ vt enfurecer

incentive /ɪnˈsentɪv/ n incentivo m

incessant /ɪnˈsesnt/ adj incesante.
~**ly** adv sin cesar

incest /ˈɪnsest/ n incesto m.
~**uous** /ɪnˈsestjʊəs/ adj incestuoso

inch /ɪntʃ/ n pulgada f; (= 2,54cm).
● vi. ~ **forward** avanzar lentamente

incidence /ˈɪnsɪdəns/ n frecuencia f

incident /ˈɪnsɪdənt/ n incidente m

incidental /ɪnsɪˈdentl/ adj (effect) secundario; (minor) incidental. ~**ly** adv a propósito

incinerat|e /ɪnˈsɪnəreɪt/ vt incinerar. ~**or** n incinerador m

incision /ɪnˈsɪʒn/ n incisión f

incite /ɪnˈsaɪt/ vt incitar. ~**ment** n incitación f

inclination /ɪnklɪˈneɪʃn/ n inclinación f. **have no** ~ **to** no tener deseos de

incline /ɪnˈklaɪn/ vt inclinar. **be** ~**d to** tener tendencia a. ● vi inclinarse. ● /ˈɪnklaɪn/ n pendiente f

inclu|de /ɪnˈkluːd/ vt incluir. ~**ding** prep incluso. ~**sion** /-ʒn/ n inclusión f. ~**sive** /-sɪv/ adj inclusivo

incognito /ɪnkɒgˈniːtəʊ/ adv de incógnito

incoherent /ɪnkəʊˈhɪərənt/ adj incoherente

incom|e /ˈɪnkʌm/ n ingresos mpl. ~**e tax** n impuesto m sobre la renta. ~**ing** adj (tide) ascendente

incomparable /ɪnˈkɒmpərəbl/ adj incomparable

incompatible /ɪnkəmˈpætəbl/ adj incompatible

incompeten|ce /ɪnˈkɒmpɪtəns/ n incompetencia f. ~**t** adj incompetente

incomplete /ɪnkəmˈpliːt/ adj incompleto

incomprehensible /ɪnkɒmprɪˈhensəbl/ adj incomprensible

inconceivable /ɪnkənˈsiːvəbl/ adj inconcebible

inconclusive /ɪnkənˈkluːsɪv/ adj no concluyente

incongruous /ɪnˈkɒŋgrʊəs/ adj incongruente

inconsiderate /ɪnkənˈsɪdərət/ adj desconsiderado

inconsisten|cy /ɪnkənˈsɪstənsɪ/ n inconsecuencia f. ~**t** adj inconsecuente. **be** ~**t with** no concordar con

inconspicuous /ɪnkənˈspɪkjʊəs/ adj que no llama la atención. ~**ly** adv sin llamar la atención

incontinent /ɪnˈkɒntɪnənt/ adj incontinente

inconvenien|ce /ɪnkənˈviːnɪəns/ adj inconveniencia f; (drawback) inconveniente m. ~**t** adj inconveniente

incorporate /ɪnˈkɔːpəreɪt/ vt incorporar; (include) incluir; (Com) constituir (en sociedad)

incorrect /ɪnkəˈrekt/ adj incorrecto

increas|e /ˈɪnkriːs/ n aumento m (in de). ● /ɪnˈkriːs/ vt/i aumentar. ~**ing** /ɪnˈkriːsɪŋ/ adj creciente. ~**ingly** adv cada vez más

incredible /ɪnˈkredəbl/ adj increíble

incredulous /ɪnˈkredjʊləs/ adj incrédulo

incriminat|e /ɪnˈkrɪmɪneɪt/ vt incriminar. ~**ing** adj comprometedor

incubat|e /'ɪŋkjʊbeɪt/ vt incubar. **~ion** /-'beɪʃn/ n incubación f. **~or** n incubadora f

incur /ɪn'kɜː(r)/ vt (pt incurred) incurrir en; contraer (debts)

incurable /ɪn'kjʊərəbl/ adj (disease) incurable; (romantic) empedernido

indebted /ɪn'detɪd/ adj. be **~ to** s.o. estar en deuda con uno

indecen|cy /ɪn'diːsnsɪ/ n indecencia f. **~t** adj indecente

indecision /ɪndɪ'sɪʒn/ n indecisión f. **~ve** /-'saɪsɪv/ adj indeciso

indeed /ɪn'diːd/ adv en efecto; (really?) ¿de veras?

indefinable /ɪndɪ'faɪnəbl/ adj indefinible

indefinite /ɪn'defɪnət/ adj indefinido. **~ly** adv indefinidamente

indelible /ɪn'delɪbl/ adj indeleble

indemni|fy /ɪn'demnɪfaɪ/ vt (insure) asegurar; (compensate) indemnizar. **~ty** /-ətɪ/ n (insurance) indemnidad f; (payment) indemnización f

indent /ɪn'dent/ vt sangrar (text). **~ation** /-'teɪʃn/ n mella f

independen|ce /ɪndɪ'pendəns/ n independencia f. **~t** adj independiente. **~tly** adv independientemente

in-depth /ɪn'depθ/ adj a fondo

indescribable /ɪndɪ'skraɪbəbl/ adj indescriptible

indestructible /ɪndɪ'strʌktɪbl/ adj indestructible

indeterminate /ɪndɪ'tɜːmɪnət/ adj indeterminado

index /'ɪndeks/ n (pl indexes) (in book) índice m; (pl indexes or indices) (Com, Math) índice m. ● vt poner índice a; (enter in index) poner en un índice. **~ finger** n

(dedo m) índice m. **~-linked** /-'lɪŋkt/ adj indexado

India /'ɪndɪə/ n la India. **~n** adj & n indio (m)

indicat|e /'ɪndɪkeɪt/ vt indicar. **~ion** /-'keɪʃn/ n indicación f. **~ive** /ɪn'dɪkətɪv/ adj & n indicativo (m). **~or** /'ɪndɪkeɪtə(r)/ n indicador m; (Auto) intermitente m

indices /'ɪndɪsiːz/ see INDEX

indict /ɪn'daɪt/ vt acusar. **~ment** n acusación f

indifferen|ce /ɪn'dɪfrəns/ n indiferencia f. **~t** adj indiferente; (not good) mediocre

indigesti|ble /ɪndɪ'dʒestəbl/ adj indigesto. **~on** /-'tʃən/ n indigestión f

indigna|nt /ɪn'dɪgnənt/ adj indignado. **~tion** /-'neɪʃn/ n indignación f

indirect /ɪndɪ'rekt/ adj indirecto. **~ly** adv indirectamente

indiscre|et /ɪndɪ'skriːt/ adj indiscreto. **~tion** /-'kreʃn/ n indiscreción f

indiscriminate /ɪndɪ'skrɪmɪnət/ adj indistinto. **~ly** adv indistintamente

indispensable /ɪndɪ'spensəbl/ adj indispensable, imprescindible

indisposed /ɪndɪ'spəʊzd/ adj indispuesto

indisputable /ɪndɪ'spjuːtəbl/ adj indiscutible

indistinguishable /ɪndɪ'stɪŋgwɪʃəbl/ adj indistinguible (from de)

individual /ɪndɪ'vɪdjʊəl/ adj individual. ● n individuo m. **~ly** adv individualmente

indoctrinat|e /ɪn'dɒktrɪneɪt/ vt adoctrinar. **~ion** /-'neɪʃn/ n adoctrinamiento m

indolen|ce /'ɪndələns/ n indolencia f. ~t adj indolente

indomitable /ɪnˈdɒmɪtəbl/ adj indómito

indoor /ˈɪndɔ:(r)/ adj interior; (clothes etc) de casa; (covered) cubierto. ~s adv dentro, adentro (LAm)

induc|e /ɪnˈdju:s/ vt inducir. ~ement n incentivo m

indulge /ɪnˈdʌldʒ/ vt satisfacer (desires); complacer (person). ● vi. ~ in permitirse. ~nce /-əns/ n (of desires) satisfacción f; (extravagance) lujo m. ~nt adj indulgente

industrial /ɪnˈdʌstrɪəl/ adj industrial; (unrest) laboral. ~ist n industrial m & f. ~ized adj industrializado

industrious /ɪnˈdʌstrɪəs/ adj trabajador

industry /ˈɪndəstrɪ/ n industria f; (zeal) aplicación f

inebriated /ɪˈni:brɪeɪtɪd/ adj beodo, ebrio

inedible /ɪnˈedɪbl/ adj incomible

ineffective /ɪnɪˈfektɪv/ adj ineficaz; (person) incompetente

ineffectual /ɪnɪˈfektʃʊəl/ adj ineficaz

inefficien|cy /ɪnɪˈfɪʃnsɪ/ n ineficacia f; (of person) incompetencia f. ~t adj ineficaz; (person) incompetente

ineligible /ɪnˈelɪdʒəbl/ adj inelegible. be ~ for no tener derecho a

inept /ɪˈnept/ adj inepto

inequality /ɪnɪˈkwɒlətɪ/ n desigualdad f

inert /ɪˈnɜ:t/ adj inerte. ~ia /ɪˈnɜ:ʃə/ n inercia f

inescapable /ɪnɪˈskeɪpəbl/ adj ineludible

inevitabl|e /ɪnˈevɪtəbl/ adj inevitable. ●n. the ~e lo inevitable. ~y adv inevitablemente

inexact /ɪnɪɡˈzækt/ adj inexacto

inexcusable /ɪnɪkˈskju:səbl/ adj imperdonable

inexpensive /ɪnɪkˈspensɪv/ adj económico, barato

inexperience /ɪnɪkˈspɪərɪəns/ n falta f de experiencia. ~d adj inexperto

inexplicable /ɪnɪkˈsplɪkəbl/ adj inexplicable

infallib|ility /ɪnfæləˈbɪlətɪ/ n infalibilidad f. ~le /ɪnˈfæləbl/ adj infalible

infam|ous /ˈɪnfəməs/ adj infame. ~y n infamia f

infan|cy /ˈɪnfənsɪ/ n infancia f. ~t n niño m. ~tile /ˈɪnfəntaɪl/ adj infantil

infantry /ˈɪnfəntrɪ/ n infantería f

infatuat|ed /ɪnˈfætjʊeɪtɪd/ adj. be ~ed with estar encaprichado con. ~ion /-ˈeɪʃn/ n encaprichamiento m

infect /ɪnˈfekt/ vt infectar; (fig) contagiar. ~ s.o. with sth contagiarle algo a uno. ~ion /-ʃn/ n infección f. ~ious /-ʃəs/ adj contagioso

infer /ɪnˈfɜ:(r)/ vt (pt inferred) deducir

inferior /ɪnˈfɪərɪə(r)/ adj & n inferior (m & f). ~ity /-ˈɒrətɪ/ n inferioridad f

inferno /ɪnˈfɜ:nəʊ/ n (pl -os) infierno m

infertil|e /ɪnˈfɜ:taɪl/ adj estéril. ~ity /-ˈtɪlətɪ/ n esterilidad f

infest /ɪnˈfest/ vt infestar

infidelity /ɪnfɪˈdelɪtɪ/ n infidelidad f

infiltrat|e /ˈɪnfɪltreɪt/ vt infiltrarse en. ● vi infiltrarse. ~or n infiltrado m

infinite /ˈɪnfɪnət/ adj infinito. ~ly

adv infinitamente

infinitesimal /ɪnfɪnɪˈtesɪml/ *adj* infinitesimal

infinitive /ɪnˈfɪnətɪv/ *n* infinitivo *m*

infinity /ɪnˈfɪnətɪ/ *n* (*infinite distance*) infinito *m*; (*infinite quantity*) infinidad *f*

infirm /ɪnˈfɜːm/ *adj* enfermizo. ~**ity** *n* enfermedad *f*

inflam|e /ɪnˈfleɪm/ *vt* inflamar. ~**mable** /ɪnˈflæməbl/ *adj* inflamable. ~**mation** /-əˈmeɪʃn/ *n* inflamación *f*

inflate /ɪnˈfleɪt/ *vt* inflar. ~**ion** /-ʃn/ *n* inflación *f*. ~**ionary** *adj* inflacionario

inflection /ɪnˈflekʃn/ *n* inflexión *f*

inflexible /ɪnˈfleksəbl/ *adj* inflexible

inflict /ɪnˈflɪkt/ *vt* infligir (on a)

influen|ce /ˈɪnfluəns/ *n* influencia *f*. under the ~**ce** (*fam, drunk*) borracho. ● *vt* influir (en). ~**tial** /-ˈenʃl/ *adj* influyente

influenza /ɪnfluˈenzə/ *n* gripe *f*

influx /ˈɪnflʌks/ *n* afluencia *f*

inform /ɪnˈfɔːm/ *vt* informar. keep ~ed tener al corriente. ● *vi*. ~ on s.o. delatar a uno

informal /ɪnˈfɔːml/ *adj* informal; (*language*) familiar. ~**ity** /-ˈmælətɪ/ *n* falta *f* de ceremonia. ~**ly** *adv* (*casually*) de manera informal; (*unofficially*) informalmente

inform|ation /ɪnfəˈmeɪʃn/ *n* información *f*. ~**ation technology** *n* informática *f*. ~**ative** *adj* /ɪnˈfɔːmətɪv/ informativo. ~**er** /ɪbˈfɔːmə(r)/ *n* informante *m*

infrared /ɪnfrəˈred/ *adj* infrarrojo

infrequent /ɪnˈfriːkwənt/ *adj* poco frecuente. ~**ly** *adv* raramente

infringe /ɪnˈfrɪndʒ/ *vt* infringir. ~

on violar. ~**ment** *n* violación *f*

infuriat|e /ɪnˈfjʊərɪeɪt/ *vt* enfurecer. ~**ing** *adj* exasperante

ingen|ious /ɪnˈdʒiːnɪəs/ *adj* ingenioso. ~**uity** /ɪndʒɪˈnjuːətɪ/ *n* ingeniosidad *f*

ingot /ˈɪŋgət/ *n* lingote *m*

ingrained /ɪnˈgreɪnd/ *adj* (*belief*) arraigado

ingratiate /ɪnˈgreɪʃɪeɪt/ *vt*. ~ o.s. with congraciarse con

ingratitude /ɪnˈgrætɪtjuːd/ *n* ingratitud *f*

ingredient /ɪnˈgriːdɪənt/ *n* ingrediente *m*

ingrowing /ˈɪngrəʊɪŋ/, **ingrown** /ˈɪngrəʊn/ *adj*. ~ **nail** *n* uñero *m*, uña *f* encarnada

inhabit /ɪnˈhæbɪt/ *vt* habitar. ~**able** *adj* habitable. ~**ant** *n* habitante *m*

inhale /ɪnˈheɪl/ *vt* aspirar. ● *vi* (*when smoking*) aspirar el humo. ~**r** *n* inhalador *m*

inherent /ɪnˈhɪərənt/ *adj* inherente. ~**ly** *adv* intrínsecamente

inherit /ɪnˈherɪt/ *vt* heredar. ~**ance** /-əns/ *n* herencia *f*

inhibit /ɪnˈhɪbɪt/ *vt* inhibir. ~**ed** *adj* inhibido. ~**ion** /-ˈbɪʃn/ *n* inhibición *f*

inhospitable /ɪnhəˈspɪtəbl/ *adj* (*place*) inhóspito; (*person*) inhospitalario

inhuman /ɪnˈhjuːmən/ *adj* inhumano. ~**e** /ɪnhjuːˈmeɪn/ *adj* inhumano. ~**ity** /ɪnhjuːˈmænətɪ/ *n* inhumanidad *f*

initial /ɪˈnɪʃl/ *n* inicial *f*. ● *vt* (*pt* initialled) firmar con iniciales. ● *adj* inicial. ~**ly** *adv* al principio

initiat|e /ɪˈnɪʃɪeɪt/ *vt* iniciar; promover (scheme etc). ~**ion** /-ˈeɪʃn/ *n* iniciación *f*

initiative /ɪˈnɪʃətɪv/ n iniciativa f.
on one's own ~ por iniciativa propia. take the ~ tomar la iniciativa

inject /ɪnˈdʒekt/ vt inyectar. **~ion**
/-ʃn/ n inyección f

injur|e /ˈɪndʒə(r)/ vt herir. **~y** n
herida f

injustice /ɪnˈdʒʌstɪs/ n injusticia f

ink /ɪŋk/ n tinta f. **~well** n tintero
m. **~y** adj manchado de tinta

inland /ˈɪnlənd/ adj interior. ● n
/ˈɪnlænd/ adv tierra adentro. **I~ Revenue** /ˈɪnlænd/ n Hacienda f

in-laws /ˈɪnlɔːz/ npl parientes mpl
políticos

inlay /ɪnˈleɪ/ vt (pt inlaid) taracear,
incrustar. ● n /ˈɪnleɪ/ n taracea f, incrustación f

inlet /ˈɪnlet/ n (in coastline) ensenada f; (of river, sea) brazo m

inmate /ˈɪnmeɪt/ n (of asylum) interno m; (of prison) preso m

inn /ɪn/ n posada f

innate /ɪˈneɪt/ adj innato

inner /ˈɪnə(r)/ adj interior; (fig) íntimo. **~most** adj más íntimo. **~tube** n cámara f

innocen|ce /ˈɪnəsns/ n inocencia
f. **~t** adj & n inocente (m & f)

innocuous /ɪˈnɒkjuəs/ adj inocuo

innovat|e /ˈɪnəveɪt/ vi innovar.
~ion /-ˈveɪʃn/ n innovación f.
~ive /ˈɪnəvətɪv/ adj innovador.
~or n innovador m

innuendo /ɪnjuːˈendəʊ/ n (pl
-oes) insinuación f

innumerable /ɪˈnjuːmərəbl/ adj
innumerable

inoculat|e /ɪˈnɒkjʊleɪt/ vt inocular. **~ion** /-ˈleɪʃn/ n inoculación f

inoffensive /ɪnəˈfensɪv/ adj inofensivo

inopportune /ɪnˈɒpətjuːn/ adj

inoportuno

input /ˈɪnpʊt/ n aportación f,
aporte m (LAm); (Comp) entrada f.
● vt (pt input, pres p inputting) entrar (data)

inquest /ˈɪnkwest/ n investigación
f judicial

inquir|e /ɪnˈkwaɪə(r)/ vt/i preguntar. **~e about** informarse de. **~y**
n pregunta f; (investigation) investigación f

inquisition /ɪnkwɪˈzɪʃn/ n inquisición f

inquisitive /ɪnˈkwɪzətɪv/ adj inquisitivo

insane /ɪnˈseɪn/ adj loco. **~ity**
/ɪnˈsænətɪ/ n locura f

insatiable /ɪnˈseɪʃəbl/ adj insaciable

inscri|be /ɪnˈskraɪb/ vt inscribir
(letters); grabar (design). **~ption**
/-ɪpʃn/ n inscripción f

inscrutable /ɪnˈskruːtəbl/ adj inescrutable

insect /ˈɪnsekt/ n insecto m.
~icide /ɪnˈsektɪsaɪd/ n insecticida f

insecur|e /ɪnsɪˈkjʊə(r)/ adj inseguro. **~ity** n inseguridad f

insensitive /ɪnˈsensɪtɪv/ adj insensible

inseparable /ɪnˈsepərəbl/ adj inseparable

insert /ˈɪnsɜːt/ n materia f insertada. ● /ɪnˈsɜːt/ vt insertar. **~ion**
/ɪnˈsɜːʃn/ n inserción f

inside /ɪnˈsaɪd/ n interior m. **~out** al revés; (thoroughly) a fondo.
● adj interior. ● adv dentro, adentro
(LAm). ● prep dentro de. **~s** npl tripas fpl

insight /ˈɪnsaɪt/ n perspicacia f.
gain an ~ into llegar a comprender bien

insignificant /ɪnsɪɡˈnɪfɪkənt/ adj insignificante

insincer|e /ɪnsɪnˈsɪə(r)/ adj poco sincero. **~ity** /-ˈserətɪ/ n falta f de sinceridad

insinuat|e /ɪnˈsɪnjʊeɪt/ vt insinuar. **~ion** /-ˈeɪʃn/ n insinuación f

insipid /ɪnˈsɪpɪd/ adj insípido

insist /ɪnˈsɪst/ vt insistir (that en que). ● vi insistir. **~ on** insistir en. **~ence** /-əns/ n insistencia f. **~ent** adj insistente. **~ently** adv con insistencia

insolen|ce /ˈɪnsələns/ n insolencia f. **~t** adj insolente

insoluble /ɪnˈsɒljʊbl/ adj insoluble

insolvent /ɪnˈsɒlvənt/ adj insolvente

insomnia /ɪnˈsɒmnɪə/ n insomnio m. **~c** /-ˈæk/ n insomne m & f

inspect /ɪnˈspekt/ vt (officially) inspeccionar; (look at closely) revisar, examinar. **~ion** /-ʃn/ n inspección f. **~or** n inspector m; (on train, bus) revisor m, inspector m (LAm)

inspir|ation /ɪnspəˈreɪʃn/ n inspiración f. **~e** /ɪnˈspaɪə(r)/ vt inspirar. **~ing** adj inspirador

instability /ɪnstəˈbɪlətɪ/ n inestabilidad f

install /ɪnˈstɔːl/ vt instalar. **~ation** /-əˈleɪʃn/ n instalación f

instalment /ɪnˈstɔːlmənt/ n (payment) plazo m; (of publication) entrega f; (of radio, TV serial) episodio m

instance /ˈɪnstəns/ n ejemplo m; (case) caso m. **for ~** por ejemplo. **in the first ~** en primer lugar

instant /ˈɪnstənt/ adj instantáneo. ● n instante m. **~aneous** /ɪnstənˈteɪnɪəs/ adj instantáneo

instead /ɪnˈsted/ adv en cambio.

~ of en vez de, en lugar de

instigat|e /ˈɪnstɪɡeɪt/ vt instigar. **~ion** /-ˈɡeɪʃn/ n instigación f

instinct /ˈɪnstɪŋkt/ n instinto m. **~ive** adj instintivo

institut|e /ˈɪnstɪtjuːt/ n instituto m. ● vt establecer; iniciar (enquiry etc). **~ion** /-ˈtjuːʃn/ n institución f. **~ional** adj institucional

instruct /ɪnˈstrʌkt/ vt instruir; (order) mandar. **~ s.o. in sth** enseñar algo a uno. **~ion** /-ʃn/ n instrucción f. **~ions** npl (for use) modo m de empleo. **~ive** adj instructivo. **~or** n instructor m

instrument /ˈɪnstrəmənt/ n instrumento m. **~al** /ɪnstrəˈmentl/ adj instrumental. **be ~al in** jugar un papel decisivo en

insubordinat|e /ɪnsəˈbɔːdɪnət/ adj insubordinado. **~ion** /-ˈneɪʃn/ n insubordinación f

insufferable /ɪnˈsʌfərəbl/ adj (person) insufrible; (heat) insoportable

insufficient /ɪnsəˈfɪʃnt/ adj insuficiente

insular /ˈɪnsjʊlə(r)/ adj insular; (narrow-minded) estrecho de miras

insulat|e /ˈɪnsjʊleɪt/ vt aislar. **~ion** /-ˈleɪʃn/ n aislamiento m

insulin /ˈɪnsjʊlɪn/ n insulina f

insult /ɪnˈsʌlt/ vt insultar. ● /ˈɪnsʌlt/ n insulto m. **~ing** /ɪnˈsʌltɪŋ/ adj insultante

insur|ance /ɪnˈʃʊərəns/ n seguro m. **~e** /ɪnˈʃʊə(r)/ vt (Com) asegurar; (Amer) see **ENSURE**

insurmountable /ɪnsəˈmaʊntəbl/ adj insuperable

intact /ɪnˈtækt/ adj intacto

integral /ˈɪntɪɡrəl/ adj integral

integrat|e /ˈɪntɪɡreɪt/ vt integrar. ● vi integrarse. **~ion** /-ˈɡreɪʃn/ n integración f

integrity /ɪn'tegrətɪ/ n integridad f

intellect /'ɪntəlekt/ n intelecto m. **~ual** /ɪntə'lektʃʊəl/ adj & n intelectual (m)

intelligen|ce /ɪn'telɪdʒəns/ n inteligencia f. **~t** adj inteligente. **~tly** adv inteligentemente

intelligible /ɪn'telɪdʒəbl/ adj inteligible

intend /ɪn'tend/ vt. ~ to do pensar hacer

intens|e /ɪn'tens/ adj intenso; (person) apasionado. **~ely** adv intensamente; (very) sumamente. **~ify** /-ɪfaɪ/ vt intensificar. ● vi intensificarse. **~ity** /-ɪtɪ/ n intensidad f

intensive /ɪn'tensɪv/ adj intensivo. ~ **care** n cuidados mpl intensivos

intent /ɪn'tent/ n propósito m. ● adj atento. ~ **on** absorto en. ~ **on doing** resuelto a hacer

intention /ɪn'tenʃn/ n intención f. **~al** adj intencional

intently /ɪn'tentlɪ/ adv atentamente

interact /ɪntər'ækt/ vi relacionarse. **~ion** /-ʃn/ n interacción f

intercept /ɪntə'sept/ vt interceptar. **~ion** /-ʃn/ n interceptación f

interchange /ɪntə'tʃeɪndʒ/ vt intercambiar. ● /'ɪntətʃeɪndʒ/ n intercambio m; (road junction) cruce m. **~able** /-'tʃeɪndʒəbl/ adj intercambiable

intercity /ɪntə'sɪtɪ/ adj rápido interurbano m

intercourse /'ɪntəkɔ:s/ n trato m; (sexual) acto m sexual

interest /'ɪntrest/ n interés m. ● vt interesar. **~ed** adj interesado. be

~ed in interesarse por. **~ing** adj interesante

interface /'ɪntəfeɪs/ n interfaz m & f; (interaction) interrelación f

interfere /ɪntə'fɪə(r)/ vi entrometerse. ~ **in** entrometerse en. ~ **with** afectar (a); interferir (radio). **~nce** /-rəns/ n intromisión f; (Radio) interferencia f

interior /ɪn'tɪərɪə(r)/ adj & n interior (m)

interjection /ɪntə'dʒekʃn/ n interjección f

interlude /'ɪntəlu:d/ n intervalo m; (theatre, music) interludio m

intermediary /ɪntə'mi:dɪərɪ/ adj & n intermediario (m)

interminable /ɪn'tɜ:mɪnəbl/ adj interminable

intermittent /ɪntə'mɪtnt/ adj intermitente. **~ly** adv con discontinuidad

intern /ɪn'tɜ:n/ vt internar. ● /'ɪntɜ:n/ n (Amer, doctor) interno m

internal /ɪn'tɜ:nl/ adj interno. **~ly** adv internamente. **I~ Revenue Service** n (Amer) Hacienda f

international /ɪntə'næʃnəl/ adj internacional

Internet /'ɪntənet/ n. the ~ el Internet

interpret /ɪn'tɜ:prɪt/ vt/i interpretar. **~ation** /-'teɪʃn/ n interpretación f **~er** n intérprete m & f

interrogat|e /ɪn'terəgeɪt/ vt interrogar. **~ion** /-'geɪʃn/ n interrogatorio m. **~ive** /-'rɒgətɪv/ adj interrogativo

interrupt /ɪntə'rʌpt/ vt/i interrumpir. **~ion** /-ʃn/ n interrupción f

intersect /ɪntə'sekt/ vt cruzar. ● vi (roads) cruzarse; (geometry) intersecarse. ~**ion** /-ʃn/ n (roads) cruce m; (geometry) intersección f

intersperse /ɪntəˈspɜːs/ vt intercalar

interstate (highway) /ˈɪntəsteɪt/ n (Amer) carretera f interestal

intertwine /ɪntəˈtwaɪn/ vt entrelazar. ● vi entrelazarse

interval /ˈɪntəvl/ n intervalo m; (theatre) descanso m. **at ~s** a intervalos

interven|e /ɪntəˈviːn/ vi intervenir. ~**tion** /-ˈvenʃn/ n intervención f

interview /ˈɪntəvjuː/ n entrevista f. ● vt entrevistar. ~**ee** /-iː/ n entrevistado m. ~**er** n entrevistador m

intestine /ɪnˈtestɪn/ n intestino m

intimacy /ˈɪntɪməsɪ/ n intimidad f

intimate /ˈɪntɪmət/ adj íntimo. ● /ˈɪntɪmeɪt/ vt (state) anunciar; (imply) dar a entender. ~**ly** /ˈɪntɪmətlɪ/ adv íntimamente

intimidat|e /ɪnˈtɪmɪdeɪt/ vt intimidar. ~**ion** /-ˈdeɪʃn/ n intimidación f

into /ˈɪntuː/ˈɪntə/ prep en; (translate) a

intolerable /ɪnˈtɒlərəbl/ adj intolerable

intoleran|ce /ɪnˈtɒlərəns/ n intolerancia f. ~**t** adj intolerante

intoxicat|e /ɪnˈtɒksɪkeɪt/ vt embriagar; (Med) intoxicar. ~**ed** adj ebrio. ~**ing** adj (substance) estupefaciente. ~**ion** /-ˈkeɪʃn/ n embriaguez f; (Med) intoxicación f

intransitive /ɪnˈtrænsɪtɪv/ adj intransitivo

intravenous /ɪntrəˈviːnəs/ adj intravenoso

intrepid /ɪnˈtrepɪd/ adj intrépido

intrica|cy /ˈɪntrɪkəsɪ/ n complejidad f. ~**te** /-ət/ adj complejo

intrigu|e /ɪnˈtriːg/ vt/i intrigar. ● /ˈɪntriːg/ n intriga f. ~**ing** /ɪnˈtriːgɪŋ/ adj intrigante

intrinsic /ɪnˈtrɪnsɪk/ adj intrínseco. ~**ally** adv intrínsecamente

introduc|e /ɪntrəˈdjuːs/ vt introducir; presentar (person). ~**tion** /ɪntrəˈdʌkʃn/ n introducción f; (to person) presentación f. ~**tory** /ɪntrəˈdʌktərɪ/ adj preliminar; (course) de introducción

introvert /ˈɪntrəvɜːt/ n introvertido m

intru|de /ɪnˈtruːd/ vi entrometerse; (disturb) importunar. ~**der** n intruso m. ~**sion** /-ʒn/ n intrusión f. ~**sive** /-sɪv/ adj impertinente

intuiti|on /ɪntjuːˈɪʃn/ n intuición f. ~**ve** /ɪnˈtjuːɪtɪv/ adj intuitivo

inundat|e /ˈɪnʌndeɪt/ vt inundar. ~**ion** /-ˈdeɪʃn/ n inundación f

invade /ɪnˈveɪd/ vt invadir. ~**r** n invasor m

invalid /ˈɪnvəlɪd/ n inválido m. ● /ɪnˈvælɪd/ adj inválido. ~**ate** /ɪnˈvælɪdeɪt/ vt invalidar

invaluable /ɪnˈvæljʊəbl/ adj inestimable, invalorable (LAm)

invariab|le /ɪnˈveərɪəbl/ adj invariable. ~**y** adv invariablemente

invasion /ɪnˈveɪʒn/ n invasión f

invent /ɪnˈvent/ vt inventar. ~**ion** /-ˈvenʃn/ n invención f. ~**ive** adj inventivo. ~**or** n inventor m

inventory /ˈɪnvəntrɪ/ n inventario m

invertebrate /ɪnˈvɜːtɪbrət/ n invertebrado m

inverted commas /ɪnvɜːtɪd ˈkɒməz/npl comillas fpl

invest /ɪnˈvest/ vt invertir. ● vi. ~ **in** invertir en

investigat|e /ɪnˈvestɪgeɪt/ vt investigar. **~ion** /-ˈgeɪʃn/ n investigación f. **under ~ion** sometido a examen. **~or** n investigador m

investment /ɪnˈvestmənt/ inversión f

investor /ɪnˈvestə(r)/ inversionista m & f

inveterate /ɪnˈvetərət/ adj inveterado

invidious /ɪnˈvɪdɪəs/ adj (hateful) odioso; (unfair) injusto

invigorating /ɪnˈvɪɡəreɪtɪŋ/ adj vigorizante; (stimulating) estimulante

invincible /ɪnˈvɪnsɪbl/ adj invencible

invisible /ɪnˈvɪzəbl/ adj invisible

invit|ation /ɪnvɪˈteɪʃn/ n invitación f. **~e** /ɪnˈvaɪt/ vt invitar; (ask for) pedir. ● /ˈɪnvaɪt/ n 🔢 invitación f. **~ing** /ɪnˈvaɪtɪŋ/ adj atrayente

invoice /ˈɪnvɔɪs/ n factura f. ● vt. **~ s.o. (for sth)** pasarle a uno factura (por algo)

involuntary /ɪnˈvɒləntərɪ/ adj involuntario

involve /ɪnˈvɒlv/ vt (entail) suponer; (implicate) implicar. **~d** in envuelto en. **~d** adj (complex) complicado. **~ment** n participación f; (relationship) enredo m

inward /ˈɪnwəd/ adj interior. ● adv hacia adentro. **~s** adv hacia dentro

iodine /ˈaɪədiːn/ n yodo m

ion /ˈaɪən/ n ion m

iota /aɪˈəʊtə/ n (amount) pizca f

IOU /aɪəʊˈjuː/ abbr (= I owe you) pagaré m

IQ abbr (= intelligence quotient) CI m, cociente m intelectual

Iran /ɪˈrɑːn/ n Irán m. **~ian** /ɪˈreɪnɪən/ adj & n iraní (m)

Iraq /ɪˈrɑːk/ n Irak m. **~i** adj & n iraquí (m & f)

irate /aɪˈreɪt/ adj colérico

Ireland /ˈaɪələnd/ n Irlanda f

iris /ˈaɪərɪs/ n (of eye) iris m; (flower) lirio m

Irish /ˈaɪərɪʃ/ adj irlandés. ● n (language) irlandés m. npl. **the ~** (people) los irlandeses. **~man** /-mən/ n irlandés m. **~woman** n irlandesa f

iron /ˈaɪən/ n hierro m; (appliance) plancha f. ● adj de hierro. ● vt planchar. □ **~ out** vt allanar

ironic /aɪˈrɒnɪk/ adj irónico. **~ally** adv irónicamente

ironing board /ˈaɪənɪŋ/ n tabla f de planchar, burro m de planchar (Mex)

iron: ~monger /-mʌŋɡə(r)/ n ferretero m. **~monger's** n ferretería f

irony /ˈaɪərənɪ/ n ironía f

irrational /ɪˈræʃənl/ adj irracional

irrefutable /ɪrɪˈfjuːtəbl/ adj irrefutable

irregular /ɪˈreɡjʊlə(r)/ adj irregular. **~ity** /-ˈlærətɪ/ n irregularidad f

irrelevan|ce /ɪˈreləvəns/ n irrelevancia f. **~t** adj irrelevante

irreparable /ɪˈrepərəbl/ adj irreparable

irreplaceable /ɪrɪˈpleɪsəbl/ adj irreemplazable

irresistible /ɪrɪˈzɪstəbl/ adj irresistible

irrespective /ɪrɪˈspektɪv/ adj. **~ of** sin tomar en cuenta

irresponsible /ɪrɪˈspɒnsəbl/ adj irresponsable

irretrievable /ɪrɪˈtriːvəbl/ adj irrecuperable

irreverent /ɪˈrevərənt/ adj irreverente

irrevocable /ɪˈrevəkəbl/ adj irrevocable

irrigat|e /ˈɪrɪgeɪt/ vt regar, irrigar. ~**ion** /-ˈgeɪʃn/ n riego m, irrigación f

irritable /ˈɪrɪtəbl/ adj irritable

irritat|e /ˈɪrɪteɪt/ vt irritar. ~**ed** adj irritado. ~**ing** adj irritante. ~**ion** /-ˈteɪʃn/ n irritación f

IRS abbr (Amer) see **INTERNAL REVENUE SERVICE**

is /ɪz/ see **BE**

ISDN abbr (Integrated Services Digital Network) RDSI

Islam /ˈɪzlɑːm/ n el Islam. ~**ic** /ɪzˈlæmɪk/ adj islámico

island /ˈaɪlənd/ n isla f. ~**er** n isleño m

isolat|e /ˈaɪsəleɪt/ vt aislar. ~**ion** /-ˈleɪʃn/ n aislamiento m

Israel /ˈɪzreɪl/ n Israel m. ~**i** /ɪzˈreɪlɪ/ adj & n israelí (m)

issue /ˈɪʃuː/ n tema m, asunto m; (of magazine etc) número m; (of stamps, bank notes) emisión f; (of documents) expedición f. take ~ with discrepar de. ● vt hacer público (statement); expedir (documents); emitir (stamps etc); prestar (library book)

it /ɪt/ pronoun

····▸ (as subject) generally not translated. it's huge es enorme. where is it? ¿dónde está? it's all lies son todas mentiras

····▸ (as direct object) lo (m), la (f). he read it to me lo/la leyó. give it to me dámelo/ dámela

····▸ (as indirect object) le. I gave it another coat of paint le di otra mano de pintura

····▸ (after a preposition) generally not translated. there's nothing behind it no hay nada detrás

! Note, however, that in some cases él or ella must be used e.g. he picked up the spoon and hit me with it agarró la cuchara y me golpeó con ella

····▸ (at door) who is it? ¿quién es?. it's me soy yo; (on telephone) who is it, please? ¿quién habla, por favor?; (before passing on to sb else) ¿de parte de quién, por favor? it's Carol soy Carol (Spain), habla Carol

····▸ (in impersonal constructions) it is well known that ... bien se sabe que ... it's four o'clock son las cuatro. it's five o'clock son las cinco. it seems así parece

····▸ that's it (that's right) eso es; (that's enough, that's finished) ya está

Italian /ɪˈtæljən/ adj & n italiano (m)

italics /ɪˈtælɪks/ npl (letra f) cursiva f

Italy /ˈɪtəlɪ/ n Italia f

itch /ɪtʃ/ n picazón f. ● vi picar. I'm ~**ing** to estoy que me muero por. my arm ~**es** me pica el brazo. ~**y** adj que pica. I've got an ~**y** nose me pica la nariz

it'd /ɪtəd/ = it had, it would

item /ˈaɪtəm/ n artículo m; (on agenda) punto m. **news** ~ n noticia f. ~**ize** vt detallar

itinerary /aɪˈtɪnərərɪ/ n itinerario m

it'll /ɪtl/ = it will

its /ɪts/ adj su, sus (pl). ● pron (el)

suyo *m*, (la) suya *f*, (los) suyos *mpl*, (las) suyas *fpl*

it's /ɪts/ = **it is**, **it has**

itself /ɪt'self/ *pron* él mismo, ella misma, ello mismo; (*reflexive*) se; (*after prep*) sí mismo, sí misma

I've /aɪv/ = **I have**

ivory /'aɪvərɪ/ *n* marfil *m*. ~ **tower** *n* torre *f* de marfil

ivy /'aɪvɪ/ *n* hiedra *f*

Ivy League - the El grupo de universidades más antiguas y respetadas de EE.UU. Situadas al noreste del país, son: Harvard, Yale, Columbia, Cornell, Dartmouth College, Brown, Princeton y Pensylvania. El término proviene de la hiedra que crece en los antiguos edificios de estos establecimientos.

Jj

jab /dʒæb/ *vt* (*pt* jabbed) pinchar; (*thrust*) hurgonear. ● *n* pinchazo *m*

jack /dʒæk/ *n* (Mec) gato *m*; (socket) enchufe *m* hembra; (Cards) sota *f*. □ ~ **up** *vt* alzar con gato

jackal /'dʒækl/ *n* chacal *m*

jackdaw /'dʒækdɔː/ *n* grajilla *f*

jacket /'dʒækɪt/ *n* chaqueta *f*; (casual) americana *f*, saco *m* (LAm); (Amer, of book) sobrecubierta *f*; (of record) funda *f*, carátula *f*

jack:~ knife *vi* (lorry) plegarse. ~**pot** *n* premio *m* gordo. **hit the** ~**pot** sacar el premio gordo

jade /dʒeɪd/ *n* (stone) jade *m*

jagged /'dʒægɪd/ *adj* (edge, cut) irregular; (rock) recortado

jaguar /'dʒægjʊə(r)/ *n* jaguar *m*

jail /dʒeɪl/ *n* cárcel *m*, prisión *f*. ● *vt* encarcelar. ~**er** *n* carcelero *m*. ~**house** *n* (Amer) cárcel *f*

jam /dʒæm/ *vt* (*pt* jammed) interferir con (radio); atestar (road). ~ **sth into sth** meter algo a la fuerza en algo. ● *vi* (brakes) bloquearse; (machine) trancarse. ● *n* mermelada *f*; (fam, situation) apuro *m*

jangle /'dʒæŋgl/ *n* sonido *m* metálico (y áspero). ● *vi* hacer ruido (metálico)

janitor /'dʒænɪtə(r)/ *n* portero *m*

January /'dʒænjʊərɪ/ *n* enero *m*

Japan /dʒə'pæn/ *n* (el) Japón *m*. ~**ese** /dʒæpə'niːz/ *adj & n invar* japonés (*m*)

jar /dʒɑː(r)/ *n* tarro *m*, bote *m*. ● *vi* (*pt* jarred) (clash) desentonar. ● *vt* sacudir

jargon /'dʒɑːgən/ *n* jerga *f*

jaundice /'dʒɔːndɪs/ *n* ictericia *f*

jaunt /dʒɔːnt/ *n* excursión *f*

jaunty /'dʒɔːntɪ/ *adj* (-ier, -iest) garboso

jaw /dʒɔː/ *n* mandíbula *f*. ~**s** *npl* fauces *fpl*. ~**bone** *n* mandíbula *f*, maxilar *m*; (of animal) quijada *f*

jay /dʒeɪ/ *n* arrendajo *m*. ~**walk** *vi* cruzar la calle descuidadamente. ~**walker** *n* peatón *m* imprudente

jazz /dʒæz/ *n* jazz *m*. □ ~ **up** *vt* animar. ~**y** *adj* chillón

jealous /'dʒeləs/ *adj* celoso; (envious) envidioso. ~**y** *n* celos *mpl*

jeans /dʒiːnz/ *npl* vaqueros *mpl*, jeans *mpl*, tejanos *mpl*, pantalones *mpl* de mezclilla (Mex)

Jeep (P), **jeep** /dʒiːp/ *n* Jeep *m* (P)

jeer /dʒɪə(r)/ *vi*. ~ **at** mofarse de;

(boo) abuchear. ● *n* burla *f*; *(boo)* abucheo *m*

Jell-O /'dʒeləʊ/ *n* (P) *(Amer)* gelatina *f* (con sabor a frutas)

jelly /'dʒelɪ/ *n* (clear jam) jalea *f*; *(pudding)* see JELL-O; *(substance)* gelatina *f*. **~fish** *n* (pl invar or **-es**) medusa *f*

jeopardize /'dʒepədaɪz/ *vt* arriesgar

jerk /dʒɜːk/ *n* sacudida *f*; (sl, fool) idiota *m* & *f*. ● *vt* sacudir

jersey /'dʒɜːzɪ/ *n* (pl **-eys**) jersey *m*, suéter *m*, pulóver *m*

jest /dʒest/ *n* broma *f*. ● *vi* bromear

Jesus /'dʒiːzəs/ *n* Jesús *m*

jet /dʒet/ *n* (stream) chorro *m*; *(plane)* avión *m* (con motor a reacción); *(mineral)* azabache *m*. **~-black** /-'blæk/ *adj* azabache negro *a* invar. **~ lag** *n* jet lag *m*, desfase *f* horario. **have ~ lag** estar desfasado. **~-propelled** /-prə'peld/ *adj* (de propulsión) a reacción

jettison /'dʒetɪsn/ *vt* echar al mar; *(fig, discard)* deshacerse de

jetty /'dʒetɪ/ *n* muelle *m*

Jew /dʒuː/ *n* judío *m*

jewel /'dʒuːəl/ *n* joya *f*. **~ler** *n* joyero *m*. **~lery** *n* joyas *fpl*

Jewish /'dʒuːɪʃ/ *adj* judío

jiffy /'dʒɪfɪ/ *n* momentito *m*. **do sth in a ~** hacer algo en un santiamén

jig /dʒɪg/ *n* (dance) giga *f*

jigsaw /'dʒɪgsɔː/ *n*. **~** (puzzle) rompecabezas *m*

jilt /dʒɪlt/ *vt* dejar plantado

jingle /'dʒɪŋgl/ *vt* hacer sonar. ● *vi* tintinear. ● *n* tintineo *m*; *(advert)* jingle *m* (publicitario)

job /dʒɒb/ *n* empleo *m*, trabajo *m*; *(piece of work)* trabajo *m*. **it is a**

good ~ that menos mal que. **~less** *adj* desempleado

jockey /'dʒɒkɪ/ *n* jockey *m*

jocular /'dʒɒkjʊlə(r)/ *adj* jocoso

jog /dʒɒg/ *vt* (pt jogged) empujar; refrescar (memory). ● *vi* hacer footing, hacer jogging. **~er** *n* persona *f* que hace footing. **~ging** *n* footing *m*, jogging *m*. **go ~ging** salir a hacer footing o jogging

join /dʒɔɪn/ *vt* (link) unir; hacerse socio de (club); hacerse miembro de (political group); alistarse en (army); reunirse con (another person). ● *n* juntura. ● *vi*. **~ together** (parts) unirse; (roads etc) empalmar; (rivers) confluir. □ **~ in** *vi* participar (en). □ **~ up** *vi* (Mil) alistarse. **~er** *n* carpintero *m*

joint /dʒɔɪnt/ *adj* conjunto. ● *n* *(join)* unión *f*, junta *f*; (in limbs) articulación *f*; *(Culin)* trozo *m* de carne (para asar). **out of ~** descoyuntado. **~ account** cuenta *f* conjunta. **~ly** *adv* conjuntamente. **~ owner** *n* copropietario *m*.

joist /dʒɔɪst/ *n* viga *f*

jok|e /dʒəʊk/ *n* (story) chiste *m*; *(practical joke)* broma *f*. ● *vi* bromear. **~er** *n* bromista *m* & *f*; *(Cards)* comodín *m*. **~y** *adj* guasón

jolly /'dʒɒlɪ/ *adj* (-ier, -iest) alegre. ● *adv* ① muy

jolt /dʒɒlt/ *vt* sacudir. ● *vi* (vehicle) dar una sacudida. ● *n* sacudida *f*

jostle /'dʒɒsl/ *vt* empujar. ● *vi* empujarse

jot /dʒɒt/ *n* pizca *f*. ● *vt* (pt jotted). □ **~ down** *vt* apuntar (rápidamente). **~ter** *n* bloc *m*

journal /'dʒɜːnl/ *n* (diary) diario *m*; *(newspaper)* periódico *m*; *(magazine)* revista *f*. **~ism** *n* periodismo *m*. **~ist** *n* periodista *m* & *f*

journey /'dʒɜːnɪ/ n viaje m. go on a ~ hacer un viaje. ●vi viajar

jovial /'dʒəʊvɪəl/ adj jovial

joy /dʒɔɪ/ n alegría f. ~ful adj feliz. ~ous adj feliz. ~rider n joven m que roba un coche para dar una vuelta. ~stick n (in aircraft) palanca f de mando; (Comp) mando m, joystick m

jubila|nt /'dʒuːbɪlənt/ adj jubiloso. ~tion /-'leɪʃn/ n júbilo m

jubilee /'dʒuːbɪliː/ n aniversario m especial

Judaism /'dʒuːdeɪɪzəm/ n judaísmo m

judge /dʒʌdʒ/ n juez m. ●vt juzgar. ~ment n juicio m

judicia|l /dʒuː'dɪʃl/ adj judicial. ~ry /-ərɪ/ n judicatura f

judo /'dʒuːdəʊ/ n judo m

jug /dʒʌg/ n jarra f

juggernaut /'dʒʌgənɔːt/ n camión m grande

juggle /'dʒʌgl/ vi hacer malabarismos. ●vt hacer malabarismos con. ~r n malabarista m & f

juic|e /dʒuːs/ n jugo m, zumo m. ~y adj jugoso, zumoso; (story etc) 🗓 picante

jukebox /'dʒuːkbɒks/ n máquina f de discos, rocola f (LAm)

July /dʒuː'laɪ/ n julio m

jumble /'dʒʌmbl/ vt. ~ (up) mezclar. ●n (muddle) revoltijo m. ~ sale n venta f de objetos usados

jumbo /'dʒʌmbəʊ/ adj gigante. ~ jet n jumbo m

jump /dʒʌmp/ vt saltar. ~ rope (Amer) saltar a la comba, saltar a la cuerda. ~ the gun obrar prematuramente. ~ the queue colarse. ●vi saltar; (start) sobresaltarse; (prices) alzarse. ~ at an opportunity apresurarse a aprovechar

una oportunidad. ●n salto m; (start) susto m; (increase) aumento m. ~er n jersey m, suéter m, pulóver m; (Amer, dress) pichi m, jumper m & f (LAm). ~er cables (Amer), ~ leads npl cables mpl de arranque. ~ rope (Amer) comba f, cuerda f, reata f (Mex). ~suit n mono m. ~y adj nervioso

junction /'dʒʌŋkʃn/ n (of roads, rails) cruce m; (Elec) empalme m

June /dʒuːn/ n junio m

jungle /'dʒʌŋgl/ n selva f, jungla f

junior /'dʒuːnɪə(r)/ adj (in age) más joven (to que); (in rank) subalterno. ●n menor m

junk /dʒʌŋk/ n trastos mpl viejos; (worthless stuff) basura f. ●vt 🗓 tirar. ~ food n comida f basura, alimento m chatarra (Mex). ~ie /'dʒʌŋkɪ/ n 🗓 drogadicto m, yonqui m & f 🗓. ~ mail n propaganda f que se recibe por correo. ~ shop n tienda f de trastos viejos

junta /'dʒʌntə/ n junta f militar

jupiter /'dʒuːpɪtə(r)/ n Júpiter m

jurisdiction /dʒʊərɪs'dɪkʃn/ n jurisdicción f

jur|or /'dʒʊərə(r)/ n (miembro m de un) jurado m. ~y n jurado m

just /dʒʌst/ adj (fair) justo. ●adv exactamente, justo; (barely) justo; (only) sólo, solamente. ~ as tall tan alto (as como). ~ listen! ¡escucha! he has ~ arrived acaba de llegar, recién llegó (LAm)

justice /'dʒʌstɪs/ n justicia f. J~ of the Peace juez m de paz

justif|iable /dʒʌstɪ'faɪəbl/ adj justificable. ~iably adv con razón. ~ication /dʒʌstɪfɪ'keɪʃn/ n justificación f. ~y /'dʒʌstɪfaɪ/ vt justificar

jut /dʒʌt/ vi (pt jutted). ~ (out)

sobresalir

juvenile /'dʒuːvənaɪl/ adj juvenil; (childish) infantil. ● n (Jurid) menor m & f

Kk

kaleidoscope /kə'laɪdəskəʊp/ n caleidoscopio m

kangaroo /kæŋgə'ruː/ n canguro m

karate /kə'rɑːtɪ/ n kárate m, karate m (LAm)

keel /kiːl/ n (of ship) quilla f. □ ~ **over** vi volcar(se)

keen /kiːn/ adj (-er, -est) (interest, feeling) vivo; (wind, mind, analysis) penetrante; (eyesight) agudo; (eager) entusiasta. I'm ~ **on** golf me encanta el golf. **he's** ~ **on** Shostakovich le gusta Shostakovich. ~**ly** adv vivamente; (enthusiastically) con entusiasmo. ~**ness** n intensidad f; (enthusiasm) entusiasmo m.

keep /kiːp/ vt (pt kept) guardar; cumplir (promise); tener (shop, animals); mantener (family); observar (rule); (celebrate) celebrar; (delay) detener; (prevent) impedir. ● vi (food) conservarse; (remain) quedarse; (continue) seguir. ~ **doing** seguir haciendo. ● n subsistencia f; (of castle) torreón m. **for** ~**s** 🄸 para siempre. □ ~ **back** vt retener. ● vi no acercarse. □ ~ **in** vt no dejar salir. □ ~ **off** vt mantenerse alejado de (land). '~ **off the grass**' 'prohibido pisar el césped'. □ ~ **on** vi seguir. ~ **on doing sth**

seguir haciendo. □ ~ **out** vt no dejar entrar. □ ~ **up** vt mantener. □ ~ **up with** vt estar al día en

kennel /'kenl/ n casa f del perro; (Amer, for boarding) residencia f canina. ~**s** n invar residencia f canina

kept /kept/ see **KEEP**

kerb /kɜːb/ n bordillo m (de la acera), borde m de la banqueta (Mex)

kerosene /'kerəsiːn/ n queroseno m

ketchup /'ketʃʌp/ n salsa f de tomate

kettle /'ketl/ n pava f, tetera f (para calentar agua)

key /kiː/ n llave f; (of computer, piano) tecla f; (Mus) tono m. **be off** ~ no estar en el tono. ● adj clave. □ ~ **in** vt teclear. ~**board** n teclado m. ~**hole** n ojo m de la cerradura. ~**ring** n llavero m

khaki /'kɑːkɪ/ adj caqui

kick /kɪk/ vt dar una patada a (person); patear (ball). ● vi dar patadas; (horse) cocear. ● n patada f; (of horse) coz f; (fam, thrill) placer m. □ ~ **out** vt 🄸 echar. □ ~ **up** vt armar (fuss etc). ~**off** n (in Sport) saque m inicial. ~ **start** vt arrancar (con el pedal de arranque) (engine)

kid /kɪd/ n (young goat) cabrito m; (fam, child) niño m, chaval m, escuincle m (Mex). ● vt (pt **kidded**) tomar el pelo a. ● vi bromear

kidnap /'kɪdnæp/ vt (pt **kidnapped**) secuestrar. ~**per** n secuestrador m. ~**ping** n secuestro m

kidney /'kɪdnɪ/ n riñón m

kill /kɪl/ vt matar; (fig) acabar con. ● n matanza f. □ ~ **off** vt matar. ~**er** n asesino m. ~**ing** n matanza f; (murder) asesinato m. **make a**

~ing (*fig*) hacer un gran negocio

kiln /kɪln/ *n* horno *m*

kilo /'ki:ləʊ/ *n* (*pl* -os) kilo *m*. **~gram(me)** /'kɪləgræm/ *n* kilogramo *m*. **~metre** /'kɪləmi:tə(r)/, /kɪ'lɒmɪtə(r)/ *n* kilómetro *m*. **~watt** /'kɪləwɒt/ *n* kilovatio *m*

kilt /kɪlt/ *n* falda *f* escocesa

kin /kɪn/ *n* familiares *mpl*

kind /kaɪnd/ *n* tipo *m*, clase *f*. ~ **of** (*fam, somewhat*) un poco. **in** ~ en especie. **be two of a** ~ ser tal para cual. ● *adj* amable

kindergarten /'kɪndəgɑːtn/ *n* jardín *m* de infancia

kind-hearted /kaɪnd'hɑːtɪd/ *adj* bondadoso

kindle /'kɪndl/ *vt* encender

kind|ly *adj* (**-ier, -iest**) bondadoso. ● *adv* amablemente; (*please*) haga el favor de. **~ness** *n* bondad *f*; (*act*) favor *m*

king /kɪŋ/ *n* rey *m*. **~dom** *n* reino *m*. **~fisher** *n* martín *m* pescador. **~-size(d)** *adj* extragrande

kink /kɪŋk/ *n* (*in rope*) vuelta *f*, curva *f*; (*in hair*) onda *f*. **~y** *adj* 🔢 pervertido

kiosk /'kiːɒsk/ *n* quiosco *m*

kipper /'kɪpə(r)/ *n* arenque *m* ahumado

kiss /kɪs/ *n* beso *m*. ● *vt* besar. ● *vi* besarse

kit /kɪt/ *n* avíos *mpl*. **tool** ~ caja *f* de herramientas. □ ~ **out** *vt* (*pt* kitted) equipar

kitchen /'kɪtʃɪn/ *n* cocina *f*

kite /kaɪt/ *n* cometa *f*, papalote *m* (*Mex*)

kitten /'kɪtn/ *n* gatito *m*

knack /næk/ *n* truco *m*

knapsack /'næpsæk/ *n* mochila *f*

knead /niːd/ *vt* amasar

knee /niː/ *n* rodilla *f*. **~cap** *n* rótula *f*

kneel /niːl/ *vi* (*pt* kneeled or knelt). ~ (**down**) arrodillarse; (*be on one's knees*) estar arrodillado

knelt /nelt/ *see* KNEEL

knew /njuː/ *see* KNOW

knickers /'nɪkəz/ *npl* bragas *fpl*, calzones *mpl* (*LAm*), pantaletas *fpl* (*Mex*)

knife /naɪf/ *n* (*pl* knives) cuchillo *m*. ● *vt* acuchillar

knight /naɪt/ *n* caballero *m*; (*Chess*) caballo *m*. ● *vt* conceder el título de Sir a. **~hood** *n* título *m* de Sir

knit /nɪt/ *vt* (*pt* knitted or knit) hacer, tejer (*LAm*). ● *vi* tejer, hacer punto. ~ **one's brow** fruncir el ceño. **~ting** *n* tejido *m*, punto *m*. **~ting needle** *n* aguja *f* de hacer punto, aguja *f* de tejer

knives /naɪvz/ *see* KNIFE

knob /nɒb/ *n* botón *m*; (*of door, drawer etc*) tirador *m*. **~bly** *adj* nudoso

knock /nɒk/ *vt* golpear; (*criticize*) criticar. ● *vi* golpear; (*at door*) llamar, golpear (*LAm*). ● *n* golpe *m*. □ ~ **about** *vt* maltratar. □ ~ **down** *vt* derribar; atropellar (person). □ ~ **off** *vt* hacer caer. ● *vi* (*fam, finish work*) terminar, salir del trabajo. □ ~ **out** *vt* (*by blow*) dejar sin sentido; (*eliminate*) eliminar. □ ~ **over** *vt* tirar; atropellar (person). **~er** *n* aldaba *f*. **~-kneed** /-'niːd/ *adj* patizambo. **~out** *n* (*Boxing*) nocaut *m*

knot /nɒt/ *n* nudo *m*. ● *vt* (*pt* knotted) anudar

know /nəʊ/ *vt* (*pt* knew) saber; (*be acquainted with*) conocer. **let s.o.** ~ **sth** decirle algo a uno;

(*warn*) avisarle algo a uno. ● vi saber. ~ how to do sth saber hacer algo. ~ about entender de (cars etc). ~ of saber de. ● n. be in the ~ estar enterado. ~-all n sabelotodo m & f. ~-how n know-how m, conocimientos mpl y experiencia. ~ingly adv a sabiendas. ~-it-all n (Amer) see **~ALL**

knowledge /'nɒlɪdʒ/ n saber m; (*awareness*) conocimiento m; (*learning*) conocimientos mpl. ~able adj informado

known /nəʊn/ see **KNOW**. ● adj conocido

knuckle /'nʌkl/ n nudillo m. □ ~ **under** vi someterse

Korea /kə'rɪə/ n Corea f. ~n adj & n coreano (m)

kudos /'kjuːdɒs/ n prestigio m

L

lab /læb/ n 🔟 laboratorio m

label /'leɪbl/ n etiqueta f. ● vt (pt labelled) poner etiqueta a; (*fig, describe as*) tachar de

laboratory /lə'bɒrətərɪ/ n laboratorio m

laborious /lə'bɔːrɪəs/ adj penoso

labour /'leɪbə(r)/ n trabajo m; (*workers*) mano f de obra; (*Med*) parto m. in ~ de parto. ● vi trabajar. ● vt insistir en. L~ n el partido m laborista. ● adj laborista. ~er n peón m

lace /leɪs/ n encaje m; (*of shoe*) cordón m, agujeta f (Mex). ● vt (*fasten*) atar

lacerate /'læsəreɪt/ vt lacerar

lack /læk/ n falta f. for ~ of por falta de. ● vt faltarle a uno. he ~s confidence le falta confianza en sí mismo. ~ing adj. be ~ing faltar. be ~ing in no tener

lad /læd/ n muchacho m

ladder /'lædə(r)/ n escalera f (de mano); (*in stocking*) carrera f. ● vt hacerse una carrera en. ● vi hacérsele una carrera a

laden /'leɪdn/ adj cargado (with de)

ladle /'leɪdl/ n cucharón m

lady /'leɪdɪ/ n señora f; (*young*) señorita f. ~bird n, ~bug n (Amer) mariquita f, catarina f (Mex). ~-in-waiting n dama f de honor. ~like adj fino

lag /læg/ vi (pt lagged). ~ (behind) retrasarse. ● vt revestir (pipes). ● n (*interval*) intervalo m

lager /'lɑːgə(r)/ n cerveza f (rubia)

lagging /'lægɪŋ/ n revestimiento m

lagoon /lə'guːn/ n laguna f

laid /leɪd/ see **LAY**

lain /leɪn/ see **LIE¹**

lair /leə(r)/ n guarida f

lake /leɪk/ n lago m

lamb /læm/ n cordero m

lame /leɪm/ adj (-er, -est) cojo, rengo (LAm); (*excuse*) pobre, malo

lament /lə'ment/ n lamento m. ● vt lamentar. ~able /'læməntəbl/ adj lamentable

lamp /læmp/ n lámpara f

lamp: ~post n farol m. ~shade n pantalla f

lance /lɑːns/ n lanza f

land /lænd/ n tierra f; (*country*) país m; (*plot*) terreno m. ● vt desembarcar; (*obtain*) conseguir; dar (blow). ● vi (*from ship*) desembarcar; (aircraft) aterrizar. □ ~ **up** vi ir a parar. ~**ing** n desembarque m; (by aircraft) aterrizaje m; (top of stairs) descanso m. ~**lady** n casera f; (of inn) dueña f. ~**lord** n casero m, dueño m; (of inn) dueño m. ~**mark** n punto m destacado. ~**scape** /-skeip/ n paisaje m. ~**slide** n desprendimiento m de tierras; (Pol) victoria f arrolladora

lane /lein/ n (path, road) camino m, sendero m; (strip of road) carril m

language /ˈlæŋgwɪdʒ/ n idioma m; (speech, style) lenguaje m

lank /læŋk/ adj (hair) lacio. ~**y** adj (-ier, -iest) larguirucho

lantern /ˈlæntən/ n linterna f

lap /læp/ n (of body) rodillas fpl; (Sport) vuelta f □ ~ **up** vt (pt lapped) beber a lengüetazos; (fig) aceptar con entusiasmo. ● vi (waves) chapotear

lapel /ləˈpel/ n solapa f

lapse /læps/ vi (decline) degradarse; (expire) caducar; (time) transcurrir. ~ **into** silence callarse. ● n error m; (of time) intervalo m

laptop /ˈlæptɒp/ n (computer) laptop m, portátil m

lard /lɑːd/ n manteca f de cerdo

larder /ˈlɑːdə(r)/ n despensa f

large /lɑːdʒ/ adj (-er, -est) grande, (before singular noun) gran. ● n. at ~ en libertad. ~**ly** adv en gran parte

lark /lɑːk/ n (bird) alondra f; (joke) broma f; (bit of fun) travesura f. □ ~ **about** vt hacer el tonto ①

larva /ˈlɑːvə/ n (pl -vae /-viː/) larva f

laser /ˈleɪzə(r)/ n láser m. ~ **beam** n rayo m láser. ~ **printer** n impresora f láser

lash /læʃ/ vt azotar. □ ~ **out** vi atacar. ~ **out against** vt atacar. ● n latigazo m; (eyelash) pestaña f; (whip) látigo m

lashings /ˈlæʃɪŋz/ npl. ~ **of** (fam, cream etc) montones de

lass /læs/ n muchacha f

lasso /læˈsuː/ n (pl -os) lazo m

last /lɑːst/ adj último; (week etc) pasado. ~ **Monday** el lunes pasado. ~ **night** anoche. ● adv por último; (most recently) la última vez. he came ~ llegó el último. ● n último m; (remainder) lo que queda. ~ **but one** penúltimo. at (long) ~ por fin. ● vi/t durar. □ ~ **out** vi sobrevivir. ~**ing** adj duradero. ~**ly** adv por último

latch /lætʃ/ n pestillo m

late /leɪt/ adj (-er, -est) (not on time) tardío; (recent) reciente; (former) antiguo, ex. **be** ~ llegar tarde. in ~ **July** a fines de julio. the ~ **Dr Phillips** el difunto Dr. Phillips. ● adv tarde. ~**ly** adv últimamente

latent /ˈleɪtnt/ adj latente

later /ˈleɪtə(r)/ adv más tarde

lateral /ˈlætərəl/ adj lateral

latest /ˈleɪtɪst/ adj último. ● n. at the ~ a más tardar

lathe /leɪð/ n torno m

lather /ˈlɑːðə(r)/ n espuma f

Latin /ˈlætɪn/ n (language) latín m. ● adj latino. ~ **America** n América f Latina, Latinoamérica f. ~ **American** adj & n latinoamericano f

latitude /ˈlætɪtjuːd/ n latitud m

latter /ˈlætə(r)/ adj último; (of two) segundo. ● n. the ~ éste m, ésta f, éstos mpl, éstas fpl

laugh /lɑːf/ vi reír(se). ~ **at** reírse de. ● n risa f. ~**able** adj ridículo. ~**ing stock** n hazmerreír m. ~**ter**

n risas *fpl*

launch /lɔ:ntʃ/ *vt* lanzar; botar (new vessel). ● *n* lanzamiento *m*; (of new vessel) botadura; (boat) lancha *f* (a motor). **~ing pad**, **~ pad** *n* plataforma *f* de lanzamiento

laund|er /'lɔ:ndə(r)/ *vt* lavar (y planchar). **~erette** /-et/, **L~romat** /'lɔ:ndrəmæt/ (Amer) (P) *n* lavandería *f* automática. **~ry** *n* (place) lavandería *f*; (dirty clothes) ropa *f* sucia; (clean clothes) ropa *f* limpia

lava /'lɑ:və/ *n* lava *f*

lavatory /'lævətərɪ/ *n* (cuarto *m* de) baño *m*. **public ~** servicios *mpl*, baños *mpl* (LAm)

lavish /'lævɪʃ/ *adj* (lifestyle) de derroche; (meal) espléndido; (production) fastuoso. ● *vt* prodigar (on a)

law /lɔ:/ *n* ley *f*; (profession, subject of study) derecho *m*. **~ and order** *n* orden *m* público. **~ court** *n* tribunal *m*

lawn /lɔ:n/ *n* césped *m*, pasto *m* (LAm). **~mower** *n* cortacésped *f*, cortadora *f* de pasto (LAm)

lawsuit /'lɔ:su:t/ *n* juicio *m*

lawyer /'lɔjə(r)/ *n* abogado *m*.

lax /læks/ *adj* descuidado; (morals etc) laxo

laxative /'læksətɪv/ *n* laxante *m*

lay /leɪ/ *see* LIE. ● *vt* (*pt* laid) poner (also table, eggs); tender (trap); formar (plan). **~ hands on** echar mano a. **~ hold of** agarrar. ● *adj* (non-clerical) laico; (opinion etc) profano. □ **~ down** *vt* dejar a un lado; imponer (condition). **~ into** *vt* 🗙 dar una paliza a. □ **~ off** *vt* despedir (worker). *vi* 🗓 terminar. **~ on** *vt* (provide) proveer. □ **~ out** *vt* (design) disponer; (display) exponer; gastar (money). **~about**

n holgazán. **~-by** *n* área *f* de reposo

layer /'leɪə(r)/ *n* capa *f*.

layette /leɪ'et/ *n* canastilla *f*

layman /'leɪmən/ *n* (*pl* -men) lego *m*

layout /'leɪaʊt/ *n* disposición *f*

laz|e /leɪz/ *vi* holgazanear; (relax) descansar. **~iness** *n* pereza *f*. **~y** *adj* perezoso. **~ybones** *n* holgazán *m*

lead¹ /li:d/ *vt* (*pt* led) conducir; dirigir (team); llevar (life); encabezar (parade, attack). **I was led to believe that** ... me dieron a entender que .... *vi* (go first) ir delante; (in race) aventajar. ● *n* mando *m*; (clue) pista *f*; (leash) correa *f*; (wire) cable *m*. **be in the ~** llevar la delantera

lead² /led/ *n* plomo *m*; (of pencil) mina *f*. **~en** *adj* (sky) plomizo; (weight) de plomo

lead: /li:d/ **~er** *n* jefe *m* (Pol) líder *m* & *f*; (of gang) cabecilla *m*. **~ership** *n* dirección *f*. **~ing** *adj* principal; (in front) delantero

leaf /li:f/ *n* (*pl* leaves) hoja *f*. □ **~ through** *vi* hojear. **~let** /'li:flɪt/ *n* folleto *m*. **~y** *adj* frondoso

league /li:g/ *n* liga *f*. **be in ~ with** estar aliado con

leak /li:k/ *n* (hole) agujero *m*; (of gas, liquid) escape *m*; (of information) filtración *f*; (in roof) gotera *f*; (in boat) vía *f* de agua. ● *vi* gotear; (liquid) salirse; (boat) hacer agua. ● *vt* perder; (information). **~y** *adj* (receptacle) agujereado; (roof) que tiene goteras

lean /li:n/ *vt* (*pt* leaned *or* leant /lent/) *vt* apoyar. ● *vi* inclinarse. □ **~ against** *vt* apoyarse en. □ **~ on** *vt* apoyarse en. □ **~ out** *vt* asomarse (of a). □ **~ over** *vi* inclinarse. ● *adj* (-er, -est) (person) delgado;

(animal) flaco; (meat) magro. **~ing** adj inclinado. **~-to** n colgadizo m

leap /li:p/ vi (pt leaped or leapt /lept/) saltar. ●n salto m. **~frog** n. play **~frog** saltar al potro, jugar a la pídola, brincar al burro (Mex). ●vi (pt -frogged) saltar. **~ year** n año m bisiesto

learn /lɜ:n/ vt/i (pt learned or learnt) aprender (to do a hacer). **~ed** /-ɪd/ adj culto. **~er** n principiante m & f; (apprentice) aprendiz m. **~ing** n saber m. **~ing curve** n curva f del aprendizaje

lease /li:s/ n arriendo m. ●vt arrendar

leash /li:ʃ/ n correa f

least /li:st/ adj (smallest amount of) mínimo; (slightest) menor; (smallest) más pequeño. ●n. the ~ lo menos. at ~ por lo menos. not in the ~ en absoluto. ●adv menos

leather /'leðə(r)/ n piel f, cuero m

leave /li:v/ vt (pt left) dejar; (depart from) salir de. ~ alone dejar de tocar (thing); dejar en paz (person). ●vi marcharse; (train) salir. ●n permiso m. ~ **behind** vt dejar. □ ~ **out** vt omitir. □ ~ **over** vt. be left over quedar. on ~ (Mil) de permiso

leaves /li:vz/ see LEAF

lecture /'lektʃə(r)/ n conferencia f; (Univ) clase f; (rebuke) sermón m. ●vi dar clase. ●vt (scold) sermonear. **~r** n conferenciante m & f, conferencista m & f (LAm); (Univ) profesor m universitario

led /led/ see LEAD¹

ledge /ledʒ/ n cornisa f; (of window) alféizar m

leek /li:k/ n puerro m

leer /lɪə(r)/ vi. ~ at mirar impúdicamente. ●n mirada impúdica f

left /left/ see LEAVE. adj izquierdo. ●adv a la izquierda. ●n izquierda f. ~-**handed** /-'hændɪd/ adj zurdo. **luggage** n consigna f. **~overs** npl restos mpl. **~wing** /-'wɪŋ/ adj izquierdista

leg /leg/ n pierna f; (of animal, furniture) pata f; (of pork) pernil m; (of lamb) pierna f; (of journey) etapa f. on its last ~s en las últimas. pull s.o.'s ~ ⒤ tomarle el pelo a uno

legacy /'legəsi/ n herencia f.

legal /'li:gl/ adj (permitted by law) lícito; (concerning by law) legal; (system etc) jurídico. **~ity** /li:'gælətɪ/ n legalidad f. **~ize** vt legalizar. **~ly** adv legalmente

legend /'ledʒənd/ n leyenda f. **~ary** adj legendario

legible /'ledʒəbl/ adj legible

legislat|e /'ledʒɪsleɪt/ vi legislar. **~ion** /-'leɪʃn/ n legislación f

legitimate /lɪ'dʒɪtɪmət/ adj legítimo

leisure /'leʒə(r)/ n ocio m. at your ~ cuando le venga bien. **~ly** adj lento, pausado

lemon /'lemən/ n limón m. **~ade** /-'neɪd/ n (fizzy) gaseosa f (de limón); (still) limonada f

lend /lend/ vt (pt lent) prestar. **~ing** n préstamo m

length /leŋθ/ n largo m; (of time) duración f; (of cloth) largo m. at a ~ (at last) por fin. at (great) ~ detalladamente. **~en** /'leŋθən/ vt alargar. ●vi alargarse. **~ways** adv a lo largo. **~y** adj largo

lenient /'li:nɪənt/ adj indulgente

lens /lenz/ n lente f; (of camera) objetivo m. (contact) **~es** npl (optics) lentillas fpl, lentes mpl de contacto (LAm)

lent /lent/ see LEND

Lent /lent/ n cuaresma f

Leo /'liːəʊ/ n Leo m

leopard /'lepəd/ n leopardo m

leotard /'liːətɑːd/ n malla f

lesbian /'lezbɪən/ n lesbiana f.
● adj lesbiano

less /les/ adj & n & adv & prep
menos. ~ **than** menos que; (with
numbers) menos de. ~ **and** ~
cada vez menos. none the ~ sin
embargo. ~**en** vt/i disminuir

lesson /'lesn/ n clase f

lest /lest/ conj no sea que (+ subjunctive)

let /let/ vt (pt let, pres p letting)
dejar; (lease) alquilar. ~ **me** do it
déjame hacerlo. ● modal verb. ~'**s**
go! ¡vamos!, ¡vámonos! ~'**s** see
(vamos) a ver. ~'**s** **talk/drink**
hablemos/bebamos. □ ~ **down** vt
bajar; (deflate) desinflar; (fig) defraudar. □ ~ **go** vt soltar. □ ~ **in** vt
dejar entrar. □ ~ **off** vt disparar
(gun); (cause to explode) hacer explotar; hacer estallar (firework);
(excuse) perdonar. □ ~ **out** vt dejar
salir. □ ~ **through** vt dejar pasar.
□ ~ **up** vi disminuir. ~**down** n
desilusión f

lethal /'liːθl/ adj (dose, wound)
mortal; (weapon) mortífero

letharg|ic /lɪ'θɑːdʒɪk/ adj letár-
gico. ~**y** /'leθədʒɪ/ n letargo m

letter /'letə(r)/ n (of alphabet)
letra f; (written message) carta f. ~
bomb n carta f bomba. ~**box** n
buzón m. ~**ing** n letras fpl

lettuce /'letɪs/ n lechuga f

let-up /'letʌp/ n interrupción f

leukaemia /luː'kiːmɪə/ n leucemia f

level /'levl/ adj (flat, even) plano,

parejo (LAm); (spoonful) raso. ~
with (at same height) al nivel de.
● n nivel m. ● vt (pt levelled) nivelar; (aim) apuntar. ~ **crossing** n
paso m a nivel, crucero m (Mex)

lever /'liːvə(r)/ n palanca f. ● vt
apalancar. ~ **open** abrir haciendo
palanca. ~**age** /-ɪdʒ/ n apalanca-
miento m

levy /'levɪ/ vt imponer (tax). ● n
impuesto m

lewd /luːd/ adj (-er, -est) lascivo

liab|ility /laɪə'bɪlətɪ/ n responsa-
bilidad f; (fam, disadvantage) lastre
m. ~**ilities** npl (debts) deudas fpl.
~**le** /'laɪəbl/ adj. be ~**le** to do
tener tendencia a hacer. ~**le** for
responsable de. ~**le** to susceptible
de; expuesto a (fine)

liais|e /lɪ'eɪz/ vi actuar de enlace
(with con). ~**on** /-ɒn/ n enlace m

liar /'laɪə(r)/ n mentiroso m

libel /'laɪbl/ n difamación f. ● vt (pt
libelled) difamar (por escrito)

liberal /'lɪbərəl/ adj liberal; (generous) generoso. L~ (Pol) del Partido
Liberal. ● n liberal m & f. ~**ly** adv li-
beralmente; (generously) generosa-
mente

liberat|e /'lɪbəreɪt/ vt liberar.
~**ion** /-'reɪʃn/ n liberación f

liberty /'lɪbətɪ/ n libertad f. take
liberties tomarse libertades. take
the ~ of tomarse la libertad de

Libra /'liːbrə/ n Libra f

librar|ian /laɪ'breərɪən/ n biblio-
tecario m. ~**y** /'laɪbrərɪ/ n biblioteca f

Library of Congress La *i*
biblioteca nacional de
EEUU, situada en Washington DC.
Fundada por el Congreso *Congress*, alberga más de ochenta

millones de libros en 470 idiomas, y otros objetos.

lice /laɪs/ *see* **LOUSE**

licence /'laɪsns/ *n* licencia *f*, permiso *m*

license /'laɪsns/ *vt* autorizar. ●*n* (Amer) *see* **LICENCE**. ~ **number** *n* (Amer) (número *m* de) matrícula *f*. ~ **plate** *n* (Amer) matrícula *f*, placa *f* (LAm)

lick /lɪk/ *vt* lamer; (sl, defeat) dar una paliza a. ●*n* lametón *m*

licorice /'lɪkərɪs/ *n* (Amer) regaliz *m*

lid /lɪd/ *n* tapa *f*; (eyelid) párpado *m*

lie¹ /laɪ/ *vi* (*pt* **lay**, *pp* **lain**, *pres p* **lying**) echarse, tenderse; (be in lying position) estar tendido; (be) estar, encontrarse. □ ~ **low** quedarse escondido. □ ~ **down** *vi* echarse, tenderse

lie² /laɪ/ *n* mentira *f*. ●*vi* (*pt* **lied**, *pres p* **lying**) mentir

lie-in /laɪ'ɪn/ *n*. **have a** ~ quedarse en la cama

lieutenant /leftˈenənt/ *n* (Mil) teniente *m*

life /laɪf/ *n* (*pl* **lives**) vida *f*. ~ **belt** *n* salvavidas *m*. ~**boat** *n* lancha *f* de salvamento; (on ship) bote *m* salvavidas. ~**buoy** *n* boya *f* salvavidas. ~ **coach** *n* coach *m & f*; personal. ~**guard** *n* salvavidas *m & f*, socorrista *m & f*. ~ **jacket** *n* chaleco *m* salvavidas. ~**less** *adj* sin vida. ~**like** *adj* verosímil. ~**line** *n* cuerda *f* de salvamento; (fig) tabla *f* de salvación. ~**long** *adj* de toda la vida. ~ **preserver** *n* (Amer, buoy) *see* ~**BUOY**; (Amer) *see* ~ **JACKET**. ~ **ring** *n* (Amer) *see* **BELT**. ~**saver** *n* (person) salvavidas *m & f*; (fig) salvación *f*. ~**size(d)** *adj* (de)

tamaño natural. ~**time** *n* vida *f*. ~ **vest** *n* (Amer) *see* ~ **JACKET**

lift /lɪft/ *vt* levantar. ●*vi* (fog) disiparse. ●*n* ascensor *m*. **give a** ~ to s.o. llevar a uno en su coche, dar aventón a uno (Mex). □ ~ **up** *vt* levantar. ~**off** *n* despegue *m*

light /laɪt/ *n* luz *f*; (lamp) lámpara *f*, luz *f*; (flame) fuego *m*. **come to** ~ salir a la luz. **have you got a** ~? ¿tienes fuego? **the** ~**s** *npl* (traffic signals) el semáforo; (on vehicle) las luces. ●*adj* (-er, -est) (in colour) claro; (not heavy) ligero. ●*vt* (*pt* lit or lighted) encender, prender (LAm); (illuminate) iluminar. ●*vi* encenderse, prenderse (LAm). □ ~ **up** *vt* iluminar. ●*vi* iluminarse. ~ **bulb** *n* bombilla *f*, foco *m* (Mex). ~**en** *vt* (make less heavy) aligerar, aliviar (LAm); (give light to) iluminar; (make brighter) aclarar. ~**er** *n* (for cigarettes) mechero *m*, encendedor *m*. ~**hearted** /-'hɑːtɪd/ *adj* alegre. ~**house** *n* faro *m*. ~**ly** *adv* ligeramente

lightning /'laɪtnɪŋ/ *n*. **flash of** ~ relámpago *m*. ●*adj* relámpago

lightweight *adj* ligero, liviano (LAm)

like /laɪk/ *adj* parecido. ●*prep* como. ●*conj* 1 como. ●*vt*. **I** ~ **chocolate** me gusta el chocolate. **they** ~ **swimming** (a ellos) les gusta nadar. **would you** ~ **a coffee?** ¿quieres un café?. ~**able** *adj* simpático.

like|lihood /'laɪklɪhʊd/ *n* probabilidad *f*. ~**ly** *adj* (-ier, -iest) probable. **he is** ~**ly to come** es probable que venga. ●*adv* probablemente. **not** ~**ly!** ¡ni hablar! ~**n** *vt* comparar (to con, a). ~**ness** *n* parecido *m*. **be a good** ~**ness** parecerse mucho. ~**wise**

adv (*also*) también; (*the same way*) lo mismo

liking /'laɪkɪŋ/ *n* (*for thing*) afición *f*; (*for person*) simpatía *f*

lilac /'laɪlək/ *adj* lila. ● *n* lila *f*; (*color*) lila *m*

lily /'lɪlɪ/ *n* lirio *m*; (*white*) azucena *f*

limb /lɪm/ *n* miembro *m*. **out on a ∼** aislado

lime /laɪm/ *n* (*white substance*) cal *f*; (*fruit*) lima *f*. **∼light** *n*. **be in the ∼light** ser el centro de atención

limerick /'lɪmərɪk/ *n* quintilla *f* humorística

limit /'lɪmɪt/ *n* límite *m*. ● *vt* limitar. **∼ation** /-'teɪʃn/ *n* limitación *f*. **∼ed** *adj* limitado. **∼ed company** *n* sociedad *f* anónima

limousine /'lɪməziːn/ *n* limusina *f*

limp /lɪmp/ *vi* cojear, renguear (LAm). ● *n* cojera *f*, renguera *f* (LAm). **have a ∼** cojear. ● *adj* (-er, -est) flojo

linden /'lɪndn/ *n* (Amer) tilo *m*

line /laɪn/ *n* línea *f*; (*track*) vía *f*; (*wrinkle*) arruga *f*; (*row*) fila *f*; (*of poem*) verso *m*; (*rope*) cuerda *f*; (*of goods*) surtido *m*; (Amer, *queue*) cola *f*. **stand in ∼** (Amer) hacer cola. **get in ∼** (Amer) ponerse en la cola. **cut in ∼** (Amer) colarse. **in ∼ with** de acuerdo con. ● *vt* forrar (*skirt, box*); bordear (*streets etc*). □ **∼ up** *vi* alinearse; (*in queue*) hacer cola. *vt* (*form into line*) poner en fila; (*align*) alinear. **∼d** /laɪnd/ *adj* (*paper*) con renglones; (*with fabric*) forrado

linen /'lɪnɪn/ *n* (*sheets etc*) ropa *f* blanca; (*material*) lino *m*

liner /'laɪnə(r)/ *n* (*ship*) transatlántico *m*

linger /'lɪŋgə(r)/ *vi* tardar en mar-

charse. **∼ (on)** (*smells etc*) persistir. □ **∼ over** *vt* dilatarse en

lingerie /'læŋʒərɪ/ *n* lencería *f*

linguist /'lɪŋgwɪst/ *n* políglota *m & f*; lingüista *m & f*. **∼ic** /lɪŋ 'gwɪstɪk/ *adj* lingüístico. **∼ics** *n* lingüística *f*

lining /'laɪnɪŋ/ *n* forro *m*

link /lɪŋk/ *n* (*of chain*) eslabón *m*; (*connection*) conexión *f*; (*bond*) vínculo *m*; (*transport, telecommunications*) conexión *f*, enlace *m*. ● *vt* conectar; relacionar (*facts, events*). □ **∼ up** *vt/i* conectar

lino /'laɪnəʊ/ *n* (*pl* -os) linóleo *m*

lint /lɪnt/ *n* (Med) hilas *fpl*

lion /'laɪən/ *n* león *m*. **∼ess** /-nɪs/ *n* leona *f*

lip /lɪp/ *n* labio *m*; (*edge*) borde *m*. **∼read** *vi* leer los labios. **∼salve** *n* crema *f* para los labios. **∼service** *n*. **pay ∼service** to aprobar de boquilla, aprobar de los dientes para afuera (Mex). **∼stick** *n* lápiz *m* de labios

liqueur /lɪ'kjʊə(r)/ *n* licor *m*

liquid /'lɪkwɪd/ *adj & n* líquido (*m*)

liquidate /'lɪkwɪdeɪt/ *vt* liquidar

liquidize /'lɪkwɪdaɪz/ *vt* licuar. **∼r** *n* licuadora *f*

liquor /'lɪkə(r)/ *n* bebidas *fpl* alcohólicas

liquorice /'lɪkərɪs/ *n* regaliz *m*

liquor store *n* (Amer) tienda *f* de bebidas alcohólicas

lisp /lɪsp/ *n* ceceo *m*. **speak with a ∼** cecear. ● *vi* cecear

list /lɪst/ *n* lista *f*. ● *vt* hacer una lista de; (*enter in a list*) inscribir. ● *vi* (*ship*) escorar

listen /'lɪsn/ *vi* escuchar. **∼ in (to)** escuchar. **∼ to** escuchar. **∼er** *n* oyente *m & f*

listless /'lɪstlɪs/ adj apático

lit /lɪt/ see LIGHT

literacy /'lɪtərəsɪ/ n alfabetismo m

literal /'lɪtərəl/ adj literal. ∼**ly** adv literalmente

literary /'lɪtərərɪ/ adj literario

literate /'lɪtərət/ adj alfabetizado

literature /'lɪtərətʃə(r)/ n literatura f; (fig) folletos mpl

lithe /laɪð/ adj ágil

litre /'liːtə(r)/ n litro m

litter /'lɪtə(r)/ n basura f; (of animals) camada f. ● vt ensuciar; (scatter) esparcir. ∼**ed with** lleno de. ∼ **bin** n papelera f. ∼**bug**, ∼**lout** n persona f que tira basura en lugares públicos

little /'lɪtl/ adj pequeño; (not much) poco. a ∼ water un poco de agua. ● pron poco, poca. a ∼ un poco. ● adv poco. ∼ **by** ∼ poco a poco. ∼ **finger** n (dedo m) meñique m

live /lɪv/ vt/i vivir. □ ∼ **down** vt lograr borrar. □ ∼ **off** vt vivir a costa de (family, friends); (feed on) alimentarse de. □ ∼ **on** vt (feed on, so on) vivir de. vi (memory) seguir presente; (tradition) seguir existiendo. □ ∼ **up** vt. ∼ **it up** 🄸 darse la gran vida. □ ∼ **up to** vt vivir de acuerdo con; cumplir (promise). ● /laɪv/ adj vivo; (wire) con corriente; (broadcast) en directo

livelihood /'laɪvlɪhʊd/ n sustento m

lively /'laɪvlɪ/ adj (-ier, -iest) vivo

liven up /'laɪvn/ vt animar. ● vi animar(se)

liver /'lɪvə(r)/ n hígado m

lives /laɪvz/ see LIFE

livestock /'laɪvstɒk/ n animales mpl (de cría); (cattle) ganado m

livid /'lɪvɪd/ adj lívido; (fam, angry) furioso

living /'lɪvɪŋ/ adj vivo. ● n vida f. make a ∼ ganarse la vida. ∼ **room** n salón m, sala f (de estar), living m (LAm)

lizard /'lɪzəd/ n lagartija f; (big) lagarto m

load /ləʊd/ n (also Elec) carga f; (quantity) cantidad f; (weight, strain) peso m. ∼**s of** 🄸 montones de. ● vt cargar. ∼**ed** adj cargado

loaf /ləʊf/ n (pl loaves) pan m; (stick of bread) barra f de pan. ● vi. ∼ (**about**) holgazanear

loan /ləʊn/ n préstamo m. on ∼ prestado. ● vt prestar

loath|e /ləʊð/ vt odiar. ∼**ing** n odio m (of a). ∼**esome** /-səm/ adj repugnante

lobby /'lɒbɪ/ n vestíbulo m; (Pol) grupo m de presión. ● vt ejercer presión sobre. ● vi. ∼ **for** sth ejercer presión para obtener algo

lobe /ləʊb/ n lóbulo m

lobster /'lɒbstə(r)/ n langosta f, bogavante m

local /'ləʊkl/ adj local. ∼ (**phone**) **call** llamada f urbana. ● n (fam, pub) bar m. **the** ∼**s** los vecinos mpl. ∼ **government** n administración f municipal. ∼**ity** /-'kælətɪ/ n localidad f. ∼**ization** n localización f. ∼**ly** adv (live, work) en la zona

locat|e /ləʊ'keɪt/ vt (situate) situar, ubicar (LAm); (find) localizar, ubicar (LAm). ∼**ion** /-ʃn/ n situación f, ubicación f (LAm). **on** ∼**ion** fuera del estudio. **to film on** ∼**ion** in Andalusia rodar en Andalucía

lock /lɒk/ n (of door etc) cerradura f; (on canal) esclusa f; (of hair) mechón m. ● vt cerrar con llave. ● vi cerrarse con llave. □ **~ in** vt encerrar. □ **~ out** vt cerrar la puerta a. □ **~ up** vt encerrar (person); cerrar con llave (building)

locker /'lɒkə(r)/ n armario m, locker m (LAm). **~ room** n (Amer) vestuario m, vestidor m (Mex)

locket /'lɒkɪt/ n medallón m

lock|out /'lɒkaʊt/ n cierre m patronal, paro m patronal (LAm). **~smith** n cerrajero m

locomotive /ləʊkə'məʊtɪv/ n locomotora f

lodg|e /lɒdʒ/ n (of porter) portería f. ● vt alojar; presentar (complaint). **~er** n huésped m. **~ings** n alojamiento m; (room) habitación f alquilada

loft /lɒft/ n desván m, altillo m (LAm)

lofty /'lɒftɪ/ adj (-ier, -iest) elevado; (haughty) altanero

log /lɒg/ n (of wood) tronco m; (as fuel) leño m; (record) diario m. sleep like a **~** dormir como un tronco. ● vt (pt logged) registrar. □ **~ in**, **~ on** vi (Comp) entrar (al sistema). □ **~ off**, **~ out** vi (Comp) salir (del sistema)

logarithm /'lɒgərɪðəm/ n logaritmo m

loggerheads /'lɒgəhedz/ npl. be at **~** with estar a matar con

logic /'lɒdʒɪk/ adj lógica f. **~al** adj lógico. **~ally** adv lógicamente

logistics /lə'dʒɪstɪks/ n logística f. ● npl (practicalities) problemas mpl logísticos

logo /'ləʊgəʊ/ n (pl -os) logo m

loin /lɔɪn/ n (Culin) lomo m. **~s** npl entrañas fpl

loiter /'lɔɪtə(r)/ vi perder el tiempo

loll /lɒl/ vi repantigarse

loll|ipop /'lɒlɪpɒp/ n pirulí m. **~y** n polo m, paleta f (helada) (LAm)

London /'lʌndən/ n Londres m. ● adj londinense. **~er** n londinense m & f

lone /ləʊn/ adj solitario. **~ly** adj (-ier, -iest) solitario. feel **~ly** sentirse muy solo. **~r** n solitario m. **~some** /-səm/ adj solitario

long /lɒŋ/ adj (-er, -est) largo. a **~** time mucho tiempo. how **~** is it? ¿cuánto tiene de largo? ● adv largo/mucho tiempo. as **~** as (while) mientras; (provided that) con tal que (+ subjunctive). before **~** dentro de poco. so **~!** ¡hasta luego! so **~** as (provided that) con tal que (+ subjunctive). □ **~ for** vt anhelar. **~ to** do estar deseando hacer. **~distance** /-'dɪstəns/ adj de larga distancia. **~distance phone call** llamada f de larga distancia, conferencia f. **~er** adv. no **~er** ya no. **~haul** /-'hɔːl/ adj de larga distancia. **~ing** n anhelo m, ansia f

longitude /'lɒŋgɪtjuːd/ n longitud f

long: **~ jump** n salto m de longitud. **~playing record** n elepé m. **~range** adj de largo alcance. **~sighted** /-'saɪtɪd/ adj hipermétrope. **~term** adj a largo plazo. **~winded** /-'wɪndɪd/ adj prolijo

loo /luː/ n 🅸 váter m, baño m (LAm)

look /lʊk/ vt mirar; representar (age). ● vi mirar; (seem) parecer; (search) buscar. ● n mirada f; (appearance) aspecto m. good **~s** belleza f. □ **~ after** vt cuidar (person); (be responsible for) encargarse de. □ **~ at** vt mirar; (consider) considerar. □ **~ down on** vt despre-

loom | low

ciar. □ ~ **for** vt buscar. □ ~ **forward to** vt esperar con ansia. □ ~ **into** vt investigar. □ ~ **like** vt parecerse a. □ ~ **on** vi mirar. □ ~ **out** vi tener cuidado. □ ~ **out for** vt buscar; (watch) tener cuidado con. □ ~ **round** vi volver la cabeza. □ ~ **through** vt hojear. □ ~ **up** vt buscar (word); (visit) ir a ver. □ ~ **up to** vt admirar. **~alike** n ① doble m & f. **~-out** n (Mil, person) vigía m. be on the ~out for andar a la caza de. **~s** npl belleza f

loom /luːm/ n telar m. ● vi aparecerse

looney, loony /'luːnɪ/ adj & n ✕ chiflado (m) ①, loco (m)

loop /luːp/ n (shape) curva f; (in string) lazada f. ● vt hacer una lazada con. **~hole** n (in rule) escapatoria f

loose /luːs/ adj (-er, -est) suelto; (garment, thread, hair) flojo; (inexact) vago; (not packed) suelto. be at a ~ end no tener nada que hacer. **~ly** adv sueltamente; (roughly) aproximadamente. **~n** vt aflojar

loot /luːt/ n botín m. ● vt/i saquear. **~er** n saqueador m

lop /lɒp/ vt (pt lopped). **~ off** cortar

lop-sided /-'saɪdɪd/ adj ladeado

lord /lɔːd/ n señor m; (British title) lord m. **(good) L~!** ¡Dios mío! the L~ el Señor. the (House of) L~s la Cámara de los Lores

lorry /'lɒrɪ/ n camión m. ~ **driver** n camionero m

lose /luːz/ vt/i (pt lost) perder. **~r** n perdedor m

loss /lɒs/ n pérdida f. be at a ~ estar perplejo. be at a ~ for words no encontrar palabras

lost /lɒst/ see **LOSE**. ● adj perdido. **get** ~ perderse. ~ **property** n, ~ **and found** (Amer) oficina f de objetos perdidos

lot /lɒt/ n (fate) suerte f; (at auction) lote m; (land) solar m. a ~ (of) muchos. quite a ~ of ① bastante. **~s (of)** ① muchos. **they ate the** ~ se lo comieron todo

lotion /'ləʊʃn/ n loción f

lottery /'lɒtərɪ/ n lotería f

loud /laʊd/ adj (-er, -est) fuerte; (noisy) ruidoso; (gaudy) chillón. **out** ~ en voz alta. **~hailer** /-'heɪlə(r)/ n megáfono m. **~ly** adv (speak) en voz alta; (shout) fuerte; (complain) a voz en grito. **~speaker** /-'spiːkə(r)/ n altavoz m, altoparlante m (LAm)

lounge /laʊndʒ/ vi repantigarse. ● n salón m, sala f (de estar), living m (LAm)

lous|e /laʊs/ n (pl lice) piojo m. **~y** /'laʊzɪ/ adj (-ier, -iest) (sl, bad) malísimo

lout /laʊt/ n patán m

lov|able /'lʌvəbl/ adj adorable. **~e** /lʌv/ n amor m; (tennis) cero m. **be in ~e (with)** estar enamorado (de). **fall in ~e (with)** enamorarse (de). ● vt querer, amar (person). **I ~e milk** me encanta la leche. **~e affair** n aventura f, amorío m

lovely /'lʌvlɪ/ adj (-ier, -iest) (appearance) precioso, lindo (LAm); (person) encantador, amoroso (LAm)

lover /'lʌvə(r)/ n amante m & f

loving /'lʌvɪŋ/ adj cariñoso

low /ləʊ/ adj & adv (-er, -est) bajo. ● vi (cattle) mugir. **~er** vt bajar. **~er o.s.** envilecerse. **~-level** adj a bajo nivel. **~ly** adj (-ier, -iest) humilde

loyal /'lɔɪəl/ adj leal, fiel. **~ty** n lealtad f. **~ty card** tarjeta f de fidelidad

lozenge /'lɒzɪndʒ/ n (shape) rombo m; (tablet) pastilla f

LP abbr (= **long-playing record**) elepé m

Ltd /'lɪmɪtɪd/ abbr (= **Limited**) S.A., Sociedad Anónima

lubricate /'lu:brɪkeɪt/ vt lubricar

lucid /'lu:sɪd/ adj lúcido

luck /lʌk/ n suerte f **good ~!** ¡(buena) suerte! **~ily** adv por suerte. **~y** adj (-ier, -iest) (person) con suerte. **be ~y** tener suerte. **~y number** número m de la suerte

lucrative /'lu:krətɪv/ adj lucrativo

ludicrous /'lu:dɪkrəs/ adj ridículo

lug /lʌg/ vt (pt **lugged**) 🄸 arrastrar

luggage /'lʌgɪdʒ/ n equipaje m. **~ rack** n rejilla f

lukewarm /'lu:kwɔ:m/ adj tibio; (fig) poco entusiasta

lull /lʌl/ vt (soothe, send to sleep) adormecer; (calm) calmar. ● n periodo m de calma

lullaby /'lʌləbaɪ/ n canción f de cuna

lumber /'lʌmbə(r)/ n trastos mpl viejos; (wood) maderos mpl. ● vt. **~ s.o. with sth** 🄸 endilgar algo a uno. **~jack** n leñador m

luminous /'lu:mɪnəs/ adj luminoso

lump /lʌmp/ n (swelling) bulto m; (as result of knock) chichón m; (in liquid) grumo m; (of sugar) terrón m. ● vt. **~ together** agrupar. **~ it** 🄸 aguantarse. **~ sum** n suma f global. **~y** adj (sauce) grumoso; (mattress, cushions) lleno de protuberancias

lunacy /'lu:nəsɪ/ n locura f

lunar /'lu:nə(r)/ adj lunar

lunatic /'lu:nətɪk/ n loco m

lunch /lʌntʃ/ n comida f, almuerzo m. **have ~** comer, almorzar

luncheon /'lʌntʃən/ n comida f, almuerzo m. **~ voucher** n vale m de comida

lung /lʌŋ/ n pulmón m

lunge /lʌndʒ/ n arremetida f. ● vi. **~ at** arremeter contra

lurch /lɜ:tʃ/ vi tambalearse. ● n. **leave in the ~** dejar plantado

lure /ljʊə(r)/ vt atraer

lurid /'ljʊərɪd/ adj (colour) chillón; (shocking) morboso

lurk /lɜ:k/ vi merodear; (in ambush) estar al acecho

luscious /'lʌʃəs/ adj delicioso

lush /lʌʃ/ adj exuberante

lust /lʌst/ n lujuria f; (craving) deseo m. ● vi. **~ after** codiciar

lute /lu:t/ n laúd m

Luxembourg, Luxemburg
/'lʌksəmbɜ:g/ n Luxemburgo m

luxuriant /lʌg'zjʊərɪənt/ adj exuberante

luxur|ious /lʌg'zjʊərɪəs/ adj lujoso. **~y** /'lʌkʃərɪ/ n lujo m. ● adj de lujo

lying /'laɪɪŋ/ see **LIE¹, LIE²**. ● n mentiras fpl. ● adj mentiroso

lynch /lɪntʃ/ vt linchar

lyric /'lɪrɪk/ adj lírico. **~al** adj lírico. **~s** npl letra f

Mm

MA /em'eɪ/ abbr see **MASTER**

mac /mæk/ n 🛈 impermeable m

macabre /mə'kɑːbrə/ adj macabro

macaroni /mækə'rəʊnɪ/ n macarrones mpl

mace /meɪs/ n (staff) maza f; (spice) macis f. **M~** (P) (Amer) gas m para defensa personal

machine /mə'ʃiːn/ n máquina f. **~ gun** n ametralladora f. **~ry** n maquinaria f; (working parts, fig) mecanismo m

mackintosh /'mækɪntɒʃ/ n impermeable m

macro /'mækrəʊ/ n (pl -os) (Comp) macro m

macrobiotic /mækrəʊbaɪ'ɒtɪk/ adj macrobiótico

mad /mæd/ adj (madder, maddest) loco; (fam, angry) furioso. be ~ about estar loco por

madam /'mædəm/ n señora f

mad: **~cap** adj atolondrado. **~ cow disease** f enfermedad f de las vacas locas. **~den** vt (make mad) enloquecer; (make angry) enfurecer

made /meɪd/ see **MAKE**. **~-to-measure** hecho a (la) medida

mad: **~house** n manicomio m. **~ly** adv (interested, in love etc) locamente; (frantically) como un loco. **~man** /-mən/ n loco m. **~ness** n locura f

Madonna /mə'dɒnə/ n. the ~ (Relig) la Virgen

maestro /'maɪstrəʊ/ n (pl maes-tri /-striː/ or -os) maestro m

Mafia /'mæfɪə/ n mafia f

magazine /mægə'ziːn/ n revista f; (of gun) recámara f

magenta /mə'dʒentə/ adj magenta, morado

maggot /'mægət/ n gusano m

magic /'mædʒɪk/ n magia f. ● adj mágico. **~al** adj mágico. **~ian** /mə'dʒɪʃn/ n mago m

magistrate /'mædʒɪstreɪt/ n juez m que conoce de faltas y asuntos civiles de menor importancia

magnet /'mægnɪt/ n imán m. **~ic** /-'netɪk/ adj magnético; (fig) lleno de magnetismo. **~ism** n magnetismo m. **~ize** vt imantar, magnetizar

magnif|ication /mægnɪfɪ'keɪʃn/ n aumento m. **~y** /'mægnɪfaɪ/ vt aumentar. **~ying glass** n lupa f

magnificen|ce /mæg'nɪfɪsns/ adj magnificencia f. **~t** adj magnífico

magnitude /'mægnɪtjuːd/ n magnitud f

magpie /'mægpaɪ/ n urraca f

mahogany /mə'hɒgənɪ/ n caoba f

maid /meɪd/ n (servant) criada f, sirvienta f; (girl, old use) doncella f. old ~ solterona f

maiden /'meɪdn/ n doncella f. ● adj (voyage) inaugural. ~ **name** n apellido m de soltera

mail /meɪl/ n correo m; (armour) (cota f de) malla f. ● adj correo. ● vt echar al correo (letter); (send) enviar por correo. **~box** n (Amer) buzón m. **~ing list** n lista f de direcciones. **~man** /-mən/ n (Amer) cartero m. **~ order** n venta f por correo

maim /meɪm/ vt mutilar

main /meɪn/ n. (water/gas) n cañería f principal. **in the ~** en su mayor parte. **the ~s** npl (Elec) la red f de suministro. ● adj principal. **~ course** n plato m principal, plato m fuerte. **~ frame** n (Comp) unidad f central. **~land** n. **the ~land** la masa territorial de un país excluyendo sus islas. ● adj. **~land China** (la) China continental. **~ly** adv principalmente. **~ road** n carretera f principal. **~stream** adj (culture) establecido. **~ street** n calle f principal

maint|ain /meɪnˈteɪn/ vt mantener. **~enance** /ˈmeɪntənəns/ n mantenimiento m

maisonette /meɪzəˈnet/ n (small house) casita f; (part of house) dúplex m

maize /meɪz/ n maíz m

majestic /məˈdʒestɪk/ adj majestuoso

majesty /ˈmædʒəstɪ/ n majestad f

major /ˈmeɪdʒə(r)/ adj (important) muy importante; (Mus) mayor. **a ~ road** una calle prioritaria. ● n comandante m & f, mayor m & f (LAm). ● vi. **~ in** (Amer, Univ) especializarse en

Majorca /məˈjɔːkə/ n Mallorca f

majority /məˈdʒɒrətɪ/ n mayoría f. ● adj mayoritario

make /meɪk/ vt (pt made) hacer; (manufacture) fabricar; ganar (money); tomar (decision); llegar a (destination). ● s.o. do sth obligar a uno a hacer algo. **be made of** estar hecho de. **I ~ it two o'clock** yo tengo las dos. ● believe fingir. ● do (manage) arreglarse. **~ do with** (content o.s.) contentarse con. **~ it** llegar; (succeed) tener éxito. **■ ~ for** vt dirigirse a. **~ good** vt compensar; (repair) reparar. **□ ~ off** vi

escaparse (with con). **□ ~ out** vt distinguir; (understand) entender; (write out) hacer; (assert) dar a entender. ● vi (cope) arreglárselas. **□ ~ up** vt (constitute) formar; (prepare) preparar; inventar (story); **~ it up** (become reconciled) hacer las paces. **□ ~ up** (one's face) maquillarse. **□ ~ up for** vt compensar. **~-believe** adj fingido, simulado. ● n ficción f. **~over** n (Amer) maquillaje m. **~r** n fabricante m & f. **~shift** adj (temporary) provisional, provisorio (LAm); (improvised) improvisado. **~up** n maquillaje m. **put on ~up** maquillarse.

making /ˈmeɪkɪŋ/ n. **he has the ~s of** tiene madera de. **in the ~** en vías de formación

maladjusted /mæləˈdʒʌstɪd/ adj inadaptado

malaria /məˈleərɪə/ n malaria f, paludismo m

Malaysia /məˈleɪzɪə/ n Malasia f. **~n** adj & n malaisio (m)

male /meɪl/ adj macho; (voice, attitude) masculino. ● n macho m; (man) varón m

malevolent /məˈlevələnt/ adj malévolo

malfunction /mælˈfʌŋkʃn/ vi fallar, funcionar mal

malic|e /ˈmælɪs/ n mala intención f, maldad f. **bear s.o. ~e** guardar rencor a uno. **~ious** /məˈlɪʃəs/ adj malintencionado. **~iously** adv con malevolencia

malignant /məˈlɪɡnənt/ adj maligno

mallet /ˈmælɪt/ n mazo m

malnutrition /mælnjuːˈtrɪʃn/ n desnutrición f

malpractice /mælˈpræktɪs/ n mala práctica f (en el ejercicio de una profesión)

malt /mɔːlt/ n malta f

Malt|a /ˈmɔːltə/ n Malta f ~**ese**
/-ˈtiːz/ adj & n maltés (m)

mammal /ˈmæml/ n mamífero m

mammoth /ˈmæməθ/ n mamut
m. ● adj gigantesco

man /mæn/ n (pl men /men/)
hombre m; (Chess) pieza f. ~ **in
the street** hombre m de la calle.
● vt (pt manned) encargarse de
(switchboard); tripular (ship); servir
(guns)

manacles /ˈmænəklz/ n (for
wrists) esposas fpl; (for legs) grillos
mpl

manag|e /ˈmænɪdʒ/ vt dirigir; ad-
ministrar (land, finances); (handle)
manejar. ● vi (Com) dirigir; (cope)
arreglárselas. ~**e to** do lograr
hacer. ~**eable** adj (task) posible de
alcanzar; (size) razonable.
~**ement** n dirección f. ~**er** n director m; (of shop) encargado m; (of
soccer team) entrenador m, director
m técnico (LAm). ~**eress** /-ˈres/ n
encargada f. ~**erial** /-ˈdʒɪəriəl/ adj
directivo, gerencial (LAm).~**ing
director** n director m ejecutivo

mandate /ˈmændeɪt/ n mandato m

mandatory /ˈmændətərɪ/ adj
obligatorio

mane /meɪn/ n (of horse) crin(es)
f(pl); (of lion) melena f

mangle /ˈmæŋɡl/ n rodillo m (es-
curridor). ● vt destrozar

man: ~**handle** vt mover a
pulso; (treat roughly) maltratar.
~**hole** n registro m. ~**hood** n
madurez f; (quality) virilidad f.
~-**hour** n hora f hombre.
~-**hunt** n persecución f

mania /ˈmeɪnɪə/ n manía f. ~**c**

manicure /ˈmænɪkjʊə(r)/ n manicura f, manicure f (LAm)

manifest /ˈmænɪfest/ adj manifiesto. ● vt manifestar. ~**ation**
/-ˈsteɪʃn/ n manifestación f

manifesto /mænɪˈfestəʊ/ n (pl
-os) manifiesto m

manipulat|e /məˈnɪpjʊleɪt/ vt
manipular. ~**ion** /-ˈleɪʃn/ n mani-
pulación f. ~**ive** /-lətɪv/ adj mani-
pulador

man: ~**kind** n humanidad f.
~**ly** adj viril. ~-**made** adj artificial

manner /ˈmænə(r)/ n manera f;
(demeanour) actitud f; (kind) clase
f. ~**ed** adj amanerado. ~**s** npl modales mpl, educación f. **bad** ~**s**
mala educación

manoeuvre /məˈnuːvə(r)/ n maniobra f. ● vt/i maniobrar

manor /ˈmænə(r)/ n. ~ **house**
casa f solariega

manpower n mano f de obra

mansion /ˈmænʃn/ n mansión f

man: ~-**size(d)** adj grande.
~**slaughter** n homicidio m sin
premeditación

mantelpiece /ˈmæntlpiːs/ n repisa f de la chimenea

manual /ˈmænjʊəl/ adj manual.
● n (handbook) manual m

manufactur|e /mænjʊ
ˈfæktʃə(r)/ vt fabricar. ● n fabricación f. ~**r** n fabricante m & f

manure /məˈnjʊə(r)/ n estiércol m

manuscript /ˈmænjʊskrɪpt/ n
manuscrito m

many /ˈmenɪ/ adj & pron muchos,
muchas. ~ **people** mucha gente.
a great/good ~ muchísimos. **how**
~? ¿cuántos? **so** ~ tantos. **too** ~
demasiados

map /mæp/ n mapa m; (of streets etc) plano m

mar /mɑː(r)/ vt (pt marred) estropear

marathon /ˈmærəθən/ n maratón m & f

marble /ˈmɑːbl/ n mármol m; (for game) canica f

march /mɑːtʃ/ vi (Mil) marchar. ~ **off** vi irse. ● n marcha f

March /mɑːtʃ/ n marzo m

march-past /ˈmɑːtʃpɑːst/ n desfile m

mare /meə(r)/ n yegua f

margarine /mɑːdʒəˈriːn/ n margarina f

margin /ˈmɑːdʒɪn/ n margen f. ~**al** adj marginal

marijuana /mærɪˈhwɑːnə/ n marihuana f

marina /məˈriːnə/ n puerto m deportivo

marine /məˈriːn/ adj marino. ● n (sailor) infante m de marina

marionette /mærɪəˈnet/ n marioneta f

marital status /mærɪtl ˈsteɪtəs/ n estado m civil

mark /mɑːk/ n marca f; (stain) mancha f; (School) nota f; (target) blanco m. ● vt (indicate) señalar, marcar; (stain) manchar; corregir (exam). ~ **time** marcar el paso. □ ~ **out** vt (select) señalar; (distinguish) distinguir. ~**ed** adj marcado. ~**edly** /-kɪdlɪ/ adv marcadamente. ~**er** n marcador m. ~**er** (pen) n rotulador m, marcador m (LAm)

market /ˈmɑːkɪt/ n mercado m. **on the** ~ en venta. ● vt comercializar. ~ **garden** n huerta f. ~**ing** n marketing m

marking /ˈmɑːkɪŋ/ n marcas fpl; (on animal, plant) mancha f

marksman /ˈmɑːksmən/ n (pl -men) tirador m. ~**ship** n puntería f

marmalade /ˈmɑːməleɪd/ n mermelada f (de cítricos)

maroon /məˈruːn/ adj & n granate (m). ● vt abandonar (en una isla desierta)

marquee /mɑːˈkiː/ n toldo m, entoldado m; (Amer, awning) marquesina f

marriage /ˈmærɪdʒ/ n matrimonio m; (ceremony) casamiento m

married /ˈmærɪd/ adj casado; (life) conyugal

marrow /ˈmærəʊ/ n (of bone) tuétano m; (vegetable) calabaza f verde alargada. ~ **squash** n (Amer) calabaza f verde alargada

marry /ˈmærɪ/ vt casarse con; (give or unite in marriage) casar. ● vi casarse. **get married** casarse (con)

Mars /mɑːz/ n Marte m

marsh /mɑːʃ/ n pantano m

marshal /ˈmɑːʃl/ n (Mil) mariscal m; (Amer, police chief) jefe m de policía. ● vt (pt marshalled) reunir; poner en orden (thoughts)

marsh: ~**mallow** /-ˈmæləʊ/ n malvavisco m, bombón m (LAm). ~**y** adj pantanoso

martial /ˈmɑːʃl/ adj marcial. ~ **arts** npl artes fpl marciales. ~ **law** n ley f marcial

martyr /ˈmɑːtə(r)/ n mártir m & f

marvel /ˈmɑːvl/ n maravilla f. ● vi (pt marvelled) maravillarse (at de). ~**lous** adj maravilloso

Marxis|m /ˈmɑːksɪzəm/ n marxismo m. ~**t** adj & n marxista (m & f)

marzipan /ˈmɑːzɪpæn/ n mazapán m

mascara /mæˈskɑːrə/ n rímel® m

mascot /ˈmæskɒt/ n mascota f

masculin|e /ˈmæskjʊlɪn/ adj & n masculino (m). **~ity** /-ˈlɪnɪtɪ/ n masculinidad f

mash /mæʃ/ n (Brit ▣, potatoes) puré m de patatas, puré m de papas (LAm). ● vt hacer puré de, moler (Mex). **~ed potatoes** n puré m de patatas, puré m de papas (LAm)

mask /mɑːsk/ n máscara f; (Sport) careta f. ● vt ocultar

masochis|m /ˈmæsəkɪzəm/ n masoquismo m. **~t** n masoquista m & f. **~tic** /-ˈkɪstɪk/ adj masoquista

mason /ˈmeɪsn/ n (stone ~) mampostero m. M**~** (freemason) masón m. **~ry** /ˈmeɪsnrɪ/ n albañilería f

masquerade /mɑːskəˈreɪd/ n mascarada f. ● vi. **~ as** hacerse pasar por

mass /mæs/ n masa f; (Relig) misa f; (large quantity) montón m. the **~es** las masas. ● vi concentrarse

massacre /ˈmæsəkə(r)/ n masacre f, matanza f. ● vt masacrar

mass|age /ˈmæsɑːʒ/ n masaje m. ● vt masajear. **~eur** /mæˈsɜː(r)/ n masajista m. **~euse** /mæˈsɜːz/ n masajista f

massive /ˈmæsɪv/ adj masivo; (heavy) macizo; (huge) enorme

mass: **~ media** n medios mpl de comunicación. M**~-produce** /-prəˈdjuːs/ vt fabricar en serie

mast /mɑːst/ n mástil m; (for radio, TV) antena f repetidora

master /ˈmɑːstə(r)/ n amo m; (expert) maestro m; (in secondary school) profesor m; (of ship) capitán m; (master copy) original m. **~'s degree** master m, maestría f. M**~ of** Arts (MA) poseedor m de una maestría en filosofía y letras. M**~ of Science** (MSc) poseedor m de una maestría en ciencias. ● vt llegar a dominar. **~ key** n llave f maestra. **~mind** n cerebro m. ● vt dirigir. **~piece** n obra f maestra. **~stroke** n golpe m de maestro. **~y** n dominio m; (skill) maestría f

masturbat|e /ˈmæstəbeɪt/ vi masturbarse. **~ion** /-ˈbeɪʃn/ n masturbación f

mat /mæt/ n estera f; (at door) felpudo m. ● adj (Amer) see MATT

match /mætʃ/ n (Sport) partido m; (for fire) cerilla f, fósforo m (LAm), cerillo m (Mex); (equal) igual m. ● vt emparejar; (equal) igualar; (clothes, colours) hacer juego con. ● vi hacer juego. **~box** n caja f de cerillas, caja f de fósforos (LAm), caja f de cerillos (Mex). **~ing** adj que hace juego. **~stick** n cerilla f, fósforo m (LAm), cerillo m (Mex)

mate /meɪt/ n (of person) pareja f; (of animals, male) macho m; (of animals, female) hembra f; (assistant) ayudante m; (▣, friend) amigo m, cuate m (Mex); (Chess) (jaque m) mate m. ● vi aparearse

material /məˈtɪərɪəl/ n material m; (cloth) tela f. ● adj material. **~istic** /-ˈlɪstɪk/ adj materialista. **~ize** vi materializarse. **~s** npl materiales mpl

matern|al /məˈtɜːnl/ adj maternal. **~ity** /-ətɪ/ n maternidad f. ● adj (ward) de obstetricia; (clothes) premamá, de embarazada

math /mæθ/ n (Amer) see MATHS

mathematic|ian /mæθəməˈtɪʃn/ n matemático m. **~al** /-ˈmætɪkl/ adj matemático. **~s** /-ˈmætɪks/ n matemática(s) f(pl)

maths /mæθs/ n matemática(s) f(pl)

matinée, matinee /'mætɪneɪ/ n (Theatre) función f de tarde; (Cinema) primera sesión f (de la tarde)

matrices /'meɪtrɪsiːz/ see **MATRIX**

matriculat|e /mə'trɪkjʊleɪt/ vi matricularse. **~ion** /-'leɪʃn/ n matrícula f

matrimon|ial /mætrɪ'məʊnɪəl/ adj matrimonial. **~y** /'mætrɪmənɪ/ n matrimonio m

matrix /'meɪtrɪks/ n (pl matrices) matriz f

matron /'meɪtrən/ n (married, elderly) matrona f; (in school) ama f de llaves; (former use, in hospital) enfermera f jefe

matt, matte (Amer) /mæt/ adj mate

matted /'mætɪd/ adj enmarañado y apelmazado

matter /'mætə(r)/ n (substance) materia f; (affair) asunto m; (pus) pus m. **as a ~ of fact** en realidad. **no ~** no importa. **what is the ~?** ¿qué pasa? **to make ~s worse** para colmo (de males). ● vi importar. **it doesn't ~** no importa. **~-of-fact** /-əv'fækt/ adj (person) práctico

mattress /'mætrɪs/ n colchón m

matur|e /mə'tjʊə(r)/ adj maduro. ● vi madurar. **~ity** n madurez f

maudlin /'mɔːdlɪn/ adj llorón

maul /mɔːl/ vt atacar (y herir)

mauve /məʊv/ adj & n malva (m)

maverick /'mævərɪk/ n inconformista m & f

maxim /'mæksɪm/ n máxima f

maxim|ize /'mæksɪmaɪz/ vt maximizar. **~um** /-əm/ adj & n máximo (m)

may /meɪ/.

past **might**

auxiliary verb

····▸ (expressing possibility) **he ~ come** puede que venga, es posible que venga. **it ~ be true** puede ser verdad. **she ~ not have seen him** es posible que o puede que no la haya visto

····▸ (asking for or giving permission) **~ I smoke?** ¿se puede fumar? **~ I have your name and address, please?** ¿quiere darme su nombre y dirección, por favor?

····▸ (expressing a wish) **~ he be happy** que sea feliz

····▸ (conceding) **he ~ not have much experience, but he's very hardworking** no tendrá mucha experiencia, pero es muy trabajador. **that's as ~ be** puede ser

····▸ **I ~ as well stay** más vale quedarme

May /meɪ/ n mayo m

maybe /'meɪbɪ/ adv quizá(s), tal vez, a lo mejor

May Day n el primero de mayo

mayhem /'meɪhem/ n caos m

mayonnaise /meɪə'neɪz/ n mayonesa f, mahonesa f

mayor /meə(r)/ n alcalde m, alcaldesa f. **~ess** /-ɪs/ n alcaldesa f

maze /meɪz/ n laberinto m

me /miː/ pron me; (after prep) mí. **he knows ~** me conoce. **it's ~** soy yo

meadow /'medəʊ/ n prado m, pradera f

meagre /'miːgə(r)/ adj escaso

meal /miːl/ n comida f. **~time** n
hora f de comer

mean /miːn/ vt (pt meant) (intend) tener la intención de, querer;
(signify) querer decir, significar. **~**
to do tener la intención de hacer.
~ well tener buenas intenciones.
be meant for estar destinado a.
● adj (-er, -est) (miserly) tacaño;
(unkind) malo; (Math) medio. ● n
media f; (average) promedio m

meander /mɪˈændə(r)/ vi (river)
serpentear

meaning /ˈmiːnɪŋ/ n sentido m.
~ful adj significativo. **~less** adj sin
sentido

meanness /ˈmiːnnɪs/ n (miserliness) tacañería f; (unkindness) maldad f

means /miːnz/ n medio m. by **~**
of por medio de, mediante. by all
~ por supuesto. by no **~** de ninguna manera. ● npl (wealth) medios
mpl, recursos mpl. **~ test** n investigación f de ingresos

meant /ment/ see MEAN

meantime /ˈmiːntaɪm/ adv mientras tanto, entretanto. ● n. in the
~ mientras tanto, entretanto

meanwhile /ˈmiːnwaɪl/ adv
mientras tanto, entretanto

measl|es /ˈmiːzlz/ n sarampión m.
~y /ˈmiːzlɪ/ adj 🖭 miserable

measure /ˈmeʒə(r)/ n medida f;
(ruler) regla f. ● vt/i medir. □ **~ up**
to vt estar a la altura de. **~ment** n
medida f

meat /miːt/ n carne f. **~ball** n albóndiga f. **~y** adj (taste, smell) a
carne; (soup, stew) con mucha
carne

mechan|ic /mɪˈkænɪk/ n mecánico m. **~ical** adj mecánico. **~ics** n
mecánica f. **~ism** /ˈmekənɪzəm/ n

mecanismo m. **~ize** /ˈmekənaɪz/ vt
mecanizar

medal /ˈmedl/ n medalla f. **~list**
/ˈmedəlɪst/ n medallista m & f. be a
gold **~list** ganar una medalla de
oro

meddle /ˈmedl/ vi meterse, entrometerse (in en). **~ with** (tinker)
toquetear

media /ˈmiːdɪə/ see MEDIUM.
● npl. the **~** los medios de comunicación

mediat|e /ˈmiːdɪeɪt/ vi mediar.
~ion /-ˈeɪʃn/ n mediación f. **~or** n
mediador m

medical /ˈmedɪkl/ adj médico;
(student) de medicina. ● n revisión
m médica

medicat|ed /ˈmedɪkeɪtɪd/ adj medicinal. **~ion** /-ˈkeɪʃn/ n medicación f

medicin|al /mɪˈdɪsɪnl/ adj medicinal. **~e** /ˈmedsɪn/ n medicina f

medieval /medɪˈiːvl/ adj medieval

mediocre /miːdɪˈəʊkə(r)/ adj mediocre

meditat|e /ˈmedɪteɪt/ vi meditar.
~ion /-ˈteɪʃn/ n meditación f

Mediterranean /medɪtə
ˈreɪnɪən/ adj mediterráneo. ● n. the
~ el Mediterráneo

medium /ˈmiːdɪəm/ n (pl media)
medio m. happy **~** término m
medio. ● adj mediano. **~-size(d)**
/-saɪz(d)/ adj de tamaño mediano

medley /ˈmedlɪ/ n (Mus) popurrí
m; (mixture) mezcla f

meek /miːk/ adj (-er, -est) dócil

meet /miːt/ vt (pt met) encontrar;
(bump into s.o.) encontrarse con;
(fetch) ir a buscar; (get to know, be
introduced to) conocer. ● vi encontrarse; (get to know) conocerse;
(have meeting) reunirse. **~ up** vi

encontrarse (with con). □ ~ **with**
vt ser recibido con; (*Amer, meet*) en-
contrarse con. ~**ing** n reunión f; (*accidental between two people*) encuentro m

megabyte /'megabaɪt/ n (*Comp*)
megabyte m, megaocteto m

megaphone /'megafəʊn/ n megáfono m

melancholic /melən'kɒlɪk/ adj
melancólico. ~**y** /'melənkɒlɪ/ n
melancolía f. ● adj melancólico

mellow /'meləʊ/ adj (-er, -est)
(*fruit*) maduro; (*sound*) dulce;
(*colour*) tenue; (*person*) apacible

melodrama /'melədrɑːmə/ n
melodrama m. ~**tic** /melədrə-
'mætɪk/ adj melodramático

melody /'melədɪ/ n melodía f

melon /'melən/ n melón m

melt /melt/ vt (*make liquid*) derretir; fundir (metals). ● vi (*become liquid*) derretirse; (metals) fundirse.
□ ~ **down** vt fundir

member /'membə(r)/ n miembro
m & f; (*of club*) socio m. ~ of **staff**
empleado m. **M~ of Congress** n
(*Amer*) miembro m & f del Congreso.
M~ of Parliament n diputado m.
~**ship** n calidad f de socio; (*members*) socios mpl, membresía f (*LAm*)

membrane /'membreɪn/ n membrana f

memento /mɪ'mentəʊ/ n (pl -os
or -oes) recuerdo m

memo /'meməʊ/ n (pl -os) memorándum m, memo m

memoir /'memwɑː(r)/ n memoria f

memorable /'memərəbl/ adj memorable

memorandum /memə-
'rændəm/ n (pl -ums or -da /-də/)
memorándum m

memorial /mɪ'mɔːrɪəl/ n monumento m. ● adj conmemorativo

memorize /'meməraɪz/ vt aprender de memoria. ~**y** /'memərɪ/ n
(*faculty*) memoria f; (*thing remembered*) recuerdo m. **from** ~ **y** de
memoria. **in** ~**y of** a la memoria de

men /men/ *see* MAN

menace /'menəs/ n amenaza f;
(*fam, nuisance*) peligro m público.
● vt amenazar. ~**ing** adj amenazador

mend /mend/ vt reparar; arreglar
(garment). ~ **one's ways** enmendarse. ● n remiendo m. **be on the**
~ ir mejorando

menfolk /'menfəʊk/ n hombres
mpl

menial /'miːnɪəl/ adj servil

meningitis /menɪn'dʒaɪtɪs/ n
meningitis f

menopause /'menəpɔːz/ n menopausia f

menstruate /'menstrʊeɪt/ vi
menstruar. ~**ion** /-'eɪʃn/ n menstruación f

mental /'mentl/ adj mental; (*hospital*) psiquiátrico. ~**ity** /-'tælətɪ/ n
mentalidad f. ~**ly** adv mentalmente. **be** ~**ly ill** ser un enfermo
mental

mention /'menʃn/ vt mencionar.
don't ~ **it!** ¡no hay de qué! ● n
mención f

mentor /'mentɔː(r)/ n mentor m

menu /'menjuː/ n menú m

meow /mɪ'aʊ/ n & vi *see* MEW

mercenary /'mɜːsɪnərɪ/ adj & n
mercenario (m)

merchandise /'mɜːtʃəndaɪz/ n
mercancías fpl, mercadería f (*LAm*)

merchant /'mɜːtʃənt/ n comerciante m. ● adj (ship, navy) mercante. **~ bank** n banco m mercantil

merci|ful /'mɜːsɪfl/ adj misericordioso. **~less** adj despiadado

mercury /'mɜːkjʊrɪ/ n mercurio m. M~ (planet) Mercurio m

mercy /'mɜːsɪ/ n compasión f. at the ~ of a merced de

mere /mɪə(r)/ adj simple. **~ly** adv simplemente

merge /mɜːdʒ/ vt unir; fusionar (companies). ● vi unirse; (companies) fusionarse. **~r** n fusión f

meridian /mə'rɪdɪən/ n meridiano m

meringue /mə'ræŋ/ n merengue m

merit /'merɪt/ n mérito m. ● vt (pt merited) merecer

mermaid /'mɜːmeɪd/ n sirena f

merr|ily /'merəlɪ/ adv alegremente. **~iment** /'merɪmənt/ n alegría f. **~y** /'merɪ/ adj (-ier, -iest) alegre. make a ~ divertirse. **~y-go-round** n tiovivo m, carrusel m (LAm). **~y-making** n jolgorio m

mesh /meʃ/ n malla f

mesmerize /'mezməraɪz/ vt hipnotizar; (fascinate) cautivar

mess /mes/ n desorden m; (dirt) suciedad f; (Mil) rancho m. make a ~ of estropear. □ ~ **up** vt desordenar; (dirty) ensuciar; estropear (plans). □ ~ **about** vi tontear. □ ~ **with** vt (tinker with) manosear

mess|age /'mesɪdʒ/ n mensaje m; (when phoning) recado m. **~enger** /'mesɪndʒə(r)/ n mensajero m

Messiah /mɪ'saɪə/ n Mesías m

Messrs /'mesəz/ npl. ~ Smith los señores Smith, los Sres. Smith

messy /'mesɪ/ adj (-ier, -iest) en desorden; (dirty) sucio

met /met/ see **MEET**

metabolism /mɪ'tæbəlɪzəm/ n metabolismo m

metal /'metl/ n metal. ● adj de metal. **~lic** /mə'tælɪk/ adj metálico

metaphor /'metəfə(r)/ n metáfora f. **~ical** /-'fɒrɪkl/ adj metafórico

mete /miːt/ vt. ~ **out** repartir; dar (punishment)

meteor /'miːtɪə(r)/ n meteoro m. **~ic** /-'ɒrɪk/ adj meteórico. **~ite** /'miːtɪəraɪt/ n meteorito m

meteorolog|ical /miːtɪərə'lɒdʒɪkl/ adj meteorológico. **~ist** /-'rɒlədʒɪst/ n meteorólogo m. **~y** /-'rɒlədʒɪ/ n meteorología f

meter /'miːtə(r)/ n contador m, medidor m (LAm); (Amer) see **METRE**

method /'meθəd/ n método m. **~ical** /mɪ'θɒdɪkl/ adj metódico. M~ist /'meθədɪst/ adj & n metodista (m & f)

methylated /'meθɪleɪtɪd/ adj. ~ **spirit(s)** n alcohol m desnaturalizado

meticulous /mɪ'tɪkjʊləs/ adj meticuloso

metre /'miːtə(r)/ n metro m

metric /'metrɪk/ adj métrico

metropoli|s /mɪ'trɒpəlɪs/ n metrópoli(s) f

mettle /'metl/ n. be on one's ~ (fig) estar dispuesto a dar lo mejor de sí

mew /mjuː/ n maullido m. ● vi maullar

Mexic|an /'meksɪkən/ adj & n mejicano (m), mexicano (m). **~o** /-kəʊ/ n Méjico m, México m

miaow /miː'aʊ/ n & vi see **MEW**

mice /maɪs/ see **MOUSE**

mickey /'mɪkɪ/ n. take the ~ out of 🆃 tomar el pelo a

micro... /'maɪkrəʊ/ *pref* micro...

microbe /'maɪkrəʊb/ *n* microbio *m*

micro: **∼chip** *n* pastilla *f*. **∼film** *n* microfilme *m*. **∼light** *n* aeroligero *m*. **∼phone** *n* micrófono *m*. **∼processor** /-'prəʊsesə(r)/ *n* microprocesador *m*. **∼scope** *n* microscopio *m*. **∼scopic** /-'skɒpɪk/ *adj* microscópico. **∼wave** *n* microonda *f*. **∼wave oven** *n* horno *m* de microondas

mid- /mɪd/ *pref.* **in ∼ air** en pleno aire. **in ∼ March** a mediados de marzo

midday /mɪd'deɪ/ *n* mediodía *m*

middle /'mɪdl/ *adj* de en medio. ● *n* medio *m*. **in the ∼ of** en medio de. **∼-aged** /-'eɪdʒd/ *adj* de mediana edad. **M∼ Ages** *npl* Edad *f* Media. **∼ class** *n* clase *f* media. **∼-class** *adj* de la clase media. **M∼ East** *n* Oriente *m* Medio. **∼eman** *n* intermediario *m*. **∼e name** *n* segundo nombre *m*. **∼ing** *adj* regular

midge /mɪdʒ/ *n* mosquito *m*

midget /'mɪdʒɪt/ *n* enano *m*. ● *adj* minúsculo

Midlands /'mɪdləndz/ *npl* región *f* central de Inglaterra

midnight /'mɪdnaɪt/ *n* medianoche *f*

midriff /'mɪdrɪf/ *n* diafragma *m*

midst /mɪdst/ *n*. **in our ∼** entre nosotros. **in the ∼ of** en medio de

midsummer /mɪd'sʌmə(r)/ *n* pleno verano *m*; (*solstice*) solsticio *m* de verano

midway /'mɪdweɪ/ *adv* a mitad de camino

Midwest /mɪd'west/ región *f* central de los EE.UU.

midwife /'mɪdwaɪf/ *n* comadrona *f*, partera *f*

midwinter /mɪd'wɪntə(r)/ *n* pleno invierno *m*

might /maɪt/ *see* MAY. ● *n* (*strength*) fuerza *f*; (*power*) poder *m*. **∼y** *adj* (*strong*) fuerte; (*powerful*) poderoso. ● *adv* 🄸 muy

migraine /'miːgreɪn/ *n* jaqueca *f*

migra|nt /'maɪgrənt/ *adj* migratorio. ● *n* (*person*) emigrante *m & f*. **∼te** /maɪ'greɪt/ *vi* emigrar. **∼tion** /-'greɪʃn/ *n* migración *f*

mild /maɪld/ *adj* (*-er, -est*) (*person*) afable; (*climate*) templado; (*slight*) ligero; (*taste, manner*) suave

mildew /'mɪldjuː/ *n* moho *m*; (*on plants*) mildiu *m*, mildiú *m*

mildly /'maɪldlɪ/ *adv* (*gently*) suavemente; (*slightly*) ligeramente

mile /maɪl/ *n* milla *f*. **∼s better** 🄸 mucho mejor. **∼s too big** 🄸 demasiado grande. **∼age** /-ɪdʒ/ *n* (*loosely*) kilometraje *m*. **∼ometer** /maɪ'lɒmɪtə(r)/ *n* (*loosely*) cuentakilómetros *m*. **∼stone** *n* mojón *m*; (*event, stage, fig*) hito *m*

militant /'mɪlɪtənt/ *adj & n* militante (*m & f*)

military /'mɪlɪtərɪ/ *adj* militar

militia /mɪ'lɪʃə/ *n* milicia *f*

milk /mɪlk/ *n* leche *f*. ● *adj* (*product*) lácteo; (*chocolate*) con leche. ● *vt* ordeñar (*cow*). **∼man** /-mən/ *n* lechero *m*. **∼ shake** *n* batido *m*, (*leche f*) malteada *f* (*LAm*), licuado *m* con leche (*LAm*). **∼y** *adj* lechoso. **M∼y Way** *n* Vía *f* Láctea

mill /mɪl/ *n* molino *m*; (*for coffee, pepper*) molinillo *m*; (*factory*) fábrica *f* de tejidos de algodón. ● *vt* moler. □ **∼ about, mill around** *vi* dar vueltas

millennium /mɪˈlenɪəm/ n (pl -ia /-ɪə/ or -iums) milenio m

miller /ˈmɪlə(r)/ n molinero m

milli... /ˈmɪlɪ/ pref mili...
~**gram(me)** n miligramo m.
~**metre** n milímetro m

milliner /ˈmɪlɪnə(r)/ n sombrerero m

million /ˈmɪlɪən/ n millón m. a ~ **pounds** un millón de libras. ~**aire** /-ˈeə(r)/ n millonario m

millstone /ˈmɪlstəʊn/ n muela f (de molino); (fig, burden) carga f

mime /maɪm/ n mímica f. ● vt imitar, hacer la mímica de. ● vi hacer la mímica

mimic /ˈmɪmɪk/ vt (pt mimicked) imitar. ● n imitador m. ~**ry** n imitación f

mince /mɪns/ vt picar, moler (LAm) (meat). **not to ~ matters/words** no andar(se) con rodeos. ● n carne f picada, carne f molida (LAm). ~ **pie** n pastelito m de Navidad (pastelito relleno de picadillo de frutos secos). ~**r** n máquina f de picar carne, máquina f de moler carne (LAm)

mind /maɪnd/ n mente f; (sanity) juicio m. **to my ~** a mi parecer. **be on one's mind** preocuparle a uno. **make up one's ~** decidirse. ● vt (look after) cuidar (de); (attend to) atender (shop). ~ **the steps!** ¡cuidado con las escaleras! **never ~ him** no le hagas caso. **I don't ~ the noise** no me molesta el ruido. **would you ~ closing the door?** ¿le importaría cerrar la puerta? ● vi. **never ~** no importa, no te preocupes. **I don't ~** (don't object) me da igual. **do you ~ if I smoke?** ¿le importa si fumo? ~**ful** adj atento (of a). ~**less** adj (activity) mecánico; (violence) ciego

mine¹ /maɪn/ poss pron (sing) mío, mía; (pl) míos, mías. **it is ~** es mío. ~ **are blue** los míos/las mías son azules. **a friend of ~** un amigo mío/una amiga mía

mine² /maɪn/ n mina f; (Mil) mina f. ● vt extraer. ~**field** n campo m de minas. ~**r** n minero m

mineral /ˈmɪnərəl/ adj & n mineral (m). ~ **water** n agua f mineral

mingle /ˈmɪŋɡl/ vi mezclarse

mini... /ˈmɪnɪ/ pref mini...

miniature /ˈmɪnɪtʃə(r)/ n miniatura f. ● adj en miniatura

mini: ~**bus** n microbús m.
~**cab** n taxi m (que se pide por teléfono)

minim|al /ˈmɪnɪml/ adj mínimo. ~**ize** vt reducir al mínimo. ~**um** /-məm/ adj & n (pl -ima /-mə/) mínimo (m)

mining /ˈmaɪnɪŋ/ n minería f. ● adj minero

miniskirt /ˈmɪnɪskɜːt/ n minifalda f

minist|er /ˈmɪnɪstə(r)/ n ministro m, secretario m (Mex); (Relig) pastor m. ~**erial** /-ˈstɪərɪəl/ adj ministerial. ~**ry** n ministerio m, secretaría f (Mex)

mink /mɪŋk/ n visón m

minor /ˈmaɪnə(r)/ adj (also Mus) menor; (injury) leve; (change) pequeño; (operation) de poca importancia. ● n menor m & f de edad. ~**ity** /maɪˈnɒrəti/ n minoría f. ● adj minoritario

minstrel /ˈmɪnstrəl/ n juglar m

mint /mɪnt/ n (plant) menta f; (sweet) pastilla f de menta; (Finance) casa f de la moneda. **in ~ condition** como nuevo. ● vt acuñar

minus /ˈmaɪnəs/ prep menos; (fam, without) sin. ● n (sign) menos *m*. five ∼ three is two cinco menos tres is igual a dos. ∼ **sign** *n* (signo *m* de) menos *m*

minute¹ /'mɪnɪt/ *n* minuto *m*. **the ∼s** *npl* (*of meeting*) el acta *f*

minute² /maɪ'njuːt/ *adj* diminuto; (*detailed*) minucioso

miracle /'mɪrəkl/ *n* milagro *m*. **∼ulous** /mɪ'rækjʊləs/ *adj* milagroso

mirage /'mɪrɑːʒ/ *n* espejismo *m*

mirror /'mɪrə(r)/ *n* espejo *m*; (*driving* ∼) (espejo *m*) retrovisor *m*. ●*vt* reflejar

mirth /mɜːθ/ *n* regocijo *m*; (*laughter*) risas *fpl*

misapprehension /mɪsæprɪ'henʃn/ *n* malentendido *m*

misbehav|e /mɪsbɪ'heɪv/ *vi* portarse mal. **∼iour** *n* mala conducta

miscalculat|e /mɪs'kælkjʊleɪt/ *vt/i* calcular mal. **∼ion** /-'leɪʃn/ *n* error *m* de cálculo

miscarr|iage /mɪs'kærɪdʒ/ *n* aborto *m* espontáneo. **∼iage of justice** *n* injusticia *f*. **∼y** *vi* abortar

miscellaneous /mɪsə'leɪnɪəs/ *adj* heterogéneo

mischie|f /'mɪstʃɪf/ *n* (*foolish conduct*) travesura *f*; (*harm*) daño *m*. **get into ∼f** hacer travesuras. **make ∼f** causar daños. **∼vous** /'mɪstʃɪvəs/ *adj* travieso; (*grin*) pícaro

misconception /mɪskən'sepʃn/ *n* equivocación *f*

misconduct /mɪs'kɒndʌkt/ *n* mala conducta *f*

misdeed /mɪs'diːd/ *n* fechoría *f*

misdemeanour /mɪsdɪ'miːnə(r)/ *n* delito *m* menor, falta *f*

miser /'maɪzə(r)/ *n* avaro *m*

miserable /'mɪzərəbl/ *adj* (*sad*) triste; (*in low spirits*) abatido;

(*wretched, poor*) mísero; (*weather*) pésimo

miserly /'maɪzəlɪ/ *adj* avariento

misery /'mɪzərɪ/ *n* (*unhappiness*) tristeza *f*; (*pain*) sufrimiento *m*

misfire /mɪs'faɪə(r)/ *vi* fallar

misfit /'mɪsfɪt/ *n* inadaptado *m*

misfortune /mɪs'fɔːtʃuːn/ *n* desgracia *f*

misgiving /mɪs'gɪvɪŋ/ *n* recelo *m*

misguided /mɪs'gaɪdɪd/ *adj* equivocado

mishap /'mɪshæp/ *n* percance *m*

misinform /mɪsɪn'fɔːm/ *vt* informar mal

misinterpret /mɪsɪn'tɜːprɪt/ *vt* interpretar mal

misjudge /mɪs'dʒʌdʒ/ *vt* juzgar mal; (*miscalculate*) calcular mal

mislay /mɪs'leɪ/ *vt* (*pt* mislaid) extraviar, perder

mislead /mɪs'liːd/ *vt* (*pt* misled /mɪs'led/) engañar. **∼ing** *adj* engañoso

mismanage /mɪs'mænɪdʒ/ *vt* administrar mal. **∼ment** *n* mala administración *f*

misplace /mɪs'pleɪs/ *vt* (*lose*) extraviar, perder

misprint /'mɪsprɪnt/ *n* errata *f*

miss /mɪs/ *vt* (*fail to hit*) no dar en; (*regret absence of*) echar de menos, extrañar (*LAm*); perder (train, party); perder (chance). ●**the point** no comprender. ●*vi* errar el tiro, fallar; (*bullet*) no dar en el blanco. ●*n* fallo *m*, falla *f* (*LAm*); (*title*) señorita *f*. □ ∼ **out** *vt* saltarse (line). **∼out on sth** perderse algo

misshapen /mɪs'ʃeɪpən/ *adj* deforme

missile /'mɪsaɪl/ *n* (*Mil*) misil *m*

m

missing | moisture

missing /ˈmɪsɪŋ/ adj (lost) perdido. be ~ faltar. go ~ desaparecer. ~ person desaparecido m

mission /ˈmɪʃn/ n misión f. ~ary /ˈmɪʃənərɪ/ n misionero m

mist /mɪst/ n neblina f; (at sea) bruma f. □ ~ **up** vi empañarse

mistake /mɪˈsteɪk/ n error m. make a ~ cometer un error. by ~ por error. ● vt (pt mistook, pp mistaken) confundir. ~ **for** confundir con. ~**n** /-ən/ adj equivocado. be ~**n** equivocarse

mistletoe /ˈmɪsltəʊ/ n muérdago m

mistreat /mɪsˈtriːt/ vt maltratar

mistress /ˈmɪstrɪs/ n (of house) señora f; (lover) amante f

mistrust /mɪsˈtrʌst/ vt desconfiar de. ● n desconfianza f. ~**ful** adj desconfiado

misty /ˈmɪstɪ/ adj (-ier, -iest) neblinoso; (day) de neblina. it's ~ hay neblina

misunderstand /mɪsʌndəˈstænd/ vt (pt -stood) entender mal. ~**ing** n malentendido m

misuse /mɪsˈjuːz/ vt emplear mal; malversar (funds). ● /mɪsˈjuːs/ n mal uso m; (unfair use) abuso m; (of funds) malversación f

mite /maɪt/ n (insect) ácaro m

mitten /ˈmɪtn/ n mitón m

mix /mɪks/ vt mezclar. ~ (o mezclarse; (go together) combinar. ~ **with** tratarse con (people). ● n mezcla f. □ ~ **up** vt mezclar; (confuse) confundir. ~**ed** adj (school etc) mixto; (assorted) mezclado. be ~**ed up** estar confuso. ~**er** n (Culin) batidora f; (TV, machine) mezcladora f. ~**ture** /ˈmɪkstʃə(r)/ n mezcla f. ~**up** n lío m

moan /məʊn/ n gemido m. ● vi

gemir; (complain) quejarse (about de)

moat /məʊt/ n foso m

mob /mɒb/ n turba f. ● vt (pt mobbed) acosar

mobil|e /ˈməʊbaɪl/ adj móvil. ~**e home** n caravana f fija, trailer m (LAm). ~**e (phone)** n (teléfono m) móvil m, (teléfono m) celular m (LAm). ● n móvil m. ~**ize** /ˈməʊbɪlaɪz/ vt movilizar. ● vi movilizarse

mock /mɒk/ vt burlarse de. ● adj (anger) fingido; (exam) de práctica. ~**ery** /ˈmɒkərɪ/ n burla f. make a ~**ery of sth** ridiculizar algo

model /ˈmɒdl/ n (example) modelo m; (mock-up) maqueta f; (person) modelo m. ● adj (exemplary) modelo; (car etc) en miniatura. ● vt (pt modelled) modelar. ~ **s.o. on** s.o. tomar a uno como modelo

modem /ˈməʊdem/ n (Comp) módem m

moderat|e /ˈmɒdərət/ adj & n moderado (m). ● /ˈmɒdəreɪt/ vt moderar. ~**ely** /ˈmɒdərətlɪ/ adv (fairly) medianamente. ~**ion** /-ˈreɪʃn/ n moderación f. in ~**ion** con moderación

modern /ˈmɒdn/ adj moderno. ~**ize** vt modernizar

modest /ˈmɒdɪst/ adj modesto. ~**y** n modestia f

modif|ication /mɒdɪfɪˈkeɪʃn/ n modificación f. ~**y** /-faɪ/ vt modificar

module /ˈmɒdjuːl/ n módulo m

moist /mɔɪst/ adj (-er, -est) húmedo. ~**en** /ˈmɔɪsn/ vt humedecer

moistur|e /ˈmɔɪstʃə(r)/ n humedad f. ~**ize** vt hidratar. ~**izer**, ~**izing cream** n crema f hidratante

mole /məʊl/ n (animal) topo m; (on skin) lunar m

molecule /ˈmɒlɪkjuːl/ n molécula f

molest /məˈlest/ vt abusar (sexualmente) de

mollify /ˈmɒlɪfaɪ/ vt aplacar

mollusc /ˈmɒləsk/ n molusco m

mollycoddle /ˈmɒlɪkɒdl/ vt mimar

molten /ˈməʊltən/ adj fundido; (lava) líquido

mom /mɒm/ n (Amer, 🄵) mamá f 🄵

moment /ˈməʊmənt/ n momento m. at the ~ en este momento. for the ~ de momento. ~ary /ˈməʊməntərɪ/ adj momentáneo

momentous /məˈmentəs/ adj trascendental

momentum /məˈmentəm/ n momento m; (speed) velocidad f

mommy /ˈmɒmɪ/ n (Amer, fam) mamá m 🄵

monarch /ˈmɒnək/ n monarca m. ~y n monarquía f

monastery /ˈmɒnəstərɪ/ n monasterio m

Monday /ˈmʌndeɪ/ n lunes m

money /ˈmʌnɪ/ n dinero m, plata f (LAm). ~box n hucha f, alcancía f (LAm). ~ order n giro m postal

mongrel /ˈmʌŋɡrəl/ n perro m mestizo, chucho m 🄵

monitor /ˈmɒnɪtə(r)/ n (Tec) monitor m. ● vt observar (elections); seguir (progress); (electronically) monitorizar, escuchar

monk /mʌŋk/ n monje m. ~fish n rape m

monkey /ˈmʌŋkɪ/ n mono m. ~nut n cacahuete m, cacahuate m (Mex), maní m (LAm). ~wrench n

llave f inglesa

mono /ˈmɒnəʊ/ n monofonía f

monologue /ˈmɒnəlɒɡ/ n monólogo m

monopol|ize /məˈnɒpəlaɪz/ vt monopolizar; acaparar (conversation). ~y n monopolio m

monoton|e /ˈmɒnətəʊn/ n tono m monocorde. ~ous /məˈnɒtənəs/ adj monótono. ~y n monotonía f

monsoon /mɒnˈsuːn/ n monzón m

monst|er /ˈmɒnstə(r)/ n monstruo m. ~rous /-strəs/ adj monstruoso

month /mʌnθ/ n mes m. £200 a ~ 200 libras mensuales or al mes. ~ly adj mensual. ~ly payment mensualidad f, cuota f mensual (LAm). ● adv mensualmente

monument /ˈmɒnjʊmənt/ n monumento m. ~al /-ˈmentl/ adj monumental

moo /muː/ n mugido m. ● vi mugir

mood /muːd/ n humor m. be in a good/bad ~ estar de buen/mal humor. ~y adj (-ier, -iest) temperamental; (bad-tempered) malhumorado

moon /muːn/ n luna f. ~light n luz f de la luna. ~lighting n pluriempleo m. ~lit adj iluminado por la luna; (night) de luna

moor /mʊə(r)/ n páramo m; (of heather) brezal m. ● vt amarrar. ~ing n (place) amarradero m. ~ings npl (ropes) amarras fpl

moose /muːs/ n invar alce m americano

mop /mɒp/ n fregona f, trapeador m (LAm); (of hair) pelambrera f. ● vt (pt mopped). ~ (up) limpiar

mope /məʊp/ vi estar abatido

moped /ˈməʊped/ n ciclomotor m

m

moral /'mɒrəl/ adj moral. ●n (of tale) moraleja f

morale /mə'rɑːl/ n moral f

moral|ity /mə'rælətɪ/ n moralidad f. **~ly** adv moralmente. **~s** npl moralidad f

morbid /'mɔːbɪd/ adj morboso

more /mɔː(r)/ adj más. two ~ bottles dos botellas más. ●pron más. you ate ~ than me comiste más que yo. some ~ más. ~ than six más de seis. the ~ he has, the ~ he wants cuánto más tiene, más quiere. ●adv más. ~ and ~ cada vez más. ~ or less más o menos. once ~ una vez más. she doesn't live here any ~ ya no vive aquí. **~over** /mɔː'rəʊvə(r)/ adv además

morgue /mɔːg/ n depósito m de cadáveres, morgue f (LAm)

morning /'mɔːnɪŋ/ n mañana f; (early hours) madrugada f. at 11 o'clock in the ~ a las once de la mañana. in the ~ por la mañana, en la mañana (LAm). tomorrow/ yesterday ~ mañana/ayer por la mañana or (LAm) en la mañana. (good) ~! ¡buenos días!

Morocc|an /mə'rʊkən/ adj & n marroquí (m & f). **~o** /-kəʊ/ n Marruecos m

moron /'mɔːrɒn/ n imbécil m & f

morose /mə'rəʊs/ adj taciturno

Morse /mɔːs/ n Morse m. in ~ (code) n en (código) morse

morsel /'mɔːsl/ n bocado m

mortal /'mɔːtl/ adj & n mortal (m). **~ity** /-'tælətɪ/ n mortalidad f

mortar /'mɔːtə(r)/ n (all senses) mortero m

mortgage /'mɔːgɪdʒ/ n hipoteca f. ●vt hipotecar

mortify /'mɔːtɪfaɪ/ vt darle mucha

vergüenza a

mortuary /'mɔːtjʊərɪ/ n depósito m de cadáveres, morgue f (LAm)

mosaic /məʊ'zeɪk/ n mosaico m

mosque /mɒsk/ n mezquita f

mosquito /mɒs'kiːtəʊ/ n (pl -oes) mosquito m, zancudo m (LAm)

moss /mɒs/ n musgo m

most /məʊst/ adj la mayoría de, la mayor parte de. ~ days casi todos los días. ●pron la mayoría, la mayor parte. at ~ como máximo. make the ~ of aprovechar al máximo. ●adv más; (very) muy; (Amer, almost) casi. **~ly** adv principalmente

MOT n. ~ (test) ITV f, inspección f técnica de vehículos

motel /məʊ'tel/ n motel m

moth /mɒθ/ n mariposa f de la luz, palomilla f; (in clothes) polilla f

mother /'mʌðə(r)/ n madre f. ●vt mimar. **~-in-law** (pl **~s-in-law**) suegra f. **~land** n patria f. **~ly** adj maternal. **~-of-pearl** n nácar m, madreperla f. **M~'s Day** n el día m de la Madre. **~-to-be** n futura madre f. **~ tongue** n lengua f materna

motif /məʊ'tiːf/ n motivo m

motion /'məʊʃn/ n movimiento m; (proposal) moción f. put or set in ~ poner algo en marcha. ●vt/i. ~ (to) s.o. to hacerle señas a uno para que. **~less** adj inmóvil

motiv|ate /'məʊtɪveɪt/ vt motivar. **~ation** /-'veɪʃn/ n motivación f. **~e** /'məʊtɪv/ n motivo m

motley /'mɒtlɪ/ adj variopinto

motor /'məʊtə(r)/ n motor m. ●adj motor; (fem) motora, motriz. **~ bike** n 🔳 motocicleta f, moto f 🔳. **~ boat** n lancha f a motor. **~ car** n automóvil m. **~ cycle** n motocicleta f. **~cyclist** n motociclista *m* & *f*. **~ing** automovilismo *m*. **~ist** *n* automovilista *m* & *f*. **~way** *n* autopista *f*

motto /'mɒtəʊ/ *n* (*pl* -oes) lema *m*

mould /məʊld/ *n* molde *m*; (*fungus*) moho *m*. ●*vt* moldear; formar (*character*). **~ing** *n* (*on wall etc*) moldura *f*. **~y** *adj* mohoso

moult /məʊlt/ *vi* mudar de pelo/piel/plumas

mound /maʊnd/ *n* montículo *m*; (*pile, fig*) montón *m*

mount /maʊnt/ *vt* montar (horse); engarzar (gem); preparar (attack). ●*vi* subir, crecer. ●*n*. montura *f*; (*mountain*) monte *m*. □ **~ up** *vi* irse acumulando

mountain /'maʊntɪn/ *n* montaña *f*. **~eer** /maʊntɪ'nɪə(r)/ *n* alpinista *m* & *f*. **~eering** *n* alpinismo *m*. **~ous** *adj* montañoso

mourn /mɔːn/ *vt* llorar. ●*vi* lamentarse. **~ for** s.o. llorar a uno. **~er** *n* doliente *m* & *f*. **~ful** *adj* triste. **~ing** *n* duelo *m*, luto *m*. **be in ~ing** estar de duelo

mouse /maʊs/ *n* (*pl* mice) ratón *m*. **~trap** *n* ratonera *f*

mousse /muːs/ *n* (*Culin*) mousse *f* or *m*; (*for hair*) mousse *f*

moustache /mə'stɑːʃ/ *n* bigote *m*

mouth /maʊθ/ *n* boca *f*; (*of cave*) entrada *f*; (*of river*) desembocadura *f*. **~ful** *n* bocado *m*. **~organ** *n* armónica *f*. **~wash** *n* enjuague *m* bucal

move /muːv/ *vt* mover; (*relocate*) trasladar; (*with emotion*) conmover; (*propose*) proponer. **~ the television** cambiar de lugar de la televisión. **~ house** mudarse de casa. ●*vi* moverse; (*be in motion*) estar en movimiento; (*take action*) tomar medidas. ●*n* movimiento *m*; (*in*

game) jugada *f*; (*player's turn*) turno *m*; (*removal*) mudanza *f*. □ **~ away** *vi* alejarse. □ **~ in** *vi* instalarse. □ **~ in with s.o.** irse a vivir con uno. □ **~ over** *vi* correrse. **~ment** *n* movimiento *m*

movie /'muːvɪ/ *n* (*Amer*) película *f*. **the ~s** *npl* el cine. **~ camera** *n* (*Amer*) tomavistas *m*, filmadora *f* (*LAm*)

moving /'muːvɪŋ/ *adj* en movimiento; (*touching*) conmovedor

mow /məʊ/ *vt* (*pt* mowed or mown /məʊn/) cortar (lawn); segar (hay). □ **~ down** *vt* acribillar. **~er** *n* (*for lawn*) cortacésped *m*

MP *abbr see* **MEMBER OF PARLIAMENT**

Mr /'mɪstə(r)/ *abbr* (*pl* Messrs) (= Mister) Sr. **~ Coldbeck** Sr. Coldbeck

Mrs /'mɪsɪz/ *abbr* (*pl* Mrs) (= Missis) Sra. **~ Andrews** Sra. Andrews

Ms /mɪz/ *abbr* (title of married or unmarried woman)

MSc *abbr see* **MASTER**

much /mʌtʃ/ *adj* & *pron* mucho, mucha. ●*adv* mucho; (*before pp*) muy. **~ as** por mucho que. **~ the same** más o menos lo mismo. **how ~?** ¿cuánto?. **so ~** tanto. **too ~** demasiado

muck /mʌk/ *n* estiércol *m*; (*fam, dirt*) mugre *f*. □ **~ about** *vi* 🅸 tontear

mud /mʌd/ *n* barro *m*, lodo *m*

muddle /'mʌdl/ *vt* embrollar. ●*n* desorden *m*; (*mix-up*) lío *m*. □ **~ through** *vi* salir del paso

muddy *adj* lodoso; (hands etc) cubierto de lodo. **~guard** *n* guardabarros *m*, salpicadera *f* (*Mex*)

muffle /'mʌfl/ *vt* amortiguar (sound). **~r** *n* (*scarf*) bufanda *f*;

(*Amer, Auto*) silenciador *m*

mug /mʌg/ *n* taza *f* (*alta y sin platillo*), tarro *m* (*Mex*); (*for beer*) jarra *f*; (*fam, face*) cara *f*, jeta *f* 🖾; (*fam, fool*) idiota *m & f*. ● *vt* (*pt* **mugged**) asaltar. **~ger** *n* asaltante *m & f* **~ging** *n* asalto *m*

muggy /ˈmʌgɪ/ *adj* bochornoso

mule /mjuːl/ *n* mula *f*

mull /mʌl/ (*Amer*), **~ over** *vt* reflexionar sobre

multi|coloured /mʌltɪˈkʌləd/ *adj* multicolor. **~national** /-ˈnæʃənl/ *adj* & *n* multinacional (*f*)

multipl|e /ˈmʌltɪpl/ *adj* múltiple. ● *n* múltiplo *m*. **~ication** /mʌltɪplɪˈkeɪʃn/ *n* multiplicación *f* **~y** /ˈmʌltɪplaɪ/ *vt* multiplicar. ● *vi* (*Math*) multiplicar; (*increase*) multiplicarse

multitude /ˈmʌltɪtjuːd/ *n*. a **~** of problems múltiples problemas

mum /mʌm/ *n* 🖾 mamá *f* 🖾

mumble /ˈmʌmbl/ *vt* mascullar. ● *vi* hablar entre dientes

mummy /ˈmʌmɪ/ *n* (*fam, mother*) mamá *f* 🖾; (*archaeology*) momia *f*

mumps /mʌmps/ *n* paperas *fpl*

munch /mʌntʃ/ *vt/i* mascar

mundane /mʌnˈdeɪn/ *adj* mundano

municipal /mjuːˈnɪsɪpl/ *adj* municipal

mural /ˈmjʊərəl/ *adj* & *n* mural (*f*)

murder /ˈmɜːdə(r)/ *n* asesinato *m*. ● *vt* asesinar. **~er** *n* asesino *m*

murky /ˈmɜːkɪ/ *adj* (*-ier, -iest*) turbio

murmur /ˈmɜːmə(r)/ *n* murmullo *m*. ● *vt/i* murmurar

musc|le /ˈmʌsl/ *n* músculo *m*. **~ular** /ˈmʌskjʊlə(r)/ *adj* muscular; (*arm, body*) musculoso

muse /mjuːz/ *vi* meditar (**on** sobre)

museum /mjuːˈzɪəm/ *n* museo *m*

mush /mʌʃ/ *n* papilla *f*

mushroom /ˈmʌʃrʊm/ *n* champiñón *m*; (*in botany*) seta *f*. ● *vi* aparecer como hongos

mushy /ˈmʌʃɪ/ *adj* blando

music /ˈmjuːzɪk/ *n* música *f*. **~al** *adj* musical. ● *n* musical *m*. **~ian** /mjuːˈzɪʃn/ *n* músico *m*

Muslim /ˈmʊzlɪm/ *adj* & *n* musulmán (*m*)

mussel /ˈmʌsl/ *n* mejillón *m*

must /mʌst/ *modal verb* deber, tener que; (*expressing supposition*) deber (de). **he ~ be old** debe (de) ser viejo. **I ~ have done it** debo (de) haberlo hecho. ● *n*. **be a ~** ser imprescindible

mustache /ˈmʌstæʃ/ *n* (*Amer*) bigote *m*

mustard /ˈmʌstəd/ *n* mostaza *f*

muster /ˈmʌstə(r)/ *vt* reunir

musty /ˈmʌstɪ/ *adj* (*-ier, -iest*) que huele a humedad

mutation /mjuːˈteɪʃn/ *n* mutación *f*

mute /mjuːt/ *adj* mudo

mutilate /ˈmjuːtɪleɪt/ *vt* mutilar

mutiny /ˈmjuːtɪnɪ/ *n* motín *m*. ● *vi* amotinarse

mutter /ˈmʌtə(r)/ *vt/i* murmurar

mutton /ˈmʌtn/ *n* carne *f* de ovino

mutual /ˈmjuːtʃʊəl/ *adj* mutuo; (*fam, common*) común

muzzle /ˈmʌzl/ *n* (*snout*) hocico *m*; (*device*) bozal *m*

my /maɪ/ *adj* (*sing*) mi; (*pl*) mis

myself /maɪˈself/ *pron* (*reflexive*) me; (*used for emphasis*) yo mismo *m*, yo misma *f*. **I cut** ∼ **me** corté. **I made it** ∼ lo hice yo mismo/misma. **I was by** ∼ estaba solo/sola

myster|ious /mɪˈstɪərɪəs/ *adj* misterioso. ∼**y** /ˈmɪstərɪ/ *n* misterio *m*

mystical /ˈmɪstɪkl/ *adj* místico

mystify /ˈmɪstɪfaɪ/ *vt* dejar perplejo

mystique /mɪˈstiːk/ *n* mística *f*

myth /mɪθ/ *n* mito *m*. ∼**ical** *adj* mítico. ∼**ology** /mɪˈθɒlədʒɪ/ *n* mitología *f*

Nn

N *abbr* (= north) N

nab /næb/ *vt* (*pt* nabbed) (*sl, arrest*) pescar; (*snatch*) agarrar

nag /næg/ *vt* (*pt* nagged) fastidiar; (*scold*) estarle encima a. ● *vi* criticar

nail /neɪl/ *n* clavo *m*; (*of finger, toe*) uña *f*. ∼ **polish** esmalte *m* para las uñas. ● *vt*. ∼ (**down**) clavar

naive /naɪˈiːv/ *adj* ingenuo

naked /ˈneɪkɪd/ *adj* desnudo. **to the** ∼ **eye** a simple vista

name /neɪm/ *n* nombre *m*; (*of book, film*) título *m*; (*fig*) fama *f*. **my** ∼ **is Chris** me llamo Chris. **good** ∼ buena reputación. ● *vt* ponerle nombre a; (*appoint*) nombrar. **a man** ∼**d Jones** un hombre llamado Jones. **she was** ∼**d after or** (*Amer*) **for her grandmother** le pusieron el nombre de su abuela. ∼**less** *adj* anónimo. ∼**ly** *adv* a saber. ∼**sake** *n* (*person*) tocayo *m*

nanny /ˈnænɪ/ *n* niñera *f*

nap /næp/ *n* (*sleep*) sueñecito *m*; (*after lunch*) siesta *f*. **have a** ∼ echarse un sueño

napkin /ˈnæpkɪn/ *n* servilleta *f*

nappy /ˈnæpɪ/ *n* pañal *m*

narcotic /nɑːˈkɒtɪk/ *adj & n* narcótico (*m*)

narrat|e /nəˈreɪt/ *vt* narrar. ∼**ive** /ˈnærətɪv/ *n* narración *f*. ∼**or** /nə ˈreɪtə(r)/ *n* narrador *m*

narrow /ˈnærəʊ/ *adj* (-**er**, -**est**) estrecho, angosto (*LAm*). **have a** ∼ **escape** salvarse de milagro. ● *vt* estrechar; (*limit*) limitar. ● *vi* estrecharse. ∼**ly** *adv* (*just*) por poco. ∼**-minded** /-ˈmaɪndɪd/ *adj* de miras estrechas

nasal /ˈneɪzl/ *adj* nasal; (*voice*) gangoso

nasty /ˈnɑːstɪ/ *adj* (-**ier**, -**iest**) desagradable; (*spiteful*) malo (**to** con); (*taste, smell*) asqueroso; (*cut*) feo

nation /ˈneɪʃn/ *n* nación *f*

national /ˈnæʃənl/ *adj* nacional. ● *n* ciudadano *m*. ∼ **anthem** himno *m* nacional. ∼**ism** *n* nacionalismo *m*. ∼**ity** /næʃəˈnælətɪ/ *n* nacionalidad *f*. ∼**ize** *vt* nacionalizar. ∼**ly** *adv* a escala nacional

---

National Trust Fundación británica cuyo objetivo es la conservación de lugares de interés histórico o de belleza natural. Se financia mediante legados y subvenciones privadas. Es la mayor propietaria de tierras de Gran Bretaña. En Escocia, es independiente y recibe el nombre de *National Trust for Scotland*. ***i***

---

nationwide /ˈneɪʃnwaɪd/ *adj & adv* a escala nacional

native /ˈneɪtɪv/ *n* natural *m & f*. **be**

a ~ of ser natural de. ● adj nativo; (country, town) natal; (language) materno; (plant, animal) autóctono. N~ **American** indio m americano

nativity /nə'tɪvətɪ/ n. the N~ la Natividad f

NATO /'neɪtəʊ/ abbr (= **North Atlantic Treaty Organization**) OTAN f

natter /'nætə(r)/ 🔟 vi charlar. ● n charla f

natural /'nætʃərəl/ adj natural. ~ **history** n historia f natural. ~**ist** n naturalista m & f. ~**ized** adj (citizen) naturalizado. ~**ly** adv (of course) naturalmente; (by nature) por naturaleza

nature /'neɪtʃə(r)/ n naturaleza f; (of person) carácter m; (of things) naturaleza f

naught /nɔːt/ n cero m

naughty /'nɔːtɪ/ adj (-ier, -iest) malo, travieso

nausea /'nɔːzɪə/ n náuseas fpl. ~**ous** /-ɪəs/ adj nauseabundo

nautical /'nɔːtɪkl/ adj náutico. ~ **mile** n milla f marina

naval /'neɪvl/ adj naval; (officer) de marina

nave /neɪv/ n nave f

navel /'neɪvl/ n ombligo m

naviga|ble /'nævɪɡəbl/ adj navegable. ~**te** /'nævɪɡeɪt/ vt navegar por (sea etc); gobernar (ship). ● vi navegar. ~**tion** /-'ɡeɪʃn/ n navegación f. ~**tor** n oficial m & f de derrota

navy /'neɪvɪ/ n marina f de guerra. ~ **(blue)** a & n azul (m) marino

NE abbr (= **north-east**) NE

near /nɪə(r)/ adv cerca. draw ~ acercarse. ● prep. ~ **(to)** cerca de. go ~ **(to)** sth acercarse a algo.

● adj cercano. ● vt acercarse a. ~**by** adj cercano. ~**ly** adv casi. he ~**ly** died por poco se muere, casi se muere. not ~**ly** ni con mucho. ~**sighted** /-'saɪtɪd/ adj miope, corto de vista

neat /niːt/ adj (-er, -est) (person) pulcro; (room etc) bien arreglado; (ingenious) hábil; (whisky, gin) solo; ; (Amer fam, great) fantástico 🔟. ~**ly** adv pulcramente; (organized) cuidadosamente

necessar|ily /nesə'serɪlɪ/ adv necesariamente. ~**y** /'nesəserɪ/ adj necesario

necessit|ate /nə'sesɪteɪt/ vt exigir. ~**y** /nɪ'sesətɪ/ n necesidad f. the bare ~**ies** lo indispensable

neck /nek/ n (of person, bottle, dress) cuello m; (of animal) pescuezo m. ~ **and** ~ a la par, parejos (LAm). ~**lace** /'nekləs/ n collar m. ~**line** n escote m

nectar /'nektə(r)/ n néctar m

nectarine /'nektərɪn/ n nectarina f

née /neɪ/ adj de soltera

need /niːd/ n necesidad f (for de). ● vt necesitar; (demand) exigir. you ~ not speak no tienes que hablar

needle /'niːdl/ n aguja f. ● vt (fam, annoy) pinchar

needless /'niːdlɪs/ adj innecesario

needlework /'niːdlwɜːk/ n labores fpl de aguja; (embroidery) bordado m

needy /'niːdɪ/ adj (-ier, -iest) necesitado

negative /'negətɪv/ adj negativo. ● n (of photograph) negativo m; (no) negativa f

neglect /nɪ'glekt/ vt descuidar (house); desatender (children); no cumplir con (duty). ● n negligencia *f.* (state of) ∼ abandono *m.* ∼**ful** *adj* negligente

neglig|ence /'neglidʒəns/ *n* negligencia *f*, descuido *m.* ∼**ent** *adj* negligente. ∼**ible** /'neglidʒəbl/ *adj* insignificante

negotia|ble /nɪ'gəʊʃəbl/ *adj* negociable. ∼**te** /nɪ'gəʊʃɪeɪt/ *vt/i* negociar. ∼**tion** /-'eɪʃn/ *n* negociación *f.* ∼**tor** *n* negociador *m*

neigh /neɪ/ *vi* relinchar

neighbour /'neɪbə(r)/ *n* vecino *m.* ∼**hood** *n* vecindad *f*, barrio *m.* **in the** ∼**hood of** alrededor de. ∼**ing** *adj* vecino

neither /'naɪðə(r)/ *adj.* ∼ **book** ninguno de los libros. ●*pron* ninguno, -na. ●*conj.* **neither**...**nor** ni...ni. ∼ **do I** yo tampoco

neon /'niːɒn/ *n* neón *m.* ●*adj* (lamp etc) de neón

nephew /'nevjuː/ *n* sobrino *m*

Neptune /'neptjuːn/ *n* Neptuno *m*

nerv|e /nɜːv/ *n* nervio *m*; (*courage*) valor *m*; (*calm*) sangre *f* fría; (*fam, impudence*) descaro *m.* ∼**es** *npl* (before exams etc) nervios *mpl.* **get on s.o.'s** ∼**es** ponerle los nervios de punta a uno. ∼**e-racking** *adj* exasperante. ∼**ous** /'nɜːvəs/ *adj* nervioso. **be/feel** ∼**ous** estar nervioso. ∼**ousness** *n* nerviosismo *m.* ∼**y** /'nɜːvi/ *adj* nervioso; (*Amer fam*) descarado

nest /nest/ *n* nido *m.* ●*vi* anidar

nestle /'nesl/ *vi* acurrucarse

net /net/ *n* red *f.* **the N**∼ (*Comp*) la Red. ●*vt* (*pt* netted) pescar (con red) (fish). ●*adj* neto. ∼**ball** *n* especie de baloncesto

Netherlands /'neðələndz/ *npl.* **the** ∼ los Países Bajos

netting /'netɪŋ/ *n* redes *fpl.* **wire** ∼ tela *f* metálica

nettle /'netl/ *n* ortiga *f*

network /'netwɜːk/ *n* red *f*; (*TV*) cadena *f*

neuro|sis /njʊə'rəʊsɪs/ *n* (*pl* -oses /-siːz/) neurosis *f.* ∼**tic** /-'rɒtɪk/ *adj* & *n* neurótico (*m*)

neuter /'njuːtə(r)/ *adj* & *n* neutro (*m*). ●*vt* castrar (animals)

neutral /'njuːtrəl/ *adj* neutral; (colour) neutro; (*Elec*) neutro. ∼ (gear) (*Auto*) punto *m* muerto. ∼**ize** *vt* neutralizar

neutron /'njuːtrɒn/ *n* neutrón *m*

never /'nevə(r)/ *adv* nunca; (*more emphatic*) jamás; (*fam, not*) no. ∼ **again** nunca más. **he** ∼ **smiles** no sonríe nunca, nunca sonríe. **I** ∼ **saw him** 🄸 no lo vi. ∼**-ending** *adj* interminable. ∼**theless** /-ðə'les/ *adv* sin embargo, no obstante

new /njuː/ *adj* (-er, -est) nuevo. ∼**born** *adj* recién nacido. ∼**comer** *n* recién llegado *m.* ∼**fangled** /-'fæŋgld/ *adj* (*pej*) moderno. ∼**ly** *adv* recién. ∼**ly-weds** *npl* recién casados *mpl*

news /njuːz/ *n.* **a piece of** ∼ una noticia. **good/bad** ∼ buenas/malas noticias. **the** ∼ (*TV, Radio*) las noticias. ∼**agent** *n* vendedor *m* de periódicos. ∼**caster** *n* locutor *m.* ∼**dealer** *n* (*Amer*) see **AGENT.** ∼**flash** *n* información *f* de última hora. ∼**letter** *n* boletín *m*, informativo *m.* ∼**paper** *n* periódico *m*, diario *m.* ∼**reader** *n* locutor *m*

newt /njuːt/ *n* tritón *m*

New Year /njuː'jɪə(r)/ *n* Año *m* Nuevo. **N**∼**'s Day** *n* día *m* de Año Nuevo. **N**∼**'s Eve** *n* noche *f* vieja, noche *f* de fin de Año

New Zealand /njuː'ziːlənd/ *n* Nueva Zeland(i)a *f*

next /nekst/ *adj* próximo; (week,

month etc) que viene, próximo; (adjoining) vecino; (following) siguiente. ● adv luego, después. ~ to al lado de. **when you see me** ~ **la próxima vez que me veas.** ~ **to nothing** casi nada. ~ **door** al lado (to de). ~**-door** adj de al lado. ~ **of kin** n familiar(es) m(pl) más cercano(s)

nib /nɪb/ n plumilla f

nibble /'nɪbl/ vt/i mordisquear. ● n mordisco m

Nicaragua /nɪkə'rægjuə/ n Nicaragua f. ~**n** adj & n nicaragüense (m & f)

nice /naɪs/ adj (-er, -est) agradable; (likeable) simpático; (kind) amable; (weather, food) bueno. **we had a** ~ **time** lo pasamos bien. ~**ly** adv (kindly) amablemente; (politely) con buenos modales

niche /nɪtʃ, niːʃ/ n nicho m

nick /nɪk/ n corte m pequeño. **in the** ~ **of time** justo a tiempo. ● vt (sl, steal) afanar ⊠

nickel /'nɪkl/ n (metal) níquel m; (Amer) moneda f de cinco centavos

nickname /'nɪkneɪm/ n apodo m. ● vt apodar

nicotine /'nɪkətiːn/ n nicotina f

niece /niːs/ n sobrina f

niggling /'nɪglɪŋ/ adj (doubt) constante

night /naɪt/ n noche f; (evening) tarde f. **at** ~ por la noche, de noche. **good** ~ ¡buenas noches! ● adj nocturno, de noche. ~**cap** n (drink) bebida f (tomada antes de acostarse). ~**club** n club m nocturno. ~**dress** n camisón m. ~**fall** n anochecer m. ~**gown**, ~**ie** /'naɪti/ ⊡ n camisón m. ~**life** n vida f nocturna. ~**ly** adj de todas

las noches. ~**mare** n pesadilla f. ~**school** n escuela f nocturna. ~**time** n noche f. ~**watchman** n sereno m

nil /nɪl/ n nada f; (Sport) cero m

nimble /'nɪmbl/ adj (-er, -est) ágil

nine /naɪn/ adj & n nueve (m). ~**teen** /naɪn'tiːn/ adj & n diecinueve (m). ~**teenth** adj decimonoveno. ● n diecinueveavo m. ~**tieth** /'naɪntɪəθ/ adj nonagésimo. ● n noventavo m. ~**ty** adj & n noventa (m)

ninth /naɪnθ/ adj & n noveno (m)

nip /nɪp/ vt (pt nipped) (pinch) pellizcar; (bite) mordisquear. ● vi (fam, rush) correr

nipple /'nɪpl/ n (of woman) pezón m; (of man) tetilla f; (of baby's bottle) tetina f, chupón m (Mex)

nippy /'nɪpɪ/ adj (-ier, -iest) (fam, chilly) fresquito

nitrogen /'naɪtrədʒən/ n nitrógeno m

no /nəʊ/ adj ninguno, (before masculine singular noun) ningún. **I have** ~ **money** no tengo dinero. **there's** ~ **food left** no queda nada de comida. **it has** ~ **windows** no tiene ventanas. **I'm** ~ **expert** no soy ningún experto. ~ **smoking** prohibido fumar. ~ **way!** ⊡ ¡ni hablar! ● adv & int no. ● n (pl **noes**) no m

noble /'nəʊbl/ adj (-er, -est) noble. ~**man** /-mən/ n noble m

nobody /'nəʊbədɪ/ pron nadie. **there's** ~ **there** no hay nadie

nocturnal /nɒk'tɜːnl/ adj nocturno

nod /nɒd/ vt (pt nodded). ~ **one's head** asentir con la cabeza. ● vi (in agreement) asentir con la cabeza; (in greeting) saludar con la cabeza.

◻ ~ **off** vi dormirse

nois|e /nɔɪz/ n ruido m. ~**ily** adv ruidosamente. ~**y** adj (-ier, -iest) ruidoso. it's too ~y here hay demasiado ruido aquí

nomad /'nəʊmæd/ n nómada m & f. ~**ic** /-'mædɪk/ adj nómada

no man's land n tierra f de nadie

nominat|e /'nɒmɪneɪt/ vt (put forward) proponer; postular (LAm); (appoint) nombrar. ~**ion** /-'neɪʃn/ n nombramiento m; (Amer, Pol) proclamación f

non-... /nɒn/ pref no ...

nonchalant /'nɒnʃələnt/ adj despreocupado

non-committal /nɒnkə'mɪtl/ adj evasivo

nondescript /'nɒndɪskrɪpt/ adj anodino

none /nʌn/ pron ninguno, ninguna. there were ~ left no quedaba ninguno/ninguna. ~ of us ninguno de nosotros. ● adv no, de ninguna manera. he is ~ the happier no está más contento

nonentity /nɒ'nentətɪ/ n persona f insignificante

non-existent /nɒnɪg'zɪstənt/ adj inexistente

nonplussed /nɒn'plʌst/ adj perplejo

nonsens|e /'nɒnsns/ n tonterías fpl, disparates mpl. ~**ical** /-'sensɪkl/ adj disparatado

non-smoker /nɒn'sməʊkə(r)/ n no fumador m. I'm a ~ no fumo

non-stop /nɒn'stɒp/ adj (train) directo; (flight) sin escalas. ● adv sin parar; (by train) directamente; (by air) sin escalas

noodles /'nuːdlz/ npl fideos mpl

nook /nʊk/ n rincón m

noon /nuːn/ n mediodía m

no-one /'nəʊwʌn/ pron nadie

noose /nuːs/ n soga f

nor /nɔː(r)/ conj ni, tampoco. neither blue ~ red ni azul ni rojo. he doesn't play the piano, ~ do I no sabe tocar el piano, ni yo tampoco

norm /nɔːm/ n norma f

normal /'nɔːml/ adj normal. ~**cy** n (Amer) normalidad f. ~**ity** /-'mælətɪ/ n normalidad f. ~**ly** adv normalmente

north /nɔːθ/ n norte m. ● adj norte. ● adv hacia el norte. **N~ America** n América f del Norte, Norteamérica f **N~ American** adj & n norteamericano (m). ~**east** n nor(d)este m. ● adj nor(d)este. ● adv (go) hacia el nor(d)este. it's ~east of Leeds está al nor(d)este de Leeds. ~**erly** /'nɔːðəlɪ/ adj (wind) del norte. ~**ern** /'nɔːðən/ adj del norte. ~**erner** n norteño m. **N~ern Ireland** n Irlanda f del Norte. **N~ Sea** n mar m del Norte. ~**ward** /'nɔːθwəd/, ~**wards** adv hacia el norte. ~**west** n noroeste m. ● adj noroeste. ● adv hacia el noroeste

Norw|ay /'nɔːweɪ/ n Noruega f. ~**egian** /-'wiːdʒən/ adj & n noruego (m)

nose /nəʊz/ n nariz f. ~**bleed** n hemorragia f nasal. ~**dive** vi descender en picado, descender en picada (LAm)

nostalgi|a /nɒ'stældʒə/ n nostalgia f. ~**c** adj nostálgico

nostril /'nɒstrɪl/ n ventana f de la nariz f

nosy /'nəʊzɪ/ adj (-ier, -iest) 🄸 entrometido, metiche (LAm)

not /nɒt/

Cuando **not** va precedido del verbo auxiliar **do** or **have** o de un verbo modal como **should** etc, se suele emplear la forma contraída **don't, haven't, shouldn't** etc

adverb

····▸ no. I don't know no sé. ∼ yet todavía no. ∼ me yo no

····▸ (*replacing a clause*) I suppose ∼ supongo que no. of course ∼ por supuesto que no. are you going to help me or ∼? ¿me vas a ayudar o no?

····▸ (*emphatic*) ni. ∼ a penny more! ¡ni un penique más!

····▸ (*in phrases*) certainly ∼ de ninguna manera . ∼ you again! ¡tú otra vez!

notabl|e /ˈnəʊtəbl/ *adj* notable; (*author*) distinguido. ∼y /ˈnəʊtəblɪ/ *adv* notablemente; (*in particular*) particularmente

notch /nɒtʃ/ *n* muesca *f*. □ ∼ **up** *vt* apuntarse

note /nəʊt/ *n* (*incl Mus*) nota *f*; (*banknote*) billete *m*. take ∼s tomar apuntes. ●*vt* (*notice*) observar; (*record*) anotar. □ ∼ **down** *vt* apuntar. ∼**book** *n* cuaderno *m*. ∼**d** *adj* célebre. ∼**paper** *n* papel *m* de carta(s)

nothing /ˈnʌθɪŋ/ *pron* nada. he eats ∼ no come nada. for ∼ (*free*) gratis; (*in vain*) en vano. ∼ else nada más. ∼ much happened no pasó gran cosa. he does ∼ but complain no hace más que quejarse

notice /ˈnəʊtɪs/ *n* (*sign*) letrero *m*;

(*item of information*) anuncio *m*; (*notification*) aviso *m*; (*of termination of employment*) preaviso *m*; (*of dismissal*) despido *m*. take ∼ of hacer caso a (person). ●*vt* notar. ●*vi* darse cuenta. ∼**able** *adj* perceptible. ∼**ably** *adv* perceptiblemente. ∼**board** *n* tablón *m* de anuncios, tablero *m* de anuncios (*LAm*)

notif|ication /nəʊtɪfɪˈkeɪʃn/ *n* notificación *f*. ∼**y** /ˈnəʊtɪfaɪ/ *vt* informar; (*in writing*) notificar. ∼**y** s.o. of sth comunicarle algo a uno

notion /ˈnəʊʃn/ *n* (*concept*) concepto *m*; (*idea*) idea *f*

notorious /nəʊˈtɔːrɪəs/ *adj* notorio

notwithstanding /nɒtwɪθ ˈstændɪŋ/ *prep* a pesar de. ●*adv* no obstante

nougat /ˈnuːɡɑː/ *n* turrón *m*

nought /nɔːt/ *n* cero *m*

noun /naʊn/ *n* sustantivo *m*, nombre *m*

nourish /ˈnʌrɪʃ/ *vt* alimentar. ∼**ment** *n* alimento *m*

novel /ˈnɒvl/ *n* novela *f*. ●*adj* original, novedoso. ∼**ist** *n* novelista *m* & *f*. ∼**ty** *n* novedad *f*

November /nəʊˈvembə(r)/ *n* noviembre *m*

novice /ˈnɒvɪs/ *n* principiante *m* & *f*

now /naʊ/ *adv* ahora. ∼ and again, ∼ and then de vez en cuando. ∼ right ∼ ahora mismo. from ∼ on a partir de ahora. ●*conj*. ∼ (that) ahora que. ∼**adays** /ˈnaʊədeɪz/ *adv* hoy (en) día

nowhere /ˈnəʊweə(r)/ *adv* por ninguna parte, por ningún lado; (*after motion towards*) a ninguna

parte, a ningún lado

nozzle /'nɒzl/ n (on hose) boca f; (on fire extinguisher) boquilla f

nuance /'njuːɑːns/ n matiz m

nuclear /'njuːklɪə(r)/ adj nuclear

nucleus /'njuːklɪəs/ n (pl -lei /-lɪaɪ/) núcleo m

nude /njuːd/ adj & n desnudo (m). in the ~ desnudo

nudge /nʌdʒ/ vt codear (ligeramente). ● n golpe m (suave) con el codo

nudi|st /'njuːdɪst/ n nudista m & f. ~ty /'njuːdəti/ n desnudez f

nuisance /'njuːsns/ n (thing, event) molestia f, fastidio m; (person) pesado m

null /nʌl/ adj nulo

numb /nʌm/ adj entumecido. go ~ entumecerse ●vt entumecer

number /'nʌmbə(r)/ n número m; (telephone number) número m de teléfono. a ~ of people varias personas. ●vt numerar; (count, include) contar. ~plate n matrícula f, placa f (LAm)

numer|al /'njuːmərəl/ n número m. ~ical /njuː'merɪkl/ adj numérico. ~ous /'njuːmərəs/ adj numeroso

nun /nʌn/ n monja f

nurse /nɜːs/ n enfermero m, enfermera f; (nanny) niñera f. ●vt cuidar; abrigar (hope etc)

nursery /'nɜːsəri/ n (for plants) vivero m; (day ~) guardería f. ~ rhyme n canción f infantil. ~ school n jardín m de infancia, jardín m infantil (LAm)

nursing home /'nɜːsɪŋ/ n (for older people) residencia f de ancianos (con mayor nivel de asistencia médica)

nut /nʌt/ n fruto m seco (nuez,

almendra, avellana etc); (Tec) tuerca f. ~case n chiflado m. ~crackers npl cascanueces m. ~meg /-meg/ n nuez f moscada

nutri|ent /'njuːtrɪənt/ n nutriente m. ~tion /njuː'trɪʃn/ n nutrición f. ~tious /njuː'trɪʃəs/ adj nutritivo

nuts /nʌts/ adj (fam, crazy) chiflado

nutshell /'nʌtʃel/ n cáscara f de nuez. in a ~ en pocas palabras

NW abbr (= **north-west**) NO

nylon /'naɪlɒn/ n nylon m

Oo

oaf /əʊf/ n zoquete m

oak /əʊk/ n roble m

OAP /əʊeɪ'piː/ abbr (= **old-age pensioner**) n pensionista m & f, pensionado m

oar /ɔː(r)/ n remo m

oasis /əʊ'eɪsɪs/ n (pl oases /-siːz/) oasis m

oath /əʊθ/ n juramento m

oat|meal /'əʊtmiːl/ n harina f de avena; (Amer, flakes) avena f (en copos). ~s /əʊts/ npl avena f

obedien|ce /əʊ'biːdɪəns/ n obediencia f. ~t adj obediente. ~tly adv obedientemente

obese /əʊ'biːs/ adj obeso. ~ity n obesidad f

obey /əʊ'beɪ/ vt/i obedecer

obituary /ə'bɪtʃʊəri/ n nota f necrológica, obituario m

object /'ɒbdʒɪkt/ n objeto m; (aim) objetivo m. ●/əb'dʒekt/ vi oponerse (to a). ~ion /əb'dʒekʃn/ n objeción f. ~ionable adj censurable; (unpleasant) desagradable. ~ive /əˈbdʒektɪv/ adj n objetivo (m)

oblig|ation /ɒblɪˈɡeɪʃn/ n obligación f. be under an ~ation to estar obligado a. ~atory /əˈblɪɡatrɪ/ adj obligatorio. ~e /əˈblaɪdʒ/ vt obligar. I'd be much ~ed if you could help me le quedaría muy agradecido si pudiera ayudarme. ● vi hacer un favor. ~ing adj atento

oblique /əˈbliːk/ adj oblicuo

obliterate /əˈblɪtəreɪt/ vt arrasar; (erase) borrar

oblivio|n /əˈblɪvɪən/ n olvido m. ~us /-vɪəs/ adj (unaware) inconsciente (to, of de)

oblong /ˈɒblɒŋ/ adj oblongo. ● n rectángulo m

obnoxious /əbˈnɒkʃəs/ adj odioso

oboe /ˈəʊbəʊ/ n oboe m

obscen|e /əbˈsiːn/ adj obsceno. ~ity /əbˈsenətɪ/ n obscenidad f

obscur|e /əbˈskjʊə(r)/ adj oscuro. ● vt ocultar; impedir ver claramente (issue). ~ity n oscuridad f

obsequious /əbˈsiːkwɪəs/ adj servil

observ|ant /əbˈzɜːvənt/ adj observador. ~ation /ɒbzəˈveɪʃn/ n observación f. ~atory /əbˈzɜːvatrɪ/ n observatorio m. ~e /əbˈzɜːv/ vt observar. ~er n observador m

obsess /əbˈses/ vt obsesionar. ~ed /əbˈsest/ adj obsesionado. ~ion /-ʃn/ n obsesión f. ~ive adj obsesivo

obsolete /ˈɒbsəliːt/ adj obsoleto

obstacle /ˈɒbstəkl/ n obstáculo m

obstina|cy /ˈɒbstɪnəsɪ/ n obstinación f. ~te /-ət/ adj obstinado. ~tely adv obstinadamente

obstruct /əbˈstrʌkt/ vt obstruir; bloquear (traffic). ~ion /-ʃn/ n obstrucción f

obtain /əbˈteɪn/ vt conseguir, obtener. ~able adj asequible

obtrusive /əbˈtruːsɪv/ adj (presence) demasiado prominente; (noise) molesto

obtuse /əbˈtjuːs/ adj obtuso

obvious /ˈɒbvɪəs/ adj obvio. ~ly adv obviamente

occasion /əˈkeɪʒn/ n ocasión f. ~al adj esporádico. ~ally adv de vez en cuando

occult /ɒˈkʌlt/ adj oculto

occup|ant /ˈɒkjʊpənt/ n ocupante m & f. ~ation /ɒkjʊˈpeɪʃn/ n ocupación f. ~ier /ˈɒkjʊpaɪə(r)/ n ocupante m & f. ~y /ˈɒkjʊpaɪ/ vt ocupar. keep o.s. ~ied entretenerse

occur /əˈkɜː(r)/ vi (pt occurred) tener lugar, ocurrir; (change) producirse; (exist) encontrarse. it ~red to me that se me ocurrió que. ~rence /əˈkʌrəns/ n (incidence) incidencia f. it is a rare ~rence no es algo frecuente

ocean /ˈəʊʃn/ n océano m

o'clock /əˈklɒk/ adv. it is 7 ~ son las siete. it's one ~ es la una

octagon /ˈɒktəɡən/ n octágono m

octave /ˈɒktɪv/ n octava f

October /ɒkˈtəʊbə(r)/ n octubre m

octopus /ˈɒktəpəs/ n (pl -puses) pulpo m

odd /ɒd/ adj (-er, -est) extraño, raro; (number) impar; (one of pair) desparejado. smoke the ~ cigarette fumarse algún que otro cigarrillo. fifty-~ unos cincuenta, cincuenta y pico. the ~ one out la excepción. ~ity n (thing) rareza f;

(*person*) bicho *m* raro. **~ly** *adv* de una manera extraña. **~ly enough** por extraño que parezca. **~ment** *n* retazo *m*. **~s** *npl* probabilidades *fpl*, (*in betting*) apuesta *f*. **be at ~s** estar en desacuerdo. **~s and ends** *mpl* ⚀ cosas *fpl* sueltas

odious /'əʊdɪəs/ *adj* odioso

odometer /ɒ'dɒmətə(r)/ *n* (*Amer*) cuentakilómetros *m*

odour /'əʊdə(r)/ *n* olor *m*

---

of /ɒv/əv/ *preposition*

····▸ de. **a pound of cheese** una libra de queso. **it's made of wood** es de madera. **a girl of ten** una niña de diez años

····▸ (*in dates*) de. **the fifth of November** el cinco de noviembre

····▸ (*Amer, when telling the time*) **it's ten (minutes) of five** son las cinco menos diez, son diez para las cinco (*LAm*)

❗ **of** is not translated in cases such as the following: **a colleague of mine** un colega mío; **there were six of us** *éramos seis*; **that's very kind of you** *es Ud muy amable*

---

off /ɒf/ *prep* (*from*) de. **he picked it up ~ the floor** lo recogió del suelo; (*distant from*) **just ~ the coast of Texas** a poca distancia de la costa de Tejas. **2 ft ~ the ground** a dos pies del suelo; (*absent from*) **I've been ~ work for a week** hace una semana que no voy a trabajar. ● *adv* (*removed*) **the lid was ~** la tapa no estaba puesta; (*distant*) **some way ~** a cierta distancia; (*leaving*) **I'm ~** me voy; (*switched off*) (light, TV) apa-

gado; (water) cortado; (*cancelled*) (match) cancelado; (*not on duty*) (day) libre. ● *adj.* **be ~** (meat) estar malo, estar pasado; (milk) estar cortado. **~-beat** *adj* poco convencional. **~ chance** *n.* **on the ~ chance** por si acaso

---

---

offen|ce /ə'fens/ *n* (breach of law) infracción *f*; (criminal *~ce*) delito *m*; (cause of outrage) atentado *m*; (Amer, attack) ataque *m*. **take ~ce** ofenderse. **~d** *vt* ofender. **~der** *n* delincuente *m* & *f*. **~sive** /-sɪv/ *adj* ofensivo; (disgusting) desagradable

offer /'ɒfə(r)/ *vt* ofrecer. **~ to do sth** ofrecerse a hacer algo. ● *n* oferta *f*. **on ~** de oferta

offhand /ɒf'hænd/ *adj* (brusque) brusco. **say sth in an ~ way** decir algo a la ligera. ● *adv* de improviso

office /'ɒfɪs/ *n* oficina *f*; (post) cargo *m*. **doctor's ~** (Amer) consultorio *m*, consulta *m*. **~ block** *n* edificio *m* de oficinas **~r** *n* oficial *m* & *f*; (police *~r*) policía *m* & *f*; (as form of address) agente

offici|al /ə'fɪʃl/ *adj* oficial. ● *n* funcionario *m* del Estado; (of party, union) dirigente *m* & *f*. **~ally** *adv* oficialmente. **~ous** /ə'fɪʃəs/ *adj* oficioso

offing /'ɒfɪŋ/ *n.* **in the ~** en perspectiva

off: ~**-licence** n tienda f de vinos y licores. ~**-putting** adj (disconcerting) desconcertante; (disagreeable) desagradable. ~**set** vt (pt -set, pres p -setting) compensar. ~**shore** adj (breeze) que sopla desde la tierra; (drilling) offshore; (well) submarino. ● adv a un lugar de mano de obra barata. ~**side** /ɒf'saɪd/ adj (Sport) fuera de juego. ~**spring** n invar prole f. ~**-stage** /-'steɪdʒ/ adv fuera del escenario. ~**-white** adj color hueso

often /'ɒfn/ adv a menudo, con frecuencia. how ~? ¿con qué frecuencia? more ~ con más frecuencia

ogle /'əʊɡl/ vt comerse con los ojos

ogre /'əʊɡə(r)/ n ogro m

oh /əʊ/ int ¡ah!; (expressing dismay) ¡ay!

oil /ɔɪl/ n aceite m; (petroleum) petróleo m. ● vt lubricar. ~**field** n yacimiento m petrolífero. ~**painting** n pintura f al óleo; (picture) óleo m. ~ **rig** n plataforma f petrolífera. ~**y** adj (substance) oleaginoso; (food) aceitoso

ointment /'ɔɪntmənt/ n ungüento m

OK /əʊ'keɪ/ int ¡vale!, ¡de acuerdo!, ¡bueno! (LAm). ● adj ~, thanks bien, gracias. the job's ~ el trabajo no está mal

old /əʊld/ adj (-er. -est) viejo; (not modern) antiguo; (former) antiguo; an ~ friend un viejo amigo. how ~ is she? ¿cuántos años tiene? she is ten years ~ tiene diez años. his ~ er sister su hermana mayor. ~ **age** n vejez f. ~**-fashioned** /-'fæʃənd/ adj anticuado

olive /'ɒlɪv/ n aceituna f.

Olympic /ə'lɪmpɪk/ adj olímpico. the ~s npl, the ~ **Games** npl los Juegos Olímpicos

omelette /'ɒmlɪt/ n tortilla f francesa, omelette m (LAm)

omen /'əʊmen/ n agüero m

omi|ssion /ə'mɪʃn/ n omisión f. ~**t** /ə'mɪt/ vt (pt omitted) omitir

on /ɒn/ prep en, sobre; (about) sobre. ~ foot a pie. ~ Monday el lunes. ~ seeing al ver. I heard it ~ the radio lo oí por la radio. ● adv (light etc) encendido, prendido (LAm); (machine) en marcha; (tap) abierto. ~ and ~ sin cesar. and so ~ y así sucesivamente. have a hat ~ llevar (puesto) un sombrero. further ~ un poco más allá. what's ~ at the Odeon? ¿qué dan en el Odeon? go ~ continuar. later ~ más tarde

once /wʌns/ adv una vez; (formerly) antes. at ~ inmediatamente. ~ upon a time there was... érase una vez.... ~ and for all de una vez por todas. ● conj una vez que

one /wʌn/ adj uno, (before masculine singular noun) un. the ~ person I trusted la única persona en la que confiaba.● n uno m. ~ by ~ uno a uno.. ● pron uno (m), una (f). the blue ~ el/la azul. this ~ éste/ésta. ~ another el uno al otro

onerous /'ɒnərəs/ adj (task) pesado

one: ~**self** /-'self/ pron (reflexive) se; (after prep) sí (mismo); (emphatic use) uno mismo, una misma. by ~**self** solo. ~**-way** adj (street) de sentido único; (ticket) de ida, sencillo

onion /'ʌnɪən/ n cebolla f

online /ɒn'laɪn/ adj en línea

onlooker /ˈɒnlʊkə(r)/ n espectador m

only /ˈəʊnlɪ/ adj único. she's an ~ child es hija única. ● adv sólo, solamente. ~ **just** (barely) apenas. I've ~ **just** arrived acabo de llegar. ● conj pero, sólo que

onset /ˈɒnset/ n comienzo m; (of disease) aparición f

onshore /ˈɒnʃɔː(r)/ adj (breeze) que sopla desde el mar; (oil field) en tierra

onslaught /ˈɒnslɔːt/ n ataque m

onus /ˈəʊnəs/ n responsabilidad f

onward(s) /ˈɒnwəd(z)/ adj & adv hacia adelante

ooze /uːz/ vt/i rezumar

opaque /əʊˈpeɪk/ adj opaco

open /ˈəʊpən/ adj abierto; (question) discutible. ● n. in the ~ al aire libre. ● vt/i abrir. ~**ing** n abertura f; (beginning) principio m. ~**ly** adv abiertamente. ~**-minded** /-ˈmaɪndɪd/ adj de actitud abierta

> **Open University** La universidad a distancia británica, fundada en 1969. La enseñanza se imparte fundamentalmente por correspondencia, mediante materiales impresos, material enviado por internet y programas de televisión emitidos por la BBC. También hay cursos de verano a los que algunos de los alumnos deben asistir. No se exigen calificaciones académicas para su ingreso.

opera /ˈɒprə/ n ópera f

operate /ˈɒpəreɪt/ vt manejar, operar (Mex) (machine). ● vi funcionar; (company) operar. ~ **(on)** (Med) operar (a)

operatic /ɒpəˈrætɪk/ adj ope-

rístico

operation /ɒpəˈreɪʃn/ n operación f; (Mec) funcionamiento m; (using of machine) manejo m. he had an ~ lo operaron. in ~ en vigor. ~**al** adj operacional

operative /ˈɒpərətɪv/ adj. be ~ estar en vigor

operator n operador m

opinion /əˈpɪnɪən/ n opinión f. in my ~ en mi opinión, a mi parecer

opponent /əˈpəʊnənt/ n adversario m; (in sport) contrincante m & f

opportune /ˈɒpətjuːn/ adj oportuno. ~**ist** /ɒpəˈtjuːnɪst/ n oportunista m & f. ~**ity** /ɒpəˈtjuːnətɪ/ n oportunidad f

oppos|e /əˈpəʊz/ vt oponerse a. be ~**ed** to oponerse a, estar en contra de. ~**ing** adj opuesto. ~**ite** /ˈɒpəzɪt/ (contrary) opuesto; (facing) de enfrente. ● n. the ~**ite** lo contrario. quite the ~**ite** al contrario. ● adv enfrente. ● prep enfrente de. ~**ite number** n homólogo m. ~**ition** /ɒpəˈzɪʃn/ n oposición f; (resistance) resistencia f

oppress /əˈpres/ vt oprimir. ~**ion** /-ʃn/ n opresión f. ~**ive** adj (cruel) opresivo; (heat) sofocante

opt /ɒpt/ vi. ~ to optar por ~. □ ~ **out** vi decidir no tomar parte

optic|al /ˈɒptɪkl/ adj óptico. ~**ian** /ɒpˈtɪʃn/ n óptico m

optimis|m /ˈɒptɪmɪzəm/ n optimismo m. ~**t** n optimista m & f. ~**tic** /-ˈmɪstɪk/ adj optimista

option /ˈɒpʃn/ n opción f. ~**al** adj facultativo

or /ɔː(r)/ conj o; (before o- and ho-) u; (after negative) ni. ~ **else** si no, o bien

oral /ˈɔːrəl/ adj oral. ● n ⊞ examen m oral

orange /'ɒrɪndʒ/ n naranja f; (colour) naranja m. ● adj naranja. ~ade /-'eɪd/ n naranjada f

orbit /'ɔːbɪt/ n órbita f ● vt orbitar

orchard /'ɔːtʃəd/ n huerto m

orchestra /'ɔːkɪstrə/ n orquesta f; (Amer, in theatre) platea f. ~l /-'kestrəl/ adj orquestal. ~te /-eɪt/ vt orquestar

orchid /'ɔːkɪd/ n orquídea f

ordain /ɔː'deɪn/ vt (Relig) ordenar; (decree) decretar

ordeal /ɔː'diːl/ n dura prueba f

order /'ɔːdə(r)/ n orden m; (Com) pedido m; (command) orden f. in ~ that para que. in ~ to para. ● vt (command) ordenar, mandar; (Com) pedir; (in restaurant) pedir, ordenar (LAm); encargar (book); llamar, ordenar (LAm) (taxi). ~ly adj ordenado. ● n camillero m

ordinary /'ɔːdɪnrɪ/ adj corriente; (average) medio; (mediocre) ordinario

ore /ɔː(r)/ n mena f

organ /'ɔːgən/ n órgano m

organ|ic /ɔː'gænɪk/ adj orgánico. ~ism /'ɔːgənɪzəm/ n organismo m. ~ist /'ɔːgənɪst/ n organista m & f. ~ization /ɔːgənaɪ'zeɪʃn/ n organización f. ~ize /'ɔːgənaɪz/ vt organizar. ~izer n organizador m

orgasm /'ɔːgæzəm/ n orgasmo m

orgy /'ɔːdʒɪ/ n orgía f

Orient /'ɔːrɪənt/ n Oriente m. ~al /-'entl/ adj oriental

orientat|e /'ɔːrɪənteɪt/ vt orientar. ~ion /-'teɪʃn/ n orientación f

origin /'ɒrɪdʒɪn/ n origen m. ~al /ə'rɪdʒənl/ adj original. ~ally adv originariamente. ~ate /ə'rɪdʒɪneɪt/ vi. ~ate from provenir de

ornament /'ɔːnəmənt/ n adorno m. ~al /-'mentl/ adj de adorno

ornate /ɔː'neɪt/ adj ornamentado; (style) recargado

ornithology /ɔːnɪ'θɒlədʒɪ/ n ornitología f

orphan /'ɔːfn/ n huérfano m. ● vt. be ~ed quedar huérfano. ~age /-ɪdʒ/ n orfanato m

orthodox /'ɔːθədɒks/ adj ortodoxo

oscillate /'ɒsɪleɪt/ vi oscilar

ostentatious /ɒsten'teɪʃəs/ adj ostentoso

osteopath /'ɒstɪəpæθ/ n osteópata m & f

ostracize /'ɒstrəsaɪz/ vt hacerle vacío a

ostrich /'ɒstrɪtʃ/ n avestruz m

other /'ʌðə(r)/ adj & pron otro. ~ than aparte de. the ~ one el otro. ~wise adv de lo contrario, si no

otter /'ɒtə(r)/ n nutria f

ouch /aʊtʃ/ int ¡ay!

ought /ɔːt/ modal verb. I ~ to see it debería verlo. he ~ to have done it debería haberlo hecho

ounce /aʊns/ n onza f (= 28.35 gr.)

our /'aʊə(r)/ adj (sing) nuestra, nuestra, (pl) nuestros, nuestras. ~s /'aʊəz/ poss pron (sing) nuestro, nuestra; (pl) nuestros, nuestras. ~s is red el nuestro es rojo. a friend of ~s un amigo nuestro. ~selves /-'selvz/ pron (reflexive) nos; (used for emphasis and after prepositions) nosotros mismos, nosotras mismas. we behaved ~selves nos portamos bien. we did it ~selves lo hicimos nosotros mismos/nosotras mismas

oust /aʊst/ vt desbancar; derrocar (government)

out /aʊt/ adv (outside) fuera, afuera

outer | oven

(*LAm*). (*not lighted, not on*) apagado; (*in blossom*) fuera; (*in error*) equivocado. he's ~ (*not at home*) no está; be ~ to estar resuelto a. ~ **of** *prep* (*from inside*) de; (*outside*) fuera, afuera (*LAm*). five ~ of six cinco de cada seis. made ~ of hecho de. we're ~ of bread nos hemos quedado sin pan. ~**break** *n* (*of war*) estallido *m*; (*of disease*) brote *m*. ~**burst** *n* arrebato *m*. ~**cast** *n* paria *m & f.* ~**come** *n* resultado *m.* ~**cry** *n* protesta *f.* ~**dated** /-'dertid/ *adj* anticuado. ~**do** /-'du:/ *vt* (*pt* -did, *pp* -done) superar. ~**door** *adj* (*clothes*) de calle; (*pool*) descubierto. ~**doors** /-'dɔːz/ *adv* al aire libre

outer /'aʊtə(r)/ *adj* exterior

out: ~**fit** *n* equipo *m*; (*clothes*) conjunto *m.* ~**going** *adj* (*minister* etc) saliente; (*sociable*) abierto. ~**goings** *npl* gastos *mpl.* ~**grow** /-'ɡrəʊ/ *vt* (*pt* -grew, *pp* -grown) crecer más que (*person*). he's ~**grown** his new shoes se han quedado pequeños los zapatos nuevos. ~**ing** *n* excursión *f.*

outlandish /aʊt'lændɪʃ/ *adj* extravagante

out: ~**law** *n* forajido *m.* • *vt* proscribir. ~**lay** *n* gastos *mpl.* ~**let** *n* salida *f*; (*Com*) punto *m* de venta; (*Amer, Elec*) toma *f* de corriente. ~**line** *n* contorno *m*; (*summary*) resumen *m*; (*plan of project*) esquema *m.* • *vt* trazar; (*summarize*) esbozar. ~**live** /-'lɪv/ *vt* sobrevivir a. ~**look** *n* perspectivas *fpl*; (*attitude*) punto *m* de vista. ~**lying** *adj* alejado. ~**number** /-'nʌmbə(r)/ *vt* superar en número. ~**of-date** *adj* (*ideas*) desfasado; (*clothes*) pasado de moda. ~**patient** *n* paciente *m* externo.

~**post** *n* avanzada *f.* ~**put** *n* producción *f*; (*of machine, worker*) rendimiento *m.* ~**right** *adv* completamente; (*frankly*) abiertamente; (*kill*) en el acto. • *adj* completo; (*refusal*) rotundo. ~**set** *n* principio *m.* ~**side** *adj* & *n* exterior (*m*). at the ~ como máximo. • /-'saɪd/ *adv* fuera, afuera (*LAm*). • *prep* fuera de. ~**size** *adj* de talla gigante. ~**skirts** *npl* afueras *fpl.* ~**spoken** /-'spəʊkn/ *adj* directo, franco. ~**standing** /-'stændɪŋ/ *adj* excepcional; (*debt*) pendiente. ~**stretched** /aʊt'stretʃt/ *adj* extendido. ~**strip** /-'strɪp/ *vt* (*pt* -stripped) (*run faster than*) tomarle la delantera a; (*exceed*) sobrepasar. ~**ward** /-wəd/ *adj* (*appearance*) exterior; (*sign*) externo; (*journey*) de ida. ~**wardly** *adv* por fuera, exteriormente. ~(**s**) *adv* hacia afuera. ~**weigh** /-'weɪ/ *vt* ser mayor que. ~**wit** /-'wɪt/ *vt* (*pt* -witted) burlar

oval /'əʊvl/ *adj* ovalado, oval. • *n* óvalo *m*

> **Oval Office** El Despacho *i*
> Oval es el despacho oficial
> del Presidente de los Estados Uni-
> dos, ubicado en el ala oeste de la
> Casa Blanca. La forma oval fue
> determinada por George Wash-
> ington, lo que le permitiría tener
> contacto visual con todos durante
> las reuniones. Originariamente,
> quería que todas las habitaciones
> de la Casa Blanca fueran ovales,
> pero pronto comprendió que este
> diseño era poco práctico.

ovary /'əʊvəri/ *n* ovario *m*

ovation /əʊ'veɪʃn/ *n* ovación *f*

oven /'ʌvn/ *n* horno *m*

over /'əʊvə(r)/ prep por encima de; (across) al otro lado de; (during) durante; (more than) más de. ~ **and above** por encima de. • adv por encima; (ended) terminado; (more) más; (in excess) de sobra. ~ **again** otra vez. ~ **and** ~ una y otra vez. ~ **here** por aquí. ~ **there** por allí. **all** ~ (finished) acabado; (everywhere) por todas partes

over... /'əʊvə(r)/ pref excesivamente, demasiado

over: ~**all** /-ɔːl/ adj global; (length, cost) total. • adv en conjunto. /'əʊvərɔːl/ n, ~**alls** npl mono m, overol m (LAm); (Amer, dungarees) peto m, overol m.
~**awe** /-ɔː/ vt intimidar. ~**balance** /-'bæləns/ vi perder el equilibrio. ~**bearing** /-'beərɪŋ/ adj dominante. ~**board** adv (throw) por la borda. ~**cast** /-kɑːst/ adj (day) nublado; (sky) cubierto. ~**charge** /-'tʃɑːdʒ/ vt cobrarle de más a. ~**coat** n abrigo m.
~**come** /-'kʌm/ vt (pt -came, pp -come) superar, vencer. ~**crowded** /-'kraʊdɪd/ adj abarrotado (de gente). ~**do** /-'duː/ vt (pt -did, pp -done) exagerar; (Culin) recocer. ~**dose** n sobredosis f.
~**draft** n descubierto m.
~**draw** /-'drɔː/ vt (pt -drew, pp -drawn) girar en descubierto. ~**drawn** tener un descubierto.
~**due** /-'djuː/ adj. the book is a month ~**due** el plazo de devolución del libro venció hace un mes.
~**estimate** /-'estɪmeɪt/ vt sobreestimar. ~**flow** /-'fləʊ/ vi desbordarse. • n /-fləʊ/ (excess) exceso m; (outlet) rebosadero m. ~**flow car park** n estacionamiento m extra (LAm), aparcamiento m extra (Esp). ~**grown** /-'grəʊn/ adj demasiado grande; (garden) lleno de maleza. ~**haul** /-'hɔːl/ vt revisar.
• /-hɔːl/ n revisión f. ~**head** /-'hed/ adv por encima. • /-hed/ adj de arriba. ~**heads** /-hedz/ npl.
~**head** n (Amer) gastos mpl indirectos. ~**hear** /-'hɪə(r)/ vt (pt -heard) oír por casualidad.
~**joyed** /-'dʒɔɪd/ adj encantado.
~**land** a/adv por tierra. ~**lap** /-'læp/ vi (pt -lapped) traslaparse.
~**leaf** /-'liːf/ adv al dorso. ~**load** /-'ləʊd/ vt sobrecargar. ~**look** /-'lʊk/ vt (room) dar a; (not notice) pasar por alto; (disregard) disculpar. ~**night** /-'naɪt/ adv durante la noche. stay ~**night** quedarse a pasar la noche. • adj (journey) de noche; (stay) de una noche.
~**pass** n paso m elevado, paso m a desnivel (Mex). ~**pay** /-'peɪ/ vt (pt -paid) pagar demasiado.
~**power** /-'paʊə(r)/ vt dominar (opponent); (emotion) abrumar.
~**powering** /-'paʊərɪŋ/ adj (smell) muy fuerte; (desire) irrestible.
~**priced** /-'praɪst/ adj demasiado caro. ~**rated** /-'reɪtɪd/ adj sobrevalorado. ~**react** /-rɪ'ækt/ vi reaccionar en forma exagerada.
~**ride** /-'raɪd/ vt (pt -rode, pp -ridden) invalidar. ~**riding** /-'raɪdɪŋ/ adj dominante. ~**rule** /-'ruːl/ vt anular; rechazar (objection). ~**run** /-'rʌn/ vt (pt -ran, pp -run, pres p -running) invadir; exceder (limit). ~**seas** /-'siːz/ adj (trade) exterior; (investments) en el exterior; (visitor) extranjero.
• adv al extranjero. ~**see** /-'siː/ vt (pt -saw, pp -seen) supervisar.
~**seer** /-sɪə(r)/ n capataz m & f, supervisor m. ~**shadow** /-'ʃædəʊ/ vt eclipsar. ~**shoot** /-'ʃuːt/ vt (pt -shot) excederse. ~**sight** n descuido m. ~**sleep** /-'sliːp/ vi (pt

-slept) quedarse dormido. **~step** /'step/ *vt* (*pt* **-stepped**) sobrepasar. **~step the mark** pasarse de la raya

overt /əʊvɜːt/ *adj* manifiesto

over:: ~take /-'teɪk/ *vt*/*i* (*pt* **-took**, *pp* **-taken**) sobrepasar; (*Auto*) adelantar, rebasar (*Mex*). **~throw** /-'θrəʊ/ *vt* (*pt* **-threw**, *pp* **-thrown**) derrocar. **~time** *n* horas *fpl* extra

overture /'əʊvətjʊə(r)/ *n* obertura *f*

over:: ~turn /-'tɜːn/ *vt* darle la vuelta a. ● *vi* volcar. **~weight** /-'weɪt/ *adj* gordo. be **~weight** pesar demasiado. **~whelm** /-'welm/ *vt* aplastar; (*with emotion*) abrumar. **~whelming** *adj* aplastante; (*fig*) abrumador. **~work** /-'wɜːk/ *vt* hacer trabajar demasiado. ● *vi* trabajar demasiado. ● *n* agotamiento *m*

owe /əʊ/ *vt* deber. **~ing** to debido a

owl /aʊl/ *n* búho *m*

own /əʊn/ *adj* propio. my **~** house mi propia casa. ● *pron*. it's my **~** es mío (propio)/mía (propia). on one's **~** solo. get one's **~** back 🔲 desquitarse. ● *vt* tener. □ **~ up** *vi*. 🔲 confesarse culpable. **~er** *n* propietario, dueño *m*. **~ership** *n* propiedad *f*

oxygen /'ɒksɪdʒən/ *n* oxígeno *m*

grandes esfuerzos para atraer a estudiantes de todos los medios sociales.

oyster /'ɔɪstə(r)/ *n* ostra *f*

P

p *abbr* (= **pence, penny**) penique(s) (*m*(*pl*))

p. (*pl* **pp.**) (= **page**) pág., p.

pace /peɪs/ *n* paso *m*. keep **~** with s.o. seguirle el ritmo a uno. ● *vi*. **~ up and down** andar de un lado para otro. **~maker** *n* (*runner*) liebre *f*; (*Med*) marcapasos *m*

Pacific /pə'sɪfɪk/ *n*. the **~** (Ocean) el (Océano) Pacífico *m*

pacif|ist /'pæsɪfɪst/ *n* pacifista *m* & *f*. **~y** /'pæsɪfaɪ/ *vt* apaciguar

pack /pæk/ *n* fardo *m*; (*of cigarettes*) paquete *m*, cajetilla *f*; (*of cards*) baraja *f*; (*of hounds*) jauría *f*; (*of wolves*) manada *f*. a **~ of lies** una sarta de mentiras. ● *vt* empaquetar; hacer (*suitcase*); (*press down*) apisonar. ● *vi* hacer la maleta, empacar (*LAm*). **~age** /-ɪdʒ/ *n* paquete *m*. **~age holiday** *n* vacaciones *fpl* organizadas. **~ed** /pækt/ *adj* lleno (de gente). **~et** /'pækɪt/ *n* paquete *m*

pact /pækt/ *n* pacto *m*, acuerdo *m*

pad /pæd/ *n* (*for writing*) bloc *m*. **shoulder ~s** hombreras *fpl*. ● *vt* (*pt* **padded**) rellenar

paddle /'pædl/ *n* pala *f*. ● *vi* mojarse los pies; (*in canoe*) remar (con pala)

paddock /'pædək/ *n* prado *m*

o
p

padlock /'pædlɒk/ n candado m.
● vt cerrar con candado

paed|iatrician /ˌpiːdɪə'trɪʃn/ n
pediatra m & f. **~ophile** /'piːdəfaɪl/
n pedófilo m

pagan /'peɪɡən/ adj & n pagano (m)

page /peɪdʒ/ n página f; (attendant) paje m; (in hotel) botones m.
● vt llamar por megafonía/por
buscapersonas, vocear (LAm)

paid /peɪd/ see PAY. ● adj. put **~**
to 🅣 acabar con

pail /peɪl/ n balde m, cubo m

pain /peɪn/ n dolor m. I have a **~**
in my back me duele la espalda.
m, be in **~** tener dolores. be a **~**
in the neck 🅣 ser un pesado;
(thing) ser una lata. ● vt doler.
~ful adj doloroso. it's very **~ful**
duele mucho. **~killer** n analgésico m. **~less** adj indoloro. **~stak-
ing** /'peɪnzteɪkɪŋ/ adj concienzudo

paint /peɪnt/ n pintura f. ● vt/i (pintar. **~er** n pintor m. **~ing** n (medium) pintura f; (picture) cuadro m

pair /peə(r)/ n par m; (of people)
pareja f. a **~** of trousers unos
pantalones. □ **~off**, **~ up** vi formar parejas

pajamas /pə'dʒɑːməz/ npl (Amer)
pijama m

Pakistan /ˌpɑːkɪ'stɑːn/ n Pakistán
m. **~i** adj & n paquistaní (m & f)

pal /pæl/ n 🅣 amigo m

palace /'pælɪs/ n palacio m

palat|able /'pælətəbl/ adj agrada-
ble. **~e** /'pælət/ n paladar m

pale /peɪl/ adj (-er, -est) pálido. go
~, turn **~** palidecer. **~ness** n pa-
lidez f

Palestin|e /'pælɪstaɪn/ n Palestina
f. **~ian** /-'stɪnɪən/ adj & n palestino
(m)

palette /'pælɪt/ n paleta f

palm /pɑːm/ n palma f. □ **~ off** vt
encajar (on a). **P~ Sunday** n Domingo m de Ramos

palpable /'pælpəbl/ adj palpable

palpitat|e /'pælpɪteɪt/ vi palpitar.
~ion /-'teɪʃn/ n palpitación f

pamper /'pæmpə(r)/ vt mimar

pamphlet /'pæmflɪt/ n folleto m

pan /pæn/ n cacerola f; (for frying)
sartén f

panacea /ˌpænə'sɪə/ n panacea f

Panama /'pænəmɑː/ n Panamá m.
~nian /-'meɪnɪən/ adj & n panameño (m)

pancake /'pænkeɪk/ n crep(e) m,
panqueque m (LAm)

panda /'pændə/ n panda m

pandemonium /ˌpændɪ
'məʊnɪəm/ n pandemonio m

pander /'pændə(r)/ vi. **~ to s.o.** to
consentirle los caprichos a uno

pane /peɪn/ n vidrio m, cristal m

panel /'pænl/ n panel m; (group of
people) jurado m. **~ling** n paneles
mpl

pang /pæŋ/ n punzada f

panic /'pænɪk/ n pánico m. ● vi (pt
panicked) dejarse llevar por el pánico. **~-stricken** adj aterrorizado

panorama /ˌpænə'rɑːmə/ n panorama m. **~ic** /-'ræmɪk/ adj pano-
rámico

pansy /'pænzɪ/ n (flower) pensamiento m

pant /pænt/ vi jadear

panther /'pænθə(r)/ n pantera f

panties /'pæntɪz/ npl bragas fpl,
calzones mpl (LAm), pantaletas fpl
(Mex)

pantihose /'pæntɪhəʊz/ npl see
PANTYHOSE

pantomime /'pæntəmaɪm/ n
pantomima f

pantry /'pæntrɪ/ n despensa f

pants /pænts/ npl (man's) calzoncillos mpl; (woman's) bragas fpl, calzones mpl (LAm), pantaletas fpl (Mex); (Amer, trousers) pantalones mpl

pantyhose /'pæntɪhəʊz/ npl (Amer) panty m, medias fpl, pantimedias fpl (Mex)

paper /'peɪpə(r)/ n papel m; (newspaper) diario m, periódico m; (exam) examen m; (document) documento m. ●vt empapelar, tapizar (Mex). ~back n libro m en rústica. ~ clip n sujetapapeles m, clip m. ~weight n pisapapeles m. ~work n papeleo m, trabajo m administrativo

parable /'pærəbl/ n parábola f

parachut|e /'pærəʃu:t/ n paracaídas m. ●vi saltar en paracaídas. ~ist n paracaidista m & f

parade /pə'reɪd/ n desfile m; (Mil) formación f. ●vi desfilar. ●vt hacer alarde de

paradise /'pærədaɪs/ n paraíso m

paraffin /'pærəfɪn/ n queroseno m

paragraph /'pærəgrɑːf/ n párrafo m

Paraguay /'pærəgwaɪ/ n Paraguay m. ~an adj & n paraguayo (m)

parallel /'pærəlel/ adj paralelo. ●n paralelo m; (line) paralela f

paraly|se /'pærəlaɪz/ vt paralizar. ~sis /pə'ræləsɪs/ n (pl -ses /-si:z/) parálisis f

parameter /pə'ræmɪtə(r)/ n parámetro m

paranoia /pærə'nɔɪə/ n paranoia f

parapet /'pærəpɪt/ n parapeto m

paraphernalia /pærəfə'neɪlɪə/ n trastos mpl

parasite /'pærəsaɪt/ n parásito m

paratrooper /'pærətru:pə(r)/ n paracaidista m (del ejército)

parcel /'pɑːsl/ n paquete m

parch /pɑːtʃ/ vt resecar. be ~ed 🔢 estar muerto de sed

parchment /'pɑːtʃmənt/ n pergamino m

pardon /'pɑːdn/ n perdón m; (Jurid) indulto m. I beg your ~. (I beg your) ~? ¿cómo?, ¿mande? (Mex). ●vt perdonar; (Jurid) indultar. ~ me? (Amer) ¿cómo?

parent /'peərənt/ n (father) padre m; (mother) madre f. my ~s mis padres. ~al /pə'rentl/ adj de los padres

parenthesis /pə'renθəsɪs/ n (pl -theses /-si:z/) paréntesis m

parenthood /'peərənthʊd/ n el ser padre/madre

Paris /'pærɪs/ n París m

parish /'pærɪʃ/ n parroquia f; (municipal) distrito m. ~ioner /pə'rɪʃənə(r)/ n feligrés m

park /pɑːk/ n parque m. ~-and-ride n estacionamiento m disuasorio (LAm), aparcamiento m disuasorio (Esp). ●vt/i aparcar, estacionar (LAm)

parking /'pɑːkɪŋ/ n: ~ lot n (Amer) aparcamiento m, estacionamiento m (LAm). ~ meter n parquímetro m

parkway /'pɑːkweɪ/ n (Amer) carretera f ajardinada

parliament /'pɑːləmənt/ n parlamento m. ~ary /-'mentrɪ/ adj parlamentario

---

Parliament El Parlamento *i* británico, el más alto organismo legislativo. Está formado por la Cámara de los Lores y la Cámara de los Comunes. La primera, consta de 703 miembros, en la mayoría nombrados, con un número de cargos hereditarios, lo que es objeto de reforma en la actualidad. La Cámara de los Comunes consta de 659 miembros elegidos por el pueblo. Ver ▷ DÁIL ÉIREANN, ▷ SCOTTISH PARLIAMENT, ▷ WELSH ASSEMBLY.

parlour /'pɑ:lə(r)/ n salón m

parochial /pə'rəʊkɪəl/ adj (fig) provinciano

parody /'pærədɪ/ n parodia f. ● vt parodiar

parole /pə'rəʊl/ n libertad f condicional

parrot /'pærət/ n loro m, papagayo m

parsley /'pɑ:slɪ/ n perejil m

parsnip /'pɑ:snɪp/ n pastinaca f

part /pɑ:t/ n parte f; (of machine) pieza f; (of serial) episodio m; (in play) papel m; (Amer, in hair) raya f **take** ~ in tomar parte en, participar en. **for the most** ~ en su mayor parte. ● adv en parte. ● vt separar. ● vi separarse. □ ~ **with** vt desprenderse de

partial /'pɑ:ʃl/ adj parcial. **be** ~ **to** tener debilidad por. ~**ly** adv parcialmente

participa|nt /pɑ:'tɪsɪpənt/ n participante m & f. ~**te** /-peɪt/ vi participar. ~**tion** /-'peɪʃn/ n participación f

particle /'pɑ:tɪkl/ n partícula f

particular /pə'tɪkjʊlə(r)/ adj particular; (precise) meticuloso; (fastidious) quisquilloso. **in** ~ en particular. ● n detalle m. ~**ly** adv particularmente; (specifically) específicamente

parting /'pɑ:tɪŋ/ n despedida f; (in hair) raya f. ● adj de despedida

partition /pɑ:'tɪʃn/ n partición f; (wall) tabique m. ● vt dividir

partly /'pɑ:tlɪ/ adv en parte

partner /'pɑ:tnə(r)/ n socio m; (Sport) pareja f. ~**ship** n asociación f; (Com) sociedad f

partridge /'pɑ:trɪdʒ/ n perdiz f

part-time /pɑ:t'taɪm/ adj & adv a tiempo parcial, de medio tiempo (LAm)

party /'pɑ:tɪ/ n reunión f, fiesta f; (group) grupo m; (Pol) partido m; (Jurid) parte f

pass /pɑ:s/ vt (hand, convey) pasar; (go past) pasar por delante de; (overtake) adelantar, rebasar (Mex); (approve) aprobar (exam, bill, law); pronunciar (judgement). ● vi pasar; (pain) pasarse; (Sport) pasar la pelota. □ ~ **away** vi fallecer. □ ~ **down** vt transmitir. □ ~ **out** vi desmayarse. □ ~ **round** vt distribuir. □ ~ **up** vt 🔢 dejar pasar. ● n (permit) pase m; (ticket) abono m; (in mountains) puerto m, desfiladero m; (Sport) pase m; (in exam) aprobado m. **make a** ~ **at** 🔢 intentar besar. ~**able** adj pasable; (road) transitable

passage /'pæsɪdʒ/ n (voyage) travesía f; (corridor) pasillo m; (alleyway) pasaje m; (in book) pasaje m

passenger /'pæsɪndʒə(r)/ n pasajero m

passer-by /pɑ:sə'baɪ/ n (pl passers-by) transeúnte m & f

passion /'pæʃn/ n pasión f. ~**ate** /-ət/ adj apasionado. ~**ately** adv apasionadamente

passive /'pæsɪv/ adj pasivo

Passover /'pɑ:səʊvə(r)/ n Pascua f de los hebreos

pass: ~**port** n pasaporte m. ~**word** n contraseña f

past /pɑːst/ adj anterior; (life) pasado; (week, year) último. **in times** ~ en tiempos pasados. • n pasado m. **in the** ~ (formerly) antes, antiguamente. • prep por delante de; (beyond) más allá de. **it's twenty** ~ **four** son las cuatro y veinte. • adv. **drive** ~ pasar en coche. **go** ~ pasar

paste /peɪst/ n pasta f; (glue) engrudo m; (wallpaper ~) pegamento m; (jewellery) estrás m

pastel /'pæstl/ adj & n pastel (m)

pasteurize /'pɑːstʃəraɪz/ vt pasteurizar

pastime /'pɑːstaɪm/ n pasatiempo m

pastry /'peɪstrɪ/ n masa f; (cake) pastelito m

pasture /'pɑːstʃə(r)/ n pasto(s) mpl

pasty /'pæstɪ/ n empanadilla f, empanada f (LAm)

pat /pæt/ vt (pt patted) darle palmaditas. • n palmadita f; (of butter) porción f

patch /pætʃ/ n (on clothes) remiendo m, parche m; (over eye) parche m. **a bad** ~ una mala racha. • vt remendar. □ ~ **up** vt hacerle un arreglo a

patent /'peɪtnt/ adj patente. • n patente f. • vt patentar. ~ **leather** n charol m. ~**ly** adv. **it's obvious that...** está clarísimo que...

patern|al /pə'tɜːnl/ adj paterno. ~**ity** /-ətɪ/ n paternidad f

path /pɑːθ/ n (pl -s /pɑːðz/) sendero m; (Sport) pista f; (of rocket) trayectoria f; (fig) camino m

pathetic /pə'θetɪk/ adj (pitiful) patético; (excuse) pobre. **don't be so**

~ **no seas tan pusilánime**

patien|ce /'peɪʃns/ n paciencia f. ~**t** adj & n paciente (m & f). **be** ~**t with s.o.** tener paciencia con uno. ~**tly** adv pacientemente

patio /'pætɪəʊ/ n (pl -os) patio m

patriot /'pætrɪət/ n patriota m & f. ~**ic** /-'ɒtɪk/ adj patriótico. ~**ism** n patriotismo m

patrol /pə'trəʊl/ n patrulla f. • vt/i patrullar

patron /'peɪtrən/ n (of the arts) mecenas m & f; (of charity) patrocinador m; (customer) cliente m & f. ~**age** /'pætrənɪdʒ/ n (sponsorship) patrocinio m; (of the arts) mecenazgo m. ~**ize** /'pætrənaɪz/ vt ser cliente de; (fig) tratar con condescendencia. ~**izing** adj condescendiente

pattern /'pætn/ n diseño m; (sample) muestra f; (in dressmaking) patrón m

paunch /pɔːntʃ/ n panza f

pause /pɔːz/ n pausa f. • vi hacer una pausa

pave /peɪv/ vt pavimentar; (with flagstones) enlosar. ~**ment** n pavimento m; (at side of road) acera f, banqueta f (Mex)

paving stone /'peɪvɪŋstəʊn/ n losa f

paw /pɔː/ n pata f

pawn /pɔːn/ n (Chess) peón m; (fig) títere m. • vt empeñar. ~**broker** n prestamista m & f

pay /peɪ/ vt (pt paid) pagar; prestar (attention); hacer (compliment, visit). ~ **cash** pagar al contado. • vi pagar; (be profitable) rendir. • n paga f. **in the** ~ **of** al servicio de. □ ~ **back** vt devolver; pagar (loan). □ ~ **in** vt ingresar, depositar (LAm). □ ~ **off** vt cancelar, saldar (debt). vi valer la pena. □ ~ **up** vi pagar. **~able** adj pagadero. **~ment** n pago m. **~roll** n nómina f

pea /piː/ n guisante m, arveja f (LAm), chícharo m (Mex)

peace /piːs/ n paz f. ~ **of mind** tranquilidad f. **~ful** adj tranquilo. **~maker** n conciliador m

peach /piːtʃ/ n melocotón m, durazno m (LAm)

peacock /'piːkɒk/ n pavo m real

peak /piːk/ n cumbre f; (of career) apogeo m; (maximum) máximo m. ~ **hours** npl horas fpl de mayor demanda (o consumo etc)

peal /piːl/ n repique m. ~s **of laughter** risotadas fpl

peanut /'piːnʌt/ n cacahuete m, maní m (LAm), cacahuate m (Mex)

pear /peə(r)/ n pera f. ~ (**tree**) peral m

pearl /pɜːl/ n perla f

peasant /'peznt/ n campesino m

peat /piːt/ n turba f

pebble /'pebl/ n guijarro m

peck /pek/ vt picotear. ● n picotazo m; (kiss) besito m

peculiar /pɪ'kjuːlɪə(r)/ adj raro; (special) especial. **~ity** /-'ærətɪ/ n rareza f; (feature) particularidad f

pedal /'pedl/ n pedal m. ● vi pedalear

pedantic /pɪ'dæntɪk/ adj pedante

peddle /'pedl/ vt vender por las calles

pedestal /'pedɪstl/ n pedestal m

pedestrian /pɪ'destrɪən/ n peatón m. ~ **crossing** paso m de peatones. ● adj pedestre; (dull) prosaico

pedigree /'pedɪgriː/ linaje m; (of animal) pedigrí m. ● adj (animal) de raza

peek /piːk/ vi mirar a hurtadillas

peel /piːl/ n piel f, cáscara f. ● vt pelar (fruit, vegetables). ● vi pelarse

peep /piːp/ vi. ~ **at** echarle un vistazo a. ● n (look) vistazo m; (bird sound) pío m

peer /pɪə(r)/ vi mirar. ~ **at** escudriñar. ● n (equal) par m & f; (contemporary) coetáneo m; (lord) par m. **~age** /-ɪdʒ/ n nobleza f

peg /peg/ n (in ground) estaca f; (on violin) clavija f; (for washing) pinza f; (hook) gancho m; (for tent) estaquilla f. **off the ~** de confección. ● vt (pt **pegged**) sujetar (con estacas, etc); fijar (precios)

pejorative /pɪ'dʒɒrətɪv/ adj peyorativo, despectivo

pelican /'pelɪkən/ n pelícano m

pellet /'pelɪt/ n bolita f; (for gun) perdigón m

pelt /pelt/ n pellejo m. ● vt. ~ **s.o. with** sth lanzarle algo a uno. ● vi. ~ **with rain**, ~ **down** llover a cántaros

pelvis /'pelvɪs/ n pelvis f

pen /pen/ (for writing) pluma f; (ballpoint) bolígrafo m; (sheep ~) redil m; (cattle ~) corral m

penal /'piːnl/ adj penal. **~ize** vt sancionar. **~ty** /'penltɪ/ n pena f; (fine) multa f; (in soccer) penalty m; (in US football) castigo m. **~ty kick** n (in soccer) penalty m

penance /'penəns/ n penitencia f

pence /pens/ see PENNY

pencil /'pensl/ n lápiz m. ● vt (pt **pencilled**) escribir con lápiz. **~sharpener** n sacapuntas m

pendulum /'pendjʊləm/ n péndulo m

penetrat|e /'penɪtreɪt/ vt/i penetrar. **~ing** adj penetrante. **~ion**

/ɪ'treɪʃn/ n penetración f

penguin /'peŋgwɪn/ n pingüino m

penicillin /penɪ'sɪlɪn/ n penicilina f

peninsula /pə'nɪnsjʊlə/ n península f

penis /'piːnɪs/ n pene m

pen: ~**knife** /'pennaɪf/ n (pl pen-knives) navaja f. ~**name** n seudónimo m

penn|iless /'penɪlɪs/ adj sin un céntimo. ~**y** /'peni/ n (pl pennies or pence) penique m

pension /'penʃn/ n pensión f; (for retirement) pensión f de jubilación. ~**er** n jubilado m

pensive /'pensɪv/ adj pensativo

Pentecost /'pentɪkɒst/ n Pentecostés m

penthouse /'penthaʊs/ n penthouse m

pent-up /pent'ʌp/ adj reprimido; (confined) encerrado

penultimate /pen'ʌltɪmət/ adj penúltimo

people /'piːpl/ npl gente f; (citizens) pueblo m. ~ **say** (that) se dice que, dicen que. English ~ los ingleses. young ~ los jóvenes. the ~ (nation) el pueblo. ● vt poblar

pepper /'pepə(r)/ n pimienta f; (vegetable) pimiento m. ● vt (intersperse) salpicar (with de). ~**box** n (Amer) pimentero m. ~**corn** n grano m de pimienta. ~**mint** n menta f; (sweet) caramelo m de menta. ~**pot** n pimentero m

per /pɜː(r)/ prep por. ~ **annum** al año. ~ **cent** see **PERCENT**. ~ **head** por cabeza, por persona. ten miles ~ **hour** diez millas por hora

perceive /pə'siːv/ vt percibir; (notice) darse cuenta de

percent, per cent /pə'sent/ n

(no pl) porcentaje m. ● adv por ciento. ~**age** /-ɪdʒ/ n porcentaje m

percepti|ble /pə'septəbl/ adj perceptible. ~**on** /-ʃn/ n percepción f. ~**ve** /-tɪv/ adj perspicaz

perch /pɜːtʃ/ n (of bird) percha f; (fish) perca f. ● vi (bird) posarse. ~ **on** (person) sentarse en el borde de

percolat|e /'pɜːkəleɪt/ vi filtrarse. ~**or** n cafetera f eléctrica

percussion /pə'kʌʃn/ n percusión f

perfect /'pɜːfɪkt/ adj perfecto; (place, day) ideal. ● vt /pə'fekt/ perfeccionar. ~**ion** /pə'fekʃn/ n perfección f. to ~**ion** a la perfección. ~**ly** /'pɜːfɪktlɪ/ adv perfectamente

perform /pə'fɔːm/ vt desempeñar (function, role); ejecutar (task); realizar (experiment); representar (play); (Mus) interpretar. ~ **an operation** (Med) operar. ● vi (actor) actuar; (musician) tocar; (produce results) (vehicle) responder; (company) rendir. ~**ance** /-əns/ n ejecución f; (of play) representación f; (of actor, musician) interpretación f; (of team) actuación f; (of car) rendimiento m. ~**er** n (actor) actor m; (entertainer) artista m & f

perfume /'pɜːfjuːm/ n perfume m

perhaps /pə'hæps/ adv quizá(s), tal vez, a lo mejor

peril /'perəl/ n peligro m. ~**ous** adj arriesgado, peligroso

perimeter /pə'rɪmɪtə(r)/ n perímetro m

period /'pɪərɪəd/ n período m; (in history) época f; (lesson) clase f; (Amer, Gram) punto m; (menstruation) período m, regla f. ● adj de (la) época. ~**ic** /-'ɒdɪk/ adj periódico. ~**ical** /pɪərɪ'ɒdɪkl/ n revista f.

P

peripheral /pə'rɪfərəl/ adj secundario; (Comp) periférico. **~y** /pə'rɪfərɪ/ n periferia f

peripher|al /pə'rɪfərəl/ adj secundario; (Comp) periférico. **~y** /pə'rɪfərɪ/ n periferia f

perish /'perɪʃ/ vi perecer; (rot) deteriorarse. **~able** adj perecedero. **~ing** adj 🄘 glacial

perjur|e /'pɜːdʒə(r)/ vr. **~ o.s.** perjurarse. **~y** n perjurio m

perk /pɜːk/ n gaje m. □ **~ up** vt reanimar. vi reanimarse

perm /pɜːm/ n permanente f. ● vt have one's hair **~ed** hacerse la permanente

permanen|ce /'pɜːmənəns/ n permanencia f. **~t** adj permanente. **~tly** adv permanentemente

permissible /pə'mɪsəbl/ adj permisible

permission /pə'mɪʃn/ n permiso m

permit /pə'mɪt/ vt (pt permitted) permitir. ● /'pɜːmɪt/ n permiso m

peroxide /pə'rɒksaɪd/ n peróxido m

perpendicular /pɜːpən'dɪkjʊlə(r)/ adj & n perpendicular (f)

perpetrat|e /'pɜːpɪtreɪt/ vt cometer. **~or** n autor m

perpetua|l /pə'petʃʊəl/ adj perpetuo. **~te** /pə'petʃʊeɪt/ vt perpetuar

perplex /pə'pleks/ vt dejar perplejo. **~ed** adj perplejo

persecut|e /'pɜːsɪkjuːt/ vt perseguir. **~ion** /-'kjuːʃn/ n persecución f

persever|ance /pɜːsɪ'vɪərəns/ n perseverancia f. **~e** /pɜːsɪ'vɪə(r)/ vi perseverar, persistir

Persian /'pɜːʃn/ adj persa. **the ~ Gulf** n el golfo Pérsico

persist /pə'sɪst/ vi persistir.

~ence /-əns/ n persistencia f. **~ent** adj persistente; (continual) continuo

person /'pɜːsn/ n persona f. **in ~** en persona. **~al** adj personal; (call) particular; (property) privado. **~al assistant** n secretario m personal. **~ality** /-'næləti/ n personalidad f. **~ally** adv personalmente. **~nel** /pɜːsə'nel/ n personal m. **P~** (department) sección f de personal

perspective /pə'spektɪv/ n perspectiva f

perspir|ation /pɜːspə'reɪʃn/ n transpiración f. **~e** /pəs'paɪə(r)/ vi transpirar

persua|de /pə'sweɪd/ vt convencer, persuadir. **~e s.o. to do sth** convencer a uno para que haga algo. **~sion** n /-ʃn/ persuasión f. **~sive** /-sɪv/ adj persuasivo

pertinent /'pɜːtɪnənt/ adj pertinente. **~ly** adv pertinentemente

perturb /pə'tɜːb/ vt perturbar

Peru /pə'ruː/ n el Perú m

peruse /pə'ruːz/ vt leer cuidadosamente

Peruvian /pə'ruːvɪən/ adj & n peruano (m)

perver|se /pə'vɜːs/ adj retorcido; (stubborn) obstinado. **~sion** n perversión f. **~t** /pə'vɜːt/ vt pervertir. ● /'pɜːvɜːt/ n pervertido m

pessimis|m /'pesɪmɪzəm/ n pesimismo m. **~t** n pesimista m & f. **~tic** /-'mɪstɪk/ adj pesimista

pest /pest/ n plaga f; (🄘, person, thing) peste f

pester /'pestə(r)/ vt importunar

pesticide /'pestɪsaɪd/ n pesticida f

pet /pet/ n animal m doméstico; (favourite) favorito m. ● adj preferido. **my ~ hate** lo que más odio. ● vt (pt petted) acariciar

petal /'petl/ n pétalo m

petition /pɪˈtɪʃn/ n petición f
pet name n apodo m
petrified /ˈpetrɪfaɪd/ adj (terrified)
muerto de miedo; (rock) petrificado
petrol /ˈpetrəl/ n gasolina f. ~
pump n surtidor m. ~ **station** n
gasolinera f. ~ **tank** n depósito m
de gasolina ~**eum** /pɪˈtrəʊliəm/ n
petróleo m.
petticoat /ˈpetɪkəʊt/ n enagua f;
(slip) combinación f
petty /ˈpetɪ/ adj (-ier, -iest) insignificante; (mean) mezquino. ~**y
cash** n dinero m para gastos menores
petulant /ˈpetjʊlənt/ adj irritable
pew /pjuː/ n banco m (de iglesia)
phantom /ˈfæntəm/ n fantasma m
pharma|ceutical /ˌfɑːmə
ˈsjuːtɪkl/ adj farmacéutico. ~**cist**
/ˈfɑːməsɪst/ n farmacéutico m. ~**cy**
/ˈfɑːməsɪ/ n farmacia f
phase /feɪz/ n etapa f. □ ~ **out** vt
retirar progresivamente
PhD abbr (= Doctor of Philosophy) n doctorado m; (person)
Dr., Dra.
pheasant /ˈfeznt/ n faisán m
phenomen|al /fɪˈnɒmɪnl/ adj fenomenal. ~**on** /-mən/ n (pl -ena
/-ɪnə/) fenómeno m
philistine /ˈfɪlɪstaɪn/ adj & n filisteo (m)
philosoph|er /fɪˈlɒsəfə(r)/ n filósofo m. ~**ical** /-əˈsɒfɪkl/ adj filosófico. ~**y** /fɪˈlɒsəfɪ/ n filosofía f
phlegm /flem/ n flema f. ~**atic**
/fleɡˈmætɪk/ adj flemático
phobia /ˈfəʊbɪə/ n fobia f
phone /fəʊn/ n 🔊 teléfono m.
● vt/i llamar (por teléfono). ~ **back**
(call again) volver a llamar; (return

call) llamar (más tarde). ~ **book** n
guía f telefónica, directorio m
(LAm). ~ **booth**, ~ **box** n cabina f
telefónica. ~ **call** n llamada f (telefónica). ~ **card** n tarjeta f telefónica. ~ **number** n número m de
teléfono
phonetic /fəˈnetɪk/ adj fonético.
~**s** n fonética f.
phoney /ˈfəʊnɪ/ adj (-ier, -iest) 🔊
falso
phosph|ate /ˈfɒsfeɪt/ n fosfato m.
~**orus** /ˈfɒsfərəs/ n fósforo m.
photo /ˈfəʊtəʊ/ n (pl -os) 🔊 foto f.
take a ~ sacar una foto. ~**copier**
/-kɒpɪə(r)/ n fotocopiadora f.
~**copy** n fotocopia f. ● vt fotocopiar. ~**genic** /-ˈdʒenɪk/ adj fotogénico. ~**graph** /-ɡrɑːf/ n fotografía
f. ● vt fotografiar, sacarle una fotografía a. ~**grapher** /fəˈtɒɡrəfə(r)/
n fotógrafo m. ~**graphic** /-ˈɡræfɪk/
adj fotográfico. ~**graphy** /fə
ˈtɒɡrəfɪ/ n fotografía f
phrase /freɪz/ n frase f. ● vt expresar. ~ **book** n manual m de conversación
physi|cal /ˈfɪzɪkl/ adj físico. ~**cian** /fɪˈzɪʃn/ n médico m. ~**cist**
/ˈfɪzɪsɪst/ n físico m. ~**cs** /ˈfɪzɪks/ n
física f. ~**ology** /fɪzɪˈɒlədʒɪ/ n fisiología f. ~**otherapist** /fɪzɪəʊ
ˈθerəpɪst/ n fisioterapeuta m & f.
~**otherapy** /fɪzɪəʊˈθerəpɪ/ n fisioterapia f. ~**que** /fɪˈziːk/ n físico m
pian|ist /ˈpɪənɪst/ n pianista m & f.
~**o** /pɪˈænəʊ/ n (pl -os) piano m
pick /pɪk/ (tool) pico m. ● vt escoger; cortar (flowers); recoger (fruit,
cotton); abrir con una ganzúa
(lock). ~ a quarrel buscar camorra. ~ **holes in** criticar. □ **on** vt
meterse con. □ **out** vt escoger;
(identify) reconocer. □ **up** vt re-

coger; (*lift*) levantar; (*learn*) aprender; adquirir (habit, etc); contagiarse de (illness). • *vi* mejorar; (*sales*) subir. **~axe** *n* pico *m*

picket /'pɪkɪt/ *n* (*group*) piquete *m*. **~ line** *n* piquete *m*. • *vt* formar un piquete frente a

pickle /'pɪkl/ *n* (*in vinegar*) encurtido *m*; (*Amer, gherkin*) pepinillo *m*; (*relish*) salsa *f* (*a base de encurtidos*). • *vt* encurtir

pick: **~pocket** *n* carterista *m* & *f.* **~-up** *n* (*truck*) camioneta *f*

picnic /'pɪknɪk/ *n* picnic *m*

picture /'pɪktʃə(r)/ *n* (*painting*) cuadro *m*; (*photo*) foto *f*; (*drawing*) dibujo *m*; (*illustration*) ilustración *f*; (*film*) película *f*; (*fig*) descripción *f*. • *vt* imaginarse. **~sque** /-'resk/ *adj* pintoresca

pie /paɪ/ *n* empanada *f*; (*sweet*) pastel *m*, tarta *f*

piece /piːs/ *n* pedazo *m*, trozo *m*; (*part of machine*) pieza *f*; (*coin*) moneda *f*; (*in chess*) figura *f*. a **~** of advice un consejo. a **~** of furniture un mueble. a **~** of news una noticia. take to **~s** desmontar. □ **~ together** *vt* juntar. **~meal** *adj* gradual; (*unsystematic*) poco sistemático. • *adv* poco a poco

pier /pɪə(r)/ *n* muelle *m*; (*with amusements*) paseo con atracciones sobre un muelle

pierc|e /pɪəs/ *vt* perforar. **~ing** *adj* penetrante

piety /'paɪətɪ/ *n* piedad *f*

pig /pɪg/ *n* cerdo *m*, chancho *m* (LAm)

pigeon /'pɪdʒɪn/ *n* paloma *f*; (*Culin*) pichón *m*. **~hole** *n* casillero *m*; (*fig*) casilla *f*

piggy /'pɪgɪ/ *n* cerdito *m*. **~back**

n. give s.o. a **~back** llevar a uno a cuestas. **~ bank** *n* hucha *f*

pig-headed /-'hedɪd/ *adj* terco

pigment /'pɪgmənt/ *n* pigmento *m*

pig|sty /'pɪgstaɪ/ *n* pocilga *f*. **~tail** *n* (*plait*) trenza *f*; (*bunch*) coleta *f*

pike /paɪk/ *n invar* (*fish*) lucio *m*

pilchard /'pɪltʃəd/ *n* sardina *f*

pile /paɪl/ *n* (*heap*) montón *m*; (*of fabric*) pelo *m*. **~ it** on exagerar. • *vi* amontonarse. □ **~ up** *vt* amontonar. • *vi* amontonarse. **~s** /paɪlz/ *npl* (*Med*) almorranas *fpl*. **~-up** *n* choque *m* múltiple

pilgrim /'pɪlgrɪm/ *n* peregrino. **~age** /-ɪdʒ/ *n* peregrinación *f*

pill /pɪl/ *n* pastilla *f*

pillar /'pɪlə(r)/ *n* columna *f*. **~ box** *n* buzón *m*

pillow /'pɪləʊ/ *n* almohada *f*. **~case** *n* funda *f* de almohada

pilot /'paɪlət/ *n* piloto *m*. • *vt* pilotar. **~ light** *n* fuego *m* piloto

pimple /'pɪmpl/ *n* grano *m*, espinilla *f* (LAm)

pin /pɪn/ *n* alfiler *m*; (*Mec*) perno *m*. **~s and needles** hormigueo *m*. • *vt* (*pt* pinned) prender con alfileres; (*fix*) sujetar

PIN /pɪn/ *n* (= **personal identification number**) NIP *m*

pinafore /'pɪnəfɔː(r)/ *n* delantal *m*. **~ dress** *n* pichi *m*, jumper *m* & *f* (LAm)

pincers /'pɪnsəz/ *npl* tenazas *fpl*

pinch /pɪntʃ/ *vt* pellizcar; (*fam, steal*) hurtar. • *vi* (shoe) apretar. • *n* pellizco *m*; (*small amount*) pizca *f*. at a **~** si fuera necesario

pine /paɪn/ *n* pino *m*. • *vi*. **~ for** sth suspirar por algo. □ **~ away** *vi* languidecer de añoranza. ~apple /'paɪræpl/ n piña f

ping-pong /'pɪŋpɒŋ/ n ping-pong m

pink /pɪŋk/ adj & n rosa (m), rosado (m)

pinnacle /'pɪnəkl/ n pináculo m

pin: ~point vt determinar con precisión f. ~stripe n raya f fina

pint /paɪnt/ n pinta f (= 0.57 litros)

pioneer /paɪə'nɪə(r)/ n pionero m

pious /'paɪəs/ adj piadoso

pip /pɪp/ n (seed) pepita f; (Mus) caramillo m; (for smoking) pipa f. ● vt llevar por tuberías. ~dream n ilusión f. ~line n conducto m; (for oil) oleoducto m. in the ~line en preparación f

piping /'paɪpɪŋ/ n tubería f. ● adv. ~ hot muy caliente, hirviendo

pira|cy /'paɪərəsɪ/ n piratería f. ~te /'paɪərət/ n pirata m

Pisces /'paɪsiːz/ n Piscis m

piss /pɪs/ vi ⊠ mear. □ ~ off vi ⊠. ~ off! ¡vete a la mierda! ~ed /pɪst/ adj (⊠, drunk) como una cuba; (Amer, fed up) cabreado

pistol /'pɪstl/ n pistola f

piston /'pɪstən/ n pistón m

pit /pɪt/ n hoyo m; (mine) mina f; (Amer, in fruit) hueso m

pitch /pɪtʃ/ n (substance) brea f; (degree) grado m; (Mus) tono m; (Sport) campo m; (throw) lanzar; armar (tent). ● vi (ship) cabecear. ~black /-'blæk/ adj oscuro como boca de lobo. ~er n jarra f

pitfall /'pɪtfɔːl/ n trampa f

pith /pɪθ/ n (of orange, lemon) médula f; (fig) meollo m

pitiful /'pɪtɪfl/ adj lastimoso

pittance /'pɪtns/ n miseria f

pity /'pɪtɪ/ n lástima f, pena f; (compassion) piedad f. it's a ~ you can't come es una lástima que no puedas venir. ● vt tenerle lástima f

pivot /'pɪvət/ n pivote m. ● vi pivotar; (fig) depender (on de)

placard /'plækɑːd/ n pancarta f; (sign) letrero m

placate /plə'keɪt/ vt apaciguar

place /pleɪs/ n lugar m; (seat) asiento m; (in firm, team) puesto m; (fam, house) casa f. feel out of ~ sentirse fuera de lugar. take ~ tener lugar. ● vt poner, colocar; (identify) identificar. be ~d (in race) colocarse. ~mat n mantel m individual

placid /'plæsɪd/ adj plácido

plague /pleɪg/ n peste f; (fig) plaga f. ● vt atormentar

plaice /pleɪs/ n invar platija f

plain /pleɪn/ adj (-er, -est) (clear) claro; (simple) sencillo; (candid) franco; (ugly) feo. in ~ clothes de civil. ● n llanura f. ~ly adv claramente; (frankly) francamente; (simply) con sencillez

plaintiff /'pleɪntɪf/ n demandante m & f

plait /plæt/ vt trenzar. ● n trenza f

plan /plæn/ n plan m; (map) plano m; (of book, essay) esquema f. ● vt (pt planned) planear; planificar (strategies). I'm ~ning to go to Greece pienso ir a Grecia

plane /pleɪn/ n (tree) plátano m; (level) nivel m; (aircraft) avión m; (tool) cepillo m. ● vt cepillar

planet /'plænɪt/ n planeta m. ~ary adj planetario

plank /plæŋk/ n tabla f

planning /'plænɪŋ/ n planificación f. family ~ planificación familiar. **town** ~ urbanismo m

plant /plɑːnt/ n planta f; (Mec) maquinaria f; (factory) fábrica f. ● vt plantar; (place in position) colocar. ~**ation** /plænˈteɪʃn/ n plantación f

plaque /plæk/ n placa f

plasma /ˈplæzmə/ n plasma m

plaster /ˈplɑːstə(r)/ n yeso m; (on walls) revoque m; (sticking plaster) tirita f (℗), curita f (℗) (LAm); (for setting bones) yeso m, escayola f. ● vt revocar; rellenar con yeso (cracks)

plastic /ˈplæstɪk/ adj & n plástico (m)

Plasticine /ˈplæstɪsiːn/ n (℗) plastilina f (℗)

plastic surgery /plæstɪk ˈsɜːdʒərɪ/ n cirugía f estética

plate /pleɪt/ n plato m; (of metal) chapa f; (silverware) vajilla f de plata; (in book) lámina f. ● vt recubrir (with de)

platform /ˈplætfɔːm/ n plataforma f; (Rail) andén m

platinum /ˈplætɪnəm/ n platino m

platitude /ˈplætɪtjuːd/ n lugar m común

platonic /pləˈtɒnɪk/ adj platónico

plausible /ˈplɔːzəbl/ adj verosímil; (person) convincente

play /pleɪ/ vt jugar a (game, cards); jugar a, jugar (LAm) (football, chess); tocar (instrument); (act role) representar el papel de. ● vi jugar. ● n juego m; (drama) obra f de teatro. □ ~ **down** vt minimizar. □ ~ **up** vi 🔽 (child) dar guerra; (car, TV) no funcionar bien. ~**er** n jugador m; (Mus) músico m. ~**ful** adj juguetón. ~**ground** n parque m de juegos infantiles; (in school) patio m de recreo. ~**group** n jardín m de la infancia. ~**ing**

card n naipe m. ~**ing field** n campo m de deportes. ~**pen** n corralito m. ~**wright** /-raɪt/ n dramaturgo m

plc abbr (= **public limited company**) S.A.

plea /pliː/ n súplica f; (excuse) excusa f; (Jurid) defensa f

plead /pliːd/ vt (Jurid) alegar; (as excuse) pretextar. ● vi suplicar. ~ **with** suplicarle a. ~ **guilty** declararse culpable

pleasant /ˈpleznt/ adj agradable

please /pliːz/ int por favor. ● vt complacer; (satisfy) contentar. ● vi agradar; (wish) querer. ~**d** adj (satisfied) satisfecho; (happy) contento. ~**ed with** satisfecho de. ~**ing** adj agradable; (news) grato. ~**ure** /ˈpleʒə(r)/ n placer m

pleat /pliːt/ n pliegue m

pledge /pledʒ/ n cantidad f prometida

plentiful /ˈplentɪfl/ adj abundante. ~**y** /ˈplentɪ/ n abundancia f. ● pron. ~**y of** muchos, -chas; (of sth uncountable) mucho, -cha

pliable /ˈplaɪəbl/ adj flexible

pliers /ˈplaɪəz/ npl alicates mpl

plight /plaɪt/ n situación f difícil

plimsolls /ˈplɪmsəlz/ npl zapatillas fpl de lona

plod /plɒd/ vi (pt **plodded**) caminar con paso pesado

plot /plɒt/ n complot m; (of novel etc) argumento m; (piece of land) parcela f. ● vt (pt **plotted**) tramar; (mark out) trazar. ● vi conspirar

plough /plaʊ/ n arado m. ● vt/i arar. □ ~ **into** vt estrellarse contra. □ ~ **through** vt avanzar laboriosamente por

ploy /plɔɪ/ n treta f

pluck /plʌk/ vt arrancar; depilarse

(eyebrows); desplumar (bird). ~ **up** courage to armarse de valor para. ● n valor m. ~**y** adj (-**ier**, -**iest**) valiente

plug /plʌg/ n (in bath) tapón m; (Elec) enchufe m; (spark ~) bujía f. ● vt (pt **plugged**) tapar; (fam, advertise) hacerle propaganda a. □ ~ **in** vt (Elec) enchufar. ~**hole** n desagüe m

plum /plʌm/ n ciruela f

plumage /'pluːmɪdʒ/ n plumaje m

plumb|er /'plʌmə(r)/ n fontanero m, plomero m (LAm). ~**ing** n instalación f sanitaria, instalación f de cañerías

plume /pluːm/ n pluma f

plump /plʌmp/ adj (-**er**, -**est**) rechoncho

plunge /plʌndʒ/ vt hundir (knife); (in water) sumergir; (into state, condition) sumir. ● vi zambullirse; (fall) caer. ● n zambullida f

plural /'plʊərəl/ n plural m. ● adj en plural

plus /plʌs/ prep más. ● adj positivo. ● n signo m de más; (fig) ventaja f

plush /plʌʃ/ adj lujoso

Pluto /'pluːtəʊ/ n Plutón m

plutonium /pluː'təʊnɪəm/ n plutonio m

ply /plaɪ/ vt manejar (tool); ejercer (trade). ~ **s.o. with drink** dar continuamente de beber a uno. ~**wood** n contrachapado m

p.m. abbr (= **post meridiem**) de la tarde

pneumatic drill /njuː'mætɪk/ adj martillo m neumático

pneumonia /njuː'məʊnjə/ n pulmonía f

poach /pəʊtʃ/ vt escalfar (egg); cocer (fish etc); (steal) cazar furtivamente. ~**er** n cazador m furtivo

PO box /piː'əʊ/ n Apdo. postal

pocket /'pɒkɪt/ n bolsillo m; (of air, resistance) bolsa f. ● vt poner en el bolsillo. ~**book** n (notebook) libro m de bolsillo; (Amer, wallet) cartera f; (Amer, handbag) bolso m, cartera f (LAm), bolsa f (Mex). ~**money** n dinero m de bolsillo, mesada f (LAm)

pod /pɒd/ n vaina f

poem /'pəʊɪm/ n poema f

poet /'pəʊɪt/ n poeta m. ~**ic** /-'etɪk/ adj poético. ~**ry** /'pəʊɪtrɪ/ n poesía f

poignant /'pɔɪnjənt/ adj conmovedor

point /pɔɪnt/ n (dot, on scale) punto m; (sharp end) punta f; (in time) momento m; (statement) observación; (in agenda, in discussion) punto m; (Elec) toma f de corriente. **to the** ~ pertinente. **up to a** ~ hasta cierto punto. **be on the** ~ **of** estar a punto de. **get to the** ~ ir al grano. **there's no** ~ **(in)** arguing no sirve de nada discutir. ● vt (aim) apuntar; (show) indicar. ● vi señalar. □ ~ **at/to sth** señalar algo. □ ~ **out** vt señalar. ~**-blank** adj & adv a quemarropa. ~**ed** adj (chin, nose) puntiagudo; (fig) mordaz. ~**less** adj inútil

poise /pɔɪz/ n porte m; (composure) desenvoltura f

poison /'pɔɪzn/ n veneno m. ● vt envenenar. ~**ous** adj venenoso; (chemical etc) tóxico

poke /pəʊk/ vt empujar; atizar (fire). ● vi hurgar; (pry) meterse. ● n golpe m. □ ~ **about** vi fisgonear. ~**r** /'pəʊkə(r)/ n atizador m; (Cards) póquer m

poky /'pəʊkɪ/ adj (-**ier**, -**iest**) diminuto

P

Poland /ˈpəʊlənd/ n Polonia f

polar /ˈpəʊlə(r)/ adj polar. ~ **bear** n oso m blanco

pole /pəʊl/ n palo m; (fixed) poste m; (for flag) mástil m; (in geography) polo m

police /pəˈliːs/ n policía f. ~**man** /-mən/ n policía m, agente m. ~ **station** n comisaría f. ~**woman** n policía f, agente f

policy /ˈpɒlɪsɪ/ n política f; (insurance) póliza f (de seguros)

polish /ˈpɒlɪʃ/ n (for shoes) betún m; (furniture ~) cera f para muebles; (floor ~) abrillantador m de suelos; (shine) brillo m; (fig) finura f. ● vt darle brillo a; limpiar (shoes); (refine) pulir. □ ~ **off** vt despachar. ~**ed** adj pulido

Polish /ˈpəʊlɪʃ/ adj & n polaco (m)

polite /pəˈlaɪt/ adj cortés. ~**ly** adv cortésmente. ~**ness** n cortesía f

politic|al /pəˈlɪtɪkl/ adj político. ~**ian** /pɒlɪˈtɪʃn/ n político m. ~s /ˈpɒlɪtɪks/ n política f

poll /pəʊl/ n elección f; (survey) encuesta f. ● vt obtener (votes)

pollack /ˈpɒlæk/ n abadejo m

pollen /ˈpɒlən/ n polen m

polling booth n cabina f de votar

pollut|e /pəˈluːt/ vt contaminar. ~**ion** /-ʃn/ n contaminación f

polo /ˈpəʊləʊ/ n polo m. ~ **neck** n cuello m vuelto

poly|styrene /pɒlɪˈstaɪriːn/ n poliestireno m. ~**thene** /ˈpɒlɪθiːn/ n plástico, polietileno m

pomp /pɒmp/ n pompa f. ~**ous** adj pomposa

pond /pɒnd/ n (natural) laguna f; (artificial) estanque m

ponder /ˈpɒndə(r)/ vt considerar. ~**ous** adj pesado

pony /ˈpəʊnɪ/ n poni m. ~-**tail** n cola f de caballo

poodle /ˈpuːdl/ n caniche m

pool /puːl/ n charca f; (artificial) estanque m; (puddle) charco m. (common fund) fondos mpl comunes; (snooker) billar m americano. (**swimming**) ~ n piscina f, alberca f (Mex). ~**s** npl quinielas fpl. ● vt aunar

poor /pʊə(r)/ adj (-er, -est) pobre; (quality, diet) malo. be in ~ health estar mal de salud. ~**ly** adj 🔳 malito. ● adv mal

pop /pɒp/ n (Mus) música f pop; (Amer fam, father) papá m. ● vt (pt popped) hacer reventar; (put) poner. □ ~ **in** vi (visit) pasar por. □ ~ **out** vi (person) salir un rato. □ ~ **up** vi surgir, aparecer

popcorn /ˈpɒpkɔːn/ n palomitas fpl

pope /pəʊp/ n papa m

poplar /ˈpɒplə(r)/ n álamo m (blanco)

poppy /ˈpɒpɪ/ n amapola f

popular /ˈpɒpjʊlə(r)/ adj popular. ~**ity** /-ˈlærətɪ/ n popularidad f. ~**ize** vt popularizar

populat|e /ˈpɒpjʊleɪt/ vt poblar. ~**ion** /-ˈleɪʃn/ n población f

pop-up /ˈpɒpʌp/ n ventana f emergente, pop-up m

porcelain /ˈpɔːsəlɪn/ n porcelana f

porch /pɔːtʃ/ n porche m

porcupine /ˈpɔːkjʊpaɪn/ n puerco m espín

pore /pɔː(r)/ n poro m

pork /pɔːk/ n carne f de cerdo m, carne f de puerco m (Mex)

porn /pɔːn/ n 🔳 pornografía f. ~**ographic** /-əˈgræfɪk/ adj pornográfico. ~**ography** /pɔːˈnɒɡrəfɪ/ n pornografía f

porpoise /'pɔːpəs/ n marsopa f

porridge /'pɒrɪdʒ/ n avena f (cocida)

port /pɔːt/ n puerto m; (Naut) babor m; (Comp) puerto m; (Culin) oporto m

portable /'pɔːtəbl/ adj portátil

porter /'pɔːtə(r)/ n (for luggage) maletero m; (concierge) portero m

porthole /'pɔːthəʊl/ n portilla f

portion /'pɔːʃn/ n porción f; (part) parte f

portrait /'pɔːtrɪt/ n retrato m

portray /pɔː'treɪ/ vt representar. ∼al n representación f

Portugal /'pɔːtjʊɡl/ n Portugal m. ∼uese /-'ɡiːz/ adj & n portugués (m)

pose /pəʊz/ n pose f, postura f. ● vt representar (threat); plantear (problem, question). ● vi posar. ∼as hacerse pasar por

posh /pɒʃ/ adj 🔲 elegante

position /pə'zɪʃn/ n posición f; (job) puesto m; (situation) situación f. ● vt colocar

positive /'pɒzətɪv/ adj positivo; (real) auténtico; (certain) seguro. ● n (Photo) positiva f. ∼ly adv positivamente

possess /pə'zes/ vt poseer. ∼ion /-ʃn/ n posesión f; (Jurid) bien m. ∼ive adj posesivo

possibility /pɒsə'bɪlətɪ/ n posibilidad f. ∼le /'pɒsəbl/ adj posible. ∼ly adv posiblemente

post /pəʊst/ n (pole) poste m; (job) puesto m; (mail) correo m. ● vt echar al correo (letter); (send) enviar por correo. keep s.o. ∼ed mantener a uno al corriente

post... /pəʊst/ pref post, pos

post: ∼age n /-ɪdʒ/ /-ɪdʒ/ franqueo m. ∼al adj postal. ∼al

order n giro m postal. ∼ **box** n buzón m. ∼**card** n (tarjeta f) postal f. ∼**code** n código m postal

poster /'pəʊstə(r)/ n cartel m, póster m

posterity /pɒs'terətɪ/ n posteridad f

posthumous /'pɒstjʊməs/ adj póstumo

post: ∼**man** /-mən/ n cartero m. ∼**mark** n matasellos m

post mortem /pəʊst'mɔːtəm/ n autopsia f

post office n oficina f de correos, correos mpl, correo m (LAm)

postpone /pəʊst'pəʊn/ vt aplazar, posponer. ∼**ment** n aplazamiento m

postscript /'pəʊstskrɪpt/ n posdata f

posture /'pɒstʃə(r)/ n postura f

posy /'pəʊzɪ/ n ramillete m

pot /pɒt/ n (for cooking) olla f; (for jam, honey) tarro m; (for flowers) tiesto m; (in pottery) vasija f. ∼s and pans cacharros mpl

potato /pə'teɪtəʊ/ n (pl -oes) patata f, papa f (LAm)

potent /'pəʊtnt/ adj potente; (drink) fuerte

potential /pəʊ'tenʃl/ adj & n potencial (m). ∼**ly** adv potencialmente

pot: ∼**hole** n cueva f subterránea; (in road) bache m. ∼**holing** n espeleología f

potion /'pəʊʃn/ n poción f

pot-shot n tiro m al azar

potter /'pɒtə(r)/ n alfarero m. ● vi hacer pequeños trabajos agradables. ∼**y** n (pots) cerámica f; (workshop, craft) alfarería f

potty /'pɒtɪ/ adj (-ier, -iest) 🔲

chiflado. ● n orinal m

pouch /paʊtʃ/ n bolsa f pequeña; (for correspondence) valija f

poultry /'pəʊltrɪ/ n aves fpl de corral

pounce /paʊns/ vi saltar. ~ on abalanzarse sobre

pound /paʊnd/ n (weight) libra f (= 454g); (money) libra f (esterlina); (for cars) depósito m. ● vt (crush) machacar. ● vi aporrear; (heart) palpitar; (sound) retumbar

pour /pɔː(r)/ vt verter; echar (salt). ~ (out) servir (drink). ● vi (blood) manar; (water) salir; (rain) llover a cántaros. □ ~ out vi (people) salir en tropel. ~ing adj. ~ing rain lluvia f torrencial

pout /paʊt/ vi hacer pucheros

poverty /'pɒvətɪ/ n pobreza f

powder /'paʊdə(r)/ n polvo m; (cosmetic) polvos mpl. ● vt empolvar. ~ one's face ponerse polvos en la cara. ~y adj con polvo

power /paʊə(r)/ n poder m; (energy) energía f; (electricity) electricidad f; (nation) potencia f. ● vt. ~ed by impulsado por. □ ~ cut n apagón m. ~ed adj con motor. ~ful adj poderoso. ~less adj impotente. ~ plant, ~-station n central f eléctrica

PR = public relations

practicable /'præktɪkəbl/ adj practicable

practical /'præktɪkl/ adj práctico. ~ joke n broma f. ~ly adv prácticamente

practi|ce /'præktɪs/ n práctica f; (custom) costumbre f; (exercise) ejercicio m; (Sport) entrenamiento m; (clients) clientela f he's out of ~ce le falta práctica. in ~ce (in fact) en la práctica. ~se /'præktɪs/

vt practicar; ensayar (act); ejercer (profession). ● vi practicar; (professional) ejercer. ~tioner /-'tɪʃənə(r)/ n médico m

prairie /'preərɪ/ n pradera f

praise /preɪz/ vt (Relig) alabar; (compliment) elogiar. ● n (credit) elogios mpl. ~worthy adj loable

pram /præm/ n cochecito m

prank /præŋk/ n travesura f

prawn /prɔːn/ n gamba f, camarón m (LAm)

pray /preɪ/ vi rezar (for por). ~er /preə(r)/ n oración f

pre.. /priː/ pref pre...

preach /priːtʃ/ vt/i predicar. ~er n predicador m; (Amer, minister) pastor m

pre-arrange /priːə'reɪndʒ/ vt concertar de antemano

precarious /prɪ'keərɪəs/ adj precario. ~ly adv precariamente

precaution /prɪ'kɔːʃn/ n precaución f

precede /prɪ'siːd/ vt preceder. ~nce /'presədəns/ n precedencia f. ~nt /'presədənt/ n precedente m

preceding /prɪ'siːdɪŋ/ adj anterior

precept /'priːsept/ n precepto m

precinct /'priːsɪŋkt/ n recinto m; (Amer, police district) distrito m policial; (Amer, voting district) circunscripción f. **pedestrian** ~ zona f peatonal. ~s (of city) límites mpl

precious /'preʃəs/ adj precioso. ● adv 🆃 muy

precipice /'presɪpɪs/ n precipicio m

precipitate /prɪ'sɪpɪteɪt/ vt precipitar. ● /prɪ'sɪpɪtət/ n precipitado m. ● /prɪ'sɪpɪtət/ adj precipitado

precis|e /prɪ'saɪs/ adj (accurate)

exacto; (*specific*) preciso; (*meticulous*) minucioso. **~ely** adv con precisión. **~!** ¡exacto! **~ion** /-'sɪʒn/ precisión f

preclude /prɪ'kluːd/ vt excluir

precocious /prɪ'kəʊʃəs/ adj precoz. **~ly** adv precozmente

preconce|ived /priːkən'siːvd/ adj preconcebido. **~ption** /-'sepʃn/ n preconcepción f

precursor /priː'kɜːsə(r)/ n precursor m

predator /'predətə(r)/ n depredador m. **~y** adj predador

predecessor /'priːdɪsesə(r)/ n predecesor m, antecesor m

predicament /prɪ'dɪkəmənt/ n aprieto m

predict /prɪ'dɪkt/ vt predecir. **~ion** /-ʃn/ n predicción f

preen /priːn/ vt arreglar. **~ o.s.** atildarse

prefab /'priːfæb/ n 🔢 casa f prefabricada. **~ricated** /-'fæbrɪkeɪtɪd/ adj prefabricado

preface /'prefəs/ n prefacio m; (*to event*) prólogo m

prefect /'priːfekt/ n (*Schol*) monitor m; (*official*) prefecto m

prefer /prɪ'fɜː(r)/ vt (*pt preferred*) preferir. **~ sth to sth** preferir algo a algo. **~able** /'prefrəbl/ adj preferible. **~ence** /'prefrəns/ n preferencia f. **~ential** /-ə'renʃl/ adj preferente

pregnan|cy /'pregnənsɪ/ n embarazo m. **~t** adj embarazada

prehistoric /priːhɪ'stɒrɪk/ adj prehistórico

prejudge /priː'dʒʌdʒ/ vt juzgar de antemano

prejudice /'predʒʊdɪs/ n prejuicio m. ● vt predisponer; (*harm*) perjudicar. **~d** adj lleno de prejuicios

preliminary /prɪ'lɪmɪnərɪ/ adj preliminar

prelude /'preljuːd/ n preludio m

premature /'premətjʊə(r)/ adj prematuro

premeditated /priː'medɪteɪtɪd/ adj premeditado

premier /'premɪə(r)/ n (*Pol*) primer ministro m

première /'premɪeə(r)/ n estreno m

premise /'premɪs/ n premisa f. **~s** /'premɪsɪz/ npl local m. **on the ~s** en el local

premium /'priːmɪəm/ n (*insurance ~*) prima f de seguro. **be at a ~** escasear

premonition /priːmə'nɪʃn/ n premonición f, presentimiento m

preoccup|ation /priːɒkjʊ 'peɪʃn/ n (*obsession*) obsesión f; (*concern*) preocupación f. **~ied** /-'ɒkjʊpaɪd/ adj absorto; (*worried*) preocupado

preparat|ion /prepə'reɪʃn/ n preparación f. **~ions** npl preparativos mpl. **~ory** /prɪ'pærətrɪ/ adj preparatorio

prepare /prɪ'peə(r)/ vt preparar. ● vi prepararse. ● adj preparado (*willing*). **be ~d to** estar dispuesto a

preposition /prepə'zɪʃn/ n preposición f

preposterous /prɪ'pɒstərəs/ adj absurdo

prerequisite /priː'rekwɪzɪt/ n requisito m esencial

prerogative /prɪ'rɒgətɪv/ n prerrogativa f

Presbyterian /prezbɪ'tɪərɪən/ adj & n presbiteriano m

prescri|be /prɪ'skraɪb/ vt prescribir; (*Med*) recetar. **~ption** /-'ɪpʃn/ n (*Med*) receta f

p

presence /'prezns/ n presencia f. ~ of mind presencia f de ánimo

present /'preznt/ n (gift) regalo m; (current time) presente m. at ~ actualmente. for the ~ por ahora. ● adj presente. ● /prɪ'zent/ vt presentar; (give) obsequiar. ~ s.o. with obsequiar a uno con. ~able /prɪ'zentəbl/ adj presentable. ~ation /prezn'teɪʃn/ n presentación f; (ceremony) ceremonia f de entrega. ~er /prɪ'zentə(r)/ n presentador m. ~ly /'prezntlɪ/ adv dentro de poco

preserv|ation /prezə'veɪʃn/ n conservación f. ~ative /prɪ'zɜːvətɪv/ n conservante m. ~e /prɪ'zɜːv/ vt conservar; (maintain) mantener; (Culin) hacer conserva de. ● n coto m; (jam) confitura f. wildlife ~e (Amer) reserva f de animales

preside /prɪ'zaɪd/ vi presidir. ~ over presidir

presiden|cy /'prezɪdənsɪ/ n presidencia f. ~t n presidente m. ~tial /-'denʃl/ adj presidencial

press /pres/ vt apretar; prensar (grapes); (put pressure on) presionar; (iron) planchar. be ~ed for time andar escaso de tiempo. ● vi apretar; (time) apremiar; (fig) urgir. ● n (Mec, newspapers) prensa f; (printing) imprenta f. ● vi ~ on seguir adelante (with con). ~ conference n rueda f de prensa. ~ cutting n recorte m de periódico. ~ing n urgente. ~-up n flexión f, fondo m

pressur|e /'preʃə(r)/ n presión f. ● vt presionar. ~e-cooker n olla f a presión. ~ize vt presionar

prestige /pre'stiːʒ/ n prestigio m. ~ious /-'stɪdʒəs/ adj prestigioso

presum|ably /prɪ'zjuːməblɪ/ adv. ~... supongo que..., me imagino

que... ~e /prɪ'zjuːm/ vt suponer. ~ptuous /prɪ'zʌmptʃʊəs/ adj impertinente

presuppose /priːsə'pəʊz/ vt presuponer

preten|ce /prɪ'tens/ n fingimiento m; (claim) pretensión f; (pretext) pretexto m. ~d /-'tend/ vt/i fingir. ~sion /-'tenʃən/ n pretensión f. ~tious /-'tenʃəs/ adj pretencioso

pretext /'priːtekst/ n pretexto m

pretty /'prɪtɪ/ adj (-ier, -iest) adv bonito, lindo (esp LAm)

prevail /prɪ'veɪl/ vi predominar; (win) prevalecer. □ ~ on vt persuadir

prevalen|ce /'prevələns/ n (occurrence) preponderancia f; (predominance) predominio m. ~t adj extendido

prevent /prɪ'vent/ vt (hinder) impedir; (forestall) prevenir, evitar. ~ion /-ʃn/ n prevención f. ~ive adj preventivo

preview /'priːvjuː/ n preestreno m; (trailer) avance m

previous /'priːvɪəs/ adj anterior. ~ to antes de. ~ly adv antes

prey /preɪ/ n presa f. bird of ~ ave f de rapiña

price /praɪs/ n precio m. ● vt fijar el precio de. ~less adj inestimable; (fam, amusing) muy divertido. ~y adj 🔟 carito

prick /prɪk/ vt/i pinchar. ● n pinchazo m

prickl|e /'prɪkl/ n (thorn) espina f; (of animal) púa f; (sensation) picor m. ~y adj espinoso; (animal) con púas; (touchy) quisquilloso

pride /praɪd/ n orgullo m. ● vr. ~ o.s. on enorgullecerse de

priest /priːst/ n sacerdote m. ~hood n sacerdocio m

prim /prɪm/ adj (primmer, prim-mest) mojigato; (affected) remilgado

primar|ily /'praɪmərɪlɪ/ adv en primer lugar. ~**y** /'praɪmərɪ/ adj (principal) primordial; (first, basic) primario. ~ **school** n escuela f primaria

prime /praɪm/ vt cebar (gun); (prepare) preparar; aprestar (surface). ● adj principal; (first rate) excelente. ~ **minister** n primer ministro m. ● n. be in one's ~ estar en la flor de la vida. ~**r** n (paint) imprimación f

primeval /praɪ'miːvl/ adj primigenio

primitive /'prɪmɪtɪv/ adj primitivo

primrose /'prɪmrəʊz/ n primavera f

prince /prɪns/ n príncipe m. ~**ss** /prɪn'ses/ n princesa f

principal /'prɪnsəpl/ adj principal. ● n (of school) director m; (of university) rector m. ~**ly** /'prɪnsɪpəlɪ/ adv principalmente

principle /'prɪnsəpl/ n principio m. in ~ en principio. on ~ por principio

print /prɪnt/ vt imprimir; (write in capitals) escribir con letras de molde. ~**ed matter** n impresos mpl. ● n (characters) letra f; (picture) grabado m; (Photo) copia f; (fabric) estampado m. in ~ (published) publicado; (available) a la venta. out of ~ agotado. ~**er** /'prɪntə(r)/ n impresor m; (machine) impresora f. ~**ing** n impresión f; (trade) imprenta f. ~**out** n listado m

prion /'praɪɒn/ n prión m

prior /'praɪə(r)/ n prior m. ● adj previo. ~ **to** antes de. ~**ity** /praɪ'ɒrɪtɪ/ n prioridad f. ~**y** n priorato m

prise /praɪz/ vt. ~ **open** abrir haciendo palanca

prison /'prɪzn/ n cárcel m. ~**er** n prisionero m; (in prison) preso m; (under arrest) detenido m. ~ **officer** n funcionario m de prisiones

priva|cy /'prɪvəsɪ/ n privacidad f. ~**te** /'praɪvɪt/ adj privado; (confidential) personal; (lessons, house) particular. in ~**te** en privado; (secretly) en secreto. ● n soldado m raso. ~**te detective** n detective m & f privado. ~**tely** adv en privado. ~**tion** /praɪ'veɪʃn/ n privación f

privilege /'prɪvɪlɪdʒ/ n privilegio m. ~**d** adj privilegiado. be ~**d to** tener el privilegio de

prize /praɪz/ n premio m. ● adj (idiot etc) de remate. ● vt estimar

pro /prəʊ/ n. ~**s and cons** los pros m y los contras

probab|ility /prɒbə'bɪlɪtɪ/ n probabilidad f. ~**le** /'prɒbəbl/ adj probable. ~**ly** adv probablemente

probation /prə'beɪʃn/ n período m de prueba; (Jurid) libertad f condicional

probe /prəʊb/ n sonda f; (fig) investigación f. ● vt sondar. ● vi. ~ **into** investigar

problem /'prɒbləm/ n problema m. ● adj difícil. ~**atic** /-'mætɪk/ adj problemático

procedure /prə'siːdʒə(r)/ n procedimiento m

proceed /prə'siːd/ vi proceder; (move forward) avanzar. ~**ings** npl (report) actas fpl; (Jurid) proceso m. ~**s** /'prəʊsiːdz/ npl. the ~**s** lo recaudado

process /'prəʊses/ n proceso m. in the ~ **of** en vías de. ● vt tratar; revelar (photo); tramitar (order).

∼ion /prəˈseɪn/ n desfile m; (Relig) procesión f. ∼or n procesador m. food ∼ procesador m de alimentos

procla|im /prəˈkleɪm/ vt proclamar. ∼mation /prɒkləˈmeɪʃn/ n proclamación f

procure /prəˈkjʊə(r)/ vt obtener

prod /prɒd/ vt (pt prodded) (with sth sharp) pinchar; (with elbow) darle un codazo a. ● n (with sth sharp) pinchazo m; (with elbow) codazo m

produc|e /prəˈdjuːs/ vt producir; surtir (effect); sacar (gun); producir (film); poner en escena (play). ● /ˈprɒdjuːs/ n productos mpl. ∼er /prəˈdjuːsə(r)/ n (TV, Cinema) productor m; (in theatre) director m; (manufacturer) fabricante m & f. ∼t /ˈprɒdʌkt/ n producto m. ∼tion /prəˈdʌkʃn/ n (manufacture) fabricación f; (output) producción f; (of play) producción f. ∼tive /prəˈdʌktɪv/ adj productivo. ∼tivity /prɒdʌkˈtɪvəti/ n productividad f

profess /prəˈfes/ vt profesar; (pretend) pretender. ∼ion /-ˈfeʃn/ n profesión f. ∼ional adj & n profesional (m & f). ∼or /prəˈfesə(r)/ n catedrático m; (Amer) profesor m

proficien|cy /prəˈfɪʃənsi/ n competencia f. ∼t adj competente

profile /ˈprəʊfaɪl/ n perfil m

profit /ˈprɒfɪt/ n (Com) ganancia f; (fig) provecho m. ● vi. ∼ from sacar provecho de. ∼able adj provechoso

profound /prəˈfaʊnd/ adj profundo. ∼ly adv profundamente

profus|e /prəˈfjuːs/ adj profuso. ∼ely adv profusamente

prognosis /prɒgˈnəʊsɪs/ n (pl -oses) pronóstico m

program /ˈprəʊgræm/ n (Comp)

programa m; (Amer, course) curso m. ∼me /ˈprəʊgræm/ n programa m. ● vt (pt -med) programar. ∼mer n programador m

progress /ˈprəʊgres/ n progreso m; (development) desarrollo m. make ∼ hacer progresos. in ∼ en curso. ● /prəˈgres/ vi hacer progresos; (develop) desarrollarse. ∼ion /prəˈgreʃn/ n progresión f; (advance) evolución f. ∼ive /prəˈgresɪv/ adj progresivo; (reforming) progresista. ∼ively adv progresivamente

prohibit /prəˈhɪbɪt/ vt prohibir; (prevent) impedir. ∼ive adj prohibitivo

project /prəˈdʒekt/ vt proyectar. ● vi (stick out) sobresalir. ● /ˈprɒdʒekt/ n proyecto m; (Schol) trabajo m; (Amer, housing ∼) complejo m de viviendas subvencionadas. ∼or /prəˈdʒektə(r)/ n proyector m

prolific /prəˈlɪfɪk/ adj prolífico

prologue /ˈprəʊlɒg/ n prólogo m

prolong /prəˈlɒŋ/ vt prolongar

prom /prɒm/ n (Amer) baile m del colegio. ∼enade /prɒməˈnɑːd/ n paseo m marítimo. ● vi pasearse

> **Prom** En EE.UU. un prom 🛈 es un baile que se celebra para los estudiantes que terminan el High School. En Londres the Proms son una serie de conciertos de música clásica, durante los cuales una gran parte del público permanece de pie. Tienen lugar en el Albert Hall en el verano, durante ocho semanas. Oficialmente, son conocidos como los Henry Wood Promenade Concerts, en memoria de su fundador.

prominen|ce /'prɒmɪnəns/ n prominencia f; (fig) importancia f. **~t** adj prominente; (important) importante; (conspicuous) destacado

promiscu|ity /prɒmɪ'skjuːətɪ/ n promiscuidad f. **~ous** /prə'mɪskjʊəs/ adj promiscuo

promis|e /'prɒmɪs/ n promesa f. • vt/i prometer. **~ing** adj prometedor; (future) halagüeño

promot|e /prə'məʊt/ vt promover; promocionar (product); (in rank) ascender. **~ion** /-'məʊʃn/ n promoción f; (in rank) ascenso m

prompt /prɒmpt/ adj (punctual) puntual. • adv en punto. • n (Comp) presto m. • vt incitar; apuntar (actor). **~ly** adv puntualmente

prone /prəʊn/ adj (tendido) boca abajo. be **~ to** ser propenso a

pronoun /'prəʊnaʊn/ n pronombre m

pronounc|e /prə'naʊns/ vt pronunciar; (declare) declarar. **~ement** n declaración f. **~ed** adj pronunciado; (noticeable) marcado

pronunciation /prənʌnsɪ'eɪʃn/ n pronunciación f

proof /pruːf/ n prueba f, pruebas fpl; (of alcohol) graduación f normal. **~** adj. **~** against de a prueba de. **~-reading** n corrección f de pruebas

propaganda /prɒpə'gændə/ n propaganda f

propagate /'prɒpəgeɪt/ vt propagar. • vi propagarse

propel /prə'pel/ vt (pt propelled) propulsar. **~ler** n hélice f

proper /'prɒpə(r)/ adj correcto; (suitable) apropiado; (Gram) propio; (fam, real) verdadero. **~ly** adv correctamente; (eat, work) bien

property /'prɒpətɪ/ n propiedad f; (things owned) bienes mpl. • adj inmobiliario

prophe|cy /'prɒfəsɪ/ n profecía f. **~sy** /'prɒfɪsaɪ/ vt/i profetizar. **~t** /'prɒfɪt/ n profeta m. **~tic** /prə'fetɪk/ adj profético

proportion /prə'pɔːʃn/ n proporción f. **~al** adj, **~ate** /-ət/ adj proporcional

propos|al /prə'pəʊzl/ n propuesta f; (of marriage) proposición f matrimonial. **~e** /prə'pəʊz/ vt proponer. • vi. **~e to** s.o. hacerle una oferta de matrimonio a una. **~ition** /prɒpə'zɪʃn/ n propuesta f; (offer) oferta f

proprietor /prə'praɪətə(r)/ n propietario m

pro rata /prəʊ'rɑːtə/ adv a prorrata

prose /prəʊz/ n prosa f

prosecut|e /'prɒsɪkjuːt/ vt procesar (for por); (carry on) proseguir. **~ion** /-'kjuːʃn/ n proceso m. the **~** (side) la acusación. **~or** n fiscal m & f; (in private prosecutions) abogado m de la acusación

prospect /'prɒspekt/ n (possibility) posibilidad f (of de); (situation envisaged) perspectiva f. **~s** (chances) perspectivas fpl. **~ive** /prə'spektɪv/ adj posible; (future) futuro. **~or** /prə'spektə(r)/ n prospector m. **~us** /prə'spektəs/ n folleto m informativo

prosper /'prɒspə(r)/ vi prosperar. **~ity** /-'sperətɪ/ n prosperidad f. **~ous** adj próspero

prostitut|e /'prɒstɪtjuːt/ n prostituta f. **~ion** /-'tjuːʃn/ n prostitución f

prostrate /'prɒstreɪt/ adj postrado

p

protagonist /prəˈtægənɪst/ n protagonista m & f

protect /prəˈtekt/ vt proteger. **∼ion** /-ʃn/ n protección f. **∼ive** adj protector. **∼or** n protector m

protein /ˈprəʊtiːn/ n proteína f

protest /ˈprəʊtest/ n protesta f. in **∼ (against)** en señal de protesta (contra). under **∼** bajo protesta. ● /prəˈtest/ vt/i protestar

Protestant /ˈprɒtɪstənt/ adj & n protestante (m & f)

protester /prəˈtestə(r)/ n manifestante m & f

protocol /ˈprəʊtəkɒl/ n protocolo m

protrud|e /prəˈtruːd/ vi sobresalir. **∼ing** adj (chin) prominente. **∼ing eyes** ojos saltones

proud /praʊd/ adj orgulloso. **∼ly** adv con orgullo; (arrogantly) orgullosamente

prove /pruːv/ vt probar; demostrar (loyalty). ● vi resultar. **∼n** adj probado

proverb /ˈprɒvɜːb/ n refrán m, proverbio m

provide /prəˈvaɪd/ vt proporcionar; dar (accommodation). **∼ s.o. with sth** proveer a uno de algo. ● vi. **∼ for** (allow for) prever; mantener (person). **∼d** conj. **∼d (that)** con tal de que, siempre que

providen|ce /ˈprɒvɪdəns/ n providencia f. **∼tial** /-ˈdenʃl/ adj providencial

providing /prəˈvaɪdɪŋ/ conj. **∼ that** con tal de que, siempre que

provinc|e /ˈprɒvɪns/ n provincia f; (fig) competencia f. **∼ial** /prəˈvɪnʃl/ adj provincial

provision /prəˈvɪʒn/ n provisión f; (supply) suministro m; (stipulation) disposición f. **∼s** npl provisiones fpl, víveres mpl. **∼al** adj provisional

provo|cation /prɒvəˈkeɪʃn/ n provocación f. **∼cative** /-ˈvɒkətɪv/ adj provocador. **∼ke** /prəˈvəʊk/ vt provocar

prow /praʊ/ n proa f

prowess /ˈpraʊɪs/ n destreza f; (valour) valor m

prowl /praʊl/ vi merodear. **∼er** n merodeador m

proximity /prɒkˈsɪmətɪ/ n proximidad f

prude /pruːd/ n mojigato m

pruden|ce /ˈpruːdəns/ n prudencia f. **∼t** adj prudente. **∼tly** adv prudentemente

prudish /ˈpruːdɪʃ/ adj mojigato

prune /pruːn/ n ciruela f pasa. ● vt podar

pry /praɪ/ vi curiosear. **∼ into sth** entrometerse en algo. vt (Amer) see PRISE

PS n (postscript) P.D.

psalm /sɑːm/ n salmo m

psychiatr|ic /saɪkɪˈætrɪk/ adj psiquiátrico. **∼ist** /saɪˈkaɪətrɪst/ n psiquiatra m & f. **∼y** /saɪˈkaɪətrɪ/ n psiquiatría f

psychic /ˈsaɪkɪk/ adj para(p)sicológico

psycho|analysis /saɪkəʊəˈnæləsɪs/ n (p)sicoanálisis m. **∼logical** /saɪkəˈlɒdʒɪkl/ adj (p)sicológico. **∼logist** /saɪˈkɒlədʒɪst/ n (p)sicólogo m. **∼logy** /saɪˈkɒlədʒɪ/ n (p)sicología f. **∼therapy** /-ˈθerəpɪ/ n (p)sicoterapia f

pub /pʌb/ n bar m

pub En Gran Bretaña, establecimiento donde se vende cerveza y otras bebidas (alcohólicas y no alcohólicas) para consumir en el local. *Pub* es la forma abreviada de *public house*. Suelen ofrecer comidas y una variedad de juegos, especialmente dardos, billar etc. Recientemente, las horas en que pueden abrir dependen de la licencia, siendo lo normal de 11 - 23 horas.

puberty /ˈpjuːbətɪ/ n pubertad f

pubic /ˈpjuːbɪk/ adj pubiano, púbico

public /ˈpʌblɪk/ adj público. ● n tabernero m. ~**ation** /-ˈkeɪʃn/ n publicación f. ~ **holiday** n día m festivo, día m feriado (*LAm*). ~ **house** n bar m. ~**ity** /pʌbˈlɪsətɪ/ n publicidad f. ~**ize** /ˈpʌblɪəsaɪz/ vt hacer público. ~**ly** adv públicamente. ~ **school** n colegio m privado; (*Amer*) instituto m, escuela f pública

public school En Inglaterra y Gales, un colegio privado para alumnos de edades comprendidas entre los 13 y 18 años. La mayoría de estos colegios tiene régimen de internado y a menudo son mixtos. En EE.UU. y Escocia, el término se utiliza para referirse a un colegio estatal.

publish /ˈpʌblɪʃ/ vt publicar. ~**er** n editor m. ~**ing** n publicación f. ~**ing house** editorial f.

pudding /ˈpʊdɪŋ/ n postre m; (*steamed*) budín m

puddle /ˈpʌdl/ n charco m

Puerto Ric|an /pwɜːtəʊˈriːkən/ adj & n portorriqueño (m), puertorriqueño (m). ~**o** /-əʊ/ n Puerto Rico m

puff /pʌf/ n (*of wind*) ráfaga f; (*of*

smoke) nube f; (*action*) soplo m; (*on cigarette*) chupada f, calada f. ● vi/i soplar. ~ **at** dar chupadas a (pipe). ~ **out** (*swell up*) inflar, hinchar. ~**ed** adj (*out of breath*) sin aliento. ~ **paste** (*Amer*), ~ **pastry** n hojaldre m. ~**y** adj hinchado

pull /pʊl/ vt tirar de, jalar (*LAm*); desgarrarse (muscle). ~ **a face** hacer una mueca. ~ **a fast one** hacer una mala jugada. ● vi tirar, jalar (*LAm*). ● n tirón m, jalón m (*LAm*); (*pulling force*) fuerza f; (*influence*) influencia f. □ ~ **away** vi (*Auto*) alejarse. □ ~ **back** vi retirarse. □ ~ **down** vt echar abajo (building); (*lower*) bajar. □ ~ **in** vi (*Auto*) parar. □ ~ **off** vt (*remove*) quitar; (*achieve*) conseguir. □ ~ **out** vt sacar; retirar (team). vi salirse. □ ~ **through** vi recobrar la salud. □ ~ **up** vi (*Auto*) parar. vt (*uproot*) arrancar; (*reprimand*) regañar

pullover /ˈpʊləʊvə(r)/ n suéter m, pulóver m, jersey m

pulp /pʌlp/ n pulpa f; (*for paper*) pasta f

pulpit /ˈpʊlpɪt/ n púlpito m

pulse /pʌls/ n (*Med*) pulso m; (*Culin*) legumbre f

pummel /ˈpʌml/ vt (*pt* pummelled) aporrear

pump /pʌmp/ n bomba f; (*for petrol*) surtidor m. ● vt sacar con una bomba. □ ~ **up** vt inflar

pumpkin /ˈpʌmpkɪn/ n calabaza f

pun /pʌn/ n juego m de palabras

punch /pʌntʃ/ vt darle un puñetazo a; (*perforate*) perforar; hacer (hole). ● n puñetazo m; (*vigour*) fuerza f; (*device*) perforadora f; (*drink*) ponche m. □ ~ **in** vi (*Amer*) fichar (*al entrar al trabajo*). ~ **out** vi (*Amer*) fichar (*al salir del trabajo*)

punctual /ˈpʌŋktʃʊəl/ adj puntual. ~**ity** /-ˈælətɪ/ n puntualidad f. ~**ly** adv puntualmente

punctuat|e /ˈpʌŋktʃʊeɪt/ vt puntuar. ~**ion** /-ˈeɪʃn/ n puntuación f

puncture /ˈpʌŋktʃə(r)/ n (in tyre) pinchazo m. have a ~ pinchar. ● vi pincharse

punish /ˈpʌnɪʃ/ vt castigar. ~**ment** n castigo m

punk /pʌŋk/ n punk m & f, punki m & f; (Music) punk m; (Amer, hoodlum) vándalo m

punt /pʌnt/ n (boat) batea f. ~**er** n apostante m & f

puny /ˈpjuːnɪ/ adj (-ier, -iest) enclenque

pup /pʌp/ n cachorro m

pupil /ˈpjuːpl/ n alumno m; (of eye) pupila f

puppet /ˈpʌpɪt/ n marioneta f, títere m; (glove ~) títere m

puppy /ˈpʌpɪ/ n cachorro m

purchase /ˈpɜːtʃəs/ vt adquirir. ● n adquisición f. ~**r** n comprador m

pur|e /ˈpjʊə(r)/ adj (-er, -est) puro. ~**ity** n pureza f

purgatory /ˈpɜːɡətrɪ/ n purgatorio m

purge /pɜːdʒ/ vt purgar. ● n purga f

purif|ication /pjʊərɪfɪˈkeɪʃn/ n purificación f. ~**y** /ˈpjʊərɪfaɪ/ vt purificar

purist /ˈpjʊərɪst/ n purista m & f

puritan /ˈpjʊərɪtən/ n puritano m. ~**ical** /-ˈtænɪkl/ adj puritano

purple /ˈpɜːpl/ adj morado. ● n morado m, púrpura f

purport /pəˈpɔːt/ vt. ~ **to be** pretender ser

purpose /ˈpɜːpəs/ n propósito m; (determination) resolución f. on ~ a propósito. **serve a** ~ servir de algo. ~**ful** adj (resolute) resuelto. ~**ly** adv a propósito

purr /pɜː(r)/ vi ronronear

purse /pɜːs/ n monedero m; (Amer) bolso m, cartera f (LAm), bolsa f (Mex)

pursu|e /pəˈsjuː/ vt perseguir, continuar con (course of action). ~**it** /pəˈsjuːt/ n persecución f; (pastime) actividad f

pus /pʌs/ n pus m

push /pʊʃ/ vt empujar; apretar (button). ● vi empujar. ● n empujón m; (effort) esfuerzo m. □ ~ **back** vt hacer retroceder. □ ~ **off** vi ⓧ largarse. ~**chair** n sillita f de paseo, carreola f (Mex). ~**y** adj (pej) ambicioso

pussy /ˈpʊsɪ/ (pl -**sies**), **pussycat** /ˈpʊsɪkæt/ n ① minino m

put /pʊt/ vt (pt put, pres p **putting**) poner; (with care, precision) colocar; (inside sth) meter; (express) decir. □ ~ **across** vt comunicar. □ ~ **away** vt guardar. □ ~ **back** vt volver a poner; retrasar (clock). □ ~ **by** vt guardar; ahorrar (money). □ ~ **down** vt (on a surface) dejar; colgar (phone); (suppress) sofocar; (write) apuntar; (kill) sacrificar. □ ~ **forward** vt presentar (plan); proponer (candidate); adelantar (clocks); adelantar (meeting). □ ~ **in** vt (instal) poner; presentar (claim). □ ~ **in for** solicitar. □ ~ **off** vt aplazar, posponer; (disconcert) desconcertar. □ ~ **on** vt (wear) ponerse; poner (CD, music); encender (light). □ ~ **out** vt (extinguish) apagar; (inconvenience) incomodar; extender (hand); (disconcert) desconcertar. □ ~ **through** vt (phone) poner, pasar (to con). □ ~ **up** vt levantar; aumentar (rent); subir (price); poner (sign); alojar (guest). □ ∼ **up with** vt aguantar, soportar

putrid /'pju:trɪd/ adj putrefacto

putt /pʌt/ n (golf) golpe m suave

puzzle /'pʌzl/ n misterio m; (game) rompecabezas m. • vt dejar perplejo. ∼**ed** adj (expression) de desconcierto. I'm ∼**ed** about it me tiene perplejo. ∼**ing** adj incomprensible; (odd) curioso

pygmy /'pɪgmɪ/ n pigmeo m

pyjamas /pə'dʒɑːməz/ npl pijama m, piyama m or f (LAm)

pylon /'paɪlɒn/ n pilón m

pyramid /'pɪrəmɪd/ n pirámide f

python /'paɪθn/ n pitón m

Qq

quack /kwæk/ n (of duck) graznido m; (person) charlatán m. ∼ **doctor** n curandero m

quadrangle /'kwɒdræŋgl/ n cuadrilátero m

quadruped /'kwɒdruped/ n cuadrúpedo m

quadruple /'kwɒdrʊpl/ adj & n cuádruplo (m). • vt cuadruplicar

quagmire /'kwægmaɪə(r)/ n lodazal m

quail /kweɪl/ n codorniz f

quaint /kweɪnt/ adj (-er, -est) pintoresco; (odd) curioso

quake /kweɪk/ vi temblar. • n □ terremoto m

qualification /kwɒlɪfɪ'keɪʃn/ n título m; (requirement) requisito m; (ability) capacidad f; (Sport) clasifica-

ción f; (fig) reserva f. ∼**ied** /'kwɒlɪfaɪd/ adj cualificado; (with degree, diploma) titulado; (competent) capacitado. ∼**y** /'kwɒlɪfaɪ/ vt calificar; (limit) limitar. • vi titularse; (Sport) clasificarse. ∼**y for sth** (be entitled to) tener derecho a algo

qualitative /'kwɒlɪtətɪv/ adj cualitativo. ∼**y** /'kwɒlɪtɪ/ n calidad f; (attribute) cualidad f

qualm /kwɑːm/ n reparo m

quandary /'kwɒndrɪ/ n dilema m

quantify /'kwɒntɪfaɪ/ vt cuantificar. ∼**ty** /-tɪ/ n cantidad f

quarantine /'kwɒrəntiːn/ n cuarentena f. • vt poner en cuarentena

quarrel /'kwɒrəl/ n pelea f. • vi (pt quarrelled) pelearse, discutir. ∼**some** /-səm/ adj pendenciero

quarry /'kwɒrɪ/ n (excavation) cantera f; (prey) presa f

quart /kwɔːt/ n cuarto m de galón

quarter /'kwɔːtə(r)/ n cuarto m; (of year) trimestre m; (district) barrio m. **a ∼ of an hour** un cuarto de hora. • vt dividir en cuartos; (Mil) acuartelar. ∼**-final** n cuarto m de final. ∼**ly** adj trimestral. • adv trimestralmente

quartz /kwɔːts/ n cuarzo m

quay /kiː/ n muelle m

queasy /'kwiːzɪ/ adj mareado

queen /kwiːn/ n reina f. ∼ **mother** n reina f madre

queer /kwɪə(r)/ adj (-er, -est) extraño

quench /kwentʃ/ vt quitar (thirst); sofocar (desire)

query /'kwɪərɪ/ n pregunta f. • vt preguntar; (doubt) poner en duda

quest /kwest/ n busca f

question /'kwestʃən/ n pregunta f; (for discussion) cuestión f. **in ∼** en cuestión. **out of the ∼** imposi-

p
q

ble. without ~ sin duda. ●vt
hacer preguntas a; (police etc) interrogar; (doubt) poner en duda.
~able adj discutible. ~ mark n
signo m de interrogación. ~naire
/-'neə(r)/ n cuestionario m

queue /kjuː/ n cola f. ●vi (pres p
queuing) hacer cola

quibble /'kwɪbl/ vi discutir; (split
hairs) sutilizar

quick /kwɪk/ adj (-er, -est) rápido.
be ~! ¡date prisa! ●adv rápido.
~en vt acelerar. ● vi acelerarse.
~ly adv rápido. ~sand n arena f
movediza. ~-tempered /-'tempəd/
adj irascible

quid /kwɪd/ n invar £ libra f (esterlina)

quiet /'kwaɪət/ adj (-er, -est) tranquilo; (silent) callado; (discreet) discreto. ● n tranquilidad f. ●vt/i
(Amer) see QUIETEN. ~en vt calmar.
● n calmarse. ~ly adv tranquilamente; (silently) silenciosamente;
(discreetly) discretamente. ~ness n
tranquilidad f

quilt /kwɪlt/ n edredón m. ~ed adj
acolchado

quintet /kwɪn'tet/ n quinteto m

quirk /kwɜːk/ n peculiaridad f

quit /kwɪt/ vt (pt quitted) dejar. ~
doing (Amer, cease) dejar de hacer.
●vi (give in) abandonar; (stop)
parar; (resign) dimitir

quite /kwaɪt/ adv bastante; (completely) totalmente; (really) verdaderamente. ~ (so)! ¡claro! ~ a
few bastantes

quits /kwɪts/ adj. be ~ estar en
paz. call it ~ darlo por terminado

quiver /'kwɪvə(r)/ vi temblar

quiz /kwɪz/ n (pl quizzes) serie f
de preguntas; (game) concurso m.
●vt (pt quizzed) interrogar. ~zical
/-ɪkl/ adj burlón

quota /'kwəʊtə/ n cuota f

quot|ation /kwəʊ'teɪʃn/ n cita f;
(price) presupuesto m. ~ation
marks npl comillas fpl. ~e /kwəʊt/
vt citar; (Com) cotizar. ● n 🅳 cita f;
(price) presupuesto m. **in ~es** npl
entre comillas

....

Rr

....

rabbi /'ræbaɪ/ n rabino m

rabbit /'ræbɪt/ n conejo m

rabi|d /'ræbɪd/ adj feroz; (dog) ra-
bioso. ~es /'reɪbiːz/ n rabia f

race /reɪs/ n (in sport) carrera f;
(ethnic group) raza f. ●vt hacer correr (horse). ●vi (run) correr, ir corriendo; (rush) ir de prisa.
~course n hipódromo m. ~horse
n caballo m de carreras. ~rela-
tions npl relaciones fpl raciales.
~track n hipódromo m

racial /'reɪʃl/ adj racial

racing /'reɪsɪŋ/ n carreras fpl. ~
car n coche m de carreras

racis|m /'reɪsɪzəm/ n racismo m.
~t adj & n racista (m & f)

rack¹ /ræk/ n (shelf) estante m;
(for luggage) rejilla f; (for plates)
escurreplatos m. ●vt. ~ one's
brains devanarse los sesos

rack² /ræk/ n. go to ~ and ruin
quedarse en la ruina

racket /'rækɪt/ n (for sports) raqueta; (din) alboroto m; (swindle)
estafa f. ~eer /-ə'tɪə(r)/ n estafador m

racy /'reɪsɪ/ adj (-ier, -iest) vivo

radar /'reɪdɑː(r)/ n radar m

radian|ce /'reɪdɪəns/ n resplandor m. **~t** adj radiante

radiat|e /'reɪdɪeɪt/ vt irradiar. ● vi divergir. **~ion** /-'eɪʃn/ n radiación f. **~or** n radiador m

radical /'rædɪkl/ adj & n radical (m)

radio /'reɪdɪəʊ/ n (pl -os) radio f or m. ● vt transmitir por radio. **~active** /reɪdɪəʊˈæktɪv/ adj radiactivo. **~activity** /-'tɪvətɪ/ n radiactividad f

radish /'rædɪʃ/ n rábano m

radius /'reɪdɪəs/ n (pl -dii /-dɪaɪ/) radio m

raffle /'ræfl/ n rifa f

raft /rɑːft/ n balsa f

rafter /'rɑːftə(r)/ n cabrio m

rag /ræg/ n andrajo m; (for wiping) trapo m. in **~s** (person) andrajoso

rage /reɪdʒ/ n rabia f; (fashion) moda f. ● vi estar furioso; (storm) bramar

ragged /'rægɪd/ adj (person) andrajoso; (clothes) hecho jirones

raid /reɪd/ n (Mil) incursión f; (by police etc) redada f; (by thieves) asalto m. ● vt (Mil) atacar; (police) hacer una redada en; (thieves) asaltar. **~er** n invasor m; (thief) ladrón m

rail /reɪl/ n barandilla f; (for train) riel m; (rod) barra f. by **~** por ferrocarril. **~ing** n barandilla f; (fence) verja f. **~road** (Amer), **~way** n ferrocarril m. **~way station** n estación f de ferrocarril

rain /reɪn/ n lluvia f. ● vi llover. **~bow** /-bəʊ/ n arco m iris. **~coat** n impermeable m. **~fall** n precipitación f. **~y** adj (-ier, -iest) lluvioso

raise /reɪz/ vt levantar; (breed) criar; obtener (money etc); formular (question); plantear (problem);

subir (price). ● n (Amer) aumento m

raisin /'reɪzn/ n (uva f) pasa f

rake /reɪk/ n rastrillo m. ● vt rastrillar; (search) buscar en. □ **~ up** vt remover

rally /'rælɪ/ vt reunir; (revive) reanimar. ● n reunión f; (Auto) rally m

ram /ræm/ n carnero m. ● vt (pt rammed) (thrust) meter por la fuerza; (crash into) chocar con

RAM /ræm/ n (Comp) RAM f

rambl|e /'ræmbl/ n excursión f a pie. ● vi ir de paseo; (in speech) divagar. □ **~e on** vi divagar. **~er** n excursionista m & f. **~ing** adj (speech) divagador

ramp /ræmp/ n rampa f

rampage /ræm'peɪdʒ/ vi alborotarse. ● /'ræmpeɪdʒ/ n. go on the **~** alborotarse

ramshackle /'ræmʃækl/ adj desvencijado

ran /ræn/ see RUN

ranch /rɑːntʃ/ n hacienda f

random /'rændəm/ adj hecho al azar; (chance) fortuito. ● n. at **~** al azar

rang /ræŋ/ see RING²

range /reɪndʒ/ n alcance m; (distance) distancia f; (series) serie f; (of mountains) cordillera f; (extent) extensión f; (Com) surtido m; (stove) cocina f económica. ● vi extenderse; (vary) variar. **~r** n guardabosque m

rank /ræŋk/ n posición f, categoría f; (row) fila f; (for taxis) parada f. the **~** and file la masa f. **~s** npl soldados mpl rasos. ● adj (-er, -est) (smell) fétido; (fig) completo. ● vt clasificar. ● vi clasificarse

ransack /'rænsæk/ vt registrar; (pillage) saquear

ransom /'rænsəm/ n rescate m.

r

hold s.o. to ~ exigir rescate por uno. ● vt rescatar; (*redeem*) redimir

rant /rænt/ vi despotricar

rap /ræp/ n golpe m seco. ● vt/i (pt rapped) golpear

rape /reɪp/ vt violar. ● n violación f

rapid /ˈræpɪd/ adj rápido. ~s npl rápidos mpl

rapist /ˈreɪpɪst/ n violador m

rapture /ˈræptʃə(r)/ n éxtasis m. ~ous /-rəs/ adj extático

rare /reə(r)/ adj (-er, -est) raro; (*Culin*) poco hecho. ~fied /ˈreərɪfaɪd/ adj enrarecido. ~ly adv raramente

raring /ˈreərɪŋ/ adj 🔢. ~ to impaciente por

rarity /ˈreərətɪ/ n rareza f

rascal /ˈrɑːskl/ n granuja m & f

rash /ræʃ/ adj (-er, -est) precipitado, imprudente. ● n erupción f

rasher /ˈræʃə(r)/ n loncha f

rashly /ˈræʃlɪ/ adv precipitadamente, imprudentemente

rasp /rɑːsp/ n (*file*) escofina f

raspberry /ˈrɑːzbrɪ/ n frambuesa f

rat /ræt/ n rata f

rate /reɪt/ n (*ratio*) proporción f; (*speed*) velocidad f; (*price*) precio m; (*of interest*) tipo m. at any ~ de todas formas. at this ~ así. ~s npl (*taxes*) impuestos mpl municipales. ● vt valorar; (*consider*) considerar. ● vi ser considerado

rather /ˈrɑːðə(r)/ adv mejor dicho; (*fairly*) bastante; (*a little*) un poco. ● int claro. I would ~ not prefiero no

rating /ˈreɪtɪŋ/ n clasificación f; (*sailor*) marinero m; (*number, TV*) índice m

ratio /ˈreɪʃɪəʊ/ n (pl -os) proporción f

ration /ˈræʃn/ n ración f. ~s npl (*provisions*) víveres mpl. ● vt racionar

rational /ˈræʃənəl/ adj racional. ~ize vt racionalizar

rattle /ˈrætl/ vi traquetear. ● vt (*shake*) agitar; 🔢 desconcertar. ● n traqueteo m; (*toy*) sonajero m. □ ~ off vt (*fig*) decir de corrida

raucous /ˈrɔːkəs/ adj estridente

ravage /ˈrævɪdʒ/ vt estragar

rave /reɪv/ vi delirar; (*in anger*) despotricar. ~ about sth poner a algo por las nubes

raven /ˈreɪvn/ n cuervo m

ravenous /ˈrævənəs/ adj voraz; (*person*) hambriento. be ~ morirse de hambre

ravine /rəˈviːn/ n barranco m

raving /ˈreɪvɪŋ/ adj. ~ mad loco de atar

ravishing /ˈrævɪʃɪŋ/ adj (*enchanting*) encantador

raw /rɔː/ adj (-er, -est) crudo; (*sugar*) sin refinar; (*inexperienced*) inexperto. ~ deal n tratamiento m injusto, injusticia f. ~ materials npl materias fpl primas

ray /reɪ/ n rayo m

raze /reɪz/ vt arrasar

razor /ˈreɪzə(r)/ n navaja f de afeitar; (*electric*) maquinilla f de afeitar

Rd /rəʊd/ abbr (= Road) C/, Calle f

re /riː/ prep con referencia a. ● pref re.

reach /riːtʃ/ vt alcanzar; (*extend*) extender; (*arrive at*) llegar a; (*achieve*) lograr; (*hand over*) pasar, dar. ● vi extenderse. ● n alcance m. within ~ of al alcance de; (*close to*) a corta distancia de. □ ~ out vi alargar la mano

react /rɪˈækt/ vi reaccionar. **~ion** /rɪˈækʃn/ n reacción f. **~ionary** adj & n reaccionario (m). **~or** /rɪˈæktə(r)/ n reactor m

read /riːd/ vt (pt read /red/) leer; (study) estudiar; (interpret) interpretar. ● vi leer; (instrument) indicar. □ **~ out** vt leer en voz alta. **~able** adj (clear) legible. **~er** n lector m

readily /ˈredɪlɪ/ adv (willingly) de buena gana; (easily) fácilmente

reading /ˈriːdɪŋ/ n lectura f

readjust /riːəˈdʒʌst/ vt reajustar. ● vi readaptarse (to a)

ready /ˈredɪ/ adj (-ier, -iest) listo, preparado. get **~** prepararse. **~-made** adj confeccionado

real /rɪəl/ adj verdadero. ● adv (Amer fam) verdaderamente. **~ estate** n bienes mpl raíces, propiedad f inmobiliaria. **~ estate agent** see REALTOR. **~ism** n realismo m. **~ist** n realista m & f. **~istic** /-ˈlɪstɪk/ adj realista. **~ity** /rɪˈælətɪ/ n realidad f. **~ization** /rɪəlaɪˈzeɪʃn/ n comprensión f. **~ize** /ˈrɪəlaɪz/ vt darse cuenta de; (fulfil, Com) realizar. **~ly** /ˈrɪəlɪ/ adv verdaderamente

realm /relm/ n reino m

realtor /ˈriːəltə(r)/ n (Amer) agente m inmobiliario

reap /riːp/ vt segar; (fig) cosechar

reappear /riːəˈpɪə(r)/ vi reaparecer

rear /rɪə(r)/ n parte f de atrás. ● adj posterior, trasero. ● vt (bring up, breed) criar. ● vi **~ (up)** (horse) encabritarse

rearguard /ˈrɪəɡɑːd/ n retaguardia f

rearrange /riːəˈreɪndʒ/ vt arreglar de otra manera

reason /ˈriːzn/ n razón f, motivo m. within **~** dentro de lo razona-

ble. ● vi razonar. **~able** adj razonable. **~ing** n razonamiento m

reassur|ance /riːəˈʃʊərəns/ n promesa f tranquilizadora; (guarantee) garantía f. **~e** /riːəˈʃʊə(r)/ vt tranquilizar

rebate /ˈriːbeɪt/ n (discount) rebaja f

rebel /ˈrebl/ n rebelde m & f. ● /rɪˈbel/ vi (pt rebelled) rebelarse. **~lion** /rɪˈbelɪən/ n rebelión f. **~lious** adj rebelde

rebound /rɪˈbaʊnd/ vi rebotar; (fig) recaer. ● /ˈriːbaʊnd/ n rebote m

rebuff /rɪˈbʌf/ vt rechazar. ● n desaire m

rebuild /riːˈbɪld/ vt (pt rebuilt) reconstruir

rebuke /rɪˈbjuːk/ vt reprender. ● n reprimenda f

recall /rɪˈkɔːl/ (call s.o. back) llamar; (remember) recordar. ● n /ˈriːkɔːl/ (of goods, ambassador) retirada f; (memory) memoria f

recap /ˈriːkæp/ vt/i (pt recapped) 🗉 resumir

recapitulate /riːkəˈpɪtʃʊleɪt/ vt/i resumir

recapture /riːˈkæptʃə(r)/ vt recobrar; (recall) hacer revivir

recede /rɪˈsiːd/ vi retroceder

receipt /rɪˈsiːt/ n recibo m. **~s** npl (Com) ingresos mpl

receive /rɪˈsiːv/ vt recibir. **~r** n (of stolen goods) perista m & f; (part of phone) auricular m

recent /ˈriːsnt/ adj reciente. **~ly** adv recientemente

recept|ion /rɪˈsepʃn/ n recepción f; (welcome) acogida f. **~ionist** n recepcionista m & f. **~ive** /-tɪv/ adj receptivo

recess /rɪˈses/ n hueco m; (holiday)

r

vacaciones *fpl.* ~**ion** /rɪˈseʃn/ *n* recesión *f*

recharge /riːˈtʃɑːdʒ/ *vt* cargar de nuevo, recargar

recipe /ˈresəpɪ/ *n* receta *f*. ~ **book** *n* libro *m* de cocina

recipient /rɪˈsɪpɪənt/ *n* recipiente *m* & *f*; (*of letter*) destinatario *m*

recit|al /rɪˈsaɪtl/ *n* (*Mus*) recital *m*. ~**e** /rɪˈsaɪt/ *vt* recitar; (*list*) enumerar

reckless /ˈreklɪs/ *adj* imprudente. ~**ly** *adv* imprudentemente

reckon /ˈrekən/ *vt/i* calcular; (*consider*) considerar; (*think*) pensar. □ ~ **on** *vt* (*rely*) contar con

reclaim /rɪˈkleɪm/ *vt* reclamar; recuperar (*land*)

reclin|e /rɪˈklaɪn/ *vi* recostarse. ~**ing** *adj* acostado; (*seat*) reclinable

recluse /rɪˈkluːs/ *n* ermitaño *m*

recogni|tion /rekəgˈnɪʃn/ *n* reconocimiento *m*. beyond ~**tion** irreconocible. ~**ze** /ˈrekəgnaɪz/ *vt* reconocer

recoil /rɪˈkɔɪl/ *vi* retroceder. ● /ˈriːkɔɪl/ *n* (*of gun*) culatazo *m*

recollect /rekəˈlekt/ *vt* recordar. ~**ion** /-ʃn/ *n* recuerdo *m*

recommend /rekəˈmend/ *vt* recomendar. ~**ation** /-ˈdeɪʃn/ *n* recomendación *f*

reconcile /ˈrekənsaɪl/ *vt* reconciliar (*people*); conciliar (*facts*). ~**e** o.s. resignarse (to a). ~**iation** /-sɪlɪˈeɪʃn/ *n* reconciliación *f*

reconnaissance /rɪˈkɒnɪsns/ *n* reconocimiento *m*

reconnoitre /rekəˈnɔɪtə(r)/ *vt* (*pres p* -**tring**) (*Mil*) reconocer

re: ~**consider** /riːkənˈsɪdə(r)/ *vt* volver a considerar. ~**construct** /riːkənˈstrʌkt/ *vt* reconstruir

record /rɪˈkɔːd/ *vt* (*in register*) registrar; (*in diary*) apuntar; (*Mus*) grabar. ● /ˈrekɔːd/ *n* (*document*) documento *m*; (*of events*) registro *m*; (*Mus*) disco *m*; (*Sport*) récord *m*. off the ~ en confianza. ~**er** /rɪˈkɔːdə(r)/ *n* registrador *m*; (*Mus*) flauta *f* dulce. ~**ing** /rɪˈkɔːdɪŋ/ *n* grabación *f*. ~**-player** /ˈrekɔːd-/ *n* tocadiscos *m invar*

recount /rɪˈkaʊnt/ *vt* contar, relatar

re-count /riːˈkaʊnt/ *vt* volver a contar; recontar (votes). ● /ˈriːkaʊnt/ *n* (*Pol*) recuento *m*

recover /rɪˈkʌvə(r)/ *vt* recuperar. ● *vi* reponerse. ~**y** *n* recuperación *f*

recreation /rekrɪˈeɪʃn/ *n* recreo *m*. ~**al** *adj* de recreo

recruit /rɪˈkruːt/ *n* recluta *m*. ● *vt* reclutar; contratar (staff). ~**ment** *n* reclutamiento *m*

rectang|le /ˈrektæŋgl/ *n* rectángulo *m*. ~**ular** /-ˈtæŋgjʊlə(r)/ *adj* rectangular

rectify /ˈrektɪfaɪ/ *vt* rectificar

rector /ˈrektə(r)/ *n* párroco *m*; (*of college*) rector *m*. ~**y** *n* rectoría *f*

recuperat|e /rɪˈkuːpəreɪt/ *vt* recuperar. ● *vi* reponerse. ~**ion** /-ˈreɪʃn/ *n* recuperación *f*

recur /rɪˈkɜː(r)/ *vi* (*pt* recurred) repetirse. ~**rence** /rɪˈkʌrns/ *n* repetición *f*. ~**rent** /rɪˈkʌrənt/ *adj* repetido

recycle /riːˈsaɪkl/ *vt* reciclar

red /red/ *adj* (redder, reddest) rojo. ● *n* rojo. be in the ~ estar en números rojos. ~**den** *vi* enrojecerse. ~**dish** *adj* rojizo

redecorate /riːˈdekəreɪt/ *vt* pintar de nuevo

rede|em /rɪˈdiːm/ *vt* redimir. ~**mption** /-ˈdempʃn/ *n* redención *f*

red: ~**-handed** /-'hændɪd/ adj.
catch s.o. ~**handed** agarrar a uno
con las manos en la masa. ~
herring n (fig) pista f falsa.
~**-hot** adj al rojo vivo. ~ **light** n
luz f roja

redo /riː'duː/ vt (pt **redid**, pp **re-**
done) rehacer

redouble /rɪ'dʌbl/ vt redoblar

red tape /red'teɪp/ n (fig) papeleo m

reduc|e /rɪ'djuːs/ vt reducir; aliviar
(pain). • vi (Amer, slim) adelgazar.
~**tion** /rɪ'dʌkʃn/ n reducción f

redundan|cy /rɪ'dʌndənsɪ/ n su-
perfluidad f; (unemployment) despido m. ~**t** superfluo. she was
made ~**t** la despidieron por reducción de plantilla

reed /riːd/ n caña f; (Mus) lengüeta f

reef /riːf/ n arrecife m

reek /riːk/ n mal olor m. • vi. ~
(of) apestar a

reel /riːl/ n carrete m. • vi dar vueltas; (stagger) tambalearse. □ ~ **off**
vt (fig) enumerar

refectory /rɪ'fektərɪ/ n refecto-
rio m

refer /rɪ'fɜː(r)/ vt (pt **referred**) remitir. • vi referirse. ~ **to** referirse
a; (consult) consultar. ~**ee** /refə
'riː/ n árbitro m; (for job) referencia
f. • vi (pt **refereed**) arbitrar. ~**ence**
/'refrəns/ n referencia f. ~**ence**
book n libro m de consulta. **in** ~
to, with ~ **to** con referencia a;
(Com) respecto a. ~**endum** /refə
'rendəm/ n (pl -ums or -da) referéndum m

refill /riː'fɪl/ vt volver a llenar.
• /'riːfɪl/ n recambio m

refine /rɪ'faɪn/ vt refinar. ~**d** adj
refinado. ~**ry** /-ərɪ/ n refinería f

reflect /rɪ'flekt/ vt reflejar. • vi re-
flejarse; (think) reflexionar. □ ~
badly upon perjudicar. ~**ion** /-ʃn/
n reflexión f; (image) reflejo m.
~**or** n reflector m

reflex /'riːfleks/ adj & n reflejo (m).
~**ive** /rɪ'fleksɪv/ adj (Gram) reflexivo

reform /rɪ'fɔːm/ vt reformar. • vi
reformarse. n reforma f

refrain /rɪ'freɪn/ n estribillo m. • vi
abstenerse (from de)

refresh /rɪ'freʃ/ vt refrescar. ~**ing**
adj refrescante. ~**ments** npl (food
and drink) refrigerio m

refrigerat|e /rɪ'frɪdʒəreɪt/ vt re-
frigerar. ~**or** n frigorífico m, refrigerador m (LAm)

refuel /riː'fjuːəl/ vt/i (pt **refuelled**)
repostar

refuge /'refjuːdʒ/ n refugio m.
take ~ refugiarse. ~**e** /refjuˈdʒiː/
n refugiado m

refund /rɪ'fʌnd/ vt reembolsar.
• /'riːfʌnd/ n reembolso m

refusal /rɪ'fjuːzl/ n negativa f

refuse /rɪ'fjuːz/ vt rehusar. • vi ne-
garse. • /'refjuːs/ n residuos mpl

refute /rɪ'fjuːt/ vt refutar

regain /rɪ'geɪn/ vt recobrar

regal /'riːgl/ adj real

regard /rɪ'gɑːd/ vt considerar;
(look at) contemplar. **as** ~**s** en lo
que se refiere a. • n (consideration)
consideración f; (esteem) estima f.
~**s** npl saludos mpl. **kind** ~**s** recuerdos. ~**ing** prep en lo que se
refiere a. ~**less** adv a pesar de
todo. ~**less of** sin tener en cuenta

regatta /rɪ'gætə/ n regata f

regime /reɪ'ʒiːm/ n régimen m

regiment /'redʒɪmənt/ n regimiento m. ~**al** /-'mentl/ adj del regimiento

r

region /'riːdʒən/ n región f. **in the ~ of** alrededor de. **~al** adj regional

register /'redʒɪstə(r)/ n registro m. ● vt registrar; matricular (vehicle); declarar (birth); certificar (letter); facturar (luggage). ● vi (enrol) inscribirse; (fig) producir impresión

registrar /redʒɪ'strɑː(r)/ n secretario m del registro civil; (Univ) secretario m general

registration /redʒɪ'streɪʃn/ n registro m; (in register) inscripción f. **~ number** n (Auto) (número de) matrícula f

registry /'redʒɪstrɪ/ n. **~ office** n registro m civil

regret /rɪ'gret/ n pesar m; (remorse) arrepentimiento m. ● vt (pt regretted) lamentar. **I ~ that** siento (que). **~table** adj lamentable

regula|r /'regjʊlə(r)/ adj regular; (usual) habitual. ● n 🔲 cliente m habitual. **~rity** /-'lærətɪ/ n regularidad f. **~rly** adv con regularidad. **~te** /'regjʊleɪt/ vt regular; (rule) regla f. **~tion** /-'leɪʃn/ n regulación f; (rule) regla f.

rehears|al /rɪ'hɜːsl/ n ensayo m. **~e** /rɪ'hɜːs/ vt ensayar

reign /reɪn/ n reinado m. ● vi reinar

reindeer /'reɪndɪə(r)/ n invar reno m

reinforce /riːɪn'fɔːs/ vt reforzar. **~ment** n refuerzo m

reins /reɪnz/ npl riendas fpl

reiterate /riː'ɪtəreɪt/ vt reiterar

reject /rɪ'dʒekt/ vt rechazar. ● /'riːdʒekt/ n producto m defectuoso. **~ion** /rɪ'dʒekʃn/ n rechazo m; (after job application) respuesta f negativa

rejoice /rɪ'dʒɔɪs/ vi regocijarse

rejoin /rɪ'dʒɔɪn/ vt reunirse con

rejuvenate /rɪ'dʒuːvəneɪt/ vt rejuvenecer

relapse /rɪ'læps/ n recaída f. ● vi recaer; (into crime) reincidir

relat|e /rɪ'leɪt/ vt contar; (connect) relacionar. ● vi relacionarse (to con). **~ed** adj emparentado; (ideas etc) relacionado. **~ion** /rɪ'leɪʃn/ n relación f; (person) pariente m & f. **~ionship** n relación f; (blood tie) parentesco m; (affair) relaciones fpl. **~ive** /'relətɪv/ n pariente m & f. ● adj relativo. **~ively** adv relativamente

relax /rɪ'læks/ vt relajar. ● vi relajarse. **~ation** /-'seɪʃn/ n relajación f; (rest) descanso m; (recreation) recreo m. **~ing** adj relajante

relay /'riːleɪ/ n relevo m. **~ (race)** n carrera f de relevos. ● /rɪ'leɪ/ vt transmitir

release /rɪ'liːs/ vt soltar; poner en libertad (prisoner); estrenar (film); (Mec) soltar; publicar (news). ● n liberación f; (of film) estreno m; (record) disco m nuevo

relent /rɪ'lent/ vi ceder. **~less** adj implacable; (continuous) incesante

relevan|ce /'reləvəns/ n pertinencia f. **~t** adj pertinente

relia|bility /rɪlaɪə'bɪlətɪ/ n fiabilidad f. **~ble** /rɪ'laɪəbl/ adj (person) de confianza; (car) fiable. **~nce** /rɪ'laɪəns/ n dependencia f; (trust) confianza f. **~nt** /rɪ'laɪənt/ adj confiado

relic /'relɪk/ n reliquia f

relie|f /rɪ'liːf/ n alivio m; (assistance) socorro m. **be on ~f** (Amer) recibir prestaciones de la seguridad social. **~ve** /rɪ'liːv/ vt aliviar; (take over from) relevar. **~ved** adj aliviado. **feel ~ved** sentir un gran alivio

religio|n /rɪ'lɪdʒən/ n religión f. **~us** /rɪ'lɪdʒəs/ adj religioso

relinquish /rɪ'lɪŋkwɪʃ/ vt abandonar, renunciar

relish /'relɪʃ/ n gusto m; (Culin) salsa f. ● vt saborear

reluctan|ce /rɪ'lʌktəns/ n desgana f. **~t** adj mal dispuesto. **be ~t to** no tener ganas de. **~tly** adv de mala gana

rely /rɪ'laɪ/ vi. **~ on** contar con; (trust) fiarse de; (depend) depender

remain /rɪ'meɪn/ vi (be left) quedar; (stay) quedarse; (continue to be) seguir. **~der** n resto m. **~s** npl restos mpl; (left-overs) sobras fpl

remand /rɪ'mɑːnd/ vt. **~ in custody** mantener bajo custodia. ● n. **on ~** en prisión preventiva

remark /rɪ'mɑːk/ n observación f. ● vt observar. **~able** adj notable

remarry /riː'mærɪ/ vi volver a casarse

remedy /'remədɪ/ n remedio m. ● vt remediar

remember /rɪ'membə(r)/ vt acordarse de, recordar. ● vi acordarse

remind /rɪ'maɪnd/ vt recordar. **~er** n recordatorio m

reminisce /remɪ'nɪs/ vi rememorar los viejos tiempos. **~nces** /-ənsɪz/ npl recuerdos mpl. **~nt** /-'nɪsnt/ adj. **be ~nt of** recordar

remnant /'remnənt/ n resto m; (of cloth) retazo m; (trace) vestigio m

remorse /rɪ'mɔːs/ n remordimiento m. **~ful** adj arrepentido. **~less** adj implacable

remote /rɪ'məʊt/ adj remoto. **~ control** n mando a distancia.

~ly adv remotamente

remov|able /rɪ'muːvəbl/ adj (detachable) de quita y pon; (handle) desmontable. **~al** n eliminación f; (from house) mudanza f. **~e** /rɪ'muːv/ vt quitar; (dismiss) destituir; (get rid of) eliminar

render /'rendə(r)/ vt rendir (homage); prestar (help etc). **~ sth useless** hacer que algo resulte inútil

rendezvous /'rɒndɪvuː/ n (pl -vous /-vuːz/) cita f

renegade /'renɪɡeɪd/ n renegado

renew /rɪ'njuː/ vt renovar; (resume) reanudar. **~al** n renovación f

renounce /rɪ'naʊns/ vt renunciar a

renovat|e /'renəveɪt/ vt renovar. **~ion** /-'veɪʃn/ n renovación f

renown /rɪ'naʊn/ n renombre m. **~ed** adj de renombre

rent /rent/ n alquiler m. ● vt alquilar. **~al** n alquiler m. **car ~** (Amer) alquiler m de coche

renunciation /rɪnʌnsɪ'eɪʃn/ n renuncia f

reopen /riː'əʊpən/ vt volver a abrir. **~ v** rebrirse

reorganize /riː'ɔːɡənaɪz/ vt reorganizar

rep /rep/ n (Com) representante m & f

repair /rɪ'peə(r)/ vt arreglar, reparar; arreglar (clothes, shoes). ● n reparación f; (patch) remiendo m. **in good ~** en buen estado. **it's beyond ~** ya no tiene arreglo

repatriat|e /riː'pætrɪeɪt/ vt repatriar

repay /riː'peɪ/ vt (pt repaid) reembolsar; pagar (debt); corresponder a (kindness). **~ment** n pago m

repeal /rɪ'piːl/ vt revocar. ● n revocación f

repeat /rɪ'piːt/ vt repetir. ● vi repetir(se). ● n repetición f. **~edly** adv repetidas veces

repel /rɪ'pel/ vt (pt repelled) repeler. **~lent** adj repelente

repent /rɪ'pent/ vi arrepentirse. **~ant** adj arrepentido

repercussion /riːpə'kʌʃn/ n repercusión f

repertoire /'repətwɑː(r)/ n repertorio m

repetition /repɪ'tɪʃn/ n repetición f. **~ious** /-'tɪʃəs/ adj. **~ive** /rɪ'petɪtɪv/ adj repetitivo

replace /rɪ'pleɪs/ vt reponer; cambiar (battery); (take the place of) sustituir. **~ment** n sustitución f; (person) sustituto m

replay /'riːpleɪ/ n (Sport) repetición f del partido; (recording) repetición f inmediata

replenish /rɪ'plenɪʃ/ vt reponer

replica /'replɪkə/ n réplica f

reply /rɪ'plaɪ/ vt/i responder, contestar. **~ to sth** responder a algo, contestar algo. ● n respuesta f

report /rɪ'pɔːt/ vt (reporter) informar sobre; informar de (accident); (denounce) denunciar. ● vi informar; (present o.s.) presentarse. ● n informe m; (Schol) boletín m de notas; (rumour) rumor m; (in newspaper) reportaje m. **~ card** (Amer) n boletín m de calificaciones. **~edly** adv según se dice. **~er** n periodista m & f, reportero m

reprehensible /reprɪ'hensəbl/ adj reprensible

represent /reprɪ'zent/ vt representar. **~ation** /-'teɪʃn/ n representación f. **~ative** adj representativo. ● n representante m & f; (Amer, in government) diputado m

repress /rɪ'pres/ vt reprimir. **~ion** /-ʃn/ n represión f. **~ive** adj represivo

reprieve /rɪ'priːv/ n indulto m; (fig) respiro m. ● vt indultar

reprimand /'reprɪmɑːnd/ vt reprender. ● n represión f

reprisal /rɪ'praɪzl/ n represalia f

reproach /rɪ'prəʊtʃ/ vt reprochar. ● n reproche m. **~ful** adj de reproche

reproduce /riːprə'djuːs/ vt producir. ● vi reproducirse. **~tion** /-'dʌkʃn/ n reproducción f. **~tive** /-'dʌktɪv/ adj reproductor

reprove /rɪ'pruːv/ vt reprender

reptile /'reptaɪl/ n reptil m

republic /rɪ'pʌblɪk/ n república f. **~an** adj & n republicano (m). R**~** adj & n (in US) republicano (m)

repugnance /rɪ'pʌgnəns/ n repugnancia f. **~t** adj repugnante

repulse /rɪ'pʌls/ vt rechazar, repulsar. **~ion** /-ʃn/ n repulsión f. **~ive** adj repulsivo

reputable /'repjʊtəbl/ adj acreditado, reputado. **~ation** /repjʊ'teɪʃn/ n reputación f

request /rɪ'kwest/ n petición f. ● vt pedir

require /rɪ'kwaɪə(r)/ vt requerir; (need) necesitar; (demand) exigir. **~d** adj necesario. **~ment** n requisito m

rescue /'reskjuː/ vt rescatar, salvar. ● n rescate m. **~r** n salvador m

research /rɪ'sɜːtʃ/ n investigación f. ● vt investigar. **~er** n investigador m

resemblance /rɪ'zembləns/ n parecido m. **~e** /rɪ'zembl/ vt parecerse a

resent /rɪ'zent/ vt guardarle rencor a (person). she **~ed** his success le molestaba que él tuviera éxito. ~**ful** *adj* resentido. ~**ment** *n* resentimiento *m*

reserv|ation /rezə'veɪʃn/ *n* reserva *f*; (*booking*) reserva *f*. ~**e** /rɪ 'zɜːv/ *vt* reservar. ● *n* reserva *f*; (*in sports*) suplente *m & f*. ~**ed** *adj* reservado. ~**oir** /'rezəvwɑː(r)/ *n* embalse *m*

reshuffle /riː'ʃʌfl/ *n* (*Pol*) reorganización *f*

resid|ence /'rezɪdəns/ *n* residencia *f*. ~**t** *adj & n* residente (*m & f*). ~**tial** /rezɪ'denʃl/ *adj* residencial

residue /'rezɪdjuː/ *n* residuo *m*

resign /rɪ'zaɪn/ *vt/i* dimitir. ~ **o.s. to** resignarse a. ~**ation** /rezɪg 'neɪʃn/ *n* resignación *f*; (*from job*) dimisión *f*. ~**ed** *adj* resignado

resilien|ce /rɪ'zɪliəns/ *n* elasticidad *f*; (*of person*) resistencia *f*. ~**t** *adj* elástico; (*person*) resistente

resin /'rezɪn/ *n* resina *f*

resist /rɪ'zɪst/ *vt* resistir. ● *vi* resistirse. ~**ance** *n* resistencia *f*. ~**ant** *adj* resistente

resolut|e /'rezəluːt/ *adj* resuelto. ~**ion** /-'luːʃn/ *n* resolución *f*

resolve /rɪ'zɒlv/ *vt* resolver. ~ **to do** resolver a hacer. ● *n* resolución *f*

resort /rɪ'zɔːt/ *n* recurso *m*; (*place*) lugar *m* turístico. **in the last** ~ como último recurso. □ ~ **to** *vt* recurrir a.

resource /rɪ'sɔːs/ *n* recurso *m*. ~**ful** *adj* ingenioso

respect /rɪ'spekt/ *n* (*esteem*) respeto *m*; (*aspect*) respecto *m*. **with** ~ **to** con respecto a. ● *vt* respetar. ~**able** *adj* respetable. ~**ful** *adj* respetuoso. ~**ively** *adv* respectivamente

respiration /respə'reɪʃn/ *n* respiración *f*

respite /'respaɪt/ *n* respiro *m*

respon|d /rɪ'spɒnd/ *vi* responder. ~**se** /rɪ'spɒns/ *n* respuesta *f*; (*reaction*) reacción *f*

responsib|ility /rɪspɒnsə'bɪləti/ *n* responsabilidad *f*. ~**le** /rɪ 'spɒnsəbl/ *adj* responsable; (*job*) de responsabilidad. ~**ly** *adv* con formalidad

responsive /rɪ'spɒnsɪv/ *adj* que reacciona bien. ~ **to** sensible a

rest /rest/ *vt* descansar; (*lean*) apoyar. ● *vi* descansar; (*lean*) apoyarse. ● *n* descanso *m*; (*Mus*) pausa *f*; (*remainder*) resto *m*, lo demás; (*people*) los demás, los otros *mpl*. **to have a** ~ tomarse un descanso. □ ~ **up** (*Amer*) descansar

restaurant /'restərɒnt/ *n* restaurante *m*

rest|ful *adj* sosegado. ~**ive** *adj* impaciente. ~**less** *adj* inquieto

restor|ation /restə'reɪʃn/ *n* restablecimiento *m*; (*of building, monarch*) restauración *f*. ~**e** /rɪ'stɔː(r)/ *vt* restablecer; restaurar (*building*); devolver (confidence, health)

restrain /rɪ'streɪn/ *vt* contener. ~ **o.s.** contenerse. ~**ed** *adj* (*moderate*) moderado; (*in control of self*) comedido. ~**t** *n* restricción *f*; (*moderation*) compostura *f*

restrict /rɪ'strɪkt/ *vt* restringir. ~**ion** /-ʃn/ *n* restricción *f*. ~**ive** *adj* restrictivo

rest room *n* (*Amer*) baño *m*, servicio *m*

result /rɪ'zʌlt/ *n* resultado *m*. **as a** ~ **of** como consecuencia de. ● *vi*. ~ **from** resultar de. ~ **in** dar como resultado

resume /rɪ'zjuːm/ *vt* reanudar. ● *vi* reanudarse

résumé /'rezjuːmeɪ/ *n* resumen *m*;

(*Amer, CV*) currículum *m*, historial *m* personal

resurrect /rezə'rekt/ *vt* resucitar. **~ion** /-ʃn/ *n* resurrección *f*

resuscitat|e /rɪ'sʌsɪteɪt/ *vt* resucitar. **~ion** /-'teɪʃn/ *n* resucitación *f*

retail /'riːteɪl/ *n* venta *f* al por menor. ● *adj & adv* al por menor. ● *vt* vender al por menor. ● *vi* venderse al por menor. **~er** *n* minorista *m & f*

retain /rɪ'teɪn/ *vt* retener; conservar (heat)

retaliat|e /rɪ'tælɪeɪt/ *vi* desquitarse; (*Mil*) tomar represalias. **~ion** /-'eɪʃn/ *n* represalias *fpl*

retarded /rɪ'tɑːdɪd/ *adj* retrasado

rethink /riː'θɪŋk/ *vt* (*pt* **rethought**) reconsiderar

reticen|ce /'retɪsns/ *n* reticencia *f*. **~t** *adj* reticente

retina /'retɪnə/ *n* retina *f*

retinue /'retɪnjuː/ *n* séquito *m*

retir|e /rɪ'taɪə(r)/ *vi* (*from work*) jubilarse; (*withdraw*) retirarse; (*go to bed*) acostarse. **~ed** *adj* jubilado. **~ement** *n* jubilación *f*. **~ing** *adj* retraído

retort /rɪ'tɔːt/ *vt/i* replicar. ● *n* réplica *f*

retrace /riː'treɪs/ *vt*. **~ one's steps** volver sobre sus pasos

retract /rɪ'trækt/ *vt* retirar (statement). ● *vi* retractarse

retrain /riː'treɪn/ *vi* hacer un curso de reciclaje

retreat /rɪ'triːt/ *vi* retirarse. ● *n* retirada *f*; (*place*) refugio *m*

retrial /riː'traɪəl/ *n* nuevo juicio *m*

retriev|al /rɪ'triːvl/ *n* recuperación *f*. **~e** /rɪ'triːv/ *vt* recuperar. **~er** *n* (*dog*) perro *m* cobrador

retro|grade /'retrəɡreɪd/ *adj* re-

trógrado. **~spect** /-spekt/ *n*. **in ~** en retrospectiva. **~spective** /-'spektɪv/ *adj* retrospectivo

return /rɪ'tɜːn/ *vi* volver, regresar; (symptom) reaparecer. ● *vt* devolver; corresponder a (affection). ● *n* regreso *m*, vuelta *f*; (*Com*) rendimiento *m*; (*to owner*) devolución *f*. **in ~ for** a cambio de. **many happy ~s!** ¡feliz cumpleaños! **~ ticket** *n* billete *m* or (*LAm*) boleto *m* de ida y vuelta, boleto *m* redondo (*Mex*). **~s** *npl* (*Com*) ingresos *mpl*

reun|ion /riː'juːnɪən/ *n* reunión *f*. **~ite** /riːju:'naɪt/ *vt* reunir

rev /rev/ *n* (*Auto, fam*) revolución *f*. ● *vt/i*. **~ (up)** (*pt* **revved**) (*Auto, fam*) acelerar(se)

reveal /rɪ'viːl/ *vt* revelar. **~ing** *adj* revelador

revel /'revl/ *vi* (*pt* **revelled**) tener un jolgorio. **~ in** deleitarse en. **~ry** *n* jolgorio *m*

revelation /revə'leɪʃn/ *n* revelación *f*

revenge /rɪ'vendʒ/ *n* venganza *f*. **take ~** vengarse. ● *vt* vengar

revenue /'revənju:/ *n* ingresos *mpl*

revere /rɪ'vɪə(r)/ *vt* venerar. **~nce** /'revərəns/ *n* reverencia *f*

Reverend /'revərənd/ *adj* reverendo

reverent /'revərənt/ *adj* reverente

reverie /'revərɪ/ *n* ensueño *m*

revers|al /rɪ'vɜːsl/ *n* inversión *f*. **~e** /rɪ'vɜːs/ *adj* inverso. ● *n* contrario *m*; (*back*) revés *m*; (*Auto*) marcha *f* atrás. ● *vt* invertir; anular (decision); (*Auto*) dar marcha atrás a. ● *vi* (*Auto*) dar marcha atrás

revert /rɪ'vɜːt/ *vi*. **~ to** volver a; (*Jurid*) revertir a

review /rɪ'vjuː/ *n* revisión *f*; (*Mil*)

revista f; (of book, play, etc) crítica f. ● vt examinar (situation); reseñar (book, play, etc); (Amer, for exam) repasar

revis|e /rɪ'vaɪz/ vt revisar; (Schol) repasar. **~ion** /rɪ'vɪʒn/ n revisión f; (Schol) repaso m

revive /rɪ'vaɪv/ vt resucitar (person)

revolt /rɪ'vəʊlt/ vi sublevarse. ● n revuelta f. **~ing** adj asqueroso

revolution /revə'luːʃn/ n revolución f. **~ary** adj & n revolucionario (m). **~ize** vt revolucionar

revolv|e /rɪ'vɒlv/ vi girar. **~er** n revólver m. **~ing** /rɪ'vɒlvɪŋ/ adj giratorio

revue /rɪ'vjuː/ n revista f

revulsion /rɪ'vʌlʃn/ n asco m

reward /rɪ'wɔːd/ n recompensa f. ● vt recompensar. **~ing** adj gratificante

rewrite /riː'raɪt/ vt (pt rewrote, pp rewritten) volver a escribir or redactar; (copy out) escribir otra vez

rhetoric /'retərɪk/ n retórica f. **~al** /rɪ'tɒrɪkl/ adj retórico

rheumatism /'ruːmətɪzəm/ n reumatismo m

rhinoceros /raɪ'nɒsərəs/ n (pl -oses or invar) rinoceronte m

rhubarb /'ruːbɑːb/ n ruibarbo m

rhyme /raɪm/ n rima f; (poem) poesía f. ● vt/i rimar

rhythm /'rɪðəm/ n ritmo m. **~ic(al)** /'rɪðmɪk(l)/ adj rítmico

rib /rɪb/ n costilla f.

ribbon /'rɪbən/ n cinta f.

rice /raɪs/ n arroz m. **~ pudding** n arroz con leche

rich /rɪtʃ/ adj (-er, -est) rico. ● n ricos mpl. **~es** npl riquezas fpl

ricochet /'rɪkəʃeɪ/ vi rebotar

rid /rɪd/ vt (pt rid, pres p ridding) librar (of de). **get ~ of** deshacerse de. **~dance** /'rɪdns/ n. **good riddance!** ¡adiós y buen viaje!

ridden /'rɪdn/ see RIDE

riddle /'rɪdl/ n acertijo m. ● vt acribillar. **be ~d** with estar lleno de

ride /raɪd/ vi (pt rode, pp ridden) (on horseback) montar a caballo; (go) ir (en bicicleta, a caballo etc). ● vt montar a (horse); ir en (bicycle); (Amer) ir en (bus, train); recorrer (distance). ● n (on horse) cabalgata f; (in car) paseo m en coche. **take s.o. for a 🔲** engañarle a uno. **~r** n (on horse) jinete m; (cyclist) ciclista m & f

ridge /rɪdʒ/ n (of hills) cadena f; (hilltop) cresta f

ridicul|e /'rɪdɪkjuːl/ n burlas fpl. ● vt ridiculizar. **~ous** /rɪ'dɪkjələs/ adj ridículo

rife /raɪf/ adj difundido

rifle /'raɪfl/ n fusil m

rift /rɪft/ n grieta f; (fig) ruptura f

rig /rɪg/ vt (pt rigged) (pej) amañar. ● n (at sea) plataforma f de perforación. □ **~ up** vt improvisar

right /raɪt/ adj (correct) correcto; (morally) bueno; (not left) derecho; (suitable) adecuado. **be ~** (person) tener razón; (clock) estar bien. **it is ~** (just, moral) es justo. **put ~** rectificar. **the ~ person for the job** la persona indicada para el puesto. ● n (entitlement) derecho m; (not left) derecha f; (not evil) bien m. **~ of way** (Auto) prioridad f. **be in the ~** tener razón. **on the ~** a la derecha. ● vt enderezar; (fig) reparar. ● adv a la derecha; (directly) derecho; (completely) completamente. **~ angle** n ángulo m recto.

r

~ **away** adv inmediatamente.
~**eous** /ˈraɪtʃəs/ adj recto; (cause)
justo. ~**ful** /ˈraɪtfl/ adj legítimo.
~**handed** /-ˈhændɪd/ adj diestro.
~**hand man** n brazo m derecho.
~**ly** adv justamente. ~ **wing** adj
(Pol) derechista

rigid /ˈrɪdʒɪd/ adj rígido

rig|orous /ˈrɪɡərəs/ adj riguroso.
~**our** /ˈrɪɡə(r)/ n rigor m

rim /rɪm/ n borde m; (of wheel)
llanta f; (of glasses) montura f

rind /raɪnd/ n corteza f; (of fruit)
cáscara f

ring[1] /rɪŋ/ n (circle) círculo m;
(circle of metal etc) aro m; (on finger) anillo m; (on finger with stone)
sortija f; (Boxing) cuadrilátero m;
(bullring) ruedo m; (for circus) pista
f; • vt cercar

ring[2] /rɪŋ/ n (of bell) toque m; (tinkle) tintineo m; (telephone call) llamada f. • vt (pt **rang**, pp **rung**)
hacer sonar; (telephone) llamar por
teléfono. ~ **the bell** tocar el timbre. • vi sonar. ~ **back** vt/i volver a
llamar. □ ~ **up** vt llamar por teléfono

ring:: ~**leader** /ˈrɪŋliːdə(r)/ n
cabecilla m & f. ~ **road** n carretera f de circunvalación

rink /rɪŋk/ n pista f

rinse /rɪns/ vt enjuagar. • n acla-
rado m; (of dishes) enjuague m; (for
hair) tintura f (no permanente)

riot /ˈraɪət/ n disturbio m; (of
colours) profusión f. **run** ~ desen-
frenarse. • vi causar disturbios

rip /rɪp/ vt (pt **ripped**) rasgar. • vi
rasgarse. n rasgón m. □ ~ **off** vt
(pull off) arrancar; (🔲, cheat)
robar

ripe /raɪp/ adj (-er, -est) maduro. •
~**n** /ˈraɪpn/ vt/i madurar

rip-off /ˈrɪpɒf/ n timo m

ripple /ˈrɪpl/ n (on water) onda f

ris|e /raɪz/ vi (pt **rose**, pp **risen**)
subir; (sun) salir; (river) crecer;
(prices) subir; (land) elevarse; (get
up) levantarse. • n subida f; (land)
altura f; (increase) aumento m; (to
power) ascenso m. **give** ~**e to** oca-
sionar. ~**er** n. **early** ~**er** n madru-
gador m. ~**ing** n. • adj (sun) na-
ciente; (number) creciente; (prices)
en alza

risk /rɪsk/ n riesgo m. • vt arriesgar. ~**y** adj (-ier, -iest) arriesgado

rite /raɪt/ n rito m

ritual /ˈrɪtjʊəl/ adj & n ritual (m)

rival /ˈraɪvl/ adj & n rival (m). ~**ry**
n rivalidad f

river /ˈrɪvə(r)/ n río m

rivet /ˈrɪvɪt/ n remache m. ~**ing**
adj fascinante

road /rəʊd/ n (in town) calle f; (between towns) carretera f; (route,
way) camino m. ~ **map** n mapa m
de carreteras. ~**side** n borde m de
la carretera. ~**works** npl obras fpl.
~**worthy** adj (vehicle) apto para
circular

roam /rəʊm/ vi vagar

roar /rɔː(r)/ n rugido m; (laughter)
carcajada f. • vt/i rugir. ~ **past** (ve-
hicles) pasar con estruendo. ~
with laughter reírse a carcajadas.
~**ing** adj (trade etc) activo

roast /rəʊst/ vt asar; tostar (coffee). • adj & n asado (m). ~ **beef** n
rosbif m

rob /rɒb/ vt (pt **robbed**) atracar,
asaltar (bank); robarle a (person).
~ **of** (deprive of) privar de. ~**ber**
n ladrón m; (of bank) atracador m.
~**bery** n robo m; (of bank)
atraco m

robe /rəʊb/ n bata f; (Univ etc)

toga f

robin /'rɒbɪn/ n petirrojo m

robot /'rəʊbɒt/ n robot m

robust /rəʊ'bʌst/ adj robusto

rock /rɒk/ n roca f; (crag, cliff) peñasco m. ● vt mecer; (shake) sacudir. ● vi mecerse; (shake) sacudirse. ● n (Mus) música f rock. ~**-bottom** /-'bɒtəm/ adj 🄣 bajísimo

rocket /'rɒkɪt/ n cohete m

rock: ~**ing-chair** n mecedora f. ~**y** adj (-ier, -iest) rocoso; (fig, shaky) bamboleante

rod /rɒd/ n vara f; (for fishing) caña f; (metal) barra f

rode /rəʊd/ see RIDE

rodent /'rəʊdnt/ n roedor m

rogue /rəʊg/ n pícaro m

role /rəʊl/ n papel m

roll /rəʊl/ vt hacer rodar; (roll up) enrollar; allanar (lawn); aplanar (pastry). ● vi rodar; (ship) balancearse; (on floor) revolcarse. be ~**ing in money** 🄣 nadar en dinero. ● n rollo m; (of ship) balanceo m; (of drum) redoble m; (of thunder) retumbo m; (bread) panecillo m, bolillo m (Mex). □ ~ **over** vi (turn over) dar una vuelta. □ ~ **up** vt enrollar; arremangar (sleeve). vi 🄣 llegar. ~**-call** n lista f

roller /'rəʊlə(r)/ n rodillo m; (wheel) rueda f; (for hair) rulo m. R~ **blades** npl (P) patines mpl en línea. ~**-coaster** n montaña f rusa. ~**-skate** n patín m de ruedas. ~**-skating** patinaje m (sobre ruedas)

rolling /'rəʊlɪŋ/ adj ondulado. ~**-pin** n rodillo m

ROM /rɒm/ n (= read-only memory) ROM f

Roman /'rəʊmən/ adj & n romano (m). ~ **Catholic** adj & n católico (m) (romano)

romance /rəʊ'mæns/ n novela f romántica; (love) amor m; (affair) aventura f

Romania /ruː'meɪnɪə/ n Rumania f, Rumanía f. ~**n** adj & n rumano (m)

romantic /rəʊ'mæntɪk/ adj romántico

Rome /rəʊm/ n Roma f

romp /rɒmp/ vi retozar

roof /ruːf/ n techo m, tejado m; (of mouth) paladar m. ● vt techar. ~**rack** n baca f. ~**top** n tejado m

rook /rʊk/ n grajo m; (in chess) torre f

room /ruːm/ n cuarto m, habitación f; (bedroom) dormitorio m; (space) espacio m; (large hall) sala f. ~**y** adj espacioso

roost /ruːst/ vi posarse. ~**er** n gallo m

root /ruːt/ n raíz f. take ~ echar raíces; (idea) arraigarse. ● vi echar raíces. ~ **about** vi hurgar. ~ **for** vt 🄣 alentar. □ ~ **out** vt extirpar

rope /rəʊp/ n cuerda f. know the ~**s** estar al corriente. ● vt atar; (Amer, lasso) enlazar. □ ~ **in** vt agarrar

rose[1] /rəʊz/ n rosa f; (nozzle) roseta f

rose[2] /rəʊz/ see RISE

rosé /'rəʊzeɪ/ n (vino m) rosado m

rot /rɒt/ vt (pt rotted) pudrir. ● vi pudrirse. ● n putrefacción f

rota /'rəʊtə/ n lista f (de turnos)

rotary /'rəʊtərɪ/ adj rotatorio

rotat|e /rəʊ'teɪt/ vt girar; (change round) alternar. ● vi girar; (change round) alternarse. ~**ion** /-ʃn/ n rotación f

rote /rəʊt/ n. by ~ de memoria

rotten /'rɒtn/ adj podrido; 🄣 pé-

r

simo 🔲; (weather) horrible

rough /rʌf/ adj (-er, -est) áspero;
(person) tosco; (bad) malo;
(ground) accidentado; (violent) brutal; (approximate) aproximado; (diamond) bruto. ● adv duro. ~
draft borrador m. ● vt. ~ it vivir
sin comodidades. **~age** /'rʌfɪdʒ/ n
fibra f. **~-and-ready** adj improvisado. **~ly** adv bruscamente; (more
or less) aproximadamente

roulette /ruː'let/ n ruleta f

round /raʊnd/ adj (-er, -est) redondo. ● n círculo m; (of visits,
drinks) ronda f; (of competition)
vuelta f; (Boxing) asalto m. ● prep alrededor de. ● adv alrededor. ~
about (approximately) aproximadamente. come ~ to, go ~ to (a
friend etc) pasar por casa de. ● vt
doblar (corner). □ ~ **off** vt terminar; redondear (number). □ ~ **up**
vt redondear (cattle); hacer una redada de (suspects). **~about** n tiovivo m,
carrusel m (LAm); (for traffic) glorieta f, rotonda f. ● adj in directo.
~ **trip** n viaje m de ida y vuelta.
~up n resumen m; (of suspects)
redada f

rous|e /raʊz/ vt despertar. **~ing**
adj enardecedor

route /ruːt/ n ruta f; (Naut, Aviat)
rumbo m; (of bus) línea f

routine /ruː'tiːn/ n rutina f. ● adj
rutinario

row¹ /raʊ/ n fila f. ● vi remar

row² /raʊ/ n (fam, noise) bulla f
🔲; (quarrel) pelea f. ● vi 🔲 pelearse

rowboat /'raʊbəʊt/ (Amer) n bote
m de remos

rowdy /'raʊdɪ/ adj (-ier, -iest) n
escandaloso, alborotado

rowing /'raʊɪŋ/ n remo m. ~

boat n bote m de remos

royal /'rɔɪəl/ adj real. **~ist** adj & n
monárquico (m). **~ly** adv magnífi-
camente. ~**ty** n realeza f

rub /rʌb/ vt (pt rubbed) frotar.
□ ~ **out** vt borrar

rubber /'rʌbə(r)/ n goma f, caucho m, hule m (Mex); (eraser) goma
f (de borrar). ~ **band** n goma f
(elástica). ~**-stamp** vt (fig) autorizar. **~y** adj parecido al caucho

rubbish /'rʌbɪʃ/ n basura f; (junk)
trastos mpl; (fig) tonterías fpl. ~ **bin**
n cubo m de la basura, bote m de
la basura (Mex). **~y** adj sin valor

rubble /'rʌbl/ n escombros mpl

ruby /'ruːbɪ/ n rubí m

rucksack /'rʌksæk/ n mochila f

rudder /'rʌdə(r)/ n timón m

rude /ruːd/ adj (-er, -est) grosero,
mal educado; (improper) indecente;
(brusque) brusco. **~ly** adv grosera-
mente. **~ness** n mala educación f

rudimentary /ruːdɪ'mentrɪ/ adj
rudimentario

ruffian /'rʌfɪən/ n rufián m

ruffle /'rʌfl/ vt despeinar (hair);
arrugar (clothes)

rug /rʌg/ n alfombra f, tapete m
(Mex); (blanket) manta f de viaje

rugged /'rʌgɪd/ adj (coast) escarpado; (landscape) escabroso

ruin /'ruːɪn/ n ruina f. ● vt arruinar;
(spoil) estropear

rul|e /ruːl/ n regla f; (Pol) dominio
m. **as a** ~ por regla general. ● vt
gobernar; (master) dominar; (Jurid)
dictaminar. ~**e out** vt descartar.
~**ed paper** n papel m rayado. **~er**
n (sovereign) soberano m & f; (leader)
gobernante m & f; (measure) regla f.
~ing adj (class) dirigente. ● n decisión f

rum /rʌm/ n ron m

rumble /'rʌmbl/ *vi* retumbar; (stomach) hacer ruidos

rummage /'rʌmɪdʒ/ *vi* hurgar

rumour /'ruːmə(r)/ *n* rumor *m*. ● *vt*. it is ~ed that se rumorea que

rump steak /rʌmpsteɪk/ *n* filete *m* de cadera

run /rʌn/ *vi* (*pt* ran, *pp* run, *pres p* running) correr; (water) correr; (*function*) funcionar; (*melt*) derretirse; (makeup) correrse; (colour) desteñir; (bus etc) circular; (in election) presentarse. ● *vt* correr (race); dirigir (business); correr (risk); (move, pass) pasar; tender (wire); preparar (bath). ● *n* a temperature tener fiebre. ● *n* corrida *f*, carrera *f*; (outing) paseo *m* (en coche); (ski) pista *f*. in the long ~ a la larga. be on the ~ estar prófugo. □ ~ away *vi* huir, escaparse. □ ~ down *vi* bajar corriendo; (battery) descargarse. *vt* (Auto) atropellar; (belittle) denigrar. □ ~ in *vi* entrar corriendo. □ ~ into *vt* toparse con (friend); (hit) chocar con. □ ~ off *vt* sacar (copies). □ ~ out *vi* salir corriendo; (liquid) salirse; (fig) agotarse. □ ~ out of *vt* quedarse sin. □ ~ over *vt* (Auto) atropellar. □ ~ through *vt* (review) repasar; (rehearse) repasar. □ ~ up *vt* ir acumulando (bill). *vi* subir corriendo. ~away *n* fugitivo *m*. ~ down *adj* (person) agotado

rung¹ /rʌŋ/ *n* (of ladder) peldaño *m*

rung² /rʌŋ/ *see* RING

run: ~ner /'rʌnə(r)/ *n* corredor *m*; (on sledge) patín *m*. ~ner bean *n* judía *f* escarlata. ~nerup *n*. be ~er-up quedar en segundo lugar. ~ning *n*. be in the ~ning tener posibilidades de ganar. ● *adj* (water) corriente; (commentary) en directo. four times ~ning cuatro veces seguidas. ~ny /'rʌnɪ/ *adj* líquido; (nose) que moquea. ~way *n* pista *f* de aterrizaje

rupture /'rʌptʃə(r)/ *n* ruptura *f*. ● *vt* romper

rural /'rʊərəl/ *adj* rural

ruse /ruːz/ *n* ardid *m*

rush /rʌʃ/ *n* (haste) prisa *f*; (crush) bullicio *m*; (plant) junco *m*. ● *vi* precipitarse. ● *vt* apresurar; (Mil) asaltar. ~-hour *n* hora *f* punta, hora *f* pico (LAm)

Russia /'rʌʃə/ *n* Rusia *f*. ~n *adj* & *n* ruso (*m*)

rust /rʌst/ *n* orín *m*. ● *vt* oxidar. ● *vi* oxidarse

rustle /'rʌsl/ *vt* hacer susurrar; (Amer) robar. ● *vi* susurrar. □ ~ up *vt* 🔳 preparar

rust: ~proof *adj* inoxidable. ~y (-ier, -iest) oxidado

rut /rʌt/ *n* surco *m*. be in a ~ estar anquilosado

ruthless /'ruːθlɪs/ *adj* despiadado

rye /raɪ/ *n* centeno *m*

r
s

Ss

S *abbr* (= south) S

sabotage /'sæbətɑːʒ/ *n* sabotaje *m*. ● *vt* sabotear. ~eur /-'tɜː(r)/ *n* saboteador *m*

saccharin /'sækərɪn/ *n* sacarina *f*

sachet /'sæʃeɪ/ *n* bolsita *f*

sack /sæk/ *n* saco *m*. get the ~ 🔳 ser despedido. ● *vt* 🔳 despedir, echar

sacrament /'sækrəmənt/ n sacramento m

sacred /'seɪkrɪd/ adj sagrado

sacrifice /'sækrɪfaɪs/ n sacrificio m. ● vt sacrificar

sacrileg|e /'sækrɪlɪdʒ/ n sacrilegio m. ~**ious** /-'lɪdʒəs/ adj sacrílego

sad /sæd/ adj (sadder, saddest) triste. ~**den** vt entristecer

saddle /'sædl/ n silla f de montar. ● vt ensillar (horse). ~ **s.o.** with sth (fig) endilgar algo a uno

sadist /'seɪdɪst/ n sádico m. ~**tic** /sə'dɪstɪk/ adj sádico

sadly /'sædlɪ/ adv tristemente; (fig) desgraciadamente. ~**ness** n tristeza f

safe /seɪf/ adj (-er, -est) seguro, (out of danger) salvo; (cautious) prudente. ~ **and sound** sano y salvo. ● n caja f fuerte. ~**guard** n salvaguardia f ● vt salvaguardar. ~**ly** adv sin peligro; (in safe place) en lugar seguro. ~**ty** n seguridad f. ~**ty belt** n cinturón m de seguridad. ~**ty pin** n imperdible m

sag /sæg/ vi (pt sagged) (ceiling) combarse; (bed) hundirse

saga /'sɑːgə/ n saga f

Sagittarius /sædʒɪ'teərɪəs/ n Sagitario m

said /sed/ see SAY

sail /seɪl/ n vela f; (trip) paseo m (en barco). **set** ~ zarpar. ● vi navegar; (leave) partir; (Sport) practicar la vela; (fig) deslizarse. **go** ~**ing** salir a navegar. ● vt gobernar (boat). ~**boat** n (Amer) barco m de vela. ~**ing** n (Sport) vela f ~**ing boat** n, ~**ing ship** n barco m de vela. ~**or** n marinero m

saint /seɪnt//sənt/ n santo m. ~**ly**

adj santo

sake /seɪk/ n. **for the** ~ **of** por. **for God's** ~ por el amor de Dios

salad /'sæləd/ n ensalada f. ~ **bowl** n ensaladera f. ~ **dressing** n aliño m

salary /'sælərɪ/ n sueldo m

sale /seɪl/ n venta f; (at reduced prices) liquidación f. **for** ~ (sign) se vende. **be for** ~ estar a la venta. **be on** ~ (Amer, reduced) estar en liquidación. ~**able** adj vendible. (for sale) estar a la venta. ~**s clerk** n (Amer) dependiente m, dependienta f. ~**sman** /-mən/ n vendedor m; (in shop) dependiente m. ~**swoman** n vendedora f; (in shop) dependienta f

saliva /sə'laɪvə/ n saliva f

salmon /'sæmən/ n invar salmón m

saloon /sə'luːn/ n (on ship) salón m; (Amer, bar) bar m; (Auto) turismo m

salt /sɔːlt/ n sal f. ● vt salar. ~**cellar** n salero m. ~**y** adj salado

salute /sə'luːt/ n saludo m. ● vt saludar. ● vi hacer un saludo

Salvadorean, Salvadorian /sælvə'dɔːrɪən/ adj & n salvadoreño (m)

salvage /'sælvɪdʒ/ vt salvar

salvation /sæl'veɪʃn/ n salvación f

same /seɪm/ adj igual (as que); (before noun) mismo (as que). **at the** ~ **time** al mismo tiempo. ● pron. **the** ~ lo mismo. **all the** ~ de todas formas. ● adv. **the** ~ igual

sample /'sɑːmpl/ n muestra f. ● vt degustar (food)

sanct|ify /'sæŋktɪfaɪ/ vt santificar. ~**ion** /'sæŋkʃn/ n sanción f. ● vt sancionar. ~**uary** /'sæŋktʃʊərɪ/ n (Relig) santuario m; (for wildlife) reserva f; (*refuge*) asilo m

sand /sænd/ n arena f ● vt pulir (floor). ~ **down** vt lijar (wood)

sandal /'sændl/ n sandalia f

sand: ~**castle** n castillo m de arena. ~**paper** n papel m de lija. ● vt lijar. ~**storm** n tormenta f de arena

sandwich /'sænwɪdʒ/ n bocadillo m, sandwich m. ● vt. be ~ed between (person) estar apretujado entre

sandy /'sændɪ/ adj arenoso

sane /seɪn/ adj (-er, -est) (person) cuerdo; (*sensible*) sensato

sang /sæŋ/ see SING

sanitary /'sænɪtrɪ/ adj higiénico; (system etc) sanitario. ~ **towel**, ~ **napkin** n (Amer) compresa f (higiénica)

sanitation /sænɪ'teɪʃn/ n higiene f; (drainage) sistema m sanitario

sanity /'sænɪtɪ/ n cordura f

sank /sæŋk/ see SINK

Santa (Claus) /'sæntə(klɔːz)/ n Papá m Noel

sap /sæp/ n (in plants) savia f. ● (pt sapped) minar

sapling /'sæplɪŋ/ n árbol m joven

sapphire /'sæfaɪə(r)/ n zafiro m

sarcas|m /'sɑːkæzəm/ n sarcasmo m. ~**tic** /-'kæstɪk/ adj sarcástico

sardine /sɑː'diːn/ n sardina f

sash /sæʃ/ n (over shoulder) banda f; (round waist) fajín m.

sat /sæt/ see SIT

SAT abbr (Amer) (Scholastic Aptitude Test); (Brit) (Standard Assessment Task)

satchel /'sætʃl/ n cartera f

satellite /'sætəlaɪt/ n & a satélite (m). ~ **TV** n televisión f por satélite

satin /'sætɪn/ n raso m ● adj de raso

satire /'sætaɪə(r)/ n sátira f. ~**ical** /sə'tɪrɪkl/ adj satírico. ~**ize** /'sætəraɪz/ vt satirizar

satis|faction /sætɪs'fækʃn/ n satisfacción f. ~**factorily** /-'fæktərɪlɪ/ adv satisfactoriamente. ~**factory** /-'fæktərɪ/ adj satisfactorio. ~**fy** /'sætɪsfaɪ/ vt satisfacer; (convince) convencer. ~**fying** adj satisfactorio

satphone /'sætfəʊn/ n teléfono m satélite

saturat|e /'sætʃəreɪt/ vt saturar. ~**ed** adj saturado; (drenched) empapado

Saturday /'sætədeɪ/ n sábado m

Saturn /'sætən/ n Saturno m

sauce /sɔːs/ n salsa f; (cheek) descaro m. ~**pan** /'sɔːspən/ n cazo m, cacerola f. ~**r** /'sɔːsə(r)/ n platillo m

saucy /'sɔːsɪ/ adj (-ier, -iest) descarado

Saudi /'saʊdɪ/ adj & n saudita (m & f). ~ **Arabia** /-ə'reɪbɪə/ n Arabia f Saudí

sauna /'sɔːnə/ n sauna f

saunter /'sɔːntə(r)/ vi pasearse

sausage /'sɒsɪdʒ/ n salchicha f

savage /'sævɪdʒ/ adj salvaje; (fierce) feroz. ● n salvaje m & f. ● vt atacar. ~**ry** n ferocidad f

sav|e /seɪv/ vt (rescue) salvar; ahorrar (money, time); (prevent) evitar; (Comp) guardar. ● n (football) parada f. ● prep salvo, excepto. ~ **up** vi/t ahorrar. ~**er** n ahorrador m. ~**ing** n ahorro m. ~**ings** npl ahorros mpl

saviour /'seɪvɪə(r)/ n salvador m

savour /'seɪvə(r)/ vt saborear. ~**y** adj (appetizing) sabroso; (not sweet) no dulce

s

saw /sɔː/ *see* SEE¹

saw² /sɔː/ *n* sierra *f.* ● *vt* (*pt* sawed, *pp* sawn) serrar. **~dust** *n* serrín *m.* **~n** /sɔːn/ *see* SAW²

saxophone /ˈsæksəfəʊn/ *n* saxofón *m,* saxófono *m*

say /seɪ/ *vt/i* (*pt* said /sed/) decir; rezar (prayer). ● *n.* have a ~ expresar una opinión; (*in decision*) tener voz en capítulo. have no ~ no tener ni voz ni voto. **~ing** *n* refrán *m*

scab /skæb/ *n* costra *f;* (*fam, blackleg*) esquirol *m*

scaffolding /ˈskæfəldɪŋ/ *n* andamios *mpl*

scald /skɔːld/ *vt* escaldar

scale /skeɪl/ *n* (*also Mus*) escala *f;* (*of fish*) escama *f.* ● *vt* (*climb*) escalar. **~ down** *vt* reducir (a escala) (drawing); recortar (operation). **~s** *npl* (*for weighing*) balanza *f,* peso *m*

scallion /ˈskæljən/ *n* (*Amer*) cebolleta *f*

scalp /skælp/ *vt* quitar el cuero cabelludo a. ● *n* cuero *m* cabelludo

scamper /ˈskæmpə(r)/ *vi.* **~ away** irse correteando

scan /skæn/ *vt* (*pt* scanned) escudriñar; (*quickly*) echar un vistazo a; (*radar*) explorar

scandal /ˈskændl/ *n* escándalo *m;* (*gossip*) chismorreo *m.* **~ize** *vt* escandalizar. **~ous** *adj* escandaloso

Scandinavia /skændɪˈneɪvɪə/ *n* Escandinavia *f.* **~n** *adj* & *n* escandinavo (*m*)

scant /skænt/ *adj* escaso **~y** *adj* (*-ier, -iest*) escaso

scapegoat /ˈskeɪpgəʊt/ *n* cabeza *f* de turco

scar /skɑː(r)/ *n* cicatriz *f*

scarc|e /skeəs/ *adj* (*-er, -est*) escaso. be **~e** escasear. make o.s.

~e 🔲 mantenerse lejos. **~ely** *adv* apenas. **~ity** *n* escasez *f*

scare /skeə(r)/ *vt* asustar. be **~d** tener miedo. be **~d** of sth tenerle miedo a algo. ● *n* susto *m.* **~crow** *n* espantapájaros *m*

scarf /skɑːf/ *n* (*pl* scarves) bufanda *f;* (*over head*) pañuelo *m*

scarlet /ˈskɑːlət/ *adj* escarlata *f.* **~ fever** *n* escarlatina *f*

scarves /skɑːvz/ *see* SCARF

scary /ˈskeərɪ/ *adj* (*-ier, -iest*) que da miedo

scathing /ˈskeɪðɪŋ/ *adj* mordaz

scatter /ˈskætə(r)/ *vt* (*throw*) esparcir; (*disperse*) dispersar. ● *vi* dispersarse. **~ed** /ˈskætəd/ *adj* disperso; (*occasional*) esporádico

scavenge /ˈskævɪndʒ/ *vi* escarbar (en la basura)

scenario /sɪˈnɑːrɪəʊ/ *n* (*pl* -os) perspectiva *f;* (*of film*) guión *m*

scen|e /siːn/ *n* escena *f;* (*sight*) vista *f;* (*fuss*) lío *m.* behind the **~es** entre bastidores. **~ery** /ˈsiːnərɪ/ *n* paisaje *m;* (*in theatre*) decorado *m.* **~ic** /ˈsiːnɪk/ *adj* pintoresco

scent /sent/ *n* olor *m;* (*perfume*) perfume *m;* (*trail*) pista *f.* (*make fragrant*) perfumar

sceptic /ˈskeptɪk/ *n* escéptico *m.* **~al** *adj* escéptico. **~ism** /-sɪzəm/ *n* escepticismo *m*

sceptre /ˈseptə(r)/ *n* cetro *m*

schedule /ˈʃedjuːl, ˈskedjuːl/ *n* programa *f;* (*timetable*) horario *m.* behind **~** atrasado. it's on **~** va de acuerdo a lo previsto. ● *vt* proyectar. **~d flight** *n* vuelo *m* regular

scheme /skiːm/ *n* proyecto *m;* (*plot*) intriga *f.* ● *vi* (*pej*) intrigar

schizophrenic /skɪtsəˈfrenɪk/ *adj* & *n* esquizofrénico (*m*)

scholar /ˈskɒlə(r)/ *n* erudito *m.*

~**ly** adj erudito. ~**ship** n erudición f; (grant) beca f

school /sku:l/ n escuela f; (Univ) facultad f. ● adj (age, holidays, year) escolar. ● vt instruir; (train) capacitar. ~**boy** n colegial m. ~**girl** n colegiala f. ~**ing** n instrucción f. ~**master** n (primary) maestro m; (secondary) profesor m. ~**mistress** n (primary) maestra f; (secondary) profesora f. ~**teacher** n (primary) maestro m; (secondary) profesor m.

scien|ce /'saɪəns/ n ciencia f. ~ **study** ~**ce** estudiar ciencias. ~**ce fiction** n ciencia f ficción. ~**tific** /-'tɪfɪk/ adj científico. ~**tist** /'saɪəntɪst/ n científico m

scissors /'sɪsəz/ npl tijeras fpl

scoff /skɒf/ vt 🔢 zamparse. ● vi. ~ **at** mofarse de

scold /skəʊld/ vt regañar

scoop /sku:p/ n pala f; (news) primicia f. ¤ ~ **out** vt sacar; excavar (hole)

scooter /'sku:tə(r)/ n escúter m; (for child) patinete m

scope /skəʊp/ n alcance m; (opportunity) oportunidad f

scorch /skɔ:tʃ/ vt chamuscar. ~**ing** adj 🔢 de mucho calor

score /skɔ:(r)/ n tanteo m; (Mus) partitura f; (twenty) veintena f. **on that** ~ en cuanto a eso. **know the** ~ 🔢 saber cómo son las cosas. ● vt marcar (goal); anotarse (points); (cut, mark) rayar; conseguir (success). ● vi marcar

scorn /skɔ:n/ n desdén m. ● vt desdeñar. ~**ful** adj desdeñoso

Scorpio /'skɔ:pɪəʊ/ n Escorpio m, Escorpión m

scorpion /'skɔ:pɪən/ n escorpión m

Scot /skɒt/ n escocés m. ~**ch**

/skɒtʃ/ n whisky m, güisqui m

scotch /skɒtʃ/ vt frustrar; acallar (rumours)

Scotch tape n (Amer) celo m, cinta f Scotch

Scot: ~**land** /'skɒtlənd/ n Escocia f. ~**s** adj escocés. ~**tish** adj escocés

scoundrel /'skaʊndrəl/ n canalla f

scour /'skaʊə(r)/ vt fregar; (search) registrar. ~**er** n estropajo m

scourge /skɜ:dʒ/ n azote m

scout /skaʊt/ n explorador m. **Boy S**~ explorador m

scowl /skaʊl/ n ceño m fruncido. ● vi fruncir el ceño

scram /skræm/ vi 🔢 largarse

scramble /'skræmbl/ vi (clamber) gatear. ● n (difficult climb) subida f difícil; (struggle) rebatiña f. ~**d egg** n huevos mpl revueltos

scrap /skræp/ n pedacito m; (fam, fight) pelea f. ● vt (pt scrapped) desechar. ~**book** n álbum m de recortes. ~**s** npl sobras fpl

scrape /skreɪp/ n (fig) apuro m. ● vt raspar; (graze) rasparse; (rub) rascar. ¤ ~ **through** vi/t aprobar por los pelos (exam). ¤ ~ **together** vt reunir. ~**r** n rasqueta f

scrap: ~**heap** n montón m de deshechos. ~ **yard** n chatarrería f

scratch /skrætʃ/ n rayar (furniture, record); (with nail etc) arañar; rascarse (itch). • vi arañar. • n rayón m; (from nail etc) arañazo m. **start from** ~ empezar desde cero. **be up to** ~ dar la talla

scrawl /skrɔːl/ n garabato m. • vt/i garabatear

scream /skriːm/ vt/i gritar. • n grito m

screech /skriːtʃ/ vi chillar; (brakes etc) chirriar. • n chillido m; (of brakes etc) chirrido m

screen /skriːn/ n pantalla f; (folding) biombo m. • vt (hide) ocultar; (protect) proteger; proyectar (film)

screw /skruː/ n tornillo m. • vt atornillar. □ ~ **up** vt atornillar; entornar (eyes); torcer (face); (sl, ruin) fastidiar. ~**driver** n destornillador m

scribble /ˈskrɪbl/ vt/i garabatear. • n garabato m

script /skrɪpt/ n escritura f; (of film etc) guión m

scroll /skrəʊl/ n rollo m (de pergamino). □ ~ **down** vi retroceder la pantalla. □ ~ **up** vi avanzar la pantalla

scrounge /skraʊndʒ/ vt/i gorronear. ~**r** n gorrón m

scrub /skrʌb/ n (land) maleza f. • vt/i (pt scrubbed) fregar

scruff /skrʌf/ n. **by the** ~ **of the** neck por el pescuezo. • adj (-ier, -iest) desaliñado

scrup|le /ˈskruːpl/ n escrúpulo m. ~**ulous** /-jələs/ adj escrupuloso

scrutin|ize /ˈskruːtɪnaɪz/ vt escudriñar; inspeccionar (document). ~**y** /ˈskruːtɪni/ n examen m minucioso

scuffle /ˈskʌfl/ n refriega f

sculpt /skʌlpt/ vt/i esculpir. ~**or** n escultor m. ~**ure** /-tʃə(r)/ n escultura f. • vt/i esculpir

scum /skʌm/ n espuma f; (people, pej) escoria f

scupper /ˈskʌpə(r)/ vt echar por tierra (plans)

scurry /ˈskʌri/ vi corretear

scuttle /ˈskʌtl/ n cubo m del carbón. • vt barrenar (ship). • vi. ~ **away** escabullirse rápidamente

scythe /saɪð/ n guadaña f

SE abbr (= **south-east**) SE

sea /siː/ n. **at** ~ en el mar; (fig) confuso. **by** ~ por mar. ~**food** n mariscos mpl. ~ **front** n paseo m marítimo, malecón m (LAm). ~**gull** n gaviota f. ~**horse** n caballito m de mar

seal /siːl/ n sello m; (animal) foca f. • vt sellar

sea level n nivel m del mar

sea lion n león m marino

seam /siːm/ n costura f; (of coal) veta f

seaman /ˈsiːmən/ n (pl -men) marinero m

seamy /ˈsiːmi/ adj sórdido

seance /ˈseɪɑːns/ n sesión f de espiritismo

search /sɜːtʃ/ vt registrar; buscar en (records). • vi buscar. • n (for sth) búsqueda f; (of sth) registro m; (Comp) búsqueda f. **in** ~ **of** en busca de. □ ~ **for** vt buscar. ~ **engine** n buscador m. ~**ing** adj penetrante. ~**light** n reflector m. ~ **party** n partida f de rescate

sea: ~**shore** n orilla f del mar. ~**sick** adj mareado. **be** ~**sick** marearse. ~**side** n playa f

season /ˈsiːzn/ n estación f; (period) temporada f. **high/low** ~

temporada f alta/baja. ● vt (Culin) sazonar. ∼al adj estacional; (demand) de estación. ∼ed adj (fig) avezado. ● n condimento m. ∼ticket n abono m (de temporada)

seat /siːt/ n asiento m; (place) lugar m; (in cinema, theatre) localidad f; (of trousers) fondillos mpl. take a ∼ sentarse. ● vt sentar; (have seats for) (auditorium) tener capacidad para; (bus) tener asientos para. ∼belt n cinturón m de seguridad

sea: ∼ trout n reo m. ∼-urchin n erizo m de mar. ∼weed n alga f marina. ∼worthy adj en condiciones de navegar

seclu|ded /sɪˈkluːdɪd/ adj aislado

second /ˈsekənd/ adj & n segundo (m). on ∼ thoughts pensándolo bien. ● adv (in race etc) en segundo lugar. ● vt secundar. ∼s npl (goods) artículos mpl de segunda calidad; (fam, more food) have ∼s repetir. ● /sɪˈkɒnd/ vt (transfer) trasladar temporalmente. ∼ary /ˈsekəndrɪ/ adj secundario. ∼ary school n instituto m (de enseñanza secundaria)

second: ∼-class adj de segunda (clase). ∼-hand adj de segunda mano. ∼ly adv en segundo lugar. ∼-rate adj mediocre

secre|cy /ˈsiːkrəsɪ/ n secreto m. ∼t adj & n secreto (m). in ∼t en secreto

secretar|ial /sekrəˈteərɪəl/ adj de secretario; (course) de secretariado. ∼y /ˈsekrətrɪ/ n secretario m. S∼y of State (in UK) ministro m; (in US) secretario m de Estado

secretive /ˈsiːkrɪtɪv/ adj reservado

sect /sekt/ n secta f. ∼arian

/-ˈteərɪən/ adj sectario

section /ˈsekʃn/ n sección f; (part) parte f

sector /ˈsektə(r)/ n sector m

secular /ˈsekjʊlə(r)/ adj secular

secur|e /sɪˈkjʊə(r)/ adj seguro; (shelf) firme. ● vt asegurar; (obtain) obtener. ∼ely adv seguramente. ∼ity n seguridad f; (for loan) garantía f

sedat|e /sɪˈdeɪt/ adj reposado. ● vt sedar. ∼ion /sɪˈdeɪʃn/ n sedación f. ∼ive /ˈsedətɪv/ adj & n sedante (m)

sediment /ˈsedɪmənt/ n sedimento m

seduc|e /sɪˈdjuːs/ vt seducir. ∼er n seductor m. ∼tion /sɪˈdʌkʃn/ n seducción f. ∼tive /sɪˈdʌktɪv/ adj seductor

see /siː/ ● vt (pt saw, pp seen) ver; (understand) comprender; (escort) acompañar. ∼ing that visto que. ∼ you later! ¡hasta luego! ● vi ver. □ ∼ off vt (say goodbye to) despedirse de. □ ∼ through vt llevar a cabo; calar (person). □ ∼ to vt ocuparse de

seed /siːd/ n semilla f; (fig) germen m; (Amer, pip) pepita f. go to ∼ granar; (fig) echarse a perder. ∼ling n planta f de semillero. ∼y adj (-ier, -iest) sórdido

seek /siːk/ vt (pt sought) buscar; pedir (approval). □ ∼ out vt buscar

seem /siːm/ vi parecer

seen /siːn/ see SEE

seep /siːp/ vi filtrarse

see-saw /ˈsiːsɔː/ n balancín m

seethe /siːð/ vi (fig) estar furioso. I was seething with anger me hervía la sangre

see-through /ˈsiːθruː/ adj transparente

segment /ˈsegmənt/ n segmento

m; (of orange) gajo *m*

segregat|e /'segrɪgeɪt/ *vt* segregar. **~ion** /-'geɪʃn/ *n* segregación *f*

seiz|e /siːz/ *vt* agarrar; (*Jurid*) incautar. **~e on** *vi* aprovechar (chance). □ **~e up** *vi* (*Tec*) agarrotarse. **~ure** /'siːʒə(r)/ *n* incautación *f*; (*Med*) ataque *m*

seldom /'seldəm/ *adv* rara vez

select /sɪ'lekt/ *vt* escoger; (*Sport*) seleccionar. ● *adj* selecto; (*exclusive*) exclusivo. **~ion** /-ʃn/ *n* selección *f*. **~ive** *adj* selectivo

self /self/ *n* (*pl* **selves**). he's his old **~** again vuelve a ser el de antes. **~-addressed** *adj* con el nombre y la dirección del remitente. **~-catering** *adj* con facilidades para cocinar. **~-centred** *adj* egocéntrico. **~-confidence** *n* confianza *f* en sí mismo. **~-confident** *adj* seguro de sí mismo. **~-conscious** *adj* cohibido. **~-contained** *adj* independiente. **~-control** *n* dominio *m* de sí mismo. **~-defence** *n* defensa *f* propia. **~-employed** *adj* que trabaja por cuenta propia. **~-evident** *adj* evidente. **~-important** *adj* presumido. **~-indulgent** *adj* inmoderado. **~-interest** *n* interés *m* (personal). **~-ish** *adj* egoísta. **~-ishness** *n* egoísmo *m*. **~-pity** *n* autocompasión *f*. **~-portrait** *n* autorretrato *m*. **~-respect** *n* amor *m* propio. **~-righteous** *adj* santurrón. **~-sacrifice** *n* abnegación *f*. **~-satisfied** *adj* satisfecho de sí mismo. **~-serve** (*Amer*), **~-service** *adj* & *n* autoservicio (*m*). **~-sufficient** *adj* independiente

sell /sel/ *vt* (*pt* **sold**) vender. ● *vi* venderse. **~ off** *vt* liquidar. ● **~ out** *vi*. we've sold out of gloves los guantes están agotados. **~-by**

date *n* fecha *f* límite de venta. **~er** *n* vendedor *m*

Sellotape /'seləteɪp/ *n* (®) celo *m*, cinta *f* Scotch

sell-out /'selaʊt/ *n* (*performance*) éxito *m* de taquilla; (*fam, betrayal*) capitulación *f*

semblance /'sembləns/ *n* apariencia *f*

semester /sɪ'mestə(r)/ *n* (*Amer*) semestre *m*

semi... /'semɪ/ *pref* semi...

semi|breve /-briːv/ *n* redonda *f*. **~circle** *n* semicírculo *m*. **~colon** /-'kəʊlən/ *n* punto *m* y coma. **~detached** /-dɪ'tætʃt/ *adj* (house) adosado. **~final** /-'faɪnl/ *n* semifinal *f*

seminar /'semɪnɑː(r)/ *n* seminario *m*

senat|e /'senɪt/ *n* senado *m*. the S**~e** (*Amer*) el Senado. **~or** /-ətə(r)/ *n* senador *m*

send /send/ *vt/i* (*pt* **sent**) mandar, enviar. □ **~ away** *vt* despedir. □ **~ away for** *vt* pedir (por correo). □ **~ for** *vt* enviar a buscar. □ **~ off for** *vt* pedir (por correo). □ **~ up** *vt* 🅣 parodiar. **~er** *n* remitente *m*. **~-off** *n* despedida *f*

senile /'siːnaɪl/ *adj* senil

senior /'siːnɪə(r)/ *adj* mayor; (*in rank*) superior; (*partner etc*) principal. ● *n* mayor *m* & *f*. **~ citizen** *n* jubilado *m*. **~ high school** *n* (*Amer*) colegio *m* secundario. **~ity** /-'ɒrəti/ *n* antigüedad *f*

sensation /sen'seɪʃn/ *n* sensación *f*. **~al** *adj* sensacional

sens|e /sens/ *n* sentido *m*; (*common sense*) juicio *m*; (*feeling*) sensación *f*. make **~e** *vt* tener sentido. make **~e of** sth entender algo. **~eless** *adj* sin sentido. **~ible**

/'sensəbl/ adj sensato; (clothing) práctico. **~itive** /'sensɪtɪv/ adj sensible; (touchy) susceptible. **~itivity** /-'tɪvɪtɪ/ n sensibilidad f. **~ual** /'senʃʊəl/ adj sensual. **~uous** /'sensʊəs/ adj sensual

sent /sent/ see SEND

sentence /'sentəns/ n frase f; (judgment) sentencia f; (punishment) condena f. ● vt. ~ **to** condenar a

sentiment /'sentɪmənt/ n sentimiento m; (opinion) opinión f. **~al** /-'mentl/ adj sentimental. **~ality** /-'tælətɪ/ n sentimentalismo m

sentry /'sentrɪ/ n centinela f

separa|ble /'sepərəbl/ adj separable. **~te** /'seprət/ adj separado; (independent) independiente. ● /'sepəreɪt/ separar. ● vi separarse. **~tely** /'sepərətlɪ/ adv por separado. **~tion** /-'reɪʃn/ n separación f. **~tist** /'sepərətɪst/ n separatista m & f

September /sep'tembə(r)/ n se(p)tiembre m

septic /'septɪk/ adj séptico.

sequel /'si:kwəl/ n continuación f; (later events) secuela f

sequence /'si:kwəns/ n sucesión f; (of film) secuencia f

Serb /sɜːb/ adj & n see SERBIAN. **~ia** /'sɜːbɪə/ n Serbia f **~ian** adj & n serbio (m)

serenade /serə'neɪd/ n serenata f. ● vt dar serenata a

serene /sɪ'riːn/ adj sereno

sergeant /'sɑːdʒənt/ n sargento m

serial /'sɪərɪəl/ n serie f. **~ize** vt serializar

series /'sɪəriːz/ n serie f

serious /'sɪərɪəs/ adj serio. **~ly** adv seriamente; (ill) gravemente. take **~ly** tomar en serio

sermon /'sɜːmən/ n sermón m

serum /'sɪərəm/ n (pl -a) suero m

servant /'sɜːvənt/ n criado m

serve /sɜːv/ vt servir; servir a (country); cumplir (sentence). ~ **as** servir de. **it ~s you right** ¡bien te lo mereces! ● vi servir; (in tennis) sacar. ● n (in tennis) saque m. **~r** n (Comp) servidor m

service /'sɜːvɪs/ n servicio m; (of car etc) revisión f. ● vt revisar (car etc). ~ **charge** n (in restaurant) servicio m. **~s** npl (Mil) fuerzas fpl armadas. ~ **station** n estación f de servicio

serviette /sɜːvɪ'et/ n servilleta f

servile /'sɜːvaɪl/ adj servil

session /'seʃn/ n sesión f

set /set/ vt (pt set, pres p setting) poner; poner en hora (clock etc); fijar (limit etc); (typeset) componer. ~ **fire to** prender fuego a. ~ **free** vt poner en libertad. ● vi (sun) ponerse; (jelly) cuajarse. ● n serie f; (of cutlery etc) juego m; (in tennis) set m; (TV, Radio) aparato m; (in theatre) decorado m; (of people) círculo m. ● adj fijo. **be ~ on** estar resuelto a. □ ~ **back** vt (delay) retardar; (fam, cost) costar. □ ~ **off** vi salir. vt hacer sonar (alarm); hacer explotar (bomb). □ ~ **out** vt exponer (argument). vi (leave) salir. □ ~ **up** vt establecer. **~back** n revés m

settee /se'tiː/ n sofá m

setting /'setɪŋ/ n (of dial, switch) posición f

settle /'setl/ vt (arrange) acordar; arreglar (matter); resolver (dispute); pagar (bill); saldar (debt). ● vi (live) establecerse. □ ~ **down** vi calmarse; (become more responsible) sentar (la) cabeza. □ ~ **for** vt aceptar. □ ~ **up** vi arreglar cuentas. **~ment** n establecimiento m; (agreement) acuerdo m; (of debt) liquidación f; (colony) colonia f. **~r** n colono m

set: ~to n pelea f. **~up** n ① sistema m; (con) tinglado m

seven /'sevn/ adj & n siete (m). **~teen** /sevn'ti:n/ adj & n diecisiete (m). **~teenth** adj & n decimoséptimo (m). ● n diecisietavo m. **~th** adj & n séptimo (m). **~tieth** /'sevəntɪɪθ/ adj septuagésimo. ● n setentavo m. **~ty** /'sevntɪ/ adj & n setenta (m)

sever /'sevə(r)/ vt cortar; (fig) romper

several /'sevrəl/ adj & pron varios

sever|e /sɪ'vɪə(r)/ adj (-er, -est) severo; (serious) grave; (weather) riguroso. **~ely** adv severamente. **~ity** /sɪ'verətɪ/ n severidad f; (seriousness) gravedad f

sew /səʊ/ vt/i (pt sewed, pp sewn, or sewed) coser. □ **~ up** vt coser

sew|age /'su:ɪdʒ/ n aguas fpl residuales. **~er** /'su:ə(r)/ n cloaca f

sewing /'səʊɪŋ/ n costura f. **~machine** n máquina f de coser

sewn /səʊn/ see **sew**

sex /seks/ n sexo m. have **~** tener relaciones sexuales. ● adj sexual. **~ist** adj & n sexista (m & f). **~ual** /'sekʃʊəl/ adj sexual. **~ual intercourse** n relaciones fpl sexuales. **~uality** /-'ælətɪ/ n sexualidad f. **~y** adj (-ier, -iest) excitante, sexy, provocativo

shabby /'ʃæbɪ/ adj (-ier, -iest) (clothes) gastado; (person) pobremente vestido

shack /ʃæk/ n choza f

shade /ʃeɪd/ n sombra f; (of colour) tono m; (for lamp) pantalla f; (nuance) matiz m; (Amer, over window) persiana f

shadow /'ʃædəʊ/ n sombra f. ● vt (follow) seguir de cerca a. **~y** adj (fig) vago

shady /'ʃeɪdɪ/ adj (-ier, -iest) sombreado; (fig) turbio; (character) sospechoso

shaft /ʃɑ:ft/ n (of arrow) astil m; (Mec) eje m; (of light) rayo m; (of lift, mine) pozo m

shaggy /'ʃægɪ/ adj (-ier, -iest) peludo

shake /ʃeɪk/ vt (pt shook, pp shaken) sacudir; agitar (bottle); (shock) desconcertar. **~ hands with** estrechar la mano a. **~ one's head** negar con la cabeza; (Amer, meaning yes) asentir con la cabeza. ● vi temblar. □ **~ off** vi deshacerse de. ● n sacudida f

shaky /'ʃeɪkɪ/ adj (-ier, -iest) tembloroso; (table etc) inestable

shall /ʃæl/ modal verb. we **~** see veremos. **~** we go to the cinema? ¿vamos al cine?

shallow /'ʃæləʊ/ adj (-er, -est) poco profundo; (fig) superficial

sham /ʃæm/ n farsa f. ● adj fingido

shambles /'ʃæmblz/ npl (fam, mess) caos m

shame /ʃeɪm/ n (feeling) vergüenza f. what a **~**! ¡qué lástima! ● vt avergonzar. **~ful** adj vergonzoso. **~less** adj desvergonzado

shampoo /ʃæm'pu:/ n champú m. ● vt lavar

shan't /ʃɑ:nt/ = **shall not**

shape /ʃeɪp/ n forma f. ● vt formar; determinar (future). ● vi tomar forma. **~less** adj informe

share /ʃeə(r)/ n porción f; (Com) acción f. ● vt compartir; (divide) dividir. ● vi compartir. **~ in sth** participar en algo. □ **~ out** vt repartir. **~holder** n accionista m & f. **~out**

n reparto *m*

shark /ʃɑːk/ *n* tiburón *m*

sharp /ʃɑːp/ *adj* (-er, -est) (knife etc) afilado; (pin etc) puntiagudo; (pain, sound) agudo; (taste) ácido; (bend) cerrado; (contrast) marcado; (clever) listo; (Mus) sostenido. ● *adv* en punto. at seven o'clock ~ a las siete en punto. ● *n* (Mus) sostenido *m*. ~**en** *vt* afilar; sacar punta a (pencil). ~**ener** *n* (Mec) afilador *m*; (for pencils) sacapuntas *m*. ~**ly** *adv* bruscamente

shatter /ˈʃætə(r)/ *vt* hacer añicos. he was ~ed by the news la noticia lo dejó destrozado. ● *vi* hacerse añicos. ~**ed** /ˈʃætəd/ *adj* (exhausted) agotado

shav|e /ʃeɪv/ *vt* afeitar, rasurar (Mex). ● *vi* afeitarse, rasurarse (Mex). ● *n* afeitada *f*, rasurada *f* (Mex). have a ~e afeitarse. ~**er** *n* maquinilla *f* (de afeitar). ~**ing brush** *n* brocha *f* de afeitar. ~**ing cream** *n* crema *f* de afeitar

shawl /ʃɔːl/ *n* chal *m*

she /ʃiː/ *pron* ella

sheaf /ʃiːf/ *n* (pl sheaves /ʃiːvz/) gavilla *f*

shear /ʃɪə(r)/ *vt* (pp shorn or sheared) esquilar. ~**s** /ʃɪəz/ *npl* tijeras *fpl* grandes

shed /ʃed/ *n* cobertizo *m*. ● *vt* (pt shed, pres p shedding) perder; derramar (tears); despojarse de (clothes). ~ **light on** arrojar luz sobre

she'd /ʃiː(ə)d/ = **she had**, **she would**

sheep /ʃiːp/ *n* invar oveja *f*. ~**dog** *n* perro *m* pastor. ~**ish** *adj* avergonzado

sheer /ʃɪə(r)/ *adj* (as intensifier) puro; (steep) perpendicular

sheet /ʃiːt/ *n* sábana *f*; (of paper) hoja *f*; (of glass) lámina *f*; (of ice) capa *f*

shelf /ʃelf/ *n* (pl shelves) estante *m*. a set of shelves unos estantes

shell /ʃel/ *n* concha *f*; (of egg) cáscara *f*; (of crab, snail, tortoise) caparazón *m* or *f*; (explosive) proyectil *m*, obús *m*. ● *vt* pelar (peas etc); (Mil) bombardear

she'll /ʃiː(ə)l/ = **she had**, **she would**

shellfish /ˈʃelfɪʃ/ *n* invar marisco *m*; (collectively) mariscos *mpl*

shelter /ˈʃeltə(r)/ *n* refugio *m*. take ~ refugiarse. ● *vt* dar cobijo a (fugitive); (protect from weather) resguardar. ● *vi* refugiarse. ~**ed** /ˈʃeltəd/ *adj* (spot) abrigado; (life) protegido

shelv|e /ʃelv/ *vt* (fig) dar carpetazo a. ~**ing** *n* estantería *f*

shepherd /ˈʃepəd/ *n* pastor *m*. ~**ess** /-ˈdes/ *n* pastora *f*

sherbet /ˈʃɜːbət/ *n* (Amer, water ice) sorbete *m*

sheriff /ˈʃerɪf/ *n* (in US) sheriff *m*

sherry /ˈʃerɪ/ *n* (vino *m* de) jerez *m*

she's /ʃiːz/ = **she is**, **she has**

shield /ʃiːld/ *n* escudo *m*. ● *vt* proteger

shift /ʃɪft/ *vt* cambiar; correr (furniture etc). ● *vi* (wind) cambiar; (attention, opinion) pasar a; (Amer, change gear) cambiar de velocidad. ● *n* cambio *m*; (work) turno *m*; (workers) tanda *f*. ~**y** *adj* (-ier, -iest) furtivo

shilling /ˈʃɪlɪŋ/ *n* chelín *m*

shimmer /ˈʃɪmə(r)/ *vi* rielar, relucir

shin /ʃɪn/ *n* espinilla *f*

shine /ʃaɪn/ *vi* (pt shone) brillar.

s

•*vt* sacar brillo a. **~ a light on sth** alumbrar algo con una luz. •*n* brillo *m*

shingle /'ʃɪŋgl/ *n* (*pebbles*) guijarros *mpl*

shin|ing /'ʃaɪnɪŋ/ *adj* brillante. **~y** /'ʃaɪnɪ/ *adj* (**-ier, -iest**) brillante.

ship /ʃɪp/ *n* barco *m*, buque *m*. •*vt* (*pt* **shipped**) transportar; (*send*) enviar; (*load*) embarcar. **~building** *n* construcción *f* naval. **~ment** *n* envío *m*. **~ping** *n* envío *m*; (*ships*) barcos *mpl*. **~shape** *adj* limpio y ordenado. **~wreck** *n* naufragio *m*. **~wrecked** *adj* naufragado. **be ~wrecked** naufragar. **~yard** *n* astillero *m*

shirk /ʃɜːk/ *vt* esquivar

shirt /ʃɜːt/ *n* camisa *f*. **in ~-sleeves** en mangas de camisa

shit /ʃɪt/ *n & int* (*vulgar*) mierda *f*. •*vi* (*vulgar*) (*pt* **shat**, *pres p* **shitting**) cagar

shiver /'ʃɪvə(r)/ *vi* temblar. •*n* escalofrío *m*

shoal /ʃəʊl/ *n* banco *m*

shock /ʃɒk/ *n* (*of impact*) choque *m*; (*of earthquake*) sacudida *f*; (*surprise*) shock *m*; (*scare*) susto *m*; (*Elec*) descarga *f*; (*Med*) shock *m*. **get a ~** llevarse un shock. •*vt* escandalizar; (*apall*) horrorizar. **~ing** *adj* escandaloso; Ⓔ espantoso

shod /ʃɒd/ *see* SHOE

shoddy /'ʃɒdɪ/ *adj* (**-ier, -iest**) mal hecho, de pacotilla

shoe /ʃuː/ *n* zapato *m*; (*of horse*) herradura *f*. •*vt* (*pt* **shod**, *pres p* **shoeing**) herrar (*horse*). **~horn** *n* calzador *m*. **~lace** *n* cordón *m* (de zapato). **~ polish** *n* betún *m*

shone /ʃɒn/ *see* SHINE

shoo /ʃuː/ *vt* ahuyentar

shook /ʃʊk/ *see* SHAKE

shoot /ʃuːt/ *vt* (*pt* **shot**) disparar; rodar (*film*). •*vi* (*hunt*) cazar. •*n* (*of plant*) retoño *m*. □ **~ down** *vt* derribar. □ **~ out** *vi* (*rush*) salir disparado. □ **~ up** *vi* (*prices*) dispararse; (*grow*) crecer mucho

shop /ʃɒp/ *n* tienda *f*. **go to the ~s** ir de compras. **talk ~** hablar del trabajo. •*vi* (*pt* **shopping**) hacer compras. **go ~ping** ir de compras. □ **~ around** *vi* buscar el mejor precio. **~ assistant** *n* dependiente *m*, dependienta *f*, empleado *m*, empleada *f* (*LAm*). **~keeper** *n* comerciante *m*, tendero *m*. **~lifter** *n* ladrón *m* (que roba en las tiendas). **~lifting** *n* hurto *m* (en las tiendas). **~per** *n* comprador *m*. **~ping** *n* (*purchases*) compras *fpl*. **do the ~ping** hacer la compra, hacer el mandado (*Mex*). **~ping bag** *n* bolsa *f* de la compra. **~ping cart** *n* (*Amer*) carrito *m* (de la compra). **~ping centre**, **~ping mall** (*Amer*) *n* centro *m* comercial. **~ping trolley** *n* carrito *m* de la compra. **~ steward** *n* enlace *m* sindical. **~ window** *n* escaparate *m*, vidriera *f* (*LAm*), aparador *m* (*Mex*)

shore /ʃɔː(r)/ *n* orilla *f*

shorn /ʃɔːn/ *see* SHEAR

short /ʃɔːt/ *adj* (**-er, -est**) corto; (*not lasting*) breve; (*person*) bajo; (*curt*) brusco. **a ~ time ago** hace poco. **be ~ of time/money** andar corto de tiempo/dinero. **Mick is ~ for Michael** Mick es el diminutivo de Michael. •*adv* (*stop*) en seco. **we never went ~ of food** nunca nos faltó comida. •*n*. **in ~** en resumen. **~age** /-ɪdʒ/ *n* escasez *f*, falta *f*. **~bread** *n* galleta *f* (de mantequilla). **~ circuit** *n* cortocircuito *m*. **~coming** *n* defecto *m*. **~ cut** *n* atajo *m*. **~en** *vt* acortar.

∼hand n taquigrafía f. **∼ly** adv (soon) dentro de poco. **∼ly before midnight** poco antes de la medianoche. **∼s** npl pantalones m cortos, shorts mpl; (Amer, underwear) calzoncillos mpl. **∼-sighted** /-'saɪtɪd/ adj miope

shot /ʃɒt/ see **SHOOT**. ●n (from gun) disparo m; tiro m; (in soccer) tiro m, disparo m; (in other sports) tiro m; (Photo) foto f. **be a good/ poor ∼** ser un buen/mal tirador. **be off like a ∼** salir disparado. **∼gun** n escopeta f

should /ʃʊd, ʃəd/ modal verb. I **∼ go** debería ir. **you ∼n't have said that** no deberías haber dicho eso. I **∼ like to see her** me gustaría verla. **if he ∼ come** si viniese

shoulder /'ʃəʊldə(r)/ n hombro m. ●vt cargar con (responsibility); ponerse al hombro (burden). **∼blade** n omóplato m

shout /ʃaʊt/ n grito m. ●vt/i gritar. **∼ at s.o.** gritarle a uno

shove /ʃʌv/ n empujón m. ●vt empujar; (fam, put) poner. ●vi empujar. □ **∼ off** vi 🇮 largarse

shovel /'ʃʌvl/ n pala f. ●vt (pt shovelled) palear (coal); espalar (snow)

show /ʃəʊ/ vt (pt showed, pp shown) mostrar; (on display) exponer; poner (film). I'll **∼ you** to your room acompañar a uno a su cuarto. ●vi (be visible) verse. ●n muestra f; (exhibition) exposición f; (in theatre) espectáculo m; (on TV, radio) programa m; (ostentation) pompa f. **be on ∼** estar expuesto. □ **∼ off** vt (pej) lucir, presumir de. vi presumir, lucirse. □ **∼ up** vi (be visible) notarse; (arrive) aparecer. vt (reveal) poner de manifiesto; (embarrass) hacer quedar mal. **∼case**

n vitrina f. **∼down** n confrontación f

shower /'ʃaʊə(r)/ n (of rain) chaparrón m; (for washing) ducha f. **have a ∼**, **take a ∼** ducharse. ●vi ducharse

showjumping n concursos mpl hípicos.

shown /ʃəʊn/ see **SHOW**

show: ∼-off n fanfarrón m. **∼room** n sala f de exposición f. **∼y** adj (-ier, -iest) llamativo; (attractive) ostentoso

shrank /ʃræŋk/ see **SHRINK**

shred /ʃred/ n pedazo m; (fig) pizca f. ●vt (pt shredded) hacer tiras; destruir, triturar (documents). **∼der** n (for paper) trituradora f; (for vegetables) cortadora f

shrewd /ʃruːd/ adj (-er, -est) astuto

shriek /ʃriːk/ n chillido m; (of pain) alarido m. ●vt/i chillar

shrift /ʃrɪft/ n. **give s.o. short ∼** despachar a uno con brusquedad. **give sth short ∼** desestimar algo de plano

shrill /ʃrɪl/ adj agudo

shrimp /ʃrɪmp/ n gamba f, camarón m (LAm); (Amer, large) langostino m

shrine /ʃraɪn/ n (place) santuario m; (tomb) sepulcro m

shrink /ʃrɪŋk/ vt (pt shrank, pp shrunk) encoger. ●vi encogerse; (amount) reducirse; retroceder (recoil)

shrivel /'ʃrɪvl/ vi (pt shrivelled). **∼ (up)** (plant) marchitarse; (fruit) resecarse y arrugarse

shroud /ʃraʊd/ n mortaja f; (fig) velo m. ●vt envolver

Shrove /ʃrəʊv/ n. **∼ Tuesday** n martes m de carnaval

s

shrub /ʃrʌb/ n arbusto m

shrug /ʃrʌg/ vt (pt **shrugged**) encogerse de hombros

shrunk /ʃrʌŋk/ see **SHRINK**. **~en** adj encogido

shudder /'ʃʌdə(r)/ vi estremecerse. ● n estremecimiento m

shuffle /'ʃʌfl/ vi andar arrastrando los pies. ● vt barajar (cards). **~ one's feet** arrastrar los pies

shun /ʃʌn/ vt (pt **shunned**) evitar

shunt /ʃʌnt/ vt cambiar de vía

shush /ʃʊʃ/ int ¡chitón!

shut /ʃʌt/ vt (pt **shut**, pres p **shutting**) cerrar. ● vi cerrarse. ● adj. **be ~** estar cerrado. □ **~ down** vt/i cerrar. □ **~ up** vi cerrar; (fig) hacer callar. vi callarse. **~ter** n contraventana f; (Photo) obturador m

shuttle /'ʃʌtl/ n lanzadera f; (by air) puente m aéreo; (space **~**) transbordador m espacial. ● vi. **~ (back and forth)** ir y venir. **~cock** n volante m. **~ service** n servicio m de enlace

shy /ʃaɪ/ adj (-er, -est) tímido. ● vi (pt **shied**) asustarse. **~ness** n timidez f

sick /sɪk/ adj enfermo; (humour) negro; (fam, fed up) harto. **be ~** estar enfermo; (vomit) vomitar. **be ~ of** (fig) estar harto de. **feel ~** sentir náuseas. **get ~** (Amer) caer enfermo, enfermarse (LAm). **~ leave** n permiso m por enfermedad, baja f por enfermedad. **~ly** /'sɪklɪ/ adj (-lier, -liest) enfermizo; (taste, smell etc) nauseabundo. **~ness** /sɪknəs/ n enfermedad f

side /saɪd/ n lado m; (of hill) ladera f; (of person) costado m; (team) equipo m; (fig) parte f. **~ by ~** uno al lado del otro. **take ~s** tomar partido. ● adj lateral. □ **~**

with vt ponerse de parte de. **~board** n aparador m. **~ dish** n acompañamiento m. **~effect** n efecto m secundario; (fig) consecuencia f indirecta. **~line** n actividad f suplementaria. **~ road** n calle f secundaria. **~step** vt eludir. **~track** vt desviar del tema. **~walk** n (Amer) acera f, vereda f (LAm), banqueta f (Mex). **~ways** adj & adv de lado

siding /'saɪdɪŋ/ n apartadero m

sidle /'saɪdl/ vi. **~ up to s.o.** acercarse furtivamente a uno

siege /siːdʒ/ n sitio m

sieve /sɪv/ n tamiz m. ● vt tamizar, cernir

sift /sɪft/ vt tamizar, cernir. ● vi. **~ through sth** pasar algo por el tamiz

sigh /saɪ/ n suspiro. ● vi suspirar

sight /saɪt/ n (spectacle) espectáculo m; (on gun) mira f. **at first ~** a primera vista. **catch ~ of** ver; (in distance) avistar. **lose ~ of** perder de vista. **see the ~s** visitar los lugares de interés. **within ~ of** (near) cerca de. ● vt ver; divisar (land). **~seeing** n. **go ~ing** ir a visitar los lugares de interés. **~seer** /-siːə(r)/ n turista m & f

sign /saɪn/ n (indication) señal f, indicio m; (gesture) señal f, seña f; (notice) letrero m; (astrological) signo m. ● vt firmar. □ **~ on** vi (for unemployment benefit) anotarse para recibir el seguro de desempleo

signal /'sɪgnəl/ n señal f. ● vt (pt **signalled**) señalar. ● vi. **~ (to s.o.)** hacer señas (a uno); (Auto) poner el intermitente, señalizar

signature /'sɪgnətʃə(r)/ n firma f. **~ tune** n sintonía f

significan|ce /sɪɡˈnɪfɪkəns/ n importancia f. **~t** adj (important) importante. **(fact)** significativo

signify /ˈsɪɡnɪfaɪ/ vt significar

signpost /ˈsaɪnpəʊst/ n señal f, poste m indicador

silen|ce /ˈsaɪləns/ n silencio m. ● vt hacer callar. **~cer** n (on gun and on car) silenciador m. **~t** adj silencioso; (film) mudo. **remain ~t** quedarse callado. **~tly** adv silenciosamente

silhouette /ˌsɪluːˈet/ n silueta f. ● vt. **be ~d** perfilarse (against contra)

silicon /ˈsɪlɪkən/ n silicio m. **~ chip** n pastilla f de silicio

silk /sɪlk/ n seda f. **~y** adj (of silk) de seda; (like silk) sedoso

silly /ˈsɪlɪ/ adj (-ier, -iest) tonto

silt /sɪlt/ n cieno m

silver /ˈsɪlvə(r)/ n plata f. ● adj de plata. **~-plated** adj bañado en plata, plateado. **~ware** /-weə(r)/ n platería f

SIM card n tarjeta f SIM

similar /ˈsɪmɪlə(r)/ adj parecido, similar. **~arity** /-ˈlærɪtɪ/ n parecido m. **~arly** adv de igual manera. **~e** /ˈsɪmɪlɪ/ n símil m

simmer /ˈsɪmə(r)/ vt/i hervir a fuego lento. □ **~ down** vi calmarse

simple /ˈsɪmpl/ adj (-er, -est) sencillo, simple; (person) (humble) simple; (backward) simple. **~e-minded** /-ˈmaɪndɪd/ adj ingenuo. **~icity** /-ˈplɪsɪtɪ/ n simplicidad f, sencillez f. **~ify** /ˈsɪmplɪfaɪ/ vt simplificar. **~y** adv sencillamente, simplemente; (absolutely) realmente

simulate /ˈsɪmjʊleɪt/ vt simular

simultaneous /ˌsɪmlˈteɪnɪəs/ adj simultáneo. **~ly** adv simultáneamente

sin /sɪn/ n pecado m. ● vi (pt sinned) pecar

since /sɪns/

● preposition desde. he's been living here **~** 1991 vive aquí desde 1991. **~** Christmas desde Navidad. **~** then desde entonces. I haven't been feeling well **~** Sunday desde el domingo que no me siento bien. how long is it **~** your interview? ¿cuánto (tiempo) hace de la entrevista?

● adverb desde entonces. I haven't spoken to her **~** no he hablado con ella desde entonces

● conjunction

····▸ desde que. I haven't seen her **~** she left no la he visto desde que se fue. **~** coming to Manchester desde que vine (or vino etc) a Manchester. it's ten years **~** he died hace diez años que se murió

····▸ (because) como, ya que. **~** it was quite late, I decided to stay como o ya que era bastante tarde, decidí quedarme

sincere /sɪnˈsɪə(r)/ adj sincero. **~ely** adv sinceramente. yours **~ely, ~ely (yours)** (in letters) (saluda) a usted atentamente. **~ity** /-ˈserɪtɪ/ n sinceridad f

sinful /ˈsɪnfl/ adj (person) pecador; (act) pecaminoso

sing /sɪŋ/ vt/i (pt sang, pp sung) cantar

singe /sɪndʒ/ vt (pres p singeing) chamuscar

singer /ˈsɪŋə(r)/ n cantante m & f

single /ˈsɪŋɡl/ adj solo; (not

double) sencillo; (unmarried) soltero; (bed, room) individual, de una plaza (LAm); (ticket) de ida, sencillo. not a ~ house ni una sola casa. every ~ day todos los días sin excepción. ●n (ticket) billete m sencillo, boleto m de ida (LAm). □~ out vt escoger; (distinguish) distinguir. ~-handed /-'hændɪd/ adj & adv sin ayuda. ~s npl (Sport) individuales mpl

singular /'sɪŋɡjʊlə(r)/ n singular f. ●adj singular; (unusual) raro; (noun) en singular

sinister /'sɪnɪstə(r)/ adj siniestro

sink /sɪŋk/ vt (pt sank, pp sunk) hundir. ●vi hundirse. ●n fregadero m (Amer, in bathroom) lavabo m, lavamanos m. □~ in vi penetrar

sinner /'sɪnə(r)/ n pecador m

sip /sɪp/ n sorbo m. ●vt (pt sipped) sorber

siphon /'saɪfən/ n sifón m. ~ (out) sacar con sifón. □~ off vt desviar (money).

sir /sɜː(r)/ n señor m. S~ n (title) sir m. Dear S~, (in letters) De mi mayor consideración.

siren /'saɪərən/ n sirena f

sister /'sɪstə(r)/ n hermana f; (nurse) enfermera f jefe. ~-in-law n (pl ~s-in-law) cuñada f

sit /sɪt/ vi (pt sat, pres p sitting) sentarse; (committee etc) reunirse en sesión. be ~ting estar sentado. ●vt sentar; hacer (exam). □~ back vi (fig) relajarse. □~ down vi sentarse. be ~ting down estar sentado. □~ up vi (from lying) incorporarse; (straighten back) ponerse derecho. ~-in n (strike) encierro m, ocupación f

site /saɪt/ n emplazamiento m; (piece of land) terreno m; (archaeo-

logical) yacimiento m. **building** ~ n solar m. ●vt situar

sit: ~ting n sesión f; (in restaurant) turno m. ~**ting room** n sala f de estar, living m

situat|e /'sɪtjʊeɪt/ vt situar. ~**ion** /-'eɪʃn/ n situación f

six /sɪks/ adj & n seis (m). ~**teen** /sɪk'stiːn/ adj & n dieciséis (m). ~**teenth** adj decimosexto. ●n dieciseisavo m. ~**th** adj & n sexto (m). ~**tieth** /'sɪkstɪɪθ/ adj sexagésimo. ●n sesentavo m. ~**ty** /'sɪkstɪ/ adj & n sesenta (m)

size /saɪz/ n tamaño m; (of clothes) talla f; (of shoes) número m; (of problem, operation) magnitud f. what ~ do you take? (clothes) ¿qué talla tiene?; (shoes) ¿qué número calza? □~ up vt 🗊 evaluar (problem); calar (person)

sizzle /'sɪzl/ vi crepitar

skat|e /skeɪt/ n patín m.●vi patinar. ~**eboard** n monopatín m, patineta f (Mex). ~**er** n patinador m. ~**ing** n patinaje m. ~**ing-rink** n pista f de patinaje

skeleton /'skelɪtn/ n esqueleto m. ~ **key** n llave f maestra

sketch /sketʃ/ n (drawing) dibujo m; (rougher) esbozo m; (TV, Theatre) sketch m. ●vt esbozar. ●vi dibujar. ~**y** adj (-ier, -iest) incompleto

ski /skiː/ n (pl skis) esquí m. ●vi (pt skied, pres p skiing) esquiar. go ~**ing** ir a esquiar

skid /skɪd/ vi (pt skidded) patinar. ●n patinazo m

ski: ~**er** n esquiador m. ~**ing** n esquí m

skilful /'skɪlfl/ adj diestro

ski-lift /'skiːlɪft/ n telesquí m

skill /skɪl/ n habilidad f; (technical) destreza f. ~**ed** adj hábil; (worker) cualificado

skim /skɪm/ vt (pt skimmed) espumar (soup); desnatar, descremar (milk); (glide over) pasar casi rozando. ~ **milk** (Amer), ~**med milk** n leche f desnatada, leche f descremada. ~ **through** vt leer por encima

skimp /skɪmp/ vi. ~ **on sth** escatimar algo. ~**y** adj (-ier, -iest) escaso; (skirt, dress) brevísimo

skin /skɪn/ n piel f. ● vt (pt skinned) despellejar. ~**-deep** adj superficial. ~**-diving** n submarinismo m. ~**ny** adj (-ier, -iest) flaco

skip /skɪp/ vi (pt skipped) vi saltar; (with rope) saltar a la comba, saltar a la cuerda. ● vt saltarse (chapter); faltar a (class). ● n brinco m; (container) contenedor m (para escombros). ~**per** n capitán m. ~**ping-rope**, ~**rope** (Amer) n comba f, cuerda f de saltar, reata f (Mex)

skirmish /ˈskɜːmɪʃ/ n escaramuza f

skirt /skɜːt/ n falda f. ● vt bordear; (go round) ladear. ~**ing-board** n rodapié m, zócalo m

skittle /ˈskɪtl/ n bolo m

skive off /skaɪv/ (vi 🇬🇧, disappear) escurrir el bulto; (stay away from work) no ir a trabajar

skulk /skʌlk/ vi (hide) esconderse. ~ **around** vi merodear

skull /skʌl/ n cráneo m; (remains) calavera f

sky /skaɪ/ n cielo m. ~**lark** n alondra f. ~**light** n tragaluz m. ~ **marshal** n guardia m armado a bordo. ~**scraper** n rascacielos m

slab /slæb/ n (of concrete) bloque m; (of stone) losa f

slack /slæk/ adj (-er, -est) flojo; (person) poco aplicado; (period) de poca actividad. ● vi flojear. ~**en** vt aflojar. ● vi (person) descansar. □ ~**en off** vt/i aflojar

slain /sleɪn/ see SLAY

slake /sleɪk/ vt apagar

slam /slæm/ vt (pt slammed). ~ **the door** dar un portazo. ~ **the door shut** cerrar de un golpe. ~ **on the brakes** pegar un frenazo; (sl, criticize) atacar violentamente. ● vi cerrarse de un portazo

slander /ˈslɑːndə(r)/ n calumnia f. ● vt difamar

slang /slæŋ/ n argot m

slant /slɑːnt/ vt inclinar. ● n inclinación f

slap /slæp/ vt (pt slapped) (on face) pegarle una bofetada a; (put) tirar. ~ **s.o. on the back** darle una palmada a uno en la espalda. ~ n bofetada f; (on back) palmada f. ● adv de lleno. ~**dash** adj descuidado; (work) chapucero

slash /slæʃ/ vt acuchillar; (fig) rebajar drásticamente. ● n cuchillada f

slat /slæt/ n tablilla f

slate /sleɪt/ n pizarra f. ● vt 🇬🇧 poner por los suelos

slaughter /ˈslɔːtə(r)/ vt matar salvajemente; matar (animal). ● n carnicería f; (of animals) matanza f

slave /sleɪv/ n esclavo m. ● vi ~ (away) trabajar como un negro. ~**-driver** n 🇬🇧 negrero m. ~**ry** /-ərɪ/ n esclavitud f

slay /sleɪ/ vt (pt slew, pp slain) dar muerte a

sleazy /ˈsliːzɪ/ adj (-ier, -iest) 🇬🇧 sórdido

sled /sled/ (Amer), **sledge** /sledʒ/ n trineo m

sledge-hammer n mazo m, almádena f

sleek /sliːk/ adj (-er, -est) liso, brillante

sleep /sliːp/ n sueño m. go to ∼ dormirse. ● vi (pt slept) dormir. ∼ off poder alojar. ∼er n (on track) traviesa f, durmiente m. be a light/ heavy ∼er tener el sueño ligero/ pesado. ∼ing bag n saco m de dormir. ∼ing pill n somnífero m. ∼less adj. have a ∼less night pasar la noche en blanco. ∼walk vi caminar dormido. ∼y adj (-ier, -iest) soñoliento. be/feel ∼y tener sueño

sleet /sliːt/ n aguanieve f

sleeve /sliːv/ n manga f; (for record) funda f, carátula f. up one's ∼ en reserva. ∼less adj sin mangas

sleigh /sleɪ/ n trineo m

slender /'slendə(r)/ adj delgado; (fig) escaso

slept /slept/ see SLEEP

slew /sluː/ see SLAY

slice /slaɪs/ n (of ham) lonja f; (of bread) rebanada f; (of meat) tajada f; (of cheese) trozo m; (of sth round) rodaja f. ● vt cortar (en rebanadas, tajadas etc)

slick /slɪk/ adj (performance) muy pulido. ● n. (oil) ∼ marea f negra

slid|e /slaɪd/ vt (pt slid) deslizar. ● vi (intentionally) deslizarse; (unintentionally) resbalarse. ● n resbalón m; (in playground) tobogán m, resbaladilla f (Mex); (for hair) pasador m, broche m (Mex); (Photo) diapositiva f. ∼ing scale n escala f móvil

slight /slaɪt/ adj (-er, -est) ligero; (slender) delgado. ● vt desairar. ● n desaire m. ∼est adj mínimo. not in the ∼est en absoluto. ∼ly adv un poco, ligeramente

slim /slɪm/ adj (slimmer, slim-

mest) delgado. ● vi (pt slimmed) (become slimmer) adelgazar; (diet) hacer régimen

slim|e /slaɪm/ n limo m; (of snail, slug) baba f. ∼y adj viscoso; (fig) excesivamente obsequioso

sling /slɪŋ/ n (Med) cabestrillo m. ● vt (pt slung) lanzar

slip /slɪp/ vt (pt slipped) deslizar. ∼ s.o.'s mind olvidársele a uno. ● vi resbalarse. it ∼ped out of my hands se me resbaló de las manos. he ∼ped out the back door se deslizó por la puerta trasera ● n resbalón m; (mistake) error m; (petticoat) combinación f; (paper) trozo m. give s.o. the ∼ lograr zafarse de uno. ∼ of the tongue n lapsus m linguae. □ ∼ away vi escabullirse. □ ∼ up vi 𝕋 equivocarse

slipper /'slɪpə(r)/ n zapatilla f

slippery /'slɪpərɪ/ adj resbaladizo

slip: ∼ road n rampa f de acceso. ∼shod /'slɪpʃɒd/ adj descuidado. ∼-up n 𝕋 error m

slit /slɪt/ n raja f; (cut) corte m. ● vt (pt slit, pres p slitting) rajar; (cut) cortar

slither /'slɪðə(r)/ vi deslizarse

slobber /'slɒbə(r)/ vi babear

slog /slɒg/ vt (pt slogged) golpear. ● vi caminar trabajosamente. ● n golpetazo m; (hard work) trabajo m penoso. □ ∼ away vi sudar tinta 𝕋

slogan /'sləʊgən/ n eslogan m

slop /slɒp/ vt (pt slopped) derramar. ● vi derramarse

slop|e /sləʊp/ vi inclinarse. ● vt inclinar. ● n declive m, pendiente f. ∼ing adj inclinado

sloppy /'slɒpɪ/ adj (-ier, -iest) (work) descuidado; (person) desaliñado

slosh /slɒʃ/ vi 🅣 chapotear

slot /slɒt/ n ranura f. ●vt (pt slotted) encajar

slot-machine n distribuidor m automático; (for gambling) máquina f tragamonedas

slouch /slaʊtʃ/ vi andar cargado de espaldas; (in chair) repanchigarse

Slovak /'sləʊvæk/ adj & n eslovaco (m). ~**ia** n Eslovaquia f

slovenly /'slʌvnlɪ/ adj (work) descuidado; (person) desaliñado

slow /sləʊ/ adj (-er, -est) lento. be ~ (clock) estar atrasado. in ~ motion a cámara lenta. ●adv despacio. ●vt retardar. ●vi ir más despacio. □ ~ **down**, ~ **up** vt retardar. vi ir más despacio. ~**ly** adv despacio, lentamente

sludge /slʌdʒ/ n fango m

slug /slʌg/ n babosa f. ~**gish** adj lento

slum /slʌm/ n barrio m bajo

slumber /'slʌmbə(r)/ vi dormir

slump /slʌmp/ n baja f repentina; (in business) depresión f. ●vi desplomarse

slung /slʌŋ/ see SLING

slur /slɜː(r)/ vt (pt slurred) ~ one's words arrastrar las palabras. ●n. a racist ~ un comentario racista

slush /slʌʃ/ n nieve f medio derretida. ~ **fund** n fondo m de reptiles

sly /slaɪ/ adj (slyer, slyest) (crafty) astuto. ●n. on the ~ a hurtadillas. ~**ly** adv astutamente

smack /smæk/ n manotazo m. ●adv 🅣 ~ **in the middle** justo en el medio. he went ~ **into** a tree se dio contra un árbol. ●vt pegarle a (con la mano)

small /smɔːl/ adj (-er, -est) pequeño, chico (LAm). ●n. the ~ of the back la región lumbar. ~ **ads** npl anuncios mpl (clasificados), avisos mpl (clasificados) (LAm). ~**change** n suelto m. ~**pox** /-pɒks/ n viruela f. ~ **talk** n charla f sobre temas triviales

smart /smɑːt/ adj (-er, -est) elegante; (clever) listo; (brisk) rápido. ●vi escocer. □ ~**en up** vt arreglar. vi (person) mejorar su aspecto, arreglarse. ~**ly** adv elegantemente; (quickly) rápidamente

smash /smæʃ/ vt romper; (into little pieces) hacer pedazos; batir (record). ●vi romperse; (collide) chocar (into con). ●n (noise) estrépito m; (collision) choque m; (in sport) smash m. □ ~ **up** vt destrozar. ~**ing** adj 🅣 estupendo

smattering /'smætərɪŋ/ n nociones fpl

smear /smɪə(r)/ vt untar (with de); (stain) manchar (with de); (fig) difamar. ●n mancha f

smell /smel/ n olor m; (sense) olfato m. ●vt (pt smelt) oler; (animal) olfatear. ●vi oler. ~ **of** sth oler a algo. ~**y** adj maloliente. be ~**y** oler mal

smelt /smelt/ see SMELL. ●vt fundir

smile /smaɪl/ n sonrisa f. ●vi sonreír. ~ **at s.o.** sonreírle a uno

smirk /smɜːk/ n sonrisita f (de suficiencia etc)

smith /smɪθ/ n herrero m

smithereens /smɪðə'riːnz/ npl. smash sth to ~ hacer algo añicos

smock /smɒk/ n blusa f, bata f

smog /smɒg/ n smog m

smoke /sməʊk/ n humo m. ●vt fumar (tobacco); ahumar (food).

● vi fumar. **∼eless** adj que arde sin humo. **∼er** n fumador m. **∼y** adj (room) lleno de humo

smooth /smuːð/ adj (-er, -est) (texture/stone) liso; (skin) suave; (movement) suave; (sea) tranquilo. ● vt alisar. □ **∼ out** vt allanar (problems). **∼ly** adv suavemente; (without problems) sin problemas

smother /ˈsmʌðə(r)/ vt asfixiar (person). **∼ s.o. with kisses** cubrir a uno de besos

smoulder /ˈsməʊldə(r)/ vi arder sin llama

smudge /smʌdʒ/ n borrón m. ● vi tiznarse

smug /smʌɡ/ adj (smugger, smuggest) pagado de sí mismo; (expression) de suficiencia

smuggle /ˈsmʌɡl/ vt pasar de contrabando. **∼er** n contrabandista m & f. **∼ing** n contrabando m

snack /snæk/ n tentempié m. **∼ bar** n cafetería f

snag /snæɡ/ n problema m

snail /sneɪl/ n caracol m. **at a ∼'s pace** a paso de tortuga

snake /sneɪk/ n culebra f, serpiente f

snap /snæp/ vt (pt snapped) (break) romper. **∼ one's fingers** chasquear los dedos. ● vi romperse; (dog) intentar morder; (say) contestar bruscamente. **∼ at** (dog) intentar morder; (say) contestar bruscamente. ● n chasquido m; (Photo) foto f ● adj instantáneo. □ **∼ up** vt no dejar escapar (offer). **∼py** adj (-ier, -iest) ⊞ rápido. **make it ∼py!** ¡date prisa! **∼shot** n foto f

snare /sneə(r)/ n trampa f

snarl /snɑːl/ vi gruñir

snatch /snætʃ/ vt. **∼ sth from s.o.** arrebatarle algo a uno; (steal)

robar. ● n (short part) fragmento m

sneak /sniːk/ n soplón m. ● vi (past & pp sneaked or ⊞ snuck). **∼ in** entrar a hurtadillas. **∼ off** escabullirse. **∼ers** /ˈsniːkəz/ npl zapatillas fpl de deporte. **∼y** adj artero

sneer /snɪə(r)/ n expresión f desdeñosa. ● vi hacer una mueca de desprecio. **∼ at** hablar con desprecio a

sneeze /sniːz/ n estornudo m. ● vi estornudar

snide /snaɪd/ adj insidioso

sniff /snɪf/ vt oler. ● vi sorberse la nariz

snigger /ˈsnɪɡə(r)/ n risilla f. ● vi reírse (por lo bajo)

snip /snɪp/ vt (pt snipped) dar un tijeretazo a. ● n tijeretazo m

sniper /ˈsnaɪpə(r)/ n francotirador m

snippet /ˈsnɪpɪt/ n (of conversation) trozo m. **∼s of information** datos mpl aislados

snivel /ˈsnɪvl/ vi (pt snivelled) lloriquear

snob /snɒb/ n esnob m & f. **∼bery** n esnobismo m. **∼bish** adj esnob

snooker /ˈsnuːkə(r)/ n snooker m

snoop /snuːp/ vi ⊞ husmear

snooze /snuːz/ n sueñecito m. ● vi dormitar

snore /snɔː(r)/ n ronquido m. ● vi roncar

snorkel /ˈsnɔːkl/ n esnórkel m

snort /snɔːt/ n bufido m. ● vi bufar

snout /snaʊt/ n hocico m

snow /snəʊ/ n nieve f. ● vi nevar. **be ∼ed in** estar aislado por la nieve. **be ∼ed under with work** estar agobiado de trabajo. **∼ball** n bola f de nieve. **∼drift** n nieve f amontonada. **∼fall** n nevada f

~flake n copo m de nieve. ~man n muñeco m de nieve. ~plough n quitanieves m. ~storm n tormenta f de nieve. ~y adj (day, weather) nevoso; (landscape) nevado

snub /snʌb/ vt (pt **snubbed**) desairar. ● n desaire m. ~-**nosed** adj chato

snuck /snʌk/ see **SNEAK**

snuff out /snʌf/ vt apagar (candle)

snug /snʌg/ adj (**snugger, snuggest**) cómodo; (tight) ajustado

snuggle (up) /snʌgl/ vi acurrucarse

so /səʊ/ adv (before a or adv) tan; (thus) así; and ~ on, and ~ forth etcétera (etcétera). I think ~ creo que sí. or ~ más o menos. ~ long! ¡hasta luego! ● conj (therefore) así que. ~ am I yo también. ~ as to para. ~ far adv (time) hasta ahora. ~ far as I know que yo sepa. ~ that conj para que.

soak /səʊk/ vt remojar. ● vi remojarse. □ ~ **in** vi penetrar. □ ~ **up** vt absorber. ~**ing** adj empapado.

so-and-so /səʊənsəʊ/ n fulano m

soap /səʊp/ n jabón m. ● n enjabonar. ~ **opera** n telenovela f, culebrón m. ~ **powder** n jabón m en polvo. ~**y** adj jabonoso

soar /sɔː(r)/ vi (bird/plane) planear; (rise) elevarse; (price) dispararse. ~**ing** adj (inflation) galopante

sob /sɒb/ n sollozo m. ● vi (pt **sobbed**) sollozar

sober /səʊbə(r)/ adj (not drunk) sobrio

so-called /səʊkɔːld/ adj denominado; (expert) supuesto

soccer /sɒkə(r)/ n fútbol m, futbol m (Mex)

sociable /səʊʃəbl/ adj sociable

social /səʊʃl/ adj social; (sociable) sociable. ~**ism** n socialismo m. ~**ist** adj & n socialista (m & f). ~**ize** vt socializar. ~ **security** n seguridad f social. ~ **worker** n asistente m social

society /səsaɪətɪ/ n sociedad f

sociolog|ical /səʊsɪəlɒdʒɪkl/ adj sociológico. ~**ist** /-ɒlədʒɪst/ n sociólogo m. ~**y** /-ɒlədʒɪ/ n sociología f

sock /sɒk/ n calcetín m

socket /sɒkɪt/ n (of joint) hueco m; (of eye) cuenca f; (wall plug) enchufe m; (for bulb) portalámparas m

soda /səʊdə/ n soda f. ~-**water** n soda f

sodium /səʊdɪəm/ n sodio m

sofa /səʊfə/ n sofá m

soft /sɒft/ adj (-er, -est) blando; (light, colour) suave; (gentle) dulce, tierno; (not strict) blando. ~ **drink** n refresco m. ~**en** /sɒfn/ vt ablandar; suavizar (skin). ● vi ablandarse. ~**ly** adv dulcemente; (speak) bajito. ~**ware** f /weə(r)/ n software m

soggy /sɒgɪ/ adj (-ier, -iest) empapado

soil /sɔɪl/ n tierra f; (Amer, dirt) suciedad f. ● vt ensuciar

solar /səʊlə(r)/ adj solar

sold /səʊld/ see **SELL**

solder /sɒldə(r)/ vt soldar

soldier /səʊldʒə(r)/ n soldado m. □ ~ **on** vi 🏴 seguir al pie del cañon

sole /səʊl/ n (of foot) planta f; (of shoe) suela f. ● adj único, solo. ~**ly** adv únicamente

solemn /sɒləm/ adj solemne

solicitor /səlɪsɪtə(r)/ n abogado m; (notary) notario m

solid /sɒlɪd/ adj sólido; (gold etc)

s

macizo; (*unanimous*) unánime; (*meal*) sustancioso. ● *n* sólido *m*. **~s** *npl* alimentos *mpl* sólidos.

~arity /sɒlɪˈdærətɪ/ *n* solidaridad *f*. **~ify** /səˈlɪdɪfaɪ/ *vi* solidificarse

solitary /ˈsɒlɪtrɪ/ *adj* solitario

solitude /ˈsɒlɪtjuːd/ *n* soledad *f*

solo /ˈsəʊləʊ/ *n* (*pl* -os) (*Mus*) solo *m*. **~ist** *n* solista *m & f*

solstice /ˈsɒlstɪs/ *n* solsticio *m*

solu|ble /ˈsɒljʊbl/ *adj* soluble. **~tion** /səˈluːʃn/ *n* solución *f*

solve /sɒlv/ *vt* solucionar (problem); resolver (mystery). **~nt** /-vənt/ *adj & n* solvente (*m*)

sombre /ˈsɒmbə(r)/ *adj* sombrío

---

some /sʌm//səm/

● adjective

····▸ (*unspecified number*) unos, unas. he ate ~ olives comió unas aceitunas

····▸ (*unspecified amount*) *not translated.* I have to buy ~ bread tengo que comprar pan. would you like ~ coffee? ¿quieres café?

····▸ (*certain, not all*) algunos, -nas. I like ~ modern writers algunos escritores modernos me gustan

····▸ (*a little*) algo de. I eat ~ meat, but not much como algo de carne, pero no mucho

····▸ (*considerable amount of*) we've known each other for ~ time ya hace tiempo que nos conocemos

····▸ (*expressing admiration*) that's ~ car you've got! ¡vaya coche que tienes!

● pronoun

····▸ (*a number of things or people*) algunos, -nas, unos, unas. ~ are mine and ~ aren't algunos *or* unos son míos y otros no. aren't there any apples? we bought ~ yesterday ¿no hay manzanas? compramos algunas ayer

····▸ (*part of an amount*) he wants ~ quiere un poco. ~ of what he said parte *or* algo de lo que dijo

····▸ (*certain people*) algunos, -nas . ~ say that... algunos dicen que...

● adverb

····▸ (*approximately*) unos, unas, alrededor de. there were ~ fifty people there había unas cincuenta personas, había alrededor de cincuenta personas

---

some: ~body /-bədɪ/ *pron* alguien. **~how** *adv* de algún modo. **~how or other** de una manera u otra. **~one** *pron* alguien

somersault /ˈsʌməsɔːlt/ *n* salto *m* mortal. ● *vi* dar un salto mortal

some: ~thing *pron* algo *m*. **~thing like** (*approximately*) alrededor de. **~time** *adj* ex. ● *adv* algún día. **~time** next week un día de la semana que viene. **~times** *adv* a veces. **~what** *adv* un tanto. **~where** *adv* en alguna parte, en algún lado

son /sʌn/ *n* hijo *m*

sonata /səˈnɑːtə/ *n* sonata *f*

song /sɒŋ/ *n* canción *f*

sonic /ˈsɒnɪk/ *adj* sónico

son-in-law /ˈsʌnɪnlɔː/ *n* (*pl* sons-in-law) yerno *m*

sonnet /ˈsɒnɪt/ *n* soneto *m*

son of a bitch *n* (*pl* sons of bitches) (*esp Amer sl*) hijo *m* de puta

soon /suːn/ adv (-er, -est) pronto; (in a short time) dentro de poco. ~ after poco después. ~er or later tarde o temprano. as ~ as en cuanto; as ~ as possible lo antes posible. the ~er the better cuanto antes mejor

soot /sʊt/ n hollín m

sooth|e /suːð/ vt calmar; aliviar (pain). ~ing adj (medicine) calmante; (words) tranquilizador

sooty /ˈsʊtɪ/ adj cubierto de hollín

sophisticated /səˈfɪstɪkeɪtɪd/ adj sofisticado; (complex) complejo

sophomore /ˈsɒfəmɔː(r)/ n (Amer) estudiante m & f de segundo curso (en la universidad)

sopping /ˈsɒpɪŋ/ adj. ~ (wet) empapado

soppy /ˈsɒpɪ/ adj (-ier, -iest) 🛈 sentimental

soprano /səˈprɑːnəʊ/ n (pl -os) soprano f

sordid /ˈsɔːdɪd/ adj sórdido

sore /sɔː(r)/ adj (-er, -est) dolorido; (Amer fam, angry) be ~ at s.o. estar picado con uno. ~ throat n dolor m de garganta. I've got a ~ throat me duele la garganta. • n llaga f

sorrow /ˈsɒrəʊ/ n pena f, pesar m

sorry /ˈsɒrɪ/ adj (-ier, -ier) arrepentido; (wretched) lamentable. I'm ~ lo siento. be ~ for s.o. (pity) compadecer a uno. I'm ~ you can't come siento que no puedas venir. say ~ pedir perdón. ~! (apologizing) ¡lo siento! ¡perdón!. ~? (asking s.o. to repeat) ¿cómo?

sort /sɔːt/ n tipo m, clase f; (fam, person) tipo m. a ~ of una especie de. • vt clasificar. □ ~ out vt (or-

ganize) ordenar; organizar (finances); (separate out) separar; solucionar (problem)

so-so /ˈsəʊsəʊ/ adj regular

soufflé /ˈsuːfleɪ/ n suflé m

sought /sɔːt/ see SEEK

soul /səʊl/ n alma f

sound /saʊnd/ n sonido m; (noise) ruido m. • vt tocar. • vi sonar; (seem) parecer (as if). it ~s interesting suena interesante.. • adj (-er, -est) sano; (argument) lógico; (secure) seguro. • adv. ~ asleep profundamente dormido. ~ **barrier** n barrera f del sonido. ~**ly** adv sólidamente, (asleep) profundamente. ~**proof** adj insonorizado. ~**track** n banda f sonora

soup /suːp/ n sopa f

sour /ˈsaʊə(r)/ adj (-er, -est) agrio; (milk) cortado

source /sɔːs/ n fuente f

south /saʊθ/ n sur m. • adj sur a invar; (wind) del sur. • adv (go) hacia el sur. it's ~ of está al sur de. S~ **Africa** n Sudáfrica f. S~ **America** n América f (del Sur), Sudamérica f. S~ **American** adj & n sudamericano (m). ~-**east** n sudeste m, sureste m. ~**erly** /ˈsʌðəlɪ/ (wind) del sur. ~**ern** /ˈsʌðən/ adj del sur, meridional. ~**erner** n sureño m. ~**ward** /-wəd/, ~**wards** adv hacia el sur. ~-**west** n sudoeste m, suroeste m

souvenir /suːvəˈnɪə(r)/ n recuerdo m

sovereign /ˈsɒvrɪn/ n & a soberano (m)

Soviet /ˈsəʊvɪət/ adj (History) soviético. the ~ **Union** n la Unión f Soviética

sow¹ /səʊ/ vt (pt sowed, pp sowed or sown /səʊn/) sembrar

s

sow[2] /sau/ n cerda f

soy (esp Amer), **soya** /'sɔɪə/ n. ~ **bean** n soja f

spa /spɑː/ n balneario m

space /speɪs/ n espacio m; (room) espacio m, lugar m. ● adj (research etc) espacial. ● vt espaciar. □ ~ **out** vt espaciar. ~**craft**, ~**ship** n nave f espacial

spade /speɪd/ n pala f. ~**s** npl (Cards) picas fpl

spaghetti /spə'getɪ/ n espaguetis mpl

Spain /speɪn/ n España f

spam /spæm/ n (Comp) correo m basura

span /spæn/ n (of arch) luz f; (of time) espacio m; (of wings) envergadura f. ● vt (pt spanned) extenderse sobre. ● adj see **SPICK**

Spaniard /'spænjəd/ n español m

spaniel /'spænjəl/ n perdiguero m

Spanish /'spænɪʃ/ adj español; (language) castellano, español. ● n (language) castellano m, español m. npl. the ~ (people) los españoles

spank /spæŋk/ vt pegarle a (en las nalgas)

spanner /'spænə(r)/ n llave f

spare /speə(r)/ vt. if you can ~ the time si tienes tiempo. can you ~ me a pound? ¿tienes una libra que me des? ~ no effort no escatimar esfuerzos. have money to ~ tener dinero de sobra. ● adj (not in use) de más; (replacement) de repuesto; (free) libre. ~ **part** n repuesto m. ~ **room** n cuarto m de huéspedes. ~ **time** n tiempo m libre. ~ **tyre** n neumático m de repuesto

sparingly /'speərɪŋlɪ/ adv (use) con moderación

spark /spɑːk/ n chispa f. ● vt provocar (criticism); suscitar (interest). ~**ing plug** n (Auto) bujía f

sparkl|e /'spɑːkl/ vi centellear. ● n destello m. ~**ing** adj centelleante; (wine) espumoso

spark plug n (Auto) bujía f

sparrow /'spærəʊ/ n gorrión m

sparse /spɑːs/ adj escaso. ~**ly** adv escasamente

spasm /'spæzəm/ n espasmo m; (of cough) acceso m. ~**odic** /-'mɒdɪk/ adj espasmódico; (Med) irregular

spat /spæt/ see **SPIT**

spate /speɪt/ n racha f

spatial /'speɪʃl/ adj espacial

spatter /'spætə(r)/ vt salpicar (with de)

spawn /spɔːn/ n huevas fpl. ● vt generar. ● vi desovar

speak /spiːk/ vt/i (pt spoke, pp spoken) hablar. ~ for s.o. hablar en nombre de uno. □ ~ **up** vi hablar más fuerte. ~**er** n (in public) orador m; (loudspeaker) altavoz m; (of language) hablante m & f

spear /spɪə(r)/ n lanza f. ~**head** vt (lead) encabezar

special /'speʃl/ adj especial. ~**ist** /'speʃəlɪst/ n especialista m & f. ~**ity** /-ɪ'ælətɪ/ n especialidad f. ~**ization** /-əlaɪ'zeɪʃn/ n especialización f. ~**ize** /-əlaɪz/ vi especializarse. ~**ized** adj especializado. ~**ly** adv especialmente. ~**ty** n (Amer) especialidad f

species /'spiːʃiːz/ n especie f

specif|ic /spə'sɪfɪk/ adj específico. ~**ically** adv específicamente; (state) explícitamente. ~**ication** /-ɪ'keɪʃn/ n especificación f. ~**y** /'spesɪfaɪ/ vt especificar

specimen /'spesɪmɪn/ n muestra f

speck /spek/ n (of dust) mota f; (in distance) punto m

specs /speks/ npl 🄸 see **SPEC-TACLES**

spectac|le /'spektəkl/ n espectáculo m. ~**les** npl gafas fpl, lentes fpl (LAm), anteojos mpl (LAm). ~**ular** /-'tækjʊlə(r)/ adj espectacular

spectator /spek'teɪtə(r)/ n espectador m

spectr|e /'spektə(r)/ n espectro m. ~**um** /'spektrəm/ n (pl -**tra** /-trə/) espectro m; (of views) gama f

speculat|e /'spekjʊleɪt/ vi especular. ~**ion** /-'leɪʃn/ n especulación f. ~**or** n especulador m

sped /sped/ see **SPEED**

speech /spi:tʃ/ n (faculty) habla f; (address) discurso m. ~**less** adj mudo

speed /spi:d/ n velocidad f; (rapidity) rapidez f. ●vi (pt **speeded**) (drive too fast) ir a exceso de velocidad. □ ~ **off**, ~ **away** (pt **sped**) vi alejarse a toda velocidad. □ ~ **by** (pt **sped**) vi (time) pasar volando. □ ~ **up** (pt **speeded**) vt acelerar. vi acelerarse. ~**boat** n lancha f motora. ~ **camera** n cámara f de control de velocidad. ~ **dating** n cita f flash, speed dating m. ~ **limit** n velocidad f máxima. ~**ometer** /spi:'dɒmɪtə(r)/ n velocímetro m. ~**way** n (Amer) autopista f. ~**y** adj (-**ier**, -**iest**) rápido

spell /spel/ n (magic) hechizo m; (of weather, activity) período m. go through a bad ~ pasar por una mala racha. ●vt/i (pt **spelled** or **spelt**) escribir. □ ~ **out** vt deletrear; (fig) explicar. ~**checker** n corrector m ortográfico. ~**ing** n ortografía f

spellbound /'spelbaʊnd/ adj em-belesado

spelt /spelt/ see **SPELL**

spend /spend/ vt (pt **spent** /spent/) gastar (money); pasar (time); dedicar (care). ●vi gastar dinero

sperm /spɜ:m/ n (pl **sperms** or **sperm**) esperma f; (individual) espermatozoide m

spew /spju:/ vt/i vomitar

spher|e /sfɪə(r)/ n esfera f. ~**ical** /'sferɪkl/ adj esférico

spice /spaɪs/ n especia f

spick /spɪk/ adj. ~ **and span** limpio y ordenado

spicy /'spaɪsɪ/ adj picante

spider /'spaɪdə(r)/ n araña f

spike /spaɪk/ n (of metal etc) punta f. ~**y** adj puntiagudo

spill /spɪl/ vt (pt **spilled** or **spilt**) derramar. ●vi derramarse. □ ~ **over** (container) desbordarse; (liquid) rebosar

spin /spɪn/ vt (pt **spun**, pres p **spinning**) hacer girar; hilar (wool); centrifugar (washing). ●vi girar. ●n. give sth a ~ hacer girar algo. go for a ~ (Auto) ir a dar un paseo en coche

spinach /'spɪnɪdʒ/ n espinacas fpl

spindly /'spɪndlɪ/ adj larguirucho

spin-drier /spɪn'draɪə(r)/ n centrifugadora f (de ropa)

spine /spaɪn/ n columna f vertebral; (of book) lomo m; (on animal) púa f. ~**less** adj (fig) sin carácter

spinning wheel /'spɪnɪŋ/ n rueca f

spin-off /'spɪnɒf/ n resultado m indirecto; (by-product) producto m derivado

spinster /'spɪnstə(r)/ n soltera f

spiral /'spaɪərəl/ adj espiral;

(shape) de espiral. ● *n* espiral *f.* ● *vi* (*pt* spiralled) (unemployment) escalar; (prices) dispararse. ~ **staircase** *n* escalera *f* de caracol

spire /'spaɪə(r)/ *n* aguja *f*

spirit /'spɪrɪt/ *n* espíritu *m.* be in good ~s estar animado. in low ~s abatido. ~ed *adj* animado, fogoso. ~s *npl* (drinks) bebidas *fpl* alcohólicas (de alta graduación). ~ual /'spɪrɪtjuəl/ *adj* espiritual

spit /spɪt/ *vt* (*pt* spat or (Amer) spit, *pres p* spitting) escupir. ● *vi* escupir. it's ~ting caen algunas gotas. ● *n* saliva *f*; (for roasting) asador *m*

spite /spaɪt/ *n* rencor *m.* in ~ of a pesar de. ● *vt* fastidiar. ~ful *adj* rencoroso

spittle /'spɪtl/ *n* baba *f*

splash /splæʃ/ *vt* salpicar. ● *vi* (person) chapotear. ● *n* salpicadura *f.* a ~ of paint un poco de pintura. □ ~ **about** *vi* chapotear. □ ~ **down** *vi* (spacecraft) amerizar. □ ~ **out** *vi* gastarse un dineral (on en)

splend|id /'splendɪd/ *adj* espléndido. ~our /-ə(r)/ *n* esplendor *m*

splint /splɪnt/ *n* tablilla *f*

splinter /'splɪntə(r)/ *n* astilla *f.* ● *vi* astillarse

split /splɪt/ *vt* (*pt* split, *pres p* splitting) partir; fisionar (atom); reventar (trousers); (divide) dividir. ● *vi* partirse; dividirse. a ~ting headache un dolor de cabeza espantoso. ● *n* (in garment) descosido *m*; (in wood, glass) rajadura *f.* □ ~ **up** *vi* separarse. ~ **second** *n* fracción *f* de segundo

splutter /'splʌtə(r)/ *vi* chisporrotear; (person) farfullar

spoil /spɔɪl/ *vt* (*pt* spoilt or spoiled) estropear, echar a perder; (indulge) consentir, malcriar. ~s *npl*

botín *m.* ~-**sport** *n* aguafiestas *m & f*

spoke[1] /spəʊk/ *see* SEE SPEAK

spoke[2] /spəʊk/ *n* (of wheel) rayo *m*

spoken /spəʊkən/ *see* SPEAK

spokesman /'spəʊksmən/ *n* (*pl* -men) portavoz *m*

sponge /spʌndʒ/ *n* esponja *f.* ● *vt* limpiar con una esponja. □ ~ **off,** ~ **on** *vt* vivir a costillas de. ~ **cake** *n* bizcocho *m*

sponsor /'spɒnsə(r)/ *n* patrocinador *m*; (of the arts) mecenas *m & f*; (surety) garante *m.* ● *vt* patrocinar. ~**ship** *n* patrocinio *m*; (of the arts) mecenazgo *m*

spontaneous /spɒn'teɪnɪəs/ *adj* espontáneo. ~**ously** *adv* espontáneamente

spoof /spu:f/ *n* [1] parodia *f*

spooky /'spu:kɪ/ *adj* (-ier, -iest) [1] espeluznante

spool /spu:l/ *n* carrete *m*

spoon /spu:n/ *n* cuchara *f.* ~**ful** *n* cucharada *f*

sporadic /spə'rædɪk/ *adj* esporádico

sport /spɔ:t/ *n* deporte *m.* ~s **car** *n* coche *m* deportivo. ~s **centre** *n* centro *m* deportivo. ~**sman** /-mən/ *n,* (*pl* -men), ~**swoman** *n* deportista *f*

spot /spɒt/ *n* mancha *f*; (pimple) grano *m*; (place) lugar *m*; (in pattern) lunar *m.* be in a ~ [1] estar en apuros. **on the** ~ allí mismo; (decide) en ese mismo momento. ● *vt* (*pt* spotted) manchar; (fam, notice) ver, divisar; descubrir (mistake). ~ **check** *n* control *m* hecho al azar. ~**less** *adj* (clothes) impecable; (house) limpísimo. ~**light** *n* reflector *m*; (in theatre) foco *m*

~**ted** adj moteado; (material) de lunares. ~**ty** adj (-ier, -iest) (skin) lleno de granos; (youth) con la cara llena de granos

spouse /spaʊz/ n cónyuge m & f

spout /spaʊt/ n pico m; (jet) chorro m

sprain /spreɪn/ vt hacerse un esguince en. ● n esguince m

sprang /spræŋ/ see **SPRING**

spray /spreɪ/ n (of flowers) ramillete m; (from sea) espuma f; (liquid in spray form) espray m; (device) rociador m. ● vt rociar

spread /spred/ vt (pt spread) (stretch, extend) extender; desplegar (wings); difundir (idea, news). ~ **butter on a piece of toast** untar una tostada con mantequilla. ● vi extenderse; (disease) propagarse; (idea, news) difundirse. ● n (of ideas) difusión f; (of disease, fire) propagación f; (fam, feast) festín m. □ ~ **out** vi (move apart) desplegarse

spree /spriː/ n. **go on a shopping** ~ ir de expedición a las tiendas

sprightly /ˈspraɪtlɪ/ adj (-ier, -iest) vivo

spring /sprɪŋ/ n (season) primavera f; (device) resorte m; (in mattress) muelle m, resorte m (LAm); (elasticity) elasticidad f; (water) manantial m. ● adj primaveral. ● vi (pt sprang, pp sprung) saltar; (issue) brotar. ~ **from sth** (problem) provenir de algo. □ ~ **up** vi surgir. ~**board** n trampolín m. ~**-clean** /ˈkliːn/ vi hacer una limpieza general. ~ **onion** n cebolleta f. ~ **time** n primavera f. ~**y** adj (-ier, -iest) (mattress, step) mullido

sprinkle /ˈsprɪŋkl/ vt salpicar; (with liquid) rociar. ● n salpicadura f. ~ (of liquid) rociada f. ~**r** n rega-

dera f

sprint /sprɪnt/ n carrera f corta. ● vi (Sport) esprintar; (run fast) correr. ~**er** n corredor m

sprout /spraʊt/ vi brotar. ● n brote m. (**Brussels**) ~**s** npl coles fpl de Bruselas

sprung /sprʌŋ/ see **SPRING**

spud /spʌd/ n 🄵 patata f, papa f (LAm)

spun /spʌn/ see **SPIN**

spur /spɜː(r)/ n espuela f; (stimulus) acicate m. **on the** ~ **of the moment** sin pensarlo. ● vt (pt spurred) ~ (**on**) espolear; (fig) estimular

spurn /spɜːn/ vt desdeñar; (reject) rechazar

spurt /spɜːt/ vi (liquid) salir a chorros. ● n chorro m; (of activity) racha f

spy /spaɪ/ n espía m & f. ● vt descubrir, ver. ● vi espiar. ~ **on s.o.** espiar a uno

squabble /ˈskwɒbl/ vi reñir

squad /skwɒd/ n (Mil) pelotón m; (of police) brigada f; (Sport) equipo m. ~ **car** n coche m patrulla. ~**ron** /ˈskwɒdrən/ n (Mil, Aviat) escuadrón m; (Naut) escuadra f

squalid /ˈskwɒlɪd/ adj miserable

squall /skwɔːl/ n turbión m

squalor /ˈskwɒlə(r)/ n miseria f

squander /ˈskwɒndə(r)/ vt derrochar; desaprovechar (opportunity)

square /skweə(r)/ n cuadrado m; (in town) plaza f. ● adj cuadrado; (meal) decente; (fam, old-fashioned) chapado a la antigua. ● vt (settle) arreglar; (Math) elevar al cuadrado. ● vi (agree) cuadrar. ~ **up** vi arreglar cuentas (with con). ~**ly** adv directamente

squash /skwɒʃ/ vt aplastar; (sup-

s

press) acallar. ● _n._ it was a terrible
~ íbamos (or iban) terriblemente
apretujados; (_drink_) **orange** ~ naranjada _f_; (_Sport_) squash _m_; (_vege-
table_) calabaza _f._ ~**y** _adj_ blando

squat /skwɒt/ _vi_ (_pt_ **squatted**) ponerse en cuclillas; (_occupy illegally_)
ocupar sin autorización. ● _adj_ rechoncho y bajo. ~**ter** _n_ ocupante
_m_ & _f_ ilegal, okupa _m_ & _f_

squawk /skwɔːk/ _n_ graznido _m._
● _vi_ graznar

squeak /skwiːk/ _n_ chillido _m_; (_of
door_) chirrido _m._ ● _vi_ chillar; (_door_)
chirriar; (_shoes_) crujir. ~**y** _adj_ chi-
rriante

squeal /skwiːl/ _n_ chillido _m_. ● _vi_
chillar

squeamish /ˈskwiːmɪʃ/ _adj_ impresionable, delicado

squeeze /skwiːz/ _vt_ apretar; expri-
mir (_lemon etc.) ● _vi._ ~ **in** meterse. ● _n_ estrujón _m_; (_of hand_)
apretón _m_

squid /skwɪd/ _n_ calamar _m_

squiggle /ˈskwɪgl/ _n_ garabato _m_

squint /skwɪnt/ _vi_ bizquear; (_try-
ing to see_) entrecerrar los ojos. ● _n_
estrabismo _m_

squirm /skwɜːm/ _vi_ retorcerse

squirrel /ˈskwɪrəl/ _n_ ardilla _f._

squirt /skwɜːt/ _vt_ (_liquid_) echar un
chorro de. ● _vi_ salir a chorros. ● _n_
chorrito _m_

St /sənt/ _abbr_ (= **saint**) /sənt/ S,
San(to); (= **street**) C/, Calle _f_

stab /stæb/ _vt_ (_pt_ **stabbed**) apuñalar. ● _n_ puñalada _f_; (_pain_) punzada
_f._ **have a** ~ **at sth** intentar algo

stabili|ty /stəˈbɪləti/ _n_ estabilidad
_f._ ~**ze** /ˈsteɪbɪlaɪz/ _vt/i_ estabilizar

stable /ˈsteɪbl/ _adj_ (**-er**, **-est**) estable. ● _n_ caballeriza _f_, cuadra _f_

stack /stæk/ _n_ montón _m._ ● _vt._ ~

(**up**) amontonar

stadium /ˈsteɪdɪəm/ _n_ (_pl_ **-diums**
or **-dia** /-dɪə/) estadio _m_

staff /stɑːf/ _n_ (_stick_) palo _m_; (_em-
ployees_) personal _m_, personal _m_
docente. ~ **member of**
~ un empleado

stag /stæg/ _n_ ciervo _m_. ~**night**,
~**party** _n_ (_before wedding_) fiesta _f_
de despedida de soltero; (_men-only
party_) fiesta _f_ para hombres

stage /steɪdʒ/ _n_ (_in theatre_) escenario _f_; (_platform_) plataforma _f_;
(_phase_) etapa _f._ **the** ~ (_profession,
medium_) el teatro. ● _vt_ poner en
escena (_play_); (_arrange_) organizar;
(_pej_) orquestar. ~**coach** _n_ diligen-
cia _f_

stagger /ˈstægə(r)/ _vi_ tambalearse. ● _vt_ dejar estupefacto; esca-
lonar (_holidays etc._). ~**ing** _adj_
asombroso

stagna|nt /ˈstægnənt/ _adj_ estan-
cado. ~**te** /stægˈneɪt/ _vi_ estancarse

staid /steɪd/ _adj_ serio, formal

stain /steɪn/ _vt_ manchar; (_colour_)
teñir. ● _n_ mancha _f_; (_dye_) tintura _f._
~**ed glass window** _n_ vidriera _f_ de
colores. ~**less steel** _n_ acero _m_ inoxidable. ~ **remover** _n_ quitaman-
chas _m_

stair /steə(r)/ _n_ escalón _m._ ~**s** _npl_
escalera _f._ ~**case**, ~**way** _n_ escalera _f_

stake /steɪk/ _n_ estaca _f_; (_wager_)
apuesta _f_; (_Com_) intereses _mpl._ **be
at** ~ estar en juego. ● _vt_ estacar;
jugarse (_reputation_). ~ **a claim** reclamar

stala|ctite /ˈstæləktaɪt/ _n_ estalac-
tita _f._ ~**gmite** /ˈstæləgmaɪt/ _n_ es-
talagmita _f_

stale /steɪl/ _adj_ (**-er**, **-est**) no
fresco; (_bread_) duro; (_smell_) vi-

ciado. ~**mate** n (Chess) ahogado m; (deadlock) punto m muerto

stalk /stɔːk/ n tallo m. ● vt acechar. ● vi irse indignado

stall /stɔːl/ n (in stable) compartimiento m; (in market) puesto m. ~**s** npl (in theatre) platea f, patio m de butacas. ● vt parar (engine). ● vi (engine) pararse; (fig) andar con rodeos

stallion /ˈstæljən/ n semental m

stalwart /ˈstɔːlwət/ adj (supporter) leal, incondicional

stamina /ˈstæmɪnə/ n resistencia f

stammer /ˈstæmə(r)/ vi tartamudear. ● n tartamudeo m

stamp /stæmp/ vt (with feet) patear; (press) estampar; (with rubber stamp) sellar; (fig) señalar. ● n sello m, estampilla f (LAm), timbre m (Mex); (on passport) sello m; (with foot) patada f; (mark) marca f, señal f. □ ~ **out** vt (fig) erradicar. ~**ed addressed envelope** n sobre m franqueado con su dirección

stampede /stæmˈpiːd/ n estampida f. ● vi salir en estampida

stance /stɑːns/ n postura f

stand /stænd/ vi (pt stood) estar de pie, estar parado (LAm); (be) ponerse de pie, pararse; (be) encontrarse; (Pol) presentarse como candidato (for en). the offer ~**s** la oferta sigue en pie. □ ~ **to reason** ser lógico. ● vt (endure) soportar; (place) colocar. ~ **a chance** tener una posibilidad. ● n posición f, postura f; (for lamp etc) pie m, sostén m; (at market) puesto m; (booth) quiosco m; (Sport) tribuna f. **make a ~ against** sth oponer resistencia a algo. □ ~ **back** vi apartarse. □ ~ **by** vi estar preparado. vt (support) apoyar. □ ~ **down** vi retirarse. □ ~

for vt significar. □ ~ **in for** vt suplir a. □ ~ **out** vi destacarse. □ ~ **up** vi ponerse de pie, pararse (LAm). □ ~ **up for** vt defender. ~ **up for oneself** defenderse. □ ~ **up to** vt resistir a

standard /ˈstændəd/ n norma f; (level) nivel m; (flag) estandarte m. ● adj estándar a invar, normal. ~**ize** vt estandarizar. ~ **lamp** n lámpara f de pie. ~**s** npl principios mpl

stand: ~**by** n (at airport) standby m. **be on ~by** (police) estar en estado de alerta. ~**in** n suplente m & f. ~**ing** adj de pie, parado (LAm); (permanent) permanente f. ● n posición f; (prestige) prestigio m. ~**off** n (Amer, draw) empate m; (deadlock) callejón m sin salida. ~**point** n punto m de vista. ~**still** n. **be at a ~still** estar paralizado. **come to a ~still** (vehicle) parar; (city) quedar paralizado

stank /stæŋk/ see STINK

staple /ˈsteɪpl/ adj principal. ● n grapa f. ● vt sujetar con una grapa. ~**r** n grapadora f

star /stɑː(r)/ n (incl Cinema, Theatre) estrella f; (asterisk) asterisco m. ● vi (pt starred). ~ **in** a film protagonizar una película. ~**board** n estribor m

starch /stɑːtʃ/ n almidón m; (in food) fécula f. ● vt almidonar. ~**y** (food) adj a base de féculas

stardom /ˈstɑːdəm/ n estrellato m

stare /steə(r)/ n mirada f fija. ● vi. ~ **(at)** mirar fijamente

starfish /ˈstɑːfɪʃ/ n estrella f de mar

stark /stɑːk/ adj (-er, -est) escueto. ● adv completamente

starling /ˈstɑːlɪŋ/ n estornino m

s

starry /ˈstɑːrɪ/ adj estrellado

start /stɑːt/ vt empezar, comenzar; encender (engine); arrancar (car); (cause) provocar; abrir (business). ● vi empezar; (car etc) arrancar; (jump) dar un respingo. **to ~ with** (as linker) para empezar. **~ off by doing sth** empezar por hacer algo. ● n principio m, (Sport) ventaja f; (jump) susto m. **make an early ~** (on journey) salir temprano. **~er** n (Auto) motor m de arranque; (Culin) primer plato m. **~ing-point** n punto m de partida

startle /ˈstɑːtl/ vt asustar

starv|ation /stɑːˈveɪʃn/ n hambre f, inanición f. **~e** /stɑːv/ vt hacer morir de hambre. ● vi morirse de hambre. **I'm ~ing** me muero de hambre

state /steɪt/ n estado m. **to be in a ~** estar agitado. **the S~** los Estados mpl Unidos. ● vt declarar; expresar (views); (fix) fijar. **~ del Estado;** (Schol) público; (with ceremony) de gala. **~ly** adj (-ier, -iest) majestuoso. **~ly home** n casa f solariega. **~ment** n declaración f; (account) informe m. **~sman** /-mən/ n estadista m

static /ˈstætɪk/ adj estacionario. ● n (interference) estática f

station /ˈsteɪʃn/ n estación f; (on radio) emisora f; (TV) canal m. ● vt colocar; (Mil) estacionar. **~ary** adj estacionario. **~er's (shop)** n papelería f. **~ery** n artículos mpl de papelería. **~ wagon** n (Amer) ranchera f, (coche m) familiar m, camioneta f (LAm)

statistic /stəˈtɪstɪk/ n estadística f. **~al** adj estadístico. **~s** n (science) estadística f

statue /ˈstætʃuː/ n estatua f

stature /ˈstætʃə(r)/ n talla f, estatura f

status /ˈsteɪtəs/ n posición f social; (prestige) categoría f; (Jurid) estado m

statut|e /ˈstætʃuːt/ n estatuto m. **~ory** /-ʊtrɪ/ adj estatutario

staunch /stɔːntʃ/ adj (-er, -est) leal

stave /steɪv/ n (Mus) pentagrama m. □ **~ off** vt evitar

stay /steɪ/ n (of time) estancia f, estadía f (LAm); (Jurid) suspensión f. ● vi quedarse; (reside) alojarse. **I'm ~ing in a hotel** estoy en un hotel. □ **~ in** vi quedarse en casa. □ **~ up** vi quedarse levantado

stead /sted/ n. **in s.o.'s ~** en lugar de uno. **stand s.o. in good ~** resultarle muy útil a uno. **~ily** adv firmemente; (regularly) regularmente. **~y** adj (-ier, -iest) firme; (regular) regular; (flow) continuo; (worker) serio

steak /steɪk/ n. **a ~** un filete. **some ~** carne para guisar

steal /stiːl/ vt (pt stole, pp stolen) robar. □ **~ in** vi entrar a hurtadillas

stealth /stelθ/ n. **by ~** sigilosamente. **~y** adj sigiloso

steam /stiːm/ n vapor m. **let off ~** (fig) desahogarse. ● vt (cook) cocer al vapor. ● vi echar vapor. □ **~ up** vi empañarse. **~ engine** n máquina f de vapor. **~er** n (ship) barco m de vapor. **~roller** n apisonadora f. **~y** adj lleno de vapor

steel /stiːl/ n acero m. ● vt. ~ **o.s.** armarse de valor. ~ **industry** n industria f siderúrgica

steep /stiːp/ ● adj (-er, -est) empinado; (increase) considerable; (price) 𝕀 excesivo

steeple /'stiːpl/ n aguja f, campanario m

steeply /'stiːplɪ/ adv abruptamente; (increase) considerablemente

steer /stɪə(r)/ vt dirigir; gobernar (ship). ● vi (in ship) estar al timón. ~ **clear of** evitar. **~ing** n (Auto) dirección f. **~ing wheel** n volante m

stem /stem/ ● n (of plant) tallo m; (of glass) pie m; (of word) raíz f. ● vt (pt stemmed) contener (bleeding). ● vi. ~ **from** provenir de

stench /stentʃ/ n hedor m

stencil /'stensl/ n plantilla f

stenographer /ste'nɒɡrəfə(r)/ n estenógrafo f

step /step/ vi (pt stepped). ~ **in** sth pisar algo. □ ~ **aside** vi hacerse a un lado. □ ~ **down** vi retirarse. □ ~ **in** vi (fig) intervenir. □ ~ **up** vt intensificar; redoblar (security). ● n paso m; (stair) escalón m; (fig) medida f. **take ~** tomar medidas. **be in** ~ llevar el paso. **be out of** ~ no llevar el paso. **~brother** n hermanastro m. **~daughter** n hijastra f. **~father** n padrastro m. **~ladder** n escalera f de tijera. **~mother** n madrastra f. **~ping-stone** n peldaño m. **~sister** n hermanastra f. **~son** n hijastro m

stereo /'sterɪəʊ/ n (pl -os estéreo m. ● adj estéreo a invar. **~type** n estereotipo m

sterile /'steraɪl/ adj estéril. **~ize**

/'sterɪlaɪz/ vt esterilizar

sterling /'stɜːlɪŋ/ n libras fpl esterlinas. ● adj (pound) esterlina

stern /stɜːn/ n (of boat) popa f. ● adj (-er, -est) severo

stethoscope /'steθəskəʊp/ n estetoscopio m

stew /stjuː/ vt/i guisar. ● n estofado m, guiso m

steward /'stjuːəd/ n administrador m; (on ship) camarero m; (air steward) sobrecargo m, aeromozo m (LAm). **~ess** /-'des/ n camarera f; (on aircraft) auxiliar f de vuelo, azafata f

stick /stɪk/ n palo m; (for walking) bastón m; (of celery etc) tallo m. ● vt (pt stuck) (glue) pegar; (fam, put) poner; (thrust) clavar; (fam, endure) soportar. ● vi pegarse; (jam) atascarse. □ ~ **out** vi sobresalir. □ ~ **to** vt ceñirse a. □ ~ **up for** vt 𝕀 defender. **~er** n pegatina f. **~ing plaster** n esparadrapo m; (individual) tirita f, curita f (LAm). **~ler** /'stɪklə(r)/ n. **be a ~ler for** insistir en. **~y** /'stɪkɪ/ adj (-ier, -iest) (surface) pegajoso; (label) engomado

stiff /stɪf/ adj (-er, -est) rígido; (joint, fabric) tieso; (muscle) entumecido; (difficult) difícil; (manner) estirado; (drink) fuerte. **have a ~ neck** tener tortícolis. **~en** vi (become rigid) agarrotarse; (become firm) endurecerse. **~ly** adv rígidamente

stifl|e /'staɪfl/ vt sofocar. **~ing** adj sofocante

stiletto (heel) /stɪ'letəʊ/ n (pl -os) tacón m de aguja

still /stɪl/ adj inmóvil; (peaceful) tranquilo; (drink) sin gas. **sit ~,** **stand ~** quedarse tranquilo. ● adv todavía, aún; (nevertheless) sin em-

s

bargo. **~born** adj nacido muerto. **~ life** n (pl **-s**) bodegón m. **~ness** n tranquilidad f

stilted /'stɪltɪd/ adj rebuscado; (conversation) forzado

stilts /stɪlts/ npl zancos mpl

stimul|ant /'stɪmjʊlənt/ n estimulante m. **~ate** /-leɪt/ vt estimular. **~ation** /-'leɪʃn/ n estímulo m. **~us** /-əs/ n (pl **-li** /-laɪ/) estímulo m

sting /stɪŋ/ n picadura f; (organ) aguijón m. ● vt/i (pt **stung**) picar

stingy /'stɪndʒɪ/ adj (**-ier, -iest**) tacaño

stink /stɪŋk/ n hedor m. ● vi (pt **stank** or **stunk**, pp **stunk**) apestar, oler mal

stipulat|e /'stɪpjʊleɪt/ vt/i estipular. **~ion** /-'leɪʃn/ n estipulación f

stir /stɜː(r)/ vt (pt **stirred**) remover, revolver; (move) agitar; estimular (imagination). ● vi moverse. **~ up** trouble armar lío ⊞. ● n revuelo m, conmoción f

stirrup /'stɪrəp/ n estribo m

stitch /stɪtʃ/ n (in sewing) puntada f; (in knitting) punto m; (pain) dolor m costado. **be in ~es** desternillarse de risa. ● vt coser

stock /stɒk/ n (Com, supplies) existencias fpl; (Com, variety) surtido m; (livestock) ganado m; (Culin) caldo m. **~s and shares, ~s and bonds** (Amer) acciones fpl. **out of ~** agotado. **take ~ of sth** (fig) hacer un balance de algo. ● adj estándar a invar. (fig) trillado. ● vt surtir, abastecer (with de). □ **~ up** vi abastecerse (with de). **~broker** /-brəʊkə(r)/ n corredor m de bolsa. **S~ Exchange** n bolsa f. **~ing** n media f. **~pile** n reservas fpl. ● vt almacenar. **~still** adj inmóvil.

~-taking n (Com) inventario m. **~y** adj (**-ier, -iest**) bajo y fornido

stodgy /'stɒdʒɪ/ (**-dgier, -dgiest**) adj pesado

stoke /stəʊk/ vt echarle carbón (or leña) a

stole /stəʊl/ see STEAL

stolen /'stəʊlən/ see STEAL

stomach /'stʌmək/ n estómago m. ● vt soportar. **~ache** n dolor m de estómago

ston|e /stəʊn/ n piedra f; (in fruit) hueso m; (weight, pl **stone**) unidad de peso equivalente a 14 libras o 6,35 kg. ● adj de piedra. ● vt apedrear. **~e-deaf** adj sordo como una tapia. **~y** adj (silence) sepulcral

stood /stʊd/ see STAND

stool /stuːl/ n taburete m

stoop /stuːp/ vi agacharse; (fig) rebajarse. ● n. **have a ~** ser cargado de espaldas

stop /stɒp/ vt (pt **stopped**) (halt, switch off) parar; (cease) terminar; (prevent) impedir; (interrupt) interrumpir. **~ doing sth** dejar de hacer algo. **~ it!** ¡basta ya! ● vi (bus) parar, detenerse; (clock) pararse. **it's ~ped raining** ha dejado de llover. ● n (bus etc) parada f; (break on journey) parada f. **put a ~ to sth** poner fin a algo. **come to a ~** detenerse. **~gap** n remedio m provisional. **~over** n escala f. **~page** /'stɒpɪdʒ/ n suspensión f; paradero m (LAm); (of work) huelga f, paro m (LAm); (interruption) interrupción f. **~per** n tapón m. **~watch** n cronómetro m

storage /'stɔːrɪdʒ/ n almacenamiento m

store /stɔː(r)/ n provisión f; (depot) almacén m; (Amer, shop)

tienda f; (fig) reserva f. **in** ~ en reserva. ●vt (for future) poner en reserva; (in warehouse) almacenar. □ ~ **up** vt (fig) ir acumulando.

~keeper n (Amer) tendero m, comerciante m & f. **~room** n almacén m; (for food) despensa f

storey /'stɔːrɪ/ n (pl -eys) piso m, planta f

stork /stɔːk/ n cigüeña f

storm /stɔːm/ n tempestad f. ●vi rabiar. ●vt (Mil) asaltar. **~y** adj tormentoso; (sea, relationship) tempestuoso

story /'stɔːrɪ/ n historia f; (in newspaper) artículo m; (rumour) rumor m; (Ⓘ, lie) mentira f, cuento m. **~-teller** n cuentista m & f

stout /staʊt/ adj (-er, -est) robusto, corpulento. ●n cerveza f negra

stove /staʊv/ n estufa f

stow /staʊ/ vt guardar; (hide) esconder. □ ~ **away** vi viajar de polizón. **~away** n polizón m & f

straggl|e /'stræɡl/ vi rezagarse. **~y** adj desordenado

straight /streɪt/ adj (-er, -est) recto; (tidy) en orden; (frank) franco; (hair) lacio; (Ⓘ, conventional) convencional. **be** ~ estar derecho. ●adv (sit up) derecho; (direct) directamente; (without delay) inmediatamente. ~ **away** en seguida, inmediatamente. ~ **on** todo recto. ~ **out** sin rodeos. ●n recta f. **~en** vt enderezar. □ ~**en up** vt ordenar. **~forward** /-'fɔːwəd/ adj franco; (easy) sencillo

strain /streɪn/ n (tension) tensión f; (injury) torcedura f. ●vt forzar (voice, eyesight); someter a demasiada tensión (relations); (sieve) colar. ~ **one's back** hacerse daño en la espalda. ~ **a muscle** hacerse

un esguince. **~ed** adj forzado; (relations) tirante. **~er** n colador m. **~s** npl (Mus) acordes mpl

strait /streɪt/ n estrecho m. **be in dire ~s** estar en grandes apuros. **~jacket** n camisa f de fuerza

strand /strænd/ n (thread) hebra f. **a ~ of hair** un pelo. ●vt. **be ~ed** (ship) quedar encallado. **I was left ~ed** me abandonaron a mi suerte

strange /streɪndʒ/ adj (-er, -est) raro, extraño; (not known) desconocido. **~ly** adv de una manera rara. **~ly enough** aunque parezca mentira. **~r** n desconocido m; (from another place) forastero m

strangle /'stræŋɡl/ vt estrangular

strap /stræp/ n correa f; (of garment) tirante m. ●vt (pt strapped) atar con una correa

strat|egic /strə'tiːdʒɪk/ adj estratégico. **~egy** /'strætɪdʒɪ/ n estrategia f

straw /strɔː/ n paja f; (drinking ~) pajita f, paja f, popote m (Mex). **the last ~** el colmo. **~berry** /-bərɪ/ n fresa f; (large) fresón m

stray /streɪ/ vi (wander away) apartarse; (get lost) extraviarse; (deviate) desviarse (from de). ●adj (animal) (without owner) callejero; (lost) perdido. ●n (without owner) perro m/gato m callejero; (lost) perro m/gato m perdido

streak /striːk/ n lista f, raya f; (in hair) reflejo m; (in personality) veta f

stream /striːm/ n arroyo m; (current) corriente f. **a ~ of abuse** una sarta de insultos. ●vi correr. □ ~ **out** vi (people) salir en tropel. **~er** n (paper) serpentina f; (decoration) banderín m. **~line** vt dar línea aerodinámica a; (simplify) racionalizar. **~lined** adj aerodinámico

s

street /striːt/ n calle f. ~car n
(Amer) tranvía m. ~ **lamp** n farol m.
~ **map**, ~ **plan** n plano m

strength /streŋθ/ n fuerza f; (of
wall etc) solidez f. ~**en** vt reforzar
(wall); fortalecer (muscle)

strenuous /'strenjʊəs/ adj enérgico; (arduous) arduo; (tiring) fati-
goso

stress /stres/ n énfasis f; (Gram)
acento m; (Mec, Med, tension) tensión f. ● vt insistir en

stretch /stretʃ/ vt estirar; (extend)
extender; forzar (truth); estirar (resources). ● vi estirarse; (when
sleepy) desperezarse; (extend) extenderse; (be elastic) estirarse. ● n
(period) período m; (of road) tramo
m. at a ~ sin parar. □ ~ **out** vi
(person) tenderse. ~**er** n camilla f

strict /strikt/ adj (-er, -est) estricto; (secrecy) absoluto. ~**ly** adv
con severidad; (rigorously) termi-
nantemente. ~**ly speaking** en
rigor

stridden /'stridn/ see STRIDE

stride /straid/ vi (pt strode, pp
stridden) andar a zancadas. ● n
zancada f. **take sth in one's** ~
tomarse algo con calma. ~**nt**
/'straidnt/ adj estridente

strife /straif/ n conflicto m

strike /straik/ vt (pt struck) golpear; encender (match); encontrar
(gold, oil); (clock) dar. it ~**s me** as
odd me parece raro. ● vi golpear;
(go on strike) declararse en huelga;
(be on strike) estar en huelga; (attack) atacar; (clock) dar la hora. ● n
(of workers) huelga f, paro m; (attack) ataque m. **come out on** ~ ir
a la huelga. □ ~ **off**, ~ **out** vt tachar. ~ **up a friendship** trabar
amistad. ~**r** n huelguista m & f;
(Sport) artillero m

striking /'straikiŋ/ adj (resemblance) sorprendente; (colour) llamativo

string /striŋ/ n cordel m, mecate
m (Mex); (Mus) cuerda f; (of lies,
pearls) sarta f; (of people) sucesión
f. □ ~ **along** vt 🆸 engañar

stringent /'strindʒənt/ adj riguroso

strip /strip/ vt (pt stripped) desnudar (person); deshacer (bed). ● vi
desnudarse. ● n tira f; (of land)
franja f. ~ **cartoon** n historieta f

stripe /straip/ n raya f. ~**d** adj a
rayas, rayado

strip lighting n luz f fluorescente

strive /straiv/ vi (pt strove, pp
striven). ~ **to** esforzarse por

strode /strəʊd/ see STRIDE

stroke /strəʊk/ n golpe m; (in
swimming) brazada f; (Med) ataque
m de apoplejía; (of pen etc) trazo m;
(of clock) campanada f; (caress) caricia f. **a** ~ **of luck** un golpe de
suerte. ● vt acariciar

stroll /strəʊl/ vi pasearse. ● n
paseo m. ~**er** n (Amer) sillita f de
paseo, cochecito m

strong /strɒŋ/ adj (-er, -est)
fuerte. ~**hold** n fortaleza f; (fig)
baluarte m. ~**ly** adv (greatly) fuertemente; (protest) enérgicamente;
(deeply) profundamente. ~**room** n
cámara f acorazada

strove /strəʊv/ see STRIVE

struck /strʌk/ see STRIKE

structur|al /'strʌktʃərəl/ adj es-
tructural. ~**e** n /'strʌktʃə(r)/ n estructura f

struggle /'strʌgl/ vi luchar;
(thrash around) forcejear. ● n
lucha f

strum /strʌm/ vt (pt strummed)

rasguear

strung /strʌŋ/ *see* STRING

strut /strʌt/ *n* (*in building*) puntal *m*. ● *vi* (*pt* strutted) pavonearse

stub /stʌb/ *n* (*of pencil, candle*) cabo *m*; (*counterfoil*) talón *m*; (*of cigarette*) colilla. □ ~ **out** (*pt* stubbed) *vt* apagar

stubble /'stʌbl/ *n* rastrojo *m*; (*beard*) barba *f* de varios días

stubborn /'stʌbən/ *adj* terco

stuck /stʌk/ *see* STICK. ● *adj*. the drawer is ~ el cajón se ha atascado. the door is ~ la puerta se ha atrancado. ~**-up** *adj* estirado

stud /stʌd/ *n* tachuela *f*; (*for collar*) gemelo *m*.

student /'stju:dənt/ *n* estudiante *m & f*; (*at school*) alumno *m*. ~ **driver** *n* (*Amer*) persona que está aprendiendo a conducir

studio /'stju:dɪəʊ/ *n* (*pl* -os) estudio *m*. ~ **apartment**, ~ **flat** *n* estudio *m*

studious /'stju:dɪəs/ *adj* estudioso

study /'stʌdɪ/ *n* estudio *m*. ● *vt/i* estudiar

stuff /stʌf/ *n* 🔲 cosas *fpl*. what's this ~ called? ¿cómo se llama esta cosa?. ● *vt* rellenar; disecar (*animal*); (*cram*) atiborrar; (*put*) meter de prisa. ~ **o.s.** 🔲 darse un atracón. ~**ing** *n* relleno *m*. ~**y** *adj* (-ier, -iest) mal ventilado; (*old-fashioned*) acartonado. it's ~ y in here está muy cargado el ambiente

stumble /'stʌmbl/ *vi* tropezar. ~ **across**, ~ **on** *vt* dar con. ~**ing-block** *n* tropiezo *m*, impedimento *m*

stump /stʌmp/ *n* (*of limb*) muñón *m*; (*of tree*) tocón *m*

stun /stʌn/ *vt* (*pt* stunned) (*daze*)

aturdir; (*bewilder*) dejar atónito. ~**ning** *adj* sensacional

stung /stʌŋ/ *see* STING

stunk /stʌŋk/ *see* STINK

stunt /stʌnt/ *n* 🔲 ardid *m* publicitario. ● *vt* detener, atrofiar. ~**ed** *adj* (*growth*) atrofiado; (*body*) raquítico. ~**man** *n* especialista *m*. ~**woman** *n* especialista *f*

stupendous /stju:'pendəs/ *adj* estupendo

stupid /'stju:pɪd/ *adj* (*foolish*) tonto; (*unintelligent*) estúpido. ~**ity** /-'pɪdətɪ/ *n* estupidez *f*. ~**ly** *adv* estúpidamente

stupor /'stju:pə(r)/ *n* estupor *m*

sturdy /'stɜ:dɪ/ *adj* (-ier, -iest) robusto

stutter /'stʌtə(r)/ *vi* tartamudear. ● *n* tartamudeo *m*

sty /staɪ/ *n* (*pl* sties) pocilga *f*; (*Med*) orzuelo *m*

style /staɪl/ *n* estilo *m*; (*fashion*) moda *f*; (*design, type*) diseño *m*. in ~ a lo grande. ● *vt* diseñar. ~**ish** *adj* elegante. ~**ist** *n* estilista *m & f*. hair ~**ist** estilista *m & f*

stylus /'staɪləs/ *n* (*pl* -uses) aguja *f* (de tocadiscos)

suave /swɑ:v/ *adj* elegante y desenvuelto

subconscious /sʌb'kɒnʃəs/ *adj &* *n* subconsciente (*m*)

subdivide /sʌbdɪ'vaɪd/ *vt* subdividir

subdued /səb'dju:d/ *adj* apagado

subject /'sʌbdʒɪkt/ *adj* sometido. ~ **to** sujeto a. ● *n* (*theme*) tema *m*; (*Schol*) asignatura *f*, materia *f* (*LAm*); (*Gram*) sujeto *m*; (*Pol*) súbdito *m*. ● /səb'dʒekt/ *vt* someter. ~**ive** /səb'dʒektɪv/ *adj* subjetivo

subjunctive /səb'dʒʌŋktɪv/ *adj &*

n subjuntivo (*m*)

sublime /sə'blaim/ *adj* sublime

submarine /sʌbmə'ri:n/ *n* submarino *m*

submerge /səb'mɜ:dʒ/ *vt* sumergir. ● *vi* sumergirse

submi|ssion /səb'miʃn/ *n* sumisión *f*. **~t** /səb'mit/ *vt* (*pt* submitted) (*subject*) someter; presentar (application). ● *vi* rendirse

subordinate /sə'bɔ:dɪnət/ *adj* & *n* subordinado (*m*). ● /sə'bɔ:dɪneɪt/ *vt* subordinar

subscri|be /səb'skraib/ *vi* suscribir. **~be to** suscribirse a (magazine). **~ber** *n* suscriptor *m*. **~ption** /-rɪpʃn/ *n* (*to magazine*) suscripción *f*

subsequent /'sʌbsɪkwənt/ *adj* posterior, subsiguiente. **~ly** *adv* posteriormente

subside /səb'said/ *vi* (land) hundirse; (flood) bajar; (storm, wind) amainar. **~nce** /'sʌbsɪdəns/ *n* hundimiento *m*

subsidiary /səb'sɪdɪərɪ/ *adj* secundario; (subject) complementario. ● *n* (Com) filial

subsid|ize /'sʌbsɪdaɪz/ *vt* subvencionar, subsidiar (LAm). **~y** /'sʌbsədɪ/ *n* subvención *f*, subsidio *m*

substance /'sʌbstəns/ *n* sustancia *f*

substandard /sʌb'stændəd/ *adj* de calidad inferior

substantial /səb'stænʃl/ *adj* (sturdy) sólido; (meal) sustancioso; (considerable) considerable

substitut|e /'sʌbstɪtju:t/ *n* (person) substituto *m*; (thing) sucedáneo *m*. ● *vt/i* sustituir. **~ion** /-'tju:ʃn/ *n* sustitución *f*

subterranean /sʌbtə'reɪnjən/

adj subterráneo

subtitle /'sʌbtaɪtl/ *n* subtítulo *m*

subtle /'sʌtl/ *adj* (-er, -est) sutil; (tactful) discreto. **~ty** *n* sutileza *f*

subtract /səb'trækt/ *vt* restar. **~ion** /-ʃn/ *n* resta *f*

suburb /'sʌbɜ:b/ *n* barrio *m* residencial de las afueras, colonia *f*. the **~s** las afueras *fpl*. **~an** /sə'bɜ:bən/ *adj* suburbano. **~ia** /sə'bɜ:bɪə/ *n* zonas residenciales de las afueras de una ciudad

subversive /səb'vɜ:sɪv/ *adj* subversivo

subway /'sʌbweɪ/ *n* paso *m* subterráneo; (Amer) metro *m*

succeed /sək'si:d/ *vi* (plan) dar resultado; (person) tener éxito. **~ in doing** lograr hacer. ● *vt* suceder

success /sək'ses/ *n* éxito *m*. **~ful** *adj* (person) de éxito, exitoso (LAm). the **~ful** applicant el candidato que obtenga el puesto. **~fully** *adv* satisfactoriamente. **~ion** /-ʃn/ *n* sucesión *f*. for 3 years in **~ion** durante tres años consecutivos. in rapid **~ion** uno tras otro. **~ive** *adj* sucesivo. **~or** *n* sucesor *m*

succulent /'sʌkjʊlənt/ *adj* suculento

succumb /sə'kʌm/ *vi* sucumbir

such /sʌtʃ/ *adj* tal (+ noun), tan (+ adj). **~ a big house** una casa tan grande. **~ and** tal o cual. **~ as como**. **~ as it is** tal como es

suck /sʌk/ *vt* chupar (sweet, thumb); sorber (liquid). □ **~ up** *vt* (vacuum cleaner) aspirar; (pump) succionar. □ **~ up to** *vt* 🅸 dar coba a. **~er** *n* (plant) chupón *m*; (fam, person) imbécil *m*

suckle /sʌkl/ *vt* amamantar

suction /'sʌkʃn/ *n* succión *f*

sudden /'sʌdn/ *adj* repentino. **all of a** ~ de repente. ~**ly** *adv* de repente.

suds /sʌds/ *npl* espuma *f* de jabón

sue /su:/ *vt* (*pres p* **suing**) demandar (**for** por)

suede /sweɪd/ *n* ante *m*

suet /'su:ɪt/ *n* sebo *m*

suffer /'sʌfə(r)/ *vt* sufrir; (*tolerate*) aguantar. ● *vi* sufrir; (*be affected*) resentirse

suffic|e /sə'faɪs/ *vi* bastar. ~**ient** /sə'fɪʃnt/ *adj* suficiente, bastante. ~**iently** *adv* (lo) suficientemente

suffix /'sʌfɪks/ *n* (*pl* -**ixes**) sufijo *m*

suffocat|e /'sʌfəkeɪt/ *vt* asfixiar. ● *vi* asfixiarse. ~**ion** /-'keɪʃn/ *n* asfixia *f*

sugar /'ʃʊɡə(r)/ *n* azúcar *m* & *f*. ~**bowl** *n* azucarero *m*. ~**y** *adj* azucarado.

suggest /sə'dʒest/ *vt* sugerir. ~**ion** /-tʃən/ *n* sugerencia *f*

suicid|al /su:ɪ'saɪdl/ *adj* suicida. ~**e** /'su:ɪsaɪd/ *n* suicidio *m*. **commit** ~**e** suicidarse

suit /su:t/ *n* traje *m*; (*woman's*) traje *m* de chaqueta; (*Cards*) palo *m*; (*Jurid*) pleito *m*. ● *vt* venirle a, convenirle a; (*clothes*) quedarle bien a; (*adapt*) adaptar. **be** ~**ed to** (*thing*) ser apropiado para. **I'm not** ~**ed to** this kind of work no sirvo para este tipo de trabajo. ~**able** *adj* apropiado, adecuado. ~**ably** *adv* (*dressed*) apropiadamente; (*qualified*) adecuadamente. ~**case** *n* maleta *f*, valija *f* (*LAm*)

suite /swi:t/ *n* (*of furniture*) juego *m*; (*of rooms*) suite *f*

sulk /sʌlk/ *vi* enfurruñarse

sullen /'sʌlən/ *adj* hosco

sulphur /'sʌlfə(r)/ *n* azufre *m*. ~**ic acid** /sʌl'fjʊərɪk/ *n* ácido *m*

sulfúrico

sultan /'sʌltən/ *n* sultán *m*

sultana /sʌl'tɑːnə/ *n* pasa *f* de Esmirna

sultry /'sʌltrɪ/ *adj* (-**ier**, -**iest**) (weather) bochornoso; (*fig*) sensual

sum /sʌm/ *n* (*of money*) suma *f*, cantidad *f*; (*Math*) suma *f*. ● □ ~ **up** (*pt* **summed**) *vt* resumir. ● *vi* recapitular

summar|ily /'sʌmərɪlɪ/ *adv* sumariamente. ~**ize** *vt* resumir. ~**y** *n* resumen *m*

summer /'sʌmə(r)/ *n* verano *m*. ~ **camp** (*in US*) colonia *f* de vacaciones. ~**time** *n* verano *m*. ~**y** *adj* veraniego

summer camp En EE.UU., es el campamento de verano, aspecto muy importante en la vida de muchos niños. Las actividades al aire libre se practican en un ambiente natural entre las que se incluyen natación, montañismo, supervivencia al aire libre. En estos campamentos miles de estudiantes trabajan como supervisores.

summit /'sʌmɪt/ *n* (*of mountain*) cumbre *f*. ~ **conference** *n* conferencia *f* cumbre

summon /'sʌmən/ *vt* llamar; convocar (meeting, s.o. to meeting); (*Jurid*) citar. □ ~ **up** *vt* armarse de. ~**s** *n* (*Jurid*) citación *f*. ● *vt* citar

sumptuous /'sʌmptjʊəs/ *adj* suntuoso

sun /sʌn/ *n* sol *m*. ~**bathe** *vi* tomar el sol, asolearse (*LAm*). ~**beam** *n* rayo *m* de sol. ~**burn** *n* quemadura *f* de sol. ~**burnt** *adj* quemado por el sol

Sunday /'sʌndeɪ/ *n* domingo *m*

sunflower /'sʌnflaʊə(r)/ n gira-sol m

sung /sʌŋ/ see SING

sunglasses /'sʌnglɑːsɪz/ npl gafas fpl de sol, lentes mpl de sol (LAm)

sunk /sʌŋk/ see SINK. ~en /'sʌŋkən/ ● adj hundido

sun: ~light n luz f del sol. ~ny adj (-ier, -iest) (day) de sol; (place) soleado. it is ~ny hace sol. ~rise n. at ~rise al amanecer. salida f del sol. ~roof n techo m corredizo. ~set n puesta f del sol. ~shine n sol m. ~stroke n insolación f. ~tan n bronceado m. get a ~tan broncearse. ~tan lotion n bronceador m

super /'suːpə(r)/ adj 🄳 genial, super a invar

superb /suːˈpɜːb/ adj espléndido

supercilious /suːpəˈsɪlɪəs/ adj desdeñoso

superficial /suːpəˈfɪʃl/ adj superficial

superfluous /suːˈpɜːfluəs/ adj superfluo

superhighway /'suːpəhaɪweɪ/ n (Amer, Auto) autopista f; (Comp) information ~ autopista f de la comunicación

superhuman /suːpəˈhjuːmən/ adj sobrehumana

superintendent /suːpərɪn'tendənt/ n director m; (Amer, of building) portero m; (of police) comisario m; (in US) superintendente m & f

superior /suːˈpɪərɪə(r)/ adj & n superior (m). ~ity /-ˈɒrətɪ/ n superioridad f

superlative /suːˈpɜːlətɪv/ adj inigualable. ● n superlativo m

supermarket /'suːpəmɑːkɪt/ n supermercado m

supernatural /suːpəˈnætʃrəl/ adj sobrenatural

superpower /'suːpəpaʊə(r)/ n superpotencia f

supersede /suːpəˈsiːd/ vt reemplazar, sustituir

supersonic /suːpəˈsɒnɪk/ adj supersónico

superstitio|n /suːpəˈstɪʃn/ n superstición f. ~us adj /-əs/ supersticioso

supervis|e /'suːpəvaɪz/ vt supervisar. ~ion /-ˈvɪʒn/ n supervisión f. ~or n supervisor m

supper /'sʌpə(r)/ n cena f (ligera), comida f (ligera) (LAm)

supple /sʌpl/ adj flexible

supplement /'sʌplɪmənt/ n suplemento m; (to diet, income) complemento m. ● vt complementar (diet, income). ~ary /-ˈmentərɪ/ adj suplementario

suppl|ier /sə'plaɪə(r)/ n (Com) proveedor m. ~y /sə'plaɪ/ vt suministrar; proporcionar (information). ~y s.o. with sth (equipment) proveer a uno de algo; (in business) abastecer a uno de algo. ● n suministro m. ~y and demand oferta y demanda. ~ies npl provisiones mpl, víveres mpl; (Mil) pertrechos mpl. office ~ies artículos mpl de oficina

support /sə'pɔːt/ vt (hold up) sostener; (back) apoyar; mantener (family). ● n apoyo m; (Tec) soporte m. ~er n partidario m; (Sport) hincha m & f

suppos|e /sə'pəʊz/ vt suponer, imaginarse; (think) creer. I'm ~ed to start work at nine se supone que tengo que empezar a trabajar a las nueve. ~edly adv supuestamente. ~ition /sʌpə'zɪʃn/ n suposición f

suppress /sə'pres/ vt reprimir (feelings); sofocar (rebellion). ~**ion** /-ʃn/ n represión f

suprem|acy /suː'preməsɪ/ n premacía f. ~**e** /suː'priːm/ adj supremo

sure /ʃʊə(r)/ adj (-er, -est) seguro. make ~ that asegurarse de que. ● adv ¡claro!. ~**ly** adv (undoubtedly) seguramente; (gladly) desde luego. ~**ly** you don't believe that! ¡no te creerás eso! ~**ty** /-ətɪ/ n garantía f

surf /sɜːf/ n oleaje m; (foam) espuma f. ● vi hacer surf. ● vt (Comp) surfear, navegar

surface /'sɜːfɪs/ n superficie f. ● adj superficial. ● vt recubrir (with de). ● vi salir a la superficie; (problems) aflorar

surfboard /'sɜːfbɔːd/ n tabla f de surf

surfeit /'sɜːfɪt/ n exceso m

surf: ~**er** n surfista m & f; (Internet) navegador m. ~**ing** n surf m

surge /sɜːdʒ/ vi (crowd) moverse en tropel; (sea) hincharse. ● n oleada f; (in demand, sales) aumento m

surg|eon /'sɜːdʒən/ n cirujano m. ~**ery** n cirugía f; (consulting room) consultorio m; (consulting hours) consulta f. ~**ical** adj quirúrgico

surly /'sɜːlɪ/ adj (-ier, -iest) hosco

surmise /sə'maɪz/ vt conjeturar

surmount /sə'maʊnt/ vt superar

surname /'sɜːneɪm/ n apellido m

surpass /sə'pɑːs/ vt superar

surplus /'sɜːpləs/ adj & n excedente (m)

surpris|e /sə'praɪz/ n sorpresa f. ● vt sorprender. ~**ed** adj sorpren-

dido. ~**ing** adj sorprendente. ~**ingly** adv sorprendentemente

surrender /sə'rendə(r)/ vt entregar. ● vi rendirse. ● n rendición f

surreptitious /sʌrəp'tɪʃəs/ adj furtivo

surround /sə'raʊnd/ vt rodear; (Mil) rodear, cercar. ~**ing** adj circundante. ~**ings** npl alrededores mpl; (environment) ambiente m

surveillance /sɜː'veɪləns/ n vigilancia f

survey /'sɜːveɪ/ n inspección f; (report) informe m; (general view) vista f general. ● /sə'veɪ/ vt inspeccionar; (measure) medir; (look at) contemplar. ~**or** n topógrafo m, agrimensor m; (of building) perito m

surviv|al /sə'vaɪvl/ n supervivencia f. ~**e** /sə'vaɪv/ vt/i sobrevivir. ~**or** n superviviente m & f

susceptible /sə'septəbl/ adj. ~ to propenso a

suspect /sə'spekt/ vt sospechar; sospechar de (person). ● /'sʌspekt/ adj & n sospechoso (m)

suspen|d /sə'spend/ vt suspender. ~**ders** npl (Amer, braces) tirantes mpl. ~**se** /-s/ n (in film etc) suspense m, suspenso m (LAm). keep s.o. in ~**se** mantener a uno sobre ascuas. ~**sion** /-ʃn/ n suspensión f. ~**sion bridge** n puente m colgante

suspici|on /sə'spɪʃn/ n (belief) sospecha f; (mistrust) desconfianza f. ~**ous** /-ʃəs/ adj desconfiado; (causing suspicion) sospechoso

sustain /sə'steɪn/ vt sostener; mantener (conversation, interest); (suffer) sufrir

SW abbr (= south-west) SO

swab /swɒb/ n (specimen) muestra f, frotis m

swagger /'swægə(r)/ vi pavonearse

swallow /'swɒləʊ/ vt/i tragar. ● n trago m; (bird) golondrina f.

swam /swæm/ see **SWIM**

swamp /swɒmp/ n pantano m, ciénaga f. ● vt inundar. ~y adj pantanoso

swan /swɒn/ n cisne m

swap /swɒp/ vt/i (pt swapped) intercambiar. ~ sth for sth cambiar algo por algo. ● n cambio m

swarm /swɔːm/ n enjambre m. ● vi (bees) enjambrar; (fig) hormiguear

swarthy /'swɔːðɪ/ adj (-ier, -iest) moreno

swat /swɒt/ vt (pt swatted) matar (con matamoscas etc)

sway /sweɪ/ vi balancearse; (gently) mecerse; (influence) influir en

swear /sweə(r)/ vt/i (pt swore, pp sworn) jurar. ~word n palabrota f

sweat /swet/ n sudor m, transpiración f. ● vi sudar

sweat|er /'swetə(r)/ n jersey m, suéter m. ~shirt n sudadera f. ~suit n (Amer) chándal m, equipo m de deportes

swede /swiːd/ n nabo m sueco

Swede /swiːd/ n sueco m. ~n /'swiːdn/ n Suecia f. ~ish adj sueco. ● n (language) sueco m. ● npl. the ~ (people) los suecos

sweep /swiːp/ vt (pt swept) barrer; deshollinar (chimney). ● vi barrer. ● n barrido m. ~ away (carry away) arrastrar; (abolish) erradicar. ~er n barrendero m. ~ing adj (gesture) amplio; (changes) radical; (statement) demasiado general

sweet /swiːt/ adj (-er, -est) dulce;

(fragrant) fragante; (pleasant) agradable; (kind, gentle) dulce; (cute) rico. **have a ~ tooth** ser dulcero. ● n caramelo m, dulce m (Mex); (dish) postre m. ~en vt endulzar. ~heart n enamorado m; (as form of address) amor m. ~ly adv dulcemente. ~ potato n boniato m, batata f, camote m LAm

swell /swel/ vt (pt swelled, pp swollen or swelled) hinchar; (increase) aumentar. ● vi hincharse; (increase) aumentar. ● adj (Amer fam) fenomenal. ● n (of sea) oleaje m. ~ing n hinchazón m

sweltering /'sweltərɪŋ/ vi sofocante

swept /swept/ see **SWEEP**

swerve /swɜːv/ vi virar bruscamente

swift /swɪft/ adj (-er, -est) veloz, rápido; (reply) rápido. ● n (bird) vencejo m. ~ly adv rápidamente

swig /swɪg/ vt (pt swigged). ● n beber a grandes tragos. ● n 🔲 trago m

swim /swɪm/ vi (pt swam, pp swum) nadar. ● n baño m. ~mer n nadador m. ~ming n natación f. ~ming bath(s) n(pl) piscina f cubierta, alberca f techada (Mex). ~ming pool n piscina f, alberca f (Mex). ~ming trunks npl bañador m, traje m de baño ~suit n traje m de baño, bañador m

swindle /'swɪndl/ vt estafar. ● n estafa f. ~r n estafador m

swine /swaɪn/ npl cerdos mpl. ● n (pl swine) (fam, person) canalla m & f. ~ fever n fiebre f porcina

swing /swɪŋ/ vt (pt swung) balancear; (object on rope) hacer oscilar. ● vi (dangle) balancearse; (swing on a swing) columpiarse; (pendulum) oscilar. **~ open/shut** abrirse/cerrarse. ●n oscilación f, vaivén m; (seat) columpio m; (in opinion) cambio m. **in full ~** en plena actividad

swipe /swaɪp/ vt darle un golpe a; (fam, snatch) birlar. ●n golpe m.

Swiss /swɪs/ adj suizo (m). ●npl. **the ~** los suizos

switch /swɪtʃ/ n (Elec) interruptor m; (exchange) intercambio m; (Amer, Rail) agujas fpl. ●vt cambiar; (deviate) desviar. □ **~ off** vt (Elec) apagar (light, TV, heating); desconectar (electricity). □ **~ on** vt encender, prender (LAm); arrancar (engine). **~board** n centralita f

Switzerland /'swɪtsələnd/ n Suiza f

swivel /'swɪvl/ vi (pt swivelled) girar. ●vt hacer girar

swollen /'swəʊlən/ see **SWELL**. ●adj hinchado

swoop /swuːp/ vi (bird) abatirse; (police) llevar a cabo una redada. ●n (of bird) descenso m en picado or (LAm) en picada; (by police) redada f

sword /sɔːd/ n espada f

swore /swɔː(r)/ see **SWEAR**

sworn /swɔːn/ see **SWEAR**. ●adj (enemy) declarado; (statement) jurado

swot /swɒt/ vt/i (pt swotted) (Schol, fam) empollar, estudiar como loco. ●n (Schol, fam) empollón m, matado m (Mex)

swum /swʌm/ see **SWIM**

swung /swʌŋ/ see **SWING**

syllable /'sɪləbl/ n sílaba f

syllabus /'sɪləbəs/ n (pl -buses) plan m de estudios; (of a particular subject) programa m

symbol /'sɪmbl/ n símbolo m. **~ic(al)** /-'bɒlɪk(l)/ adj simbólico. **~ism** n simbolismo m. **~ize** vt simbolizar

symmetr|ical /sɪ'metrɪkl/ adj simétrico. **~y** /'sɪmɪtrɪ/ n simetría f

sympath|etic /sɪmpə'θetɪk/ adj comprensivo; (showing pity) compasivo. **~ize** /'sɪmpəθaɪz/ vi comprender; (commiserate) **~ize with** s.o. compadecer a uno. **~y** /'sɪmpəθɪ/ n comprensión f; (pity) compasión f; (condolences) pésame m

symphony /'sɪmfənɪ/ n sinfonía f

symptom /'sɪmptəm/ n síntoma m. **~atic** /-'mætɪk/ adj sintomático

synagogue /'sɪnəgɒg/ n sinagoga f

synchronize /'sɪŋkrənaɪz/ vt sincronizar

syndicate /'sɪndɪkət/ n agrupación f; (Amer, TV) agencia f de distribución periodística

synonym /'sɪnənɪm/ n sinónimo m. **~ous** /-'nɒnɪməs/ adj sinónimo

syntax /'sɪntæks/ n sintaxis f

synthesi|s /'sɪnθəsɪs/ n (pl -theses /-siːz/) síntesis f. **~ze** /-aɪz/ vt sintetizar

synthetic /sɪn'θetɪk/ adj sintético

syringe /'sɪrɪndʒ/ n jeringa f, jeringuilla f

syrup /'sɪrəp/ n (sugar solution) almíbar m; (with other ingredients) jarabe m; (medicine) jarabe m

system /'sɪstəm/ n sistema m, método m; (Tec, Mec, Comp) sistema m. **the digestive ~** el aparato digestivo. **~atic** /-ə'mætɪk/ adj sistemático. **~atically** /-ə'mætɪklɪ/ adv sistemáticamente. **~s analyst** n analista m & f de sistemas

Tt

tab /tæb/ n (flap) lengüeta f; (label) etiqueta f

table /'teɪbl/ n mesa f; (list) tabla f. ~**cloth** n mantel m. ~ **mat** n salvamanteles m. ~**spoon** n cuchara f grande; (measure) cucharada f (grande)

tablet /'tæblɪt/ n pastilla f; (pill) comprimido m

table tennis n tenis m de mesa, ping-pong m

tabloid /'tæblɔɪd/ n tabloide m

taboo /tə'buː/ adj & n tabú (m)

tacit /'tæsɪt/ adj tácito

taciturn /'tæsɪtɜːn/ adj taciturno

tack /tæk/ n tachuela f; (stitch) hilván m. ● vt clavar con tachuelas; (sew) hilvanar. ● vi (Naut) virar □ ~ **on** vt añadir

tackle /'tækl/ n (equipment) equipo m; (soccer) entrada f fuerte; (US football, Rugby) placaje m. fishing ~ aparejo m de pesca. ● vt abordar (problem); (in soccer) entrarle a; (in US football, Rugby) placar

tacky /'tækɪ/ adj pegajoso

tact /tækt/ n tacto m. ~**ful** adj diplomático

tactic|al /'tæktɪkl/ adj táctico. ~s npl táctica f

tactless /'tæktləs/ adj indiscreto

tadpole /'tædpəʊl/ n renacuajo m

tag /tæg/ n (label) etiqueta f □ ~ **along** (pt tagged) vt 🗓 seguir

tail /teɪl/ n (of horse, fish, bird) cola f; (of dog, pig) rabo m. ~**s** npl (tail-coat) frac m; (of coin) cruz f ● vt seguir. □ ~ **off** vi disminuir.

tailor /'teɪlə(r)/ n sastre m. ~**ed** /'teɪləd/ adj entallado. ~**-made** n hecho a (la) medida

taint /teɪnt/ vt contaminar

take /teɪk/ vt (pt took, pp taken) tomar, coger (esp Spain), agarrar (esp LAm); (capture) capturar; (endure) aguantar; (require) requerir; llevar (time); tomar (bath); (medicine) llevar; aceptar (cheque). I ~ a size 10 uso la talla 14. □ ~ **after** vt parecerse a. □ ~ **away** vt llevarse; (confiscate) quitar. □ ~ **back** vt retirar (statement etc). □ ~ **in** vt achicar (garment); (understand) asimilar; (deceive) engañar. □ ~ **off** vt (remove) quitar, sacar; quitarse (shoes, jacket); (mimic) imitar. vi (aircraft) despegar. □ ~ **on** vt contratar (employee). □ ~ **out** vt sacar. □ ~ **over** vt tomar posesión de; hacerse cargo de (job). vi (assume control) asumir el poder. □ ~ **up** vt empezar a hacer (hobby); aceptar (challenge); subir (hem); llevar (time); ocupar (space). ● n (Cinema) toma f. ~**-off** n despegue m. ~**-over** n (Com) absorción f

takings /'teɪkɪŋz/ npl recaudación f; (at box office) taquilla f

talcum powder /'tælkəm/ n polvos mpl de talco, talco m (LAm)

tale /teɪl/ n cuento m

talent /'tælənt/ n talento m. ~**ed** adj talentoso

talk /tɔːk/ vt/i hablar. ~ to s.o. hablar con uno. ~ **about** hablar de. ● n conversación f; (lecture) charla f. □ ~ **over** vt discutir. ~**ative** /-ətɪv/ adj hablador

tall /tɔːl/ adj (-er, -est) alto. ~ **story** n 🗓 cuento m chino

tally /'tælɪ/ vi coincidir (with con)

talon /'tælən/ n garra f

tambourine /tæmbə'ri:n/ n pandereta f

tame /teɪm/ adj (-er, -est) (animal) (by nature) manso; (tamed) domado. ●vt domar (wild animal)

tamper /'tæmpə(r)/ vi. ~ with tocar; (alter) alterar, falsificar

tampon /'tæmpɒn/ n tampón m

tan /tæn/ vi (pt tanned) broncearse. ●n bronceado m. get a ~ broncearse. ●adj habano

tang /tæŋ/ n sabor m fuerte

tangent /'tændʒənt/ n tangente f

tangerine /tændʒə'ri:n/ n mandarina f

tangible /'tændʒəbl/ adj tangible

tangle /'tæŋgl/ vt enredar. get ~d (up) enredarse. ●n enredo m, maraña f

tango /'tæŋgəʊ/ n (pl -os) tango m

tank /tæŋk/ n depósito m; (Auto) tanque m; (Mil) tanque m

tanker /'tæŋkə(r)/ n (ship) buque m cisterna; (truck) camión m cisterna

tantrum /'tæntrəm/ n berrinche m, rabieta f

tap /tæp/ n grifo m, llave f (LAm); (knock) golpecito m. ●vt (pt tapped) (knock) dar un golpecito en; interceptar (phone). ●vi dar golpecitos (on en). ~ **dancing** n claqué m

tape /teɪp/ n cinta f; (Med) esparadrapo m. ●vt (record) grabar. ~-**measure** n cinta f métrica

taper /'teɪpə(r)/ vt afilar. ●vi afilarse. □ ~ **off** vi disminuir

tape recorder n magnetófon m, magnetófono m

tapestry /'tæpɪstrɪ/ n tapiz m

tar /tɑː(r)/ n alquitrán m. ●vt (pt

tarred) alquitranar

target /'tɑːgɪt/ n blanco m; (fig) objetivo m

tarmac /'tɑːmæk/ n pista f. **T~** n (Amer, ®) asfalto m

tarnish /'tɑːnɪʃ/ vt deslustrar; empañar (reputation)

tart /tɑːt/ n pastel m; (individual) pastelillo m; (sl, woman) prostituta f, fulana f 🖪. ●vt. ~ **o.s. up** 🖪 engalanarse. ●adj (-er, -est) ácido

tartan /'tɑːtn/ n tartán m, tela f escocesa

task /tɑːsk/ n tarea f. take to ~ reprender

tassel /'tæsl/ n borla f

taste /teɪst/ n sabor m, gusto m; (liking) gusto m. ●vt probar. ●vi. ~e of saber a. ~**eful** adj de buen gusto. ~**eless** adj soso; (fig) de mal gusto. ~**y** adj (-ier, -iest) sabroso

tat /tæt/ see **TIT FOR TAT**

tatter|ed /'tætəd/ adj hecho jirones. ~**s** /'tætəz/ npl andrajos mpl

tattoo /tæ'tu:/ n (on body) tatuaje m. ●vt tatuar

tatty /'tætɪ/ adj (-ier, -iest) gastado, estropeado

taught /tɔːt/ see **TEACH**

taunt /tɔːnt/ vt provocar mediante burlas. ●n pulla f

Taurus /'tɔːrəs/ n Tauro m

taut /tɔːt/ adj tenso

tavern /'tævən/ n taberna f

tax /tæks/ n impuesto m. ●vt imponer contribuciones a (person); gravar (thing); (strain) poner a prueba. ~**able** adj imponible. ~**ation** /-'seɪʃn/ n impuestos mpl; (system) sistema m tributario. ~ **collector** n recaudador m de impuestos. ~-**free** adj libre de impuestos

taxi /'tæksɪ/ n (pl -is) taxi m. ● vi (pt taxied, pres p taxiing) (aircraft) rodar por la pista

taxpayer /'tækspeɪə(r)/ n contribuyente m & f

tea /tiː/ n té m; (afternoon tea) merienda f, té m. **~ bag** n bolsita f de té

teach /tiːtʃ/ vt (pt taught) dar clases de, enseñar (subject); dar clase a (person). **~ school** (Amer) dar clase(s) en un colegio. ● vi dar clase(s). **~er** n profesor m; (primary) maestro m. **~ing** n enseñanza f. ● adj docente

tea: **~cup** n taza f de té. **~ leaf** n hoja f de té

team /tiːm/ n equipo m. □ **~ up** vi asociarse (with con). **~ work** n trabajo m de equipo

teapot /'tiːpɒt/ n tetera f

tear[1] /teə(r)/ vt (pt tore, pp torn) romper, rasgar. ● vi romperse, rasgarse. ● n rotura f; (rip) desgarrón m. □ **~ along** vi ir a toda velocidad. □ **~ apart** vt desgarrar. □ **~ off**, □ **~ out** vt arrancar. □ **~ up** vt romper

tear[2] /tɪə(r)/ n lágrima f. be in **~s** estar llorando. **~ful** adj lloroso (farewell) triste. **~ gas** n gas m lacrimógeno

tease /tiːz/ vt tomarle el pelo a

tea: **~ set** n juego m de té. **~spoon** n cucharita f, cucharilla f; (amount) cucharadita f

teat /tiːt/ n (of animal) tetilla f; (for bottle) tetina f

tea towel n paño m de cocina

techni|cal /'teknɪkl/ adj técnico. **~cality** n /-'kælətɪ/ n detalle m técnico. **~cally** adv técnicamente. **~cian** /tek'nɪʃn/ n técnico m.

~que /tek'niːk/ n técnica f

technolog|ical /teknə'lɒdʒɪkl/ adj tecnológico. **~y** /tek'nɒlədʒɪ/ n tecnología f

teddy bear /'tedɪ/ n osito m de peluche

tedi|ous /'tiːdɪəs/ adj tedioso. **~um** /'tiːdɪəm/ n tedio m

teem /tiːm/ vi abundar (with en), estar repleto (with de)

teen|age /'tiːneɪdʒ/ adj adolescente; (for teenagers) para jóvenes. **~ager** n adolescente m & f. **~s** /tiːnz/ npl adolescencia f

teeny /'tiːnɪ/ adj (-ier, -iest) [I] chiquito

teeter /'tiːtə(r)/ vi balancearse

teeth /tiːθ/ see **TOOTH**. **~e** /tiːð/ vi. he's **~ing** le están saliendo los dientes. **~ing troubles** npl (fig) problemas mpl iniciales

tele|communications /telɪkəmjuː'nɪkeɪʃnz/ npl telecomunicaciones fpl. **~gram** /'telɪgræm/ n telegrama m. **~pathic** /telɪ'pæθɪk/ adj telepático. **~pathy** /tə'lepəθɪ/ n telepatía f

telephon|e /'telɪfəʊn/ n teléfono m. ● vt llamar por teléfono. **~e booth**, **~e box** n cabina f telefónica. **~e call** n llamada f telefónica. **~e card** n tarjeta f telefónica. **~e directory** n guía f telefónica. **~e exchange** n central f telefónica. **~ist** /tɪ'lefənɪst/ n telefonista m & f

tele|sales /'telɪseɪlz/ npl televentas fpl. **~scope** n telescopio m. **~scopic** /-'skɒpɪk/ adj telescópico. **~text** n teletex(to) m. **~working** n teletrabajo m

televis|e /'telɪvaɪz/ vt televisar. **~ion** /'telɪvɪʒn/ n (medium) televisión f. **~ion (set)** n televisor m

telex /'teleks/ n télex m

tell /tel/ vt (pt told) decir; contar (story, joke); (distinguish) distinguir. ~ **the difference** notar la diferencia. ~ **the time** decir la hora. ● vi (produce an effect) tener efecto; (know) saber. □ ~ **off** vt regañar. ~**ing** adj revelador. ~**tale** n soplón m. ● adj revelador

telly /'teli/ n 🔲 tele f

temp /temp/ n empleado m eventual or temporal

temper /'tempə(r)/ n (mood) humor m; (disposition) carácter m; (fit of anger) cólera f. **be in a** ~ estar furioso. **lose one's** ~ perder los estribos. ~**ament** /'tempərəmənt/ n temperamento m. ~**amental** /-'mentl/ adj temperamental. ~**ate** /'tempərət/ adj templado. ~**ature** /'temprɪtʃə(r)/ n temperatura f. **have a** ~**ature** tener fiebre

tempestuous /tem'pestjʊəs/ adj tempestuoso

temple /'templ/ n templo m; (of head) sien f

tempo /'tempəʊ/ n (pl -os or tempi) ritmo m

temporar|ily /'tempərərəlɪ/ adv temporalmente, temporariamente (LAm). ~**y** /'tempərərɪ/ adj temporal, provisional; (job) eventual, temporal

tempt /tempt/ vt tentar. ~**ation** /-'teɪʃn/ n tentación f. ~**ing** adj tentador

ten /ten/ adj & n diez m

tenaci|ous /tɪ'neɪʃəs/ adj tenaz. ~**ty** /tɪ'næsɪtɪ/ n tenacidad f

tenan|cy /'tenənsɪ/ n inquilinato m. ~**t** n inquilino m, arrendatario m

tend /tend/ vi. ~ **to** tender a. ● vt cuidar (de). ~**ency** /'tendənsɪ/ n

tendencia f

tender /'tendə(r)/ adj tierno; (painful) sensible. ● n (Com) oferta f. **legal** ~ n moneda f de curso legal. ● vt ofrecer, presentar. ~**ly** adv tiernamente

tendon /'tendən/ n tendón m

tennis /'tenɪs/ n tenis m

tenor /'tenə(r)/ n tenor m

tens|e /tens/ adj (-er, -est) (taut) tenso, tirante; (person) tenso. ● n (Gram) tiempo m. ~**ion** /-ʃn/ n tensión f; (between two parties) conflicto m

tent /tent/ n tienda f (de campaña), carpa f (LAm)

tentacle /'tentəkl/ n tentáculo m

tentative /'tentətɪv/ adj (plan) provisional; (offer) tentativo; (person) indeciso

tenterhooks /'tentəhʊks/ npl. **be on** ~ estar en ascuas

tenth /tenθ/ adj & n décimo (m)

tenuous /'tenjʊəs/ adj (claim) poco fundado; (link) indirecto

tenure /'tenjʊə(r)/ n tenencia f; (period of office) ejercicio m

tepid /'tepɪd/ adj tibio

term /tɜːm/ n (of time) período m; (Schol) trimestre m; (word etc) término m. ~**s** npl condiciones fpl; (Com) precio m. **on good/bad** ~**s** en buenas/malas relaciones. ● vt calificar De

termin|al /'tɜːmɪnl/ adj terminal. ● n (transport) terminal f; (Comp, Elec) terminal m. ~**ate** /-eɪt/ vt poner fin a; poner término a (contract); (Amer, fire) despedir. ● vi terminarse. ~**ology** /-'nɒlədʒɪ/ n terminología f

terrace /'terəs/ n terraza f; (houses) hilera f de casas

terrain /tə'reɪn/ n terreno m

t

terrestrial /tɪˈrestrɪəl/ adj terrestre

terribl|e /ˈterəbl/ adj espantoso. **~y** adv terriblemente

terrif|ic /təˈrɪfɪk/ adj (fam, excellent) estupendo; (fam, huge) enorme. **~ied** /ˈterɪfaɪd/ adj aterrorizado. **~y** /ˈterɪfaɪ/ vt aterrorizar. **~ying** adj aterrador

territor|ial /terɪˈtɔːrɪəl/ adj territorial. **~y** /ˈterɪtrɪ/ n territorio m

terror /ˈterə(r)/ n terror m. **~ism** n terrorismo m. **~ist** n terrorista m & f. **~ize** vt aterrorizar

terse /tɜːs/ adj seco, lacónico

test /test/ n (of machine, drug) prueba f; (exam) prueba f, test m; (of blood) análisis m; (for eyes, hearing) examen m. ● vt probar, poner a prueba (product); hacerle una prueba a (student); evaluar (knowledge); examinar (sight)

testament /ˈtestəmənt/ n (will) testamento m. **Old/New T~** Antiguo/Nuevo Testamento

testicle /ˈtestɪkl/ n testículo m

testify /ˈtestɪfaɪ/ vt atestiguar. ● vi declarar

testimon|ial /testɪˈməʊnɪəl/ n recomendación f. **~y** /ˈtestɪmənɪ/ n testimonio m

test: **~ match** n partido m internacional. **~ tube** n tubo m de ensayo, probeta f

tether /ˈteðə(r)/ vt atar. ● n. **be at the end of one's ~** no poder más

text /tekst/ n texto m. ● vt mandar un mensaje a. **~book** n libro m de texto

textile /ˈtekstaɪl/ adj & n textil (m)

texture /ˈtekstʃə(r)/ n textura f

Thames /temz/ n Támesis m

than /ðæn, ðən/ conj que; (with quantity) de

thank /θæŋk/ vt darle las gracias a, agradecer. **~ you** gracias. **~ful** adj agradecido. **~fully** adv (happily) gracias a Dios. **~less** adj ingrato. **~s** npl agradecimiento m. **~s!** [T] ¡gracias!. **~s to** gracias a

Thanksgiving (Day) /θæŋks ˈɡɪvɪŋ/ n (in US) el día de Acción de Gracias

that /ðæt, ðət/ adj (pl those) ese, aquel, esa, aquella. ● pron (pl those) ese, aquél, esa, aquélla. **~ is** es decir. **~'s not true** eso no es cierto. **~'s why** por eso. **is ~ you?** ¿eres tú? **like ~** así. ● adv tan. ● rel pron que; (with prep) que la, que, el cual, la cual. ● conj que

thatched /θætʃt/ adj (roof) de paja; (cottage) con techo de paja

thaw /θɔː/ vt descongelar. ● vi descongelarse; (snow) derretirse. ● n deshielo m

---

the definite article

····▸ el (m), la (f), los (mpl), las (fpl), lo. **building** el edificio. **~ windows** las ventanas

! Feminine singular nouns beginning with a stressed or accented a or ha take the article el instead of la, e.g. **~ soul** el alma; **~ axe** el hacha; **~ eagle** el águila

Note that when el follows the prepositions de and a, it combines to form del and al, e.g. **of ~ group** del grupo. **I went to ~ bank** fui al banco

····▸ (before an ordinal number in

names, titles) not translated. Henry ~ Eighth Enrique Octavo. Elizabeth ~ Second Isabel Segunda

····▶ (*in abstractions*) lo. ~ im-possible lo imposible

theatr|e /'θɪətə(r)/ n teatro m; (*Amer, movie theater*) cine m. **~ical** /-'ætrɪkl/ adj teatral

theft /θeft/ n hurto m

their /ðeə(r)/ adj su, sus pl. **~s** /ðeəz/ poss pron (el) suyo m, (la) suya f, (los) suyos mpl, (las) suyas fpl

them /ðem, ðəm/ pron (accusative) los m, las f; (dative) les; (after prep) ellos m, ellas f

theme /θiːm/ n tema m. ~ **park** n parque m temático. ~ **song** n motivo m principal

themselves /ðəm'selvz/ pron ellos mismos m, ellas mismas f; (reflexive) se; (after prep) sí mismos m, sí mismas f

then /ðen/ adv entonces; (next) luego, después. **by ~** para entonces. **now and ~** de vez en cuando. **since ~** desde entonces. ● adj entonces

theology /θɪ'ɒlədʒɪ/ n teología f

theor|etical /θɪə'retɪkl/ adj teórico. **~y** /'θɪərɪ/ n teoría f

therap|eutic /θerə'pjuːtɪk/ adj terapéutico. **~ist** /'θerəpɪst/ n terapeuta m & f. **~y** /θerəpɪ/ n terapia f

there /ðeə(r)/ adv ahí; (further away) allí, ahí; (less precise, further) allá. ~ **is**, ~ **are** hay. ~ **it is** ahí está. ~ **down** ~ ahí abajo. **up** ~ ahí arriba. ● int. ~! that's the last box ¡listo! ésa es la última caja. ~, ~, don't cry! vamos, no llores. **~abouts** adv por ahí. **~fore** /-fɔː(r)/ adv por lo tanto.

thermometer /θə'mɒmɪtə(r)/ n termómetro m

Thermos /'θɜːməs/ n (®) termo m

thermostat /'θɜːməstæt/ n termostato m

thesaurus /θɪ'sɔːrəs/ n (pl -ri /-raɪ/) diccionario m de sinónimos

these /ðiːz/ adj estos, estas. ● pron éstos, éstas

thesis /'θiːsɪs/ n (pl theses /-siːz/) tesis f

they /ðeɪ/ pron ellos m, ellas f. ~ **say** that dicen or se dice que

they'd /ðeɪ(ə)d/ = they had, they would

they'll /ðeɪl/ = they will

they're /ðeə(r)/ = they are

they've /ðeɪv/ = they have

thick /θɪk/ adj (-er, -est) (layer, sweater) grueso, gordo; (sauce) espeso; (fog, smoke) espeso, denso; (fur) tupido; (fam, stupid) burro. ● adv espesamente, densamente. ● n. **in the ~ of** en medio de. **~en** vt espesar. ● vi espesarse. **~et** /-ɪt/ n matorral m. **~ness** n (of fabric) grosor m; (of paper, wood, wall) espesor m

thief /θiːf/ n (pl thieves /θiːvz/) ladrón m

thigh /θaɪ/ n muslo m

thimble /'θɪmbl/ n dedal m

thin /θɪn/ adj (thinner, thinnest) (person) delgado, flaco; (layer, slice) fino; (hair) ralo

thing /θɪŋ/ n cosa f. **it's a good ~** (that)... menos mal que.... just **the ~** exactamente lo que se necesita. **poor ~!** ¡pobrecito!

think /θɪŋk/ vt (pt thought) pensar, creer. ● vi pensar (about en); (carefully) reflexionar; (imagine) imaginarse. **I ~ so** creo que sí. ~ **of s.o.** pensar en uno. **I hadn't**

t

thought of that eso no se me ha ocurrido. **~ over** vt pensar bien. **~ up** vt idear, inventar. **~er** n pensador m. **~tank** n gabinete m estratégico

third /θɜːd/ adj tercero, (before masculine singular noun) tercer. ● n tercio m, tercera parte f. **~** (**gear**) n (Auto) tercera f. **~-rate** adj muy inferior. **T~ World** n Tercer Mundo m

thirst /θɜːst/ n sed f. **~y** adj sediento. **be ~y** tener sed

thirt|een /θɜːtiːn/ adj & n trece (m). **~teenth** adj decimotercero. ● n treceavo m **~ieth** /θɜːtɪəθ/ adj trigésimo. ● n treintavo m. **~y** /θɜːtɪ/ adj & n treinta (m)

this /ðɪs/ adj (pl these) este, esta. **~ one** éste, ésta. ● pron (pl these) éste, ésta, esto. **like ~** así

thistle /θɪsl/ n cardo m

thong /θɒŋ/ n correa f; (Amer, sandal) chancla f

thorn /θɔːn/ n espina f. **~y** adj espinoso

thorough /θʌrə/ adj (investigation) riguroso; (cleaning etc) a fondo; (person) concienzudo. **~bred** /-bred/ adj de pura sangre. **~fare** n vía f pública; (street) calle f. **no ~fare** prohibido el paso. **~ly** adv (clean) a fondo; (examine) minuciosamente; (completely) perfectamente

those /ðəʊz/ adj esos, esas, aquellos, aquellas. ● pron ésos, ésas, aquéllos, aquéllas

though /ðəʊ/ conj aunque. ● adv sin embargo. **as ~** como si

thought /θɔːt/ see **THINK**. ● n pensamiento m; (idea) idea f. **~ful** adj pensativo; (considerate) atento. **~fully** adv pensativamente; (con-siderately) atentamente. **~less** adj desconsiderado

thousand /θaʊznd/ adj & n mil (m). **~th** adj & n milésimo (m)

thrash /θræʃ/ vt azotar; (defeat) derrotar

thread /θred/ n hilo m; (of screw) rosca f. ● vt enhebrar (needle); ensartar (beads). **~bare** adj gastado, raído

threat /θret/ n amenaza f. **~en** vt/i amenazar. **~ening** adj amenazador

three /θriː/ adj & n tres (m). **~fold** adj triple. ● adv tres veces

threshold /θreʃhəʊld/ n umbral m

threw /θruː/ see **THROW**

thrift /θrɪft/ n economía f, ahorro m. **~y** adj frugal

thrill /θrɪl/ n emoción f. ● vt emocionar. **~ed** adj contentísimo (with con). **~er** n (book) libro m de suspense or (LAm) suspenso; (film) película f de suspense or (LAm) suspenso. **~ing** adj emocionante

thriv|e /θraɪv/ vi prosperar. **~ing** adj próspero

throat /θrəʊt/ n garganta f

throb /θrɒb/ vi (pt throbbed) palpitar; (with pain) dar punzadas; (engine) vibrar. **~bing** adj (pain) punzante

throes /θrəʊz/ npl. **be in one's death ~** estar agonizando

throne /θrəʊn/ n trono m

throng /θrɒŋ/ n multitud f

throttle /θrɒtl/ n (Auto) acelerador m (que se acciona con la mano). ● vt estrangular

through /θruː/ prep por, a través de; (during) durante; (by means of) a través de; (Amer, until and including) **Monday ~ Friday** de lunes a viernes. ● adv de parte a parte, de un lado a otro; (entirely) completamente; (to the end) hasta el final. be ~ (finished) haber terminado. ● adj (train etc) directo. no ~ road calle sin salida. ~out /-'aut/ prep por todo; (time) durante todo. ~out his career a lo largo de su carrera

throve /θrəʊv/ see **THRIVE**

throw /θrəʊ/ vt (pt threw, pp thrown) tirar, aventar (Mex); lanzar (grenade, javelin); (disconcert) desconcertar; 🔲 hacer (party). ● n (of ball) tiro m; (of dice) tirada f. □ ~ away vt tirar. □ ~ up vi (vomit) vomitar.

thrush /θrʌʃ/ n tordo m

thrust /θrʌst/ vt (pt thrust) empujar; (push in) clavar. ● n empujón m; (of sword) estocada f

thud /θʌd/ n ruido m sordo

thug /θʌg/ n matón m

thumb /θʌm/ n pulgar m. ● vt. ~ a lift ir a dedo. ~tack n (Amer) chincheta f, tachuela f, chinche f (Mex)

thump /θʌmp/ vt golpear. ● vi (heart) latir fuertemente. ● n golpazo m

thunder /'θʌndə(r)/ n truenos mpl, (of traffic) estruendo m. ● vi tronar. ~bolt n rayo m. ~storm n tormenta f eléctrica. ~y adj con truenos

Thursday /'θɜːzdeɪ/ n jueves m

thus /ðʌs/ adv así

thwart /θwɔːt/ vt frustrar

tic /tɪk/ n tic m

tick /tɪk/ n (sound) tic m; (insect) garrapata f, (mark) marca f, visto m, palomita f (Mex); (fam, instant) momentito m. ● vi hacer tictac. ● vt. ~ (off) marcar

ticket /'tɪkɪt/ n (for bus, train) billete m, boleto m (LAm); (for plane) pasaje m, billete m; (for theatre, museum) entrada f; (for baggage, coat) ticket m; (fine) multa f. ~ collector n revisor m. ~ office n (transport) mostrador m de venta de billetes or (LAm) boletos; (in theatre) taquilla f, boletería f (LAm)

tickle /'tɪkl/ vt hacer cosquillas a. ● n cosquilleo m. ~ish /'tɪklɪʃ/ adj. be ~ish tener cosquillas

tidal wave /'taɪdl/ n maremoto m

tide /taɪd/ n marea f. high/low ~ marea alta/baja. □ ~ over vt ayudar a salir de un apuro

tid|ily /'taɪdɪlɪ/ adv ordenadamente. ~iness n orden m. ~y adj (-ier, -iest) ordenado. ● vt/i ~y (up) ordenar, arreglar

tie /taɪ/ vt (pres p tying) atar, amarrar (LAm); hacer (knot). ● vi (Sport) empatar. ● n (constraint) atadura f; (bond) lazo m; (necktie) corbata f; (Sport) empate m. ~ in with vt concordar con. □ ~ up vt atar. be ~d up (busy) estar ocupado

tier /tɪə(r)/ n hilera f superpuesta; (in stadium etc) grada f; (of cake) piso m

tiger /'taɪgə(r)/ n tigre m

tight /taɪt/ adj (-er, -est) (clothes) ajustado, ceñido; (taut) tieso; (control) estricto; (knot, nut) apretado; (fam, drunk) borracho. ~en vt apretar. □ ~en up vt hacer más estricto. ~-fisted /-'fɪstɪd/ adj tacaño. ~ly adv bien, fuerte; (fastened) fuertemente. ~rope n cuerda f floja. ~s npl (for ballet etc) leotardo(s) m(pl); (pantyhose) medias fpl

tile /taɪl/ n (decorative) azulejo m; (on roof) teja f; (on floor) baldosa f

• vt azulejar; tejar (roof); embaldosar (floor)

till /tɪl/ prep hasta. • conj hasta que. • n caja f. • vt cultivar

tilt /tɪlt/ vt inclinar. • vi inclinarse. • n inclinación f

timber /'tɪmbə(r)/ n madera f (para construcción)

time /taɪm/ n tiempo m; (moment) momento m; (occasion) ocasión f; (by clock) hora f; (epoch) época f; (rhythm) compás m. at ~s a veces. for the ~ being de momento. from ~ to ~ de vez en cuando. have a good ~ divertirse, pasarlo bien. in a year's ~ dentro de un año. in no ~ en un abrir y cerrar de ojos. in ~ a tiempo; (eventually) con el tiempo. arrive on ~ llegar a tiempo. it's ~ we left es hora de irnos. • vt elegir el momento; cronometrar (race). ~ bomb n bomba f de tiempo. ~ly adj oportuno. ~r n cronómetro m; (Culin) avisador m; (with sand) reloj m de arena; (Elec) interruptor m de reloj. ~s /taɪmz/ prep. 2 ~ 4 is 8 2 (multiplicado) por 4 son 8. ~table n horario m

timid /'tɪmɪd/ adj tímido; (fearful) miedoso

tin /tɪn/ n estaño m; (container) lata f. ~ foil n papel m de estaño

tinge /tɪndʒ/ vt. be ~d with sth estar matizado de algo. • n matiz m

tingle /'tɪŋgl/ vi sentir un hormigueo

tinker /'tɪŋkə(r)/ vi. ~ with juguetear con

tinkle /'tɪŋkl/ vi tintinear

tinned /tɪnd/ adj en lata, enlatado

tin opener n abrelatas m

tint /tɪnt/ n matiz m

tiny /'taɪnɪ/ adj (-ier, -iest) minúsculo, diminuto

tip /tɪp/ n punta f. • vt (pt tipped) (tilt) inclinar; (overturn) volcar; (pour) verter; (give gratuity to) darle (una) propina a. □ ~ off vt avisar. □ ~ out vt verter. □ ~ over vi caerse. • n propina f; (advice) consejo m (práctico); (for rubbish) vertedero m. ~ped adj (cigarette) con filtro

tipsy /'tɪpsɪ/ adj achispado

tiptoe /'tɪptəʊ/ n. on ~ de puntillas

tiptop /'tɪptɒp/ adj 🄓 de primera. in ~ condition en excelente estado

tire /'taɪə(r)/ n (Amer) see TYRE. • vt cansar. • vi cansarse. ~d /'taɪəd/ adj cansado. get ~d cansarse. ~d of harto de. ~d out agotado. ~less adj incansable; (efforts) inagotable. ~some /-səm/ adj (person) pesado; (task) tedioso

tiring /'taɪərɪŋ/ adj cansado, cansador (LAm)

tissue /'tɪʃu:/ n (of bones, plants) tejido m; (paper handkerchief) pañuelo m de papel. ~ paper n papel m de seda

tit /tɪt/ n (bird) paro m; (🄓, breast) teta f

titbit /'tɪtbɪt/ n exquisitez f

tit for tat n: it was ~ fue ojo por ojo, diente por diente

title /'taɪtl/ n título m

to /tu:, tə/ prep a; (towards) hacia; (in order to) para; (as far as) hasta; (of) de. give it ~ me dámelo. what did you say ~ him? ¿qué le dijiste?; I don't want ~ no quiero. it's twenty ~ seven (by clock) son las siete menos veinte, son veinte para las siete (LAm). • adv. pull ~

cerrar. ~ **and fro** adv de un lado a otro

toad /təʊd/ n sapo m. ~**stool** n hongo m (no comestible)

toast /təʊst/ n pan m tostado, tostadas fpl; (drink) brindis m. **a piece of** ~ una tostada, un pan tostado (Mex). **drink a** ~ **to** brindar por. ● vt (Culin) tostar; (drink to) brindar por. ~**er** n tostadora f (eléctrica), tostador m

tobacco /tə'bækəʊ/ n tabaco m. ~**nist** /-ənɪst/ n estanquero m

toboggan /tə'bɒgən/ n toboggán m

today /tə'deɪ/ n & adv hoy (m)

toddler /'tɒdlə(r)/ n niño m pequeño (entre un año y dos años y medio de edad)

toe /təʊ/ n dedo m (del pie); (of shoe) punta f. **big** ~ dedo m gordo (del pie). **on one's** ~**s** (fig) alerta. ● vt. ~ **the line** acatar la disciplina

> **TOEFL - Test of English as a Foreign Language** ⓘ
> Un examen que, a la hora de solicitar el ingreso a una universidad americana, evalúa el dominio del inglés de aquellos estudiantes cuya lengua materna no es este idioma.

toffee /'tɒfɪ/ n toffee m (golosina hecha con azúcar y mantequilla)

together /tə'geðə(r)/ adv juntos; (at same time) a la vez. ~ **with** junto con

toil /tɔɪl/ vi afanarse. ● n trabajo m duro

toilet /'tɔɪlɪt/ n servicio m, baño m (LAm). ~ **paper** n papel m higiénico. ~**ries** /'tɔɪlɪtrɪz/ npl artículos mpl de tocador. ~ **roll** n rollo m de papel higiénico

token /'təʊkən/ n muestra f; (voucher) vale m; (coin) ficha f. ● adj simbólico

told /təʊld/ see **TELL**

tolera|ble /'tɒlərəbl/ adj tolerable; (not bad) pasable. ~**nce** /'tɒlərəns/ n tolerancia f. ~**nt** adj tolerante. ~**te** /-'reɪt/ vt tolerar. ~**tion** /-'reɪʃn/ n tolerancia f

toll /təʊl/ n (on road) peaje m, cuota f (Mex). **death** ~ número m de muertos. ~ **call** n (Amer) llamada f interurbana, conferencia f. ● vi doblar, tocar a muerto

tomato /tə'mɑːtəʊ/ n (pl -oes) tomate m, jitomate m (Mex)

tomb /tuːm/ n tumba f, sepulcro m. ~**stone** n lápida f

tomorrow /tə'mɒrəʊ/ n & adv mañana (f). **see you** ~! ¡hasta mañana!

ton /tʌn/ n tonelada f (= 1,016kg). ~**s of** 🔲 montones de. **metric** ~ tonelada f (métrica) (= 1,000kg)

tone /təʊn/ n tono m. □ ~ **down** vt atenuar; moderar (language). ~**deaf** adj que no tiene oído (musical)

tongs /tɒŋz/ npl tenacillas fpl

tongue /tʌŋ/ n lengua f. **say sth** ~ **in cheek** decir algo medio burlándose. ~**tied** adj cohibido. ~**twister** n trabalenguas m

tonic /'tɒnɪk/ adj tónico. ● n (Med, fig) tónico m. ~ **(water)** n tónica f

tonight /tə'naɪt/ adv & n esta noche (f); (evening) esta tarde (f)

tonne /tʌn/ n tonelada f (métrica)

tonsil /'tɒnsl/ n amígdala f. ~**litis** /-'laɪtɪs/ n amigdalitis f

too /tuː/ adv (excessively) demasiado; (also) también. **I'm not** ~ **sure** no estoy muy seguro. ~ **many** demasiados. ~ **much**

demasiado

took /tʊk/ *see* TAKE

tool /tu:l/ *n* herramienta *f*

tooth /tu:θ/ *n* (*pl* teeth) diente *m*; (*molar*) muela *f*. **~ache** *n* dolor *m* de muelas. **~brush** *n* cepillo *m* de dientes. **~paste** *n* pasta *f* dentífrica, pasta *f* de dientes. **~pick** *n* palillo *m* (de dientes)

top /tɒp/ *n* parte *f* superior, parte *f* de arriba; (*of mountain*) cima *f*; (*of tree*) copa *f*; (*of page*) parte *f* superior; (*lid, of bottle*) tapa *f*; (*of pen*) capuchón *m*; (*spinning* ~) trompo *m*, peonza *f*. be ~ of the class ser el primero de la clase. from ~ to bottom de arriba abajo. on ~ of encima de; (*besides*) además de. ● *adj* más alto; (*shelf*) superior; (*speed*) máximo; (*in rank*) superior; (*leading*) más destacado. ● *vt* (*pt* topped) cubrir; (*exceed*) exceder. ~ floor *n* último piso *m*. □ ~ up *vt* llenar; (*mobile phone*) recargar el saldo. ~ hat *n* chistera *f*. **~-heavy** /-ˈhevɪ/ *adj* inestable (por ser más pesado en su parte superior)

topic /ˈtɒpɪk/ *n* tema *m*. **~al** *adj* de actualidad

topless /ˈtɒpləs/ *adj* topless

topple /ˈtɒpl/ *vi* (*Pol*) derribar; (*overturn*) volcar. ● *vi* caerse

top secret /tɒpˈsiːkrɪt/ *adj* secreto, reservado

torch /tɔːtʃ/ *n* linterna *f*; (*flaming*) antorcha *f*

tore /tɔː(r)/ *see* TEAR¹

torment /ˈtɔːment/ *n* tormento *m*. ● /tɔːˈment/ *vt* atormentar

torn /tɔːn/ *see* TEAR¹

tornado /tɔːˈneɪdəʊ/ *n* (*pl* -oes) tornado *m*

torpedo /tɔːˈpiːdəʊ/ *n* (*pl* -oes) torpedo *m*. ● *vt* torpedear

torrent /ˈtɒrənt/ *n* torrente *m*. **~ial** /təˈrenʃl/ *adj* torrencial

torrid /ˈtɒrɪd/ *adj* tórrido; (*affair*) apasionado

tortoise /ˈtɔːtəs/ *n* tortuga *f*. **~shell** *n* carey *m*

tortuous /ˈtɔːtjʊəs/ *adj* tortuoso

torture /ˈtɔːtʃə(r)/ *n* tortura *f*. ● *vt* torturar

toss /tɒs/ *vt* tirar, lanzar (ball); (*shake*) sacudir. ● *vi*. ~ and turn (*in bed*) dar vueltas

tot /tɒt/ *n* pequeño *m*; (*fam, of liquor*) trago *m*. ● *vt* (*pt* totted). ~ up *vt* sumar

total /ˈtəʊtl/ *adj* & *n* total (*m*). ● *vt* (*pt* totalled) ascender a un total de; (*add up*) totalizar. **~itarian** /təʊtælɪˈteərɪən/ *adj* totalitario. **~ly** *adv* totalmente

totter /ˈtɒtə(r)/ *vi* tambalearse

touch /tʌtʃ/ *vt* tocar; (*move*) conmover; (*concern*) afectar. ● *vi* tocar; (*wires*) tocarse. ● *n* toque *m*; (*sense*) tacto *m*; (*contact*) contacto *m*. be/get/stay in ~ with estar/ponerse/mantenerse en contacto con. □ ~ down *vi* (*aircraft*) aterrizar. □ ~ up *vt* retocar. **~ing** *adj* enternecedor. **~y** *adj* quisquilloso

tough /tʌf/ *adj* (-er, -est) duro; (*strong*) fuerte, resistente; (*difficult*) difícil; (*severe*) severo. **~en**. □ ~ (up) *vt* endurecer; hacer más fuerte (person)

tour /tʊə(r)/ *n* viaje *m*, (*visit*) visita *f*; (*excursion*) excursión *f*; (*by team etc*) gira *f*. be on ~ estar de gira. ● *vt* recorrer; (*visit*) visitar. ~ guide *n* guía de turismo

tourism /ˈtʊərɪzəm/ *n* turismo *m*. **~t** /ˈtʊərɪst/ *n* turista *m* & *f*. ● *adj* turístico. **~t office** *n* oficina *f* de turismo

tournament /'tɔ:nəmənt/ n torneo m

tousle /'taʊzl/ vt despeinar

tout /taʊt/ vi. ~ (for) solicitar

tow /təʊ/ vt remolcar. ● n remolque m

toward(s) /tə'wɔ:d(z)/ prep hacia. his attitude ~ her su actitud para con ella

towel /'taʊəl/ n toalla f

tower /'taʊə(r)/ n torre f. ● vi. ~ above (building) descollar sobre; (person) destacar sobre. ~ block n edificio m or bloque m de apartamentos. ~ing adj altísimo; (rage) violento

town /taʊn/ n ciudad f; (smaller) pueblo m. go to ~ Ⓣ no escatimar dinero. ~ hall n ayuntamiento m

toxic /'tɒksɪk/ adj tóxico

toy /tɔɪ/ n juguete m. □ ~ with vt juguetear con (object); darle vueltas a (idea). ~shop n juguetería f

trace /treɪs/ n señal f, rastro m. ● vt trazar; (draw) dibujar; (with tracing paper) calcar; (track down) localizar. ~ing paper n papel m de calcar

track /træk/ n pista f, huellas fpl; (path) sendero m; (Sport) pista f. the ~(s) la vía férrea; (Rail) vía f. keep ~ of seguirle la pista a (person). ~ vt seguirle la pista a. □ ~ down vt localizar. ~ suit n equipo m (de deportes) chándal m

tract /trækt/ n (land) extensión f; (pamphlet) tratado m breve

traction /'trækʃn/ n tracción f

tractor /'træktə(r)/ n tractor m

trade /treɪd/ n comercio m; (occupation) oficio m; (exchange) cambio m; (industry) industria f. ● vt. ~ sth for sth cambiar algo por algo. ● vi

comerciar. □ ~ in vt (give in part-exchange) entregar como parte del pago. ~ mark n marca f (de fábrica). ~r n comerciante m & f. ~ union n sindicato m

tradition /trə'dɪʃn/ n tradición f. ~al adj tradicional

traffic /'træfɪk/ n tráfico m. ● vi (pt trafficked) comerciar (in en). ~ circle n (Amer) glorieta f, rotonda f. ~ island n isla f peatonal. ~ jam n embotellamiento m, atasco m. ~ lights npl semáforo m. ~ warden n guardia m, controlador m de tráfico

tragedy /'trædʒɪdɪ/ n tragedia f. ~ic /'trædʒɪk/ adj trágico

trail /treɪl/ vi arrastrarse; (lag) rezagarse. ● vt (track) seguir la pista de. ● n (left by animal, person) huellas fpl; (path) sendero m. be on the ~ of s.o./sth seguir la pista de uno/algo. ~er n remolque m; (Amer, caravan) caravana f, rulot m; (film) avance m

train /treɪn/ n (Rail) tren m; (of events) serie f; (of dress) cola f. ● vt capacitar (employee); adiestrar (soldier); (Sport) entrenar; educar (voice); guiar (plant); amaestrar (animal). ● vi estudiar; (Sport) entrenarse. ~ed adj (skilled) cualificado, calificado; (doctor) diplomado. ~ee /treɪ'ni:/ n aprendiz m; (Amer, Mil) recluta m & f. ~er n (Sport) entrenador m; (of animals) amaestrador m. ~ers npl zapatillas fpl de deporte. ~ing n capacitación f; (Sport) entrenamiento m

trait /treɪ(t)/ n rasgo m

traitor /'treɪtə(r)/ n traidor m

tram /træm/ n tranvía m

tramp /træmp/ vi. ~ (along) caminar pesadamente. ● n vagabundo m

trample /'træmpl/ vt pisotear.
● vi. ~ on pisotear

trampoline /'træmpəli:n/ n trampolín m

trance /trɑ:ns/ n trance m

tranquil /'træŋkwɪl/ adj tranquilo. **~lity** /-'kwɪləti/ n tranquilidad f; (of person) serenidad f. **~lize** /'træŋkwɪlaɪz/ vt sedar, dar un sedante a. **~lizer** n sedante m, tranquilizante m

transaction /træn'zækʃən/ n transacción f, operación f

transatlantic /trænzət'læntɪk/ adj transatlántico

transcend /træn'send/ vt (go beyond) exceder

transcript /'trænskrɪpt/ n transcripción f

transfer /træns'fɜ:(r)/ vt (pt transferred) trasladar; traspasar (player); transferir (funds, property); pasar (call). ● vi trasladarse. ● /'trænsfɜ:(r)/ n traslado m; (of player) traspaso m; (of funds, property) transferencia f; (paper) calcomanía f

transform /træns'fɔ:m/ vt transformar. **~ation** /-ə'meɪʃn/ n transformación f. **~er** n transformador m

transfusion /træns'fju:ʒn/ n transfusión f

transient /'trænzɪənt/ adj pasajero

transistor /træn'zɪstə(r)/ n transistor m

transit /'trænsɪt/ n tránsito m. **~ion** /træn'zɪʒn/ n transición f. **~ive** /'trænsɪtɪv/ adj transitivo

translat|e /trænz'leɪt/ vt traducir. **~ion** /-ʃn/ n traducción f **~or** n traductor m

transmission /træns'mɪʃn/ n

transmisión f

transmit /trænz'mɪt/ vt (pt transmitted) transmitir. **~ter** n transmisor m

transparen|cy /træns'pærənsɪ/ n transparencia f; (Photo) diapositiva f. **~t** adj transparente

transplant /træns'plɑ:nt/ vt trasplantar. ● /'trænsplɑ:nt/ n trasplante m

transport /træn'spɔ:t/ vt transportar. ● /'trænspɔ:t/ n transporte m. **~ation** /-'teɪʃn/ n transporte m

trap /træp/ n trampa f ● vt (pt trapped) atrapar; (jam) atascar; (cut off) bloquear. **~door** n trampilla f

trapeze /trə'pi:z/ n trapecio m

trash /træʃ/ n basura f; (Amer, worthless people) escoria f. **~ can** n (Amer) cubo m de la basura, bote m de la basura (Mex). **~y** adj (souvenir) de porquería; (magazine) malo

travel /'trævl/ vi (pt travelled) viajar; (vehicle) desplazarse. ● vt recorrer. ● n viajes mpl. **~ agency** n agencia f de viajes. **~ler** n viajero m. **~ler's cheque** n cheque m de viaje o viajero. **~ling expenses** npl gastos mpl de viaje

trawler /'trɔ:lə(r)/ n barca f pesquera

tray /treɪ/ n bandeja f

treacher|ous adj traidor; (deceptive) engañoso. **~y** n traición f

treacle /'tri:kl/ n melaza f

tread /tred/ vi (pt trod, pp trodden) pisar. **~ on sth** pisar algo. **~ carefully** andarse con cuidado. ● n (step) paso m; (of tyre) banda f de rodamiento

treason /'tri:zn/ n traición f

treasur|e /'treʒə(r)/ n tesoro m.

~ed /'treʒəd/ adj (possession) preciado. **~er** /'treʒərə(r)/ n tesorero m. **~y** n erario m, tesoro m. the T**~y** el fisco, la hacienda pública. Department of the T**~y** (in US) Departamento m del Tesoro

treat /tri:t/ vt tratar; (Med) tratar. **~ s.o.** (to meal etc) invitar a uno. ● n placer m; (present) regalo m

treatise /'tri:tiz/ n tratado m

treatment /'tri:tmənt/ n tratamiento m

treaty /'tri:ti/ n tratado m

treble /'trebl/ adj triple; (clef) de sol; (voice) de tiple. ● vt triplicar. ● vi triplicarse. ● n tiple m & f

tree /tri:/ n árbol m

trek /trek/ n caminata f. ● vi (pt trekked) caminar

trellis /'trelıs/ n enrejado m

tremble /'trembl/ vi temblar

tremendous /trı'mendəs/ adj formidable; (fam, huge) tremendo. **~ly** adv tremendamente

tremor /'tremə(r)/ n temblor m

trench /trentʃ/ n zanja f; (Mil) trinchera f

trend /trend/ n tendencia f; (fashion) moda f. **~y** adj (-ier, -iest) 🅣 moderno

trepidation /trepı'deıʃn/ n inquietud f

trespass /'trespəs/ vi. **~ on** entrar sin autorización (en propiedad ajena). **~er** n intruso m

trial /'traıəl/ n prueba f; (Jurid) proceso m, juicio m; (ordeal) prueba f dura. by **~** and error por ensayo y error. be on **~** estar a prueba; (Jurid) estar siendo procesado

triang|le /'traıæŋgl/ n triángulo m. **~ular** /-'æŋgjʊlə(r)/ adj triangular

trib|al /'traıbl/ adj tribal. **~e** /traıb/ n tribu f

tribulation /trıbjʊ'leıʃn/ n tribulación f

tribunal /traı'bju:nl/ n tribunal m

tributary /'trıbjʊtrı/ n (of river) afluente m

tribute /'trıbju:t/ n tributo m; (acknowledgement) homenaje m. pay **~** to rendir homenaje a

trick /trık/ n trampa f, ardid m; (joke) broma f; (feat) truco m; (in card games) baza f. play a **~** on gastar una broma a. ● vt engañar. **~ery** n engaño m

trickle /'trıkl/ vi gotear. **~ in** (fig) entrar poco a poco

trickster /'trıkstə(r)/ n estafador m

tricky /'trıkı/ adj delicado, difícil

tricycle /'traısıkl/ n triciclo m

tried /traıd/ see TRY

trifl|e /'traıfl/ n nimiedad f; (Culin) postre de bizcocho, jerez, frutas y nata. ● vi. □ **~e with** vt jugar con. **~ing** adj insignificante

trigger /'trıgə(r)/ n (of gun) gatillo m. ● vt. **~ (off)** desencadenar

trim /trım/ adj (trimmer, trimmest) (slim) esbelto; (neat) elegante. ● vt (pt trimmed) (cut) recortar; (adorn) adornar. ● n (cut) recorte m. in **~** en buen estado. **~mings** npl recortes mpl

trinity /'trınıtı/ n. the (Holy) T**~** la (Santísima) Trinidad

trinket /'trıŋkıt/ n chuchería f

trio /'tri:əʊ/ n (pl -os) trío m

trip /trıp/ (pt tripped) vt. **~ (up)** hacerle una zancadilla a, hacer tropezar a. ● vi tropezar. ● n (journey) viaje m; (outing) excursión f; (stumble) traspié m

tripe /traıp/ n callos mpl, mon-

triple | trunk

566

dongo m (LAm), pancita f (Mex);
(fam, nonsense) paparruchas fpl
triple /ˈtrɪpl/ adj triple. ● vt triplicar. ● vi triplicarse. ~t /ˈtrɪplɪt/ n
trillizo m
triplicate /ˈtrɪplɪkət/ adj triplicado. in ~ por triplicado
tripod /ˈtraɪpɒd/ n trípode m
trite /traɪt/ adj trillado
triumph /ˈtraɪʌmf/ n triunfo m.
● vi triunfar (over sobre). ~al
/-ˈʌmfl/ adj triunfal. ~ant /-ˈʌmfnt/
adj (troops) triunfador; (moment)
triunfal; (smile) de triunfo
trivial /ˈtrɪvɪəl/ adj insignificante;
(concerns) trivial. ~ity /-ˈælətɪ/ n
trivialidad f
trod, trodden /trɒd, trɒdn/ see
TREAD
trolley /ˈtrɒlɪ/ n (pl -eys) carretón
m; (in supermarket, airport) carrito
m; (for food, drink) carrito m, mesa
f rodante. ~ car n (Amer) tranvía f
trombone /trɒmˈbəʊn/ n trombón m
troop /truːp/ n compañía f; (of
cavalry) escuadrón m. ● vi ~ in entrar en tropel. ~ out salir en tropel. ~er n soldado m de caballería;
(Amer, state police officer) agente m
trophy /ˈtrəʊfɪ/ n trofeo m
tropic /ˈtrɒpɪk/ n trópico m. ~al
adj tropical. ~s npl trópicos mpl
trot /trɒt/ n trote m. ● vi (pt trot-
ted) trotar
trouble /ˈtrʌbl/ n problemas mpl;
(awkward situation) apuro m; (inconvenience) molestia f. be in ~
estar en apuros. get into ~ meterse en problemas. look for ~
buscar camorra. take the ~ to do
sth molestarse en hacer algo. ● vt
(bother) molestar; (worry) preocu-

par. ~-maker n alborotador m.
~some /-səm/ adj problemático.
~ spot n punto m conflictivo
trough /trɒf/ n (for drinking)
abrevadero m; (for feeding) come-
dero m
troupe /truːp/ n compañía f teatral
trousers /ˈtraʊzəz/ npl pantalón
m, pantalones mpl
trout /traʊt/ n (pl trout) trucha f
trowel /ˈtraʊəl/ n (garden) des-
plantador m; (for mortar) paleta f
truant /ˈtruːənt/ n. play ~ hacer
novillos
truce /truːs/ n tregua f
truck /trʌk/ n camión m; (Rail)
vagón m, furgón m; (Amer, vegetables, fruit) productos mpl de la
huerta. ~ driver, ~er n (Amer) n camionero m. ~ing n transporte m
por carretera
trudge /trʌdʒ/ vi andar penosa-
mente
true /truː/ adj (-er, -est) verdadero;
(story, account) verídico; (friend)
auténtico, de verdad. ~ to form
s.o. fiel a algo/uno. be ~ ser
cierto. come ~ hacerse realidad
truffle /ˈtrʌfl/ n trufa f; (chocolate)
trufa f de chocolate
truly /ˈtruːlɪ/ adv verdaderamente;
(sincerely) sinceramente. yours ~
(in letters) cordiales saludos
trump /trʌmp/ n (Cards) triunfo m;
(fig) baza f
trumpet /ˈtrʌmpɪt/ n trompeta f.
~er n trompetista m & f, trompeta
m & f
truncheon /ˈtrʌntʃən/ n porra f
trunk /trʌŋk/ n (of tree) tronco m;
(box) baúl m; (of elephant) trompa
f; (Amer, Auto) maletero m, cajuela f
(Mex). ~s npl bañador m, traje m

de baño

truss /trʌs/ vt. truss (up) vt atar

trust /trʌst/ n confianza f; (money, property) fondo m de inversiones; (institution) fundación f. **on** ~ a ojos cerrados; (Com) al fiado. ● vi. ~ **in s.o./sth** confiar en uno/algo. ● vt confiar en; (in negative sentences) fiarse; (hope) esperar. ~**ed** adj leal. ~**ee** /trʌˈstiː/ n fideicomisario m. ~**ful** adj confiado. ~**ing** adj confiado. ~**worthy** /-wɜːði/ adj digno de confianza

truth /truːθ/ n (pl -**s** /truːðz/) verdad f; (of account, story) veracidad f. ~**ful** adj veraz

try /traɪ/ vt (pt **tried**) intentar; probar (food, product); (be a strain on) poner a prueba; (Jurid) procesar. ~ **to do sth** tratar de hacer algo, intentar hacer algo. ~ **not to forget** procura no olvidarte. ● n tentativa f, prueba f; (Rugby) ensayo m. □ ~ **on** vt probarse (garment). □ ~ **out** vt probar. ~**ing** adj duro; (annoying) molesto

tsar /zɑː(r)/ n zar m

T-shirt /ˈtiːʃɜːt/ n camiseta f

tub /tʌb/ n cuba f; (for washing clothes) tina f; (bathtub) bañera f; (for ice cream) envase m, tarrina f

tuba /ˈtjuːbə/ n tuba f

tubby /ˈtʌbi/ adj (-**ier**, -**iest**) rechoncho

tube /tjuːb/ n tubo m; (fam, Rail) metro m; (Amer fam, television) tele f. **inner** ~ n cámara f de aire

tuberculosis /tjuːbɜːkjuˈləʊsɪs/ n tuberculosis f

tub|ing /ˈtjuːbɪŋ/ n tubería f. ~**ular** /-jʊlə(r)/ adj tubular

tuck /tʌk/ n (fold) jareta f. ● vt plegar; (put) meter. □ ~ **in(to)** vi (fam, eat) ponerse a comer. □ ~

up vt arropar (child)

Tuesday /ˈtjuːzdeɪ/ n martes m

tuft /tʌft/ n (of hair) mechón m; (of feathers) penacho m; (of grass) mata f

tug /tʌg/ vt (pt **tugged**) tirar de. ● vi. ~ **at sth** tirar de algo. ● n tirón m; (Naut) remolcador m. ~-**of-war** n juego de tira y afloja

tuition /tjuːˈɪʃn/ n clases fpl

tulip /ˈtjuːlɪp/ n tulipán m

tumble /ˈtʌmbl/ vi caerse. ● n caída f. ~-**down** adj en ruinas. ~-**drier** n secadora f. ~ **r** n (glass) vaso m (de lados rectos)

tummy /ˈtʌmi/ n 🔟 barriga f

tumour /ˈtjuːmə(r)/ n tumor m

tumult /ˈtjuːmʌlt/ n tumulto m. ~**uous** /-ˈmʌltjʊəs/ adj (applause) apoteósico

tuna /ˈtjuːnə/ n (pl **tuna**) atún m

tune /tjuːn/ n melodía f; (piece) tonada f. **be in** ~ estar afinado. **be out of** ~ estar desafinado. ● vt afinar, sintonizar (radio, TV); (Mec) poner a punto. ● vi. ~ **in (to)** sintonizar (con). □ ~ **up** vt/i afinar. ~**ful** adj melodioso. ~**r** n afinador m; (Radio) sintonizador m

tunic /ˈtjuːnɪk/ n túnica f

tunnel /ˈtʌnl/ n túnel m. ● vi (pt **tunnelled**) abrir un túnel

turban /ˈtɜːbən/ n turbante m

turbine /ˈtɜːbaɪn/ n turbina f

turbo /ˈtɜːbəʊ/ n (pl -**os**) turbo (compresor) m

turbulen|ce /ˈtɜːbjʊləns/ n turbulencia f. ~**t** adj turbulento

turf /tɜːf/ n (pl **turfs** or **turves**) césped m; (segment of grass) tepe m. □ ~ **out** vt 🔟 echar

turgid /ˈtɜːdʒɪd/ adj (language) ampuloso

turkey /'tɜːkɪ/ n (pl -eys) pavo m

Turk|ey /'tɜːkɪ/ f Turquía f. ~ish adj & n turco m (m)

turmoil /'tɜːmɔɪl/ n confusión f

turn /tɜːn/ vt hacer girar; volver (head, page); doblar (corner); (change) cambiar; (deflect) desviar. ~ sth into sth convertir or transformar algo en algo. • vi (handle) girar, dar vueltas; (person) volverse, darse la vuelta. ~ right girar or doblar or torcer a la derecha. ~ red ponerse rojo. ~ into sth convertirse en algo. • n vuelta f; (in road) curva f; (change) giro m; (sequence) turno m; (fam, of illness) ataque m. good ~ favor m. in ~ a su vez. □ ~ down vt doblar; (reduce) bajar; (reject) rechazar. □ ~ off vt cerrar (tap); apagar (light, TV, etc). vi (from road) doblar. □ ~ on vt abrir (tap); encender, prender (LAm) (light etc). □ ~ out vt apagar (light etc). vi (result) resultar. □ ~ round vi darse la vuelta. □ ~ up vi aparecer. vt (find) encontrar; levantar (collar); subir (hem); acortar (trousers); poner más fuerte (gas). ~ed-up adj (nose) respingón. ~ing n (in town) bocacalle f. we've missed the ~ing nos hemos pasado la calle (or carretera). ~ing-point n momento m decisivo.

turnip /'tɜːnɪp/ n nabo m

turn: ~over n (Com) facturación f; (of staff) movimiento m. ~pike n (Amer) autopista f de peaje. ~stile n torniquete m. ~table n platina f. ~up n (of trousers) vuelta f, valenciana f (Mex)

turquoise /'tɜːkwɔɪz/ adj & n turquesa (f)

turret /'tʌrɪt/ n torrecilla f

turtle /'tɜːtl/ n tortuga f de mar; (Amer, tortoise) tortuga f

turves /tɜːvz/ see TURF

tusk /tʌsk/ n colmillo m

tussle /'tʌsl/ n lucha f

tutor /'tjuːtə(r)/ n profesor m particular

tuxedo /tʌkˈsiːdəʊ/ n (pl -os) (Amer) esmoquin m, smoking m

TV /tiːˈviː/ n televisión f, tele f 🔲

twang /twæŋ/ n tañido m; (in voice) gangueo m

tweet /twiːt/ n piada f. • vi piar

tweezers /'twiːzəz/ npl pinzas fpl

twel|fth /twelfθ/ adj duodécimo. • n doceavo m. ~ve /twelv/ adj & n doce (m)

twent|ieth /'twentɪəθ/ adj vigésimo. • n veinteavo m. ~y /'twentɪ/ adj & n veinte (m)

twice /twaɪs/ adv dos veces. ~ as many people el doble de gente

twiddle /'twɪdl/ vt (hacer) girar

twig /twɪg/ n ramita f. • vi (pt twigged) 🔲 caer, darse cuenta

twilight /'twaɪlaɪt/ n crepúsculo m

twin /twɪn/ adj & n gemelo (m), mellizo (m) (LAm)

twine /twaɪn/ n cordel m, bramante m

twinge /twɪndʒ/ n punzada f; (of remorse) punzada f

twinkle /'twɪŋkl/ vi centellear. • n centelleo m; (in eye) brillo m

twirl /twɜːl/ vt (hacer) girar. • vi girar. • n vuelta f

twist /twɪst/ vt retorcer; (roll) enrollar; girar (knob); tergiversar (words); (distort) retorcer. ~ one's ankle torcerse el tobillo. • vi (rope, wire) enrollarse; (road, river) serpentear. • n torsión f; (curve)

Uu

vuelta f

twit /twɪt/ n ① imbécil m

twitch /twɪtʃ/ vi moverse. • n tic m

twitter /'twɪtə(r)/ vi gorjear

two /tu:/ adj & n dos (m). ~-**bit** adj (Amer) de tres al cuarto. ~-**faced** adj falso, insincero. ~**fold** adj doble. • adv dos veces. ~**pence** /'tʌpəns/ n dos peniques mpl. ~-**piece** (suit) n traje m de dos piezas. ~-**way** adj (traffic) de doble sentido

tycoon /tar'ku:n/ n magnate m

tying /'taɪɪŋ/ see TIE

type /taɪp/ n tipo m. • vt/i escribir a máquina. ~-**cast** adj (actor) encasillado. ~**script** n texto m mecanografiado, manuscrito m (de una obra, novela etc). ~**writer** n máquina f de escribir. ~**written** adj escrito a máquina, mecanografiado

typhoon /tar'fu:n/ n tifón m

typical /'tɪpɪkl/ adj típico. ~**ly** adv típicamente

typify /'tɪpɪfaɪ/ vt tipificar

typi|ng /'taɪpɪŋ/ n mecanografía f. ~**st** n mecanógrafo m

tyran|nical /tɪ'rænɪkl/ adj tiránico. ~**ny** /'tɪrənɪ/ n tiranía f. ~**t** /'taɪərənt/ n tirano m

tyre /taɪə(r)/ n neumático m, llanta f (LAm)

udder /'ʌdə(r)/ n ubre f

UFO /'ju:fəʊ/ abbr (= **unidentified flying object**) OVNI m (objeto volante no identificado)

ugly /'ʌglɪ/ adj (-ier, -iest) feo

UK /ju:'keɪ/ abbr (= **United Kingdom**) Reino m Unido

Ukraine /ju:'kreɪn/ n Ucrania f

ulcer /'ʌlsə(r)/ n úlcera f; (external) llaga f

ultimate /'ʌltɪmət/ adj final; (utmost) máximo. ~**ly** adv en última instancia; (in the long run) a la larga

ultimatum /ʌltɪ'meɪtəm/ n (pl -ums) ultimátum m

ultra... /'ʌltrə/ pref ultra... ~**violet** /-'vaɪələt/ adj ultravioleta

umbilical cord /ʌm'bɪlɪkl/ n cordón m umbilical

umbrella /ʌm'brelə/ n paraguas m

umpire /'ʌmpaɪə(r)/ n árbitro m. • vt arbitrar

umpteen /'ʌmptiːn/ adj ① trescientos ①. ~**th** adj ① enésimo

un... /ʌn/ pref in..., des..., no, poco, sin

UN /ju:'en/ abbr (= **United Nations**) ONU f (Organización de las Naciones Unidas)

unable /ʌn'eɪbl/ adj. be ~ to no poder; (be incapable of) ser incapaz de

unacceptable /ʌnək'septəbl/ adj (behaviour) inaceptable; (terms) inadmisible

unaccompanied /ʌnə
'kʌmpənɪd/ adj (luggage) no acom-
pañado; (person, instrument) solo;
(singing) sin acompañamiento

unaccustomed /ʌnəˈkʌstəmd/
adj desacostumbrado. **be ~ to**
no estar acostumbrado a

unaffected /ʌnəˈfektɪd/ adj natural

unaided /ʌnˈeɪdɪd/ adj sin ayuda

unanimous /juːˈnænɪməs/ adj
unánime. **~ly** adv unánimemente;
(elect) por unanimidad

unarmed /ʌnˈɑːmd/ adj desar-
mado

unattended /ʌnəˈtendɪd/ adj sin
vigilar

unattractive /ʌnəˈtræktɪv/ adj
poco atractivo

unavoidabl|e /ʌnəˈvɔɪdəbl/ adj
inevitable. **~y** adv. I was **~y** de-
layed no pude evitar llegar tarde

unaware /ʌnəˈweə(r)/ adj. **be ~**
of ignorar, no ser consciente de.
~s /-eəz/ adv desprevenido

unbearabl|e /ʌnˈbeərəbl/ adj in-
soportable, inaguantable. **~y** adv
inaguantablemente

unbeat|able /ʌnˈbiːtəbl/ adj
(quality) insuperable; (team) invencible. **~en** adj no vencido; (record)
insuperado

unbelievabl|e /ʌnbɪˈliːvəbl/ adj
increíble. **~y** adv increíblemente

unbiased /ʌnˈbaɪəst/ adj imparcial

unblock /ʌnˈblɒk/ vt desatascar

unbolt /ʌnˈbəʊlt/ vt descorrer el
pestillo de

unborn /ʌnˈbɔːn/ adj que todavía
no ha nacido

unbreakable /ʌnˈbreɪkəbl/ adj
irrompible

unbroken /ʌnˈbrəʊkən/ adj (in-

tact) intacto; (continuous) ininterrumpido

unbutton /ʌnˈbʌtn/ vt desabotonar, desabrochar

uncalled-for /ʌnˈkɔːldfɔː(r)/ adj
fuera de lugar

uncanny /ʌnˈkænɪ/ adj (-ier,
-iest) raro, extraño

uncertain /ʌnˈsɜːtn/ adj incierto;
(hesitant) vacilante. **be ~ of/about**
sth no estar seguro de algo. **~ty** n
incertidumbre f

uncharitable /ʌnˈtʃærɪtəbl/ adj
severo

uncivilized /ʌnˈsɪvɪlaɪzd/ adj in-
civilizado

uncle /ˈʌŋkl/ n tío m

> **Uncle Sam** Es la típica *i*
> personificación de EE.UU.,
> en que éste es representado por
> un hombre de barba blanca, ves-
> tido con los colores nacionales y
> con un sombrero de copa ador-
> nado con estrellas. Es posible que
> la imagen se haya extraído del
> cartel de reclutamiento, en 1917,
> que llevaba la leyenda: "A Ud. lo
> necesito".

unclean /ʌnˈkliːn/ adj impuro

unclear /ʌnˈklɪə(r)/ adj poco claro

uncomfortable /ʌnˈkʌmfətəbl/
adj incómodo

uncommon /ʌnˈkɒmən/ adj poco
común

uncompromising /ʌn
ˈkɒmprəmaɪzɪŋ/ adj intransigente

unconcerned /ʌnkənˈsɜːnd/ adj
indiferente

unconditional /ʌnkənˈdɪʃənl/
adj incondicional

unconnected /ʌnkəˈnektɪd/ adj
(unrelated) sin conexión. **the**

events are ~ estos acontecimientos no guardan ninguna relación (entre sí)

unconscious /ʌnˈkɒnʃəs/ adj (Med) inconsciente. **~ly** adv inconscientemente

unconventional /ʌnkənˈvenʃənl/ adj poco convencional

uncork /ʌnˈkɔːk/ vt descorchar

uncouth /ʌnˈkuːθ/ adj zafio

uncover /ʌnˈkʌvə(r)/ vt destapar; revelar (plot, scandal)

undaunted /ʌnˈdɔːntɪd/ adj impertérrito

undecided /ʌndɪˈsaɪdɪd/ adj indeciso

undeniable /ʌndɪˈnaɪəbl/ adj innegable. **~y** adv sin lugar a dudas

under /ˈʌndə(r)/ prep debajo de; (less than) menos de; (heading) bajo; (according to) según; (expressing movement) por debajo de. ● adv debajo, abajo

under... pref sub...

under: **~carriage** n tren m de aterrizaje. **~charge** vt /-ˈtʃɑːdʒ/ cobrarle de menos a. **~clothes** npl ropa f interior. **~coat**, **~coating** (Amer) n (paint) pintura f base; (first coat) primera mano f de pintura. **~cover** adj /-ˈkʌvə(r)/ secreto. **~current** n corriente f submarina. **~dog** n. **the ~dog** el que tiene menos posibilidades. **the ~dogs** npl los de abajo. **~done** adj /-ˈdʌn/ (meat) poco hecho. **~estimate** vt /-ˈestɪmeɪt/ (underrate) subestimar. **~fed** /-ˈfed/ adj subalimentado. **~foot** /-ˈfʊt/ adv debajo de los pies. **~go** vt (pt **-went**, pp **-gone**) sufrir. **~graduate** /-ˈgrædʒʊət/ n estudiante m universitario (no licenciado). **~ground**

/-ˈgraʊnd/ adv bajo tierra; (in secret) clandestinamente. ● /-ˈgraʊnd/ adj subterráneo; (secret) clandestino. ● n metro m. **~growth** /-ˈgrəʊθ/ n maleza f. **~hand** /-ˈhænd/ adj (secret) clandestino; (deceptive) fraudulento. **~lie** /-ˈlaɪ/ vt (pt **-lay**, pp **-lain**, pres p **-lying**) subyacer a. **~line** /-ˈlaɪn/ vt subrayar. **~lying** /-ˈlaɪŋ/ adj subyacente. **~mine** /-ˈmaɪn/ vt socavar. **~neath** /-ˈniːθ/ prep debajo de, abajo de (LAm). ● adv por debajo. **~paid** /-ˈpeɪd/ adj mal pagado. **~pants** npl calzoncillos mpl. **~pass** n paso m subterráneo; (for traffic) paso m inferior. **~privileged** /-ˈprɪvɪlɪdʒd/ adj desfavorecido. **~rate** /-ˈreɪt/ vt subestimar. **~rated** /-ˈreɪtɪd/ adj no debidamente apreciado. **~shirt** n (Amer) camiseta f (interior).

understand /ʌndəˈstænd/ vt (pt **-stood**) entender; (empathize with) comprender, entender. ● vi entender, comprender. **~able** adj comprensible. **~ing** adj comprensivo. ● n (grasp) entendimiento m; (sympathy) comprensión f; (agreement) acuerdo m

under: **~statement** n subestimación f. **~take** /-ˈteɪk/ (pt **-took**, pp **-taken**) emprender (task); asumir (responsibility). **~take to sth** comprometerse a hacer algo. **~taker** n director m de pompas fúnebres. **~taking** /-ˈteɪkɪŋ/ n empresa f; (promise) promesa f. **~tone** n. **in an ~tone** en voz baja. **~value** /-ˈvæljuː/ vt subvalorar. **~water** /-ˈwɔːtə(r)/ adj submarino. ● adv debajo del agua. **~wear** n ropa f interior. **~weight** /-ˈweɪt/ adj de peso más bajo que el normal. **~went** /-ˈwent/ see **UNDERGO**.

~**world** n (criminals) hampa f.

~**write** /-'raɪt/ vt (pt -wrote, pp -written) (Com) asegurar; (guarantee financially) financiar

undeserved /ʌndɪ'zɜːvd/ adj inmerecido

undesirable /ʌndɪ'zaɪərəbl/ adj indeseable

undignified /ʌn'dɪgnɪfaɪd/ adj indecoroso

undisputed /ʌndɪs'pjuːtɪd/ adj (champion) indiscutido; (facts) innegable

undo /ʌn'duː/ vt (pt -did, pp -done) desabrochar (button, jacket); abrir (zip); desatar (knot, laces)

undoubted /ʌn'dautɪd/ adj indudable. ~**ly** adv indudablemente, sin duda

undress /ʌn'dres/ vt desvestir, desnudar. ● vi desvestirse, desnudarse

undue /ʌn'dju:/ adj excesivo

undulate /'ʌndjʊleɪt/ vi ondular

unduly /ʌn'dju:lɪ/ adv excesivamente

unearth /ʌn'ɜːθ/ vt desenterrar; descubrir (document)

unearthly /ʌn'ɜːθlɪ/ adj sobrenatural. **at an** ~ **hour** a estas horas intempestivas

uneasy /ʌn'i:zɪ/ adj incómodo

uneconomic /ʌniːkə'nɒmɪk/ adj poco económico

uneducated /ʌn'edjʊkeɪtɪd/ adj sin educación

unemploy|ed /ʌnɪm'plɔɪd/ adj desempleado, parado. ~**ment** n desempleo m, paro m

unending /ʌn'endɪŋ/ adj interminable, sin fin

unequal /ʌn'i:kwəl/ adj desigual

unequivocal /ʌnɪ'kwɪvəkl/ adj inequívoco

unethical /ʌn'eθɪkl/ adj poco ético, inmoral

uneven /ʌn'i:vn/ adj desigual

unexpected /ʌnɪk'spektɪd/ adj inesperado; (result) imprevisto. ~**ly** adv (arrive) de improviso; (happen) de forma imprevista

unfair /ʌn'feə(r)/ adj injusto; improcedente (dismissal). ~**ly** adv injustamente

unfaithful /ʌn'feɪθfl/ adj infiel

unfamiliar /ʌnfə'mɪlɪə(r)/ adj desconocido. **be** ~ **with** desconocer

unfasten /ʌn'fɑːsn/ vt desabrochar (clothes); (untie) desatar

unfavourable /ʌn'feɪvərəbl/ adj desfavorable

unfeeling /ʌn'fiːlɪŋ/ adj insensible

unfit /ʌn'fɪt/ adj. **I'm** ~ no estoy en forma. ~ **for human consumption** no apto para el consumo

unfold /ʌn'fəʊld/ vt desdoblar; desplegar (wings); (fig) revelar. ● vi (leaf) abrirse; (events) desarrollarse

unforeseen /ʌnfɔː'siːn/ adj imprevisto

unforgettable /ʌnfə'getəbl/ adj inolvidable

unforgivable /ʌnfə'gɪvəbl/ adj imperdonable

unfortunate /ʌn'fɔːtʃənət/ adj desafortunado; (regrettable) lamentable. ~**ly** adv desafortunadamente; (stronger) por desgracia, desgraciadamente

unfounded /ʌn'faʊndɪd/ adj infundado

unfriendly /ʌn'frendlɪ/ adj poco amistoso; (stronger) antipático

unfurl /ʌnˈfɜːl/ vt desplegar

ungainly /ʌnˈɡeɪnlɪ/ adj desgarbado

ungrateful /ʌnˈɡreɪtfl/ adj desagradecido, ingrato

unhapp|iness /ʌnˈhæpɪnes/ n infelicidad f, tristeza f. ~y adj (-ier, -iest) infeliz, triste; (unsuitable) inoportuno. be ~y about sth no estar contento con algo

unharmed /ʌnˈhɑːmd/ adj (person) ileso

unhealthy /ʌnˈhelθɪ/ adj (-ier, -iest) (person) de mala salud; (complexion) enfermizo; (conditions) poco saludable

unhurt /ʌnˈhɜːt/ adj ileso

unification /juːnɪfɪˈkeɪʃn/ n unificación f

uniform /ˈjuːnɪfɔːm/ adj & n uniforme (m). ~ity /-ˈfɔːmətɪ/ n uniformidad f

unify /ˈjuːnɪfaɪ/ vt unir

unilateral /juːnɪˈlætərəl/ adj unilateral

unimaginable /ʌnɪˈmædʒɪnəbl/ adj inimaginable

unimaginative /ʌnɪˈmædʒɪnətɪv/ adj (person) poco imaginativo

unimportant /ʌnɪmˈpɔːtnt/ adj sin importancia

uninhabited /ʌnɪnˈhæbɪtɪd/ adj deshabitado; (island) despoblado

unintelligible /ʌnɪnˈtelɪdʒəbl/ adj ininteligible

unintentional /ʌnɪnˈtenʃənl/ adj involuntario

union /ˈjuːnjən/ n unión f; (trade union) sindicato m; (student ~) asociación f de estudiantes. U~ Jack n bandera f del Reino Unido

unique /juːˈniːk/ adj único

unison /ˈjuːnɪsn/ n. in ~ al unísono

unit /ˈjuːnɪt/ n unidad f; (of furniture etc) módulo m; (in course) módulo m

unite /juːˈnaɪt/ vt unir. ● vi unirse. U~d Kingdom n Reino m Unido. U~d Nations n Organización f de las Naciones Unidas (ONU). U~d States (of America) n Estados mpl Unidos (de América)

unity /ˈjuːnɪtɪ/ n unidad f

univers|al /juːnɪˈvɜːsl/ adj universal. ~e /ˈjuːnɪvɜːs/ n universo m

university /juːnɪˈvɜːsətɪ/ n universidad f. ● adj universitario

unjust /ʌnˈdʒʌst/ adj injusto. ~ified /-ɪfaɪd/ adj injustificado

unkind /ʌnˈkaɪnd/ adj poco amable; (cruel) cruel; (remark) hiriente

unknown /ʌnˈnəʊn/ adj desconocido

unlawful /ʌnˈlɔːfl/ adj ilegal

unleaded /ʌnˈledɪd/ adj (fuel) sin plomo

unleash /ʌnˈliːʃ/ vt soltar

unless /ʌnˈles, ənˈles/ conj a menos que, a no ser que

unlike /ʌnˈlaɪk/ prep diferente de. (in contrast to) a diferencia de. ~ly adj improbable

unlimited /ʌnˈlɪmɪtɪd/ adj ilimitado

unlisted /ʌnˈlɪstɪd/ adj (Amer) que no figura en la guía telefónica, privado (Mex)

unload /ʌnˈləʊd/ vt descargar

unlock /ʌnˈlɒk/ vt abrir (con llave)

unluck|ily /ʌnˈlʌkɪlɪ/ adv desgraciadamente. ~y adj (-ier, -iest) (person) sin suerte, desafortunado. be ~y tener mala suerte; (bring bad luck) traer mala suerte

unmarried /ʌnˈmærɪd/ adj

u

soltero

unmask /ʌnˈmɑːsk/ vt desenmascarar

unmentionable /ʌn 'menʃənəbl/ adj inmencionable

unmistakable /ʌnmɪˈsteɪkəbl/ adj inconfundible

unnatural /ʌnˈnætʃərəl/ adj poco natural; (not normal) anormal

unnecessar|ily /ʌnˈnesəsərɪlɪ/ adv innecesariamente. ~y adj innecesario

unnerve /ʌnˈnɜːv/ vt desconcertar

unnoticed /ʌnˈnəʊtɪst/ adj inadvertido

unobtainable /ʌnəbˈteɪnəbl/ adj imposible de conseguir

unobtrusive /ʌnəbˈtruːsɪv/ adj discreto

unofficial /ʌnəˈfɪʃl/ adj no oficial. ~ly adv extraoficialmente

unpack /ʌnˈpæk/ vt sacar las cosas de (bags); deshacer, desempacar (LAm) (suitcase). ● vi deshacer las maletas, desempacar (LAm)

unpaid /ʌnˈpeɪd/ adj (work) no retribuido, no remunerado; (leave) sin sueldo

unperturbed /ʌnpəˈtɜːbd/ adj impasible. he carried on ~ siguió sin inmutarse

unpleasant /ʌnˈpleznt/ adj desagradable

unplug /ʌnˈplʌg/ vt desenchufar

unpopular /ʌnˈpɒpjələ(r)/ adj impopular

unprecedented /ʌn 'presɪdentɪd/ adj sin precedentes

unpredictable /ʌnprɪˈdɪktəbl/ adj imprevisible

unprepared /ʌnprɪˈpeəd/ adj no preparado; (unready) desprevenido

unprofessional /ʌnprəˈfeʃənəl/ adj poco profesional

unprofitable /ʌnˈprɒfɪtəbl/ adj no rentable

unprotected /ʌnprəˈtektɪd/ adj sin protección; (sex) sin el uso de preservativos

unqualified /ʌnˈkwɒlɪfaɪd/ adj sin título; (fig) absoluto

unquestion|able /ʌn 'kwestʃənəbl/ adj incuestionable, innegable. ~ing (obedience) ciego; (loyalty) incondicional

unravel /ʌnˈrævl/ vt (pt unravelled) desenredar; desentrañar (mystery)

unreal /ʌnˈrɪəl/ adj irreal. ~istic /-ˈlɪstɪk/ adj poco realista

unreasonable /ʌnˈriːzənəbl/ adj irrazonable

unrecognizable /ʌnrekəɡ 'naɪzəbl/ adj irreconocible

unrelated /ʌnrɪˈleɪtɪd/ adj (facts) no relacionados (entre sí); (people) no emparentado

unreliable /ʌnrɪˈlaɪəbl/ adj (person) informal; (machine) poco fiable; (information) poco fidedigno

unrepentant /ʌnrɪˈpentənt/ adj impenitente

unrest /ʌnˈrest/ n (discontent) descontento m; (disturbances) disturbios mpl

unrivalled /ʌnˈraɪvld/ adj incomparable

unroll /ʌnˈrəʊl/ vt desenrollar. ● vi desenrollarse

unruffled /ʌnˈrʌfld/ (person) sereno

unruly /ʌnˈruːlɪ/ adj (class) indisciplinado; (child) revoltoso

unsafe /ʌnˈseɪf/ adj inseguro

unsatisfactory /ʌnsætɪs 'fæktərɪ/ adj insatisfactorio

unsavoury /ʌnˈseɪvərɪ/ adj desagradable

unscathed /ʌnˈskeɪðd/ adj ileso

unscheduled /ʌnˈʃedjuːld/ adj no programado, no previsto

unscrew /ʌnˈskruː/ vt destornillar; desenroscar (lid)

unscrupulous /ʌnˈskruːpjʊləs/ adj inescrupuloso

unseemly /ʌnˈsiːmlɪ/ adj indecoroso

unseen /ʌnˈsiːn/ adj (danger) oculto; (unnoticed) sin ser visto

unselfish /ʌnˈselfɪʃ/ adj (act) desinteresado; (person) nada egoísta

unsettle /ʌnˈsetl/ vt desestabilizar (situation); alterar (plans). ~**d** adj agitado; (weather) inestable; (undecided) pendiente (de resolución)

unshakeable /ʌnˈʃeɪkəbl/ adj inquebrantable

unshaven /ʌnˈʃeɪvn/ adj sin afeitar, sin rasurar (Mex)

unsightly /ʌnˈsaɪtlɪ/ adj feo

unskilled /ʌnˈskɪld/ adj (work) no especializado; (worker) no cualificado, no calificado

unsociable /ʌnˈsəʊʃəbl/ adj insociable

unsolved /ʌnˈsɒlvd/ adj no resuelto; (murder) sin esclarecerse

unsophisticated /ʌnsəˈfɪstɪkeɪtɪd/ adj sencillo

unsound /ʌnˈsaʊnd/ adj poco sólido

unspecified /ʌnˈspesɪfaɪd/ adj no especificado

unstable /ʌnˈsteɪbl/ adj inestable

unsteady /ʌnˈstedɪ/ adj inestable, poco firme

unstuck /ʌnˈstʌk/ adj despegado. come ~ despegarse; (fail) fracasar

unsuccessful /ʌnsəkˈsesfʊl/ adj

(attempt) infructuoso. be ~ no tener éxito, fracasar

unsuitable /ʌnˈsuːtəbl/ adj (clothing) poco apropiado, poco adecuado; (time) inconveniente. she is ~ for the job no es la persona indicada para el trabajo

unsure /ʌnˈʃʊə(r)/ adj inseguro

unthinkable /ʌnˈθɪŋkəbl/ adj inconcebible

untid|iness /ʌnˈtaɪdɪnəs/ n desorden m. ~y adj (-ier, -iest) desordenado; (appearance, writing) descuidado

untie /ʌnˈtaɪ/ vt desatar, desamarrar (LAm)

until /ənˈtɪl, ʌnˈtɪl/ prep hasta. ● conj hasta que

untold /ʌnˈtəʊld/ adj incalculable

untouched /ʌnˈtʌtʃt/ adj intacto

untried /ʌnˈtraɪd/ adj no probado

untrue /ʌnˈtruː/ adj falso

unused /ʌnˈjuːzd/ adj nuevo.
● /ʌnˈjuːst/ adj. ~ to no acostumbrado a

unusual /ʌnˈjuːʒʊəl/ adj poco común, poco corriente. it's ~ to see so many people es raro ver a tanta gente. ~ly adv excepcionalmente, inusitadamente

unveil /ʌnˈveɪl/ vt descubrir

unwanted /ʌnˈwɒntɪd/ adj superfluo; (child) no deseado

unwelcome /ʌnˈwelkəm/ adj (news) poco grato; (guest) inoportuno

unwell /ʌnˈwel/ adj indispuesto

unwieldy /ʌnˈwiːldɪ/ adj pesado y difícil de manejar

unwilling /ʌnˈwɪlɪŋ/ adj mal dispuesto. be ~ no querer

unwind /ʌnˈwaɪnd/ vt (pt unwound) desenrollar. ● vi (fam, *relax)* relajarse

unwise /ʌn'waɪz/ *adj* poco sensato

unworthy /ʌn'wɜːðɪ/ *adj* indigno

unwrap /ʌn'ræp/ *vt (pt* unwrapped) desenvolver

unwritten /ʌn'rɪtn/ *adj* no escrito; (*agreement*) verbal

up /ʌp/ *adv* arriba; (*upwards*) hacia arriba; (*higher*) más arriba. ~ **here** aquí arriba. ~ **there** allí arriba. ~ **to** hasta. he's not ~ **yet** todavía no se ha levantado. **be ~ against** enfrentarse con. **come ~** subir. **go ~** subir. he's not ~ **to the job** no tiene las condiciones necesarias para el trabajo. **it's ~ to you** depende de ti. **what's ~?** ¿qué pasa? ●*prep.* **go ~ the stairs** subir la escalera. **it's just ~ the road** está un poco más allá. ●*vt (pt* upped) aumentar. ●*n.* ~**s and downs** *npl* altibajos *mpl*; (*of life*) vicisitudes *fpl*. ~**bringing** /'ʌpbrɪŋɪŋ/ *n* educación *f*. ~**date** /ʌp'deɪt/ *vt* poner al día. ~**grade** /ʌp'greɪd/ *vt* elevar de categoría (*person*); mejorar (*equipment*). ~**heaval** /ʌp'hiːvl/ *n* trastorno *m*. ~**hill** /ʌp'hɪl/ *adv* cuesta arriba. ~**hold** /ʌp'həʊld/ *vt (pt* upheld) mantener (*principle*); confirmar (*decision*). ~**holster** /ʌp'həʊlstə(r)/ *vt* tapizar. ~**holstery** *n* tapicería *f*. ~**keep** *n* mantenimiento *m*. ~**market** /ʌp'mɑːkɪt/ *adj* de categoría

upon /ə'pɒn/ *prep* sobre. **once ~ a time** érase una vez

upper /'ʌpə(r)/ *adj* superior. ~ **class** *n* clase *f* alta

up: ~**right** *adj* vertical; (*citizen*) recto. **place sth ~right** poner algo de pie. ~**rising** /'ʌpraɪzɪŋ/ *n* levantamiento *m*. ~**roar** /'ʌp- n tu-

multo *m*

upset /ʌp'set/ *vt (pt* upset, *pres p* upsetting) (*hurt*) disgustar; (*offend*) ofender; (*distress*) alterar; desbaratar (plans). ●*adj (hurt)* disgustado; (*distressed*) alterado; (*offended*) ofendido; (*disappointed*) desilusionado. ● /'ʌpset/ *n* trastorno *m*. **have a stomach ~** estar mal de estómago

up: ~**shot** *n* resultado *m*. ~**side down** /ʌpsaɪd'daʊn/ *adv* al revés (con la parte de arriba abajo); (*in disorder*) patas arriba. **turn sth ~side down** poner algo boca abajo. ~**stairs** /ʌp'steəz/ *adv* arriba. **go ~stairs** subir. ● /'ʌpsteəz/ *adj* de arriba. ~**start** *n* advenedizo *m*. ~**state** *adv* (*Amer*). **I live ~state** vivo en el norte del estado. ~**stream** /ʌp'striːm/ *adv* río arriba. ~**take** *n.* **be quick on the ~take** agarrar las cosas al vuelo. ~**to-date** /ʌptə'deɪt/ *adj* al día; (*news*) de última hora. ~**turn** *n* repunte *m*, mejora *f*. ~**ward** /'ʌpwəd/ *adj (movement)* ascendente; (*direction*) hacia arriba. ●*adv* hacia arriba. ~**wards** *adv* hacia arriba

uranium /jʊ'reɪnɪəm/ *n* uranio *m*

Uranus /'jʊərənəs/jʊə'reɪnəs/ *n* Urano *m*

urban /'ɜːbən/ *adj* urbano

urchin /'ɜːtʃɪn/ *n* pilluelo *m*

urge /ɜːdʒ/ *vt* instar. ~ **s.o. to do sth** instar a uno a que haga algo. ●*n* impulso *m*; (*wish, whim*) ganas *fpl*. □ ~ **on** *vt* animar

urgen|cy /'ɜːdʒənsɪ/ *n* urgencia *f*. ~**t** *adj* urgente. ~**tly** *adv* urgentemente, con urgencia

urin|ate /'jʊərɪneɪt/ *vi* orinar. ~**e** /'jʊərɪn/ *n* orina *f*

Uruguay /'jʊərəgwaɪ/ *n* Uruguay

m. ~**an** *adj* & *n* uruguayo (*m*)

us /ʌs, əs/ *pron* nos; (*after prep*) nosotros *m*, nosotras *f*

US(A) /juːˈesˈeɪ/ *abbr* (= **United States (of America)**) EE.UU. (*only written*), Estados *mpl* Unidos

usage /ˈjuːzɪdʒ/ *n* uso *m*

use /juːz/ *vt* usar; utilizar (service, facilities); consumir (fuel). ● /juːs/ *n* uso *m*, empleo *m*. **be of** ~ servir. **it is no** ~ es inútil. □ ~ **up** *vt* agotar, consumir. ~**d** /juːzd/ *adj* usado. ● /juːst/ *v mod* ~ **to**. **he** ~**d to say** decía, solía decir. **there** ~**d to be** (antes) había. ● *adj*/juːst/. **be** ~**d to** estar acostumbrado a. ~**ful** /ˈjuːsfl/ *adj* útil. ~**fully** *adv* útilmente. ~**less** *adj* inútil. (person) incompetente. ~**r** /-zə(r)/ *n* usuario *m*. **drug** ~ *n* consumidor *m* de drogas

usher /ˈʌʃə(r)/ *n* (in theatre etc) acomodador *m*. □ ~ **in** *vt* hacer pasar; marcar el comienzo de (new era). ~**ette** /-ˈret/ *n* acomodadora *f*

USSR *abbr* (History) (= **Union of Soviet Socialist Republics**) URSS

usual /ˈjuːʒʊəl/ *adj* usual; (habitual) acostumbrado, habitual; (place, route) de siempre. **as** ~ como de costumbre, como siempre. ~**ly** *adv* normalmente. **he** ~**ly wakes up early** suele despertarse temprano

utensil /juːˈtensl/ *n* utensilio *m*

utilize /ˈjuːtɪlaɪz/ *vt* utilizar

utmost /ˈʌtməʊst/ *adj* sumo. ● *n*. **do one's** ~ hacer todo lo posible (**to** para)

utter /ˈʌtə(r)/ *adj* completo. ● *vt* pronunciar (word); dar (cry). ~**ly** *adv* totalmente

U-turn /ˈjuːtɜːn/ *n* cambio *m* de sentido

Vv

vacan|cy /ˈveɪkənsɪ/ *n* (job) vacante *f*; (room) habitación *f* libre. ~**t** *adj* (building) desocupado; (seat) libre; (post) vacante; (look) ausente

vacate /vəˈkeɪt/ *vt* dejar

vacation /vəˈkeɪʃn/ *n* (Amer) vacaciones *fpl*. **go on** ~ ir de vacaciones. ~**er** *n* (Amer) veraneante *m* & *f*

vaccin|ate /ˈvæksɪneɪt/ *vt* vacunar. ~**ation** /-ˈneɪʃn/ *n* vacunación *f*. ~**e** /ˈvæksiːn/ *n* vacuna *f*

vacuum /ˈvækjʊəm/ *n* vacío *m*. ~ **cleaner** *n* aspiradora *f*

vagina /vəˈdʒaɪnə/ *n* vagina *f*

vague /veɪɡ/ *adj* (-er, -est) vago; (outline) borroso; (person, expression) despistado. ~**ly** *adv* vagamente

vain /veɪn/ *adj* (-er, -est) vanidoso; (useless) vano. **in** ~ en vano

Valentine's Day /ˈvæləntaɪnz/ *n* el día de San Valentín

valiant /ˈvælɪənt/ *adj* valeroso

valid /ˈvælɪd/ *adj* válido. ~**ate** /-eɪt/ *vt* dar validez a; validar (contract). ~**ity** /-ˈɪdətɪ/ *n* validez *f*

valley /ˈvælɪ/ *n* (pl -eys) valle *m*

valour /ˈvælə(r)/ *n* valor *m*

valu|able /ˈvæljʊəbl/ *adj* valioso. ~**ables** *npl* objetos *mpl* de valor. ~**ation** /-ˈeɪʃn/ *n* valoración *f*. ~**e** /ˈvæljuː/ *n* valor *m*. ● *vt* valorar; tasar, valorar, avaluar (LAm) (property). ~**e added tax** *n* impuesto *m* sobre el valor añadido

valve /vælv/ *n* válvula *f*

vampire /ˈvæmpaɪə(r)/ *n*

vampiro m

van /væn/ n furgoneta f, camioneta f; (Rail) furgón m

vandal /'vændl/ n vándalo m. **~ism** n vandalismo m. **~ize** vt destruir

vanilla /və'nɪlə/ n vainilla f

vanish /'vænɪʃ/ vi desaparecer

vanity /'vænɪtɪ/ n vanidad f. **~ case** n neceser m

vapour /'veɪpə(r)/ n vapor m

varia|ble /'veərɪəbl/ adj variable. **~nce** /-əns/ n. at **~ce** en desacuerdo. **~nt** n variante f. **~tion** /-'eɪʃn/ n variación f

vari|ed /'veərɪd/ adj variado. **~ety** /və'raɪətɪ/ n variedad f. **~ety show** n espectáculo m de variedades. **~ous** /'veərɪəs/ adj (several) varios; (different) diversos

varnish /'vɑːnɪʃ/ n barniz m; (for nails) esmalte m. ● vt barnizar; pintar (nails)

vary /'veərɪ/ vt/i variar

vase /vɑːz/, (Amer) /veɪs/ n (for flowers) florero m; (ornamental) jarrón m

vast /vɑːst/ adj vasto, extenso; (size) inmenso. **~ly** adv infinitamente

vat /væt/ n cuba f

VAT /viːeɪ'tiː/ abbr (= value added tax) IVA m

vault /vɔːlt/ n (roof) bóveda f; (in bank) cámara f acorazada; (tomb) cripta f. ● vt/i saltar

VCR n = videocassette recorder

VDU n = visual display unit

veal /viːl/ n ternera f

veer /vɪə(r)/ vi dar un viraje, virar

vegeta|ble /'vedʒɪtəbl/ adj vegetal. ● n verdura f. **~rian** /vedʒɪ-

'teərɪən/ adj & n vegetariano (m). **~tion** /vedʒɪ'teɪʃn/ n vegetación f

vehement /'viːəmənt/ adj vehemente. **~tly** adv con vehemencia

vehicle /'viːɪkl/ n vehículo m

veil /veɪl/ n velo m

vein /veɪn/ n vena f; (in marble) veta f

velocity /vɪ'lɒsɪtɪ/ n velocidad f

velvet /'velvɪt/ n terciopelo m

vendetta /ven'detə/ n vendetta f

vend|ing machine /'vendɪŋ/ n distribuidor m automático. **~or** /'vendə(r)/ n vendedor m

veneer /və'nɪə(r)/ n chapa f, enchapado m; (fig) barniz m, apariencia f

venerate /'venəreɪt/ vt venerar

venereal /və'nɪərɪəl/ adj venéreo

Venetian blind /və'niːʃn/ n persiana f veneciana

Venezuela /venə'zweɪlə/ n Venezuela f. **~n** adj & n venezolano (m)

vengeance /'vendʒəns/ n venganza f. with a **~** (fig) con ganas

venom /'venəm/ n veneno m. **~ous** adj venenoso

vent /vent/ n (conducto m de) ventilación; (anus) respiradero m. give **~** to dar rienda suelta a. ● vt descargar

ventilat|e /'ventɪleɪt/ vt ventilar. **~ion** /-'leɪʃn/ n ventilación f

ventriloquist /ven'trɪləkwɪst/ n ventrílocuo m

venture /'ventʃə(r)/ n empresa f. ● vt aventurar. ● vi atreverse

venue /'venjuː/ n (for concert) lugar m de actuación

Venus /'viːnəs/ n Venus m

veranda /və'rændə/ n galería f

verb /vɜːb/ n verbo m. **~al** adj

verbal

verdict /'vɜːdɪkt/ n veredicto m; (opinion) opinión f

verge /vɜːdʒ/ n borde m. □ ~ **on** vt rayar en

verify /'verɪfaɪ/ vt (confirm) confirmar; (check) verificar

vermin /'vɜːmɪn/ n alimañas fpl

versatil|e /'vɜːsətaɪl/ adj versátil. ~**ity** /-'tɪlətɪ/ n versatilidad f

verse /vɜːs/ n estrofa f; (poetry) poesías fpl. ~**d** /vɜːst/ adj. be well-ed in ser muy versado en. ~**ion** /'vɜːʃn/ n versión f

versus /'vɜːsəs/ prep contra

vertebra /'vɜːtɪbrə/ n (pl -brae /-briː/) vértebra f. ~**te** /-brət/ n vertebrado m

vertical /'vɜːtɪkl/ adj & n vertical (f). ~**ly** adv verticalmente

vertigo /'vɜːtɪɡəʊ/ n vértigo m

verve /vɜːv/ n brío m

very /'verɪ/ adv muy. ~ **much** muchísimo. ~ **well** muy bien. the ~ **first** el primero de todos. ● adj mismo. the ~ **thing** exactamente lo que hace falta

vessel /'vesl/ n (receptacle) recipiente m; (ship) navío m, nave f

vest /vest/ n camiseta f; (Amer) chaleco m.

vestige /'vestɪdʒ/ n vestigio m

vet /vet/ n veterinario m; (Amer fam, veteran) veterano m. ● vt (pt vetted) someter a investigación (applicant)

veteran /'vetərən/ n veterano m

veterinary /'vetərɪnərɪ/ adj veterinario. ~ **surgeon** n veterinario m

veto /'viːtəʊ/ n (pl -oes) veto m. ● vt vetar

vex /veks/ vt fastidiar

via /'vaɪə/ prep por, por vía de

viable /'vaɪəbl/ adj viable

viaduct /'vaɪədʌkt/ n viaducto m

vibrat|e /vaɪ'breɪt/ vt/i vibrar. ~**ion** /-ʃn/ n vibración f

vicar /'vɪkə(r)/ n párroco m. ~**age** /-rɪdʒ/ n casa f del párroco

vice /vaɪs/ n vicio m; (Tec) torno m de banco

vice versa /vaɪsɪ'vɜːsə/ adv viceversa

vicinity /vɪ'sɪnɪtɪ/ n vecindad f. in the ~ of cerca de

vicious /'vɪʃəs/ adj (attack) feroz; (dog) fiero; (rumour) malicioso. ~ **circle** n círculo m vicioso

victim /'vɪktɪm/ n víctima f. ~**ize** vt victimizar

victor /'vɪktə(r)/ n vencedor m

Victorian /vɪk'tɔːrɪən/ adj victoriano

victor|ious /vɪk'tɔːrɪəs/ adj (army) victorioso; (team) vencedor. ~**y** /'vɪktərɪ/ n victoria f

video /'vɪdɪəʊ/ n (pl -os) vídeo m, video m (LAm). ~ **camera** n videocámara f. ~**(cassette) recorder** n magnetoscopio m. ~**tape** n videocassette f

vie /vaɪ/ vi (pres p **vying**) rivalizar

Vietnam /vjet'næm/ n Vietnam m. ~**ese** adj & n vietnamita (m & f)

view /vjuː/ n vista f; (mental survey) visión f de conjunto; (opinion) opinión f. in my ~ a mi juicio. in ~ of en vista de. on ~ expuesto. ● vt ver (scene, property); (consider) considerar. ~**er** n (TV) televidente m & f. ~**finder** n visor m. ~**point** n punto m de vista

vigil|ance n vigilancia f. ~**ant** adj vigilante

vigo|rous /'vɪɡərəs/ adj enérgico;

(growth) vigoroso. ~**ur** /'vɪɡə(r)/ n vigor m

vile /vaɪl/ adj (base) vil; (food) asqueroso; (weather, temper) horrible

village /'vɪlɪdʒ/ n pueblo m; (small) aldea f. ~**r** n vecino m del pueblo; (of small village) aldeano m

villain /'vɪlən/ n maleante m & f; (in story etc) villano m

vindicate /'vɪndɪkeɪt/ vt justificar

vindictive /vɪn'dɪktɪv/ adj vengativo

vine /vaɪn/ n (on ground) vid f; (climbing) parra f

vinegar /'vɪnɪɡə(r)/ n vinagre m

vineyard /'vɪnjəd/ n viña f

vintage /'vɪntɪdʒ/ n (year) cosecha f. ● adj (wine) añejo; (car) de época

vinyl /'vaɪnɪl/ n vinilo m

viola /vɪ'əʊlə/ n viola f

violat|e /'vaɪəleɪt/ vt violar. ~**ion** /-'leɪʃn/ n violación f

violen|ce /'vaɪələns/ n violencia f. ~**t** adj violento. ~**tly** adv violentamente

violet /'vaɪələt/ adj & n violeta (f); (colour) violeta (m)

violin /'vaɪəlɪn/ n violín m. ~**ist** n violinista m & f

VIP /viːaɪ'piː/ abbr (= very important person) VIP m

viper /'vaɪpə(r)/ n víbora f

virgin /'vɜːdʒɪn/ adj & n virgen (f)

Virgo /'vɜːɡəʊ/ n Virgo f

virile /'vɪraɪl/ adj viril

virtual /'vɜːtʃʊəl/ adj. traffic is at a ~ standstill el tráfico está prácticamente paralizado. ~ **reality** n realidad f virtual. ~**ly** adv prácticamente

virtue /'vɜːtʃuː/ n virtud f. by ~ of en virtud de

virtuous /'vɜːtʃʊəs/ adj virtuoso

virulent /'vɪrʊlənt/ adj virulento

virus /'vaɪərəs/ n (pl -uses) virus m

visa /'viːzə/ n visado m, visa f (LAm)

vise /vaɪs/ n (Amer) torno de banco

visib|ility /vɪzɪ'bɪlətɪ/ n visibilidad f. ~**le** /'vɪzɪbl/ adj visible; (sign, improvement) evidente

vision /'vɪʒn/ n visión f; (sight) vista f

visit /'vɪzɪt/ vt visitar; hacer una visita a (person). ● vi hacer visitas. ~ **with** s.o. (Amer) ir a ver a uno. ● n visita f. **pay s.o. a** ~ hacerle una visita a uno. ~**or** n visitante m & f; (guest) visita f

visor /'vaɪzə(r)/ n visera f

visual /'vɪʒʊəl/ adj visual. ~**ize** vt imaginar(se); (foresee) prever

vital /'vaɪtl/ adj (essential) esencial; (factor) de vital importancia; (organ) vital. ~**ity** /vaɪ'tælətɪ/ n vitalidad f

vitamin /'vɪtəmɪn/ n vitamina f.

vivacious /vɪ'veɪʃəs/ adj vivaz

vivid /'vɪvɪd/ adj vivo. ~**ly** adv intensamente; (describe) gráficamente

vivisection /vɪvɪ'sekʃn/ n vivisección f

vocabulary /və'kæbjʊlərɪ/ n vocabulario m

vocal /'vəʊkl/ adj vocal. ~**ist** n cantante m & f

vocation /vəʊ'keɪʃn/ n vocación f. ~**al** adj profesional

vociferous /və'sɪfərəs/ adj vociferador

vogue /vəʊɡ/ n moda f, boga f

voice /vɔɪs/ n voz f. ● vt expresar

void /vɔɪd/ adj (not valid) nulo. ● n vacío m

volatile /ˈvɒlətaɪl/ adj volátil; (person) imprevisible

volcan|ic /vɒlˈkænɪk/ adj volcánico. ~o /vɒlˈkeɪnəʊ/ n (pl -oes) volcán m

volley /ˈvɒlɪ/ n (pl -eys) (of gunfire) descarga f cerrada; (sport) volea f. ~ball n vóleibol m

volt /vəʊlt/ n voltio m. ~age /-ɪdʒ/ n voltaje m

volume /ˈvɒljuːm/ n volumen m; (book) tomo m

voluntar|ily /ˈvɒləntərəlɪ/ adv voluntariamente. ~y adj voluntario; (organization) de beneficencia

volunteer /vɒlənˈtɪə(r)/ n voluntario m. ● vt ofrecer. ● vi. ~ (to) ofrecerse (a)

vomit /ˈvɒmɪt/ vt/i vomitar. ● n vómito m

voracious /vəˈreɪʃəs/ adj voraz

vot|e /vəʊt/ n voto m; (right) derecho m al voto; (act) votación f. ● vi votar. ~er n votante m & f. ~ing n votación f

vouch /vaʊtʃ/ vi. ~ for s.o. responder por uno. ~er /-ə(r)/ n vale m

vow /vaʊ/ n voto m. ● vi jurar

vowel /ˈvaʊəl/ n vocal f

voyage /ˈvɔɪdʒ/ n viaje m; (by sea) travesía f

vulgar /ˈvʌlɡə(r)/ adj (coarse) grosero, vulgar; (tasteless) de mal gusto. ~ity /-ˈɡærətɪ/ n vulgaridad f

vulnerable /ˈvʌlnərəbl/ adj vulnerable

vulture /ˈvʌltʃə(r)/ n buitre m

vying /ˈvaɪɪŋ/ see VIE

Ww

W abbr (= West) O

wad /wɒd/ n (of notes) fajo m; (tied together) lío m; (papers) montón m

waddle /ˈwɒdl/ vi contonearse

wade /weɪd/ vi caminar (por el agua etc)

wafer /ˈweɪfə(r)/ n galleta f de barquillo

waffle /ˈwɒfl/ n 🔲 palabrería f. ● vi 🔲 divagar; (in essay, exam) meter paja 🔲. ● n (Culin) gofre m, wafle m (LAm)

waft /wɒft/ vi flotar

wag /wæɡ/ vt (pt wagged) menear. ● vi menearse

wage /weɪdʒ/ n sueldo m. ~s npl salario m, sueldo m. ~r n apuesta f

waggle /ˈwæɡl/ vt menear. ● vi menearse

wagon /ˈwæɡən/ n carro m; (Rail) vagón m; (Amer, delivery truck) furgoneta f de reparto

wail /weɪl/ vi llorar

waist /weɪst/ n cintura f. ~coat n chaleco m. ~line n cintura f

wait /weɪt/ vi esperar; (at table) servir. ~ for esperar. ~ on s.o. atender a uno. ~ (await) esperar (chance, turn). ~ table (Amer) servir a la mesa. I can't ~ to see him me muero de ganas de verlo. ● n espera f. lie in ~ acechar

waiter /ˈweɪtə(r)/ n camarero m, mesero m (LAm)

wait: ~ing-list n lista f de espera. ~ing-room n sala f de espera

waitress /ˈweɪtrɪs/ n camarera f,

mesera f (LAm)

waive /weɪv/ vt renunciar a

wake /weɪk/ vt (pt **woke**, pp **woken**) despertar. ● vi despertarse. ● n (Naut) estela f. **in the ~ of** como resultado de. □ **~ up** vt despertar. □ vi despertarse

Wales /weɪlz/ n (el país de) Gales

walk /wɔːk/ vi andar, caminar; (not ride) ir a pie; (stroll) pasear. ● vt andar por (streets); llevar de paseo (dog). ● n paseo m; (long) caminata f; (gait) manera f de andar. □ **~ out** vi salir; (workers) declararse en huelga. □ **~ out on** vt abandonar. **~er** n excursionista m & f

walkie-talkie /wɔːkɪˈtɔːkɪ/ n walkie-talkie m

walk: ~ing-stick n bastón m. **W~man** /-mən/ n Walkman m (P). **~-out** n retirada en señal de protesta; (strike) abandono m del trabajo

wall /wɔːl/ n (interior) pared f; (exterior) muro m

wallet /ˈwɒlɪt/ n cartera f, billetera f

wallop /ˈwɒləp/ vt (pt **walloped**) 🄵 darle un golpazo a.

wallow /ˈwɒləʊ/ vi revolcarse

wallpaper /ˈwɔːlpeɪpə(r)/ n papel m pintado

walnut /ˈwɔːlnʌt/ n nuez f; (tree) nogal m

walrus /ˈwɔːlrəs/ n morsa f

waltz /wɔːls/ n vals m. ● vi valsar

wand /wɒnd/ n varita f (mágica)

wander /ˈwɒndə(r)/ vi vagar; (stroll) pasear; (digress) divagar. ● n vuelta f, paseo m. **~er** n trotamundos m

wane /weɪn/ vi (moon) menguar; (interest) decaer. ● n. **be on the ~** (popularity) estar decayendo

wangle /ˈwæŋgl/ vt 🄵 agenciarse

want /wɒnt/ vt querer; (need) necesitar. ● vi carecer de. ● n necesidad f; (lack) falta f. **~ed** adj (criminal) buscado

war /wɔː(r)/ n guerra f. **at ~** en guerra

warble /ˈwɔːbl/ vi trinar, gorjear

ward /wɔːd/ n (in hospital) sala f; (child) pupilo m. □ **~ off** vt conjurar (danger); rechazar (attack)

warden /ˈwɔːdn/ n guarda m

warder /ˈwɔːdə(r)/ n celador m (de una cárcel)

wardrobe /ˈwɔːdrəʊb/ n armario m; (clothes) guardarropa f, vestuario m

warehouse /ˈweəhaʊs/ n depósito m, almacén m

wares /weəz/ npl mercancía(s) f(pl)

war: ~fare n guerra f. **~head** n cabeza f, ojiva f

warm /wɔːm/ adj (-er, -est) (water, day) tibio, templado; (room) caliente; (climate, wind) cálido; (clothes) de abrigo; (welcome) caluroso. **be ~** (person) tener calor. **it's ~ today** hoy hace calor. ● vt. □ **~ (up)** calentar (room); recalentar (food); (fig) animar. ● vi. **~ (up)** calentarse; (fig) animarse. **~-blooded** /-ˈblʌdɪd/ adj de sangre caliente. **~ly** adv (heartily) calurosamente. ~**th** n calor m; (of colour, atmosphere) calidez f

warn /wɔːn/ vt advertir. ~**ing** n advertencia f; (notice) aviso m

warp /wɔːp/ vt alabear. ~**ed** /'wɔːpt/ adj (wood) alabeado; (mind) retorcido

warrant /'wɒrənt/ n orden f judicial; (search ~) orden f de registro; (for arrest) orden f de arresto. • vt justificar. ~**y** n garantía f

warrior /'wɒrɪə(r)/ n guerrero m

warship /'wɔːʃɪp/ n buque m de guerra

wart /wɔːt/ n verruga f

wartime /'wɔːtaɪm/ n tiempo m de guerra

wary /'weərɪ/ adj (-ier, -iest) cauteloso. be ~ of recelar de

was /wəz, wɒz/ see **BE**

wash /wɒʃ/ vt lavar; fregar, lavar (LAm) (floor). ~ one's face lavarse la cara. • vi lavarse. • n (in washing machine) lavado m. have a ~ lavarse. I gave the car a ~ lavé el coche. □ ~ **out** vt (clean) lavar; (rinse) enjuagar. □ ~ **up** vi fregar los platos, lavar los trastes (Mex); (Amer, wash face and hands) lavarse. ~**able** adj lavable. ~**basin**, ~**bowl** (Amer) n lavabo m. ~**er** n arandela f. ~**ing** n lavado m; (dirty clothes) ropa f para lavar; (wet clothes) ropa f lavada. **do the** ~**ing** lavar la ropa, hacer la colada. ~**ing-machine** n máquina f de lavar, lavadora f. ~**ing-powder** n jabón m en polvo. ~**ing-up** n. **do the** ~**ing-up** lavar los platos, fregar (los platos). ~**ing-up liquid** n lavavajillas m. ~**out** n ⊞ desastre m. ~**room** n (Amer) baños mpl, servicios mpl

wasp /wɒsp/ n avispa f

waste /weɪst/ • adj (matter) de desecho; (land) (barren) yermo; (uncultivated) baldío. • n (of materials) desperdicio m; (of time) pérdida f; (refuse) residuos mpl. • vt despilfarrar (electricity, money); desperdiciar (talent, effort); perder (time). • vi. ~**-disposal unit** n trituradora f de desperdicios. ~**ful** adj poco económico; (person) despilfarrador. ~**-paper basket** n papelera f

watch /wɒtʃ/ vt mirar; observar (person, expression); ver (TV); (keep an eye on) vigilar; (take heed) tener cuidado con. • vi mirar. • n (observation) vigilancia f; (period of duty) guardia f; (timepiece) reloj m. □ ~ **out** vi (be careful) tener cuidado; (look carefully) estarse atento. ~**dog** n perro m guardián. ~**man** /-mən/ n (pl -men) vigilante m.

water /'wɔːtə(r)/ n agua f. • vt regar (plants etc). • vi (eyes) llorar. **make s.o.'s mouth** ~ hacérsele la boca agua, hacérsele agua la boca (LAm). ~ **down** vt diluir; aguar (wine). ~**colour** n acuarela f. ~**cress** n berro m. ~**fall** n cascada f; (large) catarata f. ~**ing-can** n regadera f. ~ **lily** n nenúfar m. ~**logged** /-lɒgd/ adj anegado; (shoes) empapado. ~**proof** adj impermeable; (watch) sumergible. ~**-skiing** n esquí m acuático. ~**tight** adj hermético; (boat) estanco; (argument) irrebatible. ~**way** n canal m navegable. ~**y** adj acuoso; (eyes) lloroso

watt /wɒt/ n vatio m

wave /weɪv/ n onda f; (of hand) señal f; (fig) oleada f. • vt agitar; (curl) ondular (hair). • vi (signal) hacer señales con la mano; ondear (flag). ~**band** n banda f de fre-

cuencia. ～**length** n longitud f de
onda

waver /'weɪvə(r)/ vi (be indecisive)
vacilar; (falter) flaquear

wavy /'weɪvɪ/ adj (-ier, -iest) ondulado

wax /wæks/ n cera f. ●vi (moon)
crecer. ～**work** n figura f de cera.
～**works** npl museo m de cera

way /weɪ/ n (route) camino m;
(manner) manera f, forma f, modo
m; (direction) dirección f; (habit)
costumbre f. **it's a long ～ from**
here queda muy lejos de aquí. **be
in the ～** estorbar. **by the ～** a
propósito. **either ～** de cualquier
manera. **give ～** (collapse) ceder,
romperse; (Auto) ceder el paso. **in a
～** en cierta manera. **in some ～s**
en ciertos modos. **make ～** dejar
paso a. **no ～!** ¡ni hablar! **on my ～**
to de camino a. **out of the ～** remoto; (extraordinary) fuera de lo
común. **that ～** por allí. **this ～**
por aquí. ～ **in** n entrada f. ～**lay**
/weɪ'leɪ/ vt (pt -laid) abordar. ～
out n salida f. ～**-out** adj ultramo-
derno, original. ～**s** npl costumbres
fpl

we /wiː/ pron nosotros m, nosotras f

weak /wiːk/ adj (-er, -est) débil;
(structure) poco sólido; (performance, student) flojo; (coffee) poco
cargado; (solution) diluido; (beer)
suave; (pej) aguado. ～**en** vt debili-
tar. ●vi (resolve) flaquear. ～**ling** n
alfeñique m. ～**ness** n debilidad f

wealth /welθ/ n riqueza f. ～**y** adj
(-ier, -iest) rico

weapon /'wepən/ n arma f. ～**s of
mass destruction** armas de destrucción masiva

wear /weə(r)/ vt (pt wore, pp
worn) llevar; vestirse de (black,
red, etc); (usually) usar. **I've got**

nothing to ～ no tengo nada que
ponerme. ●vi (through use) gastarse; (last) durar. ●n uso m; (damage) desgaste m; ～ **and tear** desgaste m natural. □ ～ **out** vt gastar;
(tire) agotar. vi gastarse

weary /'wɪərɪ/ adj (-ier, -iest) cansado. ●vt cansar. ●vi cansarse. ～
of cansarse de

weather /'weðə(r)/ n tiempo m.
what's the ～ like? ¿qué tiempo
hace?. **the ～ was bad** hizo mal
tiempo. **be under the ～** 🅵 no
andar muy bien 🅵. ●vt (survive)
sobrellevar. ～**-beaten** adj curtido.
～ **forecast** n pronóstico m del
tiempo. ～**-vane** n veleta f

weave /wiːv/ vt (pt wove, pp
woven) tejer; entretejer (threads).
～ **one's way** abrirse paso. ●vi
(person) zigzaguear; (road) serpentear. ～**r** n tejedor m

web /web/ n (of spider) telaraña f;
(of intrigue) red f. ～ **page** n página
web. ～ **site** n sitio web m

wed /wed/ vt (pt wedded) casarse
con. ●vi casarse.

we'd /wiːd/wɪəd/ = **we had, we
would**

wedding /'wedɪŋ/ n boda f, casamiento m. ～**-cake** n pastel m de
boda. ～**-ring** n anillo m de boda

wedge /wedʒ/ n cuña f

Wednesday /'wenzdeɪ/ n miércoles m

wee /wiː/ adj 🅵 pequeñito. ●n.
have a ～ 🅵 hacer pis 🅵

weed /wiːd/ n mala hierba f. ●vt
desherbar. □ ～ **out** vt eliminar.
～**killer** n herbicida m. ～**y** adj
(Amer, lanky) lar-
guirucho 🅵

week /wiːk/ n semana f. ～**day** n
día m de semana. ～**end** n fin m de
semana. ～**ly** adj semanal. ●n se-

manario m. ● adv semanalmente

weep /wiːp/ vi (pt **wept**) llorar

weigh /weɪ/ vt/i pesar. ~ **anchor** levar anclas. □ ~ **down** vt (fig) oprimir. □ ~ **up** vt pesar; (fig) considerar

weight /weɪt/ n peso m; (sport) pesa f. put on ~ engordar. lose ~ adelgazar. ~**lifting** n halterofilia f, levantamiento m de pesos

weir /wɪə(r)/ n presa f

weird /wɪəd/ adj (-er, -est) raro, extraño; (unearthly) misterioso

welcom|e /ˈwelkəm/ adj bienvenido. you're ~e! (after thank you) ¡de nada! ● n bienvenida f; (reception) acogida f. ● vt dar la bienvenida a; (appreciate) alegrarse de. ~**ing** adj acogedor

weld /weld/ vt soldar. ● n soldadura f. ~**er** n soldador m

welfare /ˈwelfeə(r)/ n bienestar m; (aid) asistencia f social. **W~ State** n estado m benefactor

well /wel/ adv (better, best) bien. ~ **done!** ¡muy bien!, ¡bravo! as ~ también. as ~ as además de. we may as ~ go tomorrow más vale que vayamos mañana. do ~ (succeed) tener éxito. very ~ muy bien. ● adj bien. I'm very ~ estoy muy bien. ● int (introducing, continuing sentence) bueno; (surprise) ¡vaya!; (indignation, resignation) bueno. ~ I never! ¡no me digas! ● n pozo m

we'll /wiːl/wɪəl/ = we will

well: ~-**behaved** /-bɪˈheɪvd/ adj que se porta bien, bueno. ~-**educated** /-ˈedjʊkeɪtɪd/ adj culto.

wellington (boot) /ˈwelɪŋtən/ n bota f de goma or de agua; (Amer, short boot) botín m

well: ~-**known** /-ˈnəʊn/ adj conocido. ~ **off** adj adinerado. ~-**stocked** /-ˈstɒkt/ adj bien provisto. ~-**to-do** /-təˈduː/ adj adinerado

Welsh /welʃ/ adj & n galés (m). the ~ n los galeses

Welsh Assembly La Asamblea Nacional de Gales empezó a funcionar, en Cardiff, en 1999. Tiene poderes limitados, por lo que no puede imponer impuestos. Consta de 60 miembros o AMs (Assembly Members); 40 elegidos directamente y el resto, de las listas regionales, mediante el sistema de representación proporcional.

went /went/ see **GO**

wept /wept/ see **WEEP**

were /wɜː(r), wə(r)/ see **BE**

we're /wɪə(r)/ = we are

west /west/ n oeste m. the W~ el Occidente m. ● adj oeste; (wind) del oeste. ● adv (go) hacia el oeste. al oeste. it's ~ of York está al oeste de York. ~**erly** /-əlɪ/ adj (wind) del oeste. ~**ern** /-ən/ adj occidental. ● n (film) película f del Oeste. ~**erner** n occidental m & f. **W~ Indian** adj & n antillano (m). **W~ Indies** npl Antillas fpl. ~**ward(s)** /-wəd(z)/.

wet /wet/ adj (wetter, wettest) mojado; (rainy) lluvioso; (fam, person) soso. '~ **paint**' 'pintura fresca'. get ~ mojarse. he got his feet ~ se mojó los pies. ● vt (pt wetted) mojar; (dampen) humedecer. ~ **o.s.** orinarse. ~**back** n espalda f mojada. ~ **blanket** n aguafiestas m & f. ~ **suit** n traje m de neopreno

w

we've /wiːv/ = we have

whack /wæk/ vt 🔟 golpear. ● n 🔟 golpe m.

whale /weɪl/ n ballena f. we had a ~ of a time 🔟 lo pasamos bomba 🔟

wham /wæm/ int ¡zas!

wharf /wɔːf/ n (pl wharves f or wharfs) muelle m.

---

what /wɒt/

● adjective

····▸ (in questions) qué. ~ perfume are you wearing? ¿qué perfume llevas?. ~ colour are the walls? ¿de qué color son las paredes?

····▸ (in exclamations) qué. ~ a beautiful house! ¡qué casa más linda!. ~ a lot of people! ¡cuánta gente!

····▸ (in indirect speech) qué. I'll ask him ~ bus to take le preguntaré qué autobús hay que tomar. do you know ~ time it leaves? ¿sabes a qué hora sale?

● pronoun

····▸ (in questions) qué. ~ is it? ¿qué es? ~ for? ¿para qué?. ~'s the problem? ¿cuál es el problema? ~'s he like? ¿cómo es? what? (say that again) ¿cómo?, ¿qué?

····▸ (in indirect questions) qué. I didn't know ~ to do no sabía qué hacer

····▸ (relative) lo que. I did ~ I could hice lo que pude. ~ I need is a new car lo que necesito es un coche nuevo

····▸ (in phrases) ~ about me? ¿y yo qué? ~ if she doesn't come? ¿y si no viene?

---

whatever /wɒtˈevə(r)/ adj cualquiera. ● pron (todo) lo que, cualquier cosa que

whatsoever /wɒtsəʊˈevə(r)/ adj & pron = whatever

wheat /wiːt/ n trigo m

wheel /wiːl/ n rueda f. at the ~ al volante. ● vt empujar (bicycle etc); llevar (en silla de ruedas etc) (person). ~barrow n carretilla f. ~chair n silla f de ruedas

wheeze /wiːz/ vi respirar con dificultad

when /wen/ adv cuándo. ● conj cuando. ~ever /-'evə(r)/ adv (every time that) cada vez que, siempre que; (at whatever time) we'll go ~ever you're ready saldremos cuando estés listo

where /weə(r)/ adv & conj donde; (interrogative) dónde. ~ are you going? ¿adónde vas? ~ are you from? ¿de dónde eres? ~abouts /-'abaʊts/ adv en qué parte. ● n paradero m. ~as /-'æz/ conj por cuanto; (in contrast) mientras (que). ~ver /weər'evə(r)/ adv (in questions) dónde; (no matter where) en cualquier parte. ● conj donde (+ subjunctive), dondequiera (+ subjunctive)

whet /wet/ vt (pt whetted) abrir (appetite)

whether /'weðə(r)/ conj si. I don't know ~ she will like it no sé si le gustará. ~ you like it or not te guste o no te guste

which /wɪtʃ/ adj (in questions) (sing) qué, cuál; (pl) qué, cuáles. ~ one cuál. ~ one of you cuál de ustedes. ● pron (in questions) (sing) cuál; (pl) cuáles; (relative) (sing) que; (pl) que; (after prep) (object) el cual, la cual, lo cual, los cuales, las cuales. ~ever /-'evə(r)/

adj cualquier. ● *pron* cualquiera que, el que, la que; (*in questions*) cuál; (*pl*) cuáles

while /waɪl/ *n* rato *m*. a ~ **ago** hace un rato. ● *conj* mientras; (*although*) aunque. □ ~ **away** *vt* pasar (*time*)

whilst /waɪlst/ *conj* see WHILE

whim /wɪm/ *n* capricho *m*

whimper /'wɪmpə(r)/ *vi* gimotear. ● *n* quejido *m*

whine /waɪn/ *vi* (person) gemir; (child) lloriquear; (dog) aullar

whip /wɪp/ *n* látigo *m*; (*for punishment*) azote *m*. ● *vt* (*pt* whipped /wɪpt/) fustigar, pegarle a (*con la fusta*) (horse); azotar (person); (*Culin*) batir

whirl /wɜːl/ *vi* girar rápidamente. ~**pool** *n* remolino *m*. ~**wind** *n* torbellino *m*

whirr /wɜː(r)/ *n* zumbido *m*. ● *vi* zumbar

whisk /wɪsk/ *vt* (*Culin*) batir. ● *n* (*Culin*) batidor *m*. ~ **away** llevarse

whisker /'wɪskə(r)/ *n* pelo *m*. ~**s** *npl* (*of cat etc*) bigotes *mpl*

whisky /'wɪskɪ/ *n* whisky *m*, güisqui *m*

whisper /'wɪspə(r)/ *vt* susurrar. ● *vi* cuchichear. ● *n* susurro *m*

whistle /'wɪsl/ *n* silbido *m*; (loud) chiflado *m*; (*instrument*) silbato *m*, pito *m*. ● *vi* silbar; (loudly) chiflar

white /waɪt/ *adj* (-er, -est) blanco. go ~ ponerse pálido. ● *n* blanco; (*of egg*) clara *f*. ~ **coffee** *n* café *m* con leche. ~-**collar worker** *n* empleado *m* de oficina. ~ **elephant** *n* objeto *m* inútil y costoso. ~-**hot** *adj* (metal) al rojo blanco. ~ **lie** *n* mentirijilla *f*. ~**n** *vt/i* blanquear. ~**wash** *n* cal *f*; (*cover-up*) tapadera

f 🔲. ● *vt* blanquear, encalar

Whitsun /'wɪtsn/ *n* Pentecostés *m*

whiz /wɪz/ *vi* (*pt* whizzed). ~ **by**, ~ **past** pasar zumbando. ~-**kid** *n* 🔲 lince *m* 🔲

who /huː/ *pron* (in questions) quién; (*pl*) quiénes; (*as relative*) que; **the girl** ~ **lives there** la chica que vive allí. **those** ~ **can't come tomorrow** los que no puedan venir mañana. ~-**ever** /huː'evə(r)/ *pron* quienquiera que; (*interrogative*) quién

whole /həʊl/ *adj*. **the** ~ **country** todo el país. **there's a** ~ **bottle left** queda una botella entera. ● *n* todo *m*, conjunto *m*; (*total*) total *m*. **on the** ~ en general. ~-**hearted** /-'hɑːtɪd/ *adj* (support) incondicional; (approval) sin reservar. ~**meal** *adj* integral. ~-**sale** *n* venta *f* al por mayor. ● *adj* & *adv* al por mayor. ~**some** /-səm/ *adj* sano

wholly /'həʊlɪ/ *adv* completamente

whom /huːm/ *pron* que, a quien; (in questions) a quién

whooping cough /'huːpɪŋ/ *n* tos *f* convulsa

whore /hɔː(r)/ *n* puta *f*

whose /huːz/ *pron* de quién; (*pl*) de quiénes. ● *adj* (in questions) de quién; (*pl*) de quiénes; (relative) cuyo; (*pl*) cuyos

why /waɪ/ *adv* por qué. ~ **not?** ¿por qué no? **that's** ~ **I couldn't go** por eso no pude ir. ● *int* ¡vaya!

wick /wɪk/ *n* mecha *f*

wicked /'wɪkɪd/ *adj* malo; (*mischievous*) travieso; (*fam*, very bad) malísimo

wicker /'wɪkə(r)/ *n* mimbre *m* & *f*. ● *adj* de mimbre. ~**work** *n* artícu-

w

los *mpl* de mimbre
wicket /'wɪkɪt/ *n* (cricket) rastrillo *m*
wide /waɪd/ *adj* (-er, -est) ancho; (range, experience) amplio; (off target) desviado. it's four metres ~ tiene cuatro metros de ancho. ● *adv.* open ~! abra bien la boca. ~ **awake** *adj* completamente despierto; (*fig*) despabilado. I left the door ~ **open** dejé la puerta abierta de par en par. ~**ly** *adv* extensamente; (believed) generalmente; (different) muy. ~**n** *vt* ensanchar. ● *vi* ensancharse. ~**spread** *adj* extendido; (*fig*) difundido
widow /'wɪdəʊ/ *n* viuda *f.* ~**er** *n* viudo *m.*
width /wɪdθ/ *n* anchura *f.* **in** ~ de ancho
wield /wi:ld/ *vt* manejar; ejercer (power)
wife /waɪf/ *n* (*pl* **wives**) mujer *f,* esposa *f*
wig /wɪg/ *n* peluca *f*
wiggle /'wɪgl/ *vt* menear. ● *vi* menearse
wild /waɪld/ *adj* (-er, -est) (animal) salvaje; (flower) silvestre; (country) agreste; (enraged) furioso; (idea) extravagante; (with joy) loco. a ~ **guess** una conjetura hecha totalmente al azar. I'm not ~ **about the idea** la idea no me enloquece. ● *adv* en estado salvaje. **run** ~ (children) criarse como salvajes. ~**s** *npl* regiones *fpl* salvajes. ~**erness** /'wɪldənɪs/ *n* páramo *m.* ~**fire** *n.* **spread like** ~**fire** correr como un reguero de pólvora. ~-**goose chase** *n* empresa *f* inútil. ~**life** *n* fauna *f.* ~**ly** *adv* violentamente; (*fig*) locamente.

will /wɪl/
● *auxiliary verb*

past **would;** contracted forms **I'll, you'll,** etc = **I will, you will,** etc.; **won't** = **will not**

····▸ (*talking about the future*)

❗ The Spanish future tense is not always the first option for translating the English future tense. The present tense of *ir* + *a* + *verb* is commonly used instead, particularly in Latin American countries. **he'll be here on Tuesday** *estará el martes,* **va a estar el martes;** **she won't agree** *no va a aceptar,* **no aceptará**

····▸ (*in invitations and requests*)
~ **you have some wine?** ¿quieres (un poco de) vino? **you'll stay for dinner, won't you?** te quedas a cenar, ¿no?
····▸ (*in tag questions*) **you** ~ **be back soon, won't you?** vas a volver pronto, ¿no?
····▸ (*in short answers*) **will it be ready by Monday? - yes, it** ~ ¿estará listo para el lunes? - sí
● *noun*
····▸ (*mental power*) voluntad *f*
····▸ (*document*) testamento *m*

willing /'wɪlɪŋ/ *adj* complaciente. ~ **to** dispuesto a. ~**ly** *adv* de buena gana
willow /'wɪləʊ/ *n* sauce *m*
will-power /'wɪlpaʊə(r)/ *n* fuerza *f* de voluntad
wilt /wɪlt/ *vi* marchitarse

win /wɪn/ vt (pt won, pres p winning) ganar; (achieve, obtain) conseguir. ● vi ganar. ● n victoria f. □ ~ **over** vt ganarse a

wince /wɪns/ vi hacer una mueca de dolor

winch /wɪntʃ/ n cabrestante m. ● vt levantar con un cabrestante

wind[1] /wɪnd/ n viento m; (in stomach) gases mpl. ~ **instrument** instrumento m de viento. ● vt dejar sin aliento

wind[2] /waɪnd/ vt (pt wound) (wrap around) enrollar; dar cuerda a (clock etc). ● vi (road etc) serpentear. □ ~ **up** vt dar cuerda a (watch, clock); (fig) terminar, concluir

winding /ˈwaɪndɪŋ/ adj tortuoso

windmill /ˈwɪndmɪl/ n molino m (de viento)

window /ˈwɪndəʊ/ n ventana f; (in shop) escaparate m, vitrina f (LAm), vidriera f (LAm), aparador m (Mex); (of vehicle, booking-office) ventanilla f; (Comp) ventana f, window m. ~ **box** n jardinera f. ~**-shop** vi mirar los escaparates. ~**sill** n alféizar m or repisa f de la ventana

wine /waɪn/ n vino m. ~**-cellar** n bodega f. ~**glass** n copa f de vino. ~**-growing** n vinicultura f. ● adj vinícola. ~ **list** n lista f de vinos. ~**-tasting** n cata f de vinos

wing /wɪŋ/ n ala f; (Auto) aleta f. under one's ~ bajo la protección de uno. ~**er** n (Sport) ala m & f. ~**s** npl (in theatre) bastidores mpl

wink /wɪŋk/ vi guiñar el ojo; (light etc) centellear. ● n guiño m. not to sleep a ~ no pegar ojo

win: ~**ner** n ganador m. ~**ning-post** n poste m de lle-

gada. ~**nings** npl ganancias fpl

wint|er /ˈwɪntə(r)/ n invierno m. ● vi invernar. ~**ry** adj invernal

wipe /waɪp/ vt limpiar, pasarle un trapo a; (dry) secar. ~ **one's nose** limpiarse la nariz. ● n. give sth a ~ limpiar algo, pasarle un trapo a algo. □ ~ **out** vt (cancel) cancelar; (destroy) destruir; (obliterate) borrar. □ ~ **up** vt limpiar

wir|e /ˈwaɪə(r)/ n alambre m; (Elec) cable m. ~**ing** n instalación f eléctrica

wisdom /ˈwɪzdəm/ n sabiduría f. ~ **tooth** n muela f del juicio

wise /waɪz/ adj (-er, -est) sabio; (sensible) prudente; (decision, choice) acertado. ~**ly** adv sabiamente; (sensibly) prudentemente

wish /wɪʃ/ n deseo m; (greeting) saludo m. make a ~ pedir un deseo. best ~**es, John** (in letters) saludos de John, un abrazo de John. ● vt desear. ~ **s.o. well** desear buena suerte a uno. I ~ I were rich jojalá fuera rico! he ~**ed** he hadn't told her lamentó habérselo dicho. ~**ful thinking** n ilusiones fpl

wistful /ˈwɪstfl/ adj melancólico

wit /wɪt/ n gracia f; (intelligence) ingenio m. be at one's ~s' end no saber qué más hacer

witch /wɪtʃ/ n bruja f. ~**craft** n brujería f

with /wɪð/ prep con; (cause, having) de. come ~ me ven conmigo. take it ~ you llévalo contigo; (formal) lléveselo consigo. the man ~ the beard el hombre de la barba. trembling ~ fear temblando de miedo

withdraw /wɪðˈdrɔː/ vt (pt withdrew, pp withdrawn) retirar. ● vi

w

apartarse. ~al n retirada f. ~n adj (person) retraído

wither /'wɪðə(r)/ vi marchitarse

withhold /wɪð'həʊld/ vt (pt withheld) retener; (conceal) ocultar (from a)

within /wɪð'ɪn/ prep dentro de. ● adv dentro. ~ sight a la vista

without /wɪð'aʊt/ prep sin. ~ paying sin pagar

withstand /wɪð'stænd/ vt (pt -stood) resistir

witness /'wɪtnɪs/ n testigo m; (proof) testimonio m. ● vt presenciar; atestiguar (signature). ~-box n tribuna f de los testigos

witt|icism /'wɪtɪsɪzəm/ n ocurrencia f. ~y /'wɪtɪ/ adj (-ier, -iest) gracioso

wives /waɪvz/ see WIFE

wizard /'wɪzəd/ n hechicero m

wizened /'wɪznd/ adj arrugado

wobbl|e /'wɒbl/ vi (chair) tambalearse; (bicycle) bambolearse; (voice, jelly, hand) temblar. ~y adj (chair etc) cojo

woe /wəʊ/ n aflicción f

woke /wəʊk/, **woken** /'wəʊkən/ see WAKE

wolf /wʊlf/ n (pl wolves /wʊlvz/) lobo m

woman /'wʊmən/ n (pl women) mujer f

womb /wu:m/ n matriz f

women /'wɪmɪn/ npl see WOMAN

won /wʌn/ see WIN

wonder /'wʌndə(r)/ n maravilla f; (bewilderment) asombro m. no ~ no es de extrañarse (that). ● vt (ask oneself) preguntarse. I ~ whose book this is me pregunto de quién será este libro; (in polite requests) I ~ if you could help

me? ¿me podría ayudar? ~ful adj maravilloso. ~fully adv maravillosamente

won't /wəʊnt/ = will not

wood /wʊd/ n madera f; (for burning) leña f; (area) bosque m. ~ed adj poblado de árboles, boscoso. ~en adj de madera. ~land n bosque m. ~wind /-wɪnd/ n instrumentos mpl de viento de madera. ~work n carpintería f; (in room etc) maderaje m. ~worm n carcoma f. ~y adj leñoso

wool /wʊl/ n lana f. pull the ~ over s.o.'s eyes engañar a uno. ~len adj de lana. ~ly adj (-ier, -iest) de lana; (unclear) vago. ● n jersey m

word /wɜ:d/ n palabra f; (news) noticia f. by ~ of mouth de palabra. I didn't say a ~ yo no dije nada. in other ~s es decir. ● vt expresar. ~ing n redacción f; (of question) formulación f. ~ proces-sor n procesador m de textos. ~y adj prolijo

wore /wɔ:(r)/ see WEAR

work /wɜ:k/ n trabajo m; (arts) obra f. be out of ~ estar sin trabajo, estar desocupado. ● vt hacer trabajar; manejar (machine). ● vi trabajar; (machine) funcionar; (student) estudiar; (drug etc) surtir efecto. □ ~ off vt desahogar. □ ~ out vt resolver (problem); (calculate) calcular; (understand) entender. ● vi (succeed) salir bien; (Sport) entrenarse. □ ~ up vt. get ~ed up exaltarse. ~able adj (project, solution) factible. ~er n trabajador m; (manual) obrero m; (in office, bank) empleado m. ~ing adj (day) laborable; (clothes etc) de trabajo. in ~ing order en estado de funcionamiento. ~ing class n clase f obrera. **~ing-class** adj de la clase obrera. **~-man** /-mən/ n (pl **-men**) obrero m. **~manship** n destreza f. **~s** npl (building) fábrica f; (Mec) mecanismo m. **~shop** n taller m

world /wɜːld/ n mundo m. out of this ~ maravilloso. ● adj mundial. W~ Cup n. the W~ Cup la Copa del Mundo. **~ly** adj mundano. **~wide** adj universal. W~ Wide Web n World Wide Web m

worm /wɜːm/ n gusano m, lombriz f

worn /wɔːn/ see WEAR. ● adj gastado. **~-out** adj gastado; (person) rendido

worr|ied /'wʌrɪd/ adj preocupado. **~y** /'wʌrɪ/ vt preocupar; (annoy) molestar. ● vi preocuparse. ● n preocupación f. **~ying** inquietante

worse /wɜːs/ adj peor. get ~ empeorar. ● adv peor; (more) más. **~n** vt/i empeorar

worship /'wɜːʃɪp/ n culto m; (title) Su Señoría. ● vt (pt worshipped) adorar

worst /wɜːst/ adj peor. he's the ~ in the class es el peor de la clase. ● adv peor. ● n. the ~ lo peor

worth /wɜːθ/ n valor m. ● adj. be ~ valer. it's ~ trying vale la pena probarlo. it was ~ my while (me) valió la pena. **~less** adj sin valor. **~while** /-'waɪl/ adj que vale la pena. **~y** /'wɜːðɪ/ adj meritorio; (respectable) respetable; (laudable) loable

would /wʊd/ modal verb. (in conditional sentences) ~ you go? ¿irías tú? he ~ come if he could vendría si pudiera. (in reported speech) I thought you'd forget pensé que te olvidarías; (in requests, invita-

tions) ~ you come here, please? ¿quieres venir aquí? ~ you switch the television off? ¿podrías apagar la televisión?; (be prepared to) he ~n't listen to me no me quería escuchar

wound¹ /wuːnd/ n herida f. ● vt herir

wound² /waʊnd/ see WIND²

wove, woven /wəʊv, 'wəʊvn/ see WEAVE

wow /waʊ/ int ¡ah!

wrangle /'ræŋgl/ vi reñir. ● n riña f

wrap /ræp/ vt (pt wrapped) envolver. ● n bata f; (shawl) chal m. **~per** n, **~ping** n envoltura f

wrath /rɒθ/ n ira f

wreak /riːk/ vt sembrar. ~ havoc causar estragos

wreath /riːθ/ n (pl **-ths** /-ðz/) corona f

wreck /rek/ n (ship) restos mpl de un naufragio; (vehicle) restos mpl de un avión siniestrado. be a nervous ~ tener los nervios destrozados. ● vt provocar el naufragio de (ship); destrozar (car); (Amer, demolish) demoler; (fig) destrozar. **~age** /-ɪdʒ/ n restos mpl; (of building) ruinas fpl

wrench /rentʃ/ vt arrancar; (sprain) desgarrarse; dislocarse (joint). ● n tirón m; (emotional) dolor m (causado por una separación); (tool) llave f inglesa

wrestl|e /'resl/ vi luchar. **~er** n luchador m. **~ing** n lucha f

wretch /retʃ/ n (despicable person) desgraciado m; (unfortunate person) desdichado m & f. **~ed** /-ɪd/ adj desdichado; (weather) horrible

wriggle /'rɪgl/ vi retorcerse. ~

w

out of escaparse de

wring /rɪŋ/ vt (pt wrung) retorcer (neck). ~ out of (obtain from) arrancar. □ ~ out vt retorcer

wrinkl|e /'rɪŋkl/ n arruga f. ●vt arrugar. ●vi arrugarse. ~y adj arrugado

wrist /rɪst/ n muñeca f. ~watch n reloj m de pulsera

writ /rɪt/ n orden m judicial

write /raɪt/ vt/i (pt wrote, pp written, pres p writing) escribir. □ ~ down vt anotar. □ ~ off vt cancelar (debt). ~-off n. the car was a ~-off el coche fue declarado un siniestro total. ~r n escritor m

writhe /raɪð/ vi retorcerse

writing /'raɪtɪŋ/ n (script) escritura f; (handwriting) letra f. in ~ por escrito. ~s npl obra f, escritos mpl. ~ desk n escritorio m. ~ pad n bloc. m. ~ paper n papel m de escribir

written /'rɪtn/ see WRITE

wrong /rɒŋ/ adj equivocado, incorrecto; (not just) injusto; (mistaken) equivocado. be ~ no tener razón; (be mistaken) equivocarse. what's ~? ¿qué pasa? it's ~ to steal robar está mal. what's ~ with that? ¿qué hay de malo en eso? ●adv mal. go ~ equivocarse; (plan) salir mal. ●n injusticia f; (evil) mal m. in the ~ equivocado. ●vt ser injusto con. ~ful adj injusto. ~ly adv mal; (unfairly) injustamente

wrote /rəʊt/ see WRITE

wrought iron /rɔːt/ n hierro m forjado

wrung /rʌŋ/ see WRING

wry /raɪ/ adj (wryer, wryest) irónico. make a ~ face torcer el gesto

Xx

xerox /'zɪərɒks/ vt fotocopiar, xerografiar

Xmas /'krɪsməs/ n abbr (Christmas) Navidad f

X-ray /'eksreɪ/ n (ray) rayo m X; (photograph) radiografía f. ~s npl rayos mpl. ●vt hacer una radiografía de

xylophone /'zaɪləfəʊn/ n xilofón m, xilófono m

Yy

yacht /jɒt/ n yate m. ~ing n navegación f a vela

yank /jæŋk/ vt 🔲 tirar de (violentamente)

Yankee /'jæŋkɪ/ n 🔲 yanqui m & f

yap /jæp/ vi (pt yapped) (dog) ladrar (con ladridos agudos)

yard /jɑːd/ n patio m; (Amer, garden) jardín m; (measurement) yarda f (= 0.9144 metre)

yarn /jɑːn/ n hilo m; (fam, tale) cuento m

yawn /jɔːn/ vi bostezar. ●n bostezo m

yeah /jeə/ adv 🔲 sí

year /jɪə(r)/ n año m. be three ~s old tener tres años. ~ly adj anual. ●adv cada año

yearn /jɜːn/ vi. ~ to do sth anhelar hacer algo. ~ for sth añorar algo. **~ing** n anhelo m, ansia f

yeast /jiːst/ n levadura f

yell /jel/ vi gritar. ● n grito m

yellow /'jeləʊ/ adj & n amarillo (m)

yelp /jelp/ n gañido m. ● vi gañir

yes /jes/ int & n sí (m)

yesterday /'jestədeɪ/ adv & n ayer (m). **the day before ~** anteayer m. **~ morning** ayer por la mañana, ayer en la mañana (LAm)

yet /jet/ adv todavía, aún; (already) ya. as **~** hasta ahora; (as a linker) sin embargo. ● conj pero

Yiddish /'jɪdɪʃ/ n yídish m

yield /jiːld/ vt (surrender) ceder; producir (crop/mineral); dar (results). ● vi ceder. **'yield'** (Amer, traffic sign) ceda el paso. ● n rendimiento m

yoga /'jəʊgə/ n yoga m

yoghurt /'jɒgət/ n yogur m

yoke /jəʊk/ n (fig also) yugo m

yokel /'jəʊkl/ n palurdo m

yolk /jəʊk/ n yema f (de huevo)

---

you /juː/ pronoun

····▸ (as the subject) (familiar form) (sing) tú, vos (River Plate and parts of Central America); (pl) vosotros, -tras (Spain), ustedes (LAm); (formal) (sing) usted; (pl) ustedes

! In Spanish the subject pronoun is usually only used to give emphasis or mark contrast.

····▸ (as the direct object) (familiar form) (sing) te; (pl) os (Spain), los, las (LAm); (formal) (sing) lo or (Spain) le, la; (pl) los or (Spain) les, las. **I love ~** te quiero

····▸ (as the indirect object) (familiar form) (sing) te; (pl) os (Spain), les (LAm); (formal) (sing) le; (pl) les. **I sent ~ the book yesterday** te mandé el libro ayer

! The pronoun se replaces the indirect object pronoun le or les when the latter is used with the direct object pronoun (lo, la etc), e.g. **I gave it to ~** se lo di

····▸ (when used after a preposition) (familiar form) (sing) ti, vos (River Plate and parts of Central America); (pl) vosotros, -tras (Spain), ustedes (LAm); (formal) (sing) usted; (pl) ustedes

····▸ (generalizing) uno, tú (esp Spain). **~ feel very proud** uno se siente muy orgulloso, te sientes muy orgulloso (esp Spain). **~ have to be patient** hay que tener paciencia

you'd /juːd/, /jʊəd/ = **you had**, **you would**

you'll /juːl/, /jʊəl/ = **you will**

young /jʌŋ/ adj (-er, -est) joven. **my ~er sister** mi hermana menor. **he's a year ~er than me** tiene un año menos que yo. **~ lady** n señorita f. **~ man** n joven m. **~ster** /-stə(r)/ n joven m

your /jɔː(r)/ adj (belonging to one person) (sing, familiar) tu; (pl, familiar) tus; (sing, formal) su; (pl, formal) sus; (belonging to more than one person) (sing, familiar) vuestro, -tra, su (LAm); (pl, familiar) vuestros, -tras, sus (LAm); (sing, formal) su; (pl, formal) sus

you're /jʊə(r)/, /jɔː(r)/ = **you are**

y

yours /jɔːz/ poss pron (belonging to one person) (sing, familiar) tuyo, -ya; (pl, familiar) tuyos, -yas; (sing, formal) suyo, -ya; (pl, formal) suyos, -yas. (belonging to more than one person) (sing, familiar) vuestro, -tra; (pl, familiar) vuestros, -tras, suyos, -yas (LAm); (sing, formal) suyo, -ya; (pl, formal) suyos, -yas. **an aunt of ~** una tía tuya/suya; **~ is here** el tuyo/la tuya/el suyo/la suya está aquí

yourself /jɔːˈself/ pron (reflexive). (emphatic use) ① tú mismo, tú misma; (formal) usted mismo, usted misma. **describe ~f** descríbete; (Ud form) descríbase. **stop thinking about ~f** ① deja de pensar en tí mismo; (formal) deje de pensar en sí mismo. **by ~f** solo, sola. **~ves** /jɔːˈselvz/ pron vosotros mismos, vosotras mismas (familiar); ustedes mismos, ustedes mismas (LAm familiar); ustedes mismos, ustedes mismas (formal); (reflexive). **behave ~ves** ¡portaos bien! (familiar); ¡pórtense bien! (formal, LAm familiar). **by ~ves** solos, solas

youth /juːθ/ n (pl youths /juːðz/) (early life) juventud f; (boy) joven m; (young people) juventud f. **~ful** adj joven, juvenil. **~ hostel** n albergue m juvenil

you've /juːv/ = **you have**

Yugoslav /ˈjuːɡəslɑːv/ adj & n yugoslavo (m). **~ia** /-ˈslɑːvɪə/ n Yugoslavia f

Zz

zeal /ziːl/ n fervor m, celo m

zeal|ot /ˈzelət/ n fanático m. **~ous** /-əs/ adj ferviente; (worker) que pone gran celo en su trabajo

zebra /ˈzebrə/ n cebra f. **~ crossing** n paso m de cebra

zenith /ˈzenɪθ/ n cenit m

zero /ˈzɪərəʊ/ n (pl -os) cero m

zest /zest/ n entusiasmo m; (peel) cáscara f

zigzag /ˈzɪɡzæɡ/ n zigzag m. ●vi (pt zigzagged) zigzaguear

zilch /zɪltʃ/ n ✕ nada de nada

zinc /zɪŋk/ n cinc m

zip /zɪp/ n cremallera f, cierre m (LAm), zíper m (Mex). ●vt. **~ (up)** cerrar (la cremallera). **Z~ code** n (Amer) código m postal. **~ fastener** n cremallera f. **~per** n/vt see **ZIP**

zodiac /ˈzəʊdɪæk/ n zodiaco m. **~al** /-ˈdaɪəkl/ adj zodiacal

zombie /ˈzɒmbɪ/ n zombi m & f

zone /zəʊn/ n zona f. **time ~** n huso m horario

zoo /zuː/ n zoo m, zoológico m. **~logical** /zuːəˈlɒdʒɪkl/ adj zoológico. **~logist** /zuːˈɒlədʒɪst/ n zoólogo m. **~logy** /zuːˈɒlədʒɪ/ n zoología f

zoom /zuːm/. ▢ **~ in** vi (Photo) hacer un zoom in (on sobre). ▢ **~ past** vi/t pasar zumbando. **~ lens** n teleobjetivo m, zoom m

zucchini /zuːˈkiːnɪ/ n (invar or **~s**) (Amer) calabacín m

Numbers/números

zero	0	cero
one (first)	1	uno (primero)
two (second)	2	dos (segundo)
three (third)	3	tres (tercero)
four (fourth)	4	cuatro (cuarto)
five (fifth)	5	cinco (quinto)
six (sixth)	6	seis (sexto)
seven (seventh)	7	siete (séptimo)
eight (eighth)	8	ocho (octavo)
nine (ninth)	9	nueve (noveno)
ten (tenth)	10	diez (décimo)
eleven (eleventh)	11	once (undécimo)
twelve (twelfth)	12	doce (duodécimo)
thirteen (thirteenth)	13	trece (decimotercero)
fourteen (fourteenth)	14	catorce (decimocuarto)
fifteen (fifteenth)	15	quince (decimoquinto)
sixteen (sixteenth)	16	dieciséis (decimosexto)
seventeen (seventeenth)	17	diecisiete (decimoséptimo)
eighteen (eighteenth)	18	dieciocho (decimoctavo)
nineteen (nineteenth)	19	diecinueve (decimonoveno)
twenty (twentieth)	20	veinte (vigésimo)
twenty-one (twenty-first)	21	veintiuno (vigésimo primero)
twenty-two (twenty-second)	22	veintidós (vigésimo segundo)
twenty-three (twenty-third)	23	veintitrés (vigésimo tercero)
twenty-four (twenty-fourth)	24	veinticuatro (vigésimo cuarto)
twenty-five (twenty-fifth)	25	veinticinco (vigésimo quinto)
twenty-six (twenty-sixth)	26	veintiséis (vigésimo sexto)
thirty (thirtieth)	30	treinta (trigésimo)

thirty-one (thirty-first)	31	treinta y uno (trigésimo primero)
forty (fortieth)	40	cuarenta (cuadragésimo)
fifty (fiftieth)	50	cincuenta (quincuagésimo)
sixty (sixtieth)	60	sesenta (sexagésimo)
seventy (seventieth)	70	setenta (septuagésimo)
eighty (eightieth)	80	ochenta (octogésimo)
ninety (ninetieth)	90	noventa (nonagésimo)
a/one hundred (hundredth)	100	cien (centésimo)
a/one hundred and one (hundred and first)	101	ciento uno (centésimo primero)
two hundred (two hundredth)	200	doscientos (ducentésimo)
three hundred (three hundredth)	300	trescientos (tricentésimo)
four hundred (four hundredth)	400	cuatrocientos (cuadringentésimo)
five hundred (five hundredth)	500	quinientos (quingentésimo)
six hundred (six hundredth)	600	seiscientos (sexcentésimo)
seven hundred (seven hundredth)	700	setecientos (septingentésimo)
eight hundred (eight hundredth)	800	ochocientos (octingentésimo)
nine hundred (nine hundredth)	900	novecientos (noningentésimo)
a/one thousand (thousandth)	1000	mil (milésimo)
two thousand (two thousandth)	2000	dos mil (dos milésimo)
a/one million (millionth)	1,000,000	un millón (millonésimo)

Verbos irregulares ingleses

Infinitivo	Pretérito	Participio pasado	Infinitivo	Pretérito	Participio pasado
be	was	been	**drive**	drove	driven
bear	bore	borne	**eat**	ate	eaten
beat	beat	beaten	**fall**	fell	fallen
become	became	become	**feed**	fed	fed
begin	began	begun	**feel**	felt	felt
bend	bent	bent	**fight**	fought	fought
bet	bet,	bet,	**find**	found	found
	betted	betted	**flee**	fled	fled
bid	bade, bid	bidden, bid	**fly**	flew	flown
bind	bound	bound	**freeze**	froze	frozen
bite	bit	bitten	**get**	got	got, gotten US
bleed	bled	bled	**give**	gave	given
blow	blew	blown	**go**	went	gone
break	broke	broken	**grow**	grew	grown
breed	bred	bred	**hang**	hung,	hung,
bring	brought	brought		hanged	hanged
build	built	built	**have**	had	had
burn	burnt,	burnt,	**hear**	heard	heard
	burned	burned	**hide**	hid	hidden
burst	burst	burst	**hit**	hit	hit
buy	bought	bought	**hold**	held	held
catch	caught	caught	**hurt**	hurt	hurt
choose	chose	chosen	**keep**	kept	kept
cling	clung	clung	**kneel**	knelt	knelt
come	came	come	**know**	knew	known
cost	cost,	cost,	**lay**	laid	laid
	costed (vt)	costed	**lead**	led	led
cut	cut	cut	**lean**	leaned,	leaned,
deal	dealt	dealt		leant	leant
dig	dug	dug	**learn**	learnt,	learnt,
do	did	done		learned	learned
draw	drew	drawn	**leave**	left	left
dream	dreamt,	dreamt,	**lend**	lent	lent
	dreamed	dreamed	**let**	let	let
drink	drank	drunk	**lie**	lay	lain

Infinitivo	Pretérito	Participio pasado	Infinitivo	Pretérito	Participio pasado
lose	lost	lost	**spend**	spent	spent
make	made	made	**spit**	spat	spat
mean	meant	meant	**spoil**	spoilt,	spoilt,
meet	met	met		spoiled	spoiled
pay	paid	paid	**spread**	spread	spread
put	put	put	**spring**	sprang	sprung
read	read	read	**stand**	stood	stood
ride	rode	ridden	**steal**	stole	stolen
ring	rang	rung	**stick**	stuck	stuck
rise	rose	risen	**sting**	stung	stung
run	ran	run	**stride**	strode	stridden
say	said	said	**strike**	struck	struck
see	saw	seen	**swear**	swore	sworn
seek	sought	sought	**sweep**	swept	swept
sell	sold	sold	**swell**	swelled	swollen,
send	sent	sent			swelled
set	set	set	**swim**	swam	swum
sew	sewed	sewn, sewed	**swing**	swung	swung
shake	shook	shaken	**take**	took	taken
shine	shone	shone	**teach**	taught	taught
shoe	shod	shod	**tear**	tore	torn
shoot	shot	shot	**tell**	told	told
show	showed	shown	**think**	thought	thought
shut	shut	shut	**throw**	threw	thrown
sing	sang	sung	**thrust**	thrust	thrust
sink	sank	sunk	**tread**	trod	trodden
sit	sat	sat	**under-**	under-	understood
sleep	slept	slept	**stand**	stood	
sling	slung	slung	**wake**	woke	woken
smell	smelt,	smelt,	**wear**	wore	worn
	smelled	smelled	**win**	won	won
speak	spoke	spoken	**write**	wrote	written
spell	spelled,	spelled,			
	spelt	spelt			

Spanish verbs

Regular verbs:

● in **-ar** (*e.g.* **comprar**)
Present; compr|o, ~as, ~a, ~amos,
~áis, ~an
Future: comprar|é, ~ás, ~á, ~emos,
~éis, ~án
Imperfect: compr|aba, ~abas, ~aba,
~ábamos, ~abais, ~aban
Preterite: compr|é, ~aste, ~ó,
~amos, ~asteis, ~aron
Present subjunctive: compr|e, ~es, ~e,
~emos, ~éis, ~en
Imperfect subjunctive: compr|ara,
~aras, ~ara, ~áramos, ~arais,
~aran
compr|ase, ~ases, ~ase, ~ásemos,
~aseis, ~asen
Conditional: comprar|ía, ~ías, ~ía,
~íamos, ~íais, ~ían
Present participle: comprando
Past participle: comprado
Imperative: compra, comprad

● in **-er** (*e.g.* **beber**)
Present: beb|o, ~es, ~e, ~emos,
~éis, ~en
Future: beber|é, ~ás, ~á, ~emos,
~éis, ~án
Imperfect: beb|ía, ~ías, ~ía, ~íamos,
~íais, ~ían
Preterite: beb|í, ~iste, ~ió, ~imos,
~isteis, ~ieron
Present subjunctive: beb|a, ~as, ~a,
~amos, ~áis, ~an
Imperfect subjunctive: beb|iera, ~ieras,
~iera, ~iéramos, ~ierais, ~ieran

beb|iese, ~ieses, ~iese, ~iésemos,
~ieseis, ~iesen
Conditional: beber|ía, ~ías, ~ía,
~íamos, ~íais, ~ían
Present participle: bebiendo
Past participle: bebido
Imperative: bebe, bebed

● in **-ir** (*e.g.* **vivir**)
Present: viv|o, ~es, ~e, ~imos, ~ís,
~en
Future: vivir|é, ~ás, ~á, ~emos,
~éis, ~án
Imperfect: viv|ía, ~ías, ~ía, ~íamos,
~íais, ~ían
Preterite: viv|í, ~iste, ~ió, ~imos,
~isteis, ~ieron
Present subjunctive: viv|a, ~as, ~a,
~amos, ~áis, ~an
Imperfect subjunctive: viv|iera, ~ieras,
~iera, ~iéramos, ~ierais, ~ieran
viv|iese, ~ieses, ~iese, ~iésemos,
~ieseis, ~iesen
Conditional: vivir|ía, ~ías, ~ía,
~íamos, ~íais, ~ían
Present participle: viviendo
Past participle: vivido
Imperative: vive, vivid

Irregular verbs:

[1] cerrar
Present: cierro, cierras, cierra,
cerramos, cerráis, cierran
Present subjunctive: cierre, cierres,
cierre, cerremos, cerréis, cierren
Imperative: cierra, cerrad

[2] contar, mover

Present: cuento, cuentas, cuenta, contamos, contáis, cuentan
muevo, mueves, mueve, movemos, movéis, mueven
Present subjunctive: cuente, cuentes, cuente, contemos, contéis, cuenten
mueva, muevas, mueva, movamos, mováis, muevan
Imperative: cuenta, contad
mueve, moved

[3] jugar

Present: juego, juegas, juega, jugamos, jugáis, juegan
Preterite: jugué, jugaste, jugó, jugamos, jugasteis, jugaron
Present subjunctive: juegue, juegues, juegue, juguemos, juguéis, jueguen

[4] sentir

Present: siento, sientes, siente, sentimos, sentís, sienten
Preterite: sentí, sentiste, sintió, sentimos, sentisteis, sintieron
Present subjunctive: sienta, sientas, sienta, sintamos, sintáis, sientan
Imperfect subjunctive: sint|iera, ~ieras, ~iera, ~iéramos, ~ierais, ~ieran
sint|iese, ~ieses, ~iese, ~iésemos, ~ieseis, ~iesen
Present participle: sintiendo
Imperative: siente, sentid

[5] pedir

Present: pido, pides, pide, pedimos, pedís, piden
Preterite: pedí, pediste, pidió, pedimos, pedisteis, pidieron

Present subjunctive: pid|a, ~as, ~a, ~amos, ~áis, ~an
Imperfect subjunctive: pid|iera, ~ieras, ~iera, ~iéramos, ~ierais, ~ieran
pid|iese, ~ieses, ~iese, ~iésemos, ~ieseis, ~iesen
Present participle: pidiendo
Imperative: pide, pedid

[6] dormir

Present: duermo, duermes, duerme, dormimos, dormís, duermen
Preterite: dormí, dormiste, durmió, dormimos, dormisteis, durmieron
Present subjunctive: duerma, duermas, duerma, durmamos, durmáis, duerman
Imperfect subjunctive: durm|iera, ~ieras, ~iera, ~iéramos, ~ierais, ~ieran
durm|iese, ~ieses, ~iese, ~iésemos, ~ieseis, ~iesen
Present participle: durmiendo
Imperative: duerme, dormid

[7] dedicar

Preterite: dediqué, dedicaste, dedicó, dedicamos, dedicasteis, dedicaron
Present subjunctive: dediqu|e, ~es, ~e, ~emos, ~éis, ~en

[8] delinquir

Present: delinco, delinques, delinque, delinquimos, delinquís, delinquen
Present subjunctive: delinc|a, ~as, ~a, ~amos, ~áis, ~an

[9] vencer, esparcir

Present: venzo, vences, vence, vencemos, vencéis, vencen
esparzo, esparces, esparce, esparcimos, esparcís, esparcen

Present subjunctive: venz|a, ~as, ~a, ~amos, ~áis, ~an
esparz|a, ~as, ~a, ~amos, ~áis, ~an

[10] rechazar

Preterite: rechacé, rechazaste, rechazó, rechazamos, rechazasteis, rechazaron
Present subjunctive: rechac|e, ~e, ~emos, ~éis, ~en

[11] conocer, lucir

Present: conozco, conoces, conoce, conocemos, conocéis, conocen
luzco, luces, luce, lucimos, lucís, lucen
Present subjunctive: conozc|a, ~as, ~a, ~amos, ~áis, ~an
luzc|a, ~as, ~a, ~amos, ~áis, ~an

[12] pagar

Preterite: pagué, pagaste, pagó, pagamos, pagasteis, pagaron
Present subjunctive: pagu|e, ~es, ~e, ~emos, ~éis, ~en

[13] distinguir

Present: distingo, distingues, distingue, distinguimos, distinguís, distinguen
Present subjunctive: disting|a, ~as, ~a, ~amos, ~áis, ~an

[14] acoger, afligir

Present: acojo, acoges, acoge, acogemos, acogéis, acogen
aflijo, afliges, aflige, afligimos, afligís, afligen
Present subjunctive: acoj|a, ~as, ~a, ~amos, ~áis, ~an

aflij|a, ~as, ~a, ~amos, ~áis, ~an

[15] averiguar

Preterite: averigüé, averiguaste, averiguó, averiguamos, averiguasteis, averiguaron
Present subjunctive: averigü|e, ~es, ~e, ~emos, ~éis, ~en

[16] agorar

Present: agüero, agüeras, agüera, agoramos, agoráis, agüeran
Present subjunctive: agüere, agüeres, agüere, agoremos, agoréis, agüeren
Imperative: agüera, agorad

[17] huir

Present: huyo, huyes, huye, huimos, huís, huyen
Preterite: huí, huiste, huyó, huimos, huisteis, huyeron
Present subjunctive: huy|a, ~as, ~a, ~amos, ~áis, ~an
Imperfect subjunctive: huy|era, ~eras, ~era, ~éramos, ~erais, ~eran
huy|ese, ~eses, ~ese, ~ésemos, ~eseis, ~esen
Present participle: huyendo
Imperative: huye, huid

[18] creer

Preterite: creí, creíste, creyó, creímos, creísteis, creyeron
Imperfect subjunctive: crey|era, ~eras, ~era, ~éramos, ~erais, ~eran
crey|ese, ~eses, ~ese, ~ésemos, ~eseis, ~esen
Present participle:
creyendo
Past participle: creído

[19] argüir

Present: arguyo, arguyes, arguye, argüimos, argüís, arguyen
Preterite: argüí, argüiste, arguyó, argüimos, argüisteis, arguyeron
Present subjunctive: arguy|a, ~as, ~a, ~amos, ~áis, ~an
Imperfect subjunctive: arguy|era, ~eras, ~era, ~éramos, ~erais, ~eran
arguy|ese, ~eses, ~ese, ~ésemos, ~eseis, ~esen
Present participle: arguyendo
Imperative: arguye, argüid

[20] vaciar

Present: vacío, vacías, vacía, vaciamos, vaciáis, vacían
Present subjunctive: vacíe, vacíes, vacíe, vaciemos, vaciéis, vacíen
Imperative: vacía, vaciad

[21] acentuar

Present: acentúo, acentúas, acentúa, acentuamos, acentuáis, acentúan
Present subjunctive: acentúe, acentúes, acentúe, acentuemos, acentuéis, acentúen
Imperative: acentúa, acentuad

[22] atañer, engullir

Preterite: atañ|í, ~iste, ~ó, ~imos, ~isteis, ~eron
engull|í ~iste, ~ó, ~imos, ~isteis, ~eron
Imperfect subjunctive: atañ|era, ~eras, ~era, ~éramos, ~erais, ~eran
atañ|ese, ~eses, ~ese, ~ésemos, ~eseis, ~esen
engull|era, ~eras, ~era, ~éramos, ~erais, ~eran

engull|ese, ~eses, ~ese, ~ésemos, ~eseis, ~esen
Present participle: atañendo
engullendo

[23] aislar, aullar

Present: aíslo, aíslas, aísla, aislamos, aisláis, aíslan
aúllo, aúllas, aúlla, aullamos, aulláis, aúllan
Present subjunctive: aísle, aísles, aísle, aislemos, aisléis, aíslen
aúlle, aúlles, aúlle, aullemos, aulléis, aúllen
Imperative: aísla, aislad
aúlla, aullad

[24] abolir

Present: abolimos, abolís
Present subjunctive: not used
Imperative: abolid

[25] andar

Preterite: anduv|e, ~iste, ~o, ~imos, ~isteis, ~ieron
Imperfect subjunctive: anduv|iera, ~ieras, ~iera, ~iéramos, ~ierais, ~ieran
anduv|iese, ~ieses, ~iese, ~iésemos, ~ieseis, ~iesen

[26] dar

Present: doy, das, da, damos, dais, dan
Preterite: di, diste, dio, dimos, disteis, dieron
Present subjunctive: dé, des, dé, demos, deis, den
Imperfect subjunctive: diera, dieras, diera, diéramos, dierais, dieran
diese, dieses, diese, diésemos, dieseis, diesen

[27] estar

Present: estoy, estás, está, estamos, estáis, están

Preterite: estuv|e, ~iste, ~o, ~imos, ~isteis, ~ieron

Present subjunctive: esté, estés, esté, estemos, estéis, estén

Imperfect subjunctive: estuv|iera, ~ieras, ~iera, ~iéramos, ~ierais, ~ieran

estuv|iese, ~ieses, ~iese, ~iésemos, ~ieseis, ~iesen

Imperative: está, estad

[28] caber

Present: quepo, cabes, cabe, cabemos, cabéis, caben

Future: cabr|é, ~ás, ~á, ~emos, ~éis, ~án

Preterite: cup|e, ~iste, ~o, ~imos, ~isteis, ~ieron

Present subjunctive: quep|a, ~as, ~a, ~amos, ~áis, ~an

Imperfect subjunctive: cup|iera, ~ieras, ~iera, ~iéramos, ~ierais, ~ieran

cup|iese, ~ieses, ~iese, ~iésemos, ~ieseis, ~iesen

Conditional: cabr|ía, ~ías, ~ía, ~íamos, ~íais, ~ían

[29] caer

Present: caigo, caes, cae, caemos, caéis, caen

Preterite: caí, caiste, cayó, caímos, caísteis, cayeron

Present subjunctive: caig|a, ~as, ~a, ~amos, ~áis, ~an

Imperfect subjunctive: cay|era, ~eras, ~era, ~éramos, ~erais, ~eran

cay|ese, ~eses, ~ese, ~ésemos, ~eseis, ~esen

Present participle: cayendo

Past participle: caído

[30] haber

Present: he, has, ha, hemos, habéis, han

Future: habr|é, ~ás, ~á, ~emos, ~éis, ~án

Preterite: hub|e, ~iste, ~o, ~imos, ~isteis, ~ieron

Present subjunctive: hay|a, ~as, ~a, ~amos, ~áis, ~an

Imperfect subjunctive: hub|iera, ~ieras, ~iera, ~iéramos, ~ierais, ~ieran

hub|iese, ~ieses, ~iese, ~iésemos, ~ieseis, ~iesen

Conditional: habr|ía, ~ías, ~ía, ~íamos, ~íais, ~ían

Imperative: he, habed

[31] hacer

Present: hago, haces, hace, hacemos, hacéis, hacen

Future: har|é, ~ás, ~á, ~emos, ~éis, ~án

Preterite: hice, hiciste, hizo, hicimos, hicisteis, hicieron

Present subjunctive: hag|a, ~as, ~a, ~amos, ~áis, ~an

Imperfect subjunctive: hic|iera, ~ieras, ~iera, ~iéramos, ~ierais, ~ieran

hic|iese, ~ieses, ~iese, ~iésemos, ~ieseis, ~iesen

Conditional: har|ía, ~ías, ~ía, ~íamos, ~íais, ~ían

Past participle: hecho

Imperative: haz, haced

[32] placer

Present subjunctive: plazca

Imperfect subjunctive: placiera, placiese

[33] poder

Present: puedo, puedes, puede, podemos, podéis, pueden

Future: podr|é, ~ás, ~á, ~emos, ~éis, ~án

Preterite: pud|e, ~iste, ~o, ~imos, ~isteis, ~ieron

Present subjunctive: pueda, puedas, pueda, podamos, podáis, puedan

Imperfect subjunctive: pud|iera, ~ieras, ~iera, ~iéramos, ~ierais, ~ieran
pud|iese, ~ieses, ~iese, ~iésemos, ~ieseis, ~iesen

Conditional: podr|ía, ~ías, ~ía, ~íamos, ~íais, ~ían

Past participle: pudiendo

[34] poner

Present: pongo, pones, pone, ponemos, ponéis, ponen

Future: pondr|é, ~ás, ~á, ~emos, ~éis, ~án

Preterite: pus|e, ~iste, ~o, ~imos, ~isteis, ~ieron

Present subjunctive: pong|a, ~as, ~a, ~amos, ~áis, ~an

Imperfect subjunctive: pus|iera, ~ieras, ~iera, ~iéramos, ~ierais, ~ieran
pus|iese, ~ieses, ~iese, ~iésemos, ~ieseis, ~iesen

Conditional: pondr|ía, ~ías, ~ía, ~íamos, ~íais, ~ían

Past participle: puesto

Imperative: pon, poned

[35] querer

Present: quiero, quieres, quiere, queremos, queréis, quieren

Future: querr|é, ~ás, ~á, ~emos, ~éis, ~án

Preterite: quis|e, ~iste, ~o, ~imos, ~isteis, ~ieron

Present subjunctive: quiera, quieras, quiera, queramos, queráis, quieran

Imperfect subjunctive: quis|iera, ~ieras, ~iera, ~iéramos, ~ierais, ~ieran
quis|iese, ~ieses, ~iese, ~iésemos, ~ieseis, ~iesen

Conditional: querr|ía, ~ías, ~ía, ~íamos, ~íais, ~ían

Imperative: quiere, quered

[36] raer

Present: raigo/rayo, raes, rae, raemos, raéis, raen

Preterite: raí, raíste, rayó, raímos, raísteis, rayeron

Present subjunctive: raig|a, ~as, ~a, ~amos, ~áis, ~an ray|a, ~as, ~a, ~amos, ~áis, ~an

Imperfect subjunctive: ray|era, ~eras, ~era, ~éramos, ~erais, ~eran
ray|ese, ~eses, ~ese, ~ésemos, ~eseis, ~esen

Present participle: rayendo

Past participle: raído

[37] roer

Present: roo, roes, roe, roemos, roéis, roen

Preterite: roí, roíste, royó, roímos, roísteis, royeron

Present subjunctive: ro|a, ~as, ~a, ~amos, ~áis, ~an

Imperfect subjunctive: roy|era, ~eras, ~era, ~éramos, ~erais, ~eran
roy|ese, ~eses, ~ese, ~ésemos, ~eseis, ~esen

Present participle: royendo

Past participle: roído

[38] saber

Present: sé, sabes, sabe, sabemos, sabéis, saben
Future: sabr|é, ~ás, ~á, ~emos, ~éis, ~án
Preterite: sup|e, ~iste, ~o, ~imos, ~isteis, ~ieron
Present subjunctive: sep|a, ~as, ~a, ~amos, ~áis, ~an
Imperfect subjunctive: sup|iera, ~ieras, ~iera, ~iéramos, ~ierais, ~ieran
sup|iese, ~ieses, ~iese, ~iésemos, ~ieseis, ~iesen
Conditional: sabr|ía, ~ías, ~ía, ~íamos, ~íais, ~ían

[39] ser

Present: soy, eres, es, somos, sois, son
Imperfect: era, eras, era, éramos, erais, eran
Preterite: fui, fuiste, fue, fuimos, fuisteis, fueron
Present subjunctive: se|a, ~as, ~a, ~amos, ~áis, ~an
Imperfect subjunctive: fu|era, ~eras, ~era, ~éramos, ~erais, ~eran
fu|ese, ~eses, ~ese, ~ésemos, ~eseis, ~esen
Imperative: sé, sed

[40] tener

Present: tengo, tienes, tiene, tenemos, tenéis, tienen
Future: tendr|é, ~ás, ~á, ~emos, ~éis, ~án
Preterite: tuv|e, ~iste, ~o, ~imos, ~isteis, ~ieron
Present subjunctive: teng|a, ~as, ~a, ~amos, ~áis, ~an
Imperfect subjunctive: tuv|iera, ~ieras, ~iera, ~iéramos, ~ierais, ~ieran

tuv|iese, ~ieses, ~iese, ~iésemos, ~ieseis, ~iesen
Conditional: tendr|ía, ~ías, ~ía, ~íamos, ~íais, ~ían
Imperative: ten, tened

[41] traer

Present: traigo, traes, trae, traemos, traéis, traen
Preterite: traj|e, ~iste, ~o, ~imos, ~isteis, ~eron
Present subjunctive: traig|a, ~as, ~a, ~amos, ~áis, ~an
Imperfect subjunctive: traj|era, ~eras, ~era, ~éramos, ~erais, ~eran
traj|ese, ~eses, ~ese, ~ésemos, ~eseis, ~esen
Present participle: trayendo
Past participle: traído

[42] valer

Present: valgo, vales, vale, valemos, valéis, valen
Future: vald|ré, ~ás, ~á, ~emos, ~éis, ~án
Present subjunctive: valg|a, ~as, ~a, ~amos, ~áis, ~an
Conditional: vald|ría, ~ías, ~ía, ~íamos, ~íais, ~ían
Imperative: vale, valed

[43] ver

Present: veo, ves, ve, vemos, veis, ven
Imperfect: ve|ía, ~ías, ~ía, ~íamos, ~íais, ~ían
Preterite: vi, viste, vio, vimos, visteis, vieron
Present subjunctive: ve|a, ~as, ~a, ~amos, ~áis, ~an
Past participle: visto

[44] yacer

Present: yazco, yaces, yace, yacemos, yacéis, yacen
Present subjunctive: yazc|a, ~as, ~a, ~amos, ~áis, ~an
Imperative: yace, yaced

[45] asir

Present: asgo, ases, ase, asimos, asís, asen
Present subjunctive: asg|a, ~as, ~a, ~amos, ~áis, ~an

[46] decir

Present: digo, dices, dice, decimos, decís, dicen
Future: dir|é, ~ás, ~á, ~emos, ~éis, ~án
Preterite: dij|e, ~iste, ~o, ~imos, ~isteis, ~eron
Present subjunctive: dig|a, ~as, ~a, ~amos, ~áis, ~an
Imperfect subjunctive: dij|era, ~eras, ~era, ~éramos, ~erais, ~eran
dij|ese, ~eses, ~ese, ~ésemos, ~eseis, ~esen
Conditional: dir|ía, ~ías, ~ía, ~íamos, ~íais, ~ían
Present participle: dicho
Imperative: di, decid

[47] reducir

Present: reduzco, reduces, reduce, reducimos, reducís, reducen
Preterite: reduj|e, ~iste, ~o, ~imos, ~isteis, ~eron
Present subjunctive: reduzc|a, ~as, ~a, ~amos, ~áis, ~an
Imperfect subjunctive: reduj|era, ~eras, ~era, ~éramos, ~erais, ~eran
reduj|ese, ~eses, ~ese, ~ésemos, ~eseis, ~esen

[48] erguir

Present: yergo, yergues, yergue, erguimos, erguís, yerguen
Preterite: erguí, erguiste, irguió, erguimos, erguisteis, irguieron
Present subjunctive: yerg|a, ~as, ~a, ~amos, ~áis, ~an
Imperfect subjunctive: irgu|iera, ~ieras, ~iera, ~iéramos, ~ierais, ~ieran
irgu|iese, ~ieses, ~iese, ~iésemos, ~ieseis, ~iesen
Present participle: irguiendo
Imperative: yergue, erguid

[49] ir

Present: voy, vas, va, vamos, vais, van
Imperfect: iba, ibas, iba, íbamos, ibais, iban
Preterite: fui, fuiste, fue, fuimos, fuisteis, fueron
Present subjunctive: vay|a, ~as, ~a, ~amos, ~áis, ~an
Imperfect subjunctive: fu|era, ~eras, ~era, ~éramos, ~erais, ~eran
fu|ese, ~eses, ~ese, ~ésemos, ~eseis, ~esen
Present participle: yendo
Imperative: ve, id

[50] oír

Present: oigo, oyes, oye, oímos, oís, oyen
Preterite: oí, oíste, oyó, oímos, oísteis, oyeron
Present subjunctive: oig|a, ~as, ~a, ~amos, ~áis, ~an
Imperfect subjunctive: oy|era, ~eras, ~era, ~éramos, ~erais, ~eran

oy|ese, ~eses, ~ese, ~ésemos,
~eseis, ~esen
Present participle: oyendo
Past participle: oído
Imperative: oye, oíd

[51] reír

Present: río, ríes, ríe, reímos, reís,
ríen
Preterite: reí, reíste, rió, reímos,
reísteis, rieron
Present subjunctive: ría, rías, ría,
riamos, riáis, rían
Present participle: riendo
Past participle: reído
Imperative: ríe, reíd

[52] salir

Present: salgo, sales, sale, salimos,
salís, salen
Future: saldr|é, ~ás, ~á, ~emos,
~éis, ~án
Present subjunctive: salg|a, ~as, ~a,
~amos, ~áis, ~an

Conditional: saldr|ía, ~ías,
~íamos, ~íais, ~ían
Imperative: sal, salid

[53] venir

Present: vengo, vienes, viene,
venimos, venís, vienen
Future: vendr|é, ~ás, ~á, ~er
~éis, ~án
Preterite: vin|e, ~iste, ~o, ~in
~isteis, ~ieron
Present subjunctive: veng|a, ~as
~amos, ~áis, ~an
Imperfect subjunctive: vin|iera, ~
~iera, ~iéramos, ~ierais, ~
vin|iese, ~ieses, ~iese, ~iés
~ieseis, ~iesen
Conditional: vendr|ía, ~ías, ~ía
~íamos, ~íais, ~ían
Present participle: viniendo
Imperative: ven, venid

Abbreviations/Abreviaturas

adjective	*adj*	adjetivo
abbreviation	*abbr/abrev*	abreviatura
adverb	*adv*	adverbio
American	*Amer*	americano
motoring	*Auto*	automóvil
British	*Brit*	británico
commerce	*Com*	comercio
computing	*Comp*	informática
conjunction	*conj*	conjunción
cookery	*Culin*	cocina
electricity	*Elec*	electricidad
Spain	*Esp*	España
feminine	*f*	femenino
familiar	*fam*	familiar
figurative	*fig*	figurado
philosophy	*Fil*	filosofía
photography	*Foto*	fotografía
grammar	*Gram*	gramática
interjection	*int*	interjección
invariable	*invar*	invariable
legal, law	*Jurid*	jurídico
Latin American	*LAm*	latinoamericano
masculine	*m*	masculino
mathematics	*Mat(h)*	matemáticas
mechanics	*Mec*	mecánica
medicine	*Med*	medicina
Mexico	*Mex*	México